The Concise Encyclopedia of Economics

The Concise Encyclopedia

of Economics | Edited by David R. Henderson

LIBERTY FUND   Indianapolis

This book is published by Liberty Fund, Inc., a foundation established to encourage study of the ideal of a society of free and responsible individuals.

𒂼𒄄

The cuneiform inscription that serves as our logo and as the design motif for our endpapers is the earliest-known written appearance of the word "freedom" (*amagi*), or "liberty." It is taken from a clay document written about 2300 B.C. in the Sumerian city-state of Lagash.

"Free Trade" is adapted from Alan S. Blinder, *Hard Heads, Soft Hearts: Tough-Minded Economics for a Just Society,* © 1988 by Alan S. Blinder. Originally published in 1988 by Addison-Wesley, and reprinted with the permission of Perseus Books Group.

"Keynesian Economics" is adapted from Alan S. Blinder, "The Rise and Fall of Keynesian Economics," *Economic Record,* December 1988. Reprinted with the permission of Blackwell.

"Marginalism" is adapted from Steven E. Rhoads, *The Economist's View of the World,* © 1985 by Cambridge University Press. Reprinted with the permission of Cambridge University Press.

Printed in the United States of America

```
c   2   3   4   5   6   7   8   9   10
p   2   3   4   5   6   7   8   9   10
```

Library of Congress Cataloging-in-Publication Data

The concise encyclopedia of economics / edited by David R. Henderson.
    p. cm.
    Includes bibliographical references and index.
    ISBN-13: 978-0-86597-665-8 (hardcover: alk. paper)
    ISBN-13: 978-0-86597-666-5 (pbk.: alk. paper)
    1. Economics—Encyclopedias.   I. Henderson, David R.
    HB61.C66   2007
    330.03—dc22

                                         2007015993

Liberty Fund, Inc.
8335 Allison Pointe Trail, Suite 300
Indianapolis, Indiana 46250-1684

To Rena and Karen

Contents

BIOGRAPHIES

APPENDIXES

Introduction

An old joke says that if you laid all the economists in the world end to end, they would not reach a conclusion. What makes the joke work are the popular perceptions that economists never agree and that economists (unlike biologists or the practitioners of any other science) do not share a common set of beliefs. Given all the conflicting pronouncements by economists that appear almost daily in the press, these perceptions are understandable. They are also dead wrong. While economists disagree on many matters, they have reached virtually unanimous agreement on a multitude of others. One purpose of this book is to illuminate the many, many areas where economists agree (while also describing where and why they disagree). The main purpose, however, is to show how economic analysis can illuminate large parts of our daily world that are otherwise a mystery.

Most of the disagreement among economists concerns "macroeconomics," which deals with nationwide or worldwide phenomena such as inflation, unemployment, and economic growth. Adherents of the various "schools" (Keynesians, monetarists, supply siders, rational expectationists, new classicals, new Keynesians, and Austrians) disagree a fair bit. Some of their disagreements reflect different judgments about the relative importance of, say, inflation versus unemployment. Others stem from basic disagreement on the ability of government policy to affect the total economy in predictable ways. Even here, though, viewpoints have converged: on macroeconomic policy, one of the big differences concerns whether the central bank should target the price level loosely or strictly—certainly not a major disparity. This encyclopedia reflects the disagreements and the points of convergence, with authors chosen from each school to explain and justify their views of how the "macro" world works. One of the most important issues in macroeconomics, incidentally, is what caused the Great Depression and what made it last so long. The article GREAT DEPRESSION lays out the author's view of the causes as well as the issues on which there is an emerging consensus.

Macroeconomics, however, is only a small part of the total science of economics. The vast majority of economic questions and public-policy issues fall in the realm of microeconomics. And the vast majority of economists agree on the underlying economics of most micro issues, including rent controls, minimum wages, and the need to reduce pollution. Some may disagree on the policy implications of the analysis, but remarkably few disagree on the analysis itself.

The early evidence that economists agree on many micro issues first became clear in the late 1970s, when the *American Economic Review*, the world's largest-circulation economics journal, published an opinion poll of 211 economists.[1] The poll found that

---

1. J. R. Kearl, Clayne L. Pope, Gordon C. Whiting, and Larry T. Wimmer, "A Confusion of Economists?" *American Economic Review* 69 (May 1979): 28–37.

98 percent agreed with the statement, "A ceiling on rents reduces the quantity and quality of housing available." Similarly, 90 percent of economists agreed that "a minimum wage increases unemployment among young and unskilled workers." And 97 percent agreed with the statement, "Tariffs and import quotas reduce general economic welfare." Another poll, reported in 1992, found somewhat less, but still fairly widespread, agreement, with 93 percent agreeing on rent ceilings, 79 percent agreeing on the minimum wage, and 92 percent agreeing on tariffs and import quotas.[2] A survey in 2000 found similar agreement. Seventy-four percent agreed about the minimum wage, and 93 percent agreed about tariffs and import quotas.[3] (The survey did not ask about rent ceilings.) The entries on those topics in this encyclopedia explain why economists are in such startling agreement on these and many other issues. See, for example, the articles on MINIMUM WAGES, PRICE CONTROLS, and RENT CONTROLS.

And this just scratches the surface of the agreement. Take one example among many: government-mandated benefits for employees. Many people believe that if the government requires employers to provide benefits that employees value at, say, two thousand dollars a year, then the employees are better off by two thousand dollars a year. Economists know better. They understand, based both on simple economic reasoning and on growing evidence, that the employees pay most of the cost of such mandates in the form of lower wages. Even more important than the fact that economists agree on this conclusion is the reasoning that gets them there. The article that lays out this issue quite clearly was written by Lawrence Summers while he was a Harvard professor. He later served as a member of the Clinton administration, which tried to mandate that employers provide health insurance for employees. Summers does an especially good job of laying out the economic reasoning, but many other economists could have reached the same conclusions by applying basic Econ 101 analytics, shifting demand and supply curves.[4]

In fact, the story of how I first had the idea for an encyclopedia of economics involves Larry Summers. It was the fall of 1982, when he was a domestic policy economist and I was a senior staff economist under Martin Feldstein, the new chairman of President Ronald Reagan's Council of Economic Advisers. Several of us would sometimes lunch together and, of course, would mix it up on various issues. Macroeconomics brought out a wide range of opinions. For instance, Larry and our colleague Paul Krugman, now a regular economics columnist with the *New York Times*, worried that the high deficits of the time would cause high inflation. Ben Zycher and Lincoln Anderson, fellow senior economists, and I were fairly confident that the policies would not cause high inflation because the Federal Reserve Board under Paul Volcker seemed to be keeping the growth of the money supply low. But on various microeconomic issues and on free trade we were almost completely unanimous. We all thought price controls are generally a bad idea. We all favored free trade and were critical of Reagan for his restrictions on Japanese auto exports to the United States. We often agreed that this or that government policy was counterproductive and that free people, left to their own devices, would work things out better than governments would. It was after one of those conversations that I started thinking that the world

2. Richard M. Alston, J. R. Kearl, and Michael B. Vaughan, "Is There a Consensus Among Economists in the 1990s?" *American Economic Review* 82 (May 1992): 203–209.

3. Dan Fuller and Doris Geide-Stevenson, "Consensus Among Economists: Revisited," *Journal of Economic Education* (Fall 2003): 369–387.

4. Lawrence H. Summers, "Some Simple Economics of Mandated Benefits," *American Economic Review* (May 1979): 177–183.

could use an encyclopedia. And an encyclopedia makes much more sense if there is agreement among the experts.

Interestingly, the difference between the liberals and the libertarians was less on the economic analysis and even the bottom-line policy conclusions than it was on our feelings about the bottom line. The libertarians—Anderson, Zycher, and I—loved it when the answer was that free markets work; and that was usually the answer. The liberals, Krugman more than Summers, seemed often upset when that was the answer; they seemed to want a big role for government.

This fact about economics has led many noneconomists who want government to restrict economic freedom to express disappointment with economists. Steven Kelman, a budget official in the Carter and Clinton administrations, wrote:

> At the government agency where I have worked and where agency lawyers and agency microeconomists interact with each other . . . the lawyers are often exasperated, not only by the frequency with which agency economists attack their proposals but also by the unanimity among the agency economists in their opposition. The lawyers tend to (incorrectly) attribute this opposition to failure to hire "a broad enough spectrum" of economists, and to beg the economists, if they can't support the lawyers' proposals, at least to give them "the best economic arguments" in favor of them. . . . The economists' answer is typically something like, "There are no good economic arguments for your proposal."[5]

So, why do people think economists disagree about everything? One reason is that the media present all economic issues as if they are inherently controversial. The issues themselves are controversial, but the economics of the issues more often are not. A journalist writing a piece on free trade versus trade barriers, for example, would be hard put to find an economist who will defend trade barriers (economists know that free trade virtually always improves a nation's economic well-being). But many journalists feel compelled to present a "balanced view." So they go to economists who work for interest groups that favor trade barriers—groups such as the National Association of Manufacturers or the AFL-CIO—to get an opinion against free trade. Or they turn to a business person or labor leader whose industry faces tough competition from imports. The result is that readers and viewers get the false impression that economists are divided on free trade. The articles in this encyclopedia, though, reflect the consensus. See, for example, FREE TRADE by Princeton economist Alan Blinder, a former Clinton administration economist, and PROTECTIONISM by noted Columbia economist Jagdish Bhagwati.

Another important source of the misimpression about economics comes from the often overlooked distinction that economists make between "positive" and "normative" analysis. Positive analysis is the application of economic postulates and principles to a question—in other words, finding out the way things *are* and why the world behaves as it does. Normative analysis, in contrast, deals with the way things *ought to be* and unavoidably involves the noneconomic value judgments of the analyst. For example, positive analysis says that licensing physicians will result in fewer doctors and higher prices for medical care. Whether states should license doctors to protect patients from quacks is a normative matter. In other words, there are no "shoulds" in purely positive economic analysis, but every economist has views on how things should be done.

In preparing this encyclopedia, the members of the Board of Editors and I tried to separate positive and normative positions, to emphasize the areas where economists

---

5. Steven Kelman, *What Price Incentives?* (Boston: Auburn House, 1981), p. 7.

agree while also specifying where and why they disagree. The goal is to communicate just how much economic analysis can teach us about the important issues we face as voters, as consumers, as employees, and as people who care about the world. As such, the encyclopedia gives a comprehensive yet readable and engaging survey of mainstream economic thought. Topics that will interest noneconomists are covered by economists who can make their ideas accessible to the general reader. The entries on CONSCRIPTION, DISCRIMINATION, HEALTH INSURANCE, INSIDER TRADING, JOB SAFETY, LIABILITY, and PHARMACEUTICALS: ECONOMICS AND REGULATION, for example, cover issues whose important economic aspects are often overlooked. Also not to be missed are SAVINGS AND LOAN CRISIS, which shows what caused, and what did not cause, that crisis; INFLATION, which gives one of the clearest expositions ever of the causes and effects of inflation; OPEC, which points out, among other things, that OPEC was an unintended consequence of President Dwight D. Eisenhower's quotas on oil imports; and RISK AND SAFETY, which gives startling statistics on the risks of various activities.

One last note. Various people who read and loved the first edition of the encyclopedia told me that they did not try to read it cover to cover, but instead hopped from interesting issue to interesting issue. I recommend that strategy.

David R. Henderson
Monterey, California
October 2005

Acknowledgments

I want to thank six people who were all a pleasure to work with and who were each important in getting this book done. First are the four members of the Board of Editors: Tyler Cowen, Bob Crandall, Kevin Hoover, and Russell Roberts. They gave me good comments and criticisms on all the articles, and their responses improved the articles immensely. I particularly want to single out Kevin Hoover, for his detailed comments and suggestions that were easy to follow and implement; and Tyler Cowen, for his incredibly quick turnaround and, well, encyclopedic knowledge. Also, Rena Henderson used her prodigious editing skills to make the articles more understandable to someone like herself, an intelligent reader with no background in economics. The sixth person is Laura Goetz of Liberty Fund, whom I have never met but who was always responsive to my questions, supportive of the project, friendly, and professional.

Alan Russell, chairman of Liberty Fund, deserves credit for thinking of putting the first edition of the encyclopedia on the Web. Andy Rutten, then an economist with Liberty Fund, and my agent, Henning Gutmann, did much of the tough work of bringing Liberty Fund and me to an agreement. I particularly appreciate Henning's persistence.

My friends gave me moral support, especially Charley Hooper, Arunas Kuciauskas, Tom Lee, François Melese, and Greg De Young. Alan Reynolds was particularly helpful, giving me quick feedback on an article on an issue I knew little about.

Doug Brook, the dean of the Graduate School of Business and Public Policy for the whole time I worked on this book, gave me more than a year of unpaid leave, allowing me to finish it.

Harry E. Teasley Jr. gave a generous gift to the Hoover Institution that allowed me to take time to complete this massive project.

Finally, I thank the authors of these excellent articles. They were willing to share their knowledge with a wider audience and to do so for a modest fee. I enjoyed working with them, getting to know them, and learning from them, particularly Paul Bergin, Bryan Caplan, Jeffrey Frankel, John Goodman, Kevin Hassett, Jonathan Macey, Bennett McCallum, Paul Rubin, Kenneth Small, John Seater, Richard Thaler, and Adam Wildavsky.

David R. Henderson
Monterey, California
December 2005

Articles

Advertising

George Bittlingmayer

Economic analysis of advertising dates to the 1930s and 1940s, when critics attacked it as a monopolistic and wasteful practice. Defenders soon emerged who argued that advertising promotes competition and lowers the costs of providing information to consumers and distributing goods. Today, most economists side with the defenders most of the time.

Advertising comes in many different forms: grocery ads that feature weekly specials, "feel-good" advertising that merely displays a corporate logo, ads with detailed technical information, and those that promise "the best." Critics and defenders have often adopted extreme positions, attacking or defending any and all advertising. But, at the very least, it seems safe to say that the information firms convey in advertising is not systematically worse than the information volunteered in political campaigns or used car ads.

Modern economics views advertising as a type of promotion, in the same vein as direct selling by salespersons and promotional price discounts. If we focus on the problems firms face in promoting their wares, rather than on advertising as an isolated phenomenon, it is easier to understand why advertising is used in some circumstances and not in others.

Scope

While advertising has its roots in the advance of literacy and the advent of inexpensive mass newspapers in the nineteenth century, modern advertising as we know it began early in the twentieth century with two new products, Kellogg cereals and Camel cigarettes. What is generally credited as the first product endorsement also stems from this period: Honus Wagner's autograph was imprinted on the Louisville Slugger in 1905.

Advertising as a percentage of GDP has stayed relatively constant since the 1920s, at roughly 2 percent. About 60 percent of advertising is national rather than local. Table 1 shows national and local expenditures since 1940. In 2002, newspapers accounted for some 19 percent of total advertising expenditures; magazines for 5 percent; broadcast and cable television for 23 percent; radio for 8 percent; direct mail for 19 percent; and miscellaneous techniques such as yellow pages, billboards, and the Goodyear blimp for the remaining 27 percent. Internet advertising accounted for 2 percent of total advertising expenditures.

One popular argument in favor of advertising is that it provides financial support for newspapers, radio, and television. In reply, critics remark that advertiser-supported radio and television programming is of low quality because it appeals to those who are easily influenced by advertising. They also charge that advertiser-supported newspapers and magazines are too reluctant to criticize products of firms that are actual or potential advertisers.

Table 1 Advertising Expenditures (billions $)

	National	Local	Total	% of GDP
1940	1.2	0.9	2.1	2.11
1950	3.3	2.4	5.7	1.98
1960	7.3	4.7	12.0	2.28
1970	11.4	8.2	19.6	1.89
1980	29.8	23.7	53.5	1.91
1990	73.6	56.3	130.0	2.24
2000	151.7	95.8	247.5	2.52
2002	145.7	91.8	237.4	2.27

Sources: Statistical Abstract of the United States, 1987, 537; and 2002, 438 and 772; U.S. Historical Statistics, Colonial Times to 1970, Series T444; and *Advertising Age*, May 6, 1991, p. 16. Numbers may not add up due to rounding.

While aggregate expenditures on advertising have remained steady as a percentage of GDP, the intensity of spending varies greatly across firms and industries (see Table 2). Many inexpensive consumer items, such as over-the-counter drugs, cosmetics, and razor blades, are heavily advertised. Advertising-to-sales ratios also are high for food products such as soft drinks, breakfast cereals, and beer. And there is remarkable stability in this pattern from country to country. A type of product that is heavily advertised in the United States tends to be heavily advertised in Europe, as well. Even within an industry, however, some firms will advertise more than others. Among pharmaceutical manufacturers, for example, Merck and Bayer spend less than 5 percent of sales on advertising, while Pfizer spends in excess of 12 percent.

The differences among industries, while stable, are deceptive. For example, automakers typically spend only 1 to 2 percent of sales on advertising, but their products are heavily promoted by the sales staffs in dealer showrooms. Similarly, industrial products are not heavily advertised because trade fairs and point-of-sale promotion are often more cost-effective than advertising. Products with relatively few customers may not be advertised at all or advertised solely in specialized publications.

Economic Function

While discussions of advertising often emphasize persuasion and the creation of brand loyalty, economists tend to emphasize other, perhaps more important, functions. The rise of the self-service store, for example, was aided by

Table 2 Advertising-to-Sales Ratios,
Top Twenty Industries, 2003

Loan brokers	38.4
Health services	32.5
Distilled and blended liquor	14.9
Miscellaneous publishing	12.9
Sugar and confectionery products	11.7
Soap, detergent, and toilet preparations	11.3
Amusement parks	10.7
Food and kindred products	10.2
Special cleaning and polishing preparations	9.7
Knitting mills	9.6
Television broadcast stations	9.3
Beverages	9.2
Water transportation	8.8
Malt beverages	8.5
Heating equipment and plumbing fixtures	8.4
Motion picture and video tape production	8.4
Rubber and plastic footwear	8.4
Games, toys, children's vehicles, except dolls	8.2
Dolls and stuffed toys	7.8
Cable and other pay TV services	7.7

Source: Advertising Age, online at: http://www.adage.com/page.cms
?pageId = 1013.

Note: Top twenty industries among the two hundred industries
spending the most on advertising.

consumer knowledge of branded goods. Before the advent of advertising, customers relied on knowledgeable shopkeepers for help in selecting products, which often were unbranded. Today, consumer familiarity with branded products is one factor making it possible for far fewer retail employees to serve the same number of customers.

Newly introduced products are typically advertised more heavily than established ones, as are products whose customers are constantly changing. For example, cosmetics, mouthwash, and toothpaste are marked by high rates of new product introductions because customers are willing to abandon existing products and try new ones. Viewed this way, consumer demand generates new products and the advertising that accompanies them, not the other way around.

In a similar vein, "noninformative," or image, advertising can be usefully thought of as something that customers demand along with the product. Customers often want to see themselves as athletic, adventuresome, or spontaneous, and vendors of beer, cars, and cell phones bundle the image and the physical product. When some custom-

ers are unwilling to pay for image, producers that choose not to advertise can supply them with a cheaper product. Often, the same manufacturer will respond to these differences in customer demands by producing both a high-priced, labeled, heavily advertised version of a product and a second, low-priced line as an unadvertised house brand or generic product. In baked goods, canned goods, and dairy products, for example, some manufacturers sell one version under their own nationally known label and another slightly different version under a particular grocery chain's private label.

Advertising messages obviously can be used to mislead, but a heavily advertised brand name limits the scope for deception and poor quality. A firm with a well-known brand suffers serious damage to an image that it has paid dearly to establish when a defective product reaches the consumer (see BRAND NAMES). Interestingly, even under central planning, officials in the Soviet Union encouraged the use of brand names and trademarks in order to monitor which factories produced defective merchandise and to allow consumers to inform themselves about products available from various sources.

Monopoly

Early opinion among many economists was summarized by Henry Simons, who wrote in 1948 that "a major barrier to really competitive enterprise and efficient service to consumers is to be found in advertising—in national advertising especially, and in sales organizations which cover great national and regional areas." Economic debate in the 1950s focused on whether advertising promotes monopoly by creating a "barrier to entry." Heavy advertising of existing brands, many economists thought, might make consumers less likely to try new brands, thus raising the cost of entry for newcomers. Other economists speculated that advertising makes consumers less sensitive to price, allowing firms that advertise to raise their prices above competitive levels.

Economic researchers addressed this issue by examining whether industries marked by heavy advertising were also more concentrated (see INDUSTRIAL CONCENTRATION) or had higher profits. The correlation between advertising intensity and industry concentration turned out to be very low and varied from sample to sample, and it is largely ignored today. What is more, early research found that high levels of advertising in an industry were associated with unstable market shares, consistent with the idea that advertising promoted competition rather than monopoly.

The idea that advertising creates monopoly was supported by studies that found high rates of return in industries with high levels of advertising. As other economists pointed out, however, the accounting rates of return used to measure profits do not treat advertising as an asset. Consequently, measured rates of return—income divided by measured assets—will often overstate profit rates for firms and industries with heavy advertising. Subsequent work showed that when attention is restricted to industries with relatively small bias in the accounting numbers, the correlation between rates of return and amount of advertising disappears. A lucky by-product of the advertising-and-profits dispute were studies that estimated depreciation rates of advertising—the rates at which advertising loses its effect. Typically, estimated rates are about 33 percent per year, though some authors have found rates as low as 5 percent.

Contrary to the monopoly explanation (and to the assertion that advertising is a wasteful expense), advertising often lowers prices. In a classic study of advertising restrictions on optometrists, Lee Benham found that eyeglass prices were twenty dollars higher (in 1963 dollars) in states banning advertising than in those that did not. Bans on price advertising, but not on other kinds of advertising, resulted in prices nearly as low as in the states without any restrictions at all. Benham argued that advertising allows high-volume, low-cost retailers to communicate effectively with potential customers, even if they cannot mention price explicitly.

The importance of price advertising, however, apparently varies with the way consumers typically obtain price information and make purchase decisions. An unpublished study by Al Ehrbar found gasoline prices to be significantly higher (about 6 percent, net of excise taxes) in communities that prohibited large price signs in gas stations.

Regulation

In the past, many professionals such as doctors, lawyers, and pharmacists succeeded in getting state legislatures to implement complete or partial bans on advertising in their professions, preventing either all advertising or advertising of prices. In recent decades court decisions have overturned these restrictions. At the federal level, the U.S. Federal Trade Commission has jurisdiction over advertising by virtue of its ability to regulate "deceptive" acts or practices. It can issue cease-and-desist orders, require corrective advertising, and mandate disclosure of certain information in ads.

The regulation of cigarette advertising has been particularly controversial. The Federal Trade Commission has required cigarette manufacturers to disclose tar and nicotine content since 1970, although it had prohibited precisely the same disclosure before that. Beginning January 1, 1971,

the federal government also banned all radio and television advertising of cigarettes. While overall cigarette advertising expenditures dropped by more than 20 percent, per capita cigarette consumption remained unchanged for many years. Critics of the regulations maintain that it was the growing evidence of the harmful effects of smoking, rather than the reduction in advertising, that ultimately led to the smaller percentage of smokers in society. The critics also contend that the advertising ban may have slowed the rate at which low-tar cigarettes were used.

Governmental Advertising

Governments have funded or mandated advertising to reduce harmful behaviors such as smoking, drunk driving, and drug use. Researchers have not devoted much attention to such efforts. One exception is California's Proposition 99, passed in 1988, which increased taxes on cigarettes from ten to thirty-five cents per package and earmarked 20 percent for educational programs, including an antismoking campaign. The one study that looked at this measure found that increased expenditures on antismoking measures were associated with declines in per capita cigarette sales.

About the Author

George Bittlingmayer is the Wagnon Distinguished Professor of Finance at the University of Kansas School of Business. He was previously an economist with the Federal Trade Commission.

Further Reading

Becker, Gary S., and Kevin M. Murphy. "A Simple Theory of Advertising as Good or Bad." *Quarterly Journal of Economics* 108 (November 1993): 941–964.

Benham, Lee. "The Effect of Advertising on the Price of Eyeglasses." *Journal of Law and Economics* 15 (October 1972): 337–352.

Borden, Neil H. *The Economic Effects of Advertising*. Chicago: Irwin, 1942.

Chaloupka, Frank J. "Public Policies and Private Anti-health Behavior." *American Economic Review* 85 (May 1995): 45–49.

Comanor, William S., and Thomas A. Wilson. "Advertising and Competition: A Survey." *Journal of Economic Literature* 17 (June 1979): 453–476.

Ekelund, Robert B. Jr., and David S. Saurman. *Advertising and the Market Process*. San Francisco: Pacific Research Institute for Public Policy, 1988.

Hu, The-Wei, Hai-Yen Sung, and Theodore E. Keeler. "The State Antismoking Campaign and the Industry Response: The Effects of Advertising on Cigarette Consumption in California." *American Economic Review* 85 (May 1995): 85–90.

4 | *Daniel A. Sumner*

Landes, Elisabeth M., and Andrew M. Rosenfield. "The Durability of Advertising Revisited." *Journal of Industrial Economics* 42 (September 1994): 263–276.

Rubin, Paul. "Regulation of Information and Advertising." In Barry Keating, ed., *A Companion to the Economics of Regulation*. London: Blackwell, 2004.

Schmalensee, Richard. *The Economics of Advertising.* Amsterdam: North-Holland, 1972.

Telser, Lester. "Advertising and Competition." *Journal of Political Economy* 72 (December 1964): 537–562.

———. "Some Aspects of the Economics of Advertising." *Journal of Business* 41 (April 1968): 166–173.

Agricultural Subsidy Programs

Daniel A. Sumner

Government intervention in food and fiber commodity markets began long ago. The classic case of farm subsidy through trade barriers is the English Corn Laws, which for centuries regulated the import and export of grain in Great Britain and Ireland. They were repealed in 1846. Modern agricultural subsidy programs in the United States began with the New Deal and the Agricultural Adjustment Act of 1933. With trade barriers already in place for agricultural commodities and everything else, this law gave the government the power to set minimum prices and included government stock acquisition, land idling, and schemes to cut supplies by destroying livestock. Land idling and livestock destruction were sometimes mandatory and sometimes induced by compensation (Benedict 1953).

Since the early 1930s, governments of wealthier countries around the world have used a dizzying array of schemes to support and subsidize farmers. In poor countries, where a large fraction of the population is engaged in farming, governments have tended to tax and regulate agriculture. As incomes grew and the population on farms dwindled in such countries as South Korea and Taiwan, those countries' governments shifted from penalizing farmers to subsidizing them and protecting them from imports. These countries, along with Japan, now have among the highest subsidy and protection rates in the world. Forms of farm support also differ by country and commodity, and different forms have different impacts on agriculture and the rest of the economy. This article reviews some of the major support forms and outlines their impacts. Although I often use the terms "support" and "subsidy" interchangeably, much government support of agriculture is not in the form of direct subsidy for farmer incomes or direct subsidy for production, but is indirect.

Economists have criticized farm subsidies on several counts. First, farm subsidies typically transfer income from consumers and taxpayers to relatively wealthy farmland owners and farm operators. Second, they impose net losses on society, often called deadweight losses, and have no clear broad social benefit (Alston and James 2002). Third, they impede movements toward more open international trade in commodities and thus impose net costs on the global economy (Johnson 1991; Sumner 2003).

Supporters of farm subsidies have argued that such programs stabilize agricultural commodity markets, aid low-income farmers, raise unduly low returns to farm investments, aid rural development, compensate for monopoly in farm input supply and farm marketing industries, help ensure national food security, offset farm subsidies provided by other countries, and provide various other services. However, economists who have tried to substantiate any of these benefits have been unable to do so (Gardner 1992; Johnson 1991; Wright 1995).

The U.S. government heavily subsidizes grains, oilseeds, cotton, sugar, and dairy products. Most other agriculture—including beef, pork, poultry, hay, fruits, tree nuts, and vegetables (accounting for about half of the total value of production)—receives only minimal government support. U.S. farm programs have cost about $20 billion per year in government budget outlays in recent years. But budget costs are not a particularly useful measure of the degree of support or subsidy. Some subsidy programs, such as import tariffs, actually generate tax revenue for the government but also impose costs on consumers that exceed the government's revenue gain. According to Organization for Economic Cooperation and Development (OECD) figures, the average rate of "producer support estimate" for the heavily supported commodities in the United States ranges from about 55 percent of the value of production for sugar to about 22 percent for oilseeds. For the less-supported commodities the rate is typically below 5 percent.

Among OECD members (a group of high-income countries), "producer support estimate" rates average about 31 percent of total revenue for the main grain, oilseed, sugar, and livestock products. These estimates aggregate into a single index a large range of government programs, including price supports and trade barriers, that transfer benefits to farm producers and landlords. This index measures the size of the transfer in money terms but does not attempt to assess the programs' effects on production or net income. The highest average rates of support are for rice (about 80 percent), where most of the support derives from trade barriers and direct payments. Support to farmers by Japan's and Korea's governments is a large part of the total world subsidy for rice. The highest national average support equivalent rates, across all major commodities, are offered in Norway, Switzerland, and Iceland, with average subsidies of about 65–75 percent of the value of production, and in Japan and Korea, with support rates of 60–65 percent. The lowest subsidy rates (less than 4 percent) are found in Australia and New Zealand. The average support rate in the European Union is about 35 percent of the value of production.

The forms of subsidy vary by country and commodity as well. The main forms of subsidy include: (1) direct payments to farmers and landlords; (2) price supports implemented with government purchases and storage; (3) regulations that set minimum prices by location, end use, or some other characteristic; (4) subsidies for such items as crop insurance, disaster response, credit, marketing, and irrigation water; (5) export subsidies; and (6) import barriers in the form of quotas, tariffs, or regulations. Often, supply control programs such as land-idling requirements, production quotas, or similar schemes accompany price supports or other programs. In addition, the governments of most wealthier nations provide aid for agricultural research and development, promotion, and some agricultural and rural infrastructure.

The impacts of the subsidies depend on their form. Farm subsidy programs typically transfer income from consumers and taxpayers to farm operators, especially to owners of farmland and other resources used in farm production. Evidence shows clearly, for example, that farm subsidies increase the rental rate on land to which rights to receive those payments are attached. In other words, subsidies to farming are often simply subsidies to landowners. For government-created assets such as production or marketing quotas or allotments, the market value is due entirely to government program benefits. When quotas limit production, commodity prices rise and raise the value of production rights assigned to quota owners. Such quota programs have often continued for decades (six decades in the case of the U.S. tobacco quota and more than three decades in the case of the California and Canadian dairy quotas). Interestingly, though, the asset price of the marketable quota is typically only four times the annual gain from owning the quota (Johnson 1991). This means that quota owners evidently are not confident that the program benefits will continue.

Farm subsidies stimulate additional production of government-favored commodities by raising incentives to use scarce land and farmer talent on some products rather than on others. The specifics of the government program determine the degree of production stimulus; real farm programs are usually much more complex than the per unit production subsidies or price supports described in textbooks. Eliminating a subsidy for just one crop would cause production of that crop to fall much more than if all crop subsidies were eliminated simultaneously. Because most farmland would remain in use, economists would expect relatively small adjustments in total U.S. agricultural production if all farm subsidies were eliminated together, although some shifts in the mix among commodities would occur.

Partly to limit the increased production caused by subsidies, the United States once required farmers to idle a part of their farmland in return for the subsidy. That practice is still used in the European Union and Japan. Recently, the United States has used three complex payment schemes simultaneously for grains, oilseeds, and cotton. First, farmers receive "direct payments," which are independent of current market prices and are based primarily on a farm's history of production of a specific supported crop. There are a number of restrictions on the use of the land that receives these payments, but farmers receive the payments even if they plant crops other than the payment crop or leave the land idle. Second, farmers receive "countercyclical payments," which are tied, inversely, to the market price of the payment crop, but which also allow planting flexibility. These two forms of payment do not require a farmer to plant a specific crop currently. However, because the continuation or increase of payments may depend on current production of that crop, they do provide an incentive to overproduce (Sumner 2003). The third form of subsidy payments, "marketing loan benefits," are inversely proportional to current market prices and are tied directly to current production of a specific crop. It is difficult to measure the degree of production inducement tied to this complex array of payments; nonetheless, economists agree that without them the production of subsidized crops would decline.

Among the most controversial aspects of farm subsidy programs in recent decades have been their impacts on international trade. D. Gale Johnson (1950) raised the issue more than fifty years ago. As globalization has increased, farm trade barriers and subsidies that block pursuit of agricultural comparative advantage have become more disruptive to normal trade relations and trade negotiations.

Farm subsidy programs, which are used by most wealthy countries, have made multilateral trade negotiations more complex and have threatened broad-based market opening. In the early years of the General Agreement on Tariffs and Trade (GATT) (the 1940s and early 1950s), the U.S. government placed its farm subsidy programs out of reach of trade negotiations and thereby thwarted liberalization in agriculture for three decades. In the 1980s, the U.S. government began to reduce the production stimulus of its own farm programs. In trade negotiations, it advocated freer trade in agriculture and stated its willingness to eliminate its own import barriers and trade-distorting farm subsidies if other nations would do the same. European nations, Japan, and Korea resisted. Nevertheless, the GATT agreement of 1994, which created the World Trade Organization (WTO), began modest progress toward liberalization. U.S. farm subsidy legislation in 1996 was consistent with gradual reform of farm subsidies. With the passage of new and more distorting farm subsidy programs in 2002, however, the United States has been a less credible bargainer in WTO negotiations, and reductions in subsidies and trade barriers have been delayed.

After the 2002 Farm Bill in the United States and initiation of the Doha round of WTO negotiations, farm subsidies became a high-profile issue for many less-developed-country participants in trade negotiations. They pointed out that the price-depressing effects of wealthy countries' farm subsidies disadvantaged their farmers. U.S. cotton subsidies are a clear example. Some of the poorest countries in West Africa have traditionally been cotton exporters. In 2001 and 2002, they faced a world price of cotton ranging from thirty-five cents to forty-five cents per pound. Meanwhile, cotton growers in the United States, the world's largest exporter, received seventy cents or more per pound from the subsidies plus the market price. Economists have estimated that U.S. exports of cotton would have been substantially lower, and the world price of cotton 10 to 15 percent higher, if U.S. cotton subsidies had been unavailable during this period. Reducing farm subsidies in the United States and other rich countries would help poor cotton growers and other farmers in poor countries, and, moreover, would begin a process of relying more on trade rather than aid for economic growth. Taxpayers in rich countries would gain in two ways: by paying lower subsidies to their farmers and by paying lower subsidies to people in poor countries. The WTO is the key forum for nations to pursue reforms of global agricultural policies, but this forum may not be sufficient.

In wealthy nations such as the United States, farm subsidies, though large in total, are relatively minor political issues for most voters. The reason is that the cost per voter, in higher taxes and higher food prices, is small. For farmers, though, the gain per person is large. Hence, the domestic political stage is set for continued transfers from a broad constituency of voters, who pay little attention to the issue, to a much smaller group, for whom farm subsidies are vital to their short-run economic well-being. This dilemma is not unique to farm subsidies, and in fact is a central concern of political economy (see POLITICAL BEHAVIOR). Nonetheless, with widespread attention currently being drawn to the issue, more people are open to understanding the damaging effects of farm subsidies.

About the Author

Daniel A. Sumner is the Frank H. Buck Jr. Chair Professor in the Department of Agricultural and Resource Economics at the University of California, Davis, and the director of the University of California Agricultural Issues Center. He was previously the assistant secretary for economics at the U.S. Department of Agriculture.

Further Reading

Alston, Julian M., and Jennifer S. James. "The Incidence of Agricultural Policy." Chapter 33 in B. L. Gardner and G. C. Rausser, eds., *Handbook of Agricultural Economics*. Vol. 2. Amsterdam: Elsevier, 2002. Pp. 1689–1749.

Benedict, Murray R. *Farm Policies of the United States, 1790–1950: A Study of Their Origins and Development*. New York: Twentieth Century Fund, 1953.

Gardner, Bruce L. "Changing Economic Perspectives on the Farm Problem." *Journal of Economic Literature* 30 (March 1992): 62–101.

Johnson, D. Gale. *Agriculture and Trade: A Study of Inconsistent Policies*. New York: John Wiley and Son, 1950.

———. *World Agriculture in Disarray*. 2d ed. London: Macmillan, 1973. 1991.

Organization of Economic Cooperation and Development. *Agricultural Policies in OECD Countries: Monitoring and Evaluation*. Paris: OECD, 2003.

Sumner, Daniel A. "Implications of the USA Farm Bill of 2002 for Agricultural Trade and Trade Negotiations." *Australian Journal of Agricultural and Resource Economics* 47, no. 1 (2003): 117–140.

Wright, B. D. "Goals and Realities for Farm Policy." In D. A. Sumner, ed., *Agricultural Policy Reform in the United States*. Washington, D.C.: AEI Press, 1995. Pp. 9–44.

Airline Deregulation

Fred L. Smith Jr.
Braden Cox

The 1978 Airline Deregulation Act partially shifted control over air travel from the political to the market sphere. The Civil Aeronautics Board (CAB), which had previously controlled entry, exit, and the pricing of airline services, as well as intercarrier agreements, mergers, and consumer issues, was phased out under the CAB Sunset Act and expired officially on December 31, 1984. The economic liberalization of air travel was part of a series of "deregulation" moves based on the growing realization that a politically controlled economy served no continuing public interest. U.S. deregulation has been part of a greater global airline liberalization trend, especially in Asia, Latin America, and the European Union.

Network industries, which are critical to a modern economy, include air travel, railroads, electrical power, and telecommunications. The air travel sector is an example of a network industry involving both flows and a grid. The flows are the mobile system elements: the airplanes, the trains, the power, the messages, and so on. The grid is the infrastructure over which these flows move: the airports and air traffic control system, the tracks and stations, the wires and cables, the electromagnetic spectrum, and so on. Network efficiency depends critically on the close coordination of grid and flow operating and investment decisions.

Under CAB regulation, investment and operating decisions were highly constrained. CAB rules limiting routes and entry and controlling prices meant that airlines were limited to competing only on food, cabin crew quality, and frequency. As a result, both prices and frequency were high, and load factors—the percentage of the seats that were filled—were low. Indeed, in the early 1970s load factors were only about 50 percent. The air transport market today is remarkably different. Because airlines compete on price, fares are much lower. Many more people fly, allowing high frequency today also, but with much higher load factors—74 percent in 2003, for example.

Airline deregulation was a monumental event. Its effects are still being felt today, as low-cost carriers (LCCs) challenge the "legacy" airlines that were in existence before deregulation (American, United, Continental, Northwest, US Air, and Delta). Indeed, the airline industry is experiencing a paradigm shift that reflects the ongoing effects of deregulation. Although deregulation affected the flows of air travel, the infrastructure grid remains subject to government control and economic distortions. Thus, airlines were only partially deregulated.

Benefits of Partial Deregulation

Even the partial freeing of the air travel sector has had overwhelmingly positive results. Air travel has dramatically increased and prices have fallen. After deregulation, airlines reconfigured their routes and equipment, making possible improvements in capacity utilization. These efficiency effects democratized air travel, making it more accessible to the general public.

Airfares, when adjusted for inflation, have fallen 25 percent since 1991, and, according to Clifford Winston and Steven Morrison of the Brookings Institution, are 22 percent lower than they would have been had regulation continued (Morrison and Winston 2000). Since passenger deregulation in 1978, airline prices have fallen 44.9 percent in real terms according to the Air Transport Association. Robert Crandall and Jerry Ellig (1997) estimated that when figures are adjusted for changes in quality and amenities, passengers save $19.4 billion dollars per year from airline deregulation. These savings have been passed on to 80 percent of passengers accounting for 85 percent of passenger miles. The real benefits of airline deregulation are being felt today as never before, with LCCs increasingly gaining market share.

The dollar savings are a direct result of allowing airlines the freedom to innovate in routes and pricing. After deregulation, the airlines quickly moved to a hub-and-spoke system, whereby an airline selected some airport (the hub) as the destination point for flights from a number of origination cities (the spokes). Because the size of the planes used varied according to the travel on that spoke, and since hubs allowed passenger travel to be consolidated in "transfer stations," capacity utilization ("load factors") increased, allowing fare reduction. The hub-and-spoke model survives among the legacy carriers, but the LCCs—now 30 percent of the market—typically fly point to point. The network hubs model offers consumers more convenience for routes, but point-to-point routes have proven less costly for airlines to implement. Over time, the legacy carriers and the LCCs will likely use some combination of point-to-point and network hubs to capture both economies of scope and pricing advantages.

The rigid fares of the regulatory era have given way to today's competitive price market. After deregulation, the airlines created highly complex pricing models that include the service quality/price sensitivity of various air travelers and offer differential fare/service quality packages designed for each. The new LCCs, however, have far simpler price structures—the product of consumers' (especially business travelers') demand for low prices, increased price transparency from online Web sites, and decreased reliance on travel agencies.

As prices have decreased, air travel has exploded. The total number of passengers that fly annually has more than doubled since 1978. Travelers now have more convenient travel options with greater flight frequency and more nonstop flights. Fewer passengers must change airlines to make a connection, resulting in better travel coordination and higher customer satisfaction.

Industry Problems after Deregulation

Although the gains of economic liberalization have been substantial, fundamental problems plague the industry. Some of these problems are transitional, the massive adjustments required by the end of a half century of strict regulation. The regulated airline monopolies received returns on capital that were supposed to be "reasonable" (comparable to what a company might expect to receive in a competitive market), but these returns factored in high costs that often would not exist in a competitive market. For example, the airlines' unionized workforce, established and strengthened under regulation and held in place by the Railway Labor Act, gained generous salaries and inefficient work rules compared with what would be expected in a competitive market. Problems remain in today's market, especially with the legacy airlines.

Health of the Industry

The airlines have not found it easy to maintain profitability. The industry as a whole was profitable through most of the economic boom of the 1990s. As the national economy slowed in 2000, so did profitability for the legacy airlines. Consumers became more price-sensitive and gravitated toward the lower-cost carriers. High labor costs and the network hub business model hurt legacy airlines' competitiveness. Hub-and-spoke systems decreased unit costs but created high fixed costs that required larger terminals, investments in information technology systems, and intricate revenue management systems. The LCCs have thus far successfully competed on price due to lower hourly employee wages, higher productivity, and no pension deficits. It remains to be seen whether the LCC cost and labor structures will change over time.

The Air Transport Association reports that the U.S. airline industry experienced net losses of $23.2 billion from 2001 through 2003, though the LCCs largely remained profitable. While the September 11, 2001, terrorist attack and its aftermath are a major factor in the industry's hardships, they only accelerated an already developing trend within the industry. The industry was experiencing net operating losses for many reasons, including the mild recession, severe acute respiratory syndrome (SARS), and the increase in LCC services and the decline in business fares relied on by legacy carriers. Higher fuel prices, residual labor union problems, fears of terrorism, and the intrusive measures that government now uses to clear travelers through security checkpoints are further drags on the industry.

Remaining Domestic Economic Controls

As a form of regulation, antitrust laws inhibit post-deregulation restructuring efforts, making it harder to bring salaries and work rules into line with the realities of a competitive marketplace. The antitrust regulatory laws inhibit the restructuring of corporations and block needed consolidation; the antitrust authorities view with suspicion ef-

forts to retain higher prices. Historically, the CAB had antitrust jurisdiction over airline mergers. When Congress disbanded the CAB in 1985, it temporarily transferred merger review authority to the Department of Transportation (DOT). In 1989, the Justice Department assumed merger review jurisdiction from the DOT that, when combined with its antitrust authority under the Sherman Act, makes it the primary antitrust regulator of the airline industry.

The Justice Department has contested past merger proposals, including Northwest's attempt to gain a controlling interest in Continental and the merger of United Airlines and US Airways. Antitrust law also applies to international alliances, arrangements that attempt to ameliorate restrictive foreign ownership and competition laws. While labor contracts, airport asset management, and other business practices are themselves high barriers to restructuring, these difficulties are magnified by antitrust regulatory hurdles. Cabotage restrictions, discussed below, also limit competition.

Reservation Systems

During the regulatory era, rates were determined politically and changed infrequently. The CAB had to approve every fare, limiting the airlines' ability to react to demand changes and to experiment with discount fares. After deregulation, airlines were free to set prices and to change them frequently. That was possible only because the airlines had earlier created computer reservation systems (CRSs) capable of keeping track of the massive inventory of seats on flights over a several-month period.

The early CRSs allowed the travel agent to designate an origin-destination pair and call up all available flights. The computer screen could show only a limited number of flights at one time, of course; thus, some rule was essential to rank-order the flights shown. CRSs were available only to travel agents and, beginning in 1984, were highly regulated to ensure open access to airlines that had not developed their own CRS system. The DOT regulations restricted private agreements for guaranteeing access. However, the growth of Internet travel sites and direct access to airline Web sites created new forms of competition to the airline reservation systems. Therefore, the DOT allowed the CRS regulations to expire in 2004.

Problems with Political Control of the Grid

A network can be efficient only if the flows and the grid interact smoothly. The massive expansion of air travel should have resulted in comparable expansions—either in the physical infrastructure or in more sophisticated grid management. Government management of the air travel grid has resulted in political compromises that cause friction with the smooth flow across the grid. Flight delays are increasing due to a lack of aviation infrastructure and the failure to allocate air capacity efficiently. The Air Transport Association estimates that delays cost airlines and passengers more than five billion dollars per year due to the increased costs for aircraft operation and ground personnel and loss of passengers' time. The FAA predicts that the number of passengers will increase by 60 percent and that cargo volume will double by 2010.

Airports

Airport construction and expansion face almost insurmountable political and regulatory hurdles. The number of federal requirements associated with airport finances has grown considerably in recent years and is tied to the awarding of grants from the federal Airport Improvement Program (AIP). Since 1978, only one major airport has been constructed (in Denver), and only a few runways have been added at congested airports. Airport construction faces significant nonpolitical barriers, such as vocal "not in my back yard" (NIMBY) opposition and environmental noise and emissions considerations. Federal law restricts the fees airports charge air carriers to amounts that are "fair and reasonable." These fee restrictions, although promoted as a way to provide nondiscriminatory access to all aircraft, limit an airport's ability to recover costs for air carriers' use of airfield and terminal facilities. Allowing airports more flexibility to price takeoffs and landings based on supply and demand would also help ease congestion at overburdened airports.

Air Traffic Control

Air traffic control involves the allocation of capacity and has a complex history of government management. Unfortunately, the Federal Aviation Administration (FAA), which manages air traffic control, made bad upgrading decisions. The advanced system funded by the FAA was more than a decade late and never performed as hoped. The result was that the airline expansion was not met by an expanded grid, and congestion occurred.

Better technology for air traffic control will help efficient navigation and routings. Global Positioning System (GPS) navigation technology holds great promise for more precise flight paths, allowing for increased airplane traffic. Ultimately, however, a privately managed system that allows for better coordination of airline investment and operation decisions will be necessary to ease congestion. Air traffic control operation is a business function distinct from the regulation of air traffic safety. Using pricing mechanisms to allocate the scarce resource of air traffic capacity would reduce congestion and more efficiently allocate resources.

Implementing cost-based structures by privatizing air traffic control is a controversial and politically daunting issue in the United States, but twenty-nine nations—including Canada—have already separated their traffic systems from their regulating agency. Air traffic control privatization will likely be driven by the decreasing ability of the Airport and Airways Trust Fund to deliver the necessary financial support.

Currently, the FAA rations flights by delay on a first-come, first-served basis—a system that creates overcrowding during peak hours. A system based on pricing at rates determined by voluntary contractual arrangements of market participants, not government regulators, would reduce this overcrowding. One of the results would be the use of "congestion pricing," such as rush hour surcharges or early bird discounts.

Airport Access

FAA rules that limit the number of hourly takeoffs and landings—called "slot" controls—were adopted in 1968 as a temporary measure to deal with congestion and delays at major airports. These artificial capacity limitations—known as the high density rule—still exist at JFK, La-Guardia, and Reagan National. However, limiting supply through governmental fiat is a crude form of demand management. Allowing increased capacity and congestion pricing, and allowing major airports to use their slots to favor larger aircraft, would lead to better results.

Remaining International and Economic Rules

International Competition

"Open Skies" agreements are bilateral agreements between the United States and other countries to open the aviation market to foreign access and remove barriers to competition. They give airlines the right to operate air services from any point in the United States to any point in the other country, as well as to and from third countries. The United States has Open Skies agreements with more than sixty countries, including fifteen of the twenty-five European Union nations. Open Skies agreements have been successful at removing many of the barriers to competition and allowing airlines to have foreign partners, access to international routes to and from their home countries, and freedom from many traditional forms of economic regulation. A global industry would work better with a globally minded set of rules that would allow airlines from one country (or investors of any sort) to establish airlines in another country (the right of establishment) and to operate domestic services in the territory of another country (cabotage). However, these agreements still fail to approximate the freedoms that most industries have when competing in other global markets.

National Ownership

National ownership laws are an archaic barrier to a more competitive air travel sector. These rules seem to reflect a concern for national security, even though many industries as strategic as the airline industry do not have such restrictions.

Federal law restricts the percentage of foreign ownership in air transportation. Only U.S.-registered aircraft can transport passengers and freight domestically. Airline citizenship registration is limited to U.S. citizens or permanent residents, partnerships in which all partners are U.S. citizens, or corporations registered in the United States in which the chief executive officer and two-thirds of the directors are U.S. citizens and where U.S. citizens hold or control 75 percent of the capital stock. Only U.S. citizens are able to obtain a certificate of public convenience and necessity, a prerequisite for operation as a domestic carrier.

Additional Problems Resulting from the 9/11 Response

After 9/11, safety and security regulation responsibilities were given to the new Transportation Security Administration (TSA) within the Department of Homeland Security. Created just months after 9/11, the TSA is an outgrowth of the belief that only the government can be entrusted to perform certain duties, especially those related to security. No one has clearly established that a government whose employees are difficult to fire, even for incompetence, will do better than a private employer who can more easily fire incompetent workers.

In September 2001, Congress passed the Air Transportation Safety and System Stabilization Act, which authorized payments of up to five billion dollars in assistance to reimburse airlines for the postattack four-day shutdown of air traffic and attributable losses through the end of 2001. It also created and authorized the Air Transportation Stabilization Board (ATSB) to provide up to ten billion dollars in loan guarantees for airlines in need of emergency capital. While the ATSB risked the kind of mission creep that is inevitable in an industry subsidy program, the deadline for applications to the ATSB has passed. Of the ten billion dollars authorized by Congress for these loan guarantees, the board actually committed less than two billion.

Conclusion

Air travel is a network industry, but only its flow element—the airlines—is economically liberalized. The industry is still structurally adjusting to a more competitive situation and remains subject to a large number of regulations. The capital, work rules, and compensation practices of the airline industry still reflect almost fifty years of political protection and control.

We are finally seeing the kinds of internal restructuring among airlines that was expected from deregulation. Yet, government still has much to do to ensure that the airline market will thrive in the future. The FAA is a command-and-control government agency ill-suited to providing air traffic control services to a dynamic industry. Land slots and airport space should be allocated using market prices instead of through administrative fiat. International competition will increase, and rules regarding national ownership need to change accordingly.

If the government deregulates the grid and transitions toward a market solution, the benefits of flow deregulation will increase, and costs for air travelers will fall even more.

About the Authors

Fred L. Smith Jr. is the president of, and Braden Cox is the technology counsel with, Competitive Enterprise Institute, a free-market public policy group based in Washington, D.C.

Further Reading

Bailey, Elizabeth E. "Airline Deregulation Confronting the Paradoxes." *Regulation: The Cato Review of Business and Government* 15, no. 3. Available online at: http://www.cato.org/pubs/regulation/regv15n3/reg15n3-bailey.html.

Button, Kenneth, and Roger Stough. *Air Transport Networks: Theory and Policy Implications.* Northampton, Mass.: Edward Elgar, 2000.

Crandall, Robert, and Jerry Ellig. *Economic Deregulation and Customer Choice.* Fairfax, Va.: Center for Market Processes, George Mason University, 1997. Available online at: http://www.mercatus.org/repository/docLib/MC_RSP_RP-Dregulation_970101.pdf.

Doganis, Rigas. *The Airport Business.* New York: Routledge, 1992.

Havel, Brian F. *In Search of Open Skies: Law and Policy for a New Era in International Aviation. A Comparative Study of Airline Deregulation in the United States and the European Union.* Boston: Kluwer Law International, 1997.

Morrison, Steven A., and Clifford Winston. "The Remaining Role for Government Policy in the Deregulated Airline Industry." In Sam Peltzman and Clifford Winston, eds., *Deregulation of Network Industries: What's Next?* Washington, D.C.: AEI Brookings Joint Center for Regulatory Studies, 2000.

Poole, Robert W. Jr., and Viggo Butler. *Airline Deregulation: The Unfinished Revolution.* December 1998. Available online at: http://cei.org/pdf/1451.pdf.

———. *How to Commercialize Air Traffic Control.* Policy Study No. 278. Los Angeles: Reason Public Policy Institute, 2001.

U.S. GAO. *Airline Deregulation: Changes in Airfares, Service, and Safety at Small, Medium-Sized, and Large Communities.* April 1996. Report online at: http://www.gao.gov/archive/1996/rc96079.pdf.

Antitrust

Fred McChesney

Origins

Before 1890, the only "antitrust" law was the common law. Contracts that allegedly restrained trade (e.g., price-fixing agreements) often were not legally enforceable, but they did not subject the parties to any legal sanctions, either. Nor were monopolies illegal. Economists generally believe that monopolies and other restraints of trade are bad because they usually reduce total output, and therefore the overall economic well-being for producers and consumers (see MONOPOLY). Indeed, the term "restraint of trade" indicates exactly why economists dislike monopolies and cartels. But the law itself did not penalize monopolies. The Sherman Act of 1890 changed all that by outlawing cartelization (every "contract, combination . . . or conspiracy" that was "in restraint of trade") and monopolization (including attempts to monopolize).

The Sherman Act defines neither the practices that constitute restraints of trade nor monopolization. The second important antitrust statute, the Clayton Act, passed in 1914, is somewhat more specific. It outlaws, for example, certain types of price discrimination (charging different prices to different buyers), "tying" (making someone who wants to buy good A buy good B as well), and mergers—but only when the effects of these practices "may be substantially to lessen competition or to tend to create a monopoly." The Clayton Act also authorizes private antitrust suits and triple damages, and exempts labor organizations from the antitrust laws.

Economists did not lobby for, or even support, the antitrust statutes. Rather, the passage of such laws is generally ascribed to the influence of populist "muckrakers" such as Ida Tarbell, who frequently decried the supposed ability of emerging corporate giants ("the trusts") to increase prices and exploit customers by reducing production. One reason most economists were indifferent to the law was their belief that any higher prices achieved by the supposed anticompetitive acts were more than outweighed by the price-reducing effects of greater operating efficiency and lower costs. Interestingly, Tarbell herself conceded, as did "trust-buster" Teddy Roosevelt, that the trusts might be more efficient producers.

Only recently have economists looked at the empirical evidence (what has happened in the real world) to see whether the antitrust laws were needed. The popular view that cartels and monopolies were rampant at the turn of the century now seems incorrect to most economists. Thomas DiLorenzo (1985) has shown that the trusts against which the Sherman Act supposedly was directed were, in fact, expanding output many times faster than overall production was increasing nationwide; likewise, the trusts' prices were falling faster than those of all enterprises nationally. In other words, the trusts were doing exactly the opposite of what economic theory says a monopoly or cartel must do to reap monopoly profits.

Anticompetitive Practices

In referring to contracts "in restraint of trade," or to arrangements whose effects "may be substantially to lessen competition or to tend to create a monopoly," the principal antitrust statutes are relatively vague. There is little statutory guidance for distinguishing benign from malign practices. Thus, judges have been left to decide which practices run afoul of the antitrust laws.

An important judicial question has been whether a practice should be treated as "per se illegal" (i.e., devoid of redeeming justification, and thus automatically outlawed) or whether it should be judged by a "rule of reason" (its legality depends on how it is used and on its effects in particular situations).

To answer such questions, judges sometimes have turned to economists for guidance. In the early years of antitrust, though, economists were of little help. They had not extensively analyzed arrangements such as tying, information sharing, resale price maintenance, and other commercial practices challenged in antitrust suits. But as the cases exposed areas of economic ignorance or confusion about different commercial arrangements, economists turned to solving the various puzzles.

Indeed, analyzing the efficiency rationale for practices attacked in antitrust litigation has dominated the intellectual agenda of economists who study what is called industrial organization. Initially, economists concluded that unfamiliar commercial arrangements that were not explicable in a model of perfect competition must be anticompetitive. In the past forty years, however, economic evaluations of various practices have changed. Economists now see that the perfect competition model relies on assumptions—such as everyone having perfect information and zero transaction costs—that are inappropriate for analyzing real-world production and distribution problems.

The use of more sophisticated assumptions in their models has led economists to conclude that many practices previously deemed suspect are not typically anticompetitive. This change in evaluations has been reflected in the courts. Per se liability has increasingly been superseded by rule-of-reason analysis reflecting the procompetitive potential of a given practice. Under the rule of reason, courts have become increasingly sophisticated in analyzing information and transaction costs and the ways that contested commercial practices can reduce them. Economists and judges alike are more sophisticated in several important areas.

Vertical Contracts
Most antitrust practitioners once believed that vertical mergers (i.e., one company acquiring another that is either a supplier or a customer) reduced competition. Today, most antitrust experts believe that vertical integration usually is not anticompetitive.

Progress in this area began in the 1950s with work by Aaron Director and the Antitrust Project at the University of Chicago. Robert Bork, a scholar involved with this project (and later the federal judge whose unsuccessful nomination to the U.S. Supreme Court caused much controversy), showed that if firm A has monopoly power, vertically integrating with firm B (or acquiring B) does not increase A's monopoly power in its own industry. Nor does it give A monopoly power in B's industry if that industry was competitive in the first place.

Lester Telser, also of the University of Chicago, showed in a famous 1960 article that manufacturers used resale price maintenance ("fair trade") not to create monopoly at the retail level, but to stimulate nonprice competition among retailers. Since retailers operating under fair trade agreements could not compete by cutting price, noted Telser, they instead competed by demonstrating the product to uninformed buyers. If the product is a sophisticated one that requires explaining to prospective buyers, resale price maintenance can be a rational—and competitive—action by a manufacturer. The same rationale can account for manufacturers' use of exclusive sales territories. This new knowledge about vertical contracts has had a large impact on judicial antitrust rulings.

Horizontal Contracts
Changes in the assessment of horizontal contracts (agreements among competing sellers in the same industry) have come more slowly. Economists remain almost unanimous in condemning all horizontal price-fixing. Many, however (e.g., Donald Dewey), have indicated that price-fixing may actually be procompetitive in some situations, a conclusion bolstered by Michael Sproul's empirical finding that in industries where the government successfully sues against price-fixing, prices increase, rather than decrease, after the suit. At a minimum, Peter Asch and Joseph Seneca have shown empirically, price-fixers have not

earned higher than normal profits. Other practices that some people believed made it easier for competitors to fix prices have been shown to have procompetitive explanations. Sharing of information among competitors, for example, may not necessarily be a prelude to price-fixing; it can instead have an independent efficiency rationale.

Perhaps the most important change in economists' understanding has occurred in the area of mergers. Particularly with the work of Joe Bain and George Stigler in the 1950s, economists (and courts) inferred a lack of competition in markets simply from the fact that an industry had a high four-firm concentration ratio (the percentage of sales accounted for by the four largest firms in the industry). But later work by economists such as Yale Brozen and Harold Demsetz demonstrated that correlations between concentration and profits either were transitory or were due more to superior efficiency than to anticompetitive conduct. Their work followed that of Oliver Williamson, who showed that even if merger caused a large increase in monopoly power, it would be efficient if it produced only slight cost reductions. As a result of this new evidence and new thinking, economists and judges no longer assume that concentration alone indicates monopoly. The various versions of the Department of Justice/Federal Trade Commission Merger Guidelines promulgated in the 1980s and revised in the 1990s have deemphasized concentration as a factor inviting government challenge of a merger.

Nonmerger Monopolization
Perhaps the most publicized monopolization case of recent years is the government's case against Microsoft, which (see Liebowitz and Margolis 2001) rested on questionable empirical claims and resulted ultimately in victory for Microsoft on most of the government's allegations. The failure of the government's case reflects a general recent decline in the importance of monopolization cases. Worries about monopoly have progressively diminished with the realization that various practices traditionally thought to be monopolizing devices (including vertical contracts, as discussed above) actually have procompetitive explanations. Likewise, belief in the efficacy of predatory pricing—cutting price below cost—as a monopolization device has diminished. Work begun by John McGee in the late 1950s (also an outgrowth of the Chicago Antitrust Project) showed that firms are highly unlikely to use predatory pricing to create monopoly. That work is reflected in several recent Supreme Court opinions, such as that in *Matsushita Electric Industrial Co. v. Zenith Radio Corp.*, where the Court wrote, "There is a consensus among commentators that predatory pricing schemes are rarely tried, and even more rarely successful."

As older theories of monopolization have died, newer

ones have been hatched. In the 1980s, economists began to lay out new monopolization models based on strategic behavior, often relying on game-theory constructs. They postulated that companies could monopolize markets by raising rivals' costs (sometimes called "cost predation"). For example, if firm A competes with firm B and supplies inputs to both itself and to B, A could raise B's costs by charging B a higher price. It remains to be seen whether economists will ultimately accept the proposition that raising a rival's costs can be a viable monopolizing strategy, or how the practice will be treated in the courts. But courts have sometimes imposed antitrust liability on firms possessing supposedly "essential facilities" when they deny competitors access to those facilities.

The recent era of antitrust reassessment has resulted in general agreement among economists that the most successful instances of cartelization and monopoly pricing have involved companies that enjoy the protection of government regulation of prices and government control of entry by new competitors. Occupational licensing and trucking regulation, for example, have allowed competitors to alter terms of competition and legally prevent entry into the market. Unfortunately, monopolies created by the federal government are almost always exempt from antitrust laws, and those created by state governments frequently are exempt as well. Municipal monopolies (e.g., taxicabs, utilities) may be subject to antitrust action but often are protected by statute.

The Effects of Antitrust

With the hindsight of better economic understanding, economists now realize that one undeniable effect of antitrust has been to penalize numerous economically benign practices. Horizontal and especially vertical agreements that are clearly useful, particularly in reducing transaction costs, have been (or for many years were) effectively banned. A leading example is the continued per se illegality of resale price maintenance. Antitrust also increases transaction costs because firms must hire lawyers and often must litigate to avoid antitrust liability.

One of the most worrisome statistics in antitrust is that for every case brought by government, private plaintiffs bring ten. The majority of cases are filed to hinder, not help, competition. According to Steven Salop, formerly an antitrust official in the Carter administration, and Lawrence J. White, an economist at New York University, most private antitrust actions are filed by members of one of two groups. The most numerous private actions are brought by parties who are in a vertical arrangement with the defendant (e.g., dealers or franchisees) and who therefore are unlikely to have suffered from any truly anticompetitive offense. Usually, such cases are attempts to convert simple contract disputes (compensable by ordinary damages) into triple-damage payoffs under the Clayton Act.

The second most frequent private case is that brought by competitors. Because competitors are hurt only when a rival is acting procompetitively by increasing its sales and decreasing its price, the desire to hobble the defendant's efficient practices must motivate at least some antitrust suits by competitors. Thus, case statistics suggest that the anticompetitive costs from "abuse of antitrust," as New York University economists William Baumol and Janusz Ordover (1985) referred to it, may actually exceed any procompetitive benefits of antitrust laws.

The case for antitrust gets no stronger when economists examine the kinds of antitrust cases brought by government. As George Stigler (1982, p. 7), often a strong defender of antitrust, summarized, "Economists have their glories, but I do not believe that antitrust law is one of them." In a series of studies done in the early 1970s, economists assumed that important losses to consumers from limits on competition existed, and constructed models to identify the markets where these losses would be greatest. Then they compared the markets where government was enforcing antitrust laws with the markets where governments *should* enforce the laws if consumer well-being was the government's paramount concern. The studies concluded unanimously that the size of consumer losses from monopoly played little or no role in government enforcement of the law. Economists have also examined particular kinds of antitrust cases brought by the government to see whether anticompetitive acts in these cases were likely. The empirical answer usually is *no*. This is true even in price-fixing cases, where the evidence indicates that the companies targeted by the government either were not fixing prices or were doing so unsuccessfully. Similar conclusions arise from studies of merger cases and of various antitrust remedies obtained by government; in both instances, results are inconsistent with antitrust's supposed goal of consumer well-being.

If public-interest rationales do not explain antitrust, what does? A final set of studies has shown empirically that patterns of antitrust enforcement are motivated at least in part by political pressures unrelated to aggregate economic welfare. For example, antitrust is useful to politicians in stopping mergers that would result in plant closings or job transfers in their home districts. As Paul Rubin documented, economists do not see antitrust cases as driven by a search for economic improvement. Rubin reviewed all articles written by economists that were cited in a leading industrial organization textbook (Scherer and Ross 1990) generally favorable to antitrust law. Per economists' evaluations, more bad than good cases were brought. "In other words," wrote Rubin, "it is highly unlikely that the net effect of actual antitrust policy is to deter inefficient behavior. . . . Factors other than a search for efficiency must be driving antitrust policy" (Rubin 1995, p. 61). What might those factors be? Pursuing a point suggested by Nobel laureate Ronald Coase (1972, 1988), William Shughart argued that economists' support for antitrust derives considerably from their ability to profit personally, in the form of full-time jobs and lucrative part-time work as experts in antitrust matters: "Far from contributing to improved antitrust enforcement, economists have for reasons of self-interest actively aided and abetted the public law enforcement bureaus and private plaintiffs in using the Sherman, Clayton and FTC Acts to subvert competitive market forces" (Shughart 1998, p. 151).

About the Author

Fred S. McChesney is the Class of 1967 James B. Haddad Professor of Law at Northwestern University School of Law and a professor in the Kellogg School of Management at Northwestern.

Further Reading

Asch, Peter, and J. J. Seneca. "Is Collusion Profitable?" *Review of Economics and Statistics* 53 (February 1976): 1–12.

Baumol, William J., and Janusz A. Ordover. "Use of Antitrust to Subvert Competition." *Journal of Law and Economics* 28 (May 1985): 247–265.

Bittlingmayer, George. "Decreasing Average Cost and Competition: A New Look at the Addyston Pipe Case." *Journal of Law and Economics* 25 (October 1982): 201–229.

Bork, Robert H. *The Antitrust Paradox: A Policy at War with Itself.* New York: Basic Books, 1978.

———. "Vertical Integration and the Sherman Act: The Legal History of an Economic Misconception." *University of Chicago Law Review* 22 (Autumn 1954): 157–201.

Brozen, Yale. "The Antitrust Task Force Deconcentration Recommendation." *Journal of Law and Economics* 13 (October 1970): 279–292.

Coase, R. H. "Industrial Organization: A Proposal for Research." In V. Fuchs, ed., *Economic Research: Retrospective and Prospect.* Vol. 3. Cambridge, Mass.: National Bureau of Economic Research. Reprinted in R. H. Coase, *The Firm, the Market and the Law.* Chicago: University of Chicago Press, 1988.

Coate, Malcolm B., Richard S. Higgins, and Fred S. McChesney. "Bureaucracy and Politics in FTC Merger Challenges." *Journal of Law and Economics* 33 (October 1990): 463–482.

Crandall, Robert W., and Clifford Winston. "Does Antitrust Policy Improve Consumer Welfare? Assessing the Evidence." *Journal of Economic Perspectives* 17, no. 4 (2003): 3–26.

Demsetz, Harold. "Industry Structure, Market Rivalry, and Public Policy." *Journal of Law and Economics* 16 (April 1973): 1–9.

Dewey, Donald. "Information, Entry and Welfare: The Case for Collusion." *American Economic Review* 69 (September 1979): 588–593.

DiLorenzo, Thomas J. "The Origins of Antitrust: An Interest-Group Perspective." *International Review of Law and Economics* 5 (June 1985): 73–90.

Liebowitz, Stan J., and Stephen E. Margolis. *Winners, Losers and Microsoft.* Rev. ed. Oakland, Calif.: Independent Institute, 2001.

McGee, John S. "Predatory Price Cutting: The Standard Oil (N.J.) Case." *Journal of Law and Economics* 1 (1958): 137–169.

Rubin, Paul H. "What Do Economists Think About Antitrust? A Random Walk down Pennsylvania Avenue." In Fred S. McChesney and William F. Shughart II, eds., *The Causes and Consequences of Antitrust: The Public-Choice Perspective.* Chicago: University of Chicago Press, 1995.

Scherer, F. M., and David Ross. *Industrial Market Structure and Economic Performance.* 3d ed. Boston: Houghton Mifflin, 1990.

Shughart, William F. II. "Monopoly and the Problem of the Economists." In Fred S. McChesney, ed., *Economic Inputs, Legal Outputs: The Role of Economists in Modern Antitrust.* New York: Wiley, 1998.

Shughart, William F. II, and Robert D. Tollison. "The Positive Economics of Antitrust Policy: A Survey Article." *International Review of Law and Economics* 5 (June 1985): 39–57.

Sproul, Michael F. "Antitrust and Prices." *Journal of Political Economy* 101 (1993): 741–754.

Stigler, George J. "The Economists and the Problem of Monopoly." In Stigler, *The Economist as Preacher and Other Essays.* Chicago: University of Chicago Press, 1982. Pp. 38–54.

———. "The Economists and the Problem of Monopoly." *American Economic Review Papers and Proceedings* 72 (May 1982): 1–11.

Telser, Lester G. "Why Should Manufacturers Want Fair Trade?" *Journal of Law and Economics* 3 (October 1960): 86–105.

Williamson, Oliver E. "Economies as an Antitrust Defense: The Welfare Tradeoffs." *American Economic Review* 58 (March 1968): 18–35.

Apartheid

Thomas W. Hazlett

The now-defunct apartheid system of South Africa presented a fascinating instance of interest-group competition for political advantage. In light of the extreme human rights abuses stemming from apartheid, it is remarkable that so little attention has been paid to the economic foundations of that torturous social structure. The conventional view is that apartheid was devised by affluent whites to suppress poor blacks. In fact, the system sprang from class warfare and was largely the creation of white workers struggling against both the black majority and white capitalists. Apartheid was born in the political victory of radical white trade unions over both of their rivals. In short, this cruelly oppressive economic system was socialism with a racist face.

The Roots of Conflict

When the British arrived in South Africa in 1796, they quickly conquered the Dutch settlement that had been established in 1652 and set up a government under the English Parliament and British common law. This liberal, individualistic regime was inherently offensive to the Afrikaners—the Dutch settlers of South Africa—who enjoyed both slavery (generally of imported Chinese and Malays) and a system of law that granted no standing to nonwhites. The Boers, as the Afrikaners were to call themselves, abhorred the intervention of the British, whom they considered agents of an imperialist power. Following Britain's abolition of South African slavery in 1834, the Afrikaners physically escaped the rule of the British crown in the Great Trek of 1835.

Moving north from Capetown and spilling the blood of several major tribes, including the fierce Zulus, the Boers founded the Transvaal and the Orange Free State (i.e., free of British domination), and proceeded to establish racist legal institutions. The Boers treated brutally, and denied rights to, the relatively few nonwhites who resided and worked in their agricultural economy.

The Capetown of nineteenth-century British rule was markedly different. That area experienced some of the most unconstrained racial mixing in the world. A large nonwhite population, the Cape Coloureds, participated in integrated schools, churches, businesses, and government institutions. And they voted. A color-blind franchise was explicitly adopted in 1854. As a port city, Capetown became internationally famous for its laissez-faire social scene (including miscegenation), rivaling New Orleans as a haven for sea-weary sailors.

The physical separation of the two European populations, as well as the small degree of interaction between the Afrikaners and the African tribes, allowed a brief and uneasy equilibrium in the mid-nineteenth century. It was not to last. When gold was discovered near the Rand River in the Transvaal in 1871 (diamonds had been found in 1866), the world's richest deposits exerted a powerful magnetic force on the tribes within the subcontinent: Afrika-ners, British, Xhosi, Sotho, and Zulu were all drawn to the profitable opportunities opening in the Witwatersrand basin.

Synergy and Competition:
The Dynamics of the Colour Bar

The South African gold rush made the natural synergy between white-owned capital and abundant black labor overpowering. The gains from cooperation between eager British investors and thousands of African workers were sufficient to bridge gaping differences in language, customs, and geography. At first, however, the white capitalist could deal directly only with the few English and Afrikaner managers and foremen who shared his tongue and work habits. But the premium such workers commanded soon became an extravagance. Black workers were becoming capable of performing industrial leadership roles in far greater numbers and at far less cost. Driven by the profit motive, the substitution of black for white in skilled and semiskilled mining jobs rose high on the agenda of the mining companies.

White workers feared the large supply of African labor as the low-priced competition that it was. Hence, white tradesmen and government officials, including police, regularly harassed African workers to discourage them from traveling to the mines and competing for permanent positions. Beginning in the 1890s, the Chamber of Mines, a group of employers, complained regularly of this systematic discrimination and attempted to secure better treatment for black workers. Their gesture was neither altruistic nor founded on liberal beliefs. Indeed, the mine owners often resorted to racist measures themselves. But here they had a clear economic incentive: labor costs were minimized where rules were color-blind. This self-interest was so powerful that it led the chamber to finance the first lawsuits and political campaigns against segregationist legislation.

Nonetheless, the state instituted an array of legal impediments to the promotion of black workers. The notorious Pass Laws sought to sharply limit the supply of nonwhite workers in "white" employment centers. Blacks were not allowed to become lawful citizens, to live permanently near their work, or to travel without government passports. This last restriction created a catch-22. If passports were issued only to those already possessing jobs, how was a nonwhite to get into the job area to procure a job so as to obtain a passport? Nonwhites also were prohibited from bringing their families while working in the mines (reinforcing the transient nature of employment).

Each restriction undercut the ability of blacks to fully establish themselves in the capitalist economy, and hence to compete with white workers on equal terms. Confined to temporary status, blacks were robbed of any realistic chance of building up the human capital to challenge their white bosses directly in the labor market.

Yet even on this decidedly unlevel playing field, the profit motive often found ways of matching white capitalists with black workers. Whites formed labor unions in the early 1900s to guard against this persistent tendency, and the South African Labour Party (SALP) was formed in 1908 to explicitly advance the interests of European workers. The SALP and the unions with which it allied, including the powerful Mine Workers' Union, were all white and avowedly socialist; the British Labour Party formed the model for the SALP. These organizations opposed any degradation of "European" or "civilized" standards in the workplace, by which they meant the advancement of blacks willing to undercut white union pay scales.

To discourage mine owners from substituting cheaper African labor for more expensive European labor, the trade unions regularly resorted to violence and the strike threat. They also turned to legislation: the Mines and Works Act of 1911 (commonly referred to as the first Colour Bar Act) used the premise of "worker safety" to institute a licensing scheme for labor. A government board was set up to certify individuals for work in "hazardous" occupations. The effect was to decertify non-Europeans, who were deemed "unqualified."

The legislative victory by the white unions froze African advances until the booming World War I demand for minerals raised employment and pay scales for all races. White workers did not object to black advancement per se, only to that which they perceived to come at their expense.

The postwar recession and the plummeting price of gold ended the tranquillity. In December 1921 the Chamber of Mines announced a plan to fire two thousand highly paid whites in semiskilled occupations and replace them with Africans. Before the planned substitution took effect, the Mine Workers' Union launched a massive strike, seizing the mines and occupying the entire Rand mining region for two months.

In a full-scale assault involving seven thousand government troops complete with tanks, artillery, and air support, the government reclaimed the Rand at a reported cost of 250 lives. Several leaders of the strike were hanged. The insurrection was sensational, as was the haunting slogan of the striking miners: "Workers of the world unite, and fight for a white South Africa." The miners saw not an ounce of irony in their "V. I. Lenin meets Lester Maddox" radicalism. They saw quite clearly, however, that the threat to their interests lay in the mutual interests of white capital and black labor.

White workers shared skin color with the capitalists, but their goals were quite different; the goal of mining and manufacturing capital was to hire cheap labor. As Africans assimilated into Western culture and the workforce, the abundance of managerial, skilled, and semiskilled talent would mushroom. The precariously privileged position of white labor would topple. These were not casual racists; they were economically vested up to their eyeballs in the policy of exclusion by skin color. Hence, the landmark election of 1924 tossed out the Smuts government—condemned by the strikers as a tool of big business—in a "white backlash" over suppression of the Rand Rebellion by Pretoria.

The Pact government, composed of Afrikaner nationalists (in the National Party) and white unionists (SALP), set an agenda of pro forma socialism that it dubbed the Civilized Labour Policy. Measures enacted in Western democracies as standard, off-the-shelf trade union legislation were adopted in South Africa, but with a racist twist. After the courts threw out the first Colour Bar Act in 1923 on a lawsuit by the Chamber of Mines, the Mines and Works Act of 1926 reestablished the Colour Bar. Like the earlier act, the new one used the pretext of "industrial safety" to keep blacks from moving into favorable job classifications. Despite the legalistic cover story, the government admitted its intent: to "counteract the force of economic advantages at present enjoyed by the native" (Doxey, 1961, p. 160).

Similarly, the Industrial Conciliation Act of 1924 authorized sector-by-sector labor union wage setting for the ostensible purpose of securing labor peace. The following year, the Wage Act extended this to the nonunionized sector. These rules amounted to race-based syndicalism.

The ebb and flow of the power of white trade unions to dictate terms to their bosses is graphically visible in the ethnic employment statistics. From 1910 to 1918 the ratio of blacks to whites employed in the mines ranged from 8 or 9 to 1. This was pushed down to 7.4 to 1 in the 1918 "status quo" agreement sought by the unions. After the Chamber of Mines suppressed the Rand Rebellion in 1922, it managed to up the ratio to 11.4 to 1. By 1929, however, the National Labour government, with its "civilized labour policy," had cut it back to 8.8 to 1. In 1953—the heyday of apartheid—the ratio was further constrained to 6.4 to 1, an incredible regulatory "achievement" considering that the natural (unregulated) advance of Africans would surely have pushed the ratio progressively higher over the passing decades.

Black trade unions were not illegal per se, but no black union was registered by the Ministry of Manpower until legislation explicitly promoting African unions was enacted in the late 1970s. Thus white workers were empowered—under the guise of the Industrial Conciliation Acts of 1924, 1936, and 1956—to solely control the terms of employment via officially sanctioned union bargaining. The enormous range of the state-backed unions' powers—setting wages, employment conditions, benefits, entry qualifications, work rules, and negotiation rights on behalf of the entire industrial economy—is staggering. But this was the level of state intervention required to supersede the profit motives of both firms and nonwhite workers. And that was the announced goal: to overrule the market forces that constantly sought to undermine "civilized standards for European workers."

Ironically, the labor market rules that were intended to raise barriers against black workers blocked the path for what were commonly called "poor whites," the lowest tier of the protected class. Hence, the final intervention of the Civilized Labour Policy was nationalization of businesses that employed large numbers of nonwhites. In a policy of "affirmative action," state-run railways and other huge state enterprises preferentially hired and promoted less skilled whites. In fact, many industries were nationalized just to impose racial preference. Merle Lipton reported that the perverse tendency toward the employment of (more expensive) whites was evident after the proclamation of the 1924 Civilized Labour Policy (Lipton 1986). Between 1924 and 1933 the number of whites employed by South African Railways rose from 4,760 to 17,783, or from 10 to 39 percent of employees, while the number of blacks fell from 37,564 to 22,008, or from 75 to 49 percent. In central and local government employment the proportion of whites rose from 45 to 64 percent while the number and percentage of blacks correspondingly fell.

From the Colour Bar to Apartheid

The Colour Bar brought labor calm because the black workers and white capitalists "taxed" by the deal lacked the requisite political muscle to disrupt the system. Moreover, a long period of South African prosperity began in the mid-1930s, fed by international demands for the country's mineral exports. Demand during World War II was particularly strong and led again to a large expansion of the mining and industrial sectors. This lured many thousands of new African workers into the wage economy. During the boom, these new workers were not substituting for white managers; indeed, the massive influx of black industrial labor prevented severe bottlenecks that would have lowered even white working-class incomes.

But mirroring the experience of a generation earlier, the postwar contraction brought an end to the comparative tranquillity. By 1948 the first signs of white unemployment sent a shock wave through the (white) electorate. Fears that "poor whites" would be passed by upwardly mobile black workers excited a radical response: the National Party was elected to implement apartheid, a newly comprehensive social policy of "separate development."

The problem apartheid attacked was circular. Economic cooperation among the races led to social integration. Social integration led to further economic cooperation because industrialists found low-wage blacks irresistible. Racists saw social separation enforced by law—apartheid—as the essential way to shore up the economic protection of white labor.

Furthermore, white farmers, wanting an artificially large supply of cheap black labor, endorsed measures limiting industrial jobs for blacks. Farmers were key allies of white labor in initiating and preserving apartheid. Indeed, the gerrymandering of parliamentary seats to grant overrepresentation to the rural sector gave the National Party its 1948 victory even though the party lost the popular vote by a substantial margin.

The ruthlessness with which South Africa applied apartheid is legendary. The Group Areas Act (1950) dictated where members of the various races could legally reside, and whole communities were brutally uprooted. The Population Registration Act (1950) gave the state bureaucratic control over the racial identity of its citizens, and in combination with the Pass Laws regulated internal travel. Government spending on education was hugely biased in favor of whites. In 1952, school spending per black child was about 5 percent of spending per white child. Africans were not allowed to own real estate. All these measures attempted to buttress the economic protectionism already enjoyed by white labor under the Colour Bar legislation.

Capitalists strongly opposed apartheid, and apartheidists strongly opposed capitalism. As historian Brian Lapping noted: "The National Party had to override some of the biggest financial, commercial and industrial interests in the state. . . . Overruling the bosses, the 'capitalists,' as both the National Party and the communists liked to call them, was popular with the party faithful" (Lapping 1987, p. 103).

The notorious Broederbond, the secret Afrikaner "brotherhood" that exercised huge influence on the racist policies of the apartheid government, stated its agenda quite succinctly in 1933: "Abolition of the exploitation by foreigners of [South Africa's] national resources . . . the nationalization of finance and the planned coordination of economic policy" (Lipton 1986, p. 29). White supremacy had its very own industrial policy.

Apartheid in Retreat

Beginning about 1970, the internal contradictions of apartheid finally caused its slow demise. After the massive legal discrimination of the early apartheid years, black income, relative to white, fell dramatically, and the advance of white workers was won. But much like the boom periods of the two world wars, the robust economic growth of the 1960s rendered apartheid's protection increasingly obsolete (many white workers no longer required all the separateness that apartheid had wrought) and exceedingly expensive (the South African economy was continually stalled by the artificial truncation of labor supply). Necessity became the mother of reform. Herbert Giliomee and Lawrence Schlemmer noted that

> as the white skilled-labor shortage worsened, the government became ever more impatient with white trade unions which were hampering the training of blacks and thus blocking black advances into skilled jobs. In 1973 it was announced that blacks, including Africans, could do skilled work in the white areas. The government did not rigorously adhere to its promise that it would consult with white trade unions before making this decision. In 1975 the defence force announced that black soldiers would enjoy the same status as whites of equal rank, and that whites would have to take orders from black officers. This broke the rule that the hierarchical structure (or ratchet) must be kept intact, with blacks always working under whites. (Giliomee and Schlemmer 1989, p. 124)

Postwar economic growth in South Africa so deeply integrated the nonwhite population within the "white" society that the very idea of "separate development" became ridiculous as a practical proposition, quite apart from its odious moral implications. Without skilled black labor, white living standards would fall precipitously. The inevitable economic synergy between the races drew people physically and socially closer together. Whereas the median white voter of the 1920s insecurely viewed black workers as substitutes, the majority of whites in the 1980s saw racial cooperation as increasingly beneficial. At the same time, the dramatic growth of an educated, urban African population, including a sizable black middle class, served to enormously raise the cost of enforcing apartheid. Indeed, the old African tribal system, which was cynically manipulated by apartheid policymakers under the notorious homelands policy, was eclipsed by the rise of urban townships closely tied to industrial job centers.

The vicissitudes of apartheid can be measured by the ratio of black income to white. From 1946 to 1960, despite a decrease in the white proportion of the population, a constant 70 percent of South Africa's national income went to whites. But between 1970 and 1980, this fell to 60 percent. Apartheid's decline can also be seen in increasing expenditures on black education: the twenty-to-one ratio in white-to-black per pupil educational spending in 1952 had shrunk to about five to one in 1987. Most evidently,

reform was seen in the elimination of the apartheid laws: the Prohibition of Mixed Marriages Act (scrapped in 1985), the abolition of the Pass Laws (1986), and the widespread elimination of "petty apartheid" (whereby separate facilities for racial groups was rigidly maintained). In 1991 President F. W. de Klerk eliminated the Group Areas and Population Registration Acts, the backbone of social apartheid. The nation turned its attention to crafting "a new South Africa," adopting a color-blind constitution guaranteeing equal rights under law to all citizens. In April 1994, Nelson Mandela—an antiapartheid activist who had spent twenty-six years in South African prisons—was elected president in South Africa's first all-race elections. Mandela's African National Congress Party won 252 of 400 seats in the national assembly, and has remained in power since Mandela stepped aside in 1999.

Did international sanctions against South Africa force Pretoria's hand in these reforms? The evidence is virtually unanimous that progress was only modestly correlated at best, and negatively correlated at worst, with such foreign campaigns. Not only did sanctions fail to lower South African trade flows from their previous levels, but GNP growth actually accelerated after the European Community and the United States imposed sanctions (in September and October 1986, respectively). Perversely, South African businesses reaped at least $5 billion to $10 billion in windfalls as Western firms disinvested at fire sale prices between 1984 and 1989.

Whatever the economic impact, the immediate political effect of sanctions was to encourage retrenchment by the Botha regime then in power. Right-wing (proapartheid) support rose sharply in the May 1987 parliamentary elections, and the National Party government responded by shelving all reforms and brutally suppressing antiapartheid dissent, initiating a state of emergency accompanied by sweeping press censorship. Only with a fading of sanctions pressures, a rebounding economy, and key changes in the international geopolitical environment (notably, the collapse of the Eastern bloc) did the course of reform reassert itself.

Apartheid was sought by those economically threatened by the synergies between black workers and white capitalists. That interest groups can so steer economic regulation as to achieve the social savagery of apartheid is a chilling lesson for those who take their politics—and hence their economics—seriously.

About the Author

Thomas W. Hazlett is a professor of law and economics at George Mason University. In 1991–1992 he was chief economist of the Federal Communications Commission.

Further Reading

Doxey, G. V. *The Industrial Colour Bar in South Africa.* Capetown: Oxford University Press, 1961.

Frederickson, G. M. *White Supremacy: A Comparative Study in American and South African History.* London: Oxford University Press, 1981.

Giliomee, Herbert, and Lawrence Schlemmer. *From Apartheid to Nation-Building.* Capetown: Oxford University Press, 1989.

Hazlett, Thomas W. "The Economic Origins of Apartheid." *Contemporary Policy Issues* 6 (October 1988): 85–104.

———. "The Effect of U.S. Economic Sanctions on South African Apartheid." Applied Public Policy Research Program Working Paper series no. 3. University of California at Davis, Institute of Governmental Affairs, 1992.

———. "Kinnock's Crowning Cheek on Apartheid." *Wall Street Journal,* December 31, 1986, p. 14.

———. "One Man, One Share: How to Privatize South Africa." *New Republic* 203 (December 31, 1990): pp. 14–15.

Hufbauer, Gary Clyde, Jeffrey J. Schott, and Kimberly Ann Elliott. *Economic Sanctions Reconsidered.* 2d ed. Washington, D.C.: Institute for International Economics, 1990.

Lapping, Brian. *Apartheid: A History.* London: Paladin Books, 1987.

Lingle, Christopher. "Apartheid as Racial Socialism." *Kyklos* 43, no. 2 (1989): 229–247.

Lipton, Merle. *Capitalism and Apartheid.* London: Wildwood Press, 1986.

———. "The Challenge of Sanctions." Paper presented to the Economic Society of South Africa, Johannesburg, September 6–7, 1989. Washington, D.C.: Investor Responsibility Research Center, 1989.

Lowenberg, Anton D. "An Economic Theory of Apartheid." *Economic Inquiry* 27, no. 1 (1989): 57–74.

Arts

Tyler Cowen

General economic principles govern the arts. Most important, artists use scarce means to achieve ends—and therefore recognize trade-offs, the defining aspects of economic behavior. Also, many other economic aspects of the arts make the arts similar to the more typical goods and services that economists analyze.

As in other economic sectors, marketplace exchange provides more choice for both consumers and producers. Adam Smith's famous maxim that the division of labor is limited by the extent of the market applies no less to the arts. Larger markets support more diverse and numerous artistic styles. The advent of musical recording, for instance, expanded the market and enabled jazz, blues, country, rag-

time, gospel, and rhythm and blues to find larger audiences. Each genre then split into diverse branches, as when rhythm and blues evolved into rock and roll, Motown, rap, soul, and so on. We find the same trends in literature. The book superstore and Amazon.com help many niche writers—not just authors of bestsellers—market their works to readers. The identification and marketing techniques of mass culture help artists to reach smaller groups of buyers, thereby giving artists a better chance to make a living from their work. In short, mass culture and niche culture are complements, not substitutes.

The arts also illustrate the more general benefits of wealth, a common theme in economics. The richer the society, the more options artists have. As wealth increases, so does the number of potential buyers, allowing artists to pick and choose their projects and to walk away if they do not like the terms of the commission. The pope had to beg Michelangelo to come back to finish the Sistine Chapel because the artist had many other potential customers at the time. Artistic freedom, while rarely absolute, is a product of prosperity.

Moreover, family wealth has also helped on the supply side. Many artists lived off family wealth for much of their careers. In France, for instance, Delacroix, Degas, Manet, Monet, Cézanne, Toulouse-Lautrec, Proust, Baudelaire, and Flaubert all relied on parental wealth to some extent. Some of these creators attacked the bourgeoisie of their time, in spite of the fact that a bourgeois society with its widespread wealth gave them their artistic freedom.

Wealth also gives rise to charity, one source of funding for the arts. In the United States, from 1965 to 1990, the number of symphony orchestras rose from 58 to nearly 300, the number of opera companies rose from 27 to more than 150, and the number of nonprofit regional theaters rose from 22 to 500. Charitable donations are key to all these artistic forms. Individual, corporate, and foundation donors make up about 45 percent of the budget for nonprofit arts institutions. Twelve percent of their income comes from foundation grants alone, two and a half times as much as from the National Endowment for the Arts and state arts councils combined.

Contrary to common opinion, the commercial incentives brought by wealth are not typically corrupting. Many artists chase profits, but the commercial and artistic impulses are not always at war. The letters of Bach, Mozart, Haydn, and Beethoven reveal that all were obsessed with earning money. Mozart wrote in one of his letters: "Believe me, my sole purpose is to make as much money as possible; for after good health it is the best thing to have." Charlie Chaplin once noted: "I went into the business for money and the art grew out of it." Many talented artists are motivated not just by narrow self-interest, but also by a desire to make money to help friends or to finance their creative urges.

The idea that the great artists in history were starving has been overplayed. No doubt many artists earn low incomes, in part because a market economy gives so many people the chance to shoot for an artistic career: the large number of would-be artists depresses wages. But many artists have earned a good living by selling their products to audiences or winning the loyalty of patrons. Michelangelo and Raphael were wealthy men in their time; indeed, most of the Italian Renaissance artists were commercially successful. More generally, most famous artists commanded high prices in their lifetimes. Shakespeare worked in the for-profit theater world and did not need patronage.

Even when artists cannot afford to make art for a living, a capitalist economy gives them the best chance of moonlighting. T. S. Eliot worked in Lloyd's bank, James Joyce taught languages, Charles Ives and Wallace Stevens were insurance executives, and William Faulkner worked in a power plant. They all managed to create, either on the job or in their spare time.

Just as technological progress has helped create new industries and more options for consumers in other areas of the economy, it does so in art also. We take cheap paper for granted, but the Renaissance arts blossomed only when paper became cheap enough for most artists to afford. The French Impressionists used new colors, based on new scientific research on chemicals, that came from the industrial revolution. Rock and roll required the electric guitar and the advanced recording studio. Whereas John Keats, Mozart, and Schubert all died young of illnesses such as tuberculosis, medical advances allow modern artists to live longer and produce more.

On the other side, economist William Baumol, one of the first to write on the economics of the arts, suggested that the performing arts are "technologically stagnant," not allowing significant productivity improvements. He noted that it still takes thirty minutes for four people to play a Mozart string quartet. As real wages rise in a growing economy, therefore, argued Baumol, the wage cost of a Mozart string quartet will rise. But Baumol ignored other aspects of technology that make such quartets more economically feasible. Modern broadcasting, for example, makes such quartets available not just to hundreds of people at a time, but to millions. And one reason this is a "golden age" for first-rate string quartets is that air travel allows them to perform around the globe and recruit members from different countries and continents. The contemporary Kronos Quartet plays both Bartok and Jimi Hendrik, relying on new ideas made possible by growing markets and technology.

The issue of free trade has long been resolved in economics: trade is good (see FREE TRADE). But only recently has the globalization of art attracted much attention. Arguing contrary to the principles of Adam Smith, many critics, such as Benjamin Barber, argue that cultural trade is bringing us a culture of the least common denominator—Reebok, McDonald's, and bad TV shows. The evidence, though, supports free trade in the arts. Trade has done much to stimulate international diversity, just as it supports diversity within the borders of a single country. The Third World has produced many notable authors and moviemakers over the last several decades. Gabriel García Márquez, Naguib Mahfouz, V. S. Naipaul, and John Woo are all products of globalized culture whose art could not have existed without significant international trade. The metal carving knife—a product of the West—is a boon for poor carvers and sculptors around the world, as acrylic paints and canvas are for new forms of the visual arts. World music blossomed in the twentieth century, most of all in open, cosmopolitan cities such as Lagos, Rio de Janeiro, and pre-Castro Havana. Many Third World creators earn their living by selling their products to wealthy Western consumers. Western purchasing power has been central to Haitian naïve art, Jamaican reggae music, Navajo weaving, and the Persian carpet boom of the late nineteenth century, among many other artistic movements.

Because trade tends to make countries more similar, nations may appear less diverse. But countries become more similar in a largely beneficial way by developing a varied menu of cultural choice. One can now buy sushi in Germany and France, but this hardly counts as cultural destruction. Individuals have greater opportunity to pursue cultural paths of their choosing. So, although differences across societies decrease, diversity within a given society increases.

Just as trade improves the arts, restrictions on trade damage them. French cultural protectionism, originally imposed by the Vichy government and the Nazis, was retained by the French after the war. Before that time, French culture, including French cinema, flourished under largely free trade conditions. As subsidies and protectionism have grown, French cinema has suffered increasing economic difficulties.

Subsidy defenders argue either that supporting the arts is intrinsically valuable or that subsidies to art bring additional social or economic benefits. Subsidy critics challenge both presumptions: relying on the market, they say, may give us a better menu of choices. Arts in the United States receive much smaller direct subsidies than do those in Western Europe. The budget for the National Endowment for the Arts has never exceeded $170 million (and was only $115 million in 2003), an amount far less than the budget of many Hollywood movies. Yet the American arts are economically healthier in many regards because of their stronger commercial roots.

Just as government regulation slowed innovation in industries such as airlines and trucking, government regulators tried to slow innovation in the arts. Fortunately, the government failed. Many of America's most significant cultural innovations—such as jazz, Hollywood, and rock and roll—flourished in the face of government opposition. At times the American government tried to censor these art forms or meted out especially harsh legal treatment to prominent creators (e.g., Alan Freed, Chuck Berry, and James Brown).

In sum, the economics of the arts reflects more general economic truths. The arts are often "special" in our hearts, but economic analysis suggests that increases in wealth, commercialization, and globalization are good both for the arts and for those who enjoy them.

About the Author
Tyler Cowen is a professor of economics at George Mason University and the director of both the James Buchanan Center and the Mercatus Center.

Further Reading
Cowen, Tyler. *Creative Destruction: How Globalization Is Shaping the World's Cultures*. Princeton: Princeton University Press, 2002.
———. *In Praise of Commercial Culture*. Cambridge: Harvard University Press, 1998.
Heilbrun, James, and Charles M. Gray. *The Economics of Art and Culture: An American Perspective*. Cambridge: Cambridge University Press, 1993.

Auctions

Leslie R. Fine

When most people hear the word "auction," they think of the open-outcry, ascending-bid (or English) auction. But this kind of auction is only one of many. Fundamentally, an auction is an economic mechanism whose purpose is the allocation of goods and the formation of prices for those goods via a process known as bidding. Depending on the properties of the bidders and the nature of the items to be auctioned, various auction structures may be either more efficient or more profitable to the seller than others. Like all well-designed economic mechanisms, the designer assumes that individuals will act strategically and may hold private information relevant to the decision at hand. Auc-

tion design is a careful balance of encouraging bidders to reveal valuations, discouraging cheating or collusion, and maximizing revenues.

William Vickrey first established the taxonomy of auctions based on the order in which the auctioneer quotes prices and the bidders tender their bids. He established four major (one-sided) auction types: (1) the ascending-bid (open, oral, or English) auction; (2) the descending-bid (Dutch) auction; (3) the first-price, sealed-bid auction; and (4) the second-price, sealed-bid (Vickrey) auction.

The Four Basic Auction Types
The most common type of auction, the English auction, is often used to sell art, wine, antiques, and other goods. In it, the auctioneer opens the bidding at a reserve price (which may be zero), the lowest price he is willing to accept for the item. Once a bidder has announced interest at that price, the auctioneer solicits further bids, usually raising the price by a predetermined bid increment. This continues until no one is willing to increase the bid any further, at which point the auction is closed and the final bidder receives the item at his bid price. Because the winner pays his bid, this type of auction is known as a first-price auction.

The Dutch auction, also a first-price auction, is descending. That is, the auctioneer begins at a high price, higher than he believes the item will fetch, then decreases the price until a bidder finally calls out, "Mine!" The bidder then receives the item at the price at which he made the call. If multiple items are offered, the process continues until all items are sold. One of the primary advantages of Dutch auctions is speed. Since there are never more bids than there are items being auctioned, the process takes relatively little time. This is one reason they are used in places such as flower markets in Holland (hence the name "Dutch").

In the English and Dutch auctions, bidders receive information as others bid (or refrain from bidding). However, in the third type of auction, known as the first-price, sealed-bid auction, this is not the case. In this mechanism, each bidder submits a single bid in a sealed envelope. Then, all of the envelopes are opened and the highest bidder is announced, and he receives the item at his bid price. This type of auction is most often used for refinancing credit and foreign exchange, among other (primarily financial) venues.

The fourth type is the second-price, sealed-bid auction, otherwise known as the Vickrey auction. As in the first-price, sealed-bid auction, bidders submit sealed envelopes in one round of bid submission. The highest bidder wins the item, but at the price offered by the second-highest bidder (or, in a multiple-item case, the highest unsuccessful bid). This type of auction is rarely used aside from setting the foreign exchange rates in some African countries.

Why So Many Auction Forms?

One might think so many canonical auction forms unnecessary, that there is always a best choice that will yield the most surplus to the seller. In fact, under some strict assumptions, the revenue equivalence theorem (also due to Vickrey) states that all four auction types will result in an identical level of revenue to the seller. However, these assumptions regarding the nature of the item's value and the risk attitudes of the bidders are very restrictive and rarely hold.

The first assumption of the theorem is that the asset being auctioned has an independent, private value to all bidders. This assumption tends to hold when the item is for personal consumption, without thought toward resale, as might be the case for furniture, art, or wine. In this case, the value of the item is considered to be personal and independent of the value others might place on it (independent, private values). The assumption does not hold when bidders perceive a value of resale, either of the item itself or of a by-product of the item. Buying land for the rights to the oil that lies beneath it would be a good example. In this case, the value is common; that is, individual bids are predicated not only on personal valuation, but also on the valuation of prospective buyers. Each bidder tries to estimate the value of an object using the same known measurements (common values), but their conclusions may vary widely.

In common-value environments, bidders may face the "winner's curse." If all of the bidders will eventually realize the same value from the item, then the primary differentiator between the bidders is their perception of that value. Absent special information about the item being purchased, the winner is the person with the largest positive error in his valuation, and, unless he is lucky, he will wind up losing money.

The second assumption of the revenue equivalence theorem is that all bidders are risk-neutral. The strict definition of risk neutrality is: given the choice between a guaranteed return r and a gamble with expected return also equal to r, the bidder is completely indifferent. The bidder who prefers the guaranteed return is said to be "risk-averse," while the bidder who prefers the gamble is said to be "risk-loving."

The style of auction a seller chooses depends on his judgment about which of these assumptions holds. If values are common rather than independent, the English auction yields higher seller revenue than the second-price, sealed-bid auction, which in turn yields higher revenues than the Dutch and first-price, sealed-bid auctions (which

are tied). The rankings illustrate the strategic advantages of increased information. Because the English auction reveals all bids to all bidders, it permits dynamic updating of personal valuation. (If I see that others believe the real estate is worth more, I too may decide it is worth more.) In comparison, bidders, recognizing the winner's curse, bid less aggressively in first-price, sealed-bid auctions and shade their bids downward. Similar reasoning applies to Dutch (descending) auctions. While the information is not updated in a second-price sealed-bid format, the winner pays the bid of the next-highest bidder, and so bidders raise bids, secure that they will not be disadvantaged if rival bids are lower.

In fact, in both the first-price, sealed-bid auction and the Dutch auction, no information is revealed and the bidder pays the value of his bid. Therefore, in terms of revenue maximization, it does not matter which of these auctions a seller chooses; nor does it matter whether the bidders have private or common values.

What about the role of risk aversion? In first-price, sealed-bid and Dutch auctions, risk aversion causes bidders to bid slightly higher than they might otherwise. Since they have only one chance to bid, fear of losing the item induces overbidding. In the English and Vickrey auctions, however, bidders are induced to bid their true valuation, regardless of risk attitudes.

Once a seller has decided on which of the four basic auction forms to use, he can use many variations within the auction to further manipulate the outcome to maximize revenue. These mechanisms can have profound, and often counterintuitive, effects on bidding behavior—and therefore on outcomes. Among the available mechanisms are reserve prices, entry fees, invited bidders only, closing rules, lot sizes, proxy bidding, bidding increment rules, and postwin payment rules.

Auction Success and Failure—An Example

The 1994 U.S. Federal Communications Commission (FCC) auctions of wireless bandwidth provide a useful example of both the successes and the failures of auction design. The auction to allocate Personal Communications Service (PCS) spectrum had four primary goals: (1) to attain efficient allocation of spectrum, (2) to encourage rapid deployment and network build out, (3) to attain diversity of ownership, and (4) to raise revenue. Goals 1, 2, and 4 are met by any well-designed auction, as the winner is the one who values the item most. PCS licenses are a classic common-values good, in that they have a common, large, but uncertain value, triggering the winner's curse.

The FCC developed an elaborate network of rules to ensure the desired outcomes. To encourage price discovery, the auction was a multiround, ascending-bid, first-price auction. The many licenses available covered the entire United States, allowing major complementarities and substitutes in this market. To allow bidding that took this into account, the auctions were simultaneous, and no auction ended until they all did (every license was open until there were no more bids on any of them). Further, because the FCC wanted to discourage bidders from sitting on the sidelines until the very end, an activity rule was imposed. These and an elaborate network of other rules were carefully balanced to ensure the desired outcome. The result was great success in maximizing revenues.

The 1994 FCC auction stumbled, however, in its goal of diversifying ownership. To achieve this goal, the FCC set aside two blocks (C and F) for entrepreneurs, female and minority-owned firms, and regional companies. To that end, the FCC took the carefully designed auction and changed it just a little bit.

Bidders in these two special blocks received a 25 percent bid credit. That is, if they bid eighty dollars for an item, the bid was treated as if they had bid one hundred dollars. Further, their deposit requirement was just one-fifth of what the other winning bidders paid. Lastly, "diversity bids" were offered a generous installment payment plan. Bidders had a month to furnish 10 percent of the bid and owed no more principal until seven years later. The interest for this loan was charged at the T-bill rate. Unfortunately, this seemingly small change had disastrous effects.

The payment policy created moral hazard (see INSURANCE) by, in effect, providing bidders with low-cost insurance against big misestimates or drops in the value of the bandwidth. Since winning bidders had to make a down payment of only 10 percent, if, after seven years, the item turned out to be worth less than 90 percent of the bid price, then the purchaser could simply default. This is precisely what happened. Companies bought the licenses and invested 10 percent, and then declared bankruptcy when the license turned out to be worth less than 90 percent of the bid. Nearly every company that won a license in the C or F blocks in the 1994 auction either went bankrupt or was bought by a larger firm. In the end, the FCC's ham-fisted pursuit of a noble goal destroyed this segment of the auction entirely. PCS auctions continue today, though they have been massively restructured.

About the Author

Leslie R. Fine is a scientist in the Information Dynamics Lab at HP Labs in Palo Alto, California.

Further Reading

Ashenfelter, Orley. "How Auctions Work for Wine and Art." *Journal of Economic Perspectives* 3 (1989): 23–26.
Kagel, J. H. "Auctions: A Survey of Experimental Research." In John H. Kagel and Alvin E. Roth, eds., *The Handbook of Experimental Economics*. Princeton: Princeton University Press, 1995. Pp. 1–86.
Klemperer, P. D., ed. *The Economic Theory of Auctions*. Cheltenham, U.K.: Edward Elgar, 1999.
McAfee, R. P., and J. McMillan. "Auctions and Bidding." *Journal of Economic Literature* 25 (1987): 699–738.
Milgrom, P. R. "Auctions and Bidding: A Primer." *Journal of Economic Perspectives* 3 (1989): 3–22.
———. "Putting Auction Theory to Work: The Simultaneous Ascending Auction." *Journal of Political Economy* 108, no. 21 (2000): 245–272.

Austrian School of Economics

Peter J. Boettke

The Austrian school of economics was founded in 1871 with the publication of Carl Menger's *Principles of Economics*. MENGER, along with WILLIAM STANLEY JEVONS and LEON WALRAS, developed the marginalist revolution in economic analysis. Menger dedicated *Principles of Economics* to his German colleague William Roscher, the leading figure in the German historical school, which dominated economic thinking in German-language countries. In his book, Menger argued that economic analysis is universally applicable and that the appropriate unit of analysis is man and his choices. These choices, he wrote, are determined by individual subjective preferences and the margin on which decisions are made (see MARGINALISM). The logic of choice, he believed, is the essential building block to the development of a universally valid economic theory.

The historical school, on the other hand, had argued that economic science is incapable of generating universal principles and that scientific research should instead be focused on detailed historical examination. The historical school thought the English classical economists mistaken in believing in economic laws that transcended time and national boundaries. Menger's *Principles of Economics* restated the classical political economy view of universal laws and did so using marginal analysis. Roscher's students, especially Gustav Schmoller, took great exception to Menger's defense of "theory" and gave the work of Menger and his followers, EUGEN BÖHM-BAWERK and Friedrich Wieser, the derogatory name "Austrian school" because of their faculty positions at the University of Vienna. The term stuck.

Since the 1930s, no economists from the University of Vienna or any other Austrian university have become leading figures in the so-called Austrian school of economics.

In the 1930s and 1940s, the Austrian school moved to Britain and the United States, and scholars associated with this approach to economic science were located primarily at the London School of Economics (1931–1950), New York University (1944–), Auburn University (1983–), and George Mason University (1981–). Many of the ideas of the leading mid-twentieth-century Austrian economists, such as LUDWIG VON MISES and F. A. HAYEK, are rooted in the ideas of classical economists such as ADAM SMITH and DAVID HUME, or early-twentieth-century figures such as KNUT WICKSELL, as well as Menger, Böhm-Bawerk, and Friedrich von Wieser. This diverse mix of intellectual traditions in economic science is even more obvious in contemporary Austrian school economists, who have been influenced by modern figures in economics. These include ARMEN ALCHIAN, JAMES BUCHANAN, RONALD COASE, Harold Demsetz, Axel Leijonhufvud, DOUGLASS NORTH, Mancur Olson, VERNON SMITH, GORDON TULLOCK, Leland Yeager, and Oliver Williamson, as well as Israel Kirzner and Murray Rothbard. While one could argue that a unique Austrian school of economics operates within the economic profession today, one could also sensibly argue that the label "Austrian" no longer possesses any substantive meaning. In this article I concentrate on the main propositions about economics that so-called Austrians believe.

The Science of Economics

Proposition 1: Only individuals choose.
Man, with his purposes and plans, is the beginning of all economic analysis. Only individuals make choices; collective entities do not choose. The primary task of economic analysis is to make economic phenomena intelligible by basing it on individual purposes and plans; the secondary task of economic analysis is to trace out the unintended consequences of individual choices.

Proposition 2: The study of the market order is fundamentally about exchange behavior and the institutions within which exchanges take place.
The price system and the market economy are best understood as a "catallaxy," and thus the science that studies the market order falls under the domain of "catallactics." These terms derive from the original Greek meanings of the word *"katallaxy"*—exchange and bringing a stranger into friendship through exchange. Catallactics focuses analytical attention on the exchange relationships that emerge in the market, the bargaining that characterizes the exchange process, and the institutions within which exchange takes place.

Proposition 3: The "facts" of the social sciences are what people believe and think.
Unlike the physical sciences, the human sciences begin with the purposes and plans of individuals. Where the purging of purposes and plans in the physical sciences led to advances by overcoming the problem of anthropomorphism, in the human sciences, the elimination of purposes and plans results in purging the science of human action of its subject matter. In the human sciences, the "facts" of the world are what the actors think and believe.

The meaning that individuals place on things, practices, places, and people determines how they will orient themselves in making decisions. The goal of the sciences of human action is intelligibility, not prediction. The human sciences can achieve this goal because we are what we study, or because we possess knowledge from within, whereas the natural sciences cannot pursue a goal of intelligibility because they rely on knowledge from without. We can understand purposes and plans of other human actors because we ourselves are human actors.

The classic thought experiment invoked to convey this essential difference between the sciences of human action and the physical sciences is a Martian observing the "data" at Grand Central Station in New York. Our Martian could observe that when the little hand on the clock points to eight, there is a bustle of movement as bodies leave these boxes, and that when the little hand hits five, there is a bustle of movement as bodies reenter the boxes and leave. The Martian may even develop a prediction about the little hand and the movement of bodies and boxes. But unless the Martian comes to understand the purposes and plans (the commuting to and from work), his "scientific" understanding of the data from Grand Central Station would be limited. The sciences of human action are different from the natural sciences, and we impoverish the human sciences when we try to force them into the philosophical/scientific mold of the natural sciences.

Microeconomics

Proposition 4: Utility and costs are subjective.
All economic phenomena are filtered through the human mind. Since the 1870s, economists have agreed that value is subjective, but, following ALFRED MARSHALL, many argued that the cost side of the equation is determined by objective conditions. Marshall insisted that just as both blades of a scissors cut a piece of paper, so subjective value and objective costs determine price. But Marshall failed to appreciate that costs are also subjective because they are themselves determined by the value of alternative uses of scarce resources. Both blades of the scissors do indeed cut

the paper, but the blade of supply is determined by individuals' subjective valuations.

In deciding courses of action, one must choose; that is, one must pursue one path and not others. The focus on alternatives in choices leads to one of the defining concepts of the economic way of thinking: opportunity costs. The cost of any action is the value of the highest-valued alternative forgone in taking that action. Since the forgone action is, by definition, never taken, when one decides, one weighs the expected benefits of an activity against the expected benefits of alternative activities.

Proposition 5: The price system economizes on the information that people need to process in making their decisions.

Prices summarize the terms of exchange on the market. The price system signals to market participants the relevant information, helping them realize mutual gains from exchange. In Hayek's famous example, when people notice that the price of tin has risen, they do not need to know whether the cause was an increase in demand for tin or a decrease in supply. Either way, the increase in the price of tin leads them to economize on its use. Market prices change quickly when underlying conditions change, which leads people to adjust quickly.

Proposition 6: Private property in the means of production is a necessary condition for rational economic calculation.

Economists and social thinkers had long recognized that private ownership provides powerful incentives for the efficient allocation of scarce resources. But those sympathetic to socialism believed that socialism could transcend these incentive problems by changing human nature. Ludwig von Mises demonstrated that even if the assumed change in human nature took place, socialism would fail because of economic planners' inability to rationally calculate the alternative use of resources. Without private ownership in the means of production, Mises reasoned, there would be no market for the means of production, and therefore no money prices for the means of production. And without money prices reflecting the relative scarcities of the means of production, economic planners would be unable to rationally calculate the alternative use of the means of production.

Proposition 7: The competitive market is a process of entrepreneurial discovery.

Many economists see competition as a state of affairs. But the term "competition" invokes an activity. If competition were a state of affairs, the entrepreneur would have no role.

But because competition is an activity, the entrepreneur has a huge role as the agent of change who prods and pulls markets in new directions.

The entrepreneur is alert to unrecognized opportunities for mutual gain. By recognizing opportunities, the entrepreneur earns a profit. The mutual learning from the discovery of gains from exchange moves the market system to a more efficient allocation of resources. Entrepreneurial discovery ensures that a free market moves toward the most efficient use of resources. In addition, the lure of profit continually prods entrepreneurs to seek innovations that increase productive capacity. For the entrepreneur who recognizes the opportunity, today's imperfections represent tomorrow's profit.[1] The price system and the market economy are learning devices that guide individuals to discover mutual gains and use scarce resources efficiently.

Macroeconomics

Proposition 8: Money is nonneutral.

Money is defined as the commonly accepted medium of exchange. If government policy distorts the monetary unit, exchange is distorted as well. The goal of monetary policy should be to minimize these distortions. Any increase in the money supply not offset by an increase in money demand will lead to an increase in prices. But prices do not adjust instantaneously throughout the economy. Some price adjustments occur faster than others, which means that relative prices change. Each of these changes exerts its influence on the pattern of exchange and production. Money, by its nature, thus cannot be neutral.

This proposition's importance becomes evident in discussing the costs of inflation. The quantity theory of money stated, correctly, that printing money does not increase wealth. Thus, if the government doubles the money supply, money holders' apparent gain in ability to buy goods is prevented by the doubling of prices. But while the quantity theory of money represented an important advance in economic thinking, a mechanical interpretation of the quantity theory underestimated the costs of inflationary policy. If prices simply doubled when the government doubled the money supply, then economic actors would anticipate this price adjustment by closely following money supply figures and would adjust their behavior accordingly. The cost of inflation would thus be minimal.

But inflation is socially destructive on several levels. First, even anticipated inflation breaches a basic trust be-

---

1. Entrepreneurship can be characterized by three distinct moments: serendipity (discovery), search (conscious deliberation), and seizing the opportunity for profit.

tween the government and its citizens because government is using inflation to confiscate people's wealth. Second, unanticipated inflation is redistributive as debtors gain at the expense of creditors. Third, because people cannot perfectly anticipate inflation and because the money is added somewhere in the system—say, through government purchase of bonds—some prices (the price of bonds, for example) adjust before other prices, which means that inflation distorts the pattern of exchange and production.

Since money is the link for almost all transactions in a modern economy, monetary distortions affect those transactions. The goal of monetary policy, therefore, should be to minimize these monetary distortions, precisely because money is nonneutral.[2]

Proposition 9: The capital structure consists of heterogeneous goods that have multispecific uses that must be aligned.

Right now, people in Detroit, Stuttgart, and Tokyo City are designing cars that will not be purchased for a decade. How do they know how to allocate resources to meet that goal? Production is always for an uncertain future demand, and the production process requires different stages of investment ranging from the most remote (mining iron ore) to the most immediate (the car dealership). The values of all producer goods at every stage of production derive from the value consumers place on the product being produced. The production plan aligns various goods into a capital structure that produces the final goods in, ideally, the most efficient manner. If capital goods were homogeneous, they could be used in producing all the final products consumers desired. If mistakes were made, the resources would be reallocated quickly, and with minimal cost, toward producing the more desired final product. But capital goods are heterogeneous and multispecific; an auto plant can make cars, but not computer chips. The intricate alignment of capital to produce various consumer goods is governed by price signals and the careful economic calculations of investors. If the price system is distorted, investors will make mistakes in aligning their capital goods. Once the error is revealed, economic actors will reshuffle their investments, but in the meantime resources will be lost.[3]

Proposition 10: Social institutions often are the result of human action, but not of human design.

Many of the most important institutions and practices are not the result of direct design but are the by-product of actions taken to achieve other goals. A student in the Midwest in January trying to get to class quickly while avoiding the cold may cut across the quad rather than walk the long way around. Cutting across the quad in the snow leaves footprints; as other students follow these, they make the path bigger. Although their goal is merely to get to class quickly and avoid the cold weather, in the process they create a path in the snow that actually helps students who come later to achieve this goal more easily. The "path in the snow" story is a simple example of a "product of human action, but not of human design" (Hayek 1948, p. 7).

The market economy and its price system are examples of a similar process. People do not intend to create the complex array of exchanges and price signals that constitute a market economy. Their intention is simply to improve their own lot in life, but their behavior results in the market system. Money, law, language, science, and so on are all social phenomena that can trace their origins not to human design, but rather to people striving to achieve their own betterment, and in the process producing an outcome that benefits the public.[4]

The implications of these ten propositions are rather radical. If they hold true, economic theory would be grounded in verbal logic and empirical work focused on historical

---

2. The search for solutions to this elusive goal generated some of the most innovative work of the Austrian economists and led to the development in the 1970s and 1980s of the literature on free banking by F. A. Hayek, Lawrence White, George Selgin, Kevin Dowd, Kurt Schuler, and Steven Horwitz.

3. Propositions 8 and 9 form the core of the Austrian theory of the business cycle, which explains how credit expansion by the government generates a malinvestment in the capital structure during the boom period that must be corrected in the bust phase. In contemporary economics, Roger Garrison is the leading expositor of this theory.

4. Not all spontaneous orders are beneficial and, thus, this proposition should not be read as an example of a Panglossian fallacy. Whether individuals pursuing their own self-interest generate public benefits depends on the institutional conditions within which they pursue their interests. Both the invisible hand of market efficiency and the TRAGEDY OF THE COMMONS are results of individuals striving to pursue their individual interests; but in one social setting this generates social benefits, whereas in the other it generates losses. New institutional economics has refocused professional attention on how sensitive social outcomes are to the institutional setting within which individuals interact. It is important, however, to realize that classical political economists and the early neoclassical economists all recognized the basic point of new institutional economists, and that it was only the mid-twentieth-century fascination with formal proofs of general competitive equilibrium, on the one hand, and the Keynesian preoccupation with aggregate variables, on the other, that tended to cloud the institutional preconditions required for social cooperation.

narratives. With regard to public policy, severe doubt would be raised about the ability of government officials to intervene optimally within the economic system, let alone to rationally manage the economy.

Perhaps economists should adopt the doctors' creed: "First do no harm." The market economy develops out of people's natural inclination to better their situation and, in so doing, to discover the mutually beneficial exchanges that will accomplish that goal. Adam Smith first systematized this message in *The Wealth of Nations*. In the twentieth century, economists of the Austrian school of economics were the most uncompromising proponents of this message, not because of a prior ideological commitment, but because of the logic of their arguments.

About the Author

Peter J. Boettke is a professor of economics at George Mason University, where he is also the deputy director of the James M. Buchanan Center for Political Economy and a senior fellow at the Mercatus Center. He is the editor of the *Review of Austrian Economics*.

Further Reading

General Reading

Boettke, P., ed. *The Elgar Companion to Austrian Economics*. Brookfield, Vt.: Edward Elgar, 1994.
Dolan, E., ed. *The Foundations of Modern Austrian Economics*. Mission, Kans.: Sheed and Ward, 1976.

Classic Readings

Böhm-Bawerk, E. *Capital and Interest*. 3 vols. 1883. South Holland, Ill.: Libertarian Press, 1956.
Hayek, F. A. *Individualism and Economic Order*. Chicago: University of Chicago Press, 1948.
Kirzner, I. *Competition and Entrepreneurship*. Chicago: University of Chicago Press, 1973.
Menger, C. *Principles of Economics*. 1871. New York: New York University Press, 1976.
Mises, L. von. *Human Action: A Treatise on Economics*. New Haven: Yale University Press, 1949.
O' Driscoll, G., and M. Rizzo. *The Economics of Time and Ignorance*. Oxford: Basil Blackwell, 1985.
Rothbard, M. *Man, Economy and State*. 2 vols. New York: Van Nostrand Press, 1962.
Vaughn, K. *Austrian Economics in America*. Cambridge: Cambridge University Press, 1994.

History of the Austrian School of Economics

Boettke, P., and Peter Leeson. "The Austrian School of Economics: 1950–2000." In Jeff Biddle and Warren Samuels, eds., *The Blackwell Companion to the History of Economic Thought*. London: Blackwell, 2003.
Hayek, F. A. "Economic Thought VI: The Austrian School."

In *International Encyclopedia of the Social Sciences*. New York: Macmillan, 1968.
Machlup, F. "Austrian Economics." In *Encyclopedia of Economics*. New York: McGraw-Hill, 1982.

Balance of Payments

Herbert Stein

Few subjects in economics have caused so much confusion—and so much groundless fear—in the past four hundred years as the thought that a country might have a deficit in its balance of payments. This fear is groundless for two reasons: (1) there never is a deficit, and (2) it would not necessarily hurt anything if there was one.

The balance-of-payments accounts of a country record the payments and receipts of the residents of the country in their transactions with residents of other countries. If all transactions are included, the payments and receipts of each country are, and must be, equal. Any apparent inequality simply leaves one country acquiring assets in the others. For example, if Americans buy automobiles from Japan, and have no other transactions with Japan, the Japanese must end up holding dollars, which they may hold in the form of bank deposits in the United States or in some other U.S. investment. The payments Americans make to Japan for automobiles are balanced by the payments Japanese make to U.S. individuals and institutions, including banks, for the acquisition of dollar assets. Put another way, Japan sold the United States automobiles, and the United States sold Japan dollars or dollar-denominated assets such as treasury bills and New York office buildings.

Although the totals of payments and receipts are necessarily equal, there will be inequalities—excesses of payments or receipts, called deficits or surpluses—in particular kinds of transactions. Thus, there can be a deficit or surplus in any of the following: merchandise trade (goods), services trade, foreign investment income, unilateral transfers (foreign aid), private investment, the flow of gold and money between central banks and treasuries, or any combination of these or other international transactions. The statement that a country has a deficit or surplus in its "balance of payments" must refer to some particular class of transactions. As Table 1 shows, in 2004 the United States had a deficit in goods of $665.4 billion but a surplus in services of $48.8 billion.

Many different definitions of the balance-of-payments deficit or surplus have been used in the past. Each definition has different implications and purposes. Until about 1973 attention was focused on a definition of the balance of payments intended to measure a country's ability to meet its obligation to exchange its currency for other currencies or for gold at fixed exchange rates. To meet this obligation, countries maintained a stock of official reserves, in the form of gold or foreign currencies, that they could use to support their own currencies. A decline in this stock was considered an important balance-of-payments deficit because it threatened the ability of the country to meet its obligations. But that particular kind of deficit, by itself, was never a good indicator of the country's financial position. The reason is that it ignored the likelihood that the country would be called on to meet its obligation and the willingness of foreign or international monetary institutions to provide support.

After 1973, interest in official reserve positions as a measure of balance of payments greatly diminished as the major countries gave up their commitment to convert their currencies at fixed exchange rates. This reduced the need for reserves and lessened concern about changes in the size of reserves. Since 1973, discussions of "the" balance-of-payments deficit or surplus usually refer to what is called the current account. This account contains trade in goods and services, investment income earned abroad, and unilateral transfers. It excludes the capital account, which includes the acquisition or sale of securities or other property.

Because the current account and the capital account add up to the total account, which is necessarily balanced, a deficit in the current account is always accompanied by an equal surplus in the capital account, and vice versa. A deficit or surplus in the current account cannot be explained or evaluated without simultaneous explanation and evaluation of an equal surplus or deficit in the capital account.

A country is more likely to have a deficit in its current account the higher its price level, the higher its gross national product, the higher its interest rates, the lower its barriers to imports, and the more attractive its investment opportunities—all compared with conditions in other countries—and the higher its exchange rate. The effects of a change in one of these factors on the current account balance cannot be predicted without considering the effect on the other causal factors. For example, if the U.S. government increases tariffs, Americans will buy fewer imports, thus reducing the current account deficit. But this reduction will occur only if one of the other factors changes to bring about a decrease in the capital account surplus. If none of these other factors changes, the reduced imports from the tariff increase will cause a decline in the demand for foreign currency (yen, deutsche marks, etc.), which in turn will raise the value of the U.S. dollar. The increase in

Table 1 The U.S. Balance of Payments, 2004

Goods	− 665.4
Services	+ 48.8
Investment income	+ 30.4
Balance on goods, services, and income	− 587.2
Unilateral transfers	− 80.9
Balance on current account	− 668.1
Nonofficial capital*	+ 270.6
Official reserve assets	+ 397.5
Balance on capital account	+ 668.1
Total balance	0

Source: U.S. Department of Commerce, *Survey of Current Business.*
Notes: Dollar amounts are in billions; + = surplus; − = deficit.
  * Includes statistical discrepancy.

the value of the dollar will make U.S. exports more expensive and imports cheaper, offsetting the effect of the tariff increase. The net result is that the tariff increase brings no change in the current account balance.

Contrary to the general perception, the existence of a current account deficit is not in itself a sign of bad economic policy or bad economic conditions. If the United States has a current account deficit, all this means is that the United States is importing capital. And importing capital is no more unnatural or dangerous than importing coffee. The deficit is a response to conditions in the country. It may be a response to excessive inflation, to low productivity, or to inadequate saving. It may just as easily occur because investments in the United States are secure and profitable. Furthermore, the conditions to which the deficit responds may be good or bad and may be the results of good or bad policy; but if there is a problem, it is in the underlying conditions and not in the deficit per se.

During the 1980s there was a great deal of concern about the shift of the U.S. current account balance from a surplus of $5 billion in 1981 to a deficit of $161 billion in 1987. This shift was accompanied by an increase of about the same amount in the U.S. deficit in goods. Claims that this shift in the international position was causing a loss of employment in the United States were common, but that was not true. In fact, between 1981 and 1987, the number of people employed rose by more than twelve million, and employment as a percentage of population rose from 60 percent to 62.5 percent.

Many people were also anxious about the other side of the accounts—the inflow of foreign capital that accompanied the current account deficit—fearing that the United States was becoming owned by foreigners. The inflow of foreign capital did not, however, reduce the assets owned by Americans. Instead, it added to the capital within the country. In any event, the amount was small relative to the U.S. capital stock. Measurement of the net amount of foreign-owned assets in the United States (the excess of foreign assets in the United States over U.S. assets abroad) is very uncertain. At the end of 1988, however, it was surely much less than 4 percent of the U.S. capital stock and possibly even zero. Later, there was fear of what would happen when the capital inflow slowed down or stopped. But after 1987 it did slow down and the economy adjusted, just as it had adjusted to the big capital inflow earlier, by a decline in the current account and trade deficits.

These same concerns surfaced again in the late 1990s and early 2000s as the current account went from a surplus of $4 billion in 1991 to a deficit of $666 billion in 2004. The increase in the current account deficit account, just as in the 1980s, was accompanied by an almost equal increase in the deficit in goods. Interestingly, the current account surpluses of 1981 and 1991 both occurred in the midst of a U.S. recession, and the large surpluses occurred during U.S. economic expansions. This makes sense because U.S. imports are highly sensitive to U.S. economic conditions, falling more than proportionally when U.S. GDP falls and rising more than proportionally when U.S. GDP rises. Just as in the 1980s, U.S. employment expanded, with the U.S. economy adding more than twenty-one million jobs between 1991 and 2004. Also, employment as a percentage of population rose from 61.7 percent in 1991 to 64.4 percent in 2000 and, although it fell to 62.3 percent in 2004, was still modestly above its 1991 level.

How about the issue of foreign ownership? By the end of 2003, Americans owned assets abroad valued at market prices of $7.86 trillion, while foreigners owned U.S. assets valued at market prices of $10.52 trillion. The net international investment position of the United States, therefore, was $2.66 trillion. This was only 8.5 percent of the U.S. capital stock.[1]

About the Author

Herbert Stein, who died in 1999, was a senior fellow at the American Enterprise Institute in Washington, D.C., and was on the board of contributors of the *Wall Street Journal*. He was chairman of the Council of Economic Advisers under Presidents Richard Nixon and Gerald Ford. The editor, David R.

1. If by capital stock we mean the net value of U.S. fixed reproducible assets, which was $31.4 trillion in 2003. See *Survey of Current Business*, September 2004, online at: http://www.bea.gov/bea/ARTICLES/2004/09September/Fixed_Assets.pdf.

Henderson, with the help of Kevin Hoover and Mack Ott, updated the data and added the last two paragraphs.

Further Reading

Dornbusch, Rudiger, Stanley Fischer, and Richard Startz. *Macroeconomics*. 9th ed. New York: McGraw-Hill Irwin, 2003. For general concepts and theory, see pp. 298–332.
Economic Report of the President. 2004. For good, clear reasoning about balance of payments, see pp. 239–264.
Survey of Current Business. Online at: http://www.bea.gov/bea/pubs.htm (for current data).

Bank Runs

George G. Kaufman

A run on a bank occurs when a large number of depositors, fearing that their bank will be unable to repay their deposits in full and on time, simultaneously try to withdraw their funds immediately. This may create a problem because banks keep only a small fraction of deposits on hand in cash; they lend out the majority of deposits to borrowers or use the funds to purchase other interest-bearing assets such as government securities. When a run comes, a bank must quickly increase its cash to meet depositors' demands. It does so primarily by selling assets, often hastily and at fire-sale prices. As banks hold little capital and are highly leveraged, losses on these sales can drive a bank into insolvency.

The danger of bank runs has been frequently overstated. For one thing, a bank run is unlikely to cause insolvency. Suppose that depositors, worried about their bank's solvency, start a run and switch their deposits to other banks. If their concerns about the bank's solvency are unjustified, other banks in the same market area will generally gain from recycling funds they receive back to the bank experiencing the run. They would do this by making loans to the bank or by purchasing the bank's assets at non-fire-sale prices. Thus, a run is highly unlikely to make a solvent bank insolvent.

Of course, if the depositors' fears are justified and the bank is economically insolvent, other banks will be unlikely to throw good money after bad by recycling their funds to the insolvent bank. As a result, the bank cannot replenish its liquidity and will be forced into default. But the run would not have caused the insolvency; rather, the recognition of the existing insolvency caused the run.

A more serious potential problem is spillover to other banks. The likelihood of this happening depends on what the "running" depositors do with their funds. They have three choices:

1. They can redeposit the money in banks that they think are safe, known as direct redeposit.

2. If they perceive no bank to be safe, they can buy treasury securities in a "flight to quality." But what do the sellers of the securities do? If they deposit the proceeds in banks they believe are safe, as is likely, this is an indirect redeposit.

3. If neither the depositors nor the sellers of the treasury securities believe that any bank is safe, they hold the funds as currency outside the banking system. A run on individual banks would then be transformed into a run on the banking system as a whole.

If the run is either type 1 or type 2, no great harm is done. The deposits and reserves are reshuffled among the banks, possibly including overseas banks, but do not leave the banking system. Temporary loan disruptions may occur because borrowers have to transfer from deposit-losing to deposit-gaining banks, and interest rates and exchange rates may change. But these costs are not the calamities that people often associate with bank runs.

Higher costs could occur in a type 3 run, because currency (an important component of bank reserves) would be removed from the banking system. Banks operate on a fractional reserve basis, which means that they hold only a fraction of their deposits as reserves. When people try to convert their deposits into currency, the money supply shrinks, dampening economic activity in other sectors. In addition, almost all banks would sell assets to replenish their liquidity, but few banks would be buying. Losses would be large, and the number of bank failures would increase.

In practice, bank failures have been relatively infrequent. From the end of the Civil War through 1920 (after the Federal Reserve was established in 1913 but before the Federal Deposit Insurance Corporation was formed in 1933), the bank failure rate was lower, on average, than that of nonbanking firms. The failure rate increased sharply in the 1920s and again between 1929 and 1933, when nearly 40 percent of U.S. banks failed. Yet, from 1875 through 1933, losses from failures averaged only 0.2 percent of total deposits in the banking system annually. Losses to depositors at failed banks averaged only a fraction of the annual losses suffered by bondholders of failed nonbanking firms.

A survey of all failures of national banks from 1865 through 1936 by J. F. T. O'Connor, comptroller of the currency from 1933 through 1938, concluded that runs were a contributing cause in less than 15 percent of the three thousand failures. The fact that the number of runs on individual banks was far greater than this means that most runs did not lead to failures.

The evidence suggests that most bank runs were then and are today type 1 or 2, and few were of the contagious type 3. Because a type 3 run—a run on the banking system—causes an outflow of currency, such a run can be identified by an increase in the ratio of currency to the money supply (most of the various measures of the money supply consist of currency in the hands of the public plus different types of bank deposits). Increases in this ratio have occurred in only four periods since the Civil War, and in only two—1893 and 1929–1933—did an unusually large number of banks fail. Thus, market forces and the banking system on its own successfully insulated runs on individual banks in most periods. Moreover, even in the 1893 and 1929–1933 incidents, the evidence is unclear whether the increase in bank failures caused the economic downturn or the economic downturn caused the bank failures. As a result of the introduction of deposit insurance in 1933, runs into currency are even less likely today. The threat of runs from perceived troubled large banks, which have sizable uninsured deposits, to perceived safe banks serves as a form of market discipline that may reduce the likelihood of runs on all banks by giving them an incentive to strengthen their financial positions.

About the Author

George G. Kaufman is the John F. Smith Professor of Finance and Economics at Loyola University in Chicago. He is also cochair of the Shadow Financial Regulatory Committee.

Further Reading

Allen, Franklin, and Douglas Gale. "Optimal Financial Crises." *Journal of Finance* 53, no. 4 (1998): 1245–1284.

Benston, George J., Robert A. Eisenbeis, Paul M. Horvitz, Edward J. Kane, and George G. Kaufman. *Perspectives on Safe and Sound Banking.* Cambridge: MIT Press, 1986.

Carlstrom, Charles T. "Bank Runs, Deposit Insurance, and Bank Regulation." Parts 1 and 2. *Federal Reserve Bank of Cleveland Economic Commentary,* February 1 and 15, 1988.

Diamond, Douglas W., and Philip H. Dydvig. "Bank Runs, Deposit Insurance and Liquidity." *Journal of Political Economy* 91, no. 3 (1983): 401–419.

Gorton, Gary. "Banking Panics and Business Cycles." *Oxford Economic Papers* 40 (December 1988): 751–781.

Kaufman, George G. "Bank Runs: Causes, Benefits and Costs." *Cato Journal* 2, no. 3 (1988): 559–588.

———. "Banking Risk in Historical Perspective." *Research in Financial Services* 1 (1989): 151–164.

Neuberger, Jonathan A. "Depositor Discipline and Bank Runs." Federal Reserve Bank of San Francisco, weekly letter, April 12, 1991.

Schumaker, Liliana. "Bank Runs and Currency Runs in a System Without a Safety Net." *Journal of Monetary Economics* 46, no. 1 (2000): 257–277.

Tallman, Ellis. "Some Unanswered Questions About Bank Panics." *Federal Reserve Bank of Atlanta Economic Review*, November/December 1988.

Bankruptcy

Todd J. Zywicki

Bankruptcy is common in America today. Notwithstanding two decades of largely uninterrupted economic growth, the annual bankruptcy filing rate has quintupled, topping 1.5 million individuals annually. Recent years also have seen several of the largest and most expensive corporate bankruptcies in history. This confluence of skyrocketing personal bankruptcies in a period of prosperity, an increasingly expensive and dysfunctional Chapter 11 reorganization system, and the macroeconomic competitive pressures of globalization has spurred legislative efforts to reform the bankruptcy code.

History of Bankruptcy

Early English bankruptcy laws were designed to assist creditors in collecting the debtor's assets, not to protect the debtor or discharge (forgive) his debts. The Bankruptcy Clause of the U.S. Constitution also reflects this procreditor purpose of early bankruptcy law. Under the Articles of Confederation, the states alone governed debtor-creditor relations. This situation led to diverse and contradictory state laws, many of which were prodebtor laws designed to favor farmers. Like other provisions of the Constitution, the enumeration of the bankruptcy power in article I, section 8 was designed to encourage the development of a commercial republic and to temper the excesses of prodebtor state legislation that proliferated under the Articles of Confederation. As James Madison observed in *Federalist* number 42:

> The power of establishing uniform laws of bankruptcy is so intimately connected with the regulation of commerce, and will prevent so many frauds where the parties or their property may lie or be removed into different States that the expediency of it [i.e., Congress's exclusive power to enact bankruptcy laws] seems not likely to be drawn into question.

The primary purpose of the Bankruptcy Clause was to protect creditors, not debtors, and in fact, debtor's prisons persisted in many states well into the eighteenth century.

During the nineteenth century, the federal government exercised its bankruptcy powers only sporadically and in response to major economic downturns. The first bankruptcy law lasted from 1800 to 1803, the second from 1841 to 1843, and the third from 1867 to 1878. During the periods without a federal bankruptcy law, debtor-creditor relations were governed solely by the states. The first permanent federal bankruptcy law was enacted in 1898 and remained in effect, with amendments, until it was replaced with a comprehensive new law in 1978, the essential structure of which remains in place today.

Because bankruptcy law intervenes only when a debtor is insolvent, nonbankruptcy and state law govern most issues relating to standard debtor-creditor relations, such as contracts, real estate mortgages, secured transactions, and collection of judgments. Federal bankruptcy law is thus a hybrid system of federal law layered on top of this foundation of state law, leading to variety in debtor-creditor regimes. Bankruptcy law is generally procedural in nature and therefore attempts to preserve nonbankruptcy substantive rights, such as whether a creditor has a valid claim to collect against the debtor in bankruptcy, unless modification is necessary to advance an overriding bankruptcy policy.

Bankruptcy Policies

Bankruptcy law serves three basic purposes: (1) to solve a collective action problem among creditors in dealing with an insolvent debtor, (2) to provide a "fresh start" to individual debtors overburdened by debt, and (3) to save and preserve the going-concern value of firms in financial distress by reorganizing rather than liquidating.

First, bankruptcy law solves a collective action problem among creditors. Nonbankruptcy debt collection law is an individualized process grounded in bilateral transactions between debtors and creditors. Outside bankruptcy, debt collection is essentially a race of diligence. Creditors able to translate their claims against the debtor into claims against the debtor's property are entitled to do so, subject to state laws that declare some of the debtor's property, such as the debtor's homestead, to be "exempt" from creditors' claims.

When a debtor is insolvent and there are not enough assets to satisfy all creditors, however, a common-pool problem arises (see TRAGEDY OF THE COMMONS). Each creditor has an incentive to try to seize assets of the debtor, even if this prematurely depletes the common pool of assets for creditors as a whole. Although creditors as a group may be better off by cooperating and working together to distribute the debtor's assets in an orderly fashion, each individual creditor has an incentive to race to grab his share. If he waits and others do not, there may not be enough assets available to satisfy his claim. Bankruptcy stops this race of diligence in favor of an orderly distribution of the debtor's assets through a collective proceeding that jointly involves anyone with a claim against the debtor. Once the debtor files for bankruptcy, all creditor collection actions are automatically "stayed," prohibiting further collection actions without permission of the bankruptcy court. In addition, any collections by creditors from an insolvent debtor in the period preceding the debtor's bankruptcy filing can be prohibited as a "preference." One interesting policy option that is not currently allowed is to allow parties to solve the common-pool problem through contract and corporate law, making bankruptcy unnecessary.

The second bankruptcy policy is the provision of a fresh start for individual debtors through a cancellation, or "discharge," of his debts in bankruptcy. Although many rationales have been offered for the fresh start, none is wholly persuasive, and none provides a compelling rationale for the current American rule that the debtor's right to a discharge is mandatory and nonwaiveable. This requirement increases the risk of lending to the debtor, raising the cost of credit for all debtors and leading to the rationing and denial of credit to high-risk borrowers. Allowing debtors to waive or modify their discharge right in some or all situations might be more efficient and better for debtors because by modifying their discharge rights, debtors could get lower interest rates or other more favorable credit terms. Indeed, the American system is unique in providing a mandatory fresh-start policy.

Personal bankruptcy filing rates have risen dramatically over the past twenty-five years, from fewer than 200,000 annual filings in 1979 to more than 1.6 million in 2004. Personal bankruptcy filing rates were traditionally caused by factors such as high personal debt rates, divorce, and unemployment. But given the unprecedented prosperity during the past twenty-five years—a period of generally low unemployment, declining divorce rate, low interest rates and rapid accumulation of household wealth due to a booming stock market and residential real estate market—this traditional model of the causes of consumer bankruptcy filings has become increasingly untenable (Zywicki 2005b). Scholars have suggested that the decline in the stigma associated with bankruptcy, changes in the relative economic benefits and costs of filing bankruptcy (especially the relaxation of the bankruptcy laws in the 1978 Bankruptcy Code), and changes in the consumer credit system itself have made individuals more willing to file bankruptcy than in the past (Zywicki 2005b). In response to this unprecedented rise in personal bankruptcies and the underlying reason for it, Congress has proposed reforms to reduce the abuse and fraud of the current system. One suggested reform is to require high-income filers to

repay some of their debts out of their future income as a condition for filing bankruptcy (Jones and Zywicki 1999).

The third bankruptcy policy is the promotion of the reorganization of firms in financial distress. A firm confronting financial problems might be worth more as a going concern than it would be if it was closed and sold piecemeal to satisfy creditors' claims. A firm's assets may be more valuable when kept together and owned by that firm than if they are liquidated and sold to a third party. Such assets could include physical assets (e.g., custom-made machinery), human capital assets (such as management or a specially skilled workforce), or particular synergies between various assets of the company (such as knowledge of how best to exploit intellectual property). Thus, maintaining the existing combination of assets as a going concern, rather than liquidating the firm, could make creditors better off. The railroads at the turn of the century exemplify this principle. Rather than liquidating them and selling off the various pieces for scrap (e.g., tearing up the tracks and selling them as scrap steel), reorganization kept the rail network in place and the trains rolling, and creditors were paid out of the operating revenues of the reorganized firm.

Other firms, however, may not be merely in financial distress. Some may be economically failed enterprises generating a value less than the opportunity costs of their assets. Economic efficiency, and concern for creditors, would require such firms to be liquidated and their assets redeployed to higher-valued uses. For instance, given the ubiquity and dominance of computers, it was obviously efficient to liquidate the venerable Smith-Corona typewriter company and allow its workers to retrain and its physical assets to be reallocated in the economy.

It is difficult to distinguish a firm in financial distress from an economically failed enterprise, and it is doubtful that the current reorganization system is very accurate at making the distinction. First, the decision whether to reorganize is made by a bankruptcy judge rather than by the market. The reorganization decision, therefore, is essentially a form of mini–central planning, with the bankruptcy judge making the planners' decision whether to allow the business to continue operating or to shut it down. As such, the decision is subject to the standard knowledge and incentive problems that plague central planning generally (see FRIEDRICH AUGUST HAYEK). Second, the decision whether to file and with which court is made by the debtor himself and the debtor's management staff, which will have obvious incentives to file in friendly courts and to push for reorganization and the preservation of their jobs. Third, the beneficiaries of reorganization efforts (incumbent management, workers, suppliers, etc.) have great incentives to participate in the bankruptcy case and to make their interests known to the judge. Secured creditors will accept a reorganization only if the company is worth more dead than alive. But unsecured creditors, who have no hope of recovering their investment if the company is killed, have an incentive to favor reorganization even if there is only a tiny probability that reorganization will work: a small probability of something is better than a certainty of nothing. Given the errors and inefficiencies inherent in the current system, some scholars have proposed replacing the current judicial-centered system or at least supplementing it with various market mechanisms. One such mechanism would be an auction of the assets of the company as a going concern (Baird 1986). Another would be ex ante collective contracts (such as provisions in a firm's corporate charter) that would apply if the firm became insolvent and would put creditors on notice about the risks of dealing with a particular company, causing them to tailor their interest rates and other credit terms accordingly.

The economic costs of inefficient reorganizations can be substantial. First, in large reorganization cases, the direct costs of bankruptcy reorganization routinely exceed several hundred million dollars in professional and other fees. Second, there is an opportunity cost associated with retaining the current allocation of assets, even if temporarily. For instance, a failing business continues to occupy its current location and to retain its workers and assets, not only slowing the reallocation of these assets to higher-valued uses in other firms and industries, but also injuring consumers, suppliers, and others.

The Future of Bankruptcy Law

The past several years have seen concerted efforts to reform the bankruptcy laws to address many of the above concerns. The anomaly of skyrocketing consumer bankruptcy filings during an era of economic prosperity has spurred widespread support for efforts to reform the consumer bankruptcy system. A few such reforms would include requiring high-income debtors who can repay a substantial portion of their debts to do so by entering a Chapter 13 repayment plan rather than filing for Chapter 7 bankruptcy, limiting repeat filings, and limiting some property exemptions. The proposed bankruptcy reform legislation would also attempt to streamline and reduce the cost and delay of corporate Chapter 11 bankruptcy proceedings, especially as they apply to small business bankruptcies.

Comprehensive bankruptcy reform legislation has been proposed in every Congress since the late 1990s but, notwithstanding overwhelming bipartisan support in both houses, has not yet been enacted. One reason is that various politicians introduced extraneous but controversial political issues; another reason is that bankruptcy professionals oppose reforms that would reduce the number of bankruptcies filed and the expense of bankruptcy proceedings.

On the other hand, the increasing pressure of economic globalization and the increasing challenges of bankruptcies involving multinational corporations have created incentives for bankruptcy reform. As investment capital increasingly flows worldwide, globalization creates strong incentives for national economies to adopt efficient economic policies, including bankruptcy policies. The current American bankruptcy system rests on investors' willingness to voluntarily continue to invest in American firms despite the danger that capital investment will be trapped in an expensive and inefficient reorganization regime if the firm fails. By contrast, some major economies, such as Germany and Japan, have introduced more flexibility into their bankruptcy systems. Although many commentators have advocated establishing a uniform transnational bankruptcy system by treaty, devising a scheme that would gain assent from member countries would be difficult. Also, such a regime would likely be subject to many of the same interest-group pressures that characterize the American regime. The competitive forces of globalization may generate, instead of a "top-down" global bankruptcy system, an efficient and spontaneous convergence of bankruptcy systems throughout the world.

About the Author

Todd J. Zywicki is a professor of law at George Mason University's School of Law and a senior research fellow of the James Buchanan Center, Program on Economics, Politics, and Philosophy. He was previously the director of the Office of Policy Planning at the Federal Trade Commission.

Further Reading

Baird, Douglas G. *Elements of Bankruptcy*. 3d ed. New York: Foundation Press, 2001.

———. "The Uneasy Case for Corporate Reorganization." *Journal of Legal Studies* 15 (1986): 127–147.

Jackson, Thomas H. *The Logic and Limits of Bankruptcy Law*. Cambridge: Harvard University Press, 1986.

Jones, Edith H., and Todd J. Zywicki. "It's Time for Means-Testing." *Brigham Young University Law Review* 1999 (1999): 177–250.

Rasmussen, Robert K. "A Menu Approach to Corporate Bankruptcy." *Texas Law Review* 71 (1992): 51–121.

Skeel, David A. Jr. *Debt's Dominion: A History of Bankruptcy Law in America*. Princeton: Princeton University Press, 2001.

White, Michelle J. "Economic Versus Sociological Approaches

to Legal Research: The Case of Bankruptcy." *Law and Society Review* 25 (1991): 685–709.

Zywicki, Todd J. "The Bankruptcy Clause." In Edwin Meese et al., ed., *The Heritage Guide to the Constitution*. Washington, D.C.: Heritage Foundation, 2005a. Pp. 112–114.

———. "An Economic Analysis of the Consumer Bankruptcy Crisis." *Northwestern University Law Review* 99, no. 4 (2005b): 1463–1541.

———. "The Past, Present, and Future of Bankruptcy Law in America." *Michigan Law Review* 101, no. 6 (2003): 2016–2036.

Behavioral Economics

Richard H. Thaler
Sendhil Mullainathan

How Behavioral Economics Differs from Traditional Economics

All of economics is meant to be about people's behavior. So, what is behavioral economics, and how does it differ from the rest of economics?

Economics traditionally conceptualizes a world populated by calculating, unemotional maximizers that have been dubbed *Homo economicus*. The standard economic framework ignores or rules out virtually all the behavior studied by cognitive and social psychologists. This "unbehavioral" economic agent was once defended on numerous grounds: some claimed that the model was "right"; most others simply argued that the standard model was easier to formalize and practically more relevant. Behavioral economics blossomed from the realization that neither point of view was correct.

The standard economic model of human behavior includes three unrealistic traits—unbounded rationality, unbounded willpower, and unbounded selfishness—all of which behavioral economics modifies.

Nobel Memorial Prize recipient Herbert Simon (1955) was an early critic of the idea that people have unlimited information-processing capabilities. He suggested the term "bounded rationality" to describe a more realistic conception of human problem-solving ability. The failure to incorporate bounded rationality into economic models is just bad economics—the equivalent to presuming the existence of a free lunch. Since we have only so much brainpower and only so much time, we cannot be expected to solve difficult problems optimally. It is eminently rational for people to adopt rules of thumb as a way to economize on cognitive faculties. Yet the standard model ignores these bounds.

Departures from rationality emerge both in judgments (beliefs) and in choices. The ways in which judgment diverges from rationality are extensive (see Kahneman et al. 1982). Some illustrative examples include overconfidence, optimism, and extrapolation.

An example of suboptimal behavior involving two important behavioral concepts, loss aversion and mental accounting, is a mid-1990s study of New York City taxicab drivers (Camerer et al. 1997). These drivers pay a fixed fee to rent their cabs for twelve hours and then keep all their revenues. They must decide how long to drive each day. The profit-maximizing strategy is to work longer hours on good days—rainy days or days with a big convention in town—and to quit early on bad days. Suppose, however, that cabbies set a target earnings level for each day and treat shortfalls relative to that target as a loss. Then they will end up quitting early on good days and working longer on bad days. The authors of the study found that this is precisely what they do.

Consider the second vulnerable tenet of standard economics, the assumption of complete self-control. Humans, even when we know what is best, sometimes lack self-control. Most of us, at some point, have eaten, drunk, or spent too much, and exercised, saved, or worked too little. Though people have these self-control problems, they are at least somewhat aware of them: they join diet plans and buy cigarettes by the pack (because having an entire carton around is too tempting). They also pay more withholding taxes than they need to in order to assure themselves a refund; in 1997, nearly ninety million tax returns paid an average refund of around $1,300.

Finally, people are boundedly selfish. Although economic theory does not rule out altruism, as a practical matter economists stress self-interest as people's primary motive. For example, the free-rider problems widely discussed in economics are predicted to occur because individuals cannot be expected to contribute to the public good unless their private welfare is thus improved. But people do, in fact, often act selflessly. In 1998, for example, 70.1 percent of all households gave some money to charity, the average dollar amount being 2.1 percent of household income.[1] Likewise, 55.5 percent of the population age eighteen or more did volunteer work in 1998, with 3.5 hours per week

This article is a revision of a manuscript originally written as an entry in the *International Encyclopedia of the Social and Behavioral Sciences*.

[1]. Data are from the *Chronicle of Philanthropy* (1999), available online at: http://philanthropy.com/free/articles/v12/i01/1201who donated.htm.

being the average hours volunteered.[2] Similar selfless behavior has been observed in controlled laboratory experiments. People often cooperate in PRISONERS' DILEMMA games and turn down unfair offers in "ultimatum" games. (In an ultimatum game, the experimenter gives one player, the proposer, some money, say ten dollars. The proposer then makes an offer of x, equal or less than ten dollars, to the other player, the responder. If the responder accepts the offer, he gets x and the proposer gets $10 - x$. If the proposer rejects the offer, then both players get nothing. Standard economic theory predicts that proposers will offer a token amount (say twenty-five cents) and responders will accept, because twenty-five cents is better than nothing. But experiments have found that responders typically reject offers of less than 20 percent (two dollars in this example).

Behavioral Finance

If economists had been asked in the mid-1980s to name a discipline within economics to which bounded rationality was least likely to apply, finance would probably have been the one most often named. One leading economist called the efficient markets hypothesis (see definition below), which follows from traditional economic thinking, the best-established fact in economics. Yet finance is perhaps the branch of economics where behavioral economics has made the greatest contributions. How has this happened?

Two factors contributed to the surprising success of behavioral finance. First, financial economics in general, and the efficient market hypothesis (see EFFICIENT CAPITAL MARKETS) in particular, generated sharp, testable predictions about observable phenomena. Second, high-quality data are readily available to test these sharp predictions.

The rational efficient markets hypothesis states that stock prices are "correct" in the sense that asset prices reflect the true or rational value of the security. In many cases, this tenet of the efficient market hypothesis is untestable because intrinsic values are not observable. In some special cases, however, the hypothesis can be tested by comparing two assets whose relative intrinsic values are known.

Consider closed-end mutual funds (Lee et al. 1991). These funds are much like typical (open-end) mutual funds, except that to cash out of the fund, investors must sell their shares on the open market. This means that the market prices of closed-end funds are determined by sup-

ply and demand rather than set equal to the value of their assets by the fund managers, as in open-end funds. Because closed-end funds' holdings are public, market efficiency would mean that the price of the fund should match the price of the underlying securities they hold (the net asset value, or NAV). Instead, closed-end funds typically trade at substantial discounts relative to their NAV, and occasionally at substantial premia. Most interesting from a behavioral perspective is that closed-end fund discounts are correlated with one another and appear to reflect individual investor sentiment. (Individual investors rather than institutions are the primary owners of closed-end funds.) Lee and his colleagues found that discounts shrank in months when shares of small companies (also owned primarily by individuals) did well and in months when there was a lot of initial public offering (IPO) activity, indicating a "hot" market. Since these findings were predicted by behavioral finance theory, they move the research beyond the demonstration of an embarrassing fact (price not equal to NAV) toward a constructive understanding of how markets work.

The second principle of the efficient market hypothesis is unpredictability. In an efficient market, it is not possible to predict future stock price movements based on publicly available information. Many early violations of this principle had no explicit link to behavior. Thus it was reported that small firms and "value firms" (firms with low price-to-earnings ratios) earned higher returns than other stocks with the same risk. Also, stocks in general, but especially stocks of small companies, have done well in January and on Fridays (but poorly on Mondays).

An early study by Werner De Bondt and Richard Thaler (1985) was explicitly motivated by the psychological finding that individuals tend to overreact to new information. For example, experimental evidence suggested that people tended to underweight base rate data (or prior information) in incorporating new data. De Bondt and Thaler hypothesized that if investors behave this way, then stocks that perform quite well over a period of years will eventually have prices that are too high because people overreacting to the good news will drive up their prices. Similarly, poor performers will eventually have prices that are too low. This yields a prediction about future returns: past "winners" ought to underperform, while past "losers" ought to outperform the market. Using data for stocks traded on the New York Stock Exchange, De Bondt and Thaler found that the thirty-five stocks that had performed the worst over the past five years (the losers) outperformed the market over the next five years, while the thirty-five biggest winners over the past five years subsequently underperformed. Follow-up studies showed that these early

2. Data are from Independent Sector (2004), available online at: http://www.independentsector.org/programs/research/volunteer_time.html.

results cannot be attributed to risk; by some measures the portfolio of losers was actually less risky than the portfolio of winners.

More recent studies have found other violations of unpredictability that have the opposite pattern from that found by De Bondt and Thaler, namely underreaction rather than overreaction. Over short periods—for example, six months to one year—stocks display momentum: the stocks that go up the fastest for the first six months of the year tend to keep going up. Also, after many corporate announcements such as large earnings changes, dividend initiations and omissions, share repurchases, and splits, the price jumps initially on the day of the announcement and then drifts slowly upward for a year or longer (see Shleifer 2000 for a nice introduction to the field).

Behavioral economists have also hypothesized that investors are reluctant to realize capital losses because doing so would mean that they would have to "declare" the loss to themselves. Hersh Shefrin and Meir Statman (1985) dubbed this hypothesis the "disposition effect." Interestingly, the tax law encourages just the opposite behavior. Yet Terrance Odean (1998) found that in a sample of customers of a discount brokerage firm, investors were more likely to sell a stock that had increased in value than one that had decreased. While around 15 percent of all gains were realized, only 10 percent of all losses were realized. Odean showed, moreover, that the loser stocks that were held underperformed the gainer stocks that were sold.

Saving

If finance was held to be the field in which a behavioral approach was least likely, a priori, to succeed, saving had to be one of the most promising. Although the standard life-cycle model of savings abstracts from both bounded rationality and bounded willpower, saving for retirement is both a difficult cognitive problem and a difficult self-control problem. It is thus perhaps less surprising that a behavioral approach has been fruitful here. As in finance, progress has been helped by the combination of a refined standard theory with testable predictions and abundant data sources on household saving behavior.

Suppose that Tom is a basketball player and therefore earns most of his income early in his life, while Ray is a manager who earns most of his income late in life. The life-cycle model predicts that Tom would save his early income to increase consumption later in life, while Ray would borrow against future income to increase consumption earlier in life. The data do not support this prediction. Instead, they show that consumption tracks income over individuals' life cycles much more closely than the stan-

dard life-cycle model predicts. Furthermore, the departures from predicted behavior cannot be explained merely by people's inability to borrow. James Banks, Richard Blundell, and Sarah Tanner (1998) showed, for example, that consumption drops sharply as individuals retire and their incomes drop because they have not saved enough for retirement. Indeed, many low- to middle-income families have essentially no savings. The primary cause of this lack of saving appears to be lack of self-control. One bit of evidence supporting this conclusion is that virtually all of Americans' saving takes place in forms that are often called "forced savings"—for example, accumulating home equity by paying the mortgage and participating in pension plans. Coming full circle, individuals may impose another type of "forced" savings on themselves—high tax withholding—so that when the refund comes, they can buy something they might not have had the willpower to save up for.

One of the most interesting research areas has been devoted to measuring the effectiveness of tax-advantaged savings programs such as individual retirement accounts (IRAs) and 401(k) plans. Consider the original IRA program of the early 1980s. This program provided tax subsidies for savings up to a threshold, often two thousand dollars per year. Because there was no tax incentive to save more than two thousand dollars per year, those saving more than the threshold should not have increased their total saving, but instead should have merely switched some money from a taxable account to the IRA. Yet, by some accounts, these programs appear to have generated substantial new savings. Some researchers argue that almost every dollar of savings in IRAs appears to represent new savings. In other words, people are not simply shifting their savings into IRAs and leaving their total behavior unchanged. Similar results are found for 401(k) plans. The behavioral explanation for these findings is that IRAs and 401(k) plans help solve self-control problems by setting up special mental accounts that are devoted to retirement savings. Households tend to respect the designated use of these accounts, and the tax penalty that must be paid if funds are removed prematurely bolsters people's self-control.[3]

An interesting flip side to IRA and 401(k) programs is that these programs have generated far less than the full participation expected. Many eligible people do not participate, forgoing, in effect, a cash transfer from the government (and in some cases from their employer). Ted

---

3. Some issues remain controversial. See the debate in the fall 1996 issue of the *Journal of Economic Perspectives.*

O'Donoghue and Matthew Rabin (1999) presented an explanation based on procrastination and hyperbolic discounting. Individuals typically show very sharp impatience for short-horizon decisions, but much more patience at long horizons. This behavior is often referred to as hyperbolic discounting, in contrast to the standard assumption of exponential discounting, in which patience is independent of horizon. In exponential models, people are equally patient at long and short horizons. O'Donoghue and Rabin argued that hyperbolic individuals will show exactly the low IRA participation that we observe. Though hyperbolic people will eventually want to participate in IRAs (because they are patient in the long run), something always comes up in the short run (where they are very impatient) that provides greater immediate reward. Consequently, they may indefinitely delay starting an IRA.

If people procrastinate about joining the savings plan, then it should be possible to increase participation rates simply by lowering the psychic costs of joining. One simple way of accomplishing this is to switch the default option for new workers. In most companies, employees who become eligible for the 401(k) plan receive a form inviting them to join; to join, they have to send the form back and make some choices. The default option, therefore, is not to join. Several firms have made the seemingly inconsequential change of switching the default: employees are enrolled into the plan unless they explicitly opt out. This change often produces dramatic increases in savings rates. For example, in one company studied by Brigitte C. Madrian and Dennis F. Shea (2000), the employees who joined after the default option was switched were 50 percent more likely to participate than the workers in the year prior to the change. The authors also found that the default asset allocation—that is, the allocation the firm made among stocks, bonds, and so on if the employee made no explicit choice—had a strong effect on workers' choices. The firm had made the default asset allocation 100 percent in a money market account, and the proportion of workers "selecting" this allocation soared.

It is possible to go further and design institutions that help people make better choices, as defined by the people who choose. One successful effort along these lines is Richard Thaler and Shlomo Benartzi's (2004) "Save More Tomorrow" program (SMarT). Under the SMarT plan, employers invite their employees to join a plan in which employees' contribution rates to their 401(k) plan increase automatically every year (say, by two percentage points). The increases are timed to coincide with annual raises, so the employee never sees a reduction in take-home pay, thus avoiding loss aversion (at least in nominal terms). In the first company that adopted the SMarT plan, the participants who joined the plan increased their savings rates from 3.5 percent to 13.6 percent after four pay raises (Thaler and Benartzi 2004).

About the Authors

Richard H. Thaler is the Ralph and Dorothy Keller Distinguished Service Professor of Economics and Behavioral Science at the University of Chicago's Graduate School of Business, where he is director of the Center for Decision Research. He is also a research associate at the National Bureau of Economic Research (NBER), where he codirects the behavioral economics project. Sendhil Mullainathan is a professor of economics at Harvard University and a research associate with the NBER. In 2002, he was awarded a grant from the MacArthur Fellows Program.

Further Reading

Banks, James, Richard Blundell, and Sarah Tanner. "Is There a Retirement-Savings Puzzle?" *American Economic Review* 88, no. 4 (1998): 769–788.

Camerer, Colin, Linda Babcock, George Loewenstein, and Richard H. Thaler. "Labor Supply of New York City Cabdrivers: One Day at a Time." *Quarterly Journal of Economics* 112, no. 2 (1997): 407–441.

Conlisk, John. "Why Bounded Rationality?" *Journal of Economic Literature* 34, no. 2 (1996): 669–700.

De Bondt, Werner F. M., and Richard H. Thaler. "Does the Stock Market Overreact?" *Journal of Finance* 40, no. 3 (1985): 793–805.

DeLong, Brad, Andrei Shleifer, Lawrence Summers, and Robert Waldman. "Noise Trader Risk in Financial Markets." *Journal of Political Economy* 98, no. 4 (1990): 703–738.

Kahneman, Daniel, and Amos Tversky. "Judgement Under Uncertainty: Heuristics and Biases." *Science* 185 (1974): 1124–1131.

———. "Prospect Theory: An Analysis of Decision Under Risk." *Econometrica* 47, no. 2 (1979): 263–291.

Kahneman, Daniel, Paul Slovic, and Amos Tversky. *Judgement Under Uncertainty: Heuristics and Biases.* Cambridge: Cambridge University Press, 1982.

Laibson, David. "Golden Eggs and Hyperbolic Discounting." *Quarterly Journal of Economics* 112, no. 2 (1997): 443–477.

Lee, Charles M. C., Andrei Shleifer, and Richard H. Thaler. "Investor Sentiment and the Closed-End Fund Puzzle." *Journal of Finance* 46, no. 1 (1991): 75–109.

Madrian, Brigitte C., and Dennis F. Shea. "The Power of Suggestion: Inertia in 401(k) Participation and Savings Behavior." *Quarterly Journal of Economics* 116, no. 4 (2000): 1149–1187.

Odean, Terrance. "Are Investors Reluctant to Realize Their Losses?" *Journal of Finance* 53, no. 5 (1998): 1775–1798.

O'Donoghue, Ted, and Matthew Rabin. "Procrastination in

Preparing for Retirement." In Henry Aaron, ed., *Behavioral Dimensions of Retirement Economics.* Washington, D.C.: Brookings Institution, 1999.

Shefrin, Hersh, and Meir Statman. "The Disposition to Sell Winners Too Early and Ride Losers Too Long: Theory and Evidence." *Journal of Finance* 40, no. 3 (1985): 777–790.

Shleifer, Andrei. *Inefficient Markets: An Introduction to Behavioral Finance.* Clarendon Lectures. Oxford: Oxford University Press, 2000.

Shleifer, Andrei, and Robert Vishny. "The Limits of Arbitrage." *Journal of Finance* 52, no. 1 (1997): 35–55.

Simon, Herbert A. "A Behavioral Model of Rational Choice." *Quarterly Journal of Economics* 69 (February 1955): 99–118.

Thaler, Richard H. "Mental Accounting and Consumer Choice." *Marketing Science* 4, no. 3 (1985): 199–214.

Thaler, Richard H., and Shlomo Benartzi. "Save More Tomorrow: Using Behavioral Economics to Increase Employee Saving." *Journal of Political Economy* 112 (February 2004): S164–S187.

Benefit-Cost Analysis

Paul R. Portney

Whenever people decide whether the advantages of a particular action are likely to outweigh its drawbacks, they engage in a form of benefit-cost analysis (BCA). In the public arena, formal BCA is a sometimes controversial technique for thoroughly and consistently evaluating the pros and cons associated with prospective policy changes. Specifically, it is an attempt to identify and express in dollar terms all of the effects of proposed government policies or projects. While not intended to be the only basis for decision making, BCA can be a valuable aid to policymakers.

Although conceived more than 150 years ago by the French engineer Jules Dupuit, BCA saw its first widespread use in the evaluation of federal water projects in the United States in the late 1930s. Since then, it has also been used to analyze policies affecting transportation, public health, criminal justice, defense, education, and the environment. Because some of BCA's most important and controversial applications have been in environmental policy, this discussion of key issues in BCA is illustrated with examples from the environmental arena.

To ascertain the net effect of a proposed policy change on social well-being, we must first have a way of measuring the gains to the gainers and the losses to the losers. Implicit in this statement is a central tenet of BCA: the effects of a policy change on society are no more or no less than the aggregate of the effects on the individuals who constitute society. Thus, if no individual would be made better

off by a policy change, there are no benefits associated with it; nor are there costs if no one is made worse off. In other words, BCA counts no values other than those held by the individual members of society.

It is equally important to note that benefits and costs, even though they are almost always expressed in dollar terms in BCA, go well beyond changes in individuals' incomes. If someone's well-being is improved because of cleaner air—through improved visibility, for instance—he experiences a benefit even though his income may not change. Similarly, an increase in pollution that puts people at higher risk of disease imposes a cost on them even though their incomes may not fall. Indeed, a person would bear a cost (be made worse off) if the pollution posed a threat to an exotic and little-known species of animal that he cared about. Some criticize BCA on the grounds that it supposedly enshrines the free market and discourages government intervention. However, BCA exists precisely because economists recognize that free markets sometimes allocate resources inefficiently, causing problems such as dirty air and water.

How, then, are benefits and costs estimated? While it is generally assumed that they are measured differently, benefits and costs are actually flip sides of the same coin. Benefits are measured by the willingness of individuals to pay for the outputs of the policy or project in question. The proper calculation of costs is the amount of compensation required to exactly offset negative consequences. Willingness to pay or compensation required should each be the dollar amount that would leave every individual just as well off following the implementation of the policy as before it.

Suppose, for example, we wished to evaluate the benefits and costs of a proposal to control air pollution emissions from a large factory. On the positive side, pollution abatement will mean reduced damage to exposed materials, diminished health risks to people living nearby, improved visibility, and even new jobs for those who manufacture pollution control equipment. On the negative side, the required investments in pollution control may cause the firm to raise the price of its products, close down several marginal operations at its plant and lay off workers, and put off other planned investments designed to modernize its production facilities.

How do we determine the willingness to pay for the favorable effects? First, it is relatively easy to value the reduced damage to materials. If, say, awnings will now last ten years rather than five years, it is straightforward to multiply the number of awnings times their price to get an idea of savings to consumers—so long as the price of awnings is not affected by the policy. If reduced pollution meant more agricultural output, it would be similarly easy to value because crops have well-defined market prices. In other words, when benefits involve marketed outputs, valuing them is not difficult.

But what about reduced health risks or improved visibility? Because these are not things that people buy and sell directly, it is much less clear how to estimate the willingness to pay (the value of the benefits). Two major techniques are available. One, called the contingent valuation method, involves asking people directly, via sophisticated questionnaires, how much they would pay for reduced health risks or improved visibility. This approach makes it possible to estimate the benefits of programs—for example, the preservation of a remote wilderness area—for which other techniques generally are inapplicable. However, this approach has its limitations. One is that it often requires individuals to place dollar values on things they are unused to viewing in economic terms. As a result, their responses may not be as reliable as we would like. Also, responses to surveys are hypothetical; economists prefer values revealed in actual market transactions.

Another approach is to observe how much people are willing to pay for goods that have an environmental quality component. For example, houses in unpolluted neighborhoods sell for more than those in polluted areas. Using statistical techniques to hold constant the other characteristics of houses and the neighborhoods in which they are located, it is possible to identify a "clean air premium." This provides important information on the value to individuals of air quality improvements. A similar approach for estimating how much people value pollution control and other public policies that reduce health risks is to estimate how much of a wage premium they are paid to work in jobs that pose health risks. Yet other techniques infer values from such things as the time and money people spend traveling to and from desirable recreation sites.

It is generally assumed that cost estimation involves a mere toting up of the expenditures that affected parties must make, as in our example of the firm controlling air pollution. As suggested above, however, matters are more complicated than this. Some firms not initially affected by regulation will incur higher costs—those purchasing the product of the regulated firm, for example. These "ripple" effects must be taken into account. Or if the polluting firm closes down some operations rather than purchase pollution control devices, its expenditures will be zero but the social costs are still positive. In such cases the costs are borne by employees, shareholders, and purchasers of its output. Unfortunately, techniques for making these more sophisticated cost estimates are still in their infancy; for this reason, virtually all BCAs still use direct expenditures as rough measures of true social costs.

Three additional issues in BCA bear mention. First, government policies or projects typically produce streams of benefits and costs over time rather than in one-shot increments. Commonly, in fact, a substantial portion of the costs is incurred early in the life of a project, while benefits may extend for many years (perhaps beginning only after some delay). Yet, because people prefer a dollar today to one ten years from now (see INTEREST RATES), BCA typically discounts future benefits and costs back to present values. Not only are there technical disagreements among economists about the interest rate (or rates) at which these future impacts should be discounted, but discounting raises ethical problems as well. At a discount rate of 10 percent, for instance, $1 million in benefits to people fifty years from now has a present value of only $8,500. This powerful effect of discounting is of concern when BCA is applied to the evaluation of policies with significant intergenerational effects, such as those pertaining to the prevention of global climate change or the disposal of high-level radioactive wastes (which will be lethal for hundreds of thousands of years).

A second sticking point in BCA is the fact that the willingness to pay for the favorable effects of a project or policy depends on the distribution of income: a billionaire would be able—and therefore willing—to pay more than a pauper for the same improvement in environmental quality, even though both cared about it with equal intensity. Some critics dislike BCA because it reduces benefits to pure dollar amounts. But BCA analysts use dollars to estimate benefits because there simply is no other way to directly measure the intensity with which people desire something.

Third, suppose that the aforementioned problems were to disappear, and that benefits and costs could be easily expressed in dollar terms and converted to present values. According to modern BCA, a project or policy would be attractive if the benefits it would produce exceed the costs. This is because, in theory, those gaining from the project could compensate those made worse off and still be better off themselves. In our factory example, for instance, those enjoying the benefits of cleaner air gain more than the losses to consumers who must pay more for the factory's output or to workers whose jobs are eliminated. Thus, the winners could compensate the losers and still come out ahead. In practice, of course, this compensation is seldom paid. Therefore, even the most efficient projects create some losers. This can undermine support for BCA in general and often makes it politically difficult to enact efficient policies—or, conversely, to block very inefficient projects, whose costs exceed benefits.

In spite of these sticking points, BCA seems to be playing an increasingly important role in government decision making. One reason may be that shunning a comprehensive, analytical approach to decision making simply because it has flaws inevitably pushes decisions back into the realm of the ad hoc and purely political. While BCA does have very real shortcomings, it appears preferable to smoke-filled rooms.

About the Author
Paul R. Portney is dean of the Eller College of Management at the University of Arizona. He was previously president and senior fellow at Resources for the Future, an environmental think tank in Washington, D.C.

Further Reading
Boardman, Anthony E., David H. Greenberg, Aidan R. Vining, and David L. Weimer. *Cost-Benefit Analysis: Concepts and Practice.* 2d ed. Upper Saddle River, N.J.: Prentice Hall, 2001.
Gramlich, Edward M. *Benefit-Cost Analysis of Government Programs.* Englewood Cliffs, N.J.: Prentice Hall, 1981.
Hammond, P. Brett, and Rob Coppock, eds. *Valuing Health Risks, Costs, and Benefits for Environmental Decision Making: Report of a Conference.* Washington, D.C.: National Academy Press, 1990.
Kneese, Allen V. *Measuring the Benefits of Clean Air and Water.* Washington, D.C.: Resources for the Future, 1984.
Kopp, Raymond, and Michael Hazilla. "Social Cost of Environmental Quality Regulations." *Journal of Political Economy* 98 (1990): 853–873.

Bonds

Clifford W. Smith

Bond markets are important components of capital markets. Bonds are fixed-income financial assets—essentially IOUs that promise the holder a specified set of payments. The value of a bond, like the value of any other asset, is the PRESENT VALUE of the income stream one expects to receive from holding the bond. This has several implications:

1. Bond prices vary inversely with market interest rates. Because the stream of promised payments usually is fixed no matter what subsequently happens to interest rates, higher rates reduce the present value of these promised payments, and thus the bond price.

2. The value of bonds falls when people come to expect higher inflation. The reason is that higher expected inflation raises market interest rates, and therefore reduces

the present value of the fixed stream of promised payments.

3. The greater the uncertainty about whether the promised payments will be made (the risk that the issuer will default on the promised payments), the lower the expected payments to bondholders and the lower the value of the bond.

4. Bonds whose payments are subjected to lower taxation provide investors with higher expected after-tax payments. Because investors are interested in after-tax income, such bonds sell for higher prices.

The major classes of bond issuers are the U.S. government, corporations, and municipal governments. The default risk and tax status differ from one kind of bond to another.

U.S. Government Bonds
The U.S. government is highly unlikely to default on promised payments to its bondholders because the government has the right to tax as well as the authority to print money. Thus, virtually all of the variation in the value of its bonds is due to changes in market interest rates. That is why most securities analysts use prices of U.S. government bonds to compute market interest rates.

Because the U.S. government's tax revenues rarely cover expenditures, it relies on debt financing for the balance. Moreover, on the occasions when the government does not have a budget deficit, it still sells new debt to refinance the old debt as it matures. Most of the debt sold by the U.S. government is marketable, meaning that it can be resold by its original purchaser. Marketable issues include treasury bills, treasury notes, and treasury bonds. The major nonmarketable federal debt sold to individuals is U.S. savings bonds.

Treasury bills have maturities of up to one year and are generally issued in denominations of $10,000. They do not have a stated coupon; that is, the government does not write a separate interest check to the owner. Instead, the U.S. Treasury sells these bills at a discount to their redemption value. The size of the discount determines the effective interest rate on the bill. For instance, a dealer might offer a bill with 120 days left until maturity at a yield of 7.48 percent. To translate this quoted yield into the price, one must "undo" this discount computation. Multiply the 7.48 by 120/360 (the fraction of the conventional 360-day year employed in this market) to obtain 2.493, and subtract that from 100 to get 97.506. The dealer is offering to sell the bond for $97.507 per $100 of face value.

Treasury notes and treasury bonds differ from treasury bills in several ways. First, their maturities generally are greater than one year. Notes have maturities of one to seven years, while bonds can be sold with any maturity, but their maturities at issue typically exceed five years. Second, bonds and notes specify periodic interest (coupon) payments as well as a principal repayment. Third, they normally are registered, meaning that the government records the name and address of the current owner. When treasury notes or bonds are sold initially, their coupon rate is typically set so that they will sell at close to their face (par) value.

Yields on bills, notes, or bonds of different maturities usually differ. (The array of rates associated with bonds of different maturities is referred to as the term structure of interest rates.) Because investors can invest either in a long-term note or in a sequence of short-term bills, expectations about future short-term rates affect current long-term rates. Thus, if the market expects future short-term rates to exceed current short-term rates, then current long-term rates would exceed current short-term rates—the term structure would have a positive slope (see Figure 1).

If, for example, the current short-term rate for a one-year T-bill is 5 percent, and the market expects the rate on a one-year T-bill sold one year from now to be 6 percent, then the current two-year rate must exceed 5 percent. If it did not, investors would expect to do better by buying one-year bills today and rolling them over into new one-year bills a year from now.

Savings bonds are offered only to individuals. Two types have been offered, both registered. Series E bonds are essentially discount bonds; investors receive no interest until the bonds are redeemed. Series H bonds pay interest semi-annually. Unlike marketable government bonds, which have fixed interest rates, rates received by savings bond holders normally are revised when market rates change. Some bonds—for instance, U.S. Treasury Inflation-Protected Securities (TIPS)—are indexed for inflation. If, for example, inflation were 10 percent per year, then the value of the bond would be adjusted to compensate for this inflation. If indexation were perfect, the change in expected payments due to inflation would exactly offset the inflation-caused change in market interest rates.

Corporate Bonds

Corporate bonds promise specified payments at specified dates. In general, the interest the bondholder receives is taxed as ordinary income. An issue of corporate bonds generally is covered by a trust indenture, a contract that promises a trustee (typically a bank or trust company) that it will comply with the indenture's provisions (or covenants). These include a promise of payment of principal and interest at stated dates, as well as other provisions such as limitations of the firm's right to sell pledged property, limitations on future financing activities, and limitations on dividend payments.

Potential lenders forecast the likelihood of default on a bond and require higher promised interest rates for higher forecasted default rates. (This difference in promised interest rates between low- and high-risk bonds of the same maturity is called a credit spread.) Bond-rating agencies (Moody's and Standard and Poor's, for example) provide an indication of the relative default risk of bonds with ratings that range from Aaa (the best quality) to C (the lowest). Bonds rated Baa and above typically are referred to as "investment grade." Below-investment-grade bonds are sometimes referred to as "JUNK BONDS." Junk bonds can carry promised yields that are three to six percentage points higher than those of Aaa bonds. They have a credit spread of three hundred to six hundred basis points, a basis point being one one-hundredth of a percentage point.

One way that corporate borrowers can influence the forecasted default rate is to agree to restrictive provisions or covenants that limit the firm's future financing, dividend, and investment activities—making it more certain that cash will be available to pay interest and principal. With a lower anticipated probability of default, buyers are willing to offer higher prices for the bonds. Corporate officers, thus, must weigh the costs of the reduced flexibility from including the covenants against the benefits of lower interest rates.

Describing all the types of corporate bonds that have been issued would be difficult. Sometimes different names are employed to describe the same type of bond, and, infrequently, the same name will be applied to two quite different bonds. Standard types include the following:

• Mortgage bonds are secured by the pledge of specific property. If default occurs, the bondholders are entitled to sell

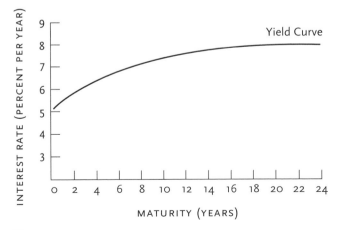

Figure 1

the pledged property to satisfy their claims. If the sale proceeds are insufficient to cover their claims, they have an unsecured claim on the corporation's other assets.

- Debentures are unsecured general obligations of the issuing corporation. The indenture will regularly limit issuance of additional secured and unsecured debt.

- Collateral trust bonds are backed by other securities (typically held by a trustee). Such bonds are frequently issued by a parent corporation pledging securities owned by a subsidiary.

- Equipment obligations (or equipment trust certificates) are backed by specific pieces of equipment (railroad rolling stock, aircraft, etc.).

- Subordinated debentures have a lower priority in bankruptcy than ordinary (unsubordinated) debentures. Junior claims are generally paid only after senior claims have been satisfied but rank ahead of preferred and common stock.

- Convertible bonds give the owner the option either to be repaid in cash or to exchange the bonds for a specified number of shares in the corporation.

Municipal Bonds

Historically, interest paid on bonds issued by state and local governments has been exempt from federal income taxes. Such interest may be exempt from state income taxes as well. For instance, the New York tax code exempts interest from bonds issued by New York and Puerto Rico municipalities. Because investors are interested in returns net of tax, municipal bonds generally have promised lower interest rates than other government bonds that have similar risk but that lack this attractive tax treatment. In 2003, the percentage difference (not the percentage point difference) between the yield on long-term U.S. government bonds and the yield on long-term municipals was about 10 percent. Thus, if an individual's marginal tax rate were higher than 10 percent, the after-tax promised return would be higher from municipal bonds than from taxable government bonds. (Although this difference might appear small, there is a credit spread in municipals just as in corporates.)

Municipal bonds typically are designated as either general obligation bonds or revenue bonds. General obligation bonds are backed by the "full faith and credit" (and thus the taxing authority) of the issuing entity. Revenue bonds are backed by a specifically designated revenue stream, such as the revenues from a designated project, authority, or agency, or by the proceeds from a specific tax.

Frequently, such bonds are issued by agencies that plan to sell their services at prices that cover their expenses, including the promised payments on the debt. In such cases, the bonds are only as good as the enterprise that backs them. In 1983, for example, the Washington Public Power Supply System (WPPSS), which Wall Street quickly nicknamed "Whoops," defaulted on $2.25 billion on its number four and number five nuclear power plants, leaving bondholders with much less than they had been promised. Industrial development bonds are used to finance the purchase or construction of facilities to be leased to private firms. Municipalities have used such bonds to subsidize businesses choosing to locate in their area by, in effect, giving them the benefit of loans at tax-exempt rates.

Some municipal bonds are still sold in bearer form; that is, possession of the bond itself constitutes proof of ownership. Historically in the United States, most public bonds (government, corporate, and municipal) were bearer bonds. Now, the Internal Revenue Service requires bonds that pay taxable interest to be sold in registered form.

About the Author

Clifford W. Smith is the Epstein Professor of Finance at the William E. Simon Graduate School of Business Administration, University of Rochester. He is an advisory editor of the *Journal of Financial Economics* and an associate editor of the *Journal of Derivatives*, the *Journal of Risk and Insurance*, and the *Journal of Financial Services Research*.

Further Reading

Brealey, Richard A., and Stewart C. Myers. *Principles of Corporate Finance*. 7th ed. Boston: McGraw-Hill/Irwin, 2003.

Peavy, John W., and George H. Hempel. "The Effect of the WPPSS Crisis on the Tax-Exempt Bond Market." *Journal of Financial Research* 10, no. 3 (1987): 239–247.

Sharpe, William F., Gordon J. Alexander, and Jeffrey V. Bailey. *Investments*. Upper Saddle River, N.J.: Prentice Hall, 1999.

Smith, Clifford W. Jr., and Jerold B. Warner. "On Financial Contracting: An Analysis of Bond Covenants." *Journal of Financial Economics* 7, no. 3 (1979): 117–161.

On the Web

http://www.Moodys.com
http://www.Investinginbonds.com

Brand Names

Benjamin Klein

Consumers pay a higher price for brand-name products than for products that do not carry an established brand name. Because this involves paying extra for what some consider an identical product that merely has been advertised and promoted, brand names may appear to be economically wasteful. This argument was behind the decision to eliminate all brand names on goods produced in the Soviet Union immediately after the 1917 Communist revolution. The problems this experiment caused—problems described by economist Marshall Goldman—suggest that brand names serve an important economic function.

When the producers of products are not identified with brand names, a crucial element of the market mechanism cannot operate because consumers cannot use their past experience to know which products to buy and which not to buy. In particular, consumers can neither punish companies that supply low-quality products by stopping their purchases nor reward companies that supply high-quality products by increasing their purchases. Thus, when all brand names, including factory production marks, were eliminated in the Soviet Union, unidentified producers manufacturing indistinguishable products each had an incentive to supply lower-quality goods. And the inability to punish these producers created significant problems for consumers.

Consumer reliance on brand names gives companies the incentive to supply high-quality products because they can take advantage of superior past performance to charge higher prices. Benjamin Klein and Keith Leffler (1981) showed that this price premium paid for brand-name products facilitates market exchange. A company that creates an established brand for which it can charge higher prices knows that if it supplies poor products and its future demand declines, it will lose the stream of income from the future price premium it would otherwise have earned on its sales. This decrease in future income amounts to a depreciation in the market value of the company's brand-name. A company's brand-name capital, therefore, is a form of collateral that ensures company performance. Companies without valuable brand names that are not earning price premiums on their products, on the other hand, have less to lose when they supply low-quality products and their demand falls. Therefore, while consumers may receive a direct benefit for the extra price they pay for brand-name products, such as the status of driving a BMW, the higher price also creates market incentives for companies with valuable brand names to maintain and improve product quality because they have something to lose if they perform poorly.

Brand-name quality assurance is especially important when consumers lack complete information about product quality at the time of purchase. Companies may take advantage of this lack of information by shaving product quality, thereby lowering costs and increasing short-term profits. A company that takes such actions, however, will experience a decrease in its future demand, and therefore in its long-term profits. The greater the value of a company's brand name—that is, the greater the present value of the extra profit a company earns on its sales—the more likely it is that this long-term negative effect on profits will outweigh any short-term positive effect and deter a policy of intentional quality deterioration. Moreover, the greater the value of a company's brand name, the more likely the company is to take quality-control precautions. To protect its brand name, a company will want to make sure its consumers are satisfied.

When it is difficult to determine the quality of a product before purchase and the consequences of poor quality are significant, it makes economic sense for consumers to rely on brand names and the company reputations associated with them. By paying more for a brand-name product in those circumstances, consumers are not acting irrationally. Consumers know that companies with established reputations for consistent high quality have more to lose if they do not perform well—namely, the loss of the ability to continue to charge higher prices. A company's high reputation indicates not only that the company has performed well in the past, but also that it will perform well in the future because it has an economic incentive to maintain and improve the quality of its products. A consumer who pays a high price for a brand-name product is paying for the assurance of increased quality.

When a company performs poorly, the brand-name, market-enforced sanction it faces is usually much greater than any court-enforced legal sanction it might face. Consider, for example, the case of defective Firestone tires on Ford Explorer sport-utility vehicles in 2000. Because consumers cannot ascertain the quality of tires by direct examination, they rely largely on the tire supplier's brand name, which was badly damaged in this case. One day after Bridgestone (Firestone's Japan-based parent company) announced the recall of the defective tires, Bridgestone's stock price dropped nearly 20 percent; it continued to fall over the next three weeks as additional information about the problem was disclosed. Overall, this amounted to a decline of nearly 40 percent in Bridgestone's stock-market value relative to the Nikkei general market index. Ford's stock price did not drop initially, but eventually it fell about 18 percent relative to the S&P 500 index over the same period as information was revealed that Ford was aware of the possibility of tire failure more than a year before the tire recall. These stock-market declines amounted to losses of about $7 billion in Bridgestone's market value and nearly $10 billion in Ford Motor Company's market value—market measures of each company's future lost profit caused by these events. These costs were substantially greater than the direct costs associated with the recall and liability litigation, estimated by Bridgestone at $754 million and by Ford at $590 million. Although these direct costs clearly were substantial, they were dwarfed by the brand-name market costs borne by Bridgestone and Ford, which were between some nine and seventeen times as large.

Similar market effects occurred in 1993 when *E. coli* bacteria in the hamburger meat purchased by Jack-in-the-Box killed four people and sickened about five hundred. Although Jack-in-the-Box reacted quickly to the food poisoning and took actions to prevent its recurrence, its stock-market value fell by more than 30 percent when this information was disclosed, or more than double the direct litigation and recall costs. Even in cases where the problem is not strictly the company's "fault," such as the 1982 Tylenol tampering cases that led to seven poisoning deaths, the $2 billion (or more than 20 percent) decline in stock-market value borne by the producer, Johnson and Johnson, was almost ten times as great as the company's direct recall and litigation costs. While the government regulates the quality of products, the regulatory cost that can be imposed on companies is generally a small fraction of the economic cost that the market imposes on poor-performing companies with established brand names. If those companies had lacked brand names, the economic punishment they suffered would have been much smaller.

Because brand-name companies have a greater incentive to ensure high quality, consumers who buy brand-name products are necessarily paying for something: the added assurance that the company has taken the necessary measures to protect its reputation for quality. Therefore, even for purchases of a "standardized" product such as aspirin, where most suppliers purchase the basic ingredient, acetylsalicylic acid, from the same manufacturer, it may make sense for consumers to purchase a higher-priced brand-name product. Consumers are not ignorant or irrational when they buy an advertised brand-name aspirin rather than a non-brand-name product at a lower price. Bottled aspirin supplied by brand-name and "non-brand-name" producers may differ technologically in dissolve rate, shelf life, and other factors. But more important, the products differ economically. A lower-priced "nonbrand" aspirin is not economically equivalent to higher-priced brand-name aspirin, because a company selling aspirin under a valuable brand name has more to lose if something goes wrong. The brand-name aspirin supplier, therefore, has a greater economic incentive to take added precautions in producing the product. Similar economic forces are at work when multiple generic drug companies produce the same drug. Because pharmacies generally have an incentive to purchase the lowest-cost generic variant, each generic company has the incentive to lower costs, including reducing its quality-control efforts, subject only to imperfect FDA audits. When companies do not earn a large price premium on their products, the potential sanction the companies face for poor quality control is much lower than the economic cost borne by brand-name companies.

Seen in this light, the question is not whether consumers are ignorant or irrational when they pay a higher price for a brand-name product, but whether they are paying too much for the additional quality assurance brand names necessarily provide. Even people who assume that all aspirin is alike spend *some* money on brand-name assurance since they do not buy "nonbrand" aspirin off the back of a pickup truck at a swap meet. Instead, they may buy "lower-brand-name" aspirin, such as aspirin carrying the brand name of a chain drugstore. It is significant, however, that consumers buy a much smaller share of such "lower-brand-name" aspirin when purchasing children's aspirin than when buying adult-dosage aspirin. Many people decide, as evidenced by their behavior, that although they are willing to purchase less brand-name assurance for themselves, they want the higher-quality assurance for their children, for whom quality-control considerations may be more important.

About the Author

Benjamin Klein is professor emeritus of economics at UCLA and director, LECG, LLC.

Further Reading

Goldman, Marshall. "Product Differentiation and Advertising: Some Lessons from the Soviet Experience." *Journal of Political Economy* 68 (1960): 346–357.

Klein, Benjamin, and Keith Leffler. "The Role of Market Forces in Assuring Contractual Performance." *Journal of Political Economy* 89 (1981): 615–641.

Mitchell, Mark. "The Impact of External Parties on Brand-Name Capital: The 1982 Tylenol Poisonings and Subsequent Cases." *Economic Inquiry* 27, no. 4 (1989): 601–618.

Bubbles

Seiji S. C. Steimetz

What Are Bubbles?

In 1996, the fledgling Internet portal Yahoo.com made its stock-market debut. This was during a time of great excitement—as well as uncertainty—about the prosperous "new economy" that the rapidly expanding Internet promised. By the beginning of the year 2000, Yahoo shares were trading at $240 each.[1] Exactly one year later, however, Yahoo's stock sold for only $30 per share. A similar story could be told for many of Yahoo's "dot-com" contemporaries—a substantial period of market-value growth during the late 1990s followed by a rapid decline as the twenty-first century approached. With the benefit of hindsight, many concluded that dot-com stocks were overvalued in the late 1990s, which created an "Internet bubble" that was doomed to burst.

Thus, as this account implies, the definition of a bubble involves some characterization of the extent to which an asset is overvalued. Let us define the "fundamental value" of an asset as the PRESENT VALUE of the stream of cash flows that its holder expects to receive. These cash flows include the series of dividends that the asset is expected to generate and the expected price of the asset when sold.[2] In an efficient market, the price of an asset is equal to its fundamental value. For instance, if a stock is trading at a price below its fundamental value, savvy investors in the market will pounce on the profit opportunity by purchasing more shares of the stock. This will bid up the stock's price until no further profits can be achieved—that is, until its price equals its fundamental value; the same mechanism works to correct stocks that are trading above their fundamental values. So, if an asset is persistently trading at a price higher than its fundamental value, we would say that its price exhibits a bubble and that the asset is overvalued by an amount equal to the bubble—the difference between the asset's trading price and its fundamental value. This definition implies that if such bubbles persist, investors are irrational in their failure to profit from the "overpriced" asset. Thus, we refer to this type of bubble as an "irrational bubble."

Over the past few decades, economists have generated a compelling amount of evidence to suggest that asset markets are remarkably efficient. These markets comprise thousands of traders who constantly seek to exploit even the smallest profit opportunities. If irrational bubbles appear, investors can use a variety of market instruments (such as options and short positions) to quickly burst them and achieve profits by doing so. Yet episodes like those of the dot-com era suggest at least the possibility that asset prices might persistently deviate from their fundamental values. Is it, then, possible that the market may at any time succumb to the "madness of crowds"?

To see how prices might persistently deviate from traditional market fundamentals, imagine that you are considering an investment in the publicly held firm Bootstrap Microdevices (BM), which is trading at fifty dollars per share. You know that BM will not declare any dividends and have ample reason to believe that one year from now BM will be trading at only ten dollars per share. Yet you also firmly believe that you can sell your BM shares in six months for one hundred dollars each. It would be entirely rational for you to purchase BM shares now and plan to sell them in six months.[3] If you did so, you and those who shared your beliefs would be "riding a bubble" and would bid up the price of BM shares in the process.

This example illustrates that if bubbles exist, they might be perpetuated in a manner that would be difficult to call irrational. The key to understanding this is in recalling that an asset's fundamental value includes its expected price when sold. If investors rationally expect an asset's selling price to increase, then including this in their assessment of the asset's fundamental value would be justified. It is possible, then, that the price of such an asset could grow and persist even if the viability of its issuing company is unlikely to support these prices indefinitely. This situation can be called a "rational bubble."[4]

Because market fundamentals are based on expectations of future events, bubbles can be identified only after the fact. For instance, it will be several years before we truly understand the impact of the Internet on our economy. It is possible that future innovations based on Internet technologies will fundamentally justify people's decision to buy and hold Yahoo shares at $240 each. In this light, it would be difficult to condemn those who paid such a price for Yahoo shares at a time when Internet usage was growing exponentially. Can bubbles, rational or otherwise, exist? An ex post examination of history's so-called famous first bubbles helps to answer this question.

Famous First Bubbles

The Tulip Bubble

Tulip bulb speculation in seventeenth-century Holland is widely recounted as a classic example of how bubbles can

---

1. This is a split-adjusted figure. The actual trading price at the time was $475 per share.

2. If the asset is to be held forever, its fundamental value is just the present value of its expected dividend stream since the present value of any dollar amount to be received an infinite number of years from now is zero.

3. In doing so, one might say that you were applying the "greater fool theory" to your investment decision, thereby building a "castle in the air."

4. Economists often refer to these types of bubble conditions as "bootstrap equilibria." High prices are thought to be held high by self-fulfilling prophecies, just as one might attempt to hold himself high off the ground by pulling up on his bootstraps.

be generated by the "madness of crowds."[5] In 1593, tulip bulbs arrived in Holland and subsequently became fashionable accessories for elite households. A handful of bulbs were infected with a virus known as mosaic, so named for the brilliant mosaic of colors exhibited by flowers from infected bulbs. These rare bulbs soon became symbols of their owners' prominence and vehicles for speculation. In 1625, an especially rare type of infected bulb called Semper Augustus sold for two thousand guilders—about $23,000 in 2003 dollars. By 1627, at least one of these bulbs was known to have sold at today's equivalent of $70,000. The growth in value of the Semper Augustus continued until a dramatic decline in early 1637, when they could not be sold for more than 10 percent of their peak value.

The dramatic rise and fall of Semper Augustus prices, and the fortunes made and lost on them, exhibited the symptoms of a classic bubble. Yet economist Peter Garber provided compelling evidence that "tulipmania" did not generate a bubble. He argued that the dynamics of bulb prices during the tulip episode were typical of even today's market for rare bulbs. It is important to note that the mosaic virus could not be systematically introduced to common bulb types. The only way to cultivate a prized Semper Augustus was to raise it from the offshoot bud of an infected mother bulb. Just as the fundamental value of a stock includes its expected stream of dividends, the fundamental value of a Semper Augustus included its expected stream of rare offspring. As the rare bulbs were introduced to the public, their growing popularity, combined with their limited supply, commanded a high price. This price was pushed up by speculators who hoped to profit from the bulb's popularity by cultivating its valuable offspring. These offspring expanded the supply of bulbs, making them less rare, and thus less valuable. Perhaps tulips' decreased popularity accelerated this downward trend in bulb prices. Interestingly, a small quantity of prototype lily bulbs sold at a 1987 Netherlands flower auction for more than $900,000 in 2003 dollars, and their offspring now sell at a tiny fraction of this price; yet no one mentions "lilymania."

The Mississippi and South Sea Bubbles

In 1717, John Law organized the Compagnie d'Occident to take over the French government's trade monopolies in Louisiana and on Canadian beaver pelts. The company was later renamed the Compagnie des Indies following a series of mergers and acquisitions, including France's Banque

Royale, whose notes were guaranteed by the crown. Eventually the company acquired the right to collect all taxes and mint new coinage, and it funded these enterprises with a series of share issues at successively higher prices. Shares sold for five hundred livres each at the company's onset, but their price increased to nearly ten thousand livres in October 1720 after these expansive moves. By September 1721, however, shares of the Compagnie des Indies fell back to their original value of five hundred livres.

Meanwhile, in England, the South Sea Company, whose only notable asset at the time was a defunct trade monopoly with the Spanish colonies in South America, had its own expansion plans. The company's goals were not as well defined as those of its French counterpart, but it managed to gain broad parliamentary support through a series of bribes and generous share allowances. In January 1720, South Sea shares sold for 120 pounds each. This price rose to 1,000 pounds by June of that year through a series of new issues. By October, however, prices fell to 290 pounds. Were Compagnie des Indies and South Sea Company shareholders riding bubbles?

Peter Garber provided a detailed account of how market fundamentals, not irrational speculation or rational bubble dynamics, might have driven these price movements. The companies started with similar plans to finance their ventures by acquiring government debt in exchange for shares. This generated streams of government cash payments, at reduced interest rates, that could be used as leverage to finance each company's commercial enterprises. With this came an extraordinary degree of visible privilege and support from their governments, extending all the way up to their royal families. The remarkable credibility of each company's potential for profit and growth may well have justified their peak share prices based on market fundamentals.

The decline of South Sea share prices began with Parliament's passage of the Bubble Act in June 1720—an act that was intended to limit the expansion of the South Sea Company's competitors. This placed downward price pressure on competitors' shares that were largely bought on margin. A wave of selling, including South Sea shares, ensued in a scramble for liquidity to meet these margins. As prices continued to drop, Parliament turned against the company and liquidated its assets.

In France, the fall of the Compagnie des Indies was more complex. At the peak of its market value, many investors wanted to convert their capital gains into the more tangible asset of gold. Of course, there was not enough gold in France at the time to satisfy all of these desires, just as there is not enough gold in the United States today to back each dollar. The Banque Royale intervened by fix-

---

5. This section is based primarily on the influential work of economist Peter Garber.

ing Compagnie share prices at nine thousand livres and exchanging its notes for Compagnie stock. Within a few months, France's money supply was effectively doubled since Banque Royale notes were considered legal tender. A period of hyperinflation ensued, followed by the company's stopgap deflationary efforts of reducing the fixed price of Compagnie shares to five thousand livres. Confidence in the company dissolved, and John Law was eventually removed from power.

This brief account shows how each company's rise and fall is traceable to events that were likely to change how investors fundamentally valued South Sea and Compagnie shares, contrary to what a bubble hypothesis would suggest. These companies were essentially performing large-scale financial experiments based on prospects for long-term growth. They ultimately failed, but they could well have shown enough promise to convince even the most incredulous investors of their potential for success. It would be difficult to characterize what may have been rational behavior ex ante as evidence of bubble formation. Indeed, John Law's operations with the Banque Royale essentially attempted to expand French commerce by expanding France's money supply. This monetary policy is one that an entire generation of Keynesian economists promoted more than two hundred years after the Mississippi and South Sea "bubbles." Yet few economists, even those highly dismissive of Keynesian economics, are willing to call Keynesians irrational.

The Modern Bubble Debate

The jury is still out on whether or not bubbles can persist in modern asset markets. Debates continue among economists even on the existence of irrational or rational bubbles. And there is often confusion in trying to distinguish irrational bubbles from rational bubbles that might be generated by investors' rational but flawed perceptions of market fundamentals. Most modern efforts focus on developing sophisticated statistical methods to detect bubbles, but none has enjoyed a consensus of support among economists.

About the Author

Seiji Steimetz is an economics professor at California State University at Long Beach. He was previously a senior consultant at Bates White LLC, an economic consulting firm.

Further Reading

Introductory

Garber, Peter. *Famous First Bubbles: The Fundamentals of Early Manias*. Cambridge: MIT Press, 2000.
Mackay, Charles. *Memoirs of Extraordinary Popular Delusions and the Madness of Crowds*. London: Office of National Illustrated Library, 1852.
Malkiel, Burton. *A Random Walk Down Wall Street: The Time-Tested Strategy for Successful Investing*. New York: Norton, 2003.
Shiller, Robert. *Irrational Exuberance*. Princeton: Princeton University Press, 2000.
Smant, David. "Famous First Bubbles or Bubble Myths Explained?" Available online at: http://www.few.eur.nl/few/people/smant/m-economics/bubbles.htm.

Advanced

Abreu, Dilip, and Markus Brunnermeier. "Bubbles and Crashes." *Econometrica* 71 (2003): 173–204.
Evans, George. "Pitfalls in Testing for Explosive Bubbles in Asset Prices." *American Economic Review* 4 (1991): 922–930.
Flood, Robert, and Robert Hodrick. "On Testing for Speculative Bubbles." *Journal of Economic Perspectives* 4 (1990): 85–101.
Garber, Peter. "Famous First Bubbles." *Journal of Economic Perspectives* 4 (1990): 35–54.
———. "Tulipmania." *Journal of Political Economy* 3 (1989): 535–560.
Shiller, Robert. "Speculative Prices and Popular Models." *Journal of Economic Perspective* 4 (1990): 55–65.
Stiglitz, Joseph. "Symposium on Bubbles." *Journal of Economic Perspectives* 4 (1990): 13–18.

Business Cycles

Christina D. Romer

The United States and all other modern industrial economies experience significant swings in economic activity. In some years, most industries are booming and unemployment is low; in other years, most industries are operating well below capacity and unemployment is high. Periods of economic prosperity are typically called expansions or booms; periods of economic decline are called recessions or depressions. The combination of expansions and recessions, the ebb and flow of economic activity, is called the business cycle.

Business cycles as we know them today were codified and analyzed by Arthur Burns and Wesley Mitchell in their 1946 book *Measuring Business Cycles*. One of Burns and Mitchell's key insights was that many economic indicators move together. During an expansion, not only does output rise, but also employment rises and unemployment falls. New construction also typically increases, and inflation may rise if the expansion is particularly brisk. Conversely, during a recession, the output of goods and services declines, employment falls, and unemployment rises; new construction also declines. In the era before World War II, prices also typically fell during a recession (i.e., inflation was negative); since the 1950s prices have continued to rise during downturns, though more slowly than during expansions (i.e., the rate of inflation falls). Burns and Mitchell defined a recession as a period when a broad range of economic indicators falls for a sustained period, roughly at least half a year.

Business cycles are dated according to when the direction of economic activity changes. The peak of the cycle refers to the last month before several key economic indicators—such as employment, output, and retail sales—begin to fall. The trough of the cycle refers to the last month before the same economic indicators begin to rise. Because key economic indicators often change direction at slightly different times, the dating of peaks and troughs is necessarily somewhat subjective. The National Bureau of Economic Research (NBER) is an independent research institution that dates the peaks and troughs of U.S. business cycles. Table 1 shows the NBER monthly dates for peaks and troughs of U.S. business cycles since 1890. Recent research has shown that the NBER's reference dates for the period before World War I are not truly comparable with those for the modern era because they were determined using different methods and data. Figure 1 shows the unemployment rate since 1948, with periods that the NBER classifies as recessions shaded in gray. Clearly, a key feature of recessions is that they are times of rising unemployment.

In many ways, the term "business cycle" is misleading. "Cycle" seems to imply that there is some regularity in the

Table 1 Business Cycle Peaks and Troughs in the United States, 1890–2004

Peak	Trough	Peak	Trough
July 1890	May 1891	May 1937	June 1938
Jan. 1893	June 1894	Feb. 1945	Oct. 1945
Dec. 1895	June 1897	Nov. 1948	Oct. 1949
June 1899	Dec. 1900	July 1953	May 1954
Sep. 1902	Aug. 1904	Aug. 1957	Apr. 1958
May 1907	June 1908	Apr. 1960	Feb. 1961
Jan. 1910	Jan. 1912	Dec. 1969	Nov. 1970
Jan. 1913	Dec. 1914	Nov. 1973	Mar. 1975
Aug. 1918	Mar. 1919	Jan. 1980	July 1980
Jan. 1920	July 1921	July 1981	Nov. 1982
May 1923	July 1924	July 1990	Mar. 1991
Oct. 1926	Nov. 1927	Mar. 2001	Nov. 2001
Aug. 1929	Mar. 1933		

timing and duration of upswings and downswings in economic activity. Most economists, however, do not think there is. As Figure 1 shows, expansions and recessions occur at irregular intervals and last for varying lengths of time. For example, there were three recessions between 1973 and 1982, but, then the 1982 trough was followed by eight years of uninterrupted expansion. The 1980 recession lasted just six months, while the 1981 recession lasted sixteen months. For describing the swings in economic activity, therefore, many modern economists prefer the term "short-run economic fluctuations" to "business cycle."

Causes of Business Cycles

Just as there is no regularity in the timing of business cycles, there is no reason why cycles have to occur at all. The prevailing view among economists is that there is a level of economic activity, often referred to as full employment, at which the economy could stay forever. Full employment refers to a level of production in which all the inputs to the production process are being used, but not so intensively that they wear out, break down, or insist on higher wages and more vacations. When the economy is at full employment, inflation tends to remain constant; only if output moves above or below normal does the rate of inflation systematically tend to rise or fall. If nothing disturbs the economy, the full-employment level of output, which naturally tends to grow as the population increases and new technologies are discovered, can be maintained forever. There is no reason why a time of full employment has to give way to either an inflationary boom or a recession.

Business cycles do occur, however, because disturbances to the economy of one sort or another push the economy above or below full employment. Inflationary booms can be generated by surges in private or public spending. For example, if the government spends a lot to fight a war but does not raise taxes, the increased demand will cause not only an increase in the output of war matériel, but also an increase in the take-home pay of defense workers. The output of all the goods and services that these workers want to buy with their wages will also increase, and total production may surge above its normal, comfortable level. Similarly, a wave of optimism that causes consumers to spend more than usual and firms to build new factories may cause the economy to expand more rapidly than normal. Recessions or depressions can be caused by these same forces working in reverse. A substantial cut in government spending or a wave of pessimism among consumers and firms may cause the output of all types of goods to fall.

Another possible cause of recessions and booms is monetary policy. The Federal Reserve System strongly influences the size and growth rate of the money stock, and

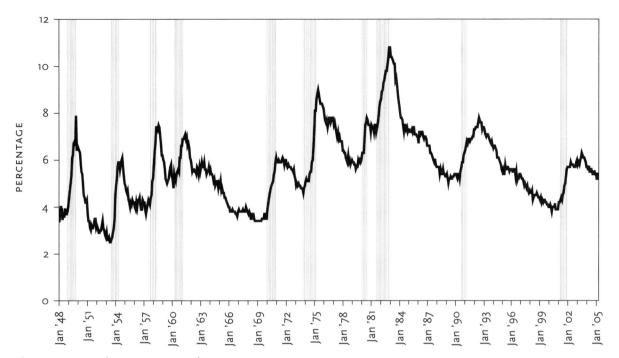

Figure 1 Unemployment Rate and Recessions
Source: The data are from the Bureau of Labor Statistics.
Note: The series graphed is the seasonally adjusted civilian unemployment rate for those age sixteen and over. The shaded areas indicate recessions.

thus the level of interest rates in the economy. Interest rates, in turn, are a crucial determinant of how much firms and consumers want to spend. A firm faced with high interest rates may decide to postpone building a new factory because the cost of borrowing is so high. Conversely, a consumer may be lured into buying a new home if interest rates are low and mortgage payments are therefore more affordable. Thus, by raising or lowering interest rates, the Federal Reserve is able to generate recessions or booms.

This description of what causes business cycles reflects the Keynesian or new Keynesian view that cycles are the result of nominal rigidities. Only when prices and inflationary expectations are not fully flexible can fluctuations in overall demand cause large swings in real output. An alternative view, referred to as the new classical framework, holds that modern industrial economies are quite flexible. As a result, a change in spending does not necessarily affect real output and employment. For example, in the new classical view a change in the stock of money will change only prices; it will have no effect on real interest rates and thus on people's willingness to invest. In this alternative framework, business cycles are largely the result of disturbances in productivity and tastes, not of changes in aggregate demand.

The empirical evidence is strongly on the side of the

view that deviations from full employment are often the result of spending shocks. Monetary policy, in particular, appears to have played a crucial role in causing business cycles in the United States since World War II. For example, the severe recessions of both the early 1970s and the early 1980s were directly attributable to decisions by the Federal Reserve to raise interest rates. On the expansionary side, the inflationary booms of the mid-1960s and the late 1970s were both at least partly due to monetary ease and low interest rates. The role of money in causing business cycles is even stronger if one considers the era before World War II. Many of the worst prewar depressions, including the recessions of 1908, 1921, and the Great Depression of the 1930s, were to a large extent the result of monetary contraction and high real interest rates. In this earlier era, however, most monetary swings were engendered not by deliberate monetary policy but by financial panics, policy mistakes, and international monetary developments.

Historical Record of Business Cycles
Table 2 shows the peak-to-trough decline in industrial production, a broad monthly measure of manufacturing and mining activity, in each recession since 1890. The industrial production series used was constructed to be comparable over time. Many other conventional macroeco-

Table 2 Peak-to-Trough Decline in Industrial Production

Year of NBER Peak	% Decline	Year of NBER Peak	% Decline
1890	−5.3	1937	−32.5
1893	−17.3	1945	−35.5
1895	−10.8	1948	−10.1
1899	−10.0	1953	−9.5
1902	−9.5	1957	−13.6
1907	−20.1	1960	−8.6
1910	−9.1	1969	−7.0
1913	−12.1	1973	−13.1
1918	−6.2	1980	−6.6
1920	−32.5	1981	−9.4
1923	−18.0	1990	−4.1
1926	−6.0	2001	−6.2
1929	−53.6		

Source: The industrial production data for 1919–2004 are from the Board of Governors of the Federal Reserve System. The series before 1919 is an adjusted and smoothed version of the Miron-Romer index of industrial production. This series is described in the appendix to "Remeasuring Business Cycles" by Christina D. Romer.

Note: The peak-to-trough decline is calculated using the actual peaks and troughs in the industrial production series. These turning points often differ from the NBER dates by a few months, and occasionally by as much as a year.

nomic indicators, such as the unemployment rate and real GDP, are not consistent over time. The prewar versions of these series were constructed using methods and data sources that tended to exaggerate cyclical swings. As a result, these conventional indicators yield misleading estimates of the degree to which business cycles have moderated over time.

The empirical record on the duration and severity of recessions over time reflects the evolution of economic policy. The recessions of the pre–World War I era were relatively frequent and quite variable in size. This is consistent with the fact that before World War I, the government had little influence on the economy. Prewar recessions stemmed from a wide range of private-sector-induced fluctuations in spending, such as investment busts and financial panics, that were left to run their course. As a result, recessions occurred frequently, and some were large and some were small.

After World War I the government became much more involved in managing the economy. Government spending

and taxes as a fraction of GDP rose substantially in the 1920s and 1930s, and the Federal Reserve was established in 1914. Table 2 makes clear that the period between the two world wars was one of extreme volatility. The declines in industrial production in the recessions of 1920, 1929, and 1937 were larger than in any recessions in the pre–World War I and post–World War II periods. A key factor in these extreme fluctuations was the replacement, by the 1920s, of some of the private-sector institutions that had helped the U.S. economy weather prewar fluctuations with government institutions that were not yet fully functional. The history of the interwar era is perhaps best described as a painful learning period for the Federal Reserve. The downturn of the mid-1940s obviously reflects the effect of World War II. The war generated an incredible boom in economic activity, as production surged in response to massive government spending. The end of wartime spending led to an equally spectacular drop in industrial production as the economy returned to more normal levels of labor and capital utilization.

Recessions in the early postwar era were of roughly the same average severity as those before World War I, although they were somewhat less frequent than in the earlier period and were more consistently of moderate size. The decreasing frequency of downturns reflects progress in economic policymaking. The Great Depression brought about large strides in the understanding of the economy and the capacity of government to moderate cycles. The Employment Act of 1946 mandated that the government use the tools at its disposal to stabilize output and employment. And indeed, economic policy since World War II has almost certainly counteracted some shocks and hence prevented some recessions. In the early postwar era, however, policymakers tended to carry expansionary policy too far, and in the process caused inflation to rise. As a result, policymakers, particularly the Federal Reserve, felt compelled to adopt contractionary policies that led to moderate recessions in order to bring inflation down. This boom-bust cycle was a common feature of the 1950s, 1960s, and 1970s.

Recessions in the United States have become noticeably less frequent and severe since the mid-1980s. The nearly decade-long expansions of the 1980s and 1990s were interrupted by only very mild recessions in 1990 and 2001. Economists attribute this moderation of cycles to a number of factors, including the increasing importance of services (a traditionally stable sector of the economy) and a decline in adverse shocks, such as oil price increases and fluctuations in consumer and investor sentiment. Most economists believe that improvements in monetary policy, particularly the end of overexpansion followed by deliberate contraction, have been a significant factor as well.

In addition to reductions in the frequency and severity of downturns over time, the effects of recessions on individuals in the United States and other industrialized countries almost surely have been lessened in recent decades. The advent of unemployment insurance and other social welfare programs means that recessions no longer wreak the havoc on individuals' standards of living that they once did.

About the Author

Christina D. Romer is a professor of economics at the University of California, Berkeley, and co-director of the Program in Monetary Economics at the National Bureau of Economic Research.

Further Reading

Burns, Arthur F., and Wesley C. Mitchell. *Measuring Business Cycles.* New York: National Bureau of Economic Research, 1946.
Friedman, Milton, and Anna Jacobson Schwartz. *A Monetary History of the United States, 1867–1960.* Princeton: Princeton University Press for NBER, 1963.
Romer, Christina D. "Changes in Business Cycles: Evidence and Explanations." *Journal of Economic Perspectives* 13 (Spring 1999): 23–44.
———. "Remeasuring Business Cycles." *Journal of Economic History* 54 (September 1994): 573–609.

Campaign Finance

Jeffrey Milyo

Conventional wisdom holds that money plays a central and nefarious role in American politics. Underlying this belief are two fundamental assumptions: (1) elective offices are effectively sold to the highest bidder, and (2) campaign contributions are the functional equivalent of bribes. Campaign finance regulations are thus an attempt to hinder the operation of this political marketplace. Of course, the scope of such regulation is itself limited by the constitutional protection of political speech, association, and the right to petition. Nevertheless, many Americans are willing to sacrifice their, and others', free-speech rights in an attempt to limit the influence of moneyed interests in politics.

One might think that the existence of a political marketplace would produce efficient policy outcomes, even if at the cost of the democratic ideals of equal representation and participation. However, PUBLIC CHOICE economists have shown that if favors are bought and sold, those who buy them often gain much per person, but their gains are more than offset by the smaller losses per person sustained by the large number of losers. So a political marketplace does not ensure efficient policies. Interestingly, though, scholarly research on the economics of campaign finance suggests that the political marketplace analogy is not a fair description of American democracy.

Electoral Effects of Campaign Spending

Every two years, public-interest groups and media pundits lament the fact that winning candidates typically far outspend their rivals. They infer from this that campaign spending drives electoral results. Most systematic studies, however, find no effect of marginal campaign spending on the electoral success of candidates.[1]

How can this be so? The best explanation to date is that competent candidates are adept at both convincing contributors to give money and convincing voters to give their vote. Consequently, the finding that campaign spending and electoral success are highly correlated exaggerates the importance of money to a candidate's chances of winning. To gauge the causal relationship between campaign spending and electoral success, it is necessary to isolate the effects of increases in campaign spending that are unrelated to a candidate's direct appeal to voters. For example, wealthy candidates are able to spend more money on their campaigns for reasons that have little to do with their popularity among voters. Consider the experience of Senator Jon Corzine (D-N.J.), who defeated a weak Republican opponent to gain election to the Senate in 2000. Corzine spent sixty million dollars, mostly from his personal fortune, on his Senate campaign. Many observers pointed to this episode as an example of how a wealthy individual can buy elective office. Despite his record spending, however, Corzine's vote total ran behind that of the average House Democrat in New Jersey and behind the Democratic nominee for president, Al Gore, even though Gore did very little campaigning in strongly Democratic New Jersey. There is even some evidence that Corzine's wealth was a liability, given that many yard signs urged his Republican opponent to "make him spend it all!"

A more systematic analysis of the electoral fortunes of wealthy candidates found no significant association between electoral or fund-raising success and personal wealth.[2] Related findings abound. For example, large cam-

---

1. Steven Levitt, "Using Repeat Challengers to Estimate the Effects of Campaign Spending on Electoral Outcomes in the U.S. House," *Journal of Political Economy* 102 (1994): 777–798.

2. Jeffrey Milyo and Timothy Groseclose, "The Electoral Effects of Incumbent Wealth," *Journal of Law and Economics* 42 (1999): 699–722.

paign war chests carried over from the previous election do not deter challengers and confer no electoral advantage on incumbents. Similarly, large fund-raising windfalls attributable to changes in campaign finance laws have been shown to be unrelated to candidates' subsequent electoral fortunes.[3] Nevertheless, no serious scholar would argue that campaign spending is unimportant. These findings do not imply that anyone running for elective office would do as well (in terms of vote share) by not spending several million dollars. Instead, the appropriate conclusion is that in the vast majority of political contests, the identity of the victor would not be different had any one candidate spent a few hundred thousand dollars more (or less).

Policy Consequences of Campaign Contributions

Are campaign contributions the functional equivalent of bribes? The conventional wisdom is that donors must get something for their money, but decades of academic research on Congress has failed to uncover any systematic evidence that this is so. Indeed, legislators tend to act in accordance with the interests of their donors, but this is not because of some quid pro quo. Instead, donors tend to give to like-minded candidates.[4] Of course, if candidates choose their policy positions in anticipation of a subsequent payoff in campaign contributions, there would be no real distinction between accepting bribes and accepting contributions from like-minded voters. However, studies of legislative behavior indicate that the most important determinants of an incumbent's voting record are constituent interests, party, and personal ideology. In election years, constituent interests become more important than in nonelection years, but overall, these three factors explain nearly all of the variation in incumbents' voting records.[5]

Most informed citizens react to these findings with incredulity. If campaign contributions do not buy favors, then why is so much money spent on politics? In fact, scholars of American politics have long noted how little is spent on politics. Consider that large firms spend ten times as much on lobbying as their employees spend on

campaign contributions through PACs, as individuals, or in the form of unregulated contributions to political parties (i.e., soft money).[6] I mention employee contributions because, contrary to the sloppy reporting that appears regularly in U.S. newspapers, corporations in the United States do not contribute to political campaigns: they are prohibited from doing so and have been so prohibited since 1907. When you read that Enron has given X million dollars to candidates, what that really means is that people who identify themselves as Enron employees have given X million dollars of their own money. In addition, political expenditures by employees of firms tend to be a fixed proportion of net revenues and do not rise and fall as relevant issues move on or off the policy agenda.[7] Neither of these facts is easily reconciled with the notion that campaign contributions are the functional equivalent of bribes. Of course, neither does this imply that campaign contributions are completely inconsequential, only that the conventional wisdom overstates their importance.

It is possible that evidence of the effect of campaign contributions may not be manifest in the roll-call votes of legislators. Scholars have long recognized that the relevant action may take place behind closed doors, where the content of legislation is determined. This is a much more difficult proposition to test, but at least one recent study has found no relationship between campaign contributions and the activities of legislators within committees.[8] More convincing would be evidence that the states with more laissez-faire campaign finance regulations adopt substantively different policies. Unfortunately, to date, no such study has been conducted.

So, why are campaign contributions not like bribes? There are several reasons: (1) federal law limits contribution amounts to federal candidates (as do most states); (2) bribery and influence peddling are illegal, so exchanges of money for campaign promises are unenforceable; (3) legislation is a collective activity, so it would be necessary to bribe a large number of legislators in order to influence policy; (4) the existence of competing interests raises the cost of trying to buy a legislative majority; (5) the existence of a muckraking press and political competition

3. Jeffrey Milyo, "The Electoral Effects of Campaign Spending in House Elections," Citizens' Research Foundation, Los Angeles, 1998.

4. Steven Levitt, "Who are PACs Trying to Influence with Contributions: Politicians or Voters?" *Economics and Politics* 10, no. 1 (1998): 19–36.

5. Steven Levitt, "How Do Senators Vote? Disentangling the Role of Party Affiliation, Voter Preferences and Senator Ideology," *American Economic Review* 86 (1996): 425–441.

6. Jeffrey Milyo, David Primo, and Timothy Groseclose, "Corporate PAC Contributions in Perspective," *Business and Politics* 2, no. 1 (2000): 75–88.

7. Stephen Ansolebehere, John M. de Figuerido, and James M. Snyder Jr., "Why Is There So Little Money in U.S. Politics?" *Journal of Economic Perspectives* 17, no. 1 (2003): 105–130.

8. Gregory Wawro, *Legislative Entrepreneurship in the United States House of Representatives* (Ann Arbor: University of Michigan Press, 2000).

means that candidates try to avoid even the appearance of impropriety; and (6) the diminishing marginal productivity of campaign spending discussed above reduces the value of any individual contribution to almost nil. This last point is perhaps the most important.

In 2000, total political spending in federal elections was about $3 billion. Contributions from individuals to candidates or parties accounted for nearly 80 percent of this total. The primary motivation for individual contributors is to support ideologically like-minded candidates, not to influence candidate positions. Further, the existence of these individual contributions drives down the marginal value of contributions from special-interest groups and hampers their ability to influence politicians.

Lessons for Reform

Political and legal decision makers have for too long considered the role of money in politics to be self-evident; this has led to a widespread and pervasive misunderstanding of the likely costs and benefits of campaign finance reform proposals. But political institutions are no less subject to scientific inquiry than are social or economic institutions. The consensus among academic researchers is that money is far less important in determining either election or policy outcomes than conventional wisdom holds it to be. Consequently, the benefits of campaign finance reforms have also been exaggerated.

There is even some reason to be concerned that ill-considered reforms will have important unintended consequences. For example, analyses of the different regulatory regimes across states reveal that limits on individual contributions are associated with reduced political competition, which is in turn associated with reduced turnout. Further, exposure to campaign advertising makes voters more knowledgeable about candidates' positions, which is not only desirable itself, but is also associated with increased voter turnout. Therefore, one unintended consequence of restrictive campaign finance reforms is to reduce voter awareness and participation. Another possibility is that reforms may reduce political accountability since incumbents can tailor reform legislation to effectively insulate themselves from viable competition.

About the Author

Jeffrey Milyo is an associate professor of economics at the University of Missouri in Columbia.

Further Reading

Ansolabehere, Stephen, John M. de Figuerido, and James M. Snyder Jr. "Why Is There So Little Money in U.S. Politics?" *Journal of Economic Perspectives* 17, no. 1 (2003): 105–130.
Levitt, Steven. "Congressional Campaign Reform." *Journal of Economic Perspectives* 9, no. 1 (1995): 183–193.
Milyo, Jeffrey. "The Political Economics of Campaign Finance." *Independent Review* 3, no. 4 (1999): 537–547.
Milyo, Jeffrey, David Primo, and Timothy Groseclose. "Corporate PAC Campaign Contributions in Perspective." *Business and Politics* 2, no. 1 (2000): 75–88.

Capital Gains Taxes

Stephen Moore

What Is Capital?

The term "capital" refers to produced goods used to produce future goods. Even a corner lemonade stand could not exist without capital; the lemons and the stand are the essential capital that makes the enterprise operate. A recent study by Dale Jorgenson of Harvard University discovered that almost half of the growth of the American economy between 1948 and 1980 was directly attributable to the increase in U.S. capital formation (with most of the rest a result of increases and improvements in the labor force).[1]

Capital can also refer to technological improvements or even the spark of an idea that leads to the creation of a new business or product. In 1975, when Bill Gates decided to form a computer software company and then brought MS-DOS to market, he created capital. Investors who had the foresight to take the risk of investing in Bill Gates's idea made fabulous amounts of money. A twenty-thousand-dollar investment in Microsoft in 1986 was worth about two million dollars in 2004.

Between 1900 and 2000, real wages in the United States quintupled from around fifteen cents an hour (worth three dollars in 2000 dollars) to more than fifteen dollars an hour. In other words, a worker in 2000 earned as much, adjusted for inflation, in twelve minutes as a worker in 1900 earned in an hour. That surge in the living standard of the American worker is explained, in part, by the increase in capital over that period. The main reason U.S. farmers and manufacturing workers are more productive, and their real wages higher, than those of most other industrial nations is that America has one of the highest ratios of capital to worker in the world. Even Americans working in the service sector are highly paid relative to workers in other nations as a result of the capital they work with. In their textbook, Nobel laureate Paul Samu-

---

1. Dale Jorgenson, *Postwar U.S. Economic Growth*, vol. 1 of *Productivity* (Cambridge: MIT Press, 1995).

elson and William D. Nordhaus noted: "Because each worker has more capital to work with, his or her marginal product rises. Therefore, the competitive real wage rises as workers become worth more to capitalists and meet with spirited bidding up of their market wage rates."[2] The capital-to-labor ratio explains roughly 95 percent of the fluctuation in wages over the past forty years. When the ratio rises, wages rise; when the ratio stays constant, wages stagnate.

What Is the Capital Gains Tax?

A capital gain is the difference between the price received from selling an asset and the price paid for it. An asset can be a home, a farm, a ranch, a family business, or a work of art, for instance.[3] In most years, slightly less than half of the capital gains that the U.S. government taxes are on the sale of corporate stock. For all the controversy surrounding the tax treatment of capital gains, that tax brings in surprisingly little revenue for the federal government. From 1990 to 1995, capital gains tax collections were between $25 billion and $40 billion a year, less than 3 percent of federal tax revenues. During the Internet boom, when stock gains were huge, capital gains tax collections peaked at $119 billion in 2000 before rapidly falling back below $50 billion (see Table 1 for a breakdown of the sources of federal revenue).

The capital gains tax is different from almost all other forms of federal taxation in that it is relatively easy to avoid. Because people pay the tax only when they sell an asset, they can legally avoid payment by holding on to their assets—a phenomenon known as the "lock-in effect."

The tax treatment of capital gains has other unique features. One is that capital gains are not indexed for inflation: the seller pays tax not only on the real gain in purchasing power, but also on the illusory gain attributable to inflation. The inflation penalty is one reason that, historically, capital gains have been taxed at lower rates than ordinary income. In fact, Alan Blinder, a former member of the Federal Reserve Board, noted in 1980 that, up until that time, "most capital gains were not gains of real purchasing power at all, but simply represented the maintenance of principal in an inflationary world."[4]

Table 1 Sources of Federal Revenue
(billions of 2003 dollars)

Capital gains tax	45
Corporate income tax	132
Individual income tax	794
Social Security taxes	713
Total revenues	1,782

Source: Historical Tables: Budget of the United States Government, Fiscal Year 2005 (Washington, D.C: Government Printing Office, 2004), Table 2.1, p. 22. Capital Gains from CBO.

Note: Columns do not add because not all sources of federal revenue are shown.

Another strange feature of the tax is that individuals are permitted to deduct only a portion of the capital losses they incur, whereas they must pay taxes on all of the gains. When taxpayers undertake risky investments, the government taxes fully any gain they realize if the investment has a positive return. But the government allows only partial tax deduction (of up to three thousand dollars per year) if the venture results in a loss. That introduces a bias in the tax code against risk-taking.[5]

One other peculiar aspect of the capital gains tax has made many economists conclude that it is economically inefficient: it is a form of double taxation on capital formation. Economists Victor Canto and Harvey Hirschorn explained:

> A government can choose to tax either the value of an asset or its yield, but it should not tax both. Capital gains are literally the appreciation in the value of an existing asset. Any appreciation reflects merely an increase in the after-tax rate of return on the asset. The taxes implicit in the asset's after-tax earnings are already fully reflected in the asset's price or change in price. Any additional tax is strictly double taxation.[6]

Take, for example, the capital gains tax paid on a pharmaceutical stock. The value of that stock equals the discounted present value of all of the company's future proceeds. If the company is expected to earn $100,000 a year for the next twenty years, the sales price of the stock will reflect those returns. The "gain" the seller realizes from

2. Paul Samuelson and William D. Nordhaus, *Economics* (New York: McGraw-Hill, 1985), p. 789.

3. Some types of capital gains are exempt from capital gains taxes. For instance, most home sales are not subject to capital gains taxes when the seller purchases another home. Moreover, pension funds, which purchase stocks and other assets, are exempt from paying taxes on capital gains.

4. Alan S. Blinder, "The Level and Distribution of Economic

Well-Being," in Martin Feldstein, ed., *The American Economy in Transition* (Chicago: University of Chicago Press, 1980), p. 48.

5. Congressional Budget Office, "Indexing Capital Gains," August 1990.

6. Victor Canto and Harvey Hirschorn, "In Search of a Free Lunch," Laffer and Canto Associates, San Diego, November 1994.

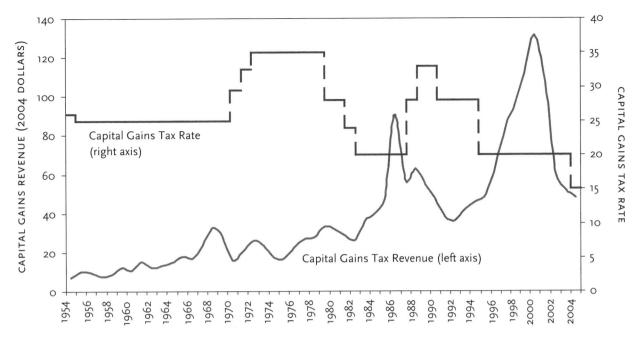

Figure 1 Capital Gains Tax and Revenue Raised

the sale of the stock will reflect those future returns, and thus the seller will pay capital gains tax on the future stream of income. But the company's future $100,000 annual returns will also be taxed when they are earned. So the $100,000 in profits is taxed twice—when the owners sell their shares of stock and when the company actually earns the income. That is why many tax analysts argue that the most equitable rate of tax on capital gains is zero.[7]

The Impact of Recent Capital Gains Tax Changes

The historical evidence suggests that when the capital gains tax is reduced, locked-in capital is liberated and, at least temporarily, the revenues from the tax rise. For example, after the 1981 capital gains tax was cut from 28 to 20 percent, real (all figures in this section are 2004 dollars) federal capital gains tax revenues leapt from $29.4 billion in 1981 to $36.6 billion by 1983—a 24 percent increase. After the capital gains tax was cut in 1997, the receipts from capital gains taxes rose from $66.9 billion in 1996 to $114.7 billion by 1999, an increase of more than 71 percent. Preliminary data suggest that the capital gains

7. See, for example, Norman B. Ture and B. Kenneth Sanden, *The Effects of Tax Policy on Capital Formation* (New York: Financial Executives Research Foundation, 1977); Jude Wanniski, "Capital Gains in a Supply Side Model," Statement before the Senate Finance Committee, February 15, 1995; and Raymond Keating, "Eliminating Capital Gains Taxes: Lifeblood for an Entrepreneurial Economy," Small Business Survival Committee, Washington, D.C., 1995.

tax cut of 2003 to a rate of 15 percent has also caused tax revenues to increase, at least in the first year (see Figure 1).

Conversely, total asset sales of taxable capital gains fell from $575 billion in 1986, the year before the capital gains rate was raised (from 20 back to 28 percent), to $246 billion in 1989. Investors were unwilling to sell stock and other taxable assets at the new higher tax rate.

Reducing the capital gains tax rate appears also to lead to higher stock prices. The stock market boomed in the 1980s after the 1981 capital gains tax cut; it boomed to new heights in the late 1990s after the Clinton capital gains rate cut, and then again in 2003 after George W. Bush signed his capital gains tax cut into law.

It may seem a paradox that a lower capital gains tax typically leads to more tax revenues collected from the tax. But, really, there is no mystery here. As mentioned, the capital gains tax is an easily avoided tax. When the tax rate is high, investors simply delay selling their assets—stocks, properties, businesses, and so on—to keep the tax collector away from their door. When the capital gains tax is cut, asset holders are more likely to sell. Moreover, because a lower capital gains tax substantially lowers the cost of capital, it encourages risk-taking and causes the economy to grow faster, thus raising all government receipts in the long term.

Capital Gains Tax Cuts and Business Creation

Past reductions in the capital gains tax rates (e.g., in 1978, 1981, and 1997) stimulated the financing and start-up of new businesses, while new business activity stalled after increases in capital gains taxes (1969 and 1986). Table 2 compares three measures of new business generation— the number of initial public stock offerings (IPOs), the dollars raised from those IPOs, and the dollars committed to venture capital firms—with fluctuations in the capital gains tax rate between 1969 and 2004.[8] New commitments to venture capital firms (in 2004 dollars) increased from $220 million in 1977, when the top marginal tax rate on capital gains was 49 percent, to $9.7 billion by 1983, when the rate had been dropped to 20 percent and the U.S. economy had started pulling out of the recession (Figure 2). That was a 4,300 percent increase in capital raised for new firms.

Venture capital funds are the economic lifeblood of high-technology companies in industries that are critical to U.S. international competitiveness: computer software, biotechnology, computer engineering, electronics, aerospace, pharmaceuticals, and so forth. The high capital gains tax rate appears to have contributed to the drying up of funding sources for those promising new frontier firms following the 1986 tax hike.[9] Significantly, the massive technology boom of the late 1990s came immediately after the 1997 capital gains tax cut, unleashing another period of venture activity (Figure 3).

Who Gains from Cuts in the Capital Gains Tax?

Any discussion of the capital gains tax inevitably leads to a discussion of which income groups will benefit most from a change in the tax policy. For example, in the 1997 debate over the capital gains tax, opponents of a rate cut maintained that almost all of the benefits would go to high-income earners. That is true of the direct effects because high-income earners also earn most of the capital gains. It is also true, however, that cuts in capital gains tax rates benefit people at all levels, mainly because of the economic growth they engender. Moreover, the gains to non-high-income families should be noted. Internal Revenue Service data indicate that in 2003, the most recent year for which these data are available, 42 percent of all returns reporting capital gains were from households with incomes below $50,000. Seventy-two percent, or 6.4 million returns, were for households with incomes below $100,000.[10] Despite this fact, overall gains are concen-

8. See Clark S. Judge, "The Tax That Ate the Economy," *Wall Street Journal*, June 24, 1991, editorial page.
9. See Coopers and Lybrand and Venture Economics, "Third Annual Economic Impact of Venture Capital Study," conducted for the National Venture Capital Association, 1993.
10. Internal Revenue Service, "Individual Income Tax Returns,

Table 2 Relationship between the Capital Gains Tax Rate and Measures of New Business Formation

Year	Top Capital Gains Rate (%)	Initial Public Offerings	Dollars Raised (millions)	Commitments to Venture Capitalists (millions)
1969	27	780	2605	506
1970	32	358	780	272
1971	39	391	1665	252
1972	45	562	2724	157
1973	45	105	330	133
1974	45	9	51	124
1975	45	14	264	20
1976	49	34	237	93
1977	49	40	151	68
1978	48	42	247	980
1979	28	103	429	449
1980	28	259	1404	961
1981	24	438	3200	1628
1982	20	198	1334	2119
1983	20	848	13168	5098
1984	20	516	3934	4590
1985	20	507	10450	3502
1986	20	953	19260	4650
1987	28	630	16380	4900
1988	33	435	5750	2100
1989	33	371	6068	2200
1990	28	276	4519	2000
1991	28	367	16420	2511
1992	28	509	23990	5178
1993	28	605	37000	4963
1994	28	500	25000	5351
1995	28	500	28000	5608
1996	28	775	50000	11278
1997	20	575	40000	17207
1998	20	350	33000	22576
1999	20	492	63000	59164
2000	20	422	97000	106,028
2001	20	91	37134.1	38,064
2002	20	81	19232.4	3,661
2003	15	81	13571.9	10,528
2004	15	242	34240.5	15,000*

* Estimated based on $11,249 through third quarter.

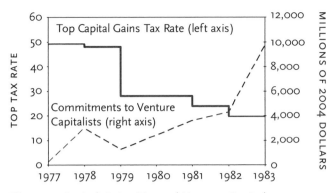

Figure 2 Capital Gains Tax and Venture Capital, 1977–1983

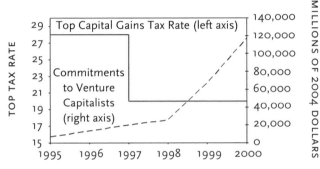

Figure 3 Capital Gains Tax and Venture Capital, 1995–2000

trated among high-income individuals, with 87 percent of overall gains going to filers with income above $100,000, and 74 percent to filers with income above $200,000. It is worth noting, however, that these numbers are misleading because they include the entire amount of the gain itself, which often represents the unlocking of value accumulated over many years. Finally, it should be noted that cuts in capital gains taxes particularly benefit the elderly. The elderly are two and a half times as likely to realize capital gains in a given year as are tax filers under the age of sixty-five. The elderly are also likely to derive a larger share of their income from capital gains than are younger workers. A study by the National Center for Policy Analysis examining IRS data from 1986 found that the average elderly tax filer had an income of $31,865, 23 percent of which was capital gains. The average nonelderly filer had an income of $26,199, 9 percent of which was from capital gains.[11]

Tax Year 2003 Preliminary Data: Selected Income and Tax Items, by Size of Adjusted Gross Income," online at: http://www.irs.gov/pub/irs-soi/03in01pd.xls.

11. John Goodman, Aldona Robbins, and Gary Robbins, "Elderly Taxpayers and the Capital Gains Tax Debate," National Center for Policy Analysis, Dallas, Texas, 1990.

Conclusion

On balance, the evidence supports the economic case for a low rate of tax on capital gains. Recent actual experience suggests that a low rate of tax on capital gains increases capital investment and new business formation. Tax revenues have surged when the capital gains rate has been cut as trillions of dollars of locked-in capital are released to be put to more productive uses.

About the Author

Stephen Moore is an editor of the *Wall Street Journal*.

Further Reading

Ivković, Zoran, James Poterba, and Scott Weisbenner. "Tax-Motivated Trading by Individual Investors." *American Economic Review* 95, no. 5 (2005): 1605–1630.

Capitalism

Robert Hessen

"Capitalism," a term of disparagement coined by socialists in the mid-nineteenth century, is a misnomer for "economic individualism," which Adam Smith earlier called "the obvious and simple system of natural liberty" (*Wealth of Nations*). Economic individualism's basic premise is that the pursuit of self-interest and the right to own private property are morally defensible and legally legitimate. Its major corollary is that the state exists to protect individual rights. Subject to certain restrictions, individuals (alone or with others) are free to decide where to invest, what to produce or sell, and what prices to charge. There is no natural limit to the range of their efforts in terms of assets, sales, and profits; or the number of customers, employees, and investors; or whether they operate in local, regional, national, or international markets.

The emergence of capitalism is often mistakenly linked to a Puritan work ethic. German sociologist Max Weber, writing in 1903, stated that the catalyst for capitalism was in seventeenth-century England, where members of a religious sect, the Puritans, under the sway of John Calvin's doctrine of predestination, channeled their energies into hard work, reinvestment, and modest living, and then carried these attitudes to New England. Weber's thesis breaks down, however. The same attitudes toward work and savings are exhibited by Jews and Japanese, whose value systems contain no Calvinist component. Moreover, Scotland in the seventeenth century was simultaneously orthodox Calvinist and economically stagnant.

A better explanation of the Puritans' diligence is that by refusing to swear allegiance to the established Church of England, they were barred from activities and professions to which they otherwise might have been drawn—land-ownership, law, the military, civil service, universities—and so they focused on trade and commerce. A similar pattern of exclusion or ostracism explains why Jews and other racial and religious minorities in other countries and later centuries tended to concentrate on retail businesses and money lending.

In early-nineteenth-century England the most visible face of capitalism was the textile factories that hired women and children. Critics (Richard Oastler and Robert Southey, among others) denounced the mill owners as heartless exploiters and described the working conditions—long hours, low pay, monotonous routine—as if they were unprecedented. Believing that poverty was new, not merely more visible in crowded towns and villages, critics compared contemporary times unfavorably with earlier centuries. Their claims of increasing misery, however, were based on ignorance of how squalid life actually had been earlier. Before children began earning money working in factories, they had been sent to live in parish poorhouses; apprenticed as unpaid household servants; rented out for backbreaking agricultural labor; or became beggars, vagrants, thieves, and prostitutes. The precapitalist "good old days" simply never existed (see INDUSTRIAL REVOLUTION AND THE STANDARD OF LIVING).

Nonetheless, by the 1820s and 1830s the growing specter of child labor and "dark Satanic mills" (poet William Blake's memorable phrase) generated vocal opposition to these unbridled examples of self-interest and the pursuit of profit. Some critics urged legislative regulation of wages and hours, compulsory education, and minimum age limits for laborers. Others offered more radical alternatives. The most vociferous were the socialists, who aimed to eradicate individualism, the name that preceded capitalism.

Socialist theorists repudiated individualism's leading tenets: that individuals possess inalienable rights, that government should not restrain individuals from pursuing their own happiness, and that economic activity should not be regulated by government. Instead, they proclaimed an organic conception of society. They stressed ideals such as brotherhood, community, and social solidarity and set forth detailed blueprints for model utopian colonies in which collectivist values would be institutionalized.

The short life span of these utopian societies acted as a brake on the appeal of socialism. But its ranks swelled after Karl Marx offered a new "scientific" version, proclaiming that he had discovered the laws of history and that socialism inevitably would replace capitalism. Beyond offering sweeping promises that socialism would create economic equality, eradicate poverty, end specialization, and abolish money, Marx supplied no details at all about how a future socialist society would be structured or would operate.

Even nineteenth-century economists—in England, America, and Western Europe—who were supposedly capitalism's defenders did not defend capitalism effectively because they did not understand it. They came to believe that the most defensible economic system was one of "perfect" or "pure" competition. Under perfect competition all firms are small scale, products in each industry are homogeneous, consumers are perfectly informed about what is for sale and at what price, and all sellers are what economists call price takers (i.e., they have to "take" the market price and cannot charge a higher one for their goods).

Clearly, these assumptions were at odds with both common sense and the reality of market conditions. Under real competition, which is what capitalism delivered, companies are rivals for sales and profits. This rivalry leads them to innovate in product design and performance, to introduce cost-cutting technology, and to use packaging to make products more attractive or convenient for customers. Unbridled rivalry encourages companies to offer assurances of security to imperfectly informed consumers, by means such as money-back guarantees or product warranties and by building customer loyalty through investing in their brand names and reputations (see ADVERTISING, BRAND NAMES, and CONSUMER PROTECTION).

Companies that successfully adopted these techniques of rivalry were the ones that grew, and some came to dominate their industries, though usually only for a few years until other firms found superior methods of satisfying consumer demands. Neither rivalry nor product differentiation occurs under perfect competition, but they happen constantly under real flesh-and-blood capitalism.

The leading American industrialists of the late nineteenth century were aggressive competitors and innovators. To cut costs and thereby reduce prices and win a larger market share, Andrew Carnegie eagerly scrapped his huge investment in Bessemer furnaces and adopted the open-hearth system for making steel rails. In the oil-refining industry, John D. Rockefeller embraced cost cutting by building his own pipeline network; manufacturing his own barrels; and hiring chemists to remove the vile odor from abundant, low-cost crude oil. Gustavus Swift challenged the existing network of local butchers when he created assembly-line meatpacking facilities in Chicago and built his own fleet of refrigerated railroad cars to deliver low-price beef to distant markets. Local merchants also were challenged by Chicago-based Sears Roebuck and Montgomery Ward, which pioneered mail-order sales on a money-back, satisfaction-guaranteed basis.

Small-scale producers denounced these innovators as

"robber barons," accused them of monopolistic practices, and appealed to Congress for relief from relentless competition. Beginning with the Sherman Act (1890), Congress enacted antitrust laws that were often used to suppress cost cutting and price slashing, based on acceptance of the idea that an economy of numerous small-scale firms was superior to one dominated by a few large, highly efficient companies operating in national markets (see ANTITRUST).

Despite these constraints, which worked sporadically and unpredictably, the benefits of capitalism were widely diffused. Luxuries quickly were transformed into necessities. At first, the luxuries were cheap cotton clothes, fresh meat, and white bread; then sewing machines, bicycles, sporting goods, and musical instruments; then automobiles, washing machines, clothes dryers, and refrigerators; then telephones, radios, televisions, air conditioners, and freezers; and most recently, TiVos, digital cameras, DVD players, and cell phones.

That these amenities had become available to most people did not cause capitalism's critics to recant, or even to relent. Instead, they ingeniously reversed themselves. Marxist philosopher Herbert Marcuse proclaimed that the real evil of capitalism is prosperity, because it seduces workers away from their historic mission—the revolutionary overthrow of capitalism—by supplying them with cars and household appliances, which he called "tools of enslavement."[1] Some critics reject capitalism by extolling "the simple life" and labeling prosperity mindless materialism. In the 1950s, critics such as John Kenneth Galbraith and Vance Packard attacked the legitimacy of consumer demand, asserting that if goods had to be advertised in order to sell, they could not be serving any authentic human needs.[2] They charged that consumers are brainwashed by Madison Avenue and crave whatever the giant corporations choose to produce and advertise, and complained that the "public sector" is starved while frivolous private desires are being satisfied. And having seen that capitalism reduced poverty instead of intensifying it, critics such as Gar Alperovitz and Michael Harrington proclaimed equality the highest moral value, calling for higher taxes on incomes and inheritances to massively redistribute wealth, not only nationally but also internationally.[3]

Capitalism is not a cure for every defect in human affairs or for eradicating all inequalities, but who ever said it was? It holds out the promise of what Adam Smith called "universal opulence." Those who demand more are likely to be using higher expectations as a weapon of criticism. For example, British economist Richard Layard recently attracted headlines and airtime with a startling revelation: money cannot buy happiness (a cliché of song lyrics and church sermons).[4] He laments that economic individualism fails to ensure the emotional satisfactions that are essential to life, including family ties, financial security, meaningful work, friendship, and good health. Instead, a capitalist society supplies new gadgets, appliances, and luxuries that arouse envy in those who cannot afford them and that inspire a ceaseless obsession with securing more among those who already own too much. Layard's long-range solutions include a revival of religion to topple the secularism that capitalism fosters, altruism to obliterate selfishness, and communitarianism to supercede individualism. He stresses the need, near-term, for robust governmental efforts to promote happiness instead of the minimalist night-watchman state that libertarian defenders of capitalism favor. He argues that low taxes are harmful to the poor because they give government inadequate revenue to provide essential services to the poor. Higher taxes really would not harm the well-to-do, he says, because money and material possessions are subject to diminishing marginal utility. If such claims have a familiar ring, it is because Galbraith made the same points fifty years ago.

Virtually all the new criticisms of capitalism are old ones repackaged as stunning new insights. One example is the attack on "globalization" (the outsourcing of service, manufacturing, and assembly jobs to foreign sites where costs are cheaper). It has been denounced as union busting, exploitative, and destructive of foreign cultures, and is damned for the loss of domestic jobs and the resulting erosion of local tax revenues. Identical complaints were voiced two generations ago when jobs began flowing from unionized New England textile factories to nonunionized southern textile mills, and then to offshore sites such as Puerto Rico.

Another "new" line of attack on capitalism has been launched by law professors Cass Sunstein and Liam Murphy and philosophers Stephen Holmes, Thomas Nagel, and Peter Singer.[5] They lament that in societies based on

1. Herbert Marcuse, "Repressive Tolerance," in Robert Paul Wolff, Barrington Moore Jr., and Marcuse, *A Critique of Pure Tolerance* (Boston: Beacon Press, 1969).

2. John Kenneth Galbraith, *The Affluent Society* (Boston: Houghton Mifflin, 1958); Vance Packard, *The Hidden Persuaders* (New York: D. McKay, 1957).

3. Gar Alperovitz, "Notes Toward a Pluralist Commonwealth," in Staughton Lynd and Alperovitz, *Strategy and Program: Two Essays Toward a New American Socialism* (Boston: Beacon Press, 1971); Michael Harrington, *Socialism Past and Future* (Boston: Little, Brown, 1989).

4. Richard Layard, *Happiness: Lessons from a New Science* (New York: Penguin Press, 2005).

5. Stephen Holmes and Cass Sunstein, *The Cost of Rights* (New

self-interest and private property, wealth earners oppose rising taxes, preferring to spend their money on themselves and leave inheritances for their children. This selfish bias leads to an impoverished public sector and to inadequate tax revenues. To justify governmental claims for higher taxes, these writers have revived an argument—attacking the legitimacy of private property and inheritance—that was advanced by institutionalist economists during the New Deal era. Government, they assert, is the ultimate source of all wealth, and so it should have first claim on wealth and earnings. "Is it really your money?" Singer asks, citing economist Herbert Simon's estimate that a flat income tax of 90 percent would be reasonable because individuals derive most of their income from the "social capital" provided by technology and by protections such as patents and copyrights, and by the physical security afforded by police, courts, and armies rather than from anything they personally do. If the "fruits of capitalism" are merely a gift of government, it is an argument that proves too much. By the same logic, individuals might be enslaved if they were not protected by government, so conscription (servitude for a brief period) would be entirely unobjectionable, as would the seizure of privately owned land to turn it over to new owners if their uses would yield higher tax revenues—exactly the basis of a 2005 Supreme Court ruling on "eminent domain."

Another persistent criticism of capitalism—the attack on corporations—harkens back to the 1930s. Critics like Ralph Nader, Mark Green, Charles Lindblom, and Robert Dahl focus their fire on giant corporations, charging that they are illegitimate institutions because they do not conform to the model of small-scale, owner-managed firms that Adam Smith extolled in 1776.[6] In fact, giant corporations are fully consistent with capitalism, which does not imply any particular configuration of firms in terms of size or legal form. They attract capital from thousands (sometimes millions) of investors who are strangers to each other and who entrust their savings to the managerial expertise of others in exchange for a share of the resulting profits.

In an influential 1932 book, *The Modern Corporation and Private Property*, Adolf A. Berle Jr. coined the phrase "splitting of the atom of ownership" to lament the fact that investment and management had become two distinct elements. In fact, the process is merely an example of the specialization of function or division of labor that occurs so often under capitalism. Far from being an abuse or defect, giant corporations are an eloquent testimonial to the ability of individuals to engage in large-scale, long-range cooperation for their mutual benefit and enrichment (see CORPORATIONS).

As noted earlier, the freedoms to invest, to decide what to produce, and to decide what to charge have always been restricted. A fully free economy, true laissez-faire, never has existed, but governmental authority over economic activity has sharply increased since the eighteenth century, and especially since the Great Depression. Originally, local authorities fixed the prices of necessities such as bread and ale, bridge and ferry tolls, or fees at inns and mills, but most products and services were unregulated. By the late nineteenth century governments were setting railroad freight rates and the prices charged by grain elevator operators, because these businesses had become "affected with a public purpose." By the 1930s the same criterion was invoked to justify price controls over milk, ice, and theater tickets. One piece of good news, though, is that a spate of deregulation in the late 1970s and the 1980s eliminated price controls on airline travel, trucking, railroad freight rates, natural gas, oil, and some telecommunications rates.

Simultaneously, from the eighteenth century on, government began to play a more active, interventionist role in offering benefits to business, such as tax exemptions, bounties or subsidies to grow certain crops, and tariff protection so domestic firms would devote capital to manufacturing goods that otherwise had to be imported. Special favors became entrenched and hard to repeal because the recipients were organized while consumers, who bore the burden of higher prices, were not.

Once safe from foreign competition behind these barriers to free trade, some U.S. producers—steel and auto manufacturers, for example—stagnated. They failed to adopt new technologies or to cut costs until low-cost, low-price overseas rivals—the Japanese, especially—challenged them for their customers. They responded initially by asking Congress for new favors—higher tariffs, import quotas, and loan guarantees—and pleading with consumers to "buy American" and thereby save domestic jobs. Slowly, but inevitably, they began the expensive process of catching up with foreign companies so they could try to recapture their domestic customers.

Today, the United States, once the citadel of capitalism, is a "mixed economy" in which government bestows favors and imposes restrictions with no clear or consistent prin-

York: Norton, 1999); Liam Murphy and Thomas Nagel, *The Myth of Ownership* (New York: Oxford University Press, 2002); Peter Singer, *The President of Good and Evil* (New York: Dutton, 2004).

6. Ralph Nader and Mark Green, *Taming the Giant Corporation* (New York: Norton, 1976); Charles Lindblom, *Politics and Markets* (New York: Basic Books, 1977); Robert Dahl, *A Preface to Economic Democracy* (Berkeley: University of California Press, 1985).

ciples in mind. As the formerly communist countries of Eastern Europe struggle to embrace free-market ideas and institutions, they can learn from the American (and British) experience about not only the benefits that flowed from economic individualism, but also the burden of regulations that became impossible to repeal and trade barriers that were hard to dismantle. If the history of capitalism proves one thing, it is that the process of competition does not stop at national borders. As long as individuals anywhere perceive a potential for profits, they will amass the capital, produce the product, and circumvent the cultural and political barriers that interfere with their objectives.

About the Author

Robert Hessen, a specialist in business and economic history, is a senior research fellow at Stanford University's Hoover Institution.

Further Reading

Berger, Peter. *The Capitalist Revolution.* New York: Basic Books, 1986.

De Soto, Hernando. *The Mystery of Capital: Why Capitalism Triumphs in the West and Fails Everywhere Else.* New York: Basic Books, 2000.

Easterbrook, Gregg. *The Progress Paradox: How Life Gets Better While People Feel Worse.* New York: Random House, 2003.

Folsom, Burton W. Jr. *The Myth of the Robber Barons: A New Look at the Rise of Big Business in America.* 3d ed. Herndon, Va.: Young America's Foundation, 1996.

Hayek, F. A., ed. *Capitalism and the Historians.* Chicago: University of Chicago Press, 1953.

Hessen, Robert. *In Defense of the Corporation.* Stanford: Hoover Institution Press, 1979.

Landes, David S. *The Wealth and Poverty of Nations: Why Some Are So Rich and Some So Poor.* New York: Norton, 1999.

McCraw, Thomas K. *Creating Modern Capitalism.* Cambridge: Harvard University Press, 1997.

Mises, Ludwig von. *The Anti-capitalistic Mentality.* Princeton: Van Nostrand, 1956.

Mueller, John. *Capitalism, Democracy, and Ralph's Pretty Good Grocery.* Princeton: Princeton University Press, 2001.

Norberg, Johan. *In Defense of Global Capitalism.* Washington, D.C.: Cato Institute, 2003.

Pipes, Richard. *Property and Freedom.* New York: Alfred A. Knopf, 2000.

Rand, Ayn. *Capitalism: The Unknown Ideal.* New York: New American Library, 1966.

Reisman, George. *Capitalism.* Ottawa, Ill.: Jameson Books, 1996.

Rosenberg, Nathan, and L. E. Birdzell Jr. *How the West Grew Rich: The Economic Transformation of the Industrial World.* New York: Basic Books, 1987.

Seldon, Arthur. *The Virtues of Capitalism.* Indianapolis: Liberty Fund, 2004.

Cartels

Andrew R. Dick

People of the same trade seldom meet together, even for merriment and diversion, but the conversation ends in a conspiracy against the public, or in some contrivance to raise prices. It is impossible indeed to prevent such meetings, by any law which either could be executed, or would be consistent with liberty and justice. But though the law cannot hinder people of the same trade from sometimes assembling together, it ought to do nothing to facilitate such assemblies; much less to render them necessary.
—Adam Smith, *An Inquiry into the Nature and Causes of the Wealth of Nations* (1776)[1]

Public policy's traditional hostility to cartels is rooted in the view, summarized by eighteenth-century economist Adam Smith, that rival sellers will almost always prefer to raise their prices in unison than to aggressively compete for customers by undercutting each other's prices. But this statement tells only half the story. The same profit motive that entices sellers to want to collude also creates strong and sometimes uncontrollable temptations to "cheat" on a cartel. This is because any individual seller can usually garner a larger share of the market and earn larger profits by undercutting the cartel's price. If enough other sellers behave in this way, however, then attempts to raise prices artificially will fail under the collective weight of cheating.[2]

To understand whether or when a cartel can avoid this problem, economists have studied two questions: (1) Why have cartels proven much more effective in some settings than in others? and (2) Why in many industries have cartels proven impossible to form in practice? In an influential article addressing these questions, Nobel laureate George Stigler identified two principal hurdles for any successful cartel: first, reaching a consensus on the terms of coordination, and, second, establishing a system to detect and punish cheating against those terms. These twin hurdles have proven to be higher in some industries than in

1. For a contrary view, see "Benign Conspiracies," *Economist,* April 9, 1997.

2. Economists refer to this breakdown of cartel pricing as a PRISONERS' DILEMMA.

others, and in many settings, sellers have found them insurmountable.

Consensus can take the form of an explicit agreement to coordinate prices, an unwritten understanding to limit competition, or simply a mutual recognition that all firms would be better off if they restrained their competitive impulses and stabilized prices. Whatever form the consensus takes, cartel members must do more than simply agree on what price to charge; they also must close off all other avenues of potential competition that could threaten the cartel's ability to increase prices. In general, therefore, a cartel must also reach consensus on what level of services to offer, what grades of quality to produce, and how to ensure that product upgrades and new product introductions do not prompt a resurgence of competition.

While building consensus might appear to be a relatively straightforward task, actual experience suggests otherwise. According to one study, failure to reach a consensus has caused the demise of roughly one out of every four attempted cartels.[3] Experience has also shown that successful cartels often find it necessary to adopt complicated and sometimes cumbersome rules to restrain competitive impulses. For example, participants in the famous electrical equipment conspiracy of the 1950s and 1960s not only fixed prices but also had to agree on how to allocate market shares and divide up the largest customers. The vitamin cartel of the 1990s, whose prosecution led to the largest antitrust fines in U.S. history, involved sellers who not only fixed prices but also rigged bids, divided up customers, and set sales quotas. The need to add layer upon layer of cartel rules not only directly complicates the process of building consensus; it also increases the likelihood that the government will learn of the illegal actions.

Once formed, a cartel must then remain vigilant against "cheating" from within its ranks and competition from outside. Experience has shown that, very frequently, the greatest threat comes from entry into the industry by sellers who choose not to follow the cartel's pricing lead. For example, an entrant might find it more profitable to undercut the cartel price if it believes it can attract a substantial number of customers. Entry has been responsible for breaking up cartels in industries ranging from ocean shipping to oil to railroads. A somewhat less prevalent cause of breakups has been underpricing by cartel participants themselves. Internal cheating has undermined cartels operating in electric turbines and railroad transportation, among other industries, when sellers could not resist the

temptation to quickly capture a large share of the market by discounting their price to a select group of major customers. Requiring audits of participants' sales, creating financial incentives for customers to report price discounts offered to them, and setting up systems to monitor emerging threats of entry are among the tools that can help cartels detect cheating.

If cheating is detected, it must then be punished to discourage repeat occurrences. Sellers will be discouraged from cheating only if their temporary gains from underpricing the cartel are outweighed by the longer-term cost of punishment. Punishment can take many forms, ranging from other sellers targeting price discounts at the offender's customers, to cutting the offender's allocated sales quota, all the way to suspending the cartel's activities for some period. In almost all instances, however, punishment will be costly not only to the offender but also to the sellers who mete out the penalties. Discipline will work, therefore, only when the cartel members believe it would be costlier to turn a blind eye to sporadic cheating than to mete out punishment as a lesson for the future. The fact that many cartels have fallen victim to cheating suggests either that the punishment was inadequate or that cartel members recognized the futility of punishment.

Economists have identified a range of conditions that tend to make forming and defending a cartel harder in particular industries, and practically impossible in some. By analyzing cartel experiences within and across industries, economists have learned that cartels tend to be less likely to form and less likely to endure in industries where:

1. Numerous small sellers currently are producing

2. Additional sellers could begin producing at relatively low start-up cost and with little delay

3. The products being sold are complex

4. A small number of large customers each purchases relatively infrequently

5. Each customer is accustomed to negotiating for its own individual price and other terms of service

6. New products or new production methods are developed frequently

To supplement these "economic" hurdles to cartel operation, governments also can take additional measures to discourage industry cartels from forming. Antitrust laws in the United States and some other countries expose cartels to criminal and civil penalties. The wave of recent high-profile cartel indictments, leading in many cases to large fines and prison sentences for corporate executives, suggests that antitrust laws may have a substantial deter-

3. Margaret C. Levenstein and Valerie Y. Suslow, "What Determines Cartel Success?" *Journal of Economic Literature* 44, no. 1 (2006): 43–95.

rence effect. Yet, at the same time, the continuing stream of prosecutions also suggests that deterrence remains incomplete.

In other instances, however, government policies have purposefully *facilitated* industries' efforts to cartelize. During the Great Depression, for example, the National Recovery Administration (NRA) imposed "Codes of Fair Competition" that exempted cartels from antitrust penalties to stop "destructive price-cutting." Throughout the late 1930s, government-encouraged cartels flourished in literally hundreds of industries ranging from steel and textiles to beer and pasta. Several of these cartels survived long after the NRA codes were struck down, which suggests that the government's actions "taught" sellers how to collude to the long-term detriment of consumers. Governments both at home and abroad also have facilitated agricultural cartels by establishing marketing boards that specify price floors or production ceilings (quotas) for particular crops.

In some industries, governmental facilitation of cartel activity has been unintentional. An infamous example originated from a decision in the early 1990s by the Danish Competition Council to collect and publish transaction prices for sellers of ready-mix concrete. Following publication of the price information, customers wound up paying 15 to 20 percent more for concrete. The government's actions made pricing more transparent among supposedly competing sellers and thereby facilitated their efforts to detect and punish those sellers who sought to undercut the cartel's fixed price. Unwitting facilitation of cartels also occurs in government procurement auctions. In an effort to discourage political corruption, many governments announce winning and losing bids after such auctions. However, this practice also broadcasts the identity of cheating sellers to members of the cartel, and thus unintentionally facilitates the detection and punishment of price cutters.[4]

Notwithstanding governments' occasional sponsorship of cartels, historical experience indicates that cartels remain rare in most industries. Even though the United States has granted broad antitrust immunity to exporting industries, for example, fewer than 5 percent have sought to fix prices to customers abroad.[5] The reluctance of most sellers to attempt a conspiracy to raise prices—even with their gov-

ernment's blessing—suggests that the economic hurdles to successful cartel operation remain high.

About the Author

Andrew Dick is a Vice President in the Competition Practice of CRA International and formerly was the acting chief of the Competition Policy Section in the U.S. Department of Justice's Antitrust Division.

Further Reading

Introductory

"After Centuries of Ripping Off Consumers, Cartels Are Suffering a Crackdown from the World's Competition Authorities." *Economist*, April 3, 2003.
Dick, Andrew R. "Identifying Contracts, Combinations and Conspiracies in Restraint of Trade." *Managerial and Decision Economics* 17 (1996): 203–216.
Levenstein, Margaret C., and Valerie Y. Suslow. "What Determines Cartel Success?" *Journal of Economic Literature* 44, no. 1 (2006): 43–95.
Posner, Richard A. *Antitrust Law: An Economic Perspective*. Chicago: University of Chicago Press, 1976. Chap. 4.

More Advanced

Albaek, Svend, Peter Mollgaard, and Per B. Overgaard. "Government-Assisted Oligopoly Coordination? A Concrete Case." *Journal of Industrial Economics* 45 (1997): 429–443.
Baker, Jonathan B. "Identifying Cartel Policing Under Uncertainty: The U.S. Steel Industry, 1933–1939." *Journal of Law and Economics* 32 (1989): S47-S76.
Dick, Andrew R. "When Are Cartels Stable Contracts?" *Journal of Law and Economics* 39 (1996): 241–283.
Scherer, Frederick M., and David Ross. *Industrial Market Structure and Economic Performance*. Boston: Houghton Mifflin, 1990. Chap. 7.
Stigler, George J. "A Theory of Oligopoly." *Journal of Political Economy* 72 (1964): 44–61.

---

4. See Armen A. Alchian, "Electrical Equipment Collusion: Why and How," in Armen A. Alchian, *Property Rights and Economic Behavior*, vol. 2 of *The Collected Works of Armen A. Alchian* (Indianapolis: Liberty Fund, 2006), pp. 429–436.

5. Andrew R. Dick, "When Are Cartels Stable Contracts?" *Journal of Law and Economics* 39 (1996): 241–283.

Charity

Russell Roberts

Let me introduce you to an acquaintance of mine: *Homo economicus,* or economic man. He is an interesting character. Economic man (it is never economic woman) is a rational, self-interested fellow always looking out for himself. He does not give to charity. Why waste money on someone other than yourself? He never leaves a tip in a restaurant unless he expects to eat there again. He never votes because his single vote is almost certain to be worthless in determining the outcome of an election, even a close one. Give blood for a blood drive? Are you crazy?

There is another name for this type of person: straw man. Why? Because economists understood long ago that altruism, fellow feeling, and caring for others are a huge part of the human enterprise. Such motives explain why we have children, do volunteer work, vote, write checks to charities, and take jobs that do not pay a lot but that are rewarding in other, nonmonetary ways.

There are many situations in which altruism is more or less irrelevant. When someone buys a house or browses the produce section at the grocery or chooses a retirement plan, narrow financial motives tend to take over. A lot of powerful predictions come from noting that people tend to act in their own narrowly defined self-interest.

But economics also has quite a bit to say about behavior that is altruistic. While the economics of altruism may seem like an oxymoron, economics is about the choices we make when we cannot have everything we want and the implications of those choices in market and nonmarket settings. As long as people do not have infinite amounts of time and money, economics will have something to say about how they behave in settings involving love and compassion, duty and honor. The essence of economics is remembering that few virtues are absolute—when they get more expensive, harder to do, or less pleasant, people will do less of them.

This richer perspective on human behavior, which allows for more complex motives than the narrowest self-interest, goes back to Adam Smith, whose underappreciated masterpiece, *The Theory of Moral Sentiments,* explores the richness of human nature. Smith understood how the power of self-interest, harnessed by competition, could make the world a better place. But he also understood that narrow self-interest in the pursuit of material well-being is only one of many human motivations.

That is not to say that economists do not recognize that some charitable giving is motivated by pecuniary self-interest. People may donate to enhance their reputation with others or for the opportunity to make social or business connections. But most of us donate to charity for the same reason that we give our money to the ice cream vendor or the car dealer—the satisfaction and pleasure we get in return make the monetary sacrifice worthwhile. That is, much of our giving stems from what might be called self-interested altruism, the joy of seeing others helped.

In 2002, individuals and corporations in America gave roughly $240 billion to charity. Is that a big number or a small one? American giving as a percentage of GDP dwarfs that of every European country, even when spending on religion is excluded. A recent study by the Johns Hopkins Comparative Nonprofit Sector Project (Salamon 2004) found that giving by American individuals and businesses, as a proportion of GDP, is eleven times that of Italy, three times that of France, seven times that of Germany, and twice that of Sweden. American giving is seven times that of Japan. Of the thirty-six developed and developing nations studied, only Israel is more generous.

Recent data suggest (Salamon 2004) that the value of time devoted to volunteering is more valuable than direct contributions of money and that some Europeans are more generous in this regard than Americans. But these data include coaching Little League and volunteering with European amateur sports clubs. And some European data include helping relatives, a category excluded from the American data. So, while volunteering is an important contribution to the fabric of life, in what follows I focus on monetary donations.

Even excluding the value of donated time, Americans donate billions more than the federal government spends on cash, food, and housing for the poor. The bulk of the money, typically about 85–90 percent, comes from individuals or bequests. What do we spend our charitable dollars on? When we think of charity, we think of helping the poor. But very little charitable giving goes to the poor. In most years, about half of all charitable giving goes to religious institutions. Most of the rest goes to education, health, the arts, and the environment. Very little of the $240 billion is what would have been called charity in, say, the nineteenth century. Almost none of it goes to feed the hungry or shelter the homeless.

The biggest recipients of United Way funds, for example, are typically the Red Cross, the YMCA, the Jewish Community Center, and the Boy Scouts. And while these groups do help the poor with some of their programs, most of their money is spent elsewhere.

Perhaps Americans are less generous than they appear to be. But economics suggests a different explanation. Charitable giving by Americans one hundred years ago was a very different picture. Back then, numerous private charities helped the destitute, the insane, the single mother, and the elderly. Some catered to the poor of specific nationalities or religions. Some provided coal in the winter or work or food or clothes. What has changed?

The simple answer is the role of the federal government in the welfare system. It is commonly believed that before the GREAT DEPRESSION, the poor, the elderly, and the vagrant had to rely on private alms. That turns out not to be true. The government has been involved in helping the poor in America since colonial times.

But the Great Depression *is* a key watershed. Before the Great Depression, public aid to the poor typically took place in almshouses or poorhouses, facilities run by the city or county where destitute people could get work and receive food and shelter in return. By all accounts, these were distinctly unpleasant places, perhaps deliberately so, as stigma was believed to be an important deterrent to dependency.

Private charities typically offered "outdoor" relief—aid "outside" the poorhouse or almshouse. It could be cash or food or coal and was doled out on a case-by-case basis.

When economic conditions worsened, private charity typically surged to deal with the increased hardship. In the severe depression of 1894, for example, the New York Association for Improving the Condition of the Poor provided $100,000 in aid to the poor of New York City. Other organizations, such as the New York World Bread Fund, the Herald Free Clothing Fund, and the East Side Relief-Work Committee, spent similar amounts. A single individual donor, Nathan Straus, was said to have contributed $100,000 by subsidizing low-cost sales of coal, food, and lodging (Closson 1894; Rezneck 1968).

But with the dramatic increase in public aid during the Great Depression, which began in late 1929, private charities were "crowded out." They could no longer successfully compete for donations with a federal government that could compel "donations" via the tax system. Table 1 shows how private charity during the Great Depression grew initially, then faded as government spending surged dramatically.

As public aid continued to grow and then remained in place, many private charities that helped the poor simply folded, presumably because they could no longer generate contributions.[1] Why give when your tax dollars already go toward the same goal? Table 2 shows how the New York Association for Improving the Condition of the Poor found its donations drying up as federal aid surged. Note the shift away from material relief—the direct transfer of money and resources—as federal aid started to grow in the early 1930s. Finally, in 1939, the association merged with another organization and focused exclusively on social services not provided by the government rather than on direct aid to the poor (see Roberts 1984 for more details).

The same phenomenon remains true today. Few private charities work with the poor, and those that do tend to work with extreme situations in which the people they are trying to help are either ineligible for public aid or uninterested in working through the public system for social or psychological reasons.

What would happen if the government were to leave charity in aid of the poor to the private sector once again? Private charity would certainly increase. But it would be

1. Mutual aid societies, a private form of social insurance, disappeared for the same reason. See Beito 1989 for more details.

Table 1 Expenditures for Relief from Public and Private Funds in 120 Urban Areas, 1929–1935 (in thousands of 1929 dollars)

	Public Funds	Private Funds
1929	33,449	10,296
1930	56,158	10,944
1931	138,874	55,663
1932	315,061	71,619
1933	557,658*	36,939
1934	835,425†	18,804
1935	1,035,206	14,536

Source: Geddes 1937.

* Excludes expenditures under the Civil Works Administration.
† Excludes expenditures under the Works Program.

Table 2 Material Relief, Expenditures, and Donations, New York Association for Improving the Condition of the Poor, 1928–1938 (in 1929 dollars)

	Material Relief	Total Expenditure	Donations*
1928	570,347	1,320,885	900,680
1929	538,167	1,397,047	827,286
1930	910,946	1,848,467	883,012
1931	1,377,964	2,518,749	1,092,823
1932	1,675,220	3,100,696	1,999,996
1933	1,415,593	2,748,344	1,712,399
1934	1,177,580	2,003,945	1,589,210
1935	1,096,386	1,931,303	1,306,765
1936	690,450	1,943,188	789,072
1937	544,153	1,848,110	855,906
1938	556,418	1,895,265	602,679

Source: Annual Reports of the association, 1928–1938.

* Excludes legacies. It is difficult to track legacies during the period.

unlikely to equal the amount of money that the government spends. Many people who are coerced into helping the poor through their taxes would be content to let others do the giving; they would give little or nothing, assuming that others would shoulder the burden. The total level of giving would thus likely be lower under a purely private system.

But the total amount of money spent on the poor is not the only measure of a social policy's success. The government system has the advantage of being able to compel people to pay their taxes. But it has the disadvantage of being inflexible and relatively stagnant. A private system of charity is likely to be smaller and more innovative.

While government welfare programs are reformed now and then, there is little political support for a radical re-ordering of responsibility away from the public sector and toward a more voluntary solution. As long as the government remains the dominant provider of aid to the poor, charity dollars in the United States will not go to the poor but will continue to provide significant support to other causes, helping the arts, museums, universities, medical research, and religion.

About the Author

Russell Roberts is a professor of economics and the J. Fish and Lillian F. Smith Distinguished Scholar at the Mercatus Center at George Mason University.

Further Reading

American Association of Fund-raising Counsel. *Giving USA.* 2003.

Beito, David T. *From Mutual Aid to the Welfare State: Fraternal Societies and Social Services, 1890–1967.* Chapel Hill: University of North Carolina Press, 1989.

Closson, Carlos Jr. "The Unemployed in American Cities, Part II." *Quarterly Journal of Economics* 8 (July 1894): 453–477.

Geddes, Anne E. *Trends in Relief Expenditures, 1910–1935.* Research Monograph 10, Works Progress Administration, Division of Social Research. Washington, D.C.: Government Printing Office, 1937.

Rezneck, Samuel. *Business Depressions and Financial Panics.* New York: Greenwood, 1968.

Roberts, Russell. "A Positive Model of Private Charity and Public Transfers." *Journal of Political Economy* 92, no. 1 (1984): 136–148.

Salamon, Lester, ed. *Global Civil Society.* Vol. 2: *Dimensions of the Non-profit Sector.* Bloomfield, Conn.: Kumarian Press, 2004.

Smith, Adam. *The Theory of Moral Sentiments.* London: A. Millar, 1790. Available online at: http://www.econlib.org/library/Smith/smMS1.html.

Warner, Amos. *American Charities.* New York: Crowell, 1908.

Communism

Bryan Caplan

Before the Russian Revolution of 1917, "socialism" and "communism" were synonyms. Both referred to economic systems in which the government owns the means of production. The two terms diverged in meaning largely as a result of the political theory and practice of Vladimir Lenin (1870–1924).

Like most contemporary socialists, Lenin believed that socialism could not be attained without violent revolution. But no one pursued the logic of revolution as rigorously as he. After deciding that violent revolution would not happen spontaneously, Lenin concluded that it must be engineered by a quasi-military party of professional revolutionaries, which he began and led. After realizing that the revolution would have many opponents, Lenin determined that the best way to quell resistance was with what he frankly called "terror"—mass executions, slave labor, and starvation. After seeing that the majority of his countrymen opposed communism even after his military triumph, Lenin concluded that one-party dictatorship must continue until it enjoyed unshakeable popular support. In the chaos of the last years of World War I, Lenin's tactics proved an effective way to seize and hold power in the former Russian Empire. Socialists who embraced Lenin's methods became known as "communists" and eventually came to power in China, Eastern Europe, North Korea, Indo-China, and elsewhere.

The most important fact to understand about the economics of communism is that communist revolutions triumphed only in heavily agricultural societies.[1] Government ownership of the means of production could not, therefore, be achieved by expropriating a few industrialists. Lenin recognized that the government would have to seize the land of tens of millions of peasants, who surely would resist. He tried during the Russian Civil War (1918–1920), but retreated in the face of chaos and five million famine deaths. Lenin's successor, Joseph Stalin, finished the job a decade later, sending millions of the more affluent peasants ("kulaks") to Siberian slave labor camps to forestall organized resistance and starving the rest into submission.

The mechanism of Stalin's "terror famine" was simple. Collectivization reduced total food production. The exiled kulaks had been the most advanced farmers, and after becoming state employees, the remaining peasants had little incentive to produce. But the government's quotas drastically increased. The shortage came out of the peasants' bellies. Robert Conquest explains:

> Agricultural production had been drastically reduced, and the peasants driven off by the millions to death and exile, with those who stayed reduced, in their own view, to serfs. But the State now controlled grain production, however reduced in quantity. And collective farming had prevailed.[2]

1. Communism was imposed on relatively advanced East Germany and Czechoslovakia by the occupying forces of the Soviet Union, not by revolution.

2. Robert Conquest, *Harvest of Sorrow* (New York: Oxford University Press, 1986), p. 187.

In the capitalist West, industrialization was a by-product of rising agricultural productivity. As output per farmer increased, fewer farmers were needed to feed the population. Those no longer needed in agriculture moved to cities and became industrial workers. Modernization and rising food production went hand in hand. Under communism, in contrast, industrialization accompanied *falling* agricultural productivity. The government used the food it wrenched from the peasants to feed industrial workers and pay for exports. The new industrial workers were, of course, former peasants who had fled the wretched conditions of the collective farms.[3]

One of the most basic concepts in economics is the production possibilities frontier (PPF), which shows feasible combinations of, for example, wheat and steel. If the frontier remains fixed, more steel means less wheat. In the noncommunist world, industrialization was a continuous outward shift of the PPF driven by technological change (Figure 1). In the communist world, industrialization was a painful movement *along* the PPF; or, to be more precise, it moved along the PPF as it shifted *in* (Figure 2).

The other distinctive feature of Soviet industrialization was that few manufactured products ever reached consumers. The emphasis was on "heavy industry" such as steel and coal. This is puzzling until one realizes that the term "industrialization" is a misnomer. What happened in the Soviet Union during the 1930s was not industrialization, but militarization, an arms build-up greater than that by any other nation in the world, including Nazi Germany.[4] Martin Malia explains:

> Contrary to the declared goals of the regime, it was the opposite of a system of production to create abundance for the eventual satisfaction of the needs of the population; it was a system of general squeeze of the population to produce capital goods for the creation of industrial power, in order to produce ever more capital goods with which to produce still further industrial might, and ultimately to produce armaments.[5]

Stalin's apologists argue that Germany forced militarization on him. In truth, Stalin not only began World War II as Hitler's active ally against Poland, but also saw the

war as a golden opportunity for communist expansion: "[T]he Soviet government made clear in its Comintern circular of September 1939 that stimulation of the 'second imperialist war' was in the interests of the Soviet Union and of world revolution, while maintaining the peace was not."[6]

Foolish as he looked after Hitler's double-cross in 1941, Stalin's assessment was correct. After World War II, the USSR installed communist regimes throughout Eastern Europe. More significantly, Japan's defeat created a power vacuum in Asia, allowing Mao Zedong to establish a Leninist dictatorship in mainland China. The European puppets closely followed the Soviet model, but their greater prewar level of development made the transition less deadly. Mao, in contrast, pursued even more radical economic policies than Stalin, culminating in the Great Leap Forward (1958–1960). Thirty million Chinese starved to death in a rerun of Soviet collectivization.

After Stalin's death in 1953, the economic policies of the Soviet Union and its European satellites moderated. Most slave laborers were released, and the camps became prisons for dissidents instead of enterprises for the cheap harvest of remote resources. Communist regimes put more emphasis on consumer goods and food production, and less on the military. But their economic pedigree remained obvious. Military strength was the priority, and consumer goods and food were an afterthought.

The most common economic criticism of the Soviet bloc has long been its failure to use incentives. This is a half-truth.[7] As Hedrick Smith explained in *The Russians*, the party leadership used incentives in the sectors where it really wanted results:

> Not only do defense and space efforts get top national priority and funding, but they also operate on a different system from the rest of the economy. Samuel Pisar, an American lawyer, writer, and consultant on East-West trade, made the shrewd observation to me that the military sector is "the only sector of the Soviet economy which operates like a market economy, in the sense that the customers pull out of the economic mechanism the kinds of weaponry they want. . . . The military, like customers in the West . . . can say, 'No, no, no, that isn't what we want.'"[8]

In a sense, the collapse of communism would not have surprised Lenin. Lenin knew that the party needed terror

3. Unluckier still were the millions of slave laborers in the mines and logging camps of Siberia. Death rates were very high. Contrary to Western impressions, most of the exiles were peasants, not former party members.

4. Stanley Payne, *A History of Fascism, 1914–1945* (Madison: University of Wisconsin Press, 1995), p. 370.

5. Martin Malia, *The Soviet Tragedy: A History of Socialism in Russia, 1917–1991* (New York: Free Press, 1994), p. 209.

6. Payne, *History of Fascism*, p. 361.

7. See Bryan Caplan, "Is Socialism Really 'Impossible'?" *Critical Review* 16, no. 1 (2004): 33–52.

8. Hedrick Smith, *The Russians* (New York: Ballantine Books, 1974), pp. 312–313.

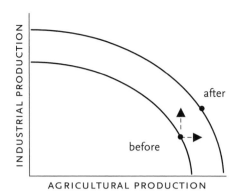

Figure 1 Normal Industrialization and the PPF

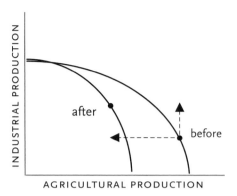

Figure 2 Communist Industrialization and the PPF

until it had solid popular support. When Mikhail Gorbachev assumed power, popular support had not materialized even in the USSR, much less in its European satellites. Gorbachev dismantled the apparatus of terror with blinding speed, undoing seven decades of intimidation in a few years. The result was the rapid end of communism in the satellites in 1989, followed by the disintegration of the Soviet Union in 1991. A patchwork quilt of nationalisms proved far more popular than Marxism-Leninism ever was.

Much, but not all, of the former Soviet bloc now has markedly more economic and political freedom—changes visible respectively in the Economic Freedom of the World (EFW) study and Freedom House (FH) country rankings (Table 1). In 1988, the republics of the Soviet Union had economic freedom scores below 1.[9] In the same year, Freedom House classified the entire Soviet bloc as "not free," except for "partly free" Poland and Hungary.

Free-market reforms have been harshly criticized, especially the drastic reforms derided as "shock therapy." But the countries that reformed the most have seen the greatest rise in their standard of living, and those that resist change continue to do poorly.[10] Critics lament large measured declines in output, but much of the "lost output" consists in products for which there was little consumer demand in the first place. Many former communist nations suffered hyperinflation, but only because—ignoring all sensible economic advice—they printed money to cover massive budget deficits. The "shock therapy" prescription

9. Online at: http://oldfraser.lexi.net/publications/books/econ_free/tables/a1-1.html.

10. Shleifer and Treisman (2003) pointed out that measured postcommunist growth is unrelated to the rate of reform, but added that measured output in unreformed nations is overstated. It follows that true output grew faster in countries that reformed more.

Table 1 The Rise in Economic Freedom (EFW) and Political Freedom (FH)

Country	2002 Economic Freedom Score	2002 Political Freedom Classification
Bulgaria	6.0	F
Czech Republic	6.9	F
Estonia	7.7	F
Hungary	7.3	F
Latvia	7.0	F
Lithuania	6.8	F
Poland	6.4	F
Romania	5.4	F
Russia	5.0	PF
Slovak Republic	6.6	F
Ukraine	5.3	PF

Sources: http://www.freetheworld.com/2004/2004dataset.xls; http://www.freedomhouse.org/ratings/allscore04.xls.

Notes: EFW scores range, 0–10, 10 being freest; Freedom House classifies countries as free (F), partly free (PF), or not free (NF).

would have been to slash government spending and/or sell more state assets.

China followed a different path away from communism. After the death of Mao in 1976, his successors essentially privatized agriculture, allowing relatively normal development to begin. Economic freedom increased significantly, but China remains a one-party dictatorship. Some attribute its impressive economic growth to this combination of moderate economic freedom and authoritarian rule. In large part, however, the growth reflects the abject poverty of Maoist China; it is easy to double production if you start near zero.

During the twentieth century, avowed socialists came to

power around the world, but only the followers of Lenin approximated the original goal of abolishing private property in the means of production. Dictatorship and terror were the necessary means, and few noncommunist politicians wholeheartedly embraced them. The communists' willingness to wage total war on their own people sets them apart.

About the Author

Bryan Caplan is an associate professor of economics at George Mason University. His Web page is www.bcaplan.com.

Further Reading

Introductory

Becker, Jasper. *Hungry Ghosts: Mao's Secret Famine.* New York: Holt, 1998.

Borkenau, Franz. *World Communism: A History of the Communist International.* New York: Norton, 1939.

Conquest, Robert. *The Harvest of Sorrow: Soviet Collectivization and the Terror-Famine.* New York: Oxford University Press, 1986.

Lenin, Vladimir. "What Is to Be Done?" In *Collected Works,* vol. 5. Moscow: Foreign Languages Publishing House, 1961. Pp. 347–530.

Malia, Martin. *The Soviet Tragedy: A History of Socialism in Russia, 1917–1991.* New York: Free Press, 1994.

Advanced

Applebaum, Anne. *Gulag: A History.* New York: Doubleday, 2003.

Courtois, Stéphane, et al. *The Black Book of Communism: Crimes, Terror, Repression.* Trans. Jonathan Murphy and Mark Kramer. Cambridge: Harvard University Press, 1999.

Fu, Zhengyuan. *Autocratic Tradition and Chinese Politics.* New York: Cambridge University Press, 1993.

Landauer, Carl. *European Socialism: A History of Ideas and Movements.* Westport, Conn.: Greenwood Press, 1976.

Mises, Ludwig von. *Socialism.* 1922. Translated from German by J. Kahane. Indianapolis: Liberty Fund, 1981.

Pipes, Richard. *The Russian Revolution.* New York: Vintage Books, 1991.

Comparative Advantage

Donald J. Boudreaux

When asked by mathematician Stanislaw Ulam whether he could name an idea in economics that was both universally true and not obvious, economist Paul Samuelson's example was the principle of comparative advantage. That principle was derived by DAVID RICARDO in his 1817 book, *Principles of Political Economy and Taxation.* Ricardo's result, which still holds up today, is that what matters is not absolute production ability but ability in producing one good relative to another.

Reckoned in physical output—for example, bunches of bananas produced per day—a producer's efficiency at growing bananas depends on the amounts of other goods and services he sacrifices by producing bananas (instead of other goods and services) compared with the amounts of other goods and services sacrificed by others who do, or who might, grow bananas. Here is a straightforward example.

Ann and Bob are the only two people on an island. They use only two goods: bananas and fish. (The assumption of two persons and two goods is made only to make the example as clear as possible; it is not essential to the outcome. The same holds for all subsequent assumptions that I make using this example.)

If Ann spends all of her working time gathering bananas, she gathers one hundred bunches per month but catches no fish. If, instead, she spends all of her working time fishing, she catches two hundred fish per month and gathers no bananas. If she divides her work time evenly between these two tasks, each month she gathers fifty bananas and catches one hundred fish. If Bob spends all of his working time gathering bananas, he gathers fifty bunches. If he spends all of his time fishing, he catches fifty fish. Table 1 shows the maximum quantities of bananas and fish that each can produce.

If Ann and Bob do not trade, then the amounts that each can consume are strictly limited to the amounts that each can produce. Trade allows specialization based on comparative advantage and thus undoes this constraint, enabling each person to consume more than each person can produce.

Suppose Ann and Bob divide their work time evenly between fishing and banana gathering. Table 2 shows the amounts that Ann and Bob each produce and consume every month.

Now Ann meets Bob and, after observing Bob's work habits, offers Bob the following deal: "I'll give you thirty-

Table 1 Production Possibilities

	Bob	Ann
Bananas	50	100
Fish	50	200

Table 2 Accounts Produced *and* Consumed before Specialization and Trade

	Bob	Ann
Bananas	25	50
Fish	25	100

seven of my fish," says Ann, "in exchange for twenty-five of your bananas." Bob accepts.

Purely for expositional simplicity, assume that both Ann and Bob want to consume the same number of bananas with trade that each consumed before trade. Table 3 shows the amounts of bananas and fish that Ann and Bob *produce* in anticipation of trading with each other. On trading day, true to their word, Ann gives Bob thirty-seven fish and Bob gives Ann twenty-five bananas. Table 4 shows the amounts of bananas and fish that Ann and Bob each *consume* with trade. Note that Ann and Bob are both better off than they were before trade. Each has the same number of bananas to consume as before, but Ann now has thirteen more fish and Bob has twelve more fish to consume. This small society—let's call it Annbobia—is wealthier by a total of twenty-five fish.

This increase in total output is not the result of any of the factors Adam Smith identified. It is the result exclusively of Ann specializing more in fishing and Bob specializing more in gathering bananas. This happy outcome occurs because in this society (here, just two people), each person concentrates more fully on producing those goods that each produces comparatively efficiently—that is, efficiently compared with others.

For each fish she catches, Ann sacrifices one-half of a banana; that is, for each fish she catches, she produces one-half fewer bananas than otherwise. For each banana

Table 3 Amounts *Produced* with Specialization and Trade

	Bob	Ann
Bananas	50	25
Fish	0	150

Table 4 Amounts *Consumed* with Specialization and Trade

	Bob	Ann
Bananas	25	50
Fish	37	113

she gathers, she sacrifices two fish. Standing alone, these numbers are meaningless. But when compared with the analogous numbers for Bob, the results tell where each person's comparative advantage exists.

For each fish Bob catches, he sacrifices one banana. So Ann's cost of producing fish is lower than Bob's—one half of a banana per fish for Ann compared with one banana per fish for Bob. Ann should specialize in fishing.

But if Ann catches fish at a lower cost than does Bob, then Bob produces bananas at a lower cost than does Ann. While Ann's cost of producing a banana is two fish, Bob's cost is only one fish. Bob should specialize in gathering bananas.

Viewed from each individual's perspective, Ann knows that each fish she catches costs her half a banana; so she is willing to sell each of her fish at any price higher than one-half of a banana. (In our example, she sold thirty-seven fish to Bob at a price of roughly two-thirds of a banana per fish.) Bob knows that each banana costs him one fish to produce, so he will sell bananas at any price higher than one fish per banana. (In our example, he sold twenty-five bananas at a price of about one and one-half fish per banana.)

There is nothing special about this particular price. Any price of fish between half a banana and one full banana will generate gains from trade for both Ann and Bob. What is important is the existence of at least one price that is mutually advantageous for both persons. And such a price (or range of prices) will exist if comparative advantage exists—which is to say, if each person has a different cost of producing each good.

When the lower-cost fisherman (Ann) produces more fish than she herself plans to consume—that is, catches fish that she intends to trade—Bob taps in to her greater efficiency at fishing. He cannot produce fish himself at a cost lower than one banana per fish, but by trading with Ann he acquires fish at a cost of two-thirds of a banana. Likewise, by trading with Bob, Ann taps in to Bob's greater efficiency at gathering bananas.

The above example, though simple, reveals comparative advantage's essential feature. Making the example more realistic by adding millions of people and millions of goods and services only increases the applicability and power of the principle, because larger numbers of people and products mean greater scope for mutually advantageous specialization and exchange.

Also, while the principle of comparative advantage is typically introduced to explain international trade, this principle is the root reason for *all* specialization and trade. Nothing about the presence or absence of a geopolitical border separating two trading parties is essential. But study of this principle *does* make clear that foreigners are willing to export only because they want to import. It is the desire for profitable exchange of goods and services that motivates all specialization and exchange.

About the Author

Donald J. Boudreaux is chairman of the economics department at George Mason University in Fairfax, Virginia. He was previously president of the Foundation for Economic Education. He blogs with Russell Roberts at http://www.cafehayek.com.

Further Reading

Boudreaux, Donald J. "Does Increased International Mobility of Factors of Production Weaken the Case for Free Trade?" *Cato Journal* 23 (Winter 2004): 373–379. Also available online at: http://www.cato.org/pubs/journal/cj23n3/cj23n3-6 .pdf.

Buchanan, James M., and Yong J. Yoon. "Globalization as Framed by the Two Logics of Trade." *Independent Review* 6 (Winter 2002): 399–405. Also available online at: http:// www.independent.org/pdf/tir/tir_06_3_buchanan.pdf.

Irwin, Douglas. *Against the Tide*. Princeton: Princeton University Press, 1996.

Jones, Ronald W. "Comparative Advantage and the Theory of Tariffs." *Review of Economic Studies* 28 (June 1961): 161–175.

Krugman, Paul. "Ricardo's Difficult Idea." Available online at: http://web.mit.edu/krugman/www/ricardo.htm.

Machlup, Fritz. *A History of Thought on Economic Integration*. New York: Columbia University Press, 1977.

Roberts, Russell D. *The Choice*. 3d ed. Englewood Cliffs, N.J.: Prentice Hall, 2006.

Ruby, Douglas. "Comparative Advantage as a Basis for Specialization and Trade." Available online at: http://www .digitaleconomist.com/ca_4010.html.

Suranovic, Steven. "The Theory of Comparative Advantage— Overview." Available online at: http://international econ.com/v1.0/ch40/40c000.html.

Competing Money Supplies

Lawrence H. White

What would be the consequences of applying the principle of laissez-faire—that is, completely free markets—to money? While the idea may seem strange to most people, economists have debated the question of competing money supplies off and on since Adam Smith's time. In recent years, trends in banking deregulation, developments in electronic payments, and episodes of dissatisfying performance by central banks (such as the Federal Reserve System in the United States) have made the question of competing money supplies topical again. Nobel laureate Friedrich A. Hayek rekindled the discussion of laissez-faire in money with his 1976 monograph *Denationalisation of Money*. Milton Friedman, in a 1986 article coauthored with Anna J. Schwartz, reconsidered the rationales he had previously accepted for governments to provide money. Other leading economists who have entertained the idea of laissez-faire in money include Gary Becker and Eugene Fama of the University of Chicago, Neil Wallace of Pennsylvania State University, and Leland B. Yeager of Auburn University.

Two sorts of monetary competition already exist today. First, private banks and financial firms compete in supplying different brands of checkable deposits and traveler's checks. They also compete in providing credit cards that are close substitutes for paying ready money. In a few corners of the world (Scotland, Northern Ireland, and Hong Kong), private banks still issue paper currency notes. Second, each national currency (such as the U.S. dollar) competes with others (such as euros and yen) to be the currency in which international contracts and portfolio assets are denominated. (Economists refer to paper money that is not convertible into an underlying asset, such as gold or silver, as a "fiat" currency.)

Much more competition in money has existed in the past. Under "free banking" systems, private banks routinely issued their own paper currencies, or "banknotes," that were redeemable for underlying "real," or "basic," monies like gold or silver. And competition among those basic monies pitted gold against silver and copper.

Today, virtually all national governments regulate and limit monetary competition. They maintain government monopolies over coinage and the issuance of paper currency and to varying degrees restrict deposit banks and other financial firms, nationalize the interbank settlement system, restrict or place special taxes on holdings of gold or of foreign-currency assets, and refuse to enforce contracts denominated in alternative currencies. In developing countries, government banks sometimes monopolize the provision of checking accounts as well.

Some economists recommend abolishing many or even all of these legal restrictions. They attribute significant inefficiency and instability in the financial system to the legal restrictions on private banks and to poor central-bank policy, and they view competition as a potential means for compelling money suppliers to be more responsive to the demands of money users. While many economists would like to restrict the discretion given to central banks, the small but growing number of free-banking advocates would like to abolish central banks entirely. Most mainstream economists, though, fear that a return to free banking would bring greater instability to the financial system.

Proponents of free banking have traditionally pointed to the relatively unrestricted monetary systems of Scotland (1716–1844), New England (1820–1860), and Canada (1817–1914) as models. Other episodes of the competitive provision of banknotes took place in Sweden, Switzerland, France, Ireland, Spain, parts of China, and Australia. In total, more than sixty episodes of competitive note issue are known, with varying amounts of legal restrictions. In all such episodes, the countries were on a gold or silver standard (except China, which used copper).

In a free banking system based on a gold standard, competing private banks would issue checking deposits and banknotes redeemable on demand for gold. In a system based on a frozen quantity of fiat dollars, as Milton Friedman and a few other economists have proposed, bank deposits and banknotes would be redeemable for government notes, as deposits are today.

Competition among banks would, history indicates, compel all banks in the system to redeem their deposits and banknotes for a common basic money, such as gold or a standard paper currency issued by the government. Banks in such a system are parts of a unified currency area; "exchange rates" among them are fixed rather than floating. Citibank's ten-dollar notes, for example, would be redeemable for ten dollars in basic money, and so would notes issued by Chase Manhattan. To attract customers, Citibank would be glad to accept deposits in Chase notes or Chase deposits, which it would then return to Chase for redemption at the clearinghouse. Given negligible risk and redemption costs (both likely under modern conditions), Citibank would even accept Chase notes at par (without a discount or fee, just as banks accept one another's checks today). Chase would do likewise. The reason is that by agreeing to accept each other's notes and checks at par, both Citibank and Chase would make their own money more useful, and therefore more widely accepted. This is not just abstract theorizing. We see par acceptance emerging historically among note-issuing banks. Similar competitive considerations have led banks more recently to form mutual acceptance networks for automatic teller machine cards, allowing customers of Citibank to get cash at Chase machines. Chase charges a fee for withdrawing Federal Reserve notes today, to cover its borrowing costs of carrying an inventory of Federal Reserve notes. Chase would not need to charge a fee for withdrawing Chase notes, because it has no borrowing costs in carrying an inventory of its own unissued notes.

What forms of money do households and business firms ordinarily use in a free banking system? When bank-notes and checks issued by any bank in the system are accepted nearly everywhere, and when banks pay interest on deposits, the public seldom feels the need to handle basic money (gold or whatever is the asset for which bank money is redeemable). Banknotes and token coins serve the need for currency. Because banknotes do not bear interest, banks compete for customers—that is, note-holding clientele—through nonprice means.

Each bank in a free banking system is constrained to limit the quantity of its liabilities (the banknotes and deposits it has issued) to the quantity the public desires to hold. When one bank accepts another bank's notes or checks, it returns them to the issuer through a cooperative interbank clearing system for redemption in basic money or in claims on the clearinghouse. An issuing bank knows that it would suffer adverse clearings and a costly loss of reserves if too many of its liabilities came into the hands of its rivals. So banks would have to carefully manage their reserve positions (the funds they use to redeem their banknotes) even if there were no central bank setting minimum reserve requirements.

Many economists (and almost everyone else) believe that a free banking system, especially one without government guarantees of deposits or banknotes, would be plagued by overissuance of banknotes, fraud, and suspensions of redeemability, all of which would give rise to runs on banks and, as a result, periodic financial panics. That would happen, the thinking goes, because the inability of any one bank to meet a run would cause runs to spread contagiously until the entire system collapsed.

The evidence from free banking systems in Scotland, Canada, Sweden, and other historical episodes does not support that conclusion. When free banking has existed, the interbank clearing system swiftly disciplined individual banks that issued more notes than their clients wished to hold. In other words, redeemability restrained the system as a whole. Fraudulent bankers did not find it easy to get their notes into circulation; bankers whose condition went from trusted to suspect found their notes being returned for redemption. Banks thus found that sound management was key to building a clientele. Clearinghouse associations policed the solvency and liquidity of their members. Runs on individual banks were not contagious; money withdrawn from suspect banks was redeposited in sounder ones. Proponents of free banking point out that the few historical episodes of contagious bank runs occurred in banking systems (like that of the United States after the Civil War) whose ill-advised legal restrictions weakened and blurred the distinctiveness of individual banks, so that troubles at one bank undermined public confidence in the entire system.

Proponents of competing money supplies have suggested several different institutional frameworks under which a competitive system could operate. A few monetary theorists, beginning with Benjamin Klein of UCLA and Friedrich Hayek, have contemplated private competition in the supply of nonredeemable "fiat" monies. We lack historical experience with such a regime, but it is doubtful that it would survive. If banks did not have to redeem their notes, they would face a strong temptation to issue money without limit. It would be too profitable for an issuer to break any promise not to overissue and depreciate its money. In contrast, where banks must redeem their notes for something, the holder of bank-issued money has a "buy-back" guarantee against depreciation.

Robert Greenfield and Leland B. Yeager, drawing on earlier work by Fischer Black, Eugene Fama, and Robert Hall, have proposed another kind of laissez-faire payments system that they claim would maintain monetary equilibrium at a stable price level. Instead of redeeming their notes for gold, silver, or government-issued paper money, banks would redeem notes and deposits for a standard "bundle" of diverse commodities. Instead of a one-dollar or one-gram-of-gold note, for example, Citibank would issue a note that could be redeemed for something worth one unit of the bundle. To avoid storage costs, people would redeem a one-bundle claim not for the actual goods that form the bundle, but rather for financial assets (e.g., treasury bonds) equal to the current market value of one bundle. There would be no basic money, such as the gold coin of old or the dollar bill of today, serving both as the accounting unit and as the redemption medium for bank liabilities. This regime also has no historical precedent. Some critics have argued that it lacks the convenience of having a standard basic money as the medium of redemption and interbank settlement.

It is more likely that a deregulated and freely competitive payments system today would resemble free banking in the traditional sense. Bank money would be redeemable for a basic money produced outside the banks. To place all forms of money beyond government manipulation, the basic money could not continue to be government fiat paper unless its stock were permanently frozen (as Milton Friedman has suggested). The most plausible—and historically precedented—way to replace the government fiat dollar is to return to a private gold coin or silver coin monetary standard. But a return to the gold standard—or to any form of free banking—seems politically implausible anytime soon.

Even so, recent developments have emphasized the continuing relevance of the question of competing money supplies. In Latin America and Russia, the U.S. dollar competes with local currencies for use in local markets. Twelve countries have combined to form the European Central Bank and its currency, the euro, but the United Kingdom and Sweden have thus far declined to join. Advocates of currency competition, whose ranks have included former U.K. prime minister Margaret Thatcher, are skeptical that a transnational supplier of money, no longer in competition with their national monies, will provide a higher-quality product.

About the Author

Lawrence H. White is the F. A. Hayek Professor of Economic History at the University of Missouri, St. Louis.

Further Reading

Dowd, Kevin. *The State and the Monetary System*. New York: St. Martin's Press, 1989.
Friedman, Milton, and Anna J. Schwartz. "Has Government Any Role in Money?" *Journal of Monetary Economics* 17, no. 1 (1986): 37–62.
Goodhart, Charles. *The Evolution of Central Banks*. Cambridge: MIT Press, 1988.
Hayek, Friedrich A. *Denationalisation of Money*. 2d ed. London: Institute of Economic Affairs, 1978.
Selgin, George A., and Lawrence H. White. "How Would the Invisible Hand Handle Money?" *Journal of Economic Literature* 32, no. 4 (1994): 1718–1749.
White, Lawrence H. *The Theory of Monetary Institutions*. Malden, Mass.: Blackwell, 1999.

Competition

Wolfgang Kasper

Economic competition takes place in markets—meeting grounds of intending suppliers and buyers.[1] Typically, a few sellers compete to attract favorable offers from prospective buyers. Similarly, intending buyers compete to obtain good offers from suppliers. When a contract is concluded, the buyer and seller exchange property rights in a good, service, or asset. Everyone interacts voluntarily, motivated by self-interest.

In the process of such interactions, much information is signaled through prices. Keen sellers cut prices to attract buyers, and buyers reveal their preferences by raising their offers to outcompete other buyers. When a deal is done,

---

1. We are not concerned here with other forms of competition, such as in sport, among political parties and interest groups, or among states in federations.

no one may be entirely happy with the agreed price, but both contract partners feel better off. If prices exceed costs, sellers make a profit, an inducement to supply more. When other competitors learn what actions lead to profits, they may emulate the original supplier. Conversely, losses tell suppliers what to abandon or modify.

Such profit-loss signals coordinate millions of sellers and buyers in the complex, evolving modern economy. The "dollar democracy" of the market ensures that buyers get more of what they want and expend fewer resources on what they do not want. Competitive prices thus work like radio signals; they are easy to perceive, and we do not need to know where they came from. There is no need to analyze all possible causes of the latest energy crisis to learn that we should scrap gas guzzlers and save electricity; and oil companies need to know only that petroleum is getting more expensive to start drilling new wells or to experiment with extracting fuel from oil shale or tar sands. Price competition informs millions of independent people in millions of markets, coordinating them effectively—as if by "an invisible hand," as Adam Smith, the father of economics, once put it.

Suppliers also engage in nonprice competition. They try to improve their products to gain a competitive advantage over their rivals. To this end, they incur the costs and risks of product innovation. This type of competition has inspired innumerable evolutionary steps—between the Wright brothers' first fence hopper and the latest Boeing 747, for example. Such competition has driven unprecedented material progress since the industrial revolution.

Differentiated products may give pioneering suppliers a "market niche." Such a niche is never entirely secure, however, since other competitors will strive to improve their own products, keeping all suppliers in a state of "creative unease."

Another tool of competition is process innovation to lower costs, which allows producers to undercut competitors on price. This kind of competitive action has given us ubiquitous two-dollar pocket calculators only a generation after the first calculators sold for three hundred times that price!

A third instrument to outcompete one's rivals is advertising to bring one's wares to buyers' attention. Suppliers also compete by offering warranties and after-sales services. This is common with complicated, durable products such as cars. It reduces the buyer's transaction costs and strengthens the supplier's competitive position.

Competition thus obliges people to remain alert and incur costs. Before one can compete effectively in a market, one needs the relevant knowledge. Buyers need to ask themselves what their requirements are, what products are available, what they can afford, and how various products compare, taking prices into account. This imposes search costs—think of the time and effort involved in buying a house, for example. Suppliers have to find out where the demand is, what technical attributes people want in their product, where to obtain the many inputs and components, how to train workers, how to distribute their wares, how to improve products and processes, how competitors will react, and much more. Such efforts—in research, development, and marketing—may be very costly and may still come to naught. For every market bonanza, there are many disappointments. And other costs arise as sellers and buyers negotiate contract details and monitor and enforce delivery.

In a dynamic, specialized economy, the costs of searching for knowledge and carrying out exchanges (called "transaction costs") tend to be high. Therefore, it is not surprising that market participants are keen to reduce transaction costs and associated risks. One method is to agree on set rules (called "institutions") that help them to economize on knowledge acquisition costs. Markets fulfill people's aspirations more effectively when there are enforced and expedient rules. Another transaction cost–saving device is to agree on open-ended, long-term relationships, such as employment contracts. Yet another is advertising, a means for sellers to inform buyers and save them some search costs. Deal making is also facilitated by intermediaries—market experts such as brokers, realtors and auctioneers.

Despite these methods of reducing transaction costs, competition is uncomfortable and costly to competitors. Some entrepreneurs enjoy the market rivalry per se. But most people are ambivalent about competition in a particular way; they would like to avoid competing on their own side of the market, but welcome competition among those they buy from or sell to. In a free society, people are, of course, entitled to rest on their laurels by not competing, but they will lose market share, and their assets will probably lose value.

To escape the competitive discipline, suppliers may try to conclude a "competitive truce," forming cartels, particularly in markets with few suppliers or suppliers who need large lumps of capital to start operating. For example, the world's airlines once formed the International Air Transport Association (IATA) cartel, which fixed airfares, schedules, and even such petty details as meal services. Cartels normally fail when a cartel member cheats on the agreed price (see CARTELS and OPEC) or when a firm not in the cartel competes by price or product innovation and established suppliers lose market share. For consumers and for the market as a whole, this cheating on cartel agreements is a boon.

The only way for cartels or monopolies to avoid competition over the long term is to obtain government protection. All too often, politicians and bureaucrats readily oblige by imposing coercive regulations. They tend to hide behind all sorts of excuses—safeguarding jobs, ensuring public health and safety, or protecting nationals from foreign competitors. Yet, in reality, inhibiting competition is most often rewarding for regulators, who obtain moral or financial support for the next election campaign or secure lucrative consultancies. Economists call this "rent seeking" and point out that it is invariably at the expense of the many buyers, who are often unaware of the costs inflicted by political interference. Interventions may offer comfort to a few suppliers, but they harm the wealth of nations, which benefits the many. Most economists, therefore, consider untrammeled competition a public good that governments should protect and cultivate. This conclusion has, for example, inspired political attempts to control mergers, monopolies, union power, and cartels through internal competition policy; and the creation of the World Trade Organization, which was formed to protect international competition from opportunistic governments.

Competition works well only if private property rights are protected and people are free to make contracts under the rule of law. Who would incur high knowledge-exploration costs knowing that the hoped-for gains might be expropriated, or that subsequent contracts to market a discovery are prohibited by regulation? That is why secure property rights, the freedom of contract, and the rule of law—in short, economic freedom—make for rapid economic growth, low unemployment, and diminishing poverty. International surveys invariably show that none of the poorest economies in the world is free, and that none of the world's freest and most competitive economies is poor.

From a society-wide viewpoint, lively market competition fulfills three vital functions:

Discovery. Human well-being can always be improved by new knowledge. Competitive rivalry among suppliers and buyers is a powerful incentive to search for knowledge. Self-interest motivates ceaseless, widespread, and often costly efforts to make the best use of one's property and skills. Central planning by government and government provision are sometimes advocated as a better means of discovering new products and processes. However, experience has shown that central committees are not sufficiently motivated and simply cannot marshal all the complex, often petty, and widely dispersed knowledge needed for broad-based progress.

Selection and peaceful coordination. Competitive "dollar voting" selects what people really want and exposes errors through the "reprimand of red ink," in the process dispersing useful knowledge. Since innovators cannot keep their discoveries secret, others see what is profitable and may emulate success. Despite occasional unsettling surprises and changing opportunities, competition fosters orderly evolution, distributing unavoidable adjustment burdens and coordinating divergent expectations. Competing and trading educates people in practicing a "commercial ethic": pragmatism in problem solving and keeping peace to get on with the job. A competitive market order thus inspires confidence, social optimism, and a can-do spirit.

Control of power. Supplier competition empowers consumers; competing employers empower workers. While some may try rent seeking, it is important that wealthy people remain exposed to competitive rivalry. Only then will they reinvest their wealth and talents in further knowledge searches, to the benefit of humankind. They will not always remain successful. Virtually none of the big American fortunes that existed in 1950 is still intact today. Competition tames concentrations of economic power and redistributes wealth. One may indeed go further and say that capitalism is legitimized by competition—the readiness of citizens of property to shoulder the costs of socially beneficial knowledge search. Socialists, with their slogan "Property is theft," will gain followers only where competition is absent or politically distorted.

Competition, as discussed here, hardly figures in standard, neoclassical economics since so-called perfect competition unrealistically assumes perfect knowledge. Yet, in reality, most economic activity is about finding and exploiting knowledge and motivating reluctant people with wealth and talents to do the same.

Senator Henry Clay was right when he told the U.S. Senate in 1832, "Of all human powers operating on the affairs of mankind, none is greater than that of competition." Indeed, competing is part and parcel of the pursuit of happiness.

About the Author

Wolfgang Kasper is an emeritus professor of economics at the University of New South Wales, Australia.

Further Reading

Gwartney, J., and R. Lawson. *Economic Freedom of the World.* Vancouver: Fraser Institute, published annually.

Hayek, F. A. "Competition as a Discovery Procedure." In F. A. Hayek, *New Studies in Philosophy, Politics, Economics and the History of Ideas.* London: Routledge and Kegan Paul, 1978. Pp. 179–190.

Kasper, W., and M. E. Streit. *Institutional Economics: Social Or-*

der and Public Policy. Cheltenham, U.K.: Edward Elgar, 1998. Especially chap. 8.

Kirzner, I. M. *How Markets Work.* London: Institute of Economic Affairs, 1997.

Conscription

Christopher Jehn

Most nations, including the United States, have used military drafts at various times. Regardless of one's views on military or defense policy, a draft has many economic aspects that are inherently unfair (and inefficient) and unacceptable to most economists. Hence, the question of whether to have a draft is really a question of whether any expected benefits outweigh those inequities.

A military draft forces people to serve in the military—something they would not necessarily choose to do. With a draft in place, the military can pay lower wages than it would take to attract a force of willing volunteers of the same size, skills, and quality. This reduction in pay is properly viewed as a tax on military personnel. The amount of the tax is simply the difference between actual pay and the pay necessary to induce individuals to serve voluntarily. If, for example, pay would have to be twenty thousand dollars per year to attract sufficient volunteers, but these volunteers are

Soldiers as Capital

The reluctance to view a man as capital is especially ruinous of mankind in wartime; here capital is protected, but not man, and in time of war we have no hesitation in sacrificing one hundred men in the bloom of their years to save one cannon.

In a hundred men at least twenty times as much capital is lost as is lost in one cannon. But the production of the cannon is the cause of an expenditure of the state treasury, while human beings are again available for nothing by means of a simple conscription order. . . .

When the statement was made to Napoleon, the founder of the conscription system, that a planned operation would cost too many men, he replied: "That is nothing. The women produce more of them than I can use."

—German economist Johann Heinrich von Thünen, in *Isolated State*, 1850.

instead drafted at twelve thousand dollars per year, the draftees each pay a tax of eight thousand dollars per year.

Before the United States abolished the draft in 1973, some of its supporters argued that an all-volunteer force (AVF) would be too expensive because the military would have to pay much higher wages to attract enlistees. But the draft does not really reduce the cost of national defense. It merely shifts part of the cost from the general public to junior military personnel (career personnel are not typically drafted). This tax is especially regressive because it falls on low-paid junior personnel, who are least able to pay. Moreover, not just draftees pay the tax; so do those who still volunteer despite the lower pay. In other words, the draft is a tax on military service, the very act of patriotism that a draft is sometimes said to encourage. The President's Commission on an All-Volunteer Force estimated that the draft tax during the Vietnam War was more than eight billion dollars per year in 2003 dollars.

Every time a draft has been imposed, the result has been lower military pay. But even in the unlikely event that military pay is not reduced, a draft would force some unwilling people to serve in order to achieve "representativeness" or "equity." In recent years, for example, some have advocated a return to conscription because today's AVF supposedly has too few college graduates or too many African Americans. How to decide which of today's volunteers to turn away is never addressed. The unwilling conscripts who replace the willing volunteers would bear a tax that no one bears in an AVF. And because these conscripts do not necessarily perform better than the volunteers they displace, this tax yields no "revenue." Because the conscripts are part of society, the tax they pay is simply a waste to the country as a whole. And some who are qualified and would like to enlist are denied and forced into jobs for which they are less well suited or that offer less opportunity.

A draft also encourages the government to misuse resources. Because draftees and other junior personnel seem cheaper than they actually are, the government may "buy" more national defense than it should, and will certainly use people, especially high-skilled individuals and junior personnel, in greater numbers than is efficient. This means that a given amount of national defense is more costly to the country than it need be.

In 1988, for example, the U.S. General Accounting Office (GAO) studied the effects of reinstituting conscription and concluded that an equally effective force under a draft would be more costly, even in a narrow budget sense, than the existing force. With a draft, a larger total force would be needed because draftees serve a shorter initial enlistment period than today's volunteers. Therefore, a larger fraction of the force would be involved in overhead activities such as training, supervising less-experienced personnel, and traveling to a first assignment. The GAO estimated that these activities would add more than four billion dollars per year (in 2003 dollars) to the defense budget.

A draft also forces some of the wrong people into the military—people who are more productive in other jobs or who have a strong distaste for military service. That has other serious consequences for the country. A draft, especially one with exemptions, causes wasteful avoidance behavior such as the unwanted schooling, emigration, early marriages, and distorted career choices of the 1950s and 1960s. A draft also weakens the military because the presence of unwilling conscripts increases turnover (conscripts reenlist at lower rates than volunteers), lowers morale, and causes discipline problems.

U.S. experience since the end of the draft in 1973 is consistent with the above reasoning. Today's military personnel are the highest quality in the nation's history. Recruits are better educated and score higher on enlistment tests than their draft-era counterparts. In 2001, 94 percent of new recruits were high school graduates, compared with about 70 percent in the draft era. More than 99 percent scored average or above on the Armed Forces Qualification Test, compared with 80 percent during the draft era. Because of that and because service members are all volunteers, the military has far fewer discipline problems, greater experience (because of less turnover), and hence more capability. So, for example, discipline rates—nonjudicial punishment and courts-martial—were down from 184 per 1,000 in 1972 to just 64 per 1,000 in 2002. And more than half of today's force are careerists—people with more than five years' experience—as compared with only about one-third in the 1950s and 1960s.

Based on this experience, almost all U.S. military leaders believe that a return to the draft could only weaken the armed forces. Nor, as mentioned, would a draft reduce the budgetary costs of the military.

For these same reasons, many countries in Europe recently have adopted an AVF or are actively considering doing so. Like the United States, the United Kingdom has had an AVF for decades. And three other large NATO countries—Spain, Italy, and, notably, France, where Napoleon invented modern conscription—recently have chosen to end conscription. Several smaller NATO members also have adopted an AVF or are considering doing so. In Germany, conscription is seen as blocking any return to twentieth-century militarism, and it provides "cheap" labor for many civilian social service agencies as well as the military. Yet some members of Germany's governing coalition also favor adopting an AVF. And of the ten Eastern Euro-

pean countries that have recently become members of NATO, six—Bulgaria, the Czech Republic, Hungary, Latvia, Slovakia, and Slovenia—plan to end conscription before 2010; and two—Romania and Lithuania—are seriously considering doing so.

These countries have elected to end conscription in part because of political pressure growing out of conscription's inequities. And in most cases they recognize as well that an AVF will lead to a more effective and, ultimately, less costly military force. While it is too soon to pronounce conscription dead in Europe, there is clearly a strong trend toward voluntarism.

In short, an all-volunteer force is both fairer and more efficient than conscription. The U.S. decision to adopt an all-volunteer force was one of the most sensible public policy changes of the last half of the twentieth century.

About the Author

Christopher Jehn is vice president for government programs at Cray Inc. He served as the assistant secretary of defense for force management and personnel from 1989 to 1993, and was assistant director for national security of the Congressional Budget Office from 1998 to 2001. He was formerly director of the Marine Corps Operations Analysis Group at the Center for Naval Analyses in Alexandria, Virginia.

Further Reading

Anderson, Martin, and Valerie Bloom, eds. *Conscription: A Select and Annotated Bibliography.* Stanford, Calif.: Hoover Institution Press, 1976.

Rostker, Bernard D. *I Want You!: The Evolution of the All-Volunteer Armed Force.* Santa Monica, Calif.: RAND Corporation, 2006.

General Accounting Office. *Military Draft: Potential Impacts and Other Issues,* Washington, D.C.: The Office, 1988.

Jehn, Christopher, and Zachary Selden. "The End of Conscription in Europe?" *Contemporary Economic Policy* 20 (Winter 2002): 101–110.

The Report of the President's Commission on an All-Volunteer Armed Force. New York: Collier Books, 1970.

Consumer Price Indexes

Michael J. Boskin

Measuring prices and their rate of change accurately is central to almost every economic issue, from the conduct of monetary policy to measuring economic progress over time and across countries to the cost and structure of indexed government spending programs and taxes. Most of us are familiar with the prices of many things we purchase.

We know what we paid recently for a pound of ground beef or a quart of milk. Renters know how much they pay in rent. Measuring prices, therefore, may seem simple and straightforward, but it is not.

The purpose of a price index is to summarize information on the prices of multiple goods and services over time. Consumer spending accounts for about two thirds of the U.S. gross domestic product (GDP). The Consumer Price Index (CPI) and the Personal Consumption Expenditure deflator (PCE) are designed to summarize information on the prices of goods purchased by consumers over time. In a hypothetical primitive society with only one good—say, one type of food—we would not need a price index; we would just follow the price of the one good. When there are many goods and services, however, we need a method for averaging the price changes or aggregating the information on the many different prices. The rate of change of prices—inflation—is important in both macro- and microeconomics. Estimating inflation and real growth, for example, requires measures of price changes, and in a flexible, dynamic modern market economy, obtaining accurate measures is complicated. A single large superstore may contain more than fifty thousand separately priced items. Within that individual store, new items are continually introduced and old items discontinued. The quality of many items improves in some objective way—greater energy efficiency, more durability, less maintenance, to name a few. Of course, many more items claim to have improved. When quality increases but the price stays the same, the real price has fallen. Even with modern scanner technology, summarizing what happened to prices in just one store over a period as short as one month is complicated. Doing so for the entire economy is vastly more complex.

To obtain information on various prices requires not only measuring the prices but also weighting the various components in the index. Weighting each price change equally would be simple but not very revealing. For example, if the price of red delicious apples fell by 5 percent and rent rose by 5 percent, such an index would suggest that there had been no change in the overall price level. But that would be silly. We need to "weight" the goods on which consumers spend more of their income more heavily than those on which they spend less.

The U.S. CPI and the Cost of Living

When economists try to measure the "true" inflation rate—the rate of change of prices—it is to answer the question, "How much more income would consumers need to be just as well off with a new set of prices as the old?" Thus, a cost-of-living concept is at the core of proper measures of prices and of changes in prices. This clearly in-

volves tracking "substitution"—that is, how consumers respond to the changes in the relative prices of various goods. It also requires measuring quality-adjusted prices. One would not want to count as inflation a major improvement in quality that resulted in a tiny price increase.

Most traditional consumer price indexes, including the CPI in the United States, measure prices with a fixed-weight system, taking the expenditure weights from some base period as given. Table 1 reports the most recent weights on very broad categories of goods from 2002; the Bureau of Labor Statistics (BLS) derives these weights from expenditure surveys that report how much consumers spent on different types of goods and services. For example, at a very broad level of aggregation, those weights are 15.6 percent for food, 6.0 percent for medical care, 40.9 percent for housing, 17.3 percent for transportation, and so on. Within each category, of course, are thousands of specific goods; for example, red delicious apples of a certain size and quality are a component of the apples subcategory, which is a component of fresh fruits, which in turn is a component of fresh fruits and vegetables.

With these expenditure weights at hand, it still takes a

Table 1 Relative Importance of Components in the Consumer Price Index (CPI-U)

Food and beverages	15.6
At home	8.3
Away from home	6.2
Alcoholic beverages	1.0
Housing (including utilities)	40.9
Apparel and services	4.2
Transportation	17.3
Vehicles	8.2
Gasoline	3.1
Other (parts, repair, insurance, public transport)	6.0
Medical care	6.0
Recreation	5.9
Education and communication	5.8
Education	2.8
Communication	3.0
Other	4.4
TOTAL:	100

Source: Consumer expenditure survey

Note: Individual items may not add to totals because of rounding.

high-quality, expensive operation to track the prices. And whose prices? For commodities purchased where and how? In the United States, there are two closely related consumer price indexes. One measures the change in a weighted average of consumer prices, with the base year expenditure weights, for a typical urban family, the so-called CPI-U. The other, not quite identical, construct is the CPI-W, which measures prices for urban wage and clerical workers. I focus here on the more widely cited CPI-U. Neither of these fixed-weight indexes accounts for substitution, the fact that consumers substitute away from goods whose prices increase more and toward goods whose prices increase less.[1]

The CPI serves, and should serve, many purposes. For example, the CPI is used to measure consumer inflation on a monthly basis; to make cost-of-living adjustments in Social Security, income tax brackets, and other government programs; to provide price data as inputs to the National Income and Product Accounts (although the Commerce Department now uses its own set of weights and methods to construct its PCE deflator from these raw data).

Figure 1 provides recent data on the U.S. CPI-U. The CPI-U sets the index = 100 for the years 1982–1984. As the figure shows, the pace of measured consumer inflation has slowed considerably relative to the 1970s and 1980s, has recently been running in very low single digits, and has had considerably less variation than in the high-inflation 1970s and early 1980s.

People change their spending patterns over time, and do so specifically in response to changes in relative prices. When the price of chicken increases, for example, people may buy more fish, and conversely. Hence the weights change, and a price index that fails to account for that—as does the fixed-weight base period CPI—overstates the true change in the cost of living.

There are two obvious approaches to weighting the prices. The first uses a fixed-base period weighting: quantity or expenditure weights remain fixed at their base period levels, and then we see what happens to the weighted average of prices as prices subsequently change. An alternative possibility is to use the expenditure weights or quantities in the second period, after the substitution. Economic theory strongly supports the idea of taking an average of these two numbers, a point originally made by the great American economist IRVING FISHER (1922). Since 2002, the BLS has computed a closely related mea-

sure called the chained-CPI; it has been rising much less rapidly than the traditional CPI-U, suggesting that the failure to account for consumer substitution explicitly is a serious weakness of the official CPI.

Similarly, *where* people make their purchases changes over time. Discount stores and online sales have become more important relative to traditional small retailers. Because price data are collected within outlets, the shift of consumer purchasing from discounters does not show up as a price decline, even though consumers reveal by their purchases that the price decline more than compensates for the potential loss of personal services. Thus, in addition to substitution bias among commodities, there is an outlet substitution bias.

Even *when* purchases are made can become important. We typically measure prices monthly, during a particular week. But if, for example, consumers get wise to post-Christmas discounts and start buying a lot more holiday items after Christmas, surveys that look solely at prices in the second week of December will miss this.

Another problem is that price data tend to be collected during the week. In the United States, about 1 percent of price quotes are collected on weekends, despite the fact that an increasing share of purchases is made on weekends and holidays (probably reflecting the increase in prevalence of two-earner couples). Because some outlets emphasize weekend sales, there may be a "when" bias as well as "what" and "where" biases. This phenomenon may explain, in part, recent research suggesting that prices rise less rapidly in data collected by scanners on actual transactions than in that collected by BLS employees gathering data on prices on shelves and racks.

Finally, an additional bias results from the difficulty of adjusting fully for quality change and the introduction of new products. In the U.S. CPI, for example, VCRs, microwave ovens, and personal computers were included a decade or more after they had penetrated the market, by which time their prices had already fallen 80 percent or more. Cellular telephones were not included in the U.S. CPI until 1998.

The CPI currently overstates inflation by 0.8–0.9 percentage points: 0.3–0.4 points are attributable to failing to account for substitution among goods; 0.1 for failing to account for substitution among retail outlets; and 0.4 for failing to account for new products. Thus, the first 0.8 or 0.9 percentage points of measured CPI inflation is not really inflation at all. This may seem small, but the bias, if left uncorrected for, say, twenty years, would cause the change in the cost of living to be overstated by 22 percent.

The U.S. CPI is one of the few economic statistics that is never revised, even if subsequent data reveal that the

1. A recent improvement by the BLS substitutes geometric for arithmetic mean formulas for aggregating at the lower levels for about 60 percent of items, thus allowing for some partial substitution.

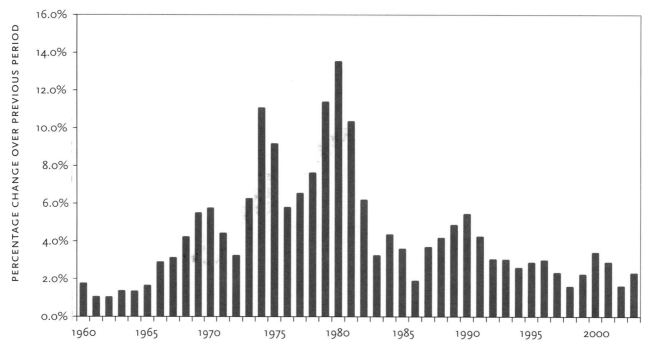

Figure 1 Percentage Change in U.S. CPI-U

published statistic is wrong. This is done because many contracts and other government programs are expressly indexed or adjusted to the CPI, and revisions would cause practical and legal complexities.

We know that different sets of consumers have different expenditure weights because they spend different fractions of their income on the various commodities: renters versus homeowners, the middle aged versus the elderly, and so on. Interestingly, most analyses find only modest differences in inflation rates across groups with different expenditure weights.

What about differences across groups in prices and rates of change of prices? For example, do the prices paid by the elderly differ from those paid by the general population? And if they do differ, have the differences changed over time? Economic theory suggests the prices will not differ much for most items, but we do not have serious empirical evidence on this score.

Thus, inflation—the rate of change of prices—is hard to measure accurately. Government statisticians in all countries, especially those at the U.S. Bureau of Labor Statistics, have made numerous important improvements over the years. Yet, new products are introduced all the time, existing ones are improved, and other products leave the market. Relative prices of various goods and services change frequently, causing consumers to change their buying patterns. Literally hundreds of thousands of goods and services are available in rich, industrialized economies. As we have become richer, our demands have shifted toward services and away from goods, and toward characteristics

of goods and services such as enhanced quality, more variety, and greater convenience. But all these factors mean that a larger fraction of what is produced and consumed in an economy today is harder to measure than it was decades ago, when a larger fraction of economic activity consisted of easy-to-measure items such as tons of steel and bushels of wheat. Thus, how to obtain information on who is buying what, where, when, why, and how, in an economy, and then to aggregate it into one or a few measures of price change raises a host of complex analytical and practical problems.

Price index research and measurement—at one time considered staid and boring—has undergone a renaissance in recent years. Price index research in academia, think tanks, and government agencies, plus practical improvements in real-time government statistics, will be an ongoing effort of major importance and immense practical consequence for many years to come.

About the Author

Michael J. Boskin is the T. M. Friedman Professor of Economics and a Hoover Institution senior fellow at Stanford University. He was chairman of the Advisory Commission on the Consumer Price Index from 1995 to 1996, and was chairman of the President's Council of Economic Advisers from 1989 to 1993.

Further Reading

Boskin, M. "Causes and Consequences of Bias in the Consumer Price Index as a Measure of the Cost of Living." *Atlantic Economic Journal* 33 (March 2005): 1–13.

Boskin, M., E. Dulberger, R. Gordon, Z. Griliches, and D. Jorgenson. "Consumer Prices, the Consumer Price Index and the Cost of Living." *Journal of Economic Perspectives* 12 (1998): 3–26.

———. "The CPI Commission: Findings and Recommendations." *American Economic Review* 87 (May 1997): 78–83.

Boskin, M., and D. Jorgenson. "Implications of Overstating Inflation for Indexing Government Programs and Understanding Economic Progress." *American Economic Review* 87 (May 1997): 89–93.

Fisher, I. *The Making of Index Numbers: A Study of Their Varieties, Tests, and Reliability.* Boston: Houghton Mifflin, 1922.

Lebow, D., and J. Rudd. "Measurement Error in the Consumer Price Index: Where Do We Stand?" *Journal of Economic Literature* 41 (March 2003): 159–201.

Stewart, K., and S. Reed. "Consumer Price Index Research Series Using Current Methods, 1978–1998." *Monthly Labor Review* 122 (June 1999): 29–38. An update is available on the BLS Web site.

For more technical discussions of the economic theory of index numbers and the important case of new products, see the following:

Diewert, E. "Exact and Superlative Index Numbers." *Journal of Econometrics* 4, no. 2 (1976): 115–145.

Hausman, J. A. "Valuation of New Goods Under Perfect and Imperfect Competition." In T. F. Bresnahan and R. J. Gordon, eds., *The Economics of New Goods.* Chicago: University of Chicago Press, 1997. P. 209.

Shapiro, M., and D. Wilcox. "Alternative Strategies for Aggregating Prices in the CPI." *Federal Reserve Bank of St. Louis Review* 79 (May/June 1997): 113–125.

Consumer Protection

Daniel B. Klein

When you buy a good or service, you rarely have perfect knowledge of its quality and safety. You are justifiably concerned about getting "ripped off." Thus the need for consumer protection.

Economic activity flourishes when consumers can trust producers, but the consumer must have grounds for trust. Consumers value, then, not only quality and safety, but also the *assurance of* quality and safety. Trust depends on assurance.

Free markets generate numerous forms of assurance. While it may be impossible to verify the quality of prospective transactions, you can often verify that of past transactions. Reports circulate in various forms—from informal gossip to carefully tended data banks and evaluations—generating a producer's reputation. "Reputation" may be defined as the relevant current opinion of the producer's trustworthiness.

Producers gain by providing assurance, so they seek to build, expand, and project a good reputation. They create and display BRAND NAMES, logos, and trademarks, umbrellas under which their transactions are grouped in the minds of consumers. They manage the extent and scope of their services to generate the repetition and pattern of dealings that give their name and reputation cogency. Once established, a good reputation can be extended to other lines of service where trust had previously been limited. Gasoline suppliers, for example, built brand names so motorists would trust the product at roadside filling stations, and then extended the trusted name to automotive services. Conversely, a producer's failings or misdeeds damage his reputation and induce consumers to shun him.

For services such as medical therapies or divorces, in which consumers and producers interact perhaps only very infrequently, the grounds for repeat dealings are thin. The demand for assurance in these cases creates opportunities for middlemen to emerge, to serve as a bridge of trust between the consumer and the producer. Consumers, for example, do not buy pharmaceuticals directly from Pfizer or Merck, but rather from established retailers. The local drug store has extended dealings with both the consumer and the producer. Also, the middleman shares some of the producer's expertise and, to some extent, serves as the consumer's knowledgeable agent. A nexus then links the parties. To the consumer, the middleman is a friend, and the manufacturer is thus like a friend of a friend. One of the important functions of all retailers, hospitals, clinics, dealers, brokers, and firms is to generate the reputational nexus that brings assurance to parties who would otherwise meet only infrequently or in isolation.

Producers typically put on their best face and will tend to conceal their failings, and this creates opportunities for a parallel industry of record-keeping, evaluation, and certification. These third-party practitioners range from neighborhood mavens to industry inspectors to product raters to medical schools. In any of these varieties, the agent may be called a "knower." Knowers have some knowledge that the consumer values but does not have. (Some use the term "certifier," but that term is too narrow.)

Sometimes, the consumer pays knowers for reporting on producers. Consumers pay Consumers Union for its magazine, *Consumer Reports;* patients pay doctors to recommend drugs; employers pay agencies to screen prospective employees; employees pay agencies to screen prospective employers; and home hunters pay agents and inspectors to evaluate properties.

Other times, the producers pay knowers. Electronics manufacturers pay Underwriters' Laboratories to evaluate the safety of their products; corporations and governments pay Moody's or Standard and Poor's to evaluate the securities they issue; corporations pay accounting firms to conduct an audit; kosher foods manufacturers pay Orthodox Union to certify their preparations; and students pay universities, institutes, and training programs to certify their abilities.

In all such cases, the producer applies to the knower and hopes to receive a certification or seal of approval that he can broadcast to prospective consumers. Word of his trustworthiness may freely flow to anyone. Consumers (or their savvy agents and middlemen) recognize such seals of approval and gain assurance of trustworthiness. The knowers, after a fashion, rent out their own good reputation to producers and have a strong incentive to do so responsibly; if they do not, other knowers may displace them. In the assurance-producing industry, as in any industry, free competition works well.

In addition to these practices, five other paths to assurance exist:

1. Producers demonstrate quality and safety and make the content of promises clear and publicly understood by such means as advertisements, displays, sales assistance, labeling and packaging, and try-out periods.

2. Traders restructure the relationship to reserve for the consumer an advantage held until the end of the relationship, by such means as warranties, guarantees, return policies, security deposits, and simply withheld payment.

3. Consumers and their agents test and monitor producers and third-party knowers using unannounced inspections, decoys, undercover operatives, investigations, and second opinions.

4. The failings of a producer are exposed by rival producers in competitive advertising, product comparisons, and contests.

5. By making visible investments that would be profitable only for a high-quality product, producers signal quality by advertising, obtaining accreditations, and making long-term investments in design, facilities, and so on.

The Internet is vastly expanding all forms of information exchange and reputation building. Critics regularly fault e-commerce for failings in privacy, security, or trust, but the pattern has been for each trouble to be fleeting. Almost as fast as the troubles emerge, entrepreneurs invent e-solutions, usually taking the form of a middleman (such as PayPal, Amazon, and eBay) service or a knower service (such as TrustE, BBBOnline, and Verisign).

On top of all these creative efforts, there is tort law and contract law, which work on the principle of allow-and-respond. That is, we are free to enter into transactions, but once authorities determine some kind of tort or undue hazard, the activity responsible is curtailed or the damages are redressed. When a surgeon cuts into the wrong organ, he is liable for damages. A quack who persists in defrauding consumers may face a court injunction on his products or services. The late political scientist Aaron Wildavsky argued that the allow-and-respond approach provides for open-ended creative developments, self-correction, and resilience.

Another form of consumer protection is government regulation. For example, the U.S. Food and Drug Administration (FDA) calls itself "the world's premier consumer protection regulatory agency." Other examples of consumer protection by regulation are occupational licensing, housing codes, the Federal Trade Commission, the Consumer Product Safety Commission, the Securities and Exchange Commission, and the National Highway Traffic Safety Administration.

These kinds of protections generally involve restrictions on freedom of producers to sell goods or services that the government has not certified. Here the principle is banned-until-permitted. The main problem with such restrictions is that, by reducing the range of choices available to consumers, they make consumers worse off. Even if some of the goods and services would have been "rip-offs," the vast majority of suppressed goods and services would have fulfilled the consumer's expectations. The case of suppression best documented by economists is the FDA's suppression of drug development and information, but economists have shed light on many other cases of suppression, such as those from licensing restrictions.

Thus, the regulations impose costs. The question is: Do they deliver benefits that redeem those costs? To assess the benefits of consumer protection laws, we need to understand how well protection is (or would be) supplied absent the governmental "protections."

In his 1962 classic, *Capitalism and Freedom,* Milton Friedman posed a fundamental challenge to occupational licensing. His challenge still stands, and, indeed, applies to all the banned-until-permitted-type regulations: even if you believe that information and assurance are, for whatever reason, inadequately supplied, that might justify, at most, a government effort to supply the missing information. Instead of occupational licensing, Friedman preferred a governmental system by which practitioners could earn state certification in the occupation, but were left free to practice and market their services even if they chose not to be state certified. Consumers would be able to choose from a free, legitimate market of plumbers, electricians, barbers, and doctors, both state certified and noncertified. Likewise, the FDA could offer safety and efficacy certification services; manufacturers could seek FDA certification if they so desired, but would be left free to produce and market the product without FDA certification. This would free consumers and their agents and knowers (doctors and pharmacists) to choose a certified or noncertified drug. Friedman, in other words, said that the supposed deficiencies could justify, at most, only governmental certification services analogous to those of Underwriters' Laboratories—that is, without compulsion. This approach would allow for competing forms of assurance; it would not lock in or privilege the governmental form. Despite the fact that Friedman's basic challenge has often been posed over the last forty-five years, to my knowledge no one has ever offered a counterargument, much less a persuasive counterargument.

About the Author

Daniel B. Klein is professor of economics at George Mason University and an associate fellow at the Ratio Institute, Stockholm, Sweden. He is the editor of *Reputation: Studies in the Voluntary Elicitation of Good Conduct* (University of Michigan Press, 1997). With Alex Tabarrok, he has applied ideas about voluntary consumer protection to issues involving the Food and Drug Administration. Klein is also editor of the online scholarly economics journal *Econ Journal Watch*.

Further Reading

Early Works

Calkins, Earnest Elmo. *Business the Civilizer.* Boston: Little, Brown, 1928. An advertising executive's earnest and highly instructive account of how businesses succeed by ensuring quality and safety.
Smith, Adam. "The Influence of Commerce on the Manners of a People." 1776. In R. L. Meek, D. D. Raphael, and P. G. Stein, eds., *Lectures on Jurisprudence.* New York: Oxford University Press, 1982.

Introductory

Klein, Daniel B. "The Demand for and Supply of Assurance." In Tyler Cowen and Eric Crampton, eds., *Market Failure or Success: The New Debate.* Cheltenham, U.K.: Edward Elgar, 2002. Pp. 172–192.
Klein, Daniel B., and Alexander Tabarrok. *Is the FDA Safe and Effective?* Oakland: Independent Institute, 2002. Online at: http://www.FDAReview.org. Summarizes how medicine proceeds without the FDA (particularly in off-label prescribing), and the strong evidence for the claim that costs of FDA restrictions are huge.
Moorhouse, John C. "Consumer Protection Regulation and Information on the Internet." In F. E. Foldvary and D. B. Klein, eds., *The Half-Life of Policy Rationales: How New Technology Affects Old Policy Issues.* New York: New York University Press, 2003. Pp. 125–143. Explains how technology is revolutionizing consumer information and how quickly things are evolving.
Poole, Robert W. Jr., ed. *Instead of Regulation: Alternatives to Federal Regulatory Agencies.* Lexington, Mass.: D.C. Heath, 1982. A landmark challenge to the then-burgeoning "consumer protection" movement, with chapters on most of the major federal agencies; still highly instructive.

Advanced

Ippolito, Pauline M., and Janis K. Pappalardo. *Advertising Nutrition and Health: Evidence from Food Advertising, 1977–1997.* Bureau of Economics Staff Report. Washington, D.C.: U.S. Federal Trade Commission, 2002. A good empirical analysis of whether and how manufacturers furnish quality information to consumers.
Svorny, Shirley. "Licensing Doctors: Do Economists Agree?" *Econ Journal Watch* 1, no. 2 (2004): 279–305. Although there is a body of economic literature on occupational licensing, the topic is much more important than the degree of interest would suggest. Because most licensing is particularistic, it is a hard topic to research. Svorny provides a comprehensive review of the judgments economists have rendered on licensing restrictions.
Wildavsky, Aaron. *Searching for Safety.* New Brunswick, N.J.: Transaction Publishers, 1988. An analysis of "anticipation" (banned-until-permitted approaches) versus "resilience" (allow-and-respond approaches).

Consumption Tax

Al Ehrbar

Some of the most significant tax changes in recent years have concerned the taxation of capital income. In 2003, Congress cut the top tax rate on dividends to 15 percent—significantly greater than the zero dividend tax that President George W. Bush wanted, but far below the 40 percent many high-income individuals paid in 2000. The 2003 tax bill also reduced the top capital gains tax from 20 percent to 15 percent. As always, political discussions of the tax cuts focused largely on who would reap the tax savings. The political wrangling obscured the real issues underlying a question that has occupied economists and tax experts for many years—whether individuals should pay any taxes at all on capital income. Strange as it may sound, most economists would agree that having zero taxes on capital income is *theoretically* the best thing to do. But many reject putting this theory into practice because they think that too much of the benefit would go to the "wrong" people, namely high-income households and the wealthy.

Those who favor eliminating taxes on capital income often couch the issue in terms of whether the government should tax income or consumption. A consumption tax— also known as an expenditures tax, consumed-income tax, or cash-flow tax—is a tax on what people spend instead of what they earn. Or, as economists Alvin Rabushka and Robert Hall put it, taxing income taxes what people contribute to the economy, while taxing consumption taxes what they take out. The United States already taxes both income and consumption, of course. For nearly a century now, the principal federal tax on individuals has been the personal income tax, which falls on both labor income (wages and salaries) and capital income (interest, dividends, and capital gains). Meanwhile, states and localities raise a large share of their revenue through sales taxes, which are taxes on consumption. The federal government also has a smattering of consumption taxes, such as the excise tax on gasoline.

Only a few advocates of a consumption tax want the federal government to replace or supplement the income tax with a national sales tax or a value-added tax (VAT) like the ones in Europe. In theory, a VAT is a tax on the difference between what a producer pays for raw materials and labor and what the producer charges for finished goods. Hence the term "value added." In practice, VAT taxes generally are applied much like sales taxes in the United States, with the government collecting a fixed percentage of the full pre-VAT selling price of a good rather than of the true value added.

Instead of moving to a VAT, most consumption tax advocates want to modify the income tax to eliminate taxes on interest, dividends, and capital gains. Achieving that goal can be done directly by cutting taxes on capital income to zero, as President Bush tried to do in the case of dividends. Alternatively, we could achieve the same result indirectly in two other ways. One is granting unlimited tax deductions for contributions to savings plans and taxing withdrawals, just as is done now with conventional individual retirement accounts (IRAs) and 401(k) plans, but without penalties for withdrawals before age fifty-nine and a half. The second is the Roth IRA structure, in which an individual gets no deduction for savings contributions but pays no taxes on withdrawals. Both conventional IRA and Roth IRA treatments are mathematically identical with a zero tax rate on capital income, as is shown below.

Why should capital income be treated differently than wages and salaries? The *economic* reason is very different from the political rhetoric. It is not to favor the rich at the expense of the working man. Nor is the principal reason to eliminate the double taxation of profits, first at the corporate level and again at the individual level as dividends or capital gains. Proponents of a consumption tax argue that it is superior to an income tax because it achieves what tax economists call "temporal neutrality." A tax is neutral (or "efficient") if it does not alter spending habits or behavior patterns from what they would be in a tax-free world, and thus does not distort the allocation of resources. No tax is completely neutral, because taxing any activity will cause people to do less of it and more of other things. For instance, the income tax creates a "tax wedge" between the value of a person's labor (the pretax wages employers are willing to pay) and what the person receives (after-tax income). As a consequence, people work less—and choose more leisure—than they would in a world with no taxes.

The case for a consumption tax is that the tax wedge created by taxing capital income does enormous long-term damage to the economy. Taxing interest, dividends, and capital gains penalizes thrift by taxing away part of the return to saving. The unavoidable result is less saving than society would choose in the absence of any taxes. The social value of saving is the market interest rate that borrowers are willing to pay for the use of resources now. Economists are confident that this is the value to society because it is a market price that reflects the desires of the various savers and borrowers. If each potential saver could collect the market interest rate, the result would be an optimal amount of saving—that is, an optimal division of resources between current consumption and future consumption. "Optimal" in this sense refers to the amount of saving that individuals, deciding freely on the basis of market prices, would choose to do on their own, rather than the amount of saving that a politician, social planner, or economist thinks they *ought* to do.

Market interest rates effectively pay people to defer consumption into the future (i.e., to save). Because the tax wedge reduces those payments, people inevitably will choose less future consumption (saving) and more current consumption. This harms the economy because less saving results in less investment, less innovation, slower growth, and lower future living standards than would be enjoyed without a tax on saving. Future consumption is reduced by both the extra current consumption *and* the forgone returns that greater saving would otherwise have produced. Some of this loss is a deadweight loss to society, that is, a loss to some that is a benefit to no one. Eliminating taxes on capital income would eliminate the tax wedge on saving, and total saving would be much closer to the optimal amount. The tax system would be "temporally" neutral in the sense that it would not affect the choice between current consumption and future consumption (saving).

To see how the tax wedge works, first consider how the income tax affects a person with $10,000 of pretax income. Assume, for simplicity, that the only tax bracket is the 35 percent top bracket in the 2003 tax law, that the pretax market interest rate on bonds is 5 percent, and that expected inflation is zero. Under the income tax, the individual pays $3,500 in taxes and can consume $6,500 of goods and services now or invest $6,500 in bonds paying 5 percent. If he saves the money, he will receive $325 in interest after one year, on which he pays $113.75 in taxes, leaving after-tax investment income of $211.25. Taxes reduce the interest rate he receives from 5 percent to just 3.25 percent. His potential consumption at the end of year one is $6,711.25.

Alternatively, if the individual puts the $6,500 in a Roth IRA and buys the same bonds, he gets the $325 in interest payments tax free and has $6,825 of potential consumption at the end of year one (assuming there are no early withdrawal penalties). The result is the same with a conventional IRA. In that case, he invests the entire $10,000 and pays no tax immediately. A year later he has $10,500—the $10,000 principal and 5 percent in interest income. If he withdraws the entire amount, he pays taxes of 35 percent on all of it, or $3,675. He is left with $6,825, the same as with the Roth IRA.

Despite its allure of eliminating the bias against saving, a true consumption tax runs into fervent opposition from some, mostly liberal, economists. As noted, their principal objection is that the greatest direct benefits of a consumption tax would go to high-income individuals. Since they are in higher tax brackets, high-income households get a greater dollar benefit from deducting savings (traditional IRA) or having after-tax contributions accumulate tax-free income (Roth IRA). In addition, high-income households have a greater ability and propensity to save, and thus are more likely to take advantage of opportunities for tax-free capital income. The counterpoints to that argument are two. First, those who pay the most in taxes inevitably will get the greatest dollar benefit from tax reductions. Second, the economic benefits from greater saving—more innovation and greater GDP growth—would be distributed to everyone in the form of a faster increase in real incomes, including wages.

The one objection to a consumption tax based on pure economics is that it would require a higher tax rate in order to raise the same revenue as an income tax that includes capital income. For this reason, a consumption tax would be less neutral between work and leisure than the current income tax. This would cause people to work less, and would increase the deadweight loss from the tax wedge on labor income. Advocates of a consumption tax maintain that the gains from additional saving and investment would greatly outweigh the losses from less work effort, though it is impossible to know with certainty whether that is correct. However, it is worth noting that the "flat tax" proposed by Alvin Rabushka and Robert Hall, which is actually a consumed-income tax, calls for a tax rate of just 19 percent.

The practical objection to a consumption tax used to be that it is too complicated to monitor the amounts that people save or dissave each year. But that actually can be done quite easily, as several decades of experience with IRAs, 401(k)s, and other special savings vehicles have shown. Moving to a complete consumption tax system for the individual tax code would entail little more than allowing universal, unlimited IRAs for everyone and doing away with penalties for early withdrawals. Individuals could continue with the IRAs and 401(k)s they currently have or roll them over into the new plans.

The new unlimited IRAs could take the form of conventional or Roth IRAs. The only genuine difference between the two—a major one—is the impact on federal tax receipts. The PRESENT VALUES of tax revenues under the two systems are essentially the same, but the timing is radically different. Under conventional IRAs, the federal treasury takes a big hit today because contributions are removed from the tax base, but future tax revenues get a boost when withdrawals are taxed. Under Roth IRAs, current tax revenues are largely unaffected, but future revenues take the hit because withdrawals are not taxed at all. Assuming that Congress could somehow achieve true fiscal discipline, it could borrow to fund deficits caused today by conventional IRAs and repay the loans with tax revenues from future IRA withdrawals. In the real world, the Roth approach has much more appeal in Washington because it produces greater revenues today.

Both conventional and Roth IRAs differ from the Bush administration's approach of directly cutting tax rates on capital income. The difference comes in the treatment of existing savings and wealth. The Bush tax cut conferred an enormous windfall on owners of existing wealth because it reduced taxes they had anticipated paying on assets they had already purchased. In other words, the cut changed the rules in their favor after the game had begun. (Owners of existing wealth actually got a second windfall in the form of an increase in stock prices in response to the reduction in dividend taxes; they would have received that type of windfall under any approach to reducing taxes on capital income.)

The IRA approach, in contrast, confers the benefit of zero taxes only on *new* saving. Under conventional IRAs, all income—from labor or capital—could be invested without going through the tax turnstile and then taxed when withdrawn. Under Roth IRAs, after-tax income from any source—labor or capital—could be invested in plans that earn tax-free capital income. Both IRA arrangements put all income on an equal tax footing, achieve temporal neutrality by cutting taxes on returns to all new saving to zero, and reduce the cost to the treasury by limiting the zero tax to returns on new saving. The Bush approach confers a significant tax advantage to existing wealth over and above the initial windfalls. Someone with $100,000 of capital income (other than interest) pays, at most, $15,000 in taxes and can invest $85,000. In contrast, an individual with high labor income has to pay $35,000 in taxes and then has only $65,000 to invest.

In 2001, the Bush administration recommended creation of lifetime savings accounts and retirement savings accounts; both are Roth-type plans with contributions of after-tax dollars. Bush proposed contribution limits of $7,500 per individual to each account, or $30,000 for a couple with no children. The administration reintroduced both plans in 2003 and 2004, but with the contribution limits reduced to $5,000 ($20,000 for the couple without children). Both proposals failed because they were opposed by liberals and by lobbies with strong vested interests in the current tax code. The lobbyists included insurance companies, which benefit from special tax treatment on what are called deferred annuities, and investment firms that administer 401(k) plans. Both feared that their plans would be eclipsed by opportunities for direct, tax-free saving by individuals. Taxation of capital income is sure to remain a highly contentious issue, and attainment of a true consumption tax is sure to remain a goal of savings-minded tax reformers.

About the Author

Al Ehrbar is a principal at EVA Advisers LLC, an investment advisory firm.

Further Reading

Bradford, David F. "U.S. Treasury Tax Policy." In *Blueprints for Basic Tax Reform.* 2d rev. ed. Washington, D.C.: U.S. Government Printing Office, 1984.

Hall, Robert T., and Alvin Rabushka. *The Flat Tax.* 2d ed. Standard, Calif.: Hoover Institution Press, 1995.

McCaffery, Edward J. *Fair Not Flat: How to Make the Tax System Better and Simpler.* Chicago: University of Chicago Press, 2002.

Corporate Financial Structure

Annette Poulsen

The Bond Market Association estimates that U.S. corporations had more than $4.5 trillion in bonds outstanding at the end of 2003, with debt averaging about 50 percent of equity (the value of the stock) from 1994 through 2003. Thus, corporations depend heavily on debt financing. One question that market participants or academic observers have not answered adequately, however, is how companies determine what fraction of their corporate activities should be funded through borrowing and what fraction through issuing stock.

In their seminal 1958 paper, Franco Modigliani and Merton Miller initiated the modern discussion of the amount of debt corporations should use (both received the Nobel Prize for this work and other contributions to economic research). The paper is so well known that, for more than thirty years, financial economists have referred to their theory as "the M&M theory."

M&M showed that the value of a firm (and of its cash flows) is independent of the ratio of debt to equity used by the firm in financing its investments. This stunning conclusion was based on certain assumptions that are not true of the real world: there are no corporate or personal taxes, people have perfect information, individuals and corporations can borrow at the same rates, and how you pay for an asset does not affect productivity. Still, it provides a jumping-off point for a better understanding of corporate debt.

Here is M&M's famous arbitrage proof in words. Think of two firms that are identical in all respects, except that one is financed completely with equity while the other uses some combination of equity and debt. Let Ms. E buy 10 percent of the all-equity firm; she buys 10 percent of the outstanding shares. Mr. D buys 10 percent of the leveraged firm; he buys 10 percent of the shares and 10 percent of the debt.

What do Ms. E and Mr. D get back for their investments? In the all-equity firm, Ms. E has a claim on 10 percent of the total profits of the firm. In the leveraged firm, however, the debt holders must receive their interest payments before the shareholders receive the remaining profits. Thus, for his share holdings, Mr. D gets 10 percent of the profits after interest payments to debt holders are subtracted. But because Mr. D also holds 10 percent of the bonds, he receives 10 percent of the profits that were paid out as interest payments. The net result for Mr. D? He receives 10 percent of the total profits, just as Ms. E does.

This reasoning led M&M to argue that the leveraged firm and the all-equity firm must have the exact same value. The value of the all-equity firm is the value of the outstanding stock. The value of the leveraged firm is the value of the outstanding stock plus the value of the outstanding debt. Because the firms are identical in the level of total profits and identical in the cash payouts paid to the investors, Ms. E and Mr. D would pay identical amounts for their respective holdings. M&M went on to show that if the leveraged and all-equity firms do not have the exact same value, arbitragers can make a guaranteed risk-free profit by selling the overvalued firm and buying the undervalued firm.

The proposition that the ratio of debt to equity is irrelevant to the value of the company is known as the irrelevance proposition. Many commentators quickly rejected the irrelevance proposition because its restrictive assumptions did not fit the real world. In 1963, Modigliani and Miller modified their discussion of corporate debt to specifically recognize corporate taxes. Under current tax regulations, interest payments made to bondholders are deducted from corporate income before computation of taxes owed. The corporate tax, then, acts like a subsidy on interest payments. If the corporate tax rate is 34 percent, then for every dollar paid in interest payments, 34 cents in corporate taxes is avoided, though those receiving the interest must pay taxes on it. In contrast, if income is paid out as dividends to shareholders, that income is taxed twice—once at the corporate level and once at the personal level. Therefore, every corporation should minimize its taxes and maximize the cash available to bond- and stockholders by financing its investments with 100 percent debt.

This result was more controversial than the first. Firms do not finance their investments with 100 percent debt. Also, there are clear patterns in financing decisions. Young firms in high-growth industries, for example, tend to use less debt, and firms in stable industries with large quantities of fixed assets tend to use more debt. The ensuing study of capital structure and corporate debt has focused on explaining these patterns and explaining why corporations are not 100 percent debt financed.

Financial economists have singled out three additional factors that limit the amount of debt financing: personal taxes, bankruptcy costs, and agency costs. Corporations trade off the benefits of government-subsidized debt against the costs of these three factors. This model of corporate financial structure is therefore called the trade-off theory.

In a 1977 article, Miller showed that considering corporate taxes in isolation is incorrect. Transferring interest payments to individuals to avoid corporate taxes does not make investors any better off if they then have to pay higher personal taxes on that interest income than the corporation and investors would have owed had the corporation not used debt. Miller argued that because tax rates on capital gains have often been lower than tax rates owed on dividend and interest income, the firm might lower the total tax bill paid by the corporation and investor combined by not issuing debt. Moreover, taxes owed on capital gains can be deferred until the realization of those gains, further lowering the effective tax rate on capital gains.

The important thrust of Miller's argument is that one must look at the interaction of both corporate and personal taxes to determine the optimal level of corporate debt. Miller showed that because of this interaction, there is an optimal level of debt (less than 100 percent) for corporations as a whole. That said, however, he also showed that for any given firm within the economy, the level of debt is again irrelevant as long as the economy-wide average is optimal.

Financial distress or bankruptcy costs may also keep firms from loading up on debt. These financial distress costs take two forms—explicit and implicit. Explicit financial distress costs include the payments made to lawyers, accountants, and so on in filing for Chapter 11 protection from creditors or in liquidation of the firm. These costs can represent a significant portion of corporate assets. Corporations also consider the indirect costs of bankruptcy, including the costs of low inventories, higher costs of inputs from suppliers who fear the company might not pay its bills next month, and the loss of customers who desire a long-term relationship with the firm. The reluctance of travelers to buy airplane tickets from airlines in financial distress or Chapter 11 situations certainly illustrates these indirect costs.

The costs of financial distress are deadweight losses to the investors of the firm: they reduce the cash flows that will eventually be paid to the bondholders and stockholders. Clearly, investors would prefer that firms stay out of financial distress so that these losses are not incurred. As the firm takes on more and more debt, however, the probability of bankruptcy increases. As the amount of debt interest increases, the chance that the firm will default on interest payments increases. These costs restrain firms from maintaining exceptionally high levels of debt.

A third factor limiting the use of debt is "agency costs." Michael Jensen and William Meckling, in a 1976 article, noted differences between the firm that is 100 percent manager owned and one in which the equity is owned partially by managers and partially by outsiders. In the latter case, the managers act as agents for the outside shareholders. Agents should run the firm to maximize its value. But managers may not be perfect agents, and they may make some decisions in their own interests rather than those of shareholders. Thus, the greater the amount of financing through debt, the greater the concentration of equity in managers' hands and the less the conflict between managers and shareholders.

However, agency costs also apply to shareholder-bondholder relations. The shareholders, through the managers, have the right to make most decisions about how to run the firm. The firm owes the bondholders fixed payments equal to the amount of money loaned to the firm, along with interest on that principal. Shareholders may adopt policies that benefit themselves at the expense of the bondholders. The possibility for such self-serving behavior is strongest when it is not clear that the firm will have sufficient cash flow to cover its interest and principal loan payments.

The most obvious action shareholders might take to benefit themselves is to pay out all of the firm's assets as dividends to themselves, leaving an empty shell for the bondholders to claim when the firm is then unable to repay its debt. Shareholders might also follow more subtle strategies. One has been called "risk shifting." A football analogy illustrates the risk-shifting concept. Woody Hayes, the legendary Ohio State University football coach known for grinding out yardage on the ground, used to say that three things can happen when you pass the ball, and two of them are bad. His philosophy is sound in a close game: it is best to play conservatively and avoid the risk of incompletion or interception. But if you are down by three touchdowns in the fourth quarter, a conservative strategy will almost certainly not win. Instead, you should throw a long pass. True, the ball might be intercepted or fall incomplete, but if you were going to lose anyway, the downside is not that bad. On the upside is the chance of a big payoff—a touchdown.

How does this relate to shareholders and bondholders? If the firm is unlikely to be able to cover its obligations, making the stock worthless, shareholders may throw the long pass—that is, take on risky projects that have big payoffs but high probability of failure. If the project fails, bondholders lose, but the shareholders are no worse off because their claims were worthless anyway. But if the project succeeds, the shareholders will be the major beneficiaries.

A third strategy that may be costly to bondholders is underinvestment on the part of stockholders. If the firm is close to being unable to meet its obligations to bondholders, shareholders may not be willing to put more equity into the firm to fund money-making projects. The reason is that any profits from the new projects are likely to go to bondholders rather than being returned to stockholders. While bondholders would be better off if the projects were undertaken, stockholders will not be willing to pay for them.

All three strategies—paying out large dividends, risk shifting, and underinvestment—are more likely the more indebted is the firm. Lenders know this. Therefore, those who organize the firm, wanting to attract lenders, rationally limit the debt. Bond covenants exist to restrict these games that shareholders might play, but bond contracts cannot prevent all eventualities. An interesting development of the 1980s, however, was the "poison put." In reaction to the large leveraged buyouts of the 1980s, many companies introduced these poison puts to protect bondholders in the event of a leveraged transaction. Bondholders generally have the right to "put" the bonds to the company and have them repurchased at face value plus, possibly, a small premium if the company takes on a lot of new debt that reduces the chance that the current bondholders will be paid off. These developments illustrate the dynamic nature of corporate finance.

Some researchers have argued that the trade-off theory does not adequately reflect the reality of how managers make financing decisions. An alternative model of financial structure is the "pecking order" model, according to which managers use external financing only when there is insufficient internal financing. In addition, managers prefer to issue debt over equity, if possible, at a reasonable cost of financing. The rationale for the pecking order model is that it is difficult for managers to inform the outside market of the true value of the firm. Thus, there is "asymmetric information" about the value of any securities the firm might issue. Equity, which represents a residual claim on the firm's assets after all debt holders have been paid, is especially subject to the asymmetric information problem. Since potential investors cannot adequately value stock, it would generally be sold at a price below the price the managers think appropriate. Rather than sell stock too cheaply, therefore, managers who need external financing will prefer to issue debt.

John Graham and Campbell Harvey (2001) surveyed chief financial officers to gather information about their perspective on the determinants of their firms' financial structure and found support for both the trade-off theory and the pecking order view. They also noted, however, that in many cases, the survey responses were inconsistent with these theories, and they questioned whether the theories were inadequate or if managers were simply ignoring them.

Those attempting to understand the determinants of corporate financing decisions in the United States have looked at empirical regularities among firms for guidance. For example, researchers have found that firms with relatively higher marginal tax burdens are more likely to use debt, thereby taking advantage of the interest tax shield, and firms with more nondebt tax shields, such as depreciation, will use less debt. However, firms that are more likely to face the possibility of financial distress (such as firms with intangible assets or uncertain future cash flows) are more likely to avoid debt in their financing and emphasize equity claims that could not force them into bankruptcy. In addition, firms that may have higher agency costs are also more likely to emphasize equity (see Harris and Raviv 1991).

Interestingly, many of the same regularities in U.S. capital structure exist in other countries. For example, according to Raghuram Rajan and Luigi Zingales (1995), the tax level in a country and the enforcement of bankruptcy laws (and therefore the costs of financial distress) are important determinants of a country's aggregate debt level. Asli Demirguc-Kunt and Vojislav Maksimovic (1999) showed that firms in countries with stronger legal systems use more external financing and long-term debt than firms in countries with less-developed legal systems.

Researchers continue to investigate the theory of capital structure and the determinants of financing policy around the world. Intercountry comparisons have helped us understand how differences in laws and differences in firms affect firms' financing policies. An important extension of the global research is investigation of how a country's financial development influences its economic growth.

About the Author

Annette Poulsen holds the Augustus H. "Billy" Sterne Chair of Banking and Finance at the University of Georgia's Terry College of Business. She was formerly acting chief economist at the Securities and Exchange Commission.

Further Reading

Bond Market Association. *Research Quarterly*, various issues. Online at: http://www.bondmarkets.com.

Demirguc-Kunt, Asli, and Vojislav Maksimovic. "Institutions, Financial Markets, and Firm Debt Maturity." *Journal of Financial Economics* 54 (1999): 295–336.

Graham, John, and Campbell Harvey. "The Theory and Practice of Corporate Finance: Evidence from the Field." *Journal of Financial Economics* 60 (May/June 2001): 187–243.

Harris, Milton, and Artur Raviv. "The Theory of Capital Structure." *Journal of Finance* 46 (March 1991): 297–355.

Jensen, Michael, and William Meckling. "Theory of the Firm: Managerial Behavior, Agency Costs and Ownership Structure." *Journal of Financial Economics* 3 (October 1976): 305–360.

Lehn, Kenneth, and Annette Poulsen. "Contractual Resolution of Bondholder-Stockholder Conflicts in Leveraged Buyouts." *Journal of Law and Economics* 34 (October 1991): 645–673.

Miller, Merton. "Debt and Taxes." *Journal of Finance* 32 (May 1977): 261–276.

———. "Leverage." *Journal of Finance* 46 (June 1991): 479–488.

Modigliani, Franco, and Merton Miller. "Corporate Income Taxes and the Cost of Capital: A Correction." *American Economic Review* 53 (June 1963): 433–443.

———. "The Cost of Capital, Corporation Finance and the Theory of Investment." *American Economic Review* 48 (June 1958): 261–297.

Rajan, Raghuram, and Luigi Zingales. "What Do We Know About Capital Structure? Some Evidence from International Data." *Journal of Finance* 50 (December 1995): 1421–1460.

Warner, Jerold B. "Bankruptcy Costs: Some Evidence." *Journal of Finance* 32 (May 1977): 337–348.

Corporate Governance

Randall S. Kroszner

The governance of corporations encompasses a wide range of checks and balances that affect the monitoring and incentives of firms' management. Sound corporate governance is particularly important when a firm's managers are not the owners. Without appropriate corporate governance, nonowner managers might not work very hard to maximize profits for shareholders and instead might spend money on perks and pursue the quiet life—or some other goal near and dear to the hearts of the managers such as personal profit maximization involving theft or fraud. The difference between the goals of the principals (i.e., owners) and the goals of their agents (i.e., managers) is typically called the "agency problem." Aligning the incentives of the managers so that they act in the interest of the owners rather than themselves is the core challenge of corporate governance.

In their classic 1932 book, Adolf Berle and Gardiner Means warned that the separation of ownership and control in the modern corporation "destroys the very foundation on which the economic order of the past three centuries has rested . . . it is rapidly increasing, and appears to be an inevitable development" of the modern corporate system (p. 8). Many contemporary scholars, such as Jensen (1989, 1993) and Roe (1990, 1994), have voiced similar concerns but argue that the problem is not inherent in capitalism; instead, they maintain that tax incentives, antitrust policies, regulations, and political pressures to adopt antitakeover statues that protect incumbent managers have led to what Mark Roe (1994) calls "strong managers and weak owners."[1]

[1]. An often-cited regulation is the Glass-Steagall Act, which forced the separation of commercial banking from investment banking and equity ownership, causing the United States to develop a much more fragmented financial system and system of corporate governance than in "universal" banking countries such as Germany (Kroszner 1996; Kroszner and Rajan 1994, 1997).

Recent research has shown, however, that the separation of ownership and control has not increased since the 1930s. In fact, managerial ownership of publicly traded firms has increased, not decreased (see Holderness et al. 1999). The average percentage of common stock held by a firm's officers and directors as a group rose from 13 percent in 1935 to 21 percent in 1995. Median holdings doubled from 7 percent to 14 percent. While the very largest firms had similar ownership percentages in both time periods, the average weighted by firm size was higher in 1995 than in 1935. In terms of real—that is, inflation-adjusted—1995 dollars, insiders' holdings were, on average, four times as high in 1995 as in 1935, rising from eighteen million dollars to seventy-three million. For all firm sizes, there was an increase in ownership by firms' officers and directors. Thus, managers generally have larger ownership stakes in the firms they manage today than in the past.

Managerial ownership, however, is but one of many devices that can help to align the incentives of managers and owners. Firms typically adopt a number of internal control and incentive mechanisms that can mitigate the agency problem. Bonuses and stock options, in addition to ownership stakes, tie the managers' compensation to the performance of the firm. An informed, independent-minded board of directors also can directly monitor and discipline managers, since the board has the power to hire and fire top management. Firms that may be particularly difficult for outsiders in the market to monitor—for example, firms whose cash flows and earnings are highly variable—tend to use more of these internal incentive-alignment devices than firms that can more easily be monitored by outsiders, such as firms in very stable industries with little innovation (see, e.g., Demsetz and Lehn 1985; Holderness et al. 1999).

In addition, external market forces can help to rein in agency costs. In a competitive market, for example, firms that are better run—that is, firms that more effectively pursue the shareholders' goal of profit maximization—tend to drive out firms that are less well managed. While competition in the market for the firm's output is important, it may not be sufficient to ensure incentive alignment and protection of shareholders. Another market force is the so-called MARKET FOR CORPORATE CONTROL. That is, outsiders can buy or take control of poorly managed firms and replace the managers and the system of corporate governance. Although the threat of takeovers imposes a valuable check on managers, it does not ensure that agency costs will be kept to a minimum, particularly when laws and regulations, such as the Williams Act and state antitakeover statutes, can reduce the effectiveness of the takeover market.

The legal environment thus affects the disciplinary impact of both market forces and internal incentive-alignment devices. Obviously, poor alignment between the incentives of managers and investors increases the risks faced by shareholders. To the extent that they are aware of these risks, investors and potential investors would require a higher rate of return to compensate for the heightened possibility of misfeasance and malfeasance, thereby increasing the cost of capital for such a firm. Research over the past decade has focused on how stronger legal protections for minority investors and other similar reforms, for example, can significantly reduce corporations' costs of obtaining outside financing, thereby improving corporate performance and capacity for growth (see La Porta et al. 1999, 2000, and 2002).

The financial reporting scandals that came to light during 2001 and 2002 have led to a reevaluation of the effectiveness of the corporate governance system in the United States and to significant responses by both the private markets and lawmakers and regulators.

Consider first the private market responses. After a firm's accounting problems are revealed, the market reacts by sharply reducing the firm's stock price. Interestingly, private market participants, not government regulatory agencies, discovered the problems in "scandal" firms such as Enron in 2001 and 2002. In addition, directors of firms associated with accounting problems or firms identified by watchdogs as being on boards of firms with poor governance practices are punished in the managerial labor market: they get fewer directorships (Wu 2004).

The private self-regulatory organizations such as the New York Stock Exchange (NYSE) and the National Association of Securities Dealers (NASD) have a strong incentive to maintain the confidence of investors in publicly traded firms. These organizations have changed their corporate governance requirements for firms listed on their exchanges. The new requirements mandate that a majority of directors be "independent" and that key committees of the board be formed of independent directors, not the executives of the firm. Also, the NYSE and NASD now require the independent directors to meet at least once per year without the executives on the board (i.e., without the "insiders"). Such changes are intended to increase confidence that the boards of the firms listed on these exchanges are actively monitoring and disciplining firm managers.

The government also responded to the corporate scandals with the Sarbanes-Oxley Act, the most sweeping changes in corporate governance legislation since the 1930s, and a sharp increase in funding for the Securities and Exchange Commission (SEC). Three basic economic principles that should guide any reforms to support effective corporate governance are: (1) accuracy and accessibility of information on a timely basis, (2) management accountability, and (3) auditor independence.

First, to act as effective monitors and provide discipline, private market participants must have accurate information about firms provided on a timely basis. Firms have an incentive to provide information to build confidence and reduce their cost of capital. Sarbanes-Oxley and the rules the SEC has adopted to implement the legislation have mandated, for example, more rapid disclosure of insider transactions. In addition, financial analysts and auditors must provide more information about potential conflicts of interest so that market participants have more information on which to judge the accuracy of the reports from both the firm and the analysts.

Second, managers must be held responsible for their actions, in particular if they commit fraud or cheat shareholders. Increasing funding for enforcement and increasing sanctions against wrongdoing should, in principle, reduce the incentive for a manager to undertake a bad act. Sarbanes-Oxley, for instance, significantly increased the maximum of both monetary sanctions and prison terms for fraud and various violations of securities laws. Along with a large rise in the SEC budget, enforcement has been enhanced by the creation of the Corporate Fraud Task Force to coordinate the expenditures and actions of the SEC, the Department of Justice, and other agencies. In addition, Sarbanes-Oxley clarifies and creates specific responsibilities for top officers, such as the requirement that the chief executive officer (CEO) and chief financial officer (CFO) personally certify the accuracy and completeness of the firm's financial reports.

The fundamental economic idea behind the principle of management accountability thus is that a higher likelihood of being caught and held responsible accompanied by higher penalties will increase the cost (or reduce the benefit) of bad behavior, and hence will result in less of it. The key to making such reforms effective is that they not go so far as to make managers so risk averse—so concerned that their acts could be subject to legal sanction even if they are undertaken in good faith but turn out badly—that managers simply minimize the possibility of a lawsuit rather than maximize firm profits. Legal actions stemming from this changed regulatory environment have only begun to work their way through the courts, so the jury is still out on assessing whether the changes have struck the right balance.[2]

Third, to enhance confidence that the financial reports contain accurate information, it is valuable for the auditor to be perceived as not subject to conflicts of interest that might compromise the auditor's independence and as exercising appropriate care and diligence in auditing the firm's accounts. The Sarbanes-Oxley Act created a new agency, the Public Company Accounting Oversight Board, to monitor and regulate auditors of publicly traded firms. This board sets standards for auditor conduct and can sanction auditors who do not meet the standards.

One new responsibility for the external auditor under section 404 of the act, for example, is to attest to the effectiveness of the internal control procedures of each firm. In particular, the implementation of section 404 has generated much controversy, due to both the uncertainty of what standards should be applied by the auditor and to the costs of implementation. A survey by Financial Executives International of CFOs at firms with average annual revenues of $5 billion suggests that total direct costs of compliance with section 404 in its first year of implementation averaged $4.36 million per firm (see Kroszner 2005). Most CFOs in the survey predicted that compliance costs will decline in the future. It is too early to determine whether this greater scrutiny of internal procedures will reduce the likelihood of fraud or misconduct sufficiently to outweigh its costs.

Responses by both the private sector and by the lawmakers and regulators should be evaluated over time as data about the costs and benefits can be estimated, particularly since many of the changes enacted in 2002 have yet to be fully implemented. In conducting such cost-benefit analyses of the regulatory changes, it is imperative to specify clearly what the "baseline" comparison is (see Kroszner 2005). Two considerations are particularly important to keep in mind here. First, no regulation can prevent all fraud—ethics cannot simply be enacted at the stroke of a pen—and costs of attempting to ensure that no fraud ever occurs would be prohibitive. Second, even if there had been no formal legal and regulatory changes, firms, markets, and self-regulatory organizations would

---

2. Part of the motivation for requiring financial expertise and

independence of board members on particular committees was to increase scrutiny of management—that is, the likelihood of detection—to reduce the ability and incentives of managers to engage in fraud. Some, such as William Niskanen (2005), have questioned the effectiveness of these provisions: "In 2000, the Enron board was judged one of the five best boards in the country by *Chief Executive* magazine. The Enron board met all the requirements of the [Sarbanes-Oxley Act], and the audit board was unusually well qualified. . . . All of the audit committee members were independent" (pp. 91 and 340).

have responded—and did respond—to perceived problems. To raise capital, firms have to be credible in the market. Even without legislative change, the private sector would have generated pressures for additional expenditures by firms on auditing and monitoring systems to enhance their credibility with investors. The relevant benchmark for measuring the cost of the Sarbanes-Oxley Act thus would not be "business as usual" in pre-Enron 2001, but what the private sector would have generated in response to demands for greater monitoring and credibility.

About the Author

Randall Kroszner is a member of the Federal Reserve Board of Governors. He was previously a professor of economics at the University of Chicago Graduate School of Business, director of the Stigler Center for the Study of the Economy and the State, and editor of the *Journal of Law and Economics*.

Further Reading

Berle, Adolf A. Jr., and Gardiner C. Means. *The Modern Corporation and Private Property.* New York: Macmillan, 1932.

Demsetz, Harold, and Kenneth Lehn. "The Structure of Corporate Ownership: Causes and Consequences." *Journal of Political Economy* 93 (1985): 1155–1177.

Holderness, Clifford G., Randall S. Kroszner, and Dennis P. Sheehan. "Were the Good Old Days That Good? Changes in Managerial Stock Ownership Since the Great Depression." *Journal of Finance* 54 (1999): 435–469.

Jensen, Michael C. "Eclipse of the Public Corporation." *Harvard Business Review* 67 (1989): 61–74.

———. "The Modern Industrial Revolution, Exit and the Failure of Internal Control Systems." *Journal of Finance* 48 (1993): 831–880.

Kroszner, Randall S. "The Economics of Corporate Governance Reform." *Journal of Applied Corporate Finance* 16, nos. 2–3 (2004) 42–50.

———. "Evaluating Section 404 of the Sarbanes-Oxley Act Concerning Internal Controls." Shadow Financial Regulatory Committee Statement no. 219, May 16, 2005.

———. "The Evolution of Universal Banking and Its Regulation in Twentieth Century America." In Anthony Saunders and Ingo Walter, eds., *Universal Banking: Financial System Design Reconsidered.* Chicago: Irwin, 1996. Pp. 70–99.

Kroszner, Randall S., and Raghuram G. Rajan. "Is the Glass-Steagall Act Justified? A Study of the U.S. Experience with Universal Banking Before 1933." *American Economic Review* 84 (September 1994): 810–832.

———. "Organization Structure and Credibility: Evidence from Commercial Bank Securities Activities before the Glass-Steagall Act." *Journal of Monetary Economics* 39, no. 3 (August 1997): 475–516.

La Porta, Raphael, Florencio Lopez-de-Silanes, and Andrei Shleifer. "Corporate Ownership Around the World." *Journal of Finance* 54 (1999): 471–517.

———. "Investor Protection and Corporate Valuation." *Journal of Finance* 57 (2002): 1147–1170.

La Porta, Raphael, Florencio Lopez-de-Silanes, Andrei Shleifer, and R. Vishny. "Investor Protection and Corporate Governance." *Journal of Financial Economics* 58 (2000): 3–27.

Niskanen, William A., ed. *After Enron: Lessons for Public Policy.* Lanham, Md.: Rowman and Littlefield, 2005.

Roe, Mark J. "Political and Legal Constraints on Ownership and Control of Public Companies." *Journal of Financial Economics* 27 (1990): 7–42.

———. *Strong Managers, Weak Owners: The Political Roots of American Corporate Finance.* Princeton: Princeton University Press, 1994.

Wu, YiLin. "The Impact of Public Opinion on Board Structure Changes, Director Career Progression, and CEO Turnover." *Journal of Corporate Finance* 10 (2004): 199–227.

Corporate Taxation

Rob Norton

The corporate income tax is the most poorly understood of all the major methods by which the U.S. government collects money. Most economists concluded long ago that it is among the least efficient and least defensible taxes. Although they have trouble agreeing on—much less measuring with any precision—who actually bears the burden of the corporate income tax, economists agree that it causes significant distortions in economic behavior. The tax is popular with the person in the street, who believes, incorrectly, that it is paid by corporations. Owners and managers of corporations often assume, just as incorrectly, that the tax is simply passed along to consumers. This very vagueness about who pays the tax accounts for its continued popularity among politicians.

The federal corporate income tax differs from the individual income tax in two major ways. First, it is a tax not on gross income but on net income, or profits, with permissible deductions for most costs of doing business. Second, it applies only to businesses that are chartered as corporations—not to partnerships or sole proprietorships. The federal tax is levied at different rates on different brackets of income: 15 percent on taxable income under $50,000, 25 percent on income between $50,000 and $75,000, and rates ranging from 34 to 39 percent on income above that. The lower-bracket rates benefit small corporations. Of the 4.8 million corporate tax returns filed in 1998, more than 90 percent were from corporations with assets of less than $1 million. The lower rates, however, had little economic significance. More than 91 percent of all corporate tax revenue came from the 1.5 percent of corporations with assets greater than $10 million.

States levy further income taxes on corporations, at rates generally ranging from 3 to 12 percent. Because states typically permit deductions for federal taxes paid, net rates range from 1.9 to 4.9 percent. Some localities tax corporations as well. One main reason that state and local corporate income taxes remain low is that corporations can easily relocate out of states that impose unusually high taxes.

How the corporate income tax arose and how it has survived over the decades is a case study of the perniciousness of bad ideas, of why tax systems are often so much worse than they need be, and of how little influence the economics profession has over government policy. Except for emergency taxes in wartime, corporate profits were first taxed in 1909, when Congress enacted a 1 percent tax on corporation income. The rate rose to 12.5 percent a decade later, and progressive rates—that is, rates that increase with income—were added in 1932. Surtaxes on corporate income were added for "excess profits" and "war profits" during both world wars. The highest peacetime rate, 52.8 percent, was reached in the 1960s.

In the 1940s and early 1950s, the corporate income tax provided about a third of federal revenues, and as recently as 1966, the proportion was 23 percent. It declined steadily for the next twenty years, reaching a nadir of 6.2 percent in 1983. This was partly by design: Congress cut the top corporate tax rates from 52.8 percent in 1969 to 46 percent in 1979, and during much of that time, tax law permitted relatively generous deductions for capital expenditures, either through accelerated depreciation schedules or through such devices as investment tax credits, so that the average tax rate paid by corporations fell even more sharply. Recent research has found that an equally important reason for the relative decline in corporate tax revenue is that U.S. corporations became less profitable. Corporate profits as a percentage of corporate assets, which averaged nearly 11 percent during the 1960s, were less than 5 percent from 1981 through 1987 and did not exceed 6.2 percent through 2000.

The Tax Reform Act of 1986 was designed to increase the share of federal revenues collected via the corporate income tax and to decrease the share from the individual income tax. While the top corporate tax rate, like the individual rate, was cut—to 34 percent—deductions for capital expenditures were severely curtailed and the investment tax credit was repealed. As a result, the effective tax rate for many corporations rose. The effort achieved its narrow goal somewhat: corporate taxes as a share of total federal receipts climbed back to more than 10 percent in the late 1980s. The top rate was raised a point, to 35 percent, in 1993, and corporate taxes rose to more than 11 percent of total revenues in the mid-1990s. As corporate profits contracted after the stock market crash of 2000 and the ensuing recession, however, so did corporate tax receipts. By 2003 they had declined to 7.4 percent.

From an economic point of view, the central problem with the corporate income tax is that, ultimately, only people can pay taxes. Economists have had great difficulty in assessing the incidence of the corporate tax—that is, determining on which groups of people the burden falls. As early as the seventeenth century, Sir William Petty, one of the progenitors of modern economics, argued that a tax on the production and sale of commodities would eventually be shifted by producers to consumers, who would pay it in the form of higher prices. Later classical economists disagreed, contending that taxes on corporate income fell on owners, making it, in effect, a tax on capital. They thought it could not be shifted because, theoretically, a corporation already charging prices that produce maximum profits could not increase prices further without reducing people's demand for its goods.

Modern economic opinion is divided on the incidence of the corporate income tax, but few economists today believe its burden falls entirely on the owners of capital. The latest thinking is that, since capital is mobile, it will flow to investments that produce the highest after-tax returns. The corporate income tax raises the cost of capital and reduces after-tax returns in the corporate sector, and thus leads to a migration of capital into noncorporate or tax-exempt sectors of the economy. This migration has two effects: it lowers the supply of capital available to corporations, and it causes a reduction in rates of return in the noncorporate sector as capital becomes more plentiful there. The ultimate effect, therefore, is to lower returns for all owners of capital across the economy. One important result of this capital migration is that the burden of the corporate income tax, over time, shifts to workers: with a smaller capital stock to employ, workers are less productive and earn lower real wages. In a 1996 survey, public finance economists were asked to estimate what percentage of the corporate income tax in the United States was ultimately borne by owners of capital. While their answers varied, the average response was 41 percent, meaning that the professional consensus is that more than half the burden is eventually shifted from owners of capital to workers or other groups.

Most economists agree that the corporate income tax causes two major inefficiencies. First, it penalizes the corporate form of business organization because income is taxed first at the corporate level and again when paid to stockholders as dividends. A traditional justification for singling out corporations is that they receive special benefits from the state and should pay for them. There are two problems with this rationale: first, if it were true, then all corporations, not just profitable ones, should pay; second, current corporate tax rates seem disproportionately high for this purpose. But the fundamental problem with this traditional justification is that it harkens back to the eighteenth century, when a corporate charter carried with it state-granted privileges such as monopoly power or exemption from specific laws. Today, corporations are created by private contract, with the government acting merely as registry and tax collector.

Recent experience shows this disincentive to the corporate form of organization at work. U.S. companies with thirty-five or fewer shareholders can elect what is called Subchapter S status. So-called S corporations have taxable income passed through to the tax returns of the owners, as in a partnership, instead of paying the corporate income tax. In the five weeks surrounding year-end 1986, after enactment of the tax reform bill, which raised the effective rate of corporate taxes, 225,000 companies elected Subchapter S status, compared with 75,000 for all of 1985.

The second major flaw in the corporate income tax is that it misallocates capital by favoring the issuance of debt over equity because interest payments are tax deductible, while dividend payments are not. This favors investments in assets more readily financed by debt, such as buildings and structures (which can be used for many purposes, and thus are more easily used as collateral for loans) over investments more logically financed by stock, such as specialized equipment or research and development. In addition, the deductibility of interest payments favors established companies over start-ups because the former can more easily issue debt securities. Some economists, focusing on this last phenomenon, have argued that this feature makes the corporate income tax a tax on entrepreneurship. During the 1980s, U.S. corporations issued huge amounts of new debt. Corporate bonds outstanding increased from less than $500 billion in 1980 to $1.4 trillion in 1988. At the same time, many corporations reduced their outstanding equity by buying back their own shares. The increased emphasis on debt financing was much more pronounced in the United States than elsewhere. In 2003, Congress took a step toward leveling the playing field by creating a special top tax rate for dividend income of 15 percent (previously, it was taxed as ordinary income at rates as high as 38.6 percent).

An additional problem with the corporate income tax is the way it is levied on multinational companies. The U.S. government taxes income earned both in the United States and abroad. Many other countries have more "territorial" tax regimes, which, in effect, tax only domestic income. The United States does grant tax credits, which allow companies to reduce their tax burdens by the amount of taxes paid to other governments, and other loopholes have been added over the decades, but the system has led to enormous complexity, especially for companies that have many operations and subsidiary companies abroad. Profits for subsidiaries are taxed only when they are returned, or repatriated, to the parent company, creating incentives for companies to reinvest foreign profits outside the United States and necessitating vast amounts of record-keeping.

The corporate income tax has survived all efforts to reform, repeal, or replace it, and there is little reason to expect a change in the near future. The simplest fix would be to equalize the treatment of interest and dividends, either by allowing corporations to deduct dividends or by granting an offsetting deduction or credit to stockholders. Most other large industrialized nations use the latter method. A more far-reaching reform, one recommended by economists for decades, would be to completely integrate the corporate and individual income taxes. One way to do this would be to treat corporations as partnerships for tax purposes (i.e., treat all corporations like S corporations), imputing all the profits to shareholders and taxing them under the individual income tax. The chief objection to this approach is that stockholders would face a tax liability for profits not distributed as dividends by the corporation. Several integration schemes have been proposed and rejected in the past. Many economists have recommended changing the tax rules for multinationals to eliminate the taxing of overseas profits, both for simplicity's sake and to improve the competitiveness of U.S. companies.

The arguments in favor of leaving the corporate income tax alone are politically compelling. For one thing, the tax has a proven ability to raise revenue, an important consideration for a nation that has run chronic budget deficits. For another, the old aphorism that "an old tax is a good tax" has some validity. Any major change in the tax code changes expectations and imposes new costs and complications during the transition period. But the most compelling rationale for the corporate income tax is the difficulty in assessing its incidence. Since no political constituency sees itself as the primary payer of the tax, none is willing to lobby aggressively for change. Indeed, the art of taxation, as seventeenth-century French administrator Jean-Baptiste Colbert reportedly said, "consists in so plucking the goose as to obtain the largest possible amount of feathers with the smallest possible amount of hissing." Judged solely by this standard, the corporate income tax has worked well.

About the Author

Rob Norton is an author and consultant. He was previously the economics editor of *Fortune* magazine.

Further Reading

Congressional Budget Office. *The Incidence of the Corporate Income Tax*. Washington, D.C.: U.S. Government Printing Office, 1996.

Economic Report of the President. Washington, D.C.: U.S. Government Printing Office, 2004.

Eden, Lorraine, ed. *Retrospectives on Public Finance*. Durham: Duke University Press, 1991.

Musgrave, Richard A., and Peggy B. Musgrave. *Public Finance in Theory and Practice*. 5th ed. New York: McGraw-Hill, 1989.

National Bureau of Economic Research. *Tax Policy and the Economy*. Vols. 1–5. Cambridge: NBER, 1987–1991.

Rosen, Harvey S. *Public Finance*. 6th ed. Boston: McGraw-Hill/Irwin, 2002.

Stiglitz, Joseph E. *Economics of the Public Sector*. 2d ed. New York: Norton, 1988.

Treubert, Patrice, and William P. Jauquet. *Corporation Income Tax Returns, 1998*. U.S. Internal Revenue Service.

Corporations

Robert Hessen

Corporations are easier to create than to understand. Because corporations arose as an alternative to partnerships, they can best be understood by comparing these competing organizational structures.

The presumption of partnership is that the investors will directly manage their own money rather than entrusting that task to others. Partners are "mutual agents," meaning that each is able to sign contracts that are binding on all the others. Such an arrangement is unsuited for strangers or those who harbor suspicions about each other's integrity or business acumen. Hence the transfer of partnership interests is subject to restrictions.

In a corporation, by contrast, the presumption is that the shareholders will not personally manage their money. Instead, a corporation is managed by directors and officers who need not be investors. Because managerial authority is concentrated in the hands of directors and officers, shares are freely transferable unless otherwise agreed. They can be sold or given to anyone without placing other investors at the mercy of a new owner's poor judgment. The splitting of management and ownership into two distinct functions is the salient feature of the corporation.

To differentiate it from a partnership, a corporation should be defined as a legal and contractual mechanism for creating and operating a business for profit, using capital from investors that will be managed on their behalf by directors and officers. To lawyers, however, the classic definition is Chief Justice John Marshall's 1819 remark that "a corporation is an artificial being, invisible, intangible, and existing only in contemplation of law."[1] But Marshall's definition is useless because it is a metaphor; it makes a corporation a judicial hallucination.

Recent writers who have tried to recast Marshall's metaphor into a literal definition say that a corporation is an entity (or a fictitious legal person or an artificial legal being) that exists independent of its owners. The entity notion is metaphorical too and violates Occam's razor, the principle that explanations should be concise and literal.

Attempts by economists to define corporations have been equally unsatisfactory. In 1917 Joseph S. Davis wrote: "A corporation [is] a group of individuals authorized by law to act as a unit."[2] This definition is defective because it also fits partnerships and labor unions, which are not corporations. Economist Jonathan Hughes wrote that a corporation is a "multiple partnership" and that "the privilege of incorporation is the gift of the state to collective business ventures."[3] Economist Robert Heilbroner wrote that a corporation is "an entity created by the state," granted a charter that enables it to exist "in its own right as a 'person' created by law."[4]

But charters enacted by state legislatures literally ceased to exist in the mid-nineteenth century. The actual procedure for creating a corporation consists of filing a registration document with a state official (like recording the use of a fictitious business name), and the state's role is purely formal and automatic. To call incorporation a "privilege" implies that individuals have no right to create a corporation. But why is government permission needed? Who would be wronged if businesses adopted corporate features by contract? Whose rights would be violated if a firm declared itself to be a unit for the purposes of suing and being sued or holding and conveying title to property, or that it would continue in existence despite the death or withdrawal of its officers or investors, or that its shares are freely transferable, or if it asserted limited liability for its

1. *Dartmouth College v. Woodward*, 4 Wheat. 518, 636, 4 L.Ed. 629, 659, 1819.

2. *Essays on the Earlier History of American Corporations*, vol. 1 (Cambridge: Harvard University Press, 1917), p. 5.

3. *American Economic History*, 2d ed. (Glenview, Ill.: Scott Foresman, 1983), p. 129.

4. *The Economic Transformation of America* (New York: Harcourt, Brace, Jovanovich, 1977), p. 99.

debt obligations? (Liability for torts is a separate issue; see Hessen 1979, pp. 18–21.) If potential creditors find any of these features objectionable, they can negotiate to exclude or modify them.

Economists invariably declare limited liability to be the crucial corporate feature. According to this view the corporation, as an entity, contracts debts in "its" own name, not the shareholders', who are not responsible for its debts. But there is no need for such mental gymnastics because limited liability actually involves an implied contract between shareholders and outside creditors. By incorporating (i.e., complying with the registration procedure prescribed by state law) and then by using the symbols "Inc." or "Corp.," shareholders are warning potential creditors that they do not accept unlimited personal liability, that creditors must look only to the corporation's assets (if any) for satisfaction of their claims. This process, known as "constructive notice," offers an easy means of economizing on transactions costs. It is an alternative to negotiating explicit limited-liability contracts with each creditor.

Creditors, moreover, are not obligated to accept limited liability. Professor Bayless Manning observed that "as a part of the bargain negotiated when the corporation incurs the indebtedness, the creditor may, of course, succeed in extracting from a shareholder (or someone else who wants to see the loan go through) an outside pledge agreement, guaranty, endorsement, or the like that will have the effect of subjecting non-corporate assets to the creditor's claim against the corporation" (1977, p. 7). This familiar pattern explains why limited liability is likely to be a mirage or delusion for a new, untested business, and thus also explains why some enterprises are not incorporated despite the ease of creating a corporation.

Another myth is that limited liability explains why corporations were able to attract vast amounts of capital from nineteenth-century investors to carry out America's industrialization. In fact, the industrial revolution was carried out chiefly by partnerships and unincorporated joint stock companies, and rarely by corporations. The chief sources of capital for the early New England textile corporations were the founders' personal savings, money borrowed from banks, the proceeds from state-approved lotteries, and the sale of bonds and debentures.

Even in the late nineteenth century, none of the giant industrial corporations drew equity capital from the general investment public. They were privately held and, to expand, drew primarily on retained earnings. (The largest enterprise, Carnegie Brothers, was organized as a limited partnership association in the Commonwealth of Pennsylvania, a status that did not inhibit its ability to own properties or sell steel in other states.)

External financing through the sale of common stock was nearly impossible in the nineteenth century because of asymmetric information—that is, the inability of outside investors to gauge which firms were likely to earn a profit, and thus to calculate what would be a reasonable price to pay for shares. Instead, founders of corporations often gave away shares as a bonus to those who bought bonds, which were less risky because they carried underlying collateral, a fixed date of redemption, and a fixed rate of return. Occasionally, wealthy local residents bought shares, not primarily as investments for profit, but rather as a public-spirited gesture to foster economic growth in a town or region. The idea that limited liability would have been sufficient to entice outside investors to buy common stock is counterintuitive. The assurance that one could lose only one's total investment is hardly a persuasive sales pitch.

No logical necessity links partnerships with unlimited liability or corporations with limited liability. Legal rules do not suddenly spring into existence full grown; instead, they arise in a particular historical context. Unlimited liability for partners dates back to medieval Italy, when partnerships were family based, personal and business funds were intermingled, and family honor required payment of debts owed to creditors, even if it meant that the whole debt would be paid by one or two partners instead of being shared proportionally by them all.

Well into the twentieth century, American judges ignored the historical circumstances in which unlimited liability became the custom and later the legal rule. Hence they repeatedly rejected partners' contractual attempts to limit their liability. Only near midcentury did state legislatures grudgingly begin enacting "close corporation" statutes for businesses that would be organized as partnerships if courts were willing to recognize the contractual nature of limited liability. These quasi corporations have nearly nothing in common with corporations financed by outside investors and run by professional managers.

Any firm, regardless of size, can be structured as a corporation, a partnership, a limited partnership, or even one of the rarely used forms—a business trust or an unincorporated joint stock company. Partnerships are not necessarily small scale or short-lived; they need not cease to exist when a general partner dies or withdraws. Features that are automatic or inherent in a corporation—continuity of existence, hierarchy of authority, freely transferable shares—are optional for a partnership or any other organizational form. The only exceptions arise if government restricts or forbids freedom of contract (such as the rule that denies limited liability for general partners).

As noted, the distinctive feature of corporations is that

investment and management are split into two functions. Critics call this phenomenon a "separation of ownership from control." The most influential indictment of this separation is presented in *The Modern Corporation and Private Property*, written in 1932 by Adolf A. Berle Jr. and Gardiner C. Means. Corporate officers, they claimed, had usurped authority, aided and abetted by directors who should have been the shareholders' agents and protectors.

But Berle and Mean's criticism overlooked how corporations were formed. The "Fortune 500" corporations were not born as giants. Initially, each was the creation of one or a few people who were the prime movers and promoters of the business and almost always the principal source of its original capital. They were able to "go public"—sell shares to outsiders to raise additional equity—only when they could persuade underwriters and investors that they could put new money to work at a profit.

If these firms had initially been partnerships, then the general partners could have accepted outside investors as limited partners without running any risk of losing or diluting their control over decision making. (By law, limited partners cannot participate in management or exercise any voice or vote, or else they forfeit their claim to limited liability.) A far different situation applies to corporations. Shareholders receive voting rights to elect the board of directors, and the directors, in turn, elect the officers. Although new shareholders could play an active role in managing these corporations, this happens only rarely.

When a corporation is created, its officers, directors, and shareholders usually are the same people. They elect themselves or their nominees to the board of directors and then elect themselves as corporate officers. When the corporation later goes public, the founders accept a dilution of control because they value the additional capital and because they expect to continue to control a majority of votes on the board and thus to direct the company's future policy and growth.

That the board of directors is dominated by "insiders" makes sense. The founders are the first directors; later, their places on the board are filled by the executives they groomed to succeed them. This arrangement does not injure new shareholders, who buy shares of common stock because the corporation's record of performance indicates a competent managerial system. They do not want to interfere with or dismantle the system; on the contrary, they willingly entrust their savings to it. They know that the best safeguard for their investments, if they become dissatisfied with the company's performance, is their ability to sell instantly their shares of a publicly traded corporation.

Berle and Means challenged the legitimacy of giant corporations when they charged that corporate officers had seized or usurped control from the owners—the shareholders. But the control is never seized. Instead, investors make choices along a risk-reward continuum. Bondholders are the most risk-averse; then come those who buy the intermediate-risk, nonvoting securities (debentures, convertible bonds, and preferred shares); the least risk-averse investors are those who buy common shares and stand to gain (or lose) the most.

Just as one may assume that investors know the difference between being a general partner and being a limited partner, so too they know that shareholders in a publicly traded corporation are the counterparts of limited partners, those who make passbook deposits in a bank, or those who buy shares in a mutual fund. All hope to make money on their savings as a sideline to their primary sources of income.

To look askance at executives who supply little or none of the corporation's capital, as many of the corporation's critics do, is to condemn division of labor and specialization of function. Corporate officers operate businesses whose capital requirements far exceed their personal savings or the amounts they would be willing or able to borrow. Their distinctive contribution to the enterprise is knowledge of production, marketing, and finance; administrative ability in building and sustaining a business, in directing its growth, and in leading its response to unforeseen problems and challenges.

Some critics equate large corporations with government institutions and then find them woefully deficient in living up to democratic norms (voting rights are based on number of shares owned rather than one vote per person, for example). Thus shareholders are renamed "citizens," the board of directors is "the legislature," and the officers are "the executive branch." They call the articles of incorporation a "constitution," the bylaws "private statutes," and merger agreements "treaties."

But the analogy, however ingenious, is defective. It cannot encompass all the major groups within the corporation. If shareholders are called citizens or voters, what are other suppliers of capital called? Are bondholders "resident aliens" because they cannot vote? And are those who buy convertible debentures "citizens in training" until they acquire voting rights? A belabored analogy cannot justify equating business and government.

Millions of people freely choose to invest their savings in the shares of publicly traded corporations. It is farfetched to believe that shareholders are being victimized—denied the control over corporate affairs that they expected to exercise, or being shortchanged on dividends—and yet still retain their shares and buy new shares or bid up the price of existing shares. If shareholders were victims, corporations could not possibly raise additional capital through new stock offerings. Yet they do so frequently.

Particular corporations can be mismanaged. They are sometimes too large or too diversified to operate efficiently; too slow to innovate; overloaded with debt; top-heavy with high-salaried, and sometimes dishonest, executives; or too slow to respond to challenges from domestic or foreign competitors. But this does not invalidate corporations as a class. Whatever the shortcomings of particular companies or whole industries, corporations are a superb matchmaking mechanism to bring savers (investors) and borrowers (workers and managers) together for their mutual benefit.

About the Author

Robert Hessen, a senior research fellow at the Hoover Institution, taught American business history at Columbia and Stanford universities from 1966 to 1995.

Further Reading

Bromberg, Alan R. *Crane and Bromberg on Partnership*. St. Paul, Minn.: West Publishing, 1968.
Conard, Alfred F. *Corporations in Perspective*. Mineola, N.Y.: Foundation Press, 1976.
Easterbrook, Frank, and Daniel Fischel. *The Economic Structure of Corporate Law*. Cambridge: Harvard University Press, 1991.
Hessen, Robert. *In Defense of the Corporation*. Stanford, Calif.: Hoover Institution Press, 1979.
Hovenkamp, Herbert. *Enterprise and American Law, 1836–1937*. Cambridge: Harvard University Press, 1991.
Manning, Bayless. *Legal Capital*. Mineola, N.Y.: Foundation Press, 1977.
Roe, Mark J. *Strong Managers, Weak Owners: The Political Roots of American Corporate Finance*. Princeton: Princeton University Press, 1994.

Corruption

François Melese

In the world's worst offending countries, corrupt government officials steal public money and collude with businesses to sell laws, rules, regulations, and government contracts. The World Bank reports that "higher levels of corruption are associated with lower per capita income" (World Bank 2001, p. 105). Corruption breeds poverty, and poverty kills. In other words, corruption kills.

How so? Corruption sabotages economies and undermines political institutions. Its most devastating impact is on investment. By discouraging investment, corruption crushes economic growth and slashes per capita incomes.

According to Mauro (1995), for example, if Bangladesh had cut corruption over the period 1960–1985 to the level of one of the world's cleanest countries (Singapore), it would have increased its growth rate by 1.8 percentage points per year. By 1985, its per capita income would have been more than 50 percent higher. Low-per-capita-income countries suffer higher infant mortality—54 deaths per 1,000 live births in Bangladesh versus 3 per 1,000 in Singapore—and lower average life expectancies—fifty-nine years versus eighty years (U.S. Census Bureau 2000.) Another insidious way in which corruption kills is that it skews public spending away from operating budgets such as health care and toward capital budgets—military spending, for example, where bribes are easier to extract (Klitgaard 1988; Mauro 1996; Tanzi and Davoodi 1997).

Corruption hurts investment in at least three ways. First, it increases the cost of doing business, which then raises the threshold revenues required for businesses to break even. Second, it causes producers, on the margin, to bribe officials rather than invest in cost-saving technology or new products. Third, if public funds end up in the pockets of government officials, taxes will be higher and public investment lower, hurting economic growth.

There is an important distinction between business-to-business corruption and government corruption (Melese 2002). The former is almost always either beneficial or self-correcting, while the latter is neither.

In its mildest and most benign form, business-to-business bribery facilitates communication and helps cement relationships between principals (customers) and agents (suppliers). "Facilitation payments" (anything from generous commissions to free meals and entertainment) can replace costly contingent contracts with implicit contracts that ensure quality, quantity, and meeting of schedule requirements. In such a case, business-to-business bribery has an offsetting benefit: it reduces transaction costs and greases the wheels of commerce.

Bad cases of business-to-business bribery typically involve private gains with no offsetting benefits. This more sinister form is like a worm that eats into corporate profits. For instance, by concealing debt and overstating revenues, corporate managers might boost a firm's stock price, increasing the value of their stock options. In the case of fraudulent financing and accounting, shareholders are the victims. Such corruption, if revealed early, is self-limiting because shareholders want to avoid its costs. If revealed too late, the outcome is bankruptcy. Honest and transparent market institutions are all that are required, although to say this is not to say that achieving honesty and transparency is always easy.

Government corruption, in contrast, does not involve a self-correcting market mechanism. It occurs because government officials, whether politicians or bureaucrats, have the power and discretion to grant favors in the form of subsidies, contracts, tax breaks, regulations, and permits.

Whereas government corruption is most acute in the poorest and least free countries, it is by no means limited to those countries. Take the case of a young congressman named Lyndon B. Johnson, who had built his family fortune from approximately zero in 1943 to at least fourteen million dollars by the time he was first elected U.S. president in 1964. About half his family's wealth derived from a single permit his wife held that allowed her to operate KTBC, a radio station in Austin, Texas. Johnson's wife bought the license for a very low price and then applied for permission to operate the radio station twenty-four hours a day and on a much better part of the AM band. The Federal Communications Commission granted her permission within one month. In return, Johnson helped save the FCC from budget cuts (Caro 1990, pp. 82–111). Here is a case of corruption that was probably completely legal. The key to corruption is the combination of power and discretion in the hands of government officials.

Most government corruption is "negative sum": losers lose more than winners gain. This explains the economics literature's almost exclusive focus on government corruption. Yale Law School economist Susan Rose-Ackerman, for example, author of one of the few book-length studies of the economics of corruption, devoted ten of eleven chapters to government corruption.

Government corruption allows long-established, politically connected firms to monopolize markets. Typically it is the long-established firms that figure out which government official has the power, or can obtain the power, to keep new firms from competing; then they bribe him, either with outright payments or with promises of future employment and shares. These bribes eat up some of the monopoly profits. Competition shifts from the marketplace to the political arena. Instead of investing in better products or processes, firms invest in government-sanctioned barriers (exclusive licenses, contracts, permits, etc.) or political favors (regulations, tariffs, quotas, etc.) to gain and preserve market power. Krueger (1974) and Tullock (1980) referred to this as "rent seeking," and Bhagwati (1982) introduced the term "directly unproductive profit seeking (DUP)" for it. Perhaps a better term is "privilege seeking." Nobel laureate George Stigler also pointed out that government regulation creates opportunities for corruption, which, he wrote, "turns regulations into gold" (cited in "Corporate Bribery," *Cato Policy Report,* February 1980). The LBJ example mentioned earlier illustrates the point.

Consider the poorest region on earth, sub-Saharan Africa. In many African countries, political coalitions and special interest groups enrich themselves and preserve their political power at the expense of their populations. Throughout the region, governments control many of the most valuable resources. African governments are often the primary investors, importers, and bankers in their countries and employ a large fraction of the educated labor force. This leaves few options for new businesses. Meanwhile, to preserve their grip on government, dominant political coalitions forcibly transfer income and wealth to their supporters. The results are grim. According to Transparency International's (2004) "Corruption Perceptions Index," of the sixty countries in the world that scored less than 3 (10 is highly clean and 0 highly corrupt), more than a third were from sub-Saharan Africa. Not surprisingly, therefore, the International Monetary Fund (IMF 2000) reported that the ratio of investment to GDP in sub-Saharan Africa hovered around 17 percent throughout the 1990s, well below the rate experienced by developing countries in Latin America (20–22 percent) and Asia (27–29 percent) (Hernández-Catá 2000, p. 6).

Some economists argue that paying bribes to the right officials can mitigate the harmful effects of excessive government regulation. If firms had a choice to wade through red tape or pay to circumvent it, paying bribes might actually improve efficiency and spur investment. Although this view is plausible, a pioneering study by Mauro found that corruption "is strongly negatively associated with the investment rate, regardless of the amount of red tape" (Mauro 1995, p. 695). In fact, allowing firms to pay bribes to circumvent regulations encourages public officials to create new opportunities for bribery.

Governments take various steps to make corruption unprofitable. These mostly boil down to increasing penalties or increasing the probability of detection. In the United States, both briber and recipient are subject to penalties under U.S. Code title 18, section 201 ("Bribery of public officials . . ."). The statute states that perpetrators can be "fined . . . not more than three times the monetary equivalent of the thing of value . . . or imprisoned for not more than fifteen years, or both." Surprisingly, although the 1977 Foreign Corrupt Practices Act forbids U.S. companies to make payments to foreign officials, it does not rule out "grease payments," that is, payments to speed up or otherwise facilitate international transactions (Bardhan 1997, p. 1337). The 1998 OECD anticorruption treaty follows in its footsteps. Although the treaty threatens multinationals that bribe foreign governments, the hidden danger is that it invites more creative ways to cheat. Unfortunately, government institutions such as the IMF and World Bank inadvertently contribute to corruption by lending to corrupt governments (Easterly 2002; McNab and Melese 2004).

There are three main strategies for reducing corruption. The first—and in this author's view, better—strategy is to reduce the power and discretion of public officials. The fewer rules, regulations, and contracts public officials have the discretion to write, modify, or enforce, the less opportunity there will be for corruption. The more transparent their actions and the more they have to lose, the better. In some cases, eliminating corruption is as simple as removing government, such as through deregulation or privatization. Clarke and Xu (2002) found that increasing competition reduces corruption. Mohtadi, Polasky, and Roe (2004) found that as trade barriers fall, so does corruption. Also, devolving more tax and decision-making authority to state and local governments reduces the central government's monopoly power and reduces the gains from corruption (Martinez-Vazquez and McNab 1998, 2002a, 2002b).

The second strategy, somewhat paradoxically, is to pay more to government officials who have discretion so that they will have more to lose by exercising their discretion corruptly. Under the Ch'ing dynasty, for example, district magistrates received an extra allowance called *yang-lien yin*, or "money to nourish honesty" (Bardhan 1997). Today, one of the world's cleanest countries, Singapore, pays its public officials so-called efficiency wages that always remain above prevailing wages; government officials who are tempted to be corrupt know that they will give up a lucrative job. Of course, for such incentives to work, officials must be convinced that if caught, they really will lose their jobs.

The third way to reduce bureaucratic corruption is to reduce the monopoly power of the bureaucrat. Shleifer and Vishny (1993) showed that if instead of a single corrupt official there are many competing corrupt officials, competition can cause bribes to drop to close to zero. Rose-Ackerman (1994) suggested that multiple officials with overlapping jurisdictions might help reduce corruption because the potential briber would face the costly prospect of persuading every official involved. She pointed to overlapping involvement of local, state, and federal drug enforcement agencies in helping reduce police corruption in the United States.

Competition works well if regulators monitor each other to prevent bribes or compete with each other to grant permits. Competition does not work well if permission is required of each one. If several public agents (agencies) have overlapping jurisdiction and each has veto power, this rapidly increases the cost of doing business and reduces the probability of success for legitimate projects (such as obtaining a permit to launch a new business). A simple example illustrates the point. Suppose there is a 50 percent chance that a single public agent will grant a permit. Now, if two agents must be consulted and each has the same veto power, then the probability of success drops to 25 percent; with four layers, the probability drops further to only 6.25 percent. Consider the World Bank's observation that starting a business in Mozambique takes *nineteen* steps, five months, and a year's worth of income (World Development Report 2002). Instead of protecting consumers and businesses, the danger is that competing and overlapping jurisdictions might crush market activity, investment, and economic growth.

About the Author

François Melese is an economics professor at the Defense Resources Management Institute at the Naval Postgraduate School in Monterey, California. He also lectures on international issues for the U.S. State Department and NATO.

Further Reading

Bardhan, P. "Corruption and Development: A Review of the Issues." *Journal of Economic Literature* 35 (1997): 1320–1346.

Bhagwati, J. "Directly Unproductive Profit-Seeking (DUP) Activities." *Journal of Political Economy* 90 (1982): 988–1002.

Becker, G. "Crime and Punishment: An Economic Approach." *Journal of Political Economy* 76 (1968): 169–217.

Bowles, R. "Corruption." In *Encyclopedia of Law and Economics.* University of Utrecht, Holland, 1999. Online at: http://allserv.rug.ac.be.

Caro, R. *The Years of Lyndon Johnson: Means of Ascent.* New York: Knopf, 1990.

Clarke, G., and L. Xu. "Ownership, Competition and Corruption: Bribe Takers vs. Bribe Payers." World Bank Development Research Group, Policy Research Working Paper no. 2783. February, 2002.

Easterly, W. "The Cartel of Good Intentions: Bureaucracy Versus Markets in Foreign Aid." Center for Global Development Working Paper no. 4. Center for Global Development, Washington, D.C., 2002.

Gordon, D. "Air Force Procurement: Protests Challenging Role of Biased Official Sustained." Testimony before the U.S. Senate, April 15, 2005. Government Accountability Office, GAO-05-436T, 2005.

Heritage Foundation. *Index of Economic Freedom.* Washington, D.C.: Heritage Foundation, 1997.

Hernández-Catá, Ernesto. "Raising Growth and Investment in Sub-Saharan Africa: What Can Be Done?" Policy Discussion Paper PDP/00/4 (Washington, D.C.: International Monetary Fund, 2000), p. 6.

Klitgaard, R. *Controlling Corruption.* Berkeley: University of California Press, 1988.

Krueger, A. "The Political Economy of Rent Seeking." *American Economic Review* 64, no. 3 (1974): 291–303.

Leff, N. "Economic Development Through Bureaucratic Corruption." *American Behavioral Scientist* 8, no. 3 (1964): 8–14.

Martinez-Vasquez, J., and R. McNab. "Decentralization and Governance." International Studies Program Working Paper. Andrew Young School of Policy Studies, Georgia State University, Atlanta, 2002a.

———. "Decentralization, Inflation, and Growth." International Studies Program Working Paper. Andrew Young School of Policy Studies, Georgia State University, Atlanta, 2002b.

———. "Fiscal Decentralization, Economic Growth, and Democratic Governance." International Studies Program Working Paper. Andrew Young School of Policy Studies, Georgia State University, Atlanta, 1998.

Mauro, P. "Corruption and Growth." *Quarterly Journal of Economics* 110, no. 3 (1995): 681–712.

———. "The Effects of Corruption on Growth, Investment, and Government Expenditure." IMF Working Paper 96/98. International Monetary Fund, Washington, D.C., 1996.

Mbaku, J. "Bureaucratic Corruption in Africa: The Futility of Cleanups." *Cato Journal* 16, no. 1 (1996): 99–118.

McNab, R., and F. Melese. "Corruption, International Donors, and Governance." In S. Rahid, ed., *Rotting from the Head: Donors and LDC Corruption*. Bangladesh: University Press Limited, 2004.

Melese, F. "The Problem of Corruption." *Free Market* 20, no. 6 (2002): 6–8.

Mohtadi, H., S. Polasky, and T. Roe. "Trade, Information and Corruption: A Signalling Game." Paper presented at American Economic Association meetings in Philadelphia, January 2005.

Rose-Ackerman, S. *Corruption: A Study in Political Economy.* New York: Academic Press, 1978.

———. "Reducing Bribery in the Public Sector." In D. Trang, ed., *Corruption and Democracy*. Budapest Institute for Constitutional and Legislative Policy, 1994.

Shleifer, A., and R. Vishny. "Corruption." *Quarterly Journal of Economics* 108, no. 3 (1993): 599–617.

Tanzi, V., and H. Davoodi. "Corruption, Public Investment, and Growth." IMF Working Paper WP/37/139. International Monetary Fund, Washington, D.C., 1997.

Tullock, G. "Efficient Rent-Seeking." In J. Buchanan, R. Tollison, and G. Tullock, eds., *Towards a Theory of the Rent-Seeking Society*. College Station: Texas A&M University Press, 1980.

U.S. Code (as of 1/26/98). Title 18 (Crimes and Criminal Procedures), Part 1 (Crimes), Chapter 11 (Bribery, Graft and Conflicts of Interest), Section 201 (Bribery of Public Officials and Witnesses).

Wei, S. "Corruption in Economic Development: Beneficial Grease, Minor Annoyance, or Major Obstacle?" Paper presented at the Sixth Mitsui Symposium on Economic Freedom and Development, Tokyo, June 17–18, 1999.

World Bank. *World Development Report 2002: Building Institutions for Markets.* New York: Oxford University Press, 2001.

Creative Destruction

W. Michael Cox
Richard Alm

Joseph Schumpeter (1883–1950) coined the seemingly paradoxical term "creative destruction," and generations of economists have adopted it as a shorthand description of the free market's messy way of delivering progress. In *Capitalism, Socialism, and Democracy* (1942), the Austrian economist wrote:

> The opening up of new markets, foreign or domestic, and the organizational development from the craft shop to such concerns as U.S. Steel illustrate the same process of industrial mutation—if I may use that biological term—that incessantly revolutionizes the economic structure from within, incessantly destroying the old one, incessantly creating a new one. This process of Creative Destruction is the essential fact about capitalism. (p. 83)

Although Schumpeter devoted a mere six-page chapter to "The Process of Creative Destruction," in which he described capitalism as "the perennial gale of creative destruction," it has become the centerpiece for modern thinking on how economies evolve.

Schumpeter and the economists who adopt his succinct summary of the free market's ceaseless churning echo capitalism's critics in acknowledging that lost jobs, ruined companies, and vanishing industries are inherent parts of the growth system. The saving grace comes from recognizing the good that comes from the turmoil. Over time, societies that allow creative destruction to operate grow more productive and richer; their citizens see the benefits of new and better products, shorter work weeks, better jobs, and higher living standards.

Herein lies the paradox of progress. A society cannot reap the rewards of creative destruction without accepting that some individuals might be worse off, not just in the short term, but perhaps forever. At the same time, attempts to soften the harsher aspects of creative destruction by trying to preserve jobs or protect industries will lead to stagnation and decline, short-circuiting the march of progress. Schumpeter's enduring term reminds us that capitalism's pain and gain are inextricably linked. The process of creating new industries does not go forward without sweeping away the preexisting order.

Transportation provides a dramatic, ongoing example of creative destruction at work. With the arrival of steam power in the nineteenth century, railroads swept across the United States, enlarging markets, reducing shipping costs, building new industries, and providing millions of new productive jobs. The internal combustion engine paved the way for the automobile early in the next century. The rush to put America on wheels spawned new enterprises; at one point in the 1920s, the industry had swelled to more than 260 car makers. The automobile's ripples spilled into oil, tourism, entertainment, retailing, and other industries. On the heels of the automobile, the airplane flew into our world, setting off its own burst of new businesses and jobs.

Americans benefited as horses and mules gave way to cars and airplanes, but all this creation did not come without destruction. Each new mode of transportation took a toll on existing jobs and industries. In 1900, the peak year for the occupation, the country employed 109,000 carriage and harness makers. In 1910, 238,000 Americans worked as blacksmiths. Today, those jobs are largely obsolete. After eclipsing canals and other forms of transport, railroads lost out in competition with cars, long-haul trucks, and airplanes. In 1920, 2.1 million Americans earned their paychecks working for railroads, compared with fewer than 200,000 today.

What occurred in the transportation sector has been repeated in one industry after another—in many cases, several times in the same industry. Creative destruction recognizes change as the one constant in capitalism. Sawyers, masons, and miners were among the top thirty American occupations in 1900. A century later, they no longer rank among the top thirty; they have been replaced by medical technicians, engineers, computer scientists, and others.

Technology roils job markets, as Schumpeter conveyed in coining the phrase "technological unemployment" (Table 1). E-mail, word processors, answering machines, and other modern office technology have cut the number of secretaries but raised the ranks of programmers. The birth of the Internet spawned a need for hundreds of thousands of webmasters, an occupation that did not exist as recently as 1990. LASIK surgery often lets consumers throw away their glasses, reducing visits to optometrists and opticians but increasing the need for ophthalmologists. Digital cameras translate to fewer photo clerks.

Companies show the same pattern of destruction and rebirth. Only five of today's hundred largest public companies were among the top hundred in 1917. Half of the top hundred of 1970 had been replaced in the rankings by 2000.

"The essential point to grasp is that in dealing with capitalism we are dealing with an evolutionary process," Schumpeter wrote (p. 82).

The Power of Productivity

Entrepreneurship and competition fuel creative destruction. Schumpeter summed it up as follows:

The fundamental impulse that sets and keeps the capitalist engine in motion comes from the new consumers' goods, the new methods of production or transportation, the new markets, the new forms of industrial organization that capitalist enterprise creates. (p. 83)

Entrepreneurs introduce new products and technologies with an eye toward making themselves better off—the profit motive. New goods and services, new firms, and new industries compete with existing ones in the marketplace, taking customers by offering lower prices, better performance, new features, catchier styling, faster service, more convenient locations, higher status, more aggressive marketing, or more attractive packaging. In another seemingly contradictory aspect of creative destruction, the pursuit of self-interest ignites the progress that makes *others* better off.

Producers survive by streamlining production with newer and better tools that make workers more productive. Companies that no longer deliver what consumers want at competitive prices lose customers, and eventually wither and die. The market's "invisible hand"—a phrase owing not to Schumpeter but to Adam Smith—shifts resources from declining sectors to more valuable uses as workers, inputs, and financial capital seek their highest returns.

Through this constant roiling of the status quo, creative destruction provides a powerful force for making societies wealthier. It does so by making scarce resources more productive. The telephone industry employed 421,000 switchboard operators in 1970, when Americans made 9.8 billion long-distance calls. With advances in switching technology over the next three decades, the telecommunications sector could reduce the number of operators to 156,000 but still ring up 106 billion calls. An average operator handled only 64 calls a day in 1970. By 2000, that figure had increased to 1,861, a staggering gain in productivity. If they had to handle today's volume of calls with 1970s technology, the telephone companies would need more than 4.5 million operators, or 3 percent of the labor force. Without the productivity gains, a long-distance call would cost six times as much.

The telephone industry is not an isolated example of creative destruction at work. In 1900, nearly forty of every hundred Americans worked in farming to feed a country of ninety million people. A century later, it takes just two out of every hundred workers. Despite one of history's most thorough downsizings, the country has not gone hungry. The United States enjoys agricultural plenty, producing more meat, grain, vegetables, and dairy products than ever, thanks largely to huge advances in agricultural productivity.

Table 1 Technological Unemployment

New Product	Labor Needed	Old Product	Labor Released
Automobile	Assemblers	Horse/carriage	Blacksmiths
	Designers	Train	Wainwrights
	Road builders	Boat	Drovers
	Petrochemists		Teamsters
	Mechanics		RR workers
	Truck drivers		Canalmen
Airplane	Pilots	Train	RR workers
	Mechanics	Ocean liner	Sawyers
	Flight attendants		Mechanics
	Travel agents		Ship hands
			Boilermakers
Plastics	Petrochemists	Steel	Miners
		Aluminum	Founders
		Barrels/tubs	Metalworkers
		Pottery/glass	Coopers
			Potters
			Colliers
Computer	Programmers	Adding machine	Assemblers
	Computer engineers	Slide rule	Millwrights
	Electrical engineers	Filing cabinet	Clerks
	Software designers	Paper	Tinsmiths
			Lumberjacks
Fax machine	Programmers	Express mail	Mail sorters
E-mail	Electricians	Teletype	Truck drivers
	Software designers		Typists
Telephone	Electronic engineers	Mail	Postal workers
	Operators	Telegraph	Telegraph operators
	Optical engineers	Overnight coach	Coach drivers
	Cellular technicians		
Polio vaccine	Chemists	Iron lung	Manufacturers
	Lab technicians		Attendants
	Pharmacists		
Internet	Programmers	Shopping malls	Retail salespersons
	Network operators	Libraries	Librarians
	Optical goods workers	Reference books	Encyclopedia salespersons
	Webmasters		

Resources no longer needed to feed the nation have been freed to meet other consumer demands. Over the decades, workers no longer required in agriculture moved to the cities, where they became available to produce other goods and services. They started out in foundries, meat-packing plants, and loading docks in the early days of the Industrial Age. Their grandsons and granddaughters, living in an economy refashioned by creative destruction into the Information Age, are less likely to work in those jobs. They are making computers, movies, and financial deci-

Table 2 The Churn: Recycling America's Labor

Job Destruction	Now (2002)	Then	Year
Railroad employees	111,000	2,076,000	1920
Carriage and harness makers	*	109,000	1900
Telegraph operators	*	75,000	1920
Boilermakers	*	74,000	1920
Milliners	*	100,000	1910
Cobblers	*	102,000	1900
Blacksmiths	*	238,000	1910
Watchmakers	*	101,000	1920
Switchboard (telephone) operators	119,000	421,000	1970
Farm workers	716,000	11,533,000	1910
Secretaries	2,302,000	3,871,000	1980
Metal & plastic working machine operators	286,000	715,000	1980
Optometrists	33,000	43,000	1998

Job Creation	Now (2002)	Then	Year
Airplane pilots and mechanics	255,000	0	1900
Auto mechanics	867,000	0	1900
Engineers	2,028,000	38,000	1900
Medical technicians	1,879,000	0	1910
Truck, bus, and taxi drivers	4,171,000	0	1900
Electricians	882,000	*	1900
Professional athletes	95,000	*	1920
Computer programmers/ operators/scientists	2,648,000	160,613	1970
Actors and directors	155,000	34,643	1970
Editors and reporters	280,000	150,715	1970
Medical scientists	89,000	3,589	1970
Dietitians	74,000	42,349	1970
Special education teachers	374,000	1,563	1970
Physicians	825,000	295,803	1970
Pharmacists	231,000	114,590	1970
Authors	139,000	26,677	1970
TV, stereo, and appliance salespersons	309,000	111,842	1970
Webmasters	500,000	0	1990

* Fewer than 5,000.

sions and providing a modern economy's myriad other goods and services (Table 2).

Over the past two centuries, the Western nations that embraced capitalism have achieved tremendous economic progress as new industries supplanted old ones. Even with the higher living standards, however, the constant flux of free enterprise is not always welcome. The disruption of lost jobs and shuttered businesses is immediate, while the payoff from creative destruction comes mainly in the long term. As a result, societies will always be tempted to block the process of creative destruction, implementing policies to resist economic change.

Attempts to save jobs almost always backfire. Instead of going out of business, inefficient producers hang on, at a high cost to consumers or taxpayers. The tinkering short-circuits market signals that shift resources to emerging industries. It saps the incentives to introduce new products and production methods, leading to stagnation, layoffs, and bankruptcies. The ironic point of Schumpeter's iconic phrase is this: societies that try to reap the gain of creative destruction without the pain find themselves enduring the pain but not the gain.

About the Authors

W. Michael Cox is senior vice president and chief economist at the Federal Reserve Bank of Dallas. Richard Alm is an economics writer at the Dallas Fed. They are coauthors of *Myths of Rich and Poor* (1999).

Further Reading

Cox, W. Michael, and Richard Alm. "The Churn: The Paradox of Progress." Federal Reserve Bank of Dallas, annual report, 1992.

Davis, Stevens J., John Haltwanger, and Scott Schuh. *Gross Job Creation, Gross Job Destruction.* Cambridge: MIT Press, 1996.

Schumpeter, Joseph A. *Business Cycles: A Theoretical, Historical, and Statistical Analysis of the Capitalist Process.* New York: McGraw-Hill, 1939.

———. *Capitalism, Socialism, and Democracy.* 3d ed. 1942. New York: Harper and Brothers, 1950.

———. *The Theory of Economic Development: An Inquiry into Profits, Capital, Credit, Interest, and the Business Cycle.* Cambridge: Harvard University Press, 1936.

Crime

David D. Friedman

Economists approach the analysis of crime with one simple assumption—that criminals are rational. A mugger is a mugger for the same reason I am an economist—because it is the most attractive alternative available to him. The decision to commit a crime, like any other economic decision, can be analyzed as a choice among alternative combinations of costs and benefits.

Consider, as a simple example, a point that sometimes comes up in discussions of gun control. Opponents of private ownership of handguns argue that, in violent contests between criminals and victims, the criminals usually win. A professional criminal, after all, has far more reason to learn how to use a gun than a random potential victim.

The argument is probably true, but the conclusion—that permitting both criminals and victims to have guns will help the criminals—does not follow. To see why, imagine that the result of legal handgun ownership is that one little old lady in ten chooses to carry a pistol in her purse. Further suppose that, of those who do, only one in ten, if mugged, succeeds in killing the mugger; the other nine miss, drop the gun, or shoot themselves in the foot.

On average, the muggers are winning. But also on average, each one hundred muggings of little old ladies produce one dead mugger. Very few little old ladies carry enough money to be worth one chance in a hundred of being killed. Economic theory suggests that the number of muggings will decrease—not because the muggers have all been killed, but because some of them have chosen to switch to safer professions.

If the idea that muggers are rational profit maximizers seems implausible, consider who gets mugged. If a mugger's objective is to express machismo, to prove what a he-man he is, there is very little point in mugging little old ladies. If the objective is to get money at as low a cost as possible, there is much to be said for picking the most defenseless victims they can find. In the real world, little old ladies get mugged a lot more often than football players do. Following out this line of argument, John Lott and David Mustard, in a controversial article, found that laws making it easier to get permission to legally carry a concealed firearm tended to reduce crime rates.

This is one example of a very general implication of the economic analysis of conflict. To stop someone from doing something that injures you, whether robbing your house or polluting your air, it is not necessary to make it impossible for him to do it—merely unprofitable.

Economic analysis can also be used to help understand the nature of organized crime. Newspapers, prosecutors, and the FBI often make organized crime sound almost like General Motors or IBM—a hierarchical organization with a few kingpins controlling thousands of subordinates. What we know about the economics of organizations makes this an unlikely description of real criminal organizations. One major limitation on the size of firms is the problem of control. The more layers of hierarchy there are between the president and the factory worker, the harder it is for management to monitor and control the workers. That is one reason that small firms often are more successful than large ones.

We would expect this problem to be especially severe in criminal markets. Legitimate businesses can and do make extensive use of memos, reports, job evaluations, and the like to pass information from one layer of the hierarchy to another. But the very information that a criminal uses to keep track of what his employees are doing can also be used by a district attorney to keep track of what the criminal is doing. What economists call "informational diseconomies of scale" are therefore a particularly serious problem in criminal firms, implying that such firms should, on average, tend to be smaller, not larger, than firms in other markets.

Criminal enterprises obviously are more difficult to study than ordinary ones. The work that has been done, however, such as that of Peter Reuter and Jonathan B. Rubinstein, seems to confirm what theory suggests. Criminal firms seem to be relatively small and the organization of criminal industries relatively decentralized—precisely the opposite of the pattern described in novels, movies, and the popular press. It may well be that "organized crime" is not so much a corporation as a sort of chamber of commerce for the criminal market—a network of individuals and small firms that routinely do business with each other and occasionally cooperate in their mutual interest.

Economic analysis can also be used to predict the effectiveness of law enforcement measures. Consider the current "War on Drugs." From an economic standpoint, its objective is to reduce the supply of illegal drugs, thus raising their prices and reducing the amount people wish to consume. One enforcement strategy is to pressure countries such as Colombia to prevent the production of coca, the raw material used to make cocaine.

Such a strategy, if successful, would shift coca production to whatever country is next best at producing it; since coca can be grown in many different places, this shift is not likely to result in a very large increase in cost. Published estimates suggest that the cost of producing drugs abroad and transporting them to the United States represents only about 1 percent of their street price. So, even if we succeed in doubling the cost of coca—which seems unlikely, given experience with elasticity of supply of other crops—the result would be only about a 1 percent increase in the price of cocaine and a correspondingly small decrease in the amount consumed. Thus, economic analysis suggests that pressuring other countries not to produce drugs is probably not a very effective way of reducing their use.

One interesting issue in the economic analysis of crime is the question of which legal rules are economically efficient. Loosely speaking, which rules maximize the total size of the economic pie, the degree to which people get what they want? This is relevant both to broad issues such as whether theft should be illegal and to more detailed questions, such as how to calculate the optimal punishment for a particular crime.

Consider the question of laws against theft. At first glance, it might seem that, however immoral theft may be, it is not inefficient. If I steal ten dollars from you, I am ten dollars richer and you are ten dollars poorer, so the total wealth of society is unchanged. Thus, if we judge laws solely on grounds of economic efficiency, it seems that there is no reason to make theft illegal.

That *seems* obvious, but it is wrong. Opportunities to make money by stealing, like opportunities to make money in other ways, attract economic resources. If stealing is more profitable than washing dishes or waiting on tables, workers will be attracted out of those activities and into theft. As the number of thieves increases, the returns from theft fall, both because everything easy to steal has already been stolen and because victims defend themselves against the increased level of theft by installing locks, bars, burglar alarms, and guard dogs. The process stops only when the next person who is considering becoming a thief concludes that he will be just about as well off continuing to wash dishes—that the gains from becoming a thief are about equal to the costs.

The thief who is just on the margin of being a thief pays, with his time and effort, the price of what he steals. Thus, the victim's loss is a net social loss—the thief has no equal gain to balance it. So the existence of theft makes society as a whole poorer, not because money has been transferred from one person to another, but because productive resources have been diverted out of the business of producing and into the business of stealing.

A full analysis of the cost of theft would be more complicated than this sketch, and the social cost of theft would no longer be exactly equal to the amount stolen. It would be less to the extent that people who are particularly skillful at theft earn more in that profession than they could in any other, giving them a net gain to partly balance the loss to their victims. It would be higher to the extent that theft results in additional costs, such as the cost of defensive precautions taken by potential victims. The central conclusion would, however, remain—that we will, on net, be better off if theft is illegal.

This conclusion must be qualified by the observation that, to reduce theft, we must spend resources on catching and punishing thieves. Theft is inefficient—but spending a hundred dollars to prevent a ten-dollar theft is still more inefficient. Reducing theft to zero would almost certainly cost more than it would be worth. What we want, from the standpoint of economic efficiency, is the optimal level of theft. We want to increase our expenditures on law enforcement only as long as one more dollar spent catching and punishing thieves reduces the net cost of theft by more than a dollar. Beyond that point, additional reductions in theft cost more than they are worth.

This raises a number of issues, both empirical and theoretical. The empirical issues involve an ongoing dispute about whether punishment deters crime and, if so, by how much. While economic theory predicts that there should be some deterrent effect, it does not tell us how large it should be. Isaac Ehrlich, in a widely quoted (and extensively criticized) study of the deterrent effect of capital punishment, concluded that each execution deters several murders. Other researchers have gotten very different results.

One interesting theoretical point is the question of how to choose the best combination of probability of apprehension and amount of punishment. One could imagine punishing theft by catching half the thieves and fining them a hundred dollars each, by catching a quarter and fining them two hundred each, or by catching one thief in a hundred and hanging him. How do you decide which alternative is best?

At first glance, it might seem efficient always to impose the highest possible punishment. The worse the punishment, the fewer criminals you have to catch in order to maintain a given level of deterrence—and catching criminals is costly. One reason this is wrong is that punishing criminals is also costly. A low punishment can take the form of a fine; what the criminal loses the court gains, so the net cost of the punishment is zero. Criminals generally cannot pay large fines, so large punishments take the form of imprisonment or execution, which is less efficient—nobody gets what the criminal loses and someone has to pay for the jail.

A second reason we do not want maximum punishments for all offenses is that we want to give criminals an incentive to limit their crimes. If the punishments for armed robbery and murder are the same, then the robber who is caught in the act has an incentive to kill the witness. He may get away, and, at worst, they can hang him only once.

One final interesting question is why we have criminal law at all. In our legal system, some offenses are called civil and are prosecuted by the victim, while others are called criminal and are prosecuted by the state. Why not have a pure civil system, in which robbery would be treated like trespass or breach of contract, with the victim suing the robber?

Such institutions have existed in some past societies. In fact, our present system of having the state hire professionals to pursue criminals is actually a relatively recent development in the Anglo-American legal tradition, dating back only about two hundred years. Several writers, starting with Gary Becker and George Stigler, have suggested that a movement toward a pure civil system would be desirable, whereas others, most notably William Landes and Richard Posner, have argued for the efficiency of the present division between civil and criminal law (see also LAW AND ECONOMICS).

About the Author

David D. Friedman is a professor of law and economics at Santa Clara University. His most recent book is *Law's Order: What Economics Has to Do with Law and Why It Matters.* His Web site is www.daviddfriedman.com.

Further Reading

Ayres, Ian, and John J. Donohue III. "Shooting Down the 'More Guns, Less Crime' Hypothesis." *Stanford Law Review* 55 (2003): 1193. Online at: http://islandia.law.yale.edu/ayers/Ayres_Donohue_article.pdf.

Becker, Gary S. "Crime and Punishment: An Economic Approach." *Journal of Political Economy* 76 (1968): 169–217.

Becker, Gary S., and George J. Stigler. "Law Enforcement, Malfeasance, and Compensation of Enforcers." *Journal of Legal Studies* 3 (1974): 1–18.

Benson, Bruce. *The Enterprise of Law: Justice Without the State.* San Francisco: Pacific Research Institute for Public Policy, 1990.

Ehrlich, Isaac. "The Deterrent Effect of Criminal Law Enforcement." *Journal of Legal Studies* 1 (1972): 259–276.

Friedman, David. "Efficient Institutions for the Private Enforcement of Law." *Journal of Legal Studies* 13 (1984): 379–397. Online at: http://www.daviddfriedman.com/Academic/Efficient_Inst_For_Priv_Enf/Private_Enforcement.html.

———. *Law's Order: What Economics Has to Do with Law and Why It Matters.* Princeton: Princeton University Press, 2000. Available online at: http://www.daviddfriedman.com/laws_order/index.shtml.

———. "Private Creation and Enforcement of Law—a Historical Case." *Journal of Legal Studies* 8 (1979): 399–415. Online at: http://www.daviddfriedman.com/Academic/Iceland/Iceland.html.

Landes, William M., and Richard A. Posner. "The Private Enforcement of Law." *Journal of Legal Studies* 4 (1975): 1–46.

Lott, John, and David Mustard. "Crime, Deterrence, and Right-to-Carry Concealed Handguns." 1997. Abstract online at http://papers.ssrn.com/sol3/papers.cfm?abstract_id=10129.

Reuter, Peter, and Jonathan B. Rubinstein. "Fact, Fancy, and Organized Crime." *Public Interest* 53 (Fall 1978): 45–67.

Defense

Benjamin Zycher

National defense is in many ways a public, or "collective," good, which means two things. First, consumption of the good by one person does not reduce the amount available for others to consume. Thus, all people in a nation must "consume" the same amount of national defense (the defense policies implemented by the government), although different people may value that common defense policy differently. Second, the benefits that a given person derives from the provision of a collective good do not depend on that individual's contribution to funding it. Everyone benefits, including those who pay little or no taxes.

To say that everyone gains from defense is not to say that everyone gains from government expenditures that are labeled "defense." There is no necessary connection between defense expenditures and actual improvements in protection from foreign threats. Some defense expenditures may not contribute to such security at all; some expenditures may contribute a great deal; and some expenditures may, by stirring up hornets' nests, actually reduce security.

National defense, like other public goods, has an important "free-rider" problem. That is, because people benefit whether or not they contribute toward defense, each person has an incentive to wait for others to provide the collective defense good, and thus hopes to get a "free ride." Also, because a free rider's consumption does not reduce the amount of defense available for others to consume, even those who pay have little incentive to prevent free riding by others.

As a result of such free riding, individuals acting privately to provide national defense services would produce too little from the standpoint of society as a whole. Each person would provide defense until the incremental benefits to him equaled the incremental costs. But for society as a whole—that is, for all individuals collectively—the incremental benefits would exceed the incremental costs, precisely because once an individual provides some of the collective good, all people benefit from it and no one can be excluded. This free-rider behavior yields one of the important traditional arguments for government: By imposing taxes on all individuals and then providing collective goods, government, in principle, can eliminate free-rider behavior and produce the "correct" amount of national defense and other collective goods.

How Can Government Be Induced to Provide the Optimal Amount of National Defense?

The traditional rationale for government taxation and spending on national defense is incomplete. It states that government *can* eliminate free-rider behavior—that is, achieve "efficiency" in the allocation of resources—but is silent on whether government has enough incentive to do so. Just as economists have shown that individuals acting alone have incentives to provide too few collective goods, public choice economists (see PUBLIC CHOICE) have shown that a democratic government acting under a majority decision rule also has an incentive to provide too few collective goods. The reason, in brief, is that the political majority can impose taxes on all citizens—or disproportionate taxes on the political minority—and then reduce spending on collective goods, such as national defense, while increasing spending on private (i.e. non-collective) goods that benefit the majority (or members of the majority coalition) but not the minority. Such transfer programs as Social Security and agricultural subsidies are examples of government spending on private goods.

If, however, the collective goods that government provides can be transformed into private ones—that is, if provision of collective goods yields ancillary benefits that some majority coalition of voters views as particularly beneficial to them—then the problem of governmental underprovision of collective goods can be at least partially offset. National defense spending does yield such ancillary benefits to special interests; defense contractors, defense-related workers, and communities with military bases are examples. The strong resistance from Congress that Defense Department officials encounter when they wish to close military bases—a resistance partly circumvented in recent years through the Base Realignment and Closing (BRAC) Commission process—illustrates the private benefits derived from such defense spending. Alternatively, defense spending can be bundled with such non-defense transfer programs as agricultural subsidies or water projects to induce majorities to fund sufficient amounts of such collective goods as defense.

Such interest groups benefiting from defense spending are located in a majority of congressional districts and in a majority of states. Their presence, therefore, offsets the bias toward too little defense spending under democratic institutions. Ironically, the geographic (and political) dispersion of military bases, defense contracts, and other seemingly "wasteful" dimensions of defense spending—not to mention transfer programs seemingly unrelated to defense—could make government budgeting more efficient rather than less.

Optimal Taxation When Government Provides National Defense

The traditional theory of optimal taxation (see TAXATION) posits that the kinds of taxes imposed and the rates levied should minimize economic distortions; that is, they should interfere as little as possible with the choices taxpayers make in the private sector. This traditional theory assumes implicitly that the size and composition of the government budget are independent of the kinds and magnitudes of the taxes imposed—a highly unrealistic assumption. If government programs benefit one group of voters but are financed by another, the beneficiaries will demand larger programs than would be the case if they were required to bear the tax burden themselves. For such collective goods as defense, political processes are more likely to yield the optimal amount of spending if each individual pays taxes proportional to the individual benefits derived from the defense services provided.

Some defense programs protect against the threat that foreign aggressors will kill and injure Americans or confiscate or destroy American property. Such programs defend individual liberty, political freedom, and the domestic political system against foreign threats. In addition, the U.S. defense budget is used to support many foreign policy objectives and so is dedicated, in part, to protecting foreigners and foreign-owned assets. The post–World War II commitment to NATO—however anomalous it has become with the collapse of the Soviet Union—is the most obvious example.

Nonetheless, the protection of domestic wealth from confiscation or destruction by foreigners is a large part of the service provided by national defense policy, particularly in an era characterized by important threats from international terrorists. Accordingly, a substantial part of the demand for national defense reasonably can be attributed to those U.S. residents owning assets threatened by foreign aggressors; lives (human capital) are foremost among them. Some kinds of assets are more vulnerable (or more threatened) than others: American-owned assets located overseas may be more vulnerable than identical ones in the United States, and ocean tankers that can be moved may be more vulnerable to confiscation but less vulnerable to destruction than office buildings. In any event, a rough surrogate for individual valuation of defense services may be individual wealth; accordingly, an important component of a tax system designed to yield appropriate democratic choices on the size of the defense sector is a tax on wealth. Taxes on income or consumption may provide good approximations for such a tax. Similarly, individual preferences for political freedom, for protection of the political system, and for foreign policy maneuverings are likely to be correlated positively with individual wealth. Again, taxes on wealth, income, or consumption may be appropriate, particularly if the revenues yielded by such tax instruments are earmarked for defense purposes.

International Defense Alliances

Nations facing a common threat often pool their defense efforts in alliances such as NATO. While NATO is a formal alliance, nations also can cooperate implicitly in informal alliances, sharing defense responsibilities and burdens without the trappings of an international organization. Indeed, in principle, little communication between such informal partners is necessary; each nation can undertake given defense activities knowing that the other(s) will pursue complementary activities in response. Whatever the nature of the alliance, the defense (or other) efforts aimed at common goals are, again, a collective good. Thus, nations, like individuals, face the free-rider problem and the resulting underprovision of defense. Because larger nations like the United States are likely to value the collective defense effort more highly than smaller ones like Belgium, small nations may attempt to exploit large ones by free riding on the larger countries' defense efforts. Thus, members of alliances often bargain over "burden sharing," or the specific efforts each is to make.

One problem with achieving an equitable and efficient sharing of burdens is the determination of the appropriate allocation of burdens in principle. Even if nations agree that contributions should be "proportional," the obvious question arises: proportional to what? Population, GDP, per capita GDP, and physical proximity to the perceived threat are all plausible candidates. Moreover, even if nations agree on precisely what efforts should be proportional to, alternative measures of effort can yield very different answers. One reasonable measure is military spending; another is the contribution of physical defense assets (troops, equipment, etc.). Contributions of physical assets and manpower may not be proportional to spending because of differences in valuations or pricing, differences in efficiency, and a host of other factors. For example, U.S. defense spending during the mid-1980s (while the perceived Soviet threat was substantial) was roughly 60 percent of the NATO total, while the United States provided about 46 percent of the main battle tanks and about 40 percent of the division-equivalent firepower (a measure of military effectiveness). The German Federal Republic (West Germany) provided about 8 percent of NATO spend-

ing, but about 17 percent of the main battle tanks and 13 percent of division-equivalent firepower. At the same time, the U.S. naval contribution was vastly disproportionate. Such indexes are crude, but they illustrate the difficulty of measuring relative contributions.

No definition of "fairness" in burden sharing is obviously correct, and this ambiguity inexorably creates tensions within alliances. Furthermore, citizens of one nation may value the collective defense effort less or more than do citizens of another nation, and they also may perceive the seriousness of the threat differently. That was the case in NATO for many years, as the United States and West Germany perceived a greater threat than did, say, Greece. In the counterterrorism context, U.S. contributions appear vastly disproportionate; but other nations may perceive a smaller threat and/or may believe that U.S. policy will not reduce the threat in the long run.

Dependence Versus "Vulnerability" in Foreign Defense Procurement

Modern military forces combine many kinds of manpower and physical matériel. Inevitably, some of these inputs, such as rare metals and electronic components, are purchased from foreigners because they are cheaper abroad than at home. Some worry that foreign procurement makes the United States vulnerable to a cutoff of foreign-supplied items; they fear that cuts in foreign supplies may exceed in both number and variety the potential supply reductions from domestic firms.

This view is misguided. Suppose that some defense good is purchased from foreign suppliers and that this arrangement is subject to easy but unpredictable cutoffs. Suppose, also, that such interruptions are easy to insure against, with stockpiles, alternative suppliers in other parts of the world, or excess production capacity in the United States. If so, foreign dependence does not yield vulnerability. The central question, therefore, is not the source of the defense goods but the ease with which interruptions in supply—whether foreign or domestic—can be insured against or hedged. If domestic dependence is more difficult to insure against than foreign dependence, then, ironically, domestic dependence may yield greater vulnerability.

What could make insurance more difficult for domestic purchases than for foreign ones? One possibility is the expectation of price controls during future conflicts. Producers of defense-related goods know that the prices of such goods can rise dramatically when a government at war or preparing for war increases its purchases of those goods. These price increases serve an important function: they reward domestic producers for stockpiling goods in advance, for maintaining excess production capacity, and for increasing production quickly. But domestic producers also know that governments attempting to constrain budget increases and reacting to political pressures on "war profiteering" and the like often impose explicit or implicit price controls on just such goods. The imposition of price controls on petroleum products during some past wars is but one example. Taking anticipated price controls into account, domestic producers would not invest as much in stockpiles or excess production capacity as is optimal for society. Nor are they likely to increase production as much when price controls are imposed. But governments for the most part cannot impose price controls on foreign producers. On net, therefore, foreign producers actually may have stronger incentives to stockpile and to maintain excess production capacity. The "vulnerability" issue is thus far more complex than the common foreign/domestic dependence view suggests.

Efficient Delivery of Defense Services
With the collapse of most systems of state socialism, the U.S. Department of Defense (DoD) may be the largest centrally planned economy in the world. And there is little reason to believe that central planning works better in the United States than elsewhere.

Central planning in the DoD creates the two problems common to all centrally planned systems. First, the decision makers who design weaponry or who specify the characteristics and performance features of equipment designed by contractors have relatively weak incentives to respond to their consumers' preferences. These "consumers" are the soldiers in the foxholes, the airmen facing dogfights and antiaircraft fire, and so forth. A good proxy for these ultimate consumers may be the theater commanders charged with winning battles. But few institutional incentives at the DoD systematically align the preferences of the decision makers with the preferences of even the theater commanders. The absence of a profit motive weakens incentives at the DoD to shape decisions according to the perceived preferences of users, and the pressures from Congress, while difficult to describe in simple terms, do not unambiguously move DoD decision making in that direction. The relative absence of competition in the provision of defense services weakens these incentives further.

As a result, the DoD and the individual armed services often promote weapons designs with dubious combat features and effectiveness. Consider, for example, the U.S. Air Force A-10 Warthog aircraft: the Warthog, designed for the support of U.S. Army and Marine Corps ground operations, has performed well in that mission. Yet the Air Force for years has tried to eliminate funding for the A-10 pre-

cisely because it supports the other services, and thus yields few bureaucratic benefits for the Air Force. The Air Force has preferred to use F-16s and other more glamorous aircraft for ground support, although their great speed may make these planes less suitable for such missions. One way to get weapons and other equipment that conform more to the demands of users is to give the users a larger voice or a direct veto in design decisions. This overall incentive effect should not be exaggerated—certainly the DoD civilian leadership has personal, professional, and political incentives to win conflicts and to minimize casualties—but centralized planning causes important adverse effects.

The absence of a profit motive and of an individual or group with a claim to the economic benefits from cost efficiencies weakens the DoD's incentive to minimize costs in the pursuit of given objectives. Contracts for the design and production of weaponry often are written on a cost-plus basis, under which the contractor receives a payment from the government equal to (approved) costs plus some predetermined "profit." This weakens incentives to minimize costs. On the other hand, if the contractor simply receives a fixed price for the delivery of specified defense goods, incentives to minimize costs are strengthened, but the risks of increases in the prices of inputs, unforeseen contingencies, and the like are borne by the contractor, which may not yield an efficient allocation of risk bearing.

The DoD's own incentives for efficient operations are weak relative to those in the private sector. Because the military services have sharply defined tasks with limited overlap, each service is, in effect, a "monopolist" in its defined missions. The Army, for example, is proscribed from flying fixed-wing aircraft in combat missions, thus giving the Air Force greater monopoly power in the provision of close air support for ground operations (although Army helicopter operations are an obvious substitute for many such missions). Because each service is likely to have better information than Congress about the minimum cost of providing given defense services, the services' efforts to maximize their budgets or their discretionary budgets can make national defense more costly than necessary. An important way to reduce these costs would be to have the services compete to provide various defense operations. The Army and Marine Corps could be required to compete on a much broader scale in the production of ground combat operations. The Army and the Air Force could compete in the provision of close air support for ground combat. The U.S. Navy could compete on a much broader scale with the U.S. Coast Guard in terms of sea operations, perhaps, in particular, in the context of counterterrorism efforts. Such budget competition, similar in many respects to competition in the private sector, would likely reduce the cost of defense programs.

**The Defense Establishment's
Threat to the Polity**
An armed defense establishment always poses some level of threat to the civilian government and to people's rights and liberties. The Founding Fathers recognized this threat clearly; in August 1789, when Congress was considering the Bill of Rights, Congressman Elbridge Gerry wrote, "What, sir, is the use of militia? It is to prevent the establishment of a standing army, the bane of liberty." That is why the Constitution empowers Congress "to provide and maintain a Navy," but, in contrast, only "to raise and support Armies." The founders recognized that the threat is posed mainly by a standing army, not by a permanent navy. Thus, two institutional arrangements have evolved from the earliest days of the American Republic. First, the ground forces are divided into the army, the Marine Corps, and the states' national guards; this means that any officers planning a coup must confront the potential opposition posed by the other ground combat services. Second, the Founding Fathers recognized from their own experience that an armed citizenry is better able to resist efforts of governments—of centralized military establishments—to impose autocracy or dictatorship. Accordingly, they specified the "right of the people to keep and bear arms" in the Second Amendment to the Constitution. Unlike the First Amendment, which places constraints only on the Congress, the Second Amendment decrees that the right to keep and bear arms "shall not be infringed."

Conclusion
National defense, while not a separate field of study within economics, raises a vast range of economic issues, and like other areas of public policy, is suitable for the prescriptions yielded by economic analysis.

About the Author
Benjamin Zycher is a senior fellow at the Manhattan Institute for Policy Research and was previously a senior economist with the RAND Corporation.

Further Reading

Brennan, Geoffrey, and James M. Buchanan. *The Power to Tax: Analytical Foundations of a Fiscal Constitution.* Indianapolis: Liberty Fund, 2000.
Cooper, Charles A., and Benjamin Zycher. "Perceptions of NATO Burden-Sharing." RAND Corporation paper no. R-3750-FF/RC, June 1989.
Enthoven, Alain C., and Wayne K. Smith. *How Much Is Enough? Shaping the Defense Program, 1961–1969.* New York: Harper and Row, 1971.
Halbrook, Stephen P. *That Every Man Be Armed: The Evolution of a Constitutional Right.* Albuquerque: University of New Mexico Press, 1984.
Hitch, Charles J., and Roland N. McKean. *The Economics of Defense in the Nuclear Age.* Cambridge: Harvard University Press, 1960.
LaPierre, Wayne. *Guns, Crime, and Freedom.* Washington, D.C.: Regnery, 1994.
Lott, John R. *The Bias Against Guns.* Washington, D.C.: Regnery, 2003.
Malcolm, Joyce Lee. *To Keep and Bear Arms: The Origins of an Anglo-American Right.* Cambridge: Harvard University Press, 1994.
Stockfisch, Jack A. *Plowshares into Swords: Managing the American Defense Establishment.* New York: Mason and Lipscomb, 1973.
Thompson, Earl A. "Taxation and National Defense." *Journal of Political Economy* 82, no. 4 (1974): 755–782.
Wolf, Charles Jr., and Benjamin Zycher. "European Military Prospects, Economic Constraints, and the Rapid Reaction Force." RAND Corporation paper no. MR-1416-OSD/SRF, 2001.
Zycher, Benjamin. "A Preliminary Benefit/Cost Framework for Counterterrorism Public Expenditures." RAND Corporation paper no. MR-1693-RC, 2003.
Zycher, Benjamin, Kenneth A. Solomon, and Loren Yager. "An 'Adequate Insurance' Approach to Critical Dependencies of the Department of Defense." RAND Corporation paper no. R-3880-DARPA, 1991.

Demand

David R. Henderson

One of the most important building blocks of economic analysis is the concept of demand. When economists refer to demand, they usually have in mind not just a single quantity demanded, but a demand curve, which traces the quantity of a good or service that is demanded at successively different prices.

The most famous law in economics, and the one economists are most sure of, is the law of demand. On this law is built almost the whole edifice of economics. The law of demand states that when the price of a good rises, the amount demanded falls, and when the price falls, the amount demanded rises.

Some of the modern evidence supporting the law of demand is from econometric studies which show that, all other things being equal, when the price of a good rises, the amount of it demanded decreases. How do we know that there are no instances in which the amount demanded rises and the price rises? A few instances have been cited, but most have an explanation that takes into account something other than price. Nobel laureate George Stigler responded years ago that if any economist found a true counterexample, he would be "assured of immortality, professionally speaking, and rapid promotion" (Stigler 1966, p. 24). And because, wrote Stigler, most economists would like either reward, the fact that no one has come up with an exception to the law of demand shows how rare the exceptions must be. But the reality is that if an economist reported an instance in which consumption of a good rose as its price rose, other economists would assume that some factor other than price caused the increase in demand.

The main reason economists believe so strongly in the law of demand is that it is so plausible, even to noneconomists. Indeed, the law of demand is ingrained in our way of thinking about everyday things. Shoppers buy more strawberries when they are in season and the price is low. This is evidence for the law of demand: only at the lower, in-season price are consumers willing to buy the higher amount available. Similarly, when people learn that frost will strike the orange groves in Florida, they know that the price of orange juice will rise. The price rises in order to reduce the amount demanded to the smaller amount available because of the frost. This is the law of demand. We see the same point every day in countless ways. No one thinks, for example, that the way to sell a house that has been languishing on the market is to raise the asking price. Again, this shows an implicit awareness of the law of demand: the number of potential buyers for any given house varies inversely with the asking price.

Indeed, the law of demand is so ingrained in our way of thinking that it is even part of our language. Think of what we mean by the term "on sale." We do not mean that the seller raised the price. We mean that he or she lowered it in order to increase the amount of goods demanded. Again, the law of demand.

Economists, as is their wont, have struggled to think of exceptions to the law of demand. Marketers have found them. One of the best examples involves a new car wax, which, when it was introduced, faced strong resistance until its price was raised from $.69 to $1.69. The reason, according to economist Thomas Nagle, was that buyers could not judge the wax's quality before purchasing it. Because the quality of this particular product was so important—a bad product could ruin a car's finish—consumers "played it safe by avoiding cheap products that they believed were more likely to be inferior" (Nagle 1987, p. 67).

Many noneconomists are skeptical of the law of de-

mand. A standard example they give of a good whose quantity demanded will not fall when the price increases is water. How, they ask, can people reduce their use of water? But those who come up with that example think of drinking water or household consumption as the only possible uses. Even here, there is room to reduce consumption when the price of water rises. Households can do larger loads of laundry or shower quickly instead of bathe, for example. The main users of water, however, are agriculture and industry. Farmers and manufacturers can substantially alter the amount of water used in production. Farmers, for example, can do so by changing crops or by changing irrigation methods for given crops.

What the skeptics may have in mind is not that people would not cut back their purchases at all when the price of a good increases, but that they might cut back only a little. Economists have considered this thoroughly and have developed a measure of the degree of cutback, which they call the "elasticity of demand." The elasticity of demand is the percentage change in quantity demanded divided by the percentage change in price. The greater the absolute value of this ratio, the greater is the elasticity of demand. When there is a close substitute for one firm's brand, for example, a small percentage increase in that firm's price may lead to a large percentage cut in the amount of the firm's good demanded. In such a case, economists say that the demand for the good is highly elastic. On the other hand, when there are few good substitutes for a firm's product, the firm might be able to raise its price substantially with only a small decrease in the quantity demanded resulting. In such a case, demand is said to be highly inelastic.

Interestingly, though, if a firm is in a position whereby it can increase a price substantially and reduce sales only a little, and if its owners want to maximize profits, the firm is well advised to raise the price until it reaches a portion of the demand curve where demand is elastic. Otherwise, the firm is forsaking an increase in revenue that it could have had with no increase in costs. One important implication of this fact is that the elasticity of demand in a market is a negative test for whether the firms are acting together as a monopoly. If, at the existing price, the elasticity of the market demand for the good is less than one, that is, if the demand is inelastic, then the firms are not acting monopolistically. If the elasticity of demand exceeds one—that is, if the demand is elastic—then we do not know whether they are acting monopolistically or not.

It is not just price that affects the quantity demanded. Income affects it too. As real income rises, people buy more of some goods (which economists call "normal goods") and less of others (called "inferior goods"). Urban mass transit and railroad transportation are classic examples of inferior goods. That is why the usage of both of these modes of travel declined so dramatically as postwar incomes were rising and more people could afford automobiles. Environmental quality is a normal good, and that is a major reason why Americans have become more concerned about the environment in recent decades.

Another influence on demand is the price of substitutes. When the price of Toyota Camrys rises, all else being equal, the quantity of Camrys demanded falls and the demand for Nissan Maximas, a substitute, rises. Also important is the price of complements, or goods that are used together. When the price of gasoline rises, the demand for cars falls.

About the Author

David R. Henderson is the editor of this encyclopedia. He is a research fellow with Stanford University's Hoover Institution and an associate professor of economics at the Naval Postgraduate School in Monterey, California. He was formerly a senior economist with President Ronald Reagan's Council of Economic Advisers.

Further Reading

Nagle, Thomas T. *The Strategy and Tactics of Pricing: A Guide to Profitable Decision Making.* Englewood Cliffs, N.J.: Prentice Hall, 1987.
Stigler, George J. *The Theory of Price.* 3d ed. New York: Macmillan, 1966.

Disaster and Recovery

Jack Hirshleifer

Defeated in battle and ravaged by bombing in the course of World War II, Germany and Japan nevertheless made postwar recoveries that startled the world. Within ten years these nations were once again considerable economic powers. A decade later, each had not only regained prosperity but had also economically overtaken, in important respects, some of the war's victors.

The surprising swiftness of recovery from disaster was also noted in previous eras. John Stuart Mill commented on

what has so often excited wonder, the great rapidity with which countries recover from a state of devastation; the disappearance, in a short time, of all traces of the mischiefs done by earthquakes, floods, hurricanes, and the ravages of war. An enemy lays waste a country by fire and sword, and destroys or carries away nearly all the movea-

ble wealth existing in it: all the inhabitants are ruined, and yet in a few years after, everything is much as it was before. (Mill 1896, book 1, chap. 5, para. I.5.19)

Still, successful recovery is by no means universal. The ancient Cretan civilization may or may not have been destroyed by earthquake, and the Mayan civilization by disease, but neither recovered. Most famously, of course, the centuries-long Dark Ages followed the fall of Rome.

Sociologists, psychologists, historians, and policy planners have extensively studied the nature, sources, and consequences of disaster and recovery, but the professional economic literature is distressingly sparse. As a telling example, the four thick volumes of *The New Palgrave: A Dictionary of Economics* (1987) omit these topics entirely. The words "disaster" and "recovery" do not even appear in the index of that encyclopedic work. Yet disasters are natural economic experiments; they parallel the tests to destruction from which engineers and physicists learn about the strength of materials and machines. Much light would be thrown on the normal everyday economy if we understood behavior under conditions of great stress.

The Historical Record

Although everyday small-scale tragedies like auto accidents and disabling illnesses are disastrous enough for those personally involved, our concern here is with events of larger magnitude. It is useful to distinguish between community-wide (middle-scale) calamities such as tornadoes, floods, or bombing raids, and society-wide (large-scale) catastrophes associated with widespread famine, destructive social revolution, or defeat and subjugation after total war. In community-wide disasters the fabric of the larger social order provides a safety net, whereas society-wide catastrophes threaten the very fabric itself. The former may involve hundreds or thousands of deaths; the latter, hundreds of thousands or millions. (As a special case, hyperinflations and great business depressions are society-wide events that do not directly generate massive casualties and yet still have calamitous consequences.)

Middle-scale community-wide disasters are relatively frequent events, making empirical generalizations possible. In such disasters, it has been observed, individuals and communities adapt. Survivors are not helpless victims. Very soon after the shock they begin to help themselves and one another. In the immediate postimpact period community identification is strong, promoting cooperative and unselfish efforts aimed at rescue, relief, and repair. After the San Francisco earthquake of 1989, for example, inhabitants of a poor neighborhood spontaneously helped rescue motorists trapped by a freeway collapse. And after the

Anchorage earthquake of 1964, local supermarkets kept the prices of necessities low while consumers generally cooperated by self-rationing.

On the other hand, there have been some serious instances of antisocial behavior. Notably, while goodwill and cooperation predominated in New York City during the 1965 electrical blackout, a second blackout in 1977 brought major violence and looting. Similar bad experiences occurred after Hurricane Hugo struck the Virgin Islands in 1989. Nevertheless, as Russell Dynes and Thomas E. Drabek have shown, prosocial behavior has historically predominated in such situations. Instances to the contrary, while not rare, usually have fairly evident roots—where members of a community have a strong preexisting sense of grievance, for example. As an even more reliable generalization, a crisis almost always triggers a flow of support from outside the immediate impact area, a phenomenon that has become known as "convergence behavior." Surprisingly often, recovering communities even surpass previous rates of progress, owing to the emergence of new leaders, enhanced social cohesion, and the abolition of outmoded attitudes and regulations.

As a specific instance, the fire-bomb raids on Hamburg in July and August 1943 were highly intense community-wide disasters. As normally occurs in such situations, people proved tougher than structures. The raids destroyed about 50 percent of the buildings in the city, whereas the 40,000 people killed were less than 3 percent of the population at risk. About half the survivors left the city. Some 300,000 returned in the recovery period, while around 500,000 were permanently evacuated to other areas throughout Germany. A "dead zone" of the city was closed off so that repairs could be concentrated in less seriously damaged areas. Electricity, gas, and telegraph services were all adequate within a few days after the attacks ended. Water supply remained a difficult problem, however, and tank trucks had to be used. The transit system recovered only partially because of serious damage and abnormally heavy traffic, but mainline rail service resumed in a few days. On the seventh day Hamburg's central bank reopened and business began to function normally. Hamburg was not a dead city. Within a few months, the U.S. Strategic Bombing Survey reported, the city had recovered 80 percent of its former productivity.

Now consider a truly large-scale disaster: the Bolshevik attempt to impose "war communism" in Russia from 1917 to 1921, dispensing with markets and even the use of money. The Russian economy had already headed drastically downward during the preceding civil war. Industrial production fell to only 20 percent of the prewar level, and the cultivated area in agriculture to around 70 percent. But it was only after the final Red victory that the economy, instead of recovering, went into a total downspin. Alexander Baykov quotes Lenin in this regard:

> On the economic front, in our attempt to pass over to Communism, we had suffered, by the spring of 1921, a more serious defeat than any previously inflicted on us by Kolchak, Denikin, or Pilsudsky. Compulsory requisition in the villages and the direct Communist approach to the problems of reconstruction in towns—this was the policy which . . . proved to be the main cause of a profound economic and political crisis. (Baykov 1947, p. 48)

The explanation appears to be that, initially, the Bolsheviks had established direct control only over the "commanding heights" of industry (i.e., over a relatively small number of large factories located mainly in the major cities). Elsewhere, a variety of private and cooperative arrangements kept industry and trade functioning, at least minimally. Military victory permitted the Communists to turn their attention to liquidating these remnants. In addition, many small capitalists who had stayed on in the hope of Soviet defeat finally decamped and abandoned their enterprises. Thus the paradox of economic collapse after political and military victory.

The shift in mid-1921 to the New Economic Policy (NEP), restoring monetary exchange and allowing considerable scope to private enterprise, led almost immediately to a substantial recovery. As a remarkable feature, this very recovery, by creating a demand for currency as a means of exchange, permitted the Soviets to use the printing presses to acquire resources through a vast inflation of the money supply. The NEP allowed the economy a breathing space before the introduction of the Stalinist five-year plans, with their forced drive toward collectivization and industrialization.

Factors Helping and Hindering Recovery

One factor favorable to recovery is the inevitable shift of demand from less essential wants, which then frees resources for urgent rescue, repair, and rehabilitation. On the supply side, resource imports (gifts, insurance proceeds, commercial loans, etc.) will flow into damaged areas from outside support zones. More important, especially in the long run, is reserve productive capacity. Workers put in more hours, children leave school, and the elderly return from retirement. Machines and structures can be worked harder. Resource substitution—such as tents in place of houses, or trucks for buses and trains—enlarges the availability of essentials. Finally, stifling regulation of commerce and industry can be relaxed or suspended, and socially dysfunctional activities such as crime and parasitical litigation can be placed under stricter rein.

For the middle-scale disasters the main problems have been technological and distributive (e.g., localized resource scarcities or the provision of fair compensation). But in large-scale calamities the survival of the social order itself is in question. Widespread famines, pandemics, destructive social revolutions, disastrous wars, and even severe business depressions and monetary hyperinflations all threaten the network of arrangements supporting the elaborate division of labor on which modern economies depend.

Historically, the most immediately vulnerable aspect of this division of labor has been the money-mediated exchange of food and manufactured goods between rural and urban areas. Correspondingly, the most visible symptom of breakdown is a movement of population from the cities back to the countryside, as illustrated in ancient times by the emptying of cities in the declining Roman Empire. In modern times the populations of Moscow and Petrograd fell by more than 50 percent between 1917 and 1920, during the Russian civil war. And similarly, though not to nearly so great a degree, the German and Japanese urban populations both declined substantially toward the end of and in the aftermath of World War II. And even in the United States, the 1929–1935 depression saw a pause, and to some extent a reversal, of the long-run trend toward urbanization.

Under Russian war communism this breakdown of monetary exchange was due to an ideologically driven attempt to smash the system of private incentives that had previously served to feed the cities. For Japan and Germany, a somewhat different "repressed inflation" process was at work, as had often occurred earlier—for example, during the French Revolution and in the southern Confederacy during the American Civil War.

The process begins with military or economic stresses—such as territorial losses, transportation breakdowns, or inflationary war finance measures—that inevitably entail food scarcities. The crucial false step is the introduction of price ceilings on food, with the aim of "fair shares" or simply to hold down urban unrest. But the consequence is that farmers reduce their food deliveries to the cities. Unofficial mechanisms of distribution then emerge: black markets, barter, and trekking (day trips of city dwellers to the countryside), all involving losses due to higher transaction costs. As the cities begin to lose population, industrial production declines. The government may then attempt to confiscate the crops by military force. This threatens to cause a general breakdown of food production. At this point, if not earlier, governments have his-

torically given way, for example when the Bolshevik government felt pressured to introduce the NEP. In postwar Germany and Japan, fortunately, the downward spiral had not progressed nearly so far before the Erhard (see GERMAN ECONOMIC MIRACLE) and Dodge reforms restored the functioning of the price system.

Policy Issues: The Role of Government
There is widespread agreement that government must take responsibility for maintaining and restoring the economic infrastructure—the system of law and order, plus essential transportation and communication links. For middle-scale community-wide disasters, the main policy question has been the extent to which government should engage in additional activities, at either the planning or the recovery stage, that might hamper or displace private efforts. Grants or subsidized loans subvert the motivation for private self-protection. For example, subsidized government flood insurance induces excessive construction in areas that are vulnerable to flooding. Similarly, some forms of government relief hinder the recovery of normal business. Free food distribution, for example, may slow the restoration of regular marketing channels. Also debatable is the extent to which government should provide extra incentives for disaster preparations as well as a paternalistic safety net for those who were in a position to act but failed to do so. As reviewed by George Horwich, despite the government-created disincentives for private action, commercial disaster response firms have come into existence (e.g., Disaster Masters, Inc., of New York City) together with an industry newsletter, *Hazard Monthly*.

When it comes to the large-scale society-wide disasters, however, private parties can scarcely protect themselves at all, except possibly by emigration. Historical experience suggests that recovery will hinge on the ability of government to maintain or restore property rights together with a market system that will support the economic division of labor.

Taking a broader view, the subject of disaster and recovery can be regarded as a special case within the general problem of economic development. As events in the 1980s and 1990s have forcefully demonstrated, socialism subjected the nations of Eastern Europe to decades of economic disasters. Some, such as Poland, Estonia, and the Czech Republic, are recovering well from these disasters; others, such as the Ukraine, are still struggling.

About the Author
Jack Hirshleifer (1925–2005) was a professor of economics at the University of California, Los Angeles, until his death.

Further Reading

Anderson, J. L., and Eric L. Jones. "Natural Disasters and the Historical Response." *Australian Economic History Review* 28 (1988): 3–20.

Baykov, Alexander. *The Development of the Soviet Economic System.* New York: Macmillan, 1947.

Dacy, Douglas C., and Howard Kunreuther. *The Economics of Natural Disasters.* New York: Free Press, 1969.

Douty, Christopher M. *The Economics of Localized Disasters.* New York: Arno Press, 1977.

Drabek, Thomas E. *Human System Responses to Disaster.* New York: Springer-Verlag, 1986.

Dynes, Russell R. *Organized Behavior in Disasters.* Lexington, Mass: Heath Lexington Books, 1970.

Fritz, Charles E. "Disaster." In R. K. Merton and R. A. Nisbet, eds., *Contemporary Social Problems.* New York: Harcourt, Brace, Jovanovich, 1961.

Hirshleifer, Jack. *Economic Behaviour in Adversity.* Chicago: University of Chicago Press, 1987.

Horwich, George. "Disasters and Market Response." *Cato Journal* 9 (1990): 531–555.

Iklé, Fred Charles. *The Social Impact of Bomb Destruction.* Norman: University of Oklahoma Press, 1958.

Mill, John Stuart. *Principles of Political Economy.* New York: D. Appleton, 1896.

Prince, Samuel Henry. *Catastrophe and Social Change.* New York: Columbia University Press, 1920.

Sorokin, Pitirim A. *Man and Society in Calamity.* New York: Dutton, 1942.

Discrimination

Linda Gorman

Many people believe that only government intervention prevents rampant discrimination in the private sector. Economic theory predicts the opposite: market mechanisms impose inescapable penalties on profits whenever for-profit enterprises discriminate against individuals on any basis other than productivity. Though bigoted managers may hold sway for a time, in the long run the profit penalty makes profit-seeking enterprises tenacious champions of fair treatment.

To see how this works, suppose that male and female hot-dog salesmen are equally productive and that bigoted stadium concessionaires prefer to hire men. The bigger demand for male employees will raise men's wages, meaning that the concessionaires will have to pay more to hire men than they would to hire equally productive women. The higher wages for men cause employers who insist on all-male workforces to be higher-cost producers. Unless customers are willing to pay more for a hot dog delivered by a man than by a woman, higher costs mean smaller profits.

Concessionaires interested in maximizing their profits will forgo prejudice, hire women, reduce their costs, and increase their profits. Even if all concessionaires collude in refusing to hire women, new woman-owned firms can exploit their cost advantage by selling hot dogs for less, an effective way to take away customers. Unless government steps in to protect the bigots from competition, market conditions will end up forcing firms to choose between lower profits and hiring women. Though it may take decades, lower costs for female labor will result in the expansion of equal-opportunity employers. This will increase the demand for female labor and increase women's wages. Some antiwomen owners may contrive to remain in business, but competition will make their taste for unfair discrimination expensive and will ensure that less of it will occur.

An example of the effect of market penalties on prejudicial hiring occurred in South Africa in the early 1900s. In spite of penalties threatened by government and violence threatened by white workers, South African mine owners sought to increase profits by laying off high-priced white workers in order to hire lower-priced black workers. Higher-paying jobs were reserved for whites only after white workers successfully persuaded the government to place extreme restrictions on blacks' ability to work (see APARTHEID). Market penalties for discrimination also mitigated the effects of prejudice in the McCarthy era when profit-maximizing producers defied the Motion Picture Academy's blacklist and secretly hired blacklisted screenwriters.

Although government intervention often blunts the market mechanisms that penalize bigotry, people who unequivocally support such intervention often do so because they believe that unfair discrimination exists whenever outcomes for a particular group differ from those of the population as a whole. Economist Thomas Sowell calls the idea that "various groups would be equally represented in institutions and occupations were it not for discrimination . . . the grand fallacy of our times."[1] People differ in their tastes, aptitudes, and childhood experiences, in the skills they acquire from their extended families, and in the geography they must adapt to. People who have lived in cities for generations are less likely to become farmers. Those whose families have spent generations in rural areas may

---

1. Thomas Sowell, "The Grand Fallacy: Equating Male-Female Differences in Salary with Discrimination," *Capitalism Magazine,* July 21, 2004, online edition: http://capmag.com/article.asp?ID = 3807.

be less likely to move to the city and earn the higher wages associated with urban life. The children of military officers are more likely to choose military careers than the children of Quakers. People subscribing to the grand fallacy ignore these details, preferring instead to ascribe many occupational differences to discrimination. Determined to equalize the representation of various protected groups in all spheres of social activity, they support government-sanctioned discrimination as long as it fosters their version of equality.

In the real world, distinguishing discrimination based on productivity from discrimination based on prejudice can be difficult. A business will want to hire an additional employee only if the additional revenue yielded as a result of hiring this new employee equals or exceeds his wages. This revenue is affected by his marginal output, which depends both on his ability and on the tools he has to work with. The additional product will sell for whatever price consumers are willing to pay.

If a concessionaire at a baseball stadium sells hot dogs for a dollar each and makes ten cents per sale, at a wage of five dollars per hour he will hire another hot-dog seller only if the new seller can sell at least fifty hot dogs per hour. If the concessionaire keeps all revenues in excess of his costs, he will naturally prefer employees who can sell more than fifty hot dogs an hour. Suppose the concessionaire notices that his highest producers are young males with little body fat who wear track-meet T-shirts. Suppose he also notices that the majority of those who failed to meet the fifty-hot-dogs-per-hour standard were overweight women. Faced with a choice between an overweight woman and a male runner, a rational employer would hire the man.

An exceptionally motivated overweight woman might outperform the average male runner, of course. Unfortunately, without requiring extensive physical examinations, the cost of which could wipe out much of the profits from hot-dog sales and make any hiring moot, the manager cannot separate exceptional overweight women from ordinary ones.

Lacking information about individuals, the concessionaire bases his decision on the average characteristics of the groups with which he has had experience. Most of his employees will be young, lean, fit, and male. Economists call this "statistical discrimination." The employer's workforce will look the same whether the manager discriminated fairly on the basis of real differences in productivity (no overweight woman is likely to cover as much area as a young male runner), fairly on the basis of incomplete information (the overweight woman was exceptionally fit but the manager did not know it), or unfairly on the basis of

managerial taste (the employer dislikes female employees).

Early studies of labor force discrimination typically calculated expected pay or advancement for different groups after controlling for factors thought to affect productivity, such as schooling, hours worked, and years in the labor force. Unexplained differences were generally attributed to unfair discrimination. But as is so often the case, adjustments are limited to factors that can be measured, and the omitted variables often contained important information.

In a 2005 paper on wage differentials in American labor markets, June O'Neill and Dave O'Neill provide a vivid example of how omitted information can change conclusions about discrimination in wage studies. Simple comparisons of group wages for American men suggest that Japanese, Asian Indian, and Korean men earn 15 to 25 percent more than white non-Hispanic men. Black and American Indian men earn 25 percent less. A naïve interpretation of these earnings gaps would suggest that employers discriminate against whites and blacks and in favor of Asians. But using the National Longitudinal Survey of Youth, an exceptionally detailed data set, the O'Neills show that Asian men in the United States have above-average educations. When education is taken into account, the earnings gap between Asians and whites vanishes, and the black/white wage gap shrinks substantially because whites, on average, have more education than blacks. Adding geographic location shrinks the black/white wage gap further because a much larger proportion of black men live in the South, and southern wage levels tend to be lower for everyone. Adding individual achievement test scores, which are a measure of educational quality, erases the black/white wage gap for college graduates. Agreeing with James Heckman, the O'Neills quote Heckman's conclusion that "most of the disparity in earnings between blacks and whites in the labor market of the 1990s is due to differences in the skills they bring to the market, not to discrimination in the market" (O'Neill and O'Neill 2005, p. 33; Heckman 1998, p. 101).

Studies of woman's wages that conclude women are discriminated against in U.S. labor markets are also misleading when they suffer from the bias caused by omitted information. The gap between male and female wages narrowed from about 40 percent in 1970 to about 24 percent in 2003. Claims that the 24 percent difference results from bigotry typically ignore the fact that as a group women are more likely to work part time, choose careers in lower-paying fields, work for government or a nonprofit, and have fewer years of labor market experience than men of the same age. These differences could all create a wage gap and may reflect choices made to accommodate family responsibilities. Researchers who adjust for standard factors such as education, experience, and line of work find no significant difference between the earnings of men and women who never married and never had a child.

Like those who subscribe to Sowell's grand fallacy, people seeking unmerited advantages for various groups often pressure government to legalize discrimination in their favor. They justify officially sanctioned discrimination by pointing to past wrongs—often past instances of officially sanctioned bigotry such as slavery—and claim that justice can be served only by more official discrimination, this time in their favor. But officially sanctioned discrimination harms innocent individuals, many of whom may not even have been living when past wrongs were committed. It denies advancement to those who work hard, favoring instead those who can claim membership in an officially protected group. It may also serve to protect group members who behave badly. These policies exacerbate social friction. In extreme cases, as when hiring quotas were based on caste membership and Sinhalese extraction in India and Sri Lanka, the grievance caused by such unfairness can lead to civil war.

Proponents of legalizing unfair discrimination often claim that the policies they propose are costless. But the experience of American students admitted to competitive colleges and universities under racial preferences shows that there are costs, and that some of these costs are borne by the very people whom discrimination is supposed to benefit. Some U.S. minority groups produce relatively few academically excellent students due to differences in family structure, deficiencies in K–12 education, and recent immigration. Claiming that they seek to rectify unfair societal discrimination, elite American colleges and universities have spent decades manipulating their admissions processes to ensure that entering classes contain a certain proportion of students from these minority groups. Even though the academic preparation of these preferential admissions is substantially below that of the average student admitted from other population groups, the schools that practice prejudicial admissions imply that these students will succeed if they matriculate. Overmatched academically, the supposed beneficiaries of official discrimination have dropout rates that are triple those of other students. This is a tragic result given that most of them would be perfectly capable of succeeding at less demanding schools. The preferential admissions also fail bar exams and medical licensing exams at much higher rates. Those who do graduate may have their confidence eroded by questions about whether they owe their success to discriminatory policies.

Because official discrimination costs politicians little if the discrimination is politically acceptable, government of-

The Market Resists Discrimination

The resistance of southern streetcar companies to ordinances requiring them to segregate black passengers vividly illustrates how the market motivates businesses to avoid unfair discrimination. Before the segregation laws were enacted, most streetcar companies voluntarily segregated tobacco users, not black people. Nonsmokers of either race were free to ride where they wished, but smokers were relegated to the rear of the car or to the outside platform. The revenue gains from pleased nonsmokers apparently outweighed any losses from disgruntled smokers.

Streetcar companies refused, however, to discriminate against black people because separate cars would have reduced their profits. They resisted even after the passage of turn-of-the-century laws requiring the segregation of black people. One railroad manager complained that racial discrimination increased costs because it required the company to "haul around a good deal of empty space that is assigned to the colored people and not available to both races." Racial discrimination also upset some paying customers. Black customers boycotted the streetcar lines and formed competing hack (horse-drawn carriage) companies, and many white customers refused to move to the white section.

In Augusta, Savannah, Atlanta, Mobile, and Jacksonville, streetcar companies responded by refusing to enforce segregation laws for as long as fifteen years after their passage. The Memphis Street Railway "contested bitterly," and the Houston Electric Railway petitioned the Houston City Council for repeal. A black attorney leading a court battle against the laws provided an ironic measure of the strength of the streetcar companies' resistance by publicly denying that his group "was in cahoots with the railroad lines in Jacksonville." As pressure from the government grew, however, the cost of defiance began to outweigh the market penalty on profits. One by one, the streetcar companies succumbed, and the United States stumbled further into the infamous morass of racial segregation.

From Jennifer Roback, "The Political Economy of Segregation: The Case of Segregated Streetcars." *Journal of Economic History* 56, no. 4 (December 1986): 893–917.

ficials unconstrained by considerations of profit can afford to turn a blind eye to the damage unfair discrimination causes. They often sanction damaging official discrimination to please politically powerful interest groups. At the turn of the century, for example, American blacks began to compete for previously all-white jobs. Racial animosity increased. Whites had the voting power. Thomas Sowell reports that federal civil service hiring rules were amended to require a photograph of the applicant and to allow the hiring official to choose between the three top performers on civil service tests. The number of blacks in federal employment plummeted and remained low until the civil rights movement led to affirmative action sixty years later. But even at the height of segregation, businesses in the South, by contrast, often resisted laws requiring discrimination (see sidebar).

Rather than reducing discrimination, many of the U.S. government policies adopted since segregation have simply changed the groups discriminated against. Along with real or implied hiring quotas, the restrictions created under affirmative action blunt the market mechanisms that make discrimination expensive. Barriers to hiring and firing make employers less likely to try out types of people with whom they have little experience. Minimum-wage laws and union wage scales keep wages higher than market wages, reducing the number of people employers wish to hire while simultaneously attracting more applicants. When this happens, bigots pay less for turning away applicants who match their productivity requirements but not their tastes.

About the Author

Linda Gorman is a senior fellow at the Independence Institute in Golden, Colorado. She was previously an economics professor at the Naval Postgraduate School in Monterey, California.

Further Reading

Friedman, Milton. *Capitalism and Freedom*. Chicago: University of Chicago Press, 1962.

Heckman, James. "Detecting Discrimination." *Journal of Economic Perspectives* 12, no. 2 (1998): 101–116.

O'Neill, June E., and Dave M. O'Neill. "What Do Wage Differentials Tell Us About Labor Market Discrimination?" NBER Working Paper no. 11240. National Bureau of Economic Research, Cambridge, Mass., 2005.

Scanlon, James P. "Illusions of Job Segregation." *Public Interest* 93 (Fall 1988): 54–69.

Sowell, Thomas. *Preferential Policies: An International Perspective*. New York: William Morrow, 1990.

———. *Race and Economics*. New York: Longman, 1975.

Thernstrom, Stephan, and Abigail Thernstrom. *America in Black and White, One Nation, Indivisible*. New York: Simon and Schuster, 1997.

Advanced Treatment

Becker, Gary S. *The Economics of Discrimination*. 2d ed. Chicago: University of Chicago Press, 1971.

Distribution of Income

Frank Levy

The distribution of income lies at the heart of an enduring issue in political economy—the extent to which government should redistribute income from those with more income to those with less.

Whether government should redistribute income is a normative question, and each person's answer will depend on his or her values. But for many people, answering the normative question requires understanding the facts about the current income distribution. The term "income distribution" is a statistical concept. No one person is distributing income. Rather, the income distribution arises from people's decisions about work, saving, and investment as they interact through markets and are affected by the tax system. The 1990s and early 2000s witnessed the establishment of a growing body of work, increasingly precise, describing how the income distribution has changed. This work can be summarized in three points:

- The distribution of pretax income in the United States today is highly unequal. The most careful studies suggest that the top 10 percent of households, with average income of about $200,000, received 42 percent of all pretax money income in the late 1990s. The top 1 percent of households, averaging $800,000 of income, received 15 percent of all pretax money income.

- In the longer view, the path of income inequality over the twentieth century is marked by two main events: a sharp fall in inequality around the outbreak of World War II and an extended rise in inequality that began in the mid-1970s and accelerated in the 1980s. Income inequality today is about as large as it was in the 1920s.

- Over multiple years, family income fluctuates, and so the distribution of multiyear income is moderately more equal than the distribution of single-year income.

Trends in Inequality

The most frequently cited statistics come from the U.S. Census Bureau's Current Population Survey (CPS), the monthly household survey best known as the source of the official unemployment rate. Since 1948, the March edition of the CPS has collected household income information for the previous year, as well as the personal characteristics of household members—their age, education, occupation, and industry (if they work), and other data that help give insight into changing income patterns. Although this makes the CPS an indispensable statistical source, it has disadvantages as well. The CPS uses a restricted income definition: pretax money receipts excluding capital gains. This definition is further restricted by a "cap," currently $999,999, imposed on reported annual earnings for reasons of confidentiality.[1] Together, these problems mean that CPS estimates of inequality omit the effects of taxes, nonmoney income such as government and private health insurance, and the portion of individual earnings that exceeds the cap.

A second source of inequality statistics is the U.S. Treasury's Statistics of Income (SOI), which summarizes income reported on federal income tax returns. SOI data contain no personal data on taxpayers such as age or education, and they cannot describe the precise shape of the lower part of the income distribution.[2] The strengths of SOI data are their ability to accurately describe the upper part of the distribution—SOI income data are not "capped"—and to extend this description back to 1917, thirty years before CPS statistics begin.

Table 1 contains selected information on CPS measures of family and household income inequality since World War II.[3] The upper panel describes income patterns across families: living units occupied by two or more related persons. The lower panel describes income patterns across households: all occupied living units including families, persons who live alone, unrelated roommates, and so on. To form each distribution, the sample of families (or households) is listed in order of increasing income. The Census then calculates the fraction of all family income going to the quintile (one-fifth) of families with the lowest incomes, the quintile of families with the second-lowest incomes, and so on, as well as the share going to the highest 5 percent of families (who also are included in the top quintile).

The CPS data in Table 1 trace a J-shaped evolution of post–World War II inequality. In 1947, the top quintile of families received $8.60 for every dollar of income received by the bottom quintile. This ratio fell gradually through the 1950s and 1960s until 1969, when it reached $7.25 to $1.00—the low point of inequality. Beginning in the late 1970s, the ratio began to rise again until, by 2002, it had increased to $11.36 to $1.00, significantly greater than in 1947. Household data tell a similar story.

To make these trends more concrete, Table 1 includes the 1947, 1979, and 2001 income levels that divide each quintile from the next. Similar data are presented for households, and all income levels are expressed in 2003 dollars. Between 1947 and the mid-1970s, income grew rapidly at all points in the distribution, resulting in both rising living standards and moderating inequality. After the mid-1970s, average income grew much more slowly, and the growth that did occur was concentrated in the distributions' upper half. Between 1979 and 2001, the income dividing the first and second family quintiles grew slightly, from $22,280 to $24,000 (7.7 percent), while the income dividing the fourth and fifth quintiles grew from $74,470 to $94,150 (26.4 percent). Now, as in the 1970s, a majority of families would describe themselves as middle class, but the "middle class" is now a larger, more diverse concept than it once was.[4]

Inequality estimates based on the U.S. Treasury's SOI data expand on this picture. At the outset, SOI data do not "cap" high incomes, so household income inequality as reported in the SOI is significantly larger.[5] Using "capped" statistics, the CPS reports that the top *one-fifth* of households receives 49 percent of all pretax money income. The SOI estimates, more accurately, that the top *one-tenth* of households, with average annual income of about $200,000, receives 42 percent of total pretax money income. The top 1 percent of households with average annual incomes of about $800,000 receives 15 percent of all pretax income. With their longer historical perspective, SOI statistics also show that inequality in the 1920s and 1930s was as high as it is today. Beginning in 1938, the income

---

1. That is, earnings greater than $999,999 are reported as $999,999.

2. SOI data are combined with National Income Account estimates of total personal income received in the economy to calculate the share of all personal income received by the top 1 percent of households, the top 10 percent of households, and so on. Because many lower-income households do not pay federal income taxes, the SOI cannot provide similar detail on, say, the share of income received by the 10 percent of households with the lowest incomes.

3. Household and family income data are available online at http://www.census.gov/hhes/income/histinc/histinctb.html.

4. The connection between "class" and the income distribution is complicated by the fact that the distribution includes families of all ages, ranging from married students to retirees, while our stereotype of a middle-class income is based on families in their prime earning years.

5. The SOI data are based on tax filing units, a concept that is reasonably close to the Census's definition of household.

Table 1 Family and Household Income Distributions (Census Definitions)

A. Shape of the Family Income Distribution (share of all family income going to each one-fifth [quintile] of families)

	First Quintile (Lowest Income)	Second Quintile	Third Quintile	Fourth Quintile	Fifth Quintile (Highest Income)	Top 5 percent (Contained in Fifth Quintile)	Upper bound of Quintile (2003 dollars)					Lower bound of top 5%
							[1st]	[2nd]	[3rd]	[4th]	[5th]*	
1947	5.0	11.9	17.0	23.1	43.0	17.5	$11,088	$17,893	$24,263	$34,427	na.	$56,506
1959	4.9	12.3	17.9	23.8	41.1	15.9						
1969	5.6	12.4	17.7	23.7	40.6	15.6						
1979	5.4	11.6	17.5	24.1	41.4	15.3	$23,171	$38,102	$53,979	$74,329	na.	$119,243
1989	4.6	10.6	16.5	23.7	44.6	17.9						
2001	4.2	9.7	15.4	22.9	47.7	21.0	$24,960	$42,772	$65,000	$97,916	na.	$170,668

B. Shape of the Household Income Distribution (share of all households' income going to each one-fifth [quintile] of households)[†]

	First Quintile (Lowest Income)	Second Quintile	Third Quintile	Fourth Quintile	Fifth Quintile (Highest Income)	Top 5 percent (Contained in Fifth Quintile)	Upper bound of Quintile (2003 dollars)					Lower bound of top 5%
							[1st]	[2nd]	[3rd]	[4th]	[5th]*	
1967	4.0	10.8	17.3	24.2	43.8	17.5	$14,002	$27,303	$38,766	$55,265	na.	$88,678
1979	4.2	10.3	16.9	24.7	44.0	16.4	$16,457	$30,605	$47,018	$68,318	na.	$111,445
1989	3.8	9.5	15.8	24.0	46.8	18.9						
2001	3.5	8.7	14.6	23.0	50.1	22.4	$17,970	$33,314	$53,000	$83,500	na.	$150,499

* Original table rearranged and bracketed headings added here for clarity.

[†] Data available only since 1967.

share of the top one-tenth of households fell from 43 percent to about 32 percent, where it remained until the deep blue-collar recession of the early 1980s. At that point, inequality began its return to the levels of the 1920s and early 1930s.[6]

The Causes of Inequality

In one sense, the growth of inequality in the last part of the twentieth century comes as a surprise. In the 1950s, the bottom part of the income distribution contained large concentrations of two kinds of families: farm families whose in-kind income was not counted in Census data, and elderly families, many of whom were ineligible for the new Social Security program. Over subsequent decades, farm families declined as a proportion of the population while increased Social Security benefits and an expanding

6. See Thomas Piketty and Emanuel Saez, "Income Inequality in the United States, 1913–1998," *Quarterly Journal of Economics* 118, no. 1 (2003): 1–39.

private pension system lifted elderly incomes. Both trends favored greater income equality but were outweighed by four main factors.

- *Family structure.* Over time, the two-parent, one-earner family was increasingly replaced by low-income single-parent families and higher-income two-parent, two-earner families. A part of the top quintile's increased share of income reflects the fact that the average family or household in the top quintile contains almost three times as many workers as the average family or household in the bottom quintile.

- *Trade and technology.* Trade and technology increasingly shifted demand away from less-educated and less-skilled workers toward workers with higher education or particular skills. The result was a growing earnings gap between more- and less-educated/skilled workers.

- *Expanded markets.* With improved communications and transportation, people increasingly functioned in national,

The Economic Case for Inequality of Wages and Incomes

David R. Henderson

Is inequality of wages and incomes bad? The question seems ludicrous. Of course inequality is bad, isn't it? Actually, no. What matters crucially is how the inequality came about.

Inequality of wages and incomes is clearly bad if it results from government privileges. Many people would find such an outcome unjust, but even more important to many economists is that such inequality sets up perverse incentives. Instead of producing valuable products and services for their fellow citizens, as people tend to do in free economies, people in societies based on government-granted privileges devote much of their effort to pleasing, or outright bribing, government officials. In many African countries, for example, such as Côte d'Ivoire, Ghana, and Zaire, there are stark inequalities because the government has the power to take a high percentage of the wealth of the already poor and give a large amount of it to government officials or their cronies. And in many Latin American countries, for many decades a few families have had most of the wealth and have used government power to cement their privileges.

But inequality in wages and incomes in relatively free economies serves two important social functions. First, it gives people strong incentives to produce so as to make higher incomes and wages. Second, it gives people, and not just young people, strong incentives to get training or education that will allow them to perform well in higher-wage jobs. In his January 1999 Richard T. Ely lecture, economist Finis Welch put the point as follows:

> Wages play many roles in our economy; along with time worked, they determine labor income, but they also signal relative scarcity and abundance, and with malleable skills, wages provide incentives to render the services that are most highly valued. (Welch 1999, p. 1)

Further Reading

Mbaku, John Mukum. "Bureaucratic Corruption in Africa: The Futility of Cleanups." *Cato Journal* 16, no. 1 (1996): 99–118.

Rothbard, Murray. "Egalitarianism as a Revolt against Nature." Available online at: http://www.lewrockwell.com/rothbard/rothbard31.html.

Welch, Finis. "In Defense of Inequality." *American Economic Review* 89, no. 2 (1999): 1–17.

rather than local, markets. In these broader markets, persons with unique talents could command particularly high salaries.

- *Immigration.* In 2002, immigrants who had entered the country since 1980 constituted nearly 11 percent of the labor force. A relatively high proportion of these immigrants had low levels of education and increased the number of workers competing for low-paid work.[7]

These factors, however, can explain only part of the increase in inequality. One other factor that explains the particularly high incomes of the highest-paid people is that between 1982 and 2004, the ratio of pay of chief executive officers to pay of the average worker rose from 42:1 to 301:1, and pay of other high-level managers, lawyers, and people in other fields rose substantially also.

Does Measurement Matter?

As noted above, both CPS and SOI statistics measure pretax money income. These measurements are deficient for three reasons. First, increases in governmental aid to the poor have been concentrated in nonmoney benefits such as Medicaid and food stamps and through tax credits under the Earned Income Tax Credit (EITC). Nonmoney benefits are excluded from standard statistics, and EITC tax credits are typically underreported. Second, an increasing proportion of wage-earners' total compensation goes to health insurance and pension benefits—which are not counted in standard statistics. Third, taxes themselves modify the income distribution.

The U.S. Census has attempted to correct these definition problems for recent years by estimating the household income distribution under alternative income definitions. Table 2 shows the effect in 2001 of moving from the standard Census definition (pretax money excluding capital gains) to an adjusted definition that includes the estimated effects of capital gains, taxes, the EITC, and the monetary value of private and governmental nonmoney benefits. The result is a substantial reduction in inequality, with the ratio between incomes in the top and bottom quintiles falling from $14.31:$1.00 to $10.40:$1.00. Similar adjustments for selected earlier years indicate that better income measurement reduces inequality in any single year. Even under the adjusted definition, though, the *trend* toward increasing inequality in the 1980s and 1990s remains, but at a slower pace.

7. See Robert Lerman, "U.S. Income Inequality Trends and Recent Immigration," *American Economic Review* 89, no. 2 (1999): 23–38.

Table 2 Shape of the Household Income Distribution Under Alternative Income Definitions for 2001 (share of income going to each quintile of households)

	First Quintile (Lowest Income)	Second Quintile	Third Quintile	Fourth Quintile	Fifth Quintile (Highest Income)	Upper bound of quintile (2003 dollars)			
						[1st]	[2nd]	[3rd]	[4th]*
Standard Census income[†]	3.5	8.7	14.6	23	50.1	$18,618	$34,780	$55,105	$86,914
Adjusted Census income	4.5	10.3	15.6	22.6	47	$21,334	$35,485	$51,747	$75,195

Note: Adjusted Census Income is based on pretax money income including estimated capital gains, less all taxes paid plus the estimated receipt of the Earned Income Tax Credit plus the imputed value of in-kind income from employer-provided health insurance and government nonmoney benefits like food stamps, Medicare and Medicaid, and free school lunches.

* Original table rearranged and bracketed headings added here for clarity.

[†] Standard Census Income is defined as pretax money income excluding capital gains.

Table 3 Mobility Within the Family Income Distribution

	Quintile in 1998				
	First Quintile (Lowest Income)	Second Quintile	Third Quintile	Fourth Quintile	Fifth Quintile (Highest Income)
First Quintile in 1988	53.30%	23.60%	12.40%	6.40%	4.30%
Fifth Quintile in 1988	3.00%	5.70%	14.90%	23.20%	53.20%

Source: Katherine Bradbury and Jane Katz, "Are Lifetime Incomes Growing More Unequal? New Evidence on Family Income Mobility," *Federal Reserve Bank of Boston Regional Review* 12, no. 4 (2002).

Inequality and Mobility

A second offset to estimated inequality is economic mobility. Because most family incomes increase as people's careers develop, long-run incomes are more equal than standard single-year statistics suggest. Table 3 summarizes the results of one study of recent family income mobility.[8] Among families in the bottom quintile in 1988, half were in the bottom quintile ten years later, a quarter had moved up to the second quintile, and a quarter had moved to the third or higher quintiles. Families in the fifth quintile (highest incomes) show a similar mobility over time.

About the Author

Frank Levy is the Daniel Rose Professor of Urban Economics in MIT's Department of Urban Studies and Planning.

8. Katherine Bradbury and Jane Katz, "Are Lifetime Incomes Growing More Unequal? New Evidence on Family Income Mobility," *Federal Reserve Bank of Boston Regional Review* 12, no. 4 (2002) 3–5.

Further Reading

Charles, Kerwin Kofi, and Erik Hurst. "Correlation of Wealth Across Generations." *Journal of Political Economy,* 111, no. 6 (2003): 1155–1182.

Fortin, Nicole M., and Thomas Lemeiux. "Institutional Changes and Rising Wage Inequality: Is There a Linkage?" *Journal of Economic Perspectives* 11, no. 2 (1997): 75–96.

Gottschalk, Peter. "Inequality, Income Growth and Mobility: The Basic Facts." *Journal of Economic Perspectives* 11, no. 2 (1997): 21–40.

Johnson, George E. "Changes in Earnings Inequality: The Role of Demand Shifts." *Journal of Economic Perspectives,* 11, no. 2 (1997): 41–54.

Saez, Emmanuel. "Income and Wealth Concentration in a Historical and International Perspective." In Alan J. Auerbach, David E. Card, and John M. Quigley, ed., *Public Policy and the Income Distribution.* New York: Russell Sage Foundation, 2006. Also available at http://emlab.berkeley.edu/users/saez/berkeleysympo2.pdf.

Topel, Robert. "Factor Proportions and Relative Wages: The Supply Side Determinants of Wage Inequality." *Journal of Economic Perspectives* 11, no. 2 (1997): 55–74.

Economic Freedom

Robert A. Lawson

For well over a hundred years, the economic world has been engaged in a great intellectual debate. On one side of this debate have been those philosophers and economists who advocate an economic system based on private property and free markets—or what one might call economic freedom. The key ingredients of economic freedom are personal choice, voluntary exchange, freedom to compete in markets, and protection of person and property. Institutions and policies are consistent with economic freedom when they allow voluntary exchange and protect individuals and their property.

Governments can promote economic freedom by providing a legal structure and a law-enforcement system that protect the property rights of owners and enforce contracts in an evenhanded manner. However, economic freedom also requires governments to refrain from taking people's property and from interfering with personal choice, voluntary exchange, and the freedom to enter and compete in labor and product markets. When governments substitute taxes, government expenditures, and regulations for personal choice, voluntary exchange, and market coordination, they reduce economic freedom. Restrictions that limit entry into occupations and business activities also reduce economic freedom.

Adam Smith was one of the first economists to argue for a version of economic freedom, and he was followed by a distinguished line of thinkers that includes John Stuart Mill, Ludwig von Mises, Friedrich A. Hayek, and Milton Friedman, as well as economists such as Murray Rothbard.

On the other side of this debate are people hostile to economic freedom who instead argue for an economic system characterized by centralized economic planning and state control of the means of production. Advocates of an expanded role for the state include Jean-Jacques Rousseau and Karl Marx and such twentieth-century advocates as Abba Lerner, John Kenneth Galbraith, Michael Harrington, and Robert Heilbroner. These scholars argue that free markets lead to monopolies, chronic economic crises, income inequality, and increasing degradation of the poor, and that centralized political control of people's economic lives avoids these problems of the marketplace. They deem economic life simply too important to be left up to the decentralized decisions of individuals.

In the early twentieth century, state control grew as communism and fascism spread. In the United States, the New Deal significantly expanded the role of the state in people's economic lives. In the late 1970s and early 1980s, economic freedom staged a comeback, with deregulation, privatization, and tax cuts. Of course, the major increase in economic freedom came with the fall of the Soviet Union. Today, the advocates of freedom dominate the debate. In fact, one major socialist, the late Robert Heilbroner, believed that the advocates of freedom have won (see SOCIALISM).

Substantial evidence has informed the debate. Indeed, the stark differences in the standards of living of people in economically freer systems compared with those in less-free systems have become more and more obvious: North versus South Korea, East versus West Germany, Estonia versus Finland, and Cubans living in Miami versus Cubans living in Cuba are examples. In each case, people in the freer economy have better lives, in virtually every way, than their counterparts in the less-free economies.

Measuring Economic Freedom

The above comparisons are suggestive. But is it possible to find a relationship between economic freedom and prosperity over a wider range of nations? In the 1980s, scholars began to measure and rate economies based on their degree of economic freedom. Organizations such as Freedom House, the Heritage Foundation, and the Fraser Institute, as well as individual scholars, published "economic freedom indexes" attempting to quantify economic freedom. They came up with an ambitious, and necessarily blunt, measure.

In 1996, the Fraser Institute, along with a network of other think tanks, began publishing the *Economic Freedom of the World* (EFW) annual reports, which present an economic freedom index for more than 120 nations. Using data from the World Bank, International Monetary Fund, *Global Competitiveness Report, International Country Risk Guide,* PricewaterhouseCoopers, and others, the report rates countries on a zero-to-ten scale. Higher scores indicate greater economic freedom. The overall index is based on ratings in five broad areas. Counting the various subcomponents, the EFW index uses thirty-eight distinct pieces of data. Each subcomponent is placed on a scale from zero to ten that reflects the range of the underlying data. The component ratings within each area are averaged to derive ratings for each of the five areas. In turn, the summary rating is the average of the five area ratings. The five major areas are:

- *Size of government.* To get high ratings in this area, governments must tax and spend modestly, and marginal tax rates must be relatively low. While governments are important in protecting property rights, enforcing contracts, and providing some services, as governments grow they inevitably infringe on people's economic freedom to engage in trade and enjoy the fruits of their labor.

- *Sound money.* It might not be clear at first why this is a measure of freedom rather than just a measure of good economic policy. But money would likely be sound if the government did not have a legal monopoly over the money supply (see COMPETING MONEY SUPPLIES and GOLD STANDARD). Therefore sound money is a measure of how much the government refrains from abusing its monopoly power. To get high ratings here, a country's inflation must be low and stable, and the government must permit people to own currencies of other nations.

- *Property rights and rule of law.* This area measures the consistency of a country's legal system with the protection of property, enforcement of contracts, and evenhanded application of the law. This is perhaps the most important area of economic freedom, as economic freedom requires that people be secure in their persons and physical property; it also requires a judicial system that enforces contractual agreements fairly.

- *International trade.* Countries that refrain from enacting protectionist tariffs, quotas, and capital controls get higher ratings in this area. Economic freedom means that people can engage in trade with any person of their choosing. If the government taxes or otherwise prevents people from buying or selling with people in other countries, it reduces their freedom.

- *Regulation.* Regulations such as interest-rate controls (usury laws), restrictions on bank ownership by foreigners, minimum wages, military conscription, business licensing, and price controls are included. Such controls and regulations violate the principles of economic freedom. To get high ratings, countries must refrain from such regulations, leaving people free to set prices, open businesses, and trade.

Any attempt to measure freedom on this basis inevitably omits the details. Because all these factors are weighted equally, two countries could have identical indexes in different ways: one might have high taxes but a good rule of law, while another may have low taxes but a poor legal system. An economic freedom index allows us to make broad comparisons among countries, but the index is a blunt measure.

What is the freest economy in the world? Hong Kong. Hong Kong has relatively low taxes, a good legal system, sound money, free trade, and minimal regulations; and it has had these institutions and policies in place for several decades. Other highly rated countries include Singapore, the United States, New Zealand, and the United Kingdom. Table 1 shows the economic freedom ratings of selected countries for 1980, 1990, and 2002.[1]

Singapore is an interesting case because it exhibits an odd combination of high economic freedom and considerable political and civil repression. Although economic freedom and political freedom tend to go together, especially in the long run, Singapore is an exception. It will be worth watching to see if Singapore can maintain this situation. Many scholars believe that economic freedom and political repression are an unsustainable combination.[2]

Some countries, such as Hong Kong, Singapore, and the United States, consistently registered high ratings throughout the 1980s and 1990s. Germany's economic freedom rating has also been quite steady. Germany's rating in 2002 was 7.3, compared with 7.0 in 1980. Because several other countries have made substantial improvements, however, Germany's ranking has declined, receding to twenty-second in 2002 from fifth in 1980. Likewise, because other countries have improved, France's ranking fell to forty-fourth from twenty-eighth in 1980.

Looking at some absolute scores, one can note a clear trend worldwide toward economic liberalization since 1980. The highest-rated African nation, Botswana, increased its rating from 5.0 in 1980 to 7.4 in 2002 and now ranks eighteenth in the world. Also in Africa, Mauritius's rating jumped from 4.7 in 1980 to 6.1 in 1990 and 7.2 in 2002. In Latin America, Chile's rating improved from 5.3 in 1980 to 7.3 in 2002, making it the highest-rated country in its region.

Among developed countries we also have seen some big reformers. Ireland's rating jumped from 6.2 in 1980 to 7.8 in 2002. The United Kingdom was a big gainer during the Thatcher years, when its rating rose from 6.1 in 1980 to 7.7 in 1990 and, ultimately, to 8.2. Similarly, New Zealand's economic reforms in the late 1980s and early 1990s caused its rating to increase from 6.1 in 1980 to 8.2 in 2002. While these gains are not the largest seen in the world, they do show that well-established developed economies can implement significant economic liberalization.

The world's two largest economies by population, India and China, both have low ratings. But both have made

1. A complete list of country ratings for the years 1970, 1975, 1980, 1985, 1990, 1995, and 2000 onward can be found online at http://www.freetheworld.com.

2. See "The Relation Between Economic Freedom and Political Freedom," in Milton Friedman, *Capitalism and Freedom* (Chicago: University of Chicago Press, 1962); see also Friedrich Hayek, *The Road to Serfdom* (Chicago: University of Chicago Press, 1944).

Table 1 Economic Freedom Ratings for
Selected Countries, 1980, 1990, and 2002

2002 Ranking	Country	Economic Freedom Rating		
		2002	1990	1980
1	Hong Kong	8.7	8.6	8.6
2	Singapore	8.6	8.5	7.5
3	New Zealand	8.2	7.3	6.1
3	United Kingdom	8.2	7.7	6.1
3	United States	8.2	8.1	7.4
9	Ireland	7.8	7.0	6.2
11	Estonia	7.7		
14	Iceland	7.6	6.6	4.9
18	Botswana	7.4	5.4	5.0
22	Chile	7.3	6.8	5.3
22	Germany	7.3	7.3	7.0
27	Mauritius	7.2	6.1	4.7
44	France	6.8	6.8	5.7
58	Mexico	6.5	5.7	5.1
68	India	6.3	4.8	4.9
86	Argentina	5.8	4.4	3.9
86	Indonesia	5.8	6.6	5.2
90	China	5.7	4.2	3.8
103	Romania	5.4	4.0	
114	Russia	5.0		
118	Venezuela	4.6	5.6	6.7
122	Zimbabwe	3.4	4.9	4.7

Source: Economic Freedom of the World: 2004 Annual Report, table
1.4

tremendous strides toward more economic freedom.
China's rating increased from 3.8 to 5.7, and India's rose
from 4.9 to 6.3. While their current ratings are still low by
world standards, these improvements in economic freedom have been quite substantial; both countries' economies are growing rapidly as a result.

Among the former Soviet and centrally planned economies, some have succeeded greatly in increasing economic
freedom. Estonia now ranks thirteenth in the world, having instituted nearly complete free trade, a stable monetary
policy, and considerable fiscal restraint. In 1995, it was
ranked eighty-first. Meanwhile, some of these nations have
shown little progress; Russia and Romania, for instance,
rank near the bottom of the list and show few signs of
improvement. In these countries, the near inability of the
legal system to protect property and fairly enforce con-

tracts—and the CORRUPTION this inevitably ensures—is a
particularly big problem from the standpoint of both economic freedom and economic growth.

Only a few countries have moved away from economic
freedom in the last twenty years. Zimbabwe has recently
taken a turn for the worse as the government continues to
attack property rights and impose tight controls on economic activity. Venezuela has steadily declined in its rating
(and ranking). In the early 1970s, Venezuela ranked in the
top twenty, but by 2002 it had fallen to the very bottom.

Economic Freedom and Economic Results
An economic freedom index allows researchers to examine
the empirical relationships between economic freedom
and other desirable social outcomes. The big question is:
Do countries that exhibit greater degrees of economic freedom perform better than those that do not?

Much scholarly research has been and continues to be
done to see if the index correlates with various measures
of the good society: higher incomes, economic growth, income equality, gender equality, life expectancy, and so on.
While there is scholarly debate about the exact nature of
these relationships, the results are uniform: measures of
economic freedom relate positively with these factors.

The figures that follow illustrate the simple relationship
between the economic freedom index and various measures of economic and social progress. These figures indicate the relationships that more scholarly studies have
found, but they are not conclusive evidence. Economic
growth, for example, appears to be related to both the level
of economic freedom and changes in the level of economic
freedom as well as to investment in physical and human
capital. The simple graphs on the next page are no substitute for more scholarly work.[3] Nevertheless, these simple
relationships are a starting point for examining the links
between economic freedom and economic results.

Figure 1 shows the economic freedom ratings related to
GDP per capita. The chart organizes the world into five
quintiles ordered from the countries with the least economic freedom to the countries with the most. As economic freedom increases, so does average income.

The level of economic development at any point in time
is, of course, the result of the accumulation of capital and
technology over a long period. Figure 2 illustrates the correlation between economic growth (rates of change in
GDP per capita) between 1980 and 2002 and the average
level of the economic freedom index since 1980. Figure 3

---

3. Berggren 2003 provides an excellent review of the scholarly
literature.

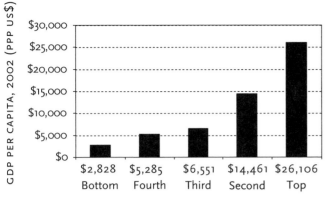

Figure 1 Economic Freedom and GDP per Capita

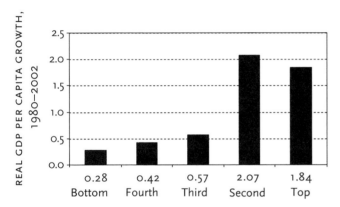

Figure 2 Economic Freedom and Economic Growth

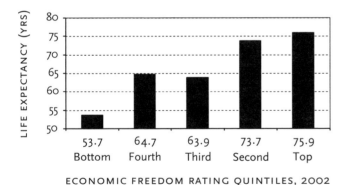

Figure 3 Economic Freedom and Life Expectancy

illustrates the large improvements in life span associated with greater economic freedom.

While there is no clear evidence that economic freedom creates greater income inequality, there is clear evidence that lowest-income people in freer countries are better off than their counterparts in less free countries. Figure 4 shows the average income level of the poorest tenth of the

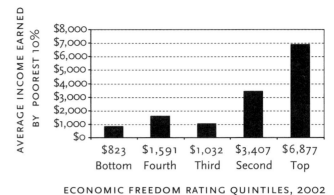

Figure 4 Economic Freedom and the Income Level of the Poor

population by economic freedom quintile. Clearly, as Adam Smith recognized more than 230 years ago, economic freedom and the economic prosperity it brings work to the advantage of the poor.

As time goes on, these measures of economic freedom will improve and our understanding of the relationship between private property and free markets and economic performance will similarly improve. But in the great debate between economic freedom and political planning, the evidence is increasingly clear. Economic freedom leads to better economic results.

About the Author

Robert A. Lawson is the George H. Moor Chair and Professor of Economics at Capital University in Columbus, Ohio. He is a coauthor of the *Economic Freedom of the World* annual reports.

Further Reading

Berggren, Niclas. "The Benefits of Economic Freedom: A Survey." *Independent Review* 8, no. 2 (2003): 193–211. Available online at: http://www.independent.org/pdf/tir/tir_08_2_berggren.pdf.

Friedman, Milton. *Capitalism and Freedom*. Chicago: University of Chicago Press, 1962.

Gwartney, James, and Robert Lawson. *Economic Freedom of the World: 2004 Annual Report*. Vancouver: Fraser Institute, 2004. Available online at: http://www.freetheworld.com.

Messick, Richard E., ed. *World Survey of Economic Freedom 1995–1996: A Freedom House Study*. New Brunswick, N.J.: Transaction Publishers, 1996.

Miles, Marc A., Edwin J. Feulner, and Mary Anastasia O'Grady. *2005 Index of Economic Freedom*. 2005. Available online at: http://www.heritage.org/research/features/index/.

Scully, G. W., and D. Slottje. "Ranking Economic Liberty Across Countries." *Public Choice* 69, no. 2 (1991): 121–152.

Economic Growth

Paul M. Romer

Compound Rates of Growth

In the modern version of an old legend, an investment banker asks to be paid by placing one penny on the first square of a chessboard, two pennies on the second square, four on the third, etc. If the banker had asked that only the white squares be used, the initial penny would have doubled in value thirty-one times, leaving $21.5 million on the last square. Using both the black and the white squares would have made the penny grow to $92 million billion.

People are reasonably good at forming estimates based on addition, but for operations such as compounding that depend on repeated multiplication, we systematically underestimate how quickly things grow. As a result, we often lose sight of how important the average rate of growth is for an economy. For an investment banker, the choice between a payment that doubles with every square on the chessboard and one that doubles with every other square is more important than any other part of the contract. Who cares whether the payment is in pennies, pounds, or pesos? For a nation, the choices that determine whether income doubles with every generation, or instead with every other generation, dwarf all other economic policy concerns.

Growth in Income per Capita

You can figure out how long it takes for something to double by dividing the growth rate into the number 72. In the twenty-five years between 1950 and 1975, income per capita in India grew at the rate of 1.8 percent per year. At this rate, income doubles every forty years because 72 divided by 1.8 equals 40. In the twenty-five years between 1975 and 2000, income per capita in China grew at almost 6 percent per year. At this rate, income doubles every twelve years.

These differences in doubling times have huge effects for a nation, just as they do for our banker. In the same forty-year time span that it would take the Indian economy to double at its slower growth rate, income would double three times—to eight times its initial level—at China's faster growth rate.

From 1950 to 2000, growth in income per capita in the United States lay between these two extremes, averaging 2.3 percent per year. From 1950 to 1975, India, which started at a level of income per capita that was less than 7 percent of that in the United States, was falling even far-

ther behind. Between 1975 and 2000, China, which started at an even lower level, was catching up.

China grew so quickly partly because it started so far behind. Rapid growth could be achieved in large part by letting firms bring in ideas about how to create value that were already in use in the rest of the world. The interesting question is why India could not manage the same trick, at least between 1950 and 1975.

Growth and Recipes

Economic growth occurs whenever people take resources and rearrange them in ways that make them more valuable. A useful metaphor for production in an economy comes from the kitchen. To create valuable final products, we mix inexpensive ingredients together according to a recipe. The cooking one can do is limited by the supply of ingredients, and most cooking in the economy produces undesirable side effects. If economic growth could be achieved only by doing more and more of the same kind of cooking, we would eventually run out of raw materials and suffer from unacceptable levels of pollution and nuisance. Human history teaches us, however, that economic growth springs from better recipes, not just from more cooking. New recipes generally produce fewer unpleasant side effects and generate more economic value per unit of raw material (see NATURAL RESOURCES).

Take one small example. In most coffee shops, you can now use the same size lid for small, medium, and large cups of coffee. That was not true as recently as 1995. That small change in the geometry of the cups means that a coffee shop can serve customers at lower cost. Store owners need to manage the inventory for only one type of lid. Employees can replenish supplies more quickly throughout the day. Customers can get their coffee just a bit faster. Although big discoveries such as the transistor, antibiotics, and the electric motor attract most of the attention, it takes millions of little discoveries like the new design for the cup and lid to double a nation's average income.

Every generation has perceived the limits to growth that finite resources and undesirable side effects would pose if no new recipes or ideas were discovered. And every generation has underestimated the potential for finding new recipes and ideas. We consistently fail to grasp how many ideas remain to be discovered. The difficulty is the same one we have with compounding: possibilities do not merely add up; they multiply.

In a branch of physical chemistry known as exploratory synthesis, chemists try mixing selected elements together at different temperatures and pressures to see what comes out. About a decade ago, one of the hundreds of compounds discovered this way—a mixture of copper, yttrium, barium, and oxygen—was found to be a superconductor at temperatures far higher than anyone had previously thought possible. This discovery may ultimately have far-reaching implications for the storage and transmission of electrical energy.

To get some sense of how much scope there is for more such discoveries, we can calculate as follows. The periodic table contains about a hundred different types of atoms, which means that the number of combinations made up of four different elements is about $100 \times 99 \times 98 \times 97 = 94,000,000$. A list of numbers like 6, 2, 1, 7 can represent the proportions for using the four elements in a recipe. To keep things simple, assume that the numbers in the list must lie between 1 and 10, that no fractions are allowed, and that the smallest number must always be 1. Then there are about 3,500 different sets of proportions for each choice of four elements, and 3,500 × 94,000,000 (or 330,000,000,000) different recipes in total. If laboratories around the world evaluated one thousand recipes each day, it would take nearly a million years to go through them all. (If you like these combinatorial calculations, try to figure out how many different coffee drinks it is possible to order at your local shop. Instead of moving around stacks of cup lids, baristas now spend their time tailoring drinks to individual palates.)

In fact, the previous calculation vastly underestimates the amount of exploration that remains to be done because mixtures can be made of more than four elements, fractional proportions can be selected, and a wide variety of pressures and temperatures can be used during mixing.

Even after correcting for these additional factors, this kind of calculation only begins to suggest the range of possibilities. Instead of just mixing elements together in a disorganized fashion, we can use chemical reactions to combine elements such as hydrogen and carbon into ordered structures like polymers or proteins. To see how far this kind of process can take us, imagine the ideal chemical refinery. It would convert abundant, renewable resources into a product that humans value. It would be smaller than a car, mobile so that it could search out its own inputs, capable of maintaining the temperature necessary for its reactions within narrow bounds, and able to automatically heal most system failures. It would build replicas of itself for use after it wears out, and it would do all of this with little human supervision. All we would have to do is get it to stay still periodically so that we could hook up some pipes and drain off the final product.

This refinery already exists. It is the milk cow. And if nature can produce this structured collection of hydrogen,

carbon, and miscellaneous other atoms by meandering along one particular evolutionary path of trial and error (albeit one that took hundreds of millions of years), there must be an unimaginably large number of valuable structures and recipes for combining atoms that we have yet to discover.

Objects and Ideas

Thinking about ideas and recipes changes how one thinks about economic policy (and cows). A traditional explanation for the persistent poverty of many less-developed countries is that they lack objects such as natural resources or capital goods. But Taiwan started with little of either and still grew rapidly. Something else must be involved. Increasingly, emphasis is shifting to the notion that it is ideas, not objects, that poor countries lack. The knowledge needed to provide citizens of the poorest countries with a vastly improved standard of living already exists in the advanced countries. If a poor nation invests in education and does not destroy the incentives for its citizens to acquire ideas from the rest of the world, it can rapidly take advantage of the publicly available part of the worldwide stock of knowledge. If, in addition, it offers incentives for privately held ideas to be put to use within its borders—for example, by protecting foreign patents, copyrights, and licenses; by permitting direct investment by foreign firms; by protecting property rights; and by avoiding heavy regulation and high marginal tax rates—its citizens can soon work in state-of-the-art productive activities.

Some ideas such as insights about public health are rapidly adopted by less-developed countries. As a result, life expectancy in poor countries is catching up with that in the leaders faster than income per capita. Yet governments in poor countries continue to impede the flow of many other ideas, especially those with commercial value. Automobile producers in North America clearly recognize that they can learn from ideas developed in the rest of the world. But for decades, car firms in India operated in a government-created protective time warp. The Hillman and Austin cars produced in England in the 1950s continued to roll off production lines in India through the 1980s. After independence, India's commitment to closing itself off and striving for self-sufficiency was as strong as Taiwan's commitment to acquiring foreign ideas and participating fully in world markets. The outcomes—grinding poverty in India and opulence in Taiwan—could hardly be more disparate.

A poor country like India can achieve enormous increases in standards of living merely by letting in the ideas held by companies from industrialized nations. With a series of economic reforms that started in the 1980s and deepened in the early 1990s, India has begun to open itself up to these opportunities. For some of its citizens, such as the software developers who now work for firms located in the rest of the world, these improvements in standards of living have become a reality. This same type of opening up is causing a spectacular transformation of life in China. Its growth in the last twenty-five years of the twentieth century was driven to a very large extent by foreign investment by multinational firms.

Leading countries like the United States, Canada, and the members of the European Union cannot stay ahead merely by adopting ideas developed elsewhere. They must offer strong incentives for discovering new ideas at home, and this is not easy to do. The same characteristic that makes an idea so valuable—everybody can use it at the same time—also means that it is hard to earn an appropriate rate of return on investments in ideas. The many people who benefit from a new idea can too easily free ride on the efforts of others.

After the transistor was invented at Bell Laboratories, many applied ideas had to be developed before this basic science discovery yielded any commercial value. By now, private firms have developed improved recipes that have brought the cost of a transistor down to less than a millionth of its former level. Yet most of the benefits from those discoveries have been reaped not by the innovating firms, but by the users of the transistors. In 1985, I paid a thousand dollars per million transistors for memory in my computer. In 2005, I paid less than ten dollars per million, and yet I did nothing to deserve or help pay for this windfall. If the government confiscated most of the oil from major discoveries and gave it to consumers, oil companies would do much less exploration. Some oil would still be found serendipitously, but many promising opportunities for exploration would be bypassed. Both oil companies and consumers would be worse off. The leakage of benefits such as those from improvements in the transistor acts just like this kind of confiscatory tax and has the same effect on incentives for exploration. For this reason, most economists support government funding for basic scientific research. They also recognize, however, that basic research grants by themselves will not provide the incentives to discover the many small applied ideas needed to transform basic ideas such as the transistor or Web search into valuable products and services.

It takes more than scientists in universities to generate progress and growth. Such seemingly mundane forms of discovery as product and process engineering or the development of new business models can have huge benefits for society as a whole. There are, to be sure, some benefits for the firms that make these discoveries, but not enough to generate innovation at the ideal rate. Giving firms tighter patents and copyrights over new ideas would increase the incentives to make new discoveries, but might also make it much more expensive to build on previous discoveries. Tighter intellectual property rights could therefore be counterproductive and might slow growth.

The one safe measure governments have used to great advantage has been subsidies for education to increase the supply of talented young scientists and engineers. They are the basic input into the discovery process, the fuel that fires the innovation engine. No one can know where newly trained young people will end up working, but nations that are willing to educate more of them and let them follow their instincts can be confident that they will accomplish amazing things.

Meta-ideas

Perhaps the most important ideas of all are meta-ideas—ideas about how to support the production and transmission of other ideas. In the seventeenth century, the British invented the modern concept of a patent that protects an invention. North Americans invented the modern research university and the agricultural extension service in the nineteenth century, and peer-reviewed competitive grants for basic research in the twentieth. The challenge now facing all of the industrialized countries is to invent new institutions that encourage a higher level of applied, commercially relevant research and development in the private sector.

As national markets for talent and education merge into unified global markets, opportunities for important policy innovation will surely emerge. In basic research, the United States is still the undisputed leader, but in key areas of education, other countries are surging ahead. Many of them have already discovered how to train a larger fraction of their young people as scientists and engineers.

We do not know what the next major idea about how to support ideas will be. Nor do we know where it will emerge. There are, however, two safe predictions. First, the country that takes the lead in the twenty-first century will be the one that implements an innovation that more effectively supports the production of new ideas in the private sector. Second, new meta-ideas of this kind will be found.

Only a failure of imagination—the same failure that leads the man on the street to suppose that everything has already been invented—leads us to believe that all of the relevant institutions have been designed and all of the policy levers have been found. For social scientists, every bit as much as for physical scientists, there are vast regions to explore and wonderful surprises to discover.

About the Author

Paul M. Romer is the STANCO 25 Professor of Economics in the Graduate School of Business at Stanford University and a senior fellow at the Hoover Institution. He also founded Aplia, a publisher of Web-based teaching tools that is changing how college students learn economics.

Further Reading

Easterly, William. *The Elusive Quest for Growth.* Cambridge: MIT Press, 2002.

Helpman, Elhanan. *The Mystery of Economic Growth.* Cambridge: Harvard University Press, 2004.

North, Douglass C. *Institutions, Institutional Change, and Economic Performance.* Cambridge: Cambridge University Press, 1990.

Olson, Mancur. "Big Bills Left on the Sidewalk: Why Some Nations Are Rich, and Others Poor." *Journal of Economic Perspectives* 10, no. 2 (1996): 3–23.

Rosenberg, Nathan. *Inside the Black Box: Technology and Economics.* Cambridge: Cambridge University Press, 1982.

Romer, Paul. "Endogenous Technological Change." *Journal of Political Economy* 98, no. 5 (1990): S71–S102.

Education

Linda Gorman

K–12

In the 1980s, economists puzzled by a decline in the growth of U.S. productivity realized that American schools had taken a dramatic turn for the worse. After rising every year for fifty years, student scores on a variety of achievement tests dropped sharply in 1967. They continued to decline through 1980. The decline was so severe, John Bishop calculates, that students graduating in 1980 had learned "about 1.25 grade-level equivalents less than those who graduated in 1967."[1] Although achievement levels began to recover in 1980, the recovery has been weak and student achievement has yet to regain 1967 levels. By the turn of the century, conservative estimates of the economic growth lost due to the academic achievement decline were on the order of 3.6 percent of the 2000 gross national product.

The characteristics of the educational productivity decline challenged widely accepted educational theories of school performance. Theorists accustomed to blaming increased poverty, family instability, large class size, and insufficient spending for poor school performance could not explain why the scores of more able students declined at least as much as those of less able ones, or why measures of inferential ability and problem solving declined more than those of simpler tasks such as arithmetic computation.

Achievement fell even though the average U.S. class size shrank from twenty-seven in 1955 to fifteen in 1995.[2] The decline affected students primarily after the third grade. First-graders continued to arrive at school better prepared than in any preceding generation. The decline was more pronounced at suburban schools than at inner-city ones, afflicted both private and public schools, and was larger for whites than for minorities in more-advanced grades.

The achievement decline cannot be blamed on inadequate spending. Between 1960 and 1995, annual per pupil spending in the United States rose from $2,122 to $6,434 in inflation-adjusted 1995 dollars.[3] By 1999, the United States was spending an average of $7,397 per K–12 student. Spending in other industrialized countries averaged $4,850. Only Switzerland, at $8,194 per pupil, spent more than the United States.[4] In industrialized countries, student scores on the Third International Mathematics and

---

1. John H. Bishop, "Is the Test Score Decline Responsible for the Productivity Growth Decline?" *American Economic Review* 79, no. 1 (1989): 178–197.

2. Darius Lakdawalla, "Quantity over Quality," *Education Next* 2, no. 3 (2002): 66–72, online edition: http://www.educationnext.org/20023/66.html; Eric A. Hanushek, "The Evidence on Class Size," Occasional Paper 98-1, W. Allen Wallis Institute of Political Economy, University of Rochester, Rochester, N.Y., 1998; Caroline M. Hoxby, "The Effects of Class Size and Composition on Student Achievement: New Evidence from Natural Population Variation," *Quarterly Journal of Economics* (November 2000): 1239–1285; Martin R. West and Ludger Woessmann, "Crowd Control," *Education Next* 3, no. 3 (2003): 56–63, online edition: http://educationnext.org/20033/56.html.

3. Eric A. Hanushek, "Deconstructing RAND," *Education Next* 1, no. 1 (2001), online edition: http://www.educationnext.org/2001sp/65.html.

4. National Center for Educational Statistics, International Comparisons of Expenditures for Education, table 40–1: Annual Expenditures on Public and Private Institutions per Student and as a Percentage of GDP, by Level of Education and Country: 1999, online at: http://nces.ed.gov/programs/coe/2003/section6/tables/t40_1.asp.

Science Studies tests are uncorrelated with spending. Though per capita U.S. spending is high and the academic achievement of its fourth-graders is above average, its eighth-graders score in the middle of the pack, and twelfth-grade achievement is consistently among the lowest of the countries studied.[5]

Achievement is also uncorrelated with spending within the United States. Although per pupil expenditures varied widely—from $4,413 to $13,577 per year in the one hundred largest districts in 2000–2001—no strong systematic relationship between spending and overall achievement has been demonstrated.[6] Nationwide, total U.S. expenditures averaged $8,859 per public school student in 2000–2001. In comparison, U.S. home-school suppliers sell complete courses for elementary or middle-school children for less than $1,000. This price includes all books, workbooks, lesson plans, tests, and supplies. It also includes the services of a remote teacher to grade monthly subject tests; of course, it does not include the cost of parents' time.

Given that the market price of home-school materials is about 10 percent of the average amount spent on a U.S. school student, it is not surprising that many private schools spend less than their public counterparts and turn out better-educated students. In 1990, a RAND Corporation study showed that Catholic high schools in New York City had higher graduation rates and better test scores than that city's public high schools despite similar student bodies drawn from rough neighborhoods. The Catholic schools excelled because they elicited dramatic performance improvements from marginal students, apparently by providing more orderly environments for learning. At $3,500 per student, the Catholic schools also spent almost 50 percent less than the public schools.[7]

Similar patterns prevail outside the United States. When researchers in India surveyed schools for the poor in 1999, they found that actual teaching activity was occurring in only 53 percent of the public schools visited. In private schools in the same area, students paid annual fees of about U.S.$10 and classroom activity was "feverish." The schools gave scholarships to exceptional students from families too poor to pay.[8] Poor Indian parents pay extra for effective private schools because they know that their children, rather than society in general, will get most of the benefit of education and that much of this benefit will be in the form of higher lifetime wages. Unlike the wealthy, the poor cannot afford to spend years in ineffective schools.

When private schooling was the rule in Britain and America, literacy was widespread even though most people attended far fewer years of school. Economist E. G. West found that, by 1869, most people in England and Wales could read and write. In 1880, when education became compulsory in Britain, about 95 percent of fifteen-year-olds were already literate. When Massachusetts began requiring compulsory education in 1852, according to Sheldon Richman, the literacy rate was already 98 percent.[9] Between 1910 and 1940, American secondary school enrollment rose from 18 to 71 percent.[10] This increase is often attributed to compulsory attendance laws and prohibitions on child labor, but economists Claudia Goldin and Lawrence Katz report that secondary schools were "already largely available and free for most students" before those laws were passed.[11] They attribute the enrollment increase to growing family wealth and the historically high returns to additional education.

Once public schools began using tax money to subsidize school tuition, schools financed and run by government began replacing private ones in both Britain and the

5. Harold R. O'Neil, Jamal Abedi, Charlotte Lee, Judy Miyoshi, and Ann Mastergeorge, *Monetary Incentives for Low-Stakes Tests* (Los Angeles: National Center for Research on Evaluation, Standards and Student Testing, University of California at Los Angeles, 2001), online at: http://nces.ed.gov/pubs2001/2001024.pdf.

6. National Center for Educational Statistics, Digest of Education Statistics, 2003, table 90, online at: http://nces.ed.gov/programs/digest/d03/tables/dt090.asp; Eric A. Hanushek and Julie A. Somers, "Schooling, Inequality, and the Impact of Government," NBER Working Paper no. 7450, National Bureau of Economic Research, Cambridge, Mass., 1999.

7. Paul Thomas Hill, Gail E. Foster, and Tamar Gendler, "High Schools with Character," Document no. R-3944-RC, RAND Corporation, Santa Monica, Calif., 1990; Peter M. Flanigan, "A School System That Works," *Wall Street Journal*, February 12, 1991; Derek A. Neal, "The Effect of Catholic Secondary Schooling

on Educational Attainment," *Journal of Labor Economics* 15, no. 1 (1997): 98–123; William H. Sander, "Catholic Grade Schools and Academic Achievement," *Journal of Human Resources* 31, no. 3 (1995): 540–548.

8. James Tooley, "Private Education: What the Poor Can Teach Us," *Policy* 18, no. 1 (2002): 18–21.

9. Edwin G. West, "The Spread of Education Before Compulsion," *Freeman*, July 1, 1996, online version: http://www.independent.org/newsroom/article.asp?id=307. West quotes Richman.

10. Claudia Goldin and Lawrence Katz, "Mass Secondary Schooling and the State: The Role of State Compulsion in the High School Movement," NBER Working Paper no. 10075, National Bureau of Research, Cambridge, Mass., 2003, p. 3.

11. Goldin and Katz, ibid., p. 28.

United States. The number of schools fell and school governance changed radically. Because the private schools depended on student tuition, they stressed items of traditional concern to parents: challenging curricula, high academic expectations, structured environments, and efficient use of class time. As public schools crowded private ones out of the market, parents dissatisfied with one school were less likely to be able to simply enroll their child in another one better suited to their needs.

As the tax-supported schools grew larger, control shifted from parents to teachers and administrators, and the focus of school governance gradually shifted from academic achievement to staff pay and working conditions. School officials sought to avoid offending any group with political power. The result was a steady decline in academic rigor featuring, as Diane Ravitch has documented, textbooks filled with banal literature, boring writing, and inaccurate content.[12]

As early as 1955, some U.S. states had begun allowing teachers' organizations to deduct dues from paychecks, bar nonunion members from teaching, and bargain collectively. The percentage of American school districts with at least 50 percent of teachers covered by collective bargaining rose from 1 percent in 1960 to 36 percent in 1992.[13] The data suggest that unionization increases school budgets, and that the increase is primarily directed to increasing teacher salaries and reducing class size to reduce workload.

Most unionized school districts in the United States set teacher pay using a "single salary schedule." Pay is determined by years of service and hours of graduate education. This equalization in pay fueled an exodus from the teaching profession between 1963 and 2000. Caroline Hoxby and Andrew Leigh found that teachers who attended colleges that required higher SAT scores for admission were the most likely to leave, presumably because they had more job opportunities outside of teaching. Overall, pay compression appears to have reduced the share of American teachers coming from colleges requiring higher average SAT scores from 5 percent to 1 percent. At the same time, the share of teachers in the lowest SAT categories rose from 16 to 36 percent.[14] As Dan Goldhaber and Dan

Player point out, single salary schedules waste money. Secondary school teachers with technical skills who leave teaching earn an average of $3,400 more a year in their new jobs than elementary school teachers who leave teaching for new jobs. School districts that pay all teachers the same wage either end up paying elementary school teachers too much or paying secondary school teachers too little. In the first case they waste money, and in the second they likely end up with secondary school teachers of lower quality.[15]

Some economists think that an increase in labor market opportunities for women means that relative teacher wages have declined and that teacher pay should be increased substantially to maintain quality.[16] But wage comparisons often ignore the fact that typical teachers work fewer than 190 days a year—including days for planning, parent conferences, and professional development—compared with 235 days per year for the average full-time U.S. worker. Teaching days are also shorter. In New York and Chicago public schools, teacher workdays are less than seven hours, including a forty-five-minute duty-free lunch period.[17] Teachers in public schools also enjoy lenient policies regarding unscheduled time off, low prices for generous health insurance, richer pensions, negligible travel requirements, and earlier retirements than private-sector employees. After accounting for differences in benefits and hours worked, economist Richard Vedder calculates that the average teacher earned an hourly wage of twenty-eight dollars in 2000. Computer programmers, accountants, mechanical engineers, registered nurses, and statisticians all made less.[18]

Current proposals for "knowledge- and skills-based" pay reforms would make public school teacher pay dependent on external pedagogical evaluations and scores on standardized tests. Like the single pay schedule, these proposals ignore labor supply and demand conditions. They also give little weight to school officials' judgments of individ-

12. Diane Ravitch, *The Language Police: How Pressure Groups Restrict What Students Learn* (New York: Knopf, 2003).

13. Caroline Minter Hoxby, "How Teachers' Unions Affect Education Production," *Quarterly Journal of Economics* 11, no. 3 (1996): 682.

14. Caroline M. Hoxby and Andrew Leigh, "Pulled Away or Pushed Out? Explaining the Decline of Teacher Aptitude in the United States." *American Economic Review* 94, no. 2 (2004): 236–240.

15. Dan Goldhaber and Dan Player, *What Different Benchmarks Suggest About How Financially Attractive It Is to Teach in Public Schools* (Madison: Consortium for Policy Research in Education, Wisconsin Center for Education Research, University of Wisconsin–Madison, 2003), p. 27.

16. Peter Temin, "Low Pay, Low Quality," *Education Next* 3, no. 3 (2003), online edition: http://www.educationnext.org/20033/8.html.

17. Michael Podgursky, "Fringe Benefits," *Education Next* 3, no. 3 (2003), online edition: http://www.educationnext.org/20033/71.html#fig1.

18. Richard Vedder, "Comparable Worth," *Education Next* 3, no. 3 (2003), online edition: http://www.educationnext.org/20033/14.html.

ual ability. State-mandated teacher certification tests are already widely in force. They appear to increase teacher wages by 3–5 percent without an observable effect on quality. It is possible that extensive reliance on time-consuming tests deters people with other job opportunities who prefer not to spend time preparing for tests.[19] In private schools, both market conditions and school administrators' perceptions of teacher quality affect pay. For example, math and science teachers at private schools typically earn 8 percent more than colleagues with similar experience.[20]

Teacher scores on tests of verbal ability correlate with student performance, as do the number of math and science courses taken by math and science teachers. Existing evidence suggests that variations in teacher quality account for 7–9 percent of the total variation in student achievement.[21] This may not sound like a large difference. But if high-quality teachers are defined as those whose students attain higher-than-expected grades, data from individual schools in the United States suggest that five years of having a teacher at the eighty-fourth quality percentile rather than at the fiftieth would completely eliminate the performance gap between poor and nonpoor children.[22]

Recent efforts to identify teacher quality using "value added" methods based on rankings derived from before-and-after student achievement test scores rest on shaky statistical foundations. No one knows how to tell how much of a student's score improvement is attributable to an individual teacher, and there is no way to know if a student who raised his score from 500 to 600 really learned less than a student who raised his score from 300 to 450.[23]

Many K–12 reformers seek to remedy the lack of accountability in government-funded schools by emphasizing parental choice via charter schools and voucher programs. Growing evidence suggests that competition does increase public-school quality. The introduction of charter schools in North Carolina apparently increased achievement in nearby public schools by about 1 percent, more than half of the recorded student achievement gain for 1999–2000.[24] Milwaukee public schools improved after vouchers were introduced. If all schools in the United States were to improve as rapidly, estimates Caroline Hoxby, "American schools could return to their 1970–71 productivity levels in under a decade" and "school productivity might be as much as 28 percent higher than it is today."[25]

Unfortunately, the American experience with voucher funding in higher education bodes ill for the long-term success of voucher funding. Grants and loans that follow students to the college of their choice, a wide choice of colleges, and providers with flexible salary schedules and the ability to hire and fire at will have not saved American higher education from recent problems with exploding costs and declining quality.

The National Association of Scholars documented the dissolution of general education requirements at the university level from 1914 to 1993.[26] In a system in which bottomless taxpayer subsidies ensure that students pay only a fraction of the costs of their college education and colleges forgo substantial revenues when a student drops out due to failing grades, American colleges and universities have limited incentive to require academic excellence or to constrain spending on amenities attractive to faculty and students.

College

According to economists Claudia Goldin and Lawrence Katz, the modern organizational structure of U.S. higher education stems from shifts in the "structure of knowledge" that occurred in the 1800s. Government funding of colleges was originally limited to producing better-educated

19. Joshua D. Angrist and Jonathan Guryan, "Does Teacher Testing Raise Teacher Quality? Evidence from State Certification Requirements," NBER Working Paper no. 9545, National Bureau of Economic Research, Cambridge, Mass., 2003.

20. Dale Ballou and Michael Podgursky, "Let the Market Decide," *Education Next* 1, no. 1 (2001), online edition: http://www.educationnext.org/2001sp/16ballou.html.

21. Eric A. Hanushek and Steven G. Rivkin, "Does Public School Competition Affect Teacher Quality?" in Caroline Minter Hoxby, ed., *The Economics of School Choice* (Chicago: University of Chicago Press, 2003), pp. 23–47, online at: http://edpro.stanford.edu/eah/papers/competition.nber.publication.pdf, p. 7. See also Christopher Jepsen and Steven Rivkin, "What Is the Tradeoff Between Smaller Classes and Teacher Quality?" NBER Working Paper no. 9205, National Bureau of Economic Research, Cambridge, Mass., 2002.

22. Eric A. Hanushek, "The Failure of Input-Based Schooling Policies," NBER Working Paper no. 9040, National Bureau of Economic Research, Cambridge, Mass., p. 42.

23. Dale Ballou, "Sizing Up Test Scores," *Education Next* 2, no. 2 (2002), online edition: http://www.educationnext.org/20022/10.html.

24. George M. Holmes, Jeff DeSimone, and Nicholas G. Rupp, "Does School Choice Increase School Quality?" NBER Working Paper no. 9683, National Bureau of Economic Research, Cambridge, Mass., May 2003.

25. Caroline Minter Hoxby, "School Choice and School Productivity (or Could School Choice Be a Tide That Lifts All Boats?)," NBER Working Paper no. 8873, National Bureau of Economic Research, Cambridge, Mass., April 2002, p. 49.

26. National Association of Scholars, *The Dissolution of General Education: 1914–1993* (Princeton: National Association of Scholars, 1996), online at: http://www.nas.org/reports/disogened/disogened_full.pdf.

grade school teachers. As science became more important in business and agriculture, state funding was expanded to produce technically trained graduates of benefit to local business interests. Between 1890 and 1940, the research university blossomed, average enrollments ballooned, and the market share of private colleges declined.[27] As government funding increased, its original intent was forgotten. In 1908, almost 30 percent of all students in the public universities were in engineering programs. By 1999, public engineering enrollment was no more than 5 percent.

By 2002–2003, state appropriations for higher education were about $63.6 billion. Most of the money went directly to the institutions themselves. Nearly two-fifths of the total revenue received by public colleges came from state appropriations. Private institutions received roughly half of their revenues from tuition income.[28] Private for-profit degree-granting institutions got about 6 percent of their revenues from governments,[29] and private not-for-profit degree-granting institutions received about 18 percent of their revenues from government through federal and state appropriations, grants, and contracts. Within this category, institutions with extensive doctoral degree programs depended on government for 28 percent of revenues, and schools offering only a baccalaureate depended on taxpayers for only 6 percent of revenues.

In return for their taxpayer funding, state college and university systems are expected to charge lower tuition. During 2002–2003, public four-year colleges charged an average list price of $4,081 per year for in-state students. Private four-year colleges charged an average of $18,273. Because students forgo state in-kind aid if they attend a private college, giving money to state colleges in return for low tuition biases students toward state institutions. In 1897, about 22 percent of higher-education students were enrolled in government-controlled institutions; in 1960 the number was 55 percent. By 1990, 68 percent of students enrolled in four-year programs were in government-supported colleges.[30]

As is the case in K–12 education, subsidizing institutions directly may have unintended consequences. Simulations by Ayşül Şahin of the Federal Reserve Bank of New York suggest that institutional subsidies in return for low tuition cause "an increase in the percentage of less able and less motivated college students" and that even highly able students respond by decreasing their effort levels.[31]

Subsidies to individual students also have unintended consequences. In the United States, mass federal subsidies for college students began in 1965, when the Higher Education Act created grants and campus programs to help poor students attend college and a loan program for middle-class students. As one would expect, federal subsidies have been systematically expanded over the last forty years in an effort to appeal to middle-class voters. More than 75 percent of federal aid to postsecondary students now underwrites loans, which appeal most strongly to middle- and upper-income students.[32] In 2003, federal spending under the Higher Education Act of 1965 reached $22.7 billion. Another program, the Hope and Lifetime Earnings tax credits, totaled $4.9 billion in 2000, the third year of the program.[33]

As federal subsidies to students have grown, American colleges have adopted pricing schemes that maximize the revenue they receive from each student. They send a prospective student individually tailored aid packages that take into account family resources, the government aid programs available, and the student's attractiveness to other schools. Colleges have little incentive to cut their costs and actively lobby government for more institutional funding and more student aid. Bridget Terry Long found that the new Hope and Lifetime Learning Tax Credits encouraged "students to attend more expensive colleges" and that some colleges responded by increasing tuition prices. They did not increase postsecondary enrollment.[34]

Aid is so generous that taxpayers are even required to subsidize child care for parents attending college. Because federal and state regulations invariably follow government funds, subsidies also increase operating costs. American

27. Claudia Goldin and Lawrence F. Katz, "The Shaping of Higher Education: The Formative Years in the United States, 1890 to 1940," Working Paper no. 6537, National Bureau of Economic Research, Cambridge, Mass., 1998.

28. Bridget Terry Long, "Does the Format of a Financial Aid Program Matter? The Effect of State In-Kind Tuition Subsidies," NBER Working Paper no. 9720, National Bureau of Economic Research, Cambridge, Mass., 2003, p. 1.

29. National Center for Education Statistics, Digest of Education Statistics, 2003, table 343, online at: http://nces.ed.gov/programs/digest/d03/tables/dt343.asp; and table 341, online at: http://nces.ed.gov/programs/digest/d03/tables/dt341.asp.

30. Goldin and Katz, "The Shaping of Higher Education," table 3.

31. Ayşül Şahin, "The Incentive Effects of Higher Education Subsidies on Student Effort," Federal Reserve Bank of New York Staff Reports, no. 192, abstract.

32. Shahira Knight, "College Affordability: Tuition Tax Credits vs. Saving Incentives," U.S. Congress, Joint Economic Committee Study, October 1997, online at: http://www.house.gov/jec/fiscal/tx-grwth/college/college.htm.

33. Bridget Terry Long, "The Impact of Federal Tax Credits for Higher Education Expenses," NBER Working Paper no. 9553, National Bureau of Economic Research, Cambridge, Mass., 2003, p. 2.

34. Long, "Impact of Federal Tax Credits," abstract.

colleges that admit students with federal funding are required to fulfill federal requirements on everything from reporting campus crime to meeting gender quotas in athletics.

In spite of their role in raising the cost of college, advocates of increased subsidies for higher education claim they are essential to ensuring equal access for everyone to the higher incomes generally associated with a college degree. Standard estimates of the rate of return to additional years of education range from 5 to 15 percent.[35] According to a 2002 Census Bureau study, people who graduated from college earned, on average, $21,800 a year more than those who did not.[36]

Unfortunately, the data on average earnings from college graduation mask the fact that those earnings disproportionately accrue to people who enter college with superior cognitive skills, particularly in mathematics.[37] Simulations by Hanushek, Leung, and Yilmaz suggest that need-based funding mechanisms allowing high-ability poor children to attend college may also benefit taxpayers by increasing economic efficiency.[38] Subsidy programs that encourage lower-ability students to incur debt in order to attend a college that increases neither their marketable skills nor their subsequent wages harm both students and taxpayers. Daniel Boothby and Geoff Rowe report that one fifth of Canadian B.A. graduates will not earn enough extra income to recover their college costs.[39]

35. Joop Hartog, "Behind the Veil of Human Capital," *OECD Observer,* no. 215 (January 1999), online at: http://www1.oecd.org/publications/observer/215/e-harto.htm as of December 5, 2004.

36. Jennifer Cheeseman Day and Eric C. Newburger, "The Big Payoff: Educational Attainment and Synthetic Estimates of Work-Life Earnings," U.S. Census Bureau, July 2002, online at: www.census.gov/prod/2002pubs/p23-210.pdf.

37. Daniel S. Hamermesh and Stephen G. Donald, "The Effect of College Curriculum on Earnings: Accounting for Non-ignorable Non-response Bias," NBER Working Paper no. w10809, National Bureau of Economic Research, Cambridge, Mass., 2004; Caroline M. Hoxby and Bridget Terry, "Explaining Rising Income and Wage Inequality Among the College-Educated," NBER Working Paper no. 6873, National Bureau of Economic Research, Cambridge, Mass., 1999.

38. Eric A. Hanushek, Charles Ka Yui Leung, and Kuzey Yilmaz, "Borrowing Constraints, College Aid, and Intergenerational Mobility," NBER Working Paper no. 10711, National Bureau of Economic Research, Cambridge, Mass., 2004.

39. Daniel Boothby and Geoff Rowe, "Rate of Return to Education: A Distributional Analysis Using the LifePaths Model," Applied Research Branch, Strategic Policy, Human Resources Development Canada, 2002, online at: http://www.hr.sdc.gc.ca/en/cs/sp/hrsd/prc/publications/research/2002-002365/page01.shtml as of December 6, 2004.

Despite lavish subsidies, only about a quarter of the U.S. population has earned a bachelor's degree. Taxpayer subsidies for higher education generally transfer income from people with lower incomes to middle-class college students. The students capture most of the gains from attending college via higher lifetime incomes. Whether such policies are fair or desirable will likely continue to provoke intense debate.

About the Author

Linda Gorman is a senior fellow at the Independence Institute, a state-based free-market think tank in Golden, Colorado. She writes frequently on education.

Efficiency

Paul Heyne

To economists, efficiency is a relationship between ends and means. When we call a situation inefficient, we are claiming that we could achieve the desired ends with less means, or that the means employed could produce more of the ends desired. "Less" and "more" in this context necessarily refer to less and more value. Thus, economic efficiency is measured not by the relationship between the physical quantities of ends and means, but by the relationship between the value of the ends and the value of the means.

Terms such as "technical efficiency" or "objective efficiency" are meaningless. From a strictly technical or physical standpoint, every process is perfectly efficient. The ratio of physical output (ends) to physical input (means) necessarily equals one, as the basic law of thermodynamics reminds us. Consider an engineer who judges one machine more efficient than another because one produces more work output per unit of energy input. The engineer is implicitly counting only the useful work done. "Useful," of course, is an evaluative term.

The inescapably evaluative nature of the concept raises a fundamental question for every attempt to talk about the efficiency of any process or institution: Whose valuations do we use, and how shall they be weighted? Economic efficiency makes use of monetary evaluations. It refers to the relationship between the monetary value of ends and the monetary value of means. The valuations that count are, consequently, the valuations of those who are willing and able to support their preferences by offering money.

From this perspective a parcel of land is used with maximum economic efficiency when it comes under the control of the party who is willing (which implies able) to pay the largest amount of money to obtain that control. The proof that a particular resource is being used efficiently is that no one is willing to pay more in order to divert it to some other use.

Those who object that this is an extremely narrow definition of efficiency often fail to recognize that every concept of efficiency has to employ some measure of value. The monetary measure used by economics turns out to be both broad and useful. It enables us to take account of and compare the evaluations made by many different persons and to respond appropriately.

What kind of structure should sit on the corner lot at Fifth and Main: a gas station, a condominium, a florist shop, or a restaurant? The owner can make a defensible decision even if everyone in town has a slightly different preference. The owner simply accepts the highest money bid that various prospective users of the land (the florist, the restaurateur, etc.) make for it. Effective social cooperation requires interpersonal comparisons of value, and monetary values supply us with a common denominator that works remarkably well.

The crucial prerequisites for the generation of these monetary values are private ownership of resources and relatively unrestricted rights to exchange ownership. When these conditions are satisfied, competing desires to use resources establish money prices that indicate each resource's value in its current use. Those who believe that particular resources would be more valuably (more efficiently) employed in some other way can raise the price and bid them away from the current users.

In the 1930s, for example, a small group of people who placed a high value on hawks bought a mountain in Pennsylvania and thereby converted it from a hawk-hunting area to a hawk sanctuary. Today our laws protect hawks and other predators, but in the 1930s hawks were in danger of extinction because they were hunted as vermin that ate chickens. If the only option for those who formed the Hawk Mountain Sanctuary Association in 1934 had been to persuade politicians and the public to change the laws, hawks could well be extinct today in that area. The association was able to save the hawks because its members demonstrated, through competing money bids, that a sanctuary was the most efficient—that is, the monetarily most valuable—use for the mountain.

Perhaps the importance of private ownership to achieving economic efficiency can be seen most clearly by looking at what happens when we try to work together without an effective system for assigning monetary value to resources. Take the example of urban automobile traffic. How can we arrive at a judgment about the overall effi-

ciency or inefficiency of the commuting process when we have to compare one person's convenience with another's delay, time saved for some with carbon monoxide inhaled by others, one person's intense dissatisfactions with another person's pleasures? To find out whether Jack values clean air more than Jill values a speedy commute requires a large set of interpersonal value indicators. Urban commuting creates congestion as well as air pollution problems in our society because we have not developed a workable procedure for weighing and comparing the positive and negative evaluations of different people.

The crucial missing element is private property. Because so many of the key resources employed by commuters are not privately owned, commuters are not required to bid for their use and to pay a price that reflects their value to others. Users pay no money prices for resources such as urban air and urban streets. Therefore, those goods are used as if they were free resources (see TRAGEDY OF THE COMMONS). But their use imposes costs on all the others who have been deprived of their use. In the absence of money prices on such scarce resources as streets and air, urban dwellers "are led by an invisible hand to promote an end that was no part of their intention," to apply Adam Smith's famous generalization. In this case, however, the end is not the public interest but a result that no one wants.

Critics of economic efficiency contend that it is a poor guide to public policy because it ignores important values other than money. They point out, for example, that the wealthy dowager who bids scarce milk away from the mother of an undernourished infant in order to wash her diamonds is promoting economic efficiency. The example is strained, not least because the pursuit of economic efficiency almost always makes milk available to the infant as well as the dowager. Most economists would agree that such dramatic examples can remind us that economic efficiency is not the highest good in life, but that does not mean we should discard the concept.

The moral intuitions that enable us to arbitrate easily between the child's hunger and the dowager's vanity cannot begin to resolve the myriad issues that arise every day as hundreds of millions of people attempt to cooperate in using scarce means with varied uses to achieve diverse ends. Moreover, the remarkable feats of social cooperation that actually make wholesome milk available to hungry infants far removed from any cows would be impossible in the absence of the monetary values that express and promote economic efficiency.

The social usefulness of well-defined property rights, free exchange, and the system of relative money prices that emerges from these conditions has perhaps been demonstrated most convincingly by the catastrophic failure in the twentieth century of the societies that tried to function without them (see SOCIALISM).

About the Author

The late Paul Heyne was a senior lecturer in economics at the University of Washington in Seattle. He held a Ph.D. in ethics and society from the Divinity School of the University of Chicago. He died in 2000.

Further Reading

Hayek, Friedrich A. "The Use of Knowledge in Society." *American Economic Review* 35, no. 4 (1945): 519–530. Reprinted in Hayek, *Individualism and Economic Order*. Chicago: University of Chicago Press, 1948.

Jouvenel, Bertrand de. "Efficiency and Amenity." Earl Grey Memorial Lecture, delivered at King's College, Newcastle upon Tyne, England, 1960. Reprinted in Kenneth J. Arrow and Tibor Scitovsky, eds., *Readings in Welfare Economics*. Homewood, Ill.: Richard D. Irwin, 1969. Pp. 100–112.

Knight, Frank H. "The Ethics of Competition." *Quarterly Journal of Economics* 37 (1923): 579–624. Reprinted in Knight, *The Ethics of Competition and Other Essays*. Chicago: University of Chicago Press, 1935.

Stroup, Richard L., and Jane S. Shaw. "The Free Market and the Environment." *Public Interest* 97 (Fall 1989): 30–43.

Efficient Capital Markets

Steven L. Jones
Jeffry M. Netter

The efficient markets theory (EMT) of financial economics states that the price of an asset reflects all relevant information that is available about the intrinsic value of the asset. Although the EMT applies to all types of financial securities, discussions of the theory usually focus on one kind of security, namely, shares of common stock in a company. A financial security represents a claim on future cash flows, and thus the intrinsic value is the PRESENT VALUE of the cash flows the owner of the security expects to receive.[1]

Theoretically, the profit opportunities represented by the existence of "undervalued" and "overvalued" stocks motivate investors to trade, and their trading moves the prices of stocks toward the present value of future cash flows. Thus, investment analysts' search for mispriced stocks and

---

[1]. For an excellent review of the debate on market efficiency, see Shiller 2003 for the behavioral finance view, and Malkiel 2003a for the proefficiency view.

their subsequent trading make the market efficient and cause prices to reflect intrinsic values. Because new information is randomly favorable or unfavorable relative to expectations, changes in stock prices in an efficient market should be random, resulting in the well-known "random walk" in stock prices. Thus, investors cannot earn abnormally high risk-adjusted returns in an efficient market where prices reflect intrinsic value.

As Eugene Fama (1991) notes, market efficiency is a continuum. The lower the transaction costs in a market, including the costs of obtaining information and trading, the more efficient the market. In the United States, reliable information about firms is relatively cheap to obtain (partly due to mandated disclosure and partly due to technology of information provision) and trading securities is cheap. For those reasons, U.S. security markets are thought to be relatively efficient.

The informational efficiency of stock prices matters in two main ways. First, investors care about whether various trading strategies can earn excess returns (i.e., "beat the market"). Second, if stock prices accurately reflect all information, new investment capital goes to its highest-valued use.

French mathematician Louis Bachelier performed the first rigorous analysis of stock market returns in his 1900 dissertation. This remarkable work documents statistical independence in stock returns—meaning that today's return signals nothing about the sign or magnitude of tomorrow's return—and this led him to model stock returns as a *random walk*, in anticipation of the EMT. Unfortunately, Bachelier's work was largely ignored outside mathematics until the 1950s. One of the first to recognize the potential information content of stock prices was John Burr Williams (1938) in his work on intrinsic value, which argues that stock prices are based on economic fundamentals. The alternative view, which dominated prior to Williams, is probably best exemplified by John Maynard Keynes's beauty contest analogy, in which each stock analyst recommends not the stock he thinks best, but rather the stock he thinks most other analysts think is best. In Keynes's view, therefore, stock prices are based more on speculation than on economic fundamentals. In the long run, prices driven by speculation may converge to those that would exist based on economic fundamentals, but, as Keynes noted in another context, "in the long run we are all dead."

Stock returns and their economic meaning received scant attention before the 1950s because there was little appreciation of the role of stock markets in allocating capital. This oversight had several contributing factors: (1) Keynes's emphasis on the speculative nature of stock prices led many to believe that stock markets were little more than "casinos," with no essential economic role; (2) many economists during the Great Depression and the immediate post–World War II era emphasized government-directed capital investment; and (3) the modern corporation, and the resulting need to raise large sums of capital, was a relatively recent development. But the invention of computing power in the 1950s, which made rigorous empirical analysis with large data sets more feasible, brought renewed attention from academic researchers.

In 1953, British statistician Maurice Kendall documented statistical independence in weekly returns from various British stock indices. Harry Roberts (1959) found similar results for the Dow Jones Industrial Index, and later, Eugene Fama (1965) provided comprehensive evidence not only of statistical independence in stock returns, but also that various techniques of "chartists" (i.e., technical analysts) had no predictive power. While this evidence was generally viewed as supporting the random walk model of stock returns, there was no formal understanding of its economic meaning, and some mistakenly took this randomness as an indication that stock returns were unrelated to fundamentals, and thus had no economic meaning or content. Fortunately, the timely work of Paul Samuelson (1965) and Benoit Mandelbrot (1966) explained that such randomness in returns should be expected from a well-functioning stock market. Their key insight was that competition implies that investing in stocks is a "fair game," meaning that a trader cannot expect to beat the market without some informational advantage. The essence of the "fair game" is that today's stock price reflects the expectations of investors given all the available information. Therefore, tomorrow's price should change only if investors' expectations of future events change, and such changes should be randomly positive or negative as long as investors' expectations are unbiased. This revelation had its roots in the developing rational expectations theory of macroeconomics, and thus, some economists refer to the EMT as the "rational markets theory." It was later recognized that the "fair game" model allows for the expectation of a positive price change, which is necessary to compensate risk-averse investors.

In 1970, Eugene Fama published his now-famous paper, "Efficient Capital Markets: A Review of Theory and Empirical Work." Fama synthesized the existing work and contributed to the focus and direction of future research by defining three different forms of market efficiency: weak form, semistrong form, and strong form. In a weak-form efficient market, future returns cannot be predicted from past returns or any other market-based indicator, such as trading volume or the ratio of puts (options to sell stocks) to calls (options to buy stocks). In a semistrong efficient market, prices reflect all publicly available information about economic fundamentals, including the public market data (in weak form), as well as the content of financial reports, economic forecasts, company announcements, and so on. The distinction between the weak and semistrong forms is that it is virtually costless to observe public market data, whereas a high level of fundamental analysis is required if prices are to fully reflect *all* publicly available information, such as public accounting data, public information regarding competition, and industry-specific knowledge. In strong form, the highest level of market efficiency, prices reflect all public and private information. This extreme form serves mainly as a limiting case because it would require even the private information of corporate officers about their own firm to be already captured in stock prices.

A simple way to distinguish among the three forms of market efficiency is to recognize that weak form precludes only technical analysis from being profitable, while semistrong form precludes the profitability of both technical and fundamental analysis, and strong form implies that even those with privileged information cannot expect to earn excess returns. Sanford Grossman and Joseph Stiglitz (1980) recognized that an extremely high level of market efficiency is internally inconsistent: it would preclude the profitable opportunities necessary to motivate the very security analysis required to produce information. Their main point is that market frictions, including the costs of security analysis and trading, limit market efficiency. Thus, we should expect to see the level of efficiency differ across markets, depending on the costs of analysis and trading. Although weak-form efficiency allows for profitable fundamental analysis, it is not difficult to imagine a market that is less than weak form but still relatively efficient in some sense. Thus, it can be useful to define the efficiency of a market in a more general, continuous sense, with faster price reaction equating to greater informational efficiency.

While most of the empirical research of the 1970s supported semistrong market efficiency, a number of apparent inconsistencies arose by the late 1970s and early 1980s. These so-called anomalies include, among others, the "small-firm effect" and the "January effect," which together document the tendency of small-capitalization stocks to earn excessive returns, especially in January. But financial economists today attribute most of the anomalies to either misspecification of the asset-pricing model or market frictions. For example, the small-firm and January effects are now commonly perceived as premiums necessary to compensate investors in small stocks, which tend to be illiquid, especially at the turn of the year. Fama (1998) also notes that the anomalies sometimes involved underreaction and sometimes overreaction and, thus, could be viewed as random occurrences that often went away when different time periods or methodologies were used.

More serious challenges to the EMT emerged from research on long-term returns. Robert Shiller (1981) argued that stock index returns are overly volatile relative to aggregate dividends, and many took this as support for Keynes's view that stock prices are driven more by speculators than by fundamentals. Related work by Werner DeBondt and Richard Thaler (1985) presented evidence of apparent overreaction in individual stocks over long horizons of three to five years. Specifically, the prices of stocks that had performed relatively well over three- to five-year horizons tended to revert to their means over the subsequent three to five years, resulting in negative excess returns; the prices of stocks that had performed relatively poorly tended to revert to their means, resulting in positive excess returns. This is called "reversion to the mean" or "mean reversion." Lawrence Summers (1986) showed that, in theory, prices could take long, slow swings away from fundamentals that would be undetectable with short-horizon returns. Additional empirical support for mispricing came from Narasimhan Jegadeesh and Sheridan Titman (1993), who found that stocks earning relatively high or low returns over three- to twelve-month intervals continued the trend over the subsequent three to twelve months.

These apparent inefficiencies contributed to the emergence of a new school of thought called behavioral finance (see BEHAVIORAL ECONOMICS), which countered the assumption of rational expectations with evidence from the field of psychology that people tend to make systematic cognitive errors when forming expectations. One such error that might explain overreaction in stock prices is the representative heuristic, which holds that individuals attempt to identify trends even where there are none and that this can lead to the mistaken belief that future patterns will resemble those of the recent past. On the other hand, momentum in stock returns may be explained by anchoring, the tendency to overweight initial beliefs and underweight the relevance of new information. It follows that momentum observed over intermediate horizons could be extrapolated over longer time horizons until overreaction develops. This does not, however, imply any easily exploitable trading strategy, because the point where momentum stops and overreaction starts will never be obvious until after the fact.

Resistance to the view that stock prices systematically overreact, as well as to the behavioral interpretation of this

evidence, came along two fronts. First, Fama and Kenneth French (1988) found that stocks earn larger returns during more difficult economic conditions when capital is relatively scarce and the default-risk premiums in interest rates are high. Higher interest rates initially drive prices down, but eventually prices recover with improved business conditions, and hence the mean-reverting pattern in aggregate returns. Second, adherents of the EMT argued that the cognitive failures of certain individuals would have little influence on stock markets because mispriced stocks should attract rational investors who buy underpriced and sell overpriced stocks.

Critics of the EMT responded to both of these charges. In response to the Fama and French evidence, James Poterba and Lawrence Summers argued that the mean-reverting pattern in aggregate index returns is too volatile to be explained by cyclical economic conditions alone. They claimed that excessive mean reversion resulted from prices straying from fundamentals, similar to Shiller's excess volatility story. As to whether the marginal trader is fully rational or subject to systematic cognitive errors, Andrei Shleifer and Robert Vishny (1997) and others noted that, while market efficiency requires traders to act quickly on their information out of fear of losing their advantage, mispricing can persist because it offers few opportunities for low-risk arbitrage trading. For example, how should one have responded during the bubble in Internet-based stocks of the late 1990s? Most of these stocks were difficult to short sell, and even if it was possible, a well-informed, fully rational short seller faced the risk that less than fully rational traders (also known as "noise traders") would continue to move prices away from fundamentals. Thus, the market will not necessarily correct as soon as rational traders recognize mispricing. Instead, the correction may come only after the mispricing becomes so large that noise traders lose confidence in the trend or rational traders act in response to the additional risk introduced by the noise traders.

The most striking examples of apparent inconsistencies with the EMT are the 1987 stock market crash and the movement of Internet stock prices beginning in the late 1990s. Some economists, admittedly a minority, believe that the 1987 crash and the Internet run-up and fall are consistent with market efficiency. For example, Mark Mitchell and Jeffry Netter (1989) argued that the large market decline in the days before the market crash in 1987 was triggered by an initially rational response to an unanticipated tax proposal, which in turn triggered a temporary liquidity crunch (or panic) due to much higher sales volumes than the market was prepared to handle. The exchanges, traders, and regulators learned from this experience, making markets more efficient. Burton Malkiel (2003a, 2003b), analyzing the Internet bubble, notes that Internet company values were difficult to determine, and while traders in most cases were wrong after the fact, there were no obvious unexploited arbitrage opportunities.

Regardless of whether it is the exception or the rule, the favorable market conditions of the late 1990s for technology and Internet-based stocks illustrate the stock market's critical role in resource allocation. A firm whose stock has appreciated rapidly finds it easier to raise additional funds through a secondary offering because higher prices mean a smaller percentage ownership of the firm needs to be offered to raise a given amount of capital. Favorable conditions also make it easier for privately held firms to raise funds through an initial public offering (IPO) of stock. Furthermore, a so-called hot IPO market entices venture capital firms to invest funds in hot industries and sectors in hopes of taking their firms public in such a favorable market. Many view these favorable market conditions as consistent with the market's valuation of growth options and the motivating incentive necessary to make the fund-raising portion of venture growth and creation possible. But while favorable market conditions can attract the investment capital necessary to grow a fledgling new industry, the market for technology and Internet-based stocks in the late 1990s appears to have overheated and, in hindsight, directed too much investment capital toward this sector. Thus, by the late 1990s, the return an investor in this sector could have rationally expected had fallen below what economic conditions could justify, as well as below what most investors actually anticipated.

While prices may take long, slow swings away from fundamentals, the EMT is still useful in at least two important ways. First, over shorter horizons, such as days, weeks, or months, there is considerable evidence that the EMT can explain the direction of stock price changes. That is, the response of stock prices to new information reasonably approximates the change in the intrinsic value of equity. Second, the EMT serves as a benchmark for how prices should behave if capital investments and other resources are to be allocated efficiently. Just how close markets come to this benchmark depends on the transparency of information, the effectiveness of regulation, and the likelihood that rational arbitragers will drive out noise traders. In fact, the informational efficiency of stock prices varies across markets and from country to country. Whatever the shortcomings of capital markets, there appears to be no better alternative means of allocating investment capital. In fact, the privatization movement of the 1990s and early 2000s suggests that most governments, including China's, now recognize this fact. Thus, academic inquiry in this area is likely to focus more on the conditions that explain and improve the informational efficiency of capital markets than on whether capital markets are efficient.

About the Authors

Steven L. Jones is an associate professor of finance at Indiana University's Kelley School of Business, Indianapolis. Jeffry M. Netter is the C. Herman and Mary Virginia Terry Chair of Business Administration in the University of Georgia's Terry College of Business. From 1986 to 1988, he was a senior research scholar at the U.S. Securities and Exchange Commission.

Further Reading

DeBondt, Werner F. M., and Richard Thaler. "Does the Stock Market Overreact?" *Journal of Finance* 40 (1985): 793–805.
Fama, Eugene F. "The Behavior of Stock Market Prices." *Journal of Business* 38 (January 1965): 34–105.
———. "Efficient Capital Markets: A Review of Empirical Work." *Journal of Finance* 25, no. 2 (1970): 383–417.
———. "Efficient Capital Markets II." *Journal of Finance* 46, no. 5 (1991): 1575–1617.
———. "Market Efficiency, Long-Term Returns, and Behavioral Finance." *Journal of Financial Economics* 49, no. 3 (1998): 283–306.
Fama, Eugene F., and Kenneth R. French. "Dividend Yields and Expected Stock Returns." *Journal of Financial Economics* 22 (October 1988): 3–25.
Grossman, Sanford J., and Joseph E. Stiglitz. "On the Impossibility of Informationally Efficient Markets." *American Economic Review* 70 (June 1980): 393–408.
Jegadeesh, Narasimhan, and Sheridan Titman. "Returns to Buying Winners and Selling Losers: Implications for Stock Market Efficiency." *Journal of Finance* 48 (March 1993): 65–91.
Kendall, Maurice. "The Analysis of Economic Time Series, Part I: Prices." *Journal of the Royal Statistical Society* 96 (1953): 11–25.
Keynes, John M. *The General Theory of Employment, Interest and Money.* New York: Harcourt, 1936.
Malkiel, Burton G. "The Efficient Market Hypothesis and Its Critics." *Journal of Economic Perspectives* 17, no. 1 (2003a): 59–82.
———. *A Random Walk down Wall Street.* 8th ed. New York: Norton, 2003b.
Mandelbrot, Benoit. "Forecasts of Future Prices, Unbiased Markets and 'Martingale Models.'" *Journal of Business*, special supplement (January 1966): 242–255.
Mitchell, Mark, and Jeffry Netter. "Triggering the 1987 Stock Market Crash: Antitakeover Provisions in the Proposed House Ways and Means Tax Bill?" *Journal of Financial Economics* 24 (1989): 37–68.
Poterba, James M., and Lawrence Summers. "Mean Reversion

in Stock Market Prices: Evidence and Implications." *Journal of Financial Economics* 22 (1987): 27–59.

Roberts, Harry. "Stock Market 'Patterns' and Financial Analysis: Methodological Suggestions." *Journal of Finance* 14 (1959): 11–25.

Samuelson, Paul. "Proof that Properly Anticipated Prices Fluctuate Randomly." *Industrial Management Review* 6 (1965): 49.

Shiller, Robert J. "Do Stock Prices Move Too Much to Be Justified by Subsequent Changes in Dividends?" *American Economic Review* 71 (June 1981): 421–435.

———. "From Efficient Markets to Behavioral Finance." *Journal of Economic Perspectives* 17, no. 1 (2003): 83–104.

Shleifer, Andrei, and Robert W. Vishny. "The Limits of Arbitrage." *Journal of Finance* 52 (March 1997): 35–55.

Summers, Lawrence. "Does the Stock Market Rationally Reflect Fundamental Values?" *Journal of Finance* 41 (July 1986): 591–601.

Williams, John Burr. *The Theory of Investment Value.* Cambridge: Harvard University Press, 1938.

Electricity and Its Regulation

Robert J. Michaels

Americans consumed 3,463 billion megawatt-hours (mwh) of electricity in 2002, with a delivered value of $249.6 billion. Thirty-seven percent of it was consumed by households, 32 percent by commercial users, and 28 percent by industrial users.[1] Adjusted for inflation, its price fell by 36 percent between 1983 and 2004.[2] Most electricity is generated when high-pressure steam rotates a turbine to induce an alternating current into a wire. In 2002, 50.1 percent of U.S. electricity was produced by coal, 17.9 by natural gas, 20.2 in nuclear units, 6.6 as hydroelectricity, and 2.3 by "renewable resources" such as wind and solar.[3] Newly generated power passes through substations that lower its voltage prior to consumption by final (retail) consumers.

1. U.S. Department of Energy, Energy Information Administration [EIA], *Electric Power Annual 2002* (December 2003), pp. 38, 40. Major portions of the remainder were used for such applications as street lighting and irrigation pumping. See http://www.eia.doe.gov/cneaf/electricity/epa/epa_sum.html.

2. EIA, Historical Statistics, online at: http://tonto.eia.doe.gov/merquery/mer_data.asp?table=T09.09, deflated by "all items" consumer price index.

3. EIA, Electric Power Annual 2002 supplementary table E5, online at: http://tonto.eia.doe.gov/merquery/mer_data.asp?table=T09.09.

Important characteristics of electricity limit the possibilities for markets. First, reserve power plants must always be operating to instantly replace generators or transmission lines that fail. Centralized control (usually by computers) is required to meet both predictable and unforeseen changes in regional conditions. Power cannot be economically stored, and area-wide blackouts occur if production either exceeds or falls short of demand for as little as a second. Second, duplication of facilities is inefficient because a single high-capacity line minimizes both capital cost per megawatt (MW) transferred and line losses due to resistance. A typical large utility (or group of them) is responsible for reliability and economical operation in its defined "control area." Each control area is interconnected with neighboring ones to facilitate emergency support, coordinated operations, and power purchases and sales. Third, an injection of power flows through the entire network according to Ohm's and Kirchoff's laws. Unlike water or gas, it cannot be directed down a single path. If a Utah generator sells power to a Wyoming user, only a small fraction of it flows directly between them. Because the power from Utah flows everywhere, it can overload lines in California and force Californians to curtail their own beneficial transactions.

Scale economies and reliability concerns left electricity dominated by large, vertically integrated utilities; that is, utilities that generated, transmitted, and distributed power. Direct competition had vanished by the 1920s as municipal franchise grants left nearly every city with a single utility. Between 1907 and 1940, all states formed regulatory commissions whose authority replaced that of cities. The reasons for the change are unclear: utilities may have sought protection from opportunistic city governments, or from competition in general. "Cost of service" regulation sets retail rates to recover expenses and give a "fair" return on capital. Problems in allocating common costs, as well as politics, allow latitude in setting rates for different customers. State regulators generally also require utilities to serve all customers and to plan facility additions in anticipation of growth. The Federal Energy Regulatory Commission (FERC) oversees "wholesale" or "bulk" transactions that occur prior to state-jurisdictional retail sales. The Federal Power Act requires that wholesale prices (including transmission charges) be cost based, but in practice, FERC simply accepts prices set by markets that meet its standards for competition. FERC's general policy has been to expand the role of markets and to decrease direct regulation subject to the law's limits, regardless of which party controls the government.

Electricity's ownership structure is complex. In 1998, America's 239 corporate utilities made 74.9 percent of retail sales; its 2,029 governmental (mostly municipal) utilities made 15.0 percent; and 912 cooperatives made 8.6 percent.[4] Most states exempt governmental utilities and cooperatives from regulation and allow them to set their own rates. Municipal utilities such as Los Angeles and San Antonio own generation and transmission, but most are small, transmission-dependent resellers of purchased power. Corporate utilities owned 66.1 percent of generating capacity in 1998, governmental utilities 10.7 percent, cooperatives 3.1 percent, and nonutility generators 11.9 percent. Federal hydroelectric facilities account for 8.2 percent of capacity.[5] Their output is preferentially allocated by law to municipals and cooperatives at below-market rates.

From the 1940s through the 1960s, regulation seemed to function well enough that few questioned its efficacy or looked to market alternatives. The states prohibited retail competition in utilities' assigned territories, but demand grew and engineering advances consistently lowered production costs of new generators. Even if utilities were operating inefficiently, consumers saw falling rates, and regulators usually allowed investors attractive returns. The industry grew more capital intensive, culminating in the 1960s with a move to nuclear generators that many expected to produce power too cheap to meter.

By the 1970s, the good times were over. Oil prices rose with OPEC, and price controls had produced shortages of natural gas. Nuclear plants experienced massive cost overruns, aggravated by the 1979 Three Mile Island accident, and consumer interests pressured regulators to disallow utilities from recovering these costs with higher rates. Technological progress in coal-fired generation slowed, and utilities became major targets of a growing environmental lobby. Environmental regulation prohibited or delayed some new plants and raised the costs of existing ones. Some regulators required demand-reduction programs in lieu of new generation, and others imposed newly politicized planning processes on their utilities.

At about this time, regulators, consumers, and utilities began reconsidering markets. Systems with high-cost, unbuilt, or delayed generators might be able to buy power more cheaply than they could produce it. New transmission and control technologies allowed reliable flows over distances of one thousand miles. Interutility exchanges grew faster than retail sales in every year between 1980 and 1998.[6] Some are under long-term contracts, while oth-

ers are daily or hourly "spot" trades. They may be for energy (flowing power) or capacity (rights to a generator's output). They can be firm (reliably backed up), interruptible, or in the form of options. Contracts for transmission service, known as "wheeling," must match delivery and receipt obligations. Beyond energy flows, since the 1970s the greater risks of unstable prices and regulatory uncertainty led to increases in generation and transmission undertaken by utility consortia.

The Public Utility Regulatory Policies Act (PURPA) of 1978 opened wholesale markets to nonutilities. Prior to PURPA, utilities could refuse to interconnect or purchase from nonutility generators at will. Part of the Carter administration's conservation policy, PURPA would encourage industrial generation from waste heat ("cogeneration") by requiring utilities to purchase it at the "avoided cost" of building and operating their own plants. The consensus in the late 1970s was that fossil fuels would remain expensive, particularly relative to the average cost of utility-owned generation fleets. This was thought to make self-supply with a fossil-fuel-burning generator uneconomic for many industrial users, the exceptions being those—thought to be few—that had high heat requirements and little choice but to get them from fossil fuels. Instead, oil prices collapsed over the 1980s, and decontrol of natural gas both ended its shortage and produced two decades of low prices. New gas-fired generators under 100 MW capacity became as cheap to operate as coal-fired plants ten times their size, and they had lower costs of environmental compliance. Experience with cogeneration led to larger nonutility plants whose output was cheaper for utilities to purchase than to generate themselves. Since 1992, utility purchases from nonutilities have grown more than twice as fast as retail sales.[7]

The Energy Policy Act of 1992 (EPAct) removed a final obstacle to generator competition by allowing FERC to order transmission owners to carry power for other wholesale parties. Nonutility generators now had access to any willing counterparty in the region, and a new industry of power marketers that handled less than 8 million mwh in 1995 traded more than 1.5 billion in 1999.[8] Transmission access allowed municipal utilities to become independent and build the power supplies they wanted. Retail customers, however, still lacked choices. They could enjoy the

4. EIA, *The Changing Structure of the Electric Power Industry 2000: An Update*, pp. 17, 28, online at: http://www.eia.doe.gov/cneaf/electricity/chg_stru_update/update2000.pdf.

5. Ibid., p. 24.

6. Ibid., p. 24.

7. Ibid., p. 23.

8. EIA, *Wholesale Competition in the U.S. Power Industry Fact Sheet* (2003), online at: http://www.eia.doe.gov/cneaf/electricity/page/fact_sheets/wholesale.html. A given megawatt of power may have passed through several marketers prior to reaching the final customer.

benefits of competition only if state regulators allowed them to leave existing utilities.

In 1994, the California Public Utilities Commission (CPUC) became the first to investigate choice for retail customers. With power costs 50 percent above the national average, even the CPUC's research staff blamed overregulation and proposed greater reliance on markets. Competitive suppliers and many retail users welcomed the proposal, but California's three large corporate utilities understandably resisted. They claimed that competitive prices would not allow them to recover about $20 billion in above-market PURPA contracts and unamortized nuclear costs. The CPUC agreed that utilities had some claim to these "stranded costs," which they had incurred in the expectation that a regulated monopoly would remain.

In 1996, California's legislature unanimously approved Assembly Bill 1890, a comprehensive but internally inconsistent compromise that authorized an Independent System Operator (ISO) to ensure nondiscriminatory use of transmission that utilities still owned but might use to stifle competition. Utilities had to divest most of their in-state gas-fired generation and were to purchase all power from markets operated by the new California Power Exchange (PX) and the ISO. They could transact for deliveries no more than a day ahead, and other risk-management activities were prohibited. Assembly Bill 1890 froze or discounted retail prices until 2002. The utilities had until then to recover most stranded costs in the difference between fluctuating wholesale prices and government-frozen retail rates. Customers choosing nonutility service were billed for their shares of stranded costs.

For two years after the markets opened in April 1998, supply and demand kept prices low and allowed utilities to recover substantial stranded costs. This ended in the summer of 2000, however. Poor snows left the Northwest with little of the surplus hydropower it normally sent south. Also, natural gas supplies became limited and expensive; because gas-fired generators tended to be the highest-marginal-cost producers, and because market prices were equal to the marginal cost of the highest-cost producer, electricity became quite expensive. Another contributing factor was the increase in the price of pollution permits by several hundred percent. California's long resistance to constructing new power plants was one factor that kept prices from their usual decline when summer 2000 ended. Allegations that generators exercised market power and traders manipulated PX and ISO rules remain in controversy and continue to be litigated. Utilities faced insolvency as rising power costs met frozen retail prices. Short-term energy prices were high everywhere in the West, but only California required its utilities to use only

short-term markets and not to pass higher prices on to customers. Dependence on short-term markets, as well as the technical nature of the rules, encouraged suppliers and utilities alike to game the system.

As California's situation deteriorated in 2000, FERC reluctantly capped short-term prices. One of its two largest utilities lost creditworthiness, and the other went bankrupt, as did the PX. State government took over power purchasing in January 2001 and, by midyear, had entered long-term contracts for most of what utilities could not produce in the plants they still owned. As new generation came online in mid-2001 and hydroelectric conditions improved, market prices fell to their precrisis levels. Again, Californians are locked into uneconomical contracts whose costs must be allocated. The state's utilities are attempting to revert to their former monopoly roles, and other interests are attempting to again involve the state in their resource planning.

California's reforms were founded on a gamble that low energy prices would allow utilities to recover their stranded costs while rates were frozen. Customers in some states that reformed more rationally are reaping substantial benefits. All large northeastern states now allow choice, as do Illinois, Ohio, Michigan, and Texas. Most northeastern states avoided California's risks by adding fixed stranded cost payoffs to everyone's bills and allowing customers access to markets that existed for years prior to reform.

Customer choice varies with market conditions. In October 2004, 78 percent of the power consumed by industrial users in New Jersey was competitively supplied, by about thirty nonutility providers.[9] Utilities have ceased supplying nearly half of the power consumed by industrial users in New York and Massachusetts.[10] Small customers can also benefit—25 percent of Pittsburgh's residential users have new suppliers.[11] New York state already has thirty-three competitive nonutility sellers vying for customers.[12] We are still a long way from fully competitive markets (and California is retrogressing), but even the limited competition available now is producing substantial benefits.[13]

9. Utilipoint International, Issue Alert 2243, October 27, 2004, online at: http://utilipoint.com/issuealert/article.asp?id=2243.

10. Figures from EIA spreadsheets online at: http://www.eia.doe.gov/cneaf/electricity/chg_str/custpart.xls.

11. Pennsylvania Office of the Consumer Advocate, April 2004, online at: http://www.oca.state.pa.us/cinfo/Stats0404.pdf.

12. Kajal Kapur, "New York Deregulation Model: Characteristics and Success," online at: http://www.energypulse.net/centers/article/article_print.cfm?a_id=750.

13. A summary of California's recent experience appears in

About the Author

Robert J. Michaels is a professor of economics at California State University, Fullerton. He has advised independent power producers, marketers, industrial users, utilities, and regulatory agencies, and testified before Congress on the issues discussed above.

Further Reading

Newbery, David M. *Privatization, Restructuring, and Regulation of Network Utilities.* Cambridge: MIT Press Reprint, 2002.

O'Donnell, Arthur. *Soul of the Grid: A Cultural Biography of the California Independent System Operator.* iUniverse, 2003.

Rothwell, Geoffrey. *Electricity Economics: Regulation and Deregulation.* New York: Wiley-IEEE, 2002.

Stoft, Steven. *Power System Economics: Designing Markets for Electricity.* New York: Wiley, 2002.

Sweeney, James. *The California Electricity Crisis.* Stanford, Calif.: Hoover Institution Press, 2002.

U.S. Department of Energy, Energy Information Administration. *The Changing Structure of the Electric Power Industry 2000: An Update.* 2002. Online at: http://www.eia.doe.gov/cneaf/electricity/chg_stru_update/update2000.pdf.

Empirics of Economic Growth

Kevin Grier

Why are some countries rich and others poor? Why do some countries experience sustained levels of high growth that propel them into the ranks of the rich while others stagnate, seemingly in perpetuity? These are perhaps the most fascinating and important questions in all of economics.

Since the late 1980s, economists have done extensive work on the determinants of ECONOMIC GROWTH. As yet, however, there are few widely agreed-on results. The lack of consensus is unfortunate because increasing the growth rates of the world's many poor countries is a primary global policy goal. We do have at least two natural experiments in which a single nation was bisected by very different forms of governments: the two Germanys from the end of World War II to reunification in 1991, and the two Koreas. In both cases, the government that allowed private property and free (at least compared with its counterpart government) enterprise oversaw an economic "miracle," while the more totalitarian governments in the pairings each produced decades of stagnation and poverty. Because,

Robert J. Michaels, "California Electricity Policy: Evolving and Retrogressing," *Natural Gas and Electricity* 21 (October 2004): 10–14.

in each case, the people and their situations were so similar before the change that split them up, we get as close as we can ever get in the real world to a laboratory experiment without a laboratory—a fact that makes these findings significant. Economists know that there is some level of government intervention so great that it stifles economic growth, causing economies under it to do poorly.

But when economists use statistical analysis on large samples, other differences between countries that are hard to measure (e.g., culture) can be relevant, and the results are not as straightforward. We can show that factors such as private property rights and lack of corruption (or, as it is sometimes called, the "rule of law") are strongly correlated with high income, but it is difficult to show that they are correlated with current growth. More on that later.

What do economists know about the causes of growth? Begin by looking at the world income distribution in the year 2000. Here, countries are the unit of analysis, which means that Uganda counts as much as China, despite China's much greater population. Most economists take this approach, although some look at either population-weighted distributions or worldwide distributions of individuals' incomes.[1]

Figure 1 displays the distribution of per capita national income in U.S. dollars adjusted for deviations from purchasing power parity for 185 countries in the year 2000. The data are from the World Bank's "World Development Indicators" online database. Ignoring the extreme outlier of Luxembourg (the $51,000 observation), the income ratio between the second-highest-income country (the United States) and the lowest-income country is about 77. There are 31 countries in the sample whose incomes are

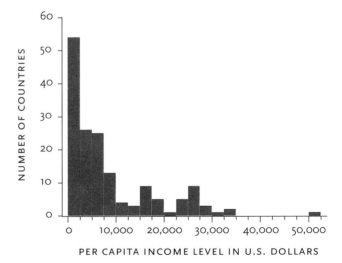

Figure 1 The World Income Distribution in 2000

1. See Sala-I-Martin 2002 for an example.

The Two Koreas and the Two Germanies: Close to a Laboratory Experiment

David R. Henderson

Economists have great difficulty determining the factors that can be shown, empirically, to affect economic growth. Many factors—economic policy, starting point, culture, and climate—can matter. So when nature presents us with experiments that are as close to laboratory experiments as we are likely to get, we should pay attention. Two such "experiments" have appeared in the last sixty years: North and South Korea and East and West Germany.

At the end of the Korean War in 1953, both North and South Korea were decimated. Both have harsh climates, and both initially had similar cultures. There was one big difference: North Koreans lived under COMMUNISM and still do, while South Koreans lived under a government that allowed property rights; was relatively open to trade; and, although it rigged the rules in favor of large corporations, was relatively open to ENTREPRENEURSHIP. In short, there was much more economic freedom in South Korea than in North Korea. The results are in. In 2004, North Korea's GDP was about $40 billion, up from $11 billion in 1953 (also in 2004 dollars). This implies an average annual growth rate of 2.6 percent, which is almost certainly an overstatement of the true North Korean growth rate because there is no good way to measure the value of output in a socialist economy. If shoes are produced but no one buys them, this counts in GDP. If one government plant produces steel that other government plants are required to take, even if it is useless, this also counts in GDP. Such surpluses of useless goods are endemic in socialist economies (see SOCIALISM). Also, the socialist planners had an incentive to overstate growth. In 2004, South Korea's GDP was about $925 billion, up from about $13.8 billion in 1953 (also in 2004 dollars). This implies an average annual growth rate of 8.6 percent, more than three times as much as North Korea's official rate.

Similarly, at the end of World War II, both East and West Germany lay in ruins. But in 1948 (see GERMAN ECONOMIC MIRACLE), West Germany slashed tax rates and ended price controls, moving from a fascist economy to a relatively free economy. East Germany, by contrast, adopted communism and did not abandon it until 1991. The results are just as stunning as in the case of the two Koreas. In 1991, East Germany's GDP (in 1990 dollars) was $86 billion, up from $51.4 billion in 1950 (also in 1990 dollars). This implies an average annual growth rate of 1.3 percent. For the same reasons as in the case of North Korea, this also is likely an overstatement. In 1991, West Germany's GDP (in 1990 dollars) was $1.24 trillion, making it the third-largest economy in the world, up from $214 billion in 1950 (also in 1990 dollars). This implies an average annual growth rate of 4.4 percent, more than three times that of East Germany.

Sources of data for the above computations:

Eberstadt, Nicholas. Private correspondence (for North Korean GDP for 1953).
Maddison, Angus. *The World Economy: Historical Statistics.* Paris: OECD, 2003. P. 28 (for East and West Germany).
The World Factbook. CIA, 2005 (for North and South Korea).

less than 5 percent of U.S. income, and 70 countries with incomes less than 10 percent of U.S. income. Income gaps this large are unprecedented in history; that is to say, the cross-country pattern of per capita incomes is diverging over time. In 1870, the corresponding income ratio was around 9, while in 1960 it was around 50.[2]

More specifically, the twenty-two highest-income countries in 1960 saw their average incomes relative to the United States rise slightly, from 69.4 percent of the U.S. level to 72.1 percent, a gain of almost 4 percent. A sample of forty-one sub-Saharan African countries saw their average relative income fall from 12 percent of the U.S. level in 1960 to 7.2 percent of the U.S. level in 2000, an average decline of 40 percent.[3] In a sample of twenty-two Latin American countries, the average country income relative to the United States fell from 27.4 percent in 1960 to 17.4 percent in 2000, about a 35 percent decline. Even Chile, a success story in the region, saw its relative level fall slightly, from 31.4 percent to 29.8 percent.[4] Only a sample of six-

2. For further details documenting the phenomenon, see Pritchett 1997.

3. Only Botswana, Cape Verde, Gabon, Mauritius, and the Seychelles showed any increases in their incomes relative to the United States over this forty-year period.

4. Chile is considered a success because, with an average annual per capita growth rate of 3.9 percent, its absolute income level (in PPP adjusted dollars) grew from $3,853 in 1960 to $9,925.5 in 2000. However, U.S. income rose from $12,272 to $33,293 over the same period.

teen Asian countries shows catch-up, with their relative average income levels more than doubling, from 11.4 percent of the U.S. level to 26.4 percent.

Consider an illustration of the importance of raising growth rates. In 1960, Bolivia ($2,354) and Malaysia ($2,120) had roughly equal per capita incomes. Over the next forty years, however, Malaysia grew at an average annual rate of about 9 percent while Bolivia's growth rate was a mere 0.5 percent. The result is that in 2000, Malaysia ($9,920) had a per capita income more than 3.5 times that of Bolivia ($2,724). Given the large number of poor countries in the world that are not currently growing much, knowing what a country can do to grow faster is vital.

At first blush, finding the determinants of growth seems simple. We simply need to figure out what the Asian countries did that Latin American and sub-Saharan African countries failed to do. Yet this task has not been easy because not all fast-growing countries have identical policies, and high-growth and low-growth countries sometimes have similar policies.

Before discussing numbers and results, though, let us examine the policy advice one would get from the most well-known and widely used theoretical model of economic growth, the neoclassical growth model (often called the Solow model after Nobel laureate Robert Solow's fundamental work). The Solow model implies that if a country's national saving rate rises, growth will temporarily rise above its long-run rate as the economy shifts to its new equilibrium. However, long-run equilibrium growth is independent of the saving rate or the population growth rate. If all countries have access to the same technology, all should have the same steady-state (long-run) growth rate.[5] If a country raises its investment rate, it will experience a period of higher-than-normal growth as the economy adjusts to its new, higher growth path; but once the adjustment has occurred, growth will revert to the steady-state level. The model, then, has two predictions. First, countries with better policies should be richer; second, countries that, for whatever reason, are far away from their steady-state income level will grow faster than countries closer to their own (possibly different) steady-state income levels.

N. G. Mankiw, David Romer, and David Weil (1992) modified the neoclassical model by adding human capital as another input into the production of national income.

In this so-called augmented Solow model, equilibrium income depends on the rate of investment in education as well as the physical capital investment rate. This opens another avenue for policy to affect wealth, as policies that increase educational investments will also make a country permanently richer and will temporarily raise its growth rate in the transition period to the new equilibrium.

Mankiw, Romer, and Weil also provided a statistical test of their model, measuring human capital investment by secondary-school enrollment rates. In their sample, this variable, a physical investment variable, and a variable related to population growth explained more than 80 percent of the cross-country variation in income. They also calculated that the rate at which a country approaches its steady state is fairly slow; only about 2 percent of the gap between the initial equilibrium and the new one is eliminated per year. This rate is generally referred to as the speed of convergence, though we should remember that the convergence concept here is conditional (relative to a country's individual steady state) rather than absolute (catching up to the richest countries). In a series of empirical papers, Robert Barro and Xavier Sala-I-Martin (1992) obtained a 2 percent convergence rate in a wide variety of samples, but even this finding has been challenged on the grounds that the studies are done with "time averaging." A numerical example illustrates the problem. Suppose that country A's annual growth rate over twenty years averages 3.5 percent and its investment rate averages 15 percent. Suppose that country B's annual growth rate over the same twenty years averages 5 percent and its investment rate averages 20 percent. Then a study of these countries will find a positive relationship between investment and growth. But what if we look beneath the averages and find that for the first ten years in country A, growth was 5 percent and the investment rate was only 10 percent and that for the next ten years, growth was down to 2 percent while the investment rate was up to 20 percent? Similarly, in country B, for the first ten years growth was 8 percent and the investment rate was 15 percent and for the next ten years, growth was down to 2 percent and the investment rate was up to 25 percent. Then for each country there would be a negative relationship between the investment rate and economic growth and "time averaging" would hide this true relationship. Most of the work finding 2 percent convergence is, unfortunately, based on time averaging.

Empirical studies of countries' growth over time—that is, studies that avoid the time-averaging problem—have shown two main differences from the work described above. First, education is generally not found to be a significant determinant of growth. This was shown first by Nazrul Islam (1995) and well documented by Lant Pritchett (2001). Sec-

5. How long countries take to get to their steady state is an important empirical question. Economists' answers vary from a very long time (thirty-seven years to get halfway there) in earlier cross-country comparisons to a much shorter time (seven years or less) in more recent work that includes a time dimension. This "speed of convergence" issue is discussed below.

ond, the convergence rate is generally estimated to be much higher than 2 percent. Islam calculated convergence rates of 4 to 6 percent, while F. Caselli, G. Esquivel, and F. Lefort (1996) obtained rates above 10 percent.

Besides potential inappropriate time averaging, there is another problem with studying countries at a point in time. Using only one observation per country in a statistical analysis requires including a large number of countries. Yet, many studies have shown that the parameters of empirical growth models vary widely across groups of countries.[6] This can cause serious problems for studying a cross section of countries at a point in time. Perhaps the most serious problem is that once the rich countries are removed from a sample, there is very little evidence of conditional convergence for the rest of the countries when one allows a time dimension in the model.

A third statistical issue that makes empirical growth research problematic is the problem of reverse causality: we are seldom sure whether the variables expected to cause growth actually do so or are themselves caused by growth. For example, some economists claim that financial development helps growth, but others argue that economic growth itself causes financial development. The same argument could be made for variables like investment, political turmoil, and even international trade. While there are statistical techniques for addressing this issue, they are especially difficult to employ in growth models, where it is hard to determine that a particular variable can legitimately be excluded.

If one ignores all three of these issues—that is to say, if one estimates cross-sectional regressions on a wide range of disparate countries and makes no allowance for the possibility of reverse causality—a few variables seem to have a significant effect on growth. Sala-I-Martin (1997) undertakes this experiment in "I Just Ran Two Million Regressions." He considers sixty-three variables that might potentially explain growth. He finds higher growth in countries that have been open to trade (as measured by the Sachs and Warner [1995] index) longer, that abide by the "rule of law," and that are more capitalistic. On the other side, he finds growth to be negatively associated with revolutions, coups, and wars. However, it is difficult to take these results at face value. Consider the finding on capitalism. Sala-I-Martin's variable for growth is the average per capita growth rate from 1960 to 1992. But his variable for capitalism is from a 1994 Freedom House document (Freedom House is an organization that rates the freedom of various countries). Literally, then, we are being told that

being capitalist in the early 1990s affected a country's growth rate in the 1950s, 1960s, and 1970s. The same type of difficulty arises in the use of the Sachs-Warner trade measure, which is constructed with data collected from 1950 to 1990. To make policy recommendations, we need to know that being open to trade today, or being capitalistic today, will increase growth in future years, and the empirical work so far does not clearly establish that claim.

All that being said, the policy variables that seem most robustly related to growth are sound macroeconomic policies (mainly stable and reasonably low inflation), openness to trade, institutional quality (i.e., little government corruption), and financial development.

One of the most interesting recent approaches to understanding what causes sustained increases in economic growth is the work by Ricardo Hausmann, Lant Pritchett, and Dani Rodrik (2004), who studied eighty-three cases in which a country rapidly increased its growth rate and sustained the increase for at least eight years. Their most statistically significant results are that a financial liberalization raises the probability of a growth increase by around 7 percent, and that a political regime change toward autocracy (from democracy or less-strict autocracy) raises the probability of increased growth by almost 11 percent. Most growth increases (which they call "growth accelerations") are unpredictable, however, and as they put it, "the vast majority of growth accelerations are unrelated to standard determinants such as political change and economic reform, and most instances of economic reform do not produce growth accelerations."[7]

Two popular candidates for factors important to economic growth are property rights and political rights. A good measure of property rights is available from the Heritage Foundation's Index of Economic Freedom, which ranks countries from one (excellent property rights, fast enforcement, no corruption, no expropriation) to five (little to no secure private property, high corruption, mostly state-owned resources, frequent expropriation).[8] A measure of political rights is taken from Freedom House's survey of freedom in the world, which ranks countries from one (free and fair elections, a competitive opposition, respect for minority political groups) to seven (political rights largely absent, oppressive regime).[9]

---

6. Kevin Grier and Gordon Tullock (1989) were perhaps the first to document this phenomenon.

7. Hausmann, Pritchett, and Rodrick, 2004, abstract. They do find that when the growth increase is accompanied by reform, it is more likely to last well beyond the eight-year window they initially chose.

8. Note that "property rights" is not the whole index, just one component of it. For more details, see http://www.heritage.org/research/features/index/chapters/Chapter_5.pdf (especially p. 72).

9. For the exact details, see the Freedom House methodology

We can take these rankings for 2000 and merge them with real per capita GDP data (again adjusted for deviations from PPP) from the Penn World Tables. This creates a sample of 120 countries for the growth rate and 123 for the 2000 income level. Doing so shows two main things: (1) for economic well-being, secure property rights are more important than political rights; and, (2) these variables explain income levels but not growth rates.

The simple correlation between the property rights variable and per capita income is −.78, while the correlation between the political rights variable and per capita income is −.59. (The negatives occur because for both measures, whether of political rights or property rights, higher numbers mean less respect for rights.) A zero would indicate no correlation between the variables, and −1 indicates perfect negative correlation. Both the correlations are sizable and significantly different from zero, but the two explanatory variables are also significantly correlated with each other (the property rights − political rights correlation is .71). A basic multiple regression can sort out the independent effects of the two variables on income. The results are as follows:

income in 2000 = 26,673 − 5,638 × property rights variable
(637)
− 471 × political rights variable
(339)

The numbers below the coefficients are their estimated standard errors; they imply that property rights is a highly significant variable, and, when it is included in the model, political rights is not significantly partially correlated with income. This simple equation accounts for about 61 percent of the variation in incomes across countries. Taken literally, every step of improvement in the secure property rights scale raises a country's per capita income by more than $5,000.[10]

For growth, as opposed to income level, the picture is quite different. The correlation between property rights and average annual growth from 1995 to 2000 is .02, and the political rights–average growth correlation is .06. In a multiple regression of income growth on the two variables, both variables are completely insignificant, either jointly or individually. Property rights do seem to matter, but mainly for being rich and not for causing higher-than-average current growth. Note that this is exactly what the neoclassical growth model would predict, in that a policy

that raises savings and investment (improving property rights) raises equilibrium income but not the long-run growth rate.

Finally, for those looking for further reading on this topic, a good starting point is the work of economists such as Stephen Durlauf, Peter Klenow, Lant Pritchett, and Dani Rodrik.[11]

About the Author

Kevin Grier is a professor of economics at the University of Oklahoma. From 1997 to 2002, he was coeditor of the *Southern Economic Journal*.

Further Reading

Barro, Robert, and X. Sala-I-Martin. "Convergence." *Journal of Political Economy* 100, no. 2 (1992): 223–251.
Caselli, F., G. Esquivel, and F. Lefort. "Re-opening the Convergence Debate: A New Look at Cross Country Growth Empirics." *Journal of Economic Growth* 1, no. 3 (1996): 363–389.
Grier, Kevin, and Gordon Tullock. "An Empirical Analysis of Cross National Economic Growth 1951–80." *Journal of Monetary Economics* 24, no. 2 (1989): 259–276.
Hausmann, Ricardo, Lant Pritchett, and Dani Rodrik. "Growth Accelerations." NBER Working Paper no. 10566, National Bureau of Economic Research, Cambridge, Mass., 2004.
Islam, Nazrul. "Growth Empirics: A Panel Data Approach." *Quarterly Journal of Economics* 110, no. 4 (1995): 1127–1170.
Klenow, Peter, and Andres Rodriguez-Clare. "Externalities and Growth." In Philippe Aghion and Steven Durlauf, eds., *Handbook of Economic Growth*. Vol. 1. Amsterdam: North-Holland, 2005.
Mankiw, N. G., David Romer, and David Weil. "A Contribution to the Empirics of Economic Growth." *Quarterly Journal of Economics* 107, no. 2 (1992): 407–437.
Pritchett, Lant. "Divergence, Big-time." *Journal of Economic Perspectives* 11, no. 3 (1997): 3–17.
———. "Where Has All the Education Gone?" *World Bank Economic Review* 15, no. 3 (2001): 367–391.
Sachs, Jeffrey, and A. Warner. "Economic Reform and the Process of Economic Integration." *Brookings Papers on Economic Activity* 1 (1995): 1–95.
Sala-I-Martin, Xavier. "I Just Ran Two Million Regressions." *American Economic Review* 87, no. 2 (1997): 178–183.
———. "The World Distribution of Income." NBER Working Paper no. 8933, National Bureau of Economic Research, Cambridge, Mass., 2002.

Web page at: http://www.freedomhouse.org/research/freeworld/2003/methodology.htm.

10. However, we have not done any work to show this equation is causal, so such an interpretation may be unwarranted.

11. This is most easily done by accessing papers on their Web sites, which are: http://www.ssc.wisc.edu/econ/Durlauf/research.html, http://www.klenow.com/, http://ideas.repec.org/e/ppr27.html, and http://ksghome.harvard.edu/~drodrik/papers.html.

Energy

Jerry Taylor
Peter Van Doren

Most of the energy consumed in America today is produced from the combustion of fossil fuels, primarily oil, coal, and natural gas. Energy can be generated, however, in any number of ways. Figure 1 indicates the sources of energy employed by the American economy as of February 2004.

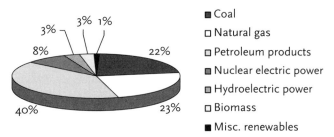

Figure 1 U.S. Energy Sources, 2004

- ■ Coal — 22%
- □ Natural gas — 23%
- □ Petroleum products — 40%
- ■ Nuclear electric power — 8%
- ▨ Hydroelectric power — 3%
- □ Biomass — 3%
- ■ Misc. renewables — 1%

The economy has become more efficient at using energy over time. In 1949, the U.S. economy required 20,620 British thermal units (Btu, a common energy measurement) to produce an inflation-adjusted dollar of domestic goods and services. By 2002, only 10,310 Btu were required to do the same.[1]

In a free market, cost dictates energy choices. Fossil fuels, for example, are economically attractive for many applications because the energy available from fossil fuels is highly concentrated, easily transportable, and cheaply extracted. Renewable energies such as wind and solar power, on the other hand, are relatively dispersed, difficult to transport, and costly to harness given the capital costs of facility construction.

Many people recommend accelerated federal subsidies and preferences for renewable energy in order to reduce America's dependence on imported oil. But such recommendations fail to appreciate the fact that energy sources are often difficult to substitute for one another. Until we see major technological advances in electric-powered vehicles and related battery systems, for example, technological breakthroughs in solar or wind power will have little, if any, impact on oil imports. That is because renewable energy is used primarily to generate electricity and cannot be used directly in transportation to replace oil: in 2002, only 2.5 percent of America's total electricity was generated

1. Energy Information Administration, "Table 1.5: Energy Consumption, Expenditures, and Emissions Indicators, 1949–2002," online at: http://www.eia.doe.gov/emeu/aer/txt/ptb0105.html.

from oil combustion.[2] The main impediment to the commercial viability of electric vehicles is the cost and operation of the vehicle's power train, not the cost of the electricity necessary as an input to that power train.

Oil Depletion

One of the recurring policy fights concerning energy is what the government should do about the depletion of economically attractive crude oil reserves. Underlying this fight, however, is a dispute about whether oil is in danger of becoming scarcer in the foreseeable future.

One camp (primarily geologists) argues that few, if any, major new oil fields remain to be found and that mathematical calculation demonstrates that production will peak at some point in the not-too-distant future and then begin a slow but steady decline.[3] Another camp (primarily economists) contends that reserves are as much an economic as a geologic phenomenon. That is, reserves are discovered and counted when it makes economic sense to find them. Thus, we do not know how much economically profitable oil has yet to be "discovered." Technological advances are adding reserves at a far greater rate than they are being depleted.[4] For example, in 1970, non-OPEC countries had about 200 billion barrels in reserves. Through 2003, they had produced 460 billion barrels and still had 209 billion barrels remaining.[5] Although the debate is inconclusive, the weight of the evidence suggests that economists have the better argument.[6]

Another dispute concerns whether price signals alone are sufficient to efficiently move from one set of energy resources to another if the need arises. Some have maintained that consumers do not change their behavior much in response to price increases. The claim is true in the short run, but not true over the course of several years. Economists estimate that a 10 percent increase in oil prices reduces the amount demanded in the short run by about 1 percent. Over the long run, however, a 10 percent increase in oil prices reduces the amount demanded by about 10 percent.[7]

2. Ninety-five billion kilowatt-hours (kWh) were generated by oil out of a total of 3,858 billion kWh in 2002. See Energy Information Administration, *Electric Power Annual 2002*, pp. 1–3.

3. Kenneth S. Deffeyes, *Hubbert's Peak: The Impending World Oil Shortage* (Princeton: Princeton University Press, 2001).

4. M. A. Adelman, *The Genie out of the Bottle: World Oil Since 1970* (Cambridge: MIT Press, 1995), pp. 11–39, and "The World Is Not Running Out of Oil," *Regulation* 27, no. 1 (2004): 16–21.

5. Adelman 2004, p. 18.

6. Robert Arnott, "Supply Side Aspects of Depletion," *Journal of Energy Literature* 8, no. 1 (2002): 3–21.

7. Adelman 1995, p. 190.

Short- and long-term responses differ because of the costs and time associated with replacing the capital stock, switching fuel sources, and adjusting manufacturing practices. Consumers generally "wait out" a price increase until they are convinced that investments in energy efficiency or fuel switching will, at the very least, pay for themselves and, at best, yield long-term gains. Although some worry that the lag between price signals and consumer response is inefficient, given the costs involved in changing consumption practices, consumer reluctance to react at the first sign of trouble is economically defensible.

The severe price implications of even modest supply disruptions have led some economists to support interventions to avoid the high prices that accompany oil supply shocks. To hedge against severe oil market disruptions, the federal government maintains the Strategic Petroleum Reserve (SPR), an inventory of 660 million barrels of oil as of mid-2004. To hedge against supply shortages and high prices in electricity markets, many states require utilities to maintain reserve generation capacity. Such interventions are not necessary because private insurance against energy price volatility is readily available in the form of commodity futures on the New York Stock Exchange and various derivative financial contracts.[8] But infrequent high energy prices are more costly politically than the hidden but constant costs of rarely utilized excess electric generation capacity and oil inventory.

How important is energy to the economy as a whole? Energy expenditures were only 7.2 percent of GDP in 2000, and oil expenditures were only 2.1 percent of GDP.[9] Some economists claim that the effect of energy price shocks on the economy is overstated and that monetary policy—not oil price shocks—deserves most of the blame for the recessions in 1973–1975, 1980, and 1990–1991.[10]

Other economists disagree.[11] Ideally, to disentangle the effect of monetary policy from oil price increases one would need episodes in which monetary policy was constant but oil prices increased. But this occurred only in 1990, and it is difficult to infer causality from one case. Thus, the debate is difficult to resolve at present.[12]

Subsidies

Are energy price signals so distorted by inappropriate government policies that they do not efficiently allocate resources? There are two fundamental complaints. The first is that government subsidies and preferences for various fuels and technologies reduce prices below market levels. The second complaint is that energy prices do not reflect the environmental damage inflicted on others by energy consumption.

Regarding the former complaint, the Energy Information Administration reports that federal energy subsidies as of 1999 were somewhere between $8.6 billion and $11.3 billion annually, or about 1 percent of total yearly energy expenditures.[13] They probably do not affect final prices because they do not affect marginal cost, and thus are simple wealth transfers from taxpayers to owners of the subsidized fuels.

The complaint about environmental damages is more serious. Economists believe that in an ideal world, taxes would be imposed on users equal to the damages imposed on others. Energy consumption would then be efficient because the external costs would be internalized in its price. However, calculating environmental costs associated with fuel use is controversial. The main difficulty is in knowing the effects of various concentrations of pollutants and hazardous substances on human health.

Figure 2 demonstrates the problem. It is a survey of the published range of external cost estimates associated with the consumption of various fuels for electricity generation. The wide disparity in published estimates in peer-reviewed journals suggests that, whatever the merits of this exercise, it is impossible at the moment to conclude scientifically what the correct tax should be.

8. Philip Verleger Jr., *Adjusting to Volatile Energy Prices* (Washington, D.C.: Institute for International Economics, 1993).

9. Energy Information Administration, *Annual Energy Review 2002,* table 1.5 p. 13. Oil expenditures are the authors' calculations using Energy Information Administration, *Monthly Energy Review,* table 1.7 (May 2004): "Products Supplied Column," and table 9.1, p. 123: "Composite Refinery Acquisition Price" and GDP data from the National Income and Product Accounts Web site at: http://www.bea.gov/bea/dn/nipaweb/index.asp.

10. The strongest argument to this effect published thus far is B. S. Bernanke, M. Gertler, and M. Watson, "Systematic Monetary Policy and the Effects of Oil Price Shocks," *Brookings Papers on Economic Activity* 1 (Washington, D.C.: Brookings Institution, 1997), pp. 91–157.

11. James D. Hamilton and Ana Maria Herrera, "Oil Shocks and Aggregate Macroeconomic Behavior: The Role of Monetary Policy," *Journal of Money, Credit, and Banking* 36 (April 2004): 265–286.

12. Donald Jones, Paul Leiby, and Inja Paik, "Oil Price Shocks and the Macroeconomy: What Has Been Learned Since 1996," *Energy Journal* 25, no. 2 (2004): 1–32.

13. U.S. Energy Information Administration, "Federal Intervention and Subsidies in Energy Markets 1999: Energy Transformation and End Use," SR/OIAF/2000–02, May 2000, p. 53.

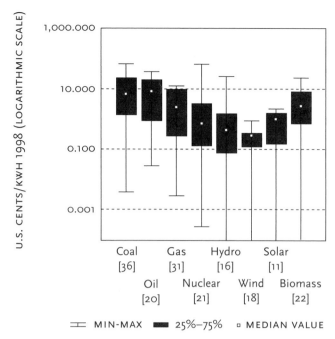

== MIN-MAX ■ 25%–75% □ MEDIAN VALUE

Figure 2 Range of External Costs Estimates

Source: Thomas Sundqvist and Patrik Soderholm, "Valuing the Environmental Impacts of Electricity Generation: A Critical Survey," *Journal of Energy Literature* 8, no. 2 (2002): 19.
Note: The figures in brackets represent the total number of observations for each fuel source. Those observations come from sixty-three externality studies; some studies have more than one observation.

A further implication of Figure 2 is worth considering. Although consumers are not explicitly taxed to reflect the "environmental externalities" associated with their energy use, the environmental costs of their energy choices are to some degree reflected in energy prices via the compliance costs associated with existing environmental regulations. Whether those regulatory costs are greater than, equal to, or less than the environmental externalities imposed by energy consumption is unclear for the same reasons that the findings reported in Figure 2 are unclear. If we accept estimates from the U.S. Environmental Protection Agency concerning the effect various energy-related pollutants have on human health, it would appear that energy prices today generally do a reasonable job of reflecting environmental costs. Economist W. Kip Viscusi et al. find that if EPA's analysis of the impact of various pollutants on human health is accurate, then coal prices are somewhat less than optimal, natural gas prices are too high, and gasoline prices are about right.[14]

Does Conservation Require Subsidies?

Some energy analysts argue that consumers invest too little in energy conservation measures such as insulation, fluorescent lights, or hybrid cars.[15] Even if that is true, can government collect and assimilate information better than people left to their own devices and then, through regulation based on that information, provide net benefits? Empirical analysis suggests that the record of government-directed conservation is rather poor.[16]

Between 1989 and 1999, for example, electric utility companies—primarily at the behest of state public utility commissions—spent $23.1 billion in the United States to subsidize ratepayer energy conservation investments. Yet a recent study found that those expenditures reduced electricity sales by only between 0.3 and 0.4 percent within their service territories and did so at an average cost of fourteen to twenty-two cents per kilowatt-hour—roughly two to three times as expensive, on average, as the energy it was attempting to conserve.[17]

Similarly, a recent study found that federal energy efficiency standards for appliances will provide net negative benefits of between $46.4 and $56.2 billion through 2050 and that those costs will be borne disproportionately by low- and middle-income households.[18]

Energy Research and Development (R&D)

Because investors cannot easily capture all the economic benefits associated with a particular technological advance, most economists agree that no government involvement

14. W. Kip Viscusi et al., "Environmentally Responsible Energy Pricing," *Energy Journal* 15, no. 2 (1994): 23–42. The authors did not consider greenhouse gas emissions in their calculations given

the uncertainty surrounding the environmental and economic ramifications of global warming.

15. Interlaboratory Working Group, *Scenarios for a Clean Energy Future* (Oak Ridge, Tenn.: Oak Ridge National Laboratory; and Berkeley, Calif.: Lawrence Berkeley National Laboratory), ORNL/CON-476 and LBNL-44029, November 2000. For an alternative view, see Mikael Togeby and Anders Larsen, "The Potential for Electricity Conservation in Industry: From Theory to Practice," in Proceedings from the eighteenth International Association for Energy Economics International Conference, *Into the 21st Century: Harmonizing Energy Policy, Environment, and Sustainable Economic Growth* (Cleveland: International Association for Energy Economics, 1995), pp. 48–55.

16. Franz Wirl, *The Economics of Conservation Programs* (Boston: Kluwer, 1997).

17. David Loughran and Jonathan Kulick, "Demand Side Management and Energy Efficiency in the United States," *Energy Journal* 25, no. 1 (2004): 19–43.

18. Ronald Sutherland, "The High Costs of Federal Energy Efficiency Standards for Residential Appliances," Policy Analysis 504, Cato Institute, December 23, 2003.

leads to a less-than-efficient level of investment in energy R&D.

The standard economic remedy is federal support of energy R&D projects. Although economists do not object to such policies on principle, they do find that government's record of support for various energy investments is dismal.[19] This has led most economists to conclude that, while there may be a "market failure" in the R&D sector, there is at least an equally serious problem of "government failure" in the "solution."[20]

Economist William Niskanen reminds us that "the case for government support of civilian R&D is that the return to the economy is greater than the return to the firm, not that government has better information on what R&D has the highest return."[21] Niskanen accordingly suggests that targeted federal R&D efforts be eliminated and replaced with a robust R&D tax credit and matching grants to universities to supplement funds raised from private sources.[22] While the idea appears meritorious, it has not attracted much political support.

Economists agree that prices allocate all resources (including energy) better than government edicts do. If politicians intervene in the energy market, manipulating price signals through tax credits is preferable to direct regulation.

CAFE Standards

An example of the economic case against direct regulation is the fuel economy standards for cars and trucks. The Congressional Budget Office estimates that increasing the Corporate Average Fuel Efficiency (CAFE) standards to achieve a 10 percent reduction in gasoline consumption would cost producers and consumers about $3.6 billion a year *more* than the value of fuel savings, or about a net cost of $228 per new vehicle sold. Achieving the same reduction through a gasoline tax increase of 46 cents per gallon would cost producers and consumers about $2.9 billion a year, or $184 per new vehicle sold.[23] While few dispute

such observations, CAFE standards are more politically palatable than gasoline taxes because the costs of the former are hidden from consumers, while the costs of the latter are not.

CAFE standards not only cost more than gasoline taxes to achieve a specific consumption reduction, they also reduce the marginal cost of driving a mile—and thus, ironically, increase vehicle miles traveled. The economics literature suggests that for every 10 percent increase in fuel efficiency through standards, people increase their miles driven by 2 percent.[24] In fact, any efficiency standard that reduces the marginal cost of consuming energy will have an analogous effect, known to economists as the "rebound effect."

One of the consequences of the rebound effect in relation to CAFE standards is a net increase in air pollution. According to one recent study, a 50 percent increase in fuel efficiency standards would reduce gasoline consumption by about 21 percent, but would increase net emissions of volatile organic compounds by 1.9 percent, nitrogen oxides by 3.4 percent, and carbon monoxide by 4.6 percent.[25]

Compensating Losers

Much of the debate about energy policy, however, is not about economic efficiency (the subject of this article so far), but about compensating losers. That is because energy prices tend to be volatile, and even minor changes in supply and demand have unusually large effects on prices in the short run. This encourages consumers to campaign for government protection from market forces when prices go up and producers to campaign for government protection from market forces when prices fall.

Past interventions driven by the desire to protect people from losses have included consumer price controls, gasoline rationing, government-managed and protected producer cartels, strict public utility regulation, fuel use mandates and prohibitions, and windfall profit taxes—all of which have been harshly criticized by economists in retrospect.[26] Interventions today are far milder, including subsidized energy services, preferences and subsidies to

19. Linda Cohen and Roger Noll, *The Technology Pork Barrel* (Washington, D.C.: Brookings Institution, 1991); U.S. General Accounting Office, "DOE's 'Success Stories' Report," GAO/RCED-96-120R, April 15, 1996; William Niskanen, "R&D and Economic Growth—Cautionary Thoughts," in Claude Barfield, ed., *Science for the 21st Century: The Bush Report Revisited* (Washington, D.C.: American Enterprise Institute, 1997), pp. 84–86.

20. Ronald Sutherland, "Time to Overhaul Federal Energy R&D," Policy Analysis 424, Cato Institute, February 7, 2002.

21. Niskanen 1997, p. 90.

22. Ibid.

23. Congressional Budget Office, "The Economic Costs of Fuel Economy Standards Versus a Gasoline Tax," December 2003.

24. David Greene, James Kahn, and Robert Gibson, "Fuel Economy Rebound Effect for U.S. Household Vehicles," *Energy Journal* 20, no. 3 (1999): 6–10.

25. Andrew Kleit, "CAFE Changes, by the Numbers," *Regulation* 25, no. 3 (2002): 35.

26. For a summary of criticisms, see Robert L. Bradley, *Oil Gas, and Government: The U.S. Experience*, vols. 1 and 2 (Lanham, Md.: Rowman and Littlefield, 1996); Richard Posner, *Natural Monopoly and Its Regulation* (Washington, D.C.: Cato Institute, 1999); and Peter Van Doren, *Politics, Markets, and Congressional Policy Choices* (Ann Arbor: University of Michigan Press, 1991).

select energy producers, largely symbolic periodic investigations of alleged industry misbehavior, and somewhat lighter public-utility regulation. Economists disagree among themselves about whether government should be shielding people from losses in the first place. However, they do agree, for the most part, that in addressing such concerns regarding energy prices, general income transfers are far more efficient and less costly than are direct regulatory interventions in particular markets.

About the Authors

Jerry Taylor is director of natural resource studies at the Cato Institute. He has testified frequently at hearings on Capitol Hill on energy and environmental policy. Peter Van Doren is editor of *Regulation* magazine and an adjunct associate professor of public policy at the University of North Carolina at Chapel Hill. He earned his Ph.D. in 1985 from Yale.

Entrepreneurship

Russell S. Sobel

An entrepreneur is someone who organizes, manages, and assumes the risks of a business or enterprise. An entrepreneur is an agent of change. Entrepreneurship is the process of discovering new ways of combining resources. When the market value generated by this new combination of resources is greater than the market value these resources can generate elsewhere individually or in some other combination, the entrepreneur makes a profit. An entrepreneur who takes the resources necessary to produce a pair of jeans that can be sold for thirty dollars and instead turns them into a denim backpack that sells for fifty dollars will earn a profit by increasing the value those resources create. This comparison is possible because in competitive resource markets, an entrepreneur's costs of production are determined by the prices required to bid the necessary resources away from alternative uses. Those prices will be equal to the value that the resources could create in their next-best alternate uses. Because the price of purchasing resources measures this opportunity cost—the value of the forgone alternatives—the profit entrepreneurs make reflects the amount by which they have increased the value generated by the resources under their control.

Entrepreneurs who make a loss, however, have reduced the value created by the resources under their control; that is, those resources could have produced more value elsewhere. Losses mean that an entrepreneur has essentially turned a fifty-dollar denim backpack into a thirty-dollar

pair of jeans. This error in judgment is part of the entrepreneurial learning, or discovery, process vital to the efficient operation of markets. The profit-and-loss system of capitalism helps to quickly sort through the many new resource combinations entrepreneurs discover. A vibrant, growing economy depends on the efficiency of the process by which new ideas are quickly discovered, acted on, and labeled as successes or failures. Just as important as identifying successes is making sure that failures are quickly extinguished, freeing poorly used resources to go elsewhere. This is the positive side of business failure.

Successful entrepreneurs expand the size of the economic pie for everyone. Bill Gates, who as an undergraduate at Harvard developed BASIC for the first microcomputer, went on to help found Microsoft in 1975. During the 1980s, IBM contracted with Gates to provide the operating system for its computers, a system now known as MS-DOS. Gates procured the software from another firm, essentially turning the thirty-dollar pair of jeans into a multibillion-dollar product. Microsoft's Office and Windows operating software now run on about 90 percent of the world's computers. By making software that increases human productivity, Gates expanded our ability to generate output (and income), resulting in a higher standard of living for all.

Sam Walton, the founder of Wal-Mart, was another entrepreneur who touched millions of lives in a positive way. His innovations in distribution warehouse centers and inventory control allowed Wal-Mart to grow, in less than thirty years, from a single store in Arkansas to the nation's largest retail chain. Shoppers benefit from the low prices and convenient locations that Walton's Wal-Marts provide. Along with other entrepreneurs such as Ted Turner (CNN), Henry Ford (Ford automobiles), Ray Kroc (McDonald's franchising), and Fred Smith (FedEx), Walton significantly improved the everyday life of billions of people all over the world.

The word "entrepreneur" originates from a thirteenth-century French verb, *entreprendre,* meaning "to do something" or "to undertake." By the sixteenth century, the noun form, *entrepreneur,* was being used to refer to someone who undertakes a business venture. The first academic use of the word by an economist was likely in 1730 by Richard Cantillon, who identified the willingness to bear the personal financial risk of a business venture as the defining characteristic of an entrepreneur. In the early 1800s, economists Jean-Baptiste Say and John Stuart Mill further popularized the academic usage of the word "entrepreneur." Say stressed the role of the entrepreneur in creating value by moving resources out of less productive areas and into more productive ones. Mill used the term "entrepreneur" in his popular 1848 book, *Principles of Political Economy*, to refer to a person who assumes both the risk and the management of a business. In this manner, Mill provided a clearer distinction than Cantillon between an entrepreneur and other business owners (such as shareholders of a corporation) who assume financial risk but do not actively participate in the day-to-day operations or management of the firm.

Two notable twentieth-century economists, Joseph Schumpeter and Israel Kirzner, further refined the academic understanding of entrepreneurship. Schumpeter stressed the role of the entrepreneur as an innovator who implements change in an economy by introducing new goods or new methods of production. In the Schumpeterian view, the entrepreneur is a disruptive force in an economy. Schumpeter emphasized the beneficial process of CREATIVE DESTRUCTION, in which the introduction of new products results in the obsolescence or failure of others. The introduction of the compact disc and the corresponding disappearance of the vinyl record is just one of many examples of creative destruction: cars, electricity, aircraft, and personal computers are others. In contrast to Schumpeter's view, Kirzner focused on entrepreneurship as a process of discovery. Kirzner's entrepreneur is a person who discovers previously unnoticed profit opportunities. The entrepreneur's discovery initiates a process in which these newly discovered profit opportunities are then acted on in the marketplace until market competition eliminates the profit opportunity. Unlike Schumpeter's disruptive force, Kirzner's entrepreneur is an equilibrating force. An example of such an entrepreneur would be someone in a college town who discovers that a recent increase in college enrollment has created a profit opportunity in renovating houses and turning them into rental apartments. Economists in the modern AUSTRIAN SCHOOL OF ECONOMICS have further refined and developed the ideas of Schumpeter and Kirzner.

During the 1980s and 1990s, state and local governments across the United States abandoned their previous focus on attracting large manufacturing firms as the centerpiece of economic development policy and instead shifted their focus to promoting entrepreneurship. This same period witnessed a dramatic increase in empirical research on entrepreneurship. Some of these studies explore the effect of demographic and socioeconomic factors on the likelihood of a person choosing to become an entrepreneur. Others explore the impact of taxes on entrepreneurial activity. This literature is still hampered by the lack of a clear measure of entrepreneurial activity at the U.S. state level. Scholars generally measure entrepreneurship by using numbers of self-employed people; the defi-

ciency in such a measure is that some people become self-employed partly to avoid, or even evade, income and payroll taxes. Some studies find, for example, that higher income tax rates are associated with higher rates of self-employment. This counterintuitive result is likely explained by the higher tax rates encouraging more tax evasion through individuals filing taxes as self-employed. Economists have also found that higher taxes on inheritance are associated with a lower likelihood of individuals becoming entrepreneurs.

Some empirical studies have attempted to determine the contribution of entrepreneurial activity to overall economic growth. The majority of the widely cited studies use international data, taking advantage of the index of entrepreneurial activity for each country published annually in the *Global Entrepreneurship Monitor*. These studies conclude that between one-third and one-half of the differences in economic growth rates across countries can be explained by differing rates of entrepreneurial activity. Similar strong results have been found at the state and local levels.

Infusions of venture capital funding, economists find, do not necessarily foster entrepreneurship. Capital is more mobile than labor, and funding naturally flows to those areas where creative and potentially profitable ideas are being generated. This means that promoting individual entrepreneurs is more important for economic development policy than is attracting venture capital at the initial stages. While funding can increase the odds of new business survival, it does not create new ideas. Funding follows ideas, not vice versa.

One of the largest remaining disagreements in the applied academic literature concerns what constitutes entrepreneurship. Should a small-town housewife who opens her own day-care business be counted the same as someone like Bill Gates or Sam Walton? If not, how are these different activities classified, and where do we draw the line? This uncertainty has led to the terms "lifestyle" entrepreneur and "gazelle" (or "high growth") entrepreneur. Lifestyle entrepreneurs open their own businesses primarily for the nonmonetary benefits associated with being their own bosses and setting their own schedules. Gazelle entrepreneurs often move from one start-up business to another, with a well-defined growth plan and exit strategy. While this distinction seems conceptually obvious, empirically separating these two groups is difficult when we cannot observe individual motives. This becomes an even greater problem as researchers try to answer questions such as whether the policies that promote urban entrepreneurship can also work in rural areas. Researchers on rural entrepreneurship have recently shown that the Internet can make it easier for rural entrepreneurs to reach a larger market. Because, as Adam Smith pointed out, specialization is limited by the extent of the market, rural entrepreneurs can specialize more successfully when they can sell to a large number of online customers.

What is government's role in promoting or stifling entrepreneurship? Because the early research on entrepreneurship was done mainly by noneconomists (mostly actual entrepreneurs and management faculty at business schools), the prevailing belief was that new government programs were the best way to promote entrepreneurship. Among the most popular proposals were government-managed loan funds, government subsidies, government-funded business development centers, and entrepreneurial curriculum in public schools. These programs, however, have generally failed. Government-funded and -managed loan funds, such as are found in Maine, Minnesota, and Iowa, have suffered from the same poor incentives and political pressures that plague so many other government agencies.

My own recent research, along with that of other economists, has found that the public policy that best fosters entrepreneurship is economic freedom. Our research focuses on the PUBLIC CHOICE reasons why these government programs are likely to fail, and on how improved "rules of the game" (lower and less complex taxes and regulations, more secure property rights, an unbiased judicial

system, etc.) promote entrepreneurial activity. Steven Kreft and Russell Sobel (2003) showed entrepreneurial activity to be highly correlated with the "Economic Freedom Index," a measure of the existence of such promarket institutions. This relationship between freedom and entrepreneurship also holds using more widely accepted indexes of entrepreneurial activity (from the *Global Entrepreneurship Monitor*) and economic freedom (from Gwartney and Lawson's *Economic Freedom of the World*) that are available selectively at the international level. This relationship holds whether the countries studied are economies moving out of socialism or economies of OECD countries. Figure 1 shows the strength of this relationship among OECD countries.

The dashed line in the figure shows the positive relationship between economic freedom and entrepreneurial activity. When other demographic and socioeconomic factors are controlled for, the relationship is even stronger. This finding is consistent with the strong positive correlation between economic freedom and the growth of per capita income that other researchers have found. One reason economic freedom produces economic growth is that economic freedom fosters entrepreneurial activity.

Economists William Baumol and Peter Boettke popularized the idea that capitalism is significantly more productive than alternative forms of economic organization because, under capitalism, entrepreneurial effort is chan-

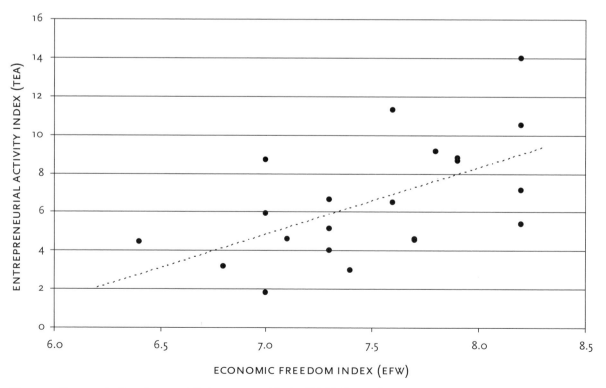

Figure 1 Economic Freedom and Entrepreneurship in OECD Countries, 2002

neled into activities that produce wealth rather than into activities that forcibly take other people's wealth. Entrepreneurs, note Baumol and Boettke, are present in all societies. In government-controlled societies, entrepreneurial people go into government or lobby government, and much of the government action that results—tariffs, subsidies, and regulations, for example—destroys wealth. In economies with limited governments and rule of law, entrepreneurs produce wealth. Baumol's and Boettke's idea is consistent with the data and research linking economic freedom, which is a measure of the presence of good institutions, to both entrepreneurship and economic growth. The recent academic research on entrepreneurship shows that, to promote entrepreneurship, government policy should focus on reforming basic institutions to create an environment in which creative individuals can flourish. That environment is one of well-defined and enforced property rights, low taxes and regulations, sound legal and monetary systems, proper contract enforcement, and limited government intervention.

About the Author

Russell S. Sobel is a professor of economics and James Clark Coffman Distinguished Chair in Entrepreneurial Studies at West Virginia University, and he was founding director of the Entrepreneurship Center there.

Further Reading

Introductory

Gwartney, James D., and Robert A. Lawson. *Economic Freedom of the World: 2002 Annual Report*. Vancouver: Fraser Institute, 2002. Information about this book can be found online at: http://www.freetheworld.com/.

Hughes, Jonathan R. T. *The Vital Few: American Economic Progress and Its Protagonists*. Exp. ed. New York: Oxford University Press, 1986.

Kirzner, Israel M. *Competition and Entrepreneurship*. Chicago: University of Chicago Press, 1973. Information about Kirzner and his works can be found online at: http://www.worldhistory.com/wiki/I/Israel-Kirzner.htm.

———. "Entrepreneurial Discovery and the Competitive Market Process: An Austrian Approach." *Journal of Economic Literature* 35, no. 1 (1997): 60–85.

Lee, Dwight R. "The Seeds of Entrepreneurship." *Journal of Private Enterprise* 7, no. 1 (1991): 20–35.

Reynolds, Paul D., Michael Hay, and S. Michael Camp. *Global Entrepreneurship Monitor*. Kansas City, Mo.: Kauffman Center for Entrepreneurial Leadership, 1999. Information about this book can be found online at: http://www.gemconsortium.org/.

Rosenberg, Nathan, and L. E. Birdzell Jr. *How the West Grew Rich*. New York: Basic Books, 1986.

Schumpeter, Joseph A. *Capitalism, Socialism, and Democracy*. New York: Harper, 1942.

———. *The Theory of Economic Development*. 1911. Cambridge: Harvard University Press, 1934. Information about Schumpeter and his works can be found online at: http://cepa.newschool.edu/het/profiles/schump.htm.

Zacharakis, Andrew L., William D. Bygrave, and Dean A. Shepherd. *Global Entrepreneurship Monitor: National Entrepreneurship Assessment: United States of America*. Kansas City, Mo.: Kauffman Center for Entrepreneurial Leadership, 2000. Information about this book can be found online at: http://www.gemconsortium.org/.

Advanced

Bates, Timothy. "Entrepreneur Human Capital Inputs and Small Business Longevity." *Review of Economics and Statistics* 72, no. 4 (1990): 551–559.

Baumol, William J. "Entrepreneurship: Productive, Unproductive and Destructive." *Journal of Political Economy* 98, no. 5 (1990): 893–921.

———. *The Free-Market Innovation Machine: Analyzing the Growth Miracle of Capitalism*. Princeton: Princeton University Press, 2002.

Blanchflower, David G., and Andrew J. Oswald. "What Makes an Entrepreneur?" *Journal of Labor Economics* 16, no. 1 (1998): 26–60.

Blau, David M. "A Time-Series Analysis of Self-Employment in the United States." *Journal of Political Economy* 95, no. 3 (1987): 445–467.

Blomstrom, Magnus, Robert E. Lipsey, and Mario Zejan. "Is Fixed Investment the Key to Economic Growth?" *Quarterly Journal of Economics* 111, no. 1 (1996): 269–276.

Boettke, Peter J. *Calculation and Coordination: Essays on Socialism and Transitional Political Economy*. New York: Routledge, 2001.

Boettke, Peter J., and Christopher J. Coyne. "Entrepreneurship and Development: Cause or Consequence?" *Advances in Austrian Economics* 6 (2003): 67–87.

Bruce, Donald. "Taxes and Entrepreneurial Endurance: Evidence from the Self-Employed." *National Tax Journal* 55, no. 1 (2002): 5–24.

Evans, David S., and Linda S. Leighton. "Some Empirical Aspects of Entrepreneurship." *American Economic Review* 79, no. 3 (1989): 519–535.

Hamilton, Barton H. "Does Entrepreneurship Pay? An Empirical Analysis of the Returns to Self Employment." *Journal of Political Economy* 108, no. 3 (2000): 604–631.

Holtz-Eakin, Douglas, David Joulfaian, and Harvey S. Rosen. "Sticking It Out: Entrepreneurial Survival and Liquidity Constraints." *Journal of Political Economy* 102, no. 1 (1994): 53–75.

Kreft, Steven F., and Russell S. Sobel. "Public Policy, Entrepreneurship, and Economic Growth." West Virginia University Entrepreneurship Center Working Paper, 2003. This article and some related research can be found online at: http://www.be.wvu.edu/ec/research.htm.

Environmental Quality

Terry L. Anderson

There are many different measures of environmental quality, and most of those in use show that environmental quality is improving. For example, from 1970 to 2000, concentrations of carbon monoxide, a pollutant, fell by 75 percent in the United States and by 95 percent in the United Kingdom. From 1975 to 2000, nitrogen oxides declined by 35 percent in the United States and by 40 percent in the United Kingdom. The percentage of beaches in Denmark not complying with local or European Union regulations fell from 14 percent in 1980 to approximately 1 percent by 2000. Between 1969 and 1994, DDT and PCB contamination of fish fell by more than 80 percent. Indeed, it is difficult to find measures indicating that environmental quality is deteriorating in countries enjoying relatively high incomes.

The correlation between environmental quality and economic growth is incontrovertible. Comparing the World Bank's environmental sustainability index with gross domestic product per capita in 117 nations shows that richer countries sustain environmental quality better than poorer countries do (see Figure 1).[1] Indeed, every systematic study of environmental indicators shows that the environment improves as incomes rise. When per capita incomes reach $4,000 to $8,000 (this would include countries such as Brazil, Ukraine, and Indonesia, for example), arsenic pollution, sulfur dioxide emissions, and deforestation decrease, while dissolved oxygen in streams, a necessary element for healthy aquatic plants and animals, increases. Nonetheless, alternate and more pessimistic views are widespread. For example, Paul and Anne Ehrlich, the modern counterparts of THOMAS ROBERT MALTHUS, write:

Humanity is now facing a sort of slow-motion environmental Dunkirk. It remains to be seen whether civilization can avoid the perilous trap it has set for itself. Unlike the troops crowding the beach at Dunkirk, civilization's fate is in its own hands; no miraculous last-minute rescue is in the cards. . . . [E]ven if humanity manages to extricate itself, it is likely that environmental events will be defining ones for our grandchildren's generation—and those events could dwarf World War II in magnitude. (Ehrlich and Ehrlich 1996, p. 11.)

Similarly, Harvard biologist Edward O. Wilson contends that "the wealth of the world, if measured by domestic product and per-capita consumption, is rising. But if calculated from the condition of the biosphere, it is falling" (2003, p. 42). From the Worldwatch Institute's assertion that "the key environmental indicators are increasingly negative" to the World Wildlife Fund's prediction that if we do not change our ways, human welfare will collapse by 2030, the view seems to be that the Earth's environment is getting worse.

The data, however, are inconsistent with this conclusion. Thanks largely to the pioneering work of the late economist Julian Simon and, more recently, to the work of statistician Bjørn Lomborg, abundant data show that we are not running out of resources, that we are not destroying our environment, and that the plight of human beings is improving rather than diminishing. Simon's confidence in challenging Ehrlich's pessimistic thinking came from his belief that people respond to scarcity by conserving on scarcer resources and by reducing waste and hence pollution.

Doubting Simon's logic and data, Bjørn Lomborg, a statistician and political scientist, set out to prove him wrong by examining reams of data on various environmental claims. These claims include: global forest cover is declining, finite resources are being depleted, global temperatures are rising due to human causes, and massive species extinctions are occurring.

Consider Lomborg's findings. Global forest cover has remained quite stable since the middle of the twentieth century. Even the Amazon forests are not declining at the alarming rates touted by doomsayers. Since the arrival of man, Amazon deforestation has been only about 14 percent, three percentage points of which have been replaced by new forests.

High oil prices in 2004 and 2005 have caused many people to fear that we will run out of energy. Long-run trends, however, suggest that such claims are exaggerated. The pessimistic view comes from the assumption that no more oil will be found. But that assumption has been

1. The World Bank's index is "a function of five phenomena: (1) the state of the environmental systems, such as air, soil, ecosystems and water; (2) the stresses on those systems, in the form of pollution and exploitation levels; (3) the human vulnerability to environmental change in the form of loss of food resources or exposure to environmental diseases; (4) the social and institutional capacity to cope with environmental challenges; and finally (5) the ability to respond to the demands on global stewardship by cooperating in collective efforts to conserve international environmental resources such as the atmosphere" in Yale Center for Environmental Law and Policy and Center for International Earth Science Information Network, *2005 Environmental Sustainability Index: Summary for Policymakers,* in collaboration with World Economic Forum and Joint Research Centre of the European Commission. Available online at: http://sedac.ciesin.columbia.edu/es/esi/, p. 4.

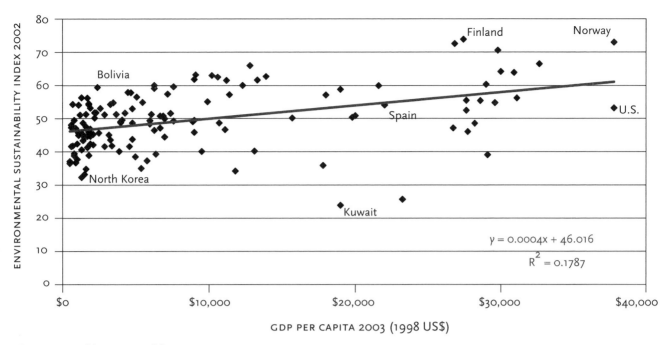

Figure 1 Wealthier Is Healthier

wrong every time it has been made. By 2003, world oil production was eighteen times its level in 1945 and yet known oil reserves were twenty-four times their 1945 level (Bradley and Fulmer 2004, p. 88). And if current oil prices prevail in the longer term, alternative sources such as shale oil will become economical with enough supply to meet current consumption for 250 years (Lomborg 2001, p. 135). For an explanation of why prices and supply are so interconnected, see NATURAL RESOURCES.

On the GLOBAL WARMING debate, there is a growing consensus that temperatures are rising, but the projected increase over a one-hundred-year period continually gets smaller as models for predicting global climate change improve. Whether and how much of the increase is anthropogenic, however, is debatable, as increases over the past century, when the human impact on the greenhouse effect has surely been the greatest, are not radically different from early global temperature increases.

Finally, claims of massive extinctions are based on projections from mathematical models rather than on data. The standard claim that we are losing forty thousand species per year comes from Cambridge scientist Norman Myers's "supposition" that if we lose one million species in twenty-five years, "this would work out . . . at an average extinction rate of 40,000 species per year, or rather over 100 species per day" (Myers 1979, p. 5). Using this number, biologist Thomas Lovejoy predicted in 1980 that we would lose 15 to 20 percent of all species by 2000 (Lovejoy 1980, p. 331). We have not. Today, the best guess is that we

will lose 0.7 percent of all species over the next fifty years (Lomborg 2004, p. 35). Some species are going extinct, but there is no empirical evidence that the extinction rate is catastrophic.

From his extensive data search, Lomborg confirmed most of Simon's findings and created a firestorm when he concluded from the data that

> children born today—in both the industrialized world and developing countries—will live longer and be healthier, they will get more food, a better education, a higher standard of living, more leisure time and far more possibilities—without the global environment being destroyed. (Lomborg 2001, p. 352)

The reason that the data do not fit the neo-Malthusian predictions is that those predictions take no account of the human ingenuity that is induced by the proper incentives. For there to be proper incentives requires the institutions of freedom—namely, private property rights and a rule of law. When the Eastern bloc countries were freed of communism, Milton Friedman believed that the key for their economic progress was "privatize, privatize, privatize" (Friedman 2002, p. xvii.) After more than a decade of experiments and a growing amount of data on what it takes to stimulate economic growth, however, Friedman modified his position, saying: "Privatization is meaningless if you don't have the rule of law. What does it mean to privatize if you do not have security of property, if you can't use property as you want to?" (Friedman 2002, p. xviii).

In other words, without the rule of law and secure property rights, growth will not occur, and without growth we will not have the ability to cope with resource scarcity and to improve environmental quality.

Using indexes of freedom to measure the sanctity of property rights and the rule of law, economists have correlated environmental quality with institutions. Madhusudan Bhattarai (2000) found that civil and political liberties, the rule of law, less-corrupt governments, and the security of property rights reduced deforestation rates in sixty-six countries across Latin America, Asia, and Africa. Seth Norton (2004) found a strong positive correlation between several measures of human well-being and varying degrees of the strength of the rule of law. For example, countries with a strong rule of law have a 45 percent lower death rate by age forty than countries with a weak rule of law; 59 percent have more access to safe drinking water; and 79 percent have lower deforestation rates.

In his book *The Ultimate Resource 2* (1998) Julian Simon built the coffin for neo-Malthusian ideas. Simon viewed human ingenuity as the ultimate resource. As he was fond of saying, "With every mouth comes two hands and a mind." The late Aaron Wildavsky shared Simon's view, saying that "scarcity has yet to win a race with creativity" (quoted in Chai and Swedlow 1998, p. 91). Both scholars understood that institutions that get the incentives right and prices that signal resource scarcity are the reasons that scarcity always loses the race. Economic prosperity emanates from the institutions of freedom—namely, private property and the rule of law—and environmental quality emanates from economic prosperity. If we can get the institutions right, we will be able to have our environmental cake and eat it too.

About the Author

Terry L. Anderson is executive director of PERC—the Property and Environment Research Center, a nonprofit institute in Bozeman, Montana, dedicated to improving environmental quality through markets; senior fellow at the Hoover Institution, Stanford University; and professor emeritus at Montana State University.

Further Reading

Anderson, Terry L., ed. *You Have to Admit It's Getting Better: From Economic Prosperity to Environmental Quality.* Stanford, Calif.: Hoover Institution Press, 2004.

Bhatarrai, Madhusudan. "The Environmental Kuznets Curve for Deforestation in Latin America, Africa, and Asia: Macroeconomic and Institutional Perspectives." Ph.D. diss., Clemson University, Clemson, S.C., 2000.

Bradley, Robert L. Jr., and Richard W. Fulmer. *Energy: The Master Resource.* Dubuque, Iowa: Kendall/Hunt Publishing, 2004.

Chai, Sun-Ki, and Brendon Swedlow. *Aaron Wildavsky: Culture and Social Theory.* New Brunswick, N.J.: Transaction Publishers, 1998.

Ehrlich, Paul R., and Ann H. Ehrlich. *Betrayal of Science and Reason: How Anti-environment Rhetoric Threatens Our Future.* Washington, D.C.: Island Press, 1996.

Friedman, Milton. "Economic Freedom Behind the Scenes." Preface to *Economic Freedom of the World: 2002 Annual Report,* by James Gwartney and Robert Lawson, with Chris Edwards, Walter Park, Veronique de Rugy, and Smitha Wagh. Vancouver, B.C.: Fraser Institute, 2002.

Lomborg, Bjørn. *The Skeptical Environmentalist: Measuring the Real State of the World.* Cambridge: Cambridge University Press, 2001.

———. "The Skeptical Environmentalist." In Terry L. Anderson, ed., *You Have to Admit It's Getting Better: From Economic Prosperity to Environmental Quality.* Stanford, Calif.: Hoover Institution Press, 2004.

Lovejoy, Thomas E. "A Projection of Species Extinctions." In Gerald O. Barney, ed., *The Global 2000 Report of the President of the United States: Entering the 21st Century I–III.* New York: Pergamon Press, 1980.

Malthus, Thomas. *Essay on the Principle of Population.* London: J. Johnson, 1798.

Myers, Norman. *The Sinking Ark: A New Look at the Problem of Disappearing Species.* Oxford: Pergamon Press, 1979.

Norton, Seth W. "Population Growth, Economic Freedom, and the Rule of Law." In Terry L. Anderson, ed., *You Have to Admit It's Getting Better: From Economic Prosperity to Environmental Quality.* Stanford, Calif.: Hoover Institution Press, 2004.

Simon, Julian L. *The Ultimate Resource 2.* Princeton: Princeton University Press, 1998.

Wilson, Edward O. *The Future of Life.* New York: Vintage Books, 2003.

Ethics and Economics

Stephen R. C. Hicks

Is capitalism good? Should we admire hard workers who are motivated to make large profits? Does competition bring out the best in people? These questions juxtapose practices and institutions that economists study (CAPITALISM, PROFITS, COMPETITION) with concepts that ethicists use (good, admirable, best).

Ethics studies values and virtues. A value is a good to be achieved or a standard of right to be followed, while a virtue is a character trait that enables one to achieve the good or act rightly. For example, a list of core goods might include wealth, love, and freedom. A corresponding list of virtues—or character traits—might include the productiveness that enables one to achieve wealth, the honesty that enables one to enjoy loving relationships, and the self-responsibility that enables one to live in freedom.

Ethical issues connect intimately with economic issues. Take the economic practice of doing a cost-benefit analysis. You could spend one hundred dollars for a night on the town, or you could donate that one hundred dollars to the reelection campaign of your favorite politician. Which option is better? The night on the town increases pleasure. A politician's successful campaign may lead to more liberty in the long term. We regularly make decisions like this, weighing our options by measuring their likely costs and likely benefits against each other.

This connects economics directly to a major issue in ethics: By what standard do we determine what counts as a benefit or a cost? A list of competing candidates for the status of ultimate value standard includes happiness, satisfying the will of God, long-term survival, liberty, duty, and equality.

Economists implicitly adopt a value framework when beginning a cost-benefit analysis. Different value commitments can lead to the same item being considered a cost from one perspective and a benefit from another. For example, those whose standard of value is increasing human happiness would count a new road to a scenic mountain vista as a benefit, while those whose standard is maintaining an unchanged natural environment would count it as a cost.

The results of economic analysis also lead directly to ethical issues. For example, one result of the nineteenth- and twentieth-century debate over capitalism and SOCIALISM is a general consensus that capitalism is effective at producing wealth and socialism is effective at keeping people poor. Advocates of capitalism use these results to argue that capitalism is good; others might respond that "socialism is good in theory, but unfortunately it is not practical." Implicit in the capitalist position is the view that practical consequences determine goodness. By contrast, implicit in the position of those who believe socialism to be an impractical moral ideal is the view that goodness is distinct from practical consequences.

This connects economics to a second major issue in ethics: Is goodness or badness determined by real-world practical consequences or by some other means, such as revelations from God, faith in authorities or authoritative institutions, appeals to rational consistency, felt senses of empathy, or an innate conscience? The point for economic analysis, most of which is a matter of understanding and predicting the consequences of various actions, is that the relevance of economic analysis to policymaking depends, in part, on what one believes is the final source of value standards.

So far, we have two questions of ethics that bear directly on economics: (1) What is the standard of good? and (2) How does one establish that something is good?

A third relevant question of ethics is: Who should be the beneficiaries of the good? A common assumption of economic analysis is that individuals are rational and self-interested. The third question focuses on self-interest. Is self-interest moral, amoral, or immoral? Is morality a matter of individuals taking responsibility for their lives and working to achieve happiness? Or is morality a matter of individuals accepting responsibility for others and being willing to forgo or sacrifice for them? This is the debate in ethics between egoism and altruism.

Strong forms of egoism hold that individuals should be self-responsible and ambitious in their pursuit of happiness, that they should treat other individuals as self-responsible trading partners, and that those who are unable to be self-responsible should be treated through voluntary charity. Strong forms of altruism argue the opposite, holding that morality is primarily a matter of helping those who are in need, that charity is more moral than trade, and that the most moral individuals will be motivated by a spirit of self-sacrifice.

For example: Carly worked hard and earned $10 million by the time she was forty. She is now in semiretirement, enjoying the good life of travel, building her dream home, managing her investments, and spending time with her family and friends. Jane, by contrast, inherited $10 million at age forty, gave $9.9 million away to charity, and lives frugally on the remaining money. Which woman is more morally admirable?

Or consider the debates over rent control and minimum wages. Economists, by a large majority, agree that such policies are not merely zero-sum, as their advocates intend, but rather negative-sum. In this encyclopedia, Walter Block (see RENT CONTROL) argues that rent controls cause landlords a loss—and also cause housing shortages that harm some of the poorest renters the most. Linda Gorman (see MINIMUM WAGES) argues that minimum wages cause employers a loss—but also destroy jobs for unskilled laborers. These unintended consequences are well known among economists, but there is little sign that rent controls and minimum wages will be abandoned anytime soon.

Why so? In the case of rent controls, part of the explanation involves the political dynamics of urban areas, in which many voters are renters: renters believe that rent control is good for them, and politicians sometimes listen to their constituents.

Yet another major part of the explanation has to do with an altruistic ethic that says that the self-interest of landlords and employers counts for little morally and may be sacrificed to help tenants and employees. The thinking is that landlords and employers are richer, and tenants and employees are poorer, and thus rich people should be willing to sacrifice profits to help out the poor if necessary. But if we cannot expect the rich to do the right thing voluntarily, then an altruistic ethic will help justify the government's mandating the sacrifice by law.

The moral difference between egoists and altruists on these economic policy issues is between those who see employers and employees as win-win trading partners and those who see employment as exploitation; and between those who see landlords and tenants as trading value to mutual benefit and those who see poor tenants vulnerable to being taken advantage of by rich landlords.

Generalizing from debates over particular policies to evaluations of economic systems as a whole, Adam Smith's famous statement about self-interest from *The Wealth of Nations* is directly relevant to our contemporary debates about the morality of capitalism:

> It is not from the benevolence of the butcher, the brewer, or the baker that we expect our dinner, but from their regard to their own interest. We address ourselves, not to their humanity but to their self-love, and never talk to them of our own necessities but of their advantages.

Smith is working out a middle ground between traditional ethical theories that have been altruistic in principle and his new (at the time) economic theory that is optimistic about the power of egoistic individuals in a free market. Smith's position is modern and egoistic in accepting that self-interest is natural and beneficial in making capitalism work well; at the same time Smith is traditionally altruistic in reserving his highest praise for those who take a disinterested perspective on their own interests and are willing to sacrifice their interests.

Bracketing Smith's view on one side is a traditional view of self-interest, one still held by most of capitalism's contemporary opponents: Self-interest is amoral or immoral because it is essentially antisocial; and because it is based on self-interest, capitalism must be a system of conflict and zero-sum transactions. And because the good of society as a whole is the standard of value, it follows that self-interest and capitalism must be restrained or sacrificed.

Smith's economic insight is to see that self-interest and capitalism do not generate social conflict. His analysis led him to see that self-interested individuals would mostly engage in win-win transactions—that the profit motive, property rights, divisions of labor, competition, and other

features of capitalism would lead to individual prosperity and social harmony. But Smith retained the traditional ethical belief that the good of society as a whole is the moral standard of value.

Bracketing Smith's view on the other side is the view—held by neo-Aristotelians and Ayn Rand, for example—that self-interest is moral and that what justifies capitalism is its protection and enabling of individuals in the pursuit of their individual lives and happiness. This position agrees essentially with Smith's *economic* analysis of capitalism as a network of win-win transactions, but not with his primary *ethical* justification.

Both ethical and economic analysis quickly become complex, and the three questions noted above provide a starting point for integrating the two fields.

Our contemporary debates over environmental values and policies can help illustrate the complex interplay. Environmental debates are about two categories of human action: resource use and waste disposal. For example, whether we are running out of trees and whether we should drill for oil in Alaska are issues of resource use; and whether toxic chemicals are poisoning a water supply and whether greenhouse gases are causing global warming are issues of waste disposal. Some issues, such as recycling, are issues of both resource use and waste disposal.

We end with the case of RECYCLING of metal drink containers as a working example. Part of the motivation for recycling may be a belief that the world is running out of a natural resource—in this case, aluminum. In part this belief depends on strictly scientific information: How much aluminum is available from the Earth? How much are we currently using? As mining and processing techniques improve, what effect will that have on the available stock of aluminum? Depending on the scientific data, one might conclude that aluminum is becoming more plentiful or scarcer (see NATURAL RESOURCES).

Another part of the recycling issue integrates economic considerations. Recycling can increase the available stock of aluminum and save space in landfills, but it also has costs: the costs of making and installing recycling bins for empty cans, the monetary and pollution costs of having recycling trucks travel through neighborhoods and businesses to collect the recyclables, the time cost of putting the cans in the right bins, the cost of reprocessing the cans to extract the raw aluminum, and so on. Whether the benefits of recycling outweigh the costs depends on the results of number crunching by economists.

Another part of the recycling issue turns on general political commitments. Given that using resources well and putting trash in its place are valuable, what social institutions should we rely on to achieve those values? Should recycling be voluntary and a matter of market incentives? Or should the government mandate recycling as part of a broader mandate to manage society's resource use and waste disposal practices? (see TRAGEDY OF THE COMMONS and FREE-MARKET ENVIRONMENTALISM).

Governing how we approach the above scientific, economic, and political issues is a set of presuppositions of ethical values. Those who think egoistically see the environment as a set of resources for humans to use for their benefit. Humans use the environment for a variety of economic and aesthetic purposes, and it is important to human health that certain standards of cleanliness are maintained. On that assumption, it makes sense to ask scientists to investigate the stock of resources and to develop techniques for extracting them. It also makes sense to ask economists to do cost-benefit analyses comparing mining and recycling to determine the most cost-effective methods of producing aluminum. The egoistic goal is to preserve, change, or use the environment in ways that increase human wealth, health, and experiences of beauty.

By contrast, strong forms of altruism when applied to environmental issues dictate different scientific and economic priorities. Altruism with respect to the environment requires that humans subordinate or sacrifice their interests to the needs of other species or to the environment as a whole. Given this perspective, the environment is something to be preserved rather than used by humans. Human self-interested values are a lower priority than the well-being of other species or the environment as a whole. Scientifically, asking researchers to find out how much aluminum is available for our use then becomes a morally suspect activity. And economically, recycling then becomes not a matter of a practice worth doing if the cost-benefit numbers work out for us but rather a duty that humans should accept no matter what the economic consequences to themselves.

About the Author

Stephen Hicks is professor in the Department of Philosophy at Rockford College and Executive Director of the Center for Ethics and Entrepreneurship. In 1994–1995 he was a visiting professor of business ethics at Georgetown University in Washington, D.C.

Further Reading

Hume, David. *A Treatise of Human Nature*. 1739–1740. Reprint. Oxford: Oxford University Press, 2000. In book III (part 1, section 1), Hume argues that there is no logical way to derive an "ought" from an "is." This implies, for example, that there is no logical connection between normative ethics and descriptive economics.

Mill, John Stuart. *On Liberty*. 1859 (many editions available). A defense of liberal society based on the argument that it realizes the utilitarian moral principle of the "greatest happiness for the greatest number." Mill's *Utilitarianism* (1861) is his argument for the "greatest happiness" principle as the ultimate standard in ethics.

Rand, Ayn. *Capitalism: The Unknown Ideal*. New York: Signet, 1967. A defense of capitalism on egoist grounds. Rand argues that what justifies capitalism morally is that it provides individuals with the liberty and property rights they need to survive and flourish self-responsibly.

Sen, Amartya. *On Ethics and Economics*. London: Blackwell, 1989. Sen criticizes standard utilitarian defenses of free markets and discusses generally the kind of theoretical ethics needed to provide a basis for welfare economics.

Smith, Adam. *The Wealth of Nations*. 1776 (many editions available). The classic early study of free markets, describing how the self-interested actions of unregulated individuals come to be coordinated to mutual benefit.

European Union

Marian L. Tupy

The European Union (EU) includes twenty-seven countries and 490 million people. In 2005, the EU had a $13 trillion (€11 trillion) economy, a single market, and for some member countries, a single currency. A growing number of political and economic decisions are made on a pan-European level in Brussels.

The origins of the EU are usually traced to the European Coal and Steel Community (1952). Heavily regulated coal and steel industries of Germany and France were to be administered by a supranational authority. Economic benefits of supranational control over one sector of the economy were expected to lead to demands for supranational management of other economic sectors. But supranationalism, characterized by bureaucratic planning and regulation, could not produce economic growth.

Ludwig Erhard's free-market reforms in West Germany in the late 1940s (see GERMAN ECONOMIC MIRACLE) provided an alternative model for development, and the resulting economic growth made a strong case for Europe-wide liberalization. The 1957 Treaty of Rome created the European Economic Community (EEC). The EEC abolished internal tariffs and quotas and established a customs union. The treaty made provisions for the eventual liberalization of movement of labor, services, and capital.

Despite the Treaty of Rome's many imperfections, the economic interdependence between nations that it produced was believed to make future armed conflict less likely. As nineteenth-century French economic journalist

Frédéric Bastiat stated, "When goods don't cross borders, soldiers will." Many of Europe's early integrationists remembered the large trade barriers of the 1930s and the collapse of international trade that followed. The new principle of economic cooperation enhanced economic efficiency and resulted in improved living standards.

The supranationalists wished to enhance European integration through a top-down approach. Europe's future social and economic development was to be managed and regulated from Brussels, the capital of Belgium. The Treaty of Rome, on the other hand, aimed at decentralization. European cooperation was to emerge "spontaneously" after barriers to interactions between social and economic actors were removed.

Development

Adam Smith observed that efficiency gains are limited by market size. International trade increases market size. Multilateral trade liberalization through the General Agreement on Tariffs and Trade (GATT) and its successor, the World Trade Organization (WTO), made great headway after World War II, substantially increasing the volume of international trade. The WTO is premised on nondiscrimination: member countries provide all other WTO members the same access to their markets (see INTERNATIONAL TRADE AGREEMENTS).

A customs union is an exception to the WTO rule. Members of a customs union may eliminate import duties on one another's goods while maintaining a unified tariff on imports from other WTO countries. The EU itself started as a customs union among Belgium, Luxembourg, France, Italy, the Netherlands, and West Germany. The United Kingdom, Ireland, and Denmark joined in 1973. Greece joined in 1981, and Spain and Portugal in 1986.

In 1986, growing global competition caused the signing of the Single European Act (SEA) and the creation of the European common market. Worldwide economic liberalization exposed Europe as an overregulated area with high unemployment and low productivity and growth. The Single European Act liberalized restrictions on merchandise transport; government procurement; and movement of services, capital, and labor. Intra-European trade has expanded: in 1960, more than 60 percent of European trade was with non-EU members, while in 2003, two-thirds of all EU trade in goods was internal. But the act also increased the European bureaucrats' power to create pan-European regulation, which reduces the possibility of policy competition within Europe.

In 1995, Austria, Finland, and Sweden became members of the EU. The Czech and Slovak Republics, Poland, Hungary, Estonia, Latvia, Lithuania, Slovenia, Cyprus, and Malta joined in 2004. Romania and Bulgaria followed in 2007.

On January 1, 1999, eleven members of the EU replaced their national currencies with a single currency, the euro (€). The monetary policies of the Eurozone members then ceased to be autonomous and are now set by the European Central Bank (ECB) in Frankfurt, Germany. The euro has reduced transaction costs and removed uncertainty created by exchange-rate fluctuations, and thus encourages additional intra-European trade and investment. However, the requirement that Eurozone members maintain the same monetary policy and the same interest rates deprives national governments of policy tools traditionally used to address their own macroeconomic problems (see MONETARY UNION).

In the past, when a country had a recession not shared by other EU countries, its central bank could expand the money supply, with the goal of boosting domestic demand and moderating the recession. With monetary policy turned over to the ECB, this kind of response is no longer possible. A common monetary policy will be useful for moderating only Europe-wide business cycle fluctuations. When European countries experience cyclical expansions and contractions at different times, the sacrifice of monetary autonomy may cost them a great deal. On the other hand, countries with loose monetary policies benefit because their governments may no longer inflate their currencies.

The EU also restricts fiscal autonomy of the member states. The growth and stability pact prohibits EU members from running an annual budget deficit of more than 3 percent of GDP. The pact is meant to ensure that fiscal irresponsibility of individual members does not endanger the stability of the single currency as a whole. However, the pact has no viable enforcement mechanism. Thus, when Germany and France violated its terms by running greater-than-allowed deficits, the EU Commission was unable to rein them in.

Another European project involves adoption of the European Constitution. The Constitution has caused much controversy. Some opponents argued that the constitution further distances the EU from the public. Others found the incorporation of the Fundamental Charter of Human Rights, which includes extensive welfare provisions, prohibitively expensive. The lack of reference to religion in general and Christianity in particular alienated the more culturally conservative members. In any case, the ratification of the Constitution is uncertain, in part because of its rejection in the French and Dutch referenda.

Harmonization

The "harmonization" debate epitomizes the tension between the two views of integration. The top-down centralists see harmonization throughout the European Union as necessary because, as they see it, the common market necessitates common rules and regulations. They also see harmonization as a way of ensuring the eventual political unification of the continent.

Others argue that it was the lack of political and economic uniformity that enabled Europe to thrive in the past. Harvard University historian David Landes writes:

> Fragmentation gave rise to competition and competition favored good care of good subjects. . . . European rulers and enterprising lords who sought to grow revenues . . . had to attract participants by the grants of franchises, freedoms and privileges—in short, by making deals. They had to persuade them to come.[1]

Decentralized political entities such as the United States still provide laboratories of social policy. Like American states today, autonomous city-states in Europe in the past offered an assortment of potential freedoms to potential émigrés. Many émigrés brought knowledge and expertise that improved the societies they joined. The top-down social harmonization in which the EU engages may prove counterproductive. Enforcement of specific social agendas breeds resentment, creates negative-sum outcomes, and intensifies political struggles.

In the past, various governments in Europe tried to gain an edge over their competitors by reducing taxes. This tax competition kept the overall level of taxation in check, just as tax competition among various U.S. states keeps state taxation in check. Yet, there are those who would like to reduce what they call "harmful tax competition."

An EU Parliament report put it bluntly. It may be necessary to harmonize business taxes, it argued, because

> cutting taxes in one country raises the competitiveness and/or attractiveness of this country relative to others. The resulting flows of goods, capital—and also, possibly, high-skilled labor—is detrimental to partner countries in terms of economic activity and in terms of tax revenues.[2]

In the atmosphere of increasing harmonization of European economies, low taxation has emerged as the most effective way for producers in various European nations to stay competitive. Tax competition is especially important to poorer EU countries burdened with excessive EU regulation. Past beneficiaries of low taxation, such as the United Kingdom and Ireland, are also likely to continue to favor tax competition.

Regulation

During the 1990s, the EU increased its regulation of production, delivery, and sale throughout the union. Legislation on worker health and safety, working hours, and mandatory leave made Europe's nonwage labor costs much higher than those in the United States and many other countries.

Some blame the governing structure of the union. The Brussels bureaucracy functions with minimal oversight by elected officials, turning out new regulations regardless of compliance costs. Over half of all regulations adopted by the British Parliament, for example, originate in Brussels. Even the former European commissioner for the internal market, Frits Bolkestein, has admitted that the EU has a "tendency to over regulate."[3] Some believe that regulations can sometimes correct market failure. But regulations also often create failure and exacerbate economic problems. The proponents of regulation are often European states with extensive welfare provisions that want to hobble competition from their less-regulated European competitors.

Overregulation complicates the EU's enlargement into the Central and Eastern European countries. Western European labor regulations, designed for wealthy societies, reduce the competitiveness of workers in these less-productive countries and may cause prolonged periods of high unemployment there. In addition, the EU Commission estimates that by 2013, new members' compliance costs with the EU environmental regulations alone will reach up to $144 billion (€120 billion). Those costs are likely to increase taxes and government debt throughout the region.

The system of quotas and subsidies presents another complicated problem. After the fall of communism, the Central and Eastern European countries adjusted to the market and became more productive. The EU now prevents them from producing "too much," reprimanding Slovakia, for example, for exceeding its steel quota.

1. David Landes, *The Wealth and Poverty of Nations* (London: Little, Brown, 1998), p. 36.

2. "The Reform of Taxation in EU Members," European Parliament, Directorate General for Research, Working Paper ECON 127 EN, 07–2001, online at: http://www.europarl.eu.int/working papers/econ/pdf/127_en.pdf.

3. "Bolkestein Accuses Commission of Over-regulating," *EUobserver,* October 13, 2003, online at: http://euobs.com/?aid = 13001 &rk = 1.

Protectionism and Redistribution

Participating countries benefit from their customs union only if their involvement creates more trade than it diverts (see INTERNATIONAL TRADE AGREEMENTS). Imagine, for example, that EU countries continue to import petroleum from the Middle East, wheat from the United States, and stereo equipment from Asia. Imagine also that they specialize further in their own production. So, instead of producing both beer and wine, the British produce beer and the French produce wine, and they trade freely with one another. In such a case, trade is created and living standards rise. But if EU members now buy expensive German barley rather than cheap American wheat because of high external tariffs or low quotas, trade is diverted and members of the customs union may be worse off.

Most previous studies have concluded that the EU is a trade-creating customs union. Excessive harmonization and overregulation, however, reduce the benefits of belonging to the EU. The Common Agricultural Policy (CAP) and other restrictions on external trade create additional inefficiencies.

The CAP subsidizes the EU's agricultural producers by about $54 billion (€45 billion) annually and keeps lower-priced imported products out. The Organization for Economic Cooperation and Development (OECD) estimates that the overall level of European government support for agricultural producers was $130 billion (€108 billion) in 2005 (www.oecd.org). The EU subsidies often lead to overproduction of agricultural commodities, some of which are then "dumped" on the global markets, depressing their global prices and creating $20 billion (€17 billion) in losses for producers in low-income countries. At the same time, the CAP keeps agricultural prices within the EU artificially high, reducing the European standard of living. According to the British think tank Policy Exchange, "EU consumers currently pay 42 percent more for agricultural products than they would if the system were dismantled." Less-well-off families, for whom food takes up a high proportion of household income, suffer disproportionately.

French economist Patrick Messerlin estimates that European trade protectionism as a whole costs Europe 5–7 percent of its annual GDP. Messerlin found that the average job saved through protectionism costs European taxpayers approximately $200,000 (€167,000) per year.

Other distributive programs in the EU include the so-called structural and cohesion funds, which subsidize low-income regions. The funds distort resource allocation and limit the movement of labor into more productive economic activities. When the funds started to be disbursed in the mid-1970s, 44 percent of the EU population lived in regions qualifying for subsidies. By 1997, that had in-

creased to almost 52 percent. The program had both failed to eliminate regional poverty and empowered special interests. Spain's government, for example, threatened to block the entire EU enlargement rather than accept a reduction in its funds.

The EU's redistributive policies will likely produce more negative-sum outcomes, discontentment, and tensions. The success of the European project may, therefore, lie in embracing a "voluntarist" Europe where individual states, businesses, and persons will be free to choose the nature and extent of their cooperation.

About the Author

Marian L. Tupy is a Policy Analyst at the Cato Institute's Center for Global Liberty and Prosperity. He earned his B.A. in international relations and classics from the University of the Witwatersrand in Johannesburg, South Africa, and his Ph.D. in international relations from the University of St. Andrews in Great Britain.

Further Reading

Bastiat, Frédéric. *The Law.* 1850.
Gillingham, John. *European Integration: 1950–2003.* Cambridge: Cambridge University Press, 2003.
Landes, David. *The Wealth and Poverty of Nations.* New York: Norton, 1998.
Messerlin, Patrick. *Measuring the Costs of Protection in Europe.* Washington, D.C.: Institute of International Economics, 2001.
Smith, Adam. *The Wealth of Nations.* 1776.
Tupy, Marian. *EU Enlargement: Costs, Benefits, and Strategies for Central and Eastern European Countries.* Cato Policy Analysis no. 489. Washington, D.C.: September 2003.
Viner, Jacob. *The Customs Union Issue.* New York: Carnegie Endowment for International Peace, 1950.

Experimental Economics

Don Coursey

When the Swedish Nobel Committee awarded the 2002 Nobel Memorial Prize in Economic Sciences to Vernon L. Smith, an economist at George Mason University, it simply affirmed what economists have long known: that experimental economics has arrived as a respected and powerful discipline within economics. The committee noted that the award was based on Smith's "having established laboratory experiments as a tool in empirical economic analysis, especially in the study of alternative market mechanisms." But what exactly are market experiments, and what can researchers learn from them? Of what importance, outside the academy, is the "study of alternative market mechanisms"?

Economic experiments are not simulations or role-playing exercises. They involve real people who make serious choices. Through their efforts, participants stand to make or lose substantial amounts of money.

The simplest form of economic transaction—and the simplest experiment to conduct—is a two-person exchange. This experiment addresses how a single buyer and seller of an item reach, or fail to reach, mutually agreeable terms of trade for that item. In this experimental setting, the researcher induces value on the item for the buyer and the seller. For example, the person assigned the role of seller might be handed a card that indicates that his cost of production for the item is $10. If he can sell the item to the buyer in the experiment for more than his cost of production, then he will be awarded the difference between his sales price and $10. Likewise, the person assigned the role of buyer might be handed a card indicating that his resale value of the item is $22. This means that if he is able to acquire the item for less than $22, he can then sell it back to the experimenter for $22 and keep the difference.

Although no actual physical object is traded, both the seller and the buyer have an incentive to behave exactly as if one were. The seller will desire a price well above $10 for his item; the buyer will wish to pay as little as possible for his. What will happen? Two outcomes are possible. Either the seller and buyer find a mutually agreeable price between $10 and $22, or they fail to reach agreement. Economics says that both sides have an incentive to make a deal, but it says nothing about how the benefits of that deal will be divided. Economics also has little to say about the frequency of occasions in which the seller and buyer part company without making a trade. Many versions of this simple experiment have been conducted to explore these empirical issues.

The simple experimental design outlined above provides a building block for all subsequent experimental market designs. After all, a market at its core is a place where bilateral trades are facilitated between multiple buyers and sellers. Suppose we want to construct a market with five sellers and five buyers. In this case, we would hand a card to each seller indicating the cost of production. For example, one seller would be given a card indicating a cost of $10. The other four sellers would have costs of $12, $14, $16, and $18. People assigned to be buyers would receive a card indicating their resale value. Continuing the example, suppose these values were $22, $20, $18, $16, and $14. Each seller and each buyer in this design would have the opportunity to make one transaction.

Given the range of values for buyers and the range of costs for sellers, what will occur when they are allowed to trade? Will sellers have the upper hand? Will all trades that might benefit both buyers and sellers occur, or will some beneficial trades fail to take place because of incomplete information or so-called market failure? When trades do take place, will they be across a wide range of prices or a narrow band?

Economic theory in its simplest incarnation of supply and demand makes a strong set of predictions. Consider a graph (see Figure 1) that has price on the vertical axis and quantity on the horizontal axis. The supply schedule answers the question: How many units would voluntarily be brought to the market at various prices? Thus, supply in this experimental structure is an ascending stair-step pattern that starts at $10 and rises $2 per step for each unit in the market. Above $18 the supply curve is vertical, for only five units can ever be purchased in this setting. Likewise, the demand schedule answers the question: How many units will be voluntarily purchased in the market at different prices? Using the same analysis as that for the sellers, we find that the demand schedule is a descending stair-step pattern that starts at $22 and falls $2 per step for each unit demanded in the market. Below a price of $14, the demand schedule also is vertical, for no more than the five units are desired in this setting. For this scenario, textbook economics predicts that equilibrium will be reached where supply equals demand. In this case, that means that four units would be traded at *the identical price of $16*.

Vernon Smith developed this basic structure for creating

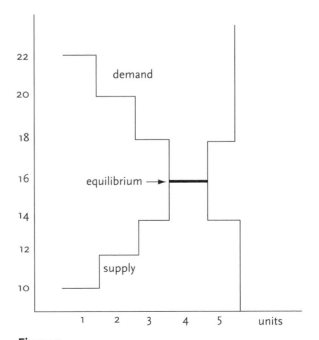

Figure 1

an experimental market in the mid-1950s. His first creative insight was motivated by the severity of the textbook prediction for all prices to be exactly $16, as noted above. He asked how everyone in the market could reach a single price. Neither the sellers, wanting high prices, nor the buyers, wanting low prices, would necessarily be happy with this outcome. In other words, how was Adam Smith's invisible hand to do its work? Vernon Smith found empirically that the market took care of both the buyers' concerns and the sellers' concerns simultaneously. This led to his first insight: a defined set of trading rules produces an efficient market price.

Smith's second creative insight was that exploring these questions could not be done in an institutional vacuum. Half of the experimental structure was missing. The sellers and buyers in this structure cannot trade unless specific rules forming the structure of a trading institution are employed. In his early work, Smith opted to use the rules of a double-oral auction. These auction rules are similar to the rules used for trading at the New York Stock Exchange or the Chicago Board of Trade. It is "double" because both sellers and buyers participate (as opposed, for example, to a silent auction at a fund-raising event, where the seller is passive). It is "oral" because the participants call out their bids and offers publicly. They do this using an important rule called the "bid-asked-price-reduction rule." What it means is that sellers call out asking prices, which are posted publicly, and all subsequent asking prices must descend from this starting asking price. On the other side of the market, once the first buyer makes his bid, all subsequent bids must ascend from this starting bid price. Trade can occur in two ways. Any buyer can accept a seller's asking price, or a seller can accept any buyer's bid.

When Smith ran these first experiments, the mechanics of the invisible hand became visible for the first time! Undergraduate student subjects produced single-price market equilibria, even though none of them desired this outcome. When they repeated the exercise, prices were even tighter around the equilibrium. The number of units being transacted was also "efficient," exhausting the gains from trade without anyone being in charge of the market.

These results came as a big surprise. Textbooks say that for the market to equilibrate, there must be perfect information. But the subjects produced market equilibria having no knowledge about others and with little experience, if any, trading in the double-oral auction. Finally, when Smith manipulated the number of sellers and buyers, he found that astoundingly small numbers of sellers and buyers—for instance, four of each—could produce competitive equilibrium. Prior to this research, the textbooks said that infinite or "numerous" numbers of each were re-

quired. Smith's early research challenged this convention and opened up the possibility that many apparently "thin" markets (having few sellers and buyers) in the real world produce competitive outcomes.

By the late 1970s Smith was examining all types of market institutions: English and Dutch single-object auctions, sealed-bid auctions, posted-offer markets (like a grocery market, where stores place take-it-or-leave-it prices), treasury bill markets, and others. Smith found a computer system at the University of Arizona that was progressive for its time, offering both real-time networking and touch-screen communication, and soon began computerizing all of his experimental markets.

I have conducted experiments of the simple-oral-double auction with groups ranging from eight-year-olds to Communists to professional traders. In every group, the auction has always produced the competitive result. It is the best economics education a student can absorb if a teacher has only one hour.

Experimental economics not only has allowed us to see how command and control regulations in the market affect behavior and produce unintended consequences, but also has helped address how public goods might be provided using market principles.

Another economist whose work on experimental economics has led to substantial insights about markets is Charles Holt of the University of Virginia. Holt, together with Anne Villamil and Loren Langan, conducted an experiment that showed that even when sellers had more than one unit of a good for sale and even when withholding output from the market could drive up the price substantially on the units they did sell, competitive pressures caused them to price at a level close to the competitive level. Work by Holt and others has also shown that when sellers can offer secret discounts from posted prices, collusive agreements tend to break down. These experiments, along with many others, buttress the late George Stigler's contention that competition is a hardy weed, not a delicate flower.

Experimental methods have been used to understand not only markets, but also politics. One leader in this area has been Charles Plott of the California Institute of Technology. Plott and Michael Levine showed that someone who rigs the agenda can push those who vote on the agenda to the outcome preferred by the rigger. The bottom line is that he who controls the agenda has a large say over the outcome.

Experimental economics is also used to solve some knotty problems in U.S. public policy. Consider two examples.

At certain times of the day in large American cities,

more jets want to land and depart than can be handled by the airport. One obvious economic solution to this problem is to auction off the right to land and take off during the congested periods so that the fixed number of scarce "slots" is sold to the highest bidders. Although this logic is correct, Vernon Smith realized that it is incomplete. The problem is not just the fact that you want to land at O'Hare airport in Chicago on Friday in the 4:00 through 5:00 P.M. time slot. Typically you want other conditions to be met as well. You might also want a slot out of O'Hare between 6:00 and 7:00 P.M. Additionally, you may be flying from Chicago to another congested airport like Atlanta, and so you will want a landing slot there as well, and so on.

At its essence, slot allocation is a problem of balancing supply and demand. But the constraints associated with so many crowded, interconnected airports with so many airlines and aircraft competing for space make the simple problem seem impossibly complex. Smith did not think so. He was able to develop a system of combined auctions that solved this problem. These auctions were exhaustively tested in his laboratory and are now used as allocation tools in national airport management.

Experimental economics has also been applied to electricity regulation. Electricity has three properties that make it different from other economic commodities. First, it is the only product for which supply and demand have to be equal at all moments in time. Electricity suppliers promise to meet the use by demanders—when you switch on your lights, you expect them to come on. Second, electricity is hard to store. Third, electricity does not really move directly from its source to its ultimate user. Rather, when electricity is provided to a power grid, the grid is like a great pond whose water level has just increased. These three factors have inhibited the trading of electricity across regions in the United States. Smith, always on the lookout for market solutions that could improve efficiency, cracked the complex technical problems associated with how to trade something so seemingly amorphous as electricity. His work in this area provided the basis for a radical new system of electricity and energy trading that swept the country during the 1990s. Smith advocated an open trading system for electricity in both the wholesale and retail markets. States that have adopted his system fully—mainly western states other than California—have benefited greatly. Other states that still use old regulatory regimes, mainly eastern states, or, like California, that applied only a partial market framework, have struggled.

The tools of experimental economics allow us not only to understand known issues with new precision, but also to discover whole new classes of otherwise unknown phenomena.

About the Author

Don Coursey is the Ameritech Professor of Public Policy Studies at the University of Chicago's Harris School of Public Policy.

Further Reading

Holt, C. A., L. Langan, and A. P. Villamil. "Market Power in Oral Double Auctions." *Economic Inquiry* 24 (1986): 107–123.

Plott, C. R. "Industrial Organization Theory and Experimental Economics." *Journal of Economic Literature* 20 (1982): 1485–1527.

Plott, C. R., and M. Levine. "A Model of Agenda Influence on Committee Decisions." *American Economic Review* 68 (1978): 146–160.

Rassenti, S. J., V. L. Smith, and R. L. Bulfin. "A Combinatorial Auction Mechanism for Airport Time Slot Allocation." *Bell Journal of Economics* 13, no. 2 (1982): 402–417.

Smith, V. L. "Economics in the Laboratory." *Journal of Economic Perspectives* 8, no. 1 (1994): 113–131.

———. "Electric Power Deregulation: Background and Prospects." *Contemporary Economic Policy* 6, no. 3 (1988) 14–24.

———. "Microeconomic Systems as an Experimental Science." *American Economic Review* 71, no. 3 (1982): 467–474.

———. "Theory, Experiment and Economics." *Journal of Economic Perspectives* 3, no. 1 (1989): 151–169.

Externalities

Bryan Caplan

Positive externalities are benefits that are infeasible to charge to provide; negative externalities are costs that are infeasible to charge to not provide. Ordinarily, as Adam Smith explained, selfishness leads markets to produce whatever people want; to get rich, you have to sell what the public is eager to buy. Externalities undermine the social benefits of individual selfishness. If selfish consumers do not *have* to pay producers for benefits, they will not pay; and if selfish producers are not paid, they will not produce. A valuable product fails to appear. The problem, as David Friedman aptly explains, "is not that one person pays for what someone else gets but that nobody pays and nobody gets, even though the good is worth more than it would cost to produce" (Friedman 1996, p. 278).

Admittedly, the real world is rarely so stark. Most people are not perfectly selfish, and it is usually feasible to charge consumers for a fraction of the benefit they receive. Due to piracy, for example, many people who enjoy a CD fail to pay the artist, which reduces the incentive to record new

CDs. But *some* incentive to record remains, because many find piracy inconvenient and others refrain from piracy because they believe it is wrong. The problem, then, is that externalities lead to what economists call *underproduction* of CDs rather than the nonexistence of CDs.

Research and development is a standard example of a positive externality, air pollution of a negative externality. Ultimately, however, the distinction is semantic. It is equivalent to say "clean air has positive externalities and so clean air is underproduced" or "dirty air has negative externalities and so dirty air is overproduced."

Economists measure externalities the same way they measure everything else: according to human beings' willingness to pay. If one thousand people would pay ten dollars each for cleaner air, there is a ten-thousand-dollar externality of pollution. If no one *minds* dirty air, conversely, no externality exists. If someone likes dirty air, this unusual person's willingness to pay for smog must be subtracted from the rest of the population's willingness to pay to curtail it.

Externalities are probably the argument for government intervention that economists most respect. Externalities are frequently used to justify the government's ownership of industries with positive externalities and prohibition of products with negative externalities. Economically speaking, however, this is overkill. If laissez-faire—that is, no government intervention—provides too little education, the straightforward solution is some form of subsidy to schooling, not government production of education. Similarly, if laissez-faire provides too much cocaine, a measured response is to tax it, not ban it completely.

Especially when faced with environmental externalities, economists have almost universally objected to government regulations that mandate specific technologies (especially "best-available technology") or business practices. These approaches make environmental cleanup much more expensive than it has to be because the cost of reducing pollution varies widely from firm to firm and from industry to industry. A more efficient solution is to issue tradable "pollution permits" that add up to the target level of emissions. Sources able to cheaply curtail their negative externalities would drastically cut back, selling their permits to less flexible polluters (Blinder 1987).[1]

While the concept of externalities is not very controversial in economics, its application is. Defenders of free markets usually argue that externalities are manageably small; critics of free markets see externalities as widespread, even ubiquitous. The most accepted examples of activities with large externalities are probably air pollution, violent and property crimes, and national defense.[2]

Other common candidates include health care, education, and the environment, but claims that these are externalities are much less tenable. Prevention and treatment of contagious disease has clear externalities, but most health care does not. Educated workers are more productive, but this benefit is hardly "external"; markets reward education with higher wages. The externalities of many environmentalist measures, including national parks, recycling, and conservation, are hard to discern. The people who enjoy national parks are visitors, who can easily be charged for admission. If the price of aluminum cans fails to spark RECYCLING, that suggests that the cost of recycling—including human effort—is less than the benefit. Similarly, as long as resources are privately owned, firms balance their current profits of logging and drilling against their future profits. If an oil driller knows that the price of oil will rise sharply in ten years, he has an incentive to conserve oil instead of selling it today.

Externalities are often blamed for "market failure," but they are also a source of government failure. Many economists who study politics decry the large negative externalities of voter ignorance. An economic illiterate who votes for protectionism hurts not just himself but also his fellow citizens (Caplan 2003; Downs 1957). Other economists believe externalities in the budget process lead to wasteful spending. A congressman who lobbies for federal funds for his district improves his chances of reelection but hurts the financial health of the rest of the nation.

Putative externalities have been found in unlikely places. Some argue that wealth itself has an externality: inflaming envy. Others maintain that there are externalities of altruism—when I give money to help the poor, everyone else who cares about the needy is better off. Defenders of Prohibition and the war on drugs emphasize the externalities of drunkenness and drug addiction, though they typically lump private costs, such as low earnings and unemployment, in with the external costs of drunk driving and violent crime. In the Big Tobacco class action suit, one of the plaintiffs' main arguments was that, given government's role in medical care, smoking costs taxpayers money.[3]

---

1. In principle, you could get the same results from pollution taxes, though these are usually more objectionable to industry than tradable permits.

2. Despite its popularity, even the national defense example can be criticized for failing to count the negative externalities of military spending on foreigners.

3. Some economists calculated, however, that the cost of treating smoking-related disorders was less than the savings attributa-

In principle, externalities could be used to rationalize censorship, persecution of religious minorities, forced veiling of women, and even South Africa's apartheid. If most people were to find Darwinism offensive, the logic of externalities would recommend a tax on Darwinian expression. Few economists have pursued such possibilities, probably out of a tacit sense that, in extreme cases, individual rights override economic efficiency.

Even from a strictly economic point of view, however, some externalities are not worth correcting. One reason is that many activities have positive and negative externalities that roughly cancel out. For example, mowing your lawn has the positive externality of improving the appearance of your neighborhood and the negative externality of creating a loud noise. A subsidy or a tax would alleviate one problem but amplify the other. To take a more controversial example, some economists question efforts to prevent GLOBAL WARMING, calculating that the benefits for people in cold climates more than balance out the costs for people in warm climates.

Another economic rationale for government inaction is as follows: sometimes an externality is large at low levels of production but rapidly fades out as the quantity increases. As long as output is high enough, such externalities can be safely ignored. For example, during a famine, doubling the supply of food has large positive externalities because starvation leads to robbery, hunger riots, and even cannibalism. During times of plenty, however, doubling the food supply would probably have no noticeable effect on crime.

Yet, it is to Nobel laureate Ronald Coase that we owe the most influential argument for letting externalities solve themselves. In "The Problem of Social Cost" (1960), Coase bypasses the earlier view that it is literally impossible to charge for some benefits. Instead, he observes that every exchange has some *transactions costs,* which vary from negligible—such as putting coins into a vending machine— to enormous—such as negotiating a contract with six billion signatories to improve air quality.

Coase drew strong implications from his commonsense observation. Instead of arguing about whether or not something is an "externality," it is more productive to ask about transactions costs. If transactions costs are reasonably low, then the affected parties negotiate tolerably efficient solutions without government intervention.

To take Coase's classic example, suppose that a railroad emits sparks on a farmer's crops. As long as transactions costs are low, the railroad and the farmer will work out a solution. Coase was particularly clever to emphasize that, in terms of economic efficiency, it does not matter whether the law sides with the railroad or the farmer. Suppose that it costs one thousand dollars to control the sparks and the lost crops are worth two thousand dollars. Even if the law sides with the railroad, the farmer will pay the railroad to control the sparks. Alternately, suppose that it costs two thousand dollars to control the sparks, the lost crops are worth only one thousand, and the law sides with the farmer. Then the railroad pays the farmer for permission to continue sparking.

Coase's argument was initially controversial. As George Stigler recounts in his autobiography, when Coase first presented his idea to a group of twenty-one colleagues, none agreed. After an evening's argument, however, Coase convinced them all. Coase's approach subsequently spread widely in both economics and law. Faced with externalities, modern analysts almost immediately inquire about transactions costs. For example, in the early 1950s, J. E. Meade advocated subsidizing apple orchards to correct for the positive externalities they provide to beekeepers. Inspired by Coase, however, Steven Cheung (1973) wrote a careful case study of the bee-apple nexus. In the real world, beekeepers and apple orchard owners do not wait for government to solve their problem. They can and do negotiate detailed contracts to deal with externalities.

Coase's approach is probably the main reason economists are skeptical of antismoking legislation. While it is costly for smokers and nonsmokers to directly negotiate with each other, the owners of bars, restaurants, and workplaces can cheaply balance their conflicting interests. If nonsmokers are willing to pay more to avoid the smell of tobacco than smokers are willing to pay to smoke, restaurants will disallow smoking—and charge a premium for their smoke-free atmosphere. If unregulated markets fail to deliver a smoke-free world, Coasean logic suggests that smokers value smoking more than nonsmokers value not being subjected to cigarette smoke.

About the Author

Bryan Caplan is an associate professor of economics at George Mason University. His Web site is www.bcaplan.com.

Further Reading

Introductory

Blinder, Alan. *Hard Heads, Soft Hearts: Tough-Minded Economics for a Just Society.* New York: Addison-Wesley, 1987.
Friedman, David. *Hidden Order: The Economics of Everyday Life.* New York: HarperBusiness, 1996.

---

ble to smokers' shorter life spans. In other words, it is *nonsmoking* that has negative externalities! (Viscusi 1994).

Landsburg, Steven. *The Armchair Economist.* New York: Free Press, 1993.

Schultze, Charles. *The Public Use of Private Interest.* Washington, D.C.: Brookings Institution Press, 1997.

Stigler, George J. *Memoirs of an Unregulated Economist.* New York: Basic Books, 1988.

Advanced

Caplan, Bryan. "The Logic of Collective Belief." *Rationality and Society* 15, no. 2 (2003): 218–242.

Cheung, Steven. "The Fable of the Bees: An Economic Investigation." *Journal of Law and Economics* 16, no. 1 (1973): 11–33.

Coase, Ronald. "The Problem of Social Cost." *Journal of Law and Economics* 3, no. 1 (1960): 1–44.

Cowen, Tyler, ed. *Public Goods and Market Failures.* New Brunswick, N.J.: Transaction Publishers, 1992.

Downs, Anthony. *An Economic Theory of Democracy.* New York: Harper, 1957.

Posner, Richard. *Economic Analysis of Law.* New York: Aspen Law and Business, 1998.

Simon, Julian. *The Ultimate Resource 2.* Princeton: Princeton University Press, 1996.

Viscusi, W. Kip. "Cigarette Taxation and the Social Consequences of Smoking." NBER Working Paper no. 4891. National Bureau of Economic Research, Cambridge, Mass., 1994.

Fascism

Sheldon Richman

As an economic system, fascism is socialism with a capitalist veneer. The word derives from *fasces,* the Roman symbol of collectivism and power: a tied bundle of rods with a protruding ax. In its day (the 1920s and 1930s), fascism was seen as the happy medium between boom-and-bust-prone liberal capitalism, with its alleged class conflict, wasteful competition, and profit-oriented egoism, and revolutionary Marxism, with its violent and socially divisive persecution of the bourgeoisie. Fascism substituted the particularity of nationalism and racialism—"blood and soil"—for the internationalism of both classical liberalism and Marxism.

Where socialism sought totalitarian control of a society's economic processes through direct state operation of the means of production, fascism sought that control indirectly, through domination of nominally private owners. Where socialism nationalized property explicitly, fascism did so implicitly, by requiring owners to use their property in the "national interest"—that is, as the autocratic authority conceived it. (Nevertheless, a few industries were operated by the state.) Where socialism abolished all market relations outright, fascism left the appearance of market relations while planning all economic activities. Where socialism abolished money and prices, fascism controlled the monetary system and set all prices and wages politically. In doing all this, fascism denatured the marketplace. Entrepreneurship was abolished. State ministries, rather than consumers, determined what was produced and under what conditions.

Fascism is to be distinguished from interventionism, or the mixed economy. Interventionism seeks to guide the market process, not eliminate it, as fascism did. Minimum-wage and antitrust laws, though they regulate the free market, are a far cry from multiyear plans from the Ministry of Economics.

Under fascism, the state, through official cartels, controlled all aspects of manufacturing, commerce, finance, and agriculture. Planning boards set product lines, production levels, prices, wages, working conditions, and the size of firms. Licensing was ubiquitous; no economic activity could be undertaken without government permission. Levels of consumption were dictated by the state, and "excess" incomes had to be surrendered as taxes or "loans." The consequent burdening of manufacturers gave advantages to foreign firms wishing to export. But since government policy aimed at autarky, or national self-sufficiency, protectionism was necessary: imports were barred or strictly controlled, leaving foreign conquest as the only avenue for access to resources unavailable domestically. Fascism was thus incompatible with peace and the international division of labor—hallmarks of liberalism.

Fascism embodied corporatism, in which political representation was based on trade and industry rather than on geography. In this, fascism revealed its roots in syndicalism, a form of socialism originating on the left. The government cartelized firms of the same industry, with representatives of labor and management serving on myriad local, regional, and national boards—subject always to the final authority of the dictator's economic plan. Corporatism was intended to avert unsettling divisions within the nation, such as lockouts and union strikes. The price of such forced "harmony" was the loss of the ability to bargain and move about freely.

To maintain high employment and minimize popular discontent, fascist governments also undertook massive public-works projects financed by steep taxes, borrowing, and fiat money creation. While many of these projects were domestic—roads, buildings, stadiums—the largest project of all was militarism, with huge armies and arms production.

The fascist leaders' antagonism to COMMUNISM has

been misinterpreted as an affinity for CAPITALISM. In fact, fascists' anticommunism was motivated by a belief that in the collectivist milieu of early-twentieth-century Europe, communism was its closest rival for people's allegiance. As with communism, under fascism, every citizen was regarded as an employee and tenant of the totalitarian, party-dominated state. Consequently, it was the state's prerogative to use force, or the threat of it, to suppress even peaceful opposition.

If a formal architect of fascism can be identified, it is Benito Mussolini, the onetime Marxist editor who, caught up in nationalist fervor, broke with the left as World War I approached and became Italy's leader in 1922. Mussolini distinguished fascism from liberal capitalism in his 1928 autobiography:

> The citizen in the Fascist State is no longer a selfish individual who has the anti-social right of rebelling against any law of the Collectivity. The Fascist State with its corporative conception puts men and their possibilities into productive work and interprets for them the duties they have to fulfill. (p. 280)

Before his foray into imperialism in 1935, Mussolini was often praised by prominent Americans and Britons, including Winston Churchill, for his economic program.

Similarly, Adolf Hitler, whose National Socialist (Nazi) Party adapted fascism to Germany beginning in 1933, said:

> The state should retain supervision and each property owner should consider himself appointed by the state. It is his duty not to use his property against the interests of others among his own people. This is the crucial matter. The Third Reich will always retain its right to control the owners of property. (Barkai 1990, pp. 26–27)

Both nations exhibited elaborate planning schemes for their economies in order to carry out the state's objectives. Mussolini's corporate state "consider[ed] private initiative in production the most effective instrument to protect national interests" (Basch 1937, p. 97). But the meaning of "initiative" differed significantly from its meaning in a market economy. Labor and management were organized into twenty-two industry and trade "corporations," each with Fascist Party members as senior participants. The corporations were consolidated into a National Council of Corporations; however, the real decisions were made by state agencies such as the Instituto per la Ricosstruzione Industriale, which held shares in industrial, agricultural, and real estate enterprises, and the Instituto Mobiliare, which controlled the nation's credit.

Hitler's regime eliminated small corporations and made membership in cartels mandatory.[1] The Reich Economic Chamber was at the top of a complicated bureaucracy comprising nearly two hundred organizations organized along industry, commercial, and craft lines, as well as several national councils. The Labor Front, an extension of the Nazi Party, directed all labor matters, including wages and assignment of workers to particular jobs. Labor conscription was inaugurated in 1938. Two years earlier, Hitler had imposed a four-year plan to shift the nation's economy to a war footing. In Europe during this era, Spain, Portugal, and Greece also instituted fascist economies.

In the United States, beginning in 1933, the constellation of government interventions known as the New Deal had features suggestive of the corporate state. The National Industrial Recovery Act created code authorities and codes of practice that governed all aspects of manufacturing and commerce. The National Labor Relations Act made the federal government the final arbiter in labor issues. The Agricultural Adjustment Act introduced central planning to farming. The object was to reduce competition and output in order to keep prices and incomes of particular groups from falling during the Great Depression.

It is a matter of controversy whether President Franklin Roosevelt's New Deal was directly influenced by fascist economic policies. Mussolini praised the New Deal as "boldly . . . interventionist in the field of economics," and Roosevelt complimented Mussolini for his "honest purpose of restoring Italy" and acknowledged that he kept "in fairly close touch with that admirable Italian gentleman." Also, Hugh Johnson, head of the National Recovery Administration, was known to carry a copy of Raffaello Viglione's pro-Mussolini book, *The Corporate State,* with him, presented a copy to Labor Secretary Frances Perkins, and, on retirement, paid tribute to the Italian dictator.

About the Author

Sheldon Richman is the editor of *The Freeman: Ideas on Liberty* at the Foundation for Economic Education in Irvington-on-Hudson, N.Y.

Further Reading

Barkai, Avraham. *Nazi Economics: Ideology, Theory, and Policy.* Trans. Ruth Hadass-Vashitz. Oxford: Berg Publishers Ltd., 1990.
Basch, Ernst. *The Fascist: His State and His Mind.* New York: Morrow, 1937.

1. "Laws decreed in October 1937 simply dissolved all corporations with a capital under $40,000 and forbade the establishment of new ones with a capital less than $20,000" (Shirer 1959, p. 262).

Diggins, John P. *Mussolini and Fascism: The View from America*. Princeton: Princeton University Press, 1972.

Flynn, John T. *As We Go Marching*. 1944. Reprint. New York: Free Life Editions, 1973.

———. *The Roosevelt Myth*. New York: Devin-Adair, 1948.

Laqueur, Walter, ed. *Fascism: A Reader's Guide*. Berkeley: University of California Press, 1976.

Mises, Ludwig von. *Omnipotent Government*. New Rochelle, N.Y.: Arlington House, 1944.

Mussolini, Benito. *Fascism: Doctrine and Institutions*. Firenze: Vallecchi, 1935.

———. *My Autobiography*. New York: Scribner's, 1928.

Pitigliani, Fauto. *The Italian Corporative State*. New York: Macmillan, 1934.

Powell, Jim. *FDR's Folly: How Roosevelt and His New Deal Prolonged the Great Depression*. New York: Crown Forum, 2003.

Shirer, William L. *The Rise and Fall of the Third Reich*. New York: Simon and Schuster, 1960.

Twight, Charlotte. *America's Emerging Fascist Economy*. New Rochelle, N.Y.: Arlington House, 1975.

Federal Reserve System

Richard H. Timberlake

The Original Federal Reserve System

Several monetary institutions appeared in the United States prior to the formation of the Federal Reserve System, or Fed. These were, in order: the constitutional gold (and bimetallic) standard, the First and Second Banks of the United States, the Independent Treasury, the National Banking System, clearinghouse associations, and the National Reserve Association. The Fed was the last such institution founded. Although it has endured, the present-day Fed would be unrecognizable to its founders.

The original Federal Reserve Act became law in December 1913. The "Federal" in the title implied that the law applied to the whole country, and "Reserve" emphasized the new institution's role as a reserve holder and reserve supplier for the commercial banking system. The twelve regional Federal Reserve Banks, according to the Federal Reserve Act, were "to furnish an elastic currency" by

discount[ing] notes, drafts, and bills of exchange arising out of actual commercial transactions. . . . The time, character, and volume of sales of [this eligible] paper . . . shall be governed with a view to accommodating commerce and business and with regard to their bearing upon the general credit situation of the country.

Conspicuously absent in the title or anywhere else in the act were the words "central bank." The primary reason for this omission was the term's unpopularity with the populist wing of the Democratic Party. Republicans had accepted the label, but, after 1912, no longer controlled either Congress or the White House. Therefore, the new institution could not be a "central bank." That term, many congressmen objected, implied monopolistic control by Wall Street bankers, who would keep interest rates "high" and conspire with speculators to cause panics. However, under Democratic sponsorship, the new institution could be an autonomous group of regional reserve-holding supercommercial banks, and the act passed through Congress in this guise.

The U.S. banking and financial system at this time had recognizable faults that some bankers, financial experts, politicians, and economists thought needed correcting. The major monetary institution of the era was the self-regulating GOLD STANDARD, which functioned much as was expected. However, the commercial banking system included both state banks—chartered by state governments—and national banks—licensed as such by the comptroller of the currency. Because of the overlap in regulatory jurisdictions, a plethora of regulations made banking operations difficult. Legal reserve requirements, for example, varied significantly at the state and national levels, and almost always made banking less flexible and more precarious. The banking system's fragility appeared whenever some random and unforeseen financial shock put undue pressure on the banking system to provide "emergency" liquidity.

The Federal Reserve System was the institutional answer to this perceived problem. Just as the gold standard worked through market forces to provide a proper quantity of gold-based money, so the new Federal Reserve Banks would augment the gold standard to ensure that the commercial banking system could issue the proper quantity of bank-created money in a timely fashion.

The twelve regional Federal Reserve Banks were to be located in major cities. Each bank was to operate autonomously in its region. A Fed Bank had a board of directors and an executive structure similar to that of any commercial bank or business firm. Commercial banks in a Federal Reserve district could become members of the Federal Reserve if they fulfilled certain requirements, including buying stock in their regional Fed Bank according to a formula based on their capital value. The Fed Bank then paid them a statutory annual return of 6 percent on the value of this stock. Member commercial banks therefore became the "stockholders" of the Fed banks.

Also included was a Federal Reserve Board located in Washington, D.C., and housed in the Treasury Department. Members of the board, appointed by the president, served staggered ten-year (later fourteen-year) terms. The board was to provide oversight and examination of the twelve Fed Banks, including the "nature and maturities of the paper and other investments owned or held by the Federal reserve banks." It could also "require Federal reserve banks to rediscount the discounted paper of other Federal reserve banks at rates of interest to be fixed by the Board." Finally, it had the power to suspend the gold reserve requirements of the twelve Fed Banks for an indefinite period.

Operations of the new Fed Banks included several important features. First, Fed Banks were to be subordinate to the gold standard, which had been in place for more than one hundred years. They were to be "lenders of last resort" and not to take the initiative in monetary affairs. They were also to be independent of political influences.

The Fed Banks' principal function was to rediscount—that is, make loans—to their member banks when the banks were short of liquidity. In keeping with the idea of a Fed Bank as a "lender of last resort," the Fed's discount rate was always supposed to be above current market rates. Bankers and politicians accepted this principle for commercial bank and central bank operations. Just as the gold standard automatically provided for the monetization of gold on fixed terms—at that time, $20.67 per ounce—so the Fed Banks were to lend money to their member banks on "eligible paper." Such paper was to be limited to short-term self-liquidating loans, bills, discounts, and advances that had appeared in conjunction with the production and marketing of real goods. This rubric, at the time known as the "commercial credit theory of banking," is also called "the real bills doctrine" and was a key factor in Federal Reserve policy for the first twenty years of the Fed's existence.

Unlike gold, which the owner could convert into money precisely according to the mint price of gold, the dollars that Fed Banks could lend to member banks on "eligible paper," or "real bills," were not specified by any formula or law. Like the gold standard, the real bills doctrine theoretically gears the production of money to the production of real goods, services, and capital. Thus, the whole strategy of the Federal Reserve System was to graft an automatic money-creating banking policy onto an automatically functioning gold standard system, with the whole money-making apparatus geared to the production of real goods and services.

The Federal Reserve System
During the 1920s
The Federal Reserve Banks became operational during World War I. Their first major task was to support the U.S. Treasury's wartime financing needs. Most of the credit they created came after the war (1918–1920) to support Liberty Loans the government floated to help finance the war and its aftermath. Their subsequent contraction of credit in 1920 contributed significantly to the recession that occurred in 1921–1922. Recovery came quickly, however, leaving the system in a position to develop certain norms of policy in the postwar period.

As the system came of age in the 1920s, both the Fed Banks and the Federal Reserve Board argued that the banks' constant presence in the money market was necessary to prevent crises. The New York and Chicago Fed Banks, the largest of the twelve, had most of the commercial banking activity in their districts, and the president of the New York Fed, Benjamin Strong, became the dominant figure in the system.

During World War I and into the 1920s, U.S. exports of goods and capital to Europe burgeoned. As gold flowed in to pay the balances on U.S. exports, member banks deposited much of it in Fed Banks. The Federal Reserve Act specified minimum reserves of 35 percent gold against member bank reserve-deposit accounts at Fed Banks, and 40 percent gold against Federal Reserve notes outstanding. By August 1929, the Fed Banks' gold holdings were $3.12 billion, double the legal requirement.

Growth in Fed Banks' excess gold reserves, formally labeled "free gold," provided a buffer for Fed policymakers. By selling off other earning assets, they could "sterilize" gold inflows so that incoming gold would not inflate the stock of common money enough to raise prices. "The" gold standard, therefore, no longer provided an effective control over the stock of U.S. money; the system was no longer autonomous and self-regulating. In place of the self-regulating gold standard were the decisions of Fed policymakers.

Throughout this era, many economists recommended that Fed policymakers use the quantity theory of money (see MONETARISM) as their guide to policy, and the Federal Reserve Bank of New York under Benjamin Strong unofficially implemented this practice for a short time (1922–1928). Most Fed officials vigorously opposed this idea, however, insisting that the compatibility of the real bills doctrine with economic productivity provided the optimal policy.

The downturn in business that became the Great Contraction of 1929–1933 began in 1928. Federal Reserve officials, and many financial analysts and politicians, believed that a financial purging of speculative and nonproductive bank credit was needed. They argued that the slackening of production in the economy indicated a diminished "need" for money. Since they had taken monetary control away from the gold standard, their faulty decision to do nothing to keep the money supply from falling allowed the recession to degenerate into a depression. As it did so through 1930 and 1931, the commercial banking system suffered three major crises. By early 1933, it and the economy were in shambles (see GREAT DEPRESSION).

The Banking Act of 1935

In 1935, Congress, at the behest of President Roosevelt, passed the Banking Act of 1935. This act converted the autonomous regional system of reserve-holding banks into a monolithic central bank with positive and deliberate control over the U.S. monetary system.

One major change was the creation of the Federal Open Market Committee (FOMC). This agency included the seven governors (as they were now labeled) of the Fed Board, the president of the New York Fed, and four of the other eleven Fed Bank presidents, who rotated membership on the committee. The FOMC controlled open market operations in government securities, which now became system-wide. Reserve Banks still set their own discount rates, but discounting never again figured prominently in Fed policies.

A 1917 amendment to the original act of 1913 had fixed member bank reserve requirements at 7, 10, and 13 percent for member banks in small to larger cities. The act of 1935 extended these percentages to a range double the original values, that is, to 7–14, 10–20, and 13–26 percent, the exact percentages to be set by decision of the Board of Governors. This change added to the board's policymaking powers. While the new act gave the Fed these additional monetary controls, it nowhere specified goals or targets for Fed policy beyond the general terms in the original act.

The Banking Act also removed the secretary of the treasury and his second-in-command, the comptroller of the currency, from the Fed Board. (They had been chairman and vice chairman of the board.) However, the board's decisions were even more under the control of the secretary of the treasury than they had been in the past. From 1935 to 1951, the secretary of the treasury, with the compliance of Fed Board Chairman Marriner Eccles, continued to dominate Fed policies.

Gold kept coming into the United States due to both the higher price (thirty-five dollars per ounce) that Congress had legislated in 1934 and the political instability in Europe. By 1936, the commercial banking system had enormous "excess" reserves—double the required amount of currency and reserve-deposit accounts with Fed Banks, which also had double the amount of required gold reserves. Observing the volume of reserves in the banking system and arguing that it would fuel inflation, the Fed Board—with the approval of the secretary of the treasury, most financial experts, and many academicians—doubled commercial bank reserve requirements in three steps: by 50 percent in August 1936, 25 percent in March 1937, and the final 25 percent in May 1937. This momentous change stifled the recovery and initiated the 1937 recession. In fact, even had the banks used all of their excess reserves to expand credit and the money supply, virtually no inflation was possible. The high unemployment of 1936 and 1937 meant that even a fully expanded banking system could not have created enough money to raise prices more than a few percent above their 1929 level. Complete economic recovery did not occur until after the start of World War II.

During World War II, the Fed concentrated on maintaining "low" interest rates so that the U.S. Treasury could sell enough bonds to finance the war. If bond prices tended to drop and interest rates on them to rise, the FOMC prevented the increase in nominal rates by using the Fed's still-abundant excess reserves to buy the securities that the markets "would not take"—at prevailing rates. Interest rates were low: 0.375 percent on the shortest-term treasury bills to 2.5 percent on long-term bonds. Commercial banks did likewise with their excess reserves. This policy pumped large quantities of inflationary new money into the monetary system. To hide inflation, the administration and Congress imposed direct controls on prices, wages, and production.

After the war ended, the Truman administration tried to continue price-wage controls, as well as its control over Fed monetary policy. However, in the mid- and late 1940s, Congress abolished most controls, then passed a resolution that reintroduced the principle of "independence" into Fed policymaking. The resolution emphasized that the Fed would be responsible for monetary policy and the U.S. Treasury for fiscal policy, and that "they should stay out of each other's backyards." It also charged both bodies to aim toward the goals specified in the Employment Act of 1946—that is, to "considerations relating to [policies'] effects on employment, production, purchasing power, and price levels." Fed and Treasury officials ratified this congressional mandate in the famous "accord" of March 1951. Around the same time, President Truman appointed William McChesney Martin chairman of the Federal Reserve Board.

The Martin Fed, 1951–1970

Under Martin's chairmanship, Fed policy became very ordinary. For sixteen years, 1951–1966, the M1 money stock increased at an average annual rate of 2.4 percent, and prices rose annually by just 1.6 percent. Most of the increase in the money stock resulted from the Fed Board's reductions of member banks' reserve requirements, which allowed the banking system to increase its deposits proportionally. By 1962, requirements were 16.5 percent for big-city member banks and 12 percent for "country" (i.e., small-town) banks. As they reached this moderate range, the Fed Board left them there and henceforth focused on open-market operations to effect monetary policy.

But starting in 1964, President Lyndon B. Johnson's government spending programs for welfare and the Vietnam War again put pressure on the Fed to keep interest rates down. The Fed yielded somewhat to administration pressure. Increases in M1 that had been between 2 and 3 percent in the early 1960s jumped to 5–8 percent from the mid-1960s to early 1970s.

Federal Reserve Policy under Arthur Burns

President Richard M. Nixon appointed Arthur Burns chairman of the Fed Board in 1970. Under Burns's chairmanship, the Fed continued its policy of "stimulation-accommodation." When a recession appeared, as occurred in 1969, the Fed increased its open-market buying activity to *stimulate* spending. Once recovery was in place, Fed policy *accommodated* revived business spending, again with open-market purchases. This combination caused higher inflation, which the Nixon administration, with Burns's blessing, sought to restrain by statutory wage and price controls—the Economic Stabilization Act, which became law in August 1971. This program failed to tame inflation. Fed policy continued in the same pattern, however, through the 1970s, reaching its climax with the inflation spike of 1979–1981.

Burns summed up the Fed's problems in 1987, as they had appeared during his tenure. "Currents of thought and the political environment they have created," he lamented, give rise to government spending programs and federal fiscal deficits. The Fed has "the power to abort the inflation" at any time, and "it has the power to end it today," he admitted. However, Burns continued,

> it is illusory to expect central banks to put an end to an inflation . . . that is continually driven by political forces. . . . Persistent inflation . . . will not be vanquished . . . until new currents of thought create a political environment in which the difficult adjustments required to end inflation can be undertaken. (Arthur F. Burns, "The Anguish of Central Banking," *Federal Reserve Bulletin,* September 1987, pp. 695–696)

Federal Reserve Policy Under Paul Volcker

President Jimmy Carter appointed Paul Volcker chairman of the Fed Board in August 1979, about a year before inflation peaked. By this time, everyone recognized the Fed's complete power to control the monetary base—that is, currency outstanding and bank reserve accounts. In addition to the base, most economists accepted and used two clas-

sifications for common money: M1, consisting of the public's holdings of currency plus checking account deposits in banks and other depository institutions; and M2, which includes M1 plus time deposits in these same institutions. These money stocks are commonly referred to as "the aggregates."

The Fed has used its power over the aggregates principally to influence short-term interest rates—the federal funds rate and the three-month treasury bill rate. Fed policymakers refer to these rates as "money market conditions." Two different indicators, therefore, react to the Fed's control over base money: the "aggregates"—money stocks M1 and M2—and "money market conditions"—the short-term interest rates noted above. Seldom can both of these indicators be appropriate policy guides simultaneously.

The inflation of the late 1970s was a result of Fed attempts to use money market conditions as a guide to policy when interest rates were responding to inflationary expectations resulting from large increases in money stocks. Pumping more money into the system to keep interest rates *down* only added to expected inflation and *increased* nominal interest rates. In October 1979, the Fed shifted to its own version of monetarism. Fed "monetarism" lasted officially only until October 1982. In practice, Fed policy never abandoned interest rate targeting and never accepted any rigorous application of true monetarism.

The Monetary Control Act of 1980

Congress passed the Depository Institutions Deregulation and Monetary Control Act (DIDMCA) in 1980. Title I of the act extended the Fed's power to specify member bank reserve requirements to include all depository institutions. This issue was contentious because Fed Banks pay zero interest on reserves; thus, the law placed what was essentially a tax on nonmember banks. Title I also extended the eligible collateral for Fed issues of federal reserve notes to include the "fully guaranteed obligations of a foreign government or the agency of a foreign government."

Title II of the DIDMCA generally deregulated and freed up operations in the financial industry. It allowed all financial institutions to provide checking account services to their customers, and it abolished interest-rate controls on deposits so that depository institutions could pay competitive interest rates on deposit accounts.

The combined effects of the new act's provisions were beneficial for the U.S. economy. Demand deposit balances were now a more attractive way to hold wealth than they had been. By 1988, the Fed had phased down reserve requirements for most demand deposits to 12 percent, where they have remained.

The resulting decline in inflation rates has prompted foreigners to hold a large but immeasurable quantity of U.S. dollars. The world's increased demand for U.S. money helped reduce inflation by decreasing the velocity of money on both M1 and M2. By 1986, inflation in the United States had ended.

Between 1985 and 1990, however, Fed policy increased the base by 9 percent per year (from $201 billion to $290 billion), while M1 increased by 7.5 percent per year (from $591 billion to $810 billion). The result was robust revenue for the U.S. Treasury, but also a resurgence of inflation by the end of the decade to annual rates of 4–5 percent.

The Greenspan Fed

In August 1987, President Ronald Reagan appointed Alan Greenspan chairman of the Federal Reserve Board. Greenspan inherited the end-of-the-decade inflation determined by the policies of his predecessor, Paul Volcker, and the FOMC. When Greenspan became chairman, he and other members of the policymaking FOMC began expressing sophisticated arguments for a monetary policy that formally concentrated on price level stability. In his reports to Congress Greenspan presented the case for such a policy on several occasions. In accordance with this prescription, the FOMC repeatedly lowered rates of growth for M1 and M2 during the 1990s. Most important, the FOMC policy directive for the day-to-day implementation of Fed policy to the Fed Bank of New York took on a new tone. Before 1988 it had stated that the FOMC "seeks monetary and financial conditions that will foster *reasonable* price level stability." But in the March 1988 directive, the FOMC deleted the modifier "reasonable." The quantity theory of money, which posits the close relationship between the quantity of money and prices, furnishes the intellectual framework for the FOMC's new emphasis.

Certain congressmen tried to formalize the FOMC's stable price level policy by means of a congressional resolution. Representative Stephen Neal, chairman of the House Subcommittee on Domestic Monetary Policy, was the major proponent of the resolution. He held hearings several times on the proposal between 1989 and 1991 and had Greenspan and several Federal Reserve Bank presidents testify on both its feasibility and its importance. However, neither the Reagan nor the Bush administration approved of their effort. Particularly if a recession is brewing, the incumbent executive inevitably wants the central bank to "lower interest rates" by (necessarily) pumping money into the system.

Nevertheless, the FOMC has continued to pursue price stability. Between 1991 and 2004, the annual inflation rate steadily declined from 4 percent to less than 2 percent. At the same time, short-term interest rates fell from 6–9 per-

cent to 1–4 percent, while long-term rates decline from 8–10 percent to 4–6 percent. These data imply the near absence of expected inflation.

The Fed's performance since 1991 has been unquestionably superior to its record at any time since 1913. However, the larger, long-run question remains: Can the Fed as an "independent" central bank maintain price stability contrary to the wishes of an executive branch that seeks to use its fiscal powers to manage the federal government's burgeoning long-term debt?

About the Author

Richard H. Timberlake is a professor of economics, retired, at the University of Georgia.

Further Reading

Friedman, M., and A. J. Schwartz. *A Monetary History of the United States, 1867–1960.* Princeton: Princeton University Press and National Bureau of Economic Research, 1963.

Goodhart, C. A. E. *The Evolution of Central Banks.* Cambridge: MIT Press, 1988.

Humphrey, T. "The Choice of a Monetary Policy Framework: Lessons from the 1920s." *Cato Journal* 21, no. 2 (2001): 285–313.

Meltzer, A. H. *A History of the Federal Reserve.* Vol. 1: 1913–1951. Chicago: University of Chicago Press, 2003.

Smith, V. C. *The Rationale of Central Banking.* Westminster: P. S. King and Son, 1936. Reprinted as *The Rationale of Central Banking and the Free Banking Alternative.* Indianapolis: Liberty Fund, 1990.

Timberlake, R. H. *Monetary Policy in the United States: An Intellectual and Institutional History.* Chicago: University of Chicago Press, 1993.

Warburton, Clark. *Depression, Inflation, and Monetary Policy: Selected Papers, 1945–1953.* Baltimore: Johns Hopkins University Press, 1966.

Financial Regulation

Bert Ely

Financial regulation in the United States, and elsewhere in the developed world, breaks down into two basic categories: safety-and-soundness regulation and compliance. While this entry focuses on U.S. financial services regulation, it broadly reflects what occurs elsewhere.

Financial institutions serve various purposes. Depository institutions (banks, savings and loans [S&Ls], and credit unions) transform liquid liabilities (checking accounts, savings accounts, and certificates of deposit that can be cashed in prior to maturity) into relatively illiquid assets, such as home mortgages, car loans, loans to finance business inventories and accounts receivable, and credit card balances. Depository institutions also operate the payments system where bank balances are shifted between parties through checks, wire transfers, and credit and debit card transactions. Insurance companies fall into two broad categories—life and health insurers, whose policies provide financial protection against death, disability, and medical bills; and property and casualty insurers, whose policies protect policyholders against losses arising from fire, natural disasters, accidents, fraud, and other calamities. Stockbrokers and related investment banking firms are central players in the capital markets where businesses raise capital and where individuals and institutional investors buy and sell shares of stock in business enterprises.

The basic goal of safety-and-soundness regulation is to protect "fixed-amount creditors" from losses arising from the insolvency of financial institutions owing those amounts, while ensuring stability within the financial system. Fixed-amount creditors are bank depositors, beneficiaries and claimants of insurance companies, and account holders at brokerage firms who are owed fixed amounts of money. Investors in a stock or bond mutual fund are not fixed-amount creditors because the value of their investments is determined solely by the market value of the fund's investments. Financial institutions with fixed-amount creditors include banks, S&Ls, credit unions, insurance companies, stockbrokers, and money-market mutual funds (MMMF). Compliance regulation broadly seeks to protect individuals from "unfair" dealing by financial institutions and in the financial markets and to impede such crimes as "money laundering," although this crime is hard to define.

Financial regulation in the United States is carried out by an alphabet soup of federal and state agencies. The federal bank regulators include the Federal Reserve System, the Federal Deposit Insurance Corporation (FDIC), the Office of the Comptroller of the Currency, the Office of Thrift Supervision, and the National Credit Union Administration. The Securities and Exchange Commission (SEC) regulates stockbrokers, MMMFs, stock and bond mutual funds, stock trading—including the stock exchanges—and financial disclosures by publicly traded corporations. State regulators oversee state-chartered banks, savings institutions, and credit unions as well as all insurance companies. State securities regulators are a junior partner to the SEC in that field.

Safety-and-Soundness Regulation

Safety-and-soundness, or solvency, regulation seeks to prevent financial institutions with fixed-amount creditors from becoming insolvent. Because government regulation cannot prevent all insolvencies, however, governments have created mechanisms to protect at least small fixed-amount creditors from any loss when a depository institution, insurance company, or brokerage firm has become insolvent—that is, has "failed." These mechanisms, such as deposit insurance, insurance guaranty funds, and investor protection funds, can properly be viewed as a product warranty for solvency regulation. That is, they protect fixed-amount creditors against losses when the "product," regulation, which is supposed to protect fixed-amount creditors, fails to prevent a financial institution's insolvency.

For the more than three centuries that banks and insurance companies have been chartered by governments, notably with the founding of the Bank of England in 1694, governments have imposed regulations to ensure that these institutions remain both solvent (the value of their assets exceeds their liabilities) and liquid (they can meet payment requests, such as checks and insurance claims, when presented). The principal solvency regulation today centers on capital regulation; that is, the financial institution must maintain a positive capital position (its assets exceed its liabilities) equal to at least a certain portion of its assets. Other solvency regulations force asset diversity by limiting loan and investment concentrations among various classes of borrowers or the amount of credit extended to any one borrower.

In 1988, banking regulators in the industrialized world began to implement a bank capital regulation, now called Basel I, which related the amount of capital a bank had to hold to the riskiness of its assets. Although Basel I was crude in many regards, many banks are financially stronger today because the amount of capital they hold bears a better relationship to the riskiness of their assets. Banking regulators are now attempting to implement a more sophisticated capital standard, called Basel II. When or if Basel II will be fully implemented is an open question.

Solvency regulations are enforced by examiners who assess the value of an institution's assets and determine the scope of its liabilities, a particularly important function in property and casualty insurance companies. A financial institution can become insolvent (its liabilities exceed the value of its assets) if it suffers a large sudden loss or a sustained period of smaller losses. Likewise, a seemingly solvent bank or insurance company can turn out to be insolvent if examiners find hidden losses—assets have been overvalued or liabilities have not been recognized. Quite often, fraud is the underlying cause of those losses.

Even honest managements can experience sudden losses if a large natural disaster causes a spike in insurance claims or if the value of loan collateral plunges. While there was some fraud in the twelve hundred S&Ls that failed during the U.S. S&L crisis of the 1980s, much of the insolvency loss in those failures arose from the collapse of real estate values, particularly in Texas. To help prevent another S&L crisis, in 1991 the U.S. Congress enacted a set of regulatory reforms, called Prompt Corrective Action, to ensure that regulators would not again drag their feet in closing insolvent banks and S&Ls. While these reforms seem to be working, they have not been tested by a full-fledged banking crisis.

Often, insolvent banks are illiquid—that is, they do not have enough cash on hand to pay customer checks and deposit withdrawals. This almost certainly is true when there is a run on the bank (see BANK RUNS). Illiquidity also can strike a solvent bank, although that is relatively rare. To prevent banking panics in the event that banks cannot honor withdrawal requests, Congress has authorized the Federal Reserve to act as a lender of last resort; that is, the Fed stands ready to lend to an illiquid bank when no one else will, provided the bank can fully collateralize its loan with high-quality assets.

MMMFs represent a special case with regard to solvency regulation and liquidity concerns. By design, MMMFs have no capital, that is, the value of their assets must always equal the face value of the shares they have issued to their shareholders; these shares usually are valued at one dollar per share. Also, MMMFs are not authorized to borrow from the Federal Reserve. SEC examiners therefore must determine that an MMMF's assets can readily be sold or redeemed for their stated value. Since MMMFs have no fixed-amount creditor protection comparable to deposit insurance, they can invest only in low-risk assets so that no MMMF will "break the buck," which could unleash a "run" on all MMMFs—that is, MMMF shareholders would attempt to cash in their MMMF shares at the same time. Given that MMMFs had $2.1 trillion of shares outstanding at the end of 2006, that is a legitimate fear. Although the Federal Reserve does not admit to this, it is widely believed that the Fed would provide emergency liquidity to the MMMFs should there be a run on them, in order to maintain the stability of the U.S. financial system, even though this action might be costly to taxpayers.

Deposit Insurance and Other Fixed-Amount Creditor Protection Schemes

Various fixed-amount creditor protection schemes have emerged in the United States, usually in response to crises arising from regulatory failures. State-provided deposit insurance dates to 1829 with the formation of the New York Safety Fund. Fourteen state deposit insurance funds eventually operated, but all had failed by the onset of the Great Depression. In 1933, following the failure of nine thousand mostly small banks in 1930–1933, Congress chartered the

FDIC. Shortly thereafter, it created the Federal Savings and Loan Insurance Corporation (FSLIC) to insure S&Ls. In the aftermath of the S&L debacle, which so far has cost taxpayers about $124 billion, Congress abolished the FSLIC and gave the FDIC responsibility for all bank and S&L deposit insurance.

While deposit insurance for credit unions (called "share insurance") started at the state level, in 1970, Congress created the National Credit Union Share Insurance Fund (NCUSIF) to give credit union members the same level of protection that bank and S&L depositors have. Today, with the exception of 175 state-chartered credit unions served by a private insurer, the federal government insures all bank, S&L, and credit union depositors.

Since 1980, the basic deposit insurance limit has been $100,000 per depositor per bank, S&L, or credit union (up from an initial $5,000 in 1934). However, because bank accounts can legally be titled in various ways, a family can hold many times that amount in insured deposits in a bank. While business deposits are insured, too, deposits in the foreign offices of U.S. banks are not. On December 31, 2006, the estimated amount of insured deposits approximated $4.6 trillion. Uninsured deposits in domestic and foreign offices of banks, S&Ls, and credit unions totaled another $3.8 trillion.

Congress intended, when it passed major deposit insurance reforms in 1991, that uninsured depositors not be protected should their bank fail. Instead, Congress wanted uninsured depositors (presumably more sophisticated than small depositors) to monitor their bank's condition and to withdraw funds from the bank if it got into trouble. In effect, bank runs are supposed to wake up regulators who fail to close a failing bank before it becomes insolvent. However, Congress's desire to share insolvency losses with uninsured depositors clashed with a real-world reality: depositor flight from a large bank could undermine confidence in large sound banks, leading to a banking collapse, a freeze-up of the payments system, and serious economic damage. Therefore, as a practical matter, the $100,000 insurance limit applies only to small banks, and not to so-called too-big-to-fail banks.

U.S. banking regulators have been loath to publicly identify America's too-big-to-fail banks, preferring to maintain the fiction that no bank is too big to fail. In its 1991 reform legislation, however, Congress included a "systemic risk" exception, which gives the regulators (with the approval of the president and the secretary of the treasury) the authority to protect all depositors (domestic and foreign) and all other creditors of a large failing bank if the regulators have determined that trying to impose losses on uninsured depositors and other creditors "would have serious adverse effects on economic conditions or financial stability." In other words, uninsured deposits are, in fact, insured if they are in a large bank.

Governments in other industrialized countries have stated their belief that some banks are too big to fail. Therefore, despite deposit insurance schemes similar to those of the United States, only large depositors in small banks have to worry about suffering a loss should their bank fail. Even then, many countries are reluctant to enforce their deposit insurance limits. Japan is an excellent example, as its government postponed implementing explicit deposit insurance limits while cleaning up its massive banking problems, without any loss to depositors.

The home countries of globally active banks—those with branches or banking subsidiaries in other countries—will find it difficult not to protect depositors and other creditors in other countries in which a troubled bank operates because of concerns of regulatory retribution if it tries to protect only home-country depositors. New Zealand, where most banking assets are controlled by very large banks headquartered elsewhere (principally Australia), is a beneficiary of this phenomenon.

Because U.S. insurance companies are chartered and regulated solely by the states, the states have assumed protection of insureds through two sets of "guaranty funds," one for life and health insurance companies and one for property and casualty companies. The types of protections and the dollar limits of those protections vary among the states. State governments' intent is to protect small insureds and those with relatively small insurance claims—a few hundred thousand dollars at most—from any loss.

Although similar to deposit insurance, guaranty funds differ in one important respect. While the FDIC and NCUSIF collect premiums in advance of the payment of losses, the guaranty funds (with the exception of New York's) collect funds from surviving insurance companies only as they make payments to insureds and claimants. Like deposit insurance, though, the guaranty funds are actuarially unsound because they do not charge risk-sensitive premiums: riskier institutions pay no more, per dollar of protection, than safer institutions.

The Securities Investor Protection Corporation (SIPC) protects customers of failed stock and bond brokerages from brokerage fraud (stolen cash and missing securities), but not from loss in the market value of securities they own. The maximum SIPC protection per customer is $500,000, including a maximum of $100,000 for cash claims.

Another federal financial insurance venture is the Pension Benefit Guaranty Corporation (PBGC). Unlike the insurance and guaranty funds described above, the PBGC is not a "product warranty" for failed regulation. Instead, it protects beneficiaries of defined-benefit pension plans that have been taken over by the PBGC because the pension plan sponsor (usually a financially troubled corporation) has gone bankrupt or out of business. Steel companies and airlines are among the firms that have dumped their unfunded pension liabilities on the PBGC. As happened with the FSLIC, federal taxpayers may eventually be forced to bail out the PBGC.

Common to all government insurance and guaranty programs is "moral hazard," the risk that the insured or guaranteed institution will make economically unwise bets because severe losses from these bets will fall on taxpayers, while owners and managers will profit from winning bets. As insurers learned long ago, properly priced insurance premiums are key to minimizing moral hazard. This moral hazard was the main cause of the S&L CRISIS in the 1980s. Unfortunately, government insurers cannot charge truly risk-sensitive premiums without experiencing severe political opposition from those who would pay high premiums because of their riskiness. Hence, moral hazard will continue to plague government insurance and guaranty programs.

Compliance Regulation
Compliance regulation seeks to ensure "fair" and nondiscriminatory treatment for customers of financial institutions and to prevent financial institutions from being used for criminal or terrorist purposes. Compliance regulation has recently become a major responsibility for the regulators and a major cost burden for financial institutions.

Congress has enacted numerous protections for customers of federally regulated financial institutions; sometimes these protections extend to other types of financial firms, such as small-loan companies. These laws include the Truth in Lending Act, the Truth in Savings Act, the Fair Credit Reporting Act, the Real Estate Settlement Procedures Act, the Expedited Funds Availability Act, and various privacy protections, to name just a few. In recent decades, Congress also has enacted legislation barring discrimination in bank lending, including the Equal Credit Opportunity Act, the Home Mortgage Disclosure Act, the Consumer Credit Protection Act, and the Community Reinvestment Act. Each new law increases compliance costs for banks and other financial institutions.

Congress enacted the Bank Secrecy Act in 1970 not to enhance secrecy but to reduce it: the act's intent was to prevent banks from being used as money-laundering conduits. Under this act, banks are required to submit Currency Transaction Reports to the Treasury Department for individual currency deposits and withdrawals exceeding ten thousand dollars unless the bank customer, such as a grocery store, regularly engages in large cash transactions with the bank. Banks also are required to submit Suspicious Activity Reports for any banking transaction that seems suspicious or out of the ordinary for that customer. According to Lawrence Lindsey, an economist and former governor of the Federal Reserve System, for the seventy-seven million currency-transaction reports filed between 1987 and 1995, the government was able to prosecute only three thousand money-laundering cases. The three thousand cases produced only 580 guilty verdicts. That amounts to more than 130,000 forms filed per conviction.

The USA PATRIOT Act, passed in the aftermath of the 2001 terrorist attacks, broadened the Bank Secrecy Act's reach. Since then, the federal government has stepped up its enforcement of the Bank Secrecy Act, including the levying of multimillion-dollar fines against banks for violations. As a result, financial institutions of all types have increased their spending on compliance. Much of the cost of this spending is borne by customers of these institutions through higher fees and lower returns.

Conclusion

While financial institution regulation has changed dramatically over the centuries, its goal has not changed: to protect fixed-amount creditors against loss should their financial institution fail and to ensure timely payment of checks, insurance claims, and other obligations of these institutions as they come due. However, financial regulation has sometimes failed badly. Hence the need for a product warranty—in the form of deposit insurance, insurance guaranty funds, and the like—to protect depositors, insureds, and brokerage customers from regulatory failure. While financial regulation seems to work well today in the industrialized world (apart from Japan), it is not a particularly efficient system, largely because it is government run. Just as other types of government activities are being privatized, perhaps the time is approaching when financial institution regulation, and its attendant financial risks, should be privatized.

About the Author

Bert Ely, the principal in Ely & Company, Inc., is a financial institutions and monetary policy consultant in Alexandria, Virginia. In 1986, he was one of the first people to publicly predict the U.S. S&L crisis.

Further Reading

The Web sites of the federal regulatory agencies named in the fourth paragraph provide substantial additional information about each agency and the institutions they regulate. The following articles provide insights into important public policy issues and debacles affecting financial institutions.

Calomiris, Charles. "Deposit Insurance: Lessons from the Record." *Federal Reserve Bank of Chicago Economic Perspectives* (May/June 1989): 10–30.
Ely, Bert. "The Fate of the State Guaranty Funds After the Advent of Federal Insurance Chartering." Paper presented at a conference sponsored by the American Enterprise Institute, June 3, 1999.
———. "Regulatory Moral Hazard: The Real Moral Hazard in Federal Deposit Insurance." *Independent Review: A Journal of Political Economy* 4, no. 2 (1999): 241–254.
Ely, Bert, and Rep. Tom Petri. "Better Banking for America: The 100 Percent Cross-Guarantee Solution." *Common Sense* (Fall 1995): 96–112.
Kaufman, George G. "The U.S. Banking Debacle of the 1980s: A Lesson in Government Mismanagement." *Freeman* 45, no. 4 (1995).
Lindsey, Lawrence B. "The Money-Laundering Conundrum: Mugging Privacy in the Assault on Crime?" In *The Future of Financial Privacy*. Washington: Competitive Enterprise Institute, 2000.

Fiscal Policy

David N. Weil

Fiscal policy is the use of government spending and taxation to influence the economy. When the government decides on the goods and services it purchases, the transfer payments it distributes, or the taxes it collects, it is engaging in fiscal policy. The primary economic impact of any change in the government budget is felt by particular groups—a tax cut for families with children, for example, raises their disposable income. Discussions of fiscal policy, however, generally focus on the effect of changes in the government budget on the overall economy. Although changes in taxes or spending that are "revenue neutral" may be construed as fiscal policy—and may affect the aggregate level of output by changing the incentives that firms or individuals face—the term "fiscal policy" is usually used to describe the effect on the aggregate economy of the overall levels of spending and taxation, and more particularly, the gap between them.

Fiscal policy is said to be tight or contractionary when revenue is higher than spending (i.e., the government budget is in surplus) and loose or expansionary when spending is higher than revenue (i.e., the budget is in deficit). Often, the focus is not on the level of the deficit, but on the *change* in the deficit. Thus, a reduction of the deficit from $200 billion to $100 billion is said to be contractionary fiscal policy, even though the budget is still in deficit.

Figure 1 shows the federal budget surplus over the period 1962–2003. The data in the figure are corrected to remove the effects of business cycle conditions. For example, in fiscal year 2003, the actual budget deficit was $375 billion, of which an estimated $68 billion was due to the lingering effects of a recession, so that the cyclically adjusted deficit was $307 billion. The data are also "standardized" to eliminate the effects of inflation and the effects of quirks in the timing of revenues and outlays, such as the receipt of payments from Desert Storm allies that arrived in the fiscal years following the war itself. Notable on the figure are the fiscal stimulus of the Vietnam War, the Kemp-Roth tax cuts of the early 1980s, and the program of tax cuts enacted under George W. Bush.

The most immediate effect of fiscal policy is to change the aggregate demand for goods and services. A fiscal expansion, for example, raises aggregate demand through one of two channels. First, if the government increases its purchases but keeps taxes constant, it increases demand directly. Second, if the government cuts taxes or increases transfer payments, households' disposable income rises, and they will spend more on consumption. This rise in consumption will in turn raise aggregate demand.

Fiscal policy also changes the composition of aggregate demand. When the government runs a deficit, it meets some of its expenses by issuing bonds. In doing so, it competes with private borrowers for money loaned by savers. Holding other things constant, a fiscal expansion will raise interest rates and "crowd out" some private investment, thus reducing the fraction of output composed of private investment.

In an open economy, fiscal policy also affects the exchange rate and the trade balance. In the case of a fiscal expansion, the rise in interest rates due to government borrowing attracts foreign capital. In their attempt to get more dollars to invest, foreigners bid up the price of the dollar, causing an exchange-rate appreciation in the short run. This appreciation makes imported goods cheaper in the United States and exports more expensive abroad, leading to a decline of the merchandise trade balance. Foreigners sell more to the United States than they buy from it and, in return, acquire ownership of U.S. assets (including government debt). In the long run, however, the accumulation of external debt that results from persistent government deficits can lead foreigners to distrust U.S. assets and can cause a depreciation of the exchange rate.

Fiscal policy is an important tool for managing the economy because of its ability to affect the total amount of output produced—that is, gross domestic product. The first impact of a fiscal expansion is to raise the demand for goods and services. This greater demand leads to increases in both output and prices. The degree to which higher

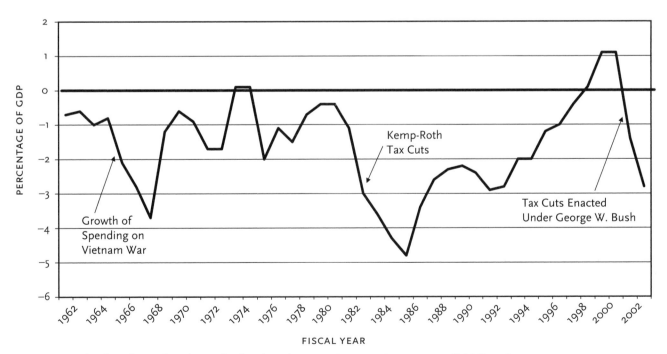

Figure 1 Cyclically Adjusted and Standardized Budget Surplus as a Percentage of GDP: 1962–2003

Source: Congressional Budget Office, Washington, D.C.

demand increases output and prices depends, in turn, on the state of the business cycle. If the economy is in recession, with unused productive capacity and unemployed workers, then increases in demand will lead mostly to more output without changing the price level. If the economy is at full employment, by contrast, a fiscal expansion will have more effect on prices and less impact on total output.

This ability of fiscal policy to affect output by affecting aggregate demand makes it a potential tool for economic stabilization. In a recession, the government can run an expansionary fiscal policy, thus helping to restore output to its normal level and to put unemployed workers back to work. During a boom, when inflation is perceived to be a greater problem than unemployment, the government can run a budget surplus, helping to slow down the economy. Such a countercyclical policy would lead to a budget that was balanced on average.

Automatic stabilizers—programs that automatically expand fiscal policy during recessions and contract it during booms—are one form of countercyclical fiscal policy. Unemployment insurance, on which the government spends more during recessions (when the unemployment rate is high), is an example of an automatic stabilizer. Similarly, because taxes are roughly proportional to wages and profits, the amount of taxes collected is higher during a boom than during a recession. Thus, the tax code also acts as an automatic stabilizer.

But fiscal policy need not be automatic in order to play a stabilizing role in business cycles. Some economists recommend changes in fiscal policy in response to economic conditions—so-called discretionary fiscal policy—as a way to moderate business cycle swings. These suggestions are most frequently heard during recessions, when there are calls for tax cuts or new spending programs to "get the economy going again."

Unfortunately, discretionary fiscal policy is rarely able to deliver on its promise. Fiscal policy is especially difficult to use for stabilization because of the "inside lag"—the gap between the time when the need for fiscal policy arises and when the president and Congress implement it. If economists forecast well, then the lag would not matter because they could tell Congress the appropriate fiscal policy in advance. But economists do not forecast well. Absent accurate forecasts, attempts to use discretionary fiscal policy to counteract business cycle fluctuations are as likely to do harm as good. The case for using discretionary fiscal policy to stabilize business cycles is further weakened by the fact that another tool, monetary policy, is far more agile than fiscal policy.

Whether for good or for ill, fiscal policy's ability to affect the level of output via aggregate demand wears off over time. Higher aggregate demand due to a fiscal stimulus, for example, eventually shows up only in higher prices and does not increase output at all. That is because, over the long run, the level of output is determined not by demand but by the supply of factors of production (capital, labor, and technology). These factors of production determine a "natural rate" of output around which business cycles and macroeconomic policies can cause only temporary fluctuations. An attempt to keep output above its natural rate by means of aggregate demand policies will lead only to ever-accelerating inflation.

The fact that output returns to its natural rate in the long run is not the end of the story, however. In addition to moving output in the short run, expansionary fiscal policy can change the natural rate, and, ironically, the long-run effects of fiscal expansion tend to be the opposite of the short-run effects. Expansionary fiscal policy will lead to higher output today, but will lower the natural rate of output below what it would have been in the future. Similarly, contractionary fiscal policy, though dampening the output level in the short run, will lead to higher output in the future.

A fiscal expansion affects the output level in the long run because it affects the country's saving rate. The country's total saving is composed of two parts: private saving (by individuals and corporations) and government saving (which is the same as the budget surplus). A fiscal expansion entails a decrease in government saving. Lower saving means, in turn, that the country will either invest less in new plants and equipment or increase the amount that it borrows from abroad, both of which lead to unpleasant consequences in the long term. Lower investment will lead to a lower capital stock and to a reduction in a country's ability to produce output in the future. Increased indebtedness to foreigners means that a higher fraction of a country's output will have to be sent abroad in the future rather than being consumed at home.

Fiscal policy also changes the burden of future taxes. When the government runs an expansionary fiscal policy, it adds to its stock of debt. Because the government will have to pay interest on this debt (or repay it) in future years, expansionary fiscal policy today imposes an additional burden on future taxpayers. Just as the government can use taxes to transfer income between different classes, it can run surpluses or deficits in order to transfer income between different generations.

Some economists have argued that this effect of fiscal policy on future taxes will lead consumers to change their saving. Recognizing that a tax cut today means higher taxes in the future, the argument goes, people will simply save the value of the tax cut they receive now in order to pay those future taxes. The extreme of this argument, known as Ricardian equivalence, holds that tax cuts will have no effect on national saving because changes in private saving will exactly offset changes in government saving. If these economists were right, then my earlier statement that budget deficits crowd out private investment would be wrong. But if consumers decide to spend some of the extra disposable income they receive from a tax cut (because they are myopic about future tax payments, for example), then Ricardian equivalence will not hold; a tax cut will lower national saving and raise aggregate demand. Most economists do not believe that Ricardian equivalence characterizes consumers' response to tax changes.

In addition to its effect on aggregate demand and saving, fiscal policy also affects the economy by changing incentives. Taxing an activity tends to discourage that activity. A high marginal tax rate on income reduces people's incentive to earn income. By reducing the level of taxation, or even by keeping the level the same but reducing marginal tax rates and reducing allowed deductions, the government can increase output. "Supply-side" economists argue that reductions in tax rates have a large effect on the amount of labor supplied, and thus on output (see SUPPLY-SIDE ECONOMICS). Incentive effects of taxes also play a role on the demand side. Policies such as investment tax credits, for example, can greatly influence the demand for capital goods.

The greatest obstacle to proper use of fiscal policy—both for its ability to stabilize fluctuations in the short run and for its long-run effect on the natural rate of output—is that changes in fiscal policy are necessarily bundled with other changes that please or displease various constituencies. A road in Congressman X's district is all the more likely to be built if it can be packaged as part of countercyclical fiscal policy. The same is true for a tax cut for some favored constituency. This naturally leads to an institutional enthusiasm for expansionary policies during recessions that is not matched by a taste for contractionary policies during booms. In addition, the benefits from expansionary policy are felt immediately, whereas its costs—higher future taxes and lower economic growth—are postponed until a later date. The problem of making good fiscal policy in the face of such obstacles is, in the final analysis, not economic but political.

About the Author

David N. Weil is a professor of economics at Brown University.

Further Reading

Nontechnical

Bartley, Robert. *Seven Fat Years*. New York: Simon and Schuster, 1992. A celebration of Ronald Reagan's fiscal policy by one of the truest believers.
Krugman, Paul. *The Great Unraveling: Losing Our Way in the New Century*. New York: Norton, 2003. An attack on the fiscal policy (and other aspects) of the George W. Bush administration.

Advanced

Barro, Robert. "The Ricardian Approach to Budget Deficits." *Journal of Economic Perspectives* 3, no. 2 (1989): 37–54.
Mankiw, N. Gregory. *Macroeconomics*. 5th ed. New York: Worth, 2003. A textbook presentation aimed at undergraduates.

Web Link

Congressional Budget Office: http://www.cbo.gov/

Fiscal Sustainability

Laurence J. Kotlikoff

The population of wealthy countries is getting much older. Between 2005 and 2035, the number of elderly in wealthy countries will more than double, but the number of workers will barely change. This historically unprecedented demographic change portends enormous fiscal stresses because of the high and growing cost of meeting government pension and health-care commitments to the elderly. Indeed, these projected payments are so high that collecting them may not be feasible, either economically or politically. The costs associated with the coming generational storm will bankrupt the governments of most wealthy countries unless major and painful adjustments are made now.

"Bankrupt" is a strong word, but entirely appropriate in this context. When countries' governments go bankrupt, they stop paying what they owe. They may default explicitly by reneging on principal and interest payments on their debt. Or they may fail to pay promised benefits and meet other spending commitments; some people regard this as default. A particularly popular way of implicitly defaulting on spending obligations and on debt is to use inflation to do the dirty work. The government simply prints the money it needs to "meet" its spending obligations. The increase in the money supply generates inflation, which waters down the real value of the government's spending and reduces the real value of its debt.

Although bankruptcies of national governments are not

common, neither are they rare. Argentina's government defaulted in 2001, and Russia's government defaulted in 1998. Before Russia, Bulgaria and other countries in Eastern Europe did likewise. In the 1970s, Israel and Bolivia took their turn at printing money to pay their bills. Going back further in time, there were the notable hyperinflations of Germany, Austria, and Hungary. Indeed, governments have engaged in official and unofficial default since at least the time of Rome's Emperor Diocletian, who ran what may well have been the mother of all hyperinflations.

One can assess whether fiscal policy is sustainable by examining the size of long-term fiscal imbalances. Doing so provides an early warning of explicit or implicit default and also indicates the magnitude of the adjustments needed to preclude default. Unfortunately, the main indicator of a country's fiscal imbalance is its annual official deficit—the difference between annual expenditures (government purchases and transfer payments) and tax and nontax receipts. The use of the deficit to assess fiscal sustainability is not simply a matter of habit. It was enshrined in the Fiscal Responsibility Act of the European Monetary Union's (EMU) Maastrict Treaty. This act limits entry to the union to countries whose deficits are less than 3 percent of GDP and imposes hypothetical penalties on EMU member nations that violate this limit. I say "hypothetical" because the treaty permits exemptions from the deficit limit that, as of 2005, appear more the rule than the exception.

But the deficit and its associated cumulate—the debt—are, economically speaking, meaningless because nothing in economic theory tells us whether any particular government receipt should be called (labeled) a "tax" or "borrowing." Nor is there anything in economic theory that can tell us whether a government payment to any entity should be labeled a "transfer payment" or "debt repayment." Thus, when the EU proclaimed that the difference between expenditures and taxes in a given year—the deficit—should be limited to 3 percent of GDP, it failed to ask itself whether there was any economic basis for distinguishing expenditures from debt repayment or taxes from borrowing.

An example helps clarify this. In 2005, the U.S. federal deficit was projected to total $325 billion. But because most people think of Social Security as a forced pension plan, we could legitimately label this year's receipts of Social Security taxes a forced loan to the government rather than taxes and label the future payments associated with these "contributions" "return of principal plus interest less an old-age tax" rather than "transfer payments." If we did so,

the U.S. deficit would amount to $1.1 trillion.[1] This alternative labeling is just as valid in terms of nomenclature and just as meaningless in terms of economics.

Because the labeling of government receipts and payments is arbitrary, governments can choose labels that generate whatever time path of deficits or surpluses they wish to report, regardless of the true underlying fiscal policy. Thus, they can announce huge surpluses precisely when they are engaging in the most fiscally irresponsible policies, and they can announce huge deficits when their policies are fiscally most conservative.

This license to define the deficit became apparent in the run-up to the introduction of the euro. France's government, for example, met the deficit limit by selling assets of state enterprises while retaining liabilities. But those manipulations were generally viewed as isolated abuses of a fundamentally sound fiscal measure. The measure is arbitrary, though. The fact that a change in words, not actions, could, from one second to the next, generate a different picture of a nation's fiscal finances should have made clear that there is, indeed, no unique way to label receipts and payments, and therefore no unique measure of the deficit.

Use of "the" deficit not only tells us nothing about the stance of current policy, it also tells us nothing about policy changes. The reason is that no one can say whether changes in the deficit arise from true changes in fiscal policy or simply a change in labeling conventions. Thus, the Bush tax cuts, which have increased the official U.S. federal deficit, can be viewed as a pure change in labels under which the government called more current receipts from the private sector "borrowing" rather than "taxes," and will call more future receipts "taxes" rather than "borrowing." And the fact that all but one lonely economist uses the former rather than the latter set of words does not endow the former set of words with any special economic content. The dictates of economic theory are not determined by majority rule.

Fiscal Relativity

I refer to the problem outlined above as "fiscal relativity" because the perception of a government's fiscal position depends on the beholder's reference point. The reason the stock of government debt and its changes over time are not well-defined economic measures is that they do not answer an economic question. An example of an economic

---

1. Note that the "old-age tax" would equal the difference between the actual payment and what would constitute interest on the "loan" given prevailing interest rates.

measure that does fit this criterion is gross domestic product, which answers the question: What is the value of all final goods and services produced by an economy in a given year?

Compare that question with the question: What are a government's official liabilities? Although the word "liabilities" has economic content, the word "official" does not. It is a legal or accounting categorization, not an economic one. And from an economics perspective, there is nothing sacrosanct about this categorization—that is, each of us is free to make up our own definition of "official liabilities."

Moreover, any allocation of official debts and assets to particular programs is entirely arbitrary. Thus, in the U.S. context, we see an endless debate about whether the Social Security Trust Fund should or should not be included in assessing Social Security's long-term underfunding. The answer is that there is no answer. Either practice is equally valid and equally meaningless. Some Americans want to claim that Social Security is in great shape because the Trust Fund is flush with government bonds that the rest of the government is responsible for paying. If they believe this, then they would have to believe that the rest of the federal government is in terrible shape because of the huge amount of money it owes the Social Security Administration. Other Americans want to claim that Social Security is in terrible shape because the bonds held in the Trust Fund are assets properly attributed to the rest of the government's fiscal operations. No one can stop either side, but that should not prevent us from recognizing that both positions are mindless.

Generational Accounting

In contrast to "official" debt, "generational accounting" answers an economic question, namely: What is the net tax burden facing future generations assuming current generations pay no more in net taxes than current policy suggests? "Net tax" refers to the actuarial present value of all future taxes minus all future transfer payments.

This question can be understood by referring to the following formulation of the government's intertemporal budget constraint, that is, its budget constraint over time:

$$A = C + D - B,$$

where A is the PRESENT VALUE of net tax payments of future generations, B is the present value of net tax payments of current generations, C is the present value of government purchases, and D is official net liabilities.

Given any labeling convention, $C + D$ can be viewed as the government's bills and B can be viewed as the amount of those bills to be paid by current generations. The value

of the difference $D - B$ is invariant to labeling conventions, but the absolute sizes of D and B are not. Since C is a well-defined measure and $D - B$, which represents the sum of explicit plus implicit debt, is also well defined, their sum, A, is itself well defined. So, different choices of labels will increase or decrease D and B by the same amount but leave A unchanged. Stated differently, you can use any labeling convention you want and still arrive at the same measure of the collective fiscal burden facing future generations. Consequently, generational accounting makes full use of "official" government statistics in determining the size of A.

Once you calculate A, you can (a) determine the lifetime net tax burden facing individual future generations assuming each pays the same lifetime net taxes on a growth-adjusted basis, and (b) compare the growth-adjusted lifetime net tax burden of future generations with that of current newborns. This comparison is label free because the lifetime net tax burden of newborns is the same, regardless of the choice of labels. "Growth adjusted" refers to having net taxes rise for each successive future generation at the rate of labor productivity growth.

If the growth-adjusted lifetime net tax burden facing future generations is larger than that facing newborns, generational policy is referred to as "imbalanced." If the burden facing future generations is larger than those generations are willing to put up with politically, fiscal policy is deemed to be both generationally imbalanced and economically unsustainable.

The Fiscal Gap

The "fiscal gap" is a closely related measure of long-term fiscal imbalances. The equation used to determine the fiscal gap, G, is given by

$$G = C + D - B - A*,$$

where $A*$ is the net tax burden that would face future generations if there were no generational imbalance, that is, if future generations were to face the same lifetime net tax bill as current newborns after adjusting for growth.

Like the imbalance in generational policy, the fiscal gap is a label-free and well-defined measure of a nation's long-term fiscal problem. In the United States, the current (2005) fiscal gap equals $65.9 trillion. This estimate comes courtesy of Jagadeesh Gokhale and Kent Smetters (2005), who based their calculation on U.S. government projections—which, incidentally, tend to be overoptimistic.

Some economists believe that if productivity in the next two decades grows at about 3 percent a year, a view Robert J. Gordon supports, then we can "grow our way out" of our fiscal problems.[2] Unfortunately, this is false. Even if productivity grows at 3 percent annually, that would only slightly improve the picture, for one simple reason: all of the spending on Social Security payments is indexed to real wages, and although Medicare spending is not indexed to real wages, real wage growth causes nonseniors to demand more and better health care, which tends to become the standard for Medicare. High-productivity growth would do much to solve the problem if and only if the U.S. government took a step similar to one that former British prime minister Margaret Thatcher took in the 1980s, namely, indexing Britain's version of Social Security benefits to consumer prices rather than to wages. Britain is almost alone in Europe in having taken care of its fiscal future.

One way to put the U.S. fiscal gap in perspective is to ask how much of a tax hike would be required to make the present value of the new taxes equal the gap. The answer is that U.S. federal personal and corporate income taxes would have to be doubled, immediately and permanently! Alternatively, the gap could be closed by immediately and permanently cutting by two-thirds the elderly's Medicare health benefits as well as their Social Security pension benefits!

Either of these policies or any combination of them would impose a huge burden on current adults. But American adults appear in no mood to endorse any fiscal adjustments that either raise their taxes or cut their benefits. Of course, what people want is often far removed from what they can get. As the government's intertemporal budget constraint reminds us, generational policy is a zero-sum game. So leaving today's "grownups" off the hook means forcing young and future Americans to pay this bill in its entirety. Such a policy is not only ethically abhorrent but also appears to be economically infeasible because it would entail a doubling of the average lifetime net tax rates levied on today's young and future generations.

Conclusion

Economic projections and measurement have now reached the point where people can understand the sustainability of fiscal policy by doing generational accounting and fiscal gap analysis. Some governments, like the United Kingdom's, are beginning to do precisely that.

About the Author

Laurence J. Kotlikoff is a professor of economics and chairman of the Department of Economics at Boston University, a research associate with the National Bureau of Economic Research, and president of Economic Security Planning, Inc. He was previously a senior economist with the President's Council of Economic Advisers.

Further Reading

Gokhale, Jagadeesh, and Kent Smetters. "Measuring Social Security's Financial Problems." NBER Working Paper no. 11060. National Bureau of Economic Research, Cambridge, Mass., 2005.
Kotlikoff, Laurence J. *Generational Policy.* Cambridge: MIT Press, 2003.
Kotlikoff, Laurence J., and Scott Burns. *The Coming Generational Storm.* Cambridge: MIT Press, 2004.

Forecasting and Econometric Models

Saul H. Hymans

An econometric model is one of the tools economists use to forecast future developments in the economy. In the simplest terms, econometricians measure past relationships among such variables as consumer spending, household income, tax rates, interest rates, employment, and the like, and then try to forecast how changes in some variables will affect the future course of others.

Before econometricians can make such calculations, they generally begin with an economic model, a theory of how different factors in the economy interact with one another. For instance, think of the economy as comprising households and business firms, as depicted in Figure 1. Households supply business firms with labor services (as tailors, accountants, engineers, etc.) and receive wages and salaries from the business firms in exchange for their labor. Using the labor services, businesses produce various outputs (clothing, cars, etc.) that are available for purchase. Households, using the earnings derived from their labor services, become the customers who purchase the output. The products the businesses produce wind up in the households, and the wage and salary payments return to the businesses in exchange for the products the households purchase.

This chain of events, as shown by the activities numbered 1–5 in Figure 1, is a description—or diagrammatic model—of the operation of a private-enterprise economy. It is obviously incomplete. There is no central bank supplying money, no banking system, and no government levying taxes, building roads, or providing education or national defense. But the essentials of the economy's pri-

2. Robert J. Gordon, "Exploding Productivity Growth: Context, Causes, and Implications," *Brookings Papers on Economic Activity* 2 (2003): 207–279.

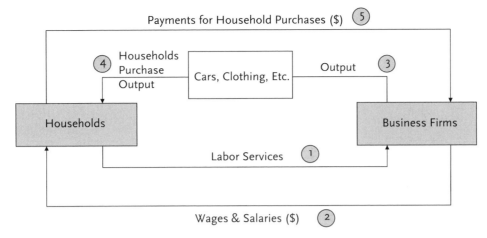

Payments for Household Purchases ($) ⑤

④ Households Purchase Output

Cars, Clothing, Etc.

Output ③

Households

Business Firms

Labor Services ①

Wages & Salaries ($) ②

Figure 1

vate sector—working, producing, and buying products and services—are represented in a useful way in Figure 1.

The diagrammatic model of Figure 1 has certain disadvantages when it comes to representing quantities such as the value of the wage and salary payments or the number of cars produced. To represent magnitudes more conveniently, economists employ a mathematical model, a set of equations that describe various relationships between variables. Consider household purchases of output, shown as activity 4 in Figure 1. If W is the value of the wages and salaries households earn, and C is household expenditures on clothing, then the equation $C = .12W$ states that households spend 12 percent of their wages and salaries on clothing. An equation could also be constructed to represent household purchases of cars or any other goods and services. Indeed, each of the activities pictured in Figure 1 can be represented in the form of an equation. Doing so may take a blend of economic theory, basic economic facts about the particular economy, and mathematical sophistication; but once done, the result would be a mathematical or quantitative economic model, which is but one important step away from an econometric model.

In the equation for clothing purchases, $C = .12W$, "12 percent" was selected purely for illustrative purposes. But if the model is to say anything useful about today's American economy, it must contain numbers (econometricians and others applying similar statistical methods refer to such numbers as "parameters") that describe what actually goes on in the real world. For this purpose, we must turn to the relevant historical data to find out what percentage of household income Americans do, in fact, typically spend on clothing.

The column headed "Total" in Table 1 shows the percentage of (after-tax) income Americans spent on clothing (including shoes) for each of the years 1995–2002. One

Table 1 Spending on Clothing and Shoes, 1995–2002

	% of Household Income	
Year	Total	Total − 100
1995	4.5	2.6
1996	4.4	2.6
1997	4.3	2.6
1998	4.2	2.7
1999	4.3	2.8
2000	4.1	2.7
2001	4.0	2.6
2002	3.9	2.6
Average	4.21	2.65

fact is immediately obvious: 12 percent was way off. If it had been left in the model, it would have led to a substantial overestimate of clothing purchases and would have been useless to understand or predict behavior in the American economy. Something closer to 4.21 percent, the average of the annual values in the "Total" column, would more accurately reflect total annual spending on clothing and shoes as a percentage of household income in the United States.

A more careful look at the facts, however, reveals that 4.21 percent may not adequately represent the actual behavior. There has been substantial annual variation—from as much 4.5 percent to as little as 3.9 percent—in household income spent on clothing and shoes. What is more, there appears to be a downward trend, with the larger percentages coming in the mid-1990s and the smaller percentages coming more recently. The following simple statistical procedure takes care of these objections. Start with total annual spending on clothing and shoes, subtract $100 billion, and then calculate the balance—annual spending on clothing and shoes *beyond* the first $100 billion—as a percentage of household income. The column headed "Total − 100" in Table 1 shows the result—a very satisfactory result, with little annual variation around the average of 2.65 percent and no apparent trend over time.

You might well wonder what this subtraction of $100 billion represents. Here is a useful way to think about it. The U.S. population averaged 277.6 million persons during 1995–2002. Therefore, the value $100 billion represents, in round numbers, $360 per person ($100 billion divided by 277.6 million persons). The facts in Table 1 suggest that an expenditure on clothing and shoes averaging about $360 per person per year is a base, or minimally acceptable, amount in the United States these days. Once that minimum is accounted for, additional purchases of clothing and shoes will amount to 2.65 percent of household income.

In other words, Americans spend more on clothing and shoes the higher their household income, but they spend at least $100 billion per year. And the best forecast of the total that will be spent is: $100 billion *plus* an additional 2.65 percent of household income. In equation form, this is represented by $C = 100 + .0265W$, a far cry from the $C = .12W$ we began with. The fact that the parameter values 100 and .0265 in the clothing equation were determined by using the relevant data is what gives us reason to believe that the equation says something meaningful about the economy. Using the data to determine or estimate all the parameter values in the model is the critical step that turns the mathematical economic model into an econometric model.

An econometric model is said to be complete if it contains just enough equations to predict values for all of the variables in the model. The equation $C = 100 + .0265W$, for example, predicts C if the value of W is known. Thus, there must be an equation somewhere in the model that determines W. If all such logical connections have been made, the model is complete and can, in principle, be used to forecast the economy or to test theories about its behavior.

Actually, no econometric model is ever truly complete. All models contain variables the model cannot predict because they are determined by forces "outside" the model. For example, a realistic model must include personal income taxes collected by the government because taxes are the wedge between the gross income earned by households and the net income (what economists call disposable income) available for households to spend. The taxes collected depend on the tax rates in the income tax laws. But the tax rates are determined by the government as a part of its fiscal policy and are not explained by the model. If the model is to be used to forecast economic activity several years into the future, the econometrician must include anticipated future tax rates in the model's information base. That requires an assumption about whether the government will change future income tax rates and, if so, when and by how much. Similarly, the model requires an assumption about the monetary policy that the central bank (the Federal Reserve System in the United States) will pursue, as well as assumptions about a host of other such "outside of the model" (or exogenous) variables in order to forecast all the "inside of the model" (or endogenous) variables.

The need for the econometrician to use the best available economic judgment about "outside" factors is inherent in economic forecasting. An econometrically based economic forecast can thus be wrong for two reasons: (1) incorrect assumptions about the "outside" or exogenous variables, which are called input errors; or (2) econometric equations that are only approximations to the truth (note that clothing purchases beyond the minimum do not amount to exactly 2.65 percent of household income every year). Deviations from the predictions of these equations are called model errors.

Most econometric forecasters believe that economic judgment can and should be used not only to determine values for exogenous variables (an obvious requirement), but also to reduce the likely size of model error. Taken literally, the equation $C = 100 + .0265W$ means that "any deviation of clothing purchases from 100 plus 2.65 percent of household income must be considered a random aberration from normal or expected behavior"—one of those inherently unpredictable vagaries of human behavior that continually trip up pollsters, economists, and others who attempt to forecast socioeconomic events.

The economic forecaster must be prepared to be wrong because of unpredictable model error. But is all model error really unpredictable? Suppose the forecaster reads reports that indicate unusually favorable consumer reaction to the latest styles in clothing. Suppose, on this basis, the forecaster believes that next year's clothing purchases are likely to exceed the usual minimum by something closer to 3 percent than to the usual 2.65 percent of household income. Should the forecaster ignore this well-founded belief that clothing sales are about to "take off," and thereby produce a forecast that is actually expected to be wrong?

The answer depends on the purpose of the forecast. If the purpose is the purely scientific one of determining how accurately a well-constructed model can forecast, the answer must be: Ignore the outside information and leave the model alone. If the purpose is the more pragmatic one of using the best available information to produce the most informative forecast, the answer must be: Incorporate the outside information into the model, even if that means effectively "erasing" the parameter value .0265 and replacing it with .0300 while generating next year's forecast. Imposing such "constant adjustments" on forecasts was at one time disparaged as entirely unscientific. These days, many researchers regard such behavior as inevitable in the social science of economic forecasting and have begun to study how best—from a scientific perspective—to incorporate such outside information.

Much of the motivation behind trying to specify the most accurately descriptive economic model, trying to determine parameter values that most closely represent economic behavior, and combining these with the best available outside information arises from the desire to produce accurate forecasts. Unfortunately, an economic forecast's accuracy is not easy to judge; there are simply too many dimensions of detail and interest. One user of the forecast may care mostly about the gross domestic product (GDP), another mostly about exports and imports, and another mostly about inflation and interest rates. Thus, the same forecast may provide very useful information to some users while being misleading to others.

For want of anything obviously superior, the most common gauge of the quality of a macroeconomic forecast is how accurately it predicts real GDP growth. Real GDP is the most inclusive summary measure of all the finished goods and services being produced within the geographic boundaries of the nation. For many purposes, there is much value in knowing with some lead time whether to expect real GDP to be increasing at a rapid rate (a booming economy with a growth rate above 4 percent), to be slowing down or speeding up relative to recent behavior, or to be slumping (a weak economy with a growth rate below 1 percent or even a recessionary economy with a negative growth rate). The information contained in Figure 2 can be used to judge, in the summary fashion just indicated, the econometric forecasting accuracy achieved by the Research Seminar in Quantitative Economics (RSQE) of the University of Michigan over the past three-plus decades.

The RSQE forecasting project, dating back to the 1950s, is one of the oldest in the United States. Figure 2 compares, for each of the years 1971–2003, the actual percentage change in real GDP (the economy's growth rate) with the RSQE forecast published in November of the preceding year. There are several ways to characterize the quality of the RSQE forecasting record. Although the forecasts missed the actual percentage change by an average of only 1.1 percentage points (measured by the average forecast

error without regard to sign), the forecast error was as small as 0.5 percentage point or less in thirteen of the thirty-three years shown. On the other hand, six years had forecast errors of 2 percentage points or more, and for 1982 and 1999, the forecast errors were 3.1 and 3.0 percentage points, respectively. But, despite some relatively large errors, there was never a boom year that RSQE forecast to be a weak year; never a weak year that RSQE forecast to be a boom year; and just a few instances—most recently, 1999 and 2001—in which the forecast really went "the wrong way" in the sense of missing badly on whether the economy's growth rate was about to increase or decrease relative to the preceding year's growth rate.

The discussion, so far, has focused on what is referred to as a structural econometric model. That is, the econometrician uses a blend of economic theory, mathematics, and information about the structure of the economy to construct a quantitative economic model. The econometrician then turns to the observed data—the facts—to estimate the unknown parameter values and turn the economic model into a structural econometric model. The term "structural" refers to the fact that the model gets its structure, or specification, from the economic theory that the econometrician starts with. The idea, for example, that spending on clothing and shoes is determined by household income comes from the core of economic theory.

Economic theories are both complex and incomplete. To illustrate:

• Does this year's spending on clothing depend only on this year's income or also on the pattern of income in recent years?

• How many years is "recent"?

• Don't other variables, such as the price of clothing relative to other consumer goods, matter as well?

This situation makes it far more difficult than implied to this point to specify the economic model one must begin with to wind up with a structural econometric model for use in forecasting. In recent years, econometricians have found that it is possible to do economic forecasting using a simpler, nonstructural, procedure without losing much forecast accuracy. Although the simpler procedure has significant costs, these costs do not show up in the normal course of forecasting. This will be explained after a quick introduction to the alternative procedure known as "time-series forecasting."

The idea of time-series forecasting is easily explained with the aid of Figure 3, which shows year-by-year changes in spending on clothing and shoes starting in 1981 and

Percent

Figure 2 RSQE Forecast Accuracy: Real GDP Growth, 1971–2003
(Actual vs. RSQE Forecast from the Preceding November)

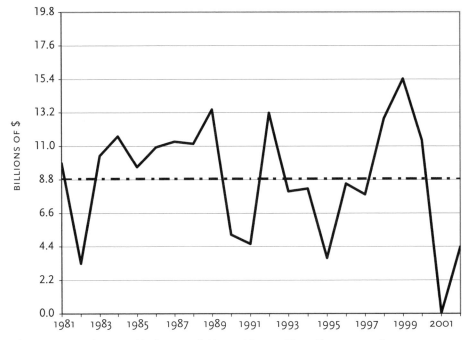

Figure 3 Spending on Clothing and Shoes, Year-to-Year Changes, 1981–2002

going through 2002. The horizontal line marks the average annual change of $8.8 billion.

Most of the year-to-year changes are in the range of $4.4–$13.2 billion, and only one change, that of 2001, is well outside that range. The year-to-year changes, in other words, appear to be stable. Some are above $8.8 billion and some are below; 1983–1988 exhibited a string of changes that were all close to $11 billion, but that was unusual. More often, one year's change is little guide to the next year's change, as the changes jump around too much. So, a forecasting rule that says next year's spending on clothing and shoes will be $8.8 billion more than this year's spending makes good sense. And that, for this simple case, is the essence of time-series forecasting. Look carefully at the historical behavior of the variable of interest, and if that behavior is characterized by some kind of stability, come up with a quantitative description of that stability and use it to construct the forecast.

It is not always easy to "see" the stability that can be counted on to provide a reliable forecast, and econometricians have developed sophisticated procedures to tease out the stability and measure it. In general, the time-series procedure and the structural model procedure seem to produce comparably good, or bad, forecasts for a year or two into the future. But the time-series procedure has the distinct advantage of being far simpler. We can forecast spending on clothing and shoes without having to worry about the theoretical relationship between spending and household income. It need not be specified and its parameters need not be estimated; just focus on the clothing variable itself.

So, where are the significant costs in using the time-series forecasting procedure? They come from the fact that the procedure gives a numerical answer and nothing else. If the user of the forecast—for example, a clothing manufacturer—asks why the forecast says what it does, the time-series econometrician can answer only, "Because that's the way spending on clothing has behaved in the past," not, "Because household income is going to rise sharply in response to an expansionary monetary policy which is being conducted in order to . . ." In short, there is no economics in the analysis in the first place. If there were, the user would be able to respond, "That makes sense; I'll plan on the basis of the forecast"; or, alternatively, "I think that forecast is too good to be true because I'm convinced that expansionary monetary policy is about to be reversed, and so I'm shaving the forecast in my planning." Time-series forecasting leaves the user "hanging": just take it or leave it.

Because many forecasters work with structural models, users can acquire not only the various numerical forecasts,

but also the economic analysis that accompanies and justifies, or explains, each forecast. A user who has to act on the basis of a forecast and can choose among the alternative forecasts available is surely getting much more information when those forecasts have a structural economic basis.

Finally, and related to the preceding discussion, structural models are the "only game in town" when it comes to the important area of econometric policy analysis or other "what if" calculations. Thus, a baseline forecast may be calculated using a structural econometric model and the best information available to the forecaster. And then someone asks, "What if Congress raises the income tax rate by five percentage points?" This single perturbation is then imposed on the original calculation, and the forecast is recalculated to show the model's evaluation of the effect on the economy of the posited change in government fiscal policy.

Economists commonly employ such calculations in the process of providing advice to businesses and units of government. The practical validity of such applications depends on how well the model's structure represents the economic behavior that is central to the "what if" question being asked. All models are merely approximations to reality; the issue is whether a given model's approximation is good enough for the question at hand. Thus, making structural models more accurate is a task of major importance. As long as model users ask "what if," structural econometric models will continue to be used and useful.

About the Author

Saul H. Hymans is an emeritus professor of economics and statistics and director of the Research Seminar in Quantitative Economics at the University of Michigan.

Further Reading

Howrey, E. Philip, Saul H. Hymans, and Michael R. Donihue. "Merging Monthly and Quarterly Forecasts: Experience with MQEM." *Journal of Forecasting* 10 (May 1991): 255–268.

Hymans, Saul H., Joan P. Crary, and Janet C. Wolfe. "The U.S. Economic Outlook for 2004–2005." In *The Economic Outlook for 2004*, Proceedings of the Fifty-first Annual Conference on the Economic Outlook, Ann Arbor, Mich., 2004. Pp. 1–84.

Kennedy, Peter. *A Guide to Econometrics*. 5th ed. Cambridge: MIT Press, 2003. Especially chaps. 18 and 19.

Klein, Lawrence R., ed. *Comparative Performance of U.S. Econometric Models*. Oxford: Oxford University Press, 1991. Especially chaps. 1, 3, 10, 11, and 12.

Klein, Lawrence R., and Richard M. Young. *An Introduction to*

Econometric Forecasting and Forecasting Models. Lexington, Mass.: Lexington Books, 1980.

Foreign Aid

Deepak Lal

Foreign aid as a form of capital flow is novel in both its magnitude and its global coverage. Though historical examples of countries paying "bribes" (see below) or "reparations" to others are numerous, the continuing large-scale transfer of capital from rich-country governments to those of poor countries is a post–World War II phenomenon. The origins of these transfers lie in the breakdown of the international capital market in the period between the two world wars and in the rivalry for political allies during the cold war.

The breakdown of the international capital market provided the impetus for the creation of the World Bank at Bretton Woods. Its purpose was to provide loans at market interest rates to poor countries that were shut out of Western capital markets—especially the largest, the United States—because of their widespread defaults in the 1930s and the imposition of the U.S. government's "blue sky" laws, which forbade U.S. financial intermediaries to hold foreign government bonds. Meanwhile, European markets were closed through exchange controls; the United Kingdom, for example, had its exchange controls until 1979. Official loans to poor countries at commercial interest rates, as laid down in the charter of the World Bank's parent, the International Bank for Reconstruction and Development, would have been justified purely on efficiency grounds to intermediate the transfer of capital from where it was less scarce to where it was scarcer.

This purely economic case was buttressed by political and, later, humanitarian justifications for concessional official flows, that is, loans with softer—that is, concessional—terms on interest and repayment. As to the political reasons for giving aid, little can be added to Lord Bauer's devastating critique (Bauer 1976) that, instead of fostering Western political interests, foreign aid abetted the formation of anti-Western coalitions of Third World states seeking "bribes" not to go communist. A statistical study concluded that "as an instrument of *political leverage,* economic aid has been unsuccessful" (Mosley 1987, p. 232). The end of the cold war has removed this political motive. Currently, advocates of foreign aid emphasize the humanitarian and economic cases, though each rationale has seen many metamorphoses.

The humanitarian case for concessional flows was based on an analogy with the Western welfare state. The idea was that just as many people favor welfare to transfer wealth from the relatively rich to the relatively poor within a country, so they favor welfare to transfer wealth from relatively rich countries to relatively poor ones. But many commentators not necessarily hostile to foreign aid—I. M. D. Little and J. Clifford, for example (Little and Clifford 1965)—emphasized that the humanitarian motives for giving aid may have justified transferring Western taxpayers' money to poor *people,* but not to poor governments: the latter may have no effect on the former. With the likes of Marcos of the Philippines, Bokassa of the Central African Republic, Abacha of Nigeria, and a host of other kleptocratic "tropical gangsters" in power (Klitgard 1990), the money may simply be stolen. According to William Easterly, despite over $2 billion in foreign aid given to Tanzania's government for roads, the roads did not improve. What increased was the bureaucracy, with the Tanzanian government producing twenty-four hundred reports a year for the one thousand donor missions that visited each year.[1] Nor can the poor of the world claim a moral *right* to welfare transfers from the rich. While recipients of domestic welfare payments depend on the existence of a national society with some commonly accepted moral standard, there is no similar international society within which a right to aid can be established (Lal 1978, 1983).

The vast majority of foreign aid has failed to alleviate poverty. It has improved the lot of poor people in a few cases. The people of Martinique, for example, are probably better off because the French government provides a very high percentage of their gross domestic product. Also, foreign aid helped wipe out river blindness in West Africa, keeping eighteen million children safe from infection.[2] But a statistical study found that foreign aid "appears to redistribute from the reasonably well-off in the West to most income groups in the Third World *except* the very poorest" (Mosley 1987, p. 23). This is consistent with the evidence from both poor and rich countries that the middle classes tend to capture government transfers (see REDISTRIBUTION). By contrast, private transfers through either traditional interfamily channels or private charities (nongovernmental organizations, or NGOs) are more efficient in targeting these transfers to the poor, as well as in delivering health care and education (Lal and Myint 1996). The centralized bureaucracies of the Western aid agencies are particularly inept in targeting these transfers to the truly

---

1. See William Easterly, "Does Foreign Aid Reach the Poor?" SAIS Lecture, December 2004, online at: http://www.sais-jhu.edu/programs/i-dev/Easterly%20Presentation.pdf.

2. Ibid.

needy because they lack local knowledge. Moreover, there is evidence that these inefficient public transfers tend to crowd out more efficient private transfers (Lal and Myint 1996). Not surprisingly, therefore, despite their claim that their mission is to alleviate Third World poverty, official aid agencies are increasingly subcontracting this role to the NGOs. Whether this official embrace of the NGOs is in the NGOs' long-term interest is arguable (Lal 1996).

The political and humanitarian justifications for foreign aid are in tatters. What of the purely economic case? One such case was the "two-gap theory," the idea that foreign aid was required to fill one of two shortfalls—in foreign exchange or savings—that depressed the growth rates of developing countries below some acceptable limit (Lal 1972). The alleged "foreign exchange" gap was based on dubious assumptions. One such assumption was "export pessimism," the idea that poor countries would not generate many exports. Many development economists held this view despite a paucity of evidence for it (Lal 2002). Because both experience and theory have shown the irrelevance of this assumption, the "foreign exchange gap" justification for foreign aid has lost all force.

Nor has the "savings gap" justification proved to be any more cogent. Contrary to the theory that foreign capital is necessary to supplement fixed and inadequate domestic savings, the savings performance of developing countries in the post–World War II period shows that nearly all of them (including those in Africa until the early 1970s) have steadily raised domestic savings rates since the 1950s (Lluch 1986). Moreover, a study of twenty-one developing countries between 1950 and 1985 confirms the common-sense expectation that differences in economic growth

rates are related more to differences in the productivity of investment than to differences in investment levels (Lal and Myint 1996). Finally, statistical studies of the effects of foreign aid on growth and poverty alleviation have not been favorable (Easterly 2001). One found that, after correcting for the link between aid and income levels and growth, the effect of aid on growth is often negative (Boone 1994) (see Figure 1). A survey of other such studies concludes that "there is now widespread skepticism that concessional assistance does have positive effects on growth, poverty reduction or environmental quality" (Gilbert et al. 1999, p. F607).

Except for sub-Saharan Africa, the World Bank finances less than 2 percent of investment in developing countries (Krueger 1998). Most of its lending continues to finance projects. The rates of return of more than 10 percent earned by these projects are not a measure of the true effects of the aid provided, because money is fungible. A government can use aid to finance a high-yielding project that it would have undertaken in any case, and then use its own resources to finance a project with a low rate of return (say, more armaments). This problem led to the growth of "program" lending, which expanded in the 1980s along with the growth of "structural adjustment" loans. Program loans were based on a mutually agreed overall economic program by the recipient government. Structural adjustment loans were given in return for specific commitments made to alter particular policies that damaged economic efficiency. Advocates of such loans hoped that by applying conditions to the program loans they could give the governments an incentive to implement better policies, by, for example, avoiding price con-

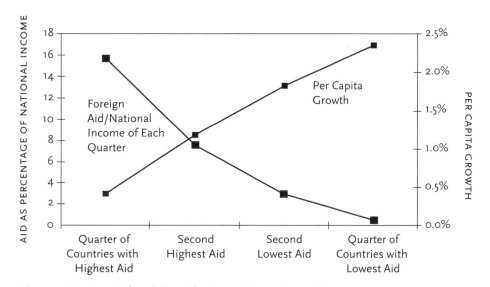

Figure 1 Foreign Aid and Growth Across Countries, 1960–2002

Source: William Easterly

trols, moving toward free trade, and reducing high marginal tax rates. That way, these advocates believed, foreign aid would improve economic conditions. But numerous studies have found that

> policy conditionality is ineffective. Not only is aid not necessarily used for what it is directly intended, but also, on average, it has no effect on growth, either directly, or indirectly through improved government policies. What matters is the policy environment, but lending appears to have little direct impact on this. (Gilbert et al. 1999, p. F619)

This is hardly surprising. As the adage has it, "You can lead a horse to the water, but you can't make him drink." Governments make all sorts of promises to get the loan, but then renege on them once they have taken the money, as President Moi of Kenya demonstrated repeatedly in the 1980s. Moreover, the aid agencies do not call their bluff, for they are part of a large international business in "poverty alleviation" from which a large number of middle-class professionals derive a good living. These "Lords of Poverty" (Hancock 1989) depend on lending as much as possible and persuading the public in rich countries that these loans will alleviate poverty. It is in the mutual interest of both the Lords of Poverty and the recalcitrant poor country governments to turn a blind eye to the nonfulfillment of the conditions on policy changes.

The latest justification for foreign aid is that, as the current ex-ante conditionality has failed, ex post conditionality should be used instead. In other words, rather than seeking promises for better future actions, governments should be judged by their past actions, and only those whose past policy environment has been better than that of their peers should receive "aid." According to this rationale, not only will the laggards have a greater incentive to improve their policies, but aid will also be more effective. There are two problems with this justification. The whole economic argument in favor of aid was to improve the economic performance of countries unable to help themselves. If the basket cases are to be left behind because of their predatory governments, what happens to the humanitarian arguments in support of aid? Second, and more important, with the opening of the world's capital markets to well-run developing countries, what incentive do these countries have to turn to the aid agencies—and their onerous procedures and conditions for loans—when they can borrow much more easily from a syndicate put together by the likes of Goldman Sachs? Any "neighborhood effects" whereby well-run countries are shunned by private capital markets because of their neighbors (as is claimed for Africa) can be readily countered by the aid agencies providing credit ratings for countries, just as Moody's does for the private sector. The large research capacity and information governments provide to the aid agencies would lend credibility to these ratings. No loans would be required.

The foreign aid programs of the last half century are a historical anomaly. They are part and parcel of the disastrous breakdown of the nineteenth-century liberal economic order during the interwar period. But just as a new liberal economic order is gradually being reconstructed—with a milestone being the collapse of the Soviet Union and its allies and their growing integration into the world economic order—the various palliatives devised to deal with the dreadful woes bred by the past century's economic breakdown are becoming more and more redundant. Whether or not there was ever a time for foreign aid, it is an idea whose time has gone.

About the Author

Deepak Lal is James S. Coleman Professor of International Development Studies, University of California at Los Angeles, and professor emeritus of political economy, University College London. He was a full-time consultant to the Indian Planning Commission (1973–1974) and has served as a consultant to the ILO, UNCTAD, OECD, UNIDO, the World Bank, and the ministries of planning in Korea and Sri Lanka. He has been a member of the U.K. Shadow Chancellor's Council of Economic Advisors since 2000, and a distinguished visiting fellow at the National Council for Economic Research, New Delhi, since 1999.

Further Reading

Bauer, P. *Dissent on Development*. 1971. Cambridge: Harvard University Press, 1976.

Boone, P. "The Impact of Foreign Aid on Savings and Growth." Mimeo, London School of Economics, London, 1994.

Collier, P., et al. "Redesigning Conditionality." *World Development* 25, no. 9 (1997): 1399–1407.

Easterly, W. *The Elusive Quest for Growth*. Cambridge: MIT Press, 2001.

Gilbert, C., A. Powell, and D. Vines. "Positioning the World Bank." *Economic Journal* 109, no. 459 (1999): F598–F633.

Hancock, G. *Lords of Poverty: The Power, Prestige, and Corruption of the International Aid Business*. London: Macmillan, 1989.

Klitgard, R. *Tropical Gangsters*. New York: Basic Books, 1990.

Krueger, A. O. "Whither the World Bank and the IMF?" *Journal of Economic Literature* 36, no. 4 (1998): 1983–2020.

Lal, D. *Against Dirigisme*. San Francisco: ICS Press, 1994.

———. "The Foreign Exchange Bottleneck Revisited: A Geometric Note." *Economic Development and Cultural Change* 20, no. 4 (1972): 720–730.

———. "Participation, Markets, and Democracy." In M. Lundahl and B. J. Nudulu, eds. *New Directions in Development Economics.* London: Routledge, 1996.

———. *The Poverty of "Development Economics."* 3d ed. London: Institute of Economic Affairs. Cambridge: Harvard University Press; Cambridge: MIT Press, 2002.

———. *Poverty, Power and Prejudice.* London: Fabian Society, 1978. Reprinted in Lal, *Against Dirigisme.* San Francisco: ICS Press, 1994.

Lal, D., and H. Myint. *The Political Economy of Poverty, Equity and Growth—A Comparative Study.* Oxford: Clarendon Press, 1996.

Little, I. M. D., and J. Clifford. *International Aid.* London: Allen and Unwin, 1965.

Lluch, C. "ICOR's, Savings Rates and the Determinants of Public Expenditure in Developing Countries." In D. Lal and M. Wolf, eds., *Stagflation and the State.* New York: Oxford University Press, 1986.

Mosley, P. *Overseas Aid.* Brighton: Wheatsheaf, 1987.

Foreign Exchange

Jeffrey A. Frankel

The foreign exchange market is the market in which foreign currency—such as the yen or euro or pound—is traded for domestic currency—for example, the U.S. dollar. This "market" is not in a centralized location; instead, it is a decentralized network that is nevertheless highly integrated via modern information and telecommunications technology.

According to a triennial survey, the average daily global turnover (i.e., amount exchanged) in traditional foreign exchange markets reached $1.9 trillion in April 2004.[1] In addition, there was $1.2 trillion of trading in derivatives such as forwards and options (see FUTURES AND OPTIONS MARKETS). In the spot market, parties contract for delivery of the foreign exchange immediately. In the forward market, they contract for delivery at some point, such as three months, in the future. In the option market, they enter a contract that allows one party to buy or sell foreign exchange in the future, but does not require it (thus the word "option"). Most of the trading is among banks, either on behalf of customers or on their own account. The counterparty to the transaction could be another dealer, another financial institution, or a nonfinancial customer. The survey reported that 89 percent of the trading involved the dollar on one side of the transaction or the other. (That the dollar is used as a "vehicle currency" explains why its trading volume is so high: someone wanting to go from the Malaysian ringgit to the South African rand passes through the dollar on the way.) Next, 37 percent of foreign exchange transactions involved the euro, 20 percent the yen, 17 percent the British pound, 6 percent the Swiss franc, 5 percent the Australian dollar, and 4 percent the Canadian dollar. London is the world's largest center for trading foreign exchange, with 31 percent of the global total turnover. Next comes New York at 19 percent, Tokyo at 8 percent, and Singapore and Frankfurt at 5 percent each.

The exchange rate is the price of foreign currency. For example, the exchange rate between the British pound and the U.S. dollar is usually stated in dollars per pound sterling ($/£); an *increase* in this exchange rate from, say, $1.80 to say, $1.83, is a *depreciation* of the dollar. The exchange rate between the Japanese yen and the U.S. dollar is usually stated in yen per dollar (¥/$); an increase in this exchange rate from, say, ¥108 to ¥110 is an *appreciation* of the dollar. Some countries "float" their exchange rate, which means that the central bank (the country's monetary authority) does not buy or sell foreign exchange, and the price is instead determined in the private marketplace. Like other market prices, the exchange rate is determined by supply and demand—in this case, supply of and demand for foreign exchange.

Some countries' governments, instead of floating, "fix" their exchange rate, at least for periods of time, which means that the government's central bank is an active trader in the foreign exchange market. To do so, the central bank buys or sells foreign currency, depending on which is necessary to peg the currency at a fixed exchange rate with the chosen foreign currency. An increase in foreign exchange reserves will add to the money supply, which could lead to inflation if it is not offset by the monetary authorities via what are called "sterilization" operations. Sterilization by the central bank means responding to increases in reserves so as to leave the total money supply unchanged. A common way to accomplish it is by selling bonds on the open market; a less common way is to increase the reserve requirements placed on commercial banks.

Still other countries follow some regime intermediate between pure fixing and pure floating (examples include bands or target zones, basket pegs, crawling pegs, and adjustable pegs). Many central banks practice "managed floating," whereby they intervene in the foreign exchange market by "leaning against the wind." To do so, a central bank sells foreign exchange when the exchange rate is going up, thereby dampening its rise, and buys when it is going down. The motive is to reduce the variability in the exchange rate. Private speculators may do the same thing:

---

1. In the most recent survey from the Bank for International Settlements, published September 2004, Basel.

such "stabilizing speculation"—buying low with the plan of selling high—is profitable if the speculators correctly anticipate the direction of future exchange rates.

Until the 1970s, exports and imports of merchandise were the most important sources of supply and demand for foreign exchange. Today, financial transactions overwhelmingly dominate. When the exchange rate rises, it is generally because market participants decided to buy assets denominated in that currency in the hope of further appreciation. Economists believe that macroeconomic fundamentals determine exchange rates in the long run. The value of a country's currency is thought to react positively, for example, to such fundamentals as an increase in the growth rate of the economy, an increase in its trade balance, a fall in its inflation rate, or an increase in its real— that is, inflation-adjusted—interest rate.

One simple model for determining the long-run equilibrium exchange rate is based on the quantity theory of money. The domestic version of the quantity theory says that a one-time increase in the money supply is soon reflected as a proportionate increase in the domestic price level. The international version says that the increase in the money supply is also reflected as a proportionate increase in the exchange rate. The exchange rate, as the relative price of money (domestic per foreign), can be viewed as determined by the demand for money (domestic relative to foreign), which is in turn influenced positively by the rate of growth of the real economy and negatively by the inflation rate.

A defect of the international quantity theory of money is that it cannot account for fluctuations in the real exchange rate as opposed to simply the nominal exchange rate. The real exchange rate is defined as the nominal exchange rate deflated by price levels (foreign relative to domestic). It is the real exchange rate that matters most for the real economy. If a currency has a high value in real terms, this means that its products are selling at less competitive prices on world markets, which will tend to discourage exports and encourage imports. If the real exchange rate were constant, then "purchasing power parity" would hold: the exchange rate would be proportionate to relative price levels. Purchasing power parity does not, in fact, hold in the short run, not even approximately, even for goods and services that are traded internationally. But purchasing power parity does tend to hold in the long run.

One elegant theory of exchange-rate determination is the late Rudiger Dornbusch's "overshooting model." In this theory, an increase in the real interest rate—due, for example, to a tightening monetary policy—causes the currency to appreciate more in the short run than it will in the long run. The explanation is that international investors will be willing to hold foreign assets, given that the rate

of return on domestic assets is higher because of the monetary tightening, only if they expect the value of the domestic currency to fall in the future. This fall in the value of the domestic currency would make up for the lower rate of return on foreign assets. The only way the value of the domestic currency will fall in the future, given that the domestic currency's value rises in the short run, is if it rises more in the short run than in the long run. Thus the term "overshooting." An advantage of this theory over the international quantity theory of money is that it can account for fluctuations in the real exchange rate.

It is extremely difficult to predict the short-run direction of exchange rates. Economists often view changes in exchange rates as following a random walk, which means that a future increase is as likely as a decrease. Short-run fluctuations are difficult to explain even after the fact. Some short-run movements no doubt reflect attempts by market participants to ascertain the future direction of macroeconomic fundamentals. But many short-run movements are hard to explain and may be due to ineffable determinants such as some vague "market sentiment" or "speculative bubbles." (Speculative bubbles are movements of the exchange rate that are not related to macroeconomic fundamentals, but instead result from self-fulfilling changes in expectations.) Those who trade foreign exchange for a living generally look at economists' models of fundamentals, when thinking about horizons of one year or longer. At horizons of a month or less, they tend to rely more on methods unrelated to economic fundamentals, such as "technical analysis." A common technical-analysis strategy is to buy currency whenever the short-run moving average rises above the long-run moving average, and sell when it goes the other way.

Exchange rate volatility is very high. During the period since the major exchange rates began to float in 1971, there have been thirty-six months in which the change in the dollar/pound rate exceeded 5 percent. These thirty-six months were 12.7 percent of the total months (through 2004). By contrast, consider the period 1955–1970, when exchange rates were "pegged" under the Bretton Woods system (named after Bretton Woods, the town in New Hampshire where a 1944 conference decided the postwar international monetary order). In only one month, which was only 0.5 percent of the total months, did the change in the dollar/pound rate exceed 5 percent. Similarly higher volatility occurred during the period 1971–2004 for the exchange rate between the dollar and the mark (later euro) and between the dollar and the yen.

Businesspeople have long been concerned that a high level of exchange-rate volatility would impose costs on importers, exporters, and those wishing to borrow or lend across national borders. Until recently, economists were skeptical of the importance of this effect. In theory, importers, exporters, and others could hedge the foreign exchange risk on the forward exchange market. And statistically it was difficult to discern that increases in exchange-rate volatility had historically been associated with decreases in trade. More recently, however, this effect has been taken more seriously. Forward exchange markets do not exist for many smaller currencies and rarely exist beyond a one-year horizon. Even when the relevant forward market does exist, there are costs to using it: transactions costs plus, perhaps, a foreign-exchange premium. Statistically, econometricians have now discovered important effects: when countries eliminate bilateral exchange-rate variability, and especially if they form a currency union, bilateral trade among the member countries rises significantly. Trade among countries that adopted the euro, for example, increased by roughly 30 percent within the first few years alone.

Given the high volatility of exchange rates, even those with strong and well-founded theories about the likely direction of future movements must acknowledge the high level of uncertainty. Indeed, differences in opinion are what give rise to much of the very high volume of trade in foreign exchange. In other words, in every transaction there is a buyer and a seller, and usually they have opposite views regarding likely future movements in the exchange rate.

The most common way of trying to ascertain the average opinion of market participants is to look at the forward exchange rate. In the forward exchange market, participants exchange dollars for foreign currency for delivery, say, one year in the future, but at a price determined today. If a currency is selling at a forward premium against the dollar—that is, the dollar price of the currency is higher on the one-year forward market than on the spot market—one could say that "the forward market thinks the currency will appreciate against the dollar" over the coming year.

Unfortunately, the forward rate seems, in practice, to be a bad predictor of the future exchange rate. The future spot rate tends to move in the *opposite* direction from that forecast by the forward rate at least as often as in the indicated direction! Researchers have never been able to decide whether this is a sign of irrationality on the part of speculators or something else. The usual technical explanation is called an "exchange-risk premium." Exchange-risk premiums are compensation that risk-averse investors require in order to expose themselves to risk. Risk premiums may be small. But they are positively influenced both by uncertainty and by the quantity of assets, such as bonds, that governments issue.

By the 1990s, the richer countries had all but eliminated capital controls—that is, restrictions on buying and selling

financial assets across their borders. The poorer countries, despite a degree of market opening, still have substantial restrictions. In the absence of barriers to movement of financial capital across borders, capital is highly mobile and financial markets are highly integrated. In this case, arbitrage is free to operate: investors buy assets in countries where they are cheap and sell them where they are expensive, and thereby bring prices into line. Arbitrage works to bring interest rates into parity across countries. The surest form of arbitrage brings about "covered interest parity": it drives the forward discount into equality with the differential in interest rates.

Covered interest arbitrage brings about covered interest parity in the absence of major transactions costs, capital controls, or other barriers to the international movement of money. Again, the definition of "covered interest parity" is that the forward discount is equal to the differential in interest rates.

It is less clear if *uncovered* interest parity holds. Under uncovered interest parity, the differential in interest rates would equal not only the forward discount but also the expected rate of future change in the exchange rate. It is hard to measure whether this condition in fact holds, because it is hard to measure investors' private expectations. One reason uncovered interest parity could easily fail is the existence of an exchange-risk premium. If uncovered interest parity holds, then countries can finance unlimited deficits by borrowing abroad, so long as they are willing and able to pay the going world rate of return. But if uncovered interest parity does not hold, then countries will find that the more they borrow, the higher the rate of interest they must pay.

About the Author

Jeffrey Frankel is the Harpel Professor of Capital Formation and Growth at Harvard University's Kennedy School of Government. He directs the program in International Finance and Macroeconomics at the National Bureau of Economic Research, where he is also a member of the Business Cycle Dating Committee. From 1996 to 1999, Professor Frankel was a member of President Bill Clinton's Council of Economic Advisers, with responsibility for international economics, macroeconomics, and the environment.

Further Reading
Dornbusch, Rudiger. "Expectations and Exchange Rate Dynamics." *Journal of Political Economy* 84 (1976): 1161–1176.
Engel, Charles. "The Forward Discount Anomaly and the Risk Premium: A Survey of Recent Evidence." *Journal of Empirical Finance* 3 (June 1996): 123–191.
Frankel, Jeffrey, and Andrew Rose. "A Survey of Empirical Research on Nominal Exchange Rates." In Gene Grossman

and Kenneth Rogoff, eds., *Handbook of International Economics.* Amsterdam: North-Holland, 1996.

Friedman, Milton. "The Case for Flexible Exchange Rates." In M. Friedman, *Essays in Positive Economics.* Chicago, University of Chicago Press, 1953. Pp. 157–203.

Meese, Richard, and Ken Rogoff. "Empirical Exchange Rate Models of the Seventies: Do They Fit out of Sample?" *Journal of International Economics* 14 (1983): 3–24.

Rogoff, Kenneth, and Maurice Obstfeld. "The Mirage of Fixed Exchange Rates." *Journal of Economic Perspectives* 9 (Fall 1995): 73–96.

Taylor, Mark. "The Economics of Exchange Rates." *Journal of Economic Literature* 33, no. 1 (1995): 13–47.

Free Market

Murray N. Rothbard

"Free market" is a summary term for an array of exchanges that take place in society. Each exchange is undertaken as a voluntary agreement between two people or between groups of people represented by agents. These two individuals (or agents) exchange two economic goods, either tangible commodities or nontangible services. Thus, when I buy a newspaper from a newsdealer for fifty cents, the newsdealer and I exchange two commodities: I give up fifty cents, and the newsdealer gives up the newspaper. Or if I work for a corporation, I exchange my labor services, in a mutually agreed way, for a monetary salary; here the corporation is represented by a manager (an agent) with the authority to hire.

Both parties undertake the exchange because each expects to gain from it. Also, each will repeat the exchange next time (or refuse to) because his expectation has proved correct (or incorrect) in the recent past. Trade, or exchange, is engaged in precisely because both parties benefit; if they did not expect to gain, they would not agree to the exchange.

This simple reasoning refutes the argument against free trade typical of the "mercantilist" period of sixteenth- to eighteenth-century Europe and classically expounded by the famed sixteenth-century French essayist Montaigne. The mercantilists argued that in any trade, one party can benefit only at the expense of the other—that in every transaction there is a winner and a loser, an "exploiter" and an "exploited." We can immediately see the fallacy in this still-popular viewpoint: the willingness and even eagerness to trade means that both parties benefit. In modern game-theory jargon, trade is a win-win situation, a "positive-sum" rather than a "zero-sum" or "negative-sum" game.

How can both parties benefit from an exchange? Each one values the two goods or services differently, and these differences set the scene for an exchange. I, for example, am walking along with money in my pocket but no newspaper; the newsdealer, on the other hand, has plenty of newspapers but is anxious to acquire money. And so, finding each other, we strike a deal.

Two factors determine the terms of any agreement: how much each participant values each good in question, and each participant's bargaining skills. How many cents will exchange for one newspaper, or how many Mickey Mantle baseball cards will swap for a Babe Ruth, depends on all the participants in the newspaper market or the baseball card market—on how much each one values the cards as compared with the other goods he could buy. These terms of exchange, called "prices" (of newspapers in terms of money, or of Babe Ruth cards in terms of Mickey Mantles), are ultimately determined by how many newspapers, or baseball cards, are available on the market in relation to how favorably buyers evaluate these goods—in shorthand, by the interaction of their supply with the demand for them.

Given the supply of a good, an increase in its value in the minds of the buyers will raise the demand for the good, more money will be bid for it, and its price will rise. The reverse occurs if the value, and therefore the demand, for the good falls. On the other hand, given the buyers' evaluation, or demand, for a good, if the supply increases, each unit of supply—each baseball card or loaf of bread—will fall in value, and therefore the price of the good will fall. The reverse occurs if the supply of the good decreases.

The market, then, is not simply an array; it is a highly complex, interacting latticework of exchanges. In primitive societies, exchanges are all barter or direct exchange. Two people trade two directly useful goods, such as horses for cows or Mickey Mantles for Babe Ruths. But as a society develops, a step-by-step process of mutual benefit creates a situation in which one or two broadly useful and valuable commodities are chosen on the market as a medium of indirect exchange. This money-commodity, generally but not always gold or silver, is then demanded not only for its own sake, but even more to facilitate a reexchange for another desired commodity. It is much easier to pay steelworkers not in steel bars but in money, with which the workers can then buy whatever they desire. They are willing to accept money because they know from experience and insight that everyone else in the society will also accept that money in payment.

The modern, almost infinite latticework of exchanges, the market, is made possible by the use of money. Each person engages in specialization, or a division of labor, producing what he or she is best at. Production begins with natural resources, and then various forms of machines and capital goods, until finally, goods are sold to the consumer. At each stage of production from natural resource to consumer good, money is voluntarily exchanged for capital goods, labor services, and land resources. At each step of the way, terms of exchanges, or prices, are determined by the voluntary interactions of suppliers and demanders. This market is "free" because choices, at each step, are made freely and voluntarily.

The free market and the free price system make goods from around the world available to consumers. The free market also gives the largest possible scope to entrepreneurs, who risk capital to allocate resources so as to satisfy the future desires of the mass of consumers as efficiently as possible. Saving and investment can then develop capital goods and increase the productivity and wages of workers, thereby increasing their standard of living. The free competitive market also rewards and stimulates technological innovation that allows the innovator to get a head start in satisfying consumer wants in new and creative ways.

Not only is investment encouraged, but perhaps more important, the price system, and the profit-and-loss incentives of the market, guide capital investment and production into the proper paths. The intricate latticework can mesh and "clear" all markets so that there are no sudden, unforeseen, and inexplicable shortages and surpluses anywhere in the production system.

But exchanges are not necessarily free. Many are coerced. If a robber threatens you with, "Your money or your life," your payment to him is coerced and not voluntary, and he benefits at your expense. It is robbery, not free markets, that actually follows the mercantilist model: the robber benefits at the expense of the coerced. Exploitation occurs not in the free market, but where the coercer exploits his victim. In the long run, coercion is a negative-sum game that leads to reduced production, saving, and investment; a depleted stock of capital; and reduced productivity and living standards for all, perhaps even for the coercers themselves.

Government, in every society, is the only lawful system of coercion. Taxation is a coerced exchange, and the heavier the burden of taxation on production, the more likely it is that economic growth will falter and decline. Other forms of government coercion (e.g., price controls or restrictions that prevent new competitors from entering a market) hamper and cripple market exchanges, while others (prohibitions on deceptive practices, enforcement of contracts) can facilitate voluntary exchanges.

The ultimate in government coercion is socialism. Under socialist central planning the socialist planning board lacks a price system for land or capital goods. As even socialists like Robert Heilbroner now admit (see SOCIALISM), the socialist planning board therefore has no way to calculate prices or costs or to invest capital so that the latticework of production meshes and clears. The experience of the former Soviet Union, where a bumper wheat harvest somehow could not find its way to retail stores, is an instructive example of the impossibility of operating a complex, modern economy in the absence of a free market. There was neither incentive nor means of calculating prices and costs for hopper cars to get to the wheat, for the flour mills to receive and process it, and so on down through the large number of stages needed to reach the ultimate consumer in Moscow or Sverdlovsk. The investment in wheat was almost totally wasted.

Market socialism is, in fact, a contradiction in terms. The fashionable discussion of market socialism often overlooks one crucial aspect of the market: When two goods are exchanged, what is really exchanged is the property titles in those goods. When I buy a newspaper for fifty cents, the seller and I are exchanging property titles: I yield the ownership of the fifty cents and grant it to the newsdealer, and he yields the ownership of the newspaper to me. The exact same process occurs as in buying a house, except that in the case of the newspaper, matters are much more informal and we can avoid the intricate process of deeds, notarized contracts, agents, attorneys, mortgage brokers, and so on. But the economic nature of the two transactions remains the same.

This means that the key to the existence and flourishing of the free market is a society in which the rights and titles of private property are respected, defended, and kept secure. The key to socialism, on the other hand, is government ownership of the means of production, land, and capital goods. Under socialism, therefore, there can be no market in land or capital goods worthy of the name.

Some critics of the free market argue that property rights are in conflict with "human" rights. But the critics fail to realize that in a free-market system, every person has a property right over his own person and his own labor and can make free contracts for those services. Slavery violates the basic property right of the slave over his own body and person, a right that is the groundwork for any person's property rights over nonhuman material objects. What is more, all rights are human rights, whether it is everyone's right to free speech or one individual's property rights in his own home.

A common charge against the free-market society is that it institutes "the law of the jungle," of "dog eat dog," that it spurns human cooperation for competition and exalts material success as opposed to spiritual values, philosophy, or leisure activities. On the contrary, the jungle is precisely a society of coercion, theft, and parasitism, a society that demolishes lives and living standards. The peaceful market competition of producers and suppliers is a profoundly cooperative process in which everyone benefits and where everyone's living standard flourishes (compared with what it would be in an unfree society). And the undoubted material success of free societies provides the general affluence that permits us to enjoy an enormous amount of leisure as compared with other societies, and to pursue matters of the spirit. It is the coercive countries with little or no market activity—the notable examples in the last half of the twentieth century were the communist countries—where the grind of daily existence not only impoverishes people materially but also deadens their spirit.

About the Author

Murray N. Rothbard, who died in 1995, was the S. J. Hall Distinguished Professor of Economics at the University of Nevada in Las Vegas. He was also the leading Austrian economist of the last half of the twentieth century. This article was edited slightly to reflect the demise of various communist countries.

Further Reading

Ballve, Faustino. *Essentials of Economics.* Irvington-on-Hudson: Foundation for Economic Education, 1963.

Hazlitt, Henry. *Economics in One Lesson.* 1946. San Francisco: Fox and Wilkes, 1996.

Mises, Ludwig von. *Economic Freedom and Intervention.* Edited by Bettina Greaves. Irvington-on-Hudson: Foundation for Economic Education, 1990.

Rockwell, Llewellyn Jr., ed. *The Economics of Liberty.* Auburn, Ala.: Ludwig von Mises Institute, 1990.

———, ed. *The Free Market Reader.* Auburn, Ala.: Ludwig von Mises Institute, 1988.

Rothbard, Murray N. *Power and Market: Government and the Economy.* 2d ed. Kansas City: Sheed, Andrews and McMeel, 1977.

———. *What Has Government Done to Our Money?* 4th ed. Auburn, Ala.: Ludwig von Mises Institute, 1990.

Free-Market Environmentalism

Richard L. Stroup

Free-market environmentalism emphasizes markets as a solution to environmental problems. Proponents argue that free markets can be more successful than government—and have been more successful historically—in solving many environmental problems.

This interest in free-market environmentalism is somewhat ironic because environmental problems have often been seen as a form of market failure (see PUBLIC GOODS and EXTERNALITIES). In the traditional view, many environmental problems are caused by decision makers who reduce their costs by polluting those who are downwind or downstream; other environmental problems are caused by private decision makers' inability to produce "public goods" (such as preservation of wild species) because no one has to pay to get the benefits of this preservation. While these problems can be quite real, growing evidence indicates that governments often fail to control pollution or to provide public goods at reasonable cost. Furthermore, the private sector is often more responsive than government to environmental demands. This evidence, which is supported by much economic theory, has led to a reconsideration of the traditional view.

The failures of centralized government control in Eastern Europe and the Soviet Union awakened further interest in free-market environmentalism in the early 1990s. As *glasnost* lifted the veil of secrecy, press reports identified large areas where brown haze hung in the air, people's eyes routinely burned from chemical fumes, and drivers had to use headlights in the middle of the day. In 1990 the *Wall Street Journal* quoted a claim by Hungarian doctors that 10 percent of the deaths in Hungary might be directly related to pollution. The *New York Times* reported that parts of the town of Merseburg, East Germany, were "permanently covered by a white chemical dust, and a sour smell fills people's nostrils."

For markets to work in the environmental field, as in any other, rights to each important resource must be clearly defined, easily defended against invasion, and divestible (transferable) by owners on terms agreeable to buyer and seller. Well-functioning markets, in short, require "3-D" property rights. When the first two are present—clear definition and easy defense of one's rights—no one is forced to accept pollution beyond the standard acceptable to the community. Local standards differ because people with similar preferences and those seeking similar opportunities often cluster together. Parts of Montana, for example, where the key economic activity is ranching, are "range country." In those areas, anyone who does not want the neighbors' cattle disturbing his or her garden has the duty to fence the garden to keep the cattle out. On the really large ranches of range country, that solution is far cheaper than fencing all the range on the ranch. But much of the state is not range country. There, the property right standards are different: It is the duty of the cattle owner to keep livestock fenced in. People in the two areas have different priorities based on goals that differ between the communities. Similarly, the "acceptable noise" standard in a vibrant neighborhood of the inner city with many young people might differ from that of a dignified neighborhood populated mainly by well-to-do retirees. "Noise pollution" in one community might be acceptable in another, because a standard that limits one limits all in the community. Those who sometimes enjoy loud music at home may be willing to accept some of it from others. Each individual has a right against invasion of himself and his property, and the courts will defend that right, but the standard that defines an unacceptable invasion can vary from one community to another. And finally, when the third characteristic of property rights—divestibility—is present, each owner has an incentive to be a good steward: preservation of the owner's wealth (the value of his or her property) depends on good stewardship.

Environmental problems stem from the absence or incompleteness of these characteristics of property rights. When rights to resources are defined and easily defended against invasion, all individuals or corporations, whether potential polluters or potential victims, have an incentive to avoid pollution problems. When air or water pollution damages a privately owned asset, the owner whose wealth is threatened will gain by seeing—in court if necessary—that the threat is abated. In England and Scotland, for example, unlike in the United States, the right to fish for sport and commerce is a privately owned, transferable right. This means that owners of fishing rights can obtain damages and injunctions against polluters of streams. Owners of these rights vigorously defend them, even though the owners are often small anglers' clubs with modest means. Fishers clearly gain, but there is a cost to them also. In 2005, for example, Internet advertisements offered fishing in the chalk streams of the River Anton, Hampshire, at 50 pounds British per day, or about $90 U.S. On the River Avon in Wiltshire, the price per day was 150 pounds, or $270. Valuable fishing rights encouraged their owners to form an association prepared to go to court when polluters violate their fishing rights. Such suits were successful well before Earth Day in 1970, and before pollution control became part of public policy. Once rights against pollution are established by precedent, as these were many years ago, going to court is seldom necessary. Potential plaintiffs who recognize they are likely to lose do not want to add court costs to their losses.

Thus, liability for pollution is a powerful motivator when a factory or other potentially polluting asset is privately owned. The case of the Love Canal, a notorious waste dump, illustrates this point. As long as Hooker Chemical Company owned the Love Canal waste site, it was designed, maintained, and operated (in the late 1940s and 1950s) in a way that met even the Environmental Protection Agency standards of 1980. The corporation wanted to avoid any damaging leaks, for which it would have to pay.

Only when the waste site was taken over by local government—under threat of eminent domain, for the cost of one dollar, and in spite of warnings by Hooker about the chemicals—was the site mistreated in ways that led to chemical leakage. The government decision makers lacked personal or corporate liability for their decisions. They built a school on part of the site, removed part of the protective clay cap to use as fill dirt for another school site, and sold off the remaining part of the Love Canal site to a developer without warning him of the dangers as Hooker had warned them. The local government also punched holes in the impermeable clay walls to build water lines and a highway. This allowed the toxic wastes to escape when rainwater, no longer kept out by the partially removed clay cap, washed them through the gaps created in the walls.

The school district owning the land had a laudable but narrow goal: it wanted to provide education cheaply for district children. Government decision makers are seldom held accountable for broader social goals in the way that private owners are by liability rules and potential profits. Of course, anyone, including private parties, can make mistakes, but the decision maker whose private wealth is on the line tends to be more circumspect. The liability that holds private decision makers accountable is largely missing in the public sector.

Nor does the government sector have the long-range view that property rights provide, which leads to protection of resources for the future. As long as the third *D*, divestibility, is present, property rights provide long-term incentives for maximizing the value of property. If I mine my land and impair its future productivity or its groundwater, the reduction in the land's value reduces my current wealth. That is because land's current worth equals the PRESENT VALUE of all future services. Fewer services or greater costs in the future mean lower value now. In fact, on the day an appraiser or potential buyer can first see that there will be problems in the future, my wealth declines. The reverse also is true: any new way to produce more value—preserving scenic value as I log my land, for example, to attract paying recreationists—is capitalized into the asset's present value.

Because the owner's wealth depends on good stewardship, even a shortsighted owner has the incentive to act as if he or she cares about the future usefulness of the resource. This is true even if an asset is owned by a corporation. Corporate officers may be concerned mainly about the short term, but as financial economists such as Harvard Business School's Michael C. Jensen have noted, even they have to care about the future. If current actions are known to cause future problems, or if a current investment promises future benefits, the stock price rises or falls to reflect the change. Corporate officers are informed by (and are judged by) these stock price changes.

This ability and incentive to engage in farsighted behavior is lacking in the political sector. Consider the example of Seattle's Ravenna Park. At the turn of the twentieth century it was a privately owned park that contained magnificent Douglas firs. A husband and wife, Mr. and Mrs. W. W. Beck, had developed it into a family recreation area that, in good weather, brought in thousands of people a day. Concern that a future owner might not take proper care of it, however, caused the local government to "preserve" this beautiful place. The owners did not want to part with it, but the city initiated condemnation proceedings and bought the park.

But since they had no personal property or income at stake, local officials allowed the park to deteriorate. In fact, the tall trees began to disappear soon after the city bought it in 1911. A group of concerned citizens brought the theft of the trees to officials' attention, but the logging continued. Gradually, the park became unattractive. By 1972 it was an ugly, dangerous hangout for drug users. The Becks, operating privately at no cost to taxpayers, but supported instead by user fees, had done a far better job of managing the park they had created.

Could parks, even national parks like Grand Canyon or Yellowstone, be run privately, by individuals, clubs, or firms, in the way the Becks ran Ravenna Park? Would park users suffer if they had to support the parks they used through fees rather than taxes? Donald Leal and Holly Fretwell studied national parks and compared certain of them with state parks nearby. The latter had similar characteristics but, unlike the national parks, were supported in large part by user fees. The comparisons were interesting. Leal and Fretwell noted, in 1997, that sixteen state park systems earned at least half their operating funds from fees. The push for greater revenue led park managers to provide better services, and more people were served. For example, in contrast to nearby national parks with similar natural features, Texas state parks offered trail runs, fun runs, "owl prowls," alligator watching, wildlife safaris, and even a longhorn cattle drive. Costs in the state parks were also lower. Park users seem happy to pay more at the parks when they enjoy more and better services.

Private individuals and groups have preserved wildlife habitats and scenic lands in thousands of places in the United States. The 2003 Land Trust Alliance Census Ta-

bles list 1,537 local, state, and regional land trusts serving this purpose.[1] Many other state and local groups have similar projects as a sideline, and national groups such as The Nature Conservancy and the Audubon Society have hundreds more. None of these is owned by the government. Using the market, such groups do not have to convince the majority that their project is desirable, nor do they have to fight the majority in choosing how to manage the site. The result, as the federal government's Council on Environmental Quality has reported, is an enormous and healthy diversity of approaches.

Nevertheless, it is important to note that the government is still involved, even in the case of privately donated and privately owned trust lands. Most of these private conservation choices benefit from tax advantages, as conservers gain charitable deductions from taxable income. Tax law, therefore, influences what sorts of donations qualify; it also increases the total amounts by rewarding all qualifying choices by tax reductions. Who gains from the increased conservation? Most often it is first and foremost the nearby landowners. When donors of trust lands retain adjacent property, they benefit from the existence of the trust lands to a degree greater than other citizens more distant. Open space usually raises the value of nearby lands.

Further, when many polluters and those who receive the pollution are involved, how can property rights force accountability? The nearest receivers may be hurt the most, and may be able to sue polluters—but not always. Consider an extreme case: the potential global warming impact of carbon dioxide produced by the burning of wood or fossil fuels. If climate change results, the effects are worldwide. Nearly everyone uses the energy from such fuels, and if the threat of global warming from a buildup of carbon dioxide turns out to be as serious as some claim, then those harmed by global warming will be hard-pressed to assert their property rights against all the energy producers or users of the world. The same is true for those exposed to pollutants produced by autos and industries in the Los Angeles air basin. Private, enforceable, and tradable property rights can work wonders, but they are not a cure-all.

Still, even the lack of property rights today does not mean that a useful property rights solution is forever impossible. Property rights tend to evolve as technology, preferences, and prices provide added incentives and new technical options. Early in American history, property rights in cattle seemed impossible to establish and enforce on the

---

1. Online at: http://www.lta.org/census/census_tables.htm.

Great Plains. But the growing value of such rights led to the use of mounted cowboys to protect herds and, eventually, barbed wire to fence the range. As economists Terry Anderson and Peter J. Hill have shown, the plains lost their status as commons and were privatized. Advances in technology may yet allow the establishment of enforceable rights to schools of whales in the oceans, migratory birds in the air, and—who knows?—even the presence of an atmosphere that clearly does not promote damaging climate change. Such is the hope of free-market environmentalism.

About the Author

Richard L. Stroup is president of the Political Economy Research Institute and visiting professor of economics at North Carolina State University, both in Raleigh, North Carolina. He is also a senior associate with the Property and Environment Research Center in Bozeman, Montana. From 1982 to 1984, he was director of the Office of Policy Analysis, U.S. Department of the Interior.

Further Reading

Anderson, Terry, and Peter J. Hill. *The Not So Wild Wild West*. Stanford, Calif.: Stanford Economics and Finance, 2004.

Anderson, Terry, and Donald Leal. *Free Market Environmentalism*. Rev. ed. New York: Palgrave, 2001.

Council on Environmental Quality. *The Fifteenth Annual Report of the Council on Environmental Quality*. 1984. Chap. 9.

Jensen, Michael C. "Agency Costs of Free Cash Flow, Corporate Finance, and Takeovers." *American Economic Review* 76, no. 2 (May 1986): 324–329.

Kensinger, John W., and John D. Martin. "The Quiet Restructuring." *Journal of Applied Corporate Finance* 1, no. 1 (1988): 16–25.

Leal, Donald, and Holly Lippke Fretwell. "Parks in Transition: A Look at State Parks." Political Economy Research Center, RS-97-1, 1997. Available online at: http://www.perc.org/publications/research/stateparks.php.

Shaw, Jane S., and Richard L. Stroup. "Gone Fishin'." *Reason* 20, no. 4 (1988): 34–37.

Stroup, Richard L. *Eco-nomics*. Washington, D.C.: Cato Institute, 2003.

———. "Rescuing Yellowstone from Politics: Expanding Parks While Reducing Conflict." In John A. Baden and Donald R. Leal, eds., *The Yellowstone Primer: Land and Resource Management in the Greater Yellowstone Ecosystem*. San Francisco: Pacific Research Institute, 1990. Pp. 169–195.

Zuesse, Eric. "The Truth Seeps Out." *Reason* 12, no. 10 (1981): 16–33. [Story about Love Canal.]

Free Trade

Alan S. Blinder

For more than two centuries economists have steadfastly promoted free trade among nations as the best trade policy. Despite this intellectual barrage, many "practical" men and women continue to view the case for free trade skeptically, as an abstract argument made by ivory tower economists with, at most, one foot on terra firma. These practical people "know" that our vital industries must be protected from foreign competition.

The divergence between economists' beliefs and those of (even well-educated) men and women on the street seems to arise in making the leap from individuals to nations. In running our personal affairs, virtually all of us exploit the advantages of free trade and comparative advantage without thinking twice. For example, many of us have our shirts laundered at professional cleaners rather than wash and iron them ourselves. Anyone who advised us to "protect" ourselves from the "unfair competition" of low-paid laundry workers by doing our own wash would be thought looney. Common sense tells us to make use of companies that specialize in such work, paying them with money we earn doing something we do better. We understand intuitively that cutting ourselves off from specialists can only lower our standard of living.

Adam Smith's insight was that precisely the same logic applies to nations. Here is how he put it in 1776:

> It is the maxim of every prudent master of a family, never to attempt to make at home what it will cost him more to make than to buy. . . . If a foreign country can supply us with a commodity cheaper than we ourselves can make it, better buy it of them with some part of the produce of our own industry, employed in a way in which we have some advantage.

Spain, South Korea, and a variety of other countries manufacture shoes more cheaply than America can. They offer them for sale to us. Shall we buy them, as we buy the services of laundry workers, with money we earn doing things we do well—like writing computer software and growing wheat? Or shall we keep "cheap foreign shoes" out and purchase more expensive American shoes instead? It is pretty clear that the nation as a whole must be worse off if foreign shoes are kept out—even though the American shoe industry will be better off.

Most people accept this argument. But they worry about what happens if another country—say, China—can make everything, or almost everything, cheaper than we can.

Will free trade with China then lead to unemployment for American workers, who will find themselves unable to compete with cheaper Chinese labor? The answer (see COMPARATIVE ADVANTAGE), which was provided by DAVID RICARDO in 1810, is *no*. To see why, let us once again appeal to our personal affairs.

Some lawyers are better typists than their secretaries. Should such a lawyer fire his secretary and do his own typing? Not likely. Though the lawyer may be better than the secretary at both arguing cases and typing, he will fare better by concentrating his energies on the practice of law and leaving the typing to a secretary. Such specialization not only makes the economy more efficient but also gives both lawyer and secretary productive work to do.

The same idea applies to nations. Suppose the Chinese could manufacture everything more cheaply than we can—which is certainly not true. Even in this worst-case scenario, there will of necessity be some industries in which China has an overwhelming cost advantage (say, toys) and others in which its cost advantage is slight (say, computers). Under free trade the United States will produce most of the computers, China will produce most of the toys, and the two nations will trade. The two countries, taken together, will get both products cheaper than if each produced them at home to meet all of its domestic needs. And, what is also important, workers in both countries will have jobs.

Many people are skeptical about this argument for the following reason. Suppose the average American worker earns twenty dollars per hour while the average Chinese worker earns just two dollars per hour. Won't free trade make it impossible to defend the higher American wage? Won't there instead be a leveling down until, say, both American and Chinese workers earn eleven dollars per hour? The answer, once again, is *no*. And specialization is part of the reason.

If there were only one industry and occupation in which people could work, then free trade would indeed force American wages close to Chinese levels if Chinese workers were as good as Americans. But modern economies are composed of many industries and occupations. If America concentrates its employment where it does best, there is no reason why American wages cannot remain far above Chinese wages for a long time—even though the two nations trade freely. A country's wage level depends fundamentally on the productivity of its labor force, not on its trade policy. As long as American workers remain more skilled and better educated, work with more capital, and use superior technology, they will continue to earn higher wages than their Chinese counterparts. If and when these advantages end, the wage gap will disappear. Trade is a mere detail that helps ensure that American labor is employed where, in Adam Smith's phrase, it has some advantage.

Those who are still not convinced should recall that China's trade surplus with the United States has been widening precisely as the wage gap between the two countries, while still huge, has been narrowing. If cheap Chinese labor was stealing American jobs, why did the theft intensify as the wage gap fell? The answer, of course, is that Chinese productivity was growing at enormous rates. The remarkable upward march of Chinese productivity both raised Chinese wages relative to American wages and turned China into a world competitor. To think that we can forestall the inevitable by closing our borders is to participate in a cruel self-deception. Nor should there be any worry about failing to forestall the inevitable. The fact that another country becomes wealthier does not mean that Americans must become poorer.

Americans should appreciate the benefits of free trade more than most people, for we inhabit the greatest free-trade zone in the world. Michigan manufactures cars; New York provides banking; Texas pumps oil and gas. The fifty states trade freely with one another, and that helps them all enjoy great prosperity. Indeed, one reason why the United States did so much better economically than Europe for more than two centuries is that America had free movement of goods and services while the European countries "protected" themselves from their neighbors. To appreciate the magnitudes involved, try to imagine how much your personal standard of living would suffer if you were not allowed to buy any goods or services that originated outside your home state.

A slogan occasionally seen on bumper stickers argues, "Buy American, save your job." This is grossly misleading for two main reasons. First, the costs of saving jobs in this particular way are enormous. Second, it is doubtful that any jobs are actually saved in the long run.

Many estimates have been made of the cost of "saving jobs" by protectionism. While the estimates differ widely across industries, they are almost always much larger than the wages of the protected workers. For example, one study in the early 1990s estimated that U.S. consumers paid $1,285,000 annually for each job in the luggage industry that was preserved by barriers to imports, a sum that greatly exceeded the average earnings of a luggage worker. That same study estimated that restricting foreign imports cost $199,000 annually for each textile worker's job that was saved, $1,044,000 for each softwood lumber job saved, and $1,376,000 for every job saved in the benzenoid chemical industry. Yes, $1,376,000 a year!

While Americans may be willing to pay a price to save jobs, spending such enormous sums is plainly irrational.

If you doubt that, imagine making the following offer to any benzenoid chemical worker who lost his job to foreign competition: we will give you severance pay of $1,376,000—not annually, but just once—in return for a promise never to seek work in the industry again. Can you imagine any worker turning down the offer? Is that not sufficient evidence that our present method of saving jobs is mad?

But the situation is actually worse, for a little deeper thought leads us to question whether any jobs are really saved overall. It is more likely that protectionist policies save some jobs by jeopardizing others. Why? First, protecting one American industry from foreign competition imposes higher costs on others. For example, quotas on imports of semiconductors sent the prices of memory chips skyrocketing in the 1980s, thereby damaging the computer industry. Steel quotas force U.S. automakers to pay more for materials, making them less competitive.

Second, efforts to protect favored industries from foreign competition may induce reciprocal actions in other countries, thereby limiting American access to foreign markets. In that case, export industries pay the price for protecting import-competing industries.

Third, there are the little-understood, but terribly important, effects of trade barriers on the value of the dollar. If we successfully restrict imports, Americans will spend less on foreign goods. With fewer dollars offered for sale on the world's currency markets, the value of the dollar will rise relative to that of other currencies. At that point unprotected industries will start to suffer because a higher dollar makes U.S. goods less competitive in world markets. Once again, America's ability to export is harmed.

On balance the conclusion seems clear and compelling: while protectionism is sold as job saving, it probably really amounts to job swapping. It protects jobs in some industries only by destroying jobs in others.

About the Author

Alan S. Blinder is the Gordon S. Rentschler Memorial Professor of Economics at Princeton University. He wrote, from 1985 to 1992, a regular economics column for *Business Week* and is the coauthor of one of the best-selling textbooks on economics. He has served as vice chairman of the Federal Reserve's Board of Governors and as a member of President Bill Clinton's Council of Economic Advisers.

Further Reading

Baldwin, Robert E. *The Political Economy of U.S. Import Policy*. Cambridge: MIT Press, 1985.
Bhagwati, Jagdish. *In Defense of Globalization*. Oxford: Oxford University Press, 2004.
Blinder, Alan S. *Hard Heads, Soft Hearts: Tough-Minded Eco-nomics for a Just Society*. Reading, Mass.: Addison-Wesley, 1987.
Destler, I. M. *American Trade Politics*. 4th ed. Washington, D.C.: Institute for International Economics, 2005.
Dixit, Avinash. "How Should the U.S. Respond to Other Countries' Trade Policies?" In Robert M. Stern, ed., *U.S. Trade Policies in a Changing World Economy*. Cambridge: MIT Press, 1987.
Hufbauer, Gary C., and Kimberly A. Elliott. *Measuring the Costs of Protection in the United States*. Washington, D.C.: Institute for International Economics, 1994.
Irwin, Douglas A. *Free Trade Under Fire*. 2d ed. Princeton: Princeton University Press, 2005.
Lawrence, Robert Z., and Robert E. Litan. *Saving Free Trade*. Washington, D.C.: Brookings Institution, 1986.

Futures and Options Markets

Gregory J. Millman

Futures Markets

In the late 1970s and early 1980s, radical changes in the international currency system and in the way the Federal Reserve managed the U.S. money supply produced unprecedented volatility in interest rates and currency exchange rates. As market forces shook the foundations of global financial stability, businesses wrestled with heretofore unimagined challenges. Between 1980 and 1985, Caterpillar, the Peoria-based maker of heavy equipment, saw exchange-rate shifts give its main Japanese competitor a 40 percent price advantage. Meanwhile, even the soundest business borrowers faced soaring double-digit interest rates. Investors clamored for dollars as commodity prices collapsed, taking whole nations down into insolvency and ushering in the Third World debt crisis.

Stymied financial managers turned to Chicago, where the traditional agricultural futures markets had only recently invented techniques to cope with financial uncertainty. In 1972, the Chicago Mercantile Exchange established the International Monetary Market to trade the world's first futures contracts for currency. The world's first interest-rate futures contract was introduced shortly afterward, at the Chicago Board of Trade, in 1975. In 1982, futures contracts on the Standard and Poor's 500 index began to trade at the Chicago Mercantile Exchange. These radically new tools helped businesses manage in a volatile and unpredictable new world order. How? Futures are standardized contracts that commit parties to buy or sell goods of a specific quality at a specific price, for delivery at a specific point in the future. The concept of buying and selling for future delivery is not in itself new. In thirteenth- and fourteenth-century Europe, buyers contracted for wool purchases one to several years forward. Cistercian monasteries that produced the wool sold forward more than their own production, expecting to buy the remainder on the market (presumably at a lower price) to satisfy their obligation. In seventeenth-century Japan, merchants bought and sold rice for future delivery. And banks have long offered their customers the opportunity to buy and sell currencies forward, with both the bank and the customer contracting today and settling their obligation in the future. But the complex legal and financial arrangements that make the modern futures market possible are thoroughly modern.

In the nineteenth century, Chicago's trading pits offered an organized venue in which farmers and other suppliers of agricultural commodities, such as warehouse owners and brokers, could remove the risk of price fluctuations from their business plans. The futures exchanges were private, member-owned organizations. Members bought "seats" on the exchange and enjoyed various trading rights. It may seem strange that markets originally established to trade agricultural commodity futures in the nineteenth century should become centers of trade for financial contracts in the twentieth. But the key to success as a trader is to understand the market; traders therefore consider themselves experts on market movements rather than authorities on minerals and crops. This is why financial futures were relatively easy to introduce to markets originally designed for agricultural commodity futures: one thing interest rates and corn have in common is a fast-changing market.

Although the underlying risks have changed, some important futures markets still operate much as they always have, with traders standing in a ring or a pit shouting buy and sell orders at each other, competing for each fraction of a cent. But electronic trading is rapidly changing how traders trade. Computer terminals linked to each other through electronic trading systems let traders access a virtual trading floor from anywhere in the world. The need to raise capital to build these systems has led several big exchanges to go public, issuing stock to investors and operating as any public corporation providing a service—the service of a market. Exchanges compete with each other to attract traders by doing a better job of providing the benefits that traders expect from a fair market.

Take futures contracts, for example. They are not contracts directly between buyers and sellers of goods. The farmer who sells a futures contract and commits to deliver corn in six months does not make his commitment to a specific corn buyer, but rather, through a broker, to the

clearinghouse of the futures exchange. The clearinghouse, another modern institution, stands between buyers and sellers and, in effect, guarantees that both buyers and sellers will receive what they have contracted for.

Thanks to the clearinghouse, the farmer does not have to be concerned about the financial stability of the buyer of the futures contract, nor does the buyer need to be concerned about the progress of any particular farmer's crop. New information about changes in supply and demand causes the prices of futures contracts to fluctuate, sometimes moving them up and down many times in a trading day. For example, news of drought or blight that may reduce the corn harvest, cutting future supplies, causes corn futures contracts to rise in price. Similarly, news of a rise in interest rates or a presidential illness can cause stock-index futures prices to fall as investors react to the prospect of difficult or uncertain times ahead. Every day, the clearinghouse tallies up and matches all contracts bought or sold during the trading session. Parties holding contracts that have fallen in price during the trading session must pay the clearinghouse a sort of security deposit called "margin." When the contracts are closed out, it is the clearinghouse that pays the parties whose contracts have gained in value. Futures trading is what economists call a zero-sum game, meaning that for every winner there is someone who loses an equal amount.

But in a fundamental economic sense, futures trading is positive sum. Both sides expect to gain, or they would not trade. Another way of saying this is that the loser may be perfectly happy to lose. That is because many businesses use futures markets as a form of insurance. A candy maker, for example, might buy sugar and cocoa futures contracts to lock in a price for some portion of its requirement for these important ingredients. The contracts are as good as physically buying the commodities and storing them. If prices rise, the futures contracts will also be more valuable. The company can choose to sell the contracts and pocket the cash, then buy the commodities from its usual suppliers at market prices, or else accept delivery of the ingredients from the seller of the contract and buy less on the market. Either way, its cost of raw materials is lower than if it had not bought the contracts. The company has cushioned itself against a price risk and does not have to worry that its production and marketing strategy will be disrupted by a sudden price increase. But what if prices fall? In that case the company loses some money on its futures contracts. But the same price decrease that causes that loss also caused something good: the company pays less for its ingredients. Remember, the purpose of buying the futures contract was to protect against something bad happening—a price rise. The bad thing did not happen; prices fell instead. The loss on the futures contract is the cost of insurance, and the company is no worse off than a person who purchases fire insurance and then does not have a fire.

The biggest users of the futures markets rely on them for risk management. That is surely one reason why defaults are rare. But there is an additional security measure between the individual trader and the clearinghouse. Buyers and sellers of futures must do business through intermediaries who are exchange members. Instead of standing between two individual traders, therefore, the clearinghouse stands between two exchange member firms. Each firm monitors its own customers and makes a "margin call" when the customer's losses make additional margin necessary. If the customer cannot pay the margin, the firm closes the account, sells off the positions, and may have to take a small loss. While firms pay attention to the credit of their customers, the clearinghouse pays attention to the credit of the firms. The clearinghouse needs to make good on a trade only if losses are so great that the exchange member firm itself fails. This happens occasionally when firms badly mismanage their risks or when a major financial crisis occurs.

Because futures contracts offer assurance of future prices and availability of goods, they provide stability in an unstable business environment. Futures have long been associated with agricultural commodities, especially grain and pork bellies, but they are now more likely to be used by bankers, airlines, and computer makers than by farmers—at least in North America and Europe. By the early 2000s, although commodities remained the mainstay of futures markets in Asia, in the developed countries of the West financial futures contracts had almost totally eclipsed commodities. The Chicago Mercantile Exchange claimed in 2004 that financial futures accounted for 99 percent of its business, and financial futures also accounted for the lion's share of business at the Chicago Board of Trade and at Euronext.liffe. (Euronext.liffe is the international derivatives business of Euronext, comprising the Amsterdam, Brussels, London, Lisbon, and Paris derivatives markets. It was formed following Euronext's purchase of the London International Financial Futures and Options Exchange [LIFFE] in 2001.) In Japan, by contrast, commodity futures trading dwarfed financial futures. This does not mean that commodities were more important than finance in the Japanese economy, of course. Financial futures got a slow start in Japan because Japanese regulations discouraged them. Traders who wanted to trade such futures had to—and did—trade them elsewhere. Thus, the first futures on Japan's Nikkei stock index traded in Singapore, and the first yen futures traded in Chicago.

Obviously, the idea of hedging against an unstable financial environment has great appeal. Companies like Caterpillar, Microsoft, or Citibank can now protect themselves against currency shifts by buying and selling futures contracts or similar instruments. Investors use contracts on interest rates, bonds, and stock indexes to protect against a decline in the value of their investments, just as farmers have long used futures to protect against a drop in the price of corn or beans.

Farmers who planted corn in the spring had no way of knowing what the price of their crop would be when they harvested in the fall. But a farmer who planted in the spring and sold a futures contract committed to deliver his grain in the fall for a definite price. Not only did he receive cash in the spring in return for his commitment, but he also received the contract price for his crop even if the market price subsequently fell because of an unexpected glut of corn. In exchange the farmer gave up the chance to get a higher price in the event of a drought or blight; he received the same fixed price for which he had contracted. In the latter case, the farmer would have netted more if he had not sold the future; however, most farmers prefer not to gamble on the corn market. Farming is risky enough, thanks to uneven rainfalls and unpredictable pests, without adding the risk of changes in market prices.

Farmers thus seek to lock in a value on their crop and are willing to pay a price for certainty. They give up the chance of very high prices in return for protection against abysmally low prices. This practice of removing risk from business plans is called hedging. As a rule of thumb, about half of the participants in the futures markets are hedgers who come to market to remove or reduce their risk.

For the market to function, however, it cannot consist only of hedgers seeking to lay off risk. There must be someone who comes to market in order to take on risk. These are the "speculators." Speculators come to market to take risk, and to make money doing it. Some speculators, against all odds, have become phenomenally wealthy by trading futures. Interestingly, even the wealthiest speculators often report having gone broke one or more times in their career. Because speculation offers the promise of astounding riches with little apparent effort, or the threat of devastating losses despite even the best efforts, it is often compared to casino gambling.

The difference between speculation in futures and casino gambling is that futures market speculation provides an important social good, namely liquidity. If it were not for the presence of speculators in the market, farmers, bankers, and business executives would have no easy and economical way to eliminate the risk of volatile prices, interest rates, and exchange rates from their business plans. Speculators, however, provide a ready and liquid market for these risks—at a price. Speculators who are willing to assume risks for a price make it possible for others to reduce their risks. Competition among speculators also makes hedging less expensive and ensures that the effect of all available information is swiftly calculated into the market price. Weather reports, actions of central banks, political developments, and anything else that can affect supply or demand in the future affect futures prices almost immediately. This is how the futures market performs its function of "price discovery."

There seems to be no limit to the potential applications of futures market technology. The New York Mercantile Exchange (NYMEX) began to trade heating oil futures in 1978. The exchange later introduced crude oil, gasoline, and natural gas futures. Airlines, shipping companies, public transportation authorities, home-heating-oil delivery services, and major multinational oil and gas companies have all sought to hedge their price risk using these futures contracts. In 1990 the NYMEX traded more than thirty-five million energy futures and option contracts.

Meanwhile, international stock market investors have discovered that stock-index futures, besides being useful for hedging, also are an attractive alternative to actually buying stocks. Because a stock-index future moves in tandem with the prices of the underlying stocks, it gives the same return as owning stocks. Yet the stock-index future is cheaper to buy and may be exempt from certain taxes and charges to which stock ownership is subject. Some large institutional investors prefer to buy German stock-index futures rather than German stocks for this very reason.

Because stock-index futures are easier to trade than actual stocks, the futures prices often change before the underlying stock prices do. In the October 1987 crash, for example, prices of stock-index futures in Chicago fell before prices on the New York Stock Exchange collapsed, leading some observers to conclude that futures trading had somehow caused the stock market crash that year. In fact, investors who wanted to sell stocks could not sell quickly and efficiently on the New York Stock Exchange and therefore sold futures instead. The futures market performed its function of price discovery more rapidly than the stock market did.

Futures contracts have even been enlisted in the fight against air pollution and the effort to curb runaway health insurance costs. When the Environmental Protection Agency decided to allow a market for sulfur dioxide emission allowances under the 1990 amendments to the Clean Air Act, the Chicago Board of Trade developed a futures contract for trading what might be called air pollution futures. The reason? If futures markets provide price discovery and liquidity to the market in emission allowances,

companies can decide on the basis of straightforward economics whether it makes sense to reduce their own emissions of sulfur dioxide and sell their emission allowance to others, or instead to sustain their current emission levels and purchase emission allowances from others.

Without a futures market it would be difficult to know whether a price offered or demanded for emissions allowances is high or low. But hedgers and speculators bidding in an open futures market will cause quick discovery of the true price, the equilibrium point at which buyers and sellers are both equally willing to transact. Similar reasoning has led to some decidedly unconventional applications of futures technology. The Iowa Electronic Market introduced political futures in 1988, and this market has generally beaten the pollsters at predicting not only the winner of the White House but also the winning margin. This makes sense because people are much more careful with information when they are betting money on it than when they are talking to a pollster. Economist Richard Roll showed that the orange juice futures market is a slightly better predictor of Florida temperatures than the National Weather Service. And in 2003, the Defense Department stirred up controversy with plans to launch what was quickly dubbed a "terrorism futures" market. The idea was to let people speculate on events in the Middle East and win real money if they made the right bet. Congressional outrage nipped that plan in the bud, but the underlying logic was sound. If futures markets are an efficient mechanism for assimilating information and assessing probabilities, why not use them for statecraft and military applications?

Option Markets
Options are among the most important inventions of contemporary finance. Whereas a futures contract commits one party to deliver, and another to pay for, a particular good at a particular future date, an option contract gives the holder the right, but not the obligation, to buy or sell. Options are attractive to hedgers because they protect against loss in value but do not require the hedger to sacrifice potential gains. Most exchanges that trade futures also trade options on futures.

There are other types of options as well. In 1973 the Chicago Board of Trade established the Chicago Board Options Exchange to trade options on stocks. The Philadelphia Stock Exchange has a thriving business in currency options. The options market owes a good deal of its success to the development of the Black-Scholes option pricing model. Developed by economists Fischer Black, Robert C. Merton, and Myron Scholes, it was first published in 1973. The model considers factors including the current price of the stock or currency, its volatility, the price at which the option allows the buyer to buy the stock or currency in the future, interest rates, and time to calculate what the option is worth. In 1997, Merton and Scholes received the Nobel Prize for this breakthrough. Fischer Black had died, and the prize cannot be awarded posthumously, but the Nobel citation said,

> Black, Merton and Scholes thus laid the foundation for the rapid growth of markets for derivatives in the last ten years. Their method has more general applicability, however, and has created new areas of research—inside as well as outside of financial economics. A similar method may be used to value insurance contracts and guarantees, or the flexibility of physical investment projects.

Not all options trade on exchanges. There is also a large, so-called over-the-counter (OTC) market in options. Participants in the OTC market include banks, investment banks, insurance companies, large corporations, and other parties. OTC options differ from exchange-traded options. Whereas exchange-traded options are standardized contracts, OTC options are usually tailored to a particular risk. If a corporation wants to hedge a stream of foreign currency revenue for five years, but exchange-traded options are available only out to six months, the corporation can use the OTC market. An insurance company or bank can design and price a five-year option on the currency in question, giving the company the right to buy or sell at a particular price during the five-year period.

Although users of the OTC options market do not access the futures exchange directly, the prices discovered on the futures exchanges are important data for determining the prices of OTC options. The liquidity and price discovery elements of futures help to keep the OTC market from getting far out of line with the futures market. When futures markets do not exist or cannot be used, hedgers pay steeply for the protection they seek.

About the Author

Gregory J. Millman is a journalist and author.

Further Reading

Hull, John C. *Options, Futures and Other Derivatives.* New York: Prentice Hall, 2002.
Miller, Merton H. *Financial Innovations and Market Volatility.* Cambridge, Mass.: Basil Blackwell, 1991.
Millman, Gregory J. *The Daytraders: The Untold Story of the Extreme Investors and How They Changed Wall Street Forever.* New York: Times Books, 1999.
———. *The Floating Battlefield: Corporate Strategies in the Currency Wars.* New York: AMACOM, 1990.
———. *The Vandals' Crown: How Rebel Currency Traders Overthrew the World's Central Banks.* New York: Free Press, 1995.
Smith, Clifford W. Jr., and Charles W. Smithson. *The Handbook of Financial Engineering.* New York: Harper, 1990.

Game Theory

Avinash Dixit
Barry Nalebuff

Game theory is the science of strategy. It attempts to determine mathematically and logically the actions that "players" should take to secure the best outcomes for themselves in a wide array of "games." The games it studies range from chess to child rearing and from tennis to takeovers. But the games all share the common feature of interdependence. That is, the outcome for each participant depends on the choices (strategies) of all. In so-called zero-sum games the interests of the players conflict totally, so that one person's gain always is another's loss. More typical are games with the potential for either mutual gain (positive sum) or mutual harm (negative sum), as well as some conflict.

Game theory was pioneered by Princeton mathematician JOHN VON NEUMANN. In the early years the emphasis was on games of pure conflict (zero-sum games). Other games were considered in a cooperative form. That is, the participants were supposed to choose and implement their actions jointly. Recent research has focused on games that are neither zero sum nor purely cooperative. In these games the players choose their actions separately, but their links to others involve elements of both competition and cooperation.

Games are fundamentally different from decisions made in a neutral environment. To illustrate the point, think of the difference between the decisions of a lumberjack and those of a general. When the lumberjack decides how to chop wood, he does not expect the wood to fight back; his environment is neutral. But when the general tries to cut down the enemy's army, he must anticipate and overcome resistance to his plans. Like the general, a game player must recognize his interaction with other intelligent and purposive people. His own choice must allow both for conflict and for possibilities for cooperation.

The essence of a game is the interdependence of player strategies. There are two distinct types of strategic interdependence: sequential and simultaneous. In the former the players move in sequence, each aware of the others' previous actions. In the latter the players act at the same time, each ignorant of the others' actions.

A general principle for a player in a sequential-move game is to look ahead and reason back. Each player should figure out how the other players will respond to his current move, how he will respond in turn, and so on. The player anticipates where his initial decisions will ultimately lead and uses this information to calculate his current best choice. When thinking about how others will respond, he must put himself in their shoes and think as they would; he should not impose his own reasoning on them.

In principle, any sequential game that ends after a finite sequence of moves can be "solved" completely. We determine each player's best strategy by looking ahead to every possible outcome. Simple games, such as tic-tac-toe, can be solved in this way and are therefore not challenging. For many other games, such as chess, the calculations are too complex to perform in practice—even with computers. Therefore, the players look a few moves ahead and try to evaluate the resulting positions on the basis of experience.

In contrast to the linear chain of reasoning for sequential games, a game with simultaneous moves involves a logical circle. Although the players act at the same time, in ignorance of the others' current actions, each must be aware that there are other players who are similarly aware, and so on. The thinking goes: "I think that he thinks that I think . . ." Therefore, each must figuratively put himself in the shoes of all and try to calculate the outcome. His own best action is an integral part of this overall calculation.

This logical circle is squared (the circular reasoning is brought to a conclusion) using a concept of equilibrium developed by the Princeton mathematician JOHN NASH. We look for a set of choices, one for each player, such that each person's strategy is best for him when all others are playing their stipulated best strategies. In other words, each picks his best response to what the others do.

Sometimes one person's best choice is the same no matter what the others do. This is called a "dominant strategy" for that player. At other times, one player has a uniformly bad choice—a "dominated strategy"—in the sense that some other choice is better for him no matter what the others do. The search for an equilibrium should begin by looking for dominant strategies and eliminating dominated ones.

When we say that an outcome is an equilibrium, there is no presumption that each person's privately best choice will lead to a collectively optimal result. Indeed, there are notorious examples, such as the PRISONERS' DILEMMA (see below), where the players are drawn into a bad outcome by each following his best private interests.

Nash's notion of equilibrium remains an incomplete solution to the problem of circular reasoning in simultane-ous-move games. Some games have many such equilibria while others have none. And the dynamic process that can lead to an equilibrium is left unspecified. But in spite of these flaws, the concept has proved extremely useful in analyzing many strategic interactions.

It is often thought that the application of game theory requires all players to be hyperrational. The theory makes no such claims. Players may be spiteful or envious as well as charitable and empathetic. Recall George Bernard Shaw's amendment to the Golden Rule: "Do not do unto others as you would have them do unto you. Their tastes may be different." In addition to different motivations, other players may have different information. When calculating an equilibrium or anticipating the response to your move, you always have to take the other players as they are, not as you are.

The following examples of strategic interaction illustrate some of the fundamentals of game theory.

The prisoners' dilemma. Two suspects are questioned separately, and each can confess or keep silent. If suspect A keeps silent, then suspect B can get a better deal by confessing. If A confesses, B had better confess to avoid especially harsh treatment. Confession is B's dominant strategy. The same is true for A. Therefore, in equilibrium both confess. Both would fare better if they both stayed silent. Such cooperative behavior can be achieved in repeated plays of the game because the temporary gain from cheating (confession) can be outweighed by the long-run loss due to the breakdown of cooperation. Strategies such as tit-for-tat are suggested in this context.

Mixing moves. In some situations of conflict, any systematic action will be discovered and exploited by the rival. Therefore, it is important to keep the rival guessing by mixing your moves. Typical examples arise in sports—whether to run or to pass in a particular situation in football, or whether to hit a passing shot crosscourt or down the line in tennis. Game theory quantifies this insight and details the right proportions of such mixtures.

Strategic moves. A player can use threats and promises to alter other players' expectations of his future actions, and thereby induce them to take actions favorable to him or deter them from making moves that harm him. To succeed, the threats and promises must be credible. This is problematic because when the time comes, it is generally costly to carry out a threat or make good on a promise. Game theory studies several ways to enhance credibility. The general principle is that it can be in a player's interest to reduce his own freedom of future action. By so doing, he removes his own temptation to renege on a promise or to forgive others' transgressions.

For example, Cortés scuttled all but one of his own ships

on his arrival in Mexico, purposefully eliminating retreat as an option. Without ships to sail home, Cortés would either succeed in his conquest or perish. Although his soldiers were vastly outnumbered, this threat to fight to the death demoralized the opposition, who chose to retreat rather than fight such a determined opponent. Polaroid Corporation used a similar strategy when it purposefully refused to diversify out of the instant photography market. It was committed to a life-or-death battle against any intruder in the market. When Kodak entered the instant photography market, Polaroid put all its resources into the fight; fourteen years later, Polaroid won a nearly billion-dollar lawsuit against Kodak and regained its monopoly market. (Polaroid's focus on instant film products later proved costly when the company failed to diversify into digital photography.)

Another way to make threats credible is to employ the adventuresome strategy of brinkmanship—deliberately creating a risk that if other players fail to act as you would like them to, the outcome will be bad for everyone. Introduced by Thomas Schelling in *The Strategy of Conflict*, brinkmanship "is the tactic of deliberately letting the situation get somewhat out of hand, just because its being out of hand may be intolerable to the other party and force his accommodation." When mass demonstrators confronted totalitarian governments in Eastern Europe and China, both sides were engaging in just such a strategy. Sometimes one side backs down and concedes defeat; sometimes tragedy results when they fall over the brink together.

Bargaining. Two players decide how to split a pie. Each wants a larger share, and both prefer to achieve agreement sooner rather than later. When the two take turns making offers, the principle of looking ahead and reasoning back determines the equilibrium shares. Agreement is reached at once, but the cost of delay governs the shares. The player more impatient to reach agreement gets a smaller share.

Concealing and revealing information. When one player knows something that others do not, sometimes he is anxious to conceal this information (his hand in poker) and at other times he wants to reveal it credibly (a company's commitment to quality). In both cases the general principle is that actions speak louder than words. To conceal information, mix your moves. Bluffing in poker, for example, must not be systematic. Recall Winston Churchill's dictum of hiding the truth in a "bodyguard of lies." To convey information, use an action that is a credible "signal," something that would not be desirable if the circumstances were otherwise. For example, an extended warranty is a credible signal to the consumer that the firm believes it is producing a high-quality product.

Recent advances in game theory have succeeded in describing and prescribing appropriate strategies in several situations of conflict and cooperation. But the theory is far from complete, and in many ways the design of successful strategy remains an art.

About the Authors
Avinash Dixit is the John J. F. Sherrerd '52 University Professor of Economics at Princeton University. Barry Nalebuff is the Milton Steinbach Professor of Management at Yale University's School of Management. They are coauthors of *Thinking Strategically*.

Further Reading
Introductory
Ankeny, Nesmith. *Poker Strategy: Winning with Game Theory.* New York: Basic Books, 1981.
Brams, Steven. *Game Theory and Politics.* New York: Free Press, 1979.
Brandenburger, Adam, and Barry Nalebuff. *Co-opetition.* New York: Doubleday, 1996.
Davis, Morton. *Game Theory: A Nontechnical Introduction.* 2d ed. New York: Basic Books, 1983.
Dixit, Avinash, and Barry Nalebuff. *Thinking Strategically: A Competitive Edge in Business, Politics, and Everyday Life.* New York: W. W. Norton, 1991.
Dixit, Avinash, and Susan Skeath. *Games of Strategy.* 2d ed. New York: W. W. Norton, 2004.
"Game Theory." Wikipedia. Online at: http://en.wikipedia.org/wiki/Game_Theory.
Luce, Duncan, and Howard Raiffa. *Games and Decisions.* New York: Wiley, 1957.
McDonald, John. *Strategy in Poker, Business and War.* New York: W. W. Norton, 1950.
Osborne, Martin. *An Introduction to Game Theory.* New York: Oxford University Press, 2003.
Porter, Michael. *Competitive Strategy.* New York: Free Press, 1982.
Raiffa, Howard. *The Art and Science of Negotiation.* Cambridge: Harvard University Press, 1982.
Riker, William. *The Art of Political Manipulation.* New Haven: Yale University Press, 1986.
Schelling, Thomas. *The Strategy of Conflict.* Cambridge: Harvard University Press, 1960.
Williams, J. D. *The Compleat Strategyst.* Rev. ed. New York: McGraw-Hill, 1966.

Advanced
Fudenberg, Drew, and Jean Tirole. *Game Theory.* Cambridge: MIT Press, 1991.
Gibbons, Robert. *Game Theory for Applied Economists.* Princeton: Princeton University Press, 1992.
Myerson, Roger. *Game Theory: Analysis of Conflict.* Cambridge: Harvard University Press, 1997.

Neumann, John von, and Oskar Morgenstern. *Theory of Games and Economic Behavior.* Princeton: Princeton University Press, 1947.

Ordeshook, Peter. *Game Theory and Political Theory.* Cambridge: Cambridge University Press, 1986.

Osborne, Martin, and Ariel Rubenstein. *A Course on Game Theory.* Cambridge: MIT Press, 1994.

Shubik, Martin. *Game Theory in the Social Sciences.* Cambridge: MIT Press, 1982.

Gender Gap

Claudia Goldin

When economists speak of the "gender gap" these days, they usually are referring to systematic differences in the outcomes that men and women achieve in the labor market. These differences are seen in the percentages of men and women in the labor force, the types of occupations they choose, and their relative incomes or hourly wages. These economic gender gaps, which were salient issues during the women's movement in the 1960s and 1970s, have been of interest to economists at least since the 1890s.

The gender gap in U.S. labor force participation has been eroding steadily for at least 110 years (see Figure 1). In 1890, 15 percent of women in the United States aged twenty-five to forty-four (all marital statuses and races) reported an occupation outside the home. This figure in-

creased to 30 percent by 1940, 47 percent by 1970, and 76 percent by 2000, when it was 93 percent for men in the same demographic groups. Whereas the trend for women was decidedly up, that for men was slightly down. As a result, the gender gap in labor force participation has greatly shrunk. By 2000, of all twenty- to sixty-four-year-olds, women made up 47 percent of the total labor force.

Advances in participation among women occurred at different times for different demographic groups. In the 1940s, for example, although the increase for the group shown in Figure 1 was not great, it was substantial for women in older age groups. Participation rates for younger (married) women grew significantly in the 1970s and 1980s. And the 1980s witnessed an increase in labor force participation of the sole group that had resisted change in previous decades—women with infants.

The gender gap that gets the most attention, however, is in earnings. The ratio of female earnings to male earnings in full-time, year-round positions has increased greatly since the 1980s, when the ratio stood at 0.6, to a ratio in excess of 0.75 (see Figure 2) today. That is, women's earnings rose from, on average, about 60 percent of what men made to about 75 percent. Although no comprehensive data exist for the period before about 1950, evidence for major sectors of the economy, when properly combined, suggests that the gender gap in earnings narrowed substantially during two earlier periods in U.S. history. Between about 1820 and 1850, an era known as the industrial revolution in America, the ratio of female-to-male full-time earnings rose from about 0.3, its level in the agricultural economy, to about 0.5 in manufacturing.

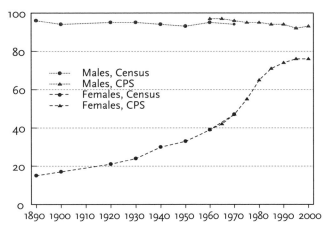

Figure 1 Labor Force Participation Rates of Men and Women, 25–44 Years Old, 1890–2000

Sources: 1890–1970, U.S. Bureau of the Census, *Historical Statistics of the United States, Colonial Times to 1970* (Washington, D.C.: U.S. Government Printing Office, 1975); and 1960 to 2000, Current Population Survey (CPS). Overlap period shows differences in the measurement of the labor force in the U.S. decennial population census and the CPS.

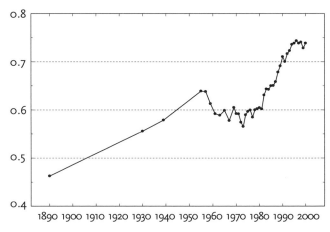

Figure 2 Ratio of Female to Male Earnings (Medians) for Full-Time, Year-Round Workers

Sources: 1890 to 1987 C. Goldin, *Understanding the Gender Gap: An Economic History of American Women* (Chicago: University of Chicago Press, 1990, fig. 3.1, p. 62); and 1988 to 2000, Current Population Survey (CPS), median for year-round, full-time workers.

From about 1890 to 1930, when the clerical and sales sectors began their ascendancy, the ratio of female earnings to male earnings again rose, from 0.46 to 0.56. But in neither of these periods did married and adult women's employment expand greatly. Yet, between 1950 and 1980, when so many married women were entering the labor force, the ratio of female earnings to male earnings for full-time, year-round employees was virtually constant, at 60 percent.

What accounts for the difference in earnings between men and women? According to the literature, observable factors that affect pay—such as education, job experience, hours of work, and so on—explain no more than 50 percent of the wage gap. The most recent studies, as reported in a review by economists Francine Blau and Lawrence Kahn (2000), found that the fraction explained is now even lower, about 33 percent. The reason is that the decrease in the gender gap in earnings was largely due to an increase in the productive attributes of women relative to men. The remainder of the gap—termed the residual—is the part that cannot be explained by observable factors. This residual could result from workers' choices or, alternatively, from economic discrimination. Surprisingly, the differing occupations of men and women explain only 10–33 percent of the difference in male and female earnings. The rest is due to differences within occupations, and part of that is due to the observable factors. In just about any year chosen, the ratio of women's to men's earnings decreases with age and rises with education. Most telling is that the ratio is higher for single than for married individuals, particularly for those without children. Family responsibilities have been an important factor in slowing women's occupational advancement over the life cycle.

Many observers have noted the paradox that as married women entered the labor force in steadily increasing numbers between 1950 and 1980, their earnings and occupational status relative to men did not improve. However, that is not as paradoxical as it might seem. Indeed, with so many new female entrants to the labor force, an economist would expect women's wages to fall (relative to men's) because of the huge increase in supply. In other words, the pay of women relative to men probably stayed constant not in spite of, but because of, the increase in the female labor force.

There is another, complementary reason why the gender gap in earnings was stagnating at the same moment that the gender gap in employment was narrowing. As more and more women entered the labor market, many of the new entrants had very little job market experience and few skills. If women tend to stay in the labor force once they enter it, the large numbers of new entrants will continually dilute the average labor market experience of all employed women. Various data demonstrate that the average job experience of employed women did not advance much from 1950 to 1980 as participation rates increased substantially. Economists James P. Smith and Michael Ward (1989) found that, among working women aged forty, for example, the average work experience in 1989 was 14.4 years, hardly any increase at all over the average experience of 14.0 years in 1950. Because earnings reflect the skills and experience of the employed, it is not surprising that the ratio of female to male earnings did not increase from 1950 to 1980.

The gender gap in earnings has decreased substantially since 1980. From 1980 to 1994, the ratio increased from 0.6 to 0.74, although the ratio has stagnated since 1994. Thus, in the fourteen years from 1980 to 1994, 35 percent of the preexisting gender gap in pay was eliminated. Moreover, these annual earnings data overstate the size of the gender gap because women who work full time actually work about 10 percent fewer hours than do men.

According to economists June O'Neill and Solomon Polachek (1993), the ratio of women's to men's pay increased for virtually all ages, all levels of education, and all levels of experience in the labor market during the 1980s. What is more, the gains occurred across all age groups. Although women in their thirties had the greatest gains relative to men their own age, the pay of older women relative to older men rose almost as much.

In this sense, the move to greater gender equality in the 1980s was remarkable. It was not merely a reflection of increased opportunities for younger or more-educated women in relation to comparable groups of men. Moreover, the increase did not occur only at the point of initial hire. It is not surprising, therefore, that conventional methods of explaining the decrease in the gender gap in earnings—those that rely on changing composition of the female workforce by education, potential job experience, occupational skill, and industry—can account for, at most, 20 percent of the increase.

Just as the stability of the earnings gap between 1950 and 1980 was probably due to the large influx of inexperienced women into the labor force, the narrowing of the gap from the 1980s to the mid-1990s may owe to the fact that female participation rates became very high. Because a larger proportion of women employed in the 1980s and 1990s were previously in the labor force, their skills and experience had expanded with time and were not greatly diluted by the addition of new entrants. The skills many of these women acquired when young enabled them to advance in ladder positions, allowing more women to have "careers," not just jobs.

Other changes also account for the decrease in the earnings gap. Educational advances, particularly among the college educated, have placed more women on a par with men. Whereas in 1960 male college graduates outnumbered females by five to three, by 1980 the numbers of female and male college graduates were equal, and today women earn 57 percent of all bachelor's degrees. College-educated women, moreover, now major in subjects very similar to those chosen by men, and they pursue advanced degrees in almost equal numbers. In the 1960s, for every hundred male recipients of professional degrees (in medicine, dentistry, law) there were fewer than five female recipients. But by 2001, women earned 46 percent of all professional degrees. That is, more than eighty females earned professional degrees for every hundred males. Young women are now forming more realistic expectations of their own futures than was the case thirty-five years ago. In 1968, only 30 percent of fifteen- to nineteen-year-old females said that they would be in the labor force at age thirty-five; by the mid-1980s, more than 80 percent thought they would be. Because the 1968 group vastly underestimated their future participation rate, they may have "underinvested" in their skills by taking academic courses that left them less prepared to compete in the job market.

To what extent has legislation narrowed the gender gap? One piece of legislation is Title VII of the Civil Rights Act of 1964, which forbids discrimination on the basis of sex in hiring, promotion, and other conditions of employment. The other is affirmative action. There is only scant evidence that either law has had any effect on the gender gap in earnings or occupations, although not enough research has been done to justify strong conclusions one way or the other.

The gender gap in employment, earnings, and occupations narrowed in various ways during the twentieth century, most especially, it seems, in the 1980s. The lessening of these gender gaps appears to have stalled in the late 1990s and has remained stalled since then. Whether or not the gap will continue to narrow and eventually disappear is uncertain and probably depends on the gender gap in time spent in child care and in the home.

About the Author

Claudia Goldin is the Henry Lee Professor of Economics at Harvard University and program director and research associate at the National Bureau of Economic Research in Cambridge, Massachusetts.

Further Reading

Blau, Francine D., and Lawrence M. Kahn. "Gender Differences in Pay." *Journal of Economic Perspectives* 14 (Autumn 2000): 75–99.
Goldin, Claudia. *Understanding the Gender Gap: An Economic History of American Women.* New York: Oxford University Press, 1990.
O'Neill, June, and Solomon Polachek. "Why the Gender Gap in Wages Narrowed in the 1980s." *Journal of Labor Economics* 11 (January 1993): 205–228.
Smith, James P., and Michael Ward. "Women in the Labor Market and in the Family." *Journal of Economic Perspectives* 3 (Winter 1989): 9–23.

German Economic Miracle

David R. Henderson

After World War II the German economy lay in shambles. The war, along with Hitler's scorched-earth policy, had destroyed 20 percent of all housing. Food production per capita in 1947 was only 51 percent of its level in 1938, and the official food ration set by the occupying powers varied between 1,040 and 1,550 calories per day. Industrial output in 1947 was only one-third its 1938 level. Moreover, a large percentage of Germany's working-age men were dead. At the time, observers thought that West Germany would have to be the biggest client of the U.S. welfare state; yet, twenty years later its economy was envied by most of the world. And less than ten years after the war people already were talking about the German economic miracle.

What caused the so-called miracle? The two main factors were currency reform and the elimination of price controls, both of which happened over a period of weeks in 1948. A further factor was the reduction of marginal tax rates later in 1948 and in 1949.

Before

By 1948 the German people had lived under price controls for twelve years and rationing for nine years. Adolf Hitler had imposed price controls on the German people in 1936 so that his government could buy war materials at artificially low prices. Later, in 1939, one of Hitler's top Nazi deputies, Hermann Goering, imposed rationing. (Roosevelt and Churchill also imposed price controls and rationing, as governments tend to do during all-out wars.) During the war, the Nazis made flagrant violations of the price controls subject to the death penalty.[1] In November 1945 the Allied Control Authority, formed by the governments

---

1. Nicholas Balabkins, *Germany Under Direct Controls* (New Brunswick, N.J.: Rutgers University Press, 1964), p. 62.

of the United States, Britain, France, and the Soviet Union, agreed to keep Hitler's and Goering's price controls and rationing in place. They also continued the Nazi conscription of resources, including labor.

Each of the Allied governments controlled a "zone" of German territory. In the U.S. zone, a cost-of-living index in May 1948, computed at the controlled prices, was only 31 percent above its level in 1938. Yet in 1947, the amount of money in the German economy—currency plus demand deposits—was five times its 1936 level. With money a multiple of its previous level but prices only a fraction higher, there were bound to be shortages. And there were.

Price controls on food made the shortages so severe that some people started growing their own food, and others made weekend treks to the countryside to barter for food. Yale University economist (and later Federal Reserve governor) Henry Wallich, in his 1955 book, *Mainsprings of the German Revival,* wrote:

> Each day, and particularly on weekends, vast hordes of people trekked out to the country to barter food from the farmers. In dilapidated railway carriages from which everything pilferable had long disappeared, on the roofs and on the running boards, hungry people traveled sometimes hundreds of miles at snail's pace to where they hoped to find something to eat. They took their wares—personal effects, old clothes, sticks of furniture, whatever bombed-out remnants they had—and came back with grain or potatoes for a week or two. (p. 65)

Barter also was so widespread in business-to-business transactions that many firms hired a "compensator," a specialist who bartered his firm's output for needed inputs and often had to engage in multiple transactions to do so. In September 1947 U.S. military experts estimated that one-third to one-half of all business transactions in the bizonal area (the U.S. and British zones) were in the form of "compensation trade" (i.e., barter).

Barter was very inefficient compared with straight purchase of goods and services for money. German economist Walter Eucken wrote that barter and self-sufficiency were incompatible with an extensive division of labor and that the economic system had been "reduced to a primitive condition" (Hazlett 1978, p. 34). The numbers bear him out. In March 1948 bizonal production was only 51 percent of its level in 1936.

The Debate

Eucken was the leader of a school of economic thought, called the Soziale Marktwirtschaft, or "social free market," based at Germany's University of Freiburg. Members of this school hated totalitarianism and had propounded their views at some risk during Hitler's regime. "During the Nazi period," wrote Henry Wallich, "the school represented a kind of intellectual resistance movement, requiring great personal courage as well as independence of mind" (p. 114). The school's members believed in free markets, along with some slight degree of progression in the income tax system and government action to limit monopoly. (Cartels in Germany had been explicitly legal before the war.) The Soziale Marktwirtschaft was very much like the Chicago school, whose budding members Milton Friedman and George Stigler also believed in a heavy dose of free markets, slight government redistribution through the tax system, and antitrust laws to prevent monopoly.

Among the members of the German school were Wilhelm Röpke and Ludwig Erhard. To clean up the postwar mess, Röpke advocated currency reform, so that the amount of currency could be in line with the amount of goods, and the abolition of price controls. Both were necessary, he thought, to end repressed inflation. The currency reform would end inflation; price decontrol would end repression.

Ludwig Erhard agreed with Röpke. Erhard himself had written a memorandum during the war laying out his vision of a market economy. His memorandum made clear that he wanted the Nazis to be defeated.

The Social Democratic Party (SPD), on the other hand, wanted to keep government control. The SPD's main economic ideologue, Dr. Kreyssig, argued in June 1948 that decontrol of prices and currency reform would be ineffective and instead supported central government direction. Agreeing with the SPD were labor union leaders, the British authorities, most West German manufacturing interests, and some of the American authorities.

The Change

Ludwig Erhard won the debate. Because the Allies wanted non-Nazis in the new German government, Erhard, whose anti-Nazi views were clear (he had refused to join the Nazi Association of University Teachers), was appointed Bavarian minister of finance in 1945. In 1947 he became the director of the bizonal Office of Economic Opportunity and, in that capacity, advised U.S. General Lucius D. Clay, military governor of the U.S. zone. After the Soviets withdrew from the Allied Control Authority, Clay, along with his French and British counterparts, undertook a currency reform on Sunday, June 20, 1948. The basic idea was to substitute a much smaller number of deutsche marks (DM), the new legal currency, for reichsmarks. The money supply would thus contract substantially so that even at the controlled prices, now stated in deutsche marks, there would be fewer shortages. The currency reform was highly complex, with many people taking a substantial reduction in their net wealth. The net result was about a 93 percent contraction in the money supply.

On that same Sunday the German Bizonal Economic Council adopted, at the urging of Ludwig Erhard and against the opposition of its Social Democratic members, a price decontrol ordinance that allowed and encouraged Erhard to eliminate price controls.

Erhard spent the summer de-Nazifying the West German economy. From June through August 1948, wrote Fred Klopstock, an economist at the Federal Reserve Bank of New York, "directive followed directive removing price, allocation, and rationing regulations" (p. 283). Vegetables, fruit, eggs, and almost all manufactured goods were freed of controls. Ceiling prices on many other goods were raised substantially, and many remaining controls were no longer enforced. Erhard's motto could have been: "Don't just sit there; undo something."

Journalist Edwin Hartrich tells the following story about Erhard and Clay. In July 1948, after Erhard, on his own initiative, abolished rationing of food and ended all price controls, Clay confronted him:

Clay: "Herr Erhard, my advisers tell me what you have done is a terrible mistake. What do you say to that?"
Erhard: "Herr General, pay no attention to them! My advisers tell me the same thing."[2]

Hartrich also tells of Erhard's confrontation with a U.S. Army colonel the same month:

Colonel: "How dare you relax our rationing system, when there is a widespread food shortage?"
Erhard: "But, Herr Oberst. I have not relaxed rationing; I have abolished it! Henceforth, the only rationing ticket the people will need will be the deutschemark. And they will work hard to get these deutschemarks, just wait and see."[3]

Of course, Erhard's prediction was on target. Decontrol of prices allowed buyers to transmit their demands to sellers, without a rationing system getting in the way, and the higher prices gave sellers an incentive to supply more.

Along with currency reform and decontrol of prices, the government also cut tax rates. A young economist named Walter Heller, who was then with the U.S. Office of Military Government in Germany and was later to be the chairman of President John F. Kennedy's Council of Economic Advisers, described the reforms in a 1949 article. To "remove the repressive effect of extremely high rates," wrote Heller, "Military Government Law No. 64 cut a wide swath

across the [West] German tax system at the time of the currency reform" (p. 218). The corporate income tax rate, which had ranged from 35 percent to 65 percent, was made a flat 50 percent. Although the top rate on individual income remained at 95 percent, it applied only to income above the level of DM250,000 annually. In 1946, by contrast, the Allies had taxed all income above 60,000 reichsmarks (which translated into about DM6,000) at 95 percent. For the median-income German in 1950, with an annual income of a little less than DM2,400, the marginal tax rate was 18 percent. That same person, had he earned the reichsmark equivalent in 1948, would have been in an 85 percent tax bracket.

After

The effect on the West German economy was electric. Wallich wrote: "The spirit of the country changed overnight. The gray, hungry, dead-looking figures wandering about the streets in their everlasting search for food came to life" (p. 71).

Shops on Monday, June 21, were filled with goods as people realized that the money they sold them for would be worth much more than the old money. Walter Heller wrote that the reforms "quickly reestablished money as the preferred medium of exchange and monetary incentives as the prime mover of economic activity" (p. 215).

Absenteeism also plummeted. In May 1948 workers had stayed away from their jobs for an average of 9.5 hours per week, partly because the money they worked for was not worth much and partly because they were out foraging or bartering for money. By October average absenteeism was down to 4.2 hours per week. In June 1948 the bizonal index of industrial production was at only 51 percent of its 1936 level; by December the index had risen to 78 percent. In other words, industrial production had increased by more than 50 percent.

Output continued to grow by leaps and bounds after 1948. By 1958 industrial production was more than four times its annual rate for the six months in 1948 preceding currency reform. Industrial production per capita was more than three times as high. East Germany's communist economy, by contrast, stagnated.

Because Erhard's ideas had worked, the first chancellor of the new Federal Republic of Germany, Konrad Adenauer, appointed him Germany's first minister of economic affairs. He held that post until 1963 when he became chancellor himself, a post he held until 1966.

The Marshall Plan

This account has not mentioned the Marshall Plan. Can't West Germany's revival be attributed mainly to that? The answer is *no.* The reason is simple: Marshall Plan aid to

---

2. Edwin Hartrich, *The Fourth and Richest Reich* (New York: Macmillan, 1980), p. 4.

3. Hartrich, *The Fourth and Richest Reich*, p. 13.

West Germany was not that large. Cumulative aid from the Marshall Plan and other aid programs totaled only $2 billion through October 1954. Even in 1948 and 1949, when aid was at its peak, Marshall Plan aid was less than 5 percent of German national income. Other countries that received substantial Marshall Plan aid exhibited lower growth than Germany.

Moreover, while West Germany was receiving aid, it was also making reparations and restitution payments well in excess of $1 billion. Finally, and most important, the Allies charged the Germans DM7.2 billion annually ($2.4 billion) for their costs of occupying Germany. (Of course, these occupation costs also meant that Germany did not need to pay for its own defense.) Moreover, as economist Tyler Cowen notes, Belgium recovered the fastest from the war and placed a greater reliance on free markets than the other war-torn European countries did, and Belgium's recovery predated the Marshall Plan.

Conclusion

What looked like a miracle to many observers was really no such thing. It was expected by Ludwig Erhard and by others of the Freiburg school who understood the damage that can be done by inflation coupled with price controls and high tax rates, and the large productivity gains that can be unleashed by ending inflation, removing controls, and cutting high marginal tax rates.

About the Author

David R. Henderson is the editor of this encyclopedia. He is a research fellow with Stanford University's Hoover Institution and an associate professor of economics at the Naval Postgraduate School in Monterey, California. He was a senior economist with the President's Council of Economic Advisers.

Further Reading

Cowen, Tyler. "The Marshall Plan: Myths and Realities." In Doug Bandow, ed., *U.S. Aid to the Developing World*. Washington, D.C.: Heritage Foundation, 1985.
Hazlett, Thomas W. "The German Non-miracle." *Reason* 9 (April 1978): 33–37.
Heller, Walter W. "Tax and Monetary Reform in Occupied Germany." *National Tax Journal* 2, no. 3 (1949): 215–231.
Hirshleifer, Jack W. *Economic Behavior in Adversity*. Chicago: University of Chicago Press, 1987.
Klopstock, Fred H. "Monetary Reform in Western Germany." *Journal of Political Economy* 57, no. 4 (1949): 277–292.
Lutz, F. A. "The German Currency Reform and the Revival of the German Economy." *Economica* 16 (May 1949): 122–142.
Mendershausen, Horst. "Prices, Money and the Distribution of Goods in Postwar Germany." *American Economic Review* 39 (June 1949): 646–672.
Wallich, Henry C. *Mainsprings of the German Revival*. New Haven: Yale University Press, 1955.

Global Warming: A Balance Sheet

Thomas Gale Moore

We live in a greenhouse world; without such gases Earth would be too cold to sustain life as we know it. Water vapor, the principal molecule that keeps us warm, accounts for almost all (98 percent) of the natural heating of the world. Other gases, such as carbon dioxide (CO_2), methane (CH_4), and nitrous oxide (N_2O), also contribute to a warmer world. Over the last three hundred years, as the world has industrialized and become more and more dependent on fossil fuels, the concentration of CO_2 in the atmosphere has increased by more than 30 percent while methane concentrations, mainly from agriculture, have increased by about 150 percent. Atmospheric scientists have predicted that increases in those greenhouse gases will lead to, or are already producing, a warmer world. The Intergovernmental Panel on Climate Change (IPCC, a UN body tasked with the science of global warming) believes that if nothing is done to slow global warming, the amount of CO_2 will have doubled by the year 2060, causing the world's temperature to rise by about 2.5°C (4.5°F).

Interestingly, Swedish scientist Svante Arrhenius, the first to predict global warming (1896), believed that it would be beneficial, especially for northern countries. In 1992, however, the fear of harm from global warming led most of the world's national governments, including the U.S. government, to sign the United Nations Framework Convention on Climate Change at the Earth Summit in Rio de Janeiro. These governments pledged to take voluntary steps to cap carbon emissions at 1990 levels by the year 2000. The U.S. Senate ratified that treaty later in 1992. International activity continued with a subsequent meeting in Berlin (1995), followed by the meeting in Kyoto (1997) that negotiated a protocol mandating emission reductions by the advanced countries of the world but exempting the rest of the globe. The Clinton administration signed the protocol, knowing that with large countries like China and India excluded, the Senate would be unlikely to ratify it. Indeed, President Clinton refused to send the protocol to the Senate for ratification, and the Senate voted 95–0 against any treaty that excluded some countries. Shortly after taking office, George W. Bush announced that the United States was withdrawing from the treaty on the grounds that the costs to the U.S. economy would be too high.

What are the likely consequences of global warming? Are they wholly bad, or are some bad effects offset by good results? Economists as well as scientists, it turns out, have a lot to contribute to this discussion.

The Pros and Cons of Global Warming

The media and many others have attributed to global warming every possible weather, from more to less climate variability, from more rainfall to more drought, and from more violent winter storms to fewer and weaker cold weather surges. But an examination of its likely effects suggests little basis for that gloomy view. According to the IPCC, global warming would warm winters more than summers, would produce more precipitation, and would lead to more of an increase in temperatures at higher latitudes—that is, in already cold regions—than at the equator.

How would climate affect economies? Climate affects principally agriculture, forestry, and fishing. For the United States, these three total less than 2 percent of the GDP. Manufacturing, most service industries, and nearly all extractive industries are immune to direct impacts from climate shifts. Factories can be built practically anywhere—in northern Sweden or in Canada, in Texas, Central America, or Mexico. Banking, insurance, medical services, retailing, education, and a wide variety of other services can prosper as well in warm climates (with air-conditioning) as in cold (with central heating). A warmer climate will lower transportation costs: less snow and ice will torment truckers and automobile drivers; fewer winter storms will disrupt air travel; bad weather in the summer has fewer disruptive effects and passes quickly; a lower incidence of storms and less fog will make shipping less risky. Higher temperatures will leave mining and the extractive industries largely unaffected; oil drilling in the northern seas and mining in the mountains might even benefit.

A few services, such as tourism, may be more susceptible to weather. A warmer climate would likely change the nature and location of pleasure trips. Many ski resorts, for example, might face less reliably cold weather and shorter seasons. Warmer conditions might also mean that fewer northerners would feel the need to vacation in Florida or the Caribbean. At the same time, new tourist opportunities might develop in Alaska, northern Canada, and other locales at higher latitudes or upper elevations. Shorter winters would benefit most outdoor recreation, such as golf, hiking, tennis, and picnicking.

In many parts of the world, warmer weather should mean longer growing seasons. If the world were to warm, the hotter climate would enhance evaporation from the seas and, in all probability, lead to more precipitation worldwide. Moreover, the enrichment of the atmosphere with CO_2 would fertilize plants, making for more vigorous growth. The IPCC assessment of warming is that "a few degrees of projected warming will lead to general increases in temperate crop yields, with some regional variation" (IPCC 2001, p. 32). Bjørn Lomborg, a Danish environmentalist and statistician, reported that with moderate adaptation by farmers, warming would boost cereal production in richer countries by 4–14 percent, while cutting them in poorer countries by 6–7 percent (2001, p. 288). The U.S. Department of Agriculture, in a cautious report, reviewed the likely influence of global warming and concluded that the overall effect on world food production would be slightly positive and that, therefore, agricultural prices would probably decrease (Kane et al. 1991).

Global warming could melt glaciers and thus cause rising sea levels, which would flood low-lying regions, including a number of islands and delta areas. The high-end estimate by the IPCC of the rise in the sea level by the year 2100 is three feet. Economists such as William Cline, William Nordhaus, and Richard Morgenstern, starting with this three-foot assumption, have estimated the costs of building dikes and levees and of the loss of land for the United States at $7–$10.6 billion annually, or about 0.1 percent of America's GDP. For some small low-lying island nations, the problems would be much more severe; in some cases they might even be completely submerged.

The Dollar Costs of Climate Change

William Cline and William Nordhaus, separately, have estimated the cost of warming of 2.5°C (4.5°F) to be about 1 percent of the U.S. GDP. Actually, though, Nordhaus calculated the cost at only 0.25 percent and then guessed, on the basis of unmeasured sectors, that the total might be as high as 1 or 2 percent. Interestingly, both Cline and Nordhaus explicitly ignored potential benefits from a warmer climate. Other economists agree that the benefits, at least to the United States and probably to most northern countries, outweigh the costs. Robert Mendelsohn of Yale University and his colleague James Neumann found that, on net, the United States would gain around 0.1–0.2 percent in GDP for the moderate warming (2.5°C) likely to occur by 2060. Even their numbers underestimate the benefits by failing to include the gain to people from enjoying warm-weather recreation.

The American public prefers warm weather to cold, a benefit generally overlooked. Thomas Moore (1998) measured Americans' preferences for climate by examining wage rates in various U.S. cities. He also looked at how death rates and hospital visits varied with climate. He found not only that people prefer warmer climates, but also that death rates and health care costs are lower in warmer climates. Based on these estimates, he concluded that the net benefits to the United States of a warmer climate could be as high as 1 percent of the GDP.

Unfortunately, some of the rest of the world, especially poor agricultural regions and those subject to flooding from rising sea levels, will suffer more from global warming. Interestingly, though, virtually all published estimates based on careful research put the cost to the world of a doubling of CO_2 at less than or equal to 1.5 percent of world income. The IPCC's Working Group III in its report to policymakers quoted estimates of the total cost from a doubling of CO_2 as "a few percent of world GDP."

Although many agree that the cost of warming, after adjustment, may be small, some observers have worried that the speed of climate change will be unprecedented, making adjustment difficult and costly. Ice core researchers have shown, however, that climate has shifted in the past as rapidly as, or more rapidly than, is predicted over the next century. In addition, the IPCC has reduced the temperature increase forecast over the next century from 5.8°F in 1990 to 3.6°F in 1995, sharply slicing the rate of change of climate. In short, there is little to fear from global warming and possibly something to gain; even the need for a "no regrets policy"—a policy with little cost but some reduction in greenhouse gases—seems negligible.

The Cost of Kyoto and of Stopping Warming

As mentioned above, most of the participating nations' governments signed the 1997 Kyoto protocol pledging that the major countries would reduce their emissions of greenhouse gases by 5 percent from their 1990 levels. Under this agreement, the United States would have had to cut its emissions by 7 percent from the 1990 levels, or about 30 percent of the emission likely by 2010, when those cuts were to be fully in place. While this treaty would have cost the United States around 3 percent of its GDP, or $300 billion, it would have had a negligible effect on slowing climate change.

Bert Bolin, former chairman of the IPCC, notes that if Kyoto were fully implemented, twenty-five years later the global temperature would be cut "by less than 0.1 degree C, which would not be detectable." Lomborg estimates that the world climate will increase by 1.92°C by 2094 if nothing is done. If Kyoto is fully followed, it will take six more years to reach the same temperature. In other words, Kyoto will neither stop nor seriously slow climate change. We would need many times Kyoto to stabilize greenhouse gas concentrations in the atmosphere.

Thus, it would cost several times Kyoto, more than 10 percent of our GDP, to stop the buildup of CO_2 while, at the outside, climate change would cost only about 1 percent of U.S. income and could be beneficial.

About the Author

Thomas Gale Moore is a senior fellow at the Hoover Institution at Stanford University. Between 1985 and 1989 he was a member of President Reagan's Council of Economic Advisers.

Further Reading

Cline, William R. *The Economics of Climate Change.* Washington, D.C.: Institute for International Economics, 1992.

IPCC Working Group II. *Climate Change 2001, Impacts, Adaptation, and Vulnerability.* Cambridge: Cambridge University Press 2001.

IPCC Working Group III. "Summary for Policymakers: The Economic and Social Dimensions of Climate Change." 1995.

Kane, Sally, John Reilly, and James Tobey. *Climate Change: Economic Implications for World Agriculture.* Agricultural Economics Report no. 647, Resources and Technology Division, Economic Research Service. Washington, D.C.: U.S. Department of Agriculture, 1991.

Lomborg, Bjørn. *The Skeptical Environmentalist: Measuring the Real State of the World.* Cambridge: Cambridge University Press, 2001.

Mendelsohn, Robert, and James E. Neumann. *The Impact of Climate Change on the United States Economy.* Cambridge: Cambridge University Press, 1999.

Morgenstern, Richard. "Towards a Comprehensive Approach to Global Climate Change Mitigation." *American Economic Review* 81 (May 1991): 140–145.

Moore, Thomas Gale. *Climate of Fear: Why We Shouldn't Worry About Global Warming.* Washington, D.C.: Cato Institute, 1998.

———. "Health and Amenity Effects of Global Warming." *Economic Inquiry* 36 (July 1998): 471–488.

Nordhaus, William D. *Managing the Global Commons.* Cambridge: MIT Press, 1994.

———. "To Slow or Not to Slow: The Economics of the Greenhouse Effect." *Economic Journal* 101 (July 1991): 920–937.

Nordhaus, William D., and Joseph Boyer. *Warming the World: Economic Models of Global Warming.* Cambridge: MIT Press, 2000.

Schelling, Thomas. "Some Economics of Global Warming." *American Economic Review* 82 (March 1992): 1–14.

Relevant Web Sites

http://www.enviroliteracy.org/. Provides excellent information and links to solid information on a variety of environmental areas, including climate change. Although intended for high school teachers, it provides material at various levels.

http://yosemite.epa.gov/oar/globalwarming.nsf/content/index.html. The official Environmental Protection Agency site. It provides charts and thumbnail coverage of various aspects of climate change.

http://www.ipcc.ch/. The official Web site of the Intergovern-
    mental Panel on Climate Change with their reports.
http://www.globalwarming.org/. The site of the Cooler Heads
    Coalition, an industry-funded group that is skeptical about
    the significance of the issue.

Gold Standard

Michael D. Bordo

The gold standard was a commitment by participating countries to fix the prices of their domestic currencies in terms of a specified amount of gold. National money and other forms of money (bank deposits and notes) were freely converted into gold at the fixed price. England adopted a de facto gold standard in 1717 after the master of the mint, Sir Isaac Newton, overvalued the guinea in terms of silver, and formally adopted the gold standard in 1819. The United States, though formally on a bimetallic (gold and silver) standard, switched to gold de facto in 1834 and de jure in 1900 when Congress passed the Gold Standard Act. In 1834, the United States fixed the price of gold at $20.67 per ounce, where it remained until 1933. Other major countries joined the gold standard in the 1870s. The period from 1880 to 1914 is known as the classical gold standard. During that time, the majority of countries adhered (in varying degrees) to gold. It was also a period of unprecedented economic growth with relatively free trade in goods, labor, and capital.

The gold standard broke down during World War I, as major belligerents resorted to inflationary finance, and was briefly reinstated from 1925 to 1931 as the Gold Exchange Standard. Under this standard, countries could hold gold or dollars or pounds as reserves, except for the United States and the United Kingdom, which held reserves only in gold. This version broke down in 1931 following Britain's departure from gold in the face of massive gold and capital outflows. In 1933, President Franklin D. Roosevelt nationalized gold owned by private citizens and abrogated contracts in which payment was specified in gold. Between 1946 and 1971, countries operated under the Bretton Woods system. Under this further modification of the gold standard, most countries settled their international balances in U.S. dollars, but the U.S. government promised to redeem other central banks' holdings of dollars for gold at a fixed rate of thirty-five dollars per ounce. Persistent U.S. balance-of-payments deficits steadily reduced U.S. gold reserves, however, reducing confidence in the ability of the United States to redeem its currency in gold. Finally, on August 15, 1971, President Richard M. Nixon announced that the United States would no longer redeem currency for gold. This was the final step in abandoning the gold standard.

Widespread dissatisfaction with high inflation in the late 1970s and early 1980s brought renewed interest in the gold standard. Although that interest is not strong today, it seems to strengthen every time inflation moves much above 5 percent. This makes sense: whatever other problems there were with the gold standard, persistent inflation was not one of them. Between 1880 and 1914, the period when the United States was on the "classical gold standard," inflation averaged only 0.1 percent per year.

How the Gold Standard Worked

The gold standard was a domestic standard regulating the quantity and growth rate of a country's money supply. Because new production of gold would add only a small fraction to the accumulated stock, and because the authorities guaranteed free convertibility of gold into nongold money, the gold standard ensured that the money supply, and hence the price level, would not vary much. But periodic surges in the world's gold stock, such as the gold discoveries in Australia and California around 1850, caused price levels to be very unstable in the short run.

The gold standard was also an international standard determining the value of a country's currency in terms of other countries' currencies. Because adherents to the standard maintained a fixed price for gold, rates of exchange between currencies tied to gold were necessarily fixed. For example, the United States fixed the price of gold at $20.67 per ounce, and Britain fixed the price at £3 17s. 10½ per ounce. Therefore, the exchange rate between dollars and pounds—the "par exchange rate"—necessarily equaled $4.867 per pound.

Because exchange rates were fixed, the gold standard caused price levels around the world to move together. This comovement occurred mainly through an automatic balance-of-payments adjustment process called the price-specie-flow mechanism. Here is how the mechanism worked. Suppose that a technological innovation brought about faster real economic growth in the United States. Because the supply of money (gold) essentially was fixed in the short run, U.S. prices fell. Prices of U.S. exports then fell relative to the prices of imports. This caused the British to demand more U.S. exports and Americans to demand fewer imports. A U.S. balance-of-payments surplus was created, causing gold (specie) to flow from the United Kingdom to the United States. The gold inflow increased the U.S. money supply, reversing the initial fall in prices. In the United Kingdom, the gold outflow reduced the money supply and, hence, lowered the price level. The net result was balanced prices among countries.

The fixed exchange rate also caused both monetary and

nonmonetary (real) shocks to be transmitted via flows of gold and capital between countries. Therefore, a shock in one country affected the domestic money supply, expenditure, price level, and real income in another country.

The California gold discovery in 1848 is an example of a monetary shock. The newly produced gold increased the U.S. money supply, which then raised domestic expenditures, nominal income, and, ultimately, the price level. The rise in the domestic price level made U.S. exports more expensive, causing a deficit in the U.S. balance of payments. For America's trading partners, the same forces necessarily produced a balance-of-trade surplus. The U.S. trade deficit was financed by a gold (specie) outflow to its trading partners, reducing the monetary gold stock in the United States. In the trading partners, the money supply increased, raising domestic expenditures, nominal incomes, and, ultimately, the price level. Depending on the relative share of the U.S. monetary gold stock in the world total, world prices and income rose. Although the initial effect of the gold discovery was to increase real output (because wages and prices did not immediately increase), eventually the full effect was on the price level alone.

For the gold standard to work fully, central banks, where they existed, were supposed to play by the "rules of the game." In other words, they were supposed to raise their discount rates—the interest rate at which the central bank lends money to member banks—to speed a gold inflow, and to lower their discount rates to facilitate a gold outflow. Thus, if a country was running a balance-of-payments deficit, the rules of the game required it to allow a gold outflow until the ratio of its price level to that of its principal trading partners was restored to the par exchange rate.

The exemplar of central bank behavior was the Bank of England, which played by the rules over much of the period between 1870 and 1914. Whenever Great Britain faced a balance-of-payments deficit and the Bank of England saw its gold reserves declining, it raised its "bank rate" (discount rate). By causing other interest rates in the United Kingdom to rise as well, the rise in the bank rate was supposed to cause the holdings of inventories and other investment expenditures to decrease. These reductions would then cause a reduction in overall domestic spending and a fall in the price level. At the same time, the rise in the bank rate would stem any short-term capital outflow and attract short-term funds from abroad.

Most other countries on the gold standard—notably France and Belgium—did not follow the rules of the game. They never allowed interest rates to rise enough to decrease the domestic price level. Also, many countries frequently broke the rules by "sterilization"—shielding the domestic money supply from external disequilibrium by buying or selling domestic securities. If, for example, France's central bank wished to prevent an inflow of gold from increasing the nation's money supply, it would sell securities for gold, thus reducing the amount of gold circulating.

Yet the central bankers' breaches of the rules must be put into perspective. Although exchange rates in principal countries frequently deviated from par, governments rarely debased their currencies or otherwise manipulated the gold standard to support domestic economic activity. Suspension of convertibility in England (1797–1821, 1914–1925) and the United States (1862–1879) did occur in wartime emergencies. But, as promised, convertibility at the original parity was resumed after the emergency passed. These resumptions fortified the credibility of the gold standard rule.

Performance of the Gold Standard

As mentioned, the great virtue of the gold standard was that it assured long-term price stability. Compare the aforementioned average annual inflation rate of 0.1 percent between 1880 and 1914 with the average of 4.1 percent between 1946 and 2003. (The reason for excluding the period from 1914 to 1946 is that it was neither a period of the classical gold standard nor a period during which governments understood how to manage monetary policy.)

But because economies under the gold standard were so vulnerable to real and monetary shocks, prices were highly unstable in the short run. A measure of short-term price instability is the coefficient of variation—the ratio of the standard deviation of annual percentage changes in the price level to the average annual percentage change. The higher the coefficient of variation, the greater the short-term instability. For the United States between 1879 and 1913, the coefficient was 17.0, which is quite high. Between 1946 and 1990 it was only 0.88. In the most volatile decade of the gold standard, 1894–1904, the mean inflation rate was 0.36 and the standard deviation was 2.1, which gives a coefficient of variation of 5.8; in the most volatile decade of the more recent period, 1946–1956, the mean inflation rate was 4.0, the standard deviation was 5.7, and the coefficient of variation was 1.42.

Moreover, because the gold standard gives government very little discretion to use monetary policy, economies on the gold standard are less able to avoid or offset either monetary or real shocks. Real output, therefore, is more variable under the gold standard. The coefficient of variation for real output was 3.5 between 1879 and 1913, and only 0.4 between 1946 and 2003. Not coincidentally, since the government could not have discretion over monetary policy, unemployment was higher during the gold standard years. It averaged 6.8 percent in the United States between 1879 and 1913, and 5.9 percent between 1946 and 2003.

Finally, any consideration of the pros and cons of the gold standard must include a large negative: the resource cost of producing gold. Milton Friedman estimated the cost of maintaining a full gold coin standard for the United States in 1960 to be more than 2.5 percent of GNP. In 2005, this cost would have been about $300 billion.

Conclusion

Although the last vestiges of the gold standard disappeared in 1971, its appeal is still strong. Those who oppose giving discretionary powers to the central bank are attracted by the simplicity of its basic rule. Others view it as an effective anchor for the world price level. Still others look back longingly to the fixity of exchange rates. Despite its appeal, however, many of the conditions that made the gold standard so successful vanished in 1914. In particular, the importance that governments attach to full employment means that they are unlikely to make maintaining the gold standard link and its corollary, long-run price stability, the primary goal of economic policy.

About the Author

Michael D. Bordo is a professor of economics at Rutgers University. From 1981 to 1982, he directed the research staff of the executive director of the U.S. Congressional Gold Commission.

Further Reading

Bordo, Michael D. "The Classical Gold Standard—Some Lessons for Today." *Federal Reserve Bank of St. Louis Review* 63, no. 5 (1981): 2–17.
———. "Financial Crises, Banking Crises, Stock Market Crashes, and the Money Supply: Some International Evidence, 1870–1933." In Forrest Capie and Geoffrey E. Wood, eds., *Financial Crises and the World Banking System.* London: Macmillan, 1986.
Bordo, Michael D., and A. J. Schwartz, eds. *A Retrospective on the Classical Gold Standard, 1821–1931.* Chicago: University of Chicago Press, 1984. Especially "The Gold Standard and the Bank of England in the Crisis of 1847," by R. Dornbusch and J. Frenkel.
———. "Transmission of Real and Monetary Disturbances Under Fixed and Floating Rates." *Cato Journal* 8, no. 2 (1988): 451–472.
Ford, A. *The Gold Standard, 1880–1914: Britain and Argentina.* Oxford: Clarendon Press, 1962.
Officer, L. "The Efficiency of the Dollar-Sterling Gold Standard, 1890–1908." *Journal of Political Economy* 94 (1986): 1038–1073.

Government Debt and Deficits

John J. Seater

Government debt is the stock of outstanding IOUs issued by the government at any time in the past and not yet repaid. Governments issue debt whenever they borrow from the public; the magnitude of the outstanding debt equals the cumulative amount of net borrowing that the government has done. The deficit is the addition in the current period (year, quarter, month, etc.) to the outstanding debt. The deficit is negative whenever the value of outstanding debt falls; a negative deficit is called a surplus.

When the government borrows, it gives its creditors government securities stating the terms of the loan: the principal being borrowed, the interest rate to be paid on the principal, and the schedule for making the interest payments and principal repayment. The amount of outstanding securities equals the amount of debt that has not yet been repaid; that amount is called "the government debt."

Governments issue several types of debt, which can be classified in various ways. One classification is by the type of government that issued the debt. In the United States, the main divisions are federal, state, and local debt; local debt can be divided further by type of locality, such as county or city (see BONDS). A second classification of government debt is by maturity at the time of issue. When we talk about a ten-year bond or a thirty-year bond, we are talking about the length of time between the date when the bond was first issued and the date on which the principal will be repaid. Federal debt is divided into three convenient maturity categories. Treasury bills have initial maturities of one year or less ("three-month bills," "year bills," etc.); treasury notes have initial maturities between one and ten years; and treasury bonds have initial maturities longer than ten years. State and local government securities generally are just called bonds, irrespective of the initial maturity. A perpetuity is a bond with an infinite maturity, which means the principal is never repaid and interest payments are made forever. The British government once issued perpetuities, calling them "consols." A third way of classifying government securities is by the source of the revenue to repay them. "General obligation bonds" will be repaid with revenue collected by taxing the public; "revenue bonds" will be repaid with revenue collected from specific user fees, such as bridge or highway tolls. This way of classifying debt is used only for state and local debt.

In early 2004, there was about $7.1 trillion of federal debt outstanding. About half ($3.6 trillion) was held by federal agencies and trust funds, which means that the government owed half the debt to itself. Such internal debt has no implications for the economy or public welfare. The important number is the amount of federal debt held by private investors, which in early 2004 was about $3.5 trillion. Foreigners held about $1.7 trillion of that amount. State and local government debt outstanding was another $1.6 trillion, most of which was held by private investors. Thus, the total amount of privately held government debt was about $5.1 trillion. As a fraction of gross domestic product (GDP) of the U.S. economy, government debt is not especially large. As of the end of 2003, GDP was about $11.1 trillion, a little more than twice the size of the privately held government debt. In contrast, at the end of World War II, outstanding federal debt alone was slightly larger than GDP. Another interesting comparison is between government debt and private debt. Corporate debt outstanding was about $5.0 trillion at the end of 2003, almost exactly the same amount as privately held government debt. Household debt is even larger. At the end of 2003, household credit market debt stood at $9.5 trillion, nearly twice the size of privately held government debt. For some reason, attitudes toward these different stocks of debt are somewhat inconsistent. Commentators regularly express concern that the sizes of government and household debt represent a risk to the economy, yet no one seems to worry much about the size of corporate debt. In fact, household and corporate debt may represent a risk in some circumstances, but government debt essentially never does. In a deep recession, debtors may become unable to repay their debts and choose to default on them. That, in turn, can make financial institutions insolvent, leading to a collapse of the financial system and a cessation of the intermediary functions that they perform. Indeed, such a mechanism was the proximate cause for the recession of 1929 turning into the GREAT DEPRESSION of 1932. Rarely, however, does any government in the United States default on its debt; the federal government has never defaulted.

The size of the outstanding government debt is a topic of perennial interest. The obvious measurement of the debt's size is the sum of all the individual outstanding government securities. That number often is reported in newspaper accounts and political debates, but, to be useful, it must be adjusted.

The most important adjustment is for INFLATION. The nominal value of a bond is the price in dollars that it would fetch on the open market. The real value of that same bond is the number of units of output that it can buy. If chocolate bars cost twenty-five cents apiece, then the real value of a ten-dollar bond is forty chocolate bars. If, however, the prices of all goods double, so that chocolate bars now cost fifty cents each, then the real value of the same ten-dollar bond is cut in half, and the bond now buys only twenty

chocolate bars. The bond's nominal value is unchanged by inflation, but its real value is changed. Real, not nominal, values are what matters because people are interested in how many goods they can buy with the wealth their bonds represent—which is precisely what the real value measures.

Adjusting official debt and deficit figures for inflation can make a big difference to measurements of the debt's size. For example, the official statistics report a federal surplus of $6.6 billion for 1947. Inflation that year was nearly 15 percent, however, and this inflation reduced the value of the huge outstanding debt by about $11.4 billion. That reduction was equivalent to a further surplus because it reduced the real value of what the federal government owed its creditors. The true surplus, therefore, was about $18 billion, nearly three times as high as the official figure. Throughout the 1970s, while the official federal deficit was positive every year, the inflation-corrected deficit was negative (i.e., there was a real surplus) in exactly half those years.

Another adjustment is for changes in interest rates. The value of outstanding debt changes as market interest rates change, but newspaper accounts usually report par values, which do not adjust for interest rate changes. Market values do account for interest rate changes and can be quite different from par values. To see what is involved, suppose that you buy a one-year $5,000 municipal bond (equivalently, you make a loan of $5,000 to the city that issued the bond) at 11:00 A.M. The bond carries an interest rate of 10 percent, which means you will be paid $500 in interest when the bond matures one year from now. At 11:05 A.M., the Federal Reserve announces a change in monetary policy that causes one-year interest rates to fall to 9 percent. Your bond now is worth more than it was when you bought it five minutes ago; that is, you could now sell the bond to someone else for more than $5,000. The reason is that anyone who wants to lend $5,000 for one year now will find that new bonds pay only 9 percent, meaning an interest payment in one year of $450. Your "old" bond, however, has a 10 percent rate locked in and will pay $500 interest for sure. That makes your bond's market value higher than its par value of $5,000.

Conversion to market value can raise or lower the size of the outstanding debt. The market value of outstanding debt will be greater than the par value if interest rates have fallen on average since the debt was issued and will be smaller than the par value if rates have risen. The difference between par value and market value of the outstanding debt is typically a few percentage points. Unfortunately, market values for the total outstanding government debt are not readily available. Governments do not report them, which is why newspaper reports rarely mention them.

More important than the sheer size of government debt are the debt's effects on the economy. Economists do not fully agree on what those effects are. When the government borrows, it promises to repay the lender. To make those repayments the government ultimately will have to raise extra taxes, beyond what it needs to pay for its other activities. The economic effect of government debt depends heavily on how taxpayers perceive those future taxes. Perceptions are difficult to measure, and neither economists nor others understand exactly how people form their perceptions.

To see what is at issue, consider a simple example. Suppose that every year the government buys $100 billion worth of goods and services and pays for them entirely by collecting taxes. Households pay the government $100 billion in tax revenue, and the government uses the revenue to buy goods and services. Revenue equals expenditure, so the government's budget is balanced. Suppose the government suddenly decides to change the way it finances its expenditures, but not the amount spent. In the first year, the government reduces taxes by $10 billion and replaces the lost revenue by selling $10 billion worth of bonds that mature in one year and carry an interest rate of 10 percent a year. In the second year, the bonds mature, and the government pays the $10 billion principal and the $1 billion of interest. Taxes in the first year are $10 billion lower, but in the second year they are $11 billion higher. How does this temporal rearrangement of tax collections affect people? In the first year, people hand over the same revenue to the government as they did when they paid taxes; the difference is that $10 billion of it is now in the form of a loan that will be repaid in the second year with an extra $1 billion in interest. On this account, people may feel richer because they seem to be paying less in total taxes over the two periods. When the second year arrives, however, people will find that they have nothing extra at all because, to pay the $11 billion in principal and interest, the government must raise taxes by exactly $11 billion, which cancels the payment of the principal and interest. The government giveth with one hand and taketh away with the other. The net result is that people do not get back the $10 billion they lent the government, and the loan is equivalent to having paid the $10 billion in taxes in the first year. This same result emerges from any maturity of debt, whether it is a one-year bond, as in the previous example, a ten-year bond, or even a perpetuity.

The crucial factor in determining how bond finance affects the economy is whether people recognize what is going to happen over time. If everybody foresees that future taxes will nullify future payments of principal and interest, then bond finance is equivalent to tax finance, and government debt has no effect on anything important. This property is known as "Ricardian equivalence," after David Ricardo, the economist who first discussed it. If people do not foresee all the future taxes implied by government debt, then they feel wealthier when the debt is issued but poorer in the future when, unexpectedly, they have to pay higher taxes to finance the principal and interest payments. So, what do people expect? Unfortunately, there is no reliable way to discover people's expectations about taxes, and we have to use other methods to learn the effect of government debt on the economy. Even though economists have been studying this issue for more than twenty years, they have not yet reached a consensus. Direct measures of the effect of debt on economic activity are straightforward in principle but difficult to construct in practice. Overall, though, the evidence favors approximate Ricardian equivalence.

If government debt is equivalent to taxation, then most of the public discussion of the "deficit problem" is misplaced. Under equivalence, government deficits merely rearrange the timing of tax collections in a way that people can anticipate and offset; no important economic effects arise. With incomplete equivalence, deficits affect the economy, but the effects are complicated. For example, suppose people do not recognize any of the future taxes implied by current deficits. In that case, partially replacing current tax collections with borrowing makes people feel wealthier today, which induces them to spend more; however, the taxes needed to repay the debt will eventually have to be collected. Because no one anticipated them, they will come as a surprise, inducing people unexpectedly to spend less in whatever period the taxes are levied. A deficit or surplus thus has effects not just in the period when the deficit or surplus occurs, but also in subsequent periods. Predicting the magnitude and timing of the sequence of effects is difficult.

A related issue is the desirability of deliberately using deficits to influence the path of the economy. Under full equivalence of deficit and tax finance, no such thing can be done, of course, because deficits do not affect anything important. Under incomplete equivalence, though, deficits do have effects, as we have just seen. Therefore, it might seem desirable to run up deficits in recessions to encourage people to spend more and to run up surpluses in booms to restrain spending. One problem is that these seemingly desirable effects arise only because people fail to perceive the future taxes implied by deficits; that is, deficits have effects only when they fool people into thinking they suddenly have become wealthier (and conversely for surpluses). Is it desirable to influence the path of the economy by using a policy that is effective only because it deliberately misleads the public? Such a proposition seems difficult to justify. Another problem is that any desirable effects are accompanied by other effects that might not be deemed desirable. When equivalence is incomplete, changing the stock of debt outstanding also changes the interest rate in the same direction. In particular, running a deficit in a recession would raise interest rates, which would reduce investment and economic growth, which in turn would reduce output in the future. Thus, using deficits to stimulate the economy now to ameliorate a recession comes at the cost of reducing output later. Whether that is a good exchange is not obvious and requires justification.

About the Author

John Seater is a professor of economics in the College of Management at North Carolina State University and a Sloan Fellow of the Wharton Financial Institutions Center of the University of Pennsylvania. He was formerly a senior economist in the Research Department of the Federal Reserve Bank of Philadelphia.

Further Reading

Barro, Robert J. "The Ricardian Approach to Budget Deficits." *Journal of Economic Perspectives* 3 (Spring 1989): 37–54.
Butkiewicz, James L. "The Market Value of Outstanding Government Debt: Comment." *Journal of Monetary Economics* 11 (May 1983): 373–379.
Cox, W. Michael. "The Behavior of Treasury Securities: Monthly, 1942–1984." *Journal of Monetary Economics* 16 (September 1985): 227–240.
Eisner, Robert. "Budget Deficits: Rhetoric and Reality." *Journal of Economic Perspectives* 3 (Spring 1989): 73–93.
Ricciuti, Roberto. "Assessing Ricardian Equivalence." *Journal of Economic Surveys* 17 (February 2003): 55–78.
Seater, John J. "The Market Value of Outstanding Government Debt, 1919–1975." *Journal of Monetary Economics* 8 (July 1981): 85–101.
———. "Ricardian Equivalence." *Journal of Economic Literature* 31 (March 1993): 142–190.

Government Growth

Robert Higgs

A modern government is not a single, simple thing. It consists of many institutions, agencies, and activities and includes many separate actors—legislators, administrators, judges, and various ordinary employees. These actors act somewhat independently, and even, at times, at cross-purposes. Because government is complex, no single measure suffices to capture its true "size." Each of the commonly employed measures has serious shortcomings and sometimes can be misleading. Nevertheless, the various measures reveal at least something about the size of government. The most common measure used by economists

is government expenditure as a percentage of gross domestic product (GDP). Sometimes, net national product or national income is used, which make more defensible denominators. Table 1 sketches the long-run growth of government in six countries in terms of this measure.

As the table shows, government expenditures have grown enormously during the past century. As late as 1913, for example, even in a group of seventeen economically advanced countries, government expenditures averaged only about 13 percent of GDP. At most (in Austria, France, and Italy), they came to just 17 percent, and for the United States they were less than 8 percent. Taxation and government employment were at similarly low levels. In contrast, by 1996, government expenditures in the same seventeen countries had reached nearly 46 percent of GDP. Sweden's were the highest, at more than 64 percent, and U.S. expenditures reached more than 32 percent.[1] Taxation, government employment, and other aspects of government had expanded similarly. Moreover, governments have vastly increased the scope and societal penetration of their regulation in ways that spending measures do not reflect. In the United States, for example, private individuals and firms spend hundreds of billions of dollars each year to comply with government regulations aimed at reducing air and water pollution, lowering health risks, and eliminating workplace discrimination against women and members of various ethnic and other protected groups.

Though imperfect, the measures illustrated in the table reflect the size of government. However, they have only a rough association with its scope—that is, the number of

Table 1 Government Expenditure as a Percentage of GDP

	France	Germany	Sweden	Japan	United Kingdom	United States
Circa 1870	12.6	10.0	—	8.8	9.4	7.3
1913	17.0	14.8	10.4	8.3	12.7	7.5
1920	27.6	25.0	10.9	14.8	26.2	12.1
1937	29.0	34.1	16.5	25.4	30.0	19.7
1960	34.6	32.4	31.0	17.5	32.2	27.0
1980	46.1	47.9	60.1	32.0	43.0	31.4
1990	49.8	45.1	59.1	31.3	39.9	32.8
1996	55.0	49.1	64.1	35.9	43.0	32.4

Source: Vito Tanzi and Ludger Schuknecht, *Public Spending in the 20th Century: A Global Perspective* (New York: Cambridge University Press, 2000), p. 6.

1. Vito Tanzi and Ludger Schuknecht, *Public Spending in the 20th Century: A Global Perspective* (New York: Cambridge University Press, 2000), pp. 6–7.

separate matters the government tries to influence or control. Over the very long run, governments have increased in both size and scope, but in any particular short period, the two measures may diverge widely. Likewise, we need to consider, apart from either size or scope, the government's power—its authority and capacity to bring coercive force to bear effectively. Again, over the very long run, most governments have increased in size, scope, and power, but the three dimensions have grown at different rates in particular short intervals. To some extent, governments may substitute growth in one dimension for growth in another; they may augment, say, their scope or power rather than their size. Eventually, however, an increase in one dimension tends to lead to increases in the others. Passage of the Social Security Act in 1935, for example, increased the power and scope of the U.S. government, but not until two decades later did the operation of the Social Security system begin to have a major effect on the magnitude of federal spending.

Crises and the Growth of Government

Superimposed on the century-long trend to bigger government—measured by size, scope, and power—are several episodes of extraordinarily rapid growth associated with crises, especially the two world wars and the Great Depression. Although much of the wartime expansion of government was reversed when the wars ended, not all of it was, and thus each episode had a "ratchet effect," lifting the size of government to a permanently higher level. Wartime expansions of government power tended to become lodged in the statute books, administrative decisions, and judicial rulings, and these legacies fostered the growth of government even during peacetime. New York City's rent controls, for example, date from World War II (see RENT CONTROL). Moreover, crisis-driven changes in the prevailing ideology supported greater long-term growth of government. Many who had opposed "big government" in the United States as late as 1930, for example, became convinced by the fifteen years of activist government during the Great Depression and World War II that government should play a much larger role in economic affairs. One upshot was the Employment Act of 1946, by which the federal government pledged itself to continuing management of the national economy.

Crises promoted the growth of government in other countries, as well. During both world wars, all the belligerents adopted extraordinary measures of economic control to mobilize resources and place them at the government's disposal for war purposes. These measures included price, wage, and rent controls; inflationary increases in the money stock; physical allocations of raw materials and commodities; conscription of labor; industrial takeovers; rationing of consumer goods and transportation services; financial and exchange controls; vast increases in government spending and employment; and increased tax rates and the imposition of new kinds of taxation. On each occasion, the war left institutional and ideological legacies that promoted the subsequent resort to similar measures even during peacetime. As Bruce Porter wrote, "The mass state, the regulatory state, the welfare state—in short, the collectivist state that reigns in Europe today—is an offspring of the total warfare of the industrial age."[2]

The Great Depression elicited similar responses, especially in the United States under Franklin D. Roosevelt's New Deal. Many current welfare-state and regulatory institutions—the Social Security system, the Securities and Exchange Commission, the National Labor Relations Act, to name but a few—originated with the New Deal. Later crises, such as the social and political turbulence associated with the civil rights revolution and the Vietnam War between the early 1960s and the early 1970s, likewise contributed significantly to the expansion of the welfare state, spawning, for example, Medicare, Medicaid, and a host of welfare, antidiscrimination, and environmental regulatory programs that remain in force today.

Trends and crises interact. Because trends bring about the particular preconditions on which each crisis bursts, they affect how each crisis unfolds. And because each crisis leaves the long-run condition of the economic and political systems altered, it affects later trends. Although many economists have dismissed crisis events as "aberrations" or statistical "outliers" in the growth of government, this practice is a serious mistake: the long run, after all, is nothing more than a series of short runs.

Structural Changes Promoting the Growth of Government

In the nineteenth century, a number of interrelated "modernizing" changes began to accelerate: industrialization, urbanization, the relative decline of agricultural output and employment, and a variety of significant improvements in transportation and communication. As these developments proceeded, masses of people, though made better off in the long run, experienced tremendous changes in their way of life. In response, they sought government assistance in order to gain from, or at least to minimize their losses from, the social and economic transformations that swept them along.

2. Bruce Porter, *War and the Rise of the State: The Military Foundations of Modern Politics* (New York: Free Press, 1994), p. 192.

The ongoing structural changes altered the perceived costs and benefits of collective action for all sorts of latent special-interest groups. Thus, for example, the gathering of large workforces in urban factories, mills, and commercial facilities created greater potential for the successful organization of labor unions and working-class political parties. New means of transportation and communication—the railroad and the telegraph, later the telephone and the automobile—reduced the costs of organizing agrarian protest movements and agrarian populist political parties. Urbanization created new demands for government provision of infrastructure such as paved streets, lighting, sewerage, and pure water supply. All such events tended to alter the configuration of political power, encouraging, enlarging, and strengthening various special-interest groups.

The structural transformations, in addition to increasing the demand for government, also increased the supply. When, for example, more people received their income in pecuniary payments traceable in business accounts, as opposed to unrecorded farm income in kind, governments found it easier to collect income taxes. The modern welfare state is often seen as originating in Imperial Germany in the 1880s, when Otto von Bismarck established compulsory accident, sickness, and old-age insurance to divert workers from revolutionary socialism and to purchase their loyalty to the Kaiser's regime. The lesson was not lost on governments elsewhere, and, by 1914, most other Western European countries had enacted similar programs. The U.S. government caught up in 1935, after such policies had been adopted at state and local levels earlier in the twentieth century.

From the mid-nineteenth century onward, collectivist ideologies of various stripes, especially certain forms of socialism, gained greater intellectual and popular followings. Traditional conservatism and classical liberalism increasingly fell out of favor and, with a lag, suffered losses in their political influence. By the early twentieth century, the intellectual cutting edge in all the economically advanced countries had become more or less socialistic (in the United States, in greater part, "Progressive"). The masses also had become more supportive of various socialist or Progressive schemes, from regulation of railway rates to municipal operation of utilities to outright takeovers of industry on a national scale. Not until the 1970s did this collectivist ideological tide begin to turn, and even now, collectivism remains the reigning mode of thought for most intellectuals and political leaders. In the United States, politicians who call themselves conservative today would have been regarded as socialists a century ago. Indeed, quadrennial Socialist Party candidate

Norman Thomas announced in 1956 that he would no longer run for president because even the Republican Party had adopted all of his socialist proposals. And the scope of government has grown enormously since 1956.

Political developments mirrored the changes in the economy and in the dominant ideology. Throughout the nineteenth and twentieth centuries, democracy tended to gain ground. The franchise was widened, and more popular parties, including frankly socialist parties and labor parties closely allied with the unions, gained greater representation in legislatures at all levels of government—more so, however, in Europe than in the United States. Everywhere, the trend toward universal manhood suffrage and, eventually, women's suffrage became seemingly irresistible. We might note that even Adolf Hitler came to power via the ballot box.

Modernizing economic transformation, collectivist ideological drift, and democratic political reconfiguration tended to bring about a changing balance of forces that favored, not always but as a rule, increases in the size, scope, and power of government.

Where We Stand

For more than half a century, the political economy of the economically advanced countries has been rife with interest groups seeking policies that make government bigger. The old fundamental checks on such growth—vestigial allegiance to classical liberal ideology and, in the United States, a Constitution long understood as placing limits on the government's role in economic life—have more or less dissolved as significant obstacles. Intellectual developments during the past thirty years, however, have revived the classical liberals' hope that, ultimately, they may be able to stem the ongoing growth of government that now seems to be an inherent aspect of the workings of the modern political economy.

About the Author
Robert Higgs is senior fellow in political economy at the Independent Institute and editor of the *Independent Review*.

Further Reading
Higgs, Robert. *Crisis and Leviathan: Critical Episodes in the Growth of American Government.* New York: Oxford University Press, 1987.
———. "Eighteen Problematic Propositions in the Analysis of the Growth of Government." *Review of Austrian Economics* 5 (1991): 3–40.
———. "The Ongoing Growth of Government in the Economically Advanced Countries." *Advances in Austrian Economics* 8 (2005): 279–300.

Holcombe, Randall G. *From Liberty to Democracy: The Trans-formation of American Government.* Ann Arbor: University of Michigan Press, 2002.

Jouvenel, Bertrand de. *On Power: The Natural History of Its Growth.* Indianapolis: Liberty Fund, 1993. Originally published in French in 1945.

Mueller, Dennis C. "The Size of Government." In Dennis C. Mueller, *Public Choice II.* New York: Cambridge University Press, 1989. Pp. 320–347.

Porter, Bruce. *War and the Rise of the State: The Military Foundations of Modern Politics.* New York: Free Press, 1994.

Tanzi, Vito, and Ludger Schuknecht. *Public Spending in the 20th Century: A Global Perspective.* New York: Cambridge University Press, 2000.

Twight, Charlotte. *Dependent on D.C.: The Rise of Federal Control over the Lives of Ordinary Americans.* New York: Palgrave, 2002.

Great Depression

Gene Smiley

A worldwide depression struck countries with market economies at the end of the 1920s. Although the Great Depression was relatively mild in some countries, it was severe in others, particularly in the United States, where, at its nadir in 1933, 25 percent of all workers and 37 percent of all nonfarm workers were completely out of work. Some people starved; many others lost their farms and homes. Homeless vagabonds sneaked aboard the freight trains that crossed the nation. Dispossessed cotton farmers, the "Okies," stuffed their possessions into dilapidated Model Ts and migrated to California in the false hope that the posters about plentiful jobs were true. Although the U.S. economy began to recover in the second quarter of 1933, the recovery largely stalled for most of 1934 and 1935. A more vigorous recovery commenced in late 1935 and continued into 1937, when a new depression occurred. The American economy had yet to fully recover from the Great Depression when the United States was drawn into World War II in December 1941. Because of this agonizingly slow recovery, the entire decade of the 1930s in the United States is often referred to as the Great Depression.

The Great Depression is often called a "defining moment" in the twentieth-century history of the United States. Its most lasting effect was a transformation of the role of the federal government in the economy. The long contraction and painfully slow recovery led many in the American population to accept and even call for a vastly expanded role for government, though most businesses resented the growing federal control of their activities. The federal government took over responsibility for the elderly

population with the creation of Social Security and gave the involuntarily unemployed unemployment compensation. The Wagner Act dramatically changed labor negotiations between employers and employees by promoting unions and acting as an arbiter to ensure "fair" labor contract negotiations. All of this required an increase in the size of the federal government. During the 1920s, there were, on average, about 553,000 paid civilian employees of the federal government. By 1939 there were 953,891 paid civilian employees, and there were 1,042,420 in 1940. In 1928 and 1929, federal receipts on the administrative budget (the administrative budget excludes any amounts received for or spent from trust funds and any amounts borrowed or used to pay down the debt) averaged 3.80 percent of GNP while expenditures averaged 3.04 percent of GNP. In 1939, federal receipts were 5.50 percent of GNP, while federal expenditures had tripled to 9.77 percent of GNP. These figures provide an indication of the vast expansion of the federal government's role during the depressed 1930s.

The Great Depression also changed economic thinking. Because many economists and others blamed the depression on inadequate demand, the Keynesian view that government could and should stabilize demand to prevent future depressions became the dominant view in the economics profession for at least the next forty years. Although an increasing number of economists have come to doubt this view, the general public still accepts it.

Interestingly, given the importance of the Great Depression in the development of economic thinking and economic policy, economists do not completely agree on what caused it. Recent research by Peter Temin, Barry Eichengreen, David Glasner, Ben Bernanke, and others has led to an emerging consensus on why the contraction began in 1928 and 1929. There is less agreement on why the contraction phase was longer and more severe in some countries and why the depression lasted so long in some countries, particularly the United States.

The Great Depression that began at the end of the 1920s was a worldwide phenomenon. By 1928, Germany, Brazil, and the economies of Southeast Asia were depressed. By early 1929, the economies of Poland, Argentina, and Canada were contracting, and the U.S. economy followed in the middle of 1929. As Temin, Eichengreen, and others have shown, the larger factor that tied these countries together was the international gold standard.

By 1914, most developed countries had adopted the gold standard with a fixed exchange rate between the national currency and gold—and therefore between national currencies. In World War I, European nations went off the gold standard to print money, and the resulting price inflation drove large amounts of the world's gold to banks in the United States. The United States remained on the gold standard without altering the gold value of the dollar. Investors and others who held gold sent their gold to the United States, where gold maintained its value as a safe and sound investment. At the end of World War I, a few countries, most notably the United States, continued on the gold standard while others temporarily adopted floating exchange rates. The world's international finance center had shifted from London to New York City, and the British were anxious to regain their old status. Some countries pledged to return to the gold standard with devalued currencies, while others followed the British lead and aimed to return to gold at prewar exchange rates.

This was not possible, however. Too much money had been created during the war to allow a return to the gold standard without either large currency devaluations or price deflations. In addition, the U.S. gold stock had doubled to about 40 percent of the world's monetary gold. There simply was not enough monetary gold in the rest of the world to support the countries' currencies at the existing exchange rates. As a result, the leading nations established a gold exchange system whereby the governments of the United States and Great Britain would be willing, at all times, to redeem the dollar and the pound for gold, and other countries would hold much of their international reserves in British pounds or U.S. dollars.

The demand for gold increased as countries returned to the gold standard. Because the franc was undervalued when France returned to the gold standard in June 1928, France began to receive gold inflows. The undervalued franc made French exports less expensive in foreign countries' currencies and made foreign imports into France more expensive in francs. As French exports rose and French imports fell, their international accounts were balanced by gold shipped to France. France's government, contrary to the tenets of the gold standard, did not use these inflows to expand its money supply. In 1928, the Federal Reserve System raised its discount rate—that is, the rate it charged on loans to member banks—in order to raise interest rates in the United States, which would stem the outflow of American gold and dampen the booming stock market. As a result, the United States began to receive shipments of gold. By 1929, as countries around the world lost gold to France and the United States, these countries' governments initiated deflationary policies to stem their gold outflows and remain on the gold standard. These deflationary policies were designed to restrict economic activity and reduce price levels, and that is exactly what they did. Thus began the worldwide Great Depression.

The onset of the contraction led to the end of the stock-market boom and the crash in late October 1929. However, the stock market collapse did not cause the depression; nor can it explain the extraordinary length and depth of the American contraction. In most countries, such as Britain, France, Canada, the Netherlands, and the Nordic countries, the depression was less severe and shorter, often ending by 1931. Those countries did not have the banking and financial crises that the United States did, and most left the gold standard earlier than the United States did. In the United States, in contrast, the contraction continued for four years from the summer of 1929 through the first quarter of 1933. During that time real GNP fell 30.5 percent, wholesale prices fell 30.8 percent, and consumer prices fell 24.4 percent.

In previous depressions, wage rates typically fell 9–10 percent during a one- to two-year contraction; these falling wages made it possible for more workers than otherwise to keep their jobs. However, in the Great Depression, manufacturing firms kept wage rates nearly constant into 1931, something commentators considered quite unusual. With falling prices and constant wage rates, real hourly wages rose sharply in 1930 and 1931. Though some spreading of work did occur, firms primarily laid off workers. As a result, unemployment began to soar amid plummeting production, particularly in the durable manufacturing sector, where production fell 36 percent between the end of 1929 and the end of 1930 and then fell another 36 percent between the end of 1930 and the end of 1931.

Why had wages not fallen as they had in previous contractions? One reason was that President Herbert Hoover prevented them from falling. He had been appalled by the wage rate cuts in the 1920–1921 depression and had preached a "high wage" policy throughout the 1920s. By the late 1920s, many business and labor leaders and academic economists believed that policies to keep wage rates high would maintain workers' level of purchasing, providing the "steadier" markets necessary to thwart economic contractions. When President Hoover organized conferences in December 1929 to urge business, industrial, and labor leaders to hold the line on wage rates and dividends, he found a willing audience. The highly protective Smoot-Hawley Tariff, passed in mid-1930, was supposed to provide protection from lower-cost imports for firms that maintained wage rates. Thus, it was not until well into 1931 that the steadily deteriorating business conditions led the boards of directors of a number of larger firms to begin significant wage rate cuts, often over the protest of the firms' top executives, who had pledged to maintain wage rates.

The Smoot-Hawley Tariff was another piece of Hoover's strategy. Though there was not a general call for tariff increases, Hoover proposed it in 1929 as a means of aiding farmers. He quickly lost control of the bill and it ended up protecting American businesses in general with much less real protection for farmers. Many of the tariff increases in the Smoot-Hawley Tariff were quite large; for example, the tariff on Canadian hard winter wheat rose 40 percent, and that on scientific glass instruments rose from 65 percent to 85 percent. Overall on dutiable imports the tariff rate rose from 40.1 percent to 53.21 percent. There was some explicit retaliation for the American tariff increases such as Spain's Wais Tariff. Some other countries' planned tariff increases were encouraged and probably expedited by the action of the United States.

Firms also heeded Hoover's call to let the contraction fall on profits rather than on dividends. Dividends in 1930 were almost as large as in 1929, but undistributed corporate profits plummeted from $2.8 billion in 1929 to − $2.6 billion in 1930. (These numbers may sound small, but compared with the 1929 U.S. GNP of $103.1 billion, they were substantial.) The value of firms' securities fell sharply, leading to a significant deterioration in the portfolios of banks. As conditions worsened and banks' losses increased, bank runs and bank failures increased. The first major bank runs and failures occurred in the Southeast in November 1930; these were followed by more runs and failures in December. There was another flurry of bank runs and bank failures in the late spring and early summer of 1931. After Great Britain left the gold standard in September 1931, the Federal Reserve System initiated relatively large increases in the discount rate to stem the gold outflow. Overseas investors in nations still on the gold standard expected the United States to either devalue the dollar or go off the gold standard as Great Britain had done. The result would be that the dollars they held, or their dollar-denominated securities, would be worth less. To prevent this they sold dollars to obtain gold from the United States. The Fed's policy moves gave overseas investors confidence that the United States would honor its gold commitment. The rise in American interest rates also made it more costly to sell American assets for dollars to redeem in gold. The resulting rise in interest rates caused not only more business failures, but also a sharp rise in bank failures. In the late spring and early summer of 1932, the Federal Reserve System finally undertook open market purchases, bringing some signs of relief and possible recovery to the beleaguered American economy.

Hoover's fiscal policy accelerated the decline. In December 1929, as a means of demonstrating the administration's faith in the economy, Hoover had reduced all 1929 income tax rates by 1 percent because of the continuing budget surpluses. By 1930 the surplus had turned into a deficit that grew rapidly as the economy contracted. By the end of 1931 Hoover had decided to recommend a large tax increase in an attempt to balance the budget; Congress approved the tax increase in 1932. Personal exemptions were reduced sharply to increase the number of taxpayers, and rates were sharply increased. The lowest marginal rate rose from 1.125 percent to 4.0 percent, and the top marginal rate rose from 25 percent on taxable income in excess of $100,000 to 63 percent on taxable income in excess of $1 million as the rates were made much more progressive. We now understand that such a huge tax increase does not promote recovery during a contraction. By reducing households' disposable income, it led to a reduction in household spending and a further contraction in economic activity.

The Fed's expansionary monetary policy ended in the early summer of 1932. After his election in November 1932, President-elect Roosevelt refused to outline his policies or endorse Hoover's, and he refused to deny that he would devalue the dollar against gold after he took office in March 1933. Bank runs and bank failures resumed with a vengeance, and American dollars began to be redeemed for gold as the gold outflow resumed. As financial conditions worsened in January and February 1933, state governments began declaring banking holidays, closing down states' entire financial sectors. Roosevelt's national banking holiday stopped the runs and banking failures and finally ended the contraction.

Between 1929 and 1933, 10,763 of the 24,970 commercial banks in the United States failed. As the public increasingly held more currency and fewer deposits, and as banks built up their excess reserves, the money supply fell 30.9 percent from its 1929 level. Though the Federal Reserve System did increase bank reserves, the increases were far too small to stop the fall in the money supply. As businesses saw their lines of credit and money reserves fall with bank closings, and consumers saw their bank deposit wealth tied up in drawn-out bankruptcy proceedings, spending fell, worsening the collapse in the Great Depression.

The national banking holiday ended the protracted banking crisis, began to restore the public's confidence in banks and the economy, and initiated a recovery from April through September 1933. President Roosevelt came into office proposing a New Deal for Americans, but his advisers believed, mistakenly, that excessive competition had led to overproduction, causing the depression. The centerpieces of the New Deal were the Agricultural Adjustment Act (AAA) and the National Recovery Administration (NRA), both of which were aimed at reducing production and raising wages and prices. Reduced production, of course, is what happens in depressions, and it never made sense to try to get the country out of depression by reducing production further. In its zeal, the administration apparently did not consider the elementary impossibility of raising *all* real wage rates and *all* real prices.

The AAA immediately set out to slaughter six million baby pigs and reduce breeding sows to reduce pork production and raise prices. Since cotton plantings were thought to be excessive, cotton farmers were paid to plow under one-quarter of the forty million acres of cotton to reduce marketed production to boost prices. Most of the payments went to the landowners, not the tenants, making conditions desperate for tenant farmers. Though landowners were supposed to share the payments with their tenant farmers, they were not legally obligated to do so and most did not. As a result, tenant farmers, and especially black tenants, who were more easily discriminated against, received none of the payments and less or no income from cotton production after large portions of the crop were plowed under. Where persuasion was ineffective in inducing the many independent farmers to reduce production, the federal government intended to mandate production cutbacks and purchase the product to take it off the market and raise prices.

The NRA was a vast experiment in cartelizing American industry. Code authorities in each industry were set up to determine production and investment, as well as to standardize firm practices and costs. The entire apparatus was aimed at raising prices and reducing, not increasing, production and investment. As the NRA codes began to take effect in the fall of 1933, they had precisely that effect. The recovery that had seemed so promising in the summer largely stopped, and there was little increase in economic activity from the fall of 1933 through midsummer 1935. Enforcement of the codes was sporadic, disagreement over the codes increased, and, in smaller, more competitive industries, fewer firms adhered to the codes. The Supreme Court ruled the NRA unconstitutional on May 27, 1935, and the AAA unconstitutional on January 6, 1936. Released from the shackles of the NRA, American industry began to expand production. By the fall of 1935 a vigorous recovery was under way.

The introduction of the NRA had initially brought about a sharp increase in money and real wage rates as firms attempted to comply with the NRA's blanket code. As firms' enthusiasm for the NRA waned, money wage rates increased little and real average wage rates actually fell slightly in 1934 and early 1935. In addition, many workers decided not to join independent labor unions. These factors helped the recovery. Unhappy with the lack of union power, however, Senator Robert Wagner, in the summer of 1935, authored the National Labor Relations Act to ensure that union members could force other workers to join

their unions with a simple majority vote, thus effectively monopolizing the labor force. Internal dissension and the new Congress of Industrial Organizations' (CIO) development of strategies to use the new law kept labor unions from taking advantage of the new act until late in 1936. In the first half of 1937, the CIO's massive organizing drives led to labor union recognition at many large firms. Generally, the new contracts raised hourly wage rates and created overtime wage rates as real hourly labor costs surged.

Several other factors also pushed up real labor costs. One factor was the new Social Security taxes instituted in 1936 and 1937. Also, Roosevelt had pushed through a new tax on undistributed corporate profits, expecting this to cause firms to pay out undistributed profits in dividends. Though some firms did pay out part of the retained earnings in larger dividends, others, such as the firms in the steel industry, also paid bonuses and raised wage rates to avoid paying their retained earnings in new taxes. As these three policies came together, real hourly labor costs jumped without corresponding increases in demand or prices, and firms responded by reducing production and laying off employees.

The second major policy change was in monetary policy. Following the end of the contraction, banks, as a precaution against bank runs, had begun to hold large excess reserves. Officials at the Federal Reserve System knew that if banks used a large percentage of those excess reserves to increase lending, the money supply would quickly expand and price inflation would follow. Their studies suggested that the excess reserves were distributed widely across banks, and they assumed that these reserves were due to the low level of loan demand. Because banks were not borrowing at the discount window and the Fed had no bonds to sell on the open market, its only tool to reduce excess reserves was the new one of varying reserve requirements. Between August 1, 1936, and May 1, 1937, in three steps, the Fed doubled reserve requirements for all classes of member banks, wiping out much of the excess reserves, especially at the larger banks. The banks, burned by their lack of excess reserves in the early 1930s, responded by beginning to restore the excess reserves, which entailed reducing loans. Within eighteen months, excess reserves were almost as large as before the reserve requirement increases, and, necessarily, the stock of money was lower.

By June 1937, the recovery—during which the unemployment rate had fallen to 12 percent—was over. Two policies, labor cost increases and a contractionary monetary policy, caused the economy to contract further. Although the contraction ended around June 1938, the ensuing recovery was quite slow. The average rate of unemployment for all of 1938 was 19.1 percent, compared with an average unemployment rate for all of 1937 of 14.3 percent. Even in 1940, the unemployment rate still averaged 14.6 percent.

Why was the recovery from the Great Depression so slow? A number of economists now argue that the NRA and monetary policy were important factors. Some maintain that Roosevelt's vacillating policies and new federal regulations hindered recovery (Gary Dean Best, Richard Vedder and Lowell Gallaway, and Gary Walton), while others emphasize monetary factors (Milton Friedman and Anna Schwartz, Christian Saint-Etienne, and Barry Eichengreen). The New Deal's NRA has received much criticism (Gary Dean Best, Gene Smiley, Richard Vedder and Lowell Gallaway, Gary Walton, and Michael Weinstein). A now discredited explanation from Alvin Hansen argued that the United States had exhausted its investment opportunities. E. Cary Brown, Larry Peppers, and Thomas Renaghan emphasize federal fiscal policies that were a drag on the return to full employment. Michael Bernstein argues that investment problems retarded the recovery because the older established industries could not generate sufficient investment while newer, growing industries had trouble obtaining investment funds in the depressed environment. Alexander Field argues that the uncontrolled housing investment of the 1920s severely reduced housing investment in the 1930s.

One of the most coherent explanations, which pulls together several of these themes, is what economic historian Robert Higgs calls "regime uncertainty." According to Higgs, Roosevelt's New Deal led business leaders to question whether the current "regime" of private property rights in their firms' capital and its income stream would be protected. They became less willing, therefore, to invest in assets with long lives. Roosevelt had first suspended the antitrust laws so that American businesses would cooperate in government-instigated cartels; he then switched to using the antitrust laws to prosecute firms for cooperating. New taxes had been imposed, and some were then removed; increasing regulation of businesses had reduced businesses' ability to act independently and raise capital; and new legislation had reduced their freedom in hiring and employing labor. Public opinion surveys of business at the end of the 1930s provided evidence of this regime uncertainty. Public opinion polls in March and May 1939 asked whether the attitude of the Roosevelt administration toward business was delaying recovery, and 54 and 53 percent, respectively, said *yes* while 26 and 31 percent said *no*. Fifty-six percent believed that in ten years there would be more government control of business while only 22 percent thought there would be less. Sixty-five percent of executives surveyed thought that the Roosevelt administration policies had so affected business confidence that the recovery had been seriously held back. Initially many firms were reluctant to engage in war contracts. The vast majority believed that Roosevelt's administration was strongly antibusiness, and this discouraged practical cooperation with Washington on rearmament.

It is commonly argued that World War II provided the stimulus that brought the American economy out of the Great Depression. The number of unemployed workers declined by 7,050,000 between 1940 and 1943, but the number in military service rose by 8,590,000. The reduction in unemployment can be explained by the draft, not by the economic recovery. The rise in real GNP presents similar problems. Most estimates show declines in real consumption spending, which means that consumers were worse off during the war. Business investment fell during the war. Government spending on the war effort exceeded the expansion in real GNP. These figures are suspect, however, because we know that government estimates of the value of munitions spending, to name one major area, were increasingly exaggerated as the war progressed. In fact, the extensive price controls, rationing, and government control of production render data on GNP, consumption, investment, and the price level less meaningful. How can we establish a consistent price index when government mandates eliminated the production of most consumer durable goods? What does the price of, say, gasoline mean when it is arbitrarily held at a low level and gasoline purchases are rationed to address the shortage created by the price controls? What does the price of new tires mean when no new tires are produced for consumers? For consumers, the recovery came with the war's end, when they could again buy products that were unavailable during the war and unaffordable during the 1930s.

Could the Great Depression happen again? It could, but such an event is unlikely because the Federal Reserve Board is unlikely to sit idly by while the money supply falls by one-third. The wisdom gained in the years since the 1930s probably gives our policymakers enough insight to make decisions that will keep the economy out of such a major depression.

About the Author

Gene Smiley is an emeritus professor of economics at Marquette University.

Further Reading

Bernstein, Michael. *The Great Depression: Delayed Recovery and Economic Change in America, 1929–1939.* New York: Cambridge University Press, 1987.

Best, Gary Dean. *Pride, Prejudice, and Politics: Roosevelt Versus Recovery, 1933–1938.* New York: Praeger, 1991.

Bordo, Michael D., Claudia Goldin, and Eugene N. White, eds. *The Defining Moment: The Great Depression and the American Economy in the Twentieth Century.* Chicago: University of Chicago Press, 1998.

Brown, E. Cary. "Fiscal Policy in the Thirties: A Reappraisal." *American Economic Review* 46 (December 1956): 857–879.

Brunner, Karl, ed. *The Great Depression Revisited.* Boston: Martinus Nijhoff, 1981.

Cole, Harold L., and Lee E. Ohanian. "New Deal Policies and the Persistence of the Great Depression: A General Equilibrium Analysis." *Journal of Political Economy* 112 (August 2004): 779–816.

Eichengreen, Barry. *Golden Fetters: The Gold Standard and the Great Depression, 1919–1939.* New York: Oxford University Press, 1992.

Field, Alexander J. "Uncontrolled Land Development and the Duration of the Depression in the United States." *Journal of Economic History* 52 (June 1992): 785–805.

Friedman, Milton, and Anna Jacobson Schwartz. *A Monetary History of the United States, 1867–1960.* Princeton: Princeton University Press, 1963.

Glasner, David. *Free Banking and Monetary Reform.* New York: Cambridge University Press, 1989.

Hall, Thomas, and J. David Ferguson. *The Great Depression: An International Disaster of Perverse Economic Policies.* Ann Arbor: University of Michigan Press, 1998.

Hansen, Alvin. *Full Recovery or Stagnation?* New York: Norton, 1938.

Higgs, Robert. *Crisis and Leviathan: Critical Episodes in the Growth of American Government.* New York: Oxford University Press, 1987.

———. "Regime Uncertainty: Why the Great Depression Lasted So Long and Why Prosperity Returned After the War." *Independent Review* 1 (Spring 1997): 561–590.

———. "Wartime Prosperity? A Reassessment of the U.S. Economy in the 1940s." *Journal of Economic History* 52 (March 1992): 41–60.

O'Brien, Anthony Patrick. "A Behavioral Explanation for Nominal Wage Rigidity During the Great Depression." *Quarterly Journal of Economics* 104 (November 1989): 719–735.

Peppers, Larry. "Full-Employment Surplus Analysis and Structural Change: The 1930s." *Explorations in Economic History* 10 (Winter 1973): 197–210.

Renaghan, Thomas. "A New Look at Fiscal Policy in the 1930s." *Research in Economic History* 11 (1988): 171–183.

Saint-Etienne, Christian. *The Great Depression, 1929–1938: Lessons for the 1980s.* Stanford: Hoover Institution Press, 1984.

Smiley, Gene. *Rethinking the Great Depression: A New View of Its Causes and Consequences.* Chicago: Ivan R. Dee, 2002.

Temin, Peter. *Did Monetary Forces Cause the Great Depression?* New York: Norton, 1976.

———. *Lessons from the Great Depression.* Cambridge: MIT Press, 1989.

———. "Socialism and Wages in the Recovery from the Great Depression in the United States and Germany." *Journal of Economic History* 50 (June 1990): 297–308.

Temin, Peter, and Barrie Wigmore. "The End of One Big Deflation." *Explorations in Economic History* 27 (October 1990): 483–502.

Vedder, Richard K., and Lowell P. Gallaway. *Out of Work: Unemployment and Government in Twentieth-Century America.* New York: Holmes and Meier, 1993.

Walton, Gary M., ed. *Regulatory Change in an Atmosphere of Crisis: Current Implications of the Roosevelt Years.* New York: Academic Press, 1979.

Weinstein, Michael. *Recovery and Redistribution Under the NIRA.* Amsterdam: North-Holland, 1980.

Wright, Gavin. "The Political Economy of New Deal Spending: An Econometric Analysis." *Review of Economics and Statistics* 56 (February 1974): 30–38.

Health Care

Michael A. Morrisey

Is Health Care Different?

Health care is different from other goods and services: the health care product is ill-defined, the outcome of care is uncertain, large segments of the industry are dominated by nonprofit providers, and payments are made by third parties such as the government and private insurers. Many of these factors are present in other industries as well, but in no other industry are they *all* present. It is the interaction of these factors that tends to make health care unique.

Even so, it is easy to make too much of the distinctiveness of the health care industry. Various players in the industry—consumers and providers, to name two—respond to incentives just as in other industries.

Federal and state governments are a major health care spender. Together they account for 46 percent of national health care expenditures; nearly three-quarters of this is attributable to Medicare and Medicaid. Private health insurance pays for more than 35 percent of spending, and out-of-pocket consumer expenditures account for another 14 percent.[1]

Traditional national income accounts substantially understate the role of government spending in the health care sector. Most Americans under age sixty-five receive their health insurance through their employers. This form of employee compensation is not subject to income or payroll taxes, and as a result, the tax code subsidizes employer

1. Katharine Levit et al., "Health Spending Rebound Continues in 2002," *Health Affairs* 23, no. 1 (2004): 147–159.

purchase of employee health insurance. The Joint Economic Committee of the U.S. Congress estimated that in 2002, the federal tax revenue forgone as a result of this tax "subsidy" equaled $137 billion.[2]

Risk and Insurance

Risk of illness and the attendant cost of care lead to the demand for health insurance. Conventional economics argues that the probability of purchasing health insurance will be greater when the consumer is particularly risk averse, when the potential loss is large, when the probability of loss is neither too large nor too small, and when incomes are lower. The previously mentioned tax incentive for the purchase of health insurance increases the chances that health insurance will be purchased. Indeed, the presence of a progressive income tax system implies that higher income consumers will buy even more insurance.

The 2002 Current Population Survey reports that nearly 83 percent of the under-age-sixty-five population in the United States had health insurance. More than three-quarters of these people had coverage through an employer, fewer than 10 percent purchased coverage on their own, and the remainder had coverage through a government program. Virtually all of those aged sixty-five and older had coverage through Medicare. Nonetheless, approximately 43.3 million Americans did not have health insurance in 2002.[3]

The key effect of health insurance is to lower the out-of-pocket price of health services. Consumers purchase goods and services up to the point where the marginal benefit of the item is just equal to the value of the resources given up. In the absence of insurance a consumer may pay sixty dollars for a physician visit. With insurance the consumer is responsible for paying only a small portion of the bill, perhaps only a ten-dollar copay. Thus, health insurance gives consumers an incentive to use health services that have only a very small benefit even if the full cost of the service (the sum of what the consumer and the insurer must pay) is much greater. This overuse of medical care in response to an artificially low price is an example of "moral hazard" (see INSURANCE).

Strong evidence of the moral hazard from health insurance comes from the RAND Health Insurance Experiment, which randomly assigned families to health insurance plans with various coinsurance and deductible amounts. Over the course of the study, those required to pay none of the bill used 37 percent more physician services than those who paid 25 percent of the bill. Those with "free care" used 67 percent more than those who paid virtually all of the bill. Prescription drugs were about as price sensitive as physician services. Hospital services were less price sensitive, but ambulatory mental health services were substantially more responsive to lower prices than were physician visits.[4]

Is the Spending Worth It?

National health care spending in 2002 was $1.55 trillion, 14.9 percent of GDP. By comparison, the manufacturing sector constituted only 12.9 percent of GDP. Adjusted for inflation, health care spending in the United States increased by nearly 102 percent over the 1993–2002 period. Hospital services reflect 31 percent of spending; professional services, 22 percent; and drugs, medical supplies, and equipment reflect nearly 14 percent.

David Cutler and Mark McClellan note that between 1950 and 1990 the PRESENT VALUE of per person medical spending in the United States increased by $35,000 and life expectancy increased by seven years. An additional year of life is conventionally valued at $100,000, and so, using a 3 percent real interest rate, the present value of the extra years is $135,000. Thus the extra spending on medical care is worth the cost if medical spending accounts for more than one-quarter ($35,000/$130,000) of the increase in longevity. Researchers have found that the substantial improvements in the treatment of heart attacks and low-birth-weight births over this period account, just by themselves, for one-quarter of the overall mortality reduction. Thus, the increased health spending seems to have been worth the cost.[5] This does not mean that there is no moral hazard. Much spending is on things that have no effect on mortality and little effect on quality of life, and these are encouraged when the patient pays only a fraction of the bill.

Taxes and Employer-Sponsored Health Insurance

There are three reasons why most people under age sixty-five get their health insurance through an employer. First, employed people, on average, are healthier than those who

2. U.S. Congress, Joint Economic Committee, "How the Tax Exclusion Shaped Today's Private Health Insurance Market," December 17, 2003.

3. Paul Fronstin, "Sources of Health Insurance and Characteristics of the Uninsured: Analysis of the March 2003 Current Population Survey," *EBRI Issue Brief,* no. 264 (Washington, D.C.: Employee Benefit Research Institute, 2003).

4. Joseph P. Newhouse et al., *Free for All? Lessons from the RAND Health Insurance Experiment* (Cambridge: Harvard University Press, 1993).

5. David A. Cutler and Mark McClellan, "Is Technology Change in Medicine Worth It?" *Health Affairs* 20, no.5 (2001): 11–29.

are unemployed; therefore, they have fewer insurance claims. Second, the sales and administrative costs of group policies are lower. Third, health insurance premiums paid by an employer are not taxed. Thus, employers and their employees have a strong incentive to substitute broader and deeper health insurance coverage for money wages. Someone in the 27 percent federal income tax bracket, paying 5 percent state income tax and 7.65 percent in Social Security and Medicare taxes, would find that an extra dollar of employer-sponsored health insurance effectively costs him less than sixty-one cents.

Workers, not employers, ultimately pay for the net-of-taxes cost of employer-sponsored health insurance. Employees are essentially paid the value of what they produce. Compensation can take many forms: money wages, vacation days, pensions, and health insurance coverage. If health insurance is added to the compensation bundle or if the health insurance becomes more expensive, something else must be removed from the bundle. Perhaps the pension plan is reduced; perhaps a wage increase is smaller than it otherwise would have been.

A recent study demonstrates the effects of rising insurance premiums on wages and other benefits in a large firm. This firm provided employees with wages and "benefits credits" that they could spend on health insurance, pensions, vacation days, and so on. Workers could trade wages for additional benefits credits, and vice versa. Health insurance premiums on all plans increased each year. When all health insurance premiums increased, the workers switched to relatively less expensive health plans, took fewer other benefits, and reduced their take-home pay. A 10 percent increase in health insurance premiums led to increased insurance expenditures of only 5.2 percent because many workers shifted to relatively cheaper health plans offered by the employer. The bulk of these higher expenditures (71 percent) was paid for with lower take-home pay; 29 percent by giving up some other benefits.[6] Thus, if insurance premiums increased, on average, by $200, the typical worker spent $104 more on coverage and paid for this by reducing take-home pay by $74 and giving up $30 in other benefits.

These so-called compensating wage differentials, reductions in wages due to higher nonwage benefits, have important policy implications. They imply, for example, that a governmental requirement that all employers provide health insurance will result in lower wages for the affected workers.

Growth and Effects of Managed Care
The health care industry has undergone fundamental changes since 1990 as a result, in large part, of the growth of managed care. As recently as 1993, 49 percent of insured workers had coverage through a conventional insurance plan; in 2002 only 5 percent did so. The rest were in health maintenance organizations (HMOs), preferred provider organizations (PPOs), or other forms of managed care. Unlike conventional insurance plans, managed care plans provide coverage only for care received from a selected set of providers in a community. The basic idea with managed care is to limit the moral hazard that comes from overuse of health care, thus keeping insurance premiums lower than otherwise and potentially making the insured person, his employer, and the insurance company better off. An HMO typically provides coverage only if the care is delivered by a member of its hospital, physician, or pharmacy panel. PPOs allow subscribers to use nonpanel providers, but only if the subscriber pays a higher out-of-pocket price. Conventional plans allow subscribers to use any licensed provider in the community, usually for the same out-of-pocket price.

Managed care changed the nature of competition among providers. Prior to the growth of managed care, hospitals competed for patients (and their physicians) by providing higher-quality care, more amenities, and more services. This so-called medical arms race resulted in the unusual economic circumstance that more hospitals in a market resulted in higher, not lower, prices. Conventional insurers (as well as government programs) essentially paid providers on a cost basis. The more that was spent, the more that was received. So providers rationally competed along dimensions that mattered. Managed care changed this by the use of "selective contracting." Not every provider in the community got a contract from the managed care plan. Contracts were awarded based on quality, amenities, services, and *price*. Research has demonstrated that in the presence of selective contracting, the usual laws of economics apply: the presence of more providers in a market results in lower prices, more idle capacity results in lower prices, and a larger market share on the part of an insurer results in lower prices paid to providers. As a consequence, health care costs increased less rapidly than they otherwise would have and health care markets have become much more competitive.[7]

6. Dana P. Goldman, N. Sood, and Arlene A. Leibowitz, "The Reallocation of Compensation in Response to Health Insurance Premium Increases," NBER Working Paper no. 9540, National Bureau of Economic Research, Cambridge, Mass., 2003.

7. Michael A. Morrisey, "Competition in Hospital and Health Insurance Markets: A Review and Research Agenda," *Health Services Research* 36, no. 1, pt. 2 (2001): 191–221.

The Inefficiency of Socialized Medicine

Patricia M. Danzon

Although other countries with more centralized government control over health budgets appear to have controlled costs more successfully, that does not mean that they have produced a more efficient result. In any case, reported statistics may be misleading. Efficient resource allocation requires that resources be spent on medical care as long as the marginal benefit exceeds the marginal cost. Marginal benefits are very hard to measure, but certainly they include more subjective values than the crude measures of morbidity and mortality that are widely used in international comparisons.

In addition to forgone benefits, government health care systems have hidden costs. Any insurance system, public or private, must raise revenues, pay providers, control moral hazard, and bear some nondiversifiable risk. In a private insurance market such as that in the United States, the costs of performing these functions can be measured by insurance overhead costs of premium collection, claims administration, and return on capital. Public monopoly insurers must also perform these functions, but their costs tend to be hidden and do not appear in health expenditure accounts. Tax financing entails deadweight costs that have been estimated at more than seventeen cents per dollar raised—far higher than the 1 percent of premiums required by private insurers to collect premiums.

The use of tight physician fee schedules gives doctors incentives to reduce their own time and other resources per patient visit; patients must therefore make multiple visits to receive the same total care. But these hidden patient time costs do not appear in standard measures of health care spending.

Both economic theory and a careful review of the evidence that goes beyond simple accounting measures suggest that a government monopoly of financing and provision achieves a less efficient allocation of resources to medical care than would a well-designed private market system. The performance of the current U.S. health care system does not provide a guide to the potential functioning of a well-designed private market system. Cost and waste in the current U.S. system are unnecessarily high because of tax and regulatory policies that impede efficient cost control by private insurers, while at the same time the system fails to provide for universal coverage.

Excerpt from Patricia M. Danzon, "Health Care Industry," in David R. Henderson, ed., *The Fortune Encyclopedia of Economics* (New York: Warner Books, 1993), 679–680.

Managed care savings have been called illusionary. The plans have been accused of enrolling healthier individuals and providing less intense care. It is true that managed care plans disproportionately attract healthier subscribers. If this was all there was to managed care, the differences in costs between managed care and conventional coverage *would* be illusionary. However, a 2001 study demonstrates that the innovation offered by managed care is its ability to negotiate lower prices. The authors examined the mix of enrollees, the service intensity, and the prices paid for care among Massachusetts public employees in conventional and HMO plans. The focus was on enrollees with one of eight medical conditions. Across these eight conditions, the HMOs had per capita plan costs that were $107 lower, on average. Fifty-one percent of the difference was attributable to the younger, healthier individuals the HMOs enrolled; 5 percent was attributable to less-intense treatments; and 45 percent of the difference was attributable to lower negotiated prices. The conventional plan paid more than $72,600, on average, for coronary artery bypass graft surgery while the HMO plans in the study, on average, paid less than $52,000.[8]

Selective contracting arguably led to the slower rate of increase in health insurance premiums through the mid-1990s. Since that time insurance premiums have increased more rapidly. Health economists believe that this change is a result of consumers' unwillingness to accept the limited provider choice that comes with selective contracting, as well as from the reduction in competition that has resulted from consolidation in the health care industry.

Government-Provided Health Insurance

Medicare is a federal tax-subsidy program that provides health insurance for some forty million persons aged sixty-five and older in the United States. Medicare Part A, which

---

8. Daniel Altman et al., "Enrollee Mix, Treatment Intensity, and Cost in Competing Indemnity and HMO Plans," *Journal of Health Economics* 22, no. 1 (2003): 23–45.

provides hospital and limited nursing home care, is funded by payroll taxes imposed on both employees and employers. Part B covers physician services. Beneficiaries pay 25 percent of these costs through a monthly premium; the other 75 percent of Part B costs is paid from general tax revenues. Part C, now called "Medicare-Advantage," allows beneficiaries to join Medicare-managed care plans. These plans are paid from Part A and Part B revenues. Part D is the new Medicare prescription drug program enacted in 2003 but not fully implemented until 2006.

In 1983 Medicare began paying hospitals on a diagnosis-related group (DRG) basis; that is, payments were made for more than five hundred specific inpatient diagnoses. Prior to DRGs, hospitals were paid on an allowable cost basis. The DRG system changed the economic incentives facing hospitals, reduced the average length of stay, and reduced Medicare expenditures relative to the old system. In 1999 Medicare began paying physicians based on a fee schedule derived from a resource-based relative value scale (RBRVS) that ranks procedures based on their complexity, effort, and practice costs. As such, the RBRVS harkens back to the discredited labor theory of value. Medicare payments, therefore, do not necessarily reflect market prices and are likely to over- or underpay providers relative to a market or competitive bidding approach. Thus, it is not surprising that physicians have argued that the system pays less than costs and some have begun to refuse to accept new Medicare patients. Moreover, the Medicare program effectively prohibits physicians from accepting payments higher than the fee schedule from Medicare beneficiaries. The result is a system of price controls that will result in shortages whenever the fee schedule is below the market-clearing price.

Medicaid, a federal-state health care program for the poor, covers more than forty million people. The federal government pays 50–85 percent of the cost of the program depending on the relative per capita income of the state. States have considerable flexibility in determining eligibility and the extent of coverage within broad federal guidelines. Medicaid is essentially three distinct programs—one for low-income pregnant women and children, one for the disabled, and one for nursing home care for the elderly. Approximately 47 percent of recipients are children, but the aged and disabled receive more than 70 percent of the payments. Much of this is due to nursing home expenditures; Medicaid provides approximately 40 percent of nursing home revenue.

State governments have gamed the system to obtain federal matching Medicaid funds. The state would tax a hospital or nursing home based on Medicaid days of care or the number of licensed beds. It would then match the taxes with federal matching dollars at a ratio of two to one or three to one, and essentially return the taxed dollars to the provider. When the federal government said this was not permissible, the states dropped the taxes and asked for "provider contributions" from the hospitals, nursing homes, and so on. Most states used the new federal money for health care services. Others simply reduced general fund expenditures by the amount of the new federal dollars—essentially using federal Medicaid dollars to fund road construction and other state functions. Neither "taxes" nor "contributions" may now be used. The states do, however, funnel state mental health and other state health program dollars through Medicaid to take advantage of the matching grants.

The expansion of the Medicaid program, particularly for children, also has had the effect of crowding out private coverage. One estimate suggests that for each two new Medicaid children enrolled, one child lost private coverage.[9]

Regulation and the Health Care Market

The health care industry is one of the most heavily regulated industries in the United States. These regulations stem from efforts to ensure quality, to facilitate the government's role as purchaser of care, and to respond to provider efforts to increase the demand for their services. Hospitals and nursing homes are licensed by the state and must comply with quality and staffing requirements to maintain eligibility for participation in federal programs. Physicians and other health professionals are licensed by the states. Prescription drugs and medical devices are regulated by the Food and Drug Administration (see PHARMACEUTICALS: ECONOMICS AND REGULATION). Some state governments require government permission before allowing a hospital or nursing home to be built or extensively changed. All of the above regulations restrict supply and raise the price of health care; interestingly, those who lobby for such regulations are medical providers, not consumers, presumably because they want to limit competition.

Some state governments limit the extent to which managed care plans may selectively contract with providers. All state governments have imposed laws governing the content of insurance packages and the factors that may be used to determine insurance rates. While these may enhance quality, they do impose costs that raise the price of health insurance and increase the number of uninsured.

9. David Cutler and Jonathan Gruber, "Medicaid and Private Health Insurance: Evidence and Implications," *Health Affairs* 16, no. 1 (1997): 194–200.

In testimony before the Joint Economic Committee of the Congress, one analyst reported the annual net cost of regulation in the health care industry to be $128 billion.[10]

Industry Structure

In 2002, there were 4,949 nonfederal short-term hospitals in the United States. Over the last decade the hospital sector has been consolidating: the number of hospitals declined by 6.4 percent and hospital beds per capita declined by more than 18 percent.[11] In addition, the sector has been reorganizing itself into systems of hospitals that are commonly owned or managed. Nearly 46 percent of hospitals were part of a system in 2002, up from only 32 percent in 1994. The hospital sector has long been dominated by not-for-profit organizations. Only 14.4 percent of the industry is legally for-profit; this ratio has been constant for the last decade. There is some evidence that the consolidation and reorganization have been a reaction to the competition generated by the selective contracting actions of managed care. In 2001, the average cost of a stay at a government hospital was $7,400—24 percent more than at a private for-profit hospital. A study released in 2000 found that for-profit hospitals offer better-quality care.[12]

There were 272 private sector physicians per 100,000 population in the United States in 2002, an 8 percent increase since 1993, but a decline since 2000. There has been a steady decline in the proportion of physicians in solo practice; by 2001 more than three-quarters of physicians were in group practice or were employees.[13] Physicians have been accused of inducing demand for their services because of the information asymmetry they hold relative to their patients. However, this argument has lost much of its impact in the last decade. Physicians' inflation-adjusted average income has declined. Primary care physician incomes declined by 6.4 percent between 1995 and 1999, and specialist income declined by 4 percent.[14]

Industry Outlook

The industry is faced with rising health care costs and an increasing number of uninsured. In the private sector the cost increases have led to an interest in consumer-directed health care. The idea is to provide health insurance payments only for expenditures in excess of a high deductible. The expectation is that consumers who must pay the full price for most health services will buy such services only when the expected benefits are at least equal to the full costs. Others see the reemergence of more aggressive selective contracting by managed care firms as a way to keep costs under control. The government is expected to be more aggressive in promoting competition among providers as well.

The retirement of the baby boom generation will put more pressure on Medicare. Indeed, the Medicare trustees reported in 2004 that the costs of the Medicare program will exceed those of Social Security by 2024. Medicare Part A—hospital coverage—is estimated to be unable to cover its expenses starting in 2019.[15] Interestingly, the 5 percent of Medicare fee-for-service beneficiaries who die each year account for one-fourth of all Medicare inpatient expenditures.[16] Tax increases, benefit reductions, and/or wholesale reform of the program will have to occur. The number of uninsured will increase if health insurance continues to be more expensive. Some have proposed expansions of existing public programs; others have proposed "refundable" tax credits as a means of subsidizing targeted groups.[17] Still others argue for reductions in regulations and a greater reliance on consumer-directed health plans as a means of lowering costs and expanding insurance coverage (see HEALTH INSURANCE).

About the Author

Michael A. Morrisey is a professor of health economics in the School of Public Health and director of the Lister Hill Center for Health Policy at the University of Alabama at Birmingham.

10. Christopher J. Conover, Testimony before the Joint Economic Committee, U.S. Congress, May 13, 2004.

11. American Hospital Association, *Hospital Statistics 2004* (Chicago: AHA, 2004).

12. Mark McClellan and Douglas Staiger, "Comparing Hospital Quality at For-Profit and Not-for-Profit Hospitals," NBER Working Paper no. 7324, National Bureau of Economic Research, Cambridge, Mass., 2000.

13. Kaiser Family Foundation, *Trends and Indicators in the Changing Health Care Marketplace, 2004 Update,* May 19, 2004, online at: http://www.kff.org/insurance/7031/index.cfm.

14. Marie C. Reed and Paul B. Ginsburg, *Behind the Times: Physician Income, 1995–1999,* Center for Studying Health System Change, Data Bulletin 24, March 2003.

15. Centers for Medicare and Medicaid Services, *2004 Annual Report of the Board of Trustees of the Federal Hospital Insurance and Federal Supplementary Medical Insurance Trust Funds,* March 23, 2004, online at: http://www.cms.hhs.gov/publications/trusteesreport/2004/secib.asp.

16. Amber E. Barnato, Mark B. McClellan, Christopher R. Kagay, and Alan M. Garber, "Trends in Inpatient Treatment Intensity Among Medicare Beneficiaries at the End of Life," *Health Services Research* 39, no. 2 (2004): 363–376.

17. Mark V. Pauly and John S. Hoff, *Responsible Tax Credits for Health Insurance* (Washington, D.C.: AEI Press, 2002).

Further Reading

Dranove, David. *The Economic Evolution of American Health Care: From Marcus Welby to Managed Care.* Princeton: Princeton University Press, 2000.

Morrisey, Michael A. "Competition in Hospital and Health Insurance Markets: A Review and Research Agenda." *Health Services Research* 36, no. 1, pt. 2 (2001): 191–221.

———. *Cost Shifting in Health Care: Separating Evidence from Rhetoric.* Washington, D.C.: AEI Press, 1994.

Pauly, Mark V. *Health Benefits at Work: An Economic and Political Analysis of Employment-Based Health Insurance.* Ann Arbor: University of Michigan Press, 2000.

Pauly, Mark V., and John S. Hoff. *Responsible Tax Credits for Health Insurance.* Washington, D.C.: AEI Press, 2002.

Health Insurance

John C. Goodman

The Birth of the "Blues"

In the 1930s and 1940s, a competitive market for health insurance developed in many places in the United States. Typically, premiums tended to reflect risks, and insurers aggressively monitored claims to keep costs down and prevent abuses. Following World War II, however, the market changed radically. Hospitals had created Blue Cross in 1939, and doctors started Blue Shield at about the same time. Under pressure from hospital and physician organizations, the "Blues" won competitive advantages from state governments and special discounts from medical providers. Once the Blues had used these advantages to gain a monopoly, the medical community was in a position to refuse to deal with commercial insurers unless they adopted many of the same practices followed by the Blues. The federal government also later adopted some of these practices through its Medicare (for the elderly) and Medicaid (for the poor) programs.[1]

Cost-Plus Finance

Four characteristics of Blue Cross/Blue Shield health insurance fundamentally shaped the way Americans paid for health care in the postwar period.

First, hospitals were reimbursed on a cost-plus basis. If Blue Cross patients accounted for 40 percent of a hospi-

1. John C. Goodman and Gerald L. Musgrave, *Patient Power: Solving America's Health Care Crisis* (Washington, D.C.: Cato Institute, 1992); and John C. Goodman, *Regulation of Medical Care: Is the Price Too High?* (San Francisco: Cato Institute, 1980).

tal's total patient days, Blue Cross was expected to pay for 40 percent of the hospital's total costs. If Medicare patients accounted for one-third of patient days, Medicare paid one-third of the total costs. Other insurers reimbursed hospitals in much the same way. For the most part, physicians and hospital managers were free to incur costs as they saw fit. The role of insurers was to pay the bills with few questions asked.

Second, the philosophy of the Blues was that health insurance should cover all medical costs—even routine checkups and diagnostic procedures. The early Blue plans had no deductibles and no copayments; insurers paid the total bill, and patients and physicians made choices with little interference from insurers. Therefore, health insurance was not really insurance; it was prepayment for the consumption of medical care.

Third, the Blues priced their policies based on "community rating." In the early days, this meant that everyone in a given geographical area was charged the same price for health insurance, regardless of age, sex, occupation, or any other factor related to differences in real health risks. Even though a sixty-year-old can be expected to incur four times the health care costs of a twenty-five-year-old, for example, both paid the same premium. In this way, higher-risk people were undercharged and lower-risk people were overcharged.

Fourth, instead of pricing their policies to generate reserves that would pay bills not presented until future years (as life insurers and property and casualty insurers do), the Blues adopted a pay-as-you-go approach to insurance. This meant that each year's premium income paid for that year's health care costs. If a policyholder developed an illness that required treatment over several years, in each successive year insurers had to collect additional premiums from all policyholders to pay those additional costs.

Even though most health care and most health insurance were provided privately, the U.S. health care system developed into a regulated, institutionalized market dominated by nonprofit bureaucracies. Such a market is very different from a truly competitive market. Indeed, the primary reason that the medical community created the Blues was to avoid the consequences of a competitive market—including vigorous price competition and careful oversight of provider behavior by third-party payers.

One area where consumers become immediately aware that the medical marketplace is different is that of hospital prices. Even today, most patients cannot find out in advance what even routine surgical procedures will cost them. When discharged, they receive lengthy itemized bills that are difficult for even physicians to understand. Thus, the buyers (i.e., the patients) of hospital services cannot discover the price prior to buying and cannot understand the charge after making the purchase.

Contrast this experience with the market for cosmetic surgery. Because neither public nor private insurance any longer covers cosmetic surgery, patients pay with their own funds. And even though many parties are involved in supplying the service (physician, nurse, anesthetist, and the hospital), patients are quoted a single package price in advance. Moreover, during the past decade, the real price of cosmetic surgery actually fell, while prices of other medical services rose faster than the rate of inflation. Consumers spending their own money have achieved something that few health insurers have.[2]

Managed Care

For all its faults, the cost-plus approach to health care finance worked tolerably well until the establishment of Medicare and Medicaid in 1965. These two programs unleashed a tidal wave of new demand. Partly in response, an era of technological innovation emerged with opportunities to spend expanding in every direction. Since there were no market-based mechanisms to deal with these pressures, double-digit increases in annual health care spending were inevitable.

The system began to unravel in the 1970s and 1980s. Large employers began to manage their own health care plans, started paying hospitals based on set charges rather than on costs, and negotiated price discounts. Through the Medicare program, the federal government began paying hospitals fixed prices for surgical procedures (the Prospective Payment System). Health maintenance organizations (HMOs) emerged as competitors to traditional fee-for-service insurance.

In 1980, fewer than ten million people were enrolled in HMOs. Today, more than seventy-four million are, about one in four Americans. Three-fourths of all employees with health insurance are covered by some type of managed care.[3] What difference has this change made?

First of all, it has meant fewer choices for patients and doctors. Only a few years ago, a person with private health insurance could see any doctor, enter any hospital, or (with a prescription) obtain any drug. Today, things are different. In general, patients must choose from a list of approved doctors covered by their health plans. But because employers switch health plans and employees often switch jobs, long-term relationships between patients and physicians are

hard to form. Moreover, many people cannot see a specialist without a referral from a "gatekeeper" family physician or even get treatment at a hospital emergency room without prior (telephone) approval from their managed care organization. Patients who fail to follow the rules may have to pay part or all of the bill out of their own pockets.

Under managed care, doctors' choices have been curtailed even more than patients' choices. Not long ago, most doctors ordered tests, prescribed drugs, admitted patients to hospitals or referred them to specialists, and performed procedures based on their own experience and professional judgment. No longer. Now doctors who want to be on the "approved" list must agree to practice medicine based on a health plan's guidelines. For most doctors, the guidelines mean fewer tests, fewer referrals, and fewer hospital admissions. By the end of the 1990s, though, managed care plans faced a backlash from patients and doctors. Politicians threatened to create a patients' bill of rights. In response, the plans began to loosen their control over patient access to specialists and expensive treatments, and the rate of increase in health care costs began to rise.

Consumer-Driven Health Care

As the twenty-first century began, many large employers and some large health insurers became convinced that a market-based solution was the answer to U.S. health care problems. Consumer-driven health care (CDHC), defined narrowly, refers to health plans in which employees have personal health accounts from which they pay medical expenses directly. The phrase is sometimes used more loosely to refer to defined contribution health plans under which employees receive a fixed-dollar contribution from an employer to choose among various plans. Those who opt for plans with rich benefits pay more of their own money in addition to the employer's contribution, while those who choose bare-bones health plans contribute less of their own money.

As early as 1996, a federal pilot program was launched, allowing the self-employed and employees of small businesses to have tax-free Medical Savings Accounts (MSAs) in conjunction with high-deductible health insurance.[4] In 2002, a U.S. Treasury Department ruling allowed large companies to implement similar plans, called Health Reimbursement Arrangements (HRAs).[5] And, as of January

2. Devon Herrick, "Why Are Health Costs Rising?" Brief Analysis no. 437, National Center for Policy Analysis, May 7, 2003.

3. "The InterStudy Competitive Edge 13.1, Part II: HMO Industry Report," InterStudy Publications, 2002.

4. NCPA Staff, "A Brief History of Health Savings Accounts," Brief Analysis no. 481, National Center for Policy Analysis, August 13, 2004.

5. Devon Herrick, "Health Reimbursement Arrangements: Making a Good Deal Better," Brief Analysis no. 438, National Center for Policy Analysis, May 8, 2003.

1, 2004, all nonelderly Americans who have high-deductible health insurance can also have Health Savings Accounts (HSA).[6]

Regardless of the acronym, the idea behind all these efforts is pretty much the same: to empower individual patients and encourage them to make the tough choices between health care and other uses of their money. The proponents expect to unleash into the medical marketplace an army of savvy consumers who can compare prices, investigate quality, bargain for services, and so on. Among the expected responses of suppliers are "focus factories"—highly efficient producers who specialize in treating only a few diseases. Yet, even if consumer-driven health care performs as well as advertised, five serious problems with the health care system remain.

Problem One: Medicare and Medicaid
While change has been rapid and swift in the private sector, government programs have been slow to evolve. Medicare today still resembles the Blue Cross plan that it copied forty years ago. That is why the program does not cover prescription drugs, although a partial drug benefit is being phased in. Medicare will pay to amputate the leg of a diabetic, but will not pay for the chronic care that would have made the amputation unnecessary. It will pay for hospitalization for a stroke victim, but will not pay for drugs that might have prevented the stroke in the first place. Medicaid, whose program specifics differ from state to state, exhibits similar inefficiencies.

One-third of Medicare dollars go for patients in the last two years of life; and because Medicare is use-it-or-lose-it, the only way to get more benefits is to consume more care. There has been some movement toward private-sector options. Roughly one in six seniors is enrolled in a private-sector HMO; under Medicaid, it is close to one in two. However, there are no HSA accounts available in either program, other than a very limited pilot program for the chronically disabled.[7]

These two enormously expensive programs are the fastest-growing programs at the state and federal levels. Medicare costs one thousand dollars for every person in the country, or roughly four thousand dollars for a family of four. Medicaid costs even more. As a result, many families pay more in taxes for other people's health insurance than they pay for their own.

Problem Two: Private Sector Spending
Medical research has pushed the boundaries of what doctors can do for us in every direction. As a result, we could probably spend the entire gross domestic product on health care in useful ways:[8]

- The Cooper Clinic in Dallas now offers a comprehensive checkup (with a full body scan) for about $2,500. If everyone in America took advantage of this opportunity, the U.S. annual health care bill would increase by one-half.

- More than nine hundred diagnostic tests can be done on blood alone, and one does not need too much imagination to justify, say, $5,000 worth of tests each year. But if everyone did that, U.S. health care spending would double.

- Americans purchase nonprescription drugs almost twelve billion times a year, and almost all of these are for self-medication. If everyone sought a physician's advice before making such purchases, we would need twenty-five times the current number of primary care physicians.

- Some 1,100 tests can be done on our genes to determine if we have a predisposition toward one disease or another. At, say, $1,000 a test, it would cost more than $1 million for a patient to run the full gamut. But if every American did so, the total cost would be about thirty times the nation's total output of goods and services.

Note that these are all examples of information collection; carrying them out would not cure a single disease or treat an actual illness. If, in the process of performing all these tests, something that warranted treatment was found, spending would be even more.

The spread of HSAs will encourage people to make choices between health care and other uses of money, but HSAs are designed mainly for small-dollar expenses. A possible solution for high-dollar expenses is to adopt the casualty model of insurance familiar to homeowners and automobile buyers. Insurance pays for the repair of a hail-

6. John C. Goodman, "Health Savings Accounts Will Revolutionize American Health Care," Brief Analysis no. 464, National Center for Policy Analysis, January 15, 2004.

7. Arkansas and Florida tested a program, often referred to as "cash and counseling" whereby selected Medicaid home care patients were allowed to control a portion of the funds used to pay their home care provider. The results were that providers were more attentive to the needs of patients who controlled the funds to pay for their own care. The patients also found the program to be beneficial. Even those patients who subsequently dropped out still had positive things to say about the program. For instance, see Leslie Foster et al., "Improving the Quality of Medicaid Per-

sonal Assistance Through Consumer Direction," *Health Affairs*, Web Exclusive W3–162, March 26, 2003.

8. John C. Goodman, Gerald L. Musgrave, and Devon M. Herrick, *Lives at Risk: Single-Payer National Health Insurance around the World* (Lanham, Md.: Rowman and Littlefield, 2004).

damaged roof, but the homeowners are usually free to up-grade (or downgrade), and roof repairers function as the homeowners' agents rather than as agents of the insurers.[9]

Problem Three: Lack of Health Insurance

About forty-five million Americans do not have health insurance, and that number, though not the percentage of the population, has been rising.[10] Approximately 75 percent of episodes without health care coverage are over within one year. About 91 percent are over within two years. Less than 3 percent (2.5 percent) last longer than three years.[11]

At least four government policies have contributed to this problem and made it much worse than it needs to be. The first is the tax law. Most people with private health insurance receive health insurance as an untaxed fringe benefit. Middle-income employees effectively avoid a 25 percent income tax, a 15.3 percent tax for Social Security (half of which is paid by employers), and perhaps another 5 or 6 percent state and local income tax. Thus, almost half of every dollar spent on health insurance through employers is a cost to government. In contrast, most of the uninsured do not have access to tax-subsidized insurance. To become insured, they must first pay taxes and then purchase the insurance with what is left over.[12]

A second source of the problem is the extensive system of free care for uninsured people who cannot pay their medical bills. Several studies estimate that we are spending about one thousand dollars per uninsured person per year in unreimbursed medical care, a practice that clearly rewards people who are uninsured by choice.[13] A sensible solution would be to use the free-care money to subsidize (say, through a tax credit) private health insurance premiums for the uninsured. However, the local governments that maintain the health care safety net do not have that option.

A third source of the problem is state government regulations, including laws that mandate what is covered under health insurance plans. Under these laws, insurers are required to cover services ranging from acupuncture to in vitro fertilization, and providers ranging from chiropractors to naturopaths. Coverage for heart transplants is mandated in Georgia, and for liver transplants in Illinois. Mandates cover marriage counseling in California, pastoral counseling in Vermont, and sperm bank deposits in Massachusetts. Studies estimate that as many as one in four uninsured people have been priced out of the market by such regulations.[14]

A fourth problem (discussed below) is that legislation has made it increasingly easy for people to obtain insurance after they get sick.

Problem Four: Lack of Portability

One disadvantage of employer-based insurance is that employees must switch health plans whenever they switch employers. In the old fee-for-service days, this defect imposed less of a hardship because employees were generally free to see any doctor under any plan. Today, however, changing jobs often means changing doctors as well. For an employee or family member with a health problem, that means no continuity of care. Individually owned insurance that travels with employees as they move from job to job would allow employees to establish long-term relations both with insurers and with doctors. Yet, portable health insurance is largely impossible under federal tax and employee benefit laws. The reason: in order to get tax-subsidized insurance, most people must obtain it through an employer; but employers are not allowed to buy individually owned insurance for their employees with pretax dollars.

Problem Five: Lack of Actuarially Priced Insurance

An increasingly common feature of insurance markets is "guaranteed issue" regulation, which forces insurers to sell to all applicants, no matter how sick or how well they are. Perversely, this practice, when combined with community

9. John C. Goodman, "Designing Health Insurance for the Information Age," in Regina E. Herzlinger, ed., *Consumer-Driven Health Care: Implications for Providers, Payer, and Policymakers* (San Francisco: John Wiley and Sons, 2004).

10. Carmen DeNavas-Walt, Bernadette D. Proctor, and Robert J. Mills, "Income, Poverty, and Health Insurance Coverage in the United States: 2003," Current Population Reports P60–226, U.S. Census Bureau, August 2004.

11. Robert J. Mills and Shailesh Bhandari, "Health Insurance Coverage in the United States: 2002," Current Population Reports P60–223, U.S. Census Bureau, September 2003, figure 7.

12. Mark V. Pauly, *Health Benefits at Work: An Economic and Political Analysis of Employment-Based Health Insurance* (Ann Arbor: University of Michigan Press, 1997).

13. Jack Hadley and John Holahan, "How Much Medical Care Do the Uninsured Use, and Who Pays for It?" *Health Affairs*, Web Exclusive, February 12, 2003. Also see Texas State Comptroller's Office, "Texas Estimated Health Care Spending on the Uninsured," Texas Comptroller of Public Accounts, State of Texas, 1999, online at: www.window.state.tx.us/uninsure.

14. John C. Goodman and Gerald L. Musgrave, "Freedom of Choice in Health Insurance," NCPA Policy Report no. 134, National Center for Policy Analysis, November 1988; and Gail A. Jensen and Michael A. Morrisey, "Mandated Benefit Laws and Employer-Sponsored Health Insurance," Health Insurance Association of America, January 1999.

rating, encourages healthy people to avoid high premiums and stay uninsured. After all, why buy health insurance today if you know you can buy it for the same price after you get sick? Under "pure" community rating, insurers charge the same price to every policyholder, regardless of age, sex, or any other indicator of health risk. Despite the fact that health costs for a sixty-year-old male are typically three to four times as high as those for a twenty-five-year-old male, both pay the same premium. "Modified" community rating allows for price differences based on age and sex, but not on health status.

Ironically, many large corporations community rate insurance premiums to their own employees, even though not required to do so by law. To the extent that employees pay part of the premiums for these plans, the premiums tend to be the same for everyone, regardless of expected costs. Whether in the marketplace or inside a corporation, distortions in prices produce distortions in results. People who are overcharged tend to underinsure. People who are undercharged tend to overinsure. In general, people cannot make rational choices about risk if risks are not accurately priced.

About the Author

John C. Goodman is the president of the National Center for Policy Analysis, a Dallas-based think tank. In 1988 he won the Duncan Black Award for the best article in public choice economics.

Further Reading

Goodman, John C. *Regulation of Medical Care: Is the Price Too High?* San Francisco: Cato Institute, 1980.
Goodman, John C., and Gerald L. Musgrave. *Patient Power: Solving America's Health Care Crisis.* Washington, D.C.: Cato Institute, 1992.
Goodman, John C., Gerald L. Musgrave, and Devon M. Herrick. *Lives at Risk: Single-Payer National Health Insurance Around the World.* Lanham, Md.: Rowman and Littlefield, 2004.
Herzlinger, Regina E., ed. *Consumer-Driven Health Care: Implications for Providers, Payers, and Policy-Makers.* San Francisco: John Wiley and Sons, 2004.
———. *Market-Driven Health Care: Who Wins, Who Loses in the Transformation of America's Largest Service Industry.* Cambridge, Mass.: Perseus Books, 1999.
Pauly, Mark V., and John S. Hoff. *Responsible Tax Credits for Health Insurance.* Washington, D.C.: AEI Press, 2002.

Housing

Benjamin Powell
Edward Stringham

The average U.S. consumer now enjoys a larger and higher-quality home than ever before. In 2001, the average home was 1,693 square feet, while in 1960 it was less than 1,200 square feet. In 2001, 58 percent of homes had three or more bedrooms, and 57 percent had 1.5 or more bathrooms. Compare that with 1970, when fewer than half of homes had three or more bedrooms and only 30 percent had 1.5 or more bathrooms. Housing amenities have also improved. In 2001, 76 percent of homes had a washing machine, 73 percent had a dryer, 56 percent had a dishwasher, and 44 percent had a kitchen sink garbage disposal; 58 percent of homes had a garage, and 80 percent had an outdoor deck or patio. In 2001, 82 percent of homes had some form of air-conditioning and 55 percent had central air; in 1970, only 36 percent of homes had air-conditioning and 11 percent had central air. Housing has improved almost across the board. Now, 98.7 percent of homes have complete plumbing that includes sinks, hot water, and flush toilets compared with 93.5 percent thirty years ago. The improvement has been especially dramatic for low-income households. University of California at Berkeley professors Quigley and Raphael (2003) report that the percentage of homes occupied by the poorest one-fifth of income earners that have incomplete plumbing declined from 40 percent in 1963 to essentially zero today.

While the size and quality of homes have increased, so have prices. Between 1970 and 2001, the median price of owner-occupied housing rose from $78,051 to $123,887 (in 2001 dollars), leading a number of groups to declare a national affordability crisis. But despite noticeable price increases, housing is not necessarily unaffordable. The U.S. Census's 2001 *American Housing Survey* estimates the cost of owning the median home at $725 per month. If 30 percent of income is spent on housing, any household earning $29,000 per year can purchase the median home. Median household income in the United States is much higher, at $41,994, and so spending $8,700 per year on the median home is well within reach. Although a nationwide affordability crisis does not exist, the numbers in certain regions are less rosy. In many areas of California and the Northeast, for example, housing is much more expensive than in the rest of the United States.

Most commentators attribute the elevated prices to high demand for scarce land. A number of economists, however, point to another explanation. High prices may not be due to intrinsically valuable land but, instead, to housing regulations such as restrictions on density, height, and design; building fees; slow approval processes; restrictions on growth; and preservation laws. One way of measuring whether high prices are due to regulations or high demand for land is to look at how much increased lot size increases the value of a home. If land scarcity drives housing prices, doubling the lot size would increase the difference between construction costs and home value by 100 percent. But Edward Glaser and Joseph Gyourko (2002) found that consumers in most cities value homes on twenty-thousand-square-foot lots by only ten to twenty thousand dollars more than they do equivalent homes on ten-thousand-square-foot lots.

This indicates that intrinsically valuable land is not the main cause of high prices. Economists who have studied the issue conclude that the scarcest input for housing is government permission to build. Econometric estimates indicate that only 10 percent of the gap between construction costs and home prices is caused by intrinsically high land prices; the other 90 percent is caused by zoning and land-use regulations. Glaser and Gyourko conclude that "land-use regulation is responsible for high housing costs where they exist" (p. 30). Another study reached the same conclusion using a different methodology. Stephen Malpezzi (1996) constructed an index of seven different land-use regulatory variables and ranked fifty-six different metropolitan areas according to how strictly land use was regulated. Regulatory variables included measures such as changes in length of approval time, time required to get land rezoned, amount of acreage zoned for residential development, and percentage of zoning changes approved. Malpezzi found that a change from a lightly regulated environment to a heavily regulated one increased home values by 51 percent and decreased the number of permits to build by 42 percent. Home ownership rates also declined by about ten percentage points. Regardless of methodology, evidence shows that areas with high levels of regulation have higher housing prices, higher rents, and lower home ownership rates.

Although no national affordable housing crisis exists, prices are quite high in some high-regulation jurisdictions. In Santa Clara County, California, for example, the median price of a newly constructed home in 2003 was more than $638,000. Assuming a family can spend 30 percent of its income on a mortgage, even with low 5 percent interest rates a family must earn more than $135,000 per year to afford the median-priced new home. If the above estimates are correct, regulations such as urban growth boundaries, moratoriums on building permits, environmental regulations, and other restrictions raise home prices as much as $300,000 in this county. Put another way, the portion of purchase price paid by residents of Santa Clara County due to regulation is almost enough to buy three complete homes of median value elsewhere in the United States.

In addition to land-use restrictions, governments drive up housing prices for lower-income families by dictating improvements in housing quality that the families might not otherwise choose. Governments do this by, for example, setting minimum lot sizes. Also, the federal government's urban renewal program between 1949 and the early 1970s destroyed more than 600,000 low-income dwellings, replacing them with 250,000 homes that were mostly for middle- and upper-income buyers (O'Sullivan 1996). Martha Burt's 1992 study found that urban renewal's destruction of low-quality, low-cost residential hotel rooms in U.S. central cities contributed to the rise of homelessness.

Real federal outlays for housing have steadily increased since the early 1960s to reach their current level of approximately thirty billion dollars per year. Today, approximately 6 million renter households receive federal housing subsidies, and 1.5 million households live in public housing. But the public sector lacks a profit incentive, and government programs are highly inefficient. One study estimated that for every hundred dollars of government spending on housing production, housing worth only forty-three dollars to the residents is produced (Mayo 1986). Because residents of public housing do not own it—and, indeed, no one owns it—public housing usually deteriorates rapidly through poor upkeep, in many cases becoming uninhabitable within twenty years. Some of the worst effects of public housing have been on the very residents the housing was created to help. Public housing projects are often plagued by high crime, and are thus considered undesirable places to live. In contrast, private developers and landlords have an incentive to make sure customers are satisfied: they lose business otherwise.

Recognizing that government is not a particularly good landlord, many policymakers are looking for other "affordable" housing solutions. At the local level, inclusionary zoning is becoming increasingly popular. The word "inclusionary" actually refers to price controls on a percentage of new homes. Builders and subsequent owners are forced to price the homes so they are "affordable" to people at specific income levels. In Tiburon, California, for example, where the median price of existing homes exceeds $1 million, builders are required to sell 10 percent of new homes for $109,825 or less. Inclusionary zoning is most popular in California, Maryland, and New Jersey. A nationwide 1991 survey found that 9 percent of cities larger than 100,000 had inclusionary zoning, and the number is increasing rapidly. In 1990, roughly thirty jurisdictions in

California had inclusionary zoning; the number had increased to more than one hundred by 2004.

Inclusionary zoning produces negative effects similar to those caused by other price controls. Price controls restrict the supply of new homes and actually make housing less affordable. Because builders are forced to sell a portion of a development at a loss, inclusionary zoning functions as a tax on new construction. Estimates of the level of the tax in California cities such as Portola Valley are above $200,000 per market-rate home. To maintain normal profit margins, builders end up passing the tax on to landowners and other home buyers. Elasticities of supply and demand determine exactly how the burden is split, but the result is almost certainly higher home prices.

Inclusionary zoning also leads to less construction. In the forty-five San Francisco Bay Area cities for which data are available, new construction fell by 31 percent in the year following the adoption of inclusionary zoning (Powell and Stringham 2004). In some cases, inclusionary zoning halts development completely. The experience of Watsonville, California, illustrates this effect. In 1990, Watsonville's inclusionary zoning ordinance imposed price controls on 25 percent of new homes. Between 1990 and 1999, with the exception of a few small nonprofit developments, almost no new construction occurred. The law was finally revised in 1999 because, in the words of Watsonville Mayor Judy Doering-Nielsen, "There was an incredible pent-up demand. Our inclusionary housing ordinance was so onerous that developers wouldn't come in." Jan Davison, director of the city's Redevelopment and Housing Department, commented that the inclusionary zoning law "was so stringent, and land costs were so high, that few units were produced," but "[it] was completely redone in 2000, and we got more units produced" (Morgan 2003). Watsonville reduced the number of units under price controls from 25 percent of all developments to 15 percent on smaller developments and 20 percent on developments of fifty units or more. In the three years after easing requirements, the city's housing stock increased by 12 percent.

In addition to restricting supply, inclusionary zoning produces a number of other undesirable effects. Price controls exacerbate shortages, decrease mobility, and are a poor way of helping those most in need. Because inclusionary zoning comes with restrictions on resale, it prevents equity appreciation and leads families to live in the homes longer than they would otherwise. This takes homes off the market and does not help other low-income families who are seeking to buy homes. Even if a family's income has considerably increased, owners of price-controlled homes are less able to move because price controls prevent their homes from appreciating at market rates. These residents are stuck with an asset that they cannot fully cash out and cannot even pass on to their children unless those children also meet low-income guidelines. This creates an incentive for owners to evade the law and resell or sublet their units at market rates. Governments then must spend resources supervising the price controls.

Interestingly, even high-priced construction benefits all consumers. When a high-income household moves into a high-priced new home, it vacates its old home for someone else. That family, in turn, vacates its old residence, freeing it up for someone else. Economists call this process "filtering" because as new homes are built, the existing stock "filters down" to lower-income households. A classic study, *New Homes and Poor People*, looked at the chain of existing home sales in thirteen different cities and found that each new home generated an average of 3.5 moves. Even though new housing tends to be higher priced, low-income households make up to 14 percent of the moves generated by new housing. According to Malpezzi and Green (1996), "to the extent that a city makes it easy for *any* type of housing to be built, it will also enhance the available stock of low-cost housing" (p. 1811, italics added). When new construction is prevented or slowed, this process is stifled. Without new homes, high-income buyers bid up prices on existing homes, thus making all housing less affordable. A sure way to make housing more affordable is to reduce zoning regulations and other restrictions on new construction.

Despite the regulations, the U.S. housing market is quite resilient. Ninety-eight percent of Americans live in privately owned and constructed homes. The size and quality of these homes have increased substantially over the past few decades. Some cities, such as Houston, Texas, have gone without zoning, and some, such as Celebration, Florida, are almost entirely privately planned. Developments such as Santana Row in San Jose, California, now provide streets, parks, and even private security. A shift away from government planning to private planning is positive for renters and homebuyers (Beito et al. 2002).

About the Authors

Benjamin Powell is an assistant professor of economics at San Jose State University and the director of the Center for Entrepreneurial Innovation at the Independent Institute. Edward Stringham is an assistant professor of economics at San Jose State University.

Further Reading

Beito, David, Peter Gordon, and Alexander Tabarrok. *The Voluntary City: Choice, Community, and Civil Society.* Ann Arbor: University of Michigan Press, 2002.

Burt, Martha. *Over the Edge: The Growth of Homelessness During the 1980s*. New York: Russell Sage Foundation, 1992.

Glaeser, Edward, and Joseph Gyourko. "Zoning's Steep Price." *Regulation* (Fall 2002): 24–30.

Green, Richard, and Stephen Malpezzi. *A Primer on U.S. Housing Markets and Housing Policy*. Washington, D.C.: Urban Institute Press, 2003.

Lansing, John, Charles Clifton, and James Morgan. *New Homes and Poor People*. Ann Arbor: Institute for Social Research, 1969.

Malpezzi, Stephen. "Housing Prices, Externalities, and Regulation in U.S. Metropolitan Areas." *Journal of Housing Research* 7, no. 2 (1996): 209–241.

Malpezzi, Stephen, and Richard Green. "What Has Happened to the Bottom of the U.S. Housing Market?" *Urban Studies* 33, no. 10 (1996): 1807–1820.

Mayo, Stephen. "Sources of Inefficiency in Subsidized Housing Programs: A Comparison of U.S. and German Experience." *Journal of Urban Economics* 20 (1986): 229–249.

Morgan, Terri. "Loosened Rules Lure Developers to Watsonville." *San Jose Mercury News*, October 18, 2003.

O'Sullivan, Arthur. *Urban Economics*. Chicago: Irwin/McGraw-Hill, 1996.

Powell, Benjamin, and Edward Stringham. *Housing Supply and Affordability: Do Affordable Housing Mandates Work?* Policy Study no. 318. Reason Public Policy Institute, 2004.

Quigley, John, and Steven Raphael. "Is Housing Unaffordable? Why Isn't It More Affordable?" *Journal of Economic Perspectives* 18, no. 1 (2004): 191–214.

U.S. Census Bureau. *Annual Housing Survey, 1973: United States and Regions*. Washington, D.C.: U.S. Census Bureau, 1975.

———. *American Housing Survey for the United States: 2001*. Washington, D.C.: U.S. Census Bureau, 2002.

Human Capital

Gary S. Becker

To most people, capital means a bank account, a hundred shares of IBM stock, assembly lines, or steel plants in the Chicago area. These are all forms of capital in the sense that they are assets that yield income and other useful outputs over long periods of time.

But such tangible forms of capital are not the only type of capital. Schooling, a computer training course, expenditures on medical care, and lectures on the virtues of punctuality and honesty are also capital. That is because they raise earnings, improve health, or add to a person's good habits over much of his lifetime. Therefore, economists regard expenditures on education, training, medical care, and so on as investments in human capital. They are

called human capital because people cannot be separated from their knowledge, skills, health, or values in the way they can be separated from their financial and physical assets.

Education, training, and health are the most important investments in human capital. Many studies have shown that high school and college education in the United States greatly raise a person's income, even after netting out direct and indirect costs of schooling, and even after adjusting for the fact that people with more education tend to have higher IQs and better-educated, richer parents. Similar evidence covering many years is now available from more than a hundred countries with different cultures and economic systems. The earnings of more-educated people are almost always well above average, although the gains are generally larger in less-developed countries.

Consider the differences in average earnings between college and high school graduates in the United States during the past fifty years. Until the early 1960s, college graduates earned about 45 percent more than high school graduates. In the 1960s, this premium from college education shot up to almost 60 percent, but it fell back in the 1970s to less than 50 percent. The fall during the 1970s led some economists and the media to worry about "overeducated Americans." Indeed, in 1976, Harvard economist Richard Freeman wrote a book titled *The Overeducated American*. This sharp fall in the return to investments caused doubt about whether education and training really do raise productivity or simply provide signals ("credentials") about talents and abilities.

But the monetary gains from a college education rose sharply again during the 1980s, to the highest level since the 1930s. Economists Kevin M. Murphy and Finis Welch have shown that the premium on getting a college education in the 1980s was above 65 percent. This premium continued to rise in the 1990s, and in 1997 it was more than 75 percent. Lawyers, accountants, engineers, and many other professionals experienced especially rapid advances in earnings. The earnings advantage of high school graduates over high school dropouts has also greatly increased. Talk about overeducated Americans has vanished, replaced by concern about whether the United States provides adequate quality and quantity of education and other training.

This concern is justified. Real wage rates of young high school dropouts have fallen by more than 25 percent since the early 1970s. This drop is overstated, though, because the inflation measure used to compute real wages overstates the amount of inflation over that time (see CONSUMER PRICE INDEXES). Real wages for high school dropouts stayed constant from 1995 to 2004, which means, given the price index used to adjust them, that these wages have increased somewhat.

Thinking about higher education as an investment in human capital helps us understand why the fraction of high school graduates who go to college increases and decreases from time to time. When the benefits of a college degree fell in the 1970s, for example, the fraction of white high school graduates who started college fell—from 51 percent in 1970 to 46 percent in 1975. Many educators expected that enrollments would continue to decline in the 1980s, partly because the number of eighteen-year-olds was declining, but also because college tuition was rising rapidly. They were wrong about whites. The fraction of white high school graduates who entered college rose steadily in the 1980s, reaching 60 percent in 1988, and caused an absolute increase in the number of whites enrolling despite the smaller number of college-aged people. That percentage kept increasing to an all-time high of 67 percent in 1997 and then declined slightly to 64 percent in 2000.

This makes sense. The benefits of a college education, as noted, increased in the 1980s and 1990s. Tuition and fees did rise by about 39 percent from 1980 to 1986, and by 20 percent more from 1989 to 2000 in real, inflation-adjusted terms (again, using the faulty price indexes available). But tuition and fees are not, for most college students, the major cost of going to college. On average, three-fourths of the private cost of a college education—the cost borne by the student and the student's family—is the income that college students give up by not working. A good measure of this "opportunity cost" is the income that a newly minted high school graduate could earn by working full time. During the 1980s and 1990s, this forgone income rose only about 4 percent in real terms. Therefore, even a 67 percent increase in real tuition costs in twenty years translated into an increase of just 20 percent in the average student's total cost of a college education.

The economics of human capital also account for the fall in the fraction of black high school graduates who went on to college in the early 1980s. As UCLA economist Thomas J. Kane has pointed out, costs rose more for black college students than for whites. That is because a higher percentage of blacks are from low-income families, and therefore had been heavily subsidized by the federal government. Cuts in federal grants to them in the early 1980s substantially raised their cost of a college education. In the 1990s, however, there was a substantial recovery in the percentage of black high school graduates going on to college.

According to the 1982 "Report of the Commission on Graduate Education" at the University of Chicago, demo-graphic-based college enrollment forecasts had been wide of the mark during the twenty years prior to that time. This is not surprising to a "human capitalist." Such forecasts ignored the changing incentives—on the cost side and on the benefit side—to enroll in college.

The economics of human capital have brought about a particularly dramatic change in the incentives for women to invest in college education in recent decades. Prior to the 1960s, American women were more likely than men to graduate from high school, but less likely to go to college. Women who did go to college shunned or were excluded from math, sciences, economics, and law, and gravitated toward teaching, home economics, foreign languages, and literature. Because relatively few married women continued to work for pay, they rationally chose an education that helped in "household production"—and no doubt also in the marriage market—by improving their social skills and cultural interests.

All this has changed radically. The enormous increase in the labor participation of married women is the most important labor force change during the past twenty-five years. Many women now take little time off from their jobs, even to have children. As a result, the value to women of market skills has increased enormously, and they are bypassing traditional "women's" fields to enter accounting, law, medicine, engineering, and other subjects that pay well. Indeed, women now constitute about one-third of enrollments in business schools, more than 45 percent in law schools, and more than 50 percent in medical schools. Many home economics departments have either shut down or are emphasizing the "new home economics"—that is, the economics of whether to get married, how many children to have, and how to allocate household resources, especially time. Improvements in the economic position of black women have been especially rapid, and black women now earn almost as much as white women.[1]

Of course, formal education is not the only way to invest in human capital. Workers also learn and are trained outside schools, especially on the job. Even college graduates are not fully prepared for the labor market when they leave school and must be fitted into their jobs through formal and informal training programs. The amount of on-the-job training ranges from an hour or so at simple jobs like dishwashing to several years at complicated tasks like engineering in an auto plant. The limited data available indicate that on-the-job training is an important source of the very large increase in earnings that workers get as they

1. National Center for Education Statistics, "Educational Achievement and Black-White Inequality," NCES 2001–061, U.S. Department of Education, 2001.

gain greater experience at work. Bold estimates by Columbia University economist Jacob Mincer suggest that the total investment in on-the-job training may be well above $200 billion a year, or about 2 percent of GDP.

No discussion of human capital can omit the influence of families on the knowledge, skills, health, values, and habits of their children. Parents affect educational attainment, marital stability, propensities to smoke and to get to work on time, and many other dimensions of their children's lives.

The enormous influence of the family would seem to imply a very close relation between the earnings, education, and occupations of parents and children. Therefore, it is rather surprising that the positive relation between the earnings of parents and children is not so strong, although the relation between the years of schooling of parents and their children is stronger. For example, if fathers earn 20 percent above the mean of their generation, sons at similar ages tend to earn about 8–10 percent above the mean of theirs. Similar relations hold in Western European countries, Japan, Taiwan, and many other places. Statisticians and economists call this "regression to the mean."

The old adage of "from shirtsleeves to shirtsleeves in three generations" (the idea being that someone starts with hard work and then creates a fortune for the next generation that is then dissipated by the third generation) is no myth; the earnings of grandsons and grandparents at comparable ages are not closely related.[2] Apparently, the opportunities provided by a modern economy, along with extensive government and charitable support of education, enable the majority of those who come from lower-income backgrounds to do reasonably well in the labor market. The same opportunities that foster upward mobility for the poor create an equal amount of downward mobility for those higher up on the income ladder.

The continuing growth in per capita incomes of many countries during the nineteenth and twentieth centuries is partly due to the expansion of scientific and technical knowledge that raises the productivity of labor and other inputs in production. And the increasing reliance of industry on sophisticated knowledge greatly enhances the value of education, technical schooling, on-the-job training, and other human capital.

New technological advances clearly are of little value to countries that have very few skilled workers who know how to use them. Economic growth closely depends on the synergies between new knowledge and human capital, which is why large increases in education and training have accompanied major advances in technological knowledge in all countries that have achieved significant economic growth.

The outstanding economic records of Japan, Taiwan, and other Asian economies in recent decades dramatically illustrate the importance of human capital to growth. Lacking natural resources—they import almost all their energy, for example—and facing discrimination against their exports by the West, these so-called Asian tigers grew rapidly by relying on a well-trained, educated, hardworking, and conscientious labor force that makes excellent use of modern technologies. China, for example, is progressing rapidly by mainly relying on its abundant, hardworking, and ambitious population.

About the Author

Gary S. Becker is university professor of economics and sociology at the University of Chicago, a professor at the Graduate School of Business, and the Rose-Marie and Jack R. Anderson Senior Fellow at Stanford's Hoover Institution. He was a pioneer in the study of human capital and was awarded the 1992 Nobel Memorial Prize in Economic Sciences (see also BIOGRAPHIES section).

Further Reading

Becker, Gary S. *Human Capital: A Theoretical and Empirical Analysis, with Special Reference to Education.* 2d ed. New York: Columbia University Press for NBER, 1975.

Freeman, Richard. *The Overeducated American.* New York: Academic Press, 1976.

Kane, Thomas J. "College Attendance by Blacks Since 1970: The Role of College Cost, Family Background and the Returns to Education." *Journal of Political Economy* 102 (1994): 878–911.

Mincer, Jacob. "Investment in U.S. Education and Training." NBER Working Paper no. 4844. National Bureau of Economic Research, Cambridge, Mass., 1994.

Murphy, Kevin M., and Finis Welch. "Wage Premiums for College Graduates: Recent Growth and Possible Explanations." *Educational Researcher* 18 (1989): 17–27.

National Center for Education Statistics. "Digest of Education Statistics 2001." NCES 2002–130. U.S. Department of Education, March 2002.

———. "Paying for College—Changes Between 1990 and 2000 for Full-Time Dependent Undergraduates." NCES 2004–075. U.S. Department of Education, June 2004.

———. "Projections of Education Statistics to 2012." NCES 2002–030. U.S. Department of Education, October 2002.

"Report of the Commission on Graduate Education." *University of Chicago Record* 16, no. 2 (1982): 67–180.

Topel, Robert. "Factor Proportions and Relative Wages: The

2. Gary Solon, "Intergenerational Income Mobility in the United States," *American Economic Review* 82 (June 1992): 393–408.

Supply Side Determinants of Wage Inequality." *Journal of Economic Perspectives* II (Spring 1997): 55–74.

Welch, Finis, ed. *The Causes and Consequences of Increasing Inequality.* Bush School Series in the Economics of Public Policy. Chicago: University of Chicago Press, 2001.

Hyperinflation

Michael K. Salemi

Inflation is a sustained increase in the aggregate price level. Hyperinflation is very high inflation. Although the threshold is arbitrary, economists generally reserve the term "hyperinflation" to describe episodes when the monthly inflation rate is greater than 50 percent. At a monthly rate of 50 percent, an item that cost $1 on January 1 would cost $130 on January 1 of the following year.

Hyperinflation is largely a twentieth-century phenomenon. The most widely studied hyperinflation occurred in Germany after World War I. The ratio of the German price index in November 1923 to the price index in August 1922—just fifteen months earlier—was 1.02×10^{10}. This huge number amounts to a monthly inflation rate of 322 percent. On average, prices quadrupled each month during the sixteen months of hyperinflation.

While the German hyperinflation is better known, a much larger hyperinflation occurred in Hungary after World War II. Between August 1945 and July 1946 the general level of prices rose at the astounding rate of more than 19,000 percent per month, or 19 percent per day.

Even these very large numbers understate the rates of inflation experienced during the worst days of the hyperinflations. In October 1923, German prices rose at the rate of 41 percent per day. And in July 1946, Hungarian prices more than tripled each day.

What causes hyperinflations? No single shock, no matter how severe, can explain sustained, continuously rapid growth in prices. The world wars themselves did not cause the hyperinflations in Germany and Hungary. The destruction of resources during the wars can explain why prices in Germany and Hungary would be higher after the wars than before. But the wars themselves cannot explain why prices would continuously rise at rapid rates during hyperinflation periods.

Hyperinflations are caused by extremely rapid growth in the supply of "paper" money. They occur when the monetary and fiscal authorities of a nation regularly issue large quantities of money to pay for a large stream of government expenditures. In effect, inflation is a form of taxation in which the government gains at the expense of those who hold money while its value is declining. Hyperinflations are very large taxation schemes.

During the German hyperinflation the number of German marks in circulation increased by a factor of 7.32×10^9. In Hungary, the comparable increase in the money supply was 1.19×10^{25}. These numbers are smaller than those given earlier for the growth in prices. What does it mean when prices increase more rapidly than the supply of money?

Economists use a concept called the "real quantity of money" to discuss what happens to people's money-holding behavior when prices grow rapidly. The real quantity of money, sometimes called the "purchasing power of money," is the ratio of the amount of money held to the price level. Imagine that the typical household consumes a certain bundle of goods. The real quantity of money measures the number of bundles a household could buy with the money it holds. In low-inflation periods, a household will maintain a high real money balance because it is convenient to do so. In high-inflation periods, a household will maintain a lower real money balance to avoid the inflation "tax." They avoid the inflation tax by holding more of their wealth in the form of physical commodities. As they buy these commodities, prices rise higher and inflation increases. Figure 1 shows real money balances and inflation for Germany from the beginning of 1919 until April 1923. The graph indicates that Germans lowered real balances as inflation increased. The last months of the German hyperinflation are not pictured in the figure because the inflation rate was too high to preserve the scale of the graph.

Hyperinflations tend to be self-perpetuating. Suppose a government is committed to financing its expenditures by issuing money and begins by raising the money stock by 10 percent per month. Soon the rate of inflation will increase, say, to 10 percent per month. The government will observe that it can no longer buy as much with the money it is issuing and is likely to respond by raising money growth even further. The hyperinflation cycle has begun. During the hyperinflation there will be a continuing tug-of-war between the public and the government. The public is trying to spend the money it receives quickly in order to avoid the inflation tax; the government responds to higher inflation with even higher rates of money issue.

Most economists agree that inflation lowers economic welfare even when allowing for revenue from the inflation tax and the distortion that would be created by alternative taxes that raise the same revenue.[1]

---

1. For more on the "optimal" rate of inflation, see Timothy Cogley, "What Is the Optimal Rate of Inflation," FRSBSF Eco-

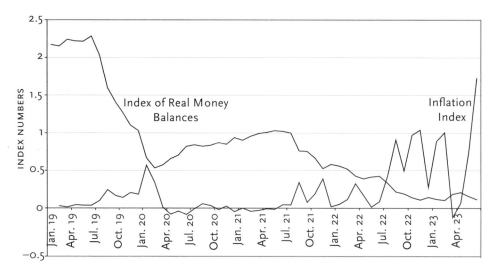

Figure 1 During the German Hyperinflation, the Real Quantity of Money Fell as Inflation Increased

How do hyperinflations end? The standard answer is that governments have to make a credible commitment to halting the rapid growth in the stock of money. Proponents of this view consider the end of the German hyperinflation to be a case in point. In late 1923, Germany undertook a monetary reform, creating a new unit of currency called the rentenmark. The German government promised that the new currency could be converted on demand into a bond having a certain value in gold. Proponents of the standard answer argue that the guarantee of convertibility is properly viewed as a promise to cease the rapid issue of money.

An alternative view held by some economists is that not just monetary reform, but also fiscal reform, is needed to end a hyperinflation. According to this view, a successful reform entails two believable commitments on the part of government. The first is a commitment to halt the rapid growth of paper money. The second is a commitment to bring the government's budget into balance. This second commitment is necessary for a successful reform because it removes, or at least lessens, the incentive for the government to resort to inflationary taxation. If the government commits to balancing its budget, people can reasonably believe that money growth will not rise again to high levels in the near future. Thomas Sargent, a proponent of the second view, argues that the German reform of 1923 was successful because it created an independent central bank that could refuse to monetize the government deficit and because it included provisions for higher taxes and lower government expenditures. Another way to look at Sar-

gent's view is that hyperinflations end when people reasonably believe that the rate of money growth will fall to normal levels both now and in the future.

What effects do hyperinflations have? One effect with serious consequences is the reallocation of wealth. Hyperinflations transfer wealth from the general public, which holds money, to the government, which issues money. Hyperinflations also cause borrowers to gain at the expense of lenders when loan contracts are signed prior to the worst inflation. Businesses that hold stores of raw materials and commodities gain at the expense of the general public. In Germany, renters gained at the expense of property owners because rent ceilings did not keep pace with the general level of prices. Costantino Bresciani-Turroni argues that the hyperinflation destroyed the wealth of the stable classes in Germany and made it easier for the National Socialists (Nazis) to gain power.

Hyperinflation reduces an economy's efficiency by driving people away from monetary transactions and toward barter. In a normal economy, using money in exchange is highly efficient. During hyperinflations people prefer to be paid in commodities in order to avoid the inflation tax. If they are paid in money, they spend that money as quickly as possible. In Germany, workers were paid twice per day and would shop at midday to avoid further depreciation of their earnings. Hyperinflation is a wasteful game of "hot potato" in which people use up valuable resources trying to avoid holding on to paper money.

Hyperinflations can lead to behavior that would be thought bizarre under normal conditions. Gerald Feldman's book *The Great Disorder* shows a photo of a small firm transporting wages in a wheelbarrow because the number of banknotes required to pay workers grew very

nomic Letter 97-27, online at: http://www.sf.frb.org/econrsrch/
wklyltr/el97-27.html.

large during the hyperinflation (Feldman 1993, p. 680). Corbis, an Internet source of photos (www.corbis.com), shows an image of a German woman burning banknotes in her stove because doing so provided more heat than using them to buy other fuel would have done. Another image shows German children playing with blocks of banknotes in the street.

More-recent examples of very high inflation have occurred mostly in Latin America and former Eastern bloc nations. Argentina, Bolivia, Brazil, Chile, Peru, and Uruguay together experienced an average annual inflation rate of 121 percent between 1970 and 1987. In Bolivia, prices increased by 12,000 percent in 1985. In Peru, a near hyperinflation occurred in 1988 as prices rose by about 2,000 percent for the year, or by 30 percent per month. However, Thayer Watkins documents that the record hyperinflation of all time occurred in Yugoslavia between 1993 and 1994.[2]

The Latin American countries with high inflation also experienced a phenomenon called "dollarization," the use of U.S. dollars in place of the domestic currency. As inflation rises, people come to believe that their own currency is not a good way to store value and they attempt to exchange their domestic money for dollars. In 1973, 90 percent of time deposits in Bolivia were denominated in Bolivian pesos. By 1985, the year of the Bolivian hyperinflation, more than 60 percent of time deposit balances were denominated in dollars.

What caused high inflation in Latin America? Many Latin American countries borrowed heavily during the 1970s and agreed to repay their debts in dollars. As interest rates rose, all of these countries found it increasingly difficult to meet their debt service obligations. The high-inflation countries were those that responded to these higher costs by printing money.

The Bolivian hyperinflation is a case in point. Eliana Cardoso explains that in 1982 Hernán Siles Suazo took power as head of a leftist coalition that wanted to satisfy demands for more government spending on domestic programs but faced growing debt service obligations and falling prices for its tin exports. The Bolivian government responded to this situation by printing money. Faced with a shortage of funds, it chose to raise revenue through the inflation tax instead of raising income taxes or reducing other government spending.

About the Author

Michael K. Salemi is an economics professor at the University of North Carolina in Chapel Hill.

2. See http://www.sjsu.edu/faculty/watkins/hyper.htm.

Further Reading

Introductory

Bresciani-Turroni, Costantino. *The Economics of Inflation: A Study of Currency Depreciation in Post-war Germany.* New York: Augustus M. Kelley, 1937. A readable classic originally written in Italian.

Cardoso, Eliana A. "Hyperinflation in Latin America." *Challenge* (January/February 1989): 11–19. Interesting and accessible.

Federal Reserve Bank of San Francisco. "The Optimal Rate of Inflation." *FRBSF Economic Letter* 97–27, September 19, 1997. A very readable overview of theoretical analyses of the welfare effects of inflation.

Feldman, Gerald. *The Great Disorder.* Oxford: Oxford University Press, 1993. Source of the wheelbarrow picture.

Graham, Frank D. *Exchange, Prices, and Production in Hyperinflation Germany, 1920–1923.* New York: Russell and Russell, 1930. Readable with a focus on data.

Holtfrerich, Carl-Ludwig. *The German Inflation 1914–1923: Causes and Effects in International Perspective.* New York: De Gruyter, 1986. Written by an economist who worked with German archives.

Sargent, Thomas J. "The Ends of Four Big Inflations." In *Rational Expectations and Inflation.* New York: Harper and Row, 1986. Sargent explains in detail why fiscal reform is needed to end hyperinflations.

Salemi, Michael, and Sarah Leak. *Analyzing Inflation and Its Control: A Resource Guide.* New York: National Council on Economic Education, 1984. Designed to help high school teachers teach about inflation.

Advanced

Bomberger, William A., and Gail E. Makinen. "The Hungarian Hyperinflation and Stabilization of 1945–1946." *Journal of Political Economy* 91 (October 1983): 801–824.

Cagan, Phillip. "The Monetary Dynamics of Hyperinflation." In Milton Friedman, ed., *Studies in the Quantity Theory of Money.* Chicago: University of Chicago Press, 1956.

Fischer, Stanley, Ratna Sahay, and Carlos A. Vegh. "Modern Hyper- and High Inflations." *Journal of Economic Literature* 40, no. 3 (2002): 837–880. A comprehensive look at modern episodes and theory.

Salemi, Michael. "Hyperinflation, Exchange Depreciation, and the Demand for Money in Post World War I Germany." Ph.D. diss., University of Minnesota, 1976.

Immigration

George J. Borjas

Immigration is once again a major component of demographic change in the United States. Since 1940, the number of legal immigrants increased at a rate of one million per decade. By 2002, approximately one million legal immigrants were being admitted each year, a rate of almost ten million for the decade (Table 1). Large numbers of illegal aliens also have entered the country. According to the official estimates of the Bureau of Citizenship and Immigration Services, there were 7 million illegal aliens in the United States in 2000, and this number grows by about 350,000 per year.

In the early 1900s, when immigration reached historically high levels, half the growth in U.S. population was due to immigration. In the 1970s, only about one-quarter of the growth in population was due to immigration. Current immigration again accounts for about half the growth in population, not only because of the large number of immigrants, but also because of the declining fertility rate of American women.

Just as numbers of immigrants have changed, so have the means of selection. Between 1924 and 1965, immigrants were selected mainly on the basis of national origin. The United Kingdom and Germany received more than 60 percent of the visas allocated outside the Western Hemisphere. (Visa applicants originating in North or South America were not subject to these quotas.) That all changed with the 1965 amendments to the Immigration and Nationality Act. Under the new system, most visas are reserved for relatives of U.S. residents. Between 2000 and 2002, for example, 63 percent of immigrants were admitted because of family ties, and an additional 10 percent were refugees.

The 1965 amendments dramatically altered the mix of immigrants (Figure 1). In the 1950s, 53 percent of immigrants originated in Europe, 25 percent in Latin America, and 6 percent in Asia. By the 1990s, only 15 percent of

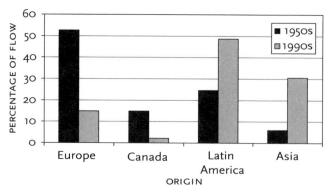

Figure 1 The Changing National Origin Mix of Legal Immigrants

immigrants originated in Europe, while 49 percent originated in Latin America and 31 percent in Asia.

The U.S. government enacted two major changes in immigration policy between 1985 and 1990. First, the 1986 Immigration Reform and Control Act granted amnesty to three million illegal aliens and introduced penalties for employers who hire undocumented workers. Although the act's purpose was to stem the illegal flow, it obviously failed in its goal. The second piece of legislation was the 1990 Immigration Act, which permits the entry of an additional 175,000 immigrants per year, with half of the extra visas reserved for skilled applicants.

Because of the increasing economic and demographic importance of immigration—and because of the national security implications of immigration in a post 9/11 world—we are now in the midst of a renewed debate over the "immigration problem." In terms of the economic impact, the debate will inevitably be guided by three issues: (1) How well do immigrants adapt to the United States? (2) What is their impact on the labor market opportunities of natives? (3) What immigration policy is most beneficial for the country?

Immigrant Performance in the Labor Market

When immigrants enter the United States, they typically lack skills—such as proficiency in the English language—that American employers value. Hence, it is not surprising that new immigrants earn less than native workers. As immigrants acquire these skills, however, their economic status catches up to that of natives (Figure 2). But because the recent immigrants are relatively less skilled than earlier waves were, the wage disadvantage of newly arrived immigrants has worsened over time. Immigrants who arrived in the late 1950s earned, on their arrival, 9 percent less than natives. The wage disadvantage for new arrivals increased to 26 percent in the late 1970s and to 28 percent in the late 1990s. Because recent immigrants start so far

Table 1 Legal Immigration to the United States, by Decade

Years	Number of Legal Immigrants (thousands)	Years	Number of Legal Immigrants (thousands)
1821–1830	143.4	1921–1930	4,107.2
1831–1840	599.1	1931–1940	528.4
1841–1850	1,713.3	1941–1950	1,035.0
1851–1860	2,598.2	1951–1960	2,515.5
1861–1870	2,314.8	1961–1970	3,321.7
1871–1880	2,812.2	1971–1980	4,493.3
1881–1890	5,246.6	1981–1990	7,338.1
1891–1900	3,687.6	1991–2000	9,095.4
1901–1910	8,795.4	2001–2002	2,128.0
1911–1920	5,735.8		

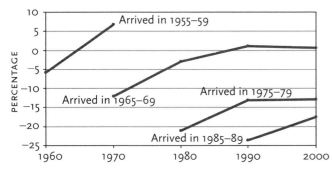

Figure 2 The Changing Wage Gap Between Immigrants and Natives as Assimilation Occurs (relative wage of immigrants who arrived when they were 25–34 years old)

behind, they do not attain wage parity with natives even after two or three decades in the United States (see Figure 1).

There are large differences in economic performance among the various national origin groups that make up the immigrant population. In 2000, immigrants from Jamaica earned 12.2 percent less than natives, and Mexican or Guatemalan immigrants earned nearly 40 percent less (Table 2). Compare these figures with immigrants from Canada or the United Kingdom, who earned almost 40 percent more than natives.

The large disparity in earnings for various nationalities

Table 2 Hourly Wage Differentials Across National Origin Groups, 2000

Country of Origin	Percentage of Immigrant Workforce Belonging to National Origin Group	Percentage Wage Gap Between Immigrant and Native Men
Canada	2.3	35.0
China	4.7	0.8
Cuba	2.8	−18.2
Dominican Republic	1.9	−31.3
El Salvador	2.9	−34.3
Germany	1.6	22.4
Guatemala	1.7	−36.9
India	4.4	35.4
Jamaica	1.6	−12.2
Korea	2.2	−0.6
Mexico	31.9	−38.4
Russia	1.9	−0.7
Sweden	0.1	45.5
United Kingdom	2.7	38.5
Vietnam	3.4	−17.6

arises partly because skills acquired in advanced, industrialized economies (such as Canada and the United Kingdom) are more easily transferable to the American labor market. But another reason is that the typical worker who emigrates from a country such as Sweden differs substantially from the typical worker who leaves Mexico. The Swedish government taxes skilled workers heavily and subsidizes the unskilled. Hence the brain drain: skilled Swedes migrate to the United States, where they can keep a larger portion of their income. In contrast, there is a great deal of income inequality in Mexico. Unskilled workers have few economic opportunities and skilled workers are well rewarded; therefore, it is the unskilled who wish to emigrate.

An important consequence of the shift toward a less-skilled immigrant flow is a sizable increase in the costs associated with welfare use among immigrants. In 1970, immigrant households were slightly less likely to receive public assistance than were native households: 5.9 percent of immigrant households received cash benefits, versus 6.0 percent of native households. By 2002, immigrant households were much more likely to receive assistance: 22.7 percent of immigrant households received some type of welfare (defined as cash benefits, Medicaid, or food stamps) versus 14.6 percent of native households.

The Impact of Immigrants on Native Earnings

There are two opposing views about how immigrants affect the labor market opportunities of natives. One view is that they have a harmful effect because immigrants and natives tend to have similar skills and compete for the same jobs, thus driving down the native wage. The other view is that the services of immigrants and natives are not interchangeable but instead complement each other. Put differently, immigrants do jobs that natives do not want to do. For instance, some immigrant groups may be unskilled but particularly adept at harvesting crops. Immigration then increases native productivity and wages because natives can specialize in tasks for which they are better suited.

The early empirical evidence on this subject seemed to indicate that immigration did not have a substantial impact on the labor market opportunities of native workers. This evidence was based on the speculation that if the services of natives and immigrants are interchangeable, natives should earn less in cities where immigrants are in abundant supply, such as Los Angeles or New York, than in cities with relatively few immigrants, such as Nashville or Pittsburgh. Although natives do earn somewhat less in cities with large immigrant populations, the correlation between the native wage and the presence of immigrants is close to zero.

Further evidence of the weak correlation comes from the Mariel boatlift. In April 1980, when Fidel Castro declared that Cubans wishing to emigrate could leave from the port of Mariel, 125,000 people accepted the offer and Miami's labor force suddenly grew by 7 percent. Yet, the trends in wages and unemployment rates in Miami between 1980 and 1985, including those of black workers, resembled those observed in comparable cities.

Such evidence, however, is not conclusive. This approach to measuring the labor market impact of immigration ignores the fact that labor and capital are mobile between cities. If an influx of immigrant workers reduced wages substantially in a particular city, native workers and some immigrants would leave that city and find work elsewhere. And natives who contemplated migrating to that city would choose another destination. Also, capital would "migrate" to cities with large numbers of unskilled immigrants, where capitalists can earn a greater return on their investment. Large-scale immigration, therefore, may not drive down wages in particular cities. Rather, its depressing effect on wages is nationwide.

Recent evidence on the *national* labor market impact of immigration is striking. The evidence indicates that the wage of the skill groups—defined in terms of educational attainment and labor market experience—that experienced the largest influx of immigrants grew most slowly over the 1960–2000 period. It has been estimated that the wages of native workers in a particular skill group will decline by about 3–4 percent for every 10-percent increase in the number of workers that can be attributed to immigration. So, for example, if there are 1,000,000 workers in a particular skill group and that group is expanded by 100,000 immigrants, the hourly wages of the entire group would fall by 3 to 4 percent.

Economic Impact of Immigration

Although the entry of immigrants reduces the wages of comparable natives, it increases slightly the income of U.S. natives overall. Using a well-known formula in economics (a variation on the theme of the so-called Harberger triangle), we can estimate that immigration increases the real income of natives, but only by about 0.2 percent. U.S. natives' economic gains from immigration, therefore, are relatively small: about $22 billion per year (in 2003 dollars). Of course, not everyone benefits equally from immigration; workers with competing skills lose, while owners of land and capital gain.

Many people believe that because a large percentage of

immigrants go on welfare, the costs to American taxpayers may wipe out the gains from immigration. Increasingly, the evidence tends to indicate that because of these fiscal impacts, immigration is essentially a wash for the U.S. economy. The National Academy of Sciences estimated in 1997 that the typical native household pays somewhere between $195 and $265 in additional taxes (in 2003 dollars) because of immigration. There are around ninety million native households in the United States, which puts the national fiscal burden somewhere between $18 billion and $24 billion per year. In the short run, therefore, there is little support for the argument that immigration is a great boon for the country. One solution would be to have a ten-year residency requirement for welfare recipients; those who planned to immigrate for welfare would then be much less inclined to do so. Welfare reform legislation passed in 1996 prohibits immigrants from receiving welfare as long as they are noncitizens. Becoming naturalized takes at least five years. This new provision in welfare eligibility may not have had the impact that the planners intended. Most large immigrant-receiving states simply ignore the federal restrictions and use their own money to pay for immigrant services.

Because the net gains from immigration depend on the skill level of immigrants, some host countries (e.g., Australia and Canada) use a "point system" to allocate visas. Applicants are graded on the basis of such factors as education, age, and occupation, and only those applicants who "pass the test" are awarded entry visas. It is not surprising that people migrating to those countries are more skilled than those admitted by the United States. The United States, in effect, is losing the competition for skilled workers in the immigration market.

Changes in U.S. immigration policy since 1965 have greatly altered the number, national origin mix, and skill composition of immigrants. Importing unskilled workers helps fill menial jobs at low wages, but these immigrants also impose substantial costs, mainly by being disproportionately on welfare. Although it is unclear that U.S. natives benefit from immigration on net, immigration does induce a sizable redistribution of wealth—away from competing workers and toward Americans who hire or use immigrant-provided services.

About the Author

George J. Borjas is the Robert W. Scrivner Professor of Economics and Social Policy at the Kennedy School of Government, Harvard University, and a research associate at the National Bureau of Economic Research. He was a member of the National Academy of Sciences panel on the demographic and economic impact of immigration.

Further Reading

Borjas, George J. *Heaven's Door: Immigration Policy and the American Economy.* Princeton: Princeton University Press, 1999.

———. "The Labor Demand Curve Is Downward Sloping: Reexamining the Impact of Immigration on the Labor Market." *Quarterly Journal of Economics* 118 (November 2003): 1335–1374.

———. "Self-Selection and the Earnings of Immigrants." *American Economic Review* 77 (September 1987): 531–553.

Card, David. "The Impact of the Mariel Boatlift on the Miami Labor Market." *Industrial and Labor Relations Review* 43 (January 1990): 245–257.

Smith, James P., and Barry Edmonston, eds. *The New Americans: Economic, Demographic, and Fiscal Effects of Immigration.* Washington, D.C.: National Academy Press, 1997.

Industrial Concentration

William F. Shughart II

"Industrial concentration" refers to a structural characteristic of the business sector. It is the degree to which production in an industry—or in the economy as a whole—is dominated by a few large firms. Once assumed to be a symptom of "market failure," concentration is, for the most part, seen nowadays as an indicator of superior economic performance. In the early 1970s, Yale Brozen, a key contributor to the new thinking, called the profession's about-face on this issue "a revolution in economics." Industrial concentration remains a matter of public policy concern even so.

The Measurement of Industrial Concentration

Industrial concentration was traditionally summarized by the concentration ratio, which simply adds the market shares of an industry's four, eight, twenty, or fifty largest companies. In 1982, when new federal merger guidelines were issued, the Herfindahl-Hirschman Index (HHI) became the standard measure of industrial concentration. Suppose that an industry contains ten firms that individually account for 25, 15, 12, 10, 10, 8, 7, 5, 5, and 3 percent of total sales. The four-firm concentration ratio for this industry—the most widely used number—is $25 + 15 + 12 + 10 = 62$, meaning that the top four firms account for 62 percent of the industry's sales. The HHI, by contrast, is calculated by summing the squared market shares of all of the firms in the industry: $25^2 + 15^2 + 12^2 + 10^2 + 10^2 + 8^2 + 7^2 + 5^2 + 5^2 + 3^2 = 1,366$. The HHI has two distinct advantages over the concentration ratio. It uses information about the relative sizes of all of an in-

dustry's members, not just some arbitrary subset of the leading companies, and it weights the market shares of the largest enterprises more heavily.

In general, the fewer the firms and the more unequal the distribution of market shares among them, the larger the HHI. Two four-firm industries, one containing equal-sized firms each accounting for 25 percent of total sales, the other with market shares of 97, 1, 1, and 1, have the same four-firm concentration ratio (100) but very different HHIs (2,500 versus 9,412). An industry controlled by a single firm has an HHI of $100^2 = 10,000$, while the HHI for an industry populated by a very large number of very small firms would approach the index's theoretical minimum value of zero.

Concentration in the U.S. Economy

According to the U.S. Department of Justice's merger guidelines, an industry is considered "concentrated" if the HHI exceeds 1,800; it is "unconcentrated" if the HHI is below 1,000. Since 1982, HHIs based on the value of shipments of the fifty largest companies have been calculated and reported in the manufacturing series of the Economic Census.[1] Concentration levels exceeding 1,800 are rare. The exceptions include glass containers (HHI = 2,959.9 in 1997), motor vehicles (2,505.8), and breakfast cereals (2,445.9). Cigarette manufacturing also is highly concentrated, but its HHI is not reported owing to the small number of firms in that industry, the largest four of which accounted for 89 percent of shipments in 1997. At the other extreme, the HHI for machine shops was 1.9 the same year.

Whether an industry is concentrated hinges on how narrowly or broadly it is defined, both in terms of the product it produces and the extent of the geographic area it serves. The U.S. footwear manufacturing industry as a whole is very unconcentrated (HHI = 317 in 1997); the level of concentration among house slipper manufacturers is considerably higher, though (HHI = 2,053.4). Similarly, al-

[1]. The Economic Census has been conducted every five years since 1967, and before that for 1954, 1958, and 1963. Prior to 1997, it was known as the Census of Manufactures. That same year, industries began being categorized according to the North American Industry Classification System (NAICS), which replaced the Standard Industrial Classification (SIC) codes used until 1992. Industrial concentration also is reported by the Economic Census on the basis of value added. Industry concentration ratios and HHIs for the 1992 and 1997 economic censuses can be accessed online at: http://www.census.gov/epcd/www/concentration.html. Information on industrial concentration is not readily available for sectors of the economy other than manufacturing.

though the national ready-mix concrete industry is unconcentrated (HHI = 29.4), concentration in that industry undoubtedly is much higher in specific cities and towns that typically are served by only a handful of such firms.

These examples suggest that concentration varies substantially across U.S. industries. Trends in concentration vary from industry to industry, but most changes in concentration proceed at a glacial pace. So, too, does aggregate concentration: the fifty largest U.S. companies accounted for 24 percent of manufacturing value added (revenue minus the costs of fuel, power, and raw materials) in 1997, the same percentage as in 1992 (and as in 1954, for that matter). On some measures—the percentages of total employment and total assets controlled by the nation's 50, 100, or 200 largest firms—industrial concentration in the United States actually has declined since World War II.

Concentration indexes calculated for a particular year conceal the identities of the industry's members. In reality, turnover among the nation's leading firms is fairly regular over long time horizons, averaging between 2 and 5 percent annually. Success at one point in time does not guarantee survival: only three of the ten largest U.S. companies in 1909 made the top one hundred list in 1987. Available concentration indexes, which are based solely on domestic manufacturing data, also ignore the global dimensions of industrial production.

The Causes and Consequences of Industrial Concentration

Some industries are more concentrated than others because of technical properties of their production technologies or unique characteristics of the markets they serve. Economies of scale, which allow firms to reduce their average costs as they increase their rates of output, favor large-scale production over small-scale production. Thus, industries for which scale economies are important (e.g., auto manufacturing and petroleum refining) are expected to be more concentrated than others in which costs do not fall as rapidly as output expands (e.g., cut-and-sew apparel manufacturing). Similarly, concentration tends to be higher in industries, such as aircraft and semiconductor manufacturing, where learning curves generate substantial production-cost savings as additional units of the original model or design are made.

Owing to so-called network effects, some goods increase in value as more people use them. Computer operating systems, word-processing software, and video recorder-players are examples of such goods, as are literal networks such as railroads, commercial air transportation, and wire line telephony. Because standard technologies and protocols that provide compatible interconnections are critical to the realization of network effects—allowing faxes to be sent and received or computer users easily to exchange files—consumers rationally favor large networks over small ones. The necessity of building networks that accommodate critical masses of users means that only a few providers will achieve dominant positions, and therefore the industry will tend to be highly concentrated. Such domination is likely to be temporary, however, since consumers will switch networks when benefits outweigh costs, as illustrated by the replacement of Beta-formatted video tapes by VHS formatted ones, which in turn are being replaced by DVDs.

Industrial concentration also is promoted by barriers to entry, which make it difficult for new firms to displace established firms. Barriers to entry are erected by government-conferred privileges such as patents, copyrights and trademarks, exclusive franchises, and licensing requirements. Existing firms may possess other advantages over newcomers, including lower costs and brand loyalty, which make entry more difficult.

The fundamental public policy question posed by industrial concentration is this: Are concentrated industries somehow less competitive than unconcentrated ones? Concentration would have adverse effects if it bred market power—the ability to charge prices in excess of costs—thereby increasing industry profits at consumers' expense. In theory, industrial concentration can facilitate the exercise of market power if the members of the industry agree to cooperate rather than compete, or if the industry's dominant firm takes the lead in setting prices that rivals follow. And, indeed, the evidence generated by hundreds of econometric studies suggests that concentrated industries are more profitable than unconcentrated ones. But that evidence begs the question. It does not tell us whether profits are higher in concentrated industries because of market power effects or because the firms in those industries use resources more efficiently (i.e., have lower costs).

Some economists have found that concentration leads to higher prices, but the link observed typically is both small (prices elevated by 1–5 percent) and statistically weak. A detailed econometric study by Sam Peltzman (1977) reaches the opposite conclusion. He reports that profits are higher in concentrated industries not because prices are higher, but because they do not decline as much as costs do as efficient firms expand their scales of operation. Analyses by Yale Brozen (1982), Harold Demsetz (1974), and others have found that the positive relation between industrial concentration and profits disappears altogether when firm size is taken into account. These results are consistent with the hypothesis that some industries are more concentrated than others because large firms have significant cost advantages over small firms. There is, in short, little unequivocal evidence that industrial concentration per se is worrisome. Just the reverse seems to be true.

Public Policies Toward Industrial Concentration

Consolidating production in the hands of fewer firms through mergers and acquisitions obviously is the most direct route to industrial concentration. Preventing transactions that, by eliminating one or more competitors, would lead to undue increases in concentration and the possible exercise of market power by the remaining firms is the mandate of the two federal antitrust agencies—the U.S. Department of Justice and the Federal Trade Commission—under section 7 of the Clayton Act (1914). That mandate was strengthened considerably by the Hart-Scott-Rodino Act (1978), which requires firms to notify the antitrust authorities of their intention to merge and then to hold the transaction in abeyance until it has been reviewed. Most transactions with summed firm values of fifteen million dollars or more had to file premerger notifications initially; in February 2001 that threshold was raised to fifty million dollars and indexed for inflation.

Two important factors that antitrust authorities consider in deciding whether to allow a proposed merger to proceed are the level of market concentration if the merger is consummated and the change in market concentration from its premerger level. (Note that the "market" considered relevant for merger analysis hardly ever corresponds to the "industry" defined by the Economic Census; antitrust markets may be defined more broadly or more narrowly; in practice, the definition of the relevant market usually is the key to whether a merger is lawful or not.) Concentration thresholds are laid out in the Justice Department's merger guidelines, first promulgated in 1968, revised substantially in 1982, and amended several times since.

The guidelines state that proposed mergers are unlikely to be challenged if the postmerger market is unconcentrated (HHI remains below 1,000). However, mergers generally will not be approved if, following consummation, market concentration falls within the 1,000–1,800 range, and the HHI increases by more than 100 points or, if the postmerger HHI is 1,800 or more, concentration increases by more than 50 points.[2] Exceptions are provided

when the merging firms can demonstrate significant cost savings, when barriers to entry are low, or when one of the merger's partners would fail otherwise. (In the European Union, by contrast, competition policy, including merger law enforcement, is shaped principally by fears of possible "abuses of dominant market positions" by large firms.)

Studies examining the enforcement of section 7 under the merger guidelines have found that they are not always followed closely. Mergers are, indeed, more likely to be challenged the greater the level of market concentration and the higher the barriers to entry are thought to be. But law enforcement also is found to be influenced significantly by political pressures on the antitrust authorities from groups that stand to lose if a merger is approved, including rivals worried that the transaction will create a more effective competitor. In fact, studies of stock-market reactions to news that a merger is likely to be challenged typically find competitors to be the main beneficiaries of such decisions.

About the Author

William F. Shughart II is F. A. P. Barnard Distinguished Professor of Economics at the University of Mississippi. He was special assistant to the director of the Federal Trade Commission's Bureau of Economics during the Reagan administration and currently is editor in chief of *Public Choice* and associate editor of the *Southern Economic Journal*.

Further Reading

Introductory

Adams, Walter, and James Brock. *The Structure of American Industry*. 11th ed. Upper Saddle River, N.J.: Pearson/Prentice Hall, 2005.
Cabral, Luís M. B. *Introduction to Industrial Organization*. Cambridge: MIT Press, 2000.
Kwoka, John E. Jr., and Lawrence J. White. *The Antitrust Revolution: Economics, Competition, and Policy*. 4th ed. New York: Oxford University Press, 2004.
Pautler, Paul A. "Evidence on Mergers and Acquisitions." *Antitrust Bulletin* 48 (Spring 2003): 119–221.
Shughart, William F. II. *Antitrust Policy and Interest-Group Politics*. New York: Quorum Books, 1990.
———. "Regulation and Antitrust." In Charles K. Rowley and Friedrich Schneider, eds., *The Encyclopedia of Public Choice*. Vol. 1. Boston: Kluwer, 2004. Pp. 263–283.

---

2. When firms with market shares of s_1 and s_2 merge, the HHI increases by $(s_1 + s_2)^2 - s_1^2 - s_2^2 = 2s_1s_2$. So, for example, if a merger is proposed between the two largest firms in the hypo-

thetical ten-firm industry described earlier, the HHI would increase by $2 \times 25 \times 15 = 750$ points (from 1,366 to 2,116). According to the guidelines, that merger would in all likelihood be challenged.

Advanced

Brozen, Yale. *Concentration, Mergers, and Public Policy.* New York: Macmillan, 1982.

Carlton, Dennis W., and Jeffrey M. Perloff. *Modern Industrial Organization.* 3d ed. Reading, Mass.: Addison-Wesley, 2000.

Coate, Malcolm B., Richard S. Higgins, and Fred S. McChesney. "Bureaucracy and Politics in FTC Merger Challenges." *Journal of Law and Economics* 33 (October 1990): 463–482.

Demsetz, Harold. "Two Systems of Belief About Monopoly." In Harvey J. Goldschmid, H. Michael Mann, and J. Fred Weston, eds., *Industrial Concentration: The New Learning.* Boston: Little, Brown, 1974.

Goldschmid, Harvey J., H. Michael Mann, and J. Fred Weston, eds. *Industrial Concentration: The New Learning.* Boston: Little, Brown, 1974.

McChesney, Fred S., and William F. Shughart II, eds. *The Causes and Consequences of Antitrust: The Public-Choice Perspective.* Chicago: University of Chicago Press, 1995.

Peltzman, Sam. "The Gains and Losses from Industrial Concentration." *Journal of Law and Economics* 20 (April 1977): 229–263.

Shy, Oz. *The Economics of Network Industries.* Cambridge: Cambridge University Press, 2001.

Stiglitz, Joseph E., and G. Frank Mathewson, eds. *New Developments in the Analysis of Market Structure.* Cambridge: MIT Press, 1986.

Industrial Revolution and the Standard of Living

Clark Nardinelli

Between 1760 and 1860, technological progress, education, and an increasing capital stock transformed England into the workshop of the world. The industrial revolution, as the transformation came to be known, caused a sustained rise in real income per person in England and, as its effects spread, in the rest of the Western world. Historians agree that the industrial revolution was one of the most important events in history, marking the rapid transition to the modern age, but they disagree vehemently about many aspects of the event. Of all the disagreements, the oldest one is over how the industrial revolution affected ordinary people, often called the working classes. One group, the pessimists, argues that the living standards of ordinary people fell, while another group, the optimists, believes that living standards rose.

At one time, behind the debate was an ideological argument between the critics (especially Marxists) and the defenders of free markets. The critics, or pessimists, saw nineteenth-century England as Charles Dickens's Coketown or poet William Blake's "dark, satanic mills," with capitalists squeezing more surplus value out of the working class with each passing year. The defenders, or optimists, saw nineteenth-century England as the birthplace of a consumer revolution that made more and more consumer goods available to ordinary people with each passing year. The ideological underpinnings of the debate eventually faded, probably because, as T. S. Ashton pointed out in 1948, the industrial revolution meant the difference between the grinding poverty that had characterized most of human history and the affluence of the modern industrialized nations. No economist today seriously disputes the fact that the industrial revolution began the transformation that has led to extraordinarily high (compared with the rest of human history) living standards for ordinary people throughout the market industrial economies.

The standard-of-living debate today is not about *whether* the industrial revolution made people better off, but about *when*. The pessimists claim no marked improvement in standards of living until the 1840s or 1850s. Most optimists, by contrast, believe that living standards were rising by the 1810s or 1820s, or even earlier.

The most influential recent contribution to the optimist position (and the center of much of the subsequent standard-of-living debate) is a 1983 paper by Peter Lindert and Jeffrey Williamson that produced new estimates of real wages in England for the years 1755 to 1851. These estimates are based on money wages for workers in several broad categories, including both blue-collar and white-collar occupations. The authors' cost-of-living index attempted to represent actual working-class budgets. Lindert's and Williamson's analyses produced two striking results. First, they showed that real wages grew slowly between 1781 and 1819. Second, after 1819, real wages grew rapidly for all groups of workers. For all blue-collar workers—a good stand-in for the working classes—the Lindert-Williamson index number for real wages rose from 50 in 1819 to 100 in 1851. That is, real wages doubled in just thirty-two years.

Other economists challenged Lindert's and Williamson's optimistic findings. Charles Feinstein produced an alternative series of real wages based on a different price index. In the Feinstein series, real wages rose much more slowly than in the Lindert-Williamsons series. Other researchers have speculated that the largely unmeasured effects of environmental decay more than offset any gains in well-being attributable to rising wages. Wages were higher in English cities than in the countryside, but rents were higher and the quality of life was lower. What proportion of the rise in urban wages reflected compensation for worsening urban squalor rather than true increases in real incomes? Williamson—using methods developed to measure the ill effects of twentieth-century cities—found that between 8 and 30 percent of the higher urban wages could be attributed to compensation for the inferior quality of life in English cities. John Brown found that much of the rise in real wages in the factory districts could be explained as compensation for poor working and living conditions. Another criticism of Lindert's and Williamson's optimistic findings is that their results were for workers who earned wages. We do not know what happened to people who worked at home or were self-employed. Because the consumption per person of tea and sugar, thought of as luxury goods at the time, failed to rise along with real wages, Joel Mokyr has suggested that workers who were not in the Lindert-Williamson sample may have suffered sufficiently deteriorating real incomes to offset rising wage income; in other words, the average person was no better off. Mokyr's explanation could also explain a lag between industrialization and the diffusion of its benefits.

What does "standard of living" mean? Economic historians would like it to mean happiness. But the impossibility of measuring happiness forces them to equate the standard of living with monetary measures such as real wages or real income. "Real income" is usually defined as money income adjusted for the cost of living, but not for effects of things such as health, longevity, unemployment, pollution, the condition of women and children, urban crowding, and the amount of leisure time. Although some new indexes attempt to capture the various dimensions of well-being, for most practical purposes real income per person remains the most telling indicator.

According to estimates by economist N. F. R. Crafts, British income per person (in 1970 U.S. dollars) rose from about $400 in 1760 to $430 in 1800, to $500 in 1830, and then jumped to $800 in 1860. (For many centuries before the industrial revolution, in contrast, periods of falling income offset periods of rising income.) Crafts's estimates indicate slow growth lasting from 1760 to 1830 followed by higher growth beginning sometime between 1830 and 1860. For this doubling of real income per person between 1760 and 1860 not to have made the lowest-income people better off, the share of income going to the lowest 65 percent of the population would have had to fall by half for them to be worse off after all that growth. It did not. In 1760, the lowest 65 percent received about 29 percent of total income in Britain; in 1860, their share was down only four percentage points to 25 percent. So the lowest 65 percent were substantially better off, with an increase in average real income of more than 70 percent.

The estimates of real income imply that a mildly optimistic conclusion on living standards is justified for the century after 1760. But the long period of slow growth makes pessimistic conclusions about shorter periods plausible. For example, did the working class become worse off during the early years of England's industrialization (1760–1830), when Crafts's estimates show real income per person growing at only about 0.3 percent annually? Growth at such a slow rate made deterioration in the lot of the working classes possible. A simple numerical illustration will show why. If we take 0.3 percent per year as the annual rate of growth of real income, average real income in 1830 would have been about 16 percent higher than in 1760. The share of total income going to the lowest 65 percent of the income distribution need only have fallen to 86 percent of its 1790 level to negate the benefit of rising average income. Most economic historians agree that the distribution of income became more unequal between 1790 and 1840. Moreover, if we add the effects of unemployment, poor harvests, war, pollution, urban crowding, and other social ills, the modest rise in average income could well have been accompanied by a fall in the standard of living of the working classes.

Other evidence supports the conclusion of slow improvement in living standards during the years of the industrial revolution. Crafts and C. K. Harley have emphasized the limited spread of modernization in England throughout most of the century of the industrial revolution. Feinstein estimated consumption per person for each decade between the 1760s and 1850s, and found only a small rise in consumption between 1760 and 1820 and a rapid rise after 1820. On the other hand, according to historians E. A. Wrigley and Roger S. Schofield, between 1781 and 1851, life expectancy at birth rose from thirty-five years to forty years, a 15 percent increase. Although this increase was modest compared with what was to come, it was nevertheless substantial.

The research of economic historians, then, has altered the old standard-of-living debate. They now seek to answer not the question of what happened to the standard of living, but the question of the effect of the industrial revolution net of other historical events. For example, the positive effect of the industrial revolution may well have been offset by the negative effect of frequent wars (the American Revolution, the Napoleonic Wars, the War of 1812) and the high taxes that accompanied them. Some economic historians include bad harvests, misguided government policies, rapid population growth, and the costs of transforming preindustrial workers into a modern labor force as additional causes of slow growth. In a counterfactual simulation, Mokyr has shown that without the technological changes of the industrial revolution, population growth could have substantially reduced real income per person between 1760 and 1830. In other words, the net effect of the industrial revolution was strongly positive but was largely offset by the negative effects of rapid population growth.

About the Author

Clark Nardinelli is an economist at the U.S. Food and Drug Administration.

Further Reading

Ashton, Thomas S. *The Industrial Revolution: 1760–1830.* London: Oxford University Press, 1948.
———. "The Standard of Life of the Workers in England, 1790–1830." In Friedrich A. Hayek, ed., *Capitalism and the Historians.* Chicago: University of Chicago Press, 1954.
Brown, John C. "The Condition of England and the Standard of Living: Cotton Textiles in the Northwest, 1806–1850." *Journal of Economic History* 50 (1990): 591–615.
Crafts, Nicholas F. R. *British Economic Growth During the Industrial Revolution.* New York: Oxford University Press, 1985.
Crafts, Nicholas F. R., and C. Knick Harley. "Output Growth and the British Industrial Revolution: A Restatement of the Crafts-Harley View." *Economic History Review* 45 (1992): 703–730.
Deane, Phyllis. *The First Industrial Revolution.* Cambridge: Cambridge University Press, 1979.
Floud, Roderick, and Paul Johnson, eds. *The Cambridge Economic History of Modern Britain.* Vol. 1: *Industrialization, 1700–1860.* Cambridge: Cambridge University Press, 2004.
Hartwell, R. M. *The Industrial Revolution and Economic Growth.* London: Methuen, 1971.
Hobsbawm, Eric. *Labouring Men: Studies in the History of Labour.* London: Weidenfeld and Nicolson, 1964.
Lindert, Peter H., and Jeffrey G. Williamson. "English Workers' Living Standard During the Industrial Revolution: A New Look." *Economic History Review* 36 (1983): 1–25.
Mokyr, Joel, ed. *The British Industrial Revolution: An Economic Perspective.* Boulder, Colo.: Westview Press, 1999.
Nardinelli, Clark. *Child Labor and the Industrial Revolution.* Bloomington: Indiana University Press, 1990.
Taylor, Arthur J., ed. *The Standard of Living in Britain in the Industrial Revolution.* London: Methuen, 1975.
Williamson, Jeffrey G. *Did British Capitalism Breed Inequality?* Boston: Allen and Unwin, 1985. Chaps. 1–4.
Wrigley, E. Anthony, and Roger S. Schofield. *The Population History of England, 1541–1871: A Reconstruction.* Cambridge: Harvard University Press, 1981.

Inflation

Lawrence H. White

Economists use the term "inflation" to denote an ongoing rise in the general level of prices quoted in units of money. The magnitude of inflation—the inflation rate—is usually reported as the annualized percentage growth of some broad index of money prices. With U.S. dollar prices rising, a one-dollar bill buys less each year. Inflation thus means an ongoing fall in the overall purchasing power of the monetary unit.

Inflation rates vary from year to year and from currency to currency. Since 1950, the U.S. dollar inflation rate, as measured by the December-to-December change in the U.S. Consumer Price Index (CPI), has ranged from a low of −0.7 percent (1954) to a high of 13.3 percent (1979). Since 1991, the rate has stayed between 1.6 percent and 3.3 percent per year. Since 1950 at least eighteen countries have experienced episodes of HYPERINFLATION, in which the CPI inflation rate has soared above 50 percent per *month*. In recent years, Japan has experienced negative inflation, or "deflation," of around 1 percent per year, as measured by the Japanese CPI. Central banks in most countries today profess concern with keeping inflation low but positive. Some specify a target range for the inflation rate, typically 1–3 percent.

Although economies on silver and gold standards sometimes experienced inflation, inflation rates in such economies seldom exceeded 2 percent per year, and the overall experience over the centuries was inflation of close to zero. Economies on paper-money standards, which all economies have today, have displayed much more inflation. As Peter Bernholz (2003, p. 1) points out, "the worst excesses of inflation occurred only in the 20th century" in countries where metallic standards were no longer in force. In 1971 the U.S. government cut the U.S. dollar's last link to gold, ending its commitment to redeem dollars for gold at a fixed rate for foreign central banks. Even among countries that have avoided hyperinflation, inflation rates have generally been higher in the period after 1971. But inflation rates in most countries have been lower since 1985 than they were in 1971–1985.

Measuring Inflation

In the United States, the inflation rate is most commonly measured by the percentage rise in the Consumer Price Index, which is reported monthly by the Bureau of Labor Statistics (BLS). A CPI of 120 in the current period means that it now takes $120 to purchase a representative basket of goods that $100 once purchased. Because the CPI basket is not identical with the specific basket of goods and services that *you* consume, the percentage rise in the CPI is, at best, only a rough approximation of the percentage rise in *your* cost of living. The same is true for any alternative measure of inflation, such as the gross domestic product deflator. The GDP deflator is arguably more representative of the economy as a whole, but is less relevant to ordinary consumers because its basket includes the prices of nonconsumer goods (such as new business equipment) that consumers do not buy, and excludes the prices of the many foreign-produced goods that consumers do buy.

Causes of Inflation

In a nutshell, inflation occurs—that is, the purchasing power of the dollar shrinks—to the extent that the nominal supply of dollars grows faster than the real demand to hold dollars. A standard approach to analyzing the connection between the money supply (M) and the general price level (P) uses an accounting identity called the "equation of exchange":

$$MV = Py$$

where V denotes the income-velocity of money (the number of times per year the average dollar turns over in transactions for final goods and services), and y denotes the economy's real income (as measured, e.g., by real GDP). Because V is *defined* as Py/M, the ratio of nominal income to money balances, the equation follows. The quantity theory of money (a better name would be "the quantity-of-money theory of the price level") says that a higher or lower level of M does not cause any permanent change in y or desired V—or, in other words, does not permanently affect the real demand to hold money. It follows that, in the long run, a larger M means a proportionally higher P. In less formal terms, putting more dollars in circulation dilutes the purchasing power of each dollar; or: prices rise when there are more dollars chasing the same amount of goods.

Thought experiments can help to illustrate the thinking behind the quantity theory. Consider an economy in which all prices are in equilibrium. Now, imagine doubling the stock of money by magically doubling the numbers on all pieces of currency and all bank account balances. All price tags must be simultaneously doubled to keep relative prices and the purchasing power of each person's (nominally doubled) money balances the same, and thus to keep the economy in equilibrium. Prices must rise in proportion to the quantity of money. For a slightly less magical case, imagine that a Federal Reserve helicopter flies across

the country and drops enough currency to double the money supply. If the people who get the new cash want to buy the same basket of goods as the population in general, a doubling of all prices is once again called for.

The real-world process by which the Fed injects new money—typically by purchasing bonds in the open market with newly created Fed liabilities—differs from these thought experiments. Among other differences, the first-round spending of the new money is on bonds, not on consumer goods in representative proportions. In the second round, the bond sellers' banks, into which the Fed has wired newly created reserves, will themselves buy additional securities (or make additional loans), expanding the banking system's deposits as they do so. The actions of the Fed (and the subsequent actions of the commercial banks) expand the supply of loanable funds and therefore may lower the real interest rate. The commercial banks' borrowers (predominantly business firms) may, at least temporarily, raise the *relative* prices of the assets they buy (business plant and equipment). Many economists assume that such relative-price effects are negligible, but others (e.g., the AUSTRIAN SCHOOL) assign them a key role in their theories of the business cycle.

For the *only* result of a real-world monetary expansion to be an exactly equiproportional rise in all prices, the spending diffusion of the new money must *not* significantly raise some prices ahead of others. This condition is sometimes described by saying that "money is neutral." In the long run, it is reasonable to assume that relative price effects largely wash out, so for understanding decade-long inflation we may abstract from them. To understand how monetary policy can drive a business cycle, however, the assumption of neutrality must be put aside.

The equation of exchange can be employed to show how the inflation rate depends on the growth rates of M, V, and y. The relationship among all four growth rates is given by the "dynamic," or growth-rate, version of the equation,

$$gM + gV = gP + gy,$$

which says: the rate of growth of the quantity of money, plus the rate of growth of the velocity of money, equals the rate of inflation plus the rate of growth of real income. The equation holds exactly for continuously compounded growth rates. For year-over-year rates it is an approximation.

The dynamic equation of exchange indicates that, as a matter of accounting, inflation depends not only on the rate of monetary expansion, but also on the rate of velocity growth and (negatively) on the rate of real income growth. Which of these three factors contributes the most to inflation in practice? The well-known monetary economist Milton Friedman (1992, p. 262) famously proclaimed: "Inflation is always and everywhere a monetary phenomenon." What he meant was that sustained inflation has historically always been due to sustained money supply growth, not to sustained velocity growth or sustained negative growth in real income.

The supporting evidence for Friedman's proposition is straightforward. For virtually any country one examines, even in a bad year real income seldom falls by more than two or three percentage points. Velocity has been known to rise over long periods, but seldom more than one percentage point year after year. When high-inflation and low-inflation countries are compared, differences in money growth are much greater from country to country than differences in either real output growth or velocity. As a result, the rate of monetary expansion is the dominant factor accounting for differences in inflation rates across countries. High-inflation countries are countries with rapid money growth. Likewise, the dominant factor accounting for different inflation rates over decades in the same country (e.g., the lower U.S. inflation rate in the 1990s compared with the 1970s) is different money growth rates. High-inflation decades are decades with rapid money growth. The dominance of money growth in accounting for inflation is especially pronounced in HYPERINFLATION.

The implication for controlling inflation is equally straightforward. Achieving zero inflation merely requires the central bank, which controls the money supply, to refrain from expanding the money supply too rapidly (more specifically, adjusting for velocity growth, expanding the money supply at a rate faster than the economy's real output of goods and services is expanding). The Federal Reserve System could maintain zero inflation ($gP = 0$), on average, by controlling growth in the stock of U.S. dollars (gM) appropriately. Central banks elsewhere in the world (Australia, Canada, the euro zone, New Zealand, Sweden, the United Kingdom) have, in recent years, each announced a target range for the inflation rate, often 1–3 percent, and have been rather successful in keeping the inflation rate within that range.

Some economists call the above analysis a "demand-pull" explanation (monetary expansion fuels spending that pulls prices up), while proposing a "cost-push" alternative. For particular episodes of inflation, they have variously blamed monopolies, labor unions, OPEC, and even the failure of the anchovy harvest off Peru for pushing up prices. The equation of exchange warns us that for a "supply shock" to account for a large rise in the *general* price level (not just a *relative* rise in some prices, such as the price of oil), the economy's output must shrink by a large percentage. In practice, "supply shock" cases are seldom large enough to account for much inflation and are typically short-lived. For example, of the 9.2 percent U.S. inflation rate in 1980 (as measured by the GDP deflator, $gP = 9.2$ percent), the negative growth of real GDP (due, in part, to the OPEC oil price shock of 1979–1980) accounted for only 0.2 percentage points ($gy = -0.2\%$). Meanwhile, growth in the money stock (M1 measure, December 1980 over December 1979) accounted for 7.0 percentage points ($gM = 7.0$ percent). Growth of approximately 2 percent in the income-velocity of M1 accounted for the remainder ($gV = 2.0$ percent). For the M2 measure of money and its velocity, the respective figures were 8.5 percent and 0.5 percent.

The equation of exchange also tells us, contrary to what some pundits used to suggest, that "too much growth" cannot be a cause of inflation. The higher the rate of real income growth (gy), the *lower* the inflation rate (gP), other things (gM and gV) being equal. If an increase in inflation is associated with an "overheating" economy (gy above its sustainable long-run trend), the explanation is that both rising inflation and a temporary spurt in real growth are effects of a previous increase in money growth.

What may look like "cost-push inflation" is often "demand-pull inflation" in disguise. Suppose that expansion of the money supply fuels an increase in demand for retail goods and services. Retailers may delay raising prices of goods already in inventory, but (owing to larger sales) place larger restocking orders with wholesalers, who do likewise, restocking from factories. Factories increase their demands for raw materials and labor, driving up material prices and wage rates. Factories may then "pass through" their cost increases to wholesalers, who do likewise to retailers. At each level, the price increase appears to be pushed by input costs. But the rise in input costs is due, ultimately, to the demand pull of money growth.

Consequences of Inflation

Inflation can do great harm. The harm is greater to the extent that the *actual* inflation rate differs from the *anticipated* inflation rate. When transactors correctly anticipate a faster decline in the purchasing power of the dollar (a higher inflation rate), the terms of contracts calling for future payments in dollars are adjusted accordingly. Borrowers and lenders who expect higher inflation agree to a higher nominal interest rate (dollars repaid over dollars lent) so as to preserve the real interest rate (purchasing power repaid over purchasing power lent) between them.

A simple expression for the relation of the nominal interest rate to the expected inflation rate is

$$(1 + i) = (1 + r) \times (1 + gP^e),$$

where i is the nominal rate, r is the real rate, and gP^e is the expected inflation rate. This equation is sometimes called the Fisher relationship, after the early-twentieth-century monetary economist IRVING FISHER. Fisher argued that the equilibrium real rate is independent of the expected inflation rate, so that increases in expected inflation are passed through entirely to the nominal rate.

Although lenders and borrowers do not suffer from a higher inflation rate when the rate is perfectly anticipated, holders of non-interest-bearing forms of money, such as currency, do. Higher anticipated inflation subjects them to the equivalent of a higher tax on their money holdings. Inflation thereby drives transactors into costly strategies for getting by with smaller currency holdings, such as making more trips to the bank to take out smaller amounts each time.

From the point of view of eliminating needless costs of economizing on cash, low inflation is clearly preferable to high inflation. But just how low is the best, or optimal, inflation rate? One proposal for achieving the "optimal" result—indeed the most widely discussed proposition in the pure theory of monetary policy—is that the inflation rate should be sufficiently negative that the nominal rate of interest is zero (on bonds of zero default risk and the shortest maturity). Any higher nominal interest rate means that currency pays a poorer return than bonds. This induces people to economize on holding cash, an action that is optimal from the individual's viewpoint but costly from society's viewpoint. From the Fisher equation it can be seen that achieving a zero nominal interest rate implies an inflation rate approximately equal to the negative of the real rate of interest, which suggests deflation of about 2–3 percent per annum.

In addition to the tax on cash balances, at least one other harm stems from higher inflation even when perfectly anticipated. With higher inflation, published prices become obsolete more quickly, and so price setters must more frequently incur the costs of adjusting nominal prices. Economists sometimes call these "menu costs" because they include reprinting restaurant menus as well as changing price tags on supermarket shelves, revising catalogs, replacing numbers on gas station price signs, and so on.

Where the tax code is not fully indexed, higher inflation increases the distorting effects of taxes. Before the U.S. income tax brackets were indexed, inflation pushed income earners with unchanged real income into brackets where they faced higher marginal income tax rates. This discouraged people from making taxable income. With indexing of federal tax brackets in 1985, this distortion disappeared. However, the capital gains tax is still levied on nominal gains, not on real—that is, inflation-adjusted—gains. The portion of your asset's nominal price rise that merely corresponds to inflation is taxed along with any real profit. The higher the inflation rate, the higher the effective tax rate on your real capital gains, even with an unchanged nominal capital gains tax rate. Higher inflation thus discourages capital formation by discouraging people from accumulating taxable assets.

Unanticipated Inflation

When the inflation rate is *incorrectly* anticipated, financial trades are upset. If the inflation rate turns out to be higher than anticipated, a borrower gets to repay in less valuable dollars, at the expense of the lender who gets less back in purchasing power than expected. If the inflation rate turns out to be lower than anticipated, the lender gains at the expense of the borrower (assuming the borrower is able to make the greater real payment). For example, the federal government, because it is the U.S. economy's biggest debtor, gains from unanticipated inflation and loses when inflation is less than anticipated. As a result, the federal government is biased toward higher inflation.

When the future inflation rate is highly uncertain, so that the risk of such gains and losses on new contracts is great, risk-averse parties shy away from making debt contracts (deposits, loans, bonds). Because inflation becomes more variable as the average inflation rate rises, high-inflation economies have stunted banking and bond markets. The real returns from holding bonds and loans of long maturities—for example, thirty-year corporate bonds or thirty-year fixed-rate mortgages—are especially sensitive to inflation variability. When an economy moves to higher and more variable inflation, therefore, such long-term contracts disappear. Long-term investments are discouraged by the greater risk in financing them.

High-inflation currencies have also stunted stock markets, although the reason why is less clear-cut. One likely reason (Aarstol 2000) is that higher inflation is associated with more "noise" in relative prices—that is, transient changes in relative prices due simply to different prices being adjusted at different speeds. Investors, therefore, cannot put as much credence in the earnings reports of companies listed on the stock exchange. High profits for a firm may be only temporary good luck owing to output prices randomly rising ahead of input prices. In such an economy, savers shy away from stock markets, as well as from bond and loan markets. They save less and divert their savings into "inflation hedges" such as houses and gold, rather than adding to the economy's stock of factories and machines. A second possible reason why inflation reduces the value of corporate shares is that the corporate income tax system in many countries is not fully indexed. Firms face higher real tax burdens as inflation rises.

In addition to hampering financial markets, the "noise" generated by high inflation means that the price system does not communicate information as well. Misinformation distorts investment and employment decisions. For all these reasons, high-inflation economies suffer poor growth. Robert Barro (1997) found in a cross-country study that an inflation rate 10 percentage points higher is associated with real growth 0.3–0.4 percentage points lower. Javier Andrés and Ignacio Hernando (1999), who studied OECD countries, report that lowering inflation by 1 percentage point will boost per capita GDP by 0.5–2.0 percent.

Does inflation have any benefits? Some Keynesian macroeconomists once believed that higher inflation could "buy" a permanent reduction in the unemployment rate, a belief that was encapsulated in early versions of the "Phillips curve." Economists now agree that no such exploitable trade-off exists; it seemed to exist in the 1960s only when higher inflation was a surprise. Surprise inflation can reduce layoffs (by making dollar sales unexpectedly high) and shorten job search (by making dollar wage offers unexpectedly high), lowering the unemployment rate below its "natural rate." When workers come to expect a high inflation rate, as they did in the 1970s, unemployment returns to its "natural rate" (see PHILLIPS CURVE). By the same logic, a surprise reduction in inflation can raise unemployment above its natural rate, making disinflation costly.

Although the consensus against high inflation is widespread, opinions vary over whether an inflation rate of 0 percent is better than a rate of +3 percent or −3 percent. There are two main cases in favor of a positive inflation rate. George Akerlof, William Dickens, and George Perry (1996) argue that zero inflation would lead to inefficiency due to wage and price stickiness. In their view, a little bit of inflation provides "grease" to the economic system. Fed governor Ben Bernanke, among others, argues that positive inflation—by keeping nominal interest rates well above their zero lower bound—preserves the Fed's ability to cut rates if looser monetary policy is needed. In favor of zero inflation, William Poole (1999) finds flaws in both of these arguments. Against the first he notes that if inflation does make nominal wage rigidity easier to live with, for that very reason it likely perpetuates the rigidity. Against

the second he counters that low interest rates do not make expansionary monetary policy ineffective. Poole favors zero inflation as the policy that minimizes uncertainty about future inflation, thereby best facilitating financial contracts; and that minimizes the distortions associated with unindexed taxes. In favor of a negative inflation rate there is the "optimum quantity of money" argument noted above for minimizing the deadweight cost of holding currency. On different grounds, George Selgin (1997) makes a case for falling prices in an economy with ongoing productivity improvements. He notes that it is beneficial to let prices of particular products fall as their unit costs fall. In his view, using monetary expansion to raise other prices, so as to produce zero or positive overall inflation, does nothing to increase efficiency but instead increases the adjustment burden placed on the price system.

About the Author

Lawrence H. White is the F. A. Hayek Professor of Economic History at the University of Missouri, St. Louis.

Further Reading

Aarstol, Michael P. "Inflation, Agency Costs, and Equity Returns." *Journal of Economics and Business* 52 (September–October 2000): 387–404.

Akerlof, George A., William T. Dickens, and George L. Perry. "The Macroeconomics of Low Inflation." *Brookings Papers on Economic Activity* 1996, no. 1: 1–59.

Andrés, Javier, and Ignacio Hernando. "Does Inflation Harm Economic Growth? Evidence from the OECD." In Martin Feldstein, ed., *The Costs and Benefits of Price Stability*. Chicago: University of Chicago Press for NBER, 1999.

Barro, Robert. *Determinants of Economic Growth: A Cross-Country Empirical Study.* Cambridge: MIT Press, 1997.

Bernholz, Peter. *Monetary Regimes and Inflation.* Cheltenham, U.K.: Edward Elgar, 2003.

Friedman, Milton. *Money Mischief: Episodes in Monetary History.* New York: Harcourt Brace Jovanovich, 1992.

McCulloch, J. Huston. *Money and Inflation: A Monetarist Approach.* 2d ed. New York: Academic Press, 1982.

Poole, William. "Is Inflation Too Low?" *Federal Reserve Bank of St. Louis Review* (July/August 1999): 3–10.

Selgin, George. *Less Than Zero: The Case for a Falling Price Level in a Growing Economy.* London: Institute of Economic Affairs, 1997.

White, Lawrence H. *The Theory of Monetary Institutions.* Oxford: Blackwell, 1999.

Information

Joseph E. Stiglitz

Since about 1970, an important strand of economic research, sometimes referred to as information economics, has explored the extent to which markets and other institutions process and convey information. Many of the problems of markets and other institutions result from costly information, and many of their features are responses to costly information.

Many of the central theories and principles in economics are based on assumptions about perfect information. Among these, three stand out: efficiency, full employment of resources, and uniform prices.

Efficiency

At least since Adam Smith, most economists have believed that competitive markets are efficient, and that firms, in pursuing their own interests, enhance the public good "as if by an invisible hand." A major achievement of economic science during the first half of the twentieth century was finding the precise sense in which that result is true. This result, known as the Fundamental Theorem of Welfare Economics, provides a rigorous analytic basis for the presumption that competitive markets allocate resources efficiently. In the 1980s economists made clear the hidden information assumptions underlying that theorem. They showed that in a wide variety of situations where information is costly (indeed, almost always), government interventions could make everyone better off if government officials had the right incentives. At the very least these results have undermined the long-standing presumption that markets are necessarily efficient.

Full Employment of Resources

A central result (or assumption) of standard economic theory is that resources are fully employed. The economy has a variety of mechanisms (savings and inventories provide buffers; price adjustments act as shock absorbers) that are supposed to dampen the effects of any shocks the economy experiences. In fact, for the past two hundred years economies have experienced large fluctuations, and there has been massive unemployment in the slumps. Though the GREAT DEPRESSION of the 1930s was the most recent prolonged and massive episode, the American economy suffered major recessions from 1979 to 1982, and many European economies experienced prolonged high unemployment rates during the 1980s. Information economics has explained why unemployment may persist and why fluctuations are so large.

The failure of wages to fall so that unemployed workers can find jobs has been explained by efficiency wage theories, which argue that the productivity of workers increases with higher wages (both because employees work harder and because employers can recruit a higher-quality labor force). If information about their workers' output were costless, employers would not pay such high wages because they could costlessly monitor output and pay accordingly. But because monitoring is costly, employers pay higher wages to give workers an incentive not to shirk.

While efficiency wage theory helps explain why unemployment may persist, other theories that focus on the implications of imperfect information in the capital markets can help explain economic volatility.

One strand of this theory focuses on the fact that many of the market's mechanisms for distributing risk, which are critical to an economy's ability to adjust to economic shocks, are imperfect because of costly information. Most notable in this respect is the failure of equity markets. In recent years less than 10 percent of new capital has been raised via equity markets. Information economics explains why. First, issuers of equity generally know more about the value of the shares than buyers do, and are more inclined to sell when they think buyers are overvaluing their shares. But most potential buyers know that this incentive exists and, therefore, are wary of buying. Second, shareholders have only limited control over managers. Information about what management is doing, or should be doing, to maximize shareholder value is costly. Thus, shareholders often limit the amount of "free cash" managers have to play with by imposing sufficient debt burdens to put managers' "backs to the wall." Managers must then exert strong efforts to meet those debt obligations and lenders will carefully scrutinize firms' behavior.

The fact that firms cannot (or choose not to) raise capital via equity markets means that if firms wish to invest more than their cash flow allows—or if they wish to produce more than they can finance out of their current working capital—they must turn to credit markets, and to banks in particular. From the firm's perspective, borrowing has one major disadvantage: it imposes a fixed obligation on the firm. If it fails to meet that obligation, the firm can go bankrupt. (By contrast, an all-equity firm cannot go bankrupt.) Firms normally take actions to reduce the likelihood of bankruptcy by acting in a risk-averse manner.

Risk-averse behavior, in turn, has two important consequences. First, it means that a firm's behavior is affected by its net-worth position. When its financial position is adversely affected, it cuts back on all its activities (since there is some risk associated with virtually all activities);

activities that are particularly risky—such as long-term investments—are cut the most.

Second, it means that if a firm perceives an increase in the risk associated with production or investment—such as when the economy appears to be going into a recession—it cuts back on those activities. Since risk perceptions are notoriously volatile, this too helps explain the economy's volatility.

Similarly, costly information explains why banks ration credit. Why ration rather than simply charge higher interest rates to higher-risk borrowers? Because often the only borrowers who will borrow at high rates are those who are the highest risk—and on whom, therefore, the lenders are most likely to lose. Also, higher interest rates may even induce borrowers to undertake greater risks.

Banks, in turn, can be viewed as highly leveraged firms that borrow from depositors. Their "production" activity is making loans (screening loan applicants, monitoring loans, etc.). When their net worth is reduced, or when they perceive that the risk from lending has increased, they (like any other risk-averse firm) cut back on their activities: they make fewer loans. But this in turn has strongly adverse effects on producing firms, particularly as the economy goes into a recession. Firms' cash flows are reduced. To maintain their production and investment levels, given their reluctance to issue equity, they turn to banks for credit. And it is precisely when they need the credit the most that banks may be cutting back their credit rather than expanding it. Thus, the recessionary pressures are exacerbated. As one might expect, these effects are particularly important for small and medium-sized firms, for which the issuing of commercial paper is not a viable alternative.

Thus, the characteristics of credit and equity markets—characteristics that can be explained by imperfect, costly, and asymmetric information—help explain the volatility of the economy. Information economics helps explain economic volatility in another important way. In standard theory, changes in economic circumstances lead to changes in wages, prices, and interest rates. Adjustments in these variables act as "shock absorbers." In fact, Keynes noted that prices, wages, and interest rates are not so flexible, and a major strand of Keynesian research has placed these rigidities at the center of macroeconomic fluctuations.

The explanation of such rigidities remains controversial, however. Perhaps the most convincing explanation is that firms are uncertain of the consequences of their actions, and the larger the change in any action, the more uncertain they feel. The greater their perceived uncertainty, the more conservative their actions. They change prices and wages only slowly because the consequences of changing them are so uncertain.

Uniform Prices

A third major principle of economics (besides the efficiency of market economies and the fact that resources, including labor, are fully utilized) is referred to as the "Law of the Single Price." Under this law, there is a uniform price in the market, and price differences are quickly eliminated by arbitrage. In fact, many markets are marked by noticeable differences in prices. The differences in observed prices and wages are far larger than can be accounted for simply by differences in attributes of, say, location, differences in quality, and nonpecuniary characteristics of jobs. As GEORGE STIGLER pointed out in a seminal article in 1962, costly information provides a ready explanation: arbitrage is costly. It is costly for consumers to search for the lowest price or the highest-paying jobs.

But the consequences of imperfect information are even more fundamental. Firms recognize that consumers and workers face costly searches. In some special cases this may lead each firm, less concerned about losing customers or workers to rivals, to raise its price or lower its wage.

In some cases it has been shown that even though there are many firms, prices might be raised to the monopoly level even when search costs are very small. To see why, consider a case where all firms charged the same price. If any firm were to raise its price just a little—by an amount less than the cost to customers of switching to another firm—that firm would lose no customers. Thus, so long as the price is below the monopoly price, it pays that firm to raise its price by a little. But it pays each firm to do so: all raise their prices—and the process continues until the monopoly price is reached.

In other cases it has been shown that markets create their own "noise," so that an equilibrium in which all firms charge the same price cannot exist. If all firms were charging the same price (and there was, accordingly, no need to search for the store with the lowest price), it would pay some firm to raise its price to exploit those who are particularly price insensitive because their search costs are high.

Many market institutions, practices, and structures can be viewed as the economy's responses to these informational problems. We have already noted three of these: the prevalence of the use of credit rather than equity as a source of finance for new investment; the widespread occurrence of credit rationing; and the fact that firms pay wages higher than strictly necessary in order to obtain workers, both to enable them to acquire a higher-quality labor force and to induce them to work harder.

Three other market responses to costly information are particularly important. First, firms need to have reputations so that customers know they will not be cheated, and workers need reputations so firms know that they will not shirk (see BRAND NAMES). This means that firms and workers must have an incentive to maintain their reputations. Usually, the most severe punishment a customer can impose on a firm that has sold her a shoddy product is to stop dealing with the firm and to tell her friends and associates. The most severe punishment a firm can impose on a worker who has shirked in performing duties is to fire the worker. But in traditional economic theory neither of these acts would make much difference: firms make zero profits at the margin, and workers are paid their opportunity cost (i.e., the amount they could earn elsewhere). Therefore, there is no difference between the wage paid by the firm and what they could obtain elsewhere.

Thus, for reputation mechanisms to work, firms must receive some profits at the margin, and workers must receive wages in excess of their opportunity costs. The presence and importance of these higher-than-normal profits and wages, though long recognized, had not been previously explained.

A second response to imperfect information is ADVERTISING. Because information is costly, both suppliers and demanders must spend resources to acquire and disseminate information. Just as customers search for the lowest price and workers search for the highest wage, stores advertise to provide information to potential customers concerning the location, price, availability, and qualities of their products.

Middlemen are a third example of a market response to costly information. Much popular literature vilifies the role of the middleman. Press reports point out the huge difference between the prices received by farmers and the prices paid by customers, suggesting that evil middlemen are engaged in robbing farmers and consumers. But middlemen provide a vital function in ensuring that goods are delivered where they are wanted. They are in the business of ensuring the efficient allocation of the economy's scarce resources. For the most part, competition in this sector is keen. The fact that so much is paid for these services reflects their value in allocating resources efficiently. The fact that there are often high profits simply reflects the ability of some individuals to perform those services much better than others.

The standard theorems that underlie the presumption that markets are efficient are no longer valid once we take into account the fact that information is costly and imperfect. To some, this has suggested a switch to the Austrian approach, most forcefully developed during the 1940s and later by FRIEDRICH HAYEK and his followers. They have not attempted to "defend" markets by the use of theorems. Instead, they see markets as institutions that have evolved to solve information problems. According to Hayek, neoclassical economics got itself into trouble by assuming perfect information to begin with. A much better approach, wrote Hayek, is to assume the world we have, one in which everyone has only a little information. The great virtue of free markets, he wrote, is that they allow each person to efficiently use his own information, and do not require that anyone have all the information. In this sense, Hayek noted, government planning requires the impossible— that a small body of officials have all this information.

The new information economics substantiates Hayek's contention that central planning faces problems because it requires an impossible agglomeration of information. It agrees with Hayek that the virtue of markets is that they make use of the dispersed information held by different participants in the market. But information economics does not agree with Hayek's assertion that markets act efficiently.

The fact that markets with imperfect information do not work perfectly provides a rationale for potential government actions. The older theory said that no government, no matter how well organized, could do better than markets. If that was true, then we had little need to inquire into the nature of government. The modern theory says that government might improve on matters, but to ascertain whether or not this is the case requires a closer examination of how governments actually behave, or might behave under various rules.

The modern study of political economy has uncovered many inefficiencies associated with government behavior, just as the modern study of firms has uncovered many inefficiencies associated with market behavior. An important line of research has focused on identifying how government differs intrinsically from other organizations in the economy (their powers and constraints, including the limitations on information that they face and their powers and incentives to acquire information) and, based on these distinctive features, on determining the appropriate economic roles of governments and markets.

About the Author

Joseph E. Stiglitz is an economics professor at Columbia University. He was previously chief economist at the World Bank and chairman of President Bill Clinton's Council of Economic Advisers. In 1979 he received the American Economic Association's John Bates Clark Award, given every two years to the economist under age forty who is judged to have made the most significant contribution to economics. He is a founding editor of the AEA's *Journal of Economic Perspectives*. He shared the Nobel memorial prize in economic sciences in 2001 (see also BIOGRAPHIES section).

Further Reading

Hayek, Friedrich. *Individualism and Economic Order*. Chicago: University of Chicago Press, 1948.

———. "The Use of Knowledge in Society." *American Economic Review* 35 (1945): 519–553.

Stiglitz, Joseph E. "The Causes and Consequences of the Dependence of Quality on Prices." *Journal of Economic Literature* 25 (March 1987): 1–48.

———. "Information and Economic Analysis." In Michael Parkin and A. R. Nobay, eds., *Current Economic Problems.* Cambridge: Cambridge University Press, 1975.

———. "Information and Economic Analysis: A Perspective." *Economic Journal* 95, supplement: Conference Papers (1985): 21–41.

———. "On the Economic Role of the State." In A. Heertje, ed., *The Economic Role of the State.* Oxford: Blackwell, 1989.

Information and Prices

Donald J. Boudreaux

Modern economists excel at identifying theoretical reasons why markets might fail. While these theories may temper uncritical views of the market, it is important to note that markets do, in fact, work incredibly well. Indeed, markets work so thoroughly and quietly that their success too often goes unnoticed.

Consider that the number of different ways to arrange, even in a single dimension, a mere twenty items is far greater than the number of seconds in ten billion years. Now consider that the world contains *trillions* of different resources: my labor, iron ore, Hong Kong harbor, the stage at the Met, countless stands of pine trees, fertile Russian plains, orbiting satellites, automobile factories—the list is endless. The number of different ways to use, combine, and recombine these resources is unimaginably colossal.

And almost all of these ways are useless.

It would be a mistake, for example, to combine Arnold Schwarzenegger with medical equipment and have him perform brain surgery. Likewise, it would be a genuine shame to use the fruit of Chateau Petrus's vines to make grape juice.

Only a tiny fraction of all the possible ways to allocate resources is useful. How can we discover these ways?

Random chance clearly will not work. Nor will central planning—which is really just a camouflaged method of relying on random chance. It is impossible for a central planning body even to survey the full set of possible resource arrangements, much less to rank these according to how well each will serve human purposes.

That citizens of modern market societies eat and bathe regularly; wear clean clothes; drive automobiles; fly to Rome, Italy, or Branson, Missouri, for holidays; and chat routinely on cell phones is powerful evidence that our economy is amazingly well arranged. An effective means must be at work to ensure that some of the relatively very few patterns of resource use that are beneficial are actually used (rather than any of the 99.9999999 + percent of resource-use patterns that would be either useless or calamitous).

The decentralized price system is that means. Critical to its functioning is the institution of private property with its associated duties and rights, including the duty to avoid physically harming and taking other people's property, and the right to exchange property and its fruits at terms agreed on voluntarily.

Each person seeks to use every parcel of his property in ways that yield him maximum benefit, either by consuming it most effectively according to his own subjective judgment or by employing it most effectively ("profitably") in production. Market prices are vital to making such decisions.

Vital Role of Prices

Market prices are vital because they condense, in as objective a form as possible, information on the value of alternative uses of each parcel of property. Nearly every parcel of property has alternative uses. For example, a plot of land can be used to site a pumpkin patch, a restaurant, a suite of physicians' offices, or any of many other things.

If this plot of land is to be used beneficially rather than wastefully, those responsible for deciding how it will be used must be able to determine the likely worth of each possible alternative. Making such determinations requires reliable information. And market prices are a marvelously compact and reliable source of such information.

Offers on the land from potential buyers or renters combine with the current owner's assessment of the value of the land to him to create a price for the land. Each potential user values the land by at least as much as he is willing to bid. The more intense the bidding, the more likely that each bid will reflect the maximum value each bidder places on the land. Of course, the market prices of goods or services that can be produced with the land are an especially important source of information exploited by potential users of the land to determine how much each will bid.

If the land's current owner cannot use it in a way that promises him as much value as he can get by selling it, he will sell to the buyer offering the highest price. If a commercial developer purchases the land as a site for doctors' offices, it is because this buyer observed that the rents for office space currently paid by physicians are sufficiently high to justify his purchase of the land, construction of the buildings, and purchase and assembly of all other inputs necessary to create a suite of medical offices.

The fact that the developer outbid pumpkin farmers, restaurateurs, and all other potential users of the land shows that this particular piece of land is now best used as a site for medical offices—or at least this is the best bet in an inherently uncertain world. Existing, actual prices guided him to this decision and guided others to avoid bidding more for the land than it is likely to be worth to each of them.

If consumers valued pumpkins with sufficiently greater intensity, the market price of pumpkins would have been high enough to inform pumpkin farmers that it was worthwhile to outbid any other potential user. Similarly, if, in the future, consumers come to value pumpkins more highly—or if, say, a remarkable new cure-all pill is invented that significantly reduces people's demand for physician services—pumpkin farmers might then find it worthwhile to buy the land, raze the medical offices, and plant pumpkins.

Equilibrium Prices Unnecessary

Nothing about market prices requires that they be "correct" in the sense of being the prices that would exist in general competitive equilibrium. All that is required for the best achievable economic outcomes is that actual prices give producers and consumers sufficiently reliable information and incentives to help them to coordinate their actions—to use resources in ways that are mutually beneficial relative to all other possible ways currently within human purview.

Mistakes will be made and changes will occur that continually reveal some uses of resources to be less desirable than other perceived possible uses. Producers and consumers continually respond to this information by adjusting their decisions at the margin. Prices change accordingly. Each adjustment tends to improve resource use. Such decentralized, local adjustments that improve resource use are the best that humans can achieve. Comparing this ongoing market process of adjustment, mutual accommodation, and improvement in resource use to a hypothetical "perfect" equilibrium state of allocation only courts misunderstanding. The fact that real-world markets do not achieve all imaginable gains and eradicate all vestiges of human ignorance and error is simply irrelevant, for no set of actual institutions can achieve such a fantastical outcome.

Of course, for this process to work, prices must reflect the relevant costs and benefits. If people do not take account of substantial costs of their actions, they will act in inappropriate ways. They will either engage in too much of an action (if the ignored effects are costs imposed on third parties) or too little of it (if the ignored effects are benefits enjoyed by third parties). The well-recognized existence of EXTERNALITIES creates, at least in theory, a situation that can be remedied by wise government regulation, taxation, or subsidization.

Even in the face of significant externalities, however, one method of government intervention remains especially suspect—namely, price controls. Any arbitrary floors or ceilings placed by government on prices will either prevent better prices from emerging or—if the market is infected by significant externalities—mask the problems that can be solved only by changing the underlying demand or supply conditions (see, e.g., RENT CONTROL).

By far the most important way to ensure that the forces of demand and supply result in prices that encourage useful coordination of economic plans is to keep property private, divisible, and transferable. The actual result of this ongoing series of decentralized resource-use decisions guided by actual market prices is a commercial economy of enormous productivity and prosperity for nearly every human touched by it.

About the Author

Donald J. Boudreaux is chairman of the economics department at George Mason University in Fairfax, Virginia. He was previously president of the Foundation for Economic Education. He blogs with Russell Roberts at http://cafehayek.type pad.com/.

Further Reading

Alchian, Armen A. "Property Rights." In this volume, below, and online at: http://www.econlib.org/library/Enc/Property Rights.html.

Arrow, Kenneth J. "Toward a Theory of Price Adjustment." In Moses Abramovitz, ed., *The Allocation of Economic Resources*. Stanford: Stanford University Press, 1959.

Coase, Ronald H. "The Marginal Cost Controversy." In Ronald H. Coase, ed., *The Firm, the Market, and the Law*. Chicago: University of Chicago Press, 1988.

Hayek, F. A. "The Use of Knowledge in Society." In Hayek, *Individualism and Economic Order*. Chicago: University of Chicago Press, 1948.

Kirzner, Israel M. *How Markets Work: Disequilibrium, Entrepreneurship, and Discovery*. New Delhi: Centre for Civil Society, 1997.

Machovec, Frank M. *Perfect Competition and the Transformation of Economics*. London: Routledge, 1995.

Read, Leonard E. "I, Pencil." *The Freeman*. Reprinted in Leonard E. Read, *Anything That's Peaceful: The Case for the Free Market*. Irvington-on-Hudson, N.Y.: Foundation for Economic Education, 1998. Online at: http://www.econlib .org/library/Essays/rdPncl1.html.

Schumpeter, Joseph A. "Can Capitalism Survive?" In Schumpeter, *Capitalism, Socialism, and Democracy.* New York: Harper and Brothers, 1942.

Stigler, George J. "Competition." In Stigler, *The Organization of Industry.* Homewood, Ill.: Irwin, 1968.

Innovation

Timothy Sandefur

"Innovation": creativity; novelty; the process of devising a new idea or thing, or improving an existing idea or thing. Although the word carries a positive connotation in American culture, innovation, like all human activities, has costs as well as benefits. These costs and benefits have preoccupied economists, political philosophers, and artists for centuries.

Nature and Effects

Innovation can turn new concepts into realities, creating wealth and power. For example, someone who discovers a cure for a disease has the power to withhold it, give it away, or sell it to others.[1] Innovations can also disrupt the status quo, as when the invention of the automobile eliminated the need for horse-powered transportation.

JOSEPH SCHUMPETER coined the term "CREATIVE DESTRUCTION" to describe the process by which innovation causes a free market economy to evolve.[2] Creative destruction occurs when innovations make long-standing arrangements obsolete, freeing resources to be employed elsewhere, leading to greater economic EFFICIENCY. For example, when a business manager installs a new machine that replaces manual laborers, the laborers who lose their jobs are now free to put their labor into another enterprise, resulting in more productivity. In fact, in many cases, the number of jobs available will actually increase because the machinery is introduced.

Henry Hazlitt provides the example of cotton-spinning machinery introduced in England in the 1760s.[3] At the time, the English textile industry employed some 7,900 people, and many workers protested the introduction of machinery out of fear for their livelihoods. But in 1787

there were 320,000 workers in the English textile industry. Although the introduction of machinery caused temporary discomfort to some workers, the machinery increased the aggregate wealth of society by decreasing the cost of production. Amazingly, concerns over technology and job loss in the textile industry continue today. One report notes that the introduction of new machinery in American textile mills between 1972 and 1992 coincided with a greater than 30 percent decrease in the number of textile jobs. However, that decrease was offset by the creation of new jobs. The authors conclude that "there is substantial entry into the industries, job creation rates are high, and productivity dynamics suggest surviving plants have emerged all the stronger while it has been the less productive plants that have exited."[4]

According to Schumpeter, the process of technological change in a free market consists of three parts: invention (conceiving a new idea or process), innovation (arranging the economic requirements for implementing an invention), and diffusion (whereby people observing the new discovery adopt or imitate it). These stages can be observed in the history of several famous innovations. The Xerox photocopier was invented by Chester Carlson,[5] a patent attorney frustrated by the difficulty of copying legal documents.[6] After several years of tedious work, Carlson and a physicist friend successfully photocopied a phrase on October 22, 1938. But industry and government were not interested in further development of the invention. In 1944, the nonprofit Battelle Corporation,[7] dedicated to helping inventors, finally showed interest. It and the Haloid Company (later called Xerox) invested in further development. Haloid announced the successful development of a photocopier on October 22, 1948, but the first commercially available copier was not sold until 1950. After another $16 million was invested in developing the photocopier concept, the Xerox 915 became the first simple push-button plain-paper copier. An immense success, it earned Carlson more than $150 million.[8] In the following years, competing firms began selling copiers, and other inventions, such as the fax machine, adapted the technology.

---

1. See, e.g., Jane S. Smith, *Patenting the Sun: Polio and the Salk Vaccine* (New York: Anchor, 1991).

2. Joseph Schumpeter, *Capitalism, Socialism, and Democracy,* 3d ed. (New York: Harper, 1975), chap.7, online at: http://transcriptions.english.ucsb.edu/archive/courses/liu/english25/materials/schumpeter.html.

3. Henry Hazlitt, *Economics in One Lesson* (New York: Three Rivers Press, 1979) chap. 7.

4. Jim Levinsohn and Wendy Petropoulos, "Creative Destruction or Just Plain Destruction? The U.S. Textile and Apparel Industries Since 1972" (2000), online at: http://www.nber.org/~confer/2000/itifoo/levinsohn.pdf.

5. See http://www.lib.rochester.edu/index.cfm?PAGE=399.

6. See http://www.ideafinder.com/history/inventors/carlson.htm.

7. See http://www.battelle.org/.

8. See Frederic M. Scherer, *Industrial Market Structure and Economic Performance* (Chicago: Rand McNally, 1970), chap. 15.

Schumpeter limited his analysis of innovation to its economic aspects, but Friedrich Hayek pointed out that the same process takes place at the level of social mores and political philosophy. Hayek and his contemporary Karl Popper developed the political theory of the "open society," stressing the importance of innovation for the discovery and testing of social values.[9] In Hayek's words, "the existence of individuals and groups simultaneously observing partially different rules provides the opportunity for the selection of the more effective ones."[10] This process, however, creates discomfort as well.

Reasons for Opposing Innovation

The discomfort that innovation generates has led many people to condemn it outright or to try to regulate it. Reasons for opposing innovation range from the practical concern that unforeseen consequences of untried innovations might cause disaster—as when a new drug causes unpredicted side effects—to immediate self-interest of those who benefit from the status quo—as when film studios sought to stifle the development of the home video recorder, which, they thought, threatened their profits.[11] Likewise, dictatorships bar demonstrations and elections to prevent the dictator from losing authority. More theoretical concerns that, by altering the state of affairs, moral and social rules will also be upset can lead to regulation of innovation. Leon Kass, for example, argues that innovations in medical science will destroy important social and moral values such as respect for nature.[12] In *The Republic,* Plato declared that in the ideal commonwealth, governing authorities would "be watchful against innovations in music and gymnastics counter to the established order, and to the best of their power guard against them . . . [f]or the modes of music are never disturbed without unsettling the most political and social conventions."[13] Opponents of in-

novation are frequently motivated by a desire to preserve a stable social order, often on the grounds that permanency is the essential goal of political society.

Innovation in technology upsets established orders no less than innovation in social mores does because technology and social mores are often intertwined. The introduction of steam power, firearms, and alcohol to Native Americans during the nineteenth century severely disrupted their ancient traditions. The introduction of technology into the workplace has often been a target of anti-innovation criticism. Household tools that reduced the amount of housework traditionally done by women enabled them to leave the home and enter the workforce in competition with men.[14] One result was the passage of legislation barring women from certain professions, supposedly to protect them but in reality because, as the president of the International Cigar Makers Union admitted in 1879, "We cannot drive the females out of the trade, but we can restrict this daily quota of labor through factory laws."[15]

Reasons for Innovation

Defenders of innovation, whom Virginia Postrel calls "dynamists,"[16] argue that innovation is essential for solving problems that impose significant social and personal costs. For example, humans lived with disease and starvation for most of recorded history, but technological advancement has led to cures for many of these diseases and improved the production of food, with beneficial consequences for a great many people. The introduction of labor-saving technology was essential to this process even though it initially caused disruption by costing the jobs of manual laborers.

Moreover, some defenders of innovation point out that some of what opponents see as "costs" of innovation are in reality benefits. C. P. Snow, for example, argues in *The Two Cultures* that opponents of innovation tend to overlook the suffering of disenfranchised groups, or even to romanticize it. Postrel criticizes Leon Kass's views on medical science on these grounds, arguing that it is morally wrong to regard suffering and illness as essential parts of human experience that ought to be preserved.[17] By contrast, de-

9. On Popper, see http://www.eeng.dcu.ie/~tkpw/; also see Karl Popper, *The Open Society and Its Enemies,* 5th ed. (Princeton: Princeton University Press, 1966).

10. Friedrich Hayek, *The Constitution of Liberty* (Chicago: University of Chicago Press, 1960), p. 63.

11. *Sony v. Universal Studios,* 464 U.S. 417 (1984), online at: http://caselaw.lp.findlaw.com/scripts/getcase.pl?court=us&vol=464&invol=417.

12. See, e.g., Leon Kass, *The New Biology: What Price the Relief of Man's Estate?* (American Association for the Advancement of Science, 1971); online at: http://www.alteich.com/links/kass.htm.

13. *The Republic* 4.424b (trans. Benjamin Jowett), online at: http://www.perseus.tufts.edu/cgi-bin/ptext?doc=Perseus%3Atext%3A1999.01.0168. See also *Laws* 2.656d et seq. (trans. Benjamin Jowett), online at: http://www.perseus.tufts.edu/cgi-bin/ptext?doc=Perseus%3Atext%3A1999.01.0166; http://www.utm.edu/research/iep/p/plato.htm.

14. See http://college.hmco.com/history/readerscomp/rcah/html/ah_093200_womenandthew.htm.

15. Quoted in Jo Freeman, "The Revolution for Women in Law and Public Policy," in Jo Freeman, ed., *Women: A Feminist Perspective,* 5th ed. (Mountain View, Calif.: Mayfield, 1995), online at: http://www.jofreeman.com/lawandpolicy/revlaw.htm.

16. See Virginia Postrel, *The Future and Its Enemies* (New York: Free Press, 1998).

17. See http://www.dynamist.com/articles-speeches/forbes/

fenders of innovation often see it as beneficial for innovation to disrupt social orders they see as unjust; in *The Hunchback of Notre Dame,* for example, Victor Hugo dramatizes the importance of the printing press in disrupting the unjust social order of the middle ages.[18]

As with social disruption, dynamists regard the economic disruption caused by innovation as a benefit to the consumer and as an important step in the pursuit of economic efficiency. In short, dynamists tend to favor innovation out of a humanistic concern for the survival and flourishing of individuals.

Requirements for Innovation

There are two common sayings about innovation. The first is that "if you build a better mousetrap, the world will beat a path to your door." In a seminal work on innovation, economist Jacob Schmookler gave credence to this view when he compared the rates at which patents were issued with the amount of investment in new technologies. Schmookler concluded that innovation is driven almost exclusively by economic demand: people engage in innovation out of a belief that the economic returns will be greater than its costs.[19] But some economists criticize his approach as overly simplistic, particularly for ignoring factors independent of economics that heavily influence how innovation happens.[20] Mere demand for a new product or service is not enough to bring an innovation about.

The other common saying holds that "necessity is the mother of invention." But the reality is that *leisure* is the mother of innovation. In economic terms, surplus capital provides the necessary time and startup costs for implementing a new idea (see INVESTMENT).[21] Because a new product or service, or even a new social more, might not succeed, a potential innovator must assemble the resources to permit him to begin implementation without a guaranteed return on the investment. The ability to assemble and invest capital is therefore indispensable for innovation of any sort, and capital is available only when some people have enough wealth to permit innovators to spend their time thinking creatively.

But the mere availability of capital is not sufficient for innovation. Capital must also be mobile and stable (see PROPERTY RIGHTS). Hernando de Soto explains that even in places where entrepreneurship is strong and capital is available, capital cannot serve the needs of potential innovators unless it is in a mobile form that allows various types of wealth to be converted into credit. This mobility includes "property document[s]" such as title deeds, which "represent the invisible potential that is locked up in the assets we accumulate."[22] Stability of capital is provided by the rule of law,[23] by which the use of coercion in society is made regular and predictable. If investments cannot be insured against expropriation, possessors of capital are less likely to take the risk of investing in an innovation. Nations lacking a stable rule of law, including property rights, tend to be less prosperous and to have less innovation.[24]

Paul Romer, a leading scholar of economic growth, has explained that innovation results from a combination of growth-fostering social institutions and new ideas.[25] Because ideas, unlike objects, can be shared by many at the same time, they greatly increase the speed of technological advancement. Capital, social institutions, and new technology, therefore, do not alone cause growth; they must be combined with the ability and willingness to think and act creatively (see ENTREPRENEURSHIP), which in turn means that innovation has philosophical and psychological requirements.[26] The ability to think creatively requires epistemological tools such as the scientific method, by which an innovator can approach a problem and begin the process of solving it. Philosophies that have not produced such tools, such as dogmatic religions, tend to retard technological innovation. As Nathan Rosenberg and L. E. Birdzell note, the scientific method provided Western civilization with an indispensable tool in its creation of prosperity.[27] David Landes's book *The Wealth and Poverty of*

prodeath.html; http://www.dynamist.com/articles-speeches/opeds/latcells.html.

18. See especially chap. 23, online at: http://www.gutenberg.org/etext/6539.

19. Jacob Schmookler, *Invention and Economic Growth* (Cambridge: Harvard University Press, 1966).

20. See, e.g., http://www.compilerpress.atfreeweb.com/Anno%20Rosenberg%20Science,%20Invention%20and%20Economic%20Growth%20EJ%201974.htm.

21. See http://www.informationweek.com/803/romer.htm.

22. Hernando de Soto, *The Mystery of Capital* (New York: Basic Books, 2000), p. 7; on de Soto, see http://www.worldpress.org/Americas/1602.cfm.

23. See further Hayek, *Constitution of Liberty*, p. 205–233.

24. See http://www.econlib.org/library/Enc/PropertyRights.html; http://fte.org/capitalism/lessons/02/outline/; http://www.hoover.stanford.edu/publications/books/fulltext/better/143.pdf.

25. See http://www.stanford.edu/~promer/Econgro.htm; http://www.reason.com/0112/fe.rb.post.shtml.

26. See http://www.compilerpress.atfreeweb.com/Anno%20Romer%20Why,%20Indeed,%20in%20America%20Theory,%20History,%20and%20the%20Origins%20of%20Modern%20AER%201996.htm; http://arnoldkling.com/~arnoldsk/aimst4/aimst420.html.

27. Nathan Rosenberg and L. E. Birdzell Jr., *How the West Grew*

Nations emphasizes that, in addition to geographical and other circumstantial causes, innovation has important ethical and metaphysical foundations. Societies in which innovation is seen as a sinful disruption of the proper cosmological order, or in which individuals are punished or shunned for thinking differently than others, are also unlikely to experience innovation. On the other hand, early America, for example, prospered in large part because it was "a seed bed of democracy and enterprise" wherein "equality bred self-esteem, ambition, a readiness to enter and compete in the marketplace, a spirit of individualism and contentiousness."[28]

Some economists argue that larger firms have an advantage in introducing innovative goods and services, as they can afford to invest in developing a possibly fruitless new idea—which can be very expensive.[29] RCA, for example, invested more than sixty-five million dollars in the color television, a lot of money in mid-twentieth-century dollars, before it became commercially successful. Also, some economists argue, larger firms can attract more talented employees to devise new ideas. But market dominance may not be as important as these economists suppose. Frederic Scherer notes that of sixty-one important twentieth-century inventions, more than half were devised by people who were independent of any formal research organization or who were college professors.[30] Private research and development is responsible for the telephone, the lightbulb, paper matches, and even the baby incubator, which was introduced as a carnival attraction at Coney Island.[31] Also, established firms are sometimes slow to introduce new creations: Gillette took its time introducing the stainless steel razor in the 1960s, partly out of fear that it would be so efficient that Gillette sales would decrease. (As with English textile machinery in the eighteenth cen-

tury, this fear proved groundless.)[32] And IBM delayed production of the personal computer until small upstart companies such as Apple and Commodore had introduced them successfully. Nor do long-established, wealthy firms necessarily have greater access to talent. Some Silicon Valley software companies have created workplaces designed to foster innovative talent, providing beds, foosball and Frisbee games, and snack rooms full of free food.[33] Employees of the film company Pixar work not in cubicles but in "cottages" they design themselves, so as to create an ideal environment for creative thinking.[34] An individual's willingness to entertain unorthodox ideas and confront those who oppose his innovation as immoral or unwise will also determine his ability to innovate. The creative process often involves potential embarrassment and financial ruin. In extreme cases, it may mean conflict with family, friends, and religious or social leaders. Innovation is therefore related to the psychological phenomenon of self-esteem.[35]

Political freedom is also an important ingredient. Because innovation often requires the exchange and expression of ideas, the freedom to dissent is particularly important. Also, since innovation is often encouraged by a desire for profit, secure property rights serve as an incentive by ensuring that innovators are secure in the fruits of their labor. Scientific, as well as artistic or philosophical, innovation tends to be greater in countries with greater political freedom. Moreover, political freedom requires an innovation to satisfy the consumer, rather than the political authorities, if it is to succeed. Although economist Kenneth Arrow argued in the 1960s that free markets tend to underinvest in innovation out of fear of the risk involved, Rosenberg and Birdzell contend that Western nations prospered precisely because "the response of the market was *the* test of the success or failure of an innovation," an effect that "was intensified by the Western practice of leaving the losers to bear their own losses, which were often substantial. This use of a competitive spur to stimulate change was a marked departure from tradition, for societies and their rulers have always strongly resisted change unless it enhanced the ruler's

Rich: The Economic Transformation of the Industrial World (New York: Basic Books, 1987), pp. 250–257.

28. David S. Landes, *The Wealth and Poverty of Nations* (New York: Norton, 1999), p. 297. See further Jacob Bronowski, *Science and Human Values* (New York: Harper, 1965); W. J. F. Jenner, *The Tyranny of History: The Roots of China's Crisis* (New York: Viking, 1992).

29. See, e.g., Kenneth Arrow, "Economic Welfare and the Allocation of Resources for Invention," in Richard Nelson, ed., *The Rate of Inventive Activity* (Princeton: Princeton University Press, 1962).

30. Scherer, *Industrial Market Structure and Economic Performance*.

31. See http://www.matchcovers.com/first100.htm; http://xroads.virginia.edu/~UG02/altman/coney_island_webpage/coney_island_webpage/babies.html.

32. See http://www.time.com/time/archive/printout/0,23657,870492,00.html.

33. See http://www.santacruzsentinel.com/archive/2003/November/02/biz/stories/01biz.htm.

34. See http://www.boingboing.net/2005/03/16/pixars_groovy_noncub.html.

35. Nathaniel Branden, *Self-Esteem at Work: How Confident People Make Powerful Companies* (San Francisco: Jossey-Bass, 1998), p. 69.

own power and well-being."[36] In Rosenberg and Birdzell's view, the potential risks of innovation help to ensure that capital is more wisely invested in a free economy than it would be in a command economy.

The prospect of monopoly profits is a particularly important incentive to innovation. A "new mousetrap" gives its producer an advantage against competitors, at least until the competitors imitate the innovation. As Schumpeter writes, "Every successful corner may spell monopoly for the moment."[37] One example of how innovations often begin with a desire for monopoly profits is the movie industry. In the early days of motion pictures, entrepreneur Adolph Zukor began Paramount Pictures. Like many other movie studios, Paramount integrated the entire film production process, from script writing to filming to distribution to movie theaters owned by the film company itself.[38] Because motion pictures were still a relatively new idea, it made sense for a single firm to both produce and show movies—just as broadcast television networks were sometimes owned by the same companies that manufactured televisions.[39] An antitrust lawsuit ended the movie studios' ownership of theaters in 1948,[40] but actual monopolies have also assisted innovation in some cases. One legal device designed to encourage innovation is the patent, a legal monopoly giving the holder the exclusive right to profit from the implementation of an idea. Any person who attempts to profit from the sale of something covered by another's patent can be prosecuted and forced to disgorge his profits.

Yet, while the possibility of temporary monopoly may attract innovation, a permanent monopoly can stifle it. "A company which already dominates the market it supplies has little to gain by speeding up the introduction of product improvements," writes Scherer. Hence patents are granted only for a limited time. This ensures that firms must continue to satisfy the consumer if they are to maintain their market dominance: "If their market position is threatened by the introduction of the smaller innovator, they have a great deal to lose by running a poor second:

the larger share they would otherwise enjoy."[41] Besides IBM and Apple, the history of innovation is replete with examples. Henry Ford's failure to introduce the electric starter gave the Dodge Brothers an opportunity to compete against the Model T. When the management of Ben Franklin thrift stores rejected the marketing ideas of employee Sam Walton in the 1960s, he went on to found Wal-Mart on his own.[42]

About the Author

Timothy Sandefur is the lead attorney in the Economic Liberty Project at the Pacific Legal Foundation in Sacramento, California. He is also a contributing editor of *Liberty* magazine.

Insider Trading

Stanislav Dolgopolov

"Insider trading" refers to transactions in a company's securities, such as stocks or options, by corporate insiders or their associates based on information originating within the firm that would, once publicly disclosed, affect the prices of such securities. Corporate insiders are individuals whose employment with the firm (as executives, directors, or sometimes rank-and-file employees) or whose privileged access to the firm's internal affairs (as large shareholders, consultants, accountants, lawyers, etc.) gives them valuable information. Famous examples of insider trading include transacting on the advance knowledge of a company's discovery of a rich mineral ore (*Securities and Exchange Commission v. Texas Gulf Sulphur Co.*), on a forthcoming cut in dividends by the board of directors (*Cady, Roberts & Co.*), and on an unanticipated increase in corporate expenses (*Diamond v. Oreamuno*). Although insider trading typically yields significant profits, these transactions are still risky. Much trading by insiders, though, is due to their need for cash or to balance their portfolios. The above definition of insider trading excludes transactions in a company's securities made on nonpublic "outside" information, such as the knowledge of forthcoming market-wide or industry developments or of competitors' strategies and products. Such trading on information originating outside the company is generally not covered by insider trading regulation.

---

36. Arrow, "Economic Welfare and the Allocation of Resources for Invention"; Rosenberg and Birdzell, *How the West Grew Rich,* p. 23.

37. Schumpeter, *Capitalism, Socialism, and Democracy,* p. 102.

38. Kevin Starr, *Inventing The Dream: California Through the Progressive Era* (New York: Oxford University Press, 1985), pp. 312–333.

39. See http://members.aol.com/cingram/television/dumont.htm.

40. See http://www.cobbles.com/simpp_archive/paramount case_6supreme1948.htm.

41. Scherer, *Industrial Market Structure and Economic Performance,* p. 368.

42. See http://www.anbhf.org/laureates/swalton.html.

Insider trading is quite different from market manipu-lation, disclosure of false or misleading information to the market, or direct expropriation of the corporation's wealth by insiders. It also should be noted that transactions based on unequally distributed information are common and of-ten legal in labor, commodities, and real estate markets, to name a few. Nevertheless, many people still find insider trading in corporate securities objectionable. One objec-tion is that it violates the fiduciary duties that corporate employees, as agents, owe to their principals, the share-holders (Wilgus 1910). A related objection is that, because managers control the production of, disclosure of, and ac-cess to inside information, they can transfer wealth from outsiders to themselves in an arbitrary and hidden way (Brudney 1979; Clark 1986). The economic rationale ad-vanced for prohibiting insider trading is that such trading can adversely affect securities markets (Khanna 1997) or decrease the firm's value (Haft 1982).

Regulation of insider trading began in the United States at the turn of the twentieth century, when judges in several states became willing to rescind corporate insiders' trans-actions with uninformed shareholders. One of the earliest (and unsuccessful) federal attempts to regulate insider trading occurred after the 1912–1913 congressional hear-ings before the Pujo Committee, which concluded that "the scandalous practices of officers and directors in spec-ulating upon inside and advance information as to the ac-tion of their corporations may be curtailed if not stopped." The Securities Acts of 1933–1934, passed by the U.S. Con-gress in the aftermath of the stock market crash, though aimed primarily at prohibiting fraud and market manip-ulation, also targeted insider trading. This federal legisla-tion mandated disgorgement of profits made by corporate insiders on round-trip transactions (a purchase and later sale or a sale and later purchase) effected within six months, required disclosure of past inside transactions, and prohibited insiders from selling "borrowed" shares of their companies. However, the Securities Acts did not con-tain a broad prohibition of insider trading as such.

Broader enforcement of restrictions on insider trading began only in the 1960s, when the U.S. Securities and Exchange Commission (SEC) prosecuted the *Cady, Roberts* and *Texas Gulf Sulphur* cases using Rule 10b-5, a catch-all provision against securities fraud. In those and subse-quent cases that shaped the evolution of the general in-sider trading prohibition, the SEC based its justification for regulation on the unfairness of unequal access to in-formation, the violation of fiduciary duties by insiders, and the misappropriation of information as a form of property. The U.S. Congress and the SEC increased penalties for the use of inside information, extended the prohibition into derivatives markets, proscribed selective disclosure of in-formation, and even placed restrictions on the use of cer-tain types of "outside" information, dealing mainly with takeovers pursued by third parties. Nevertheless, federal legislators have never defined insider trading; in the 1980s, the SEC actually opposed efforts to do so. Since the U.S. Supreme Court decided *United States v. O'Hagan* in 1997, however, the judicial definition of proscribed activi-ties has become fairly clear: it includes trading by corpo-rate insiders and their associates on inside information as well as trading by individuals who misappropriate certain types of "outside" information from third parties.

As of 2004, at least ninety-three countries, the vast ma-jority of nations that possess organized securities markets, had laws regulating insider trading. Several factors explain the rapid emergence of such regulation, particularly dur-ing the last twenty years: namely, the growth of the secu-rities industry worldwide, pressures to make national se-curities markets look more attractive in the eyes of outside investors, and the pressure the SEC exerted on foreign lawmakers and regulators to increase the effectiveness of domestic enforcement by identifying and punishing of-fenders and their associates operating outside the United States. In some countries, insider trading had been regu-lated through private means before the arrival of public regulation, as the examples of the United Kingdom's City Code on Takeovers and Mergers and the German Volun-tary Insider Trading Guidelines show. At the same time, the effectiveness of the insider trading prohibition and the commitment to enforcing it have been low in most coun-tries (Bhattacharya and Daouk 2002).

Who benefits from regulation of insider trading? One group of beneficiaries is market professionals—broker-dealers, securities analysts, floor traders, arbitrageurs, and institutional investors. The reason is that they are "next in line" for trading profits, as they possess an advantage over public investors in collecting and analyzing information (Haddock and Macey 1987). Regulation also, of course, benefits the regulators—that is, the SEC—by giving that agency greater power, prestige, and budget (Bainbridge 2002). However, the benefits from insider trading laws to small shareholders, the alleged primary beneficiaries, have been extensively debated.

Henry G. Manne popularized the economic analysis of insider trading (Manne 1966), although a similar book-length attempt by Frank P. Smith is dated a quarter cen-tury earlier (Smith 1941). The major public policy ques-tions economists and legal scholars have tried to answer are: How extensive should restrictions on insider trading be and should they be mandatory through the means of public regulation or voluntary by individual companies and securities exchanges? Empirical research has focused on the profitability of insiders' transactions, the effects of insider trading on securities prices and transaction costs, and the effectiveness of regulation. Such studies have had one common methodological problem: precise data on illegal insider trading, as opposed to disclosed insiders' transactions, are, by their very nature, not readily available.

Many researchers argue that trading on inside information is a zero-sum game, benefiting insiders at the expense of outsiders. But most outsiders who bought from or sold to insiders would have traded anyway, and possibly at a worse price (Manne 1970). So, for example, if the insider sells stock because he expects the price to fall, the very act of selling may bring the price down to the buyer. In such a case, the buyer who would have bought anyway actually gains. But this does not mean that no one loses because of insider trading, although such losses are likely to be diffuse and not easily traceable (Wang and Steinberg 1996). The outsiders who lose in such a situation are buyers on the margin, who would not have bought unless the insider had sold and brought the price down slightly, and sellers who sold for less or could not sell at all. Consequently, some commentators argue that such systematic diversion of wealth from outsiders to insiders may decrease the share price and raise the corporate cost of capital (Mendelson 1969). However, long-term shareholders, as opposed to those speculating on short-term price movements, are rarely adversely affected by insider trading because the probability is low that such trading would affect the timing of their transactions and the corresponding market price (Manne 1966).

A controversial case is that of abstaining from trading on the basis of inside information (Fried 2003). For example, an insider who had planned to sell stock but abstains on the basis of positive inside information thereby marginally prevents a potential buyer from getting a better deal on the stock. In a sense, the insider's abstention transfers wealth from the potential buyer to himself, although this does not happen consistently. Yet, it is clearly infeasible to monitor and prosecute insiders for *not* trading.

There is little disagreement that insider trading makes securities markets more efficient by moving the current market price closer to the future postdisclosure price. In other words, insiders' transactions, even if they are anonymous, signal future price trends to others and make the current stock price reflect relevant information sooner. Accurately priced stocks give valuable signals to investors and ensure more efficient allocation of capital. The controversial question is whether insider trading is more or less effective than public disclosure. Insider trading's advan-

tage is that it introduces individual profit motives, does not directly reveal sensitive intercorporate information, and mitigates the management's aversion to disclosing negative information (Carlton and Fischel 1983; Scott 1980). Insider trading's potential disadvantage is that it may be a more ambiguous and less reliable signal than disclosure (Cox 1986). Empirical work demonstrates that insider trading does move prices in the correct direction (Meulbroek 1992). Some researchers argue, though, that this additional price accuracy only redistributes wealth instead of making the process of capital allocation more efficient, because insider trading speeds up the process by only a few days or weeks without affecting the long-run attractiveness of a company as an investment (Klock 1994).

Probably the most controversial issue in the economic analysis of insider trading is whether it is an efficient way to pay managers for their entrepreneurial services to the corporation. Some researchers believe that insider trading gives managers a monetary incentive to innovate, search for, and produce valuable information, as well as to take risks that increase the firm's value (Carlton and Fischel 1983; Manne 1966). Researchers have also pointed out that compensation in the form of insider trading is "cheap" for long-term shareholders because it does not come from corporate profits (Hu and Noe 1997). Their opponents contend that insider trading has some downside incentives and is likely to reward mere access to information rather than its production. The argument is that allowing insider trading may encourage managers to disclose information prematurely (Bainbridge 2002) or delay disclosure in order to arrange stock trades (Schotland 1967), to delay transmitting information to corporate decision makers (Haft 1982), to pursue excessively risky projects that increase trading profits but reduce corporate value (Easterbrook 1981), to increase tolerance for bad corporate performance by allowing insiders to profit on negative developments (Cox 1986), and to determine their compensation unilaterally (Clark 1986). This controversy has not been resolved and is difficult to test empirically.

Another economic argument for insider trading is that it provides efficient compensation to holders of large blocks of stock (Demsetz 1986; Thurber 1994). Such shareholders, who provide valuable corporate monitoring and sometimes cannot diversify their portfolios easily—and thus bear the disproportionate risk of price fluctuations—are compensated by trading on inside information. However, proponents of regulation point out that such an arrangement would allow large shareholders to transfer wealth from smaller shareholders to themselves in an arbitrary fashion and, possibly, provoke conflicts between these two groups (Maug 2002). This concern may explain why the SEC, in 2000, adopted Regulation FD (FD stands for "full disclosure") banning selective disclosure of information by corporations to large shareholders and securities analysts.

A common contention is that the presence of insider trading decreases public confidence in, and deters many potential investors from, equity markets, making them less liquid (Loss 1970). But the possibility of trading with better-informed insiders would likely cause investors to discount the security's price for the amount of expected loss rather than refusing to buy the security (Carney 1987). Empirical comparisons across countries do not clearly demonstrate that stricter enforcement of insider trading regulation has directly caused more widespread participation in equities markets. Another argument is that insider trading harms market liquidity by increasing transaction costs. The alleged reason is that market makers—specialized intermediaries who provide liquidity by continuously buying and selling securities, such as NYSE specialists or NASDAQ dealers—consistently lose from trading with insiders and recoup their losses by increasing their bid-ask spread (the differential between buying and selling prices) (Bagehot 1971). Yet, the lack of actual lawsuits by market makers, except in options markets, is strong evidence that insider trading is not a real concern for them. Moreover, econometric attempts to find a relationship between the bid-ask spread and the risk of insider trading have been inconsistent and unreliable (Dolgopolov 2004).

Empirical research generally supports skepticism that regulation of insider trading has been effective in either the United States or internationally, as evidenced by the persistent trading profits of insiders, behavior of stock prices around corporate announcements, and relatively infrequent prosecution rates (Bhattacharya and Daouk 2002; Bris 2005). Even in the United States, disclosed trading by corporate insiders generally yields them abnormal profits (Pettit and Venkatesh 1995). Thus, insider trading regulation may affect the behavior of certain categories of traders, but it does not eliminate profits from trading on private information. The likely explanation for the fact that profits remain is that the regulation shifts insiders' emphasis from legal to illegal trading, changes insiders' trading strategies, or transfers profits to market professionals. For these reasons, some scholars doubt the value of such laws to public investors; moreover, enforcement is costly and could be dangerously selective.

Several researchers have proposed that market professionals (notably, securities analysts) be allowed to trade on inside information (Goshen and Parchomovsky 2001). These researchers reason that such professionals enjoy economies of scale and scope in processing firm-specific and external information and are removed from corporate decision making. Therefore, allowing market professionals to trade on inside information would create more liquidity in securities markets and stimulate competition in the acquisition of information. The related argument is that the "outside" search for information is more socially valuable, even if it is occasionally more costly, and that trading by corporate insiders may crowd out securities research on external factors (Khanna 1997). Thus, the proponents of regulation argue that unrestricted insider trading would adversely affect the process of gathering and disseminating information by the securities industry, and this point of view has some empirical support (Bushman et al. 2005). On the other hand, permitting insiders to trade on inside information may allow companies to pay managers less because they have insider-trading opportunities. In fact, there is evidence from Japan and the United States that the cash portion of executive salaries is lower when potential trading profits are higher (Hebner and Kato 1997; Roulstone 2003). If market professionals could trade legally on private information but insiders could not, public shareholders would still lose, while being unable to recoup their trading losses in the form of higher corporate profits because of lower managerial compensation (Haddock and Macey 1987).

Despite numerous and extensive debates, economists and legal scholars do not agree on a desirable government policy toward insider trading. On the one hand, absolute information parity is clearly infeasible, and information-based trading generally increases the pricing efficiency of financial markets. Information, after all, is a scarce economic good that is costly to produce or acquire, and its subsequent use and dissemination are difficult to control. On the other hand, insider trading, as opposed to other forms of informed trading, may produce unintended adverse consequences for the functioning of the corporate enterprise, the market-wide system of publicly mandated disclosure, or the market for information. While the effects of insider trading on securities prices and insiders' profits have been extensively studied empirically, the incentive effects of insider trading and its impact on the inner functioning of corporations are not well known. It also should be considered that individual firms have an incentive to weigh negative and positive consequences of insider trading and decide, through private contracting, whether to allow it. The case for having public regulation of insider trading must, therefore, rest on such factors as inefficiency of private enforcement or insider trading's overall adverse impact on securities markets.

About the Author

Stanislav Dolgopolov is a John M. Olin Fellow in Law and Economics at the University of Michigan Law School.

Further Reading

Introductory

Brudney, Victor. "Insiders, Outsiders, and Informational Advantages Under the Federal Securities Laws." *Harvard Law Review* 93 (1979): 322–376.

Carlton, Dennis W., and Daniel R. Fischel. "The Regulation of Insider Trading." *Stanford Law Review* 35 (1983): 857–895.

Haft, Robert J. "The Effect of Insider Trading Rules on the Internal Efficiency of the Large Corporation." *Michigan Law Review* 80 (1982): 1051–1071.

Hu, Jie, and Thomas H. Noe. "The Insider Trading Debate." *Federal Reserve Bank of Atlanta Economic Review* 82 (4th Quarter 1997): 34–45.

Klock, Mark. "Mainstream Economics and the Case for Prohibiting Insider Trading." *Georgia State University Law Review* 10 (1994): 297–335.

Manne, Henry G. *Insider Trading and the Stock Market*. New York: Free Press, 1966.

Wang, William K. S., and Marc I. Steinberg. *Insider Trading*. Boston: Little, Brown, 1996.

Advanced

Bagehot, Walter [pseudonym for Jack L. Treynor]. "The Only Game in Town." *Financial Analysts Journal* 27 (March–April 1971): 12–14, 22.

Bainbridge, Stephen M. *Corporation Law and Economics*. New York: Foundation Press, 2002.

Bhattacharya, Utpal, and Hazem Daouk. "The World Price of Insider Trading." *Journal of Finance* 57 (2002): 75–108.

Bris, Arturo. "Do Insider Trading Laws Work?" *European Financial Management* 11 (2005): 267–312.

Bushman, Robert M., Joseph D. Piotroski, and Abbie J. Smith. "Insider Trading Restrictions and Analysts' Incentives to Follow Firms." *Journal of Finance* 60 (2005): 35–66.

Carney, William J. "Signaling and Causation in Insider Trading." *Catholic University Law Review* 36 (1987): 863–898.

Clark, Robert Charles. *Corporate Law*. Boston: Little, Brown, 1986.

Cox, James D. "Insider Trading and Contracting: A Critical Response to the 'Chicago School.'" *Duke Law Journal* 1986 (1986): 628–659.

Demsetz, Harold. "Corporate Control, Insider Trading, and Rates of Return." *American Economic Review* 76 (1986): 313–316.

Dolgopolov, Stanislav. "Insider Trading and the Bid-Ask Spread: A Critical Evaluation of Adverse Selection in Market Making." *Capital University Law Review* 33 (2004): 83–180.

Easterbrook, Frank H. "Insider Trading, Secret Agents, Evidentiary Privileges, and the Production of Information." *Supreme Court Review* 1981 (1981): 309–365.

Fried, Jesse M. "Insider Abstention." *Yale Law Journal* 113 (2003): 455–492.

Goshen, Zohar, and Gideon Parchomovsky. "On Insider Trading, Markets, and 'Negative' Property Rights in Information." *Virginia Law Review* 87 (2001): 1229–1277.

Haddock, David D., and Jonathan R. Macey. "Regulation on Demand: A Private Interest Model, with an Application to Insider Trading Regulation." *Journal of Law and Economics* 30 (1987): 311–352.

Hebner, Kevin J., and Takao Kato. "Insider Trading and Executive Compensation: Evidence from the U.S. and Japan." *International Review of Economics and Finance* 6 (1997): 223–237.

Khanna, Naveen. "Why Both Insider Trading and Non-mandatory Disclosures Should Be Prohibited." *Managerial and Decision Economics* 18 (1997): 667–679.

Loss, Louis. "The Fiduciary Concept as Applied to Trading by Corporate 'Insiders' in the United States." *Modern Law Review* 33 (1970): 34–52.

Manne, Henry G. "Insider Trading and Law Professors." *Vanderbilt Law Review* 23 (1970): 547–590.

Maug, Ernst. "Insider Trading Legislation and Corporate Governance." *European Economic Review* 46 (2002): 1569–1597.

Mendelson, Morris. "The Economics of Insider Trading Reconsidered." *University of Pennsylvania Law Review* 117 (1969): 470–492.

Meulbroek, Lisa K. "An Empirical Analysis of Illegal Insider Trading." *Journal of Finance* 47 (1992): 1661–1699.

Pettit, R. Richardson, and P. C. Venkatesh. "Insider Trading and Long-Run Return Performance." *Financial Management* 24 (Summer 1995): 88–105.

Roulstone, Darren T. "The Relation Between Insider-Trading Restrictions and Executive Compensation." *Journal of Accounting Research* 41 (2003): 525–551.

Schotland, Roy A. "Unsafe at Any Price: A Reply to Manne, *Insider Trading and the Stock Market*." *Virginia Law Review* 53 (1967): 1425–1478.

Scott, Kenneth E. "Insider Trading: Rule 10b-5, Disclosure and Corporate Policy." *Journal of Legal Studies* 9 (1980): 801–818.

Smith, Frank P. *Management Trading: Stock-Market Prices and Profits*. New Haven: Yale University Press, 1941.

Thurber, Stephen. "The Insider Trading Compensation Contract as an Inducement to Monitoring by the Institutional Investor." *George Mason University Law Review* 1 (1994): 119–134.

Wilgus, H. L. "Purchase of Shares of Corporation by a Director from a Shareholder." *Michigan Law Review* 8 (1910): 267–297.

Insurance

Richard Zeckhauser

Insurance plays a central role in the functioning of modern economies. Life insurance offers protection against the economic impact of an untimely death; health insurance covers the sometimes extraordinary costs of medical care; and bank deposits are insured by the federal government. In each case, the insured pays a small premium in order to receive benefits should an unlikely but high-cost event occur.

Insurance issues, traditionally a stodgy domain, have become subjects for intense debate and concern in recent years. How to provide health insurance for the significant portion of Americans not now covered is a central political issue. Some states, attempting to hold back the tide of higher costs, have placed severe limits on auto insurance rates and have even sought refunds from insurers. And ways to cover losses from terrorism have become a major issue. Temporarily, in response to the massive losses of 9/11, the federal government adopted a heavily subsidized three-year program for reinsuring terror-related building losses. (The program was extended.) In theory, the government can recoup some losses after the fact by levying a surcharge on the premiums of surviving firms.

The Basics

An understanding of insurance must begin with the concept of risk—that is, the variation in possible outcomes of a situation. A's shipment of goods to Europe might arrive safely or be lost in transit. B may incur zero medical expenses in a good year, but if she is struck by a car they could be upward of $100,000. We cannot eliminate risk from life, even at extraordinary expense. Paying extra for double-hulled tankers still leaves oil spills possible. The only way to eliminate auto-related injuries is to eliminate automobiles.

Thus, the effective response to risk combines two elements: efforts or expenditures to lessen the risk, and the purchase of insurance against whatever risk remains. Consider A's shipment of, say, $1 million in goods. If the chance of loss on each trip is 3 percent, the loss will be $30,000 (3 percent of $1 million), on average. Let us assume that A can ship by a more costly method and cut the risk by one percentage point, thus saving $10,000, on average. If the additional cost of this shipping method is less than $10,000, it is a worthwhile expenditure. But if cutting risk by a further percentage point will cost $15,000, it sacrifices resources.

To deal with the remaining 2 percent risk of losing $1 million, A should think about insurance. To cover administrative costs, the insurer might charge $25,000 for a risk that will incur average losses of no more than $20,000. From A's standpoint, however, the insurance may be worthwhile because it is a comparatively inexpensive way to deal with the potential loss of $1 million. Note the important economic role of such insurance: without it, A might not be willing to risk shipping goods in the first place.

In exchange for a premium, the insurer will pay a claim should a specified contingency—such as death, medical bills, or, in this instance, shipment loss—arise. The insurer—whether a corporation with diversified ownership or a mutual company made up of the insureds themselves—is able to offer such protection against financial loss by pooling the risks from a large group of similarly situated individuals or firms. The laws of probability ensure that only a tiny fraction of these insured shipments will be lost, or only a small fraction of the insured population will face expensive hospitalization in a year. If, for example, each of 100,000 individuals independently faces a 1 percent risk in a year, on average, 1,000 will have losses. If each of the 100,000 people paid a premium of $1,000, the insurance company would have collected a total of $100 million. Leaving aside administrative costs, this is enough to pay $100,000 to anyone who had a loss. But what would happen if 1,100 people had losses? The answer, fortunately, is that such an outcome is exceptionally unlikely. Insurance works through the magic of the law of large numbers. This law assures that when a large number of people face a low-probability event, the proportion experiencing the event will be close to the expected proportion. For instance, with a pool of 100,000 people who each face a 1 percent risk, the law of large numbers says that 1,100 people or more will have losses only one time in one thousand.

In many cases, however, the risks to different individuals are not independent. In a hurricane, airplane crash, or epidemic, many may suffer at the same time. Insurance companies spread such risks not only across individuals, but also across good years and bad, building up reserves in the good years to deal with heavier claims in bad ones. For further protection, they also diversify across lines, selling both health and homeowners' insurance, for example.

The risks normally insured are unintentional, either due to the actions of nature or the inadvertent consequences of human activity. Terrorism creates a new model for insurance for three reasons: (1) The losses are man-made and intentional. (2) Massive numbers of people and structures could be harmed. (Theft losses fall in the first category, but not in the second.) (3) Historical experience does not provide a yardstick for assessing likely risk levels. Nuclear war presented equivalent challenges in the twentieth century. Had there been a significant nuclear war, insurance companies simply would not have paid. The losses would have been too massive to pay out of assets, and many of the assets underlying the insurance would have been destroyed. In time, appropriate insurance arrangements for this new category of massive risk will be developed.

The Identity and Behavior of the Insured

An economist views insurance as being like most other commodities. It obeys the laws of supply and demand, for example. However, it is unlike many other commodities in one important respect: the cost of providing insurance depends on the identity of the purchaser. A year of health insurance for an eighty-year-old costs more to provide than one for a fifty-year-old. It costs more to provide auto insurance to teenagers than to middle-aged people. If a company mistakenly sells health policies to old folks at a price appropriate for young folks, it will assuredly lose money, just as a restaurant will lose if it sells twenty-dollar steak dinners for ten dollars. The restaurant would lure lots of steak eaters. So, too, would the insurance company attract large numbers of older clients. Because of the differential cost of providing coverage, and because customers search for their lowest price, insurance companies go to great pains to set different premiums for different groups, depending on the risks each will impose.

Recognizing that the identity of the purchaser affects the cost of insurance, insurers must be careful to whom they offer insurance at a particular price. Those high-risk individuals whose knowledge of their risk is better than that of the insurers will step forth to purchase, knowing that they are getting a good deal. This is a process called adverse selection, which means that the mix of purchasers will be adverse to the insurer.

What leads to this adverse selection is asymmetric information: potential purchasers have more information than the sellers. The potential purchasers have "hidden" information that relates to their particular risk, and those whose information is unfavorable are thus most likely to purchase. For example, if an insurer determined that 1 percent of fifty-year-olds would die in a year, it might establish a premium of $12 per $1,000 of coverage—$10 to cover claims and $2 to cover administrative costs. The insurer might naively expect to break even. However, insureds who ate poorly or who engaged in high-risk professions or whose parents had died young might have an annual risk of mortality of 3 percent. They would be most

likely to purchase insurance. Health fanatics, by contrast, might forgo life insurance because for them it is a bad deal. Through adverse selection, the insurer could end up with a group whose expected costs were, say, $20 per $1,000 rather than the $10 per $1,000 for the population as a whole; at a $12 price, the insurer would lose money.

The traditional approach to the adverse selection problem is to inspect each potential insured. Individuals taking out substantial life insurance must submit to a medical exam. Fire insurance might be granted only after a check of the alarm and sprinkler systems. But no matter how careful the inspection, some information will remain hidden, and a disproportionately high number of those choosing to insure will be high risk. Therefore, insurers routinely set high rates to cope with adverse selection. Alas, such high rates discourage ordinary-risk buyers from buying insurance.

Though this problem of adverse selection is best known in insurance problems, it applies broadly across economics. Thus, a company that "insures" its salesmen by offering a relatively high salary compared with commission will end up with many salesmen who are not confident of their abilities. Colleges that insure their students by offering many pass-fail courses can expect weaker students to enroll.

Moral Hazard or Hidden Action

Once insured, an individual has less incentive to avoid the risk of a bad outcome. A person with automobile collision insurance, for example, is more likely to venture forth on an icy night. Federal pension insurance induces companies to underfund (see PENSIONS) and weakens the incentives for their employees to complain. Federally subsidized flood insurance encourages citizens to build homes on floodplains. Insurers use the term "moral hazard" to describe this phenomenon. It means, simply, that insured people undertake actions they would otherwise avoid. Stated in less judgmental language, people respond to incentives. In the above salesman example, not only are low-quality salesmen enticed to join, but all salesmen, even those of high quality, are given an incentive to be less productive.

Ideally, the insurer would like to be able to monitor the insured's behavior and take appropriate action. Flood insurance might not be sold to new residents of a floodplain. Collision insurance might not pay off if it can be proven that the policyholder had been drinking or had otherwise engaged in reckless behavior. But given the difficulty of monitoring many actions, insurers accept that once policies are issued, behavior will change adversely, and more claims will be made.

The moral hazard problem is often encountered in areas that, at first glance, do not seem associated with traditional insurance. Products covered under optional warranties tend to get abused, as do autos that are leased with service contracts.

Equity Issues

The same insurance policy will have different costs for serving individuals whose behavior or underlying characteristics may differ. Because these cost differences influence pricing, some people see an equity dimension to insurance. Some think, for example, that urban drivers should not pay much more than rural drivers to protect themselves from auto liability, even though urban driving is riskier. But if prices are not allowed to vary in relation to risk, insurers will seek to avoid various classes of customers altogether, and availability will be restricted. When sellers of health insurance are not allowed to find out if potential clients are HIV-positive, for example, insurance companies often respond by refusing to insure, say, never-married men over age forty.

Equity issues in insurance are addressed in a variety of ways in the real world. Most employers cross-subsidize health insurance, providing the same coverage at the same price to older, higher-risk workers and younger, lower-risk ones. Sometimes the government provides the "insurance" itself, although the federal government's Medicare and Social Security programs are really a combined tax and subsidy scheme—one that gives a bigger benefit to those who live longer. The government's decision not to tax employer-provided health insurance as income acts like a subsidy. In pursuit of equity, governments may set insurance rates, as many states do with auto insurance. The traditional public-interest argument for government rate regulation is that it serves to control a monopoly. But this argument fails with auto insurance: in most regulated insurance markets, there are dozens of competing insurers. Insurance rates are regulated to help some groups—usually those imposing high risks—at the expense of others. The Massachusetts auto insurance market provides an example. High-cost drivers are subsidized at the expense of all other drivers. Thus, inexperienced, occasional drivers in Massachusetts paid, on average, $1,967 for insurance in 2004 compared with $1,114 for experienced drivers. In contrast, in neighboring Connecticut, where such cross-subsidies were not imposed, the respective rates are $3,518 and $845.

Such practices raise a new class of equity issues. Should the government force people who live quiet, low-risk lives to subsidize the high-risk fringe? Most people's response to this question depends on whether they think people can control risks. Because most of us think we should not encourage people to engage in behavior that is costly to the system, we conclude, for example, that nonsmokers should not have to pay for smokers. The question becomes more complex when it comes to health care premiums for, say, gay men or recovering alcoholics, whose health care costs are likely to be greater than average. Moral judgments inevitably creep into such discussions. And sometimes the facts lead to disquieting considerations. Smokers, for example, tend to die early, reducing expected costs for Social Security. Should they, therefore, pay lower Social Security taxes? Black men have shorter lives than white men. Should black men pay lower Social Security taxes?

Government's Role in Insurance

Government plays four major roles with insurance: (1) Government writes it directly, as with Social Security, terrorism reinsurance, and pension guarantees—via the Pension Benefit Guaranty Corporation (PBGC)—should a corporation fail. (2) Government subsidizes insurance: quite explicitly in some programs, such as federal flood insurance, but only de facto in other cases (e.g., the PBGC has a large projected deficit). (3) Government mandates a residual market for high risks (e.g., Florida's program for hurricanes or many states' programs for high-risk drivers). Governments hold down prices in such markets either by creating a state fund to cover losses or by requiring insurers who participate in the voluntary market to pick up a certain portion of this high-risk market. (4) Government regulates matters such as premiums, insurance company solvency (to make sure that insureds get paid), and permissible criteria for pricing insurance (e.g., for auto insurance, race and ethnicity are banned everywhere; Michigan bans geographic designations smaller than a city).

Property liability insurance is regulated at the state level, providing many opportunities to compare the efficacy of alternative approaches. The three main regulatory approaches to pricing have been: (1) prior approval (regulators must approve rates before they go in effect); (2) use and file (companies set rates, but regulators can disallow them subsequently if they are found excessive); and (3) open competition (a market-based system in which rates are deemed not excessive as long as there is competition). Empirical studies conflict as to whether regulation leads to lower prices.

Government participates far more in insurance markets than in typical markets. The two great dangers with government participation in insurance arise when, as is common, the goals for participation remain vague (e.g., promoting the insured activity, redistributing income, or spreading risk effectively), or when its expected cost is not recognized in budgets. With insurance, as with all government endeavors, the citizenry deserves to know both the rationale and the cost.

Conclusion

The traditional role of insurance remains the essential one recognized centuries ago: that of spreading risk among similarly situated individuals. Insurance works most effectively when losses are not under the control of individuals (thus avoiding moral hazard) and when the losses are readily determined (lest significant transactions costs associated with lawsuits become a burden).

Individuals and firms insure against their most major risks—high health costs, the inability to pay depositors—which often are politically salient issues as well. Not surprisingly, government participation—as a setter of rates, as a subsidizer, and as a direct provider of insurance services—has become a major feature in insurance markets. Its highly subsidized terrorism reinsurance provides a dramatic example. Political forces may sometimes triumph over sound insurance principles, but such victories are Pyrrhic. In a sound market, we must recognize that with insurance, as with bread and steel, the cost of providing it must be paid.

About the Author

Richard Zeckhauser is the Frank P. Ramsey Professor of Political Economy at Harvard University's John F. Kennedy School of Government. He writes frequently on risk-related issues. Practicing what he preaches, in 2003 and 2004 he came in second and third in two different U.S. national bridge championships.

Further Reading

Arrow, Kenneth J. "The Economics of Agency." In John W. Pratt and Richard J. Zeckhauser, eds., *Principals and Agents: The Structure of Business.* Boston: Harvard Business School Press, 1985.
———. *Essays in the Theory of Risk-Bearing.* Amsterdam: North-Holland, 1971.
Cutler, David, and Richard Zeckhauser. "The Anatomy of Health Insurance." In Joseph P. Newhouse and Anthony Culyer, eds., *The Handbook of Health Economics.* New York: Elsevier, 2000.
———. "Extending the Theory to Meet the Practice of Insurance." In Robert E. Litan and Richard Herring, eds., *Brookings-Wharton Papers on Financial Services.* Washington, D.C.: Brookings Institution Press, 2004. Pp. 1–53.
Gollier, Christian. *The Economics of Risk and Time.* Cambridge: MIT Press, 2001.
Huber, Peter W. *Liability: The Legal Revolution and Its Consequences.* New York: Basic Books, 1988.

Intellectual Property

Stan Liebowitz

Intellectual property is normally defined as the set of products protected under laws associated with copyright, patent, trademark, industrial design, and trade secrets. The U.S. Constitution expressly allows for intellectual property protection, albeit for a limited time, in the form of protection of "writings and discoveries" in order to promote "science and useful arts." This article focuses on the two most important categories: copyright and patent law.

Copyright, which covers the expression of ideas (e.g., through words or music), currently lasts for the rest of the author's life plus seventy years (or ninety-five years after publication if the product is a "work-for-hire"). But the protection is very narrow. If someone else should, by a remarkable coincidence, write exactly the same song or story as you without ever coming into contact with your work, your prior copyright does not prevent him from selling his work. Copyright currently exists on a work without any effort on the part of the author to attain copyright and without any requirement of quality or originality.

Patents, in contrast, last for twenty years and apply to inventions. The protection, although shorter, is broader than that of copyright. If someone else independently creates a duplicate of your invention after you have patented yours, your patent can make his invention worthless since he will not have the legal right to sell his version. This may be true even if his invention is slightly different from yours. For this reason, being the first to patent a valuable idea is very important, and "patent races," as competitors vie to be first, can be a wasteful use of resources. Unlike copyright, getting the legal patent from the patent office requires spending resources, and before a patent is granted, the ideas that are to be patented must pass several legal hurdles regarding their originality and quality.

Although expression and invention must be transformed into physical embodiments before they can have market value, they can also exist, and indeed must originally exist, in the creator's mind. As such, traditional laws of property, which require physicality, do not apply. Traditional laws of economics, such as the assumption of scarcity, also seem not to apply because individual expressions and ideas cannot be used up.

Economists have a term for goods that cannot be used up—"nonrivalrous consumption" (sometimes known as "public goods")—and these goods require a different form of analysis than more typical economic goods. In particular, the prices individual consumers are willing to pay are summed to arrive at an overall demand for the intellectual product, a process known as the vertical addition of demands. This differs from the more traditional summation of quantities each individual demands at various prices—horizontal addition—to derive the market demand for rivalrous goods.

There is no practical mechanism for the ideal production of nonrivalrous goods, as Kenneth Arrow concluded in his classic 1962 article. Harold Demsetz properly noted, though, in his classic 1969 critique, that efficiency does not require perfection, and so markets might still produce these goods efficiently. The difficulty of ideally producing nonrivalrous goods is contained in the well-known trade-off between production and consumption, to which we now turn.

The Consumption-Production Trade-off

The fact that ideas and expressions do not get used up allows for an unusual result in terms of the "efficient," or ideal, level of consumption. I will illustrate the example with a creative expression, but it applies equally well to ideas that are patented.

Since my listening to a song does not reduce your ability to listen to the same song, efficient consumption of that song, *once it has been produced,* is to allow everyone who has a positive value of the song that is greater than the cost of transmitting the song (often assumed to be zero) to consume the song.

This is a quite remarkable result. Typical goods, such as apples, are scarce, meaning that there are fewer in existence than the number that potential consumers would wish to eat if apples were freely available; thus, some rationing mechanism, such as price, must be used to determine who gets the apples. Efficient consumption requires that consumers who value the apples more get them and consumers who value them less go without. The correct *allocation* of apples is important in achieving efficiency.

The ability of one unit of a nonrivalrous good to provide for the entire set of users turns usual rules of consumption efficiency on their head. Everyone, today and in every future generation to come, without limit, can listen to Beethoven's Ninth Symphony. There is no *allocation* problem to be solved. Thus, efficient consumption of Beethoven's Ninth, if transmittal costs are zero, requires that everyone who places a positive value on hearing the symphony be allowed to listen to it.

This would seem to imply that everyone should be allowed to consume all the products that are normally copy-righted, and everyone should be allowed to use the ideas that are normally protected by patent. But there is a fly in this ointment, which is why I used the term "trade-off" in this section's heading.

The requirement that all potential consumers be allowed to consume the intellectual products puts some serious restrictions on the price(s) that can be charged for the product. If consumers have differing values for the good, but the producer (creator) can charge each potential consumer a price slightly below the maximum price that consumers are willing to pay, then all potential consumers would consume the product and efficiency would be achieved, a result known as perfect price discrimination. But if, more realistically, the producer is unable to charge different prices to different potential customers, then no matter what price the producer picks, some potential consumers will be priced out of the market—unless the producer picks a price of zero.

A zero price, alas, provides the producer with no revenue. If producers receive no revenue, then there is little reason to believe that production will occur. This, then, is the problem brought about if one attempts to achieve efficient consumption: there is nothing for potential consumers to consume since nothing will be produced at a price of zero. Reducing consumptive efficiency is the cost involved in allowing for increased creation of ideas. As government increases the production of creative ideas by giving producers of these ideas more and more control over the production of the embodiments of these ideas, the consumption of these embodiments becomes less and less efficient.

The application of this trade-off occurs when the competitive model is grafted onto these ideas. If anyone can make a copy (embodiment) of an idea or expression without the permission of the original creator, the price of embodiments would be expected to drop to zero (plus the transmission/reproduction costs), leaving nothing for the creator.

Therefore, if markets are to be used to provide producers with a pecuniary incentive to create intellectual products, creators must be given some degree of control over the use of their products, prohibiting others from copying their ideas or expressions. This is where copyrights and patents come in.

This prohibition on copying is generally referred to as a "monopoly," although for many intellectual products the term is not economically correct. As Edmund Kitch (2000) correctly pointed out, providing property rights does not confer economic monopoly—which would imply that consumers have only a small number of alternative products that are not very good substitutes. In reality, the "monopoly" conferred by copyright is no greater than the monopoly that each worker has on his or her efforts, or that each firm has on products bearing its name. The monopoly created by patent law would generally be somewhat stronger than for copyright law because it is a realistic possibility that others would have independently created the same idea, but the patent eliminates the use of such independent creations. Nevertheless, competition is still possible between the patent holder and other ideas or technologies not limited by the particular patent.

Intellectual property protection, then, can be seen to create two countervailing results. First, it provides authors and inventors the wherewithal to receive remuneration for their activities, which has the beneficial impact of increasing the production of expressions and ideas. On the other hand, copyright and patent laws allow the owners of the intellectual properties to charge positive prices for their use, restricting the usage and consumption of these ideas below their ideal levels.

Several simplifications in the above story weaken its generality. First, it is not clear that competition will remove all revenues from creators. Although profits will be competed to zero in the long run, the long run does not happen instantaneously. Because the creator is usually the first to market, that temporal advantage would allow the creator to generate some revenue above the cost of reproduction.

Second, the extent to which copyright owners require remuneration to create their artistic works is not clear. The claim that creative production requires remuneration of the producers is fully consistent with the usual market principles. Adam Smith's famous maxim that production does not come from the "benevolence" of butchers, bakers, or brewers, but instead derives from their self-interested behavior, certainly has a plethora of empirical evidence to support it.

Nevertheless, it has often been argued that artistic creation is often undertaken for reasons having little to do with pecuniary rewards. The idea that artists require payment seems antithetical to various romantic notions of "art." (Inventors, on the other hand, are usually thought to be less interested in "creation for creation's sake" and, as such, are usually assumed to require compensation.) Even if one does not subscribe to the romantic view of art, however, the fame from creating successful works can bring its own rewards and often the ability to generate additional revenues in other markets (such as concerts for musicians).

The Optimal Term

One of the most important aspects of intellectual property is its limited term. In principle, economic efficiency would require that the length of protection be the minimum nec-

essary to provide the author/creator with the incentive to create the product. (An additional problem with patents is the proper "scope" of the patent.) In this way, the restriction on consumption would be minimized, and yet the creator would receive sufficient remuneration to produce the product. This would require a different term for each intellectual product. Composers (or recording artists) who could make money by performing at concerts, for example, would not need as long a copyright term as composers who do not concertize.

Although attractive in theory, such an approach does not appear practical and has not been used. The question, then, becomes what the efficient terms for patent and copyright might be—5 years, 50 years, 150 years? This has led to much debate, but no consensus.

The problem with determining the optimal term of intellectual property protection is that no one knows any of the key pieces of information needed to determine the optimal term. These include how much incentive is required to induce creators to create, the size of the harm from reduced consumption during the term of the intellectual property law, the size of the revenues generated during the term of protection that can be used to pay the creator, and future interest rates. No one has these facts, and the difficulty in learning them is such that we may never be in a position to determine the optimal term with any precision.

Alternatives to Intellectual Property

Because of the imperfections of market-based intellectual property systems, various alternatives have been proposed. In most of these alternative systems, the government funds creators. The advantage of such a system is that competition would drive the price of the intellectual products down to their transmission/reproduction costs, and no consumers would be denied the product because the price was above the transmission/reproduction costs. Of course, the funding of these products through tax revenues (see TAXATION) causes its own set of inefficiencies that might otherwise appear to be hidden from view, and there is no reason to believe that the inefficiencies from the tax code will be less than the inefficiencies from having too few users of intellectual products.

An even more serious problem with this system is caused by the government's need to decide how much revenue to pay to creators. Even a well-intentioned government would have great difficulty determining the optimal size of the pot to be shared by various authors/creators. Even though the market-based system of intellectual property is imperfect in generating revenues, it is far more likely to track the direction and size of the "optimal" market than will even the best-intentioned efforts of the government. The reason is simple: without a market to provide guidance, it is virtually impossible to divine even a rough approximation of the prices and quantities that would be found in an ideal market.

A final problem with this solution is determining which authors and which inventions should be most richly rewarded. For material such as books and music, it might not be too difficult to get some measure of relative sales of reproductions, and from that to determine the relative payments to be made to authors since one can examine the market shares of the sales of reproductions. Determining the relative market value of inventions would be much more difficult if the government were to just grant rewards for inventive activity.

One interesting idea to overcome this difficulty in valuing patents was suggested by Michael Kremer (1998), who proposed that the government purchase patents and then put them in the public domain. In his model the government determines the value of the patent by holding an auction. The high bidder occasionally gets the patent (to keep bidders honest), but most of the time the government takes the patent, and the current patent holder can refuse the price if he thinks it is too low. This plan solves the underconsumption problem and allows follow-on innovations to occur more easily. Unfortunately, it introduces its own distortion through the use of taxes to pay for this scheme. Further, it is susceptible to gaming whereby the original patent owner pays others to overbid for his patents, and it is susceptible to the government overpaying when the patent owner has negative inside information about the value of the patent.

Finally, all of this assumes that a government-run intellectual property system is well intentioned and insulated from political considerations. Given our understanding of government regulation of markets (see PUBLIC CHOICE), it seems fair to say that politics will certainly enter these decisions and that the bureaucrats in charge of these agencies will be influenced by the various parties involved. Giving away other people's money is not a job that mere mortals are likely to accomplish without a good deal of political influence, if not outright corruption.

Current Controversies

The reliance on property rights comes to the fore in the current controversy surrounding file sharing. Several prominent legal academics, following the lead of Lawrence Lessig (2001), have suggested that traditional copyright protection of music (and movies) be discarded and replaced with an organization along the lines of ASCAP or BMI, which would collect monies from income taxes or taxes in markets such as ISPs or blank CDs and distribute the monies to creators. This model, most fully developed by William Fisher (2004), is still a variant of the government provision discussed above, with all of its limitations. It is possible, however, that file sharing cannot be controlled and that the market for sound recordings and movies might essentially vanish. In that case, some alternative is probably better than nothing, although government provision can, in principle, create losses greater than the vanishing of the market.

The specter of digital rights management (DRM), which would allow copyright owners to monitor and control use of their works through software built into a work, has also created a stir. A traditional defense against charges of copyright infringement is "fair use," which is intended to allow actions such as copying part of another work in an academic analysis or criticism. Many legal academics have decried the possible loss of fair use that would occur if the software required payment for uses that were previously deemed "fair." The concern over fair use appears to be overstated because one of the purposes of fair use, to allow usage when the costs of transacting exceed the value of the transaction, no longer holds under DRM. Further, if someone wishes to use a snippet of someone else's work in an academic article, that would still be allowed, although the words might have to be hand copied instead of electronically cut and pasted.

Another recent controversy surrounds the Sonny Bono Copyright Term Extension Act of 1998, which retroactively increased copyright protection from fifty years to seventy years after the death of the author. The act was challenged as being unconstitutional. A group of seventeen famous economists (Akerlof et al. 2002) wrote a brief in that case criticizing the efficiency of the act. Part of their criticism had to do with the retroactive increase in copyright for old works. After all, increasing the term of copyright for already created works cannot increase the number of already created works, although it would increase the harm from having some consumers priced out of the market. The other part of their criticism had to do with the extension of the copyright term. In their view, the present value of the additional revenues fifty-plus years down the road was too small to have an impact on the production of new creations, and thus served no purpose. Stan Liebowitz and Stephen Margolis (2005) criticized this brief on several grounds. First, they argued that one reason to allow current copyright holders to control stewardship over already created works is to reduce externalities, for example, by preventing overuse of certain copyrighted characters that lowers their social value the way overuse of the same house style can lower the value of a neighborhood. Second, even a small increase in expected revenues can have a relatively large impact on the number of new creations (relative to the present value of future deadweight losses), as long as the elasticity of supply is not zero, a factor the seventeen economists ignored. Third, a high percentage of best-sellers, which are responsible for a majority of trade sales, remain in print for more than sixty years, thus indicating that the copyright extension would be expected to have an impact on incentives to create.

About the Author

Stan Liebowitz is an economist in the Business School of the University of Texas at Dallas and director of the Center for the Analysis of Property Rights and Innovation.

Further Reading

Akerlof, George A., et al. Brief as Amici Curiae in support of Petitioners at 12, Eldred v. Ashcroft, no. 01-618 (2002). Available online at: http://www.aei-brookings.org/admin/authorpdfs/page.php?id=16.

Arrow, Kenneth J. "Economic Welfare and the Allocation of Resources for Invention." In R. Nelson, ed., *The Rate and Direction of Inventive Activity*. Princeton: Princeton University Press, 1962.

Demsetz, Harold. "Information and Efficiency: Another Viewpoint." *Journal of Law and Economics* 12 (1969): 1–22.

Fisher, William. *Promises to Keep*. Stanford: Stanford University Press, 2004.

Kitch, Edmund W. "Elementary and Persistent Errors in the Economic Analysis of Intellectual Property." *Vanderbilt Law Review* 53 (November 2000): 1727.

Kremer, Michael. "Patent Buyouts: A Mechanism for Encouraging Innovation." *Quarterly Journal of Economics* 113 (November 1998): 1137–1167.

Lessig, Lawrence. *The Future of Ideas*. New York: Vintage Books, 2001.

Liebowitz, Stan J., and Stephen E. Margolis. "Seventeen Famous Economists Weigh in on Copyright: The Role of Theory, Empirics, and Network Effects." *Harvard Journal of Law and Technology* 18 (Spring 2005): 435–457.

Interest Rates

Burton G. Malkiel

The rate of interest measures the percentage reward a lender receives for deferring the consumption of resources until a future date. Correspondingly, it measures the price a borrower pays to have resources now.

Suppose I have $100 today that I am willing to lend for one year at an annual interest rate of 5 percent. At the end of the year, I get back my $100 plus $5 interest (0.05 × 100), for a total of $105. The general relationship is:

$$\text{Money Today} (1 + \text{interest rate}) = \text{Money Next Year}$$

We can also ask a different question: What is the most I would pay today to get $105 next year? If the rate of interest is 5 percent, the most I would pay is $100. I would not pay $101, because if I had $101 and invested it at 5 percent, I would have $106 next year. Thus, we say that the value of money in the future should be discounted, and $100 is the "discounted present value" of $105 next year. The general relationship is:

$$\text{Money Today} = \frac{\text{Money Next Year}}{(1 + \text{interest rate})}$$

The higher the interest rate, the more valuable is money today and the lower is the present value of money in the future.

Now, suppose I am willing to lend my money out for a second year. I lend out $105, the amount I have next year, at 5 percent and have $110.25 at the end of year two. Note that I have earned an extra $5.25 in the second year because the interest that I earned in year one also earns interest in year two. This is what we mean by the term "compound interest"—the interest that money earns also earns interest. Albert Einstein is reported to have said that compound interest is the greatest force in the world. Money left in interest-bearing investments can compound to extremely large sums.

A simple rule, the rule of 72, tells how long it takes your money to double if it is invested at compound interest. The number 72 divided by the interest rate gives the approximate number of years it will take to double your money. For example, at a 5 percent interest rate, it takes about fourteen years to double your money (72 ÷ 5 = 14.4), while at an interest rate of 10 percent, it takes about seven years.

There is a wonderful actual example of the power of compound interest. Upon his death in 1791, Benjamin Franklin left $5,000 to each of his favorite cities, Boston and Philadelphia. He stipulated that the money should be invested and not paid out for one hundred to two hundred years. At one hundred years, each city could withdraw $500,000; after two hundred years, they could withdraw the remainder. They did withdraw $500,000 in 1891; they invested the remainder and, in 1991, each city received approximately $20,000,000.

What determines the magnitude of the interest rate in an economy? Let us consider five of the most important factors.

1. *The strength of the economy and the willingness to save.* Interest rates are determined in a free market where supply and demand interact. The supply of funds is influenced by the willingness of consumers, businesses, and governments to save. The demand for funds reflects the desires

of businesses, households, and governments to spend more than they take in as revenues. Usually, in very strong economic expansions, businesses' desire to invest in plants and equipment and individuals' desire to invest in housing tend to drive interest rates up. During periods of weak economic conditions, business and housing investment falls and interest rates tend to decline. Such declines are often reinforced by the policies of the country's central bank (the Federal Reserve in the United States), which attempts to reduce interest rates in order to stimulate housing and other interest-sensitive investments.

2. *The rate of inflation.* People's willingness to lend money depends partly on the inflation rate. If prices are expected to be stable, I may be happy to lend money for a year at 4 percent because I expect to have 4 percent more purchasing power at the end of the year. But suppose the inflation rate is expected to be 10 percent. Then, all other things being equal, I will insist on a 14 percent rate on interest, ten percentage points of which compensate me for the inflation.[1] Economist IRVING FISHER pointed out this fact almost a century ago, distinguishing clearly between the real rate of interest (4 percent in the above example) and the nominal rate of interest (14 percent in the above example), which equals the real rate plus the expected inflation rate.

3. *The riskiness of the borrower.* I am willing to lend money to my government or to my local bank (whose deposits are generally guaranteed by the government) at a lower rate than I would lend to my wastrel nephew or to my cousin's risky new venture. The greater the risk that my loan will not be paid back in full, the larger is the interest rate I will demand to compensate me for that risk. Thus, there is a risk structure to interest rates. The greater the risk that the borrower will not repay in full, the greater is the rate of interest.

4. *The tax treatment of the interest.* In most cases, the interest I receive from lending money is fully taxable. In certain cases, however, the interest is tax free. If I lend to my local or state government, the interest on my loan is free of both federal and state taxes. Hence, I am willing to accept a lower rate of interest on loans that have favorable tax treatment.

---

1. Actually, I will insist on 14.4 percent, 4 percent to compensate me for the inflation-caused loss of principal and 0.4 percent to compensate me for the inflation-caused loss of real interest. The general relationship is given by the mathematical formula: $1 + i = (1 + r) \times (1 + p)$, where i is the nominal interest rate (the one we observe), r is the real interest rate (the one that would exist if inflation were expected to be zero), and p is the expected inflation rate.

5. *The time period of the loan.* In general, lenders demand a higher rate of interest for loans of longer maturity. The interest rate on a ten-year loan is usually higher than that on a one-year loan, and the rate I can get on a three-year bank certificate of deposit is generally higher than the rate on a six-month certificate of deposit. But this relationship does not always hold; to understand the reasons, it is necessary to understand the basics of bond investing.

Most long-term loans are made via bond instruments. A BOND is simply a long-term IOU issued by a government, a corporation, or some other entity. When you invest in a bond, you are lending money to the issuer. The interest payments on the bond are often referred to as "coupon" payments because up through the 1950s, most bond investors actually clipped interest coupons from the bonds and presented them to their banks for payment. (By 1980 bonds with actual coupons had virtually disappeared.) The coupon payment is fixed for the life of the bond. Thus, if a one-thousand-dollar twenty-year bond has a fifty-dollar-per-year interest (coupon) payment, that payment never changes. But, as indicated above, interest rates do change from year to year in response to changes in economic conditions, inflation, monetary policy, and so on. The price of the bond is simply the discounted present value of the fixed interest payments and of the face value of the loan payable at maturity. Now, if interest rates rise (the discount factor is higher), then the present value, or price, of the bond will fall. This leads to three basic facts facing the bond investor:

1. If interest rates rise, bond prices fall.

2. If interest rates fall, bond prices rise.

3. The longer the period to maturity of the bond, the greater is the potential fluctuation in price when interest rates change.

If you hold a bond to maturity, you need not worry if the price bounces around in the interim. But if you have to sell prior to maturity, you may receive less than you paid for the bond. The longer the maturity of the bond, the greater is the risk of loss because long-term bond prices are more volatile than shorter-term issues. To compensate for that risk of price fluctuation, longer-term bonds usually have higher interest rates than shorter-term issues. This tendency of long rates to exceed short rates is called the risk-premium theory of the yield structure. This relationship between interest rates for loans or bonds and various terms to maturity is often depicted in a graph showing interest rates on the vertical axis and term to maturity on the horizontal. The general shape of that graph is called the shape of the yield curve, and typically the curve is rising. In other words, the longer term the bond, the greater is the interest rate. This typical shape reflects the risk premium for holding longer-term debt.

Long-term rates are not always higher than short-term rates, however. Expectations also influence the shape of the yield curve. Suppose, for example, that the economy has been booming and the central bank, in response, chooses a restrictive monetary policy that drives up interest rates. To implement such a policy, central banks sell short-term bonds, pushing their prices down and interest rates up. Interest rates, short term and long term, tend to rise together. But if bond investors believe such a restrictive policy is likely to be temporary, they may expect interest rates to fall in the future. In such an event, bond prices can be expected to rise, giving bondholders a capital gain. Thus long-term bonds may be particularly attractive during periods of unusually high short-term interest rates, and in bidding for these long-term bonds, investors drive their prices up and their yields down. The result is a flattening, and sometimes even an inversion, in the yield curve. Indeed, there were periods during the 1980s when U.S. Treasury securities yielded 10 percent or more and long-term interest rates (yields) were well below shorter-term rates.

Expectations can also influence the yield curve in the opposite direction, making it steeper than is typical. This can happen when interest rates are unusually low, as they were in the United States in the early 2000s. In such a case, investors will expect interest rates to rise in the future, causing large capital losses to holders of long-term bonds. This would cause investors to sell long-term bonds until the prices came down enough to give them higher yields, thus compensating them for the expected capital loss. The result is long-term rates that exceed short-term rates by more than the "normal" amount.

In sum, the term structure of interest rates—or, equivalently, the shape of the yield curve—is likely to be influenced both by investors' risk preferences and by their expectations of future interest rates.

About the Author

Burton G. Malkiel, the Chemical Bank Chairman's Professor of Economics at Princeton University, is the author of the widely read investment book *A Random Walk down Wall Street*. He was previously dean of the Yale School of Management and William S. Beinecke Professor of Management Studies there. He is also a past member of the Council of Economic Advisers and a past president of the American Finance Association.

Further Reading

Fabozzi, Frank J. *Bond Markets, Analysis and Strategies*. 4th ed. New York: Prentice Hall, 2000.
Fisher, Irving. *The Theory of Interest*. 1930. Reprint. Brookfield, Vt.: Pickering and Chatto, 1997.
Patinkin, Don. "Interest." In *International Encyclopedia of the Social Sciences*. Vol. 7. New York: Macmillan, 1968.

International Capital Flows

Mack Ott

International capital flows are the financial side of international trade.[1] When someone imports a good or service, the buyer (the importer) gives the seller (the exporter) a monetary payment, just as in domestic transactions. If total exports were equal to total imports, these monetary transactions would balance at net zero: people in the country would receive as much in financial flows as they paid out in financial flows. But generally the trade balance is not zero. The most general description of a country's balance of trade, covering its trade in goods and services, income receipts, and transfers, is called its current account balance. If the country has a surplus or deficit on its current account, there is an offsetting net financial flow consisting of currency, securities, or other real property ownership claims. This net financial flow is called its capital account balance.

When a country's imports exceed its exports, it has a current account deficit. Its foreign trading partners who hold net monetary claims can continue to hold their claims as monetary deposits or currency, or they can use the money to buy other financial assets, real property, or equities (stocks) in the trade-deficit country. Net capital flows comprise the sum of these monetary, financial, real property, and equity claims. Capital flows move in the *opposite* direction to the goods and services trade claims that give rise to them. Thus, a country with a current account deficit

---

1. Technically, the sum of capital account, financial account, and reserve flows finances the current account. The financial account—portfolio investment and direct investment—accounts for 90 percent of the financing while the capital account—payments for buildings and nonproduced fixed assets such as land—constitutes a minor part of the financing of the current account, typically less than 10 percent; a miniscule residual amount is accounted for by flows of currencies between central banks. It is traditional to refer to the financial side of the balance of payments as the capital account, and, except where it is necessary to maintain the distinction, "capital account" and "financial account" are used here interchangeably. Further analyses of capital flows, their accounting, and their relation to trade and international investment are contained in the NBER volume edited by Martin Feldstein (1999).

necessarily has a capital account surplus. In balance-of-payments accounting terms, the current-account balance, which is the total balance of internationally traded goods and services, is just offset by the capital-account balance, which is the total balance of claims that domestic investors and foreign investors have acquired in newly invested financial, real property, and equity assets in each others' countries. While all the above statements are true by definition of the accounting terms, the data on international trade and financial flows are generally riddled with errors, generally because of undercounting. Therefore, the international capital and trade data contain a balancing error term called "net errors and omissions."

Because the capital account is the mirror image of the current account, one might expect total recorded world trade—exports plus imports summed over all countries—to equal financial flows—payments plus receipts. But in fact, during 1996–2001, the former was $17.3 trillion, more than three times the latter, at $5.0 trillion.[2] There are three explanations for this. First, many financial transactions between international financial institutions are cleared by netting daily offsetting transactions. For example, if on a particular day, U.S. banks have claims on French banks for $10 million and French banks have claims on U.S. banks for $12 million, the transactions will be cleared through their central banks with a recorded net flow of only $2 million from the United States to France even though $22 million of exports was financed. Second, since the 1970s, there have been sustained and unexplained balance-of-payments discrepancies in both trade and financial flows; part of these balance-of-payments anomalies is almost certainly due to unrecorded capital flows. Third, a huge share of export and import trade is intrafirm transactions; that is, flows of goods, material, or semifinished parts (especially automobiles and other nonelectronic machinery) between parent companies and their subsidiaries. Compensation for such trade is accomplished with accounting debits and credits within the firms' books and does not require actual financial flows. Although data on such intrafirm transactions are not gen-

erally available for all industrial countries, intrafirm trade for the United States in recent years accounts for 30–40 percent of exports and 35–45 percent of imports.[3]

The bulk of capital flows are transactions between the richest nations. In 2003, of the more than $6.4 trillion in gross financial transactions, about $5.4 trillion (84 percent) involved the 24 industrial countries and almost $1.0 trillion (15 percent) involved the 162 less-developed countries (LDCs) or economic territories, with the rest, less than 1 percent, accounted for by international organizations.[4] The shares of both industrial nations and the international organizations have been receding from their highs in 1998: 90 percent for industrial nations and 5 percent for the international organizations. In that year the combination of the Russian debt default and ruble devaluation, the south Asia financial crisis, and the lingering uncertainty about financial consequences of the return of Hong Kong to Chinese sovereignty in July 1997 drove the LDC share down to 5 percent of world capital flows.[5] In the more tranquil five years following these crises, 1999–2003, LDC financial transactions involving mainland China and Hong Kong averaged 28 percent of the LDC total, and adding Taiwan, Singapore, and Korea brings the share to 53 percent of the developing-country transactions. Of the remaining forty-seven percentage points of developing-country transactions, Europe (primarily Russia, Turkey, Poland, and the Czech Republic) and the Western Hemisphere (primarily Mexico, Brazil, and Chile) each accounted for about sixteen percentage points, with the Middle East and Africa combining for the remaining sixteen percentage points.

Financing Trade in Goods, Services, and Assets

Figure 1 shows that most financial flows involve industrial countries whose gross flows (credits plus debits) during 1995–2003 averaged $4.9 trillion per year. Capital flows

3. William J. Zeile, "U.S. Affiliates of Foreign Companies: Operations in 2001," *Survey of Current Business* 83 (August 2003): 50.

4. These international organizations are primarily the International Monetary Fund, the World Bank, other regional development banks, and the United Nations. The use of "involved" rather than "between" is important as many transactions *involving* LDCs were *between* an LDC and an industrial country. Still, the overall magnitudes clearly imply that the overwhelming majority of financial transactions involve industrial countries rather than LDCs.

5. In 1998, capital flows of Hong Kong amounted to more than 7 percent of the world total as inflows to Hong Kong financial assets and outflows from its liabilities each amounted to fifteen times their levels in succeeding years.

2. Note that these are financial transactions entailing a purchase/sale of a security or real asset, not currency exchanges. The Bank of International Settlements estimated the daily volume in currency transactions to be $1.2 trillion in 2001. Thus, the daily flow through currency markets is nearly one-third of the annual volume in financial flows. Unless otherwise noted, these and other data cited in this article are drawn from the International Monetary Fund's *Balance of Payments Statistics* for May 2005. For nearly all international or regional data, the most recent observations are for 2002 or 2003.

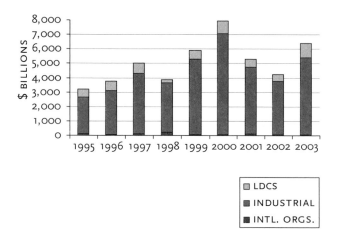

Figure 1 World Financial Flows

involving industrial countries comprised about 90 percent of total transactions, with LDCs and international organizations accounting for the remainder. Perhaps more significant, these gross flows were about ten times the net capital flows, reflecting the netting out of the vast majority of financial flows.

While much international trade is financed by offsetting trade flows, ultimately net trade balances must be financed by net financial flows. As Figure 2 shows, the United States has had large current-account deficits, primarily due to its deficit on merchandise trade; the non-U.S. industrial countries have had large trade surpluses; and LDCs, in aggregate, shifted from trade deficits to growing trade surpluses at the end of the twentieth century.

Net capital and financial flows finance these net trade imbalances, which, while primarily between industrial counties in gross terms, increasingly flowed, on net, from both developing and non-U.S. industrial countries to the United States. Reflecting their shift from trade deficits to trade surpluses at the end of the twentieth century, LDCs became net suppliers of capital in 1999 (Figure 3).

Figures 2 and 3 contain two glaring anomalies. First, Figure 2 shows that the U.S. current account deficit is far larger than the sum of the current account surpluses of the other industrial countries and the LDCs. This implies that the world has been running a current account deficit with itself, something that is logically impossible because the sum of all transactions across all countries—with exports positive and imports negative—must be zero. That is, an export from China to France is an import by France from China. Because the world is a closed system (no country trades with Mars), if trade data were accurate, the sum of world trade in goods and services (including income and transfers) would be zero. Yet, according to the *recorded* data, the world ran a current account deficit averaging more than $95 billion annually during 1995–2003. Combined with estimated errors and omissions, these missing data constitute omitted exports and financial flows well in excess of $100 billion per year.[6] Second, Figure 3 shows that the sum of capital outflows from the non-U.S. industrial countries and LDCs is far smaller than the reported inflow of capital to the United States. Thus, the world ran a substantial capital surplus—again, a logical impossibility (no borrowing from Mars). Although there

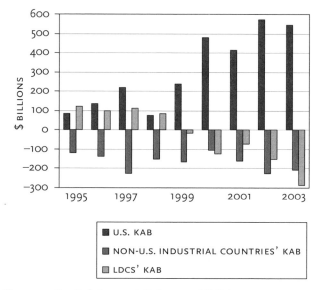

Figure 3 Capital Account Balances (KABs)

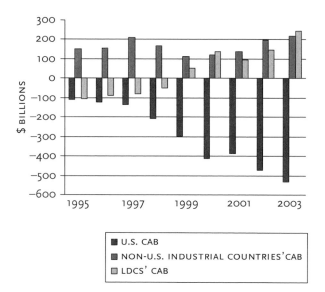

Figure 2 Current Account Balances (CABs)

6. This is not a recent problem: the first IMF report on this issue, appearing in 1987 (*Report on the World Current Account Discrepancy*), observed that a substantial discrepancy had existed since the 1970s.

is no agreed-upon explanation for these discrepancies, there are two possible reasons, depending on whether or not U.S. data on earnings from foreign direct investment are accurate.

First, if the U.S. data are correct, then, because the sum of the U.S. current account deficit in Figure 2 and its capital account surplus in Figure 3 is close to zero, there must be underreported exports to the United States from the non-U.S. industrial countries and the LDCs, balanced by unreported financial flows from them to the United States.

Alternatively, suppose that the U.S. data on foreign direct investment earnings are not accurate, in particular that U.S. net income from its direct investments has been underreported.[7] Reporting these earnings at their higher actual level would result in a reduction of the U.S. current account deficit (due to the increased income from "renting" capital to foreigners) and an equal reduction of the U.S. capital-account surplus.[8]

The available evidence makes the second explanation more likely than the first.

Composition of Capital and Financial Flows

Trade imbalances are financed by offsetting capital and financial flows, which generate changes in net foreign assets. These payments can be any combination of the following:

- capital investments
- portfolio investments in either debt or equity securities
- direct investment in domestic firms (FDI) including start-ups
- changes in international reserves[9]

As Table 1 shows, industrial countries financed their current account balances primarily with financial flows

other than direct investment or reserve flows. Indeed, while the industrial countries were importing capital in the form of other financial flows, they were at the same time exporting capital as investors in the form of foreign direct investment (outflow of capital indicated by minus sign). The flow of net direct investment from industrial countries averaged − $115 billion during the nine years shown in Table 1 and was directed primarily to developing countries. These capital outflows were an important component of financing investment in the LDCs, where the foreign direct investment inflows averaged $154 billion, positive numbers indicating an inflow.

The difference between the industrial country outflow and the developing country inflow was primarily due to foreign direct investment in the United States, which averaged − $36 billion; that is, investors in LDCs were making substantial investments in the United States, much of it reflecting capital flight from insecure financial markets in LDCs to the greater security of property rights in industrial countries. Because financial claims may be short term or long term, real or financial, the key to development is to raise long-term investments as a percentage of capital inflows into LDCs.[10] Foreign direct investment—distinguished from portfolio investment by the investor's substantial ownership share (>10 percent)—implies a greater commitment to a long-term interest in the investment project and an active interest in managing the project. While the United States has been, along with developing countries, the major recipient of direct investment inflows, it is also a major supplier of foreign direct investment.

As Table 1 shows, flows of net investment from industrial countries to LDCs were substantial and were a major impulse to their growth; however, much of industrial and developing country investment was funneled to the United States. Of these capital flows from LDCs to the United States, a substantial share has been purchases of U.S. government debt taken up by LDCs as reserve assets; LDCs' central banks buy and hold a great amount of U.S. debt as international reserves to back their domestic currencies. Purchases of such reserve assets, primarily short-term U.S. Treasury bills, amounted to more than $1 trillion during 1997–2003, with $340 billion in 2003 alone.

The non-U.S. industrial countries—particularly France, Japan, the Netherlands, Switzerland, and the United Kingdom—have been the primary net investors; these five countries supplied the largest part of direct investment during the period 1995–2003, equivalent to 76 percent of the annual net direct investment of all LDCs over this pe-

7. In 1984 former Federal Reserve Board governor H. Robert Heller testified to Congress that "there is some reason to believe that the bulk of unrecorded transactions is due to an underreporting of receipts of service items such as reinvested earnings abroad, investment income and fees. Consequently, the U.S. current account deficit, if measured properly, is likely to have been substantially smaller than indicated by the officially reported data" (Heller 1984, p. 67). Correspondingly, U.S. merchandise trade data have long been suspect in underreporting both merchandise exports and interest income (see Ott 1987).

8. There would be corresponding reductions in industrial country and LDC balances reducing their current account balance and increasing their capital account balance.

9. International reserve assets consist of foreign exchange holdings (currency and short-term assets) that are held by public (central bank and government) or private individuals and firms.

10. See Chuhan et al. 1996 for a discussion of the importance of long-term capital investment flows to LDC development.

Table 1 Current Account Financing ($ Billions)

	1995	1996	1997	1998	1999	2000	2001	2002	2003
					Industrial Countries				
Current Account Balance Financing	42	33	73	−41	−186	−292	−249	−276	−314
Net foreign direct investment	−106	−115	−133	−153	−172	18	−100	−77	−202
Reserves	−78	−77	−23	7	−40	−45	−27	−66	−166
Other financial and capital flows	162	205	168	73	282	413	394	496	714
Net errors and omissions	−20	−47	−84	114	116	−93	−18	−77	−32
					LDCs				
Current Account Balance Financing	−104	−88	−81	−51	52	136	94	148	245
Net foreign direct investment	103	120	155	165	191	169	179	136	141
Reserves	−112	−112	−83	−48	−110	−127	−129	−204	−340
Other financial and capital flows	140	100	50	−29	−94	−149	−122	−86	−85
Net errors and omissions	−28	−20	−41	−37	−38	−30	−22	5	39

Notes: Capital flows indicate investments and borrowings of all terms, ranging from currency holdings and short-term lending to long-term bonds or equity investments. Capital inflows (borrowings and investments) are indicated by positive numbers while capital outflows (lending and investments) are indicated by negative numbers.

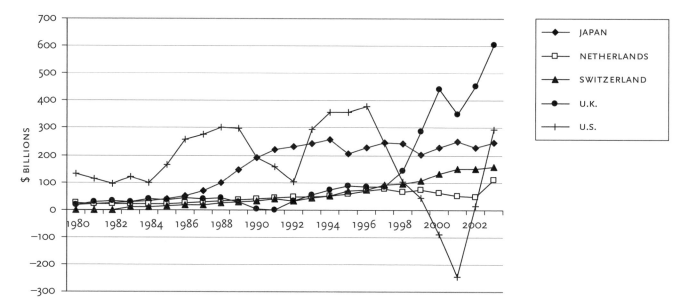

Figure 4 Net Foreign Direct Investment Positions of the Largest Industrial Countries

riod.[11] The distribution of this net foreign direct investment (inflows) was not uniform across LDCs. Almost half of total net direct investment in developing countries was invested in three LDCs: China with 26 percent, Brazil with 13 percent, and Mexico with 8 percent. At the other end of the spectrum, the countries of sub-Saharan Africa accounted, in total, for only 5 percent of total direct investment in LDCs.

Contemporary Versus Historical Capital and Financial Flows

Over the past two hundred years, the world's dominant international investors have been the Western European nations, particularly the United Kingdom, the Nether-

11. Germany was a major supplier of direct investment funds in the first half of this period, but from 2000 forward it became, like the United States, a beneficiary of net direct investment inflows—during 2000–2003, net inflows of foreign direct investment to Germany totaled $171 billion.

lands, and Switzerland. Capital from these countries was invested in their own and other European colonies and in other developing nations, first in the Western Hemisphere and, more recently, worldwide, particularly in China and Brazil. During the nineteenth century, the British financed the transcontinental railroads in the United States and Canada and built vast agricultural plantations in Africa and Asia. Today, Great Britain and the Netherlands remain, as they have from colonial times, among the largest direct investors in the United States: Britain is largest, followed by Japan, Germany, the Netherlands, and France. After World War I, the United States emerged as the world's predominant direct investor and, in gross terms, remains so. As of 2003, U.S. foreign direct assets were more than twice those of the United Kingdom, the next largest asset holder at $2.7 trillion, while U.S. foreign direct investment liabilities were $2.4 trillion, implying a net FDI position of $300 billion. During the past two decades, the United Kingdom again became the world's largest net foreign direct investor, with about $600 billion in net holdings at exchange rates prevailing in 2003. Following the United Kingdom in order are the United States, Japan, Switzerland, and the Netherlands. As Figure 4 shows, foreign direct investment flows have cumulated to huge international holdings by these five principal investors.[12]

About the Author

Mack Ott is an international economic consultant whose major assignments have been in the former Soviet Union countries, the Balkans, and Egypt. During 2003 and 2004 he was macroeconomic adviser to the chief economist of Nigeria and to the West African Monetary Institute. He has also been a U.S. Treasury adviser to the Ministry of Finance of Saudi Arabia.

Further Reading

Chuhan, Punan, Gabriel Perez-Quiros, and Helden Popper. "International Capital Flows—Do Short-Term Investment and Direct Investment Differ?" World Bank Policy Research Paper no. 1669, 1996.

Feldstein, Martin, ed. International Capital Flows. Chicago: University of Chicago Press for NBER, 1999.

Heller, H. Robert. "Statement of H. Robert Heller, Vice President of Bank of America NT&SA." In The Foreign Trade Dilemma: Fact and Fiction. Hearing before the Joint Economic Committee, 98th Congress. Washington, D.C.: U.S. Government Printing Office, 1984. Pp. 48–70.

International Monetary Fund. Report on the World Current Account Discrepancy. September 1987.

Ott, Mack. "Have U.S. Exports Been Larger than Reported?" St. Louis Federal Reserve Bank Review (September/October 1987).

Zeile, William. "U.S. Affiliates of Foreign Companies: Operations in 2001." Survey of Current Business 83 (August 2003): pp. 38–56.

International Trade

Arnold Kling

On the topic of international trade, the views of economists tend to differ from those of the general public. There are three principle differences. First, many noneconomists believe that it is more advantageous to trade with other members of one's nation or ethnic group than with outsiders. Economists see all forms of trade as equally advantageous. Second, many noneconomists believe that exports are better than imports for the economy. Economists believe that all trade is good for the economy. Third, many noneconomists believe that a country's balance of trade is governed by the "competitiveness" of its wage rates, tariffs, and other factors. Economists believe that the balance of trade is governed by many factors, including the above, but also including differences in national saving and investment.

The noneconomic views of trade all seem to stem from a common root: the tendency for human beings to emphasize tribal rivalries. For most people, viewing trade as a rivalry is as instinctive as rooting for their national team in Olympic basketball.

To economists, Olympic basketball is not an appropriate analogy for international trade. Instead, we see international trade as analogous to a production technique. Opening up to trade is equivalent to adopting a more efficient technology. International trade enhances efficiency by allocating resources to increase the amount produced for a given level of effort. Classical liberals, such as Richard Cobden, believed that free trade could bring about world peace by substituting commercial relationships among individuals for competitive relationships between states.[1]

History of Trade Theory

David Ricardo developed and published one of the first theories of international trade in 1817. "England," he wrote,

---

12. Figure 4 also shows an implausible variability in the U.S. net position during 1996–2003—another aspect, perhaps, of unreported capital flows.

1. See http://www.independent.org/students/garvey/essay.asp?id=1381.

may be so circumstanced, that to produce the cloth may require the labour of 100 men for one year; and if she attempted to make the wine, it might require the labour of 120 men for the same time. . . .

To produce the wine in Portugal, might require only the labour of 80 men for one year, and to produce the cloth in the same country, might require the labour of 90 men for the same time. It would therefore be advantageous for her to export wine in exchange for cloth. This exchange might even take place, notwithstanding that the commodity imported by Portugal could be produced there with less labour than in England.[2]

If a painter takes twenty hours to paint a house, and a surgeon could do the job in fifteen hours, it still makes sense for the surgeon to hire the painter. The surgeon can earn enough money in a few hours of surgery to pay for the entire house-painting job. We say that the surgeon's comparative advantage is in doing surgery, while the painter's comparative advantage is in painting houses. Ricardo's theory of comparative advantage explains why a surgeon will hire a house painter and why a lawyer will hire a secretary.

The opportunity to trade with the painter enables the surgeon to paint her house by doing a few hours of surgery. Similarly, international trade enables one country to obtain cloth more cheaply by specializing in the production of wine and trading for cloth, rather than producing both goods for itself.

What determines the pattern of specialization and trade? In the 1920s, Eli Heckscher and Bertil Ohlin offered one theory, called the factor proportions model. The idea is that a country with a high ratio of labor to capital will tend to export goods that are labor-intensive, and vice versa.

The Ricardo and Heckscher-Ohlin theories tend to predict clear patterns of specialization in trade. A country will focus on one type of industry for exports and another type of industry for imports. In fact, the types of industries in which a country exports and the types in which it imports are not dramatically different. This fact has led to the emphasis on another theory of trade, developed by Paul Krugman and others. The idea is that patterns of specialization develop almost by accident and that these patterns persist because of positive feedback. This is known as the increasing-returns model of international trade. "Increasing returns" means that the more of something you produce, the more efficient you get at producing it.

In the United States, for example, Detroit became an automobile-manufacturing center. Once the first large automaker located in Detroit, it was natural that other auto companies would be started there because it was easier to find employees with the right skills. Likewise, people with the skills to produce movies were first located in Hollywood. It became uneconomical to try to build an auto plant in Hollywood or a movie studio in Detroit. Thus, Detroit became an exporter of automobiles, and Hollywood became an exporter of movies. The same model of efficiency explains the international arena—why, for example, the Swiss specialize in watches and the Japanese in portable music players.

Gains from Trade

All of the economic theories of international trade suggest that it enhances efficiency. In this regard, international trade is like a new technology. It adds to the productive capacity of all countries that engage in trade. Some of the efficiency is due to comparative advantage, as in the Ricardo and Heckscher-Ohlin theories. In addition, some efficiency comes from taking advantage of increasing returns.

Trade based on comparative advantage should tend to benefit small countries more than large countries. That is because the benefits of comparative advantage are proportional to the difference between the relative prices in world markets and the relative prices that would prevail in home markets without trade. If that difference is large, then a country earns a large advantage from trade. If that difference is small, then there is only a small advantage from trade. Small countries are more likely than large countries to find that relative prices in the world market differ significantly from what would prevail in their home markets.

Another benefit from trade is that it promotes dynamism and innovation within an economy. Improvements in manufacturing quality and productivity in the United States in recent decades have been credited, in part, to the pressure of competition from Japan and elsewhere.

An economy that is closed to trade is one in which inefficient industries and laggard firms are well protected. In fact, studies suggest that barriers to trade are a major cause of extreme underdevelopment. The countries that are most closed to trade tend to be the poorest in the world. Countries that have reduced trade barriers and increased the share of imports and exports in their economies tend to be among the fastest-growing nations.

According to a World Bank study, twenty-four developing countries that became more integrated into the world economy in the 1980s and 1990s had higher income growth, longer life expectancy, and better schooling. Per capita income in these countries, home to half the world's

2. Quoted from http://www.econlib.org/library/Ricardo/ricP .html.

population, grew by an average of 5 percent in the 1990s compared with only 2 percent in rich countries. China, India, Hungary, and Mexico are among the countries that adopted policies that allowed their people to take advantage of global markets. As a result, they sharply increased the amount of their GDP accounted for by trade. Real wages in these countries rose and the number of poor people fell.

The study also points out that two billion people—particularly in sub-Saharan Africa, the Middle East, and the former Soviet Union—are in countries being left behind. These countries' integration into the world economy has not increased, and their ratio of trade to GDP has stagnated or fallen. Their economies have generally contracted, poverty has increased, and education levels have risen less rapidly than in the more globalized countries.[3]

Another report notes that exports plus imports as a share of output among the richest countries rose from 32.3 percent to 37.9 percent between 1990 and 2001. Moreover, among developing countries, that share rose from 33.8 percent to 48.9 percent over that period. The success of India and China recently, and Japan, Taiwan, South Korea, and other countries in the 1970s and 1980s, is due in large part to trade.[4]

The OECD countries, which together have more than $25 trillion in GDP, account for most of world trade. Poor countries account for less than $300 billion in GDP, which is less than one-tenth of world output, and thus account for only a miniscule fraction of world trade.

Purchasing Power Parity

If goods were perfectly tradable across borders, with no trade barriers or transactions costs, then there would be no reason for prices to differ. This gives rise to the idea of purchasing power parity, a theory of exchange-rate adjustment based on the law of one price.

If the same good sells for one hundred dollars in the United States and one hundred euros in Europe, then according to the law of one price the exchange rate between dollars and euros ought to be one. The theory of purchasing power parity is that this relationship holds for an overall market basket of goods and services.

Empirical tests tend to show only a weak tendency for exchange rates to move in the direction of purchasing power parity. This means that cross-border trade is not nearly friction free. The failure of purchasing power parity to hold, except perhaps in the long run, indicates that

transportation costs, language-translation costs, and other factors limit the integration of global markets.

Capital Flows and the Balance of Trade

In 2000, U.S. exports were $1.1 trillion and U.S. imports were close to $1.5 trillion. The excess of imports over exports is called a current account deficit. What caused this deficit? Modern economists believe that the trade surplus and capital flows are mutually determined. When a nation's domestic saving (personal saving plus retained earnings of corporations) exceeds the domestic uses of saving (financing its private investment and its government budget deficit), then that nation will run a trade surplus, and vice versa.

Imagine that all international trade took place in the form of barter of goods and services. If you wanted to buy a Japanese car, you would have to offer something of equivalent value in return. In that case, trade in goods and services would have to balance, and there would be no trade deficits.

To obtain a Japanese car without trading goods and services, the Japanese have to accept financial assets in exchange for cars. These assets could be dollars, shares of U.S. companies, corporate bonds or other private debt instruments, or U.S. government debt. A country that is accumulating foreign assets will necessarily run a trade surplus. A country that is selling assets to foreigners will necessarily run a trade deficit. A country will accumulate assets when its domestic saving is greater than its domestic uses of saving. A country will sell assets when its national saving is insufficient for its domestic uses of saving.

Typically, one would expect wealthy countries to have excess saving and to invest in capital-poor countries. From this perspective, it is an anomaly that the United States is a capital importer and China is a capital exporter. However, the United States is a relatively attractive country in which to invest, and American policies tend to encourage consumption rather than saving.

Conclusion

Economic theory indicates that international trade raises the standard of living. A comparison between the performance of open and closed economies confirms that the benefits of trade in practice are significant.

About the Author

Arnold Kling is the author of *Learning Economics,* a nonmathematical introduction to economics. He was an economist at the Federal Reserve and at Freddie Mac before founding Homefair.com in 1994. His personal Web site is http://arnold kling.com.

3. See http://econ.worldbank.org/prr/globalization/.

4. See http://www1.worldbank.org/economicpolicy/globalization/documents/AssessingGlobalizationP1.pdf.

Further Reading

On the differences between economists and noneconomists on international trade, see Bryan Caplan, "Straight Talk About Economic Literacy." Online at: http://www.mercatus.org/publications/pubid.3320/pub_detail.asp.

On the history of trade theory, see Steven Suranovic, *International Trade Theory and Policy Analysis*. Online at: http://internationalecon.com/v1.0/toc.html.

On capital flows and the balance of trade, see Arnold Kling, "The Balance of Saving." Online at: http://www.techcentralstation.com/111803C.html. Reprinted in *Learning Economics*. Online at: http://arnoldkling.com/econ/book/contents.html.

For the relationship between trade and jobs, see "Remarks by Vice Chairman Roger W. Ferguson, Jr. at the Conference on Trade and the Future of American Workers, Washington, D.C." Online at: http://www.federalreserve.gov/boarddocs/speeches/2004/20041007/default.htm.

For the effects of globalization and trade on the standard of living in developed and underdeveloped countries, see the World Bank's *Assessing Globalization*. Online at: http://www1.worldbank.org/economicpolicy/globalization/documents/AssessingGlobalizationP1.pdf.

For the argument that underdevelopment reflects trade and regulatory barriers, see Stephen L. Parente and Edward C. Prescott. *Barriers to Riches*. Cambridge: MIT Press, 2000.

For more on purchasing power parity, see Ken Rogoff. "The Purchasing Power Parity Puzzle." *Journal of Economic Literature* 34 (June 1996): 647–668. Online at: http://www.economics.harvard.edu/~krogoff//JEL1996.pdf.

International Trade Agreements

Douglas A. Irwin

Ever since Adam Smith published *The Wealth of Nations* in 1776, the vast majority of economists have accepted the proposition that free trade among nations improves overall economic welfare. Free trade, usually defined as the absence of tariffs, quotas, or other governmental impediments to international trade, allows each country to specialize in the goods it can produce cheaply and efficiently relative to other countries. Such specialization enables all countries to achieve higher real incomes.

Although free trade provides overall benefits, removing a trade barrier on a particular good hurts the shareholders and employees of the domestic industry that produces that good. Some of the groups that are hurt by foreign competition wield enough political power to obtain protection against imports. Consequently, barriers to trade continue to exist despite their sizable economic costs. According to

the U.S. International Trade Commission, for example, the U.S. gain from removing trade restrictions on textiles and apparel would have been almost twelve billion dollars in 2002 alone. This is a net economic gain after deducting the losses to firms and workers in the domestic industry. Yet, domestic textile producers have been able to persuade Congress to maintain tight restrictions on imports.

While virtually all economists think free trade is desirable, they differ on how best to make the transition from tariffs and quotas to free trade. The three basic approaches to trade reform are unilateral, multilateral, and bilateral.

Some countries, such as Britain in the nineteenth century and Chile and China in recent decades, have undertaken unilateral tariff reductions—reductions made independently and without reciprocal action by other countries. The advantage of unilateral free trade is that a country can reap the benefits of free trade immediately. Countries that lower trade barriers by themselves do not have to postpone reform while they try to persuade other nations to follow suit. The gains from such trade liberalization are substantial: several studies have shown that income grows more rapidly in countries open to international trade than in those more closed to trade. Dramatic illustrations of this phenomenon include China's rapid growth after 1978 and India's after 1991, those dates indicating when major trade reforms took place.

For many countries, unilateral reforms are the only effective way to reduce domestic trade barriers. However, multilateral and bilateral approaches—dismantling trade barriers in concert with other countries—have two advantages over unilateral approaches. First, the economic gains from international trade are reinforced and enhanced when many countries or regions agree to a mutual reduction in trade barriers. By broadening markets, concerted liberalization of trade increases competition and specialization among countries, thus giving a bigger boost to efficiency and consumer incomes.

Second, multilateral reductions in trade barriers may reduce political opposition to free trade in each of the countries involved. That is because groups that otherwise would oppose or be indifferent to trade reform might join the campaign for free trade if they see opportunities for exporting to the other countries in the trade agreement. Consequently, free trade agreements between countries or regions are a useful strategy for liberalizing world trade.

The best possible outcome of trade negotiations is a multilateral agreement that includes all major trading countries. Then, free trade is widened to allow many participants to achieve the greatest possible gains from trade. After World War II, the United States helped found the General Agreement on Tariffs and Trade (GATT), which quickly became the world's most important multilateral trade arrangement.

The major countries of the world set up the GATT in reaction to the waves of protectionism that crippled world trade during—and helped extend—the Great Depression of the 1930s. In successive negotiating "rounds," the GATT substantially reduced the tariff barriers on manufactured goods in the industrial countries. Since the GATT began in 1947, average tariffs set by industrial countries have fallen from about 40 percent to about 5 percent today. These tariff reductions helped promote the tremendous expansion of world trade after World War II and the concomitant rise in real per capita incomes among developed and developing nations alike. The annual gain from removal of tariff and nontariff barriers to trade as a result of the Uruguay Round Agreement (negotiated under the auspices of the GATT between 1986 and 1993) has been put at about $96 billion, or 0.4 percent of world GDP.

In 1995, the GATT became the World Trade Organization (WTO), which now has more than 140 member countries. The WTO oversees four international trade agreements: the GATT, the General Agreement on Trade in Services (GATS), and agreements on trade-related intellectual property rights and trade-related investment (TRIPS and TRIMS, respectively). The WTO is now the forum for members to negotiate reductions in trade barriers; the most recent forum is the Doha Development Round, launched in 2001.

The WTO also mediates disputes between member countries over trade matters. If one country's government accuses another country's government of violating world trade rules, a WTO panel rules on the dispute. (The panel's ruling can be appealed to an appellate body.) If the WTO finds that a member country's government has not complied with the agreements it signed, the member is obligated to change its policy and bring it into conformity with the rules. If the member finds it politically impossible to change its policy, it can offer compensation to other countries in the form of lower trade barriers on other goods. If it chooses not to do this, then other countries can receive authorization from the WTO to impose higher duties (i.e., to "retaliate") on goods coming from the offending member country for its failure to comply.

As a multilateral trade agreement, the GATT requires its signatories to extend most-favored-nation (MFN) status to other trading partners participating in the WTO. MFN status means that each WTO member receives the same tariff treatment for its goods in foreign markets as that extended to the "most-favored" country competing in the same market, thereby ruling out preferences for, or discrimination against, any member country.

Although the WTO embodies the principle of nondiscrimination in international trade, article 24 of the GATT permits the formation of free-trade areas and "customs unions" among WTO members. A free-trade area is a group of countries that eliminate all tariffs on trade with each other but retain autonomy in determining their tariffs with nonmembers. A customs union is a group of countries that eliminate all tariffs on trade among themselves but maintain a common external tariff on trade with countries outside the union (thus technically violating MFN).

The customs union exception was designed, in part, to accommodate the formation of the European Economic Community (EC) in 1958. The EC, originally formed by six European countries, is now known as the EUROPEAN UNION (EU) and includes twenty-seven European countries. The EU has gone beyond simply reducing barriers to trade among member states and forming a customs union. It has moved toward even greater economic integration by becoming a common market—an arrangement that eliminates impediments to the mobility of factors of production, such as capital and labor, between participating countries. As a common market, the EU also coordinates and harmonizes each country's tax, industrial, and agricultural policies. In addition, many members of the EU have formed a single currency area by replacing their domestic currencies with the euro.

The GATT also permits free-trade areas (FTAs), such as the European Free Trade Area, which is composed primarily of Scandinavian countries. Members of FTAs eliminate tariffs on trade with each other but retain autonomy in determining their tariffs with nonmembers.

One difficulty with the WTO system has been the problem of maintaining and extending the liberal world trading system in recent years. Multilateral negotiations over trade liberalization move very slowly, and the requirement for consensus among the WTO's many members limits how far agreements on trade reform can go. As Mike Moore, a recent director-general of the WTO, put it, the organization is like a car with one accelerator and 140 hand brakes. While multilateral efforts have successfully reduced tariffs on industrial goods, it has had much less success in liberalizing trade in agriculture, textiles, and apparel, and in other areas of international commerce. Recent negotiations, such as the Doha Development Round, have run into problems, and their ultimate success is uncertain.

As a result, many countries have turned away from the multilateral process toward bilateral or regional trade agreements. One such agreement is the North American Free Trade Agreement (NAFTA), which went into effect in January 1994. Under the terms of NAFTA, the United

States, Canada, and Mexico agreed to phase out all tariffs on merchandise trade and to reduce restrictions on trade in services and foreign investment over a decade. The United States also has bilateral agreements with Israel, Jordan, Singapore, and Australia and is negotiating bilateral or regional trade agreements with countries in Latin America, Asia, and the Pacific. The European Union also has free-trade agreements with other countries around the world.

The advantage of such bilateral or regional arrangements is that they promote greater trade among the parties to the agreement. They may also hasten global trade liberalization if multilateral negotiations run into difficulties. Recalcitrant countries excluded from bilateral agreements, and hence not sharing in the increased trade these bring, may then be induced to join and reduce their own barriers to trade. Proponents of these agreements have called this process "competitive liberalization," wherein countries are challenged to reduce trade barriers to keep up with other countries. For example, shortly after NAFTA was implemented, the EU sought and eventually signed a free-trade agreement with Mexico to ensure that European goods would not be at a competitive disadvantage in the Mexican market as a result of NAFTA.

But these advantages must be offset against a disadvantage: by excluding certain countries, these agreements may shift the composition of trade from low-cost countries that are not party to the agreement to high-cost countries that are.

Suppose, for example, that Japan sells bicycles for fifty dollars, Mexico sells them for sixty dollars, and both face a twenty-dollar U.S. tariff. If tariffs are eliminated on Mexican goods, U.S. consumers will shift their purchases from Japanese to Mexican bicycles. The result is that Americans will purchase from a higher-cost source, and the U.S. government receives no tariff revenue. Consumers save ten dollars per bicycle, but the government loses twenty dollars. Economists have shown that if a country enters such a "trade-diverting" customs union, the cost of this trade diversion may exceed the benefits of increased trade with the other members of the customs union. The net result is that the customs union could make the country worse off.

Critics of bilateral and regional approaches to trade liberalization have many additional arguments. They suggest that these approaches may undermine and supplant, instead of support and complement, the multilateral WTO approach, which is to be preferred for operating globally on a nondiscriminatory basis. Hence, the long-term result of bilateralism could be a deterioration of the world trading system into competing, discriminatory regional trading blocs, resulting in added complexity that complicates the smooth flow of goods between countries. Furthermore, the reform of such issues as agricultural export subsidies cannot be dealt with effectively at the bilateral or regional level.

Despite possible tensions between the two approaches, it appears that both multilateral and bilateral/regional trade agreements will remain features of the world economy. Both the WTO and agreements such as NAFTA, however, have become controversial among groups such as antiglobalization protesters, who argue that such agreements serve the interests of multinational corporations and not workers, even though freer trade has been a time-proven method of improving economic performance and raising overall incomes. To accommodate this opposition, there has been pressure to include labor and environmental standards in these trade agreements. Labor standards include provisions for minimum wages and working conditions, while environmental standards would prevent trade if environmental damage was feared.

One motivation for such standards is the fear that unrestricted trade will lead to a "race to the bottom" in labor and environmental standards as multinationals search the globe for low wages and lax environmental regulations in order to cut costs. Yet there is no empirical evidence of any such race. Indeed, trade usually involves the transfer of technology to developing countries, which allows wage rates to rise, as Korea's economy—among many others—has demonstrated since the 1960s. In addition, rising incomes allow cleaner production technologies to become affordable. The replacement of pollution-belching domestically produced scooters in India with imported scooters from Japan, for example, would improve air quality in India.

Labor unions and environmentalists in rich countries have most actively sought labor and environmental standards. The danger is that enforcing such standards may simply become an excuse for rich-country protectionism, which would harm workers in poor countries. Indeed, people in poor countries, whether capitalists or laborers, have been extremely hostile to the imposition of such standards. For example, the 1999 WTO meeting in Seattle collapsed in part because developing countries objected to the Clinton administration's attempt to include labor standards in multilateral agreements.

A safe prediction is that international trade agreements will continue to generate controversy.

About the Author

Douglas A. Irwin is a professor of economics at Dartmouth College. He formerly served on the staff of the President's

Council of Economic Advisers and on the Federal Reserve Board.

Further Reading

Bhagwati, Jagdish, ed. Going Alone: *The Case for Relaxed Reciprocity in Freeing Trade.* Cambridge: MIT Press, 2002.

Bhagwati, Jagdish, and Arvind Panagariya eds. *The Economics of Preferential Trade Agreements.* Washington, D.C.: AEI Press, 1996.

Irwin, Douglas A. *Against the Tide: An Intellectual History of Free Trade.* Princeton: Princeton University Press, 1996.

———. *Free Trade Under Fire.* 2d ed. Princeton: Princeton University Press, 2005.

U.S. International Trade Commission. *The Economic Effects of Significant U.S. Import Restraints.* Fourth update. USITC Publication no. 3701. June 2004.

Wacziarg, Romain, and Karen H. Welch. "Trade Liberalization and Growth: New Evidence." NBER Working Paper no. 10152. National Bureau of Economic Research, Cambridge, Mass., 2003.

Internet

Stan Liebowitz

The Internet and Economics

"The Internet changes everything"—or so we were told at the height of the Internet craze. According to a prominent *Wall Street Journal* article titled "Goodbye Supply and Demand," one of the changes it was claimed to have brought about was a transformation of the basic economic forces at work in the economy. After the fact, we know that the Internet did not change everything, and it certainly did not change the fundamental economic forces that underlie the workings of markets. Many economists did not believe that the Internet, or any mere change in technology, could alter the fundamental laws of markets that have been established over the last three centuries.

The Internet's main function is to reduce the cost of transmitting information, and that is really all it does. Since the Internet only moves electrical pulses from one location to another, it is capable only of transmitting products that can be digitized—and that comes down to various forms of information (including digitized entertainment).

The fact that we can describe what the Internet does in such a brief sentence does not undercut its value as a technology. Not only does it allow the economy to benefit directly from the decreased costs of information transmittal, but also it allows markets to function more efficiently.

Information in the hands of consumers allows them to better choose their products. Anyone who has tried to purchase a car and has consulted the Edmunds or Autobytel Web sites can testify to the wealth of free information available. Stock trackers can do research more easily and collect real-time quotes, something inconceivable for a typical investor before the Internet. Anyone interested in product or market information can quickly find it with search engines such as Google, although this information has not prevented consumers from sometimes overbidding for items on eBay. In addition, many Web sites allow consumers to help other prospective consumers by providing feedback on products.

By reducing the cost of transmitting information, the Internet has also revolutionized some markets, making some local markets into national markets (as with used car parts from scrap yards) and national markets into international markets. It has also allowed people to stay in almost constant contact with friends using instant messaging, has fostered the creation of virtual communities interested in particular topics, and has allowed people with enough energy and interest to become "broadcasters" of information via Web sites and blogs (Web logs).

But despite these changes in marketplace information, the Internet does not change the underlying market forces. The bursting of the bubble—the deflating of the lofty market capitalizations of firms related in any way to the Internet—was itself the most pedestrian case of time-honored economic forces coming to the fore. The law of demand states that the price the marginal consumer is willing to pay declines as the output increases, holding other things constant. This means that price falls as supply increases. Applied to investment, it means that returns fall as the level of investment increases.

Because expectations for the Internet were so high and so widely held, firms promising to use the Internet in their business plans drew a tremendous amount of investment. Some of these business plans were just so much thin air with no potential for any profit. But even companies whose business plans made sense were unable to translate them into profits when a dozen other firms were investing in the same idea. So much investment money was thrown at "Internet" firms that the rate of return was negative.

Of course, consumers benefit from these new investments even if the investors do not. This is also consistent with simple microeconomics, which teaches that although the price falls as supply increases, the benefit to consumers increases.

Some relatively new economic concepts predating the Internet were often used in discussions of the Internet. These concepts—network effects, winner take all, lock-in, first mover wins—are often misunderstood. The last two on the list, as they are commonly used, are not supported in the economics literature.

Concepts Associated with the Internet

Network Effects

Many products and firms associated with the Internet are thought to have an economic property known as "network effects." Network effects are present when a product becomes more useful to consumers as the number of other people using it increases. For example, the owner of a fax machine benefits from the fact that there are many other people with fax machines.

While some products associated with e-commerce did have network effects, many products did not have even the slightest trace of them. Most Internet retailers, for example, had no network effects to speak of. Take the example of E-toys. Although consumers were unlikely to care about the size of the network—how many other consumers were using E-toys—many pundits assumed that any business conducted over a network had network effects.

Winner Take All

When network effects are strong, firms with large networks have an advantage over those with small networks. Everything else being equal, consumers should be willing to pay more to join a large network. This advantage of large over small is referred to as winner take all, even though consumers tend to have differentiated tastes and market shares are almost never 100 percent. This is an advantage of size on the demand side, whereas such advantages had previously been thought most likely to arise on the supply side, when firms had economies of scale.

Could the transformation of business from brick and mortar to Internet-based turn an industry that was not previously winner take all into one that was? For the large number of Internet firms that did not enjoy network effects, the answer had to be *no*. Even for those that had network effects, it need not be, and generally was not, true that the network effects would be strong enough to convert an otherwise typical firm facing the law of diminishing returns into an increasing-returns firm.

Nevertheless, there can be cases where network effects help create winner-take-all characteristics. The software industry might fit that description, although network effects probably play second fiddle to traditional economies of scale—caused by large fixed costs—in creating winner-take-all conditions. The network effects associated with businesses such as eBay, where consumers value having many choices, might be responsible for winner-take-all results.

The Concepts of Lock-in and First Mover Wins

Winner-take-all markets do not require that the same winner keep winning time after time. It is possible that there will be swift leadership changes whenever a better challenger enters the market.

The concept of lock-in as it is most commonly used—that is, a strong version of lock-in—suggests otherwise. According to the strong version, the winner not only takes all, but also continues to do so even in the face of a better rival. The theory of just why this would be so has to do with a particular type of coordination problem associated with network effects.

Whenever consumers attempt to determine which brand or type of product to buy in network markets, they need to take account of the strength or size of the competing networks. For example, a consumer in the early 1980s determining whether to buy a VHS or Beta VCR would normally have considered the prospective size of the two networks.

Strong lock-in proposes a tantalizing possibility. Every consumer might know that a better technology exists, but because they all fear that other consumers will not switch, everyone remains with the inferior product. Nevertheless, strong lock-in ignores the possibility that consumers will expect others to pick the better product or that the producer of the better product might engage in practices to convince consumers to switch, such as low pricing or performance guarantees.

If the strong lock-in held, then firms would succeed by getting to market first and largely ignoring relative quality because even with a significantly better product a challenger could not dislodge the incumbent. This is the genesis of the first-mover-wins doctrine. This thinking led to the massive frenzied investments that occurred during the Internet bubble and played an important role in the Microsoft antitrust case.

Although this form of lock-in is theoretically possible, before presuming that it is a serious problem we should check to see if it actually happens.

Real-World Intrusions on the Theoretical Party

There is no evidence that strong-form lock-in actually occurs. That explains why Altair, VisiCalc, and Ampex—the first firms to produce PCs, spreadsheets, and VCRs, respectively—are not today the leaders in those markets. And it explains why Apple, Lotus, and Sony, the second-generation leaders, are not the current leaders in those markets.

Some economists claim that real cases of strong lock-in do exist. The two most popular alleged examples are the typewriter keyboard and the VCR. The problem, however, is that these examples are counterfeit.

The keyboard story starts with the claim (without any supporting evidence) that to prevent jamming of the keys, the typewriter mechanics who worked on the original QWERTY (named after the upper lefthand keys) machine in the late 1800s came up with a design to slow typing down. In the 1930s, a professor of ergonomics at the University of Washington, August Dvorak, patented his own keyboard, painstakingly created from a systematic study of keyboard design. Dvorak's own research claimed that this keyboard design worked much better than the QWERTY design, but lock-in advocates give more weight to a U.S. Navy study that supposedly demonstrated that Professor Dvorak's design was indeed at least 40 percent faster than the QWERTY design.

This story is flawed in many respects. First, it ignores a heavily publicized General Services Administration (GSA) study comparing the two keyboards, which concluded that Dvorak's design was not superior to QWERTY. Second, it neglects to mention that the Navy's chief expert during its tests was Lieutenant Commander August Dvorak, the patent holder of the alternative keyboard, who was identified by the GSA study as the author of the Navy study. When Stephen Margolis and I examined the Navy study, we found several important biases and errors. Finally, the story ignores modern ergonomic studies of the keyboard that are inconsistent with the claims of Dvorak advocates.

The VHS/Beta story, claiming that Beta was the better format but that VHS was locked in, is equally flawed for many reasons, not the least of which is that Beta came first. Further, the developers of Beta and VHS had a patent-sharing agreement and used the same technology, with the two formats differing mainly in the size of the tape. This tape size, which gave VHS a longer playing time, proved crucial.

Various people have claimed that the internal combustion engine was locked in at the turn of the twentieth century, preventing steam or electric engines from taking hold. Yet, as a student of Paul David's concluded after writing his dissertation on the subject, this claim was false. So far, no examples of strong lock-in have withstood scrutiny.

In our lengthy examination of software markets, Margolis and I found that the product that wins also happens to be as good as or better than the others. A 1999 study I conducted for McKinsey produced similar results. I looked at twenty different markets, ranging from high tech, such as Web portals, to low tech, such as athletic apparel and discount retailers. The results were consistent with those found in software markets. Finally, work by Peter Golder and Gerard Tellis refutes many previous examples of purported wins by first movers.

The Internet and Business Strategy

Characteristics of Goods Likely to Sell Well over the Web
The Internet will change certain markets. It can play an important role in retailing, particularly when information is of central importance. It will likely become the primary mode of distribution for all things based on information—music, software, books, movies, travel bookings, and so on—although various copyright mechanisms need to be worked out before this becomes true in all cases.

Firms might forgo bricks and mortar if the products they sell have particular characteristics, including, low shipping costs relative to value. Since Internet firms must use delivery companies to get the product to consumers, it is important that the shipping costs not overwhelm the value of the product. The products must be nonperishable goods that can go through a delivery process without losing their value (which was why Internet grocery sales made no sense). Experience goods, which consumers can evaluate only in person, cannot be sold through a virtual experience such as the Internet; nor can goods intended for instant gratification, because shipping time removes the "instant" component of instant gratification. And of course, even brick-and-mortar firms might benefit from using the Web to promote their products or take orders.

Advertising Revenues for Web Sites
Many Web sites have had difficulty supporting themselves. Again, this was partly due to too much investment leading to too many Web sites chasing too few dollars. But there were other miscalculations as well. Although originally many sites expected to charge subscribers for use, this business model was quickly replaced by an advertising-only model adopted from the television industry.

The success over the years of television broadcasters might have provided an appealing exemplar for Web sites, but television has some advantages not shared by Web sites. First, and most important, competition is restricted in the television market since the FCC grants a limited number of licenses, allowing television stations to earn above-normal returns for many years without fear of having entry compete them away, as would happen in a competitive industry.

In addition, television has a superior advertising methodology. The advertisements are embedded in the programming in such a way that one cannot bypass the advertising while consuming the programming (short of averting one's eyes, leaving the room, or changing channels). The same is not true of most Internet advertising, although popover ads are an attempt to diminish the ease of ignoring the advertising. Further, television advertising is far more engaging than Internet advertising has been and is likely to be for the foreseeable future.

Finally, television has a larger audience—the average household still watches more than seven hours per day, with the typical person watching almost four hours per day. The most recent estimate for Internet usage (2004) is twenty-eight minutes per day per person, with projections of thirty-three minutes per day expected in 2009.[1]

The size of the relative audiences, compounded by the superior advertising capability of television, allows a simple estimation of the maximum reasonable advertising revenues from the Internet. In *Rethinking the Network Economy*, I compared the sizes of the two audiences, assuming equivalent advertising capability, and discovered that Internet advertising was already higher than could be reasonably expected. Thus, there was little room for future growth without major increases in Internet usage or more compelling advertising except for search engine advertising.

Web sites hoping to support themselves with their content, therefore, will need to rely increasingly on subscription revenues if they are to survive.

About the Author

Stan Liebowitz is an economist in the Business School of the University of Texas at Dallas and director of the Center for the Analysis of Property Rights and Innovation.

Further Reading

Overview

Liebowitz, Stan. *Rethinking the Network Economy*. New York: Amacom, 2002.

The Internet Changed Everything

Arthur, W. Brian. "Positive Feedbacks in the Economy." *Scientific American* (February 1990). Also online at: http://www.santafe.edu/arthur/Papers/Papers.html.

David, Paul A. "Clio and the Economics of QWERTY." *American Economic Review* 75 (May 1985): 332–337.

Petzinger, Thomas Jr. "So Long, Supply and Demand: There's a New Economy Out There—and It Looks Nothing Like the Old One." *Wall Street Journal*, January 3, 2000, P. S1.

1. Data from *U.S. Statistical Abstract*, table 1110: "Media Usage and Consumer Spending: 1999 to 2009," online at: http://www.census.gov/compendia/statab/tables/07s1110.xls.

Views on Network Effects

Katz, Michael L., and Carl Shapiro. "Network Externalities, Competition, and Compatibility." *American Economic Review* 75, no. 3 (1985): 424–440.

Liebowitz, S. J., and Stephen E. Margolis. "Network Externality: An Uncommon Tragedy." *Journal of Economic Perspectives* 8, no. 2 (1994): 133–150.

Evidence that Better Products Tend to Win

Golder, Peter N., and Gerard J. Tellis. *Will and Vision: How Latecomers Grow to Dominate Markets*. New York: McGraw-Hill, 2002.

Kirsch, David. "The Electric Car and the Burden of History: Automotive Systems Rivalry in America." Stanford, Department of History, 1996.

Liebowitz, Stan. "Product Quality and the Economic Performance of Firms." Report for McKinsey and Company, October 15, 1999. Available online at: http://wwwpub.utdallas.edu/~liebowit/mckinsey.pdf.

Liebowitz, Stan J., and Stephen E. Margolis. *Winners, Losers, and Microsoft*. 2d ed. Oakland, Calif.: Independent Institute, 2001. Especially chaps. 7, 8, and 9.

VanVleck, V. N. L. "Delivering Coal by Road and Rail in Britain: The Efficiency of the 'Silly Little Bobtailed' Coal Wagons." *Journal of Economic History* 57, no. 1 (1997): 139–160. March 1997.

Investment

Kevin A. Hassett

Investment is one of the most important variables in economics. On its back, humans have ridden from caves to skyscrapers. Its surges and collapses are still a primary cause of recessions. Indeed, as can be seen in Figure 1, investment has dropped sharply during almost every postwar U.S. recession. As the graph suggests, one cannot begin to project where the economy is going in the near term or the long term without having a firm grasp of the future path of investment. Because it is so important, economists have studied investment intensely and understand it relatively well.

What Is Investment?

By investment, economists mean the production of goods that will be used to produce other goods. This definition differs from the popular usage, wherein decisions to purchase stocks or bonds are thought of as investment.

Investment is usually the result of forgoing consumption. In a purely agrarian society, early humans had to choose how much grain to eat after the harvest and how much to save for future planting. The latter was investment. In a more modern society, we allocate our productive capacity to

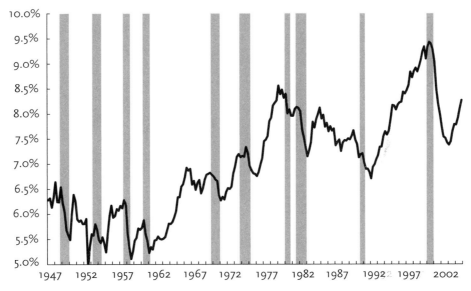

Figure 1 Investment/GDP, 1947–2004

Source: Bureau of Economic Analysis and NBER.

Note: Shaded regions represent recessions as determined by the NBER.

producing pure consumer goods such as hamburgers and hot dogs, and investment goods such as semiconductor foundries. If we create one dollar worth of hamburgers today, then our gross national product is higher by one dollar. If we create one dollar worth of semiconductor foundry today, gross national product is higher by one dollar, but it will also be higher next year because the foundry will still produce computer chips long after the hamburger has disappeared. This is how investment leads to economic growth. Without it, human progress would halt.

Investment need not always take the form of a privately owned physical product. The most common example of nonphysical investment is investment in HUMAN CAPITAL. When a student chooses study over leisure, that student has invested in his own future just as surely as the factory owner who has purchased machines. Investment theory just as easily applies to this decision. Pharmaceutical products that establish heightened well-being can also be thought of as investments that reap higher future productivity. Moreover, government also invests. A bridge or a road is just as much an investment in tomorrow's activity as a machine is. The literature discussed below focuses on the study of physical capital purchases, but the analysis is more widely applicable.

Where Do the Resources for Investment Come From?

In an economy that is closed to the outside world, investment can come only from the forgone consumption—the saving—of private individuals, private firms, or government. In an open economy, however, investment can surge at the same time that a nation's saving is low because a country can borrow the resources necessary to invest from neighboring countries. This method of financing investment has been very important in the United States. The industrial base of the United States in the nineteenth century—railroads, factories, and so on—was built on foreign finance, especially from Britain. More recently, the United States has repeatedly posted significant investment growth and very low savings. However, when investment is funded from outside, some of the future returns to capital are passed outside as well. Over time, then, a country that relies exclusively on foreign financing of investment may find that it has very little capital income with which to finance future consumption. Accordingly, the source of investment finance is an important concern. If it is financed by domestic saving, then future returns stay at home. If it is financed by foreign saving, then future returns go abroad, and the country is less wealthy than otherwise.

What Makes Investment Go Up and Down?

The theory of investment dates back to the giants of economics. IRVING FISHER, ARTHUR CECIL PIGOU, and ALFRED MARSHALL all made contributions; as did JOHN MAYNARD KEYNES, whose Marshallian user cost theory is a central feature in his *General Theory*. In addition, investment was one of the first variables studied with modern empirical techniques. Already in 1909, Albert Aftalion noted that investment tended to move with the business cycle.

Many authors, including Nobel laureate TRYGVE HAAVELMO, contributed to the advance of the investment literature after the war. Dale Jorgenson published a highly influential synthesis of this and earlier work in 1963. His neoclassical theory of investment has withstood the test of time because it allows policy analysts to predict how changes in government policy affect investment. In addition, the theory is intuitively appealing and is an essential tool for any economist.

Here is a brief sketch. Suppose you run a firm and are deciding whether to purchase a machine. What should affect your decision? The first observation is that you should purchase the machine if doing so will increase your profits. For that to happen, the revenue you earn from the machine should at least be equal to the costs. On the revenue side, the calculation is easy. If, for example, the machine will produce one thousand donuts and you can sell them at ten cents apiece, then you know, after subtracting the noncapital costs such as flour, exactly how much extra revenue the machine will produce. But what costs are associated with the machine?

Suppose the machine lasts forever, so you do not have to worry about wear and tear. If you buy the machine, then it produces donuts and the machine's manufacturer has your money. If you decide not to buy the machine, then you can put the money in the bank and earn interest. If the machine truly does not wear (i.e., depreciate) while you use it, you could, in principle, purchase the machine this year and sell it next year at the same price, and get your money back. In that case, you gain the extra revenue from selling donuts but lose the interest you could have had if you had just placed the money in the bank. You should buy the machine if the interest is less than the extra money you will make from the machine.

Jorgenson expanded this basic insight to account for the facts that the machine might wear out, the price of the machine might change, and the government imposes taxes. His "user cost" equation is a sophisticated model of investment, and economists have found that it describes investment behavior well. Specifically, a number of predictions of Jorgenson's model have been confirmed empirically. Firms buy fewer machines when their profits are taxed more and when the interest rate is high. Firms buy more machines when tax policy gives them generous tax breaks for doing so.

Investment fluctuates a lot because the fundamentals that drive investment—output prices, interest rates, and taxes—also fluctuate. But economists do not fully understand fluctuations in investment. Indeed, the sharp swings in investment that occur might require an extension to the Jorgenson theory.

Despite this, Jorgenson's theory has been a key determinant of economic policy. During the recession of 2001,

for example, the U.S. government introduced a measure that significantly increased the tax benefits to firms that purchased new machines. This tax "subsidy" to the purchases of machines was meant to stimulate investment at precisely the time that it would otherwise have plummeted. This countercyclical investment policy follows significant precedent. In 1954, accelerated depreciation was introduced, allowing investors to deduct a larger fraction of the purchase price of a machine than had previously been allowed. In 1962, President John F. Kennedy introduced an investment tax credit to stimulate investment. This credit was enacted and repealed numerous times between then and 1986, when it was finally repealed for good. In each case, the Jorgenson model provided a guide to policymakers of the likely impact of the tax change. Empirical studies have confirmed that the predicted effects occurred.

The Theoretical Frontier

In Jorgenson's user cost model, firms will purchase a machine if the extra revenue the machine generates is a smidgen more than its cost. This prediction of the model has been the subject of significant debate among economists for two main reasons. First, some economists who study recessions have found that financial constraints have affected investment. That is, they argue that sometimes firms want to purchase machines, and would make more money if they did so, but are unable to because banks will not lend them money. The extensive literature on this topic has concluded that such liquidity constraints do not significantly affect most large firms, although occasional liquidity crises cannot be ruled out. Such liquidity constraints are more likely to affect small firms.

The second extension of the basic user cost theory owes to a seminal contribution by Robert McDonald and Daniel Siegel (1986). They noted that firms do not typically purchase machines when the extra revenue is just a smidgen more than the cost, but, instead, require a bigger surplus before taking the plunge. In addition, consumers and businesses appear to be very reluctant to adopt novel technologies. McDonald and Siegel developed a model of investment that explained why. Their analysis has two key features that differ from Jorgenson's: first, the future is highly uncertain; second, a firm has to "nail down" a new machine that it purchases and cannot expect ever to be able to sell it. That is, the purchase of a machine is "irreversible."

These two features change the analysis. Consider, for example, a firm that traditionally powers its furnaces with coal deciding whether to buy a new, more energy-efficient natural gas–powered furnace that costs one hundred dollars today but has an uncertain return tomorrow. If the price of natural gas does not change, then the firm stands to make a four-hundred-dollar profit by operating the new furnace. If the price of natural gas increases, however, then the new furnace will remain idle and the firm will gain nothing from owning it. If the probability of either outcome is 0.5, then, using a zero interest rate for simplicity, the expected net present value of purchasing the machine is (Scenario 1):

$$(0.5 \times \$400) + (0.5 \times 0) - \$100 = \$100$$

Because the project has a positive expected cash flow, it might seem optimal to buy the furnace today. But it is not. Consider what happens if the firm waits until the news is revealed before deciding, as shown in Scenario 2. By waiting, the firm will actually increase its expected profit by fifty dollars. The reason the firm is better off waiting is that if the bad news happens—that is, if natural gas prices increase—the firm can avoid the loss of one hundred dollars by not purchasing the furnace at all. By waiting, the firm is acquiring better information than it would have if it bought today. Note that the two examples would have the same expected return if the firm were allowed to resell the furnace at the original purchase price if there is bad news. But this is unrealistic for two reasons: (1) many pieces of equipment are customized so that once installed they would have little or no value to anyone else; and (2) if gas prices rise, the gas-powered furnace would have little value to anyone else.

The general conclusion is that there is a gain to waiting if there is uncertainty and if the installation of the machine entails sunk costs, that is, costs that cannot be recovered once spent. Although quantifying this gain exactly is a highly mathematical exercise, the reasoning is straightforward. That would explain why firms typically want to invest only in projects that have a high expected profit.

The fact of irreversibility might explain the large fluctuations in investment that we observe. When a recession begins, firms face uncertainty. At these times, it may be optimal for each firm to wait until some of the uncertainty is resolved. When many firms do that, wild swings in investment occur. Recent work by Ricardo Caballero, Eduardo Engel, and John Haltiwanger (1995) confirms that these factors may also be important in explaining the steep drop in investment during recessions.

That economists have a fairly strong understanding of firms' investment behavior makes sense. A firm that maximizes its profits must address investment using the framework discussed in this article. If it fails to maximize profits, it is less profitable than firms that do, and will eventually disappear from the competitive marketplace. Darwinian forces weed out bad companies.

As mentioned above, investment ultimately comes from forgone consumption, either here or abroad. Consumer behavior is harder to study than firms' behavior. Market forces that drive irrational people out of the marketplace are much weaker than market forces that drive bad companies from the market. Accordingly, the study of saving behavior, that lynchpin for investment, is not nearly as advanced as that of investment. Because the saving response of consumers must be known if one is to fully understand the impact of any investment policy, and because saving behavior is so poorly understood, much work remains to be done.

Scenario 1 Expected profit if the firm buys a new gas-powered furnace today that costs $100 and has an uncertain return tomorrow.

	Tomorrow		
Today	If Good News (Probability = .5)	If Bad News (Probability = .5)	Expected Return
Pay $100	Earn $400	Earn nothing	$100

Scenario 2 Expected profit if firm waits and decides tomorrow.

	Tomorrow		
Today	If Good News (Probability = .5)	If Bad News (Probability = .5)	Expected Return
Pay nothing	Earn $400 − $100	Earn nothing	$150

About the Author

Kevin A. Hassett is the director of Economic Policy Studies and a resident scholar at the American Enterprise Institute. He was an economic adviser to the George W. Bush campaign in the 2004 presidential election and was the chief economic adviser to John McCain during the 2000 primaries. He is also a member of the Joint Committee on Taxation's Blue Ribbon Dynamic Scoring Advisory Panel and its Estimating Review Panel.

Further Reading

Aftalion, Albert. "La Réalité des surproductions générales: Essai d'une théorie des crises générales et périodiques." *Revue d'Economie Politique* (1909).

Caballero, Ricardo, Eduardo Engel, and John C. Haltiwanger. "Plant Level Adjustment and Aggregate Investment Dynamics." *Brookings Papers on Economic Activity* 2 (1995): 1–39.

Cummins, Jason G., Kevin A. Hassett, and Stephen D. Oliner. "Investment Behavior, Observable Expectations, and Internal Funds." *American Economic Review* 96, no. 3 (2006): 796–810.

Hassett, Kevin A., and R. Glenn Hubbard. "Taxes and Business Investment." In Alan Auerbach and Martin Feldstein, eds., *Handbook of Public Economics.* Vol. 3. New York: Elsevier, 2002.

Jorgenson, Dale W. "Capital Theory and Investment Behavior." *American Economic Review* 53, no. 2 (1963): 247–259.

Keynes, John Maynard. *The General Theory of Employment, Interest, and Money.* New York: Harcourt, Brace, 1936.

McDonald, Robert L., and Daniel R. Siegel. "The Value of Waiting to Invest." *Quarterly Journal of Economics* 101 (1986): 707–727.

Japan

Benjamin Powell

Following the end of the Allied occupation of Japan, real increases in GNP averaged 9.6 percent from 1952 to 1971. From 1972 to 1991, growth remained strong but less dramatic, averaging 4 percent per year. The rest of the 1990s and early 2000s have been a different story. From 1991 to 2003, real economic growth averaged just 1.2 percent per year. Why was Japan able to grow so fast for so long, and why has the subsequent slowdown lasted more than a decade?

A number of factors contributed to Japan's rapid economic growth, including its starting point. World War II ruined Japan's economy, killing millions of its people and destroying about 40 percent of its capital stock. With so much of Japan's capital stock gone, the rate of return on capital was high, and so people had a strong incentive to invest and accumulate more capital. Naturally, this increased growth rates. But this, by itself, cannot explain why Japan's growth rate was high for so long; other countries with even less capital failed to attract more and grow.

Low levels of privilege seeking also helped Japan grow. Privilege seeking occurs when a special interest group tries to obtain special privileges from the government. Because the interest group's gains are much less than the overall losses to society, lower economic growth rates occur. Mancur Olson's book *The Rise and Decline of Nations* describes how a major conflict such as World War II breaks up entrenched interest groups in losing countries and how this improves growth rates. Groups need time to reorganize and begin to seek privileges, and meanwhile, the economy grows faster. As more and more groups successfully get their special privileges, growth rates slow. Olson attributes

much of the postwar performance of Japan and other Axis powers to the breakup of interest groups.

Japan funded its investment and capital accumulation through high rates of domestic savings. Gross private savings rose from 16.5 percent of GNP between 1952 and 1954 to 31.9 percent in 1970 and 1971. Average domestic savings from 1960 through 1971 averaged 36.1 percent of national income. The United States, by comparison, averaged only 15.8 percent from 1961 to 1971. The Japanese government encouraged saving by not taxing away the incentive to save. The tax code allowed for a portion of savings to earn interest income tax free when in an employer-run savings plan. In addition, interest on the first thirteen thousand dollars in each postal savings account was tax free, and many people had multiple accounts.

But special tax treatment was not the only cause of high levels of savings and investment. The overall environment of universally low taxes and economic freedom created much of the incentive to invest. Taxes as a percentage of national income fell from 22.4 in 1951 to 18.9 in 1970. During the same period, that percentage in the United States rose from 28.5 to 31.3. Lower tax rates in Japan fueled investment because citizens had more money to invest and businesses had a greater incentive to exploit opportunities since they would reap the rewards.

Tax rates, regulations, inflation, and other measures must be examined collectively to determine the extent of government intervention in an economy. The best compilation of these measures can be found in the *Economic Freedom of the World Annual Report* (see ECONOMIC FREEDOM). In 1970, the earliest year for which a ranking is available, Japan was concluding its period of rapid growth and was the seventh-freest economy in the world.

Various observers, including Chalmers Johnson, Robert Wade, and economist Joseph Stiglitz, have attributed Japan's growth to the policies of the Ministry of International Trade and Industry (MITI). All claim that MITI helped Japan achieve a high growth rate by selectively pursuing tariffs and other industrial policies to favor particular industries.

The idea that MITI's industrial policy was a cause of Japan's growth does not bear close scrutiny. Any industrial policy that promotes one industry is necessarily a policy against other industries. For industrial planning to succeed, it must identify, better than markets do, which industries should be favored. In a free market, competitive bidding dictates how capital and labor are allocated, and profits and losses reveal what adjustments should be made. Information about which industries should exist is revealed only through the market's process. Industrial policy rigs the market to enlarge some industries at the expense of others, thus undermining the process that generates the relevant information. Industrial policy faces the same knowledge problem as socialist planning: neither central planners nor anyone else can know the optimal industrial structure before the market produces it. Attempts at industrial planning are likely to hinder development by promoting incorrect industries. MITI was no exception.

In the 1950s, MITI attempted to prevent a small firm from acquiring manufacturing rights from Western Electric to produce semiconductors. The firm persisted and was eventually allowed to acquire the technology. That firm, Sony, went on to become a highly successful consumer electronics company. MITI also attempted to prevent firms in the auto industry from entering the export market and tried to force ten firms in this industry to merge into two: Nissan and Toyota. These attempts failed, and automobile manufacturing went on to become one of Japan's most successful industries.

While striking examples exist of companies succeeding despite MITI's discouragement, evidence of successful promotion does not. Although some industries previously promoted by MITI are profitable today, that alone does not show them to be good investments. They might have evolved similarly without subsidy; and one cannot demonstrate that MITI's favoring of particular industries was better for the economy than if industrial policy had not rigged the outcome. Rigging the market process allows some companies to bid away resources that would have gone to other industries if the market had operated unencumbered. The industries discouraged by industrial policy would have better corresponded to Japan's comparative advantage because they would have obtained their resources through the competitive process without the distorting influence of government.

Despite MITI's involvement, Japan's institutional environment of relatively low government interference and high economic freedom allowed the nation to grow rapidly for a number of years. During the 1980s and 1990s, however, policies changed.

After the September 1985 Plaza Accord, in which leaders from the world's five biggest economies made agreements on economic policy, the yen appreciated and economic growth fell from 4.4 percent in 1985 to 2.9 percent in 1986. Between January 1986 and February 1987, Japan's government attempted to offset the stronger yen by easing monetary policy, reducing the discount rate from 5 percent to 2.5 percent. The stock of narrow money (M1) was expanded at an annual rate of 6.7 percent from 1986 to 1988, while broader monetary aggregates (M2) grew even faster, at an average annual rate over those two years

of 10.1 percent. Following the stimulus, asset prices in the real estate and stock markets increased, creating a financial bubble. The government responded by tightening monetary policy, raising the discount rate five times—up to 6 percent by 1990—while reducing narrow money growth to 2.3 percent in 1989 and 4.3 percent in 1990. After the tightening, stock prices and real estate prices collapsed.

The Nikkei stock-market index fell by more than 60 percent—from a high of 40,000 at the end of 1989 to below 15,000 by 1992; in May 2005, it was at about 11,000. Real estate prices also plummeted during the recession—by 80 percent from 1991 to 1998. After the onset of the recession in 1991, with the exception of a couple years of stronger growth in the mid-1990s Japan's economy has shown either slow growth or an actual contraction. Overall, real GDP grew only 1.17 percent per year from 1992 through 2003, with an even lower 0.75 percent growth rate since 1998. The unemployment rate rose from 2.1 percent in 1991 to 4.7 percent at the end of 2004. These numbers understate labor market inefficiencies because of the Japanese commitment to lifetime employment that has resulted in many unproductive workers remaining on payrolls essentially as "window sitters."

Japan's government has taken an active role in trying to get out of the depression. Unfortunately, its policies have further hampered economic recovery. Most of Japan's policies have focused on the traditional Keynesian prescription of increased government spending to boost aggregate demand for goods and services. Since 1992, Japan's government has tried ten different fiscal stimulus packages totaling more than 135 trillion yen. These packages have accounted for approximately 3 percent of the Japanese economy. None was able to cure the depression, but the spending programs have caused Japan's official public debt to exceed 150 percent of GDP, up from 40 percent before 1992 and currently higher than that of any other developed nation. While there were some temporary income tax rate cuts and revenues were falling with decreased economic activity, there were also some tax rate increases such as the two-percentage-point 1997 consumption tax increase that raised it to 5 percent.

Monetarist policies that focus on increasing the money supply to stimulate the economy have also failed. From 1995 through 2003, while central bank discount rates were often pushed down below 1 percent, the stock of narrow money (M1) was increased at an annual rate of 9.8 percent; but growth remained low and sometimes even negative. Expanding the stock of narrow money failed to produce similar increases in broader measures of money. The broader money (M2) measure increased only 2.7 percent annually during this same time. Some economists have mistakenly called the situation a liquidity trap, that is, a situation in which monetary policy is impotent because investors expect that in the future interest rates can only rise from the current low levels. But the lack of credit expansion is not due to investors' expectations of future interest rate increases. Rather, it results from the enormous amount of bad debt in the banking system. Banks have used increases in the money supply to improve their balance sheets instead of issuing more loans.

Japan's government has tried to circumvent banks' unwillingness to lend. The Fiscal Investment and Loan Program (FILP), an off-budget branch of the Japanese government, lends directly to borrowers. FILP receives most of its money from the post office savings system, which had 254.9 trillion yen in funds at year-end 2000—around 35 percent of total household deposits. FILP and the postal savings system have been disconnected since reform in April 2001, but until that point, FILP had played a role in prolonging the recession. FILP allocated funds to borrowers through the Ministry of Finance Trust Fund Bureau. Politicians in the Liberal Democratic Party (LDP) run most of the government agencies in the bureau, and the Economist Intelligence Unit reports that "FILP money is channeled towards traditional supporters of the LDP, such as those in the construction industry, and without proper consideration of the costs and benefits of specific projects" (2001, p. 30). In one instance, a $5.3 billion loan was channeled into building a high-tech bridge-tunnel spanning Tokyo Bay that will, by the government's own estimates, suffer losses until the year 2038. Thus, government direct lending does not aid economy recovery because funds are allocated to the most politically connected businessmen rather than according to consumer preferences. This leads to a higher cost of borrowing for those seeking private funds, further distorting the economy. Japan's fiscal condition also worsened because the loans are often highly risky. Once FILP and other "off-budget" debts are included, Japan's debt at year-end 2004 is estimated to exceed well over 200 percent of GDP.

The policy remedies that Japan's government has tried have all focused on increasing aggregate demand. The real problem with the Japanese economy, however, is a mismatch between the structure of production and consumers' specific demands. The structure of production was distorted away from consumer preferences when the post–Plaza Accord monetary expansion artificially depressed interest rates, thus signaling investors to undertake capital-intensive and long-time-horizon projects. When the monetary expansion stopped in the early 1990s, the boom collapsed. The Japanese government's interventions in the

economy have hampered the market's correction process by maintaining the existing structure of production against consumer wishes, thus delaying economic recovery.

Much of the government spending has been on public works benefiting the construction industry—a large, politically powerful segment of the Japanese economy. The Liberal Democratic Party, which has been dominant in Japan since 1955, has cultivated the construction companies' support through years of expensive public works programs. Almost half of the April 1998 and one-third of the November 1998 fiscal stimulus packages were spent on public works. Overall, between 1991 and 2000, the construction industry received more than fifty-nine trillion yen in orders from the government, accounting for 30 percent of all construction business. From 2001 to 2004 government has fallen to "only" 25 percent of the industry's total business. The Economist Intelligence Unit's profile notes that "generous Public works programmes have allowed many unviable construction companies to remain in business" (EIU 2001, p. 40). By keeping otherwise unviable construction companies in business, the government has hindered the market's adjustment process by maintaining a capital structure that does not reflect consumers' desires.

The government has used bailout funds and nationalization to help the banking industry. In late 1998, it set up a $514 billion bailout fund, with $214 billion designated to buy stock in troubled banks and $154 billion to nationalize, restructure, and liquidate failed banks. But nationalization and bailout funds serve only to prop up unsound financial institutions, delaying needed restructuring that would allow them to function as financial intermediaries again. The market deals with unsound banks by allowing bank failures, mergers, acquisitions, and restructuring. Some market corrections have taken place, but most bank mergers have occurred among smaller regional banks without access to bailout funds. Until the government stops intervening with bailout funds and nationalization, the process of larger bank failures and mergers will be delayed, and the time that the banks cannot function as efficient financial intermediaries will be extended.

The government has attempted to prevent the liquidation of the boom's bad investments by creating a twenty-trillion-yen credit guarantee fund to ease credit availability for companies. The Economist Intelligence Unit's profile states: "Funds disbursed under the programme are often going to companies that are not creditworthy and that would otherwise go bankrupt" (EIU 2001, p. 29). For the economy to recover, these companies must go bankrupt so that their capital and labor can be reallocated to other industries that better satisfy consumer preferences.

The repeated fiscal stimulus packages, the large amount

of money controlled by the postal savings system and allocated through FILP, and the efforts to prevent bank and business failures have all prevented the market recovery process from working in Japan. These repeated government interventions have maintained the existing structure of production, delaying its alignment to the particular demands of consumers.

In the past half century Japan has experienced both high growth and prolonged stagnation. During the period of rapid growth, despite the existence of MITI, low taxes and low levels of government intervention were the main policies driving that growth. During the prolonged stagnation of the 1990s, economic growth suffered because the opposite was true.

About the Author

Benjamin Powell is an assistant professor of economics at San Jose State University and the director of the Center for Entrepreneurial Innovation at the Independent Institute.

Further Reading

Economist Intelligence Unit. *Country Profile. Japan.* London: The Unit, 2001 and 2005.
Olson, M. *The Rise and Decline of Nations.* New Haven: Yale University Press, 1982.
World Bank. *World Development Indicators Online.* 2005. Online at: http://www.worldbank.org/data/wdi.

Critical Accounts of State Industrial Planning

Henderson, D. "Japan and the Myth of MITI." In *The Fortune Encyclopedia of Economics.* New York: Warner Books, 1993. Available online at: http://www.econlib.org/library/Enc/JapanandtheMythofMITI.html.
Powell, B. "State Development Planning: Did It Create an East Asian Miracle." *Review of Austrian Economics* 18, no. 3 (2005): 305–323.

Favorable Accounts of Industrial Planning

Johnson, C. *MITI and the Japanese Miracle: The Growth of Industrial Policy, 1925–1975.* Stanford: Stanford University Press, 1982.
Stiglitz, J. "From Miracle to Crisis to Recovery: Lessons from Four Decades of East Asian Experience." In Joseph Stiglitz and Shahid Yusuf, eds., *Rethinking the East Asian Miracle.* New York: Oxford University Press, 2001.
———. "Some Lessons from the East Asian Miracle." *World Bank Research Observer* 11, no. 2 (1996): 151–177.
Wade, R. *Governing the Market.* Princeton: Princeton University Press, 1990.

Articles on Japan's Recession

Herbener, J. "The Rise and Fall of the Japanese Miracle." Ludwig von Mises Institute, 1999. Available online at: http://www.mises.org/fullarticle.asp?control=298&id=64.

Powell, B. "Explaining Japan's Recession." *Quarterly Journal of Austrian Economics* 5, no. 2 (2002): 35–50.

Job Safety

W. Kip Viscusi

Many people believe that employers do not care about workplace safety. If the government were not regulating job safety, they contend, workplaces would be unsafe. In fact, employers have many incentives to make workplaces safe. Since the time of Adam Smith, economists have observed that workers demand "compensating differentials" (i.e., wage premiums) for the risks they face. The extra pay for job hazards, in effect, establishes the price employers must pay for an unsafe workplace. Wage premiums paid to U.S. workers for risking injury are huge; they amount to about $245 billion annually (in 2004 dollars), more than 2 percent of the gross domestic product and 5 percent of total wages paid. These wage premiums give firms an incentive to invest in job safety because an employer who makes the workplace safer can reduce the wages he pays.

Employers have a second incentive because they must pay higher premiums for workers' compensation if accident rates are high. And the threat of lawsuits over products used in the workplace gives sellers of these products another reason to reduce risks. Of course, the threat of lawsuits gives employers an incentive to care about safety only if they anticipate the lawsuits. In the case of asbestos litigation, for example, liability was deferred by several decades after the initial exposure to asbestos. Even if firms had been cognizant of the extent of the health risk—and many were not—none of them could have anticipated the shift in legal doctrine that, in effect, imposed liability retroactively. Thus, it is for acute accidents rather than unanticipated diseases that the tort liability system bolsters the safety incentives generated by the market for safety.

How well does the safety market work? For it to work well, workers must have some knowledge of the risks they face. And they do. One study of how 496 workers perceived job hazards found that the greater the risk of injury in an industry, the higher the proportion of workers in that industry who saw their job as dangerous. In industries with five or fewer disabling injuries per million hours worked, such as women's outerwear manufacturing and the communication equipment industry, only 24 percent of surveyed workers considered their jobs dangerous. But in industries with forty or more disabling injuries per million hours, such as the logging and meat products industries, 100 percent of the workers knew that their jobs were dangerous. That workers know the dangers makes sense. Many hazards, such as visible safety risks, can be readily monitored. Moreover, some dimly understood health risks are often linked to noxious exposures and dust levels that workers can monitor. Also, symptoms sometimes flag the onset of some more serious ailment. Byssinosis, for example, a disease that afflicts workers exposed to cotton dust, proceeds in stages.

Even when workers are not well informed, they do not necessarily assume that risks are zero. According to a large body of research, people systematically overestimate small risks and underestimate large ones. If workers overestimate the probability of an injury that occurs infrequently—for example, exposure to a highly publicized potential carcinogen, such as secondhand smoke—then employers will have too great an incentive to reduce this hazard. The opposite is also true: when workers underestimate the likelihood of more frequent kinds of injuries, such as falls and motor vehicle accidents on the job, employers may invest too little in preventing those injuries.

The bottom line is that market forces have a powerful influence on job safety. The $245 billion in annual wage premiums referred to earlier is in addition to the value of workers' compensation. Workers on moderately risky blue-collar jobs, whose annual risk of getting killed is 1 in 25,000, earn a premium of $280 per year. The imputed compensation per "statistical death" (25,000 times $280) is therefore $7 million. Even workers such as coal miners and firemen, who are not strongly averse to risk and who have knowingly chosen extremely risky jobs, receive compensation on the order of $1 million per statistical death.

These wage premiums are the amount workers insist on being paid for taking risks—that is, the amount workers would willingly forgo to avoid the risk. Employers will eliminate hazards only when it costs them less than what they will save in the form of lower wage premiums. For example, the employer will spend $10,000 to eliminate a risk if doing so allows the employer to pay $11,000 less in wages. Costlier reductions in risk are not worthwhile to employees (since they would rather take the risk and get the higher pay) and are not voluntarily undertaken by employers.

Other evidence that the safety market works comes from the decrease in the riskiness of jobs throughout the century. One would predict that, as workers become wealthier, they will be less desperate to earn money and will therefore demand more safety. The historical data show that this is what employees have done and that employers have responded by providing more safety. As per capita disposable income per year rose from $1,085 (in 1970 prices) in 1933

to $3,376 in 1970, death rates on the job dropped from 37 per 100,000 workers to 18 per 100,000. Since 1997, fatality rates have been less than 4 per 100,000.

The impetus for these improvements has been increased societal wealth. Every 10 percent increase in people's income leads them to increase by 6 percent the price they charge employers for bearing risk. That is, their value of statistical life increases, boosting the wages required to attract workers to risky jobs.

Despite this strong evidence that the market for safety works, not all workers are fully informed about the risks they face. They may be uninformed about little-understood health hazards that have not yet been called to their attention. But even where workers' information is imperfect, additional market forces are at work. Survey results indicate that of all workers who quit manufacturing jobs, more than one-third do so when they discover that the hazards are greater than they initially believed. Losing employees costs money. Production suffers while companies train replacements. Companies, therefore, have an incentive to provide a safe work environment, or at least to inform prospective workers of the dangers. Although the net effect of these market processes does not always ensure the optimal amount of safety, the incentives for safety are substantial.

Beginning with the passage of the Occupational Safety and Health Act of 1970, the federal government has attempted to augment these safety incentives, primarily by specifying technological standards for workplace design. These government attempts to influence safety decisions formerly made by companies generated substantial controversy and, in some cases, imposed huge costs. A particularly extreme example is the 1987 OSHA formaldehyde standard, which imposed costs of $78 billion for each life that the regulation is expected to save. Because the U.S. Supreme Court has ruled that OSHA regulations cannot be subject to a formal cost-benefit test, there is no legal prohibition against regulatory excesses. However, OSHA sometimes takes account of costs while designing regulations. For example, OSHA set the cotton dust standard at a level beyond which compliance costs would have grown explosively.

Increases in safety from OSHA's activities have fallen short of expectations. According to some economists' estimates, OSHA regulations have reduced workplace injuries by, at most, 2–4 percent. Why such a modest impact on risks? One reason is that the financial incentives for safety imposed by OSHA are comparatively small. Although total penalties have increased dramatically since 1986, they averaged less than $10 million per year for many years of the agency's operation. By 2002, the total annual OSHA penalties levied had reached $149 million. The $245 billion wage premium that workers "charge" for risk is more than sixteen hundred times as large.

The workers' compensation system that has been in place in the United States since the early twentieth century also gives companies strong incentives to make workplaces safe. Premiums for workers' compensation, which employers pay, totaled $26 billion annually as of 2001. Particularly for large firms, these premiums are strongly linked to their injury performance. Statistical studies indicate that in the absence of the workers' compensation system, workplace death rates would rise by 27 percent. This estimate assumes, however, that workers' compensation would not be replaced by tort liability or higher market wage premiums. The strong performance of workers' compensation, particularly when contrasted with the command-and-control approach of OSHA regulation, has led many economists to suggest that an injury tax be instituted as an alternative to the current regulatory standards.

The main implication of economists' analysis of job safety is that financial incentives matter and that the market for job safety is alive and well.

About the Author

W. Kip Viscusi is the University Distinguished Professor of Law, Economics, and Management at Vanderbilt University. He is the founding editor of the *Journal of Risk and Uncertainty*. Viscusi was also deputy director of President Jimmy Carter's Council on Wage and Price Stability, which was responsible for White House oversight of new regulations.

Further Reading

Morrall, John F. "Saving Lives: A Review of the Record." *Journal of Risk and Uncertainty* 27, no. 3 (2003): 221–237.
Viscusi, W. Kip. *Rational Risk Policy: The 1996 Arne Ryde Memorial Lectures*. New York: Oxford University Press, 1998.
Viscusi, W. Kip, and Joseph E. Aldy. "The Value of a Statistical Life: A Critical Review of Market Estimates Throughout the World." *Journal of Risk and Uncertainty* 27, no. 1 (2003): 5–76.

Junk Bonds

Glenn Yago

Junk bonds, also known less pejoratively as high-yield bonds, are bonds that are rated as "speculative" or "below investment" grade issues: below BBB for bonds rated by Moody's and below Baa for bonds rated by Standard and Poor's (the two main debt-rating agencies). Bond ratings measure the perceived risk that the bonds' issuer will not make interest payments or repay the principal at maturity. The riskier a bond is, other things being equal, the lower its rating. The highest-rated nondefaulted bonds are rated AAA or Aaa, and the lowest are rated C, with defaulted bonds rated D; thus, junk bonds can be rated anywhere between Baa (BB) and D. As junk bonds are perceived to be riskier than other types of debt, they typically trade at higher yields—that is, higher rates of return—than investment-grade bonds. Over the past twenty years, this difference, or spread, between junk bonds and U.S. Treasury bonds has varied between three and nine percentage points, averaging six percentage points. The debt of 95 percent of U.S. companies with revenues over $35 million (and of 100 percent of companies with revenues less than that) is rated noninvestment grade, or junk. Today, junk bond issuers that are household names include U.S. Steel, Delta, and Dole Foods. Moreover, the use of high-yield securities for corporate financing greatly expanded after the mid-1990s in Latin America, Asia, and Europe (both in transition markets in Central and Eastern Europe and in the European Union). Many high-yield bonds issued in the United States are now placed by foreign corporations spurred by privatizations, mergers and restructurings, and new technology expansions.

The history of high-yield bonds is nearly as long as the history of public capital markets, with early issuers including General Motors, IBM, J. P. Morgan's U.S. Steel in the first few decades of the twentieth century, and the United States of America soon after the nation's founding in the 1780s. The public market for new-issue junk bonds gradually atrophied, and for most of the twentieth century—up to the 1970s—all new publicly issued bonds were investment grade. The only publicly traded junk bonds were ones that had once been investment grade but had become "fallen angels," having been downgraded to junk as the financial condition of the issuer deteriorated. The interest payments on these bonds were not high, but with the bonds selling at pennies on the dollar, their yields were quite high. Companies deemed speculative grade were effectively shut out of the public capital market and had to rely on more expensive and restrictive bank loans and private placements (where bonds are sold directly to investors such as insurance companies). Interestingly, even though these private placements were riskier than the public high-yield bonds of the 1980s, they were never labeled "junk." Indeed, the label "junk" and the decision about what level of risk it applies to, though now well established, is essentially arbitrary.

Financial conditions in the United States in the 1970s set the stage for the success of the junk-bond market. The collapse of the Bretton Woods system of fixed exchange rates resulted in an upward spiral of inflation and interest rates. By the mid-1970s, three decades of interest rate stability came to an abrupt end, and short-term borrowing costs doubled in less than two years. At the same time, two oil shocks and a recession sent stock prices into a two-year slide that reduced the market value of U.S. firms by more than 40 percent. Banks curtailed lending to all but the largest and highest-rated companies, and as yields in the open market rose above government-set interest-rate ceilings on bank deposits, funds flowed out of the banking system into money market accounts. As this "credit crunch" spread, only the most creditworthy borrowers could receive credit, and, paradoxically, the most innovative companies—those with the highest returns on capital and the fastest rates of growth—had the least access to capital. From these circumstances, the contemporary high-yield securities market emerged.

If other debt is "junior" to junk bonds—that is, if junk-bond owners can be paid ahead of other debtors—then, in the event of a default, other debtors will be hurt. But these other debtors can protect themselves with debt covenants (see BONDS) that give them certain rights when junk bonds are issued in a recapitalization or merger transaction.

The market for new-issue junk bonds dramatically reopened for business in 1977 when Bear Stearns and Company underwrote the first new-issue junk bond in decades. Soon thereafter, Drexel Burnham brought the debt of seven below-investment-grade companies to market. By 1983 more than one-third of all corporate bond issues were noninvestment grade. Today, the junk-bond market, by most definitions, exceeds half a trillion dollars.

This explosive growth had several causes. High-yield bonds were extremely attractive for borrowers, as they had lower interest rates and greater liquidity than private placements, and they imposed fewer restrictions on the actions of the borrowers (restrictive covenants) than either loans or private placements. The value of high-yield bonds to investors, moreover, was strengthened by the research of W. Braddock Hickman, Thomas R. Atkinson, Orin K. Burrell, and others, who discovered that below-investment-grade debt earned a higher risk-adjusted rate of return than investment-grade bonds. In other words, the interest rate that premium junk bonds offered more than compensated investors for the added risk of default. Michael Milken trumpeted these insights to both his investor customers and entrepreneurs seeking growth capital, with stunning success. The companies Milken financed with these bonds created millions of new jobs between the 1970s and 1990s.

The 1980s saw the junk-bond market grow from $10 billion in 1979 to $189 billion in 1989, an increase of 34 percent per year. Borrowers in new and emerging industries in the 1980s included Turner Broadcasting, MCI Communications, and McCaw Cellular (now part of Cingular Wireless). As well as financing innovation, junk bonds allowed firms and industries in distress to restructure and increased efficiency through the market for corporate control. Junk bonds financed the successful restructuring of numerous manufacturing firms, including Chrysler, and funded consolidations in a host of industries. During this period, yields averaged 14.5 percent while default rates averaged just 2.2 percent—a combination that resulted in annual total returns of some 13.7 percent, on average. This period ended by 1989, when a politically driven campaign by Rudolph Giuliani and financial competitors that had previously dominated corporate credit markets against the high-yield market resulted in a temporary market collapse and the bankruptcy of Drexel Burnham. Almost overnight, the market for newly issued junk bonds disappeared, and no significant new junk issues came to market for more than a year. Investors lost 4.4 percent in 1990, the first year of negative returns in a decade.

The market rebounded sharply in 1991 with positive total returns of a stunning 40 percent. The 1990s saw the market mature with increased emphasis by traders and investors on risk and portfolio management. Junk bonds left the controversy of the 1980s behind and became just another, albeit rather profitable, asset class. Default rates fell from their 1990 and 1991 highs (10.1 and 10.3 percent, respectively) to single digits in the 1990s, with an average rate of 2.4 percent from 1992 to 2000. From 1990 to 1999, the market returned an average of 15 percent annually. During this same period, the market grew from $181 billion to $567 billion, an average annual increase of 13 percent.

From 2000 to 2002, difficulties in the telecom industry, combined with the general downturn in U.S. economic activity, resulted in high default rates and disappointing total returns in the junk-bond market. The average default rate for this short period was 9.2 percent (more than four and a half times the average rate for the period 1992–1999), and the average annual total rate of return was 0 percent. Indeed, 2002 was a record year for defaults and bankruptcies, but the number of defaults decreased dramatically in 2003. The high-yield market recovered from this downturn as the telecom defaults became a thing of the past and the U.S. economy emerged

The Strange Case of Michael Milken

David R. Henderson

A discussion of the junk-bond era of the 1980s would be incomplete without at least a brief exposition of the legal case involving Michael Milken. Press accounts at the time promoted the view that Milken had committed serious crimes. Two journalists who repeatedly made these claims were *Wall Street Journal* reporter James Stewart and *Barron's* writer Ben Stein. Stein, in fact, even claimed that Milken had run a "vast Ponzi" scheme. But there was nothing illegal about the use of junk bonds per se. Instead, Milken pled guilty to six felony counts of illegal activity, five of which had been previously understood to be simple technical violations of the law rather than actual crimes. The judge found the total economic effect of all the violations to be $318,082.

Four of the six counts involved Milken's dealings with arbitrageur Ivan Boesky. Boesky had paid Drexel, Milken's firm, $5.3 million, which was plausibly—as Milken claimed—simply the value that Drexel and Boesky placed on various reciprocal favors on a number of transactions. The government claimed, to the contrary, that the $5.3 million payment was the net amount Boesky owed after the gains and losses on various illegal securities transactions. But even if the government's claim is true (and there is no evidence that it is), Milken's "crime" was that he had not properly documented the ownership of some stock. The government never identified anyone injured by this failure to document.

The fifth count was that Milken failed to disclose an agreement with a man named David Solomon, by which Solomon would adjust some transactions prices of stocks to favor Drexel. The adjustments were small enough that they were within the bid-ask spread but large enough to keep Drexel interested in doing business with Solomon's firm, Finsbury Group Ltd. Although Milken did fail to disclose, no one was hurt by this nondisclosure.

The sixth and final count was Milken's having assisted Solomon in filing a false 1985 tax return. The problem with the government's case was that the return was not false. Solomon claimed a real economic loss, something he had the legal right to do.

Why, then, did Milken plead guilty and accept a prison sentence rather than fight the charges and pay a fine for technical violations? The reason was that an aggressive and politically ambitious prosecutor, Rudolph Giuliani, the U.S. attorney for the Southern District of New York, took extreme measures to go after Milken. Giuliani let Drexel off with a reduced penalty in return for the firm's cooperation in convicting Milken. Guiliani even invoked the Racketeer Influenced and Corrupt Organizations Act (RICO) to charge Milken with "racketeering." When RICO was passed in 1970, it was aimed at organized crime, but Giuliani used it to get Milken.

Even Milken was probably shocked, though, when Judge Kimba Wood gave him a stiff ten-year sentence. Later, Wood reduced Milken's sentence to two years, ostensibly because Milken had cooperated with the prosecution in other cases. Milken's cooperation was minimal, though, as he kept insisting on telling the whole truth, even when that damaged the government's chances in these other cases. Economist Daniel Fischel speculates that Wood had time to realize her mistake. After the initial sentencing, her colleague, Judge Louis Stanton, had stated that the tax "felony" to which Milken had pled guilty was not a felony. And Wood was aware that the Second Circuit had reversed many of Giuliani's convictions of various people who faced charges similar to Milken's.

from recession. The default rate in 2003 was 4.7 percent (down from 12.8 percent the year before), and year-to-date in 2004 was 2.41 percent. At the same time, the total rate of return for these years was 29 percent and 10.3 percent, respectively.

Despite external shocks to the market, such as the bankruptcy of Drexel Burnham, two wars in Iraq, three recessions, and the disruption of markets following the September 11, 2001, terrorist attacks, the new-issue and secondary markets recovered, issuers continued to tap the market, and institutional buyers returned. The continuing strength of the junk-bond market is based on linking the U.S. economy's need for capital with investors' need for high returns.

About the Author

Glenn Yago is director of capital studies at the Milken Institute in Santa Monica.

Further Reading

Altman, E. I., N. Hukkawala, and V. Kishore. "Defaults and Returns on High Yield Bonds." *Business Economics* 35, no. 2 (2000): 27–38.
Asquith, P., R. Gertner, and D. Scharfstein. "Anatomy of Fi-

nancial Distress: An Examination of Junk Bond Issuers."
Quarterly Journal of Economics 109 (1994): 625–634.

Atkinson, T. R. *Trends in Corporate Bond Quality*. Cambridge, Mass.: National Bureau of Economic Research, 1967.

Barnhill, T. M., W. F. Maxwell, and M. R. Shenkman. *High Yield Bonds: Market Structure, Portfolio Management and Credit Risk Management*. New York: McGraw-Hill, 1998.

Blume, Marshall E., F. Liff, and A. C. MacKinlay. "The Declining Credit Quality of U.S. Corporate Debt: Myth or Reality." *Journal of Finance* 53, no. 4 (2000): 1389–1413.

Fischel, Daniel. *Payback: The Conspiracy to Destroy Michael Milken and His Financial Revolution*. New York: Harper-Business, 1995.

Gertler, M., and C. S. Lown. "The Information in the High Yield Bond Spread for the Business Cycle: Evidence and Some Implications." *Oxford Review of Economic Policy* 15, no. 2 (1999): 132–150.

Yago, Glenn. *Junk Bonds: How High Yield Securities Restructured Corporate America*. New York: Oxford University Press, 1991.

Yago, Glenn, and Susanne Trimbath. *Beyond Junk Bonds: Expanding High Yield Markets*. New York: Oxford University Press, 2003.

Web Sites

Advantage Data: http://www.advantagedata.com
The Bond Market Association: http://www.bondmarkets.com
Financial Research Associates: http://www.frallc.com
High Yield Report: http://www.highyieldreport.com
KDP Advisor: http://www.kdpadvisor.com
Milken Institute: http://www.milkeninstitute.org
Moody's Investors Service: http://www.moodys.com
Standard and Poor's: http://www.standardandpoors.com
Strategic Research Institute: http://www.srinstitute.com

Keynesian Economics

Alan S. Blinder

Keynesian economics is a theory of total spending in the economy (called aggregate demand) and its effects on output and inflation. Although the term has been used (and abused) to describe many things over the years, six principal tenets seem central to Keynesianism. The first three describe how the economy works.

1. *A Keynesian believes that aggregate demand is influenced by a host of economic decisions—both public and private—and sometimes behaves erratically.* The public decisions include, most prominently, those on monetary and fiscal (i.e., spending and tax) policies. Some decades ago, economists heatedly debated the relative strengths of monetary and fiscal policies, with some Keynesians arguing that monetary policy is powerless, and some monetarists arguing that fiscal policy is powerless. Both of these are essentially dead issues today. Nearly all Keynesians and monetarists now believe that both fiscal and monetary policies affect aggregate demand. A few economists, however, believe in debt neutrality—the doctrine that substitutions of government borrowing for taxes have no effects on total demand (more on this below).

2. *According to Keynesian theory, changes in aggregate demand, whether anticipated or unanticipated, have their greatest short-run effect on real output and employment, not on prices.* This idea is portrayed, for example, in PHILLIPS CURVES that show inflation rising only slowly when unemployment falls. Keynesians believe that what is true about the short run cannot necessarily be inferred from what must happen in the long run, and we live in the short run. They often quote Keynes's famous statement, "In the long run, we are all dead," to make the point.

Monetary policy can produce real effects on output and employment only if some prices are rigid—if nominal wages (wages in dollars, not in real purchasing power), for example, do not adjust instantly. Otherwise, an injection of new money would change all prices by the same percentage. So Keynesian models generally either assume or try to explain rigid prices or wages. Rationalizing rigid prices is a difficult theoretical problem because, according to standard microeconomic theory, real supplies and demands should not change if all nominal prices rise or fall proportionally.

But Keynesians believe that, because prices are somewhat rigid, fluctuations in any component of spending—consumption, investment, or government expenditures—cause output to fluctuate. If government spending increases, for example, and all other components of spending remain constant, then output will increase. Keynesian models of economic activity also include a so-called multiplier effect; that is, output increases by a multiple of the original change in spending that caused it. Thus, a ten-billion-dollar increase in government spending could cause total output to rise by fifteen billion dollars (a multiplier of 1.5) or by five billion (a multiplier of 0.5). Contrary to what many people believe, Keynesian analysis does not require that the multiplier exceed 1.0. For Keynesian economics to work, however, the multiplier must be greater than zero.

3. *Keynesians believe that prices, and especially wages, respond slowly to changes in supply and demand, resulting in periodic shortages and surpluses, especially of labor.* Even Milton Friedman acknowledged that "under any conceivable institutional arrangements, and certainly under those that

now prevail in the United States, there is only a limited amount of flexibility in prices and wages."[1] In current parlance, that would certainly be called a Keynesian position.

No policy prescriptions follow from these three beliefs alone. And many economists who do not call themselves Keynesian would nevertheless accept the entire list. What distinguishes Keynesians from other economists is their belief in the following three tenets about economic policy.

4. *Keynesians do not think that the typical level of unemployment is ideal—partly because unemployment is subject to the caprice of aggregate demand, and partly because they believe that prices adjust only gradually.* In fact, Keynesians typically see unemployment as both too high on average and too variable, although they know that rigorous theoretical justification for these positions is hard to come by. Keynesians also feel certain that periods of recession or depression are economic maladies, not, as in real business cycle theory, efficient market responses to unattractive opportunities.

5. *Many, but not all, Keynesians advocate activist stabilization policy to reduce the amplitude of the business cycle, which they rank among the most important of all economic problems.* Here, however, even some conservative Keynesians part company by doubting either the efficacy of stabilization policy or the wisdom of attempting it.

This does not mean that Keynesians advocate what used to be called fine-tuning—adjusting government spending, taxes, and the money supply every few months to keep the economy at full employment. Almost all economists, including most Keynesians, now believe that the government simply cannot know enough soon enough to fine-tune successfully. Three lags make it unlikely that fine-tuning will work. First, there is a lag between the time that a change in policy is required and the time that the government recognizes this. Second, there is a lag between when the government recognizes that a change in policy is required and when it takes action. In the United States, this lag can be very long for fiscal policy because Congress and the administration must first agree on most changes in spending and taxes. The third lag comes between the time that policy is changed and when the changes affect the economy. This, too, can be many months. Yet many Keynesians still believe that more modest goals for stabilization policy—coarse-tuning, if you will—are not only defensible but sensible. For example, an economist need not have detailed quantitative knowledge of lags to prescribe a

dose of expansionary monetary policy when the unemployment rate is very high.

6. *Finally, and even less unanimously, some Keynesians are more concerned about combating unemployment than about conquering inflation.* They have concluded from the evidence that the costs of low inflation are small. However, there are plenty of anti-inflation Keynesians. Most of the world's current and past central bankers, for example, merit this title whether they like it or not. Needless to say, views on the relative importance of unemployment and inflation heavily influence the policy advice that economists give and that policymakers accept. Keynesians typically advocate more aggressively expansionist policies than non-Keynesians.

Keynesians' belief in aggressive government action to stabilize the economy is based on value judgments and on the beliefs that (a) macroeconomic fluctuations significantly reduce economic well-being and (b) the government is knowledgeable and capable enough to improve on the free market.

The brief debate between Keynesians and new classical economists in the 1980s was fought primarily over (a) and over the first three tenets of Keynesianism—tenets the monetarists had accepted. New classicals believed that anticipated changes in the money supply do not affect real output; that markets, even the labor market, adjust quickly to eliminate shortages and surpluses; and that business cycles may be efficient. For reasons that will be made clear below, I believe that the "objective" scientific evidence on these matters points strongly in the Keynesian direction. In the 1990s, the new classical schools also came to accept the view that prices are sticky and that, therefore, the labor market does not adjust as quickly as they previously thought (see NEW CLASSICAL MACROECONOMICS).

Before leaving the realm of definition, I must underscore several glaring and intentional omissions.

First, I have said nothing about the RATIONAL EXPECTATIONS school of thought. Like Keynes himself, many Keynesians doubt that school's view that people use all available information to form their expectations about economic policy. Other Keynesians accept the view. But when it comes to the large issues with which I have concerned myself, nothing much rides on whether or not expectations are rational. Rational expectations do not, for example, preclude rigid prices; rational expectations models with sticky prices are thoroughly Keynesian by my definition. I should note, though, that some new classicals see rational expectations as much more fundamental to the debate.

The second omission is the hypothesis that there is a

1. "The Role of Monetary Policy," *American Economic Review* 58, no. 1: 13.

"natural rate" of unemployment in the long run. Prior to 1970, Keynesians believed that the long-run level of unemployment depended on government policy, and that the government could achieve a low unemployment rate by accepting a high but steady rate of inflation. In the late 1960s, Milton Friedman, a monetarist, and Columbia's Edmund Phelps, a Keynesian, rejected the idea of such a long-run trade-off on theoretical grounds. They argued that the only way the government could keep unemployment below what they called the "natural rate" was with macroeconomic policies that would continuously drive inflation higher and higher. In the long run, they argued, the unemployment rate could not be below the natural rate. Shortly thereafter, Keynesians like Northwestern's Robert Gordon presented empirical evidence for Friedman's and Phelps's view. Since about 1972 Keynesians have integrated the "natural rate" of unemployment into their thinking. So the natural rate hypothesis played essentially no role in the intellectual ferment of the 1975–1985 period.

Third, I have ignored the choice between monetary and fiscal policy as the preferred instrument of stabilization policy. Economists differ about this and occasionally change sides. By my definition, however, it is perfectly possible to be a Keynesian and still believe either that responsibility for stabilization policy should, in principle, be ceded to the monetary authority or that it is, in practice, so ceded. In fact, most Keynesians today share one or both of those beliefs.

Keynesian theory was much denigrated in academic circles from the mid-1970s until the mid-1980s. It has staged a strong comeback since then, however. The main reason appears to be that Keynesian economics was better able to explain the economic events of the 1970s and 1980s than its principal intellectual competitor, NEW CLASSICAL ECONOMICS.

True to its classical roots, new classical theory emphasizes the ability of a market economy to cure recessions by downward adjustments in wages and prices. The new classical economists of the mid-1970s attributed economic downturns to people's misperceptions about what was happening to relative prices (such as real wages). Misperceptions would arise, they argued, if people did not know the current price level or inflation rate. But such misperceptions should be fleeting and surely cannot be large in societies in which price indexes are published monthly and the typical monthly inflation rate is less than 1 percent. Therefore, economic downturns, by the early new classical view, should be mild and brief. Yet, during the 1980s most of the world's industrial economies endured deep and long recessions. Keynesian economics may be theoretically un-

tidy, but it certainly predicts periods of persistent, involuntary unemployment.

According to the early new classical theorists of the 1970s and 1980s, a correctly perceived decrease in the growth of the money supply should have only small effects, if any, on real output. Yet, when the Federal Reserve and the Bank of England announced that monetary policy would be tightened to fight inflation, and then made good on their promises, severe recessions followed in each country. New classicals might claim that the tightening was unanticipated (because people did not believe what the monetary authorities said). Perhaps it was, in part. But surely the broad contours of the restrictive policies were anticipated, or at least correctly perceived as they unfolded. Old-fashioned Keynesian theory, which says that any monetary restriction is contractionary because firms and individuals are locked into fixed-price contracts, not inflation-adjusted ones, seems more consistent with actual events.

An offshoot of new classical theory formulated by Harvard's Robert Barro is the idea of debt neutrality (see GOVERNMENT DEBT AND DEFICITS). Barro argues that inflation, unemployment, real GNP, and real national saving should not be affected by whether the government finances its spending with high taxes and low deficits or with low taxes and high deficits. Because people are rational, he argues, they will correctly perceive that low taxes and high deficits today must mean higher future taxes for them and their heirs. They will, Barro argues, cut consumption and increase their saving by one dollar for each dollar increase in future tax liabilities. Thus, a rise in private saving should offset any increase in the government's deficit. Naïve Keynesian analysis, by contrast, sees an increased deficit, with government spending held constant, as an increase in aggregate demand. If, as happened in the United States in the early 1980s, the stimulus to demand is nullified by contractionary monetary policy, real interest rates should rise strongly. There is no reason, in the Keynesian view, to expect the private saving rate to rise.

The massive U.S. tax cuts between 1981 and 1984 provided something approximating a laboratory test of these alternative views. What happened? The private saving rate did not rise. Real interest rates soared. With fiscal stimulus offset by monetary contraction, real GNP growth was approximately unaffected; it grew at about the same rate as it had in the recent past. Again, this all seems more consistent with Keynesian than with new classical theory.

Finally, there was the European depression of the 1980s, the worst since the depression of the 1930s. The Keynesian explanation is straightforward. Governments, led by the British and German central banks, decided to fight inflation with highly restrictive monetary and fiscal policies. The anti-inflation crusade was strengthened by the European monetary system, which, in effect, spread the stern German monetary policy all over Europe. The new classical school has no comparable explanation. New classicals, and conservative economists in general, argue that European governments interfere more heavily in labor markets (with high unemployment benefits, for example, and restrictions on firing workers). But most of these interferences were in place in the early 1970s, when unemployment was extremely low.

About the Author

Alan S. Blinder is the Gordon S. Rentschler Memorial Professor of Economics at Princeton University. He was previously vice chairman of the Federal Reserve's Board of Governors, and before that was a member of President Bill Clinton's Council of Economic Advisers.

Further Reading

Blinder, Alan S. "Keynes After Lucas." *Eastern Economic Journal* 12, no. 3 (1986): 209–216.

———. "Keynes, Lucas, and Scientific Progress." *American Economic Review* 77, no. 2 (1987): 130–136. Reprinted in Mark Blaug, ed., *John Maynard Keynes (1833–1946)*, vol. 2. Brookfield, Vt.: Edward Elgar, 1991.

Gordon, Robert J. "What Is New-Keynesian Economics?" *Journal of Economic Literature* 28, no. 3 (1990): 1115–1171.

Keynes, John Maynard. *The General Theory of Employment, Interest, and Money*. London: Macmillan, 1936.

Mankiw, N. Gregory, and others. "A Symposium on Keynesian Economics Today." *Journal of Economic Perspectives* 7 (Winter 1993): 3–82.

Labor Unions

Morgan O. Reynolds

Although labor unions have been celebrated in folk songs and stories as fearless champions of the downtrodden working man, this is not how economists see them. Economists who study unions—including some who are avowedly prounion—analyze them as CARTELS that raise wages above competitive levels by restricting the supply of labor to various firms and industries.

Many unions have won higher wages and better working conditions for their members. In doing so, however, they have reduced the number of jobs available in unionized companies. That second effect occurs because of the basic law of demand: if unions successfully raise the price of labor, employers will purchase less of it. Thus, unions are a major anticompetitive force in labor markets. Their gains come at the expense of consumers, nonunion workers, the jobless, taxpayers, and owners of corporations.

According to Harvard economists Richard Freeman and James Medoff, who look favorably on unions, "Most, if not all, unions have monopoly power, which they can use to raise wages above competitive levels" (1984, p. 6). Unions' power to fix high prices for their members' labor rests on legal privileges and immunities that they get from government, both by statute and by nonenforcement of other laws. The purpose of these legal privileges is to restrict others from working for lower wages. As antiunion economist Ludwig von Mises wrote in 1922, "The long and short of trade union rights is in fact the right to proceed against the strikebreaker with primitive violence." Interestingly, those who are expected to enforce the laws even-handedly, the police, are themselves heavily unionized.

U.S. unions enjoy many legal privileges. Unions are immune from taxation and from antitrust laws. Companies are legally compelled to bargain with unions in "good faith." This innocent-sounding term is interpreted by the National Labor Relations Board to suppress such practices as Boulwarism, named for a former General Electric personnel director. To shorten the collective bargaining process, Lemuel Boulware communicated the "reasonableness" of GE's wage offer directly to employees, shareholders, and the public. Unions also can force companies to make their property available for union use.

Once the government ratifies a union's position as representing a group of workers, it represents them exclusively, whether or not particular employees want collective representation. In 2002, unions represented about 1.7 million waged and salaried employees who were not union members. Also, union officials can force compulsory union dues from employees—members and nonmembers alike—as a condition for keeping their jobs. Unions often use these funds for political purposes—political campaigns and voter registration, for example—unrelated to collective bargaining or to employee grievances, despite the illegality of this under federal law. Unions are relatively immune from payment of tort damages for injuries inflicted in labor disputes, from federal court injunctions, and from many state laws under the "federal preemption" doctrine. Nobel laureate Friedrich A. Hayek summed it up as follows: "We have now reached a state where [unions] have become uniquely privileged institutions to which the general rules of law do not apply" (1960, p. 267).

Labor unions cannot prosper in a competitive environment. Like other successful cartels, they depend on gov-

Unions and Exploitation of Labor, Capital, and Taxpayers

Morgan O. Reynolds

Conventional wisdom about labor exploitation can be summed up in two propositions:

- Workers and employers are natural opponents; employers have a powerful advantage and they pay employees less than they are worth.

- Public policy must tilt toward unions to help employees who are otherwise at the mercy of employers in wage bargaining.

The public has considerable sympathy for the "underpayment" thesis and even for unions as a corrective force. Consider this survey question: "Do you think that the interests of employers and employees are, by their very nature, opposed; or are they basically the same?"

	Opposed	Same
1939 Roper/Fortune	25 percent	56 percent
1994 Roper ASW	45 percent	40 percent

Yet economists point out that the U.S. labor market is highly competitive, with more than five million employers competing for labor, entrepreneurs establishing new businesses daily, and private industry hiring four million persons per month. A "powerful" employer cannot depress labor prices below the value of workers' marginal (incremental) productivity for long because other firms are attracted by the cheaper labor. The new firms hire these workers and thereby put upward pressure on the prices paid to labor until further profit from the initial exploitation of isolated labor disappears. Also, if employer clout depresses wage rates in one location, labor supply will decrease as mobile workers leave, again putting corrective, upward pressure on wage rates.

Even if monopoly demand over labor were common in the U.S. economy, policy in favor of unions would not logically follow. Promoting union monopolies on labor to counter employer monopoly on labor demand establishes "bilateral monopolies." Alternative policies that would directly address any lack of competition among employers would include removing government barriers that block new employers from entering an industry or applying antitrust law against employer cartels to fix wage rates.

Even the historical image of corporate power dominating isolated "company mining towns" is mostly fiction. Nineteenth-century Appalachian coal miners, for example, were highly mobile, and literally hundreds of companies competed in the same coal and labor markets in both company-owned and independent towns. In fact, extensive mineral deposits mined by a single company are rare.

More generally, what is at issue is the potential for owners of cooperating, complementary inputs to exploit and underpay each other. These situations are highly limited. It is much easier for a labor organization to exploit vulnerable owners of ports, mines, plants, utilities, and other massive fixed facilities than the reverse. Because labor is the most versatile and flexible input, it is much harder for owners of large fixed-capital investments to exploit labor than for labor unions to exploit business investors.

Sports teams at both the collegiate and professional levels offer rare examples of durable underpayment. Today, colleges still maintain a successful cartel to suppress the pay of college athletes below competitive levels. While there are tremendous advantages to cheating, thereby spawning "under-the-table" benefits to recruit superior athletes, the NCAA system suppresses member violations by sanctions and ultimately threatening termination of academic accreditation, thereby cutting off the elaborate network of subsidies each college depends on. By contrast, rival leagues, court rulings, and collective bargaining have broken the old system of noncompetitive salaries for professional athletes in team sports such as football, basketball, and baseball in favor of approximately competitive labor markets.

ernment patronage and protection. Worker cartels grew in surges during the two world wars and the Great Depression of the 1930s. Federal laws—the Railway Act of 1926 (amended in 1934), the Davis-Bacon Act of 1931, the Norris-LaGuardia Act of 1932, the National Labor Relations Act of 1935, the Walsh-Healy Act of 1936, the Fair Labor Standards Act of 1938, various war labor boards, and the Kennedy administration's encouragement of public-sector unionism in 1962—all added to unions' monopoly power.

Most unions in the private sector are in crafts and industries that have few companies or that are concentrated in one region of the country. This makes sense. Both factors—few employers and regionally concentrated employers—make organizing easier. Conversely, the large number of employers and the regional dispersion of employers sharply limit unionization in trade, services, and agriculture. A 2002 unionization rate of 37.5 percent in the government sector, more than four times the 8.5 percent rate in the private sector, further demonstrates that unions do best in heavily regulated, monopolistic environments. Even within the private sector, the highest unionization rates (23.8 percent) are in transportation (airlines, railroads, trucking, urban transit, etc.) and public utilities (21.8 percent), two heavily regulated industries.

What have been the economic consequences of unions? In 2002, full-time nonunion workers had usual weekly earnings of $587, 21 percent lower than the $740 earned by union members. H. Gregg Lewis's 1985 survey of two hundred economic studies concluded that unions caused their members' wages to be, on average, 14–15 percent higher than wages of similarly skilled nonunion workers. Other economists—Harvard's Freeman and Medoff, and Peter Linneman and Michael Wachter of the University of Pennsylvania—claimed that the union premium was 20–30 percent or higher during the 1980s. In a recent National Bureau of Economic Analysis study, David Blanchflower and Alex Bryson found a union wage differential of 18 percent, a relatively stable premium from 1973 through 1995.

The wage premium varies by industry and stage of the business cycle. Unions representing garment workers, textile workers, white-collar government workers, and teachers seem to have little impact on wages. But wages of unionized mine workers, building trades people, airline pilots, merchant seamen, postal workers, teamsters, rail workers, and auto and steel workers exceed wages of similarly skilled nonunion employees by 25 percent or more. During the job boom of the late 1990s, the union premium eroded, following a historical pattern. Union wage agreements tend to be relatively rigid for three years, so gains lag behind the more responsive and flexible nonunion sector during a boom. The reverse happens during an employment slump like that of the early 2000s because nonunion wage growth slumps as hiring weakens, while union wage gains march on.

The wage advantage enjoyed by union members results from two factors. First, monopoly unions raise wages above competitive levels. Second, nonunion wages fall because workers priced out of jobs by high union wages move into the nonunion sector and bid down wages there. Thus, some of the gains to union members come at the expense of those who must shift to lower-paying or less desirable jobs or go unemployed.

Despite considerable rhetoric to the contrary, unions have blocked the economic advance of blacks, women, and other minorities. That is because another of their functions, once they have raised wages above competitive levels, is to ration the jobs that remain. The union can discriminate on the basis of blood relationships or skin color rather than auctioning off (openly selling) the valuable jobs to the highest-bidding applicants. Because craft unions such as the carpenters' and railway unions have had more monopoly control over wage rates and hiring practices than industrial unions such as the auto and steel workers have had, craft unions have had more opportunities to exclude minority workers. Industrial unions have had to organize whoever was hired, and industrial companies have hired large numbers of black workers. The degree of racial discrimination exercised by union officials depends on their ability and willingness to exclude. For example, leaders at the local shop level facing contested elections and turnover in office cannot stray far from median membership preferences, while insulated top union leaders have more discretion.

Economist Ray Marshall, although a prounion secretary of labor under President Jimmy Carter, made his academic reputation by documenting how unions excluded blacks from membership in the 1930s and 1940s. Marshall also wrote of incidents in which union members assaulted black workers hired to replace them during strikes. During the 1911 strike against the Illinois Central, noted Marshall, whites killed two black strikebreakers and wounded three others at McComb, Mississippi. He also noted that white strikers killed ten black firemen in 1911 because the New Orleans and Texas Pacific Railroad had granted them equal seniority. Not surprisingly, therefore, black leader Booker T. Washington opposed unions all his life, and W. E. B. DuBois called unions the greatest enemy of the black working class. Another interesting fact: the "union label" was started in the 1880s to proclaim that a product was made by white rather than yellow (Chinese) hands. More generally, union wage rates, union-backed requirements for a license to practice various occupations, and union-backed labor regulations such as the minimum wage law and the Davis-Bacon Act continue to reduce opportunities for black youths, females, and other minorities.

The monopoly success of private-sector unions, however, has brought their decline. The silent, steady forces of the marketplace continually undermine them. Linneman and Wachter, along with economist William Carter, found that the rising union wage premium was responsible for up to 64 percent of the decline in unions' share of employment in the last twenty years. The average union wage premium for railroad workers over similarly skilled nonrailroad workers, for example, increased from 32 percent to 50 percent between 1973 and 1987; at the same time, employment on railroads declined from 520,000 to 249,000. By 2002, railroad employment had slipped to 216,000, down 13 percent since 1987, while total nonfarm employment grew 26 percent during the same period. Increased wage premiums also caused declines in union employment in construction, manufacturing, and communications. The silent, steady forces of the marketplace continually undermine labor cartels.

In recent decades, union representation of workers has declined in all private industries in the United States. A major reason is that employees do not like unions. According to a Louis Harris poll commissioned by the AFL-CIO in 1984, only one in three U.S. employees would vote for union representation in a secret ballot election. The Harris poll found, as have other surveys, that nonunion employees are more satisfied than union workers with job security, recognition of job performance, and participation in decisions that affect their jobs. And the U.S. economy's evolution toward smaller companies, the South and West, higher-technology products, and more professional and technical personnel continues to erode union membership.

In the United States, union membership in the private sector peaked at 17 million in 1970 and had fallen by nearly half—to 8.8 million—by 2002. Barring new legislation, such as a congressional proposal to ban the hiring of non-union replacement workers, private-sector membership will likely fall from 8.5 percent to 5–6 percent by 2010, no higher than the percentage a hundred years ago. While the unionization rate in government jobs may decline slightly from 37.5 percent, public-sector unions are on schedule to claim an absolute majority of union members within the next few years, thereby transforming a historically private-sector labor movement into a primarily government one. Asked in the 1920s what organized labor wanted, union leader Samuel Gompers allegedly answered, "More." Today's union leader would probably answer, "More government." That answer further exposes the deep, permanent conflict between union members and workers in general that inevitably arises when union-represented employees are paid monopoly prices for their services.

Assuming that unions continue to decline, what organizations might replace them? "Worker associations" that lack legal privileges and immunities and that must produce services of value to get members may fill the need. Such voluntary worker associations could negotiate labor contracts, serve as clearinghouses for workers to learn what their best alternatives are, monitor administration of fringe benefit plans, and administer training and benefit plans. Worker associations could also institute legal proceedings against collusion by employers, as the Major League Baseball Players' Association does so successfully

for free agents. Such services could be especially valuable to the immigrant, minority, and female workers now dominating entry into today's labor force.

About the Author

Morgan O. Reynolds is a former chief economist at the U.S. Department of Labor and a professor emeritus of economics at Texas A&M University.

Further Reading

Blanchflower, David, and Alex Bryson. "Changes over Time in Union Relative Wage Effects in the UK and the US Revisited." NBER Working Paper no. 9395. National Bureau of Economic Research, Cambridge, Mass., 2002.

Epstein, Richard A. "A Common Law for Labor Relations: A Critique of the New Deal Labor Legislation." *Yale Law Journal* 92 (July 1983): 1357–1408.

Freeman, Richard B., and James L. Medoff. *What Do Labor Unions Do?* 1984. Available online at: http://papers.nber .org/papers/w11410.

Harvard Journal of Law and Public Policy 13 (Spring 1990). Entire issue devoted to labor law.

Hayek, Friedrich A. von. *The Constitution of Liberty*. Chicago: University of Chicago Press, 1960.

Hutt, William H. *The Strike-Threat System: The Economic Consequences of Collective Bargaining*. New Rochelle, N.Y.: Arlington House, 1973.

Lewis, H. Gregg. *Union Relative Wage Effects*. Chicago: University of Chicago Press, 1986.

Linneman, Peter D., Michael L. Wachter, and William H. Carter. "Evaluating the Evidence on Union Employment and Wages." *Industrial and Labor Relations Review* 44 (October 1990): 34–53.

Marshall, F. Ray. *The Negro and Organized Labor*. New York: Wiley, 1965.

Reynolds, Morgan O. *Making America Poorer: The Cost of Labor Law*. Washington, D.C.: Cato Institute, 1987.

Troy, Leo. "Is the U.S. Unique in the Decline of Private Sector Unionism?" *Journal of Labor Research* 11 (Spring 1990): 111–143.

Law and Economics

Paul H. Rubin

"Law and economics," also known as the economic analysis of law, differs from other forms of legal analysis in two main ways. First, the theoretical analysis focuses on EFFICIENCY. In simple terms, a legal situation is said to be efficient if a right is given to the party who would be willing to pay the most for it. There are two distinct theories of legal efficiency, and law and economics scholars support arguments based on both. The positive theory of legal efficiency states that the common law (judge-made law, the main body of law in England and its former colonies, including the United States) is efficient, while the normative theory is that the law *should be* efficient. It is important that the two theories remain separate. Most economists accept both.

Law and economics stresses that markets are more efficient than courts. When possible, the legal system, according to the positive theory, will force a transaction into the market. When this is impossible, the legal system attempts to "mimic a market" and guess at what the parties would have desired if markets had been feasible.

The second characteristic of law and economics is its emphasis on incentives and people's responses to these incentives. For example, the purpose of damage payments in accident (tort) law is not to compensate injured parties, but rather to provide an incentive for potential injurers to take efficient (cost-justified) precautions to avoid causing the accident. Law and economics shares with other branches of economics the assumption that individuals are rational and respond to incentives. When penalties for an action increase, people will undertake less of that action. Law and economics is more likely than other branches of legal analysis to use empirical or statistical methods to measure these responses to incentives.

The private legal system must perform three functions, all related to property and property rights. First, the system must define property rights; this is the task of property law itself. Second, the system must allow for transfer of property; this is the role of contract law. Finally, the system must protect property rights; this is the function of tort law and criminal law. These are the major issues studied in law and economics. Law and economics scholars also apply the tools of economics, such as game theory, to purely legal questions, such as various parties' litigation strategies. While these are aspects of law and economics, they are of more interest to legal scholars than to students of the economy.

History and Significance

Modern law and economics dates from about 1960, when Ronald Coase (who later received a Nobel Prize) published "The Problem of Social Cost." Gordon Tullock and Friedrich Hayek also wrote in the area, but the expansion of the field began with Gary Becker's 1968 paper on crime (Becker also received a Nobel Prize). In 1972, Richard Posner, a law and economics scholar and the major advocate of the positive theory of efficiency, published the first edition of *Economic Analysis of Law* and founded the *Journal of Legal Studies,* both important events in the creation of

the field as a thriving scholarly discipline. Posner went on to become a federal judge while remaining a prolific scholar. An important factor leading to the spread of law and economics in the 1970s was a series of seminars and law courses for economists and economics courses for lawyers, organized by Henry Manne and funded, in part, by the Liberty Fund.

The discipline is now well established, with eight associations, including the American, Canadian, and European law and economics associations, and several journals.[1] Law and economics articles also appear regularly in the major economics journals, and the approach is common in law review articles. Most law schools have faculty trained in economics, and most offer law and economics courses. Many economics departments also teach courses in the field. A course in law and economics is very useful for undergraduates contemplating law school. Several consulting firms specialize in providing economic expertise in litigation.

Substance

Property
A legal system should provide clear definitions of property rights. That is, for any asset, it is important that parties be able to determine unambiguously who owns the asset and exactly what set of rights this ownership entails. Ideally, efficiency implies that, in a dispute regarding the ownership of a right, the right should go to the party who values it the most. But if exchanges of rights are allowed, the efficiency of the initial allocation is of secondary importance. The Coase theorem—the most fundamental result in the economic study of law—states that if rights are transferable and if transactions costs are not too large, then the exact definition of property rights is not important because parties can trade rights, and rights will move to their highest-valued uses (see EXTERNALITIES).

In many circumstances, however, who owns the right will matter. Transactions costs are never zero, and so if rights are incorrectly allocated, a costly transaction will be needed to correct this misallocation. If transactions costs are greater than the increase in value from moving the resource to the efficient owner, there may be no corrective

1. Including: *Journal of Law and Economics; Journal of Legal Studies; Journal of Law, Economics and Organization; American Law and Economics Review; International Review of Law and Economics; Supreme Court Economic Review; Research in Law and Economics; European Journal of Law and Economics.* Articles in the field are also available online at: http://ssrn.com/ and http://law.bepress.com/repository/. On the American Law and Economics Association, see: http://www.amlecon.org/.

mechanism. This can happen in any sort of economy. An extreme example is Russia, where the courts have not been able to provide clear definitions of property rights, and those persons with control of firms are not necessarily the owners. That is, those with control over a firm cannot sell it and keep the proceeds. This creates incentives for inefficient use of the assets, such as sale of valuable raw materials for below-market prices, with the proceeds deposited outside the country. In such circumstances, the Coase theorem will not operate, and correctly defining property rights becomes important. More generally, experience in Russia and its former satellites has emphasized the importance of the legal system for development of a market economy and, thus, has shown the importance of law and economics in influencing policy.

One important finding of law and economics is that, in market economies, property rights are defined efficiently in many circumstances. The characteristics of efficient property rights are universality (everything is owned), exclusivity (everything is owned by one agent), and transferability. Law and economics can also explain the results of inefficient property definitions. For example, because no one owns wild fish, the only way to own a fish is to catch it. The result is overfishing (see TRAGEDY OF THE COMMONS). INTELLECTUAL PROPERTY is an important area of current research because new copying and duplicating technologies are having profound effects on the definition of this form of property rights and on incentives for creating such property.

Contract Law

The law governing exchange is crucial for a market economy. Most of the doctrines of contract law seem consistent with economic efficiency. Law and economics study of contract law has shown that, in general, it is efficient for parties to be allowed to write their own contracts, and under normal circumstances, for courts to enforce the agreed-on terms, including the agreed-on price. The courts will generally not enforce contracts if performance would be inefficient, but, rather, will allow payment of damages. If, for example, I agree to build something for you in return for $50,000, but meanwhile costs increase so that the thing would cost me $150,000 to build, it is inefficient for me to build it. Courts, recognizing this, allow me to compensate you with a monetary payment instead. This is efficient.

Contracts and contract law are also designed to minimize problems of opportunism. The danger of opportunism arises when two parties agree to something, and one makes irreversible investments to carry out his side of the bargain. So, for example, a company invests in a railroad spur to a coal mine, making a contract in advance to ship the coal at a specific price. Once the railroad is built, the mine owner can refuse to honor his contract and can hold out for a lower shipping rate. As long as this rate exceeds the railroad's incremental costs, the railroad owner will be tempted to accept. If he does so, he will not receive the full return on the spur line that he needed to make the investment worthwhile. Doctrines such as a duty to mitigate (to reduce the harmful effects of breach of contract) are easily explained as being efficient.

However, not all doctrines are efficient. Contracting parties will sometimes specify damages (called "liquidated damages") to be paid if there is a breach. If the courts decide that these liquidated damages are too high—that they are a penalty rather than true damages—they will not enforce the amount of contractual liquidated damages. This failure to enforce agreed-on terms is a major puzzle to law and economics scholars; it appears that the courts would do better to enforce the parties' agreement, just as they do with respect to price and other terms of a contract. Here, the positive theory of the efficiency of law seems to be violated, but scholars argue that the courts should enforce these agreements.

Tort Law

Tort law and criminal law protect property rights from intentional or unintentional harm. The primary purpose of these laws is to induce potential tortfeasors (those who cause torts, or accidents) or criminals to internalize—that is, take account of—the external costs of their actions, although criminal law has other functions as well.

Tort law is part of the system of private law and is enforced through private actions. The economic analysis of tort law has stressed issues such as the distinction between negligence (a party must pay for harms only when the party failed to take adequate or efficient precautions) and strict liability (a party must pay for any injury caused by its actions). Because most accidents are caused by a joint action of injurer and victim (a driver goes too fast, and the pedestrian he hits does not look carefully), efficient rules create incentives for both parties to take care; most negligence rules (negligence, negligence with a defense of contributory negligence, comparative negligence) create exactly these incentives. Strict liability is important when the issue is not only the care used in undertaking the activity, but also whether the activity is done at all and the extent to which it is done (the level of the activity); highly dangerous activities (e.g., blasting with explosives or keeping wild animals as pets) are generally governed by strict liability.

Tort law used to be uninteresting and unimportant, dealing largely with automobile accidents. But it has become quite important in the United States in the last fifty years, because many events traditionally treated under contract law are now subject to tort law. For example, in products liability and medical malpractice cases, the parties have a preaccident relationship and so could have specified and traditionally did specify in their contracts what damages would be paid in the event of a mishap. But since about 1950, the courts have refused to honor these contracts, treating these instead as tort cases. Many observers believe that this was a fundamental error of the courts and look on it as the primary example of an inefficient doctrine in modern American law. Scholars have found that this error was caused by actions on the part of the plaintiff's bar, who were seeking to benefit themselves at the expense of the public in general. Problems are exacerbated when claims are aggregated through the mechanism of class actions.

Two factors have caused the major expansion of product liability law. One was finding relatively strict liability for "design defects" in addition to "manufacturing defects." The other was expansion of liability for "failure to warn." One result of treating these events as part of tort law is that injured parties can collect classes of damage payments (such as damages for pain and suffering and sometimes excessive punitive damages) that would be excluded by contract if contracts could be enforced. As a result, prices of many goods and services (including medical services) are driven above the value that consumers would place on them. That is why, for example, private airplanes are so expensive, and obstetricians and gynecologists are unavailable in some markets.

Criminal Law
Criminal law is enforced by the state rather than by victims. This is because efficient enforcement requires that only a fraction of criminals be caught (in order to conserve on enforcement resources) and the punishment of this fraction be multiplied to reflect the low probability of detection and conviction. If, for example, only one out of four criminals is caught and punished, then the punishment must be four times the cost of the crime in order to provide adequate deterrence.

However, most criminals do not have sufficient wealth to pay such multiplied fines, and so incarceration or other forms of nonpecuniary punishment must be used. One implication of law and economics is that a fine should be used as punishment whenever the miscreant can pay. The reason is that fines are transfers and do not create dead-weight losses (i.e., losses to some that are not gains to others); imprisonment, on the other hand, transfers virtually no wealth from the criminal but causes two forms of deadweight loss: the loss of the criminal's earning power in a legitimate job in the outside world and the cost to taxpayers of providing a prison and guards. But because so few criminals have enough wealth to pay multiplied fines, private enforcement would not be profitable for private enforcers, and so the state provides enforcement. In some circumstances, incarceration serves the additional function of incapacitation of potential wrongdoers.

Criminal law has been the subject of the most extensive empirical work in law and economics, probably because of the availability of data (see CRIME). Economic theory predicts that criminals, like others, respond to incentives, and there is unambiguous evidence that increases in the probability and severity of punishment in a jurisdiction lead to reduced levels of crime in that jurisdiction. The issue of the deterrent effect of capital punishment has been more controversial, but several recent papers using advanced econometric techniques and comprehensive data have found a significant deterrent effect; each execution deters between eight and twenty-eight murders, with eighteen being the best single estimate. No refereed empirical criticism of these papers has been published. Research on procedural rules has shown that increased rights for accused persons can lead to increases in crime. One controversial paper by John Donohue and Steven Levitt argues empirically that the easing of abortion restrictions led to a reduction in crime because unwanted children would have been more likely to become criminals. There are also major debates in the literature on the effect on crime of laws allowing easier carrying of concealed weapons. Some, such as John Lott, find significant decreases in crime from these laws, while others find much smaller effects, although there is little evidence of any increase in crime.

About the Author
Paul H. Rubin is Samuel Candler Dobbs Professor of Economics and Law at Emory University in Atlanta and editor in chief of *Managerial and Decision Economics*. Dr. Rubin was a senior staff economist with President Ronald Reagan's Council of Economic Advisers, chief economist with the U.S. Consumer Product Safety Commission, and director of Advertising Economics at the Federal Trade Commission.

Further Reading
Becker, Gary S. "Crime and Punishment: An Economic Approach." *Journal of Political Economy* 76 (1968): 169–

217. The seminal article on the economic approach to crime.

Bouckaert, Boudewijn, and Gerrit De Geest, eds. *Encyclopedia of Law and Economics*. London: Edward Elgar, 2000. Also available online: http://encyclo.findlaw.com/. Mainly for economists and legal scholars interested in exploring particular topics more deeply.

Coase, Ronald H. "The Problem of Social Cost." *Journal of Law and Economics* 3, no. 1 (1960): 1–44. The key article in law and economics and the origin of the famous Coase theorem.

Cooter, Robert D., and Thomas Ulen. *Law and Economics*. 3d ed. New York: Addison-Wesley, 1999. A textbook introduction to law and economics, mainly for economics students.

Dezhbakhsh, Hashem, Paul H. Rubin, and Joanna M. Shepherd. "Does Capital Punishment Have a Deterrent Effect? New Evidence from Post-moratorium Panel Data." *American Law and Economics Review* 5 (2003): 344–376. Source of the estimate that each execution deters an average of eighteen murders.

Donohue, John, and Steven Levitt. "Legalized Abortion and Crime." *Quarterly Journal of Economics* 116, no. 2 (2001): 379–420. Finds that much of the reduction in crime in recent years is due to the legalization of abortion.

Friedman, David D. *Law's Order: An Economic Account*. Princeton: Princeton University Press, 2000. The simplest introduction to law and economics; accessible to general readers. Available online at: http://www.daviddfriedman.com/laws_order/index.shtml.

Hayek, Friedrich. *The Constitution of Liberty*. Chicago: University of Chicago Press, 1960. More difficult reading, philosophical as well as economic.

Lott, John R. Jr., and David B. Mustard. "Crime, Deterrence and the Right-to-Carry Concealed Handguns." *Journal of Legal Studies* 26 (1997): 1–68. The original study finding that right-to-carry laws reduce crime. Although the study has been criticized, there is no evidence that these laws cause increases in crime.

Newman, Peter, ed. *New Palgrave Dictionary of Economics and the Law*. London: Macmillan, 1998. Mainly for economists and legal scholars interested in exploring particular topics more deeply.

Posner, Richard A. *Economic Analysis of Law*. 1st ed. Boston: Little, Brown, 1973; 7th ed. New York: Aspen Publishers, 2007. Both a key treatise in the field and a textbook suitable for students of both law and economics.

Rubin, Paul H. "Micro and Macro Legal Efficiency: Supply and Demand." *Supreme Court Economic Review* 13 (2005): 19–34. Describes the history of the economic analysis of efficiency in the law.

Shavell, Steven. *Foundations of Economic Analysis of Law*. Cambridge: Belknap Press of Harvard University Press, 2004. The newest comprehensive book in the field; nonmathematical but complex.

Liability

W. Kip Viscusi

Until the 1980s, property and liability insurance was a small cost of doing business. But the substantial expansion in what legally constitutes liability has greatly increased the cost of liability insurance for personal injuries. The plight of the U.S. private aircraft industry illustrates the extent of these liability costs. Although accident rates for general aviation and for small aircraft declined steadily, liability costs for the industry soared, so that by the 1990s the U.S. private aircraft industry had all but ceased production. These substantial costs arose because accident victims or their survivors began to sue aircraft companies in 90 percent of all crashes, even though pilot error is responsible for 85 percent of all accidents. Only after Congress exempted planes older than eighteen years from liability by passing the General Aviation Revitalization Act of 1994 did the industry begin to increase production. Still, output is well below its level before the rise in liability costs. In 1978, 17,811 new U.S.-manufactured general aviation airplanes were shipped, but by 1994 this amount had plummeted to 928. Though shipments have since rebounded to 2,137 airplanes in 2003, that amount is still well below the peak production years.

The consequences of liability can be substantial for industries, and some, such as the asbestos industry, have disappeared altogether because of liability costs. The U.S. vaccine industry has been hard hit by the costs associated with liability for adverse reactions to its vaccines. Indeed, much of the price of vaccines is attributable to costs of liability, which are largely shifted to consumers through higher prices because expected liability costs raise the costs of supplying vaccines. Ten of the thirteen companies manufacturing vaccines for the five serious childhood diseases exited the market because of rising liability costs.

Negligence was at one time the dominant legal criterion for determining a firm's liability. Firms were responsible for accidents arising from their products only if they did not provide an efficient level of safety (see LAW AND ECONOMICS for an explanation of how the term "efficient" is used in this case). Over the past three decades, however, broader liability doctrines, some of which have nothing to do with negligence, have placed greater responsibilities on product manufacturers. In the 1960s, courts adopted "strict liability," which required producers to pay for accident costs in a much broader range of circumstances. The asbestos litigation is perhaps the best-known example of a major line of litigation that was facilitated by the adoption of the strict liability doctrine. One of the courts' stated rationales for this expansion is that producers can serve as the insurers of the accident victims' costs and spread these costs among all consumers through a higher product price. And that is precisely what has happened.

Courts have also expanded liability by broadening the meaning of the term "design defect." This had been reflected in, for example, a surge of litigation claiming that an inadequate warning—one that does not fully inform the user of a product's risks—is enough to deem a product's design defective. A federal appeals court found Uniroyal liable for the death of a professional truck driver because it failed to warn of the risks from underinflated tires. FMC lost a product-liability suit involving a crane because there was no warning in the cab about hitting power lines with the machine. Many asbestos cases have focused on whether companies properly informed workers of the cancer risk and the need to avoid breathing asbestos dust.

Although increases in liability enhance the incentives to provide safer products, they also discourage product innovation. In a 1990 report, the National Academy of Sciences concluded that the United States had fallen a decade behind Europe in the development of new contraceptives, partly because of the chilling effect of rising liability costs (Mastroianni et al. 1990). In one case, G. D. Searle and Company spent $1.5 million in a single year to successfully defend itself against four lawsuits over its intrauterine device Copper-7. Because annual sales of the product were only $11 million, the company chose to discontinue it.

One might expect liability costs to follow the same trend as risks, but that has not happened. General liability insurance costs rose from $6.4 billion in 1980 to $22 billion in 2001. Over that same period, the overall accidental death rate per 100,000 population actually fell from 46.2 to 35.3. The accident rate per 100,000 population for the highest-accident-risk product, motor vehicles, declined from 23.5 to 15.7.

The principal components of the awards in liability suits are economic damages (lost earnings and medical expenses), compensation for noneconomic damages, and punitive damages. Economic damages have risen, in part, because the cost of medical care has risen. Noneconomic damages, chiefly from pain and suffering, have attracted the most attention from liability reformers because their conceptual basis remains ill-defined. Medical malpractice reforms, in particular, have emphasized limits on noneconomic damages. The legal criteria for pain and suffering compensation are not well articulated. They are an economic loss against which people do not usually insure.

This lack of a conceptual base has caused substantial uncertainty in determining compensation for pain and suffering. But juries seem willing to see pain and suffering almost everywhere. After an Illinois refinery explosion, for example, a jury awarded $700,000 to the victim's survivors, even though there was no evidence that the comatose victim was conscious and would have experienced any pain. The award was overturned on appeal. But the fact that such awards are granted is one reason the U.S. Department of Justice and various legal reform groups advocate schedules and limits for compensating pain and suffering. Most recently, there has been a tremendous expansion of the pain-and-suffering concept as passengers on a plane that never crashed successfully sued for the "fear of death," and witnesses of the death of a stranger successfully sued for the emotional trauma they experienced by witnessing this death. One plaintiff received an award of $1.5 million simply for the fear of a crash of a United Airlines flight.[1]

Punitive damages awards have achieved increasing prominence. While million-dollar awards were once sufficient to garner headlines, from 1985 to 2003 there were sixty-four punitive damages awards of $100 million or more, and more than 95 percent of these awards were the result of jury trials rather than bench trials. Eleven of the punitive damages awards have been at least $1 billion. These awards often bear little relationship to the value of compensatory damages, as illustrated by the punitive award of $28 billion in *Bullock v. Philip Morris*. In that individual smoker case, the compensatory damages were $650,000, producing a ratio of punitive damages to compensatory damages of forty-three thousand. In 2003, the U.S. Supreme Court attempted to rein in such excesses in *State Farm v. Campbell*, in which it indicated that the upper limit should be a single-digit ratio of punitive damages to compensatory damages.

Perhaps the most dramatic change in the character of product-liability litigation has been the emergence of mass toxic torts. Agent Orange, asbestos, and the Dalkon Shield cases are the three most notable examples of such litigation. Each involved more than 100,000 injury claimants—125,000 claimants in the Agent Orange litigation, 190,000 claimants against the Manville Corporation for asbestos exposures, 150,000 claimants in other asbestos cases, and 210,000 claimants against the Dalkon Shield. Asbestos litigation was 2 percent of federal product-liability litigation in 1975, but had risen to 61 percent by 1989. The surge in mass toxic torts has overwhelmed the

1. See *Blum v. Airport Terminal Services,* 762 S.W. 2d 67 (Mo., 1988).

courts' capacity to process these claims. After the lawsuits against companies that produced asbestos abated, a new wave of asbestos litigation began against firms that used asbestos in their production processes or in their products.

These cases are distinguished not only by their number, but also by the difficulties they create for the liability system. Due to the substantial time lags involved, causality has been difficult to determine. It is noteworthy that in the Agent Orange case, legal doctrine (*Feres v. United States*) prevented soldiers from suing the actor primarily responsible for their injuries—the federal government. Consequently, they sought compensation from the deep and more readily available pockets of Dow Chemical Company and other Agent Orange producers. The judge who presided over the Agent Orange litigation could not find any clear-cut causality between Agent Orange and the veterans' ailments and, as a result, fashioned a "compromise" settlement for $180 million.

Moreover, in the asbestos cases, liability was imposed retroactively on firms that could not have anticipated the extent of the risks or the likely litigation costs. This means that one of the main modern rationales for expanded liability—that it gives companies an incentive to avoid accidents—does not apply in the asbestos case. The viability of insuring these losses by shifting accident costs onto companies has also come under fire, as the Manville Corporation and others have reorganized under federal bankruptcy law and set up trust funds in excess of $3 billion (in the case of Manville) to cover losses that will inevitably exceed that amount.

Another recent phenomenon has been the emergence of rising liability suits to foster outcomes that are tantamount to regulatory policy changes. In the 1990s, the states sued the tobacco industry to recover the health care costs due to smoking. This litigation led to a settlement with forty-six states for $206 billion and separate settlements with four states for another $36.8 billion, for a total of $243 billion. What was distinctive about the settlement was that it was not a settlement in any conventional sense. Rather, these amounts represented the funds that would be generated by a new per-pack levy on cigarettes. In effect, the industry agreed to a new cigarette excise tax to settle the litigation. This regulation-through-litigation phenomenon is not restricted to tobacco; similar suits have been filed against the gun industry, manufacturers of lead paint, and HMOs. Such suits are controversial because high-stakes litigation is being used to force outcomes that make new regulatory and tax policies, but these efforts are not subject to legislative action and the other mechanisms that ensure broad input into policy decisions.

Periodically, there has been a surge in liability costs, leading to claims that there is a liability crisis. A number of explanations have been offered for these crises. One is that they may be caused by the so-called insurance underwriting cycle. Over the decades, insurance companies have periodically underpriced insurance as they competed for more business. When the claims on these underpriced policies generated large losses, the insurers responded by raising prices substantially. Another explanation offered is that the insurance industry may have had a capital shortfall, causing it to decrease the amount of coverage it would write. It did so, according to this explanation, by raising prices. A third explanation is that the crises were caused by changes in liability—the rise in liability costs, the increased uncertainty of the liability system, and the presence of highly correlated risks that decrease the ability of insurers to pool offsetting risks in their portfolios. The long-run nature of the rise in insurance premiums and the linkage of this increase to the surge in litigation suggest that shifts in liability doctrine are the major contributors to the rise in liability costs. Although the short-run crises have abated, a broad array of tort-reform groups, ranging from the U.S. Department of Justice to the American Law Institute, has concluded that the liability system must be restructured to provide an efficient level of deterrence, to provide appropriate incentives for the introduction of new products, and to meet the legitimate needs of accident victims.

About the Author

W. Kip Viscusi is the University Distinguished Professor of Law, Economics, and Management at Vanderbilt University. He is the founding editor of the *Journal of Risk and Uncertainty*.

Further Reading

American Law Institute. *Reporters Study, Enterprise Liability for Personal Injury.* 1991.

Manning, Richard L. "Changing Rules in Tort Law and the Market for Childhood Vaccines." *Journal of Law and Economics* 37, no. 1 (1994): 247–275.

Mastroianni, Luigi Jr., Peter J. Donaldson, and Thomas T. Kane, eds. *Developing New Contraceptives: Obstacles and Opportunities.* Washington, D.C.: National Academy of Sciences Press, 1990.

Sunstein, Cass, et al. *Punitive Damages: How Juries Decide.* Chicago: University of Chicago Press, 2002.

Viscusi, W. Kip. *Reforming Products Liability.* Cambridge: Harvard University Press, 1991.

———, ed. *Regulation Through Litigation.* Washington, D.C.: AEI-Brookings Joint Center for Regulatory Studies, 2002.

Marginal Tax Rates

Alan Reynolds

The marginal tax rate is the rate on the last dollar of income earned. This is very different from the average tax rate, which is the total tax paid as a percentage of total income earned. In 2003, for example, the United States imposed a 35 percent tax on every dollar of taxable income above $155,975 earned by a married taxpayer filing separately. But that tax bracket applied only to earnings *above* that $155,975 threshold; income below that cutoff point would still be taxed at rates of 10 percent on the first $7,000, 15 percent on the next $14,400, and so on. Depending on deductions, a taxpayer might pay a relatively modest *average* tax on total earnings, yet nonetheless face a 28–35 percent *marginal* tax on any activities that could push income higher—such as extra effort, education, entrepreneurship, or investment. Marginal decisions (such as extra effort or investment) depend mainly on marginal incentives (extra income, after taxes).

The seemingly arcane topic of marginal tax rates became the central theme of a revolution in economic policy that swept the globe during the last two decades of the twentieth century, with more than fifty nations significantly reducing their highest marginal tax rates on individual income (most of which are shown in Table 1). Tax rates on corporate income (not shown) were also reduced in most cases (e.g., to 12.5 percent in Ireland). Table 1 also shows, however, that a handful of countries did comparatively little to reduce the highest, most damaging tax rates—notably, most of Western Europe, Scandinavia, Canada, and Japan.

Why did so many other countries so dramatically reduce marginal tax rates? Perhaps they were influenced by new economic analysis and evidence from optimal tax theorists, new growth economics, and supply-side economics. But the sheer force of example may well have been more persuasive. Political authorities saw that other national governments fared better by having tax collectors claim a medium share of a rapidly growing economy (a low marginal tax) rather than trying to extract a large share of a stagnant economy (a high average tax). East Asia, Ireland, Russia, and India are a few of the economies that began expanding impressively after their governments sharply reduced marginal tax rates.

Economic Growth by Robert J. Barro and Xavier Sala-i-Martin (MIT Press, 2004, p. 514) lists among the world's twenty fastest-growing economies Taiwan, Singapore, South Korea, Hong Kong, Botswana, Thailand, Ireland, Malaysia, Portugal, Mauritius, and Indonesia. As Table 1

Table 1 Maximum Marginal Tax Rates on Individual Income

	1979	1990	2002
Argentina	45	30	35
Australia	62	48	47
Austria	62	50	50
Belgium	76	55	52
Bolivia	48	10	13
Botswana	75	50	25
Brazil	55	25	28
Canada (Ontario)	58	47	46
Chile	60	50	43
Colombia	56	30	35
Denmark	73	68	59
Egypt	80	65	40
Finland	71	43	37
France	60	52	50
Germany	56	53	49
Greece	60	50	40
Guatemala	40	34	31
Hong Kong	25*	25	16
Hungary	60	50	40
India	60	50	30
Indonesia	50	35	35
Iran	90	75	35
Ireland	65	56	42
Israel	66	48	50
Italy	72	50	52
Jamaica	58	33	25
Japan	75	50	50
South Korea	89	50	36
Malaysia	60	45	28
Mauritius	50	35	25
Mexico	55	35	40
Netherlands	72	60	52
New Zealand	60	33	39
Norway	75	54	48
Pakistan	55	45	35
Philippines	70	35	32
Portugal	84	40	40
Puerto Rico	79	43	33
Russia	NA	60	13
Singapore	55	33	26
Spain	66	56	48
Sweden	87	65	56
Thailand	60	55	37
Trinidad and Tobago	70	35	35
Turkey	75	50	45
United Kingdom	83	40	40
United States	70	33	39**

Source: PricewaterhouseCoopers; International Bureau of Fiscal Documentation.

* Hong Kong's maximum tax (the "standard rate") has normally been 15 percent, effectively capping the marginal rate at high income levels (in exchange for no personal exemptions).

** The highest U.S. tax rate of 39.6 percent after 1993 was reduced to 38.6 percent in 2002 and to 35 percent in 2003.

shows, all these countries either had low marginal tax rates to begin with (Hong Kong) or cut their highest marginal tax rates in half between 1979 and 2002 (Botswana, Mauritius, Singapore, Portugal, etc.). This might be dismissed as a remarkable coincidence were it not for a plethora of economic studies demonstrating several ways in which high marginal tax rates can adversely affect economic performance.

Numerous studies, ably surveyed by Karabegovic et. al. (2004), have found that high marginal tax rates reduce people's willingness to work up to their potential, to take entrepreneurial risks, and to create and expand a new business: "The evidence from economic research indicates that . . . high and increasing marginal taxes have serious negative consequences on economic growth, labor supply, and capital formation" (p. 15).

Federal Reserve Bank of Minneapolis senior adviser Edward Prescott, corecipient of the 2004 Nobel Prize in economics, found that the "low labor supplies in Germany, France, and Italy are due to high [marginal] tax rates" (Prescott 2004, p. 7). He noted that adult labor force participation in France has fallen about 30 percent below that of the United States, which accounts for the comparably higher U.S. living standards.

Even in the United States, marginal tax rates are really higher than statutory rates suggest. In a study aptly titled "Does It Pay to Work?" Jagadeesh Gokhale et al. (2002) include state and local taxes, the marginal impact of losing government benefits (such as Medicaid and food stamps) if income rises, the progressive nature of Social Security benefits (which are least generous to those who work the most), and the phasing out of deductions and exemptions as income rises. They conclude that even "those with earnings that exceed 1.5 times the minimum wage face marginal net taxes on full-time work above 50 percent" (Abstract). At higher incomes, the estimated federal, state, and local marginal tax rate is about 56–57 percent. Marginal tax rates are higher still, however, in countries where statutory rates are higher.

Lifetime family work effort and entrepreneurship are not the only things affected. Nobel laureate Robert Lucas emphasized the deleterious effect on economic growth of high tax rates on capital. Philip Trostel focused on the impact on human capital, finding that high marginal tax rates on labor income reduce the lifetime reward from investing time and money in education. There are evidently many channels through which high marginal tax rates may discourage additions to personal income, and thus also discourage marginal additions to national output (i.e., economic growth). As the variety among these studies suggests, each separate effect of high marginal tax rates is typically examined separately, which makes the overall economic distortions and disincentives appear less significant than if they were all combined.

Despite widespread reduction of marginal tax rates throughout the world, there remains considerable misunderstanding about what marginal tax rates are and why they matter. The common practice of measuring tax receipts as a percentage of GDP, for example, is too static. It ignores the destructive effects of tax avoidance on tax revenues, the numerator of that ratio, and on the growth of GDP, the denominator. A sizable portion of productive activity may cease, move abroad, or vanish into inefficient little "informal" enterprises. And just as so-called tax havens attract foreign investment and immigrants, countries in which the combined marginal impact of taxes and benefits is to punish success and reward indolence often face "capital flight" and a "brain drain."

OECD in Figures (2003) shows total taxes as 45.3 percent of GDP in France, compared with 29.6 percent in the United States. But it would be a mistake to conclude that the higher average tax burden in France is a result of that country's more steeply graduated income tax. French income tax rates claim half of any extra dollar at incomes roughly equivalent to $100,000 in the United States, and exceed the highest U.S. tax rates at even middling income levels. Yet these high individual income taxes account for only 18 percent of revenues in France, about 8.2 percent of GDP, while much lower individual income tax rates in the United States account for 42.4 percent of total tax receipts, or 12.5 percent of GDP. Countries such as France and Sweden do not collect high revenues from high marginal tax rates, but from flat rate taxes on the payrolls and consumer spending of people with low and middle incomes. Revenues are also high relative to GDP partly because private GDP (the tax base) has grown unusually slowly, not because tax revenues have grown particularly fast.

People react to tax incentives for the same reason they react to price incentives. Supply (of effort and investment) and demand (for government transfer payments) respond to marginal incentives. To increase income, people may have to study more, accept added risks and responsibilities, relocate, work late or take work home, tackle the dangers of starting a new business or investing in one, and so on. People earn more by producing more. Because it is easier to earn less than to earn more, marginal incentives matter.

To the extent to which a country's tax system punishes added *income* with high marginal tax rates, it must also punish added *output*—that is, economic growth.

Further Reading

Gokhale, Jagadeesh, Laurence Kotlikoff, and Alexi Sluchynsky. "Does It Pay to Work?" NBER Working Paper no. w9096. National Bureau of Economic Research, Cambridge, Mass., 2002. Online at: http://www.nber.org/papers/w9096.

Karabegovic, Amelia, Niels Veldhuis, Jason Clemens, and Keith Godin. "Do Tax Rates Matter?" *Fraser Forum,* July 2004. Online at: http://www.fraserinstitute.ca/admin/books/chapterfiles/July04ffkarabeg.pdf#.

Lucas, Robert E. Jr. "Supply-Side Economics: An Analytical Review." *Oxford Economic Papers* 42 (April 1990): 293–316. Online at: http://ideas.repec.org/a/oup/oxecpp/v42y1990i2p293-316.html.

Prescott, Edward C. "Why Do Americans Work So Much More than Europeans?" *Federal Reserve Bank of Minneapolis Quarterly Review* (July 2004). Online at: http://minneapolisfed.org/research/qr/qr2811.pdf.

Reynolds, Alan. "Crises and Recoveries: Multinational Failures and National Success." *Cato Journal* 23 (Spring/Summer 2003): 101–113. Online at: http://www.cato.org/pubs/journal/cj23n1/cj23n1-11.pdf.

———. "The Fiscal-Monetary Policy Mix." *Cato Journal* 21 (Fall 2001): 263–275. Online at: http://www.cato.org/pubs/journal/cj21n2/cj21n2-11.pdf.

———. "International Comparisons of Taxes and Government Spending." In Stephen E. Easton and Michael A. Walker, eds., *Rating Global Economic Freedom.* Vancouver: Fraser Institute, 1992. Pp. 361–388. Online at: http://oldfraser.lexi.net/publications/books/rating_econ_free/.

———. "Tax Reform in Lithuania and Around the World." Lithuanian Free Market Institute, no. 6, 1997. Online at: http://www.freema.org/NewsLetter/tax.budget/1997.6.treform.phtml.

———. "Workforce 2005: The Future of Jobs in the United States and Europe." In *OECD Societies in Transition: The Future of Work and Leisure.* Paris: OECD, 1994. Pp. 47–80. Online at: http://www.oecd.org/dataoecd/26/32/17780767.pdf.

Trostel, Philip A. "The Effect of Taxation on Human Capital." *Journal of Political Economy* 101 (1993): 327–350. Online at: http://econpapers.hhs.se/article/ucpjpolec/v_3A101_3Ay_3A1993_3Ai_3A2_3Ap_3A327-50.htm.

Marginalism

Steven E. Rhoads

Adam Smith struggled with what came to be called the paradox of "value in use" versus "value in exchange." Water is necessary to existence and of enormous value in use; diamonds are frivolous and clearly not essential. But the price of diamonds—their value in exchange—is far higher than that of water. What perplexed Smith is now rationally explained in the first chapters of every college freshman's introductory economics text. Smith had failed to distinguish between "total" utility and "marginal" utility. The elaboration of this insight transformed economics in the late nineteenth century, and the fruits of the marginalist revolution continue to set the basic framework for contemporary microeconomics.

The marginalist explanation is as follows: The total utility or satisfaction of water exceeds that of diamonds. We would all rather do without diamonds than without water. But almost all of us would prefer to win a prize of a diamond rather than an additional bucket of water. To make this last choice, we ask ourselves not whether diamonds or water give more satisfaction in total, but whether one more diamond gives greater additional satisfaction than one more bucket of water. For this marginal utility question, our answer will depend on how much of each we already have. Though the first units of water we consume every month are of enormous value to us, the last units are not. The utility of additional (or marginal) units continues to decrease as we consume more and more.

Economists believe that sensible choice requires comparing marginal utilities and marginal costs. They also think that people apply the marginalism concept regularly, even if subconsciously, in their private decisions. In southern states, for example, a much lower fraction of people buy snow shovels than in northern states. The reason is that although snow shovels cost about the same from state to state, the marginal benefit of a snow shovel is much higher in northern states. But in discussions of public-policy issues, where most of the benefits and costs do not accrue to the individual making the policy decision (e.g., subsidies for health care), the appeal of total utility and intrinsic worth as the basis for decision can mask the insights of marginalism.

Even good answers to certain grand questions give little guidance for rational public policy choices. For example, what is more important, health or recreation? If forced to choose, everyone would find health more important than recreation. But marginalism suggests that our real con-

Why Repairmen Earn More Than Child-Care Workers

David R. Henderson

Child-care workers perform important work. The total utility of their work is probably much higher than the total utility of the work performed by workers who repair air conditioners. So why do air-conditioning repairmen earn more than child-care workers? Marginalism has the answer. Suppose there are fewer children and more air conditioners than there used to be. Suppose also that for the same wage there is a surplus of child-care workers and a shortage of people who repair air conditioners. Then the wage cannot be the same. If it were, the only way to get enough air-conditioning repairmen would be to conscript them. So the only peaceful way to get the right number of child-care workers and the right number of air-conditioning workers is to let the market work. This means letting the higher supply of child-care workers drive down their wage and the lower supply of air-conditioning repairmen drive up their wage. Although the total utility of work performed by child-care workers exceeds the total utility of work performed by air-conditioning repairmen, the marginal value of the latter's utility exceeds the marginal value of the former's.

cern should be with proportion, not rank. Finding health in total to be more important than recreation in total does not imply that all diving boards should be removed from swimming pools just because a few people die in diving accidents. We need to compare the number of lives saved from fewer diving accidents, that is, the marginal benefit of getting rid of diving boards, with the pleasure given up by getting rid of diving boards, that is, the marginal cost of getting rid of diving boards. Similarly, we clearly want cleaner air and economic growth. And we want recreational opportunities in natural settings and in developed ones. But how much more? The answer will depend on the marginal value of these things compared with their marginal cost.

One writer argues that early deaths of the young are our greatest life-saving problem, and therefore the health budget should emphasize preventing the largest killers of the young, such as accidents and suicides. But even if one accepts this writer's values, his policy conclusions do not follow. We may not know how to prevent suicides at reasonable cost, but perhaps a medical breakthrough has made possible a low-cost cure for a disease that is the sixth-leading cause of death among the young. We would then save more lives among the young if we devoted more of our resources to their sixth-largest health problem rather than to their first or second. Marginalism thus requires looking at the details—looking at the marginal costs and marginal benefits of particular opportunities.

The marginalist insight also illuminates some weaknesses in the health policy outlook of those who base their position on the idea of medical needs. Because health is an essential need, many think that those with medical complaints should have free and quick access to physicians. When they think of health demand, such people think of serious, medically treatable illness. But from the viewpoint of the consumer, at least, a significant portion of demand for medical care gives very small benefits. These benefits are poorly indicated by thinking about total utility (i.e., how important health is).

In studying a number of small groups, scholars have observed the effects of insurance policy changes on the amount of health care people demanded. A few actual experiments have also been conducted. One required a group of California Medicaid beneficiaries to pay one dollar for their first two office visits each month, while a similar group continued to receive completely free service. This modest charge reduced office visits by 8 percent, and it seems unlikely that those who stopped going to doctors could not afford the one-dollar charge.

Other studies have found that even small changes in time cost can have an effect. For example, when the health facility at one college was moved so that it took twenty minutes rather than five to ten to walk there, student visits fell by nearly 40 percent. Similarly, a 10 percent increase in the travel time to outpatient clinics among a low-income urban group caused an estimated 10 percent decrease in demand for visits to physicians. Whether the health services forgone in these cases were necessary remains an open question, but surely the potential patients did not act as if they had no option other than to obtain care.

Marginalism also leads one to question the old maxim that anything worth doing at all is worth doing well. Nobel laureate James Buchanan suggested that an economist can be distinguished from a noneconomist by his reaction to that statement. Another economist actually polled a group of his fellows to judge their agreement or disagreement with this and four other maxims. "Anything worth doing . . ." was by far the least popular, with 74 percent of respondents disagreeing. A careful weighing of marginal cost implies that we should use well the money we devote to a task, but we should rarely do as much as interested professionals think necessary.

These examples apply marginalism to government expenditures directed at specific policy areas such as health care. The tax side of the budgetary equation also calls for the concept. Marginalism reminds us that when contemplating the effect of tax rates on the incentive to work, we are usually less interested in the average tax rate paid on a family's entire income than in the MARGINAL TAX RATE— the proportion of added (marginal) income that the husband or wife will pay in taxes if either works a little more. Similarly, when considering the effect of a tax cut on savings, it reminds us that we should not look at the percentage of a family's total income that is saved but rather at the percentage of any additional income received (in this case from the tax cut). Though the average national saving rate is less than 5 percent, the long-run marginal saving rate is more than double the 5 percent average rate even at the lowest income levels. In the highest income brackets the long-run marginal saving rate has been estimated to be more than 50 percent.

About the Author

Steven E. Rhoads is a professor of politics at the University of Virginia.

Further Reading

Anderson, Douglas. *Regulating Politics and Electric Utilities.* Boston: Auburn House, 1981. Chap. 4.

Cooper, Michael. "Economics of Need: The Experience of the British Health Service." In Mark Perlman, ed., *The Economics of Health and Medical Care.* New York: Wiley, 1974. Especially pp. 89–99, 105.

Kahn, Alfred. "Applications of Economics to an Imperfect World." *American Economic Review* 69 (1979): 1–13. Especially pp. 1–3.

McKenzie, Richard, and Gordon Tullock. *The New World of Economics.* New York: Irwin, 1981. Chaps. 2, 20.

Rhoads, Steven E. *The Economist's View of the World: Government, Markets and Public Policy.* Cambridge: Cambridge University Press, 1985. Chap. 3.

Market for Corporate Control

Jonathan R. Macey

Markets discipline producers by rewarding them with profits when they create value for consumers and punishing them with losses when they fail to create enough value for consumers. The disciplinarians are the consumers. The market for corporate control is no different in principle. It disciplines the managers of corporations with publicly traded stock to act in the best interests of shareholders. Here the disciplinarians are shareholders.

Firms whose share prices are lower than they could be if managed by more talented or highly motivated managers are attractive takeover targets. By buying up enough shares to vote in a new board of directors, a bidder can then replace an inefficient or ineffectual management team. The bidder profits when the new management team gets results, which come in the form of improved corporate performance, higher profits, and, ultimately, higher share prices.

Takeovers are not the only source of market discipline for companies. In particular, robust competition exists in product markets, labor markets, and capital markets for both debt and equity. Competition in these other markets disciplines managers and owners of all firms, both closely held and privately held. The market for corporate control provides an additional source of market discipline for the managers of publicly held companies.

A robust, properly functioning market for corporate control is vital to the performance of a free-enterprise economy with public corporations. A public corporation is a company whose shares are owned by the public—that is, whose shares are publicly traded. Public corporations are highly efficient and socially desirable for a number of reasons (see CORPORATIONS). Without an effective market for corporate control, however, public corporations are unlikely to perform as well as they would otherwise. Of course, private markets are remarkably flexible and diverse. Economic activity frequently is organized in private, closely held firms as well as in large publicly held companies.

Numerous studies show that shareholders in firms that are the subject of takeovers enjoy significant profits. Gains to target shareholders average 40–50 percent above the prices at which target firms' shares traded immediately prior to the takeover.

The empirical evidence on returns to bidders, however, is more ambiguous. Early studies showed relatively small (3–5 percent) gains, but later studies have shown negligible gains, and some have shown slight losses. There are two reasons for this result. The first has to do with empirical methodology: takeovers are a surprise for the target firm, and so their share prices jump suddenly on the news of a takeover. Bidders, however, often announce their plans to embark on an acquisition strategy months before they locate a suitable target, much less make an acquisition. This means that any increase in the share price of the bidding company from a particular acquisition or series of acquisitions occurs quite gradually, and is therefore hard to measure empirically. Suppose the market initially expected an acquiring firm to gain 25 percent in value from a particular acquisition program, but the firm announces a particular acquisition that promises gains of only 20 percent. The firm's share price will decline as a result, because even though the firm is performing well, it is doing a bit more poorly than expected.

The second explanation for a decline in returns to bidders is regulation. The Williams Act,[1] a federal law enacted in 1968, requires firms and individuals that make public bids for the shares of publicly traded companies (such public bids are called "tender offers") to disclose information about themselves, their sources of financing, and their plans for other companies. This regulation ostensibly was enacted to benefit target-firm shareholders by providing them with what supporters falsely claimed were much-needed disclosures. What was never made clear was why shareholders of target firms should have (or would want, much less pay for) this legal privilege. One unintended, but totally predictable, consequence of the regulations is that they deter valuable bids. Once the acquirer announces the information, other share buyers bid up the price of the target company's shares, giving a gain to the acquirer, who did all the costly research, only on his 5 percent of the shares. The Williams Act therefore acts as a strong disincentive to do the research in the first place.

Unfortunately, bidders cannot avoid the reach of the Williams Act simply by not making a public bid or tender offer. This is because another provision of the statute requires any bidder to make the same disclosures within ten days of acquiring 5 percent of the shares of a public company, regardless of how those shares were acquired.

To understand the importance of the market for corporate control, one must first understand the economics of the public corporation. Public companies can be more efficient at deploying capital than can private (also called closely held) companies, for several reasons. First, public corporations permit accumulations of a large amount of capital without government involvement. When business needs a lot of money to operate, either because there are economies of scale or scope in operation or because the business is highly capital intensive (such as manufacturing), selling shares to the public is often the only—and is generally the most efficient—way to accumulate such capital.

Second, the existence of the public corporation permits the separation of two different economic functions: investment and management. This is efficient because the people who invest often have no expertise, experience, or

inclination to manage the companies in which they invest. Many investors, such as doctors, teachers, lawyers, factory workers, and scientists, fit this description. Similarly, entrepreneurs and managers may be able to employ investors' capital effectively, but they may not have much capital themselves. Specialization, which occurs by separating the investing function from the management function, is therefore often highly efficient.

Finally, the public corporation permits more efficient risk taking in the economy. Public corporations allow for the investment of relatively small amounts of money simultaneously in many corporations, either directly or by investing in mutual funds, which in turn make investments in many companies. Because these investors enjoy the benefits of diversification, they are more willing to invest far more money at far lower expected rates of return than they would be if they had to "put all of their eggs in one basket."

But along with the massive economic and social benefits of public companies come costs. The costs that result from separating the investing and management functions are called "agency costs" because the managers and directors of public companies are the agents of the investor-shareholders. Because these agents are deploying the shareholders' money rather than their own when they manage the corporation, they can benefit themselves by acting in their own interests rather than in the interests of the shareholders.

While antifraud laws can deter managers from outright theft and fraud, it is extremely difficult for shareholders, who are widely dispersed, to detect, much less to prevent, mismanagement. Shareholders face an array of collective-action problems that prevent them from coalescing to deal with bad management. One of these problems is the "rational ignorance" phenomenon: the cost to an individual shareholder to investigate and ferret out wrongdoing in a company is far above the amount he or she stands to gain. Consequently, the shareholder remains "rationally ignorant" of what is going on.

A similar problem plaguing shareholders is the "free rider" problem: while individual shareholders must bear all of the costs of correcting managers' errors themselves, they share the benefits of such corrective action with *all* shareholders. Thus, the free-rider problem leads to less than the optimal amount of monitoring and other corrective action.

The market for corporate control is the only known antidote for all of these collective-action problems.

A market for corporate control emerges when bidders have incentives to monitor the corporate world for companies that are undervalued due to inattentive or inept managers. Bidders have such incentives in a market for

---

[1]. Its author, Harrison Williams, a U.S. senator from New Jersey, later went to prison for taking bribes.

corporate control that is unfettered by regulation because they can profit from such monitoring by buying a controlling interest in the shares of undervalued companies and displacing those managers.

Another important, but often unnoted, feature of the market for corporate control is that its very existence reduces agency costs, the costs associated with the separation of share ownership and management of the corporation that defines the publicly held company. This is the case because no incumbent target management team wants to be ignominiously thrown out of office in a hostile takeover. After all, if the managers did not like their jobs, they could just leave before being removed in a hostile takeover.

Bidders can make mistakes. This is of little concern because bidders' mistakes manifest themselves only in the form of overpayment for shares in target firms. But shareholders in the target firm benefit when this occurs because they have the opportunity to sell their shares at a premium. The only losers when this happens are the bidders themselves and the management of the target firm. But this is a risk people take when they become managers. Moreover, to the extent that such managers own shares in the companies they run, they benefit from the takeover premium just like any other shareholder.

The market for corporate control need not always involve hostile takeovers, although their possibility is critical to a properly functioning market. Firms in financial distress and firms whose managers' interests are closely aligned with shareholders' interests often will welcome friendly acquisitions. These acquisitions generally take the form of mergers in which the board of directors of one company agrees and recommends that its shareholders vote in favor of exchanging their shares to an acquirer, either for cash or for stock in the acquirer.

But no market functions costlessly, and the market for corporate control is no exception. For one thing, bidders, like other capitalists, need financing. The capital markets have been remarkably successful at generating sufficient capital to finance takeovers. For example, in April 2005, the upstart electronic stock exchange Arca/EX was able to engineer the purchase of the venerable New York Stock Exchange, and the over-the-counter market, Nasdaq, Inc., was able to borrow the one billion dollars it needed to acquire the Instinet trading system.

A major financing innovation involves the use of the assets in the target company to secure a loan to acquire the target's own shares. Transactions that involve the use of leverage, or debt, are known as leveraged buyouts, or LBOs.

Other costs associated with the market for corporate control involve the transaction costs of writing the contracts necessary to protect target-firm shareholders from collective-action problems and to align the incentives of target-firm managers and their shareholders. One potential collective-action problem facing target-firm shareholders is the "PRISONERS' DILEMMA" such shareholders face when presented with a bid for less than 100 percent of the shares in their firm. Suppose, for example, that a firm has 101 shares outstanding. The bidder owns 1 share, and the other 100 shares are divided evenly between two shareholders, Abby and Samantha. Abby and Samantha live far apart, do not know each other, and have no easy way to communicate. Suppose that the bidder makes a bid for 50, and only 50, shares of the company's stock at a price of $1.40, which is 40 percent higher than the current $1.00 price. Suppose, further, that the bidder is known to be hard-working, diligent, and honest, and, therefore, that market experts predict the firm's shares to rise to $2.00 per share when the takeover is consummated. Under these facts, the bid might not be successful because Abby and Samantha will each be better off by not selling her shares to the bidder and hoping that the other shareholder will tender her shares. One way to deal with this problem is to permit bidders to disguise their identities and to make their bids on a first-come, first-served basis. Unfortunately, the Williams Act made both of these strategies illegal.

Another, legal, way for bidders to deal with this problem is to make an offer for 100 percent of the shares in the target, and to make their bids contingent on receiving a very high percentage of the target company's shares. This strategy, while effective, is quite costly, but regulation has made other strategies difficult to implement.

Worse, if the bidder is thought to be lazy or inattentive or dishonest, rational target-firm shareholders may rush to sell their shares in what is known as a "coercive tender offer." A sort of coercion is said to occur because shareholders want to avoid winding up as minority shareholders in a firm run by an inept or unscrupulous bidder. The only way they can assure themselves of doing this is by selling their shares. If either Abby or Samantha decides to sell her shares, the other will wind up as a minority shareholder in a poorly run company.

Happily, there are many contractual solutions—called "defensive tactics"—to this collective-action problem, and managers have strong incentives to employ these contractual solutions to protect their shareholders and themselves. In fact, the real problem is not that bidders will "coerce" target firm shareholders into selling; it is that managers will engage in defensive maneuvering even when their shareholders do not want them to in order to entrench themselves in their cushy jobs at the shareholders' expense. This is why investors often criticize defensive tactics.

Some defensive tactics are quite modest and are carefully tailored to deal with the problem of coercive tender offers. "Shark repellant amendments," for example, require shareholders to vote to approve outside acquisitions by large "supermajorities" of, say, 75 percent in order to complete an acquisition. This sort of defense is ineffective at defeating bids for large blocks of shares that are in the shareholders' interest because shareholders are happy to approve such transactions.

A more controversial and potent defense is the shareholder rights plan, popularly known as the "poison pill" defense. Poison pills are rights freely distributed to target-company shareholders that give the shareholders the "right" to purchase shares in the target firm (or the bidding firm in case of a merger) at significant discounts in price when a "triggering event" occurs. A typical triggering event is someone's or some firm's accumulation of voting shares in the target above a specified threshold, such as 15 or 25 percent, without the approval of the target company's board of directors. These rights impose severe economic penalties on the hostile acquirer and usually also dilute the voting power of the acquirer's existing stake in the firm. Poison pills are effective at deterring hostile bidders because when the target-firm shareholders exercise their "rights" under these plans, they severely dilute a bidder's stake in the target. Target-firm shareholders will exercise these rights because they cannot resist the opportunity to buy shares at a huge discount to market, especially since they understand that their fellow shareholders are doing the same thing. Thus, ironically, poison pills place target-firm shareholders in the same sort of coerced, collective-action problem as the partial bids they ostensibly prevent.

Poison pills are a very popular antitakeover device. Most big companies have them, but, at least to some extent, courts police their abuse by target-company boards of directors. In addition, bidders have some strategies for dealing with poison pills: they can make a tender offer contingent on the target-company board nullifying the pill, and they can launch a proxy contest, in which they solicit target shareholders' votes to unseat the incumbent directors of the target company. By replacing the directors of the target, the bidder can take control of the board and nullify the pill itself. Another, increasingly popular way to deal with the pill is for large institutional investors to communicate to management that they disapprove of its use. However, as a policy matter, it would be better if the poison pill did not apply to all-cash bids for 100 percent of the stock in the target company because shareholders do not need poison pills to protect themselves from this type of bid.

Thus, the biggest problem with the takeover market is not the poison pill; it is the state and federal laws that impede takeovers. Delaware's antitakeover law is particularly important because most large public companies are incorporated in Delaware, and thus are subject to Delaware law. The Delaware statute prohibits a hostile acquirer from completing a takeover by merging with the target for at least three years after buying a controlling interest unless the bidder either obtains the approval of the target company's board of directors or acquires more than 85 percent of the target's stock.

Like other markets, the market for corporate control has its critics. The main criticism is that this market focuses too much attention on shareholders and not enough attention on other "constituencies" of the public corporation, such as workers and local communities. These arguments are weak for several reasons.

First, antitakeover laws are a bad way to protect these other constituencies because any protections such statutes provide create large inefficiencies by reducing the quantity and quality of the monitoring of public companies' management. Second, antitakeover statutes do not help workers or local communities or any other nonshareholder constituency; they simply entrench target-company management. Third, the empirical evidence shows that, by improving efficiency, takeovers help rather than hurt workers and local communities by promoting employment and increasing societal wealth.

Finally, no contractual agreement gave these "constituencies" any say in the takeover decision. For them to get that power, they would have to give something up, whether in wages or in other forms. The fact that they did not negotiate that power suggests that they did not value it enough to do so. In fact, those who claim to speak for them have no basis for their claim. Of course, many constituencies would want a say after all the contractual terms are negotiated. But this is no different in principle from the fact that people often want unilateral changes in contracts after the contracts have been agreed to. That does not mean they are entitled to them.

The other major criticism is that the market for corporate control causes managers and boards of public companies to focus on short-term share price performance rather than on long-term projects. This criticism is illogical. Share prices reflect the present value of future returns to shareholders and are, therefore, a measure of the long run. Successful corporate strategies, even those that are not expected to produce positive returns for years, will generate immediate increases in share prices. There is little doubt that if a major pharmaceutical company cut its research and development (R&D) budget to zero, its earnings would rise but its share price would fall. Economists have tested this theory empirically by looking at what happens to corporate expenditures on R&D after takeovers occur. If the short-run story applies, one would expect R&D to fall after a takeover. In fact, the opposite is true. Those who take over companies are usually in it for the long haul.

The market for corporate control is a critical component of a free market. Takeovers vastly improve the efficiency of public companies by providing monitoring and discipline for management and by aligning managers' incentives with those of outside investors. Regulation, often implemented at the behest of entrenched managers who want to be insulated from this market, provides no benefits to shareholders, who easily can protect themselves via contract. Such regulation impedes the market for corporate control, robs shareholders of wealth, and reduces the efficiency of private enterprise.

About the Author

Jonathan Macey is Sam Harris Professor of Corporate Law, Corporate Finance and Securities Regulation at Yale Law School.

Further Reading

Bebchuk, Lucian. "The Case Against Board Veto in Corporate Takeovers." *University of Chicago Law Review* 69 (2002): 973.

Easterbrook, Frank H., and Daniel R. Fischel. *The Economic Structure of Corporate Law.* Cambridge: Harvard University Press, 1991. This is the most comprehensive application of the "contractual" understanding of corporations and other business organizations available. It includes chapters on the corporation as a nexus of contracts, limited liability, shareholder voting, fiduciary duties, corporate control transactions, the appraisal remedy, tender offers, antitakeover statutes, close corporations, insider trading, mandatory disclosure under the securities law, and securities litigation.

———. "The Proper Role of a Target's Management in Responding to a Tender Offer." *Harvard Law Review* 94 (1981): 1161.

Jarrell, Gregg A., James Brickley, and Jeffry Netter. "The Market for Corporate Control: The Empirical Evidence Since 1980." *Journal of Economic Perspectives* 2, no. 1 (1988): 49–68.

Jensen, Michael, and Richard Ruback. "The Market for Corporate Control: The Scientific Evidence." *Journal of Financial Economics* 11 (March 1983): 5–50.

Macey, Jonathan R. "Auction Theory, MBOs and Property Rights in Corporate Assets." *Wake Forest Law Review* 25 (1990): 85.

Macey, Jonathan R., and Fred S. McChesney. "A Theoretical Analysis of Corporate Greenmail." *Yale Law Journal* 95 (1985): 113.

Manne, Henry G. "Mergers and the Market for Corporate Control." *Journal of Political Economy* 73 (1965): 110.

Romano, Roberta A. "Guide to Takeovers: Theory, Evidence, and Regulation." *Yale Journal on Regulation* 9 (1992): 119. Surveys the huge literature on mergers and acquisitions. Since "the empirical evidence is most consistent with value-maximizing, efficiency-based explanations of takeovers," Professor Romano argues that "much of the takeover regulatory apparatus [which seeks to 'thwart and burden takeovers'] is misconceived and poor public policy."

Rosett, Joshua G. "Do Union Wealth Concessions Explain Takeover Premiums? The Evidence on Contract Wages." *Journal of Financial Economics* 27 (1990): 263–282.

Marxism

David L. Prychitko

More than a century after his death, Karl Marx remains one of the most controversial figures in the Western world. His relentless criticism of capitalism and his corresponding promise of an inevitable, harmonious socialist future inspired a revolution of global proportions. It seemed that—with the Bolshevik revolution in Russia and the spread of communism throughout Eastern Europe—the Marxist dream had firmly taken root during the first half of the twentieth century.

That dream collapsed before the century had ended. The people of Poland, Hungary, Czechoslovakia, East Germany, Romania, Yugoslavia, Bulgaria, Albania, and the USSR rejected Marxist ideology and entered a remarkable transition toward private property rights and the market-exchange system, one that is still occurring. Which aspects of Marxism created such a powerful revolutionary force? And what explains its eventual demise? The answers lie in some general characteristics of Marxism—its economics, social theory, and overall vision.

Labor Theory of Value

The labor theory of value is a major pillar of traditional Marxian economics, which is evident in Marx's masterpiece, *Capital* (1867). The theory's basic claim is simple: the value of a commodity can be objectively measured by the average number of labor hours required to produce that commodity.

If a pair of shoes usually takes twice as long to produce as a pair of pants, for example, then shoes are twice as valuable as pants. In the long run, the competitive price of shoes will be twice the price of pants, *regardless of the value of the physical inputs.*

Although the labor theory of value is demonstrably false,

it prevailed among classical economists through the mid-nineteenth century. Adam Smith, for instance, flirted with a labor theory of value in his classic defense of capitalism, *The Wealth of Nations* (1776), and David Ricardo later systematized it in his *Principles of Political Economy* (1817), a text studied by generations of free-market economists.

So the labor theory of value was not unique to Marxism. Marx did attempt, however, to turn the theory against the champions of capitalism, pushing the theory in a direction that most classical economists hesitated to follow. Marx argued that the theory could explain the value of all commodities, including the commodity that workers sell to capitalists for a wage. Marx called this commodity "labor power."

Labor power is the worker's capacity to produce goods and services. Marx, using principles of classical economics, explained that the value of labor power must depend on the number of labor hours it takes society, on average, to feed, clothe, and shelter a worker so that he or she has the capacity to work. In other words, the long-run wage workers receive will depend on the number of labor hours it takes to produce a person who is fit for work. Suppose five hours of labor are needed to feed, clothe, and protect a worker each day so that the worker is fit for work the following morning. If one labor hour equaled one dollar, the correct wage would be five dollars per day.

Marx then asked an apparently devastating question: if all goods and services in a capitalist society tend to be sold at prices (and wages) that reflect their true value (measured by labor hours), how can it be that capitalists enjoy profits—even if only in the short run? How do capitalists manage to squeeze out a residual between total revenue and total costs?

Capitalists, Marx answered, must enjoy a privileged and powerful position as owners of the means of production and are therefore able to ruthlessly exploit workers. Although the capitalist pays workers the correct wage, somehow—Marx was terribly vague here—the capitalist makes workers work more hours than are needed to create the worker's labor power. If the capitalist pays each worker five dollars per day, he can require workers to work, say, twelve hours per day—a not uncommon workday during Marx's time. Hence, if one labor hour equals one dollar, workers produce twelve dollars' worth of products for the capitalist but are paid only five. The bottom line: capitalists extract "surplus value" from the workers and enjoy monetary profits.

Although Marx tried to use the labor theory of value against capitalism by stretching it to its limits, he unintentionally demonstrated the weakness of the theory's logic and underlying assumptions. Marx was correct when he claimed that classical economists failed to adequately explain capitalist profits. But Marx failed as well. By the late nineteenth century, the economics profession rejected the labor theory of value. Mainstream economists now believe that capitalists do not earn profits by exploiting workers (see PROFITS). Instead, they believe, entrepreneurial capitalists earn profits by forgoing current consumption, by taking risks, and by organizing production.

Alienation

There is more to Marxism, however, than the labor theory of value and Marx's criticism of profit seeking. Marx wove economics and philosophy together to construct a grand theory of human history and social change. His concept of alienation, for example, first articulated in his *Economic and Philosophic Manuscripts of 1844*, plays a key role in his criticism of capitalism.

Marx believed that people, by nature, are free, creative beings who have the potential to totally transform the world. But he observed that the modern, technologically developed world is apparently beyond our full control. Marx condemned the free market, for instance, as being "anarchic," or ungoverned. He maintained that the way the market economy is coordinated—through the spontaneous purchase and sale of private property dictated by the laws of supply and demand—blocks our ability to take control of our individual and collective destinies.

Marx condemned capitalism as a system that alienates the masses. His reasoning was as follows: although workers produce things for the market, market forces, not workers, control things. People are required to work for capitalists who have full control over the means of production and maintain power in the workplace. Work, he said, becomes degrading, monotonous, and suitable for machines rather than for free, creative people. In the end, people themselves become objects—robotlike mechanisms that have lost touch with human nature, that make decisions based on cold profit-and-loss considerations, with little concern for human worth and need. Marx concluded that capitalism blocks our capacity to create our own humane society.

Marx's notion of alienation rests on a crucial but shaky assumption. It assumes that people can successfully abolish an advanced, market-based society and replace it with a democratic, comprehensively planned society. Marx claimed that we are alienated not only because many of us toil in tedious, perhaps even degrading, jobs, or because by competing in the marketplace we tend to place profitability above human need. The issue is not about toil versus happiness. We are alienated, he maintained, because we have not yet designed a society that is fully planned and controlled, a society without competition, profits and losses, money, private property, and so on—a society that, Marx predicted, must inevitably appear as the world advances through history.

Here is the greatest problem with Marx's theory of alienation: even with the latest developments in computer technology, we cannot create a comprehensively planned system that puts an end to scarcity and uncertainty. But for Marxists to speak of alienation under capitalism, they must *assume* that a successfully planned world is possible. That is, Marx believed that under capitalism we are "alienated" or "separated" from our potential to creatively plan and control our collective fate. But if comprehensive socialist planning fails to work in practice—if, indeed, it is an impossibility, as we have learned from Mises and Hayek—then we cannot be "alienated" in Marx's use of the term. We cannot really be "separated" from our "potential" to comprehensively plan the economy if comprehensive planning is impossible.

Scientific Socialism

A staunch antiutopian, Marx claimed that his criticism of capitalism was based on the latest developments in science. He called his theory "scientific socialism" to clearly distinguish his approach from that of other socialists (Henri de Saint-Simon and Charles Fourier, for instance), who seemed more content to dream about some future ideal society without comprehending how existing society really worked.

Marx's scientific socialism combined his economics and philosophy—including his theory of value and the concept of alienation—to demonstrate that throughout the course of human history, a profound struggle has developed between the "haves" and the "have-nots." Specifically, Marx claimed that capitalism has ruptured into a war between two classes: the bourgeoisie (the capitalist class that owns the means of production) and the proletariat (the working class, which is at the mercy of the capitalists). Marx claimed that he had discovered the laws of history, laws that expose the contradictions of capitalism and the necessity of the class struggle.

Marx predicted that competition among capitalists would grow so fierce that, eventually, most capitalists would go bankrupt, leaving only a handful of monopolists controlling nearly all production. This, to Marx, was one of the contradictions of capitalism: competition, instead of creating better products at lower prices for consumers, in the long run creates monopoly, which exploits workers and consumers alike. What happens to the former capitalists? They fall into the ranks of the proletariat, creating a greater supply of labor, a fall in wages, and what Marx called a

growing reserve army of the unemployed. Also, thought Marx, the anarchic, unplanned nature of a complex market economy is prone to economic crises as supplies and demands become mismatched, causing huge swings in business activity and, ultimately, severe economic depressions.

The more advanced the capitalist economy becomes, Marx argued, the greater these contradictions and conflicts. The more capitalism creates wealth, the more it sows the seeds of its own destruction. Ultimately, the proletariat will realize that it has the collective power to overthrow the few remaining capitalists and, with them, the whole system.

The entire capitalist system—with its private property, money, market exchange, profit-and-loss accounting, labor markets, and so on—must be abolished, thought Marx, and replaced with a fully planned, self-managed economic system that brings a complete and utter end to exploitation and alienation. A socialist revolution, argued Marx, is inevitable.

An Appraisal

Marx was surely a profound thinker who won legions of supporters around the world. But his predictions have not withstood the test of time. Although capitalist markets have changed over the past 150 years, competition has not devolved into monopoly. Real wages have risen and profit rates have not declined. Nor has a reserve army of the unemployed developed. We do have bouts with the business cycle, but more and more economists believe that significant recessions and depressions may be more the unintended result of state intervention (through monetary policy carried out by central banks and government policies on taxation and spending) than an inherent feature of markets as such.

Socialist revolutions, to be sure, have occurred throughout the world, but never where Marx's theory had predicted—in the most advanced capitalist countries. On the contrary, socialism was forced on poor, so-called Third World countries. And those revolutions unwittingly condemned the masses to systemic poverty and political dictatorship. In practice, socialism absolutely failed to create the nonalienated, self-managed, and fully planned society. It failed to emancipate the masses and instead crushed them with statism, domination, and the terrifying abuse of state power.

Nations that have allowed for private property rights and full-blown market exchange, in contrast to those "democratic socialist republics" of the twentieth century, *have* enjoyed remarkable levels of long-term economic growth. Free-market economies lift the masses from poverty and create the necessary institutional conditions for overall political freedom.

Marx just didn't get it. Nor did his followers. Marx's theory of value, his philosophy of human nature, and his claims to have uncovered the laws of history fit together to offer a complex and grand vision of a new world order. If the first three-quarters of the twentieth century provided a testing ground for that vision, the end of the century demonstrates its truly utopian nature and ultimate unworkability.

In the wake of communism's collapse, traditional Marxism, which so many mainstream economists criticized relentlessly for decades, is now seriously questioned by a growing number of disillusioned radicals and former Marxists. Today there is a vibrant post-Marxism, associated with the efforts of those active in the scholarly journal *Rethinking Marxism,* for instance. Rather than trying to solve esoteric puzzles about the labor theory of value or offering new theoretical models of a planned economy, many of today's sharpest post-Marxists appreciate marginal analysis and the knowledge and incentive problems of collective action. In this new literature, FRIEDRICH HAYEK seems to be getting a more positive reception than Marx himself. Exactly what will come out of these developments is hard to predict, but it is unlikely to look like the Marxism of the past.

About the Author

David L. Prychitko is an economics professor at Northern Michigan University.

Further Reading

Boettke, Peter J. *The Political Economy of Soviet Socialism: The Formative Years, 1918–1928.* Boston: Kluwer, 1990.

Böhm-Bawerk, Eugen von. *Karl Marx and the Close of His System.* 1896. Reprint. Clifton, N.J.: Augustus M. Kelley, 1975.

Burczak, Theodore. *Socialism After Hayek.* Ann Arbor: University of Michigan Press, 2006.

Elliot, John E., ed. *Marx and Engels on Economics, Politics, and Society: Essential Readings with Editorial Commentary.* Santa Monica, Calif.: Goodyear, 1981.

Hayek, Friedrich A. *The Fatal Conceit: The Errors of Socialism.* Edited by W. W. Bartley III. Chicago: University of Chicago Press, 1988.

Kolakowski, Leszek. *Main Currents of Marxism.* 3 vols. New York: Oxford University Press, 1985.

Prychitko, David L. *Markets, Planning, and Democracy: Essays After the Collapse of Communism.* Northampton, Mass.: Edward Elgar, 2002.

———. *Marxism and Workers' Self-Management: The Essential Tension.* Westport, Conn.: Greenwood Press, 1991.

Mercantilism

Laura LaHaye

Mercantilism is economic nationalism for the purpose of building a wealthy and powerful state. Adam Smith coined the term "mercantile system" to describe the system of political economy that sought to enrich the country by restraining imports and encouraging exports. This system dominated Western European economic thought and policies from the sixteenth to the late eighteenth centuries. The goal of these policies was, supposedly, to achieve a "favorable" balance of trade that would bring gold and silver into the country and also to maintain domestic employment. In contrast to the agricultural system of the physiocrats or the laissez-faire of the nineteenth and early twentieth centuries, the mercantile system served the interests of merchants and producers such as the British East India Company, whose activities were protected or encouraged by the state.

The most important economic rationale for mercantilism in the sixteenth century was the consolidation of the regional power centers of the feudal era by large, competitive nation-states. Other contributing factors were the establishment of colonies outside Europe; the growth of European commerce and industry relative to agriculture; the increase in the volume and breadth of trade; and the increase in the use of metallic monetary systems, particularly gold and silver, relative to barter transactions.

During the mercantilist period, military conflict between nation-states was both more frequent and more extensive than at any other time in history. The armies and navies of the main protagonists were no longer temporary forces raised to address a specific threat or objective, but were full-time professional forces. Each government's primary economic objective was to command a sufficient quantity of hard currency to support a military that would deter attacks by other countries and aid its own territorial expansion.

Most of the mercantilist policies were the outgrowth of the relationship between the governments of the nation-states and their mercantile classes. In exchange for paying levies and taxes to support the armies of the nation-states, the mercantile classes induced governments to enact policies that would protect their business interests against foreign competition.

These policies took many forms. Domestically, governments would provide capital to new industries, exempt new industries from guild rules and taxes, establish monopolies over local and colonial markets, and grant titles and pensions to successful producers. In trade policy the government assisted local industry by imposing tariffs, quotas, and prohibitions on imports of goods that competed with local manufacturers. Governments also prohibited the export of tools and capital equipment and the emigration of skilled labor that would allow foreign countries, and even the colonies of the home country, to compete in the production of manufactured goods. At the same time, diplomats encouraged foreign manufacturers to move to the diplomats' own countries.

Shipping was particularly important during the mercantile period. With the growth of colonies and the shipment of gold from the New World into Spain and Portugal, control of the oceans was considered vital to national power. Because ships could be used for merchant or military purposes, the governments of the era developed strong merchant marines. In France, Jean-Baptiste Colbert, the minister of finance under Louis XIV from 1661 to 1683, increased port duties on foreign vessels entering French ports and provided bounties to French shipbuilders.

In England, the Navigation Act of 1651 prohibited foreign vessels from engaging in coastal trade in England and required that all goods imported from the continent of Europe be carried on either an English vessel or a vessel registered in the country of origin of the goods. Finally, all trade between England and its colonies had to be carried in either English or colonial vessels. The Staple Act of 1663 extended the Navigation Act by requiring that all colonial exports to Europe be landed through an English port before being re-exported to Europe. Navigation policies by France, England, and other powers were directed primarily against the Dutch, who dominated commercial marine activity in the sixteenth and seventeenth centuries.

During the mercantilist era it was often suggested, if not actually believed, that the principal benefit of foreign trade was the importation of gold and silver. According to this view the benefits to one nation were matched by costs to the other nations that exported gold and silver, and there were no net gains from trade. For nations almost constantly on the verge of war, draining one another of valuable gold and silver was thought to be almost as desirable as the direct benefits of trade. Adam Smith refuted the idea that the wealth of a nation is measured by the size of the treasury in his famous treatise *The Wealth of Nations,* a book considered to be the foundation of modern economic theory. Smith made a number of important criticisms of mercantilist doctrine. First, he demonstrated that trade, when freely initiated, benefits both parties. Second, he argued that specialization in production allows for economies of scale, which improves efficiency and growth. Finally, Smith argued that the collusive relationship between government and industry was harmful to the gen-

eral population. While the mercantilist policies were designed to benefit the government and the commercial class, the doctrines of laissez-faire, or free markets, which originated with Smith, interpreted economic welfare in a far wider sense of encompassing the entire population.

While the publication of *The Wealth of Nations* is generally considered to mark the end of the mercantilist era, the laissez-faire doctrines of free-market economics also reflect a general disenchantment with the imperialist policies of nation-states. The Napoleonic Wars in Europe and the Revolutionary War in the United States heralded the end of the period of military confrontation in Europe and the mercantilist policies that supported it.

Despite these policies and the wars with which they were associated, the mercantilist period was one of generally rapid growth, particularly in England. This is partly because the governments were not very effective at enforcing the policies they espoused. While the government could prohibit imports, for example, it lacked the resources to stop the smuggling that the prohibition would create. In addition, the variety of new products that were created during the industrial revolution made it difficult to enforce the industrial policies that were associated with mercantilist doctrine.

By 1860 England had removed the last vestiges of the mercantile era. Industrial regulations, monopolies, and tariffs were abolished, and emigration and machinery exports were freed. In large part because of its free trade policies, England became the dominant economic power in Europe. England's success as a manufacturing and financial power, coupled with the United States as an emerging agricultural powerhouse, led to the resumption of protectionist pressures in Europe and the arms race between Germany, France, and England that ultimately resulted in World War I.

Protectionism remained important in the interwar period. World War I had destroyed the international monetary system based on the gold standard. After the war, manipulation of the exchange rate was added to governments' lists of trade weapons. A country could simultaneously lower the international prices of its exports and increase the local currency price of its imports by devaluing its currency against the currencies of its trading partners. This "competitive devaluation" was practiced by many countries during the Great Depression of the 1930s and led to a sharp reduction in world trade.

A number of factors led to the reemergence of mercantilist policies after World War II. The Great Depression created doubts about the efficacy and stability of free-market economies, and an emerging body of economic thought ranging from Keynesian countercyclical policies to Marxist centrally planned systems created a new role for governments in the control of economic affairs. In addition, the wartime partnership between government and industry in the United States created a relationship—the military-industrial complex, in Dwight D. Eisenhower's words—that also encouraged activist government policies. In Europe, the shortage of dollars after the war induced governments to restrict imports and negotiate bilateral trading agreements to economize on scarce foreign exchange resources. These policies severely restricted the volume of intra-Europe trade and impeded the recovery process in Europe in the immediate postwar period.

The economic strength of the United States, however, provided the stability that permitted the world to emerge from the postwar chaos into a new era of prosperity and growth. The Marshall Plan provided American resources that overcame the most acute dollar shortages. The Bretton Woods agreement established a new system of relatively stable exchange rates that encouraged the free flow of goods and capital. Finally, the signing of the GATT (General Agreement on Tariffs and Trade) in 1947 marked the official recognition of the need to establish an international order of multilateral free trade.

The mercantilist era has passed. Modern economists accept Adam Smith's insight that free trade leads to international specialization of labor and, usually, to greater economic well-being for all nations. But some mercantilist policies continue to exist. Indeed, the surge of protectionist sentiment that began with the oil crisis in the mid-1970s and expanded with the global recession of the early 1980s has led some economists to label the modern pro-export, anti-import attitude "neomercantilism." Since the GATT went into effect in 1948, eight rounds of multilateral trade negotiations have resulted in a significant liberalization of trade in manufactured goods, the signing of the General Agreement on Trade in Services (GATS) in 1994, and the establishment of the World Trade Organization (WTO) to enforce the agreed-on rules of international trade. Yet numerous exceptions exist, giving rise to discriminatory anti-dumping actions, countervailing duties, and emergency safeguard measures when imports suddenly threaten to disrupt or "unfairly" compete with a domestic industry. Agricultural trade is still heavily protected by quotas, subsidies, and tariffs, and is a key topic on the agenda of the ninth (Doha) round of negotiations. And cabotage laws, such as the U.S. Jones Act, enacted in 1920 and successfully defended against liberalizing reform in the 1990s, are the modern counterpart of England's Navigation Laws. The Jones Act requires all ships carrying cargo between U.S. ports to be U.S. built, owned, and documented.

Modern mercantilist practices arise from the same source as the mercantilist policies of the sixteenth through eighteenth centuries. Groups with political power use that power to secure government intervention to protect their interests while claiming to seek benefits for the nation as a whole. In their recent interpretation of historical mercantilism, Robert B. Ekelund and Robert D. Tollison (1997) focused on the privilege-seeking activities of monarchs and merchants. The mercantile regulations protected the privileged positions of monopolists and cartels, which in turn provided revenue to the monarch or state. According to this interpretation, the reason England was so prosperous during the mercantilist era was that mercantilism was not well enforced. Parliament and the common-law judges competed with the monarchy and royal courts to share in the monopoly or cartel profits created by mercantilist restrictions on trade. This made it less worthwhile to seek, and to enforce, mercantilist restrictions. Greater monarchical power and uncertain property rights in France and Spain, by contrast, were accompanied by slower growth and even stagnation during this period. And the various cabotage laws can be understood as an efficient tool to police the trading cartels. By this view, the establishment of the WTO will have a liberalizing effect if it succeeds in raising the costs or reducing the benefits of those seeking mercantilist profits through trade restrictions.

Of the false tenets of mercantilism that remain today, the most pernicious is the idea that imports reduce domestic employment. Labor unions have used this argument to justify protection from imports originating in low-wage countries, and there has been much political and media debate about the implications of offshoring of service sector jobs for national employment. Many opponents have claimed that offshoring of services puts U.S. jobs at risk. While it does threaten some U.S. jobs, it puts no jobs at risk in the aggregate, however, but simply causes a reallocation of jobs among industries. Another mercantilist view that persists today is that a current account deficit is bad. When a country runs a current account deficit, it is either borrowing from or selling assets to the rest of the world to finance expenditure on imports in excess of export revenue. However, even when this results in an increase of net foreign indebtedness, and associated future debt-servicing requirements, it will promote economic wealth if the spending is for productive purposes that yield a greater return than is forgone on the assets exchanged to finance the spending. Many developing countries with high rates of return on capital have run current account deficits for extremely long periods while enjoying rapid growth and solvency. The United States was one of these for a large part of the nineteenth century, borrowing from English investors to build railroads (see INTERNATIONAL

CAPITAL FLOWS). Furthermore, persistent surpluses may primarily reflect a lack of viable investment opportunities at home or a growing demand for money in a rapidly developing country, and not a "mercantile" accumulation of international reserves at the expense of the trading partners.

About the Author

Laura LaHaye is an adjunct professor at the Illinois Institute of Technology. She was a visiting scholar from 2004 to 2005 at the University of Illinois in Chicago and an economics professor there from 1981 to 1990. In 1981, she was a research economist with the General Agreement on Tariffs and Trade.

Further Reading

Allen, William R. "Mercantilism." In John Eatwell, Murray Milgate, and Peter Newman, eds., *The New Palgrave: A Dictionary of Economics*. Vol. 3. London: Macmillan, 1987. Pp. 445–448.

Ekelund, Robert B. Jr., and Robert D. Tollison. *Politicized Economies: Monarchy, Monopoly and Mercantilism*. College Station: Texas A&M University Press, 1997.

Heckscher, Eli. *Mercantilism*. 2 vols. London: Allen and Unwin, 1934.

Magnusson, Lars. *Mercantilism: The Shaping of an Economic Language*. London: Routledge, 1994.

Salvatore, Dominick, ed. *The New Protectionist Threat to World Welfare*. New York: North-Holland, 1987.

Smith, Adam. *The Wealth of Nations*. Edwin Cannan edition. 1937.

Viner, Jacob. *Studies in the Theory of International Trade*. New York: Harper and Brothers, 1937.

Microeconomics

Arnold C. Harberger

Until the so-called Keynesian revolution of the late 1930s and 1940s, the two main parts of economic theory were typically labeled "monetary theory" and "price theory." Today, the corresponding dichotomy is between "macroeconomics" and "microeconomics." The motivating force for the change came from the macro side, with modern macroeconomics being far more explicit than old-fashioned monetary theory about fluctuations in income and employment (as well as the price level). In contrast, no revolution separates today's microeconomics from old-fashioned price theory; one evolved from the other naturally and without significant controversy.

The strength of microeconomics comes from the simplicity of its underlying structure and its close touch with the real world. In a nutshell, microeconomics has to do with supply and demand, and with the way they interact in various markets. Microeconomic analysis moves easily and painlessly from one topic to another and lies at the center of most of the recognized subfields of economics. Labor economics, for example, is built largely on the analysis of the supply and demand for labor of different types. The field of industrial organization deals with the different mechanisms (monopoly, cartels, different types of competitive behavior) by which goods and services are sold. International economics worries about the demand and supply of individual traded commodities, as well as of a country's exports and imports taken as a whole, and the consequent demand for and supply of foreign exchange. Agricultural economics deals with the demand and supply of agricultural products and of farmland, farm labor, and the other factors of production involved in agriculture.

Public finance looks at how the government enters the scene. Traditionally, its focus was on taxes, which automatically introduce "wedges" (differences between the price the buyer pays and the price the seller receives) and cause inefficiency. More recently, public finance has reached into the expenditure side as well, attempting to analyze (and sometimes actually to measure) the costs and benefits of various government outlays and programs.

Applied welfare economics is the fruition of microeconomics. It deals with the costs and benefits of just about anything—government projects, taxes on commodities, taxes on factors of production (corporation income taxes, payroll taxes), agricultural programs (like price supports and acreage controls), tariffs on imports, foreign exchange controls, various forms of industrial organization (like monopoly and oligopoly), and various aspects of labor market behavior (like minimum wages, the monopoly power of labor unions, and so on).

It is hard to imagine a basic course in microeconomics failing to include numerous cases and examples drawn from all of the fields listed above. This is because microeconomics is so basic. It represents the trunk of the tree from which all the listed subfields have branched.

At the root of everything is supply and demand. It is not at all farfetched to think of these as basically human characteristics. If human beings are not going to be totally self-sufficient, they will end up producing certain things that they trade in order to fulfill their demands for other things. The specialization of production and the institutions of trade, commerce, and markets long antedated the science of economics. Indeed, one can fairly say that from the very outset the science of economics entailed the study of the market forms that arose quite naturally (and without any help from economists) out of human behavior. People specialize in what they think they can do best—or more existentially, in what heredity, environment, fate, and their own volition have brought them to do. They trade their services and/or the products of their specialization for those produced by others. Markets evolve to organize this sort of trading, and money evolves to act as a generalized unit of account and to make barter unnecessary.

In this market process, people try to get the most from what they have to sell, and to satisfy their desires as much as possible. In microeconomics this is translated into the notion of people maximizing their personal "utility," or welfare. This process helps them to decide what they will supply and what they will demand.

When hybrid corn first appeared in the United States, it was in experiment stations, not on ordinary farms. But over a period of decades it became the product of choice of hundreds of thousands of farmers. At the beginning of the process, those who adopted the new hybrids made handsome profits. By the time the transition was complete, any farmer who clung stubbornly to the old nonhybrid seed was likely to be driven out of business, leaving only farmers who acted as if they were profit maximizing; the ones who did not had failed. By a very similar process new varieties of wheat spread through the Punjab and other parts of India in the 1960s, and new varieties of rice through the Philippines and the rest of East Asia. What economists call "maximizing behavior" explains the real-world behavior of these millions of farmers, whose actions increased the supply of corn, wheat, and rice, making much more of these products available to the consumers of the world at lower prices.

Similar scenarios reveal how maximizing behavior works on the demand side. Today's textiles include vast amounts of artificial fibers, nearly all of them unknown a century ago. They conquered markets for themselves, at the expense of the older natural fibers, because consumers perceived them to be either better or cheaper, or both. In the end, when old products end up on the ash heap of history, it is usually because consumers have found new products that they greatly prefer to the old ones.

The economics of supply and demand has a sort of moral or normative overtone, at least when it comes to dealing with a wide range of market distortions. In an undistorted market, buyers pay the market price up to the point where they judge further units not to be worth that price, while competitive sellers supply added units as long as they can make money on each increment. At the point where supply just equals demand in an undistorted market, the price measures both the worth of the product to buyers and the worth of the product to sellers.

That is not so when an artificial distortion intervenes. With a 50 percent tax based on selling price, an item that costs $1.50 to the buyer is worth only $1.00 to the seller.

The tax creates a wedge, mentioned earlier, between the value to the buyer and the return to the seller. The anomaly thus created could be eliminated if the distortion were removed; then the market would find its equilibrium at some price in between (say, $1.20) where the product's worth would be the same to buyers and to sellers. Whenever we start with a distortion, we can usually assert that society as a whole can benefit from its removal. This is epitomized by the fact that buyers gain as they get extra units at less than $1.50, while sellers gain as they get to sell extra units at more than $1.00.

Many different distortions can create similar anomalies. If cotton is subsidized, the price farmers get will exceed, by the amount of the subsidy, the value to consumers. Society thus stands to gain by eliminating the subsidy and moving to a price that is the same for both buyers and sellers. If price controls keep bread (or anything else) artificially cheap, the predictable result is that less will be supplied than is demanded. Nine times out of ten, the excess demand will end up being reflected in a gray or black market, whose existence is probably the clearest evidence that the official price is artificially low. In turn, economists are nearly always right when they predict that pushing prices down via price controls will end up reducing the amount supplied and generating black-market prices not only well above the official price, but also above the market price that would prevail in the absence of controls.

Official prices that are too high also produce curious results. In the 1930s the U.S. government adopted so-called parity prices for the major grains and a few other farm products. Basically, if the market price was below the parity price, the government would pay farmers the difference or buy any unsold crops at the parity price. The predictable result was production in excess of the amount demanded—leading to surpluses that were bought up (and stored) by the government. Then, in an effort to eliminate the purchase of surpluses (but without reducing the parity price), the government instituted acreage controls under which it paid farmers to take land out of production. Some people were surprised to see that a 20 percent cut in wheat acreage did not lead to a 20 percent fall in the production of wheat. The reason was that other factors of production could be (and were) used more intensively, with the result that in order to get a 20 percent cut in wheat, acreage "had to" be cut by 30–40 percent.

Economists have a better solution. Had the government given wheat farmers coupons, each of which permitted the farmer to market one bushel of wheat, wheat marketings could have been cut by the desired amount. Production inefficiencies could be avoided by allowing the farmers to buy and sell coupons among themselves. Low-cost farmers would buy coupons from high-cost farmers, thus ensuring efficient production. This is known as a "second-best" solution to a policy problem. It is second rather than first best because consumers would still be paying the artificially high parity price for wheat.

MONOPOLY represents the artificial restriction of production by an entity having sufficient "market power" to do so. The economics of monopoly are most easily seen by thinking of a "monopoly markup" as a privately imposed, privately collected tax. This was, in fact, a reality a few centuries ago when feudal rulers sometimes endowed their favorites with monopoly rights over certain products. The recipients need not ever "produce" such products themselves. They could contract with other firms to produce the good at low prices and then charge consumers what the traffic would bear (so as to maximize monopoly profit). The difference between these two prices is the "monopoly markup," which functions like a tax. In this example it is clear that the true beneficiary of monopoly power is the one who exercises it; both producers and consumers end up losing.

Modern monopolies are a bit less transparent, for two reasons. First, even though governments still grant monopolies, they usually grant them to the producers. Second, some monopolies just happen without government creating them, although these are usually short-lived. Either way, the proceeds of the monopoly markup (or tax) are commingled with the return to capital of the monopoly firms. Similarly, labor monopoly is usually exercised by unions, which are able to charge a monopoly markup (or tax), which then becomes commingled with the wages of their members. The true effect of labor monopoly on the competitive wage is seen by looking at the nonunion segment of the economy. Here, wages end up lower because the union wage causes fewer workers to be hired in the unionized firms, leaving a larger labor supply (and a consequent lower wage) in the nonunion segment.

A final example of what occurs with official prices that are too high is the phenomenon of "RENT SEEKING," which occurs when someone enters a business to earn a profit that the government has tried to make unusually high. A simple example is a city that imposes a high official meter rate for taxis but allows free entry into the taxi business. The fare must cover the cost of paying a driver plus a market rate of return on the capital costs involved. Labor and capital will flow into the cab industry until each ends up getting its expected, normal return instead of the high returns one would expect with high fares. What will adjust is simply the number of cabs and the fraction of the time they actually carry passengers. Cabs will get more for each rider, but each cab will have fewer riders.

Other situations of rent seeking occur when artificially high urban wages attract migrants from rural areas. If the wage does not adjust downward to equate supply and demand, the rate of urban unemployment will rise until further migration is deterred. Still other examples are in banking and drugs. When the "margin" in banking is set too high, new banks enter and/or branches of old ones proliferate until further entry is deterred. Artificially maintained drug prices led, in several Latin American countries (Argentina, Chile, and Uruguay before their major liberalizations of recent decades), to a pharmacy on almost every block.

Rent seeking also occurs when something of value (like import licenses or radio/TV franchises) is being given away or sold below its true value. In such cases potential buyers often spend large amounts "lobbying" to improve their chances of getting the prize. Indeed, a broad view of rent seeking easily covers most cases of lobbying (using real resources in efforts to gain legislative or executive "favors").

The great unifying principles of microeconomics are, ever and always, supply and demand. The normative overtone of microeconomics comes from the fact that competitive supply price represents value as seen by suppliers, and competitive demand price represents value as seen by demanders. The motivating force is that of human beings, always gravitating toward choices and arrangements that reflect their tastes. The miracle of it all is that on the basis of such simple and straightforward underpinnings, a rich tapestry of analysis, insights, and understanding can be woven. This brief article can only give its readers a glimpse—hopefully a tempting one—of the richness, beauty, and promise of that tapestry.

About the Author

Arnold C. Harberger is a professor of economics at the University of California in Los Angeles. He is also the Gustavus F. and Ann M. Swift Distinguished Service Professor Emeritus at the University of Chicago. He has consulted extensively on microeconomic issues for many international organizations, including the International Monetary Fund, the World Bank, and the Inter-American Development Bank; governments, including Argentina, Bolivia, Brazil, Canada, Chile, India, and Mexico; and corporations, including Bechtel International, Republic Steel, and Ontario Hydro. He was special ambassador, U.S. Department of State, in 1984 and was on a presidential mission to Poland in 1989. He was president of the Western Economic Association from 1989 to 1990, and president of the American Economic Association in 1997.

Further Reading

Alchian, Armen, and William R. Allen. *Exchange and Production.* 3d ed. Belmont, Calif.: Wadsworth, 1983.
Colander, David C. *Microeconomics.* 5th ed. Boston: McGraw-Hill/Irwin, 2004.

Friedman, David D. *Price Theory: An Intermediate Text.* 2d ed. Cincinnati: South-Western, 1990.

Hirshleifer, Jack, and David Hirshleifer. *Price Theory and Applications.* 6th ed. Upper Saddle River, N.J.: Prentice Hall, 1998.

Mankiw, N. Gregory. *Principles of Microeconomics.* 3d ed. Mason, Ohio: Thomson/South-Western, 2004.

Nicholson, Walter. *Intermediate Microeconomics and Its Applications.* 9th ed. Mason, Ohio: Thomson/South-Western, 2004.

Minimum Wages

Linda Gorman

Minimum wage laws set legal minimums for the hourly wages paid to certain groups of workers. In the United States, amendments to the Fair Labor Standards Act have increased the federal minimum wage from $.25 per hour in 1938 to $5.15 in 1997.[1] Minimum wage laws were invented in Australia and New Zealand with the purpose of guaranteeing a minimum standard of living for unskilled workers. Most noneconomists believe that minimum wage laws protect workers from exploitation by employers and reduce poverty. Most economists believe that minimum wage laws cause unnecessary hardship for the very people they are supposed to help.

The reason is simple: although minimum wage laws can set wages, they cannot guarantee jobs. In practice they often price low-skilled workers out of the labor market. Employers typically are not willing to pay a worker more than the value of the additional product that he produces. This means that an unskilled youth who produces $4.00 worth of goods in an hour will have a very difficult time finding a job if he must, by law, be paid $5.15 an hour. As Princeton economist David F. Bradford wrote, "The minimum wage law can be described as saying to the potential worker: 'Unless you can find a job paying at least the minimum wage, you may not accept employment.'"[2]

Several decades of studies using aggregate time-series data from a variety of countries have found that minimum wage laws reduce employment. At current U.S. wage levels, estimates of job losses suggest that a 10 percent in-crease in the minimum wage would decrease employment of low-skilled workers by 1 or 2 percent. The job losses for black U.S. teenagers have been found to be even greater, presumably because, on average, they have fewer skills. As liberal economist Paul A. Samuelson wrote in 1973, "What good does it do a black youth to know that an employer must pay him $2.00 per hour if the fact that he must be paid that amount is what keeps him from getting a job?"[3] In a 1997 response to a request from the Irish National Minimum Wage Commission, economists for the Organization for Economic Cooperation and Development (OECD) summarized economic research results on the minimum wage: "If the wage floor set by statutory minimum wages is too high, this may have detrimental effects on employment, especially among young people."[4] This agreement over the general effect of minimum wages is long-standing. According to a 1978 article in *American Economic Review,* 90 percent of the economists surveyed agreed that the minimum wage increases unemployment among low-skilled workers.[5]

Australia provided one of the earliest practical demonstrations of the harmful effects of minimum wage laws when the federal court created a minimum wage for unskilled men in 1921. The court set the wage at what it thought employees needed for a decent living, independent of what employers would willingly pay. Laborers whose productivity was worth less than the mandated wage could find work only in occupations not covered by the law or with employers willing to break it. Aggressive reporting of violations by vigilant unions made evasion difficult. The historical record shows that unemployment remained a particular problem for unskilled laborers for the rest of the decade.

At about the same time, a hospital in the United States fired a group of women after the Minimum Wage Board in the District of Columbia ordered that their wages be raised to the legal minimum. The women sued to halt enforcement of the minimum wage law. In 1923, the U.S. Supreme Court, in *Adkins* v. *Children's Hospital,* ruled that the minimum wage law was price fixing and that it represented an unreasonable infringement on individuals' freedom to determine the price at which they would sell their services.

1. Employment Standards Administration, U.S. Department of Labor, *History of Changes to the Minimum Wage Law,* 2003, online at: http://www.dol.gov/esa/minwage/coverage.htm.

2. "Minimum Wage vs. Supply and Demand," *Wall Street Journal,* April 24, 1996.

3. Paul Samuelson, *Economics,* 9th ed. (New York: McGraw-Hill, 1973), pp. 393–394.

4. Organization for Economic Cooperation and Development, *OECD Submission to the Irish National Minimum Wage Commission,* Labour Market and Social Policy Occasional Papers no. 28, 1997, p. 15.

5. Kearl, J. R., et al., "A Confusion of Economists?" *American Economic Review* 69 (1979): 28–37.

In addition to making jobs hard to find, minimum wage laws may also harm workers by changing how they are compensated. Fringe benefits—such as paid vacation, free room and board, inexpensive insurance, subsidized child care, and on-the-job training—are an important part of the total compensation package for many low-wage workers. When minimum wages rise, employers can control total compensation costs by cutting benefits. In extreme cases, employers convert low-wage full-time jobs with benefits to high-wage part-time jobs with no benefits and fewer hours. David Neumark and William Wascher found that a 10 percent increase in minimum wages decreased on-the-job training for young people by 1.5–1.8 percent.[6] Since on-the-job training is the way most people build their salable skills, these findings suggest that minimum wage laws also reduce future opportunities for the unskilled.

A particularly graphic example of benefits reduction occurred in 1990, when the U.S. Department of Labor ordered the Salvation Army to pay the minimum wage to voluntary participants in its work therapy programs. In exchange for processing donated goods, the programs provided participants, many of whom were homeless alcoholics and drug addicts, with a small weekly stipend and up to ninety days of food, shelter, and counseling. The Salvation Army said that the expense of complying with the minimum wage order would force it to close the programs. Ignoring both the fact that the beneficiaries of the program could leave to take higher-paying jobs at any time and the cash value of the food, shelter, and supervision, the Labor Department insisted that it was protecting workers' rights by enforcing the minimum wage. After a public outcry, the Labor Department backed down.[7] Its Wage and Hour Division Field Operations Handbook now contains a special section on minimum wage enforcement and the Salvation Army.[8]

Minimum wage increases make unskilled workers more expensive relative to all other factors of production. If skilled workers make fifteen dollars an hour and unskilled workers make three dollars an hour, skilled workers are five times as expensive as the unskilled. Imposing a minimum wage of five dollars an hour makes skilled workers relatively more attractive by making them only three times as expensive as unskilled workers. This explains why unions, whose members have historically been highly skilled and seldom hold minimum wage jobs, invariably support legislation increasing minimum wages. As in the Australian case, unions also protect themselves against competitive threats by assiduously helping labor authorities find and prosecute suspected violators.

Many employers in the U.S. construction industry have found it less expensive to hire unskilled workers at low wages and train them on the job. By accepting lower wages in return for training, unskilled workers increase their expected future income. With high minimum wages like those specified for government construction by the Davis-Bacon Act, the cost of wages and training for the unskilled may rise enough to make employers prefer more productive union members. In effect, higher minimum wages reduce the competition faced by union members while leaving the unskilled unemployed. Of course, employers may also respond to minimum wage laws by decreasing overall employment, substituting machines for people, moving production abroad, or shutting down labor-intensive businesses.

While those rendered unemployed by a minimum wage increase are largely invisible, it is easy to calculate the increased income enjoyed by those who keep their jobs after an increase. This asymmetry has led many advocates to mistakenly assume that increasing the minimum wage is an effective way to fight poverty. Using 1997 Census data, D. Mark Wilson found that only 11.7 percent of minimum-wage workers were the sole breadwinners in their families, and that more than 40 percent of the sole breadwinners earning the minimum wage were voluntary part-time workers.[9] Richard Burkhauser used 1996 U.S. Census data to identify the likely beneficiaries from the 1996 increase in the federal minimum wage. He concluded that the "20.9 percent of minimum wage workers who lived in poor families only received 16.8 percent of the benefits."[10]

6. David Neumark and William Wascher, "Minimum Wages and Training Revisited," NBER Working Paper no. 6651, National Bureau of Economic Research, Cambridge, Mass., 1998.

7. James Bovard, "How Fair Are the Fair Labor Standards," *Regulation* 18, no. 1 (1985), online at: http://www.cato.org/pubs/regulation/reg18n1d.html.

8. Section 64c06: Salvation Army says: "The Salvation Army's position is that individuals in its rehabilitation program (called 'beneficiaries') are not employees under the FLSA. Although WH may not agree with this position, do not initiate C/As until receiving clearance from both the RA and the Child Labor and Special Employment Team, NO/OEP. Advise beneficiaries who complain that this WH policy has no effect on their private-action rights under section 16(b) of the FLSA" (http://www.dol.gov/esa/whd/FOH/ch64/64c06.htm).

9. D. Mark Wilson, *Increasing the Mandated Minimum Wage: Who Pays the Price?* Backgrounder no. 1162 (Washington, D.C.: Heritage Foundation, 1998).

10. Richard V. Burkhauser, Written testimony before the Committee on Education and the Workforce, U.S. House of Representatives, 106th Congress, April 27, 1999. See also Richard V. Burkhauser, Kenneth A. Couch, and Andrew J. Glenn, "Public Policies

Additional evidence on the distributional effect of minimum wages comes from David Neumark, Mark Schweitzer, and William Wascher. Raising the minimum wage increases both the probability that a poor family will escape poverty through higher wages and the probability that another nonpoor family will become poor as minimum wage increases price it out of the labor market. They found that the unemployment caused by minimum wage increases is concentrated among low-income families. This suggests that minimum wage increases generally redistribute income among low-income families rather than moving it from those with high incomes to those with low incomes. The authors found that although some families do benefit, minimum wage increases generally increase the proportion of families that are poor and near-poor. Minimum wage increases also decrease the proportion of families with incomes between one and a half and three times the poverty level, suggesting that they make it more difficult to escape poverty.[11]

In the early 1990s, after a telephone survey of 410 fast-food restaurants in New Jersey and Pennsylvania, economists David Card and Alan B. Krueger challenged the consensus view that higher minimum wages shrink employment opportunities. Their results appeared to demonstrate that a minimum wage increase resulted in increased employment.[12] Because telephone survey data are notoriously prone to measurement error, Neumark and Wascher repeated Card and Krueger's analysis using payroll records from a similar sample of restaurants over the same time period. The results from the payroll data showed that "the minimum-wage increase led to a *decline*

in employment in New Jersey fast food restaurants relative to the Pennsylvania control group."[13] After an extended academic debate, Card and Krueger retreated from their earlier position, writing that "the increase in New Jersey's minimum wage probably had no effect on total employment in New Jersey's fast-food industry, and possibly had a small positive effect."[14]

Even without the results from the payroll data, the contrary results from the Card and Krueger study would have had a limited impact on economists' belief that increasing the minimum wage increases unemployment. As labor economist Finis Welch pointed out, the consensus theory does not predict how any one firm or industry is affected by minimum wage increases.[15] Even if nationally recognized fast-food restaurants did not reduce hiring in response to higher minimum wages, Card and Krueger were silent about what happened at less-visible businesses, such as small retailers and local pizza and sandwich shops.

Furthermore, estimates of the overall effect of minimum wage increases often lead people to overlook the fact that regional and sectoral wage differentials average together to produce the national result. A federal minimum wage of $5.15 an hour may substantially reduce employment in rural areas, where it exceeds the prevailing wage, but have little effect on employment in large cities, where almost everyone earns more. Regional studies leave little doubt that substantial increases in the minimum wage can shrink local industries and inhibit job creation in areas with market wages below the new minimum. The growth of the textile industry in the southern United States, for example, was propelled by low wages. Had the federal minimum wage been set at the wage earned by northern work-

for the Working Poor: The Earned Income Tax Credit Versus Minimum Wage Legislation," *Research in Labor Economics* 15 (1996): 65–109; Richard V. Burkhauser, Kenneth A. Couch, and David C. Wittenburg, "Who Gets What from Minimum Wage Hikes: A Re-estimation of Card and Kreuger's Distributional Analysis in *Myth and Measurement: The New Economics of the Minimum Wage,*" *Industrial and Labor Relations Review* 49, no. 3 (1996): 547–552.

11. David Neumark, Mark Schweitzer, and William Wascher, "Will Increasing the Minimum Wage Help the Poor?" *Federal Reserve Bank of Cleveland Economic Commentary,* February 1, 1999, online version at: http://www.clevelandfed.org/Research/com99/0201.pdf.

12. David Card and Alan B. Krueger, "Minimum Wages and Employment: A Case Study of the Fast-Food Industry in New Jersey and Pennsylvania," *American Economic Review* 84, no. 4 (1994): 792. A later book expanded on these results, see David Card and Alan B. Krueger, *Myth and Measurement: The New Economics of the Minimum Wage* (Princeton: Princeton University Press, 1995).

13. David Neumark and William Wascher, "Minimum Wages and Employment: A Case Study of the Fast-Food Industry in New Jersey and Pennsylvania: Comment," *American Economic Review* 90, no. 5 (2000): 1390. Researchers from the Employment Policies Institute also reported finding data errors in the Card and Krueger sample. In one Wendy's in New Jersey, for example, there were no full-time workers and thirty part-time workers in February 1992. By November 1992, the restaurant had added thirty-five full-time workers with no change in part-timers. See David R. Henderson, "The Squabble over the Minimum Wage," *Fortune,* July 8, 1996, pp. 28ff.

14. David Card and Alan B. Krueger, "Minimum Wages and Employment: A Case Study of the Fast-Food Industry in New Jersey and Pennsylvania: Reply." *American Economic Review* 90, no. 5 (2000): 1419.

15. American Enterprise Institute, "The Minimum Wage and Employment: What Research Shows," conference summaries, Washington, D.C., August 1995, online at: http://www.aei.org/cs/cs5365.htm.

ers, the migration of textile workers to the South might never have occurred.

It is also easy to overlook the fact that raising the minimum wage applicable to a relatively small proportion of occupations will not necessarily increase measured unemployment. Some people will lose their jobs in covered occupations and withdraw from the labor market entirely. They will not be included in the unemployment statistics. Others will seek jobs at lower pay in uncovered occupations. Though the labor influx reduces wages in the uncovered sector, people do have jobs, and unemployment may not change. As minimum wage laws cover more occupations, however, the shrinking uncovered sector may not be able to absorb all of the people thrown out of work. The 1989 U.S. minimum wage legislation brought us one step closer to this possibility by extending coverage to all workers engaged in interstate commerce, regardless of employer size.

The fact that gross unemployment statistics do not necessarily reflect the harm done by minimum wage laws with limited coverage probably explains the popularity of the living-wage ordinances now in vogue in American cities with strong union ties. Living-wage ordinances set minimum wages for businesses and nonprofits that receive contracts or subsidies from local government. To arrive at the appropriate minimum living wage, advocates calculate the amount required to pay for a basket of goods containing "decent" housing, child care, food, transportation, health insurance, clothing, and taxes for various family sizes. The minimum is then set at the rate that produces enough money to buy the basket when someone works forty hours a week for a year. Initial empirical studies by Neumark suggest that the trade-off between wages and employment is the same for living wages as for minimum wages.[16]

In San Francisco in 2001, passage of a living-wage law raised the compensation of airport skycaps from $4.75 an hour to $10.00 an hour plus health insurance.[17] By the end of 2002, the Economic Policy Institute, an advocacy group supported by labor unions and liberal foundations, reported that living-wage ordinances had set minimum

wages ranging from $6.25 an hour in Milwaukee to $12.00 an hour in Santa Cruz, California.[18] In September 2003, the California Assembly passed a $10 minimum-wage requirement for contractors doing business with the state.

By one reckoning, the total cost of the typical basket of worker necessities used to arrive at living-wage minimums exceeds the incomes of almost a third of all families in the United States.[19] It will not be surprising, therefore, as the number of cities with "living-wage" laws expands, to see unskilled workers harmed by falling employment, fewer entry-level jobs, and a reduction in job-related training and educational opportunities.

About the Author

Linda Gorman is a senior fellow with the Independence Institute in Golden, Colorado. She was previously an economics professor at the Naval Postgraduate School in Monterey, California.

Further Reading

Brown, Charles. "Minimum Wage Laws: Are They Overrated?" *Journal of Economic Perspectives* 2, no. 3 (1988): 133–145.
Burkhauser, Richard V., Kenneth Couch, and David C. Wittenburg. "A Reassessment of the New Economics of the Minimum Wage Literature with Monthly Data from the Current Population Survey." *Journal of Labor Economics* 18, no. 4 (2000): 653–680.
Employment Standards Administration. U.S. Department of Labor. "History of Changes to the Minimum Wage Law." Online at: http://www.dol.gov/esa/minwage/coverage.htm.
Eccles, Mary, and Richard B. Freeman. "What! Another Minimum Wage Study?" *American Economic Review* 94 (May 1982): 226–232.
Forster, Colin. "Unemployment and Minimum Wages in Australia, 1900–1930." *Journal of Economic History* 45, no. 2 (June 1985): 383–391.

16. David Neumark and Scott Adams, "Do Living Wage Ordinances Reduce Urban Poverty?" NBER Working Paper no. 7606, National Bureau of Economic Research, Cambridge, Mass., 2000; David Neumark, *How Living Wages Affect Low-Wage Workers and Low Income Families* (San Francisco: Public Policy Institute of California, 2002).

17. Adam Geller, "'Living-Wage' Laws Raise Pay for Poor but May Cost Jobs," Associated Press, September 1, 2001, online at: http://projects.is.asu.edu/pipermail/hpn/2001-September/004534.html.

18. The Economic Policy Institute received $90,000 from the NEA in 2000–2001 (Education Policy Institute, http://216.239.33.100/search?q=cache:fYjj4PUYjiYC:www.educationpolicy.org/NEAreport2000.htm+%22Economic+Policy+Institute%22+%22Form+990%22&hl=en&ie=UTF-8), and $200,000 from the Joyce Foundation (2001 Annual Report, http://www.joycefdn.org/pdf/01_AnnualReport.pdf). For a complete list of supporters in 2000, see the institute's annual report at: http://www.epinet.org/ar2000/AR00_RS3.htm. The rate is $11.00 if health benefits are included in the wage package.

19. Economic Policy Institute, Basic Family Budget Calculator, online at: http://epinet.org/, under Poverty and Family Budgets section. Fraction below living wage minimums from Heather Boushey, Chauna Brocht, Bethney Gunderson, and Jared Bernstein, *Hardships in America: The Real Story of Working Families* (Washington, D.C.: Economic Policy Institute, 2001), table 5.

Hashimoto, Masanori. "Minimum Wage Effects on Training on the Job." *American Economic Review* 72, no. 5 (1982): 1070–1087.

Neumark, David, Mark Schweitzer, and William Wascher. "Will Increasing the Minimum Wage Help the Poor?" *Federal Reserve Bank of Cleveland Economic Commentary*, February 1, 1999. Online at: http://www.clevelandfed.org/Research/com99/0201.pdf.

Neumark, David, and William Wascher. "Minimum Wages and Employment: A Case Study of the Fast-Food Industry in New Jersey and Pennsylvania: Comment." *American Economic Review* 90, no. 5 (2000): 1362–1396.

———. "Minimum Wages and Training Revisited." *Journal of Labor Economics* 19, no. 3 (2001): 563–595.

Rottenberg, Simon, ed. *The Economics of Legal Minimum Wages*. Washington, D.C.: American Enterprise Institute for Public Policy Research, 1981.

Welch, Finis. *Minimum Wages: Issues and Evidence.* Santa Monica, Calif.: RAND Corp., 1978.

Wilson, D. Mark. *Increasing the Mandated Minimum Wage: Who Pays the Price?* Backgrounder no. 1162. Washington, D.C.: Heritage Foundation, 1998.

Monetarism

Bennett T. McCallum

Monetarism is a macroeconomic school of thought that emphasizes (1) long-run monetary neutrality, (2) short-run monetary nonneutrality, (3) the distinction between real and nominal interest rates, and (4) the role of monetary aggregates in policy analysis. It is particularly associated with the writings of Milton Friedman, Anna Schwartz, Karl Brunner, and Allan Meltzer, with early contributors outside the United States including David Laidler, Michael Parkin, and Alan Walters. Some journalists—especially in the United Kingdom—have used the term to refer to doctrinal support of free-market positions more generally, but that usage is inappropriate; many free-market advocates would not dream of describing themselves as monetarists.

An economy possesses basic long-run monetary neutrality if an exogenous increase of Z percent in its stock of money would ultimately be followed, after all adjustments have taken place, by a Z percent increase in the general price level, with no effects on real variables (e.g., consumption, output, relative prices of individual commodities). While most economists believe that long-run neutrality is a feature of actual market economies, at least approximately, no other group of macroeconomists emphasizes this proposition as strongly as do monetarists. Also, some would object that, in practice, actual central banks almost never conduct policy so as to involve exogenous changes in the money supply. This objection is correct factually but irrelevant: the crucial matter is whether the supply and demand choices of households and businesses reflect concern only for the underlying quantities of goods and services that are consumed and produced. If they do, then the economy will have the property of long-run neutrality, and thus the above-described reaction to a hypothetical change in the money supply would occur.[1] Other neutrality concepts, including the natural-rate hypothesis, are mentioned below.

Short-run monetary nonneutrality obtains, in an economy with long-run monetary neutrality, if the price adjustments to a change in money take place only gradually, so that there are temporary effects on real output (GDP) and employment. Most economists consider this property realistic, but an important school of macroeconomists, the so-called real business cycle proponents, denies it.

Continuing with our list, real interest rates are ordinary ("nominal") interest rates adjusted to take account of expected inflation, as rational, optimizing people would do when they make trade-offs between present and future. As long ago as the very early 1800s, British banker and economist Henry Thornton recognized the distinction between real and nominal interest rates, and American economist Irving Fisher emphasized it in the early 1900s. However, the distinction was often neglected in macroeconomic analysis until monetarists began insisting on its importance during the 1950s. Many Keynesians did not disagree in principle, but in practice their models often did not recognize the distinction and/or they judged the "tightness" of monetary policy by the prevailing level of nominal interest rates. All monetarists emphasized the undesirability of combating inflation by nonmonetary means, such as wage and price controls or guidelines, because these would create market distortions. They stressed, in other words, that ongoing inflation is fundamentally monetary in nature, a viewpoint foreign to most Keynesians of the time.

Finally, the original monetarists all emphasized the role of monetary aggregates—such as M1, M2, and the monetary base—in monetary policy analysis, but details differed between Friedman and Schwartz, on the one hand, and Brunner and Meltzer, on the other. Friedman's striking and famous recommendation was that, irrespective of current macroeconomic conditions, the stock of money

---

1. For long-run neutrality to obtain exactly, the economy would also have to possess the "Ricardian" property that makes bond-financed changes in government taxes inconsequential (see GOVERNMENT DEBT AND DEFICITS and NEW CLASSICAL MACROECONOMICS).

should be made to grow "month by month, and indeed, so far as possible, day by day, at an annual rate of X per cent, where X is some number between 3 and 5."[2] Brunner and Meltzer also favored monetary policy rules but recognized the attractiveness of *activist* rules that relate money growth rates to prevailing economic conditions. Also, they typically concentrated on the monetary base, adjusted to reflect changes in reserve requirements, whereas Friedman was more concerned with M2 or M1 and, indeed, sought major changes in banking legislation, such as 100 percent reserve requirements on deposits, designed to make the chosen aggregate precisely controllable.

Friedman's constant-money-growth rule, rather than other equally fundamental aspects of monetarism, attracted the most attention, thereby detracting from the understanding and appreciation of monetarism. In particular, this led to the comparative neglect of Friedman's crucial "accelerationist" or "natural-rate" hypothesis, according to which there is no long-run trade-off between inflation and unemployment; that is, the long-run PHILLIPS CURVE is vertical. The no-trade-off view was also promoted by Brunner and Meltzer. Accordingly, it might be argued that the two fundamental monetarist propositions are (1) that cyclical movements in nominal income are primarily attributable to movements in the stock of money, and, (2) that there is no permanent trade-off between unemployment and inflation. Together, these lead to monetarist-style policy positions.

Monetarism's rise to intellectual prominence began with writings on basic monetary theory by Friedman and other University of Chicago economists during the 1950s, writings that were influential because of their adherence to fundamental neoclassical principles. The most outstanding in this series was Friedman's presidential address to the American Economic Association in 1967, published in 1968 as "The Role of Monetary Policy." In this paper Friedman developed the natural-rate hypothesis (which he had clearly stated two years earlier) and used it as a pillar in the argument for a constant-growth-rate rule for monetary policy. Almost simultaneously, Edmund Phelps, who was not a monetarist, developed a similar no-trade-off theory, and, within a few years, events in the world economy apparently provided dramatic empirical support.

In the late 1970s and early 1980s, after a decade of increasing influence, monetarism's reputation began to decline for three main reasons. One was the growing belief, based on plausible interpretations of experience, that

money demand is in practice highly "unstable," shifting significantly and unpredictably from one quarter to the next. The second was the rise of RATIONAL EXPECTATIONS economics, which split analysts antagonistic to Keynesian activism into distinct camps. (A majority of monetarists themselves soon embraced the rational expectations hypothesis.) The third was the Federal Reserve's famous "monetarist experiment" of 1979–1982. The latter episode warrants an extended discussion.

During the 1970s, inflation rose in the United States, as well as in many other industrial nations, to levels unprecedented on a multiyear basis during periods of relative peace. This occurred as a consequence of various "shocks"—oil price increases, the Vietnam War, and especially the 1971–1973 demise of the Bretton Woods system of fixed exchange rates (itself caused largely by the failure of the United States to maintain the gold value of the dollar). This demise left central bankers with a major new responsibility; namely, to provide a nominal anchor for national fiat currencies to replace the gold standard. The Federal Reserve announced several times during the 1970s that it intended to bring inflation under control, but various attempts were unsuccessful. Then, on October 6, 1979, the Fed, under Paul Volcker's chairmanship, announced and put into effect a new attempt involving drastically revised operating procedures that had some prominent features in common with monetarist recommendations. In particular, the Fed would try to hit specified monthly targets for the growth rate of M1, with operating procedures that emphasized control over a narrow and controllable monetary aggregate, nonborrowed reserves (i.e., bank reserves minus borrowings from the Fed). The M1 targets were intended to bring inflation down from double-digit levels to unspecified but much lower values.

In retrospect, the events that occurred from October 1979 to September 1982 are widely viewed as the crucial beginning of a necessary and successful attack on inflation that led, eventually, to the worldwide low-inflation environment of the 1990s. At the time, however, the "experiment" seemed anything but successful to many Americans. Short-term interest rates jumped dramatically in late 1979 under the tightened conditions, and 1980 witnessed a major fall in output in one quarter followed by a major jump in the next, due primarily to the imposition, and then removal, of credit controls. Finally, in 1981 and into the middle of 1982, a sustained period of monetary stringency brought about the deepest recession since the Great Depression of the 1930s and began to bring inflation down, more rapidly than many economists anticipated, toward acceptable values. Some relevant statistics, designed to put

2. Milton Friedman, *Capitalism and Freedom* (Chicago: University of Chicago Press, 1962), p. 54.

Table 1 Selected Statistics, 1960–1999, percentages (average or changes)

Year or Average Over	CPI Inflation Dec.–Dec.	Fed Funds Rate	"Real" Funds Rate	M1 Growth Rate	Adjusted M1B Growth	Unemployment Rate
1960–64	1.2	2.9	1.7	2.8	—	5.7
1965–69	3.9	5.4	1.5	5.0	—	3.8
1970–74	6.7	7.1	0.4	6.1	—	5.4
1975	6.9	5.8	−1.1	4.7	—	8.5
1976	4.9	5.0	0.1	6.7	5.8	7.7
1977	6.7	5.5	−1.2	8.0	7.9	7.1
1978	9.0	7.9	−1.1	8.0	7.2	6.1
1979	13.3	11.2	−2.1	6.9	6.8	5.8
1980	12.5	13.4	0.9	7.0	6.9	7.1
1981	8.9	16.4	7.5	6.9	2.4	7.6
1982	3.8	12.3	8.5	8.7	9.0	9.7
1983	3.8	9.1	5.3	9.8	10.3	9.6
1984	3.9	10.2	6.3	5.8	5.2	7.5
1985–89	3.7	7.8	4.1	7.7	—	6.2
1990–94	3.5	4.9	1.4	7.8	—	6.6
1995–99	2.4	5.4	3.0	−0.4	—	4.9

Sources: Economic Report of the President, 2003, except: Adjusted M1B Growth: Alfred Broaddus and Marvin Goodfriend, "Base Drift and the Longer Run M1 Growth Rate: Experience from a Decade of Monetary Targeting," *Federal Reserve Bank of Richmond Economic Review* 70 (November–December 1984), pp. 3–14.

Note: Adjustments to M1 growth rates were made and used by the Fed, at the time, to take account of estimated distortions brought about by the introduction of NOW (negotiated order of withdrawal) accounts.

the episode in perspective, are reported in Table 1. Throughout the entire episode, moreover, both interest rates and money growth rates were highly variable. To be specific, the standard deviation of monthly percentage growth rates of M1 increased from 3.73 (for the previous three years) to 8.22 for the period from October 1979 to September 1982, while the standard deviation of monthly percentage changes in the federal funds rate jumped from 2.86 to 23.1 (annualized units).

Many critics characterized the "experiment" as a macroeconomic disaster. Some believed, moreover, that it provided strong and definitive evidence invalidating monetarism—partly by showing how undesirable it was to have money growth targets and partly in showing how poor are operating procedures for controlling M1 money growth by means of tight control of a narrow monetary aggregate. Monetarists argued that the episode was actually *not* monetarist in its design because growth rates of M1 fluctuated very widely on a month-to-month basis; the operating procedures in place were, because of lagged reserve requirements, extremely poorly designed for the control of M1;

and the Fed never forswore discretionary responses to current cyclical conditions. It now seems clear that the Fed's use of a narrow monetary aggregate for week-to-week control was highly effective in terms of public relations. The reason was that it permitted the Fed to escape political responsibility for the resulting high and, therefore, unpopular interest rate levels by claiming that these were simply the consequence of market forces.[3] At the same time, by adopting a putatively monetarist approach, the Fed could at least, even if the episode was a failure, discredit monetarism and the Fed's annoying monetarist critics. As matters played out, the episode was soon seen as a strategic success, despite temporary unhappiness, and monetarism was discredited as well!

What is left today of monetarism? While some disagreement remains, certain things are clear. Interestingly, most

3. This claim was somewhat deceptive in the following way. Each period's interest rate level was indeed market determined once the quantity of nonborrowed reserves for the period was determined, but this quantity was itself set by the Fed.

of the changes to Keynesian thinking that early monetarists proposed are accepted today as part of standard macro/monetary analysis. After all, the main proposed changes were to distinguish carefully between real and nominal variables, to distinguish between real and nominal interest rates, and to deny the existence of a long-run trade-off between inflation and unemployment. Also, most research economists today accept, at least tacitly, the proposition that monetary policy is more potent and useful than fiscal policy for stabilizing the economy. There is some academic support, and a bit in central bank circles, for the real-business-cycle suggestion that monetary policy has no important effect on real variables, but this idea probably has marginal significance. It is hard to believe that the major recession of 1981–1983 in the United States was not caused largely by the Fed's deliberate tightening of 1981—a tightening that shows up in ex-post real interest rates and in M1B growth rates as adjusted by the Fed at the time (Table 1, column 6) to take account of major institutional changes.

In 2005, most academic specialists in monetary economics would probably describe their orientation as NEW KEYNESIAN. Also, monetary aggregates currently play a small or nonexistent role in the monetary policy analysis of academic and central-bank economists. In terms of its underlying scientific rationale, however, today's mainstream analysis is much closer to that of the monetarist than the Keynesian position of, for example, 1956–1978. In addition to the points noted above, current thinking clearly favors policy rules in contrast to "discretion," however defined, and stresses the central importance of maintaining inflation at quite low rates. It is only in its emphasis on monetary aggregates that monetarism is not being widely espoused and practiced today.

About the Author

Bennett T. McCallum is the H. J. Heinz Professor of Economics in the Tepper School of Business at Carnegie Mellon University. He is also a research associate of the National Bureau of Economic Research, a research adviser for the Federal Reserve Bank of Richmond, a fellow of the Econometric Society, a member of the Shadow Open Market Committee, and an honorary adviser to the Institute for Monetary and Economic Studies of the Bank of Japan.

Further Reading

Brunner, Karl, and Allan H. Meltzer. "An Aggregate Theory for a Closed Economy." In Jerome L. Stein, ed., *Monetarism*. New York: American Elsevier, 1976.
Friedman, Milton. *A Program for Monetary Stability*. New York: Fordham University Press, 1959.
———. "The Role of Monetary Policy." *American Economic Review* 58 (March 1968): 1–17.
Friedman, Milton, and Anna J. Schwartz. *A Monetary History of the United States, 1867–1960*. Princeton: Princeton University Press, 1963.
McCallum, Bennett T. *Monetary Economics: Theory and Policy*. New York: Macmillan, 1989.
Symposium: "Monetarism: Lessons from the Post-1979 Experiment." *American Economic Review Papers and Proceedings* 74 (May 1984): 382–400.
Taylor, John B., ed. *Monetary Policy Rules*. Chicago: University of Chicago Press, 1999.

Monetary Policy

James Tobin

Paul Volcker, while chairman of the Board of Governors of the FEDERAL RESERVE SYSTEM (1979–1987), was often called the second most powerful person in the United States. Volcker and company triggered the "double-dip" recessions of 1980 and 1981–1982, vanquishing the double-digit inflation of 1979–1980 and bringing the unemployment rate into double digits for the first time since 1940. Volcker then declared victory over inflation and piloted the economy through its long 1980s recovery, bringing unemployment below 5.5 percent, half a point lower than in the 1978–1979 boom.

Volcker was powerful because he was making monetary policy. His predecessors were powerful too. At least five of the previous eight postwar recessions can be attributed to their anti-inflationary policies. Likewise, Alan Greenspan's Federal Reserve bears the main responsibility for the 1990–1991 and 2001 recessions.

Central banks are powerful everywhere, although few are as independent of their governments as the Fed is of Congress and the White House. Central bank actions are the most important government policies affecting economic activity from quarter to quarter or year to year.

Monetary policy is the subject of a lively controversy between two schools of economics: MONETARIST and KEYNESIAN. Although they agree on goals, they disagree sharply on priorities, strategies, targets, and tactics. As I explain how monetary policy works, I shall discuss these disagreements. At the outset I disclose that I am a Keynesian.

Common Goals

Few monetarists or Keynesians would disagree with this dream scenario:

• First, no business cycles. Instead, production—as measured by real (inflation-corrected) gross national product—

would grow steadily, in step with the capacity of the economy and its labor force.

- Second, a stable and low rate of price inflation, preferably zero.

- Third, the highest rates of capacity utilization and employment that are consistent with a stable trend of prices.

- Fourth, high trend growth of productivity and real GDP per worker.

Monetary policies are demand-side macroeconomic policies. They work by stimulating or discouraging spending on goods and services. Economy-wide recessions and booms reflect fluctuations in aggregate demand rather than in the economy's productive capacity. Monetary policy tries to damp, perhaps even eliminate, those fluctuations. It is not a supply-side instrument. Central banks have no handle on productivity and real economic growth.

Priorities

The second and third goals frequently conflict. Should policymakers give priority to price stability or to full employment? American and European monetary policies differed dramatically after the deep 1981–1982 recession. The Fed "fine-tuned" a six-year recovery and recouped the employment and production lost in the 1980 and 1981–1982 downturns. Keeping a watchful eye on employment and output, and on wages and prices, the Fed stepped on the gas when the economic engine faltered and on the brakes when it threatened to overheat. During this catch-up recovery the economy grew at a faster rate than it could sustain thereafter. The Fed sought to slow its growth to a sustainable pace as full employment was restored.

European central banks, led by the German Bundesbank, were more conservative. They did little to help their economies catch up. They regarded active monetary stimulus as dangerously inflationary, even when their economies were barely emerging from recession. They were determined never to finance more than sustainable noninflationary growth, even temporarily. Europe recovered much more slowly than America, and its unemployment rates have ratcheted up from the 1970s.

Priorities reflect national dreams and nightmares. German horror of inflation, for example, dates from the 1923 HYPERINFLATION and from a second bout of inflation after World War II. Priorities also reflect divergent views of how economies work. European monetary authorities were acting like monetarists, Americans like Keynesians, although both would disavow the labels.

Here is the crucial issue: Expansionary monetary policy, all agree, increases aggregate spending on goods and services—by consumers, businesses, governments, and foreigners. Will these new demands raise output and employment? Or will they just raise prices and speed up inflation?

Keynesians say the answers depend on circumstances. Full employment means that everyone (allowing for persons between jobs) who is productive enough to be worth the prevailing real wage and wants a job at that wage is employed. In these circumstances more spending just brings inflation. Frequently, however, qualified willing workers are involuntarily unemployed; there is no demand for the products they would produce. More spending will put them to work. Competition from firms with excess capacity and from idle workers will keep extra spending from igniting inflation.

Monetarists answer that nature's remedy for excess supply in any market is price reduction. If wages do not adjust to unemployment, either government and union regulations are keeping them artificially high or the jobless prefer leisure and/or unemployment compensation to work at prevailing wages. Either way, the problem is not remediable by monetary policy. Injections of new spending would be futile and inflationary.

Experience, certainly in the Great Depression and also in subsequent recessions, indicates that downward adjustments of wages and prices cannot avoid damage to output and employment. [*Editor's note:* for another view, see GREAT DEPRESSION.] Moreover, wage and price cuts may actually reduce demand by generating expectations of further disinflation or deflation.

A. W. Phillips's famous curve (see PHILLIPS CURVE) showed wage inflation varying inversely with unemployment. Keynesians were tempted to interpret it as a policy trade-off: less unemployment at the cost of a finite boost in inflation. Milton Friedman convinced the economics profession in 1968 that if monetary policy persistently attempts to bring unemployment below "the natural rate of unemployment" (the rate corresponding to Keynes's "full employment"), it will only boost the inflation rate explosively. Friedman's further conclusion that monetary policy should never concern itself with unemployment, production, or other real variables has been very influential. But in situations of Keynesian slack, as recent American experience again confirms, demand expansion can improve real macroeconomic performance without accelerating prices.

Strategies

Here too the monetarist-Keynesian controversy is exemplified by Federal Reserve and Bundesbank policies in the 1980s. The issue is this: how actively and frequently should policymakers respond to observed and expected departures from their targets? Friedman wants them to follow the same routine regardless of the economic weather, increasing the money supply at a constant rate. In his view, trying to outguess the economy usually exacerbates fluctuations.

While not all monetarists endorse Friedman's rule, they do stress the importance of announced rules enabling the public to predict the central bank's behavior. In principle, announced rules need not blind policymakers to changing circumstances; they could specify in advance their responses to feedback information. But it is impossible to anticipate all contingencies. No central bank could have foreseen the OPEC shocks of the 1970s and decided its responses in advance. Any practicable rule is bound to be simple. Any reactive policy, like the Fed's fine-tuning after 1982, is bound to allow discretion.

Relation to Fiscal Policy

In monetarists' view, government budgets have important supply-side effects for good or ill but have no demand-side role unless they trigger changes in monetary policy. In Keynesian theory, fiscal policy is a distinct demand-side instrument. The government affects aggregate demand directly by its own expenditures and indirectly by its taxes.

Prior to 1981, presidents and Congresses in making annual budgets considered their macroeconomic effects. In the 1980s budget making became slow and cumbersome, and the explosion of deficits and debt made countercyclical fiscal policy very difficult. Since then, the burden of stabilization policy has fallen almost entirely on monetary policy. The one main exception, not necessarily intentional, is the timing of President George W. Bush's tax cuts, which were, in essence, activist fiscal policy after 2001.

Monetary and fiscal policies are distinct only in financially developed countries, where the government does not have to cover budget deficits by printing money but can sell obligations to pay money in the future, like U.S. Treasury bills, notes, and bonds. In the United States, Congress and the president decide on expenditure programs and tax codes and thus—subject to the vagaries of the economy—on the budget deficit (or surplus). This deficit (or surplus) adds to (or subtracts from) the federal debt accumulated from past budgets. The Federal Reserve decides how much, if any, of the debt is "monetized"—that is, takes the form of currency or its equivalent. The rest consists of interest-bearing treasury securities. Those central bank decisions are the essence of monetary policy.

Mechanics of Monetary Policy

A central bank is a "bankers' bank." The customers of the twelve Federal Reserve banks are not ordinary citizens but "banks" in the inclusive sense of all depository institu-

tions—commercial banks, savings banks, savings and loan associations, and credit unions. They are eligible to hold deposits in and borrow from Federal Reserve banks and are subject to the Fed's reserve requirements and other regulations.

At year-end 2003, federal debt outstanding was $7,001 billion, of which only 11 percent, or $753 billion, was monetized. That is, the Federal Reserve banks owned $753 billion of claims on the U.S. Treasury, against which they had incurred liabilities in currency (Federal Reserve notes) or in deposits convertible into currency on demand. Total currency in public circulation outside banks was $664 billion at year-end 2003. Banks' reserves—the currency in their vaults plus their deposits in the Fed—were $89 billion. The two together constitute the monetary base (M0 or MB), $753 billion at year-end 2003.

Banks are required to hold reserves at least equal to prescribed percentages of their checkable deposits. Compliance with the requirements is regularly tested—every two weeks for banks accounting for the bulk of deposits. Reserve tests are the fulcrum of monetary policy. Banks need "federal funds" (currency or deposits at Federal Reserve banks) to pass the reserve tests, and the Fed controls the supply. When the Fed buys securities from banks or their depositors with base money, banks acquire reserve balances. Likewise the Fed extinguishes reserve balances by selling treasury securities. These are open-market operations, the primary modus operandi of monetary policy. These transactions are supervised by the Federal Open Market Committee (FOMC), the Fed's principal policy-making organ.

A bank in need of reserves can borrow reserve balances on deposit in the Fed from other banks. Loans are made for one day at a time in the "federal funds" market. Interest rates on these loans are quoted continuously. Central bank open-market operations are interventions in this market. When the Federal Reserve (or other central bank) conducts an open-market operation, it typically buys treasury bills, paying for them with reserves, or sells them, taking reserves in payment. Open-market operations thus amount to interventions in the federal funds market. Banks can also borrow from the Federal Reserve banks themselves, at their announced discount rates, which are in practice the same at all twelve banks. The setting of the discount rate is another instrument of central bank policy. Nowadays it is secondary to open-market operations, and the Fed generally keeps the discount rate close to the federal funds market rate. However, announcing a new discount rate is often a convenient way to send a message to the money markets. In addition to its responsibilities for macroeconomic stabilization, the central bank has a traditional safety-net role in temporarily assisting individual banks and in preventing or stemming systemic panics as "lender of last resort."

Tactics: Operating Procedures

Through open-market operations, the FOMC can set a target federal funds rate and instruct its trading desk at the Federal Reserve Bank of New York to enter the market as necessary to keep the funds rate on target. The target itself is temporary; the FOMC reconsiders it every six weeks or so at its regular meetings, or sooner if financial and economic surprises occur.

An alternative operating procedure is to target a funds quantity, letting the market move the funds interest rate to whatever level equates banks' demands to that quantity. This was the Fed's practice in 1979–1982, adopted in response to monetarist complaints that the Fed had been too slow to raise interest rates in booms to check money growth and inflation. The volatility of interest rates was much greater in this regime than in the interest-rate-target regime.

How is the Fed's control of money markets transmitted to other financial markets and to the economy? How does it influence spending on goods and services? To banks, money market rates are costs of funds they could lend to their customers or invest in securities. When these costs are raised, banks raise their lending rates and become more selective in advancing credit. Their customers borrow and spend less. The effects are widespread, affecting businesses dependent on commercial loans to finance inventories; developers seeking credit for shopping centers, office buildings, and housing complexes; home buyers needing mortgages; consumers purchasing automobiles and appliances; credit card holders; and municipalities constructing schools and sewers.

Banks compete with each other for both loans and deposits. Before 1980, legal ceilings on deposit interest restricted competition for deposits, but now interest rates on certificates of deposits, savings accounts, and even checkable deposits are unregulated. Because banks' profit margins depend on the difference between the interest they earn on their loans and other assets and what they pay for deposits, the two move together.

Banks compete with other financial institutions and with open financial markets. Corporations borrow not only from banks but also from other financial intermediaries: insurance companies, pension funds, and investment companies. They sell bonds, stocks, and commercial paper in open markets, where the buyers include individuals, nonprofit institutions, and mutual funds, as well as banks. Households and businesses compare the returns and advantages of bank deposits with those of money market funds, other mutual funds, open-market securities, and other assets.

Thanks to its control of money markets and banks, the Fed influences interest rates, asset prices, and credit flows throughout the financial system. Arbitrage and competition spread increases or decreases in interest rates under the Fed's direct control to other markets. Even stock prices are sensitive, falling when yields on bonds go up, and rising when they fall.

The Fed has less control over bond yields and other long-term rates than over money market and short-term rates. Long rates depend heavily on expectations of future short rates, and thus on expectations of future Fed policies. For example, heightened expectations of future inflation or of higher federal budget deficits will raise long rates relative to short rates because the Fed has created expectations that it will tighten monetary policy in those circumstances.

Another mechanism for transmitting monetary policy to the demand for goods and services became increasingly important after 1973. Since 1973 foreign exchange rates have been allowed to float, and obstacles to international movements of funds have steadily disappeared. An increase in U.S. interest rates relative to those in Tokyo, London, and Frankfurt draws funds into dollar assets and raises the value of the dollar in terms of yen, pounds sterling, and deutsche marks. American goods become more expensive relative to foreign goods, for buyers both at home and abroad. Declines in exports and increases in imports reduce aggregate demand for domestic production. High interest rates and exchange appreciation created a large and stubborn U.S. trade deficit in 1981–1985. Since 1985, as the interest advantage of dollar assets was reduced or reversed, the dollar depreciated and the U.S. trade deficit slowly fell. A similar pattern recurred between 1995 and 2002 as the exchange rate appreciated and the trade deficit widened as a proportion of GDP by more than 50 percent compared with its 1980s nadir. As of the end of 2004, two years of depreciation of the dollar have yet to reverse the trade deficit.

Targets: Monetary Aggregates or Macroeconomic Performance?

People hold dollar currency because it is the means of payment in many transactions. But checkable deposits are usually more convenient. They are not confined to particular denominations, cannot be lost or stolen, pay interest, and generate records most of us find useful.

The use of deposits in place of currency greatly economizes on base money. The $89 billion of bank reserves at year-end 2003 supported about $629 billion in checkable deposits. (The $572 billion of other assets behind those deposits were banks' loans and investments. In this sense banks "monetize" debts of all kinds.) These deposits plus the $664 billion in circulating currency provided a stock of transactions money (M1) of $1,293 billion. But time deposits and deposit certificates, though not checkable, are close substitutes for transactions deposits in many respects. So are money market funds and other assets outside banks altogether. Consequently the Fed keeps track of a spectrum of monetary aggregates, M1, M2, M3, each more inclusive than the preceding one.

The same open-market operations that move the monetary base up and down and interest rates down and up change the quantities of M1 and other monetary aggregates. Operations that reduce federal funds rates and related short-term interest rates add to bank reserves, thus also to bank loans and deposits. In 2003 reserve requirements averaged about 10 percent of checkable deposits. Thus a one-dollar increase in the bank reserves component of the monetary base meant roughly a ten-dollar increase in the deposit component of M1. In contrast, a one-dollar increase in the currency component of the monetary base is always just a one-dollar increase in M1.

If there were no change in the ratio of deposits to currency that the public preferred in 2003, a $1.00 increase in the monetary base would mean a $1.70 increase in M1. This is the "money multiplier." It does not stay constant, for several reasons. The Fed occasionally changes the required reserve ratio. Banks sometimes hold excess reserves, and sometimes borrow reserves from the Fed. The public's demand for currency relative to deposits varies seasonally, cyclically, and randomly. In fact, the public's demand for currency relative to demand deposits has increased significantly over the past fifteen years. In 1990, the money multiplier was $2.71 per new dollar of monetary base. In 2003, it was about 40 percent smaller. This reflects developments in transactions technology and financial institutions that allow people and firms to keep more of their liquid funds in forms other than checkable deposits and still pay their bills easily. Thus, the Fed's control of M1 is imprecise, and its control of broader aggregates is still looser.

Monetarists urge the Fed to gear its operations to steady growth of a monetary aggregate, M1 or M2. Under congressional mandate the Fed twice a year announces target ranges for growth of monetary aggregates several quarters ahead. In the 1970s the FOMC tried to stay within these ranges but often missed. Monetarist criticism became especially insistent when money growth exceeded Fed targets during the oil shocks. In October 1979 Chairman Volcker warned the public that the Fed would stick to its restrictive targets for monetary aggregates until inflation was conquered. Three years later, however, the Fed stopped taking the monetary aggregates seriously.

Monetary aggregates are not important in themselves. What matters is macroeconomic performance as indicated by GDP, employment, and prices. Monetarist policies are premised on a tight linkage between the stock of money in dollars—say, M1—and the flow of spending, GDP in dollars per year. The connection between them is the velocity of money, the number of times per year an average dollar travels around the circuit and is spent on GDP. By definition of velocity, GDP equals the stock of money times its velocity. The velocity of M1 was 8.5 in 2003. If it were predictable, control of M1 would control dollar GDP too. But M1 velocity is quite volatile. For the years from 1961 to 1990, average annual velocity growth was 2.2 percent, with a standard deviation of 3.6 percent. That is, the chance was about one in three in any year that velocity would either rise by more than 5.8 percent or decline by more than 1.4 percent. For the 1991–2003 period, the average annual growth of velocity was 1.6 percent, with a standard deviation of 5.9 percent. (M2 velocity is less volatile, but M2 itself is less controllable.)

Velocity depends on the money management practices of households and businesses throughout the economy. As transactions technologies and financial institutions have evolved and an increasing array of money substitutes has arisen, velocity has become less stable and monetary aggregates have become less reliable proxies for aggregate spending and economic activity. The 1981–1982 recession was deeper than the Fed intended because the FOMC stuck stubbornly to its monetary aggregates targets while velocity was precipitously falling.

Accounting for aggregate demand as the product of a money stock and its velocity is inadequate shorthand for the complex processes by which monetary policies are transmitted—via interest rates, banks, and asset markets—to spending on GDP by households, businesses, and foreigners. The Fed does better by aiming directly at desired macroeconomic performance than by binding itself to intermediate targets.

About the Author
The late James Tobin was the Sterling Professor Emeritus of economics at Yale University. He received the Nobel Prize in economics in 1981. He was a member of President John F. Kennedy's Council of Economic Advisers. The numbers and some of the facts were updated or clarified, where needed, by Kevin D. Hoover of Duke University. Professor Hoover was careful to maintain the spirit, tone, and judgments of Professor Tobin, rather than substituting his own.

Further Reading

Ando, Albert, H. Eguchi, R. Farmer, and Y. Suzuki, eds. *Monetary Policy in Our Times*. Cambridge: MIT Press, 1985.

Friedman, Milton. "The Role of Monetary Policy." Presidential address at the Eightieth Annual Meeting of the American Economic Association, December 1967. *American Economic Review* 58, no. 1 (March 1968): 1–17.

Greider, William. *Secrets of the Temple: How the Federal Reserve Runs the Country*. New York: Simon and Schuster, 1987.

Meulendyke, Ann-Marie. *U.S. Monetary Policy and Financial Markets*. 1989. New York: Federal Reserve Bank of New York, 1998.

Samuelson, Paul A. "Money, Interest Rates and Economic Activity: Their Interrelationship in a Market Economy." In Robert C. Merton, ed., *The Collected Scientific Papers of Paul A. Samuelson*. Vol. 3. Cambridge: MIT Press, 1972. Originally published in American Bankers Association, *Proceedings of a Symposium on Money, Interest Rates, and Economic Activity*. New York, 1967.

Walsh, Carl E. *Monetary Theory and Policy*. Cambridge: MIT Press, 1998.

Monetary Union

Paul Bergin

When economists such as ROBERT MUNDELL were theorizing about optimal monetary unions in the middle of the twentieth century, most people regarded the exercise as largely hypothetical. But since many European countries established a monetary union at the end of the century, the theory of monetary unions has become much more relevant to many more people.

Definitions and Background

The ability to issue money usable for transactions is a power usually reserved by a country's central government, and it is often seen as a part of a nation's sovereignty. A monetary union, also known as a currency union or common currency area, entails multiple countries ceding control over the supply of money to a common authority. Adjusting the MONEY SUPPLY is a common tool for managing overall economic activity in a country (see MONETARY POLICY), and changes in the money supply also affect the financing of government budgets. So giving up control of a national money supply introduces new limitations on a country's economic policies.

A monetary union in many ways resembles a fixed-exchange-rate regime, whereby countries retain distinct national currencies but agree to adjust the relative supply of these to maintain a desired rate of exchange. A monetary union is an extreme form of a fixed-exchange-rate regime, with at least two distinctions. First, because the countries switch to a new currency, the cost of abandoning the new system is much higher than for a typical fixed-exchange-rate regime, giving people more confidence that the system will last. Second, a monetary union eliminates the transactions costs people incur when they need to exchange currencies in carrying out international transactions. Fixed-exchange-rate regimes have been quite common throughout recent history. The United States participated in such a regime from the 1940s until 1973; numerous Europeans participated in one until the creation of the monetary union; and many small or poor countries (Belize, Bhutan, and Botswana, to name just a few) continue to fix their exchange rates to the currencies of major trading partners.

The precedents for monetary unions prior to the current European Monetary Union are rare. From 1865 until World War I, all four members of the Latin Monetary Union—France, Belgium, Italy, and Switzerland—allowed coins to circulate throughout the union. Luxembourg shared a currency with its larger neighbor Belgium from 1992 until the formation of the broader European Monetary Union. In addition, many former colonies such as the franc zone in western Africa or other small poor countries (Ecuador and Panama) adopted the currency of a large, wealthier trading partner. But the formation of the European Monetary Union by a group of large and wealthy countries is an unprecedented experiment in international monetary arrangements.

Optimal Currency Area Theory

Forming a monetary union carries benefits and costs. One benefit is that merchants no longer need worry about unexpected movements in the exchange rate. Suppose a seller of computers in Germany must decide between buying from a supplier in the United States at a price set in dollars and a supplier in France with a price in euros, payment on delivery. Even if the U.S. supplier's price is lower once it is converted from dollars to euros at the going exchange rate, there is a risk that the dollar's value will rise before the time of payment, raising the cost of the computers in euros, and hence lowering the merchant's profits. Even if the merchant expects that the import price probably will be lower, he may decide it is not worth risking a mistake. A monetary union, like any fixed-exchange-rate regime, eliminates this risk. One effect is to promote international trade among members of the monetary union.

The same argument can be made for international investment. If a European investor is considering buying a computer manufacturing company in the United States, the value of profits converted from dollars to euros is uncertain. On the other hand, exchange-rate fluctuations could make international investment more appealing, in that they can be used strategically to lower production costs. For example, suppose the European investor above buys the computer manufacturing company in the United States, and suppose he already owns one in Europe. Then, when a dollar depreciation lowers relative production costs in the United States, he can shift production toward the U.S. facility; during times of dollar appreciation he can shift production toward the European facility. Although the overall theoretical effect on investment is unclear, international trade and investment are highly beneficial to society. To the degree that exchange-rate variability tends to discourage the volume of trade and investment, this can provide a rationale for stabilizing the exchange rate.

How strong is the effect of exchange-rate variability? Regarding trade, most empirical estimates are close enough to zero to question if there is any effect; regarding investment, estimates conflict as to whether the effect is positive or negative. The apparently small effect of exchange-rate uncertainty might be due to the fact that international financial markets provide people with opportunities to hedge against the risk of exchange-rate changes: they can buy or sell in the currency futures markets.

But recall that a monetary union goes beyond simply fixing the exchange rate, and it appears to offer additional benefits. For example, it also eliminates the need for merchants to exchange currencies and pay the associated transactions costs. Empirical evidence indicates that while simply reducing exchange-rate uncertainty may not noticeably affect trade, adopting a fully common currency can raise trade much more—approximately doubling it according to several estimates. It is not yet known whether these large effects directly reflect the reduction of transactions costs.

Balanced against the benefit of increased international trade is the cost of losing control over national monetary policy. Countries whose governments control their own money supply typically use monetary policy to influence the level of activity in the country's economy. When, for example, the United States enters the downturn of a business cycle, growth slows and unemployment rises. The U.S. Federal Reserve increases the supply of money in circulation in order to reduce the interest rate. A lower interest rate, which lowers the cost of borrowing, stimulates consumption and investment spending, boosting production and counteracting the movement toward recession. Conversely, when the United States enters a boom of a business cycle, with high inflation, it pursues the opposite monetary policy. Because a monetary union has only one money, it must agree on a single monetary policy to address the business cycles of multiple countries.

How costly this loss is depends on institutional features of the particular countries involved. If Germany and Italy tend to have recessions at the same time, they can agree more often on a single monetary policy that accommodates the needs of both countries simultaneously. Even if Germany has a recession when Italy has a boom, this asymmetry can be accommodated if newly unemployed Germans move to Italy to take the newly vacant positions. Another way to mitigate this asymmetry is if Italy transfers income to help support unemployed Germans during Germany's recessions, and vice versa during times of recession in Italy.

The European Case

Much of the theory of optimal currency areas is illustrated by the institutions of the U.S. economy, which might be viewed a type of monetary union in which fifty states have agreed to share a common currency. Although the severity of recessions in the United States can vary by region, there is significant labor mobility, with around 3 percent of the U.S. population moving from one state to another annually. Further, the federal fiscal system permits compensation across state lines. Economists have estimated that for every dollar lost in one region relative to another in a recent recession, up to thirty-five cents were transferred to the losing region from the rest of the country, in terms of lower income taxes paid to the federal government and extra unemployment benefits received.

By contrast, there is relatively little labor mobility between European countries. Only about 1 percent of Germans and Italians relocate annually between regions within their own countries, and even fewer move between the two countries. As yet, most taxes and fiscal expenditures are conducted at the national level, and so there is limited opportunity for cross-country compensation. Further, European countries have more distinct business cycles than those observed between U.S. regions.

Perhaps it is too soon to tell whether Europe satisfies the theoretical criteria for an optimal currency area. Now that the euro has been adopted, the euro-area economies may evolve to more closely match the criteria for an optimal currency area. It may be that business cycles will become more synchronized across Europe as trade linkages increase, or that labor mobility or fiscal federalism (EU transfers of wealth from one EU country to another) will develop over time. Further, it should be noted that much of the motivation for the monetary union in Europe was not economic, but political. Policymakers seem to value monetary union as a stepping-stone toward greater political integration, quite separate from its economic implications.

The development of monetary union in Europe was a gradual political process. Monetary union was a stated objective as early as 1969 (Werner Report), but it was not until 1989 that concrete steps were laid out for achieving this objective (Delors Commission). A controversial part of this process was the set of criteria for who could join the union, as set forth in the Maastricht Treaty of 1992. This included restrictions on the level of fiscal debts and deficits, as well as a requirement for exchange-rate stability and convergence of national inflation rates. The fiscal restrictions proved difficult for many of the participants and were loosely enforced. The monetary union formally began in 1999, though it was not until 2002 that the new currency began to circulate in physical form.

The European Monetary Union (EMU) has taken care in designing its institutions. The member countries' national central banks have been fused together into the European System of Central Banks, with all money-supply decisions directed solely by the European Central Bank (ECB) in Frankfurt. A governing council with representatives from each member country decides monetary policy. The ECB's charter states that controlling inflation, rather than smoothing business cycles, is its primary objective. The ECB is insulated from political pressure: the president is offered an eight-year term, and governing council members are prohibited from taking instructions from their home governments.

The European Monetary Union has experienced some bumps in the road, with an early change of president and disagreement on how strictly to enforce restrictions on the size of fiscal deficits of member countries. Depending on the experience in Europe, one might expect to see future proposals for the formation of monetary unions in other regions of the world.

About the Author

Paul Bergin is an associate professor at the University of California at Davis and a faculty research fellow at the National Bureau of Economic Research.

Further Reading

Eichengreen, Barry. "European Monetary Unification." *Journal of Economic Literature* 31 (September 1993): 1321–1357. Summary of the theory and application to the European case.

Levin, Jay H. *A Guide to the Euro.* Boston: Houghton Mifflin, 2000. Concise survey of the European case.

Mundell, Robert A. "The Theory of Optimum Currency Areas." *American Economic Review* 51 (September 1961): 717–725. Primary source for the general theory of optimal currency areas.

Money Supply

Anna J. Schwartz

What Is the Money Supply?

The U.S. money supply comprises currency—dollar bills and coins issued by the Federal Reserve System and the U.S. Treasury—and various kinds of deposits held by the public at commercial banks and other depository institutions such as thrifts and credit unions. On June 30, 2004, the money supply, measured as the sum of currency and checking account deposits, totaled $1,333 billion. Including some types of savings deposits, the money supply totaled $6,275 billion. An even broader measure totaled $9,275 billion.

These measures correspond to three definitions of money that the Federal Reserve uses: M1, a narrow measure of money's function as a medium of exchange; M2, a broader measure that also reflects money's function as a store of value; and M3, a still broader measure that covers items that many regard as close substitutes for money.

The definition of money has varied. For centuries, physical commodities, most commonly silver or gold, served as money. Later, when paper money and checkable deposits were introduced, they were convertible into commodity money. The abandonment of convertibility of money into a commodity since August 15, 1971, when President Richard M. Nixon discontinued converting U.S. dollars into gold at $35 per ounce, has made the monies of the United States and other countries into fiat money—money that national monetary authorities have the power to issue without legal constraints.

Why Is the Money Supply Important?

Because money is used in virtually all economic transactions, it has a powerful effect on economic activity. An increase in the supply of money works both through lowering interest rates, which spurs investment, and through putting more money in the hands of consumers, making them feel wealthier, and thus stimulating spending. Business firms respond to increased sales by ordering more raw materials and increasing production. The spread of business activity increases the demand for labor and raises the demand for capital goods. In a buoyant economy, stock market prices rise and firms issue equity and debt. If the money supply continues to expand, prices begin to rise, especially if output growth reaches capacity limits. As the public begins to expect inflation, lenders insist on higher interest rates to offset an expected decline in purchasing power over the life of their loans.

Opposite effects occur when the supply of money falls

or when its rate of growth declines. Economic activity declines and either disinflation (reduced inflation) or deflation (falling prices) results.

What Determines the Money Supply?

Federal Reserve policy is the most important determinant of the money supply. The Federal Reserve affects the money supply by affecting its most important component, bank deposits.

Here is how it works. The Federal Reserve requires depository institutions (commercial banks and other financial institutions) to hold as reserves a fraction of specified deposit liabilities. Depository institutions hold these reserves as cash in their vaults or Automatic Teller Machines (ATMs) and as deposits at Federal Reserve banks. In turn, the Federal Reserve controls reserves by lending money to depository institutions and changing the Federal Reserve discount rate on these loans and by open-market operations. The Federal Reserve uses open-market operations to either increase or decrease reserves. To increase reserves, the Federal Reserve buys U.S. Treasury securities by writing a check drawn on itself. The seller of the treasury security deposits the check in a bank, increasing the seller's deposit. The bank, in turn, deposits the Federal Reserve check at its district Federal Reserve bank, thus increasing its reserves. The opposite sequence occurs when the Federal Reserve sells treasury securities: the purchaser's deposits fall, and, in turn, the bank's reserves fall.

If the Federal Reserve increases reserves, a single bank can make loans up to the amount of its excess reserves, creating an equal amount of deposits. The banking system, however, can create a multiple expansion of deposits. As each bank lends and creates a deposit, it loses reserves to other banks, which use them to increase their loans and thus create new deposits, until all excess reserves are used up.

If the required reserve ratio is 10 percent, then starting with new reserves of, say, $1,000, the most a bank can lend is $900, since it must keep $100 as reserves against the deposit it simultaneously sets up. When the borrower writes a check against this amount in his bank A, the payee deposits it in his bank B. Each new demand deposit that a bank receives creates an equal amount of new reserves. Bank B will now have additional reserves of $900, of which it must keep $90 in reserves, so it can lend out only $810. The total of new loans the banking system as a whole grants in this example will be ten times the initial amount of excess reserve, or $9,000: 900 + 810 + 729 + 656.1 + 590.5, and so on.

In a system with fractional reserve requirements, an increase in bank reserves can support a multiple expansion of deposits, and a decrease can result in a multiple contraction of deposits. The value of the multiplier depends on the required reserve ratio on deposits. A high required-reserve ratio lowers the value of the multiplier. A low required-reserve ratio raises the value of the multiplier.

In 2004, banks with a total of $7 million in checkable deposits were exempt from reserve requirements. Those with more than $7 million but less than $47.6 million in checkable deposits were required to keep 3 percent of such accounts as reserves, while those with checkable accounts amounting to $47.6 million or more were required to keep 10 percent. No reserves were required to be held against time deposits.

Even if there were no legal reserve requirements for banks, they would still maintain required clearing balances as reserves with the Federal Reserve, whose ability to control the volume of deposits would not be impaired. Banks would continue to keep reserves to enable them to clear debits arising from transactions with other banks, to obtain currency to meet depositors' demands, and to avoid a deficit as a result of imbalances in clearings.

The currency component of the money supply, using the M2 definition of money, is far smaller than the deposit component. Currency includes both Federal Reserve notes and coins. The Board of Governors places an order with the U.S. Bureau of Engraving and Printing for Federal Reserve notes for all the Reserve Banks and then allocates the notes to each district Reserve Bank. Currently, the notes are no longer marked with the individual district seal. The Federal Reserve Banks typically hold the notes in their vaults until sold at face value to commercial banks, which pay private carriers to pick up the cash from their district Reserve Bank.

The Reserve Banks debit the commercial banks' reserve accounts as payment for the notes their customers demand. When the demand for notes falls, the Reserve Banks accept a return flow of the notes from the commercial banks and credit their reserves.

The U.S. mints design and manufacture U.S. coins for distribution to Federal Reserve Banks. The Board of Governors places orders with the appropriate mints. The system buys coin at its face value by crediting the U.S. Treasury's account at the Reserve Banks. The Federal Reserve System holds its coins in 190 coin terminals, which armored carrier companies own and operate. Commercial banks buy coins at face value from the Reserve Banks, which receive payment by debiting the commercial banks' reserve accounts. The commercial banks pay the full costs of shipping the coin.

In a fractional reserve banking system, drains of currency from banks reduce their reserves, and unless the

Federal Reserve provides adequate additional amounts of currency and reserves, a multiple contraction of deposits results, reducing the quantity of money. Currency and bank reserves added together equal the monetary base, sometimes known as high-powered money. The Federal Reserve has the power to control the issue of both components. By adjusting the levels of banks' reserve balances, over several quarters it can achieve a desired rate of growth of deposits and of the money supply. When the public and the banks change the ratio of their currency and reserves to deposits, the Federal Reserve can offset the effect on the money supply by changing reserves and/or currency.

If the Federal Reserve determines the magnitude of the money supply, what makes the nominal value of money in existence equal to the amount people want to hold? A change in interest rates is one way to make that correspondence happen. A fall in interest rates increases the amount of money people wish to hold, while a rise in interest rates decreases that amount. A change in prices is another way to make the money supply equal the amount demanded. When people hold more nominal dollars than they want, they spend them faster, causing prices to rise. These rising prices reduce the purchasing power of money until the amount people want equals the amount available. Conversely, when people hold less money than they want, they spend more slowly, causing prices to fall. As a result, the real value of money in existence just equals the amount people are willing to hold.

Changing Federal Reserve Techniques

The Federal Reserve's techniques for achieving its desired level of reserves—both borrowed reserves that banks obtain at the discount window and nonborrowed reserves that it provides by open-market purchases—have changed significantly over time. At first, the Federal Reserve controlled the volume of reserves and of borrowing by member banks mainly by changing the discount rate. It did so on the theory that borrowed reserves made member banks reluctant to extend loans because their desire to repay their own indebtedness to the Federal Reserve as soon as possible was supposed to inhibit their willingness to accommodate borrowers. In the 1920s, when the Federal Reserve discovered that open-market operations also created reserves, changing nonborrowed reserves offered a more effective way to offset undesired changes in borrowing by member banks. In the 1950s, the Federal Reserve sought to control what are called free reserves, or excess reserves minus member bank borrowing.

The Fed has interpreted a rise in interest rates as tighter monetary policy and a fall as easier monetary policy. But interest rates are an imperfect indicator of monetary policy.

If easy monetary policy is expected to cause inflation, lenders demand a higher interest rate to compensate for this inflation, and borrowers are willing to pay a higher rate because inflation reduces the value of the dollars they repay. Thus, an increase in expected inflation increases interest rates. Between 1977 and 1979, for example, U.S. monetary policy was easy and interest rates rose. Similarly, if tight monetary policy is expected to reduce inflation, interest rates could fall.

From 1979 to 1982, when Paul Volcker was chairman of the Federal Reserve, the Fed tried to control nonborrowed reserves to achieve its monetary target. The procedure produced large swings in both money growth and interest rates. Forcing nonborrowed reserves to decline when above target led borrowed reserves to rise because the Federal Reserve allowed banks access to the discount window when they sought this alternative source of reserves. Since then, the Federal Reserve has specified a narrow range for the federal funds rate, the interest rate on overnight loans from one bank to another, as the instrument to achieve its objectives. Although the Fed does not directly transact in the Fed funds market, when the Federal Reserve specifies a higher Fed funds rate, it makes this higher rate stick by reducing the reserves it provides the entire financial system. When it specifies a lower Fed funds rate, it makes this stick by providing increased reserves. The Fed funds market rate deviates minimally from the target rate. If the deviation is greater, that is a signal to the Fed that the reserves it has provided are not consistent with the funds rate it has announced. It will increase or reduce the reserves depending on the deviation.

The big change in Federal Reserve objectives under Alan Greenspan's chairmanship was the acknowledgment that its key responsibility is to control inflation. The Federal Reserve adopted an implicit target for projected future inflation. Its success in meeting its target has gained it credibility. The target has become the public's expected inflation rate.

History of the U.S. Money Supply

From the founding of the Federal Reserve in 1913 until the end of World War II, the money supply tended to grow at a higher rate than the growth of nominal GNP. This increase in the ratio of money supply to GNP shows an increase in the amount of money as a fraction of their income that people wanted to hold. From 1946 to 1980, nominal GNP tended to grow at a higher rate than the growth of the money supply, an indication that the public reduced its money balances relative to income. Until 1986, money balances grew relative to income; since then they have declined relative to income. Economists explain these movements by changes in price expectations, as well as by changes in interest rates that make money holding more or less expensive. If prices are expected to fall, the inducement to hold money balances rises since money will buy more if the expectations are realized; similarly, if interest rates fall, the cost of holding money balances rather than spending or investing them declines. If prices are expected to rise or interest rates rise, holding money rather than spending or investing it becomes more costly.

Since 1914 a sustained decline of the money supply has occurred during only three business cycle contractions, each of which was severe as judged by the decline in output and rise in unemployment: 1920–1921, 1929–1933, and 1937–1938. The severity of the economic decline in each of these cyclical downturns, it is widely accepted, was a consequence of the reduction in the quantity of money, particularly so for the downturn that began in 1929, when the quantity of money fell by an unprecedented one-third. There have been no sustained declines in the quantity of money in the past six decades.

The United States has experienced three major price inflations since 1914, and each has been preceded and accompanied by a corresponding increase in the rate of growth of the money supply: 1914–1920, 1939–1948, and 1967–1980. An acceleration of money growth in excess of real output growth has invariably produced inflation—in these episodes and in many earlier examples in the United States and elsewhere in the world.

Until the Federal Reserve adopted an implicit inflation target in the 1990s, the money supply tended to rise more rapidly during business cycle expansions than during business cycle contractions. The rate of rise tended to fall before the peak in business and to increase before the trough. Prices rose during expansions and fell during contractions. This pattern is currently not observed. Growth rates of money aggregates tend to be moderate and stable, although the Federal Reserve, like most central banks, now ignores money aggregates in its framework and practice. A possibly unintended result of its success in controlling inflation is that money aggregates have no predictive power with respect to prices.

The lesson that the history of money supply teaches is that to ignore the magnitude of money supply changes is to court monetary disorder. Time will tell whether the current monetary nirvana is enduring and a challenge to that lesson.

About the Author

Anna J. Schwartz is an economist at the National Bureau of Economic Research in New York. She is a distinguished fellow of the American Economic Association.

Further Reading

Eatwell, John, Murray Milgate, and Peter Newman, eds. *Money: The New Palgrave.* New York: Norton, 1989.
Friedman, Milton. *Monetary Mischief: Episodes in Monetary History.* New York: Harcourt Brace Jovanovich, 1992.
Friedman, Milton, and Anna J. Schwartz. *A Monetary History of the United States, 1867–1960.* Princeton: Princeton University Press, 1963.
McCallum, Bennett T. *Monetary Economics.* New York: Macmillan, 1989.
Meltzer, Allan H. *A History of the Federal Reserve.* Vol. 1: *1913–1951.* Chicago: University of Chicago Press, 2003.
Rasche, Robert H., and James M. Johannes. *Controlling the Growth of Monetary Aggregates.* Rochester Studies in Economies and Policy Issues. Boston: Kluwer, 1987.
Schwartz, Anna J. *Money in Historical Perspective.* Chicago: University of Chicago Press, 1987.

Monopoly

George J. Stigler

A monopoly is an enterprise that is the only seller of a good or service. In the absence of government intervention, a monopoly is free to set any price it chooses and will usually set the price that yields the largest possible profit. Just being a monopoly need not make an enterprise more profitable than other enterprises that face competition: the market may be so small that it barely supports one enterprise. But if the monopoly is in fact more profitable than competitive enterprises, economists expect that other entrepreneurs will enter the business to capture some of the higher returns. If enough rivals enter, their competition will drive prices down and eliminate monopoly power.

Before and during the period of the classical economics (roughly 1776–1850), most people believed that this process of monopolies being eroded by new competitors was pervasive. The only monopolies that could persist, they thought, were those that got the government to exclude rivals. This belief was well expressed in an excellent article on monopoly in the *Penny Cyclopedia* (1839, vol. 15, p. 741):

It seems then that the word monopoly was never used in English law, except when there was a royal grant authorizing some one or more persons only to deal in or sell a certain commodity or article. If a number of individuals were to unite for the purpose of producing any particular article or commodity, and if they should succeed in selling such article very extensively, and almost solely, such individuals in popular language would be said to have a monopoly. Now, as these individuals have no advantage given them by the law over other persons, it is clear they can only sell more of their commodity than other persons by producing the commodity cheaper and better.

Even today, most important enduring monopolies or near monopolies in the United States rest on government policies. The government's support is responsible for fixing agricultural prices above competitive levels, for the exclusive ownership of cable television operating systems in most markets, for the exclusive franchises of public utilities and radio and TV channels, for the single postal service—the list goes on and on. Monopolies that exist independent of government support are likely to be due to smallness of markets (the only druggist in town) or to rest on temporary leadership in innovation (the Aluminum Company of America until World War II).

Why do economists object to monopoly? The purely "economic" argument against monopoly is very different from what noneconomists might expect. Successful monopolists charge prices above what they would be with competition so that customers pay more and the monopolists (and perhaps their employees) gain. It may seem strange, but economists see no reason to criticize monopolies simply because they transfer wealth from customers to monopoly producers. That is because economists have no way of knowing who is the more worthy of the two parties—the producer or the customer. Of course, people (including economists) may object to the wealth transfer on other grounds, including moral ones. But the transfer itself does not present an "economic" problem.

Rather, the purely "economic" case against monopoly is that it reduces aggregate economic welfare (as opposed to simply making some people worse off and others better off by an equal amount). When the monopolist raises prices above the competitive level in order to reap his monopoly profits, customers buy less of the product, less is produced, and society as a whole is worse off. In short, monopoly reduces society's income. The following is a simplified example.

Consider the case of a monopolist who produces his product at a fixed cost (where "cost" includes a competitive rate of return on his investment) of $5 per unit. The cost is $5 no matter how many units the monopolist makes. The number of units he sells, however, depends on the price he charges. The number of units he sells at a given price depends on the "demand" schedule shown in Table 1.

The monopolist is best off when he limits production to 200 units, which he sells for $7 each. He then earns monopoly profits (what economists call "economic rent") of $2 per unit ($7 minus his $5 cost, which, again, includes

Table 1 Demand Schedule

Price	Quantity Demanded (units per year)
$7	200
$6	300
$5	420

a competitive rate of return on investment) times 200, or $400 a year. If he makes and sells 300 units at $6 each, he earns a monopoly profit of only $300 ($1 per unit times 300 units). If he makes and sells 420 units at $5 each, he earns no monopoly profit—just a fair return on the capital invested in the business. Thus, the monopolist is $400 richer because of his monopoly position at the $7 price.

Society, however, is worse off.

Customers would be delighted to buy 220 more units if the price were $5: the demand schedule tells us they value the extra 220 units at prices that do not fall to $5 until they have 420 units. Let us assume these additional 220 units have an average value of $6 for consumers. These additional 220 units would cost only $5 each, so the consumer would gain 220 × $1 of satisfaction if the competitive price of $5 were set. Because the monopolist would cover his costs of producing the extra 220 units, he would lose nothing. Producing the extra 220 units, therefore, would benefit society to the tune of $220. But the monopolist chooses not to produce the extra 220 units because to sell them at $5 apiece he would have to cut the price on the other 200 units from $7 to $5. The monopolist would lose $400 (200 units times the $2 per unit reduction in price), but consumers would gain the same $400. In other words, selling at a competitive price would transfer $400 from the monopolist to consumers and create an added $220 of value for society.

The desire of economists to have the state combat or control monopolies has undergone a long cycle. As late as 1890, when the Sherman antitrust law was passed, most economists believed that the only antimonopoly policy needed was to restrain government's impulse to grant exclusive privileges, such as that given to the British East India Company to trade with India. They thought that other sources of market dominance, such as superior efficiency, should be allowed to operate freely, to the benefit of consumers, since consumers would ultimately be protected from excessive prices by potential or actual rivals.

Traditionally, monopoly was identified with a single seller, and competition with the existence of even a few rivals. But economists became much more favorable toward antitrust policies as their view of monopoly and competition changed. With the development of the concept of perfect competition, which requires a vast number of rivals making the identical commodity, many industries became classified as oligopolies (i.e., ones with just a few sellers). And oligopolies, economists believed, surely often had market power—the power to control prices, alone or in collusion.

More recently, and at the risk of being called fickle, many economists (I am among them) have lost both our enthusiasm for antitrust policy and much of our fear of oligopolies. The declining support for antitrust policy has been due to the often objectionable uses to which that policy has been put. The Robinson-Patman Act, ostensibly designed to prevent price discrimination (i.e., companies charging different prices to different buyers for the same good) has often been used to limit rivalry instead of increase it. Antitrust laws have prevented many useful mergers, especially vertical ones. (A vertical merger is one in which company A buys another company that supplies A's inputs or sells A's output.) A favorite tool of legal buccaneers is the private antitrust suit in which successful plaintiffs are awarded triple damages.

How dangerous are monopolies and oligopolies? How much can they reap in excessive profits? Several kinds of evidence suggest that monopolies and small-number oligopolies have limited power to earn much more than competitive rates of return on capital. A large number of studies have compared the rate of return on investment with the degree to which industries are concentrated (measured by share of the industry sales made by, say, the four largest firms). The relationship between profitability and concentration is almost invariably loose: less than 25 percent of the variation in profit rates across industries can be attributed to concentration.

A more specific illustration of the effect the number of rivals has on price can be found in Reuben Kessel's study of the underwriting of state and local government bonds. Syndicates of investment bankers bid for the right to sell an issue of bonds by, say, the state of California. The successful bidder might bid 98.5 (or $985 for a $1,000 bond) and, in turn, seek to sell the issue to investors at 100 ($1,000 for a $1,000 bond). In this case the underwriter "spread" would be 1.5 (or $15 per $1,000 bond).

In a study of thousands of bond issues, after correcting for size and safety and other characteristics of each issue, Kessel found the pattern of underwriter spreads to be as shown in Table 2.

For twenty or more bidders—which is, effectively, perfect competition—the spread was ten dollars. Merely increasing the number of bidders from one to two was suf-

Natural Monopoly

David R. Henderson

The main kind of monopoly that is both persistent and not caused by the government is what economists call a "natural" monopoly. A natural monopoly comes about due to economies of scale—that is, due to unit costs that fall as a firm's production increases. When economies of scale are extensive relative to the size of the market, one firm can produce the industry's whole output at a lower unit cost than two or more firms could. The reason is that multiple firms cannot fully exploit these economies of scale. Many economists believe that the distribution of electric power (but not the production of it) is an example of a natural monopoly. The economies of scale exist because another firm that entered would need to duplicate existing power lines, whereas if only one firm existed, this duplication would not be necessary. And one firm that serves everyone would have a lower cost per customer than two or more firms.

Whether, and how, government should regulate monopoly is controversial among economists. Most favor regulation to prevent the natural monopoly from charging a monopoly price. Other economists want no regulation because they believe that even natural monopolies must face some competition (electric utilities must compete with home generation of wind power, for example, and industrial customers can sometimes produce their own power or buy it elsewhere), and they want the natural monopoly to have a strong incentive to cut costs. Besides regulating price, governments usually prevent competing firms from entering an industry that is thought to be a natural monopoly. A firm that wants to compete with the local utility, for example, cannot legally do so. Economists tend to oppose regulating entry. The reason is as follows: If the industry really is a natural monopoly, then preventing new competitors from entering is unnecessary because no competitor would want to enter anyway. If, on the other hand, the industry is not a natural monopoly, then preventing competition is undesirable. Either way, preventing entry does not make sense.

ficient to halve the excess spread over what it would be at the ten-dollar competitive level. Thus, even a small number of rivals may bring prices down close to the competitive level. Kessel's results, more than any other single study,

Table 2 Number of Bidders and Underwriter Spread

No. of Bidders	Underwriter Spread
1	$15.74
2	$12.64
3	$12.36
6	$10.71
10	$10.23

convinced me that competition is a tough weed, not a delicate flower.

If a society wishes to control monopoly—at least those monopolies that were not created by its own government—it has three broad options. The first is an antitrust policy of the American variety; the second is public regulation; and the third is public ownership and operation. Like monopoly, none of these is ideal.

Antitrust policy is expensive to enforce: the Antitrust Division of the Department of Justice had a budget of $133 million in 2004, and the Federal Trade Commission's budget was $183 million. The defendants (who also face hundreds of private antitrust cases each year) probably spend ten or twenty times as much. Moreover, antitrust is slow moving. It takes years before a monopoly practice is identified, and more years to reach a decision; the antitrust case that led to the breakup of the American Telephone and Telegraph Company began in 1974 and was under judicial administration until 1996.

Public regulation has been the preferred choice in America, beginning with the creation of the Interstate Commerce Commission in 1887 and extending down to municipal regulation of taxicabs and ice companies. Yet most public regulation has the effect of reducing or eliminating competition rather than eliminating monopoly. The limited competition—and resulting higher profits for owners of taxis—is the reason New York City taxi medallions sold for more than $150,000 in 1991 (at one point in the 1970s, a taxi medallion was worth more than a seat on the New York Stock Exchange). Moreover, regulation of "natural monopolies" (industries, usually utilities, in which the market can support only one firm at the most efficient size of operation) has mitigated some monopoly power but usually introduces serious inefficiencies in the design and operation of such utilities.

A famous theorem in economics states that a competitive enterprise economy will produce the largest possible income from a given stock of resources. No real economy meets the exact conditions of the theorem, and all real economies will fall short of the ideal economy—a difference called "market failure." In my view, however, the degree of "market failure" for the American economy is much smaller than the "political failure" arising from the imperfections of economic policies found in real political systems. The merits of laissez-faire rest less on its famous theoretical foundations than on its advantages over the actual performance of rival forms of economic organization.

About the Author

The late George J. Stigler was the Charles R. Walgreen Distinguished Service Professor, Emeritus, of Economics at the University of Chicago. He also was director of the Center for the Study of the Economy and the State. He received the Nobel Prize in economics in 1982. The editor altered the article slightly, but only to reflect new facts or to return to Stigler's original thoughts in his final draft.

Further Reading

Atkinson, Scott E., and Robert Halvorsen. "The Relative Efficiency of Public and Private Firms in a Regulated Environment." *Journal of Public Economics* 29 (April 1986): 281–294.

Barro, Robert J. "Let's Play Monopoly." *Wall Street Journal,* August 27, 1991.

Boardman, Anthony E., and Aidan R. Vining. "Ownership and Performance in Competitive Environments." *Journal of Law and Economics* 32 (April 1989): 1–34.

Bork, Robert H. *The Antitrust Paradox.* New York: Basic Books, 1978.

Harberger, Arnold C. "Monopoly and Resource Allocation." *American Economic Review* 44, no. 2 (1954): 77–87.

Kessel, Reuben. "A Study of the Effects of Competition in the Tax-Exempt Bond Market." *Journal of Political Economy* 79 (July/August 1971): 706–738.

Shepherd, William G. "Causes of Increased Competition in the U.S. Economy, 1939–80." *Review of Economics and Statistics* 64 (November 1982): 613–626.

Stigler, George J. *Memoirs of an Unregulated Economist.* New York: Basic Books, 1988. Chap. 6.

National Income Accounts

Mack Ott

National income accounts (NIAs) are fundamental aggregate statistics in macroeconomic analysis. The groundbreaking development of national income and systems of NIAs was one of the most far-reaching innovations in applied economics in the early twentieth century. NIAs provide a quantitative basis for choosing and assessing economic policies as well as making possible quantitative macroeconomic modeling and analysis. NIAs cannot substitute for policymakers' judgment or allow them to evade policy decisions, but they do provide a basis for the objective statement and assessment of economic policies.

Combined with population data, national income accounts can provide a measure of well-being through per capita income and its growth over time. Also, NIAs, combined with labor force data, can be used to assess the level and growth rate of productivity, although the utility of such calculations is limited by NIAs' omission of home production, underground activity, and illegal production. Combined with financial and monetary data, NIAs provide a guide to inflation policy. NIAs provide the basis for evaluating government policy and can rationalize political challenges to incumbents by people who are dissatisfied with measurable aspects of the government's policies. In emerging and transition economies, implementing a dependable and accurate system of NIAs is a crucial step in developing economic policy.

NIAs, to be most useful, require honest and timely publication. Long-delayed information is of no use either in making policy or in monitoring the efficacy of policies already implemented. Delay frequently implies that the government has something to hide. Indeed, once released, NIAs can enforce their own discipline. That is, obfuscation cannot be maintained by altering or exaggerating one aspect of NIAs, say investment or growth of total income, since each such number is related to others, and consistency is a check on the accuracy of the components. Because the data cannot easily be faked, autocrats are loathe to publish their countries' NIAs and either proscribe or delay their release. Turkmenistan's dictator, for example, does not report to the IMF, and the governments of Myanmar (1999) and Zimbabwe (2000) ceased reporting NIAs. Conversely, nation-states that are committed to democracy report their NIAs, warts and all—for example, Croatia or Nigeria and proto-states such as Montenegro or Kosovo—laying bare the economic policy issues that confront them.

Measuring National Income

National income is the total market value of production in a country's economy during a year. It can be measured alternatively and equivalently in three ways:

• The value of expenditures

• The value of inputs used in production

• The sum of value added at each level of production

That the first two measures are identical can be seen by considering that any good—say, a loaf of bread—can be equivalently valued as either the price that is paid for it in the market by the final consumer or as the distributed factor payments—to labor (wages) and to capital (rent, interest, and profit)—used in its production. Since national output is the sum of all production, the total value will be the same whether added up by final expenditure or by the value of inputs (including profit) used in their production. The equivalence of the last measure can be seen by noting that the value of every final good is simply the sum of the value added at each stage of production. Again, consider a loaf of bread: Its value is the sum of the value of labor at each successive stage of production and other ingredients added by the farmer (wheat production), the miller (grinding to flour), the baker (flour plus other ingredients), and the grocer (distribution services).[1]

The broadest and most widely used measure of national income is gross domestic product (GDP), the value of expenditures on final goods and services at market prices produced by domestic factors of production (labor, capital, materials) during the year. It is also the market value of these domestic-based factors (adjusted for indirect business taxes and subsidies) entering into production of final goods and services. "Gross" implies that no deduction for the reduction in the stock of plant and equipment due to wear and tear has been applied to the measurements and survey-based estimates. "Domestic" means that the GDP includes only production by factors located in the country—whether home or foreign owned. GDP includes the production and income of foreigners and foreign-owned property in the home country and excludes the production and incomes of the country's own citizens or their property located abroad. "Product" refers to the measurement of output at final prices as observed in market transactions or of the market value of factors (inclusive of taxes less subsidies) used in their creation. Only newly produced goods—including those that increase inventories—are counted in GDP. Sales of used goods and sales from inventories of goods produced in prior years are excluded, but the services of dealers, agents, and brokers in implementing these transactions are included.

Measured by expenditures, GDP is the sum of goods and services produced during the period. Total output comprises four groups' purchases of final goods and services: households purchase consumption goods; busi-

---

1. National output includes only the value of net exports. In each of these three equivalent measures, the value of imports is deducted from the value of exports.

Table 1 Percentage Shares of Components of GDP for Selected Countries, 1990–2003

Country and World Bank Income Class[1]	Household Consumption	Government Consumption	Capital Formation	Change in Inventories	Net Exports
Chile (um)	63.2	11.2	23.4	1.1	1.1
Egypt (lm)	74.6	11.1	18.9	1.8	−6.4
France (h)	54.6	23.6	19.7	0.8	1.4
Morocco (lm)	68.4	18.0	22.3	−4.2	−4.6
Nigeria (l)	73.1	5.6	7.9	1.4	12.1
Poland (um)	62.2	18.0	20.6	0.7	−1.4
Thailand (lm)	55.2	10.4	32.3	0.8	1.3
Turkey (um)	69.1	12.8	22.6	−1.0	−3.5
United States (h)	67.8	15.4	18.5	0.4	−2.1
Average	65.3	14.0	20.7	0.2	−0.2

Source: IMF International Financial Statistics, October 2004.

1. Income classes by per capita income level from World Bank indicators. The income classes are: low income (l), $765 or less; lower middle income (lm), $766–$3,035; upper middle income (um), $3,036–$9,385; and high income (h), $9,386 or more.

nesses purchase investment goods (and retain unsold production as inventory increases); governments purchase goods and services used in public administration and welfare transfers; and foreigners purchase (net) exports. There is substantial uniformity in the shares of consumption and investment (the sum of capital expenditures and inventories) across nations with quite disparate income levels. As Table 1 shows, household consumption accounts for the largest share of GDP, an average of 65 percent for the nine countries considered; when added to government consumption, the share approximates 80 percent. Investment (gross capital formation plus increases in inventories) typically accounts for around 20 percent, although rapidly developing countries such as Thailand have higher investment and lower consumption shares. With few exceptions—for example, oil-exporting countries such as Nigeria—net exports are typically within plus or minus 5 percent of GDP. Five of the countries shown had average trade deficits during the fourteen-year period.

Measured by inputs, GDP is the sum of payments to domestic factors of production—wages, salaries, rent, interest, and profit, where profit is gross of the depreciation of domestic fixed capital—plus indirect business taxes less net subsidies to business. Because the value of any good or service is the sum of its inputs plus profit, the sum of the labor services, capital services (gross profit including depreciation), and indirect taxes less net business subsidies must equal the value of output, GDP. The third method of measurement is the sum of *value added*

at each stage of production of each of these final goods and services.

The Importance of NIA Data in Policy and Development Analysis

The development of NIA statistics provided the potential for converting economic policymaking from a rule-of-thumb-based guessing game to a quantitatively based science. Yet, policy remains, in part, a normative decision process, and rival politicians, as advocates of conflicting policy agendas, frequently assess the economy's performance differently and argue for divergent policies, even when citing the same NIA data. People's disagreements often are based on the distribution of income as opposed to its average level. Nevertheless, quantitative assessments of the economy and its growth bring discipline to the discussion.

The importance of accurate and accessible NIA is implicit in an observation made by a West African policymaker: "What cannot be measured cannot be managed." Of course, implementing measurability does not imply that all economic processes are manageable; and, in the case of government expenditures, unlike the other components of GDP, there is no way to assess value from observing voluntary market transactions. Because government expenditures are neither voluntarily elicited nor priced in the market, they are valued at cost, which is primarily the cost of labor. The capital cost of the buildings and land used is not included.

Limitation of NIA as a Gauge of Welfare

Per capita GDP is frequently used as a measure of welfare, both for indicating the rate of improvement over time and for comparisons across nations. Yet per capita GDP is an imperfect indicator of welfare of the representative individual. GDP does not account for nonmarket production in the household—for example, meal preparation, cleaning, laundry, and child care. Therefore, when these activities are, because of greater labor force participation, shifted to the market—as restaurant meals and semiprepared foods in grocery stores, cleaning and laundry services, and day care—the change in the value of production is overstated due to the decline in nonmarket (household) production. Second, gray market and illegal activities—such as production and distribution of marijuana or gambling—can be significant sources of sustenance in economies but are not included. Third, in benign climates, clothing and heating are less costly, so comparing across countries (or across regions within large states) will distort the relative level of well-being. Fourth, government services, because not subject to a market test, will typically be worth less than they cost, even though cost is used as a measure of value. Fifth, per capita income—an average measure—can be a misleading image of the representative resident's well-being if the distribution of income is very unequal. A better measure is the median income level and, for many analytic purposes, the income level by quintiles of the income distribution; however, such distributional measures cannot be directly obtained from GDP data and population and require separate surveys. Another limit on per capita income as a measure of well-being is that it flies in the face of the way people think about having children. Most young couples see themselves as being better off when they have their first baby, even though the immediate impact is a 33 percent drop in the family's per capita income.

History of NIA

An indication of NIAs' impacts on economics is that the third and fifteenth Nobel Prizes in economic science were awarded largely for contributions to the development of national income statistics—to SIMON KUZNETS in 1969 and to RICHARD STONE in 1984. Their citations also noted the men's advocacy roles in persuading the United States and United Kingdom to devote adequate resources to produce and maintain timely and accurate NIA data.

Working for the U.S. Commerce Department in the 1930s, Kuznets had developed time series of national income in order to develop a quantitative basis for studying and measuring economic growth and the shifts in production from agriculture to industry to services. Interestingly, Kuznets parted with the department because it refused to include estimates of household production. PAUL SAMUELSON once quipped that the size of the U.S. GDP could be dramatically increased if housewives would simply contract out with their neighbors (reciprocally) to provide cleaning and cooking services. In fact, this very omission of household production has overstated the rise in national output of the economy due to the increase in women's labor force participation from around 25 percent in the late 1930s to about 60 percent in 2003. Kuznets also strenuously objected to counting *all* government spending on goods and services as part of GDP because he regarded most such expenditures to be intermediate, not final, products.

In contrast to Kuznets, Stone developed a double-entry accounting system, also in the 1930s and 1940s, partly driven by the British government's war effort. His social accounting matrix implemented many cross-checks on the validity of components of national income and, in so doing, derived means of measuring them. He demonstrated, empirically as well as theoretically, that national income could be measured as either the market value of final product or the total of the gross factor incomes used in producing it. Stone's structure became the foundation for the United Nations System of National Accounts (SNA), first published in 1953, providing a uniform basis for all countries to report national output. Virtually all nations now use his system of national accounts.

About the Author

Mack Ott is an international economic consultant whose major assignments have been in the former Soviet Union countries, the Balkans, and Egypt. During 2003 and 2004 he was macroeconomic adviser to the chief economist of Nigeria and to the West African Monetary Institute. He has also been a U.S. Treasury adviser to the Ministry of Finance of Saudi Arabia.

Further Reading

Kendrick, John W. "National Income and Product Accounts." In *International Encyclopedia of the Social Sciences*. New York: Macmillan and Free Press, 1968. Vol. 6, pp. 19–34.

Mankiw, N. Gregory. *Macroeconomics*. New York: Worth Publishing, 2000.

Ott, Mack. "National Income Accounts, Economic Policy Analysis and the Initial Estimates of Kosovo's GDP." *Contemporary Economic Policy* (April 2003).

Rothbard, Murray. "The Falacy of the 'Public Sector.'" *New Individualist Review* (Summer 1961): 3–7. Available online at: http://www.mises.org/rothbard/public.asp.

United Nations. *System of National Accounts 1993*. New York: United Nations, 1993.

———. *Use of the System of National Accounts in Economies in Transition.* New York: United Nations, 1996.

Natural Gas: Markets and Regulation

Robert J. Michaels

Natural gas is the commercial name for methane, a hydrocarbon produced by the same geological processes that produce oil. Relatively abundant in North America, its production and combustion have fewer adverse environmental effects than those of coal or oil. The 23.1 trillion cubic feet (TCF) of gas that Americans consumed in 2002 accounted for 30.3 percent of all their energy use (measured in British thermal units), up from 21.5 percent in 1952.[1] Households consumed 23.3 percent of delivered gas, electric utilities used 27.0 percent as generator fuel, and the remainder went to commercial and industrial users. In 2002, 3.8 TCF were imported from Canada and a negligible amount was exported.[2] The U.S. output was produced in 383,000 wells owned by hundreds of producers and was transported through 285,000 miles of interstate pipelines.[3]

Before high-pressure pipelines were developed in the 1920s, gas was either consumed in the vicinity of its production or flared off as hazardous. Today, producers and marketers use interstate pipelines for deliveries to distributors and large consumers. The Federal Energy Regulatory Commission (FERC) determines cost-based pipeline rates, but pipelines are free to discount these (which they often do) in order to attract business. The rates of most local distribution companies (LDCs) that deliver and sell gas to final users are under state regulation, and the remainder are operated by municipal governments. Thus, gas is a vertically unintegrated industry in which dependable product flows require coordination among producers, pipelines, and LDCs. Since the 1970s, the industry has relied more heavily on coordination by market forces and less

heavily on regulation, although the latter still plays a large role. Somewhat unusually, regulators themselves took major initiatives to bring competition to the industry, rather than protecting the status quo or imposing heavier regulations. The industry's evolution is a case study in the replacement of inefficient economic institutions by efficient ones and the replacement of localized markets by national and global ones.

1938–1985: Pervasive Regulation and Shortages

The Natural Gas Act of 1938 instituted pipeline regulation by the Federal Power Commission, which was reconstituted as FERC in 1978. The government justified regulation by asserting that pipelines were "natural monopolies" with scale economies so pervasive that a single line (or a handful to guarantee reliability) was the most economical link between producing and consuming areas. At the same time, state-regulated LDCs were (and continue to be) monopoly franchises with cost-based rates and the ability to pass on gas costs dollar for dollar to end-users. Until the mid-1980s, pipelines purchased gas from producers and resold it, with no markup, to LDCs.

In 1954, the Supreme Court ruled that federal regulation extended to the wellhead prices received by producers. Prices were to be determined using recorded costs. Regulators set the allowable costs of replacing exhausted wells at low levels that seriously discouraged exploration for new gas. Because oil prices remained unregulated through the 1960s (most gas is found in association with oil), gas shortages became serious only when new price controls on oil helped bring about the "energy crisis" of 1973–1975. Administrations of both political parties were unable or unwilling to acknowledge that the controls restricted the amount supplied and increased the amount demanded. Instead, they instituted direct controls on gas use, such as prohibiting construction of new gas-burning power plants, in the mistaken belief that falling reserves indicated the exhaustion of supply. In reality, reserves were falling because allowable prices were too low to make exploration profitable. Prior to 1978, intrastate markets were exempt from federal price controls, and they experienced no shortages.

1985–2000: A National Gas Market Emerges

A complex series of events in the early 1980s led FERC to lift all price controls in 1985, a promarket policy that the Supreme Court subsequently ratified. The decontrol followed on 1984's Order 436, which effectively ended the earlier role of pipelines as purchasers and resellers of gas to LDCs. Order 436 (followed by Order 636 in 1992) turned pipelines into "open access" transporters for gas owned by producers, LDCs, and others. FERC still set max-

1. U.S. Department of Energy, Energy Information Administration [EIA], table 1.3, Energy Consumption by Source, 1949–2002, updated annually, online at: http://www.eia.doe.gov/emeu/aer/txt/stb0103.xls.

2. EIA, U.S. Total Natural Gas Consumption by End Use, updated annually, online at: http://tonto.eia.doe.gov/dnav/ng/ng_cons_sum_top.asp.

3. EIA, Natural Gas Quick Stats, online at: http://www.eia.doe.gov/neic/quickfacts/quickgas.htm.

imum pipeline rates, but also left pipelines free to charge less to attract business. For the first time since the 1930s, producers and LDCs could contract for gas as they wished, sometimes with the help of a new industry of marketers. Soon these parties learned to use the new rules to trade rights to pipeline transportation among themselves and to repackage those rights into more valuable combinations. Although pipelines may be natural monopolies, exchangeable transport rights allowed competitive markets to allocate much of their capacity.

In the 1990s, open access moved downstream. A series of FERC rulings allowed large users to arrange their own transactions with producers and use interstate pipelines on the same terms as LDCs. Since FERC had given these customers new options, state regulators had difficulty cross-subsidizing small consumers by setting high LDC rates for industrial users. During the 1990s, regulators in most states with large industrial loads began to allow industrial consumers to transport their own gas purchases over LDC lines, replacing regimes in which LDCs acted as full-requirements resellers of gas to all of their customers. In at least one major metropolitan area, Atlanta, households now have a choice of gas marketers who will sell to them.

With the end of price controls the shortage of gas vanished. In real terms, the average annual wellhead price of gas peaked in 1984, when price controls were still in effect. (Regulators had raised them on several occasions following the 1973 energy crisis.) It then fell almost steadily until 1998, when it reached 46 percent of the 1984 level. After 1998, it began rising to a 2001 high equal to 89 percent of the 1984 level.[4] Instead of falling with supply exhaustion, U.S. gas consumption rose by 25 percent between 1984 and 2002.[5] As economists would predict, during the 1984–1998 period of declining prices, reserves fell to 85 percent of their 1984 levels. Over the higher-price years 1998–2002, they then rose by 13.8 percent with increased exploration and drilling.[6] Demand for gas is growing with the invention of new, environmentally clean technologies. Most important, the development of relatively small (under 200 megawatts), fuel-efficient gas-fired power plants has brought competition to the primary production of electricity in most parts of the country.

The shortages and politically determined allocations of gas that accompanied price controls are no more. Open access to pipelines and storage has brought about a nationwide market that is becoming continent-wide as Canadian gas is integrated into U.S. supplies. In the unified market, prices at different locations differ only by the cost of transporting gas between them, as long as pipeline capacity is not a constraint due to severe weather. Most gas is traded in short-term markets for delivery during the next month. Long-term contracts and large storage capacities were necessary when price controls created risk that the gas would not be delivered, but now both gas and its transportation are available on short notice. The market price of gas is more volatile than that of any other major commodity. To hedge it, a wide variety of financial derivatives is now available, many based on the New York Mercantile Exchange's futures contract, a highly successful instrument introduced in 1990. Over-the-counter derivatives also allow hedging of regional price differences and transportation costs.

2001 and Beyond: A Global Gas Market

As natural gas becomes more widely used, the low prices of the 1980s and 1990s may be vanishing. Those low prices were the favorable result of two countering forces. First, advances in drilling technology and seismic imaging sharply raised the probability that a newly drilled well would contain gas. Second, more attempts to find gas were successful, but by the 1990s, most legally accessible areas had been well probed. New wells were likely to be marginal and subject to quicker rates of production decline. As noted above, this does not indicate that the nation is "running out" of gas. Newly found reserves exceed current production, but gas will be more costly to extract from them. Environmental concerns have closed substantial parts of the country (including offshore areas) to exploration, despite evidence that gas production is compatible with the preservation of many natural environments. Gas imports from southwestern Canada have replaced some of the production decline, but that area is unlikely to contain undiscovered major fields.

Gas deposits elsewhere dwarf North America's, which has only 3.3 percent of the world's currently known total (and even less that can be reached cheaply). The coming alternative is liquefied natural gas (LNG), which can be economically transported across oceans in special tankers. LNG has been supercooled to −260°F, turning it into a liquid whose volume is 1/600 that of gas at atmospheric pressure. The LNG is offloaded to onshore storage facili-

4. Data taken from EIA, "July 2006 Monthly Energy Review," table 9.11: Natural Gas Prices, updated monthly, online at: http://tonto.eia.doe.gov/merquery/mer_data.asp?table=T09.11.

5. EIA, note 1 above.

6. EIA, Historical Natural Gas Data, Table 4.2: Crude Oil and Natural Gas Cumulative Production, Proved Reserves, and Proved Ultimate Recovery, 1977–2004, online at: http://www.eia.doe.gov/emeu/aer/txt/ptb0402.html; and EIA, Total Natural Gas, Wet After Lease Separation Total Proved Reserves, 1998–2002.

ties and sent into pipelines as necessary. LNG technology has existed for decades but has been little used because most consuming nations, until recently, had pipeline access to economical supplies. The conspicuous exception is Japan, which imports nearly all of its gas (nine TCF per year) as LNG through eighteen onshore terminals. Indonesia is currently the largest LNG producer, reflecting its proximity to Japan.[7]

Only 4 percent of world gas consumption currently moves as LNG, and LNG imports account for only 1 percent of U.S. use. The market, however, is rapidly expanding. As of December 2003, 151 LNG tankers were operating and 50 were under construction. A single tanker can carry 5 percent of the U.S. average daily consumption. The United States has four LNG terminals in operation or operable, and rising domestic prices have brought at least twenty credible proposals for additional ones. Twelve nations (including Qatar, Algeria, and Trinidad and Tobago) currently export LNG. Australia, Russia, Norway, and Egypt are constructing facilities, and numerous others will probably soon join them. The geography and politics of world gas markets will differ from world oil markets, a situation of particular interest because oil and gas are substitutes in many uses.

Because all aspects of LNG require specialized facilities, long-term contracts with inflexible prices dominate this stage of its development. Already, however, 8 percent of LNG is in short-term markets with flexible prices (often linked to oil prices), a figure that will grow with market liquidity and the development of tools for risk management. Like oil, gas will be monetized, and paper trades will supplement physical exchanges. Deliverability will be market responsive because LNG carriers, unlike pipelines, can change destinations in real time. In as little as ten years, we may see a single world price for gas, one hallmark of an efficient and competitive market.

About the Author

Robert J. Michaels is a professor of economics at California State University, Fullerton. He has served as consultant to gas producers, pipelines, and industrial gas users. He has testified before FERC, state regulatory commissions, and Congress.

Further Reading

American Gas Association. *Gas Facts.* New York: American Gas Association, annual.
Michaels, Robert J. "The New Age of Natural Gas: How the

Regulators Brought Competition." *Regulation* 16 (Winter 1993): 20–31.
Michaels, Robert J., and Arthur S. De Vany. "Market-Based Rates for Interstate Gas Pipelines: The Relevant Market and the Real Market." *Energy Law Journal* 16, no. 2 (1995): 299–346.
National Petroleum Council. *Balancing Natural Gas Policy.* September 2003.
Sturm, Fletcher J. *Trading Natural Gas: A Nontechnical Guide.* Tulsa, Okla.: PennWell Books, 1997.
Tussing, Arlon R., and Bob Tippee, eds. *The Natural Gas Industry.* Tulsa, Okla.: PennWell Books, 1995.
U.S. Department of Energy. Energy Information Administration [EIA]. *Natural Gas Annual.* Publication DOE/EIA-0131.
———. *The Global Liquefied Natural Gas Market: Status and Outlook.* December 2003.
Yergin, Daniel, and Michael Stoppard. "The Next Prize: A Global Gas Market." *Foreign Affairs* 82 (November–December 2003): 103–114.

Natural Resources

Sue Anne Batey Blackman
William J. Baumol

The earth's natural resources are finite, which means that if we use them continuously, we will eventually exhaust them. This basic observation is undeniable. But another way of looking at the issue is far more relevant to assessing people's well-being. Our exhaustible and unreproducible natural resources, if measured in terms of their prospective contribution to human welfare, can actually increase year after year, perhaps never coming anywhere near exhaustion. How can this be? The answer lies in the fact that the *effective* stocks of natural resources are continually expanded by the same technological developments that have fueled the extraordinary growth in living standards since the Industrial Revolution.

Innovation has increased the productivity of natural resources (e.g., increasing the gasoline mileage of cars). Innovation also increases the recycling of resources and reduces waste in their extraction and processing. And innovation affects the prospective output of natural resources (e.g., the coal still underneath the ground). If a scientific breakthrough in a given year increases the prospective output of the unused stocks of a resource by an amount greater than the reduction (via resources actually used up) in that year, then, in terms of human economic welfare, the stock of that resource will be larger at the end of the year than at the beginning. Of course, the remaining physical amount of the resource must continually decline,

---

7. All figures and descriptions in this paragraph and below are from Yergin and Stoppard 2003; and EIA, *The Global Liquefied Natural Gas Market,* various pages.

but it need never be exhausted completely, and its effective quantity can rise for the indefinite future. The exhaustion of a particular resource, though not impossible, is also not inevitable.

Ever since the Industrial Revolution, world demand for power and raw materials has grown at a fantastic rate. One respected observer estimates that humankind "has consumed more aluminum, copper, iron and steel, phosphate rock, diamonds, sulfur, coal, oil, natural gas, and even sand and gravel over the past century than over all earlier centuries put together," and goes on to write that "the pace continues to accelerate, so that today the world annually produces and consumes nearly all mineral commodities at record rates" (Tilton 2001, p. I-1).

Are our natural resources truly being gobbled up by an insatiable industrial world? Table 1 presents some estimates of known world reserves of five important nonfuel minerals (tin, copper, iron ore, lead, and zinc). Clearly, even though the mining of these minerals between 1950 and 2000 used up much more than the known 1950 reserves, the known supplies of these minerals were greater in 2000 than in 1950. This increase in presumably finite stocks is explained by the way data on natural resources are compiled. Each year, the U.S. Geological Survey (USGS) estimates the amounts of reserves: the quantities of mineral that can be economically extracted or produced at the time of determination (as in Table 1). Those quantities can and do rise in response to price rises and anticipated increases in demand. As previously discovered reserves of a resource grow scarce, the price rises, stimulating exploration that frequently adds new reserves faster than the previously proven reserves run out.

Clearly, data on reserves do not show whether a resource is about to run out. There is, however, another indicator of the scarcity of a resource that is more reliable: its price. If the demand for a resource is not falling, and if its price is not distorted by interference such as government intervention or international cartels, then the resource's price will rise as its remaining quantity declines. So any price rises can be interpreted as a signal that the resource is getting scarcer. If, on the other hand, the price of a resource actually falls, consistently and without regulatory interference, it is very unlikely that its effective stock is growing scarce.

H. J. Barnett and Chandler Morse (1963) found that the real cost (price) of extraction for a sample of thirteen minerals had declined for all but two (lead and zinc) between 1870 and 1956. William Baumol et al. (1989) calculated the price of fifteen resources for the period 1900–1986 and found that until the "energy crises" of the 1970s, there was a negligible upward trend in the real (inflation-adjusted) prices of coal and natural gas and virtually no increase in the price of crude oil. Petroleum prices catapulted in the 1970s and 1980s under the influence of the Organization of Petroleum Exporting Countries (OPEC). After that, as Figure 1 shows, real oil prices returned to their historical levels, until 2003, when oil prices increased significantly again. While the longer-term prospects for these prices are uncertain, new energy-producing techniques such as nuclear fusion, along with the increasing use of renewable energy sources such as wind power, solar power, and hydrogen fuel cells, may be able at least to offset the upward pressure on energy prices.

The price history of nonfuel minerals is even more striking, with the prices of almost all exhibiting a generally declining (though fluctuating) trend after correction for inflation. Zinc, for example, which cost $2,021 (in 2000 dollars) per ton in 1900, had dropped to $1,226 in 2000 (with many peaks and valleys in between). The price of lead fell overall over the century, with its 2000 price at $961 per ton compared with $2,083 in 1900. The real price of iron ore, which increased for most of the twentieth century, has now returned to its pre–World War II levels. Real copper prices have fluctuated wildly, with no upward trend. And for some minerals, such as aluminum, inflation-adjusted prices today are far lower than they were one hundred years ago (U.S. Geological Survey). The USGS mine production composite price index, which provides an overall snapshot of mineral prices, declined throughout the twentieth century, dropping from 185 in 1905 to 100 in 2000 (USGS, *Economic Drivers of Mineral Supply*, 2002, p. 63). This is hardly evidence of imminent exhaustion.

The effective stocks of a natural resource can be increased in at least three ways:

1. A technological innovation that reduces the amount of iron ore lost during mining or smelting increases the effective stock of that resource. Likewise, a new technique

Table 1 World Reserves and Cumulative Production of Selected Minerals: 1950–2000 (millions of metric tons)

Mineral	1950 Reserves	Production 1950–2000	2000 Reserves
Tin	6	11	10
Copper	100	339	340
Iron Ore	19,000	37,583	140,000
Lead	40	150	64
Zinc	70	266	190

Sources: National Commission on Supplies and Shortages, 1976; and U.S. Geological Survey, http://www.usgs.gov.

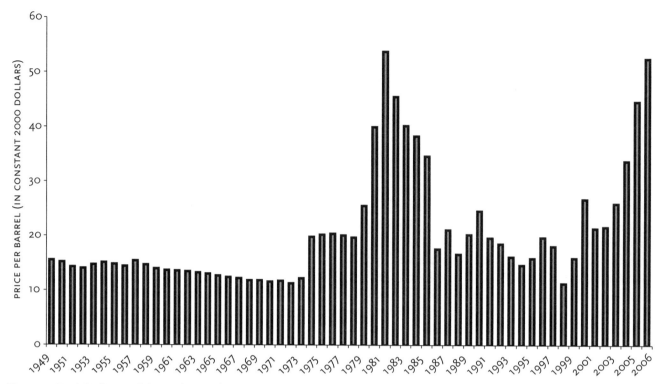

Figure 1 Real (Inflation-Adjusted) Petroleum Prices, 1949–2006

Sources: Oil prices: U.S. Department of Energy, Energy Information Administration, Annual Energy Review 2003 and Petroleum Marketing Monthly, Nov. 2004 (http://www.doe.gov); Implicit price deflator, Bureau of Economic Analysis (http//www.bea.gov).
Note: Prices are crude oil domestic first-purchase prices in constant 2000 dollars, calculated using GDP implicit price deflators.

may make it economical to force more oil out of previously abandoned wells. This decrease in waste translates directly into a rise in the effective supplies of oil. For example, say that in 1960, with known drilling techniques, only 40 percent of the oil at a site in Borger, Texas, could have been extracted at a cost ever likely to be acceptable, but by 2000 improved technology had raised this figure to 80 percent. Assume, for simplicity, that the amount of oil in Borger was 10 million barrels. Let us say that between 1960 and 2000, 5 percent of the originally available oil—500,000 barrels—has been used up. Then, by 2000, the effective supply of oil in that part of the Texas Panhandle will have risen from its initial level of 4 million barrels (40 percent of 10 million) to 7.6 million barrels (80 percent of 9.5 million), which yields a net rise of effective supply equal to 90 percent. In these cases, what occurs is not a rise in the physical quantity of oil, but an increase in the productivity of the remaining supply.

2. The (partial) substitutability within the economy of virtually all resources for others is at the heart of the second method for increasing the effective stocks of natural resources. The energy crises of the 1970s provided dramatic illustrations of the substitutability of resources.

Homeowners increased their expenditures on insulation to save on fuel costs, thus substituting fiberglass for heating oil. Newspapers even reported that the cattle drives of earlier eras were being revived, with cowhand labor substituting for gasoline. Technological innovation can reduce the cost of extracting or processing a resource. A new oil rig, for example, may require fewer labor hours to operate and use less electricity and less steel in its manufacture. Those savings of other resources can translate into savings of oil, because those other resources are thus freed up to be used elsewhere in the economy, and some of the alternative uses will entail substitution for oil. Second, technology can reduce the amount of the resource needed in a given use. Innovation in the auto industry, for example, has roughly doubled miles per gallon in all petroleum used for transportation. Scientists measure this progress as a decrease in "energy intensity," or the amount of raw energy resource required per unit of economic output. The Worldwatch Institute reported that in the United States, one unit of gross domestic product (GDP) in 2000 required less than one-fifth as much energy as it did two hundred hundred years ago (Worldwatch Institute 2001, p. 91).

3. The third way we can increase our effective stocks of

a natural resource is, of course, by technological changes that facilitate RECYCLING. Say, for example, that a new recycling technique allows copper to be reused before it is scrapped and that no such reuse was economical before. Then this technique has doubled the effective reserves of copper (aside from any resources used up in the recycling process). It is important to note, however, that recycling adopted without regard for economic considerations can actually waste resources rather than save them. For example, some researchers have found that combustion of municipal garbage to generate electricity sometimes actually uses up more energy than it produces.

These three means can all increase the effective supplies of exhaustible resources and can augment the prospective economic contribution of the current inventory of resources, perhaps more than enough to offset the consumption of resources during the same period.

Some people believe that the burst of productivity and the improvement in living standards that have occurred since the industrial revolution can be attributed to our willingness to deplete our natural heritage at the expense of future generations. But as we have seen here, rising productivity (the source of the great leap in economic growth) may actually augment humanity's stock of natural resource capital instead of depleting it, and may be able to do so, for all practical purposes, "forever." The evidence of trends in the prices of natural resources suggests that technological innovation has indeed provided continuing increases in the effective stocks of finite resources. But is there a limit to this process? Can we expect the wonders of technology to continue to wring ever more from the earth's resources? No one knows. One observer summed up the situation as follows:

> So far, the pessimists have been wrong in their predictions. But one thing is also clear: to conclude that there is no reason whatsoever to worry is tantamount to committing the same mistake the pessimists are often guilty of—that is the mistake of extrapolating past trends. The future is something inherently uncertain. . . . That the alarmists have regularly and mistakenly cried "wolf!" does not *a priori* imply that the woods are safe. (Neumayer 2000, p. 309)

More recently, accumulating evidence has led to some shift in the main focus of concern. Observers do not place primary emphasis on the prospect of total resource exhaustion. Rather, their attention has shifted to the consequences of the extraction processes—their degradation of pristine wilderness areas in places such as Alaska and the Amazon—and the effects of resource consumption on the environment overall, with the burning of fossil fuels and their connection to global warming the most critical issues. These are matters that cannot be ignored. Rational responses, however, require evaluation of the prospective costs to society of both counteraction and inaction.

About the Authors

Sue Anne Batey Blackman is senior research specialist in the Department of Economics at Princeton University. William J. Baumol is senior economist and professor emeritus at Princeton and the Harold Price Professor of Entrepreneurship and academic director of the Berkley Center for Entrepreneurial Studies at New York University's Leonard N. Stern School of Business.

Further Reading

Barnett, H. J., and Chandler Morse. *Scarcity and Growth: The Economics of Natural Resource Availability.* Baltimore: Johns Hopkins University Press for Resources for the Future, 1963.

Baumol, William J., Sue Anne Batey Blackman, and Edward N. Wolff. *Productivity and American Leadership: The Long View.* Cambridge: MIT Press, 1989. Earlier estimates in this entry are taken from Baumol, William J., and Wallace E. Oates, with Sue Anne Batey Blackman. *Economics, Environmental Policy and the Quality of Life.* Englewood Cliffs, N.J.: Prentice Hall, 1979.

Kelly, Thomas, Grecia Matos, et al. "Historical Statistics for Mineral and Material Commodities in the United States." USGS Data Series 140, 2006. Online at: http://minerals.usgs.gov/ds/2005/140/.

Krautkraemer, Jeffrey A. "Nonrenewable Resource Scarcity." *Journal of Economic Literature* 36 (December 1998): 2065–2107.

National Commission on Supplies and Shortages. *Government and the Nation's Resources.* Washington, D.C.: U.S. Government Printing Office, 1976. P. 16.

Neumayer, E. "Scarce or Abundant? The Economics of Natural Resource Availability." *Journal of Economic Surveys* 14, no. 3 (2000): 307–335.

Resources for the Future. Online at: http://www.rff.org.

Simon, Julian L., and Herman Kahn. *The Resourceful Earth.* Oxford: Basil Blackwell, 1984.

Tilton, John E. "Depletion and the Long-Run Availability of Mineral Commodities." In *Mining, Minerals and Sustainable Development.* Vol. 14, March 2001, International Institute for Environment and Development. Available online at: http://www.iied.org.

———. *On Borrowed Time? Assessing the Threat of Mineral Depletion.* Washington, D.C.: Resources for the Future Press, 2003.

U.S. Geological Survey. *Economic Drivers of Mineral Supply.* Washington, D.C.: U.S. Geological Survey, 2002. Available

online at: http://pubs.usgs.gov/of/2002of02-335/of02-335.pdf.
———. *Mineral Commodity Summaries*. Published annually. Washington, D.C.: U.S. Geological Survey. Available online at: http://minerals.usgs.gov.
Worldwatch Institute. *State of the World 2001* [and following years]. Online at: http://www.worldwatch.org.

New Classical Macroeconomics

Kevin D. Hoover

After Keynesian Macroeconomics

The new classical macroeconomics is a school of economic thought that originated in the early 1970s in the work of economists centered at the Universities of Chicago and Minnesota—particularly, Robert Lucas (recipient of the Nobel Prize in 1995), Thomas Sargent, Neil Wallace, and Edward Prescott (corecipient of the Nobel Prize in 2004). The name draws on John Maynard Keynes's evocative contrast between his own macroeconomics and that of his intellectual forebears. Keynes had knowingly stretched a point by lumping his contemporaries, A. C. Pigou and Alfred Marshall, in with the older classical political economists, such as David Ricardo, and calling them all "classical."

According to Keynes, the classics saw the price system in a free economy as efficiently guiding the mutual adjustment of supply and demand in all markets, including the labor market. Unemployment could arise only because of a market imperfection—the intervention of the government or the action of labor unions—and could be eliminated through removing the imperfection. In contrast, Keynes shifted the focus of his analysis away from individual markets to the whole economy. He argued that even without market imperfections, aggregate demand (equal, in a closed economy, to consumption plus investment plus government expenditure) might fall short of the aggregate productive capacity of its labor and capital (plant, equipment, raw material, and infrastructure). In such a situation, unemployment is largely involuntary—that is, workers may be unemployed even though they are willing to work at a wage lower than the wage the firms pay their current workers.

Later Keynesian economists achieved a measure of reconciliation with the classics. PAUL SAMUELSON argued for a "neoclassical synthesis" in which classical economics was viewed as governing resource allocation when the economy was kept, through judicious government policy, at full employment. Other Keynesian economists sought to explain consumption, investment, the demand for money, and other key elements of the aggregate Keynesian model in a manner consistent with the assumption that individuals behave optimally. This was the program of "microfoundations for macroeconomics."

Origins of the New Classical Macroeconomics

Although its name suggests a rejection of Keynesian economics and a revival of classical economics, the new classical macroeconomics began with Lucas's and Leonard Rapping's attempt to provide microfoundations for the Keynesian labor market. Lucas and Rapping applied the rule that equilibrium in a market occurs when quantity supplied equals quantity demanded. This turned out to be a radical step. Because involuntary unemployment is exactly the situation in which the amount of labor supplied exceeds the amount demanded, their analysis leaves no room at all for involuntary unemployment.

Keynes's view was that recessions occur when aggregate demand falls—largely as the result of a fall in private investment—causing firms to produce below their capacity. Producing less, firms need fewer workers, and thus employment falls. Firms, for reasons that Keynesian economists continue to debate, fail to cut wages to as low a level as job seekers will accept, and so involuntary unemployment rises. The new classicals reject this step as irrational. Involuntary unemployment would present firms with an opportunity to raise profits by paying workers a lower wage. If firms failed to take the opportunity, then they would not be optimizing. Employed workers should not be able to resist such wage cuts effectively since the unemployed stand ready to take their places at the lower wage. Keynesian economics would appear, then, to rest either on market imperfections or on irrationality, both of which Keynes denied.

These criticisms of Keynesian economics illustrate the two fundamental tenets of the new classical macroeconomics. First, individuals are viewed as optimizers: given the prices, including wage rates, they face and the assets they hold, including their education and training (or "human capital"), they choose the best options available. Firms maximize profits; people maximize utility. Second, to a first approximation, prices adjust, changing the incentives to individuals, and thereby their choices, to align quantities supplied and demanded.

Business Cycles

Business cycles pose a special challenge for new classical economists: How are large fluctuations in output compatible with the two fundamental tenets of their doctrine?

Here is how. The economy, they believe, is often buffeted by unexpected shocks. Shocks to aggregate demand are typically unanticipated changes in monetary or fiscal policy. Shocks to aggregate supply are typically changes in productivity that may result, for example, from transient changes to technology, prices of raw materials, or the organization of production. Ideally, firms would choose to produce more and to pay their workers more when the economy has been hit by favorable shocks and less when hit by unfavorable shocks. Similarly, workers would be willing to work more when productivity and wage rates are higher and to take more leisure when their rewards are lower. For both, the rule is "make hay while the sun shines."

Employment, like output, would clearly rise with favorable shocks and fall with unfavorable shocks. But having rejected the very notion of involuntary unemployment, why do new classicals think that the unemployment rate would fall in the boom and rise in the slump? When a worker is laid off, he must seek a new job. He weighs the value of taking a lower-paid job that might be easily available (a machinist might become a day laborer) against the value of a better-paid, more suitable job that is harder to find. The new classicals do not argue that the unemployed job searcher is happy with his choice: being laid off was a bad draw, and, like everyone, he prefers good luck to bad. Rather, they argue that the worker chooses what he regards as the best available option, even when the options are poor. To remain unemployed (and to show up in the unemployment statistics) is something that he chooses based on his judgment that the benefits of the search outweigh the costs; this is not an exception to the rule that amount supplied equals amount demanded.

The fact that the economy experiences good and bad shocks is not enough to explain business cycles. An adequate theory must account for persistence—the fact that business cycles typically display long runs of good times followed by shorter, but still significant, runs of bad times. Those new classicals who regard demand shocks as dominant argue that the shocks are propagated slowly. It is always costly to adjust production levels quickly. Similarly, when higher production requires new capital, it takes time to build it up. And when lower production renders existing capital redundant, it takes time to wear it out or use it up. New classicals of the "real-business-cycle school" (led by EDWARD PRESCOTT and FINN KYDLAND, corecipients of the 2004 Nobel Prize) regard changes in productivity as the driving force in business cycles. Because changes in technology may also come in waves, runs of favorable or unfavorable productivity (or technology) shocks may ac-

count for some of the persistence characteristic of business cycles.

Rational Expectations and Policy Ineffectiveness

Most economic decisions are forward looking. To know whether today is a day for work or for leisure, we need to decide whether tomorrow will be more or less productive than today; in short, we must have an expectation of the future. How should economists analyze expectations? The new classicals adopted John Muth's "rational-expectations hypothesis" (see RATIONAL EXPECTATIONS). Muth argued that an economic model in which people's expectations differ from the outcomes predicted by the model itself is poorly formulated. If the predictions of the model were correct—and therefore people's expectations were wrong—then they could use the model to correct their own expectations. To fail to do so would result in economic losses and would be irrational. At one level, Muth's hypothesis is just a technical consistency criterion for models. At another level, it appeals to the economic insight that people will not persist in easily correctable, systematic, and costly errors. The new classicals appeal implicitly (and sometimes explicitly) to Lincoln's well-known adage: "You can fool some of the people all of the time, and all of the people some of the time, but you cannot fool all of the people all of the time." They warn policymakers that a policy that depends on the assumption that the public systematically misunderstands its own interest is likely to fail.

Keynesian economists of the 1960s often appealed to the PHILLIPS CURVE, taking it to imply that monetary or fiscal policy that lowered the unemployment rate also caused a higher inflation rate. The interesting policy question was the trade-off: How much extra inflation was a one-point fall in the unemployment rate worth? The new classicals rejected the idea that there was any useful trade-off. They argued that an expansion of aggregate demand lowered unemployment only because the acceleration in prices was not anticipated. Firms that mistook higher market prices for higher real returns would be willing to produce more. Workers who mistook higher market wages for higher purchasing power would be willing, if unemployed, to take a job sooner. Increased output and lower unemployment would, however, be temporary because neither the returns to firms nor the purchasing power of workers was, corrected for inflation, really higher. As soon as they realized the mistake, firms and workers would return to old levels of production and labor supply.

What is more, having made the mistake once, they would not be easily fooled again by the same policy. The combination of rational expectations and the central tenet of new classical analysis that quantity supplied equals quantity demanded ensures that *systematic, pure* aggregate-demand policies do not have real effects on the economy. The Phillips curve trade-off can be observed in the data because some part of policy is always unanticipated. But policymakers cannot exploit it because the public will see through any systematic policy. Because it rejected the prevailing Keynesian view that monetary policy could offset a recession, this "policy-ineffectiveness proposition" became the most startling and controversial conclusion of the early new classical macroeconomics.

The policy-ineffectiveness proposition is frequently misunderstood. It is not a claim that no government policy affects the economy. Policies on government spending, for example, represent changes in the real claims the government makes on GDP and may affect output and employment. Rather, the proposition is limited to the effects of changes in government liabilities (the monetary base and the government debt) that may affect the rate of inflation. In this respect, the policy-ineffectiveness proposition is related to another new classical proposition: Ricardian equivalence (see GOVERNMENT DEBT AND DEFICITS). Ricardian equivalence is the claim that whether a given path of government expenditure is financed through taxes or debt is unimportant: substituting debt for taxes appears to increase disposable income today. But since the debt must be repaid with interest, a rational taxpayer would save the entire windfall in order to afford the future tax bill, leaving his expenditure unchanged. Ricardian equivalence remains controversial because it depends on assumptions about the public's foresight and grasp of the fiscal system closely related to the rational-expectations hypothesis and on debatable assumptions about the incidence of taxes and expenditure.

The Lucas Critique

Unanticipated policy has real effects, but, because it is unanticipated, it cannot be systematic—and therefore it cannot be used to direct the economy. The systematic element of policy can be viewed, implicitly at least, as a policy rule. Consider the Phillips curve again. How much does unemployment fall for a one-percentage-point increase in the price level? Lucas argued that the answer depends on the policy rule. If the rule had been one that held the inflation rate to zero (prices are constant), then the increase would be unanticipated and unemployment would fall. If the rule had been one that maintained a steady 1 percent rate of inflation (each year prices grow by 1 percent), then the increase would be just what systematic policy implied, the inflation would be perfectly anticipated, and unemploy-

ment would not change. And if the rule had been one that maintained a steady 2 percent rate of inflation, then a one-percentage-point increase would fall short of what had been anticipated, and unemployment would rise. These different trade-offs suggest that there is a different Phillips curve for each policy rule. A Phillips curve estimated under one policy regime would not predict accurately what would happen under a different regime.

Lucas argued that what is true of the Phillips curve in this example is true of the most important relationships in the econometric macroeconomic models used to evaluate economic policy. His analysis has come to be known as the "policy non-invariance" or "Lucas" critique.

The Legacy of the New Classical Macroeconomics

The new classicals profoundly changed the technical underpinnings of modern macroeconomics. Economists now widely accept the Lucas critique. To avoid it, economists sought ways to predict exactly how estimated relationships would change with the policy regime by integrating rational expectations and the public's response to policy rules into their models. Because rational expectations depend on the structure of the whole economy, the program of microfoundations is no longer content to look at different markets separately, but concentrates on general equilibrium among them. Dynamic models have replaced static models: policy actions cannot be evaluated merely for what they do today, but for how they change people's judgments about the future.

While few economists want to assume that the government can fool the public systematically, many remain skeptical of the rational-expectations hypothesis as a description of people's actual expectations. Some, including founding new classicals such as Sargent, have explored models of learning that emphasize that overcoming expectational errors is a process that may take some time.

Most economists, even among the new classicals, no longer accept the policy-ineffectiveness proposition. It is widely agreed that wages and prices do not move quickly and smoothly to the values needed for long-run equilibrium between quantities supplied and demanded. Consequently, even if monetary policy is ineffective in the long run, it may be of considerable use in the short run.

While optimal search and voluntary changes in labor supply may explain a large portion of routine unemployment rates, many economists question whether they explain high unemployment in recessions. Was the 25 percent unemployment rate of the Great Depression the result of a mass decision to take a vacation? New Keynesian critics typically maintain that unemployment is, in fact, characterized by wages above the level needed to clear the labor market. But what, exactly, prevents firms from taking profitable advantage of the situation remains controversial.

About the Author

Kevin D. Hoover is professor of the departments of economics and philosophy at Duke University. He is past president of the History of Economics Society, past chairman of the International Network for Economic Method, and editor of the *Journal of Economic Methodology.*

Further Reading

Hartley, James, Kevin D. Hoover, and Kevin D. Salyer, eds. *Real Business Cycles: A Reader.* London: Routledge, 1998. Important articles for and against real business cycle models, including Finn E. Kydland and Edward C. Prescott's seminal "Time to Build and Aggregate Fluctuations," and the editors' introduction that presents an accessible, critical account of the models.

Hoover, Kevin D. *The New Classical Macroeconomics: A Sceptical Inquiry.* Oxford: Blackwell, 1988. General account of the new classical economics.

Lucas, Robert E., Jr. *Studies in Business Cycle Theory.* Oxford: Blackwell, 1981. Some of Lucas's own articles are collected here, including "Econometric Testing of the Natural Rate Hypothesis," a formal but relatively accessible presentation of key new classical ideas, and "Understanding Business Cycles," which lays out the basis for the new classical theory of the business cycle.

Lucas, Robert E., Jr., and Thomas J. Sargent, eds. *Rational Expectations and Econometric Practice.* London: Allen and Unwin, 1981. Many key articles covering the first decade of the new classical school, including Muth's original article on rational expectations, Sargent and Wallace's articles on the policy-ineffectiveness proposition, and Lucas and Sargent's new classical manifesto, "After Keynesian Macroeconomics."

Sheffrin, Steven M. *Rational Expectations.* 2d ed. Cambridge: Cambridge University Press, 1996. General account of the new classical economics.

New Keynesian Economics

N. Gregory Mankiw

New Keynesian economics is the school of thought in modern macroeconomics that evolved from the ideas of John Maynard Keynes. Keynes wrote *The General Theory of Employment, Interest, and Money* in the 1930s, and his influence among academics and policymakers increased through the 1960s. In the 1970s, however, new classical economists such as Robert Lucas, Thomas J. Sargent, and Robert Barro called into question many of the precepts of the Keynesian revolution. The label "new Keynesian" describes those economists who, in the 1980s, responded to this new classical critique with adjustments to the original Keynesian tenets.

The primary disagreement between new classical and new Keynesian economists is over how quickly wages and prices adjust. New classical economists build their macroeconomic theories on the assumption that wages and prices are flexible. They believe that prices "clear" markets—balance supply and demand—by adjusting quickly. New Keynesian economists, however, believe that market-clearing models cannot explain short-run economic fluctuations, and so they advocate models with "sticky" wages and prices. New Keynesian theories rely on this stickiness of wages and prices to explain why involuntary unemployment exists and why monetary policy has such a strong influence on economic activity.

A long tradition in macroeconomics (including both Keynesian and monetarist perspectives) emphasizes that monetary policy affects employment and production in the short run because prices respond sluggishly to changes in the money supply. According to this view, if the money supply falls, people spend less money and the demand for goods falls. Because prices and wages are inflexible and do not fall immediately, the decreased spending causes a drop in production and layoffs of workers. New classical economists criticized this tradition because it lacks a coherent theoretical explanation for the sluggish behavior of prices. Much new Keynesian research attempts to remedy this omission.

Menu Costs and Aggregate-Demand Externalities

One reason prices do not adjust immediately to clear markets is that adjusting prices is costly. To change its prices, a firm may need to send out a new catalog to customers, distribute new price lists to its sales staff, or, in the case of a restaurant, print new menus. These costs of price adjustment, called "menu costs," cause firms to adjust prices intermittently rather than continuously.

Economists disagree about whether menu costs can help explain short-run economic fluctuations. Skeptics point out that menu costs usually are very small. They argue that these small costs are unlikely to help explain recessions, which are very costly for society. Proponents reply that "small" does not mean "inconsequential." Even though menu costs are small for the individual firm, they could have large effects on the economy as a whole.

Proponents of the menu-cost hypothesis describe the situation as follows. To understand why prices adjust slowly, one must acknowledge that changes in prices have externalities—that is, effects that go beyond the firm and its customers. For instance, a price reduction by one firm benefits other firms in the economy. When a firm lowers the price it charges, it lowers the average price level slightly and thereby raises real income. (Nominal income is determined by the money supply.) The stimulus from higher income, in turn, raises the demand for the products of all firms. This macroeconomic impact of one firm's price adjustment on the demand for all other firms' products is called an "aggregate-demand externality."

In the presence of this aggregate-demand externality, small menu costs can make prices sticky, and this stickiness can have a large cost to society. Suppose General Motors announces its prices and then, after a fall in the money supply, must decide whether to cut prices. If it did so, car buyers would have a higher real income and would therefore buy more products from other companies as well. But the benefits to other companies are not what General Motors cares about. Therefore, General Motors would sometimes fail to pay the menu cost and cut its price, even though the price cut is socially desirable. This is an example in which sticky prices are undesirable for the economy as a whole, even though they may be optimal for those setting prices.

The Staggering of Prices

New Keynesian explanations of sticky prices often emphasize that not everyone in the economy sets prices at the same time. Instead, the adjustment of prices throughout the economy is staggered. Staggering complicates the setting of prices because firms care about their prices relative to those charged by other firms. Staggering can make the overall level of prices adjust slowly, even when individual prices change frequently.

Consider the following example. Suppose, first, that price setting is synchronized: every firm adjusts its price on the first of every month. If the money supply and aggregate demand rise on May 10, output will be higher from May 10 to June 1 because prices are fixed during this interval. But on June 1 all firms will raise their prices in response to the higher demand, ending the three-week boom.

Now suppose that price setting is staggered: half the firms set prices on the first of each month and half on the fifteenth. If the money supply rises on May 10, then half of the firms can raise their prices on May 15. Yet because half of the firms will not be changing their prices on the fifteenth, a price increase by any firm will raise that firm's

relative price, which will cause it to lose customers. Therefore, these firms will probably not raise their prices very much. (In contrast, if all firms are synchronized, all firms can raise prices together, leaving relative prices unaffected.) If the May 15 price setters make little adjustment in their prices, then the other firms will make little adjustment when their turn comes on June 1, because they also want to avoid relative price changes. And so on. The price level rises slowly as the result of small price increases on the first and the fifteenth of each month. Hence, staggering makes the price level sluggish, because no firm wishes to be the first to post a substantial price increase.

Coordination Failure

Some new Keynesian economists suggest that recessions result from a failure of coordination. Coordination problems can arise in the setting of wages and prices because those who set them must anticipate the actions of other wage and price setters. Union leaders negotiating wages are concerned about the concessions other unions will win. Firms setting prices are mindful of the prices other firms will charge.

To see how a recession could arise as a failure of coordination, consider the following parable. The economy is made up of two firms. After a fall in the money supply, each firm must decide whether to cut its price. Each firm wants to maximize its profit, but its profit depends not only on its pricing decision but also on the decision made by the other firm.

If neither firm cuts its price, the amount of real money (the amount of money divided by the price level) is low, a recession ensues, and each firm makes a profit of only fifteen dollars.

If both firms cut their price, real money balances are high, a recession is avoided, and each firm makes a profit of thirty dollars. Although both firms prefer to avoid a recession, neither can do so by its own actions. If one firm cuts its price while the other does not, a recession follows. The firm making the price cut makes only five dollars, while the other firm makes fifteen dollars.

The essence of this parable is that each firm's decision influences the set of outcomes available to the other firm. When one firm cuts its price, it improves the opportunities available to the other firm, because the other firm can then avoid the recession by cutting its price. This positive impact of one firm's price cut on the other firm's profit opportunities might arise because of an aggregate-demand externality.

What outcome should one expect in this economy? On the one hand, if each firm expects the other to cut its price, both will cut prices, resulting in the preferred outcome in which each makes thirty dollars. On the other hand, if each firm expects the other to maintain its price, both will maintain their prices, resulting in the inferior solution, in which each makes fifteen dollars. Hence, either of these outcomes is possible: there are multiple equilibria.

The inferior outcome, in which each firm makes fifteen dollars, is an example of a coordination failure. If the two firms could coordinate, they would both cut their price and reach the preferred outcome. In the real world, unlike in this parable, coordination is often difficult because the number of firms setting prices is large. The moral of the story is that even though sticky prices are in no one's interest, prices can be sticky simply because price setters expect them to be.

Efficiency Wages

Another important part of new Keynesian economics has been the development of new theories of unemployment. Persistent unemployment is a puzzle for economic theory. Normally, economists presume that an excess supply of labor would exert a downward pressure on wages. A reduction in wages would in turn reduce unemployment by raising the quantity of labor demanded. Hence, according to standard economic theory, unemployment is a self-correcting problem.

New Keynesian economists often turn to theories of what they call efficiency wages to explain why this market-clearing mechanism may fail. These theories hold that high wages make workers more productive. The influence of wages on worker efficiency may explain the failure of firms to cut wages despite an excess supply of labor. Even though a wage reduction would lower a firm's wage bill, it would also—if the theories are correct—cause worker productivity and the firm's profits to decline.

There are various theories about how wages affect worker productivity. One efficiency-wage theory holds that high wages reduce labor turnover. Workers quit jobs for many reasons—to accept better positions at other firms, to change careers, or to move to other parts of the country. The more a firm pays its workers, the greater their incentive to stay with the firm. By paying a high wage, a firm reduces the frequency of quits, thereby decreasing the time spent hiring and training new workers.

A second efficiency-wage theory holds that the average quality of a firm's workforce depends on the wage it pays its employees. If a firm reduces wages, the best employees may take jobs elsewhere, leaving the firm with less-productive employees who have fewer alternative opportunities. By paying a wage above the equilibrium level, the firm may avoid this adverse selection, improve the average quality of its workforce, and thereby increase productivity.

A third efficiency-wage theory holds that a high wage improves worker effort. This theory posits that firms cannot perfectly monitor the work effort of their employees and that employees must themselves decide how hard to work. Workers can choose to work hard, or they can choose to shirk and risk getting caught and fired. The firm can raise worker effort by paying a high wage. The higher the wage, the greater is the cost to the worker of getting fired. By paying a higher wage, a firm induces more of its employees not to shirk, and thus increases their productivity.

A New Synthesis

During the 1990s, the debate between new classical and new Keynesian economists led to the emergence of a new synthesis among macroeconomists about the best way to explain short-run economic fluctuations and the role of monetary and fiscal policies. The new synthesis attempts to merge the strengths of the competing approaches that preceded it. From the new classical models it takes a variety of modeling tools that shed light on how households and firms make decisions over time. From the new Keynesian models it takes price rigidities and uses them to explain why monetary policy affects employment and production in the short run. The most common approach is to assume monopolistically competitive firms (firms that have market power but compete with other firms) that change prices only intermittently.

The heart of the new synthesis is the view that the economy is a dynamic general equilibrium system that deviates from an efficient allocation of resources in the short run because of sticky prices and perhaps a variety of other market imperfections. In many ways, this new synthesis forms the intellectual foundation for the analysis of monetary policy at the Federal Reserve and other central banks around the world.

Policy Implications

Because new Keynesian economics is a school of thought regarding macroeconomic theory, its adherents do not necessarily share a single view about economic policy. At the broadest level, new Keynesian economics suggests—in contrast to some new classical theories—that recessions are departures from the normal efficient functioning of markets. The elements of new Keynesian economics—such as menu costs, staggered prices, coordination failures, and efficiency wages—represent substantial deviations from the assumptions of classical economics, which provides the intellectual basis for economists' usual justification of laissez-faire. In new Keynesian theories recessions are caused by some economy-wide market failure.

Thus, new Keynesian economics provides a rationale for government intervention in the economy, such as countercyclical monetary or fiscal policy. This part of new Keynesian economics has been incorporated into the new synthesis that has emerged among macroeconomists. Whether policymakers should intervene in practice, however, is a more difficult question that entails various political as well as economic judgments.

About the Author

N. Gregory Mankiw is a professor of economics at Harvard University. From 2003 to 2005, he was the chairman of President George W. Bush's Council of Economic Advisers.

Further Reading

Clarida, Richard, Jordi Gali, and Mark Gertler. "The Science of Monetary Policy: A New Keynesian Perspective." *Journal of Economic Literature* 37 (1999): 1661–1707.

Goodfriend, Marvin, and Robert King. "The New Neoclassical Synthesis and the Role of Monetary Policy." In Ben S. Bernanke and Julio Rotemberg, eds., *NBER Macroeconomics Annual 1997*. Cambridge: MIT Press, 1997. Pp. 231–283.

Mankiw, N. Gregory, and David Romer, eds. *New Keynesian Economics*. 2 vols. Cambridge: MIT Press, 1991.

OPEC

Benjamin Zycher

Few observers and even few experts remember that the Organization of Petroleum Exporting Countries (OPEC) was created in response to the 1959 imposition of import quotas on crude oil and refined products by the United States. In 1959, the U.S. government established the Mandatory Oil Import Quota program (MOIP), which restricted the amount of imported crude oil and refined products allowed into the United States and gave preferential treatment to oil imports from Canada, Mexico, and, somewhat later, Venezuela. This partial exclusion of Persian Gulf oil from the U.S. market depressed prices for Middle Eastern oil; as a result, oil prices "posted" (paid to the selling nations) were reduced in February 1959 and August 1960.

In September 1960, four Persian Gulf nations (Iran, Iraq, Kuwait, and Saudi Arabia) and Venezuela formed OPEC in order to obtain higher prices for crude oil. By 1973, eight other nations (Algeria, Ecuador, Gabon, Indonesia, Libya, Nigeria, Qatar, and the United Arab Emirates) had joined OPEC; Ecuador withdrew at the end of 1992, and Gabon withdrew in 1994.

The collective effort to raise oil prices was unsuccessful during the 1960s; real (i.e., inflation-adjusted) world market prices for crude oil fell from $9.78 (in 2004 dollars) in 1960 to $7.08 in 1970. However, real prices began to rise slowly in 1971 and then increased sharply in late 1973 and 1974, from roughly $10.00 per barrel to more than $36.00 per barrel in the wake of the 1973 Arab-Israeli ("Yom Kippur") War.

Despite what many noneconomists believe, the 1973–1974 price increase was not caused by the oil "embargo" (refusal to sell) that the Arab members of OPEC directed at the United States and the Netherlands. Instead, OPEC reduced its production of crude oil, raising world market prices sharply. The embargo against the United States and the Netherlands had no effect whatsoever: people in both nations were able to obtain oil at the same prices as people in all other nations. This failure of the embargo was predictable, in that oil is a "fungible" commodity that can be resold among buyers. An embargo by sellers is an attempt to raise prices for some buyers but not others. Only one price can prevail in the world market, however, because differences in prices will lead to arbitrage: that is, a higher price in a given market will induce other buyers to resell oil into the high-price market, thus equalizing prices worldwide.

Nor, as is commonly believed, did OPEC cause oil shortages and gasoline lines in the United States. Instead, the shortages were caused by price and allocation controls on crude oil and refined products, imposed originally by President Richard Nixon in 1971 as part of the Economic Stabilization Program. Although the price controls allowed the price of crude oil to rise, it was not allowed to rise to free-market levels. Thus, the price controls caused the amount people wanted to consume to exceed the amount available at the legal maximum prices. Shortages were the inevitable result. Moreover, the allocation controls distorted the distribution of supplies; the government based allocations on consumption patterns observed before the sharp increase in prices. The higher prices, for example, reduced long-distance driving and agricultural fuel consumption, but the use of historical consumption patterns resulted in a relative oversupply of gasoline in rural areas and a relative undersupply in urban ones, thus exacerbating the effects of the price controls themselves. Countries whose governments did not impose price controls, such as (then West) Germany and Switzerland, did not experience shortages and queues.

OPEC is in many ways a CARTEL—a group of producers that attempts to restrict output in order to raise prices above the competitive level. The decision-making center of OPEC is the Conference, comprising national delegations at the level of oil minister, which meets twice each year to decide overall oil output—and thus prices—and to assign output quotas for the individual members. Those quotas are upper limits on the amount of oil each member is allowed to produce. The Conference also may meet in special sessions when deemed necessary, particularly when downward pressure on prices becomes acute.

OPEC faces the classic cartel enforcement problem: overproduction and price cheating by members. At the higher cartel price, less oil is demanded; output quotas are necessary in that each member of OPEC has an incentive to sell more than its quota by "shaving" (cutting) its price because the cost of producing an additional barrel of oil usually is well below the cartel price. The methods available to engage in such cheating are numerous: sellers can extend credit to buyers for periods longer than the standard thirty days, sell higher grades (or blends) of oil for prices applicable to lower grades, give transportation credits, offer buyers side payments or rebates, and so on.

This tendency of individual producers to cheat on a cartel agreement is a long-standing feature of OPEC behavior. Individual producers usually have exceeded their production quotas, and so official OPEC prices have been somewhat unstable. But unlike the classic "textbook" cartel, OPEC is unusual in that one producer—Saudi Arabia—is much larger than the others. This condition has caused Saudi Arabia to serve, from time to time, as the OPEC "swing" producer—that is, the producer that adjusts its output in order to preserve the official price in the world market. One reason the Saudis have so acted is that downward pressure on the official price imposes larger total losses on them than on the other OPEC producers in the short run. The Saudis, in their efforts to defend the official OPEC price, have periodically reduced their sales, at times dramatically, thus reducing their revenues substantially. In 1983, 1984, and 1986, for example, the Saudis produced only about 3.5 million barrels per day, despite their (then) production capacity of about 10 million barrels per day.

How successful has OPEC been since the early 1970s? Not as successful as many observers believe. Except in the wake of the 1979 Iranian upheaval, and in market anticipation of a possible destruction of substantial reserves in the 1990–1991 and 2003 Gulf wars, real prices of crude oil fell from 1974 through 2003. Prices increased in 2004 and (thus far) 2005, but this has little to do with the effectiveness of OPEC as a cartel. The causes of the 2004 and 2005 price increases were increased demand in Asia; production problems in Venezuela, Nigeria, and other producing regions; a weakening dollar; and an increased terrorist threat to oil production and transport facilities. Over the longer time frame, prices began declining rapidly in

the early 1980s, after the Reagan administration ended the price and allocation regulations, which, because of their specific design, increased the U.S. demand for foreign oil. The Saudis then concluded that lower prices and higher production would further their interests; world market prices (in 2004 dollars) fell from $62.76 per barrel in 1981 to $44.89 in 1984, $21.84 in 1986, and $21.39 in 1988. Indeed, prices even unadjusted for inflation often have declined, from $34.28 in 1981 to $14.96 in 1988. Table 1 shows price data; Table 2 contains current estimated reserves, official production capacity, reported production levels, and OPEC production quotas.

This longer-term downward trend in prices has yielded increased tensions between two rival groups within OPEC. The price "hawks"—for the most part nations with smaller reserves relative to population—have pressed for lower output and higher prices; the principal hawks within OPEC have been Iran and Iraq before the overthrow of the Baathist regime of Saddam Hussein. The price "doves"—for the most part nations with larger reserves relative to

Table 1 World Crude Oil Prices (U.S. dollars per barrel)

Year	Nominal Price	In Year 2004 Dollars	Year	Nominal Price	In Year 2004 Dollars
1965	1.80	8.64	1985	27.53	42.74
1966	1.80	8.41	1986	14.38	21.84
1967	1.80	8.15	1987	18.42	27.24
1968	1.80	7.82	1988	14.96	21.39
1969	1.80	7.45	1989	18.20	25.08
1970	1.80	7.08	1990	23.81	31.59
1971	2.24	8.39	1991	20.05	25.70
1972	2.48	8.90	1992	19.37	24.27
1973	3.29	11.18	1993	17.07	20.91
1974	11.58	36.09	1994	15.98	19.16
1975	11.53	32.84	1995	17.18	20.19
1976	12.38	33.34	1996	20.81	24.00
1977	13.30	33.67	1997	19.30	21.89
1978	13.60	32.17	1998	13.11	14.71
1979	30.03	65.60	1999	18.25	20.18
1980	35.69	71.48	2000	28.26	30.59
1981	34.28	62.76	2001	22.95	24.26
1982	31.76	54.81	2002	24.10	25.06
1983	28.77	47.76	2003	28.50	29.10
1984	28.06	44.89	2004	36.20	36.20

Source: U.S. Energy Information Administration, U.S. Departments of Commerce and Labor.

Table 2 Crude Oil Reserves, Production Capacity, and Production

Nation	Reserves[1]	Production Capacity[2]	Production[3]	Quota[4]
Algeria	11.8	1,305	1,305	878
Indonesia	4.7	960	960	1,425
Iran	125.8	3,900	3,900	4,037
Iraq	115.0	1,900	1,900	n.a.
Kuwait[5]	101.5	2,500	2,500	2,207
Libya	39.0	1,600	1,600	1,473
Nigeria	32.3	2,300	2,300	2,265
Qatar	15.2	800	800	713
Saudi Arabia[5]	261.9	11,000	9,500	8,937
United Arab Emirates	97.8	2,500	2,450	2,400
Venezuela	77.2	2,600	2,600	3,165
OPEC total	882.2	31,365	29,815	27,500
World total	1,277.7	87,200	85,000	n.a.

Source: U.S. Energy Information Administration.

Note: Totals may not sum due to rounding. Production capacity and production figures are subject to some dispute.

    1. Billions of barrels as of January 1, 2005.

    2. Maximum sustainable, thousands of barrels per day as of March 2005.

    3. Thousands of barrels per day as of March 2005.

    4. Thousands of barrels per day as of March 16, 2005.

    5. Includes half the Neutral Zone.

    n.a.: not applicable.

population—have argued for higher output and lower prices, so as to preserve over the longer term their oil markets, and thus the economic value of their oil resources. The principal doves within OPEC are Saudi Arabia, Kuwait, and the United Arab Emirates.

Relatively lower prices serve the interests of the OPEC doves because oil consumers have responded to prior price increases by finding ways to reduce oil consumption below levels that otherwise would have prevailed. For example, U.S. energy use per dollar of gross domestic product (2004 dollars) in 1970 was about 17,000 Btu. By 1988, after the price increases of 1973 and 1979, it had declined to about 11,600 Btu, and by 2003 it had declined further to about 8,900 Btu. Thus, the price doves, led by Saudi Arabia, generally resisted pressures for relatively higher prices.

Over the long run, the real prices of natural resources and commodities usually fall, largely because of technological advances. Crude oil is no exception. From about $47 per barrel (2004 dollars) in the late 1860s, prices fell to about $28 in 1920, about $13 in 1950, about $12 in 1960, and about $7 in 1970. The price increases of the 1970s and the first half of the 2000s are relatively recent phenomena, and historical patterns suggest that they will not be long-lived. Technological advances in seismic exploration have dramatically reduced the cost of finding new reserves, thus greatly increasing oil reserves; proven world crude oil reserves have doubled since 1980. Horizontal drilling and other new techniques have reduced the cost of producing known reserves, while other technological improvements yield both substitutes for oil and ways to use less oil to achieve given ends.

Moreover, advances in technology over time similarly will reduce prices for such substitute fuels as natural gas, thus exerting continuing downward pressure on crude oil prices. Also, an increasing willingness to devote resources toward environmental improvement suggests that the market for crude oil may decline relative to those for such "cleaner" energy sources as natural gas and nuclear power, unless other technological advances yield substantial improvement in the ability to use oil cleanly. Accordingly, the demand for crude oil over the long term may decline relative to the demand for competing fuels, just as wood gradually gave way to coal—which in turn gave way to oil. These long-term market forces suggest that the economic power of OPEC inexorably will erode.

About the Author

Benjamin Zycher is the president of Benjamin Zycher Economics Associates, Inc., and a senior fellow at the Manhattan Institute for Policy Research. From 1981 to 1983, he was the senior economist for energy with President Ronald Reagan's Council of Economic Advisers.

Further Reading

Adams, Neal. *Terrorism and Oil.* Tulsa, Okla.: PennWell, 2003.

Adelman, Morris A. *The Economics of Petroleum Supply.* Cambridge: MIT Press, 1993.

———. *Genie out of the Bottle: World Oil Since 1970.* Cambridge: MIT Press, 1995.

Bradley, Robert L. Jr. *The Mirage of Oil Protection.* Lanham, Md.: University Press of America, 1988.

———. *Oil, Gas, and Government: The U.S. Experience.* Lanham, Md.: Rowman and Littlefield, 1996.

Yergin, Daniel. *The Prize.* New York: Free Press, 1992.

Zycher, Benjamin. "A Counterintuitive Perspective on Energy Policy." United Nations Economic Commission for Europe, Briefing, November 2002.

———. "Emergency Management." In S. Fred Singer, ed., *Free Market Energy.* New York: Universe Books, 1984.

Opportunity Cost

David R. Henderson

When economists refer to the "opportunity cost" of a resource, they mean the value of the next-highest-valued alternative use of that resource. If, for example, you spend time and money going to a movie, you cannot spend that time at home reading a book, and you cannot spend the money on something else. If your next-best alternative to seeing the movie is reading the book, then the opportunity cost of seeing the movie is the money spent plus the pleasure you forgo by not reading the book.

The word "opportunity" in "opportunity cost" is actually redundant. The cost of using something is already the value of the highest-valued alternative use. But as contract lawyers and airplane pilots know, redundancy can be a virtue. In this case, its virtue is to remind us that the cost of using a resource arises from the value of what it could be used for instead.

This simple concept has powerful implications. It implies, for example, that even when governments subsidize college education, most students still pay more than half of the cost. Take a student who annually pays $4,000 in tuition at a state college. Assume that the government subsidy to the college amounts to $8,000 per student. It looks as if the cost is $12,000 and the student pays less than half. But looks can be deceiving. The true cost is $12,000 plus the income the student forgoes by attending school rather than working. If the student could have earned $20,000 per year, then the true cost of the year's schooling is $12,000 plus $20,000, for a total of $32,000. Of this $32,000 total, the student pays $24,000 ($4,000 in tuition plus $20,000 in forgone earnings). In other words, even with a hefty state subsidy, the student pays 75 percent of the whole cost. This explains why college students at state universities, even though they may grouse when the state government raises tuitions by, say, 10 percent, do not desert college in droves. A 10 percent increase in a $4,000 tuition is only $400, which is less than a 2 percent increase in the student's overall cost (see HUMAN CAPITAL).

What about the cost of room and board while attending school? This is not a true cost of attending school at all because whether or not the student attends school, the student still has expenses for room and board.

About the Author

David R. Henderson is the editor of this encyclopedia. He is a research fellow with Stanford University's Hoover Institution and an associate professor of economics at the Naval Post-graduate School in Monterey, California. He was formerly a senior economist with President Ronald Reagan's Council of Economic Advisers.

Further Reading

Alchian, Armen. "Cost." In *Encyclopedia of the Social Sciences.* New York: Macmillan. Vol. 3, pp. 404–415.
Buchanan, J. M. *Cost and Choice.* Chicago: Markham. 1969. Republished as Midway Reprint. Chicago: University of Chicago Press, 1977.

Pensions

Henry McMillan

A private pension plan is an organized program to provide retirement income for a firm's workers. Some 56.7 percent of full-time, full-year wage and salary workers in the United States participate in employment-based pension plans (EBRI Issue Brief, October 2003). Private trusteed pension plans receive special tax treatment and are subject to eligibility, coverage, and benefit standards. Private pensions have become an important financial intermediary in the United States, with assets totaling $3.0 trillion at year-end 2002, while state and local government retirement funds totaled $1.967 trillion. By comparison, all New York Stock Exchange (NYSE) listed stocks totaled $9.557 trillion at year-end 2002. In other words, private and local government pension plan assets are large enough to purchase about 60 percent of all stocks listed on the NYSE.

For individuals, future pension benefits provided by employers substitute for current wages and personal saving. A person would be indifferent between pension benefits and personal saving for retirement if each provided the same retirement income at the same cost of forgone current consumption. Tax advantages, however, create a bias in favor of saving through organized pension plans administered by the employee's firm and away from direct saving.

For a firm, pension plans serve two primary functions: first, pension benefits substitute for wages; second, pensions can provide firms with a source of financing because pension benefits need not require current cash payments. The current U.S. tax code provides additional advantages for using pension plans to finance operations.

Basic Features of U.S. Pension Plans

Virtually all private plans satisfy federal requirements for favorable tax treatment. The tax advantages are three: (1) pension costs of a firm are, within limits, tax deductible;

(2) investment income of a pension fund is tax exempt; and (3) pension benefits are taxed when paid to retirees, not when earned by workers.

To qualify for these tax advantages, pension plan benefits must not discriminate in favor of highly compensated employees, and plan obligations must be satisfied through an organized funding program (see McGill et al. 1996 for further details on these and other institutional features).

Benefits are calculated through formulas established in the pension plan. There are two primary plan types: defined contribution and defined benefit.

Defined Contribution Plans

Defined contribution (DC) plans specify (define) a firm's payments (contribution) to the pension fund. The funds are allocated to individual employees, much like a bank account or mutual fund. When the individual reaches retirement age, he or she usually can take the accumulated money as a lump-sum payment or use it to purchase a retirement annuity. Special cases of defined contribution plans include Internal Revenue Code (IRC) sections 401(k), 403(b), and 457 plans.

For example, suppose a DC pension plan specifies that 5 percent of a worker's salary be contributed each year to a pension fund. Suppose the worker starts at age thirty-five, retires at age sixty-five, and earns $50,000 annually. Then the firm's annual contribution would be $2,500 (5 percent of $50,000). If the fund earns 7 percent annually, the worker would have $244,277 in the pension fund at retirement, which could purchase a twenty-year annuity paying $22,727 annually.

Defined Benefit Plans

A defined benefit (DB) plan specifies (defines) the monthly payment (benefit) a retiree receives instead of the annual contribution the employer makes. The benefit is typically specified in terms of years of service and percentage of salary. For example, a plan might specify that a worker will receive 1.5 percent of his or her average monthly salary in the last five years of service, times years of service. If the worker began at thirty-five, retired at sixty-five, and earned an average of $50,000 in the last five years, the annual retirement payment would be $22,500 (45 percent of $50,000). The worker's firm must pay the promised benefit, either by taking money from the pension fund annually or by purchasing an annuity for the worker from an insurance company. For the pension expense to be tax deductible, the firm must establish an actuarial funding program designed to accumulate enough assets to provide promised benefits.

An actuarial funding program combines data on plan specifications, employee characteristics, and pension fund size with assumptions about future interest, salary, turnover, death, and disability rates. Given these assumptions and data, an actuary estimates the firm's future pension obligations and an annual payment schedule to satisfy those obligations. Different interest rate and salary assumptions can have a substantial effect on annual contributions, given a plan's characteristics and an actuarial funding method. A rule of thumb is that an increase of the valuation interest rate by one percentage point will lower pension liabilities by 15 percent, holding all else constant.

Similarly, different actuarial funding methods can substantially affect required and allowable contributions in any given year, even with the same plan characteristics and actuarial assumptions. For example, when Financial Accounting Standards Board Statement no. 87 specified a particular actuarial method for financial disclosure, this raised pension expenses by nine million dollars for Firestone but lowered expenses by forty million dollars for Goodyear when first applied in 1986 (Bleiberg 1988). Federal law, regulations, and accounting standards have reduced the latitude available in the choice of assumptions and in funding methods.

Defined benefit plans are more common among large firms, unionized labor forces, and public-sector employees. Defined contribution plans are smaller, on average, but more numerous, and they frequently supplement an existing defined benefit plan. Defined contribution plans have been growing more rapidly, possibly because government regulation has made defined benefit plans relatively more costly to operate, especially for small firms.

Hybrid Plans

Hybrid plans combine elements of defined benefit and defined contribution plans. The most common type is known as a cash balance plan. Benefits are defined in a manner similar to that of a defined benefit plan. However, a cash balance is established for each employee, which is really just a bookkeeping device to track benefit accruals. An employee who leaves the firm before retirement is permitted to take the cash balance on leaving.

Plan Termination

Pension plans can be terminated. With defined contribution plans, the firm merely passes the pension fund management to an insurance company and stops making future contributions. Terminating a defined benefit plan is more complicated and controversial since pension fund assets do not necessarily equal the present value of pension benefits. If assets exceed promised benefits, the excess assets may revert to the employer, subject to certain tax penalties. If a company fails and its pension assets fall short of obligations, deficiencies are partially insured by the Pension Benefit Guaranty Corporation (PBGC), a federal corporation established by the Employee Retirement Income Security Act of 1974 (ERISA). Recent large terminations of pension plans by LTV Steel, TWA, and Polaroid, coupled with the stock market decline, have moved the PBGC from a surplus to a deficit position.

Economic Issues

A basic premise of the extensive economic literature on pension policy in the United States is that pension benefits are not free goods: they are provided to workers as substitutes for current wages. Economists have found that the higher a person's marginal tax rate, the higher his pension is likely to be as a percentage of his wages. This makes sense because pensions are, in part, a means of tax avoidance. Also, the higher an individual's income, the higher his pension benefit will be as a percentage of current income. So, if a person's income doubles, the pension portion of his current total compensation might rise from, say, 8 to 12 percent.

How do firms choose how much to fund pension plans and what kinds of assets to invest in? For defined contribution plans, the first half of the question is simple: the employer has to make the promised contribution (e.g., 5 percent of salary or wages) each year and has no other funding decisions to make. Thus, the only ongoing issue for a defined contribution plan is how to invest the assets. Standard portfolio theory suggests that workers would be best off with some well-diversified combination of stocks, bonds, and treasury bills. The relative weights on the portfolios would depend on the worker's tolerance for risk: the more risk the worker wants to take, the higher the proportion in stock. Because attitudes toward risk differ among individuals and for any one individual as he ages, defined contribution plans frequently allow participants to allocate their contributions among a handful of mutual funds.

For defined benefit plans the answers to both parts of the question are much more complex. In practice, most pension plans are roughly "fully funded" (meaning that assets equal the present value of benefits already earned by workers), and the pension fund is split equally between stocks and bonds. Economists are not sure why this is so but have come up with two possible explanations. The first assumes that the firm owns the pension fund. If so, the firm should choose the funding and portfolio strategy with the highest net present value to it. This leads to two polar-opposite solutions: underfund and buy risky assets, or overfund and buy high-grade bonds.

Why does the first strategy—underfunding and buying risky assets—make sense? Under federal law, a firm can terminate its pension plans without further cost only if the pension fund is greater than accrued benefits or if the firm is bankrupt. In the latter case, the PBGC absorbs the excess liability up to a certain maximum. The insurance premium the firm pays the PBGC bears no relation to the riskiness of its pension fund investments and only limited relation to its funding ratio—the ratio of pension fund assets to pension liabilities. (The basic premium is nineteen dollars per participant with an incremental nine dollars per thousand dollars of unfunded vested benefits.) Therefore, the government's insurance plan gives the firm an incentive to fund the pension plan only to the minimum required, to substitute pension benefits for wages as much as workers will allow, and then to invest the fund in risky assets such as stock or junk bonds. If the investment works out, the firm gains. If the investment fails, the government and the firm's workers lose. Note the similarity to federal deposit insurance: both create an incentive to invest in risky assets because the government (actually, the taxpayer) covers losses.

Now for the second strategy—overfunding and buying bonds. This makes sense as a way of reducing taxes for stockholders. Stockholders can reduce their taxes by shifting highly taxed assets out of their taxable personal portfolio and into the tax-exempt pension fund portfolio. This strategy works if stockholders implicitly own the pension fund and can claim those funds later by reducing funding. Furthermore, stockholders can increase their wealth by issuing debt on the corporate account (which is tax deductible at the corporate tax rate) and investing the proceeds in bonds owned by the pension fund. The overfunding strategy works best for ongoing plans because when plans terminate, the reversion of excess pension fund assets to the firm is subject to a stiff excise tax that ranges from 20 percent to 50 percent, depending on the circumstances.

Because one strategy leads to investment in stocks and junk bonds and the other leads to investment in low-risk bonds, firms might be following a mix of the two strategies. This could explain the roughly fifty-fifty split in pension plans' investments. Alternatively, the fifty-fifty split may simply reflect the "risk-averse" behavior of plan trustees as fiduciaries attempting to satisfy ERISA's "prudent person" investment standards.

Another explanation for this split is based on the idea

that workers, as well as employers, implicitly own the pension fund by sharing in pension fund performance. How? While total pension benefits are allocated by a defined benefit formula, the size of total benefits implicitly depends on fund performance. In such a case, balanced investments serve workers' aggregate interests because they share in good and bad pension fund performance.

Why would firms allow workers to own the pension fund? One reason, in the case of salaried employees, would be to signal to the employees that it is safe for them to make a long-term commitment to the firm. For union employees, the firm might be concerned that the union will hold out for high wages that, in the long run, will drive the firm out of business. The firm wants its workers to have a strong interest in its long-term survival. If their pension plan is underfunded, workers will have such an interest because they can collect their full benefits only if the firm survives. These incentives are weaker for overfunded defined benefit plans or for defined contribution plans (which must always be fully funded). This can explain why union plans have been almost exclusively of the defined benefit variety and, prior to ERISA, were 30 percent less funded than nonunion plans.

About the Author

Henry McMillan is senior vice president of Pacific Life Insurance. He was previously an economist with the Securities and Exchange Commission and a business economics professor at the Graduate School of Management of the University of California, Irvine. His views do not necessarily reflect the views of Pacific Life or its staff.

Further Reading

Black, F. "The Tax Consequences of Long-Run Pension Policy." *Financial Analysts Journal* (July–August 1980): 21–28.
Bleiberg, D. "Less than Zero." *Financial Analysts Journal* (March–April 1988): 13–15.
Bodie, Z. "Pensions as Retirement Income Insurance." *Journal of Economic Literature* 28, no. 1 (1990): 28–49.
Copeland, Craig. *Employment-based Retirement and Pension Plan Participation: Declining Levels and Geographic Differences.* Employee Benefit Research Institute Issue Brief no. 262. Washington, D.C.: EBRI, 2003.
Ippolito, Richard. *Pension Plans and Employee Performance: Evidence, Analysis, and Policy.* Chicago: University of Chicago Press, 1998.
———. *Pensions, Economics, and Public Policy.* Homewood, Ill.: Dow-Jones Irwin, 1986.
Leibowitz, Martin, Stanley Kogelman, and Lawrence Bader. "Asset Allocation Under Shortfall Constraint." *Journal of Portfolio Management* (Winter 1996): 18–23.
McGill, Dan, Kyle Brown, John Haley, and Sylvester Schieber. *Fundamentals of Private Pensions.* 7th ed. Philadelphia: University of Pennsylvania Press, 1996.
Mitchell, Olivia, ed. *Innovations in Retirement Financing.* Philadelphia: Pension Research Council Publications, 2002.
Sharpe, W. "Corporate Pension Funding Policy." *Journal of Financial Economics* 3, no. 2 (1976): 183–193.

Pharmaceuticals: Economics and Regulation

Charles L. Hooper

Pharmaceuticals are unique in their combination of extensive government control and extreme economics, that is, high fixed costs of development and relatively low incremental costs of production.

Regulation

The Food and Drug Administration (FDA) is the U.S. government agency charged with ensuring the safety and efficacy of the medicines available to Americans. The government's control over medicines has grown in the last hundred years from literally nothing to far-reaching, and now pharmaceuticals are among the most-regulated products in this country. The two legislative acts that are the main source of the FDA's powers both followed significant tragedies.

In 1937, to make a palatable liquid version of its new antibiotic drug sulfanilamide, the Massengill Company carelessly used the solvent diethylene glycol, which is also used as an antifreeze.[1] Elixir Sulfanilamide killed 107 people, mostly children, before it was quickly recalled; Massengill was successfully sued and the chemist responsible committed suicide. This tragedy led to the Food, Drug, and Cosmetic Act of 1938, which required that drugs be proven safe prior to marketing.[2] In the next infamous tragedy, more than ten thousand European babies were born deformed after their mothers took thalidomide as a tranquilizer to alleviate morning sickness.[3] This led to the Kefauver-Harris Amendments of 1962, which required

1. Philip J. Hilts, *Protecting America's Health: The FDA, Business, and One Hundred Years of Regulation* (New York: Alfred A. Knopf, 2003), pp. 89–90.
2. Daniel B. Klein and Alexander Tabarrok, FDAReview.org, Independent Institute, online under "History" at: http://www.FDAReview.org/history.shtml#fifth.
3. "THALOMID (Thalidomide): Balancing the Benefits and the Risks," Celgene Corporation, p. 2, online at: www.sanmateo.org/rimm/Tali_benefits_risks_celgene.pdf.

that efficacy be proven prior to marketing. Note that even though thalidomide's problem was clearly one of safety, an issue for which the FDA already had regulations, the laws were changed to add proof of efficacy.

Many people are unaware that most of the drugs, foods, herbs, and dietary supplements that Americans consume have been neither assessed nor approved by the FDA. Some are beyond the scope of the FDA's regulatory authority—if no specific health claims are made—and some are simply approved drugs being used in ways the FDA has not approved. Such "off-label" uses by physicians are widespread and can reach up to 90 percent in some therapeutic areas.[4] Although the FDA tolerates off-label usage, it forbids pharmaceutical companies from promoting such applications of their products.

Problems, sometimes serious, can arise even after FDA approval. Baycol (cerivastatin), Seldane (terfenadine), Vioxx (rofecoxib), and "Fen Phen" (fenfluramine and phentermine) are well-known examples of FDA-approved drugs that their manufacturers voluntarily withdrew after the drugs were found to be dangerous to some patients. Xalatan (latanoprost) for glaucoma caused 3–10 percent of users' blue eyes to turn permanently brown. This amazing side effect was uncovered only after the drug was approved as "safe and effective." One group of researchers estimated that 106,000 people died in 1994 alone from adverse reactions to drugs the FDA deemed "safe."[5]

One problem with the 1962 Kefauver-Harris Amendments was the additional decade of regulatory delay they created for new drugs. For example, one researcher estimated that ten thousand people died unnecessarily each year while beta blockers languished at the FDA, even though they had already been approved in Europe. The FDA has taken a "guilty until proven innocent" approach rather than weighing the costs and benefits of such delays. Just how cautious should the FDA be? Thalidomide and sulfanilamide demonstrate the potential benefit of delays, while a disease such as lung cancer, which kills an American every three minutes, highlights the costs.

In 1973, economist Sam Peltzman examined the pre- and post-1962 market to estimate the effect of the FDA's new powers and found that the number of new drugs had been reduced by 60 percent. He also found little evidence to suggest a decline in the proportion of inefficacious

drugs reaching the market.[6] From 1963 through 2003, the number of new drugs approved each year approximately doubled, but pharmaceutical R&D expenditures grew by a factor of twenty.[7]

One result of the FDA approach is the very high, perhaps excessive, level of evidence required before drugs can be marketed legally. In December 2003, an FDA advisory committee declined to endorse the use of aspirin for preventing initial myocardial infarctions (MIs), or heart attacks.[8] Does this mean that aspirin, which is approved for prevention of second heart attacks, does not work to prevent first heart attacks? No. One of the panelists, Dr. Joseph Knapka, stated: "As a scientist, I vote no. As a heart patient, I would probably say yes." In other words, he had two standards. One standard is the scientific proof that aspirin works beyond any reasonable doubt. By this standard, the data on fifty-five thousand patients fall short.[9] The other standard is measured by our choices in the real world. By this standard, aspirin passes easily. "The question today isn't, does aspirin work? We know it works, and we certainly know it works in a net benefit to risk positive sense in the secondary prevention setting," said panelist Thomas Fleming, chairman and professor of the Department of Biostatistics at the University of Washington, who also voted no.[10]

When our medical options are left to the scientific experts at a government agency, that agency has a bias toward conservatism. The FDA is acutely aware that of the two ways it can fail, approving a bad drug is significantly worse for its employees than failing to approve a good drug. Approving a bad drug may kill or otherwise harm patients, and an investigation of the approval process will lead to finger pointing. As former FDA employee Henry Miller put it, "This kind of mistake is highly visible and has immediate consequences—the media pounces, the public denounces, and Congress pronounces."[11] Such an outcome

4. Alexander Tabarrok, "The Anomaly of Off-Label Drug Prescriptions," Independent Institute Working Paper no. 10, December 1999.

5. Lazarov, Jason, et al. "Incidence of Adverse Drug Reactions in Hospitalized Patients." *Journal of the American Medical Association* 279, no. 15 (1998): 1200–1205.

6. Peltzman, Sam. An Evaluation of Consumer Protection Legislation: The 1962 Drug Amendments. *Journal of Political Economy* 81, no. 5 (1973): 1049–1091.

7. *Parexel's Pharmaceutical R&D Statistical Sourcebook 2004–2005* (Waltham, Mass.: Parexel International Corporation, 2004), p. 9.

8. "Broader Use for Aspirin Fails to Win Backing," *Wall Street Journal*, December 9, 2003, p. D9.

9. This 55,000 is the total number of patients tested in five published clinical trials of the use of aspirin to prevent initial non-fatal myocardial infraction.

10. Food and Drug Administration, Center for Drug Evaluation and Research, Cardiovascular and Renal Drugs Advisory Committee meeting, Monday, December 8, 2003, Gaithersburg, Md.

11. Henry I. Miller, M.D., *To America's Health: A Proposal to Re-*

is highly emotional and concrete, while not approving a good drug is intellectual and abstract. Who would have benefited and by how much? Who will know enough to complain that she was victimized by being denied such a medicine?

The FDA's approach also curtails people's freedom. The available medicines are what the FDA experts think we should have, not what *we* think we should have. It is common to picture uneducated patients blindly stumbling about the complexities of medical technology. While this certainly happens, it is mitigated by the expertise of caregivers (such as physicians), advisers (such as medical thought leaders), and watchdogs (such as the media), which comprise a surprisingly large support group. Of course, not all patients make competent decisions at all times, but FDA regulation treats all patients as incompetent.

A medicine that may work for one person at a certain dose at a certain time for a given disease may not work if any of the variables changes. Thalidomide, though unsafe for fetuses, is currently being studied for a wide range of important diseases and was even approved by the FDA in 1998, after four decades of being banned, for a painful skin condition of leprosy.[12] Similarly, finasteride is used in men to shrink enlarged prostate glands and to prevent baldness, but women are forbidden even to work in the finasteride factory due to the risk to fetuses. Also, the FDA pulled Propulsid (cisapride), a heartburn drug, from the market in March 2000 after eighty people who took it died from an irregular heartbeat. But for patients with cerebral palsy Propulsid is a miracle drug that allows them to digest food without extreme pain.[13] What is a poison for one person may be a lifesaver for another.

Economists have long recognized that good decisions cannot be made without considering the affected person's unique characteristics. But the FDA has little knowledge of a given individual's tolerance for pain, fear of death, or health status. So the decisions the FDA makes on behalf of individuals are imperfect because the agency lacks fundamental information. Economist Ludwig von Mises made this same argument in its universal form when he identified the Achilles' heel of socialism: centralized governments are usually incapable of making good decisions for their citizens because they lack most of the relevant information.

Some economists have proposed that the FDA continue to evaluate and approve new drugs, but that the drugs be made available—if the manufacturer wishes—during the approval process.[14] The FDA could rate or grade drugs and put stern warnings on unapproved drugs and drugs that appear to be riskier. Economists expect that cautious drug companies and patients would simply wait for FDA approval, while some patients would take their chances. Such a solution is PARETO optimal, in that everyone is at least as satisfied as under the current system. Cautious patients get the safety of FDA approval while patients who do not want to wait don't have to.

Economics

A study by Joseph DiMasi, an economist at the Tufts Center for the Study of Drug Development in Boston, found that the cost of getting one new drug approved was $802 million in 2000 U.S. dollars.[15] Most new drugs cost much less, but his figure adds in each successful drug's prorated share of failures. Only one out of fifty drugs eventually reaches the market.

Why are drugs so expensive to develop? The main reason for the high cost is the aforementioned high level of proof required by the Food and Drug Administration. Before it will approve a new drug, the FDA requires pharmaceutical companies to carefully test it in animals and then humans in the standard phases 0, I, II, and III process. The path through the FDA's review process is slow and expensive. The ten to fifteen years required to get a drug through the testing and approval process leaves little remaining time on a twenty-year patent.

Although new medicines are hugely expensive to bring to market, they are cheap to manufacture. In this sense, they are like DVD movies and computer software. This means that a drug company, to be profitable or simply to break even, must price its drugs well above its production costs. The company that wishes to maximize profits will set high prices for those who are willing to pay a lot and low prices that at least cover production costs for those willing to pay a little. That is why, for example, Merck priced its anti-AIDS drug, Crixivan, to poor countries in

form the Food and Drug Administration (Stanford, Calif.: Hoover Institution Press, 2000), p. 42.

12. "FDA Gives Restricted Approval to Thalidomide," CNN News, July 16, 1998.

13. "Drug Ban Brings Misery to Patient," Associated Press, November 11, 2000.

14. Klein and Tabarrok, FDAReview.org, online under "Reform Options" at http://www.fdareview.org/reform.shtml#5; David R. Henderson, *The Joy of Freedom: An Economist's Odyssey* (New York: Prentice Hall, 2002), pp. 206–207, 278–279.

15. Joseph A. DiMasi, Ronald W. Hansen, and Henry G. Grabowski, "The Price of Innovation: New Estimates of Drug Development Costs," *Journal of Health Economics* 22 (2003): 151–185.

Africa and Latin America at $600 while charging relatively affluent Americans $6,099 for a year's supply.

This type of customer segmentation—similar to that of airlines—is part of the profit-maximizing strategy for medicines. In general, good customer segmentation is difficult to accomplish. Therefore, the most common type of pharmaceutical segmentation is charging a lower price in poorer countries and giving the product free to poor people in the United States through patient assistance programs.

What complicates the picture is socialized medicine, which exists in almost every country outside the United States—and even, with Medicare and Medicaid, in the United States. Because governments in countries with socialized medicine tend to be the sole bargaining agent in dealing with drug companies, these governments often set prices that are low by U.S. standards. To some extent, this comes about because these governments have monopsony power—that is, monopoly power on the buyer's side—and they use this power to get good deals. These governments are, in effect, saying that if they cannot buy it cheaply, their citizens cannot get it.

These low prices also come about because governments sometimes threaten drug companies with compulsory licensing (breaking a patent) to get a low price. This has happened most recently in South Africa and Brazil with AIDS drugs. This violation of INTELLECTUAL PROPERTY rights can bring a seemingly powerful drug company into quick compliance. When faced with a choice between earning nothing and earning something, most drug companies choose the latter.

The situation is a PRISONERS' DILEMMA. Everyone's interest is in giving drug companies an adequate incentive to invest in new drugs. To do so, drug companies must be able to price their drugs well above production costs to a large segment of the population. But each individual government's narrow self-interest is to set a low price on drugs and let people in other countries pay the high prices that generate the return on R&D investments. Each government, in other words, has an incentive to be a free rider. And that is what many governments are doing. The temptation is to cease having Americans bear more than their share of drug development by having the U.S. government set low prices also. But if Americans also try to free ride, there may not be a ride.

Governments are not the only bulk purchasers. The majority of pharmaceuticals in the United States are purchased by managed-care organizations (MCOs), hospitals, and governments, which use their market power to negotiate better prices. These organizations often do not take physical possession of the drugs; most pills never pass through the MCO's hands, but instead go from manufacturer to wholesaler to pharmacy to patient. Therefore, manufacturers rebate money—billions of dollars—to compensate for purchases made at list prices. Managed-care rebates are given with consideration; they are the result of contracts that require performance. For example, a manufacturer will pay an HMO a rebate if it can keep a drug's prescription market share above the national level. These rebates average 10–40 percent of sales. The net result is that the neediest Americans, frequently those without insurance, pay the highest prices, while the most powerful health plans and government agencies pay the lowest.

Pharmaceutical companies would like to help poor people in the United States, but the federal government and, to a much lesser extent, health plans have tied their hands. Drug companies can and do give drugs away free through patient assistance programs, but they cannot sell them at very low prices because the federal government requires drug companies to give the huge Medicaid program their "best prices." If a drug company sells to even one customer at a very low price, it also has to sell at the same price to the 5–40 percent of its customers covered by Medicaid.

Drug prices are regularly attacked as "too high." Yet, cheaper over-the-counter drugs, natural medicines, and generic versions of off-patent drugs are ubiquitous, and many health plans steer patients toward them. Economic studies have shown that even the newer, more expensive drugs are usually worth their price and are frequently cheaper than other alternatives. One study showed that each dollar spent on vaccines reduced other health care costs by $10. Another study showed that for each dollar spent on newer drugs, $6.17 was saved.[16] Therefore, health plans that aggressively limited their drug spending ended up spending *more* over all.

Most patients do not pay retail prices because they have some form of insurance. In 2003, before a law was passed that subsidizes drugs for seniors, 75–80 percent of seniors had prescription drug insurance. Insured people pay either a flat copayment, often based on tiers (copayment levels set by managed-care providers that involve a low payment for generic drugs and a higher payment for brand-name drugs) or a percentage of the prescription cost. On average, seniors spend more on entertainment than they do on drugs and medical supplies combined. But for the uninsured who are also poor and sick, drug prices can be a devastating burden. The overlap of the 20–25 percent who lack drug insurance and the 10 percent who pay more than five thousand dollars per year—approximately 2 percent

16. Frank R. Lichtenberg, "Benefits and Costs of Newer Drugs: An Update," NBER Working Paper no. 8996, National Bureau of Economic Research, Cambridge, Mass., 2002.

are in both groups—is where we find the stories of people skimping on food to afford their medications. The number of people in both groups is actually lower than 2 percent because of the numerous patient assistance programs offered by pharmaceutical companies. For all the talk of lower drug prices, what people really want is lower risk through good insurance.

Insurance lowers an individual's risk and, consequently, increases the demand for pharmaceuticals. By spending someone else's money for a good chunk of every pharmaceutical purchase, individuals become less price sensitive. A two-hundred-dollar prescription for a new medicine is forty times as expensive as a five-dollar generic, but its copay may be only three times the generic's copay. The marginal cost to patients of choosing the expensive product is reduced, both in absolute and relative terms, and patients are thus more likely to purchase the expensive drug and make purchases they otherwise would have skipped. The data show that those with insurance consume 40–100 percent more than those without insurance.

Drugs account for a small percentage of overall health-care spending. In fact, branded pharmaceuticals are about 7 percent and generics 3 percent of total U.S. health-care costs.[17] The tremendous costs involved with illnesses— even if they are not directly measured—are the economic and human costs of the diseases themselves, not the drugs.

About the Author

Charles L. Hooper is president of Objective Insights, a company that consults for pharmaceutical and biotech companies. He is a visiting fellow with the Hoover Institution.

Further Reading

Bast, Joseph L., Richard C. Rue, and Stuart A. Wesbury Jr. *Why We Spend Too Much on Health Care and What We Can Do About It.* Chicago: Heartland Institute, 1993.
DiMasi, Joseph A., Ronald W. Hansen, and Henry G. Grabowski. "The Price of Innovation: New Estimates of Drug Development Costs." *Journal of Health Economics* 22, no. 2 (2003): 151–185.
Higgs, Robert, ed. *Hazardous to Our Health? FDA Regulation of Health Care Products.* Oakland, Calif.: Independent Institute, 1995.
Hilts, Philip J. *Protecting America's Health: The FDA, Business, and One Hundred Years of Regulation.* New York: Alfred A. Knopf, 2003.
Klein, Daniel B., and Alexander Tabarrok. FDAReview.org. Oakland, Calif.: Independent Institute. Online at: http://www.fdareview.org/.

17. The Centers for Medicare and Medicaid Services (CMS), January 8, 2004.

Miller, Henry I. *To America's Health: A Proposal to Reform the Food and Drug Administration.* Stanford, Calif.: Hoover Institution Press, 2000.

Phillips Curve

Kevin D. Hoover

The Phillips curve represents the relationship between the rate of inflation and the unemployment rate. Although he had precursors, A. W. H. Phillips's study of wage inflation and unemployment in the United Kingdom from 1861 to 1957 is a milestone in the development of macroeconomics. Phillips found a consistent inverse relationship: when unemployment was high, wages increased slowly; when unemployment was low, wages rose rapidly.

Phillips conjectured that the lower the unemployment rate, the tighter the labor market and, therefore, the faster firms must raise wages to attract scarce labor. At higher rates of unemployment, the pressure abated. Phillips's "curve" represented the average relationship between unemployment and wage behavior over the business cycle. It showed the rate of wage inflation that would result if a particular level of unemployment persisted for some time.

Economists soon estimated Phillips curves for most developed economies. Most related general price inflation, rather than wage inflation, to unemployment. Of course, the prices a company charges are closely connected to the wages it pays. Figure 1 shows a typical Phillips curve fitted to data for the United States from 1961 to 1969. The close fit between the estimated curve and the data encouraged many economists, following the lead of Paul Samuelson and Robert Solow, to treat the Phillips curve as a sort of menu of policy options. For example, with an unemployment rate of 6 percent, the government might stimulate the economy to lower unemployment to 5 percent. Figure 1 indicates that the cost, in terms of higher inflation, would be a little more than half a percentage point. But if the government initially faced lower rates of unemployment, the costs would be considerably higher: a reduction in unemployment from 5 to 4 percent would imply more than twice as big an increase in the rate of inflation—about one and a quarter percentage points.

At the height of the Phillips curve's popularity as a guide to policy, Edmund Phelps and Milton Friedman independently challenged its theoretical underpinnings. They argued that well-informed, rational employers and workers would pay attention only to real wages—the inflation-adjusted purchasing power of money wages. In their view, real wages would adjust to make the supply of labor equal

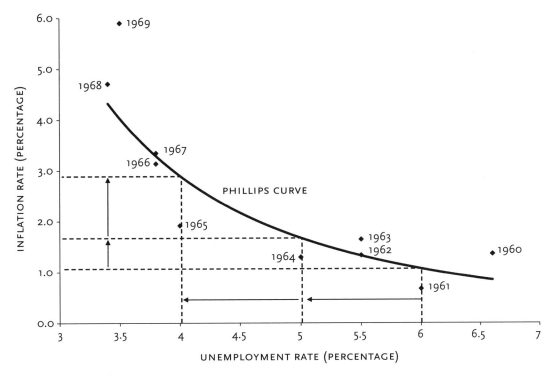

Figure 1 The Phillips Curve, 1961–1969

Source: Bureau of Labor Statistics.

Note: Inflation based on the Consumer Price Index.

to the demand for labor, and the unemployment rate would then stand at a level uniquely associated with that real wage—the "natural rate" of unemployment.

Both Friedman and Phelps argued that the government could not permanently trade higher inflation for lower unemployment. Imagine that unemployment is at the natural rate. The real wage is constant: workers who expect a given rate of price inflation insist that their wages increase at the same rate to prevent the erosion of their purchasing power. Now, imagine that the government uses expansionary monetary or fiscal policy in an attempt to lower unemployment below its natural rate. The resulting increase in demand encourages firms to raise their prices faster than workers had anticipated. With higher revenues, firms are willing to employ more workers at the old wage rates and even to raise those rates somewhat. For a short time, workers suffer from what economists call money illusion: they see that their money wages have risen and willingly supply more labor. Thus, the unemployment rate falls. They do not realize right away that their purchasing power has fallen because prices have risen more rapidly than they expected. But, over time, as workers come to anticipate higher rates of price inflation, they supply less labor and insist on increases in wages that keep up with inflation. The real wage is restored to its old level, and the unem-

ployment rate returns to the natural rate. But the price inflation and wage inflation brought on by expansionary policies continue at the new, higher rates.

Friedman's and Phelps's analyses provide a distinction between the "short-run" and "long-run" Phillips curves. So long as the average rate of inflation remains fairly constant, as it did in the 1960s, inflation and unemployment will be inversely related. But if the average rate of inflation changes, as it will when policymakers persistently try to push unemployment below the natural rate, after a period of adjustment, unemployment will return to the natural rate. That is, once workers' expectations of price inflation have had time to adjust, the natural rate of unemployment is compatible with any rate of inflation. The long-run Phillips curve could be shown on Figure 1 as a vertical line above the natural rate. The original curve would then apply only to brief, transitional periods and would shift with any persistent change in the average rate of inflation. These long-run and short-run relations can be combined in a single "expectations-augmented" Phillips curve. The more quickly workers' expectations of price inflation adapt to changes in the actual rate of inflation, the more quickly unemployment will return to the natural rate, and the less successful the government will be in reducing unemployment through monetary and fiscal policies.

The 1970s provided striking confirmation of Friedman's and Phelps's fundamental point. Contrary to the original Phillips curve, when the average inflation rate rose from about 2.5 percent in the 1960s to about 7 percent in the 1970s, the unemployment rate not only did not fall, it actually rose from about 4 percent to above 6 percent.

Most economists now accept a central tenet of both Friedman's and Phelps's analyses: there is some rate of unemployment that, if maintained, would be compatible with a stable rate of inflation. Many, however, call this the "nonaccelerating inflation rate of unemployment" (NAIRU) because, unlike the term "natural rate," NAIRU does not suggest that an unemployment rate is socially optimal, unchanging, or impervious to policy.

A policymaker might wish to place a value on NAIRU. To obtain a simple estimate, Figure 2 plots changes in the rate of inflation (i.e., the acceleration of prices) against the unemployment rate from 1976 to 2002. The expectations-augmented Phillips curve is the straight line that best fits the points on the graph (the regression line). It summarizes the rough inverse relationship. According to the regression line, NAIRU (i.e., the rate of unemployment for which the change in the rate of inflation is zero) is about 6 percent. The slope of the Phillips curve indicates the speed of price adjustment. Imagine that the economy is at

NAIRU with an inflation rate of 3 percent and that the government would like to reduce the inflation rate to zero. Figure 2 suggests that contractionary monetary and fiscal policies that drove the average rate of unemployment up to about 7 percent (i.e., one point above NAIRU) would be associated with a reduction in inflation of about one percentage point per year. Thus, if the government's policies caused the unemployment rate to stay at about 7 percent, the 3 percent inflation rate would, on average, be reduced one point each year—falling to zero in about three years.

Using similar, but more refined, methods, the Congressional Budget Office estimated (Figure 3) that NAIRU was about 5.3 percent in 1950, that it rose steadily until peaking in 1978 at about 6.3 percent, and that it then fell steadily to about 5.2 by the end of the century. Clearly, NAIRU is not constant. It varies with changes in so-called real factors affecting the supply of and demand for labor such as demographics, technology, union power, the structure of taxation, and relative prices (e.g., oil prices). NAIRU should not vary with monetary and fiscal policies, which affect aggregate demand without altering these real factors.

The expectations-augmented Phillips curve is a fundamental element of almost every macroeconomic forecasting model now used by government and business. It is accepted by most otherwise diverse schools of macroeco-

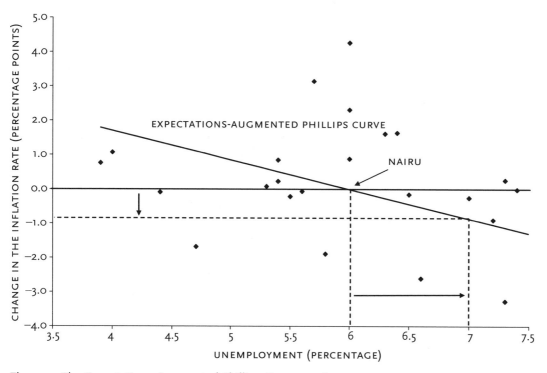

Figure 2 The Expectations-Augmented Phillips Curve, 1976–2002

Source: Bureau of Labor Statistics.
Note: Inflation based on the Consumer Price Index.

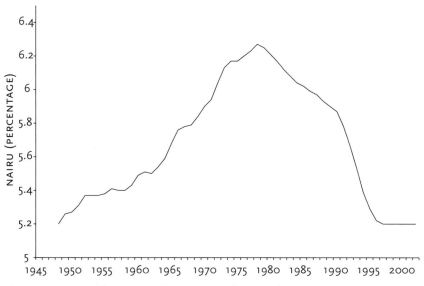

Figure 3 Nonaccelerating Inflation Rate of Unemployment
Source: Congressional Budget Office.

nomic thought. Early new classical theories assumed that prices adjusted freely and that expectations were formed rationally—that is, without *systematic* error. These assumptions imply that the Phillips curve in Figure 2 should be very steep and that deviations from NAIRU should be short-lived (see NEW CLASSICAL MACROECONOMICS and RATIONAL EXPECTATIONS). While sticking to the rational-expectations hypothesis, even new classical economists now concede that wages and prices are somewhat sticky. Wage and price inertia, resulting in real wages and other relative prices away from their market-clearing levels, explain the large fluctuations in unemployment around NAIRU and slow speed of convergence back to NAIRU.

Some "new Keynesian" and some free-market economists hold that, at best, there is only a weak tendency for an economy to return to NAIRU. They argue that there is no natural rate of unemployment to which the actual rate tends to return. Instead, when actual unemployment rises and remains high for some time, NAIRU also rises. The dependence of NAIRU on actual unemployment is known as the hysteresis hypothesis. One explanation for hysteresis in a heavily unionized economy is that unions directly represent the interests only of those who are currently employed. Unionization, by keeping wages high, undermines the ability of those outside the union to compete for employment. After prolonged layoffs, employed union workers may seek the benefits of higher wages for themselves rather than moderating their wage demands to promote the rehiring of unemployed workers. According to the hysteresis hypothesis, once unemployment becomes high—

as it did in Europe in the recessions of the 1970s—it is relatively impervious to monetary and fiscal stimuli, even in the short run. The unemployment rate in France in 1968 was 1.8 percent, and in West Germany, 1.5 percent. In contrast, since 1983, both French and West German unemployment rates have fluctuated between 7 and 11 percent. In 2003, the French rate stood at 8.8 percent and the German rate at 8.4 percent. The hysteresis hypothesis appears to be more relevant to Europe, where unionization is higher and where labor laws create numerous barriers to hiring and firing, than it is to the United States, with its considerably more flexible labor markets. The unemployment rate in the United States was 3.4 percent in 1968. U.S. unemployment peaked in the early 1980s at 10.8 percent and fell back substantially, so that by 2000 it again stood below 4 percent.

Modern macroeconomic models often employ another version of the Phillips curve in which the output gap replaces the unemployment rate as the measure of aggregate demand relative to aggregate supply. The output gap is the difference between the actual level of GDP and the potential (or sustainable) level of aggregate output expressed as a percentage of potential. This formulation explains why, at the end of the 1990s boom when unemployment rates were well below estimates of NAIRU, prices did not accelerate. The reasoning is as follows. Potential output depends not only on labor inputs, but also on plant and equipment and other capital inputs. At the end of the boom, after nearly a decade of rapid investment, firms found themselves with too much capital. The excess capacity raised potential output, widening the output gap and reducing the pressure on prices.

Many articles in the conservative business press criticize the Phillips curve because they believe it both implies that growth causes inflation and repudiates the theory that excess growth of money is inflation's true cause. But it does no such thing. One can believe in the Phillips curve and still understand that increased growth, all other things equal, will reduce inflation. The misplaced criticism of the Phillips curve is ironic since Milton Friedman, one of the coinventors of its expectations-augmented version, is also the foremost defender of the view that "inflation is always, and everywhere, a monetary phenomenon."

The Phillips curve was hailed in the 1960s as providing an account of the inflation process hitherto missing from the conventional macroeconomic model. After four decades, the Phillips curve, as transformed by the natural-rate hypothesis into its expectations-augmented version, remains the key to relating unemployment (of capital as well as labor) to inflation in mainstream macroeconomic analysis.

About the Author

Kevin D. Hoover is professor in the departments of economics and philosophy at Duke University. He is past president of the History of Economics Society, past chairman of the International Network for Economic Method, and editor of the *Journal of Economic Methodology*.

Further Reading

Cross, Rod, ed. *Unemployment, Hysteresis, and the Natural Rate Hypothesis*. Oxford: Blackwell, 1988.

Friedman, Milton. "The Role of Monetary Policy." *American Economic Review* 58, no. 1 (1968): 1–17.

Lucas, Robert E. Jr. "Econometric Testing of the Natural Rate Hypothesis." In Otto Eckstein, ed., *The Econometrics of Price Determination*. Washington, D.C.: Federal Reserve System, 1972.

Phelps, Edmund S. "Phillips Curves, Expectations of Inflation and Optimal Employment over Time." *Economica*, n.s., 34, no. 3 (1967): 254–281.

Phillips, A. W. H. "The Relation Between Unemployment and the Rate of Change of Money Wage Rates in the United Kingdom, 1861–1957." *Economica*, n.s., 25, no. 2 (1958): 283–299.

Samuelson, Paul A., and Robert M. Solow. "Analytical Aspects of Anti-inflation Policy." *American Economic Review* 50, no. 2 (1960): 177–194.

Sheffrin, Steven M. *Rational Expectations*. 2d ed. Cambridge: Cambridge University Press, 1996.

Symposium: "The Natural Rate of Unemployment." *Journal of Economic Perspectives* 11, no. 1 (1997): 3–108.

Political Behavior

Richard L. Stroup

The fact of scarcity, which exists everywhere, guarantees that people will compete for resources. Markets are one way to organize and channel this competition. Politics is another. People use both markets and politics to get resources allocated to the ends they favor. Even in a democracy, however, political activity is startlingly different from voluntary exchange in markets.

People can accomplish many things in politics that they could not accomplish in the private sector. Some of these are vital to the broader community's welfare, such as control of health-threatening air pollution from myriad sources affecting millions of individuals or the provision of national defense. Other public-sector actions, such as subsidies to farmers and restrictions on the number of taxicabs in a city, provide narrow benefits that fall far short of their costs.

In democratic politics, rules typically give a majority coalition power over the entire society. These rules replace the rule of willing consent and voluntary exchange that exists in the marketplace. In politics, people's goals are similar to the goals they have as consumers, producers, and resource suppliers in the private sector, but people participate instead as voters, politicians, bureaucrats, and lobbyists. In the political system, as in the marketplace, people are sometimes (but not always) selfish. In all cases, they are narrow: how much they know and how much they care about other people's goals is necessarily limited.

An advocate of the homeless working in the political arena typically lobbies for a shift of funding (reflecting a move of real resources) from other missions to help poor people who lack housing. The views of such a person, while admirable, are narrow. He or she prefers that the government (and other givers) allocate more resources to meet his or her goals, even though it means fewer resources for the goals of others. Similarly, a dedicated professional, such as the director of the National Park Service, however unselfish, pushes strongly for shifting government funds away from other uses and toward expanding and improving the national park system. His or her priority is to get more resources allocated to parks, even if goals espoused by others, such as helping the poor, necessarily suffer. Passionate demands for funding and for legislative favors (inevitably at the expense of other people's goals) come from every direction.

Political rules determine how these competing demands, which far exceed the government's ability to provide them, will be arbitrated. The rules of the political game are critical. Is the government purely democratic or a representative democracy? Who can vote? Over what domain of issues can the government make decisions? How much of the society's output is available for diversion to political allocation? The rules provide answers to these questions, influencing not only who gets what from society's product, but also how big the product itself will be and how much of it is diverted from the production of goods and services and devoted instead to influencing the political game.

Why do individuals and groups often seek their aims in the political sector rather than in markets? The motives range from public spirited to narrowly selfish:

- Political solutions can compel people, on threat of prison or worse, to financially support politically chosen goals. This solves the financial "free rider" problem caused by the fact that with solely voluntary provision, even citizens who do not pay for national defense or for, say, a sculpture in the town square can potentially benefit from the expenditures of those who do.

- Imperfections in the legal protection of one's rights, such as one's right to be safe from harmful air pollutants, or even one's civil rights, can be addressed politically.

- Even in a democracy, political action can allow one group to benefit at the expense mainly of the rest of society. Except for gifts and unintended spillovers, this does not happen in a free market with protected property rights, where those who pay *are* the ones who benefit, and transfers such as gifts are strictly voluntary. (Political victories, however, are often costly to those who win them; lobbying is not free.)

Some aspects of the political process, however, work against those who pursue their goals via the political route:

- One Congress or legislature cannot bind the next, and so a political solution, other than the grant or sale of private rights, lasts only as long as the political muscle of those who push it. Any political program, land allocation, or treaty can be reversed as political pressures change. In other words, a political solution cannot be purchased: it can only be rented. A political act is inherently less secure than a private purchase or trust arrangement, if property rights are secure.

- Truly innovative activity is often difficult to sell to the majority of the political group, such as the Congress or a specific committee, which must agree to the proposed action. In the free market, on the other hand, innovations typically are funded when only a few entrepreneurs and capi-

talists believe in them because only their capital, not that of all taxpayers, is at risk.

For ordinary citizens who are not politically active, political activity has very different consequences from market activity. Although such citizens may benefit from political action that others take, they are bound by all and must pay for some political outcomes, whether in their own interest or not. Ordinary citizens are outside the political process except when they vote and when they have concentrated, or special, interests and are politically well organized. Dairy farmers, for example, typically know little or nothing about how much they pay to operate the national park system or whether the parks are well managed. However, they are keenly informed about the federal milk program, which restricts milk production and keeps milk prices high. Thus, they do not have an incentive to act politically to control the costs of the national park system, but they do have an incentive to act to expand the milk program. Their counterparts, such as conservation advocates eager to expand the national park system, know little about the costs they are bearing to support the milk program and concentrate instead on expanding the park system and its budget.

Although political activity has benefits as well as costs, political behavior causes some predictable problems for citizens in general:

- One-to-a-citizen ballot votes, the currency of the formal democratic marketplace, do not allow voters to show the intensity of their preferences, as dollar votes do when citizens focus their budgets—some spending more on housing, others on entertainment, education, or their favorite charity.

- The voter purchases a large bundle of policies and cannot pick and choose. In a representative government, the voters select a single candidate (the "bundle") to represent them on many different issues. Voters cannot vote for the position of one candidate on issue A, the position of another on issue B, and so on, as they do routinely when shopping for thousands of items in the marketplace. In a representative democracy, fine-tuning one's expression at the ballot box is impossible.

- An individual voter has virtually no chance of casting the decisive vote in an election. Even among the more than four thousand elections held each decade to fill the U.S. House of Representatives, a race decided by less than one hundred votes is newsworthy at the national level, and a recount is normally conducted. Moreover, the cost of an uninformed or mistaken vote that did make a difference would be spread among other citizens. This differs from the cost of a mistaken personal purchase, the full burden of which the buyer pays. People thus have little incentive to spend valuable time and effort learning about election issues beyond their narrow personal interest, monitoring politicians' overall performance, or even voting. Instead, voters are "rationally ignorant" on most issues. Thus, it makes sense for a politician to pay attention primarily to special interests on most issues, and to use the financial support of special interests to campaign on "image" issues at election time.

• Because politicians do not sell their interests to their successors (the way the owners of companies, farms, and houses do), they have an incentive to provide current benefits while delaying costs into the future whenever possible. They have less incentive to invest today for the benefit of the future. Future voters cannot affect elections now, but will simply inherit what current voters leave to them—both debts and assets. In contrast, private assets can either be sold to benefit the owner directly or given by bequest. Only charitable instincts among voter-taxpayers (and perhaps the lobbying of special interest groups such as weapons system suppliers or owners of real estate that may go up in value if a project is built) will push for a costly project with benefits mainly in the future. Charitable instincts toward the future are present in the private sector, too (especially in private charities), and are reinforced by the fact that future productivity and profits are reflected in today's asset prices, including the stock price of a corporation.

One special interest that has gained at the expense of consumers and taxpayers is wool and mohair producers. During World War II, military planners discovered that U.S. wool producers could supply only half the wool the military wanted. Partly for this reason, and partly to give added income to wool growers, Congress passed the National Wool Act in 1954. Mohair, produced by Angora goats, had no military use but was included as an offshoot of the wool industry. Although wool was removed from the military's list of strategic materials in 1960, the program survived and continued to grow.

Under the Wool Act, growers were given subsidy checks to supplement what they received in the market for their wool. In 1990, the wool subsidy rate was 127 percent, so a farmer who got $1,000 for selling wool in the market also got a $1,270 check from the government. The subsidy rate for mohair was a much larger 387 percent. The subsidies were paid for by tariffs on imported wool. Thus, consumers were paying more for imported wool, which also drove up the market price paid for domestic wool, a close substitute. The economy operated less efficiently because less wool was imported, even though the imported wool would have cost less to produce and to buy. The subsidy program, together with the higher price caused by the wool tariff, meant that domestic land, labor, and capital resources were applied to the production of wool and mohair instead of to more valuable goods.

Nevertheless, political support for the program was strong, and Congress continued it. Thousands of very small checks were sent to small growers in every state. Almost half of the 1990 payments were less than $100. Many of those receiving them were willing to write letters and to vote for those who support the program. Nearly half of the money, though, went to the 1 percent of the growers who were the largest producers. The largest checks, nearly three hundred of them, averaged $98,000 and accounted for 27 percent of the program's 1990 cost. Recipients of these large checks could be counted on to contribute to organizing costs and to give campaign donations to members of congressional committees critical to the subsidy program. By contrast, because American taxpayers paid only a few dollars per family (Wool Act subsidies were $104 million in 1990), most taxpayers were unaware of the program and of how their elected representatives voted on it. Even though taxpayers were numerous and the Wool Act cost them a lot as a group, each taxpayer lost so little that none had an incentive to become organized or knowledgeable on the topic. Thus, the Wool Act, which harmed the interests of the great majority of voters, survived until 1996, the last year of a three-year phaseout of the program mandated by Congress in 1994. But organized interests are resilient. A subsidy program that effectively set minimum prices for both wool and mohair was part of the 2002 Farm Act and seems likely to persist for years to come.

Although such special interest groups are sometimes in line with more general interests of the citizens, there is little to confine their actions when they are not. For example, the general public wants national defense, and weapons contractors have an interest in providing the means to obtain defense. But the contractors and the government's military itself will push for far more elaborate, extensive, and costly means of defense than would a knowledgeable citizen with broader interests.

Political activity is often seen as a way to solve problems not handled well by the private sector—sometimes including everything from pollution problems and national defense to the redistribution of income to the poor. Clearly, private-sector results in each of these areas are unsatisfactory to many, and there are massive, growing political programs aimed at each of these goals. But the problems just described reduce the ability of the political system to reach the sought-after goals—or to reach any goal in a least-cost manner.

Pollution control programs, from the Clean Air and Clean Water acts to the Superfund program, have received great political support. The cost to the economy of environmental programs is generally agreed to be more than $100 billion per year. Yet political manipulation of each program is widely recognized to have led to large imperfections in handling these problems. A classic case has been the political uses of the 1977 amendments to the Clean Air Act. Bruce Ackerman and William Hassler showed that by requiring the use of expensive scrubbers on coal-fired power plants, the amendments effectively protected eastern coal interests while harming both the health and the pocketbooks of millions of Americans. Robert Crandall of the Brookings Institution showed that eastern and midwestern manufacturing interests used the same amendments to stifle competition from new Sunbelt factories. Jonathan Adler has since documented a number of similar cases in which environmental policy initiatives have produced private benefits at public cost.

Bureaucratic performance in achieving the voters' goals is also a serious concern. Leaders of government agencies make strong, consistent attempts to gain larger budgets and more regulatory authority to further their programs. They often can achieve their ends with a "can't do" stance in place of the "can do" attitude needed for market success.

A perennial case in point is the "Washington Monument strategy" of the National Park Service. At budget time, the service frequently threatens to curtail visiting hours at its most popular attractions, such as the Washington Monument, if its budget request is not met, and it threatens to blame Congress and the budget process when tourists complain. Other agencies use this and similar tactics to seek more support for their narrow programs. In doing so, too often they impose enormous costs on society. It is hard to imagine a private firm—even a large, bureaucratic one—responding to hard budget times by curtailing its most popular product or service. The private firm would lose too much business to the competition.

Summary

Political behavior in a democracy has both prospects and problems that differ from those of private, voluntary activity. Political action can force all citizens to comply with decisions made by their elected representatives. Because these political decisions are supposed to be for the benefit of all, the support of all is commanded. But because no single citizen's ballot is decisive, voters are not very effective at monitoring the intent and the efficiency of political action. Voter turnout is often low, and even very intelligent voters are notoriously uninformed on policy issues. Americans of voting age cannot, on average, even name their

congressional representative. Such results are not as strange as they may sound when the impact of political rules on individual incentives is examined.

About the Author

Richard L. Stroup is president of the Political Economy Research Institute and visiting professor of economics at North Carolina State University, both in Raleigh, North Carolina. He is also a senior associate with the Property and Environment Research Center in Bozeman, Montana. From 1982 to 1984 he was director of the Office of Policy Analysis, U.S. Department of the Interior.

Further Reading

Ackerman, Bruce A., and William T. Hassler. *Clean Coal/Dirty Air; or How the Clean Air Act Became a Multibillion-Dollar Bail-out for the High-Sulfur Coal Producers and What Should Be Done About It.* New Haven: Yale University Press, 1981.
Adler, Jonathan H. "Clean Politics, Dirty Profits: Rent-Seeking Behind the Green Curtain." In Terry L. Anderson, ed., *Political Environmentalism: Going Behind the Green Curtain.* Stanford, Calif.: Hoover Institution Press, 2000. Pp. 1–30.
Buchanan, James, and Gordon Tullock. *The Calculus of Consent.* Ann Arbor: University of Michigan Press, 1962.
Crandall, Robert W. "Economic Rents as a Barrier to Deregulation." *Cato Journal* 6, no. 1 (1986): 186–189.
Downs, Anthony. *An Economic Theory of Democracy.* New York: Harper, 1957.
Gwartney, James, Richard L. Stroup, Russell S. Sobel, and David A. Macpherson. *Economics: Private and Public Choice.* 11th ed. Mason, Ohio: Thompson South-Western, 2006.

Pollution Controls

Robert W. Crandall

There is general agreement that we must control pollution of our air, water, and land, but there is considerable dispute over how controls should be designed and how much control is enough. The pollution control mechanisms adopted in the United States have tended toward detailed regulation of technology, leaving polluters little choice in how to achieve the environmental goals. This "command-and-control" strategy needlessly increases the cost of pollution controls and may even slow our progress toward a cleaner environment.

In 1970, popular concern about environmental degradation coalesced into a major political force, resulting in President Richard Nixon's creation of the federal Environmental Protection Agency (EPA) and the first of the major federal attempts to regulate pollution directly—the Clean

Air Act Amendments of 1970. Since then, the federal role in regulating pollution has grown immensely, unleashing many regulatory responsibilities on the EPA and a cascade of regulations on local governments and the business community. But that has begun to change somewhat as environmentalists have increasingly realized that markets can work to allocate pollution reduction responsibilities efficiently among firms and across industries. Although the command-and-control approach is still the norm, environmental lobbyists and legislators have, on occasion, considered market-based approaches to pollution control. Most of the proposals for limiting global warming, for example, explicitly include market-based approaches for controlling carbon dioxide emissions.

Regulatory Standards

In virtually every antipollution law, Congress has instructed the EPA to establish and enforce specific pollution standards for individual polluters. The EPA generally bases these standards on some notion of the "best available" or "best achievable" technology for each source of pollution in each industry. Because each pollutant has many sources, the EPA often sets literally hundreds of maximum-discharge standards for any single pollutant.

Existing pollution sources (such as old factories) are generally required to meet less onerous standards than those applicable for new sources, largely because it is considered more costly to retrofit an old factory than to build pollution control devices into a new one. However, even the definition of "new" requires further regulations because the EPA must distinguish between, for example, when a utility simply repairs or refurbishes an "old" fossil-fuel-fired boiler and when it replaces enough components to make it a "new" boiler. Complicating matters further, standards for both existing and new sources are often stricter in regions with a higher-quality environment (i.e., cleaner air, cleaner water, etc.). Because the tighter standards on new or upgraded sources may reduce the incentive to replace the dirty, older facilities, in 2003 the EPA revised its rules to allow power plants and other major polluting facilities to be modernized without triggering the full panoply of "new-source review" requirements if the modernization involved did not involve a major design change and did not cost more than 20 percent of a completely new facility.

The Cost of Pollution Controls

The way pollution controls are often built into the production process makes any estimation of their cost extremely difficult. In addition, pollution controls often discourage new investment and production, but because the value of what is not produced is not seen, no one currently calculates such indirect costs. The federal government has, however, estimated a subset of costs—namely, direct expenditures on pollution controls. These expenditures cost governments and private entities an estimated $50 billion plus in 2002 alone. Some thirty-one billion dollars was spent on air-pollution abatement, seventeen billion on water-pollution controls, and eight billion for a variety of solid waste, hazardous waste, and other programs.

The most costly and complex federal pollution-control policy has been the motor vehicle emissions-control program. In order to enforce automobile standards set by Congress, the EPA must test each model line of new cars and must also test a random sample of vehicles already on the road. The EPA imposed the first federally mandated exhaust emission controls on new cars in 1967 and tightened these controls several times in the next twenty-five years. The Clean Air Act requires that emission controls on new cars work for at least the first eighty thousand miles driven or for eight years. The EPA estimated that the direct expenditures for compliance with the new-vehicle emissions standards totaled nineteen billion dollars in 2002.

Among the federally funded programs, two have been especially costly. The larger of these is the Municipal Sewage Treatment Construction Grant program begun in 1973. Through this program, the federal government directly underwrote grants totaling more than forty-three billion dollars by 1983 to pay for municipal sewage-treatment plants. Over time, the number of municipal sewage-treatment plants requiring major upgrades was reduced, and the federal contribution has now declined to less than two billion dollars per year.

The second program is better known. In 1980, Congress established the Superfund to finance the cleaning of hazardous waste sites. This program required private entities responsible for hazardous dumps to clean them up. But if these parties could not be found, the cleanup would be funded by the government through general revenues and a tax on petroleum feedstocks. In 1986, a new statute—the Superfund Amendments and Reauthorization Act—levied a federal tax on all corporations with taxable income over $2 million to help fund these remedial actions. Thus, corporations that had nothing to do with old hazardous waste sites or that do not even generate toxic waste were required to pay for the pollution others left behind. The Superfund program has been plagued with delays and a lack of detailed monitoring of its results. The EPA estimated its cost at $7.7 billion in 2002, but the EPA cannot estimate the program's benefits because it does not have the requisite evidence that the program has improved the ecosystem. Moreover, the EPA admits that it could not place a value on such improvements even if it had the requisite data.

The Economic Effects of Pollution Controls

Pollution controls divert economic resources from other economic activities, thereby reducing the potential size of measured national output. As long as the increase in the value of the environment is at least one dollar for each additional dollar spent on controls, the total value of goods, services, and environmental amenities is not reduced. Unfortunately, that seldom happens, for at least three reasons.

First, the Congress or the EPA may decide to control the wrong substances or to control some discharges too strictly. Congress's own Office of Technology Assessment concluded, for example, that attempting to reach the EPA's goal for urban smog reduction could cost more than $13 billion per year but result in less than $3.5 billion in improved health, agricultural, and amenity benefits. Attempting to use invariant national pollution standards to control smog, which varies substantially across geographic regions and over the seasons of the year, continues to be a very inefficient policy.

Second, regulatory standards can result in very inefficient patterns of control. Some polluters may be forced to spend twenty-five thousand dollars per ton to control the discharge of a certain pollutant, while for others the cost is only five hundred dollars per ton. Obviously, shifting the burden away from the former polluter toward the latter would result in lower total control costs for society for any given level of pollution control.

Third, pollution controls can have deleterious effects on investment in two ways. First, by making certain goods—chemicals, paper, metals, motor vehicles—more expensive to produce in the United States, they raise the prices of these goods and thereby reduce the amount of each demanded. Second, because controls are generally more onerous for new sources than for older, existing ones, managers are more likely to keep an old plant in use rather than replace it with a new, more efficient facility, even though the new facility would produce the same goods as the old one.

The command-and-control approach is flawed in other ways, too. It does little to encourage compliance beyond what is mandated. Regulations are introduced only after noticeable damage has occurred, and they may be difficult to enforce. Polluters who manage to avoid legislative scrutiny continue to pollute.

Market-Based Approach to Pollution Control

Problems like these have led policymakers to look for more efficient means of cleaning up the environment. As a result, the 1990 Clean Air Act Amendments look very different from their predecessors of the 1970s because they include market-based incentives to reduce pollution.

Market incentives are generally of two forms: pollution fees and so-called marketable permits. Pollution fees are simply taxes on polluters that penalize them in proportion to the amount they discharge into an airshed, waterway, or local landfill. Such taxes are common in Europe but have not been used in the United States. Marketable permits are essentially transferable discharge licenses that polluters can buy and sell to meet the control levels set by regulatory authorities. These permits have been used in the United States because they do not impose large taxes on a small set of polluting industries, as would be the case with pollution fees.

The 1990 Clean Air Act allows the EPA to grant "emissions permits" for certain pollutants. These are, in effect, rights to pollute that can be traded among polluters. Imagine a giant bubble that encloses all existing sources of air pollution. Within that bubble, some emitters may pollute more than the control level as long as other polluters compensate by polluting less. The government or some other state or regional authority decides on the desired level of pollution and the initial distribution of pollution rights within an industry or for a geographic region—the "bubble" that encloses these sources. Purchases and sales of permits within the "bubble" should reduce the total level of pollution to the allowable limit at the lowest total cost.

For example, a St. Louis study found that the cost of reducing particulate emissions for a paper products factory was $4 per ton, while the cost to a brewery was $600 per ton. The Clean Air Act could require St. Louis to reduce its emissions by a certain amount. Under the traditional approach, the brewery and the paper factory would each be required to cut emissions by, say, ten tons. The cost to the paper factory would be only $40, while the cost to the brewery would be $6,000. But with tradable permits, the brewery could pay the paper factory to cut emissions by twenty tons so that the brewery could continue to operate without reducing emissions at all. The net result is the same emission reduction of twenty tons as under the command-and-control approach, but the total cost to society of the reduction is only $80 instead of $6,040.

The tradable permits work. The most notable success has been in reducing sulfur dioxide emissions from electric utility plants. The 1990 Clean Air Act Amendments contained a provision that set a cap on total sulfur dioxide emissions that would decline over time to about half their 1980 level. Instead of requiring all power plants to meet a technology-based standard, electric utilities were allocated a share of the maximum allowable national emissions. They could then buy or sell emission allowances, depending on their needs and their marginal costs of abatement. The program has worked spectacularly well, reducing total control costs by an estimated $750 million to $1.5 billion per year relative to the cost of the former technology-based standards, while meeting or exceeding the environmental goals of sulfur dioxide reductions.

Marketable permits also were used to phase down the use of chlorofluorocarbons (CFCs) in order to preserve the stratospheric ozone layer and to phase out the use of lead in gasoline in the 1980s. The CFC policy was instituted in 1990 and succeeded in mitigating the opposition to a phase-down of CFCs in developed countries, particularly the United States. The lead phase-down was designed to allow smaller refineries to acquire marketable permits rather than employing technologies that the larger refineries could implement more efficiently. This program saved hundreds of millions of dollars per year, promoted technological progress, and allowed a more orderly transition of refinery capacity without sacrificing environmental quality. Protecting our environment does not have to put an end to economic progress. Free markets in permits to pollute, like free markets for other resources, can ensure that pollution is controlled at the lowest cost possible.

About the Author

Robert W. Crandall is a senior fellow at the Brookings Institution in Washington, D.C. He served as acting director of the Council on Wage and Price Stability during the Carter administration and was previously an associate professor of economics at MIT.

Further Reading

Carlson, Curtis, Dallas Butraw, Maureen Cropper, and Karen Palmer. "Sulfur Dioxide Control by Electric Utilities: What Are the Gains from Trade?" Resources for the Future, Discussion Paper 98–44, revised April 2000.
Hahn, Robert W., and Gordon L. Hester. "Where Did All the Markets Go?" *Yale Journal on Regulation* 6, no. 1 (1989): 109–153.
Newell, Richard G., and Kristen Rogers. "The Market-Based Lead Phasedown." Resources for the Future, Discussion Paper 03–37, November 2003.
Schmalensee, Richard, Paul M. Joskow, A. Denny Ellerman, Juan Pablo Montero, and Elizabeth M. Bailey. "An Interim Evaluation of Sulfur Dioxide Emissions Trading." *Journal of Economic Perspectives* 12, no. 3 (1998): 53–68.
Tietenberg, Thomas H. *Emissions Trading: An Exercise in Reforming Pollution Policy.* Washington, D.C.: Resources for the Future, 1985.
U.S. Department of Energy. Office of Environmental Analysis, Assistant Secretary for Environmental Safety and Health. *A Compendium of Options for Government Policy to Encourage* *Private Sector Responses to Potential Climate Change.* October 1989.
U.S. Environmental Protection Agency. *2003–08 Strategic Plan.* Appendix 1. 2004.
U.S. Office of Management and Budget. *2005 Report to Congress on the Costs and Benefits of Federal Regulations.* 2005.

Population

Ronald Demos Lee

The world's population increased by 50 percent between 1900 and 1950 and by 140 percent between 1950 and 2000, and is projected by the United Nations to increase by just under 50 percent between 2000 and 2050. Of the 3.44 billion increase in the number of people between 1950 and 2000, only 8 percent was in developed (i.e., rich) countries. The remaining 92 percent of the increase was in less-developed, or poor, countries (LDCs), reflecting the large difference in fertility levels and, to some degree, the different age distributions. Life expectancy in developed countries rose from 66.1 years during the period from 1950 to 1954, to 75.3 years in 2000. For LDCs, life expectancy rose from only 41.0 years during the same period to 63.0 years in 2000. Over that same time, the number of births per woman fell from 2.8 to 1.6 in developed countries and from 6.2 births per woman to 3.0 in LDCs. Birthrates in LDCs remain high enough to contribute substantially to population growth.

Population Aging

Lower birthrates and longer lives lead to "population aging" (i.e., more elderly people and fewer children). Population aging is most rapid, and has gone furthest, in the developed world. The median age in developed countries rose from 28.6 in 1950 to 37.3 in 2000, while in the United States it rose from 30.0 to 35.2. In LDCs, by contrast, the median age in 1950 was only 21.3, rising to 24.1 in 2000. Of course, individual countries vary. In Japan, Italy, and Switzerland the median age was over 40 in 2000, whereas in Uganda, Yemen, Niger, and Somalia it was under 16.

Population aging matters for many reasons, but first and foremost because of the costs of retirement (pensions and health care). In the developed countries, these costs are borne principally by the central government and funded through taxes on the working-age population. The old-age-dependency ratio—that is, the population aged 65 and over divided by the population aged 15 to 64—is a key indicator of population aging. Other things being equal, the tax rate for pensions will be proportional to this ratio.

In the developed world, this ratio has risen from .12 in 1950 to .21 today, and is projected to increase to .44 by 2050. If, in the developed countries, the elderly in 2050 are to receive the level of benefits given to the current elderly, then the level of payroll taxes needed to fund government pensions will more than double by 2050. Due to higher fertility and immigration, the U.S. population is projected to remain younger than those of other OECD countries, and the pension problem will be less severe. Health costs, however, pose an even more difficult problem because of Medicare, the socialized health-care system for the elderly in the United States. As the population ages and spending per elderly person rises, government spending on health care will likely soar.

Workers paying for the current retirees do so with the understanding that they, in turn, will collect from the next generation of workers. Population aging generates intense political pressure to modify this implicit contract with the government by such devices as delaying the age of retirement or reducing the size of the benefit. The fear of population aging is a strong political force in many developed countries, leading to policies intended to induce people to have larger families. Such policies include banning abortion and contraception (Romania), offering prizes and financial incentives for births (France), and instituting generous paid-leave policies for women who stay home to care for their babies (Sweden). Although the increased costs of the elderly are to some degree offset by declining government and private costs of raising children as the ratio of children to the working-age population declines, population aging increases the total deadweight loss, a loss that always comes about from TAXATION because most of the child costs are private, while the costs of the elderly are mainly paid by taxpayers.

The projected median age for the developed countries in 2050 (46.4 years) is only slightly higher than that for East Asia (44.3). Projected population aging is a serious problem for LDCs, just as economic development and urbanization are weakening traditional family-based support systems for the elderly.

Fluctuations in Generation Size

Fluctuations in generation size also cause problems. When a small generation pays high taxes to support a large retired one, as will soon happen in the United States, many of the smaller generation will feel unfairly burdened. Changes in generation size also affect the labor market. When the small U.S. generation born in the depressed 1930s reached the labor market in the 1950s, its small size relative to the demand for new workers brought easy employment, high wages, and rapid advancement. But when the baby-boom generation reached the labor market in the 1970s, it experienced relatively high unemployment, low wages, and slow promotion. This picture is complicated by immigration, as well as by changing patterns of international trade and education.

Population and Development

Although population aging and bulging age distributions are real concerns, many people's greater fear is that global population growth will overwhelm the capacity of economies and of the global ecosystem.

This fear of population growth is not new. THOMAS ROBERT MALTHUS and other classical economists worried that as the growing population made land increasingly scarce, rising food prices would eventually choke off further economic and population growth, leading to the "stationary state." For classical economists, natural resource constraints, particularly of land, were at the heart of the problem. But the economic importance of land has dwindled in the modern world. The share of the labor force in agriculture has declined from around 80 percent to around 5 percent in many developed countries, while industrialization has caused agricultural output to fall to even less than 5 percent of total production.

Even within agriculture, land has become less important as productivity has been boosted by other inputs, including labor, fertilizer, pesticides, insecticides, new seed varieties, irrigation, mechanical or animal draft power, and education. Contrary to the predictions of the classical economists, real food prices have historically fallen. Since 1800, for example, the price of wheat, adjusted for inflation, has fallen by about 90 percent.[1] Also contrary to the classicals' predictions, from 1961 to 2002, the world's per capita food production increased by 0.6 percent per year, for a total increase of 27 percent. The incidence of famines has diminished, not increased, and modern famines arise not from population growth but, rather, from wars (recent disturbances in Africa) and mistaken policies (e.g., the Great Leap Forward in China). Although hunger and malnutrition are serious problems in many parts of the world, they result more from poverty and uneven income distribution than from deficiencies of agricultural production due to population growth.

So the classical economists' emphasis on land as the critical limiting factor was undermined by the ability of technical progress and capital accumulation to expand output. Economists came to view natural resource constraints as unimportant. Instead, investment and capital accumulation, the creation and transfer of technology, and appro-

---

1. See Bjørn Lomborg, *The Skeptical Environmentalist*, p. 62.

priate institutions and policies (e.g., private property and free-market prices) were seen as the keys to economic development.

In the 1940s and 1950s, economists who studied population had a new concern. They argued that when population grows more rapidly, a greater proportion of current output must be set aside to create capital—housing, tools, and machinery—for new members of the population. All these investments must increase, they noted, at the same time that more children per family tend to reduce domestic saving rates. If the additional investment does not take place, they claimed, then capital will be diluted: new generations will be less well equipped than older ones. Standard economic growth models—those of Robert Solow, for example—imply that "capital dilution" should have relatively small effects: an increase in the population growth rate from 2 percent per year to 3 percent per year, for example, would eventually reduce per capita output by about 7 percent. In any event, statistical analyses of the international record did not find that more rapid population growth depressed rates of growth of per capita income. More recent studies, however, have found that in the 1980s and 1990s, population growth and growth of per capita income were negatively correlated.

Of course, per capita income is not an ideal indicator of economic well-being in any case. A couple that has an intended birth simultaneously raises its well-being and reduces its family per capita income.

While some economists were emphasizing these Malthusian views, two others, Ester Boserup and the late Julian Simon, argued forcefully that population growth has positive economic effects. Simon pointed out that another birth means another mind that can help think up ways of using resources more efficiently. More population could also stimulate investment demand, break down traditional barriers to the market economy, spur technological progress, and lead to harder work (the latter because the presence of more dependents in the household raises the marginal utility of income relative to leisure and leads to longer hours of work). They noted also that a larger population can more easily bear the costs of providing certain kinds of social infrastructure—transportation, communications, water supply, government, research—for which the need increases less than proportionately with population. Indeed, Simon argued that the ultimate resource was people, and that the world would be better off with more of them.

By the 1980s, policymakers were confused. Was population growth good? Was it bad? Did it matter at all? A reassessment in the 1980s revealed a surprisingly high degree of agreement among economists that population growth matters less than had previously been thought, in part due to the flexibility of free, competitive markets. In market economies, when population growth makes resources more scarce, the prices of those resources rise. This leads consumers to reduce their use of these resources and to find substitutes. The higher prices of resources also give producers an incentive to find new supplies and to substitute cheaper resources as inputs. But, more important, technological progress often reduces prices of resources, even in the face of higher demand (see NATURAL RESOURCES).

The real prices of most minerals have been falling historically, not rising. The total costs of natural resources as a share of national output have not been rising. The one exception is petroleum prices, but part of that is due to OPEC, not to rising population. Before OPEC exerted control on the world oil market in 1973, the real price of oil had been falling. And even at about fifty dollars a barrel in late 2004, the real price of oil is less than 60 percent of the level it reached in 1980. In 1980, Simon wagered environmentalist Paul Ehrlich that mineral prices would decline in real terms during the following decade. They agreed to follow five minerals: copper, chrome, nickel, tin, and tungsten. In 1990, Simon won the well-publicized bet and collected his money. Between 1980 and 1990, the inflation-adjusted price of all five minerals fell—copper by 18 percent, chrome by 40, nickel by 3, tin by 72, and tungsten by 57.

While economists were concluding that population growth is relatively harmless, ecologists and environmentalists such as Paul Ehrlich and Garrett Hardin sounded the population alarm. They pointed out that the biosphere provides essential, although uncounted, inputs to economic activity, and they worried that its limits and fragility place bounds on sustainable levels of production. These bounds, they said, had already been surpassed, and the global economy, they thought, was profligately consuming ecological capital rather than living off the "interest" it yielded.

Although mineral depletion is probably not the real problem, some of the ecologists' warnings appear correct. The reason, interestingly, is that many renewable resources—air, water, fisheries, land, forest cover, ozone layer, and species—are not privately owned and are not subject to the market. Instead, they are held in common. Therefore, as Garrett Hardin points out (see TRAGEDY OF THE COMMONS), no person who uses these resources takes account of the damage he or she imposes on others. Individuals and companies, for example, can sometimes dump pollution into the air and water without being made to bear the full cost of environmental degradation. The costs are passed on to society as a whole. Consequently, economic incentives encourage overuse. Because the automatic signaling mechanism of market prices is absent, price changes serve neither as an incentive for preservation nor as a signal of increasing scarcity. The problem, then, is not population per se, but rather lack of private property rights or explicit regulation of the use of the resource.

Worries about population growth have now come full circle: from the classical concern for limited land, to the emphasis on physical capital, to the more recent emphasis on human capital and the ameliorative influence of competitive markets, to beneficial aspects of population growth, and back to the natural constraints urged by ecologists. This time, however, the concern is for renewable natural resources, many of which fall outside the market. For some, the urgency of population control on ecological grounds is obvious. Others, who see potential market solutions for these resource problems, remain skeptical.

As for the more narrowly economic reasons for restraining population growth, decades of research are still inconclusive. For a few countries with very dense populations, such as Bangladesh, China, and Egypt, it seems clear that increasing population density on agricultural land contributes to rural poverty. For a few others with exceptionally rapid population growth, such as Somalia and Burkina Faso, the case is also clear. For other countries already facing rapid population aging, such as Japan, Germany, and Taiwan, higher fertility may well bring benefits.

About the Author

Ronald Demos Lee is professor of demography and the Jordan Family Professor of Economics at the University of California, Berkeley. A past president of the Population Association of America, Lee received its Mindel Sheps and Taeuber awards for population research. He is an elected member of the National Academy of Sciences and the American Association for the Advancement of Science, and a corresponding member of the British Academy. He co-chaired the National Academy of Sciences' working group on population and economic development, which produced a widely cited report in 1986.

Further Reading

Ehrlich, Paul, and Ann Ehrlich. *The Population Explosion*. New York: Simon and Schuster, 1990.
Kelley, Allen. "Economic Consequences of Population Change in the Third World." *Journal of Economic Literature* 26, no. 4 (1988): 1685–1728.
Lee, Ronald. "The Demographic Transition: Three Centuries of Fundamental Change." *Journal of Economic Perspectives* 17, no. 4 (2003): 167–190.
Lomborg, Bjørn. *The Skeptical Environmentalist: Measuring the Real State of the World*. Cambridge: Cambridge University Press, 2001.
National Academy of Sciences. *Population Growth and Economic Development: Policy Questions*. Washington, D.C.: National Academy Press, 1986.
Simon, Julian. *The Ultimate Resource*. 2d ed. Princeton: Princeton University Press, 1996.

Poverty in America

Isabel V. Sawhill

The United States produces more per capita than any other industrialized country, and in recent years governments at various levels have spent about $350 billion per year, or about 3.5 percent of gross domestic product, on programs serving low-income families.[1] Despite this, measured poverty is more prevalent in the United States than in most of the rest of the industrialized world. In the mid-1990s, the U.S. poverty rate was twice as high as in Scandinavian countries, and one-third higher than in other European countries and Japan.[2] Poverty is also as prevalent now as it was in 1973, when the incidence of poverty in America reached a postwar low of 11.1 percent. According to the Census Bureau, 37 million Americans were poor in 2005, just over 12.5 percent of the population.[3]

These official figures represent the number of people whose annual family income is less than an absolute "poverty line" developed by the federal government in the mid-1960s. The poverty line is roughly three times the annual cost of a nutritionally adequate diet. It varies by family size and is updated every year to reflect changes in the consumer price index. In 2005, the poverty line for a family of four was $19,971.[4]

The author is grateful to Melissa Cox for extensive research assistance on this article.

1. Committee on Ways and Means, U.S. House of Representatives, *2004 Green Book: Background Material and Data on Programs Within the Jurisdiction of the Committee on Ways and Means*, tables I-5 and K-9, online at: http://waysandmeans.house.gov/Documents.asp?section=813.

2. Michael Forster and Mark Pearson, "Income Distribution and Poverty in the OECD Area: Trends and Driving Forces," *OECD Economic Studies*, no. 1 (2002): 13.

3. Carmen De Navas-Walt, Bernadette D. Proctor, and Cheryl Hill Lee, "Income, Poverty and Health Insurance in the United States: 2005," U.S. Census Bureau, August 2006, p. 6, online at: http://www.census.gov/prod/2006pubs/p60-231.pdf.

4. U.S. Census Bureau, "Poverty Thresholds for 2002 by Size of Family and Number of Related Children Under 18 Years," online at: http://www.census.gov/hhes/www/poverty/threshld/thresh05.html.

Many researchers believe that the official method of measuring poverty is flawed. Some argue that poverty is a state of relative economic deprivation, that it depends not on whether income is lower than some arbitrary level but on whether it falls far below the incomes of others in the same society. But if we define poverty to mean relative economic deprivation, then no matter how wealthy everyone is, there will always be poverty. Others point out that the official measure errs by omission. For example, official poverty figures take no account of refundable tax credits or the value of noncash transfers such as food stamps and housing vouchers, which serve as income for certain purchases. Incorporating these factors into family income would have reduced the measured poverty rate by an estimated 1.9 percentage points (or by approximately 16 percent) in 2002.[5]

Official poverty figures also ignore work-related expenses that affect families' disposable incomes. Child care is a case in point. Isabel Sawhill and Adam Thomas estimated that deducting this expense from family incomes would have increased the measured poverty rate by up to one percentage point (or 8 percent) in 1998.[6] Also, smaller, more fragmented households are more common today than a few decades ago, suggesting that some poor households were formed for the privacy and autonomy of their members. To the extent that some people have willingly sacrificed their access to the economic resources of parents, spouses, or adult children, some of the increase in poverty may actually represent an improvement in well-being.

Another problem with the official measure arises from the dynamic nature of poverty. Most Americans who experience poverty do so only temporarily. In the four years from 1996 through 1999, only 2 percent of the population was poor for two years or more.[7] During the same period, 34 percent of the population was poor for at least two months.[8] In short, persistent poverty is relatively uncommon.

In recent years, income mobility has fallen slightly. According to one estimate, 40 percent of families occupied the same position in the income distribution at the beginning and end of the 1990s, compared with 36 percent in the 1970s.[9]

Another criticism of the poverty measures is that they are based on income rather than on consumption. Consumption spending may be a better measure of well-being than reported income is, although data from the consumer expenditure survey have their own limitations. Daniel Slesnick found, using consumption spending, that the poverty rate fell from 31 percent in 1949 to 13 percent in 1965 and to 2 percent at the end of the 1980s. One rough indicator of the decline in poverty is the range of items that most poor homes now contain—from color TVs to VCRs to washing machines to microwaves—compared with the relative lack of these items in poor homes in the early 1970s.[10]

Despite their flaws, the official figures are widely used to measure poverty. According to the Census Bureau, the poverty rate declined from 22.2 percent in 1960 to 12.6 percent in 2005. Most of this decline occurred in the 1960s. By 1970, the poverty rate had fallen to the current level of 12.6 percent. It then hovered between 11 and 13 percent in the 1970s, fluctuating primarily with the state of the economy.[11] A longer-term perspective leaves a more positive impression. For example, according to one estimate by Christine Ross, Sheldon Danziger, and Eugene Smolensky, more than two-thirds of the population in 1939 was poor by today's standards.[12]

The trend in poverty masks the divergent experiences of poverty among various demographic groups. The poverty rate among the elderly, for example, declined dramatically from 35.2 percent in 1959 to 10.1 percent in 2005 and is now lower than for any other age group. The poverty rate among children declined between 1959 and 1970, increased to 22.7 percent in 1993, and then fell steadily to 17.6 percent in 2005; it remains higher than poverty rates among other age groups. The poverty rate among black households has also declined over the last forty years, but at 24.9 percent in 2005 remains more than twice as high as the rate among white households.

5. Unpublished data supplied by Wendell Primus, Committee on Ways and Means, U.S. House of Representatives.

6. Isabel Sawhill and Adam Thomas, "A Hand up for the Bottom Third: Toward a New Agenda for Low-Income Working Families," Brookings Institution, 2001, online at: www.brook.edu/views/papers/sawhill/20010522.pdf.

7. John Iceland, "Dynamics of Economic Well-Being: Poverty 1996–1999," U.S. Census Bureau, July 2003, p. 4, online at: http://www.census.gov/prod/2003pubs/p70-91.pdf.

8. Ibid.

9. Katherine Bradbury and Jane Katz, "Are Lifetime Incomes Growing More Unequal?" *Federal Reserve Bank of Boston Regional Review* (4th Quarter 2002): 4.

10. W. Michael Cox and Richard Alm, *Myths of Rich and Poor* (New York: Basic Books, 1999), p. 15.

11. De Navas-Walt, et al., "Income, Poverty and Health Insurance in the United States: 2005," p. 46.

12. Christine Ross, Sheldon Danziger, and Eugene Smolensky, "The Level and Trend of Poverty in the United States, 1939–1979," *Demography* 24 (1987): 587–600.

The poverty rate for households headed by women declined from 49.4 percent in 1959 to 28.7 percent in 2005, but is still much higher than for other types of households. This higher incidence of reported poverty, together with the rising share of households headed by women, has led to what researchers call the "feminization of poverty." Between 1959 and 2005, the proportion of the poor in female-headed households rose from 17.8 percent to 31.1 percent.[13] Some of these women (about 13 percent) live with unrelated men or have unreported income from casual jobs that enable them to cope, but there is little doubt that the growth of single-parent families has contributed importantly to the rise in poverty.

Researchers have suggested a number of plausible explanations for both positive and negative trends in poverty. These explanations include changes in the composition of households, economic growth, immigration, efforts to increase the education and skills of the poor, and the structure and generosity of the welfare system.

The rapid growth of households headed by women and unrelated individuals, who typically cannot earn as much as married-couple families, has left a larger share of the population in poverty. This demographic trend has increased poverty rates among children. The proportion of children living in female-headed households doubled between 1970 and 2003, rising from 11.6 percent in 1970 to 23.6 in 2003.[14] Had that proportion remained constant since 1970, the child poverty rate would have been about 4.4 percentage points lower in 1998.[15]

The ebb and flow of the economy also influences the incidence of poverty. Researchers have found that recessions have a disproportionate impact on the poor because they cause rising unemployment, a reduction in work hours, and stagnant family incomes. The relationship between the changes in the unemployment rate and the poverty rate was stronger during the 1960s and 1990s than during the 1970s and 1980s.[16] But economic downturns have been accompanied by rising poverty rates during each of the six recessions in the past thirty years.[17]

Increased immigration and the characteristics of immigrants also affect poverty. Immigration increases the poverty rate because newly arrived immigrants are, on average, poorer than native-born citizens. Of the foreign-born population in 1999, 16.8 percent were poor, compared with 11.2 percent of native-born citizens.[18] After declining during the 1930s and 1940s, the foreign-born population surged from 4.7 percent of the American population in 1970 to 10.4 percent in 2000.[19] Immigration may also indirectly influence the incidence of poverty, because a surge in immigrants with minimal training tends to depress incomes among native workers at the bottom. For example, George Borjas attributed half of the drop in the relative wage of high school dropouts between 1980 and 1995 to immigration.[20]

Training and compensatory education programs such as the Job Corps and Head Start, designed as part of the War on Poverty to increase the skills of the poor, may also have reduced poverty. Many of these programs have not been carefully evaluated, but some of those that have are modestly successful. For example, some early education programs have had a positive effect on poor children, helping them to complete school, avoid crime, and achieve higher test scores.[21] Some employment and training programs have raised earnings for adult women, although these programs have been less helpful to adult men and young people.[22]

Finally, safety-net programs have contributed to the decline. These are typically divided into two categories: public assistance programs, such as Temporary Assistance for Needy Families, food stamps, and Medicaid, which were designed to help people who are already poor; and social insurance programs such as Social Security, unemployment insurance, and Medicare, which were designed to prevent poverty when events such as layoff or retirement

13. De Navas-Walt, et al., "Income, Poverty and Health Insurance in the United States: 2005," p. 14.

14. U.S. Census Bureau, Historical Poverty Table 10: Related Children in Female Householder Families as a Proportion of All Related Children, by Poverty Status: 1959 to 2003, online at: http://www.census.gov/hhes/poverty/histpov/hstpov10.html.

15. Adam Thomas and Isabel Sawhill, "For Richer or for Poorer: Marriage as an Antipoverty Strategy," *Journal for Policy Analysis and Management* 21, no. 4 (2002): 587–599.

16. Robert Haveman, "Poverty and the Distribution of Economic Well-Being Since the 1960s," in George L. Perry and James Tobin, eds., *Economic Events, Ideas, and Policies* (Washington, D.C.: Brookings Institution, 2000), p. 281.

17. Proctor and Dalaker, "Poverty in the United States: 2002," p. 3.

18. U.S. Census Bureau, "Profile of the Foreign-Born Population in the United States: 2000," December 2001, P23-206, p. 6.

19. Ibid., p. 9.

20. George J. Borjas, ed., *Issues in the Economics of Immigration*, National Bureau of Economic Research Conference Report (Chicago: University of Chicago Press, 2000), p. 6.

21. James J. Heckman, "Policies to Foster Human Capital," *Research in Economics* 54, no. 1 (2000): 3–56.

22. Judith M. Gueron and Gayle Hamilton, "The Role of Education and Training in Welfare Reform," Welfare Reform and Beyond Policy Brief no. 20, April 2002.

threaten a household's well-being. Expenditures on these programs totaled roughly $1,279 billion in 2002, up 160 percent in real terms since 1975.[23] However, much of this spending was for noncash assistance (especially health care) that improves the well-being of the poor but has no effect on measured poverty.

The antipoverty effectiveness of these programs is typically measured by counting the number of people with pretransfer incomes below the poverty line whose incomes are raised above the poverty line by income transfers. According to government estimates, social insurance and public assistance programs moved nearly half of the pretransfer poor above the poverty line in 2002. This implies that these programs reduce the poverty rate by ten percentage points.[24]

By ignoring the incentive effects these programs have on recipients, however, the above analysis overstates the success of safety-net programs. Specifically, means-tested cash transfers such as Aid to Families with Dependent Children (AFDC), which decline as the welfare recipient earns more reported income, have long been understood to be antiwork and antifamily. This criticism of the program led to its reform in 1996. Under the revised law, called Temporary Assistance for Needy Families (TANF), welfare mothers are required to work and federal benefits are limited to five years. Aided by a strong economy and more generous assistance for the working poor in the form of an expanded Earned Income Tax Credit and other measures, welfare reform led to a sharp fall in caseloads in the late 1990s. Employment rates among single mothers rose and child poverty fell. In addition, after increasing for decades, the share of births to unmarried mothers has leveled off and teen birth rates have declined. (The reasons for these changes in fertility are not well understood and may or may not be related to welfare reform.) Although some families are worse off as a result of welfare reform, the majority of former welfare mothers have been able to earn enough to improve their economic situation. The longer-term effects of welfare reform, especially those that might be expected in a less robust economy, are more uncertain and are likely to depend, to some extent, on the provision of additional supports such as child care for low-income working families.

U.S. poverty, measured by income, ebbs and flows with the state of the economy and with demographic shifts, especially immigration and the growth of single-parent fam-

23. Committee on Ways and Means, U.S. House of Representatives, *2004 Green Book*, tables I-5 and K-9.
24. Unpublished data supplied by Wendell Primus, Committee on Ways and Means, U.S. House of Representatives.

ilies. Policy measures—whether in the form of direct income support or education and skills training of the poor—have swum against these strong tides and have had a mixed record of success. Since the mid-1990s, policies that have both required and supported work as the best strategy for reducing poverty have had considerable success.

About the Author

Isabel V. Sawhill is a senior fellow and the Cabot Family Chair at the Brookings Institution and was previously associate director of the Office of Management and Budget during President Bill Clinton's administration.

Further Reading

Blank, Rebecca. *It Takes a Nation: A New Agenda for Fighting Poverty.* New York: Russell Sage Foundation; Princeton: Princeton University Press, 1997.
Citro, Constance, and Robert T. Michael, eds. *Measuring Poverty: A New Approach.* Washington, D.C.: National Academy Press, 1995.
Danziger, Sheldon H., and Robert Haveman, eds. *Understanding Poverty.* New York: Russell Sage Foundation; Cambridge: Harvard University Press, 2001.
Sawhill, Isabel, R. Kent Weaver, Ron Haskins, and Andrea Kane, eds. *Welfare Reform and Beyond: The Future of the Safety Net.* Washington, D.C.: Brookings Institution, 2002.
Slesnick, Daniel T. "Gaining Ground: Poverty in the Postwar United States." *Journal of Political Economy* 101, no. 1 (1993): 1–38.

Present Value

David R. Henderson

Present value is the value today of an amount of money in the future. If the appropriate interest rate is 10 percent, then the present value of $100 spent or earned one year from now is $100 divided by 1.10, which is about $91. This simple example illustrates the general truth that the present value of a future amount is less than that actual future amount. If the appropriate interest rate is only 4 percent, then the present value of $100 spent or earned one year from now is $100 divided by 1.04, or about $96. This illustrates the fact that the lower the interest rate, the higher the present value. The present value of $100 spent or earned twenty years from now is, using an interest rate of 10 percent, $100/(1.10)^{20}, or about $15. In other words, the present value of an amount far in the future is a small fraction of the amount.

The fact that a dollar one year from now is less than a

dollar today would be true even if the inflation rate were zero. The reason is that we prefer current availability to future availability: we want it now. That is why there is interest even when expected inflation is zero.

The concept of present value is very useful. One can, for example, determine what a lottery prize is really worth. The California state government advertises the worth of one of its lottery prizes as $1 million. But that is not the value of the prize. Instead, the California government promises to pay $50,000 a year for twenty years. If the discount rate is 10 percent and the first payment is received immediately, then the present value of the lottery prize is "only" $468,246.

Present value also helps us with such practical issues as the location of an airport. Suppose someone argues that an airport, say Denver International Airport, should be built twenty miles from the edge of the city because twenty-five years from now the city will have expanded to reach the airport. That means that for twenty-five years, people will spend valuable time going the long distance to and from the airport. The gain is that twenty-five years from now the airport will be appropriately situated. But because the gain from appropriately locating the airport is so far in the future, the present value of this gain is small; therefore, building the airport so far away today probably does not make sense.

About the Author

David R. Henderson is the editor of this encyclopedia. He is a research fellow at Stanford University's Hoover Institution and an associate professor of economics at the Naval Postgraduate School in Monterey, California. He was formerly a senior economist with President Ronald Reagan's Council of Economic Advisers.

Further Reading

Fisher, Irving. *The Theory of Interest*. New York: Macmillan, 1930. Online at: http://www.econlib.org/library/YPDBooks/Fisher/fshToI.html.

Price Controls

Hugh Rockoff

Governments have been trying to set maximum or minimum prices since ancient times. The Old Testament prohibited interest on loans to fellow Israelites; medieval governments fixed the maximum price of bread; and in recent years, governments in the United States have fixed the price of gasoline, the rent on apartments in New York City, and the wage of unskilled labor, to name a few. At times, governments go beyond fixing specific prices and try to control the general level of prices, as was done in the United States during both world wars and the Korean War, and by the Nixon administration from 1971 to 1973.

The appeal of price controls is understandable. Even though they fail to protect many consumers and hurt others, controls hold out the promise of protecting groups that are particularly hard-pressed to meet price increases. Thus, the prohibition against usury—charging high interest on loans—was intended to protect someone forced to borrow out of desperation; the maximum price for bread was supposed to protect the poor, who depended on bread to survive; and rent controls were supposed to protect those who were renting when the demand for apartments exceeded the supply, and landlords were preparing to "gouge" their tenants.

Despite the frequent use of price controls, however, and despite their appeal, economists are generally opposed to them, except perhaps for very brief periods during emergencies. In a survey published in 1992, 76.3 percent of the economists surveyed agreed with the statement: "A ceiling on rents reduces the quality and quantity of housing available." A further 16.6 percent agreed with qualifications, and only 6.5 percent disagreed. The results were similar when the economists were asked about general controls: only 8.4 percent agreed with the statement: "Wage-price controls are a useful policy option in the control of inflation." An additional 17.7 percent agreed with qualifications, but a sizable majority, 73.9 percent, disagreed (Alston et al. 1992, p. 204).

The reason most economists are skeptical about price controls is that they distort the allocation of resources. To paraphrase a remark by Milton Friedman, economists may not know much, but they do know how to produce a shortage or surplus. Price ceilings, which prevent prices from exceeding a certain maximum, cause shortages. Price floors, which prohibit prices below a certain minimum, cause surpluses, at least for a time. Suppose that the supply and demand for wheat flour are balanced at the current price, and that the government then fixes a lower maximum price. The supply of flour will decrease, but the demand for it will increase. The result will be excess demand and empty shelves. Although some consumers will be lucky enough to purchase flour at the lower price, others will be forced to do without.

Because controls prevent the price system from rationing the available supply, some other mechanism must take its place. A queue, once a familiar sight in the controlled economies of Eastern Europe, is one possibility. When the United States set maximum prices for gasoline in 1973 and

1979, dealers sold gas on a first-come-first-served basis, and drivers had to wait in long lines to buy gasoline, receiving in the process a taste of life in the Soviet Union. The true price of gasoline, which included both the cash paid and the time spent waiting in line, was often higher than it would have been if the price had not been controlled. In 1979, for example, the United States fixed the price of gasoline at about $1.00 per gallon. If the market price had been $1.20, a driver who bought ten gallons would apparently have saved $.20 per gallon, or $2.00. But if the driver had to wait in line for thirty minutes to buy gasoline, and if her time was worth $8.00 per hour, the real cost to her was $10.00 for the gas and $4.00 for the time, an overall cost of $1.40 per gallon. Some gasoline, of course, was held for friends, longtime customers, the politically well connected, and those who were willing to pay a little cash on the side.

The incentives to evade controls are ever present, and the forms that evasion can take are limitless. The precise form depends on the nature of the good or service, the organization of the industry, the degree of government enforcement, and so on. One of the simplest forms of evasion is quality deterioration. In the United States during World War II, fat was added to hamburger, candy bars were made smaller and of inferior ingredients, and landlords reduced their maintenance of rent-controlled apartments. The government can attack quality deterioration by issuing specific product standards (hamburger must contain so much lean meat, apartments must be painted once a year, and so on) and by government oversight and enforcement. But this means that the bureaucracy controlling prices tends to get bigger, more intrusive, and more expensive.

Sometimes more subtle forms of evasion arise. One is the tie-in sale. To buy wheat flour at the official price during World War I, consumers were often required to purchase unwanted quantities of rye or potato flour. "Forced up-trading" is another. Consider a manufacturer that produces a lower-quality, lower-priced line sold in large volumes at a small markup, and a higher-priced, higher-quality line sold in small quantities at a high markup. When the government introduces price ceilings and causes a shortage of both lines, the manufacturer may discontinue the lower-priced line, causing the consumer to "trade up" to the higher-priced line. During World War II, the U.S. government made numerous unsuccessful attempts to force clothing manufacturers to continue lower-priced lines.

Not only do producers have an incentive to raise prices, but some consumers also have an incentive to pay them. The result may be payments on the side to distributors (a bribe for the superintendent of a rent-controlled building,

for example), or it may be a full-fledged black market in which goods are bought and sold clandestinely. Prices in black markets may be above not only the official price but even the price that would prevail in a free market, because the buyers are unusually desperate and because sellers face penalties if their transactions are detected, and this risk is reflected in the price.

The obvious costs of queuing, evasion, and black markets often lead governments to impose some form of rationing. The simplest is a coupon entitling a consumer to buy a fixed quantity of the controlled good. For example, each motorist might receive a coupon permitting the purchase of one set of new tires. Rationing solves some of the shortage problems created by controls. Producers no longer find it easy to divert supplies to the black market since they must have ration tickets to match their production; distributors no longer have as much incentive to accept bribes or demand tie-in purchases; and consumers have a smaller incentive to pay high prices because they are assured a minimum amount. Rationing, as Forrest Capie and Geoffrey Wood (2002) pointed out, increases the integrity and efficiency of a system of price controls.

Rationing, however, comes at a cost. The government must undertake the difficult job of adjusting rations to reflect fluctuating supplies and demands and the needs of individual consumers. While an equal ration for each consumer makes sense in a few cases—bread in a city under siege is the classic example—most rationing programs must face the problem that consumer needs vary widely. One solution is to tailor the ration to the needs of individuals: people with a long commute to work can be given a larger ration of gasoline. In World War II, community boards in the United States had the power to issue extra rations to particularly needy individuals. The danger of favoritism and corruption in such a scheme, particularly if continued after the spirit of patriotism has begun to erode, is obvious. One way of ameliorating some of the problems created by rationing is to permit a free market in ration tickets. The free exchange of ration tickets has the advantages of providing additional income for consumers who sell their extra tickets and improving the well-being of those who buy. A "white market" in ration tickets, however, does nothing to encourage additional production, an end that can be accomplished by removing price controls. Also, a white market in ration tickets will not necessarily cause the product sold to be moved to the same regions of the country where the tickets are sold. Thus, a white market will not necessarily eliminate regional shortages.

With all of the problems generated by controls, we can well ask why they are ever imposed and why they are sometimes maintained for so long. The answer, in part, is that the public does not always see the links between controls and the problems they create. The elimination of lower-priced lines of merchandise may be interpreted simply as callous disregard for the poor rather than a consequence of controls. But price controls almost always benefit a subset of consumers who may have a particular claim to public sympathy and who, in any case, have a strong interest in lobbying for controls. Minimum-wage laws may create unemployment among the unskilled or drive them into the black market, but MINIMUM WAGES do raise the income of those poor workers who remain employed in regulated markets. Rent controls make it difficult for young people to find an apartment, but they do hold down the rent for those who already have an apartment when controls are instituted (see RENT CONTROL).

General price controls—controls on prices of many goods—are often imposed when the public becomes alarmed that inflation is out of control. In the twentieth century, war has frequently been the occasion for general price controls. Here, the case can be made that controls have a positive psychological benefit that outweighs the costs, at least in the short run. Surging inflation may lead to panic buying, strikes, animosity toward racial or ethnic minorities who are perceived as benefiting from inflation, and so on. Price controls may make a positive contribution by calming these fears, particularly if patriotism can be counted on to limit evasion. This was the limited case for controls made by Frank W. Taussig, a member of the Price Fixing Committee in World War I, in his famous essay "Price-Fixing as seen by a Price-Fixer." A somewhat similar case can be made for removing controls cautiously when suppressed inflation—that is, inflation that the government holds down forcibly by price controls—is significant. Toward the end of World War II, more than fifty leading economists, including friends of the free market such as Frank H. Knight and Henry Simons, wrote to the *New York Times* (April 9, 1946, p. 23) calling on Congress to continue controls for another year until supplies and demands were more nearly in equilibrium in order to prevent the inflationary spiral they feared would arise if controls were removed suddenly.

However, most inflation, even in wartime, is due to inflationary monetary and fiscal policies rather than to panic buying. To the extent that wartime controls suppress price increases produced by monetary and fiscal policies, controls only postpone the day of reckoning, converting what would have been a steady inflation into a period of slow inflation followed by more rapid inflation. Also, part of the apparent stability of the price indexes under wartime controls is an illusion. All of the problems with price controls—queuing, evasion, black markets, and rationing—

raise the real price of goods to consumers, and these effects are only partly taken into account when the price indexes are computed. When controls are removed, the hidden inflation is unveiled.

Inflation is extremely difficult to contain through general controls, in part because the attempt to limit control to a manageable sector of the economy is usually hopeless. John Kenneth Galbraith, in *A Theory of Price Control,* which was based on his experience as deputy administrator of the Office of Price Administration in World War II, argued that the prices of goods produced by large industrial oligopolists were relatively easy to control. These firms had large numbers of administrators who could be pressed into service—administrators who were willing, moreover, to shift their allegiance from their employers to the government, at least during the war. Galbraith overstated the market power of large firms, most of which were in highly competitive industries. But even if he had been right about these firms' market power, the problem with limiting controls to a particular sector of the economy is that when demand is surging, it tends to shift from the controlled to the uncontrolled sector, forcing prices in the uncontrolled sector to rise even faster than before. Resources follow prices, and supplies tend to rise in the uncontrolled sector at the expense of supplies in the controlled sector. Thus, a government that begins by controlling prices on selected goods tends to end with across-the-board controls. This is what happened in the United States during World War II. The attempt to confine controls to a limited sector of highly concentrated industrial firms simply did not work.

A second problem with general controls is the trade-off between the need to have a simple program generally perceived as fair and the need for sufficient flexibility to maintain efficiency. Creating an appearance of fairness requires holding most prices constant, but efficiency requires making frequent changes. Adjustments of relative prices, however, subject the bureaucracy administering controls to a barrage of lobbying and complaints of unfairness. This conflict was brought out sharply by the American experience in World War II. At first, relative prices were changed frequently on the advice of economists who maintained that this was necessary to eliminate problems in specific markets. However, mounting complaints that the program was unfair and was not stopping inflation led to President Franklin D. Roosevelt's famous "hold-the-line" order, issued in April 1943, that froze most prices. Whatever its defects as economic policy, the hold-the-line order was easy to justify to the public.

The best case for imposing general controls in peacetime turns on the possibility that controls can ease the transition from high to low inflation. If a tight monetary policy is introduced after a long period of inflation, the long-run effect will be for prices and wages to rise more slowly. But in the short run, some prices may continue to rise at the older rate. Wages also may continue to rise because of long-term contracts or because workers fail to appreciate the extent of the change in policy and, therefore, hold out for higher wages than they otherwise would. Rising wages and prices may keep output and employment below their potential. Price and wage controls may limit these temporary costs of disinflation by prohibiting wage increases that are out of line with the new trends in demand and prices. From this viewpoint, restrictive monetary policy is the operation that cures inflation, and price and wage controls are the anesthesia that suppresses the pain.

But this best case for price controls is weak. The danger is that the painkiller may be mistaken for the cure. In the eyes of the public, price controls free the monetary authority from responsibility for inflation. As a result, the pressures on the monetary authority to avoid recession may lead to a continuation or even acceleration of excessive growth in the money supply. Something very like this happened in the United States under the controls imposed by President Richard M. Nixon in 1971. Although controls were justified on the grounds that they were being used to "buy time" while more fundamental cures for inflation were put in place, monetary policy continued to be expansionary, perhaps even more so than before.

The study of price controls teaches important lessons about free competitive markets. By examining cases in which controls have prevented the price mechanism from working, we gain a better appreciation of its usual elegance and efficiency. This does not mean that there are no circumstances in which temporary controls may be effective. But a fair reading of economic history shows just how rare those circumstances are.

About the Author

Hugh Rockoff is a professor of economics at Rutgers University in New Brunswick, New Jersey, and a research associate of the National Bureau of Economic Research.

Further Reading

Alston, Richard M., J. R. Kearl, and Michael B. Vaughan. "Is There a Consensus Among Economists in the 1990's?" *American Economic Review* 82 (1992): 203–209.
Capie, Forrest, and Geoffrey Wood. "Price Controls in War and Peace: A Marshallian Conclusion." *Scottish Journal of Political Economy* 49 (2002): 39–60.
Clinard, Marshall Barron. *The Black Market: A Study of White Collar Crime.* New York: Rinehart, 1952.
Galbraith, John Kenneth. *A Theory of Price Control.* Cambridge: Harvard University Press, 1952.
Grayson, C. Jackson. *Confessions of a Price Controller.* Homewood, Ill.: Dow Jones–Irwin, 1974.
Jonung, Lars. *The Political Economy of Price Controls: The Swedish Experience 1970–1987.* Brookfield, Mass.: Avebury, 1990.
Rockoff, Hugh. *Drastic Measures: A History of Wage and Price Controls in the United States.* New York: Cambridge University Press, 1984.
Schultz, George P., and Robert Z. Aliber, eds. *Guidelines: Informal Controls and the Market Place.* Chicago: University of Chicago Press, 1966.
Taussig, Frank W. "Price-Fixing as Seen by a Price-Fixer." *Quarterly Journal of Economics* 33 (1919): 205–241.

Prisoners' Dilemma

Avinash Dixit
Barry Nalebuff

The prisoners' dilemma is the best-known game of strategy in social science. It helps us understand what governs the balance between cooperation and competition in business, in politics, and in social settings.

In the traditional version of the game, the police have arrested two suspects and are interrogating them in separate rooms. Each can either confess, thereby implicating the other, or keep silent. No matter what the other suspect does, each can improve his own position by confessing. If the other confesses, then one had better do the same to avoid the especially harsh sentence that awaits a recalcitrant holdout. If the other keeps silent, then one can obtain the favorable treatment accorded a state's witness by confessing. Thus, confession is the dominant strategy (see GAME THEORY) for each. But when both confess, the outcome is worse for both than when both keep silent. The concept of the prisoners' dilemma was developed by RAND Corporation scientists Merrill Flood and Melvin Dresher and was formalized by Albert W. Tucker, a Princeton mathematician.

The prisoners' dilemma has applications to economics and business. Consider two firms, say Coca-Cola and Pepsi, selling similar products. Each must decide on a pricing strategy. They best exploit their joint market power when both charge a high price; each makes a profit of ten million dollars per month. If one sets a competitive low price, it wins a lot of customers away from the rival. Suppose its profit rises to twelve million dollars, and that of the rival falls to seven million. If both set low prices, the profit of each is nine million dollars. Here, the low-price strategy is akin to the prisoner's confession, and the high-price akin to keeping silent. Call the former cheating, and the latter cooperation. Then cheating is each firm's dominant strategy, but the result when both "cheat" is worse for each than that of both cooperating.

Arms races between superpowers or local rival nations offer another important example of the dilemma. Both countries are better off when they cooperate and avoid an arms race. Yet the dominant strategy for each is to arm itself heavily.

On a superficial level the prisoners' dilemma appears to run counter to Adam Smith's idea of the invisible hand. When each person in the game pursues his private interest, he does not promote the collective interest of the group. But often a group's cooperation is not in the interests of society as a whole. Collusion to keep prices high, for example, is not in society's interest because the cost to consumers from collusion is generally more than the increased profit of the firms. Therefore companies that pursue their own self-interest by cheating on collusive agreements often help the rest of society. Similarly, cooperation among prisoners under interrogation makes convictions more difficult for the police to obtain. One must understand the mechanism of cooperation before one can either promote or defeat it in the pursuit of larger policy interests.

Can "prisoners" extricate themselves from the dilemma and sustain cooperation when each has a powerful incentive to cheat? If so, how? The most common path to cooperation arises from repetitions of the game. In the Coke-Pepsi example, one month's cheating gets the cheater an extra two million dollars. But a switch from mutual cooperation to mutual cheating loses one million dollars. If one month's cheating is followed by two months' retaliation, therefore, the result is a wash for the cheater. Any stronger punishment of a cheater would be a clear deterrent.

The following five points elaborate on the idea:

1. *The cheater's reward comes at once, while the loss from punishment lies in the future.* If players heavily discount future payoffs, then the loss may be insufficient to deter cheating. Thus, cooperation is harder to sustain among very impatient players (governments, for example).

2. *Punishment will not work unless cheating can be detected and punished.* Therefore, companies cooperate more when their actions are more easily detected (setting prices, for example) and less when actions are less easily detected (deciding on nonprice attributes of goods, such as repair warranties). Punishment is usually easier to arrange in smaller and closed groups. Thus, industries with few firms and less threat of new entry are more likely to be collusive.

3. *Punishment can be made automatic by following strategies like "tit for tat."* This idea was popularized by University of Michigan political scientist Robert Axelrod. Here, you cheat if and only if your rival cheated in the previous round. But if rivals' innocent actions can be misinterpreted as cheating, then tit for tat runs the risk of setting off successive rounds of unwarranted retaliation.

4. *A fixed, finite number of repetitions is logically inadequate to yield cooperation.* Both or all players know that cheating is the dominant strategy in the last play. Given this, the same goes for the second-last play, then the third-last, and so on. But in practice we see some cooperation in the early rounds of a fixed set of repetitions. The reason may be either that players do not know the number of rounds for sure, or that they can exploit the possibility of "irrational niceness" to their mutual advantage.

5. *Cooperation can also arise if the group has a large leader, who personally stands to lose a lot from outright competition and therefore exercises restraint, even though he knows that other small players will cheat.* Saudi Arabia's role of "swing producer" in the OPEC cartel is an instance of this.

About the Authors

Avinash Dixit is the John J. F. Sherrerd '52 University Professor of Economics at Princeton University. Barry Nalebuff is the Milton Steinbach Professor of Management at Yale University's School of Management. They are coauthors of *Thinking Strategically.*

Further Reading

Introductory

Axelrod, Robert. *The Evolution of Cooperation.* New York: Basic Books, 1984.

Dixit, Avinash, and Barry Nalebuff. *Thinking Strategically: A Competitive Edge in Business, Politics, and Everyday Life.* New York: W. W. Norton, 1991.

Hofstader, Douglas. "Mathamagical Themas." *Scientific American* (May 1983): 16–26.

Poundstone, William. *Prisoner's Dilemma: John von Neumann, Game Theory, and the Puzzle of the Bomb.* New York: Doubleday, 1992.

Rapoport, Anatol, and A. M. Chammah. *Prisoners' Dilemma.* Ann Arbor: University of Michigan Press, 1965.

"Prisoner's Dilemma." Wikipedia, online at: http://en .wikipedia.org/wiki/Prisoner%27s_dilemma.

Advanced

Kreps, David, Robert Wilson, Paul Milgrom, and John Roberts. "Rational Cooperation in the Finitely Repeated Prisoners' Dilemma." *Journal of Economic Theory* 27, no. 2 (August 1982): 245–252.

Milgrom, Paul. "Axelrod's The Evolution of Cooperation." *RAND Journal of Economics* 15, no. 2 (1984): 305–309.

Privatization

Robert W. Poole Jr.

"Privatization" is an umbrella term covering several distinct types of transactions. Broadly speaking, it means the shift of some or all of the responsibility for a function from government to the private sector. The term has most commonly been applied to the divestiture, by sale or long-term lease, of a state-owned enterprise to private investors. But another major form of privatization is the granting of a long-term franchise or concession under which the private sector finances, builds, and operates a major infrastructure project. A third type of privatization involves government selecting a private entity to deliver a public service that had previously been produced in-house by public employees. This form of privatization is increasingly called outsourcing. (Other forms of privatization, not discussed here, include service shedding, vouchers, and joint ventures.)

Regardless of the mode of privatization, the common motivation for engaging in all three types is to substitute more efficient business operations for what are seen as less efficient, bureaucratic, and often politicized operations in the public sector. Some have described the key difference as the substitution of competition for monopoly, though some forms of privatization may involve only one provider in a given geographic area for a specific period of time. But because government almost always operates as a monopoly provider, the decision to privatize usually means demonopolization, even if not always robust, free-market competition.

The decision to privatize usually involves money. Governments sell state-owned enterprises to obtain proceeds either for short-term budget balancing or to pay down debt. They turn to the private sector to finance and develop a major bridge or seaport when their own resources are stretched too thin. And they outsource services in the hope of saving money in their operating budgets, either to balance those budgets or to spend more on other services (and occasionally to permit tax reductions).

Classical Privatization (Asset Divestiture)

As recently as the 1970s, many major industries in OECD countries were owned by the state, in keeping with the Fabian Society's dictum that the "commanding heights" of the economy should be in government hands.[1] As is still true today of state-owned enterprises (SOEs) in China and many other developing countries, these businesses were generally run at a loss, subsidized by all the taxpayers. In other words, the value of their outputs was less than the value of their inputs, making them into value-subtracting (rather than value-adding) enterprises. The reasons for this situation were many, but generally they included explicit or implicit policy decisions that—in addition to producing whatever goods or services (cars, steel, air travel, etc.) they were set up to produce—the SOE was also intended to provide jobs, provide its output at "affordable" prices, and accomplish other ends.

The first organized effort to divest SOEs took place in Chile under the influence of the "Chicago boys" during the 1970s' Pinochet era of economic reform. But the largest and best-known effort was that of Margaret Thatcher's government in the United Kingdom during the 1980s. Thatcher succeeded in making privatization politically popular while selling off the commanding heights of the British economy: British Airways, British Airports Authority, British Petroleum, British Telecom, and several million units of public housing, to name only a few examples. Thatcher's political strategy emphasized widespread public share offerings rather than auctions to other private firms. Over the decade, this approach tripled the number of individual shareholders in Britain, giving the policy a popular base of support.

By the end of the 1980s, the sale of SOEs had gone global, inspired in part by the British example. Governments in France, Germany, Japan, Australia, Argentina, and Chile all sold numerous SOEs, and global privatization proceeds ran in the tens of billions of dollars each year. Generally speaking, companies that moved into the private sector were restructured (often with considerable loss of jobs) and turned into value-adding enterprises. In the case of public utilities (airports, electricity, water, etc.), privatization generally led to the creation of some form of regulatory oversight if the company remained a monopoly provider. The privatization wave expanded further in the 1990s, encompassing the countries emerging from communism and many more developing countries. Here, the privatization record was mixed, with many cases of less-than-transparent sale processes (to firms well connected with government officials) and a botched shares-for-debt scheme in Russia that created an instant crop of politically

---

1. The thirty member countries of the Organisation for Economic Cooperation and Development include most Western European countries, the United States, Japan, Mexico, Turkey, Canada, Australia, Poland, South Korea, the Czech Republic, the Slovak Republic, Finland, Greece, and New Zealand. The Fabian Society was a British group, whose most prominent members were George Bernard Shaw and Sidney and Beatrice Webb, that was formed in the late nineteenth century to push for socialism.

connected billionaires. Still, by the end of the decade, privatization proceeds were well above $100 billion per year, and the cumulative total for the two decades exceeded $1 trillion.

Few people today dispute the value of transforming value-subtracting SOEs into value-adding companies accountable to their shareholders. China, India, and numerous other developing countries continue to prepare and sell SOEs, though this can be a painful process in a country like China, where SOEs have historically provided extensive social welfare services, and neither the government nor the civil society has devised a safety-net alternative. In OECD countries, there are very few industrial SOEs left, although many airports, railways, motorways, and electric and water utility systems are still in state hands (but increasingly being privatized).

Infrastructure Partnerships

The idea of granting a private firm or consortium the right to develop and operate a major infrastructure project is not new. Most British and American (pre–auto era) toll roads of the eighteenth and nineteenth centuries operated on this model. So did the electric streetcar systems and the original New York subway. So, still today, do most U.S. investor-owned utilities, typically operating on fifty- or ninety-nine-year franchises. But apart from those utilities, the idea seemed to die out in most of the world for most of the twentieth century.

The governments of France and Italy revived the idea in the 1960s to develop national networks of tolled motorways, and Portugal's and Spain's governments later imitated them. These transport examples inspired the historic Channel Tunnel, a rail link between England and France built in the 1990s. Neither government was prepared to put up the estimated four billion dollars needed for the project, so an investor group eventually succeeded in winning a fifty-five-year concession agreement to do the project privately. The project cost nearly twice as much to build and is generating much less revenue than forecast. But apart from renegotiating the franchise term to ninety-nine years, the company has received no taxpayer bailout; only its investors have been on the hook for the overruns.

That example illustrates one of the principal virtues of the infrastructure franchise model. While governments typically focus on the advantage of being able to get such major projects built without adding to the government's debt, a more important benefit is risk transfer. Hapless taxpayers should not be burdened with such risks as construction cost overruns and less-than-expected traffic; those are risks the private sector can take on. But in a properly structured "public-private partnership" agreement, risks that the government is better suited to bear (policy changes, "acts of God," etc.) should remain with the public sector; otherwise, there is likely to be no private-sector partner willing to tackle the project.

This model—often called build-operate-transfer (or BOT)—went global during the 1990s, with the enthusiastic backing of the World Bank and other global development agencies. It was adopted without such prodding in most OECD countries: for example, Australia developed modern toll expressway systems in Sydney and Melbourne; Britain added major bridges and its first tolled motorway; and more than a dozen U.S. states passed transportation partnership laws to facilitate BOT toll-road projects. Development bank reports helped spread the model across South America and southern Asia, with airport, seaport, toll road, electric power, and water/wastewater projects in scores of countries. A major year-end survey in 2003 by *Public Works Financing* lists 1,369 such projects in 87 countries costing $587 billion that have been financed since 1985. Adding those in the design or proposal stage produces the larger totals of 2,701 projects in 124 countries costing $1.15 trillion.

As with the sale of SOEs, infrastructure partnerships can be done well or poorly. Developers often seek guarantees of traffic or revenue, which undercut commercial discipline and void the desired risk transfer away from taxpayers. On the other hand, political risk can be high in many countries. Governments may impose after-the-fact controls on pricing or may not allow prices to be adjusted to take into account a major devaluation (as in Argentina, where privatized utilities were caught with large debts in dollars but revenues in greatly devalued local currency), or a change of government can lead to the abrupt termination of a previously awarded concession. But despite such problems, the BOT model appears to have become a standard modus operandi in many countries in the early twenty-first century.

Outsourcing

The rationale for outsourcing is that there is a difference in principle between providing for a public service and producing that service. Government may be responsible for maintaining highways, collecting garbage, or operating recreation centers, but just like any private company it is faced with a "make or buy" decision about that service. Economic theory suggests several reasons why outsourcing might be more cost-effective than in-house provision. First, the unit of government with responsibility for the service may not be of the optimum scale to provide the service efficiently. Second, it may lack the required expertise or technology, for various reasons. Third, and probably

416 | *Robert W. Poole Jr.*

most important, a perpetual in-house monopoly will have weaker incentives to innovate in order to find more cost-effective ways to operate. Competition to be the service deliverer should produce stronger incentives.

Although outsourcing is still debated politically, the empirical question has long since been answered in its favor. In the 1970s, the National Science Foundation funded the first empirical study, examining the cost and performance of municipal garbage collection under various institutional alternatives. The researchers found that competitive contracting was clearly less costly. Further research during the 1980s and 1990s—by academics, think tanks, and the federal government's General Accounting Office—reinforced those findings across hundreds of different types of services at federal, state, and local levels of government in the United States. The findings on municipal garbage collection were replicated in a large-scale study in Canada.

During the 1980s, outsourcing became common in municipal and state governments, primarily in the Sunbelt. In California, more than seventy cities joined the California Contract Cities Association. Aiming from the outset to obtain most of their public services via contractual arrangements, these cities contracted either with private firms or with larger nearby governments. In the 1990s, outsourcing was embraced by reform mayors, both Republican and Democrat, in larger and older cities, such as Chicago, Cleveland, Indianapolis, New York, and Philadelphia.

At the federal level, the Office of Management and Budget issued government-wide policies on competitive contracting (OMB Circular A-76) during the 1960s. Aside from an effort to promote this approach aggressively during the final year of the Reagan administration (1988), outsourcing at the federal level waxed and waned until the Bush administration in 2001. Under the President's Management Agenda, "competitive sourcing" has become a White House priority, with government-wide targets for outsourcing a large fraction of the 850,000 federal positions that the agencies themselves have classified as commercial in nature.

Public employee unions have engaged in large-scale efforts to thwart outsourcing by governments. They publicize individual examples of privatizations that have gone wrong—and there definitely are such cases. Firms seeking government contracts make campaign contributions, and sometimes contracts are awarded via less-than-transparent processes. In other cases, once a firm has won a contract via a low bid, it may seek to renegotiate the contract at a higher price. And there is always the danger that once a firm becomes the incumbent provider, it will persuade public officials that, instead of going back out to bid when

the contract expires, they should simply negotiate a contract extension. All such practices undermine the competition-works-better-than-monopoly rationale for outsourcing and may reduce or eliminate the intended savings for taxpayers. Moreover, unless the government becomes skilled at writing solid and measurable performance standards into the contract, it may not be able to ensure that it is getting the full measure of services it expects at the promised lower cost.

These problems are real, but they are arguments for doing outsourcing well rather than not doing it at all. Overall, the continued spread of outsourcing and its increasingly bipartisan acceptance (e.g., by New Democrats such as David Osborne) suggest that the advantages are genuine, despite the occasional failure to do it well.

Conclusion

Privatization encompasses a variety of techniques for shifting functions that have traditionally been wholly in the public sector into the private sector to various degrees. In the case of state-owned enterprises, there is widespread consensus that steel mills, auto factories, and airlines belong in the private sector, and the first decade of the twenty-first century should see most of the remaining SOEs in these areas sold off or liquidated. The track record of large-scale private infrastructure projects is more mixed, with many of these projects (especially in poorer countries) financed with a mixture of state and private capital, which leads to blurred incentives and challenging policy questions. The next decade or two should see continued efforts to fine-tune the allocation of tasks and risks between public and private sectors in these projects.

Because public service delivery is the one area in which labor unions have been gaining ground in OECD countries during the past few decades, we can expect continued battles over outsourcing such services. Recent U.S. controversies over airport screening and air traffic control suggest that these battles will be high profile, emotional, and costly. But to the degree that competition becomes institutionalized in public-service delivery, the performance and cost-effectiveness of those services seem likely to improve, regardless of which party wins a particular competition.

Classical privatization (the sale of SOEs) became such a phenomenon in the late 1980s that several global newsletters and magazines were devoted exclusively to the subject, complete with league tables and aggregate statistics. By the twenty-first century, however, such privatization had become so commonplace that there was no longer a market for these publications. By contrast, infrastructure franchising still supports a specialized newsletter (*Public Works Financing*), and outsourcing also has a newsletter (*Privatization Watch*).

About the Author

Robert Poole founded the Reason Foundation, a public policy think tank based in Los Angeles. He is nationally known as an expert on privatization and transportation policy. He was the first person to use the term "privatization" to refer to the contracting out of public services.

Further Reading

Butler, Eamonn, and Madsen Pirie. *The Manual on Privatization*. London: Adam Smith Institute, 1990.

Eggers, William D., and John O'Leary. *Revolution at the Roots*. New York: Free Press, 1995.

Flybvjerg, Bent, et al. *Megaprojects and Risk*. Cambridge: Cambridge University Press, 2003.

Gómez-Ibáñez, José A., and John R. Meyer. *Going Private: The International Experience with Transport Privatization*. Washington, D.C.: Brookings Institution, 1993.

MacAvoy, Paul W., et al. *Privatization and State-Owned Enterprises*. Boston: Kluwer, 1989.

Osborne, David. *Reinventing Government*. New York: Plume, 1993.

Poole, Robert W. Jr. *Cutting Back City Hall*. New York: Universe Books, 1980.

Savas, E. S. *Privatization and Public-Private Partnerships*. New York: Chatham House, 2000.

Walzer, Norman, and Robin Johnson. *Local Government Innovation: Issues and Trends in Privatization and Managed Competition*. Westport, Conn.: Greenwood Press, 2000.

Vickers, J., and G. Yarrow. *Privatisation and the Natural Monopolies*. London: Public Policy Centre, 1985.

Web Sites

http://rru.worldbank.org
http://www.privatization.org
http://www.tollroadsnews.com

Productivity

Alexander J. Field

The growth of productivity—output per unit of input—is the fundamental determinant of the growth of a country's material standard of living. The most commonly cited measures are output per worker and output per hour—measures of labor productivity. One cannot have sustained growth in output per person—the most general measure of a country's material standard of living—without sustained growth in output per worker.

Increases in output per hour are the same thing as reductions in hours per unit of output. So, as labor productivity rose in the American car industry during the 1920s, it took fewer and fewer hours to assemble a Model T. The price of automobiles fell, and the real standard of living of Americans increased. This was reflected in the number of cars registered in the country, which rose from 6.7 million in 1919 to 23.1 million in 1929. As the result of productivity improvement, in other words, the number of households with access to automobile transportation more than tripled in the short span of a decade.

Recently, output per hour in the sectors of the economy producing computers and telecommunications equipment has soared. The prices of these goods have plummeted, and tens of millions of American households now have high-speed computers and cellular telephones, reflecting some of the more dramatic improvements in our standard of living in recent decades.

Productivity improvements can also take place in service sector industries, as they have recently in wholesale and retail trade and securities trading. Some of our greatest challenges and opportunities lie in the service sector. For example, if we can successfully use information technology to streamline the creation, storage, and retrieval of medical records, productivity in the health sector may rise substantially. This would mean that we could deliver more services with the resources currently deployed or the same services with fewer resources reemployed elsewhere. Either way, our standard of living would rise.

A final example: in 1790, the year of the first U.S. census, upward of 90 percent of the labor force worked in agriculture. In the year 2000, less than 1.4 percent of the labor force was so employed, still producing enough for the U.S. population to eat as well as substantial exports. Continuing improvements in labor productivity in agriculture made that possible.

If the demand for a product or service is price inelastic—that is, if a given percentage decrease in price results in a lower percentage increase in the quantity demanded—then rapid productivity improvement can result in workers having to leave the industry. The reason is that industry output, even if it has risen moderately, can now be produced with fewer workers. This eventually became true for grain farming, but not generally for computers, where the demand has been more price elastic. The relative price declines produced such a big increase in quantity demanded that industry employment has actually increased. But even in the case of grain farming, the falling food prices associated with the productivity improvement led *automatically* to increases in real income elsewhere. These increases eventually resulted in increased demand for other goods and services, leading to expansion of demand, employment, and output outside of agriculture.

Whether or not productivity improvement is associated with increasing or decreasing employment in the affected industries, and whether or not it is temporarily associated with rises in unemployment rates, such improvements are, in the long run, the basis for increases in our material well-being.

More Technical Points
In the United States, the Bureau of Labor Statistics calculates productivity measures for the private domestic economy and the private nonfarm economy, as well as for manufacturing, industries within manufacturing, and a few other subsectors. The private nonfarm economy accounts for about three-fourths of total GDP: it excludes agriculture, housing (which is entirely services and produced almost entirely by capital), and government. The private domestic economy includes agriculture. For subsectors of the economy, or for particular industries or firms, the measure of output is value added, not gross sales. The contribution to GDP (as well as gross domestic income) of any particular economic entity is gross receipts less purchased materials and contract services.

For example, if your bakery business buys flour and yeast, rents a shop and equipment, and pays for fuel, its contribution to GDP is not the sales price of the bread made, but the difference between gross revenues and purchased materials and services except hired labor. Your firm's output is what you and your employees have added to the value of the materials and services purchased from other firms. You do not get credit for what the other firms did. Increasing labor productivity in your bakery means increasing value added per worker or per hour worked.

A second important measure of productivity is called either total factor productivity, a term many economists favor, or multifactor productivity (MFP), the term the Bureau of Labor Statistics uses; the terms are interchangeable. Their rate of growth is often called the residual. MFP can be most easily understood by comparing the calculation of its growth rate with the calculation of the growth rate of output per hour (labor productivity).

If we use capital letters for levels and lower-case letters for rates of growth, Y/N can stand for the level of labor productivity, where Y is real output and N is hours; $y - n$, the growth rate of the numerator less the growth rate of the denominator, is the growth rate of labor productivity. This simply says that if output per hour is to grow, output

(the numerator) has to rise faster than hours (the denominator).

Multifactor productivity, in turn, is calculated as the difference between the growth rate of real output (y) and a weighted average of the growth rates of capital services and hours, the weights corresponding to shares in national income. Thus, if capital services and hours grew at the same rate, there would be no difference between the growth rate of multifactor productivity and the growth of labor productivity.

For example, between 1929 and 1941 in the United States—in other words, during the Great Depression—neither hours nor capital services increased measurably, but real output rose 32 percent. Because the weighted average of the growth of inputs in this instance was effectively zero, all of the growth of output (and growth in output per hour) was due to growth in multifactor productivity, which can be interpreted as a crude measure of the rate of "technical change." If output rises faster than the growth of inputs conventionally measured, then we can say that some recipes for turning inputs into output must have improved.

Total (multi) factor productivity and labor productivity are related to each other. Output per hour grows as the result of two conceptually distinct mechanisms. First, if the economy saves and invests more of its current output such that the physical capital stock rises more rapidly than the number of labor hours employed, output per hour should rise as the result of "capital deepening." Capital deepening occurs when the ratio of physical capital to labor hours rises. The idea that this positively affects labor productivity is based on the intuitive proposition that ditch diggers move more cubic meters of earth if they are using backhoes than if they use only shovels. But output per hour can also rise through the discovery of new technologies or ways of organizing production. Such discoveries contribute to growth in our measures of multifactor productivity and enable output per hour to rise even in the absence of more capital accumulation (think about the Depression example).

To return to our example of the bakery, if your firm invests in more machines so that less hand labor per loaf is required, output (value added) per hour should go up. But multifactor productivity will not necessarily rise, because your combined input measure will rise by about the same amount as output. There is another potential source, however, of increases in output per hour. If you discover a way to rearrange your labor force and equipment so that production is more efficient, or discover a great new recipe for a loaf that is equally tasty but costs you less to bake, multifactor productivity in your firm may go up, increasing your output (value added) per hour even in the absence of any capital deepening.

The bottom line: If a country wants its standard of living to rise over the long run, its labor productivity has to go up. And for that to happen, it either has to save more or innovate.

About the Author

Alexander J. Field is the Michel and Mary Orradre Professor of Economics at Santa Clara University. He is the editor of *Research in Economic History* and the executive director of the Economic History Association.

Further Reading

Abramovitz, Moses. "Resource and Output Trends in the United States since 1870." *American Economic Review* 46 (May 1956): 5–23. Important article, the first to document the rise in the value of the residual in the United States during the second quarter of the twentieth century.

Abramovitz, Moses, and Paul David. "American Macroeconomic Growth in the Era of Knowledge-Based Progress: The Long Run Perspective." In Stanley Engerman and Robert Gallman, eds., *The Cambridge Economic History of the United States*. Vol. 3. Cambridge: Cambridge University Press, 2000. Pp. 1–92. Analysis, up through 1989, extending the idea of the shift from dominance of physical capital accumulation in the nineteenth century to knowledge-based growth in the twentieth.

Field, Alexander J. "The Most Technologically Progressive Decade of the Century." *American Economic Review* 93 (September 2003): 1399–1413. Shows that the high value of the residual in the second quarter of the century was principally due to the high growth rate of MFP between 1929 and 1941.

———. "Technical Change and U.S. Economic Growth: The Interwar Period and the 1990s." In Paul Rhode and Gianni Toniolo, eds., *Understanding the 1990s: The Economy in Historical Perspective*. Cambridge: Cambridge University Press, 2005. Compares economic growth in the 1930s and the 1920s with that in the 1990s.

Gordon, Robert J. "Interpreting the 'One Big Wave' in U.S. Long Term Productivity Growth." In Bart van Ark, Simon Kuipers, and Gerard Kuper, eds., *Productivity, Technology, and Economic Growth*. Boston: Kluwer, 2000. Pp. 19–66. Argues that high rates of MFP growth in the second and third quarters of the twentieth century may have been historically unique.

Jorgenson, Dale. "Information Technology and the U.S. Economy." *American Economic Review* 91 (March 2001): 1–32. Optimistic interpretation of the effect of the IT revolution on U.S. productivity growth.

Kendrick, John. *Productivity Trends in the United States*. Princeton: Princeton University Press, 1961. Classic reference for anyone wishing to push analysis back before 1947. Detailed aggregate and sectoral estimates for the U.S. economy.

Lipsey, Richard J., and Kenneth Carlaw. "What Does Total Factor Productivity Measure?" *International Productivity Monitor* (Fall 2000): 23–28. Skeptical view of what inferences we can draw from measures of the residual.

Oliner, Steven D., and Daniel E. Sichel. "The Resurgence of Growth in the Late 1990s: Is Information Technology the Story?" *Journal of Economic Perspectives* 14 (Fall 2000): 3–22. Analysis of contribution of the IT revolution to recent productivity growth by two Federal Reserve economists.

Solow, Robert J. "Technical Change and the Aggregate Production Function." *Review of Economics and Statistics* 39 (August 1957): 312–320. Seminal article laying out the dynamics of the Solow growth model and providing a production function interpretation of growth accounting. Analyzes data from 1909 to 1949.

Web Sites

http://www.bls.gov. This is *the* Web site to visit for the latest U.S. productivity data, as well as historical data running back in some cases to 1947.

http://www.oecd.org/topicstatsportal/0,2647,en_2825_30453906_1_1_1_1_1,00.html. Provides productivity data for members of the Organisation for Economic Co-operation and Development (OECD).

Profits

Lester C. Thurow

In a capitalistic society, profits—and losses—hold center stage. Those who own firms (the capitalists) choose managers who organize production efforts so as to maximize their income (profits). Their search for profits is guided by the famous "invisible hand" of capitalism. When profits are above the normal level, they attract additional investment, either by new firms or by existing firms. New investment enters until profits are competed down to the same level the investment could earn elsewhere. In this way, high profits attract firms to invest in areas where consumers are signaling that they want the investment to occur.

Capitalists earn a return on their efforts by providing three productive inputs. First, they are willing to delay their own personal gratification. Instead of consuming all of their resources today, they save some of today's income and invest those savings in activities (plant and equipment) that will yield goods and services in the future. When sold, these future goods and services will yield profits that can then be used to finance consumption or additional investment. Put bluntly, the capitalist provides capital by not consuming. Without capital much less production could occur. As a result, some profits are effectively the "wages" paid to those who are willing to delay their own personal gratification.

Second, some profits are a return to those who take risks. Some investments make a profit and return what was invested plus a profit; others do not. When an airline goes broke, for example, the investors in the airline lose some of their wealth and become poorer. Just as underground miners, who are willing to perform a dangerous job, get paid more than those who work in safer occupations, so investors who are willing to invest in risky ventures earn more than those who invest in less risky ones. On average, those who take risks will earn a higher rate of return on their investments than those who invest more conservatively.

Third, some profits are a return to organizational ability, enterprise, and entrepreneurial energy. The entrepreneur, by inventing a new product or process, or by organizing the better delivery of an old product, generates profits. People are willing to pay the entrepreneur because he or she has invented a "better mousetrap."

Economists use the word "interest" to mean the payment for delayed gratification, and use the word "profits" to mean only the earnings that result from risk taking and from entrepreneurship. But in everyday business language the owner's return on his or her capital is also called profits. (In business language the lender's return is called interest, even though most lending also entails some risks.)

Attempts have been made to organize productive societies without the profit motive. Communism is the best recent example. But in the modern world these attempts have failed spectacularly.

While most profits flow to the three previously mentioned necessary inputs into the productive process, there are two other sources of profits. One is monopoly. A firm that has managed to establish a monopoly in producing some product or service can set a price higher than would be set in a competitive market, and thus earn higher-than-normal competitive returns. (Economists call these extra returns "economic rents.") Historically, one can find examples of monopolies that have been able to extract large amounts of income from the average consumer. One modern example is taxicab companies, which in virtually every major U.S. city outside of Washington, D.C., have persuaded the local government to limit the number of cabs that may legally be operated.

Although some monopoly profits exist in any economy, they are a very small portion of total profits in any rich society. In rich societies, most consumption consists of either luxuries or products that have close substitutes. As a result, the twentieth-century monopolist has less power to raise prices than the nineteenth-century monopolist. If the monopolistic firm does raise prices very much, the consumer simply buys something else. Professional football, for example, is a monopoly. But Americans have many ways to get pleasure without watching football. The National Football League, therefore, has some, but not much, power to raise prices above the competitive level.

"Market imperfections" provide a second source of profits. Suppose firm A sells a product for ten dollars while firm B sells the same product for eight dollars. Suppose also that many customers do not know that the product can be bought for eight dollars from firm B and, therefore, they pay ten dollars to firm A. Firm A gets an extra two dollars in profit. In a "perfect" market, where every consumer is completely informed about prices, this would not happen. But in real economies it often does. We all recall buying a product at one price only to find later that someone else was selling it for a slightly lower price. Profits from such "imperfections" certainly exist, but here again they are not a large fraction of total profits.

When it comes to actually measuring profits, some difficult accounting issues arise. Suppose one looks at the income earned by capitalists after they have paid all of their suppliers and workers. In 2004 this amounted to $3,689 billion, or 31 percent of GDP. Some of this flow of income represents a return to capital (profits). Some of it needs to be set aside, however, to replace the plant and equipment that have worn out or become obsolete during the year. It is hard to say exactly how much must be reinvested to maintain the size of the capital stock ("capital consumption allowances") because it is hard to know precisely how fast equipment is wearing out or becoming obsolete. But the Department of Commerce thought that $1,352 billion needed to be set aside to maintain the capital stock in 2004. This left $2,337 billion for other purposes.

Many capitalists are small businessmen (technically known as single proprietorships) whose "profits" include their wages. No one knows how to disentangle these two streams of income. In the corporate sector, where this problem does not exist, profits after subtracting capital consumption allowances amounted to $985 billion, or 14 percent of the GDPs produced in the corporate sector. Some of these profits, however, were paid to the government in corporate income taxes. After the payment of taxes, $716 billion, or 10 percent of the corporate GDP, was left as profits. Of this sum capitalists paid themselves $444 billion in dividends and put $272 billion back into their businesses as new investments.

Table 1 provides some information on profits in different industries. In 2005 the highest profits were earned in toi-

Table 1 Return on Stockholders' Equity, 2005 (selected industries, percentage)

Toiletries and cosmetics	41.4
Beverages (alcoholic)	32.6
Tobacco	32.1
Beverage (soft drinks)	26.2
Building materials	22.9
Food processing	21.2
Pharmaceutical	18.3
Petroleum (producing)	16.9
Petroleum (integrated)	15.5
Computer software	13.8
Medical services	13.0
Computers and peripherals	12.7
Publishing	12.3
Chemicals (specialty)	12.3
Apparel	12.0
Auto parts	11.4
Automobiles and trucks	10.0
Furniture and home furnishings	9.9
Machinery	9.3
Metal fabricating	9.2
Trucking	9.0
Aerospace and defense	8.9
Metals and mining	8.5
Chemicals (basic)	8.2
Forest products	2.5
Tire and rubber products	2.0
Precision instruments	−0.2
Electronics	−1.3
Value line market	11.6

Table 2 After-Tax Profits as Percentage of GNP for Nonfinancial Corporations, 1970–2004

1970	5.6	1980	7.5	1990	4.6	2000	4.8
1971	6.2	1981	6.8	1991	4.3	2001	3.8
1972	6.8	1982	5.0	1992	5.1	2002	4.3
1973	7.9	1983	5.3	1993	5.7	2003	5.2
1974	8.3	1984	5.6	1994	6.7	2004	5.1
1975	7.8	1985	4.4	1995	7.2		
1976	8.6	1986	3.1	1996	7.4		
1977	8.8	1987	4.5	1997	7.5		
1978	9.1	1988	5.6	1998	6.2		
1979	8.9	1989	4.7	1999	5.8		

Source: U.S. Department of Commerce, *Survey of Current Business.*

wars. Profits reached a low of 3.1 percent in 1986. Because the owners were effectively withdrawing their own capital from their businesses (substituting debt for equity), they were providing much less of the total capital stock and, therefore, earning less in profits. Profits went down as interest payments to lenders went up.

Capitalism requires profits, and profits require ownership. Property ownership generates responsibility. Two decades ago I wrote an article about communism entitled "Who Stays Up with the Sick Cow?" Without ownership the answer was too often, "No one," and the cow and communism died.

About the Author

Lester C. Thurow is the Jerome and Dorothy Lemelson Professor of Management and Economics at MIT's Sloan School of Management. In 1977 he was on the editorial board of the *New York Times*. From 1983 to 1987 he was a member of the Time Magazine Board of Economists. Shortly after graduating from Harvard, he was a staff member with President Lyndon B. Johnson's Council of Economic Advisers.

Further Reading

Knight, Frank. *Risk, Uncertainty, and Profit.* Boston: Houghton Mifflin, 1921.
Thurow, Lester. "Who Stays Up with the Sick Cow?" *New York Times Book Review,* September 7, 1986, p. 9.

letries and cosmetics (41.4 percent), the lowest in electronics materials (−1.3 percent; i.e., losses rather than profits). Over time, profits rise and fall with the onset of booms and recessions (see Table 2). After tax, corporate profits for nonfinancial corporations have ranged from above 9 percent of the GDP produced by nonfinancial corporations in 1978 to just above 3 percent in 1986. Profit rates fell in the recession of 1990–91 only to rise again in 1992. They fell again in the recession of 2000 and recovered in 2002. No matter what the year, corporate profits as a percentage of GDP are far below 45 percent, the level, according to a Gallup poll, that many college graduates believe them to be.

The mid-1980s saw a steady decline in profits as firms acquired tremendous debt in the merger and takeover

Property Rights

Armen A. Alchian

One of the most fundamental requirements of a capitalist economic system—and one of the most misunderstood concepts—is a strong system of property rights. For decades social critics in the United States and throughout the Western world have complained that "property" rights too often take precedence over "human" rights, with the result that people are treated unequally and have unequal opportunities. Inequality exists in any society. But the purported conflict between property rights and human rights is a mirage. Property rights are human rights.

The definition, allocation, and protection of property rights comprise one of the most complex and difficult sets of issues that any society has to resolve, but one that must be resolved in some fashion. For the most part, social critics of "property" rights do not want to abolish those rights. Rather, they want to transfer them from private ownership to government ownership. Some transfers to public ownership (or control, which is similar) make an economy more effective. Others make it less effective. The worst outcome by far occurs when property rights really are abolished (see TRAGEDY OF THE COMMONS).

A property right is the exclusive authority to determine how a resource is used, whether that resource is owned by government or by individuals. Society approves the uses selected by the holder of the property right with governmental administered force and with social ostracism. If the resource is owned by the government, the agent who determines its use has to operate under a set of rules determined, in the United States, by Congress or by executive agencies it has charged with that role.

Private property rights have two other attributes in addition to determining the use of a resource. One is the exclusive right to the services of the resource. Thus, for example, the owner of an apartment with complete property rights to the apartment has the right to determine whether to rent it out and, if so, which tenant to rent to; to live in it himself; or to use it in any other peaceful way. That is the right to determine the use. If the owner rents out the apartment, he also has the right to all the rental income from the property. That is the right to the services of the resources (the rent).

Finally, a private property right includes the right to delegate, rent, or sell any portion of the rights by exchange or gift at whatever price the owner determines (provided someone is willing to pay that price). If I am not allowed to buy some rights from you and you therefore are not allowed to sell rights to me, private property rights are reduced. Thus, the three basic elements of private property are (1) exclusivity of rights to choose the use of a resource, (2) exclusivity of rights to the services of a resource, and (3) rights to exchange the resource at mutually agreeable terms.

The U.S. Supreme Court has vacillated about this third aspect of property rights. But no matter what words the justices use to rationalize such decisions, the fact is that such limitations as price controls and restrictions on the right to sell at mutually agreeable terms are reductions of private property rights. Many economists (myself included) believe that most such restrictions on property rights are detrimental to society. Here are some of the reasons why.

Under a private property system the market values of property reflect the preferences and demands of the rest of society. No matter who the owner is, the use of the resource is influenced by what the rest of the public thinks is the most valuable use. The reason is that an owner who chooses some other use must forsake that highest-valued use—and the price others would pay him for the resource or for the use of it. This creates an interesting paradox: although property is called "private," private decisions are based on public, or social, evaluation.

The fundamental purpose of property rights, and their fundamental accomplishment, is that they eliminate destructive competition for control of economic resources. Well-defined and well-protected property rights replace competition by violence with competition by peaceful means.

The extent and degree of private property rights fundamentally affect the ways people compete for control of resources. With more complete private property rights, market exchange values become more influential. The personal status and personal attributes of people competing for a resource matter less because their influence can be offset by adjusting the price. In other words, more complete property rights make DISCRIMINATION more costly. Consider the case of a black woman who wants to rent an apartment from a white landlord. She is better able to do so when the landlord has the right to set the rent at whatever level he wants. Even if the landlord would prefer a white tenant, the black woman can offset her disadvantage by offering a higher rent. A landlord who takes the white tenant at a lower rent anyway pays for discriminating.

But if the government imposes rent controls that keep the rent below the free-market level, the price the landlord pays to discriminate falls, possibly to zero. The rent control does not magically reduce the demand for apartments. Instead, it reduces every potential tenant's ability to compete by offering more money. The landlord, now unable to receive the full money price, will discriminate in favor of tenants whose personal characteristics—such as age, sex, ethnicity, and religion—he favors. Now the black woman seeking an apartment cannot offset the disadvantage of her skin color by offering to pay a higher rent.

Competition for apartments is not eliminated by rent controls. What changes is the "coinage" of competition. The restriction on private property rights reduces competition based on monetary exchanges for goods and services and increases competition based on personal characteristics. More generally, weakening private property rights increases the role of personal characteristics in inducing sellers to discriminate among competing buyers and buyers to discriminate among sellers.

The two extremes in weakened private property rights are socialism and "commonly owned" resources. Under socialism, government agents—those whom the government assigns—exercise control over resources. The rights of these agents to make decisions about the property they control are highly restricted. People who think they can put the resources to more valuable uses cannot do so by purchasing the rights because the rights are not for sale at any price. Because socialist managers do not gain when the values of the resources they manage increase, and do not lose when the values fall, they have little incentive to heed changes in market-revealed values. The uses of resources are therefore more influenced by the personal characteristics and features of the officials who control them. Consider the socialist manager of a collective farm under the old Soviet communist system. By working every night for one week, he could have made, say, one million rubles of additional profit for the farm by arranging to transport the farm's wheat to Moscow before it rotted. But because neither the manager nor those who worked on the farm were entitled to keep even a portion of this additional profit, the manager was more likely than the manager of a capitalist farm to go home early and let the crops rot.

Similarly, common ownership of resources—whether in the former Soviet Union or in the United States—gives no one a strong incentive to preserve the resource. A fishery that no one owns, for example, will be overfished. The reason is that a fisherman who throws back small fish to wait until they grow is unlikely to get any benefit from his waiting. Instead, some other fisherman will catch the fish. The same holds true for other common resources whether they be herds of buffalo, oil in the ground, or clean air. All will be overused.

Indeed, a main reason for the spectacular failure of the 1980s and early 1990s economic reforms in the former Soviet Union is that resources were shifted from ownership by government to de facto common ownership. How? By making the Soviet government's revenues de facto into a common resource. Harvard economist Jeffrey Sachs, who advised the Soviet government, once pointed out that when Soviet managers of socialist enterprises were allowed to open their own businesses but still were left as managers of the government's businesses, they siphoned out the profits of the government's business into their private corporations. Thousands of managers doing this caused a large budget deficit for the Soviet government. In this case the resource that no manager had an incentive to conserve was the Soviet government's revenues. Similarly, improperly set premiums for U.S. deposit insurance gave banks and S&Ls (see SAVINGS AND LOAN CRISIS) an incentive to make excessively risky loans and to treat the deposit insurance fund as a "common" resource.

Private property rights to a resource need not be held by a single person. They can be shared, with each person sharing in a specified fraction of the market value while decisions about uses are made in whatever process the sharing group deems desirable. A major example of such shared property rights is the corporation. In a limited liability corporation, shares are specified and the rights to decide how to use the corporation's resources are delegated to its management. Each shareholder has the unrestrained right to sell his or her share. Limited liability insulates each shareholder's wealth from the liabilities of other shareholders, and thereby facilitates anonymous sale and purchase of shares.

In other types of enterprises, especially where each member's wealth will become uniquely dependent on each other member's behavior, property rights in the group endeavor are usually salable only if existing members approve of the buyer. This is typical for what are often called joint ventures, "mutuals," and partnerships.

While more complete property rights are preferable to less complete rights, any system of property rights entails considerable complexity and many issues that are difficult to resolve. If I operate a factory that emits smoke, foul smells, or airborne acids over your land, am I using your land without your permission? This is difficult to answer.

The cost of establishing private property rights—so that I could pay you a mutually agreeable price to pollute your air—may be too high. Air, underground water, and electromagnetic radiation, for example, are expensive to monitor and control. Therefore, a person does not effectively have enforceable private property rights to the quality and condition of some parcel of air. The inability to cost-effectively monitor and police uses of your resources means "your" property rights over "your" land are not as extensive and strong as they are over some other resources such as furniture, shoes, or automobiles. When private property

Property Rights for "Sesame Street"

Janet Beales Kaidantzis

Ever seen two children quarreling over a toy? Such squabbles had been commonplace in Katherine Hussman Klemp's household. But in the *Sesame Street Parent's Guide* she tells how she created peace in her family of eight children by assigning property rights to toys.

As a young mother, Klemp often brought home games and toys from garage sales. "I rarely matched a particular item with a particular child," she says. "Upon reflection, I could see how the fuzziness of ownership easily led to arguments. If everything belonged to everyone, then each child felt he had a right to use anything."

To solve the problem, Klemp introduced two simple rules: First, never bring anything into the house without assigning clear ownership to one child. The owner has ultimate authority over the use of the property. Second, the owner is not required to share. Before the rules were in place, Klemp recalls, "I suspected that much of the drama often centered less on who got the item in dispute and more on whom Mom would side with." Now, property rights, not parents, settle the arguments.

Instead of teaching selfishness, the introduction of property rights actually promoted sharing. The children were secure in their ownership and knew they could always get their toys back. Adds Klemp, "'Sharing' raised their self-esteem to see themselves as generous persons."

Not only do her children value their own property rights, but also they extend that respect to the property of others. "Rarely do our children use each other's things without asking first, and they respect a 'No' when they get one. Best of all, when someone who has every right to say 'No' to a request says 'Yes,' the borrower sees the gift for what it is and says 'Thanks' more often than not," says Klemp.

rights are unavailable or too costly to establish and enforce, substitute means of control are sought. Government authority, expressed by government agents, is one very common such means. Hence the creation of environmental laws.

Depending on circumstances, certain actions may be considered invasions of privacy, trespass, or torts. If I seek refuge and safety for my boat at your dock during a sudden severe storm on a lake, have I invaded "your" property rights, or do your rights not include the right to prevent that use? The complexities and varieties of circumstances render impossible a bright-line definition of a person's set of property rights with respect to resources.

Similarly, the set of resources over which property rights may be held is not well defined and demarcated. Ideas, melodies, and procedures, for example, are almost costless to replicate explicitly (near-zero cost of production) and implicitly (no forsaken other uses of the inputs). As a result, they typically are not protected as private property except for a fixed term of years under a patent or copyright.

Private property rights are not absolute. The rule against the "dead hand," or perpetuities, is an example. I cannot specify how resources that I own will be used in the indefinitely distant future. Under our legal system, I can specify the use only for a limited number of years after my death or the deaths of currently living people. I cannot insulate a resource's use from the influence of market values of all future generations. Society recognizes market prices as measures of the relative desirability of resource uses. Only to the extent that rights are salable are those values most fully revealed.

Accompanying and conflicting with the desire to secure private property rights for oneself is the desire to acquire more wealth by "taking" from others. This is done by military conquest and by forcible reallocation of rights to resources (also known as stealing). But such coercion is antithetical to—rather than characteristic of—a system of private property rights. Forcible reallocation means that the existing rights have not been adequately protected.

Private property rights do not conflict with human rights. They are human rights. Private property rights are the rights of humans to use specified goods and to exchange them. Any restraint on private property rights shifts the balance of power from impersonal attributes toward personal attributes and toward behavior that political authorities approve. That is a fundamental reason for preference of a system of strong private property rights: private property rights protect individual liberty.

About the Author

Armen A. Alchian is an emeritus professor of economics at the University of California, Los Angeles. Most of his major scientific contributions are in the economics of property rights.

Further Reading

Alchian, Armen. "Some Economics of Property Rights." *Il Politico* 30 (1965): 816–829.

Alchian, Armen, and Harold Demsetz. "The Property Rights Paradigm." *Journal of Economic History* 33, no. 1 (1973): 16–27.

Demsetz, Harold. "When Does the Rule of Liability Matter?" *Journal of Legal Studies* 1 (January 1972): 13–28.

Sachs, Jeffrey. Interview. *Omni* (June 1991): 98.

Siegan, Bernard. *Economic Liberties and the Constitution*. Chicago: University of Chicago Press, 1980.

Protectionism

Jagdish Bhagwati

The fact that trade protection hurts the economy of the country that imposes it is one of the oldest but still most startling insights economics has to offer. The idea dates back to the origin of economic science itself. Adam Smith's *The Wealth of Nations,* which gave birth to economics, already contained the argument for free trade: by specializing in production instead of producing everything, each nation would profit from free trade. In international economics, it is the direct counterpart to the proposition that people within a national economy will all be better off if they specialize at what they do best instead of trying to be self-sufficient.

It is important to distinguish between the case for free trade for oneself and the case for free trade for all. The former is an argument for free trade to improve one nation's own welfare (the so-called national-efficiency argument). The latter is an argument for free trade to improve every trading country's welfare (the so-called cosmopolitan-efficiency argument).

Underlying both cases is the assumption that free markets determine prices and that there are no market failures. But market failures can occur. A market failure arises, for example, when polluters do not have to pay for the pollution they produce (see EXTERNALITIES). But such market failures or "distortions" can arise from governmental action as well. Thus, governments may distort market prices by, for example, subsidizing production, as European governments have done in aerospace, as many other governments have done in electronics and steel, and as all wealthy countries' governments do in agriculture. Or governments may protect intellectual property inadequately, leading to underproduction of new knowledge; they may also overprotect it. In such cases, production and trade, guided by distorted prices, will not be efficient.

The cosmopolitan-efficiency case for free trade is relevant to issues such as the design of international trade regimes. For example, the General Agreement on Tariffs and Trade (GATT), incorporated into the World Trade Organization (WTO) in 1995, oversees world trade among member nations, just as the International Monetary Fund oversees international macroeconomics and exchange rates. The national-efficiency case for free trade concerns national trade policies; it is, in fact, Adam Smith's case for free trade. Economists typically have the national-efficiency case in mind when they discuss the advantage of free trade and the folly of protectionism.

This case, as refined greatly by economists in the postwar period, admits two main theoretical possibilities in which protection could improve a nation's economic well-being. First, as Adam Smith himself noted, a country might be able to use the threat of protection to get other countries to reduce their protection against its exports. Thus, threatened protection could be a tool to pry open foreign markets, like oysters, with "a strong clasp knife," as Lord Randolph Churchill put it in the late nineteenth century. If the protectionist threat worked, then the country using it would gain doubly: from its own free trade and from its trading partners' free trade. However, both Smith and later economists in Britain feared that such threats would not work. They feared that the protection imposed as a threat would be permanent and that the threat would not lower the other countries' trade barriers.

U.S. trade policy today is premised on a different assessment: that U.S. markets can, and should, be closed as a means of opening new markets abroad. This premise underlies sections 301–310 of the 1988 Omnibus Trade and Competitiveness Act, which permit, and sometimes even require, the U.S. government to force other countries to accept new trade obligations by threatening tariff retaliation if they do not. But those "trade obligations" do not always entail freer trade. They can, for instance, take the form of voluntary quotas on exports of certain goods to the United States. Thus, they may simply force weak nations to redirect their trade in ways that strong nations desire, cutting away at the principle that trade should be guided by market prices.

The second exception in which protection could improve a nation's economic well-being is when a country has monopoly power over a good. Since the time of Robert Torrens and John Stuart Mill—that is, since the mid-1800s—economists have argued that a country that produces a large percentage of the world's output of a good can use an "optimum" tariff to take advantage of its latent monopoly power, and thus gain more from trade. This is, of course, the same as saying that a monopolist will maximize his profits by raising his price and reducing his output.

Two objections to this second argument immediately

come to mind. First, with rare exceptions such as OPEC, few countries seem to have significant monopoly power in enough goods to make this an important, practical exception to the rule of free trade. Second, other countries might retaliate against the optimum tariff. Therefore, the likelihood of successful (i.e., welfare-increasing) exploitation of monopoly power becomes quite dubious. Several economists, among them Avinash Dixit, Gene Grossman, and Paul Krugman, made their academic reputations by finding theoretical cases in which oligopolistic markets enable governments to use import tariffs to improve national welfare; but even these researchers have advised strongly against protectionist policies. Their advice is based principally on the fact that governments would rarely have the information required to know where to apply the tariffs.

One may well think that any market failure could be a reason for protection. Indeed, economists fell into this trap for nearly two centuries, until the 1950s. Economists now argue, instead, that protection is an inappropriate and inefficient way to correct for domestic market failures. For example, if wages do not adjust quickly enough when demand for an industry's product falls, as was the case with U.S. auto workers losing out to foreign competition, the appropriate policy is for the government to intervene—or possibly to remove intervention—in the labor market, directly aiming remedial policy at the source of the problem. This is the principal insight from the post–World War II theory of commercial policy: it significantly narrows the rationale for protectionism and has revolutionized the conventional understanding of the relative merits of free trade and protectionism.

Many economists also believe that even if protection were appropriate in theory, it would in practice be "captured" by groups who would misuse it to pursue their own narrow interests instead of the national interest. One clear cost of protection is that the country imposing it forces its consumers to forgo cheap imports. But another important cost of protection may well be the lobbying costs incurred by those seeking protection. These lobbying activities, now extensively studied by economists, are variously described as RENT SEEKING or directly unproductive profit-seeking activities. They are unproductive because they produce profit or income for those who lobby, without creating valuable output for the rest of society.

Protectionism arises in ingenious ways. When free-trade advocates squelch it in one place, it pops up in another. Protectionists seem to always be one step ahead of free traders in creating new ways to protect against foreign competitors. One way is by replacing restrictions on imports with what are euphemistically called "voluntary" export restrictions (VERs) or "orderly" market arrangements

(OMAs). Instead of the importing country restricting imports with quotas or tariffs, the exporting country restricts exports. The protectionist effect is still the same. The real difference, which makes exporting nations prefer restrictions on exports to restrictions on imports, is that the VERs enable the exporters to charge higher prices and thus collect for themselves the higher prices caused by protection. That has been the case with Japan's voluntary quotas on exports of cars to the United States. The United States could have kept Japanese car imports in check by placing a tariff on them. That would have raised the price, so consumers would have bought fewer. Instead, the Japanese government limited the number of cars shipped to the United States. Since supply was lower than it would have been in the absence of the quotas, Japanese car makers were able to charge higher prices and still sell all their exports to the United States. The accrual of the resulting extra profits from the voluntary export restraint may also, ironically, have helped the Japanese auto producers find the funds to make investments that made them even more competitive.

The growth of VERs in the 1980s was a disturbing development for a second reason as well. They selectively target suppliers instead of letting the market decide who will lose when trade must be restricted. As an alternative, the United States could provide just as much protection for domestic auto makers by putting a quota or tariff on all foreign cars, letting consumers decide whether they wanted to buy fewer Japanese cars or fewer European ones. With VERs, in other words, politics replaces economic efficiency as the criterion determining who trades what.

Protectionism recently has come in another form more insidious than VERs. Economists call the new form "administered protection." Nearly all rich countries today have "fair trade" laws. The stated purpose of these laws is twofold: to ensure that foreign nations do not subsidize exports (which would distort market incentives and hence destroy efficient allocation of activity among the world's nations) and to guarantee that foreign firms do not dump their exports in a predatory fashion. National governments thus provide for procedures under which a countervailing duty (CVD) against foreign subsidy or an antidumping (AD) duty can be levied when subsidization or dumping is found to occur. These two "fair trade" mechanisms are meant to complement free trade.

In practice, however, when protectionist pressures rise, fair trade is misused to work against free trade. Thus, CVD and AD actions often are started against successful foreign firms simply to harass them and coerce them into accepting VERs. Practices that are thoroughly normal at home are proscribed as predatory when foreign firms engage in them. As one trade analyst put it, "If the same anti-dumping laws applied to U.S. companies, every after-Christmas sale in the country would be banned."

Much economic analysis shows that, in the 1980s, fair trade mechanisms turned increasingly into protectionist instruments used unfairly against foreign competition. U.S. rice producers got a countervailing duty imposed on rice from Thailand, for example, by establishing that the Thai government was subsidizing rice exports by less than 1 percent—and ignoring the fact that Thailand also imposed a 5 percent tax on exports. We usually think that a foreign firm is dumping when it sells at a lower price in our market than in its own. But the U.S. government took an antidumping action against Poland's exports of golf carts even though no golf carts were sold in Poland.

Economists have been thinking about how these fair trade mechanisms can be redesigned so as to insulate them from being "captured" and misused by special interests. Ideas include the creation of binational, as opposed to purely national, adjudication procedures that would ensure greater impartiality, as in the U.S.-Canada Free Trade Agreement, then incorporated into the enlarged North American Free Trade Agreement with Mexico. Also, greater use of WTO dispute-settlement procedures, and readier acceptance of their outcomes, is a possibility.

Increasingly, domestic producers have labeled as "unfair trade" a variety of foreign policies and institutions. Thus, opponents of the U.S.-Mexico Free Trade Agreement claimed that free trade between the two nations was impossible because of differences in Mexico's environmental and labor standards. The litany of objections to gainful free trade from these alleged sources of unfair trade (or its evocative synonym, "the absence of level playing fields") is endless. Here lies a new and powerful source of attack on the principles of free trade.

The current concerns about protectionism extend to two main issues. First, the exclusion of rich-country agricultural protectionism, chiefly in the form of production and trade subsidies exempted from GATT discipline by a waiver in 1965, is finally being challenged effectively. This is good for universal free trade. Second, economic analysts have been profoundly concerned by the proliferation of bilateral free trade agreements, now known as preferential trade agreements (PTAs), which currently number almost three hundred. Thanks to these PTAs and the massive extension of special and differential treatment to the poor countries, under which they get varying exemptions from the most-favored-nation (MFN) tariff (see INTERNATIONAL TRADE AGREEMENTS), there has now been a serious, systemic erosion of the MFN principle, which assured that every trading nation that was party to GATT would enjoy the most-favored-nation—that is, the lowest—tariff that others enjoyed. This is bad for universal free trade.

About the Author

Jagdish Bhagwati is University Professor at Columbia University and a senior fellow at the Council on Foreign Relations. He was economic policy adviser to the director general of the General Agreement on Tariffs and Trade (1991–1993) and special adviser to the UN on globalization. The *Financial Times* has called him "the doyen of economists working on international trade."

Further Reading

Bhagwati, Jagdish. *Free Trade Today*. Princeton: Princeton University Press, 2002.
———. *In Defense of Globalization*. New York: Oxford University Press, 2004.
———. *Protectionism*. Cambridge: MIT Press, 1988.
Dixit, Avinash. "International Trade Policy for Oligopolistic Industries." *Economic Journal* 94 (1983): 1–16.
Grossman, Gene. "Strategic Export Promotion: A Critique." In Paul Krugman, ed., *Strategic Trade Policy and the New International Economics*. Cambridge: MIT Press, 1986.
Krugman, Paul, ed. *Strategic Trade Policy and the New International Economics*. Cambridge: MIT Press, 1986.
World Trade Organization. *Report on the Future of the WTO*. Geneva, Switzerland, January 17, 2004.

Public Choice

William F. Shughart II

Public choice applies the theories and methods of economics to the analysis of political behavior, an area that was once the exclusive province of political scientists and sociologists. Public choice originated as a distinctive field of specialization a half century ago in the works of its founding fathers, Kenneth Arrow, Duncan Black, James Buchanan, Gordon Tullock, Anthony Downs, William Niskanen, Mancur Olson, and William Riker. Public choice has revolutionized the study of democratic decision-making processes.

Foundational Principles

As James Buchanan artfully defined it, public choice is "politics without romance." The wishful thinking it displaced presumes that participants in the political sphere aspire to promote the common good. In the conventional "public interest" view, public officials are portrayed as benevolent "public servants" who faithfully carry out the "will of the people." In tending to the public's business, voters, politicians, and policymakers are supposed somehow to rise above their own parochial concerns.

In modeling the behavior of individuals as driven by the goal of utility maximization—economics jargon for a personal sense of well-being—economists do not deny that people care about their families, friends, and community. But public choice, like the economic model of rational behavior on which it rests, assumes that people are guided chiefly by their own self-interests and, more important, that the motivations of people in the political process are no different from those of people in the steak, housing, or car market. They are the same human beings, after all. As such, voters "vote their pocketbooks," supporting candidates and ballot propositions they think will make them personally better off; bureaucrats strive to advance their own careers; and politicians seek election or reelection to office. Public choice, in other words, simply transfers the rational actor model of economic theory to the realm of politics.

Two insights follow immediately from economists' study of collective choice processes. First, the individual becomes the fundamental unit of analysis. Public choice rejects the construction of organic decision-making units, such as "the people," "the community," or "society." Groups do not make choices; only individuals do. The problem then becomes how to model the ways in which the diverse and often conflicting preferences of self-interested individuals get expressed and collated when decisions are made collectively.

Second, public and private choice processes differ, not because the motivations of actors are different, but because of stark differences in the incentives and constraints that channel the pursuit of self-interest in the two settings. A prospective home buyer, for example, chooses among the available alternatives in light of his personal circumstances and fully captures the benefits and bears the costs of his own choice. The purchase decision is voluntary, and a bargain will be struck only if both buyer and seller are made better off. If, on the other hand, a politician proposes a project that promises to protect the new homeowner's community from flooding, action depends on at least some of his neighbors voting for a tax on themselves and others. Because the project's benefits and costs will be shared, there is no guarantee that everyone's welfare will be improved. Support for the project will likely be forthcoming from the owners of houses located on the floodplain, who expect to benefit the most. Their support will be strengthened if taxes are assessed uniformly on the community as a whole. Homeowners far from the floodplain, for whom the costs of the project exceed expected benefits, rationally will vote against the proposal; if they find themselves in the minority, they will be coerced into paying for it. Unless the voting rule requires unanimous consent, which allows any individual to veto a proposal that would harm him, or unless those harmed can relocate easily to another political jurisdiction, collective decision-making processes allow the majority to impose its preferences on the minority. Public choice scholars have identified even deeper problems with democratic decision-making processes, however.

The Institutions and Mechanisms of Public Choice

It has been recognized at least since the time of the Marquis de Condorcet (1785) that voting among three or more candidates or alternatives may fail to select the majority's most preferred outcome or may be prone to vote "cycles" producing no clear winner.[1] Indeed, Kenneth Arrow's "impossibility theorem" shows that there is no mechanism for making collective choices, other than dictatorship, that translates the preferences of diverse individuals into a well-behaved social utility function. Nor has any electoral rule been found whose results cannot be manipulated either by individuals voting insincerely—that is, casting their ballots strategically for less-preferred candidates or issues in order to block even worse outcomes—or by an agenda setter who controls the order in which votes are taken.

Elections

Studying collective decision-making by committees, Duncan Black deduced what has since been called the median-voter theorem. If voters are fully informed, if their preferred outcomes can be arrayed along one dimension (e.g., left to right), if each voter has a single most-preferred outcome, and if decisions are made by simple majority rule, then the median voter will be decisive. Any proposal to the left or right of that point will be defeated by one that is closer to the median voter's preferred outcome. Because

---

1. Consider the problem of dividing $100 among three people. Suppose two of them agree to split that sum, with $60 going to one and $40 to the other. The third person, who receives nothing, has an incentive to strike a bargain with the second, offering a split of, say, $50 each, which makes them both better off than under the initial proposal. Faced with desertion, the first person can destabilize the new coalition by offering to accept $45, leaving $55 for one of the others. And so on. The game has three possible (and equally likely) outcomes in which two of the three players accept payments of $50 each, but the third player can always upset the equilibrium by cutting another deal. The same endless series of changing winning coalitions or vote "cycles" can emerge in elections involving three or more candidates or ballot issues when no one of them is strongly preferred by a simple majority of the voters.

extreme proposals lose to centrist proposals, candidates and parties in a two-party system will move to the center, and, as a result, their platforms and campaign promises will differ only slightly. Reversing 1964 presidential hopeful Barry Goldwater's catchphrase, majority-rule elections will present voters with an echo, not a choice. If the foregoing assumptions hold, the median voter's preferences also will determine the results of popular referenda. As a matter of fact, anticipating that immoderate proposals will be defeated, the designers of ballot initiatives will strive to adopt centrist language, in theory moving policy outcomes closer to the median voter's ideal point than might be expected if decisions are instead made by politically self-interested representatives.

Modeling the decision to vote in a rational choice context, Anthony Downs pointed out that the act of voting itself is irrational. That conclusion follows because the probability of an individual's vote determining an election's outcome is vanishingly small. One person's vote will tip the scales in favor of the preferred candidate or issue only if the votes of all other voters are evenly split. As the number of voters becomes large, the chances of that happening quickly approach zero, and hence the benefits of voting are likely to be less than the costs. Public choice reasoning thus predicts low rates of voter participation if voters are rational. Indeed, if there is an unsolved puzzle, it is not why turnout in U.S. elections is so low, but why it is so high.

Downs and other public choice scholars also conclude that voters in democratic elections will tend to be poorly informed about the candidates and issues on the ballot. Voter ignorance is rational because the cost of gathering information about an upcoming election is high relative to the benefits of voting. Why should a voter bother to become informed if his vote has a very small chance of being decisive? Geoffrey Brennan and Loren Lomasky, among others, have suggested that people vote because it is a low-cost way to express their preferences. In this view, voting is no more irrational than cheering for one's favorite sports team.

Legislatures

Ballot initiatives, referenda, and other institutions of direct democracy aside, most political decisions are made not by the citizenry itself, but by the politicians elected to represent them in legislative assemblies. Because the constituencies of these representatives typically are geographically based, legislative officeholders have strong incentives to support programs and policies that provide benefits to the voters in their home districts or states, no matter how irresponsible those programs and policies may be from a

national perspective. Such "pork barrel" projects are especially likely to gain a representative's endorsement when they are financed by the taxpayers in general, most of whom reside, and vote, in other districts or states.

Legislative catering to the interests of the minority at the expense of the majority is reinforced by the logic of collective action. Small, homogeneous groups with strong communities of interest tend to be more effective suppliers of political pressure and political support (votes, campaign contributions, and the like) than larger groups whose interests are more diffuse. The members of smaller groups have greater individual stakes in favorable policy decisions, can organize at lower cost, and can more successfully control the free riding that otherwise would undermine the achievement of their collective goals. Because the vote motive provides reelection-seeking politicians with strong incentives to respond to the demands of small, well-organized groups, representative democracy frequently leads to a tyranny of the minority. George Stigler, Sam Peltzman, Gary Becker, and others used that same reasoning to model the decisions of regulatory agencies as being influenced by special-interest groups' relative effectiveness in applying political pressure.

The logic of collective action explains why farmers have secured government subsidies at the expense of millions of unorganized consumers, who pay higher prices for food, and why textile manufacturers have benefited significantly from trade barriers at the expense of clothing buyers. Voted on separately, neither of those legislatively enacted special-interest measures would pass. But by means of logrolling bargains, in which the representatives of farm states agree to trade their votes on behalf of trade protectionism in exchange for pledges of support for agricultural subsidies from the representatives of textile-manufacturing states, both bills can secure a majority. Alternatively, numerous programs of this sort can be packaged in omnibus bills that most legislators will support in order to get their individual pet projects enacted. The legislative pork barrel is facilitated by rational-voter ignorance about the adverse effects of legislative decisions on their personal well-being. It also is facilitated by electoral advantages that make it difficult for challengers to unseat incumbents, who, accordingly, can take positions that work against their constituents' interests with little fear of reprisal.

Bureaucracies

Owing to the benefits of specialization and division of labor, legislatures delegate responsibility for implementing their policy initiatives to various departments and agencies staffed by career bureaucrats, who secure their positions through civil service appointment rather than by democratic election. The early public choice literature on bureaucracy, launched by William Niskanen, assumed that these agencies would use the information and expertise they gained in administering specific legislative programs to extract the largest budget possible from relatively uninformed, inexpert legislators. Budget maximization was assumed to be the bureaucracy's goal because more agency funding translates into broader administrative discretion, more opportunities for promotion, and greater prestige for the agency's bureaucrats.

More recently, public choice scholars have adopted a "congressional dominance" model of bureaucracy. In that model, government bureaus are not free to pursue their own agendas. On the contrary, agency policy preferences mirror those of the members of key legislative committees that oversee particular areas of public policy, such as agriculture, international trade, and the judiciary. These oversight committees constrain bureaucratic discretion by exercising their powers to confirm political appointees to senior agency positions, to mark up bureau budget requests, and to hold public hearings. The available evidence does suggest that bureaucratic policymaking is sensitive to changes in oversight committee membership.

Other Institutions
Public choice scholars, such as Gary Anderson, Mark Crain, William Shughart, and Robert Tollison, have not neglected the study of the other major institutions of democratic governance: the president or chief executive officer and the "independent" judiciary. They model the occupants of these positions as self-interested people who, by exercising the power to veto bills, on the one hand, and by ruling on the constitutionality of laws, on the other, add stability to democratic decision-making processes and increase the durability of the favors granted to special-interest groups and, hence, the amounts the groups are willing to pay for them.

The Lessons of Public Choice
One key conclusion of public choice is that changing the identities of the people who hold public office will not produce major changes in policy outcomes. Electing better people will not, by itself, lead to much better government. Adopting the assumption that all individuals, be they voters, politicians, or bureaucrats, are motivated more by self-interest than by public interest evokes a Madisonian perspective on the problems of democratic governance. Like that founding father of the American constitutional republic, public choice recognizes that men are not angels and focuses on the importance of the institutional rules under which people pursue their own objectives. "In framing a government which is to be administered by men over men,

the great difficulty lies in this: you must first enable the government to control the governed; and in the next place oblige it to control itself" (*Federalist*, no. 51).

Institutional problems demand institutional solutions. If, for example, democratic governments institutionally are incapable of balancing the public budget, a constitutional rule that limits increases in spending and taxes to no more than the private sector's rate of growth will be more effective in curbing profligacy than "throwing the rascals out." Given the problems endemic to majority-rule voting, public choice also suggests that care must be exercised in establishing the domains of private and collective choice; that it is not necessarily desirable to use the same voting rule for all collective decisions; and that the public's interest can be best protected if exit options are preserved by making collective choices at the lowest feasible level of political authority.

About the Author
William F. Shughart II is F. A. P. Barnard Distinguished Professor of Economics at the University of Mississippi. He is editor in chief of *Public Choice*, the field's leading scholarly journal.

Further Reading

Original Sources

Arrow, Kenneth J. *Social Choice and Individual Values*. 2d ed. 1951. New York: Wiley, 1963.
Black, Duncan. *The Theory of Committees and Elections*. 1958. Boston: Kulwer, 1987.
Buchanan, James M., and Gordon Tullock. *The Calculus of Consent: Logical Foundations of Constitutional Democracy*. Ann Arbor: University of Michigam Press, 1962.
Downs, Anthony. *An Economic Theory of Democracy*. New York: Harper, 1957.
Niskanen, William A. *Bureaucracy and Representative Government*. Chicago: Aldine, Atherton, 1971.
Olson, Mancur. *The Logic of Collective Action: Public Goods and the Theory of Groups*. Cambridge: Harvard University Press, 1965.
Riker, William H. *The Theory of Political Coalitions*. New Haven: Yale University Press, 1962.

Comprehensive Literature Reviews

Mueller, Dennis C. *Public Choice III*. Cambridge: Cambridge University Press, 2003.
Rowley, Charles K., and Friedrich Schneider, eds. *The Encyclopedia of Public Choice*. 2 vols. Boston: Kluwer, 2004.
Shughart, William F. II, and Laura Razzolini, eds. *The Elgar Companion to Public Choice*. Northampton, Mass.: Edward Elgar, 2001.

Public Goods

Tyler Cowen

Public goods have two distinct aspects: nonexcludability and nonrivalrous consumption. "Nonexcludability" means that the cost of keeping nonpayers from enjoying the benefits of the good or service is prohibitive. If an entrepreneur stages a fireworks show, for example, people can watch the show from their windows or backyards. Because the entrepreneur cannot charge a fee for consumption, the fireworks show may go unproduced, even if demand for the show is strong.

The fireworks example illustrates the related free-rider problem. Even if the fireworks show is worth ten dollars to each person, arguably few people will pay ten dollars to the entrepreneur. Each person will seek to "free ride" by allowing others to pay for the show, and then watch for free from his or her backyard. If the free-rider problem cannot be solved, valuable goods and services—ones people otherwise would be willing to pay for—will remain unproduced.

The second aspect of public goods is what economists call "nonrivalrous consumption." Assume the entrepreneur manages to exclude noncontributors from watching the show (perhaps one can see the show only from a private field). A price will be charged for entrance to the field, and people who are unwilling to pay this price will be excluded. If the field is large enough, however, exclusion is inefficient. Even nonpayers could watch the show without increasing the show's cost or diminishing anyone else's enjoyment. In other words, the relevant consumption is nonrivalrous. Nonetheless, nonexcludability is usually considered the more important of the two aspects of public goods. If the good is excludable, private entrepreneurs will try to serve as many fee-paying customers as possible, charging lower prices to some customers if need be.

One of the best examples of a public good is national DEFENSE. To the extent one person in a geographic area is defended from foreign attack or invasion, other people in that same area are likely defended also. This makes it hard to charge people for defense, which means that defense faces the classic free-rider problem. Indeed, almost all economists are convinced that the only way to provide a sufficient level of defense is to have government do it and fund defense with taxes.

Many other problems, though, that are often perceived as public-goods problems are not really, and markets handle them reasonably well. For instance, although many people think a television signal is a public good, cable television services scramble their transmissions so that nonsubscribers cannot receive broadcasts easily. In other words,

the producers have figured out how to exclude nonpayers. Both throughout history and today, private roads have been financed by tolls charged to road users. Other goods often seen as public goods, such as private protection and fire services, are frequently sold through the private sector on a fee basis. Excluding nonpayers is possible. In other cases, potentially public goods are funded by advertisements, as happens with television and radio.

Partially public goods also can be tied to purchases of private goods, thereby making the entire package more like a private good. Shopping malls, for instance, provide shoppers with a variety of services that are traditionally considered public goods: lighting, protection services, benches, and restrooms are examples. Charging directly for each of these services would be impractical. Therefore, the shopping mall finances the services through receipts from the sale of private goods in the mall. The public and private goods are "tied" together. Private condominiums and retirement communities also are market institutions that tie public goods to private services. They use monthly membership dues to provide a variety of public services.

Some public goods are provided through fame incentives or through personal motives to do a good job. The World Wide Web offers many millions of home pages and informational sites, and most of their constructors have not received any payment. The writers either want recognition or seek to reach other people for their own pleasure or to influence their thinking.

The "reciprocity motive" is another possible solution, especially in small groups. I may contribute to a collective endeavor as part of a broader strategy to signal that I am a public-minded, cooperative individual. You may then contribute in return, hoping that we develop an ongoing agreement—often implicit—to both contribute over time. The agreement can be self-sustaining if I know that my withdrawal will cause the withdrawal of others as well. A large body of anecdotal and experimental evidence suggests that such arrangements, while imperfect, are often effective. Roommates, for instance, often have implicit or explicit agreements about who will take out the trash or do the dishes. These arrangements are enforced not by contract but rather by the hope of continuing cooperation.

Other problems can be solved by defining individual property rights in the appropriate economic resource. Cleaning up a polluted lake, for instance, involves a free-rider problem if no one owns the lake. If there is an owner, however, that person can charge higher prices to fishermen, boaters, recreational users, and others who benefit from the lake. Privately owned bodies of water are common in the British Isles, where, not surprisingly, lake owners maintain quality.

Well-defined property rights can solve apparent public-goods problems in other environmental areas, such as land use and species preservation. The buffalo neared extinction and the cow did not because cows could be privately owned and husbanded for profit. It is harder to imagine easily enforceable private property rights in schools of fish. For this reason we see a mix of government regulation and privately determined quotas in that area. The depletion of fish stocks nonetheless looms as a problem, as does the more general loss of biodiversity.

For environmental problems involving the air, it is difficult to imagine how property rights could be defined and enforced effectively. Market mechanisms alone probably cannot prevent depletion of the Earth's ozone layer. In such cases economists recognize the likely necessity of a governmental regulatory solution.

Contractual arrangements can sometimes be used to overcome what otherwise would be public goods and externalities problems. If the research and development activities of one firm benefit other firms in the same industry, these firms may pool their resources and agree to a joint project (antitrust regulations permitting). Each firm will pay part of the cost, and the contributing firms will share the benefits.

Contractual arrangements sometimes fail. The costs of bargaining and striking an agreement may be very high. Some parties to the agreement may seek to hold out for a better deal, and the agreement may collapse. In other cases it is simply too costly to contact and deal with all the potential beneficiaries of an agreement. A factory, for instance, might find it impossible to negotiate directly with each affected citizen to decrease pollution.

The imperfections of market solutions to public-goods problems must be weighed against the imperfections of government solutions. Governments rely on bureaucracy, respond to poorly informed voters, and have weak incentives to serve consumers. Therefore they produce inefficiently. Furthermore, politicians may supply public "goods" in a manner to serve their own interests rather than the interests of the public; examples of wasteful government spending and pork barrel projects are legion. Government often creates a problem of "forced riders" by compelling persons to support projects they do not desire. Private means of avoiding or transforming public-goods problems, when available, are usually more efficient than governmental solutions.

About the Author

Tyler Cowen is an economics professor at George Mason University and director of the Mercatus Center and the James M. Buchanan Center.

Further Reading

Benson, Bruce. *The Enterprise of Law.* San Francisco: Pacific Research Institute for Public Policy, 1990.

Buchanan, James M. "Public Goods in Theory and Practice: A Note on the Minasian-Samuelson Discussion." *Journal of Law and Economics* 10 (October 1967): 193–197.

Cowen, Tyler, ed. *Public Goods and Market Failures.* New Brunswick, N.J.: Transaction Publishers, 1992.

Cowen, Tyler, and Eric Crampton, eds. *Market Failure or Success: The New Debate.* Cheltenham, U.K.: Edward Elgar, 2003.

Klein, Daniel. "Tie-ins and the Market Provision of Public Goods." *Harvard Journal of Law and Public Policy* 10 (Spring 1987): 451–474.

McCallum, Spencer Heath. *The Art of Community.* Menlo Park, Calif.: Institute for Humane Studies, 1970.

Minasian, Jora R. "Television Pricing and the Theory of Public Goods." *Journal of Law and Economics* 7 (October 1964): 71–80.

———. "Public Goods in Theory and Practice Revisited." *Journal of Law and Economics* 10 (October 1967): 205–207.

Samuelson, Paul A. "The Pure Theory of Public Expenditure." *Review of Economics and Statistics* 36 (1954): 387–390.

———. "Pitfalls in the Analysis of Public Goods." *Journal of Law and Economics* 10 (October 1967): 199–204.

Rational Expectations

Thomas J. Sargent

While rational expectations is often thought of as a school of economic thought, it is better regarded as a ubiquitous modeling technique used widely throughout economics.

The theory of rational expectations was first proposed by John F. Muth of Indiana University in the early 1960s. He used the term to describe the many economic situations in which the outcome depends partly on what people expect to happen. The price of an agricultural commodity, for example, depends on how many acres farmers plant, which in turn depends on the price farmers expect to realize when they harvest and sell their crops. As another example, the value of a currency and its rate of depreciation depend partly on what people expect that rate of depreciation to be. That is because people rush to desert a currency that they expect to lose value, thereby contributing to its loss in value. Similarly, the price of a stock or bond depends partly on what prospective buyers and sellers believe it will be in the future.

The use of expectations in economic theory is not new. Many earlier economists, including A. C. Pigou, John Maynard Keynes, and John R. Hicks, assigned a central role in the determination of the business cycle to people's expectations about the future. Keynes referred to this as "waves of optimism and pessimism" that helped determine the level of economic activity. But proponents of the rational expectations theory are more thorough in their analysis of expectations.

The influences between expectations and outcomes flow both ways. In forming their expectations, people try to forecast what will actually occur. They have strong incentives to use forecasting rules that work well because higher "profits" accrue to someone who acts on the basis of better forecasts, whether that someone is a trader in the stock market or someone considering the purchase of a new car. And when people have to forecast a particular price over and over again, they tend to adjust their forecasting rules to eliminate avoidable errors. Thus, there is continual feedback from past outcomes to current expectations. Translation: in recurrent situations the way the future unfolds from the past tends to be stable, and people adjust their forecasts to conform to this stable pattern.

The concept of rational expectations asserts that outcomes do not differ systematically (i.e., regularly or predictably) from what people expected them to be. The concept is motivated by the same thinking that led Abraham Lincoln to assert, "You can fool some of the people all of the time, and all of the people some of the time, but you cannot fool all of the people all of the time." From the viewpoint of the rational expectations doctrine, Lincoln's statement gets things right. It does not deny that people often make forecasting errors, but it does suggest that errors will not persistently occur on one side or the other.

Economists who believe in rational expectations base their belief on the standard economic assumption that people behave in ways that maximize their utility (their enjoyment of life) or profits. Economists have used the concept of rational expectations to understand a variety of situations in which speculation about the future is a crucial factor in determining current action. Rational expectations is a building block for the "random walk" or "efficient markets" theory of securities prices, the theory of the dynamics of hyperinflations, the "permanent income" and "life-cycle" theories of consumption, and the design of economic stabilization policies.

The Efficient Markets Theory of Stock Prices
One of the earliest and most striking applications of the concept of rational expectations is the efficient markets theory of asset prices. A sequence of observations on a variable (such as daily stock prices) is said to follow a random walk if the current value gives the best possible prediction of future values. The efficient markets theory of stock prices uses the concept of rational expectations to reach the conclusion that, when properly adjusted for discounting and dividends, stock price changes follow a random walk. The chain of reasoning goes as follows. In their efforts to forecast prices, investors comb all sources of information, including patterns that they can spot in past price movements.

Investors buy stocks they expect to have a higher-than-average return and sell those they expect to have lower returns. When they do so, they bid up the prices of stocks expected to have higher-than-average returns and drive down the prices of those expected to have lower-than-average returns. The prices of the stocks adjust until the expected returns, adjusted for risk, are equal for all stocks. Equalization of expected returns means that investors' forecasts become built into or reflected in the prices of stocks. More precisely, it means that stock prices change so that after an adjustment to reflect dividends, the time value of money, and differential risk, they equal the market's best forecast of the future price. Therefore, the only factors that can change stock prices are random factors that could not be known in advance. Thus, changes in stock prices follow a random walk.

The random walk theory has been subjected to literally hundreds of empirical tests. The tests tend to support the theory quite strongly. While some studies have found situations that contradict the theory, the theory does explain, at least to a very good first approximation, how asset prices evolve (see EFFICIENT CAPITAL MARKETS).

The Permanent Income Theory of Consumption
The Keynesian consumption function holds that there is a positive relationship between people's consumption and their income. Early empirical work in the 1940s and 1950s encountered some discrepancies in the theory, which Milton Friedman successfully explained with his celebrated "permanent income theory" of consumption. Friedman built on Irving Fisher's insight that a person's consumption ought not depend on current income alone, but also on prospects of income in the future. Friedman posited that people consume out of their "permanent income," which can be defined as the level of consumption that can be sustained while leaving wealth intact. In defining "wealth," Friedman included a measure of "human wealth"—namely, the present value of people's expectations of future labor income.

Although Friedman did not formally apply the concept of rational expectations in his work, it is implicit in much of his discussion. Because of its heavy emphasis on the role of expectations about future income, his hypothesis was a prime candidate for the application of rational expectations. In work subsequent to Friedman's, John F. Muth and Stanford's Robert E. Hall imposed rational expectations on versions of Friedman's model, with interesting results. In Hall's version, imposing rational expectations produces the result that consumption is a random walk: the best prediction of future consumption is the present level of consumption. This result encapsulates the consumption-smoothing aspect of the permanent income model and reflects people's efforts to estimate their wealth and to allocate it over time. If consumption in each period is held at a level that is expected to leave wealth unchanged, it follows that wealth and consumption will each equal their values in the previous period plus an unforecastable or unforeseeable random shock—really a forecast error.

The rational expectations version of the permanent income hypothesis has changed the way economists think about short-term stabilization policies (such as temporary tax cuts) designed to stimulate the economy. Keynesian economists once believed that tax cuts boost disposable income and thus cause people to consume more. But according to the permanent income model, temporary tax cuts have much less of an effect on consumption than Keynesians had thought. The reason is that people are basing their consumption decision on their wealth, not their current disposable income. Because temporary tax cuts are bound to be reversed, they have little or no effect on wealth, and therefore have little or no effect on consumption. Thus, the permanent income model had the effect of diminishing the expenditure "multiplier" that economists ascribed to temporary tax cuts.

The rational expectations version of the permanent income model has been extensively tested, with results that are quite encouraging. The evidence indicates that the model works well but imperfectly. Economists next extended the model to take into account factors such as "habit persistence" in consumption and the differing durabilities of various consumption goods. Expanding the theory to incorporate these features alters the pure "random walk" prediction of the theory and so helps remedy some of the empirical shortcomings of the model, but it leaves the basic permanent income insight intact.

Expectational Error Models of the Business Cycle

A long tradition in business cycle theory has held that errors in people's forecasts are a major cause of business fluctuations. This view is embodied in the PHILLIPS CURVE (the observed inverse correlation between unemployment and inflation), with economists attributing the correlation to errors people make in their forecasts of the price level.

Before the advent of rational expectations, economists often proposed to "exploit" or "manipulate" the public's forecasting errors in ways designed to generate better performance of the economy over the business cycle. Thus, Robert Hall aptly described the state of economic thinking in 1973 when he wrote:

> The benefits of inflation derive from the use of expansionary policy to trick economic agents into behaving in socially preferable ways even though their behavior is not in their own interest. . . . The gap between actual and expected inflation measures the extent of the trickery. . . . The optimal policy is not nearly as expansionary [inflationary] when expectations adjust rapidly, and most of the effect of an inflationary policy is dissipated in costly anticipated inflation.

Rational expectations undermines the idea that policymakers can manipulate the economy by systematically making the public have false expectations. Robert Lucas showed that if expectations are rational, it simply is not possible for the government to manipulate those forecast errors in a predictable and reliable way for the very reason that the errors made by a rational forecaster are inherently unpredictable. Lucas's work led to what has sometimes been called the "policy ineffectiveness proposition." If people have rational expectations, policies that try to manipulate the economy by inducing people into having false expectations may introduce more "noise" into the economy but cannot, on average, improve the economy's performance.

Design of Macroeconomic Policies

The "policy ineffectiveness" result pertains only to those economic policies that have their effects solely by inducing forecast errors. Many government policies work by affecting "margins" or incentives, and the concept of rational expectations delivers no policy ineffectiveness result for such policies. In fact, the idea of rational expectations has been used extensively in such contexts to study the design of monetary, fiscal, and regulatory policies to promote good economic performance.

The idea of rational expectations has also been a workhorse in developing prescriptions for optimally choosing monetary policy. Truman Bewley and William A. Brock have been important contributors to this literature. Bewley's and Brock's work describes precisely the contexts in which an optimal monetary arrangement involves having the government pay interest on reserves at the market rate. Their work supports, clarifies, and extends proposals to monetary reform made by Milton Friedman in 1960 and 1968.

Rational expectations has been a working assumption in recent studies that try to explain how monetary and fiscal authorities can retain (or lose) "good reputations" for their conduct of policy. This literature has helped economists understand the multiplicity of government policy strategies followed, for example, in high-inflation and low-inflation countries. In particular, work on "reputational equilibria" in macroeconomics by Robert Barro and by David Gordon and Nancy Stokey showed that the preferences of citizens and policymakers and the available production technologies and trading opportunities are not by themselves sufficient to determine whether a government will follow a low-inflation or a high-inflation policy mix. Instead, reputation remains an independent factor even after rational expectations have been assumed.

About the Author

Thomas J. Sargent is a senior fellow at Stanford's Hoover Institution and an economics professor at New York University. He is one of the pioneers in the theory of rational expectations.

Further Reading

Fischer, Stanley, ed. *Rational Expectations and Economic Policy.* Chicago: University of Chicago Press, 1980.
Lucas, Robert E. Jr. *Models of Business Cycles.* Oxford: Basil Blackwell, 1987.
Muth, John A. "Rational Expectations and the Theory of Price Movements." *Econometrica* 29, no. 6 (1961): 315–335.
Sargent, Thomas J. *Rational Expectations and Inflation.* New York: Harper and Row, 1986.
Sheffrin, Steven M. *Rational Expectations.* 2d ed. Cambridge: Cambridge University Press, 1996.

Recycling

Jane S. Shaw

Recycling is the process of converting waste products into reusable materials. Recycling differs from reuse, which simply means using a product again. According to the Environmental Protection Agency (EPA), about 30 percent of U.S. solid waste (i.e., the waste that is normally handled through residential and commercial garbage-collection systems) is recycled. About 15 percent is incinerated and about 55 percent goes into landfills.

Recycling is appealing because it seems to offer a way to simultaneously reduce the amount of waste disposed in landfills and save natural resources. During the late 1980s, as environmental concerns grew, public opinion focused on recycling as a prime way to protect the environment. Governments, businesses, and the public made strenuous efforts to recycle. By 2000, the recycling rate had nearly doubled the 1990 rate of 16 percent. A big portion of the increase has been in yard trimmings and food scraps collected for composting.

Recycling, however, is not always economically efficient or even environmentally helpful. The popular emphasis on recycling stems partly from misconceptions. One misconception is that landfills and incinerators are environmentally risky. It is true that at one time landfills were constructed to fill in swamps (sometimes to reduce insect infestation). If material leaked out from the landfill, it could contaminate nearby waters. But today landfills are sited away from wetlands. They are designed to keep their contents dry, and monitoring programs ensure that any leakage that does occur is caught before it causes harm.

Another misconception is that we are running out of landfill space. The truth is that landfills today are large enough to accommodate the solid waste produced by the United States until 2019, even if no new ones are established. Economist Daniel Benjamin (2003) reports that the fear of running out of landfill space stems from an EPA study in the 1980s that counted landfills rather than landfill capacity. In fact, the report omitted the fact that landfill space was actually increasing because sites were getting larger. Indeed, the EPA continues to publish a chart showing the declining number of landfills even while stating that "at the national level, capacity does not seem to be a problem, although regional dislocations sometimes occur" (EPA 2002, p. 14).

People also tend to overestimate how much space is required to bury our trash. Numerous studies have shown that it is not all that much. Statistician Bjørn Lomborg has calculated that a ten-mile-square, 255-foot-deep landfill could contain all the trash produced in the United States over the next century.

The Economics of Recycling

In the absence of government regulation, the economics of each material determines how much of it is recycled. For example, about 55 percent of all aluminum cans were recycled in 2000. Recycling of beverage cans goes back to 1968, when the Reynolds Metals Company started a pilot project. The chief motivation was to respond to public concerns about litter, which were spurring laws that required deposits on beverage containers. But energy prices began to rise during the 1970s and, because producing new aluminum from bauxite requires large amounts of energy, recycling aluminum cans became economically attractive.

About 56 percent of paper and cardboard was recycled

in 2000. Recycling is economically rewarding because cardboard can be made from a wide variety of used paper. In addition, because many places (such as supermarkets and discount stores) use large quantities of corrugated boxes, collection costs can be low.

In contrast, only about 9 percent of plastic packaging is recycled. Because different plastic resins cannot be mixed together and reprocessed, plastics must be separated at some point if they are to be recycled. The plastics packaging industry has developed symbols for different kinds of resins, but people do not seem eager to separate plastic. In addition, the relatively low cost of producing new plastic from oil-based petrochemicals makes recycling less economically rewarding.

Ironically, recycling does not eliminate environmental worries. Recycling is a manufacturing process and, like other manufacturing processes, can produce pollution. An EPA study of toxic chemicals found such chemicals in both recycling and virgin paper processing, and for most of the toxins studied, the recycling process had higher levels than the virgin manufacturing did. Nor will recycling more newspapers necessarily preserve trees, because many trees are grown specifically to be made into paper. A study prepared for the environmental think tank Resources for the Future estimated that if paper recycling reached high levels, demand for virgin paper would fall. As a result, writes economist A. Clark Wiseman, "some lands now being used to grow trees will be put to other uses." The impact would not be large, but it would be the opposite of what most people expect—there would be fewer trees, not more. Finally, curbside recycling programs require additional trucks, which use more energy and create more pollution.

Curbside Recycling

The private sector typically adopts recycling when and where it makes economic sense. When recycling is a government program, however, it can be costly and can waste rather than save resources. Using figures collected by Franklin Associates, Daniel Benjamin compared the costs of traditional municipal waste disposal (by landfill, but allowing residents to drop off material for recycling) and curbside recycling (where the city picks up recyclables separate from trash). He found that the curbside recycling programs cost between 35 and 55 percent more than the traditional landfill disposal. Recycling programs used "huge amounts of capital and labor," writes Benjamin. Used materials were sold, but the costs of workers and equipment vastly outweighed the revenues from their sale.

Other problems arise, too. In 2003, the citizens of Tucson, Arizona, were disturbed to learn that the city's recy-

cling contractor was landfilling glass that many of them had separated and put into recycling bins. Prices for recycled glass had fallen so low that it would have cost eighty dollars a ton to ship it to Los Angeles to find a buyer. Depositing the glass in a landfill cost only twenty-eight dollars per ton.

These facts, however, have not stopped many local governments from establishing expensive curbside programs. Seattle's city council went even further in December 2003, voting to make recycling mandatory. When the program went into effect in 2005, residents were prohibited from putting any recyclables into their trash. The city's previous method of charging residents on a per-trash-can basis (charging more for larger cans) provided an inducement to reduce waste, whether through recycling or other means, and helped boost Seattle's recycling rate to 40 percent. This was not high enough for the council, however, which made the program mandatory in hope of reaching a 60 percent recycling rate.

Recycling is not a panacea for environmental problems. It is instead only one of several means for disposing of waste. Recycling is widely used where the economics are favorable but inappropriate where they are not. Government regulations may override the economics, but only at a high cost and by requiring actions, such as curbside recycling, that people will not do voluntarily.

About the Author

Jane S. Shaw is executive vice president of the J. W. Pope Center for Higher Education Policy in Raleigh, North Carolina. She is also a senior fellow with PERC, the Property and Environment Research Center, a nonprofit institute in Bozeman, Montana. In 2003–2004 she was president of the Association of Private Enterprise Education.

Further Reading

Benjamin, Daniel K. "Eight Great Myths of Recycling." PERC Policy Series PS-28. Bozeman, Mont.: PERC—the Center for Free Market Environmentalism, 2003. Available online at: http://www.perc.org/publications/policyseries/recycling.php?s = 2.

Environmental Protection Agency. *Municipal Solid Waste in the United States: 2000 Facts and Figures.* Washington, D.C.: U.S. Government Printing Office, 2002. Available online at: http://www.epa.gov/epaoswer/non-hw/muncpl/pubs/exec-00.pdf.

Rathje, William L. "Rubbish!" *Atlantic Monthly* (December 1989): 99–109.

Tierney, John. "Recycling Is Garbage." *New York Times,* June 30, 1996, pp. 24–29ff.

"Redistribution"

Dwight R. Lee

The federal government has increasingly assumed responsibility for reducing poverty in America. Its primary approach is to expand programs that transfer wealth, supposedly from the better off to the poor. In 1962, federal transfers to individuals (not counting payments for goods and services provided or interest for money loaned) amounted to 5.2 percent of gross domestic product, or 27 percent of federal spending (Stein and Foss 1995, p. 212). By 2000, federal transfers had increased to 10.9 percent of GDP, or approximately 60 percent of federal spending; GDP was $9.82 trillion and federal spending was $1.79 trillion. These transfers are commonly referred to as government redistribution programs, presumably from the wealthy to the poor. The unstated implication is that income was originally distributed by someone. But no one distributes income. Rather, incomes are determined in the marketplace by millions of people providing and purchasing services through voluntary exchanges, and government transfers necessarily limit these exchanges. That explains the quotation marks around the term "redistribution."

Almost without exception, academic studies and journalistic accounts of government's effect on the well-being of the poor focus exclusively on the effectiveness of programs that actually transfer income to the poor. What does this leave out? It leaves out all the programs that transfer income away from the poor. To know the net amount the poor receive after considering transfers to and transfers from them, we need to consider all government transfer programs.

Such an examination yields a striking fact: most government transfers are not from the rich to the poor. Instead, government takes from the relatively unorganized (e.g., consumers and general taxpayers) and gives to the relatively organized (groups politically organized around common interests, such as the elderly, sugar farmers, and steel producers). The most important factor in determining the pattern of redistribution appears to be political influence, not poverty. Of the $1.07 trillion in federal transfers in 2000, only about 29 percent, or $312 billion, was means tested (earmarked for the poor) (Rector 2001, p. 2). The other 71 percent—about $758 billion in 2000—was distributed with little attention to need.

Take Social Security, for example. The net worth per family of the elderly is about twice that of families in general. Yet, Social Security payments transferred $406 billion in 2003 to the elderly, regardless of their wealth. Also, qualifying for Medicare requires only that one be sixty-five or older. Because this age group's poverty rate is quite low (only 10.4 percent in 2002), most of the more than $280 billion in annual Medicare benefits go to the nonpoor.

What is more, the direct transfer of cash and services is only one way that government transfers income. Another way is by restricting competition among producers. The inevitable consequence—indeed, the intended consequence—of these restrictions is to enrich organized groups of producers at the expense of consumers. Here, the transfers are more perverse than with Medicare and Social Security. They help relatively wealthy producers at the expense of relatively poor (and, in some cases, absolutely poor) consumers. Many government restrictions on agricultural production, for example, allow farmers to capture billions of consumer dollars through higher food prices (see AGRICULTURAL SUBSIDY PROGRAMS). Most of these dollars go to relatively few large farms, whose owners are far wealthier than the average taxpayer and consumer (or the average farmer). Also, wealthy farmers receive most of the government's direct agricultural subsidies.

Restrictions on imports also transfer wealth from consumers to domestic producers of the products. Again, those who receive these transfers are typically wealthier than those who pay for them. Consider, for example, the tariffs imposed on steel imports in 2002 to save steelworkers' jobs. A study done for the Consuming Industries Trade Action Coalition in 2003 found that the steel tariffs eliminated the jobs of about 200,000 U.S. workers in industries that, because of the tariffs, had to pay more for the steel needed in their production processes. This is far more jobs than were saved, because the entire American steel industry employs only 187,500 workers, only a fairly small fraction of whom would have lost their jobs without the steel tariffs. Also, consumers had to pay more for products containing steel. Since unionized steelworkers earn more than the average worker and consumer, the steel tariffs transferred wealth to a few well-paid and politically organized workers at the expense of many less-well-paid workers and consumers.

Not only do the poor receive a smaller percentage of income transfers than most people realize, but also the transfers they do get are worth less to them, dollar for dollar, than transfers going to the nonpoor. The reason is that subsidies to the poor tend to be in kind rather than in cash. Slightly over half of all the transfers targeted to the poor are in the form of medical care. In addition to medical care, the poor receive a significant proportion of their assistance for such things as housing, energy, and job training. This means that well over half of the transfers going to the poor are in-kind transfers. However, transfers that are not means tested are more likely to be in the form of cash. For example, in 2000, Social Security retirement payments were $353 billion, more than 46 percent of non-means-tested government transfers during that year. Many other non-means-tested transfers are also in the form of cash payments. Consider just a few of the farm subsidy programs. From 1995 through 2002, corn farmers received $34.5 billion in government subsidies, wheat farmers received $17.2 billion, soybean growers received almost $11 billion, and cotton farmers received $10.7 billion. When all non-means-tested cash transfers are added up, they come to more than 50 percent of all non-means-tested transfers. While in-kind transfers are worth having, economists who study poverty point out that the poor, like the rest of us, value cash more than in-kind transfers because with cash they can choose what to buy. So a higher percentage of the transfer dollars going to the nonpoor is actually *worth* a dollar to the recipients than is the case with the transfer dollars going to the poor.

The most important question, of course, is whether the poor have benefited from the large increase in the percentage of national income that has been channeled through government in the name of reducing poverty. The answer, surprising though it may seem, is that we really do not know. To determine the effect of government transfer programs on the poor, we would have to know how the poor would have fared had these programs never existed, and that is difficult to estimate with much confidence.

Most attempts to measure the benefit to the poor from government transfers compare the income of the recipients with what their incomes would be if all transfer income were eliminated. The assumption is that the entire transfer is an increase in the income of the recipients. Such studies conclude that government programs have significantly reduced the poverty rate.

But such studies overstate the benefits to the poor because they fail to account for the negative effect of the benefit programs on the income-earning actions of the beneficiaries. When, for example, transfers are means tested, recipients who work lose a large part of their transfer payment. This penalty on working has the same effect as a high marginal income tax and creates a disincentive for the poor to work their way out of poverty, trapping the most vulnerable poor into permanent dependency. Ending the transfer payment, therefore, would motivate the former recipient to earn more income. Failing to account for this higher earning in the absence of welfare payments causes analysts to overstate welfare programs' positive effect on recipients' income. In fact, ending the welfare trap

was part of the motivation for the welfare reform of 1996 (the Personal Responsibility and Work Opportunity Reconciliation Act of 1996), which limits the time an individual can remain on welfare.

The Earned Income Tax Credit program (EITC), which was expanded in the 1980s and 1990s, is an attempt to transfer income to the poor without significantly reducing their incentive to work. The EITC is a federal income tax credit that low-income workers receive through lower (in some cases negative) taxes, and which they can take as a cash refund. There is evidence that the program has increased the incentive for people on welfare to enter the workforce. But it also reduces the incentive for those already working to work as many hours as before: the more income a worker earns, the smaller the tax credit received. A clear advantage of the EITC is that it transfers income in the form of cash, with this transfer coming to about $33 billion in 2002. Workers covered by the EITC, though, receive less than this $33 billion. The reason is that the net effect of the EITC is an increase in the supply of workers, which causes wages to fall. This downward pressure on wages is not negated by the minimum wage, because more than 60 percent of the workers receiving EITC make more than the minimum. And even those at minimum wage can have their wages reduced through the loss of fringe benefits.

Although there is controversy over the magnitude, all economists agree that means-tested programs, even the EITC, create disincentives. The late Arthur Okun, President Lyndon B. Johnson's chief economist and a strong advocate of government transfers to the poor, compared transfer programs to a leaky bucket to illustrate the fact that the increase in recipient income is less than the amount transferred. Okun's bucket leaks from both ends. The higher taxes needed to pay for transfers to the poor also create disincentives for those with higher incomes to work as hard, earn as much, and invest in businesses, which can reduce not only the money available for transfers, but also economic activity and job opportunities for the poor.

Probably the best reason for believing that government transfers have done less to help the poor than most people think follows from recognizing that competition for political favor determines transfer decisions, as it does most government decisions. People are poor because they do not have the skills, drive, and connections to compete effectively in the marketplace. For those same reasons, they are unlikely to compete very effectively politically. The result is that the best-organized, and generally the wealthiest, groups consistently outcompete the poor for government transfers. For example, according to the Environmental

Working Group Farm Subsidy Database (easily found through Google), "Nationwide, ten percent of the biggest (and often most profitable) subsidized crop producers collected 71 percent of all subsidies, averaging $34,800 in annual payments between 1995 and 2002. The bottom 80 percent of the recipients saw only $846 on average per year." The same pattern occurs with contract set-asides, that is, contracts to perform services for the federal government that are set aside from the normal bidding process for particular types of business. Thomas Sowell (2004, p. 120) reports on a study that found that more than two-thirds of a random sample of minority recipients of contract set-asides by the Small Business Administration were millionaires. These are only some of many examples.

This discussion has been entirely about the effect of federal taxes and transfers on the poor, even though state and local government policies also affect income inequality. State and local programs are more difficult to discuss because there are so many of them and they differ in details, but there is little reason to believe that they are any more effective at transferring income from the wealthy to the poor than are federal programs. First, those with the skills and connections to compete best for federal programs that serve their interests are also more effective competing at the state and local levels. The best public schools, for example, are in wealthy suburbs, not inner cities. Second, state and local taxes are regressive; that is, they take a larger percentage of income from those with less income. Finally, even if they wanted to, state and local policymakers have less ability to reduce income inequality than the federal authorities because states must compete with each other for residents.

Despite the significant increase in the percentage of national income transferred through government programs since the 1960s, there is no evidence that the distribution of income (again, after taxes and transfers at all levels of government) has shifted in favor of the poor. We can never know for certain what would have happened if government transfers had not increased. But even if transfer programs have somewhat increased the share of national income going to the poor, their disincentive effects have made national income smaller than otherwise. A slightly higher share of a smaller pie could be a smaller slice.

About the Author

Dwight R. Lee is the Ramsey Professor of Economics in the Terry College of Business at the University of Georgia. In 1997–1998, he was president of the Southern Economics Association.

Further Reading

Denzau, Arthur T. *How Import Restrictions Reduce Employment.* Formal publication no. 80. St. Louis: Center for the Study of American Business, Washington University, 1987.

Haveman, Robert. *Starting Even: An Equal Opportunity Program to Combat the Nation's New Poverty.* New York: Simon and Schuster, 1988.

Okun, Arthur M. *Equality and Efficiency: The Big Tradeoff.* Washington, D.C.: Brookings Institution, 1975.

Rector, Robert. "Means Tested Welfare Spending: Past and Future Growth." In *Policy Research and Analysis.* Washington, D.C.: Heritage Foundation, 2001.

Reynolds, Morgan, and Eugene Smolensky. *Public Expenditures, Taxes, and the Distribution of Income: The United States, 1950–1970.* New York: Academic Press, 1977.

Sawhill, Isabel V. "Poverty in the U.S.: Why Is It So Persistent?" *Journal of Economic Literature* 26 (September 1988): 1073–1119.

Sowell, Thomas. *Affirmative Action Around the World: An Empirical Study.* New Haven: Yale University Press, 2004.

Stein, Herbert, and Murray Foss. *The New Illustrated Guide to the American Economy.* Washington, D.C.: AEI Press, 1995.

Tanner, Michael D. *The Poverty of Welfare: Helping Others in Civil Society.* Washington, D.C.: Cato Institute, 2003.

Tullock, Gordon. *Economics of Income Redistribution.* Boston: Kluwer–Nijhoff, 1983.

Regulation

Robert Litan

Businesses complain about regulation incessantly, but many citizens, consumer advocates, and nongovernmental organizations (NGOs) think it absolutely necessary to protect the public interest. What is regulation? Why do we have it? How has it changed? This article briefly provides some answers, concentrating on experience with regulation in the United States.

Regulation consists of requirements the government imposes on private firms and individuals to achieve government's purposes. These include better and cheaper services and goods, protection of existing firms from "unfair" (and fair) competition, cleaner water and air, and safer workplaces and products. Failure to meet regulations can result in fines, orders to cease doing certain things, or, in some cases, even criminal penalties.

Economists distinguish between two types of regulation: economic and social. "Economic regulation" refers to rules that limit who can enter a business (entry controls) and what prices they may charge (price controls). For example, taxi drivers and many professionals (lawyers, accountants, beauticians, financial advisers, etc.) must have licenses in order to do business; these are examples of entry controls. As for price controls, for many years, airlines, trucking companies, and railroads were told what prices they could charge, or at least not exceed. Companies providing local telephone service are still subject to price controls in all states.

"Social regulation" refers to the broad category of rules governing how any business or individual carries out its activities, with a view to correcting one or more "market failures." A classic way in which the market fails is when firms (or individuals) do not take account of the costs their activities may impose on third parties (see EXTERNALITIES). When this happens, the activities will be pursued too intensely or in ways that fail to stem harm to third parties. For example, left to its own devices, a manufacturing plant may spew harmful chemicals into the air and water, causing harm to its neighbors. Governments respond to this problem by setting standards for emissions or even by requiring that firms use specific technologies (such as "scrubbers" for utilities that capture noxious chemicals before steam is released into the air).

Another kind of market failure arises when firms fail to supply sufficient information for consumers or workers to make informed choices. Disclosure requirements solve this problem, at least in principle. Examples include "truth in lending" disclosures of interest rates and other pertinent features of bank loans, and required disclosures by pharmaceutical companies of the possible side effects of the drugs they sell. Although truth-in-lending disclosures seem to work well, other disclosures work less well. Few people, for example, read the voluminous package inserts that come with the drugs they take. When policymakers conclude that individuals may be unable to effectively process or act on the information that is disclosed, governments may mandate certain rules or practices. The prime examples are limits on certain chemical exposures to workers in manufacturing plants.

A large body of economic research over the past several decades has focused on regulation, and a surprising degree of consensus has emerged on several propositions. Somewhat surprisingly, policymakers have gradually paid attention to what economists have recommended and changed regulation accordingly. To be sure, policymakers have acted for other reasons, as well—because of pressure from certain segments of the business community or from NGOs. But economists have played an important role in providing intellectual justification for the changes that have been made.

First, economists have urged that price controls be confined to situations in which a market may be domi-

nated by one or perhaps two firms. Otherwise, if markets are reasonably competitive, there is no place for price regulation. Consistent with these propositions, the federal government in the late 1970s and early 1980s began dismantling price regulation of various transportation services, where there are multiple firms and thus choices for consumers (see AIRLINE DEREGULATION and SURFACE FREIGHT TRANSPORTATION DEREGULATION). Still, there are pockets of economic activity—insurance is one notable example—where some kind of price regulation remains, even though the underlying markets are fundamentally competitive.

Similarly, economists have encouraged policymakers to reduce entry controls so that any firm or individual can enter any market, except in situations where they judge that low quality should not be tolerated. For example, bank regulators no longer closely scrutinize the need for new banks before handing out charters (and instead limit their scrutiny only to whether banks have adequate initial capital and whether their owners are reputable). Licensing systems still remain, however, for doctors, lawyers, accountants, nuclear power plants, and the like because some policymakers believe that the potential damage from low-quality providers can be substantial or irreparable (see CONSUMER PROTECTION for another viewpoint).

Second, economists have urged regulators to design more efficient social regulations so that a given goal—such as clean air—can be achieved at least cost. In practical terms, this means not telling firms exactly what technologies to use (i.e., setting design standards), but instead simply giving them a standard to meet and letting them decide how to meet it (i.e., setting performance standards). In addition, economists have urged regulators to allow firms to trade their compliance status with other firms. For example, a firm that, because of a cheaper technology, can reduce the emissions of a noxious chemical to a level below the standard would be able to sell the rights to emit that shortfall to another firm whose cost of complying is higher. This reduces the total cost for a given reduction of overall emissions.

In fact, regulators have taken this advice to heart. The federal agencies governing the safety of automobiles, industrial workplaces, and the environment all have moved in the direction of regulating by performance rather than by design. The U.S. Environmental Protection Agency (EPA), in particular, has implemented emissions-trading programs for sulfur dioxide and other pollutants.

Because even a well-functioning economy will have market failures, however, there will always be a case for some regulation. In some of these cases, it is useful to think of regulation as an alternative to direct government expenditures or tax incentives. For example, to ensure cleaner air or water, the government itself could pay for or subsidize technologies to prevent emissions in the first place and then pay to clean up any residual mess that firms and individuals may leave behind. In large part because governments are unwilling to increase taxes to follow such policies, and in part because of pressure from environmental NGOs, governments tend to embrace regulation instead. For example, the EPA has introduced and enforced a series of standards for various kinds of pollutants.

Often government regulates intrusively. The EPA, for example, has compelled firms to install the best available pollution removal control technology rather than allowing firms to meet prevailing standards by changing their input mixes to prevent POLLUTION from arising in the first place. One particularly costly example is the EPA's requirement that utilities install scrubbers in their plants even if they use cheaper low-sulfur coal to minimize sulfur pollution. Eastern U.S. coal producers lobbied for this requirement because their coal was high in sulfur and the scrubbers made it less worthwhile for utilities to purchase low-sulfur coal from the western United States.[1]

Unlike direct expenditures or tax incentives, which are recorded as part of the government's budget, the spending by private firms and individuals to comply with government mandates has not, until very recently, been tallied up and still is not subject to a formal budgeting process. In 2000, the Office of Management and Budget (OMB)—which compiles the budget for direct federal expenditures—tried to add up both the compliance costs and the benefits of almost all federal regulatory activity (with exceptions for regulations issued by "independent" agencies or those not belonging to the executive branch). OMB now does this every year and has improved its methodology over time.

In its regulatory report for 2003, for example, the OMB estimated that the annual compliance costs of all new federal executive branch regulations issued during the decade 1992–2002 ranged from $38 billion to $44 billion (though the cost of preexisting regulations was estimated to exceed $200 billion). By comparison, the OMB estimated the annual benefits of these rules to total between $135 and $218 billion. It would be a mistake, however, to conclude from these aggregate figures that the benefits of all individual regulations exceed their costs. In fact, independent analysts have documented the reverse for many regulations.

To minimize the chances that agencies will issue regulations whose costs exceed their benefits, all administrations since Gerald Ford's have conducted a White House review of executive branch regulatory proposals before they become final. The institutional homes for these reviews have varied, but since Ronald Reagan's first term a suboffice of the OMB has overseen the review process. The reviewers try to ensure that regulations pass some kind of benefit-cost test before they become final, subject to the constraint that for some regulations, Congress does not allow or somehow restricts decision makers from balancing benefits against costs. This type of decision making, known as BENEFIT-COST ANALYSIS, has been required under successive Executive Orders issued by presidents from both political parties over the course of three decades.

There continues to be spirited debate—largely between economists and noneconomists—about the appropriateness of benefit-cost analysis. On the one hand, economists broadly agree that this type of analysis is necessary not only for regulatory decisions, but also for decisions about other governmental functions (direct expenditures and tax incentives) and for private-sector decisions. But, on the other hand, some benefits of government programs (regulatory and nonregulatory) cannot be quantified or expressed in monetary terms. What is the value, for example, of preserving a certain species of fish or knowing that certain lakes and rivers will not be despoiled? In such cases, advocates of benefit-cost analysis urge analysts at least to tote up compliance costs and compare them with the benefits qualitatively described, and then to decide whether the particular form of regulation is the most efficient way of achieving those benefits. This kind of analysis is called cost-effectiveness analysis.

Critics of benefit-cost analysis offer both moral and technical objections. On moral grounds, some critics argue that many objectives of regulation—such as clean air or water—are priceless, and regulators should endeavor to eliminate all pollutants regardless of the cost. Defenders of benefit-cost analysis reply that the cost of completely clean air and water would be so large that the money spent could have been used to save many lives.

Other critics raise a variety of technical objections. Perhaps the most common are those that question whether regulators can obtain unbiased estimates of benefits and costs of regulatory proposals before they actually are implemented (and even after the fact it may be difficult to sort out what is due to regulation and what is due to market pressure). In reality, however, there may not be large differences, or any difference at all, in at least the cost estimates (though estimates of benefits typically span a broader range). For example, the National Highway Traffic

1. See Bruce Ackerman and William T. Hassler, *Clean Coal/Dirty Air; or How the Clean Air Act Became a Multibillion-Dollar Bail-out for High-Sulfur Coal Producers and What Should Be Done About It* (New Haven: Yale University Press, 1981).

Safety Administration reported no range of costs for regulations governing the stability and control of medium and heavy vehicles in the mid-1990s. Similarly, the EPA reported no range in costs for regulations issued in 2001–2002 governing emissions from recreational vehicles. The OMB also provides information each year about rules for which there is no range in the cost estimates.

Although the various debates over cost-benefit analysis and how it is carried out will surely continue, some sort of centralized review of federal regulation has become sufficiently institutionalized that it is highly likely to become a permanent part of the governmental regulatory process. And as long as this occurs, it is also highly likely that decision makers, whether in the agencies or in the executive office of the president, will compare the pros and cons of regulatory proposals before they are issued. In this sense, government officials are likely to act as ordinary citizens do in their everyday lives.

About the Author

Robert Litan is vice president for research and policy at the Kauffman Foundation; senior fellow in economic studies at the Brookings Institution; and director of the AEI-Brookings Joint Center for Regulatory Studies.

Further Reading

For a thorough list of documents, articles, and monographs on the full range of regulatory issues, see http://aei-brookings.org. In addition, readers may be interested in the following:

Breyer, Stephen. *Breaking the Vicious Circle: Toward Effective Risk Regulation.* Cambridge: Harvard University Press, 1995.
Hahn, Robert W. *Risks, Costs and Lives Saved: Getting Better Results from Regulation.* Oxford: Oxford University Press, 1996.
Kelman, Steven. *What Price Incentives: Economists and the Environment.* Boston: Auburn House, 1981.
Litan, Robert E., and William D. Nordhaus. *Reforming Federal Regulation.* New Haven: Yale University Press, 1983.

Rent Control

Walter Block

New York State legislators defend the War Emergency Tenant Protection Act—also known as rent control—as a way of protecting tenants from war-related housing shortages. The war referred to in the law is not the 2003 war in Iraq, however, or the Vietnam War; it is World War II. That is when rent control started in New York City. Of course, war has very little to do with apartment shortages. On the contrary, the shortage is created by rent control, the supposed solution. Gotham is far from the only city to have embraced rent control. Many others across the United States have succumbed to the blandishments of this legislative "fix."

Rent control, like all other government-mandated price controls, is a law placing a maximum price, or a "rent ceiling," on what landlords may charge tenants. If it is to have any effect, the rent level must be set at a rate below that which would otherwise have prevailed. (An enactment prohibiting apartment rents from exceeding, say, $100,000 per month would have no effect since no one would pay that amount in any case.) But if rents are established at less than their equilibrium levels, the quantity demanded will necessarily exceed the amount supplied, and rent control will lead to a shortage of dwelling spaces. In a competitive market and absent controls on prices, if the amount of a commodity or service demanded is larger than the amount supplied, prices rise to eliminate the shortage (by both bringing forth new supply and by reducing the amount demanded). But controls prevent rents from attaining market-clearing levels and shortages result.

With shortages in the controlled sector, this excess demand spills over onto the noncontrolled sector (typically, new upper-bracket rental units or condominiums). But this noncontrolled segment of the market is likely to be smaller than it would be without controls because property owners fear that controls may one day be placed on them. The high demand in the noncontrolled segment along with the small quantity supplied, both caused by rent control, boost prices in that segment. Paradoxically, then, even though rents may be lower in the controlled sector, they rise greatly for uncontrolled units and may be higher for rental housing as a whole.

As in the case of other price ceilings, rent control causes shortages, diminution in the quality of the product, and queues. But rent control differs from other such schemes. With price controls on gasoline, the waiting lines worked on a first-come-first-served basis. With rent control, because the law places sitting tenants first in the queue, many of them benefit.

The Effects of Rent Control

Economists are virtually unanimous in concluding that rent controls are destructive. In a 1990 poll of 464 economists published in the May 1992 issue of the *American Economic Review,* 93 percent of U.S. respondents agreed, either completely or with provisos, that "a ceiling on rents reduces the quantity and quality of housing available."[1]

1. Richard M. Alson, J. R. Kearl, and Michael B. Vaughan, "Is There a Consensus Among Economists in the 1990's?" *American Economic Review* 82, no. 2 (1992): 203–209.

Similarly, another study reported that more than 95 percent of the Canadian economists polled agreed with the statement.[2] The agreement cuts across the usual political spectrum, ranging all the way from Nobel Prize winners MILTON FRIEDMAN and FRIEDRICH HAYEK on the "right" to their fellow Nobel laureate GUNNAR MYRDAL, an important architect of the Swedish Labor Party's welfare state, on the "left." Myrdal stated, "Rent control has in certain Western countries constituted, maybe, the worst example of poor planning by governments lacking courage and vision."[3] His fellow Swedish economist (and socialist) Assar Lindbeck asserted, "In many cases rent control appears to be the most efficient technique presently known to destroy a city—except for bombing."[4] That cities like New York have clearly not been destroyed by rent control is due to the fact that rent control has been relaxed over the years.[5] Rent stabilization, for example, which took the place of rent control for newer buildings, is less restrictive than the old rent control. Also, the decades-long boom in the New York City housing market is not in rent-controlled or rent-stabilized units, but in condominiums and cooperative housing. But these two forms of housing ownership grew important as a way of getting around rent control.

Economists have shown that rent control diverts new investment, which would otherwise have gone to rental

---

Rent Control:
It's Worse Than Bombing

NEW DELHI—A "romantic conception of socialism" . . . destroyed Vietnam's economy in the years after the Vietnam war, Foreign Minister Nguyen Co Thach said Friday.

Addressing a crowded news conference in the Indian capital, Mr. Thach admitted that controls . . . had artificially encouraged demand and discouraged supply. . . . House rents had . . . been kept low . . . so all the houses in Hanoi had fallen into disrepair, said Mr. Thach.

"The Americans couldn't destroy Hanoi, but we have destroyed our city by very low rents. We realized it was stupid and that we must change policy," he said.

—From a news report in *Journal of Commerce*, quoted in Dan Seligman, "Keeping Up," *Fortune*, February 27, 1989.

---

housing, toward greener pastures—greener in terms of consumer need. They have demonstrated that it leads to housing deterioration, fewer repairs, and less maintenance. For example, Paul Niebanck found that 29 percent of rent-controlled housing in the United States was deteriorated, but only 8 percent of the uncontrolled units were in such a state of disrepair. Joel Brenner and Herbert Franklin cited similar statistics for England and France.

The economic reasons are straightforward. One effect of government oversight is to retard investment in residential rental units. Imagine that you have five million dollars to invest and can place the funds in any industry you wish. In most businesses, governments will place only limited controls and taxes on your enterprise. But if you entrust your money to rental housing, you must pass one additional hurdle: the rent-control authority, with its hearings, red tape, and rent ceilings. Under these conditions is it any wonder that you are less likely to build or purchase rental housing?

This line of reasoning holds not just for you, but for everyone else as well. As a result, the quantity of apartments for rent will be far smaller than otherwise. And not so amazingly, the preceding analysis holds true not only for the case where rent controls are in place, but even where they are only threatened. The mere anticipation of controls is enough to have a chilling effect on such investment. Instead, everything else under the sun in the real estate market has been built: condominiums, office towers, hotels, warehouses, commercial space. Why? Be-

2. Walter Block and Michael A. Walker, "Entropy in the Canadian Economics Profession: Sampling Consensus on the Major Issues," *Canadian Public Policy* 14, no. 2 (1988): 137–150, online at: http://141.164.133.3/faculty/Block/Blockarticles/Entropy.htm.

3. Gunnar Myrdal, "Opening Address to the Council of International Building Research in Copenhagen," *Dagens Nyheter* (Swedish newspaper), August 25, 1965, p. 12; cited in Sven Rydenfelt, "The Rise, Fall and Revival of Swedish Rent Control," in *Rent Control: Myths and Realities*, Walter Block and Edgar Olsen, eds. (Vancouver: The Fraser Institute, 1981), p. 224.

4. Assar Lindbeck, *The Political Economy of the New Left* (New York: Harper and Row, 1972); cited in Sven Rydenfelt, "The Rise, Fall and Revival of Swedish Rent Control," in *Rent Control: Myths and Realities*, Walter Block and Edgar Olsen, eds. (Vancouver: The Fraser Institute, 1981), pp. 213, 230.

5. States New York "public advocate" Mark Green: "the number of rent-controlled apartments fell 18.2% between 1991 and 1993 and the new data we have analyzed shows an even greater decline—30%—from 1993 to 1996. Indeed, the total number of rent-controlled apartments has fallen by 75% from its peak of 285,000 in 1981" (http://www.tenant.net/Alerts/Guide/papers/mgreen1.html). This is due to the fact that when rents reach a certain level ($2,000 per month under certain conditions), apartments leave the controlled sector altogether. Inflation plus a "hot" New York City housing market have pushed many units above this level. See on this http://www.housingnyc.com/html/resources/faq/decontrol.html. Ken Rosenblum, Mike Golden, and Deborah Poole provided the above cites.

cause such investments have never been subject to rent controls, and no one fears that they ever will be. It is no accident that these facilities boast healthy vacancy rates and relatively slowly increasing rental rates, while residential space suffers from a virtual zero vacancy rate in the controlled sector and skyrocketing prices in the uncontrolled sector.

Although many rent-control ordinances specifically exempt new rental units from coverage, investors are too cautious (perhaps too smart) to put their faith in rental housing. In numerous cases housing units supposedly exempt forever from controls were nevertheless brought under the provisions of this law due to some "emergency" or other. New York City's government, for example, has three times broken its promise to exempt new or vacant units from control. So prevalent is this practice of rent-control authorities that a new term has been invented to describe it: "recapture."

Rent control has destroyed entire sections of sound housing in New York's South Bronx and has led to decay and abandonment throughout the entire five boroughs of the city. Although hard statistics on abandonments are not available, William Tucker estimates that about 30,000 New York apartments were abandoned annually from 1972 to 1982, a loss of almost a third of a million units in this eleven-year period. Thanks to rent control, and to potential investors' all-too-rational fear that rent control will become even more stringent, no sensible investor will build rental housing unsubsidized by government.

Effects on Tenants

Existing rental units fare poorly under rent control. Even with the best will in the world, the landlord sometimes cannot afford to pay his escalating fuel, labor, and materials bills, to say nothing of refinancing his mortgage, out of the rent increase he can legally charge. And under rent controls he lacks the best will; the incentive he had under free-market conditions to supply tenant services is severely reduced.

The sitting tenant is "protected" by rent control but, in many cases, receives no real rental bargain because of improper maintenance, poor repairs and painting, and grudging provision of services. The enjoyment he can derive out of his dwelling space ultimately tends to be reduced to a level commensurate with his controlled rent. This may take decades, though, and meanwhile he benefits from rent control.

In fact, many tenants, usually rich or middle-class ones who are politically connected or who were lucky enough to be in the right place at the right time, can gain a lot from rent control. Tenants in some of the nicest neigh-

borhoods in New York City pay a scandalously small fraction of the market price of their apartments. In the early 1980s, for example, former mayor Ed Koch paid $441.49 for an apartment then worth about $1,200.00 per month. Some people in this fortunate position use their apartments like hotel rooms, visiting only a few times per year.

Then there is the "old lady effect." Consider the case of a two-parent, four-child family that has occupied a ten-room rental dwelling. One by one the children grow up, marry, and move elsewhere. The husband dies. Now the lady is left with a gigantic apartment. She uses only two or three of the rooms and, to save on heating and cleaning, closes off the remainder. Without rent control she would move to a smaller accommodation. But rent control makes that option unattractive. Needless to say, these practices further exacerbate the housing crisis. Repeal of rent control would free up thousands of such rooms very quickly, dampening the impetus toward vastly higher rents.

What determines whether or not a tenant benefits from rent control? If the building in which he lives is in a good neighborhood where rents would rise appreciably if rent control were repealed, then the landlord has an incentive to maintain the building against the prospect of that happy day. This incentive is enhanced if there are many decontrolled units in the building (due to "vacancy decontrol" when tenants move out) or privately owned condominiums for which the landlord must provide adequate services. Then the tenant who pays the scandalously low rent may "free ride" on his neighbors. But in the more typical case the quality of housing services tends to reflect rental payments. This, at least, is the situation that will prevail at equilibrium.

If government really had the best interests of tenants at heart and was for some reason determined to employ controls, it would do the very *opposite* of imposing rent restrictions: it would instead control the price of every *other* good and service available, apart from residential suites, in an attempt to divert resources out of all those other opportunities and into this one field. But that, of course, would bring about full-scale socialism, the very system under which the Eastern Europeans suffered so grimly. If the government wanted to help the poor and was for some reason constrained to keep rent controls, it would do better to tightly control rents on luxury unit rentals and to eliminate rent controls on more modest dwellings—the very opposite of the present practice. Then, builders' incentives would be turned around. Instead of erecting luxury dwellings, which are now exempt, they would be led, "as if by an invisible hand," to create housing for the poor and middle classes.

Solutions

The negative consequences of rent legislation have become so massive and perverse that even many of its former supporters have spoken out against it. Instead of urging a quick termination of controls, however, some pundits would only allow landlords to buy tenants out of their controlled dwellings. That they propose such a solution is understandable. Because tenants outnumber landlords and are usually convinced that rent control is in their best interests, they are likely to invest considerable political energy in maintaining rent control. Having landlords "buy off" these opponents of reform, therefore, could be a politically effective way to end rent control.

But making property owners pay to escape a law that has victimized many of them for years is not an effective way to make them confident that rent controls will be absent in the future. The surest way to encourage private investment is to signal investors that housing will be safe from rent control. And the most effective way to do that is to eliminate the possibility of rent control with an amendment to the state constitution that forbids it. Paradoxically, one of the best ways to help tenants is to protect the economic freedom of landlords.

About the Author

Walter Block (wblock@loyno.edu) holds the Harold E. Wirth Eminent Scholar Chair in Economics at Loyola University's Joseph A. Butt, S.J., College of Business Administration.

Further Reading

Arnott, Richard. "Time for Revisionism on Rent Control?" *Journal of Economic Perspectives* 9, no. 1 (1995): 99–120.

Baird, Charles. *Rent Control: The Perennial Folly*. Washington D.C.: Cato Institute, 1980.

Block, Walter. "A Critique of the Legal and Philosophical Case for Rent Control." *Journal of Business Ethics* 40 (2002): 75–90. Online at: http://www.mises.org/etexts/rentcontrol.pdf.

Block, Walter, and Edgar Olsen, eds. *Rent Control: Myths and Realities*. Vancouver: Fraser Institute, 1981.

Brenner, Joel F., and Herbert M. Franklin. *Rent Control in North America and Four European Countries*. Rockville, Md.: Council for International Urban Liaison, 1977.

Grampp, W. S. "Some Effects of Rent Control." *Southern Economic Journal* (April 1950): 425–426.

Johnson, M. Bruce, ed. *Resolving the Housing Crisis: Government Policy, Decontrol, and the Public Interest*. San Francisco: Pacific Institute, 1982.

Niebanck, Paul L. *Rent Control and the Rental Housing Market in New York City*. New York: Housing and Development Administration, Department of Rent and Housing Maintenance, 1968.

Salins, Peter D. *The Ecology of Housing Destruction: Economic Effects of Public Intervention in the Housing Market*. New York: New York University Press, 1980.

Tucker, William. *The Excluded Americans: Homelessness and Housing Policies*. Washington, D.C.: Regnery Gateway, 1990.

Rent Seeking

David R. Henderson

"Rent seeking" is one of the most important insights in the last fifty years of economics and, unfortunately, one of the most inappropriately labeled. Gordon Tullock originated the idea in 1967, and Anne Krueger introduced the label in 1974. The idea is simple but powerful. People are said to seek rents when they try to obtain benefits for themselves through the political arena. They typically do so by getting a subsidy for a good they produce or for being in a particular class of people, by getting a tariff on a good they produce, or by getting a special regulation that hampers their competitors. Elderly people, for example, often seek higher Social Security payments; steel producers often seek restrictions on imports of steel; and licensed electricians and doctors often lobby to keep regulations in place that restrict competition from unlicensed electricians or doctors.

But why do economists use the term "rent"? Unfortunately, there is no good reason. David Ricardo introduced the term "rent" in economics. It means the payment to a factor of production in excess of what is required to keep that factor in its present use. So, for example, if I am paid $150,000 in my current job but I would stay in that job for any salary over $130,000, I am making $20,000 in rent. What is wrong with rent seeking? Absolutely nothing. I would be rent seeking if I asked for a raise. My employer would then be free to decide if my services are worth it. Even though I am seeking rents by asking for a raise, this is not what economists mean by "rent seeking." They use the term to describe people's lobbying of government to give them special privileges. A much better term is "privilege seeking."

It has been known for centuries that people lobby the government for privileges. Tullock's insight was that expenditures on lobbying for privileges are costly and that these expenditures, therefore, dissipate some of the gains to the beneficiaries and cause inefficiency. If, for example, a steel firm spends one million dollars lobbying and advertising for restrictions on steel imports, whatever money it gains by succeeding, presumably more than one million, is not a net gain. From this gain must be subtracted the one-million-dollar cost of seeking the restrictions. Although such an expenditure is rational from the narrow viewpoint of the firm that spends it, it represents a use of real resources to get a transfer from others and is therefore a pure loss to the economy as a whole.

Krueger (1974) independently discovered the idea in her study of poor economies whose governments heavily regulated their people's economic lives. She pointed out that the regulation was so extensive that the government had the power to create "rents" equal to a large percentage of national income. For India in 1964, for example, Krueger estimated that government regulation created rents equal to 7.3 percent of national income; for Turkey in 1968, she estimated that rents from import licenses alone were about 15 percent of Turkey's gross national product. Krueger did not attempt to estimate what percentage of these rents were dissipated in the attempt to get them. Tullock (1993) tentatively maintained that expenditures on rent-seeking in democracies are not very large.

About the Author

David R. Henderson is the editor of this encyclopedia. He is a research fellow with Stanford University's Hoover Institution and an associate professor of economics at the Naval Postgraduate School in Monterey, California. He was formerly a senior economist with President Ronald Reagan's Council of Economic Advisers.

Further Reading

Krueger, Anne O. "The Political Economy of the Rent-Seeking Society." *American Economic Review* 64 (1974): 291–303.
Tullock, Gordon. *Rent Seeking*. Brookfield, Vt.: Edward Elgar, 1993.
———. "The Welfare Costs of Tariffs, Monopolies and Theft." *Western Economic Journal* 5 (1967): 224–232.

Risk and Safety

Aaron Wildavsky
Adam Wildavsky

Since the late 1950s, the regulation of risks to health and safety has taken on ever-greater importance in public policy debates—and actions. In its efforts to protect citizens against hard-to-detect hazards such as industrial chemicals and against obvious hazards in the workplace and elsewhere, Congress has created or increased the authority of the Food and Drug Administration, the Environmental Protection Agency, the Occupational Health and Safety Administration, the Federal Trade Commission's Bureau of Consumer Protection, and other administrative agencies.

Activists in the pursuit of a safer society decry the damage that industrial progress wreaks on unsuspecting citizens. Opponents of the "riskless society," on the other hand, complain that government is unnecessarily proscribing free choice in the pursuit of costly protection that people do not need or want. This article describes some facts about risk and discusses some academic theories about why people on both sides of the risk debate take the positions they do.

The health of human beings is a joint product of their genetic inheritance (advice: choose healthy and long-lived parents), their way of life (the poor person who eats regularly and in moderation, exercises, does not smoke, does not drink to excess, is married, and does not worry overly much is likely to be healthier than the rich person who does the opposite), and their wealth (advice: be rich). Contrary to common opinion, living in a rich, industrialized, technologically advanced country that makes considerable use of industrial chemicals and nuclear power is a lot healthier than living in a poor, nonindustrialized nation that uses little modern technology and few industrial chemicals. That individuals in rich nations are, on average, far healthier, live far longer, and can do more of the things they want to do at corresponding ages than people in poor countries is a rule without exception.

Prosperous also means efficient. The most polluted nations in the world, many times more polluted than democratic and industrial societies, are the former communist countries of Central Europe and the Soviet Union. To produce one unit of output, communist countries used two to four times the amount of energy and material used in capitalist countries. On average, individuals unfortunate enough to live in an inefficient economy die younger and have more serious illnesses than those in Western and industrial democracies. A little richer is a lot safer. As Peter Huber demonstrated in *Regulation* magazine, "For a 45-year-old man working in manufacturing, a 15 percent increase in income has about the same risk-reducing value as eliminating all hazards—every one of them—from his workplace."

Among the many facts that might be observed from Figure 1 and Tables 1A and 1B is that longevity has increased dramatically since 1900. The trend continues if we look further back—boys born in Massachusetts in 1850 could expect to live to an average age of 38.3, girls until 40.5.

Turning to death rates, note the decline by half since 1900 of deaths from all forms of accidents and the spectacular declines in all sorts of diseases. The 88 percent drop in deaths from pneumonia and influenza is par for the course. On the other side of the ledger, cancer deaths continue to rise, though their increase has slowed, and deaths from major cardiovascular diseases remain high.

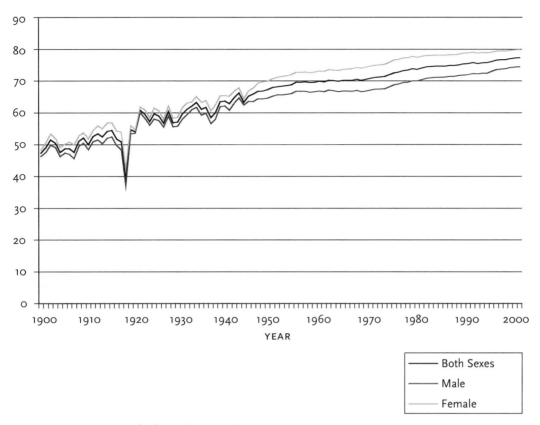

Figure 1 Expectation of Life in the United States, 1900–2000

Source: http://www.stanford.edu/group/virus/uda.

Note: The dip in life expectancy in 1918 was due to the global influenza epidemic ("pandemic"). An estimated 675,000 Americans died of influenza during the pandemic, ten times as many as in the First World War.

Why these discrepancies? Cancer is largely a disease of old age. When people died at roughly half the present life expectancy, they died before they had an opportunity, if one may call it that, to get cancer. Of course, people must die of something. Lacking other information, it is usual to classify deaths as due to heart failure, given that heart stoppage is one of the signs of death.

The most dangerous activities are precisely what we might think they are—sports such as motorcycling and parachuting and occupations such as firefighting and coal mining. However, many of the risks that people have begun to worry about in recent years are far smaller than generally perceived. However low the risk of being killed by lightning (see Table 2), the risk of getting cancer from drinking tap water (chlorine forms chloroform, which is a weak carcinogen) is even lower than that, and the harm—if any—done by pesticides in food is even less. One of the smallest risks that statisticians have measured—dying as a result of cancer caused by the release of plutonium from a deep space probe that loses control during its swing around the Earth to gain velocity and burns up in the atmosphere—measures in at three-millionths of one percent.

In its regulations specifying maximum discharges of potentially harmful substances from factories, the Environmental Protection Agency (EPA) sets a safety threshold of one additional death in a million given a lifetime of exposure. How, we might ask, did the EPA arrive at one in a million? Well, let's face it, no real man tells his girlfriend that she is one in a hundred thousand. The root of the "one in a million" standard, however, can be traced to the Food and Drug Administration's (FDA) efforts to find a number that was essentially equivalent to zero. That this is a stringent standard can be seen by noting that each of us has roughly one chance in a million of expiring every hour of every day of our lives.

Many experts argue that insisting on essentially zero risk is going too far. As John D. Graham, director of the Harvard School of Public Health's Center for Risk Analysis, wrote, "No one seriously suggested that such a stringent risk level should be applied to a hypothetical maximally exposed individual."[1] This mythical "maximally

1. John D. Graham, "Improving Chemical Risk Assessment," *Regulation* 14, no. 4 (1991): pp. 14–18; online at: http://www.cato.org/pubs/regulation/reg14n4-graham.html.

Table 1A Deaths per 100,000 U.S. Population

Cause of Death	2003	2000	1999	1998	1990	1980	1950	1945–49	1920–24	1900–04
All causes	840.4	873.1	877.0	864.7	863.8	883.4	960.1	1,000.6	1,157.4	1,621.6
Typhoid fever	*	*	*	*	*	*	0.1	0.2	7.3	26.7
Communicable diseases of childhood	*	*	*	*	*	*	1.3	2.3	33.8	65.2
Measles	*	*	*	*	*	*	0.3	0.6	7.3	10.0
Scarlet fever	*	*	*	*	*	*	0.2	0.1	4.0	11.8
Whooping cough	*	*	*	*	*	*	0.7	1.0	8.9	10.7
Diphtheria	*	*	*	*	*	*	0.3	0.7	13.7	32.7
Pneumonia and influenza	22.0	23.7	23.4	34.0	32.0	23.3	31.3	41.3	140.3	184.3
Pneumonia	21.9	23.1	22.8	33.4	31.1	22.0	26.9	37.2	105.5	161.5
Influenza	0.1	0.6	0.6	0.6	0.8	1.1	4.4	5.0	34.8	22.8
Tuberculosis	0.3	0.3	0.3	0.4	0.7	0.8	22.5	33.3	96.7	184.7
Cancer	190.7	200.9	201.6	200.3	203.2	182.5	139.8	134.0	86.9	67.7
Diabetes mellitus	25.4	25.2	25.1	24.0	19.2	15.0	16.2	24.1	17.1	12.2
Major cardiovascular diseases	289.7	319.1	327.3	326.8	347.4	434.5	510.8	493.1	369.9	359.5
Diseases of the heart	235.4	258.2	265.9	268.2	289.5	335.2	356.8	325.1	169.8	153.0
Cerebrovascular diseases	54.3	60.9	61.4	58.6	57.9	74.6	104.0	93.8	93.5	106.3
Nephritis and nephrosis	14.6	13.5	13.0	9.7	8.3	7.6	16.4	48.4	81.5	84.3

Table 1B Deaths per 1,000 U.S. Live Births

	2002	2000	1999	1998	1990	1980	1950	1945–49	1920–24	1900
Infant mortality	7.0	6.9	7.1	7.2	9.2	12.6	29.2	33.3	76.7	140.0
Neonatal mortality	4.7	4.6	4.7	4.8	5.8	8.5	20.5	22.9	39.7	n.a.
Fetal mortality	6.4	6.6	6.7	6.7	7.5	9.1	18.4	21.6	n.a.	n.a.
Maternal mortality	n.a.	0.1	0.1	0.1	0.1	0.1	0.8	1.4	6.9	7.5

Sources: National Center for Health Statistics, Leading Causes of Death series (http://www.cdc.gov/nchs/deaths.htm); U.S. Census Bureau, *Statistical Abstract of the United States* (http://www.census.gov/prod/www/statistical-abstract-us.html); National Highway Traffic Safety Administration (http://www-fars.nhtsa.dot.gov/); *Time* magazine, April 13, 1999; reported in Jim Tomlinson, *Comparing 1900 with 2000* (http://facstaff.bloomu.edu/jtomlins/comparing_1900_with_2000.htm); Centers for Disease Control and Prevention, *Morbidity and Mortality Weekly Report*, October 1, 1999 (http://www.cdc.gov/mmwr/preview/mmwrhtml/mm4838a2.htm).

Note: Due to changes in statistical methods, death rates are not always strictly comparable from year to year. In particular, a major change in the classification system took place between 1998 and 1999. The pneumonia rate in 1999, for instance, surely dropped because of the changes in classification, not because of a major medical breakthrough.

n.a. = Data not available

* = Smaller than 0.1, but not necessarily zero. For instance, in 1980 there were ten deaths ascribed to measles out of a U.S. population of about 227,000,000, a rate of .004 per 100,000.

exposed" human being is created by assuming that he or she lives within two hundred meters of the offending industrial plant, lives there for a full seventy years, remains outdoors day and night—or at least all day—and will get cancers at the same level as rodents or other small animals that are bred to be especially susceptible to such cancers and are given doses proportionally thousands of times larger than would be given to any person other than those who receive lifetime occupational exposures on the job.

Another questionable assumption is that cancer causation is a linear process, meaning that there is no safe dose and that damage occurs at a constant rate as exposure in-

Table 2 Annual Fatalities per 100,000 Persons at Risk

Activity/Event	Death Rate
Chicago crack dealer	7,000
Texas death row inmate	5,000
President of the United States—all causes	3,700
Space shuttle astronaut—shuttle accidents only	2,000
President of the United States—assassination only	1,850
U.S. population—all causes (2003)	840
Smoking one pack of cigarettes per day (all causes)	300
Sport parachuting	200
Smoking one pack of cigarettes per day (cancer)	120
Lumberjack	118
Motorcycling	65
Aerial acrobatics (planes)	65[1]
Sky diving	58
Farming	28
Mining	27
Hang gliding	26
Police officer	20
Motor vehicle accidents	15
Firefighter	10
Boating	5
One drink with alcohol per day—cancer and other adverse consequences only	5[2]
Injury at work—all jobs	4
Manufacturing	3
Hunting	3
Fires	1
Bear attacks on hikers	1[1]
1 diet drink per day (saccharin)	1[3]
Rodeo performer	1[1]
4 tbsp. peanut butter per day (aflatoxin)	0.4[3]
Cell phone use while driving	0.15
Floods	0.05
Large meteorite impact	0.04
Lightning	0.02
Chlorinated tap water	0.01[3]
Accidental reentry of a deep space probe	0.00000003

Sources: E. Crouch and R. Wilson, *Risk/Benefit Analysis*, 2d ed. (Cambridge: Harvard University Press, 2001); National Center for Health Statistics, Leading Causes of Death series (http://www.cdc.gov/nchs/deaths.htm); Bureau of Labor Statistics, survey of occupations with minimum 30 fatalities and 45,000 workers in 2002; National Center for Statistics and Analysis, Traffic Safety Facts 2003—Motorcycle (http://www-nrd.nhtsa.dot.gov/pdf/nrd-30/NCSA/TSF2003/809764.pdf); U.S. Fire Administration (http://www.usfa.fema.gov/statistics); FBI 2003 report on Law Enforcement Officers Killed and Assaulted (http://www.fbi.gov/ucr/ucr.htm); S. Levitt and S. Dubner, *Freakonomics*, New York: HarperCollins, 2005), p. 104.

Note: These figures, while the most recent available, are often from different years and are only roughly comparable.

1. Based on a small population and death rate, and so the uncertainty factor is high.

2. One drink with alcohol per day is also associated with a *reduction* in the risk of heart disease by a factor of 200 per 100,000.

3. Assumes a linear dose-response relationship. If a significant threshold or hormesis effect applies, then the risk is likely zero.

creases. This is known as the "linear no-threshold hypothesis." Scientific evidence increasingly shows that there are indeed threshold effects. Such effects were observed five hundred years ago by the physician and scientist Paracelsus, sometimes known as the father of toxicology, who noted: "Dosis facit venenum" (the dose makes the poison). One can readily observe the threshold effect in action. Consuming two gallons of 100-proof liquor in an hour would be enough to kill most of us. If the linear no-threshold hypothesis applied to alcohol, one would expect that if 256 people consumed an ounce of liquor each, then on average one of them would keel over and die. It would be only a slight exaggeration to say that were the EPA to regulate ethyl alcohol—that is, the alcohol in alcoholic beverages—the same way it regulates other chemical compounds, we would each be limited to sixteen-millionths of an ounce per lifetime.

In many cases a hormesis effect may apply as well. Hormesis is the phenomenon whereby a small dose has the opposite effect of a large dose. Many things that are bad for us in large quantities, for example, are good for us in small quantities. Some familiar examples are vitamin A, vitamin C, and aspirin.

If threshold or hormesis effects apply, then the cancers animals develop as a result of being subjected to huge doses in short periods tell us essentially nothing about the reactions of human beings. To go from mouse to man, for instance, requires statistical adjustments for the hugely different weights of the two creatures and for the hugely different doses. Many statistical models fit the data that scientists have gathered on risks. Even though these models vary in their outcomes for risk by thousands of times over, there is no scientific way of choosing among them. Only if the mechanism by which a chemical causes cancer were well known would it be possible to choose a good model. In short, current measures of risk from low-level exposures to industrial technology have no validity whatsoever. This explains why health rates keep getting better while governments estimate that safety keeps getting worse.

Why are some people frightened of certain risks while others are not? Surveys of risk perception show that knowledge of the known hazards of a technology does not determine whether or to what degree an individual thinks a given technology is safe or dangerous. This holds true not only for laymen, but also for experts in risk assessment. Thus, the most powerful factors related to how people perceive risk apparently are "trust in institutions" and "self-rated liberal and conservative identification." In other words, these findings suggest strongly that people use a framework involving their opinion of the validity of institutions in order to interpret riskiness.

According to one cultural theory, people choose what to fear as a way to defend their way of life. The theory hypothesizes that adherents of a hierarchical culture will approve of technology, provided it is certified as safe by their experts. Competitive individualists will view risk as opportunity and hence will be optimistic about technology. Egalitarians will view technology as part of the apparatus by which corporate capitalism maintains inequalities that harm society and the natural environment.

One study sought to test this theory by comparing how people rate the risks of technology compared with risks from social deviance (departures, such as criminal behavior, from widely approved norms), war, and economic decline. The results are that egalitarians fear technology immensely and think that social deviance is much less dangerous. Hierarchists, by contrast, think technology is basically good if their experts say so but that social deviance leads to disaster. And individualists think that risk takers do a lot of good for society and that if deviants don't bother them, they won't bother deviants; but they fear war greatly because it stops trade and leads to conscription. Thus, there is no such thing as a risk-averse or risk-taking personality. People who either take or avoid all risks are probably certifiably insane; neither would last long. Think of a protester against, say, nuclear power. He is evidently averse to risks posed by nuclear power, but he also throws his body on the line (i.e., takes risks in opposing it).

Other important literature pursues risk perception through what is known as cognitive psychology. Featuring preeminently the pathbreaking work of Daniel Kahneman and Amos Tversky, using mainly small-group experiments in which individuals are given tasks involving gambling, this work demonstrates that most of us are poor judges of probability. More important, perhaps, is the population's general conservatism: a great many people care more about avoiding loss than they do about making gains. Therefore, they will go to considerable lengths to avoid losses, even in the face of high probabilities of making considerable gains.

In extreme form this conservatism expresses itself as a modern variation of Pascal's wager known as the "precautionary principle." As enacted into law by the government of the city of San Francisco in 2003, it states: "Where threats of serious or irreversible damage to people or nature exist, lack of full scientific certainty about cause and effect shall not be viewed as sufficient reason for the City to postpone measures to prevent the degradation of the environment or protect the health of its citizens."

The precautionary principle is a marvelous piece of rhetoric. It places the speaker on the side of the citizen—I am acting for your health—and portrays the opponents of the contemplated ban or regulation as indifferent or hostile to the public's health. The rhetoric works in part because it assumes what actually should be proved, namely that the health effects of the regulation will be superior to the alternative. This comparison is made possible in the only possible way—by assuming that there are no health detriments from the proposed regulation.

If one is concerned primarily with health, then the question for any regulation ought to be whether the health gains associated will outweigh the health costs. This is precisely the calculation the precautionary principle says we need not make. Likewise there is no moral norm stating that health must be our only value or even our dominant value. Emphasizing a single value, to which all others must be subordinated, is a sign of fanaticism. How much is a marginal gain in health worth compared with losses in other values such as freedom, justice, and excellence? The answer will vary by individual. A Patrick Henry, for instance, will not thank you for attempts to protect life at the expense of liberty.

With regard to the consequences of technological risk, there are two major strategies for improving safety: anticipation versus resilience. The risk-averse strategy seeks to anticipate and thereby prevent harm from occurring. In order to make a strategy of anticipation effective, it is necessary to know the quality of the adverse consequence expected, its probability, and the existence of effective remedies. The knowledge requirements and organizational capacities required to make anticipation an effective strategy—to know what will happen, when, and how to prevent it without making things worse—are large, often impossibly so.

A strategy of resilience, on the other hand, requires reliance on experience with adverse consequences once they occur in order to develop a capacity to learn from the harm and bounce back. Resilience, therefore, requires the accumulation of large amounts of generalizable resources—such as organizational capacity, knowledge, wealth, energy, and communication—that can be used to craft solutions to problems that the people involved did not know would occur. Thus, a strategy of resilience requires much less predictive capacity but much more growth, not only in wealth, but also in knowledge. Hence it is not surprising that systems such as capitalism, based on incessant and decentralized trial and error, accumulate the most resources. Strong evidence from around the world demonstrates that such societies are richer and produce healthier people and a more vibrant natural environment.

About the Authors

Aaron Wildavsky, who died in 1993, was the Class of 1940 Professor of Political Science and Public Policy at the University of California at Berkeley. He wrote forty-five books, including *But Is It True? A Citizen's Guide to Environmental Health and Safety Issues, Cultural Theory* (with Richard Ellis and Michael Thompson), and *Searching for Safety*. Adam Wildavsky is a senior software engineer with Google, Inc.

Further Reading

Crouch, Edmund, and Richard Wilson. *Risk/Benefit Analysis.* 2d ed. Cambridge: Harvard University Press, 2001.

Dake, Karl, and Aaron Wildavsky. "Theories of Risk Perception: Who Fears What and Why?" *Daedalus* 119, no. 4 (1990): 41–61.

Dietz, Thomas, and Robert Rycroft. *The Risk Professionals.* New York: Russell Sage Foundation, 1987.

Douglas, Mary, and Aaron Wildavsky. *Risk and Culture.* Berkeley: University of California Press, 1982.

Kahneman, Daniel, Paul Slovic, and Amos Tversky, eds. *Judgment Under Uncertainty: Heuristics and Biases.* Cambridge: Cambridge University Press, 1982.

Kahneman, Daniel, and Amos Tversky. "Variants of Uncertainty." *Cognition* 11, no. 2 (1982): 143–157.

Keeney, Ralph L. "Mortality Risks Induced by Economic Expenditures." *Risk Analysis* 10, no. 1 (1990): 147–159.

Moronwe, Joseph G., and Edward J. Woodhouse. *Averting Catastrophe.* Berkeley: University of California Press, 1986.

Rand, Ayn, and Peter Schwartz. *Return of the Primitive: The Anti-industrial Revolution.* New York: Penguin Putnam, 1999.

Schwarz, Michael, and Michael Thompson. *Divided We Stand: Redefining Politics, Technology and Social Choice.* Philadelphia: University of Pennsylvania Press, 1990.

Slovic, Paul. "Informing and Educating the Public About Risk." *Risk Analysis* 6, no. 4 (1986): 407.

Wildavsky, Aaron. *But Is It True? A Citizen's Guide to Environmental Health and Safety Issues.* Cambridge: Harvard University Press, 1995. Published posthumously.

———. *Searching for Safety.* New Brunswick, N.J.: Transaction Press, 1988.

Sanctions

Kimberly Ann Elliott
Gary Clyde Hufbauer
Barbara Oegg

Throughout most of modern history, economic sanctions have preceded or accompanied war, often in the form of a naval blockade intended to weaken the enemy. Only when the horrors of World War I prompted President Woodrow Wilson to call for an alternative to armed conflict were economic sanctions seriously considered. (Wilson claimed that, by themselves, sanctions could be a "deadly force" and a very effective diplomatic tool.) Sanctions were subsequently incorporated as a tool of enforcement in each of the two collective security systems established in this century—the League of Nations between the two world wars and the United Nations after World War II. Following the collapse of the Soviet Union and the end of the cold war, the U.N. Security Council frequently authorized sanctions to quell civil wars and national strife, especially in Africa and Yugoslavia. However, the highest-profile U.N. sanctions were those against Iraq (1990–2003) preceding and following the first Gulf War (1991). In addition to U.N. sanctions, major powers (foremost the United States) continue to deploy unilateral economic sanctions. Since 1990, "targeted sanctions"—aimed at political leaders, drug lords, and terrorists—frequently have been used in an attempt to avoid the humanitarian fallout resulting from broad-brush sanctions.

Purposes of Economic Sanctions

The term "economic sanctions" encompasses the deliberate, government-inspired withdrawal, or threat of withdrawal, of customary trade or financial relations. ("Customary" refers to the levels of trade or financial activity that would probably have occurred in the absence of sanctions.) In this article, we discuss the use of economic sanctions to achieve *political* goals; in other words, we exclude cases of economic sanctions used to achieve *commercial* goals, such as the withdrawal of tariff protection.

The motives behind the use of sanctions parallel the three basic purposes of national criminal law: to punish, to deter, and to rehabilitate.

Individual countries, as well as various ad hoc coalitions, frequently impose sanctions to achieve a wide variety of foreign policy goals, even when the probability of forcing a change in the target country's policy is small. In addition to demonstrating resolve and signaling displeasure to the immediate transgressor, politicians may also want to posture for their domestic constituencies. It is quite clear, for example, that U.S., European, and British Commonwealth sanctions against South Africa (1985–1991), as well as U.S., European, and Japanese sanctions against Burma (1988–), were designed principally to assuage domestic constituencies, to make moral and historical statements, and to send a warning to future offenders of the international order. The effect on the specific target country was almost secondary. Sanctions played only a moderate role in ending South Africa's apartheid. Economic and political conditions inside South Africa were the most important factors influencing the outcome. Sanctions did not cause the National Party to abandon apartheid, but by adding to the already mounting costs of maintaining apartheid they accelerated the inevitable.

World leaders often decide that the obvious alternatives to economic sanctions are unsatisfactory; military action would be too massive, and diplomatic protest too meager. Sanctions can provide a satisfying theatrical display, yet avoid the high costs of war. This is not to say that sanctions are costless, just that they are often less costly than the alternatives.

Prior to the 1990s, institutionally endorsed sanctions were rare. The League of Nations imposed or threatened to impose economic sanctions only four times in the 1920s and 1930s, twice successfully. But the league faded from history when its ineffectual response failed to deter Benito Mussolini's conquest of Ethiopia in 1935 and 1936. Freed from the restraints of superpower rivalry, the United Nations played a much bigger role in international affairs in the 1990s. The new activism of the United Nations is reflected in the fact that the Security Council imposed mandatory sanctions thirteen times in response to instances of civil strife, regional aggression, or grave violations of human rights—compared with just twice (against South Africa and Rhodesia) in previous decades.[1] In many instances, however, the new threats were not of paramount concern for the major powers, and only weakly enforced arms embargoes were imposed. As a result, U.N. sanctions enjoyed limited success. With the exception of those imposed against Libya in response to Pan Am 103 terrorist attacks and, possibly, those imposed against Yugoslavia over the civil war in Bosnia, U.N. sanctions have failed to achieve their objectives. In fact, the decade-long comprehensive sanctions regime against Iraq generated considerable political backlash.

Types of Sanctions

A "sender" country tries to inflict costs on its target in two main ways: (1) with trade sanctions that limit the target country's exports or restrict its imports, and (2) with financial sanctions that impede finance (including reducing aid). Governments that impose limits on target countries' exports intend to reduce its foreign sales and deprive it of foreign exchange. Governments impose limits on their own exports to deny critical goods to the target country. If the sender country exports a large percentage of world output, this may also cause the target to pay higher prices for substitute imports, but only if the sender country also reduces its overall output. When governments impose financial sanctions by interrupting commercial finance or by

1. Since 1990, the U.N. Security Council has mandated sanctions against Iraq (1990), the former Yugoslavia (1991), Liberia (1992), Libya (1992), Somalia (1992), Angola (1993), Haiti (1993), Rwanda (1994), Sudan (1996), Sierra Leone (1997), Federal Republic of Yugoslavia/Kosovo (1998), Afghanistan (1999), and Ethiopia and Eritrea (2000).

slashing government loans to the target country's government, they intend to cause the target country to pay higher interest rates and to scare away alternative creditors. When a poor country is the target, the government imposing the sanction can use the subsidy component of official financing or other development assistance to gain further leverage.

Total embargoes are rare. Most trade sanctions are selective, affecting only one or a few goods. Thus, the economy-wide impact of the sanction may be quite limited. Because sanctions are often unilateral, the trade may be only diverted rather than cut off. Whether import prices paid by (or export prices received by) the target country increase (or decrease) after the sanctions are applied depends on the market in question. If there are many alternative markets and suppliers, the effects on prices may be very modest, and the economic impact of the sanctions will be negligible.

For example, Australia cut off shipments of uranium to France from 1983 to 1986 because of France's refusal to halt testing of nuclear weapons in the South Pacific. In 1984, however, the price of uranium oxide dropped nearly 50 percent. France was able to replace the lost supply, and at a cost lower than its contract price with the Australian mine. Because Australia was unable to find alternative buyers for all the uranium intended for France, the Australian government ultimately paid Queensland Mines $26 million in 1985 and 1986 for uranium it had contracted to sell to France.

Financial sanctions, in contrast, are usually more difficult to evade. Because sanctions are typically intended to foster or exacerbate political or economic instability, alternative financing may be hard to find and is likely to carry a higher interest rate. Private banks and investors are easily scared off by the prospect that the target country will face a credit squeeze in the future. Moreover, many sanctions involve the suspension or termination of government subsidies to poor countries—large grants of money or concessionary loans from one government to another—which may be irreplaceable.

Another important difference between trade sanctions and financial sanctions lies in the parties that are hurt by each. The pain from trade sanctions, especially export controls, usually is diffused throughout the target country's population. Indeed, political elites in the target country may *benefit* from trade sanctions by controlling lucrative black markets. Financial sanctions, on the other hand, are more likely to hit the pet projects or personal pockets of government officials who shape local policy. On the sender's side of the equation, an interruption of official aid or credit is unlikely to create the same political backlash

from domestic business firms and allies abroad as an interruption of private trade. Finally, financial sanctions, especially those involving trade finance, may interrupt trade even without the imposition of explicit trade sanctions. In practice, however, financial and trade sanctions are usually used in some combination with one another.

The ultimate form of financial and trade control is a freeze of the target country's foreign assets, such as bank accounts held in the sender country. In addition to imposing a cost on the target country, a key goal of an assets freeze is to deny an invading country the full fruits of its aggression. In the 1990 Middle East crisis, the U.S. government and its allies froze Kuwait's assets to prevent Saddam Hussein from plundering them.

Such measures were also used against Japan just before and during World War II. Increasingly concerned with Japanese military aggression in Southeast Asia, the United States gradually tightened economic sanctions imposed against Japan from July 1940 to July 1941. Initial licensing requirements for the export of arms, ammunition, and aviation fuel were followed by a total ban on exports of iron and steel scrap a few months later, and finally, in July 1941, by a freezing of Japanese assets and a tightening of the licensing requirements that de facto ended all trade with Japan, including oil exports. Despite considerable costs to its economy, Japan did not abandon its policy of expansionism but rather intensified the war efforts in the Pacific and in the end attacked Pearl Harbor in December 1941. While economic sanctions did not deter Japan, they denied vital resources to a potential enemy.

Effectiveness of Sanctions

Senders usually have multiple goals and targets in mind when they impose sanctions, and simple punishment is rarely at the top of the list. Judging the effectiveness of sanctions requires sorting out the various goals sought, analyzing whether the type and scope of the chosen sanction were appropriate to the occasion, and determining the economic and political impacts on the target country.

If governments that impose sanctions embrace contradictory goals, sanctions will usually be weak and, ultimately, ineffective. In such cases, the country or group imposing sanctions will not exert much influence on the target country. Thus, it may be the policy—not the instrument (sanctions)—that fails. For example, the Reagan and Bush administrations began economic sanctions against Panama in 1987 in an effort to destabilize the Noriega regime. But because they wanted to avoid destroying their political allies in the Panamanian business and financial sectors, they imposed sanctions incrementally and then gradually weakened them with exemptions. In the end, the sanctions proved inadequate, and the U.S. military invaded Panama and took Noriega by force.

In many cases, sanctions are imposed primarily for "signaling" purposes—for the benefit of allies, other third parties, or a domestic audience. The intended signal is not always received. Instead, it may be overwhelmed by a cacophony of protests from injured domestic parties, which may force a premature reversal of the policy. For example, American farmers howled with outrage when President Jimmy Carter embargoed grain sales to the Soviet Union following the Soviet invasion of Afghanistan. The protests, buttressed by candidate Ronald Reagan's promise to lift the embargo if elected (which he did within three months of his inauguration) undermined the seriousness of intent that Carter wanted to convey. Efforts to extend sanctions extraterritorially may produce similar effects abroad. The extraterritorial features of the U.S. Helms-Burton sanctions against Cuba provoked enormous resentment in Europe and Canada, and these features were effectively waived by Presidents Bill Clinton and George W. Bush. Sanctions imposed for symbolic purposes must be carefully crafted if they are to convey the intended signal.

Sanctions intended to change the government of a target country are even more difficult to design. In such cases, sanctions must be imposed as quickly and comprehensively as possible. A strategy of "turning the screws" gives the target leaders time to adjust by finding alternative suppliers or markets, by building new alliances, and by mobilizing domestic opinion in support of its policies. Great Britain, followed by the United Nations, adopted a slow and deliberate strategy in response to Ian Smith's "unilateral declaration of independence" in Rhodesia in 1965. Aided by hesitation and delays, the Smith regime was able to use import substitution, smuggling, and other circumvention techniques to fend off black majority rule for more than a decade.

Our assessment of nearly two hundred observations of economic sanctions imposed since World War I indicates that economic sanctions tend to be most effective at modifying the target country's behavior under the following conditions:

1. The goal is relatively modest: winning the release of a political prisoner versus overthrowing the regime of Saddam Hussein, for example. Less ambitious goals may be achieved with more modest sanctions; this also lessens the importance of multilateral cooperation, which is often difficult to obtain. Finally, if the stakes are small, there is less chance that a rival power will step in with offsetting assistance.

2. The target is much smaller than the country imposing

sanctions, economically weak, and politically unstable. The average sender's economy in the 198 episodes studied was 245 times as large as the economy of the average target. (Moreover, this calculation excludes 21 instances in which a major power targeted a microstate, and the GDP ratio exceeded 2000.)

3. The sanctions are imposed quickly and decisively to maximize impact. The average cost to the target as a percentage of GNP in successful cases was 2.6 percent and in failures was only 1.5 percent (excluding Iraq), while successful sanctions lasted an average of only three years, versus eight years for failures.

4. The sender avoids high economic or political costs to itself.

It is obvious from these prescriptions that effective sanctions, in the sense of coercing a change in target country policy, are achieved infrequently. Economic sanctions were relatively effective tools of foreign policy in the first two decades after World War II: they achieved their stated goals in nearly half the cases (twenty-seven successes out of sixty-one cases). The evolution of the world economy, however, has narrowed the circumstances in which unilateral economic leverage can be effectively applied, and only one in five unilateral U.S. sanctions after 1970 scored as a success (ten successes out of fifty-two cases). For multilateral sanctions, increasing economic interdependence acts as a double-edged sword. It increases the latent power of economic sanctions because countries are more dependent on international trade and financial flows. But it also means wider sources of supply and greater access to markets and, thus, the possibility that a greater number of neutral countries can undermine the economic impact of a sanctions effort should they choose to do so. Since 1970, over a third of multilateral sanctions in which the United States participated scored as a success (twenty successes out of fifty-three cases).

Iraq, the United Nations, and the Future of Sanctions

During most of the 1990s, the Iraqi sanctions regime, the most comprehensive U.N. sanctions to date, dominated the debate about the effectiveness of economic sanctions, their humanitarian impact, and the morality of the "deadly weapon." Economic sanctions, enforcement of no-fly zones, and occasional use of military force provided leverage for U.N. weapons inspectors to uncover and have destroyed Iraq's stockpile of weapons of mass destruction (WMD) and related facilities. While the U.S. goal of regime change was achieved only with military force, U.N. inspections and the denial of oil revenues, despite widespread smuggling and manipulation of the oil-for-food program, clearly helped in containing Iraq's WMD capabilities. However, this success came at a high price in terms of humanitarian effects inside Iraq.[2] In fact, the decade-long sanctions regime generated considerable domestic political backlash in most Western nations as well as Arab countries and illustrates how concerns about humanitarian and third-country effects of sanctions can undermine the political unity required for the effective implementation of multilateral sanctions. The effectiveness of a sanctions regime depends partly on how it addresses humanitarian issues. Although virtually all sanctions regimes launched during the 1990s allowed trade in humanitarian goods, the "blunt weapon" of an almost-comprehensive embargo inevitably hurt those at the bottom of the economic heap. In response to these concerns, practitioners and scholars alike have sought ways to fine-tune sanctions to concentrate their force against those in power.

Targeted sanctions such as arms embargoes, travel bans, and asset freezes are intended to focus their impact on leaders, political elites, and segments of society believed to be responsible for the objectionable behavior. The goal is to fashion a more useful foreign policy tool while inflicting smaller economic costs on civilian populations, third states, and sender countries.

In addition, many issues formerly considered internal affairs of the state became legitimate concerns of the international community in the post–Cold War era. U.N. sanctions against Somalia, Liberia, Rwanda, Sierra Leone, and the Federal Republic of Yugoslavia were all linked to instances of civil war and internal strife. As a consequence, U.N. sanctions initiated in the 1990s were frequently targeted against internal actors. In the case of U.S. and U.N. sanctions against Haiti, not only were imports of oil and arms prohibited, but also sanctions were aimed directly at the members of the military junta and their families. Overseas bank accounts and other financial assets of people involved in the coup were frozen, private flights to and from Haiti were banned, and visas of military junta leaders and their families were revoked. U.N. Security Council actions in Angola focus on one particular internal actor— UNITA. When UNITA renounced U.N.-supervised elections and resumed military activities in 1993, the United

Nations placed an arms and oil embargo on UNITA. The initial embargo was followed by a travel ban for senior UNITA officials and their families in 1997 and, finally, a ban on all financial transactions with UNITA, a mandated freeze of UNITA financial assets, and an embargo on imports of diamonds not certified by the Angolan government.

Targeted sanctions operate at a level of intervention and discrimination in the internal affairs of states that was unknown in previous decades. No longer is the targeted state seen as a single-purpose unitary actor. Instead, it is seen as a geographic location of discordant groups. Setting aside the question of the effectiveness of targeted sanctions in reaching their stated goals, these measures also depart from the traditional sanctions philosophy that civilian pain leads to political change. Because targeted sanctions focus on certain groups and individuals within the targeted country, they assume that the leaders do not represent the population and can actually be separated from them.

Nevertheless, targeted U.N. sanctions enjoyed only limited success. The U.N. system lacks the formal mechanisms, the technical resources, and the financial capacity to effectively administer and monitor sanctions. U.N. sanctions committees, created to monitor the implementation, are established on an ad hoc basis for each sanctions episode. Sanctions committees vary significantly in extent and effectiveness, depending both on the extent of the cohesion (or division) within the Security Council and on the political and geographic circumstances of the target country. The "Sanctions Assistance Missions" (SAMs) deployed along the borders of Yugoslavia illustrate how U.N. member states can cooperate to better implement comprehensive sanctions. Despite the best efforts, however, Yugoslavia's geography made evasion relatively easy.

Similarly, the effectiveness of U.N. arms embargoes in ending conflicts remains elusive. U.N. resolutions are often deliberately vague, leaving wide room for diverging interpretations by member states. Weak enforcement, poor monitoring, and dire conditions in bordering countries all work to undermine arms embargoes. Trafficking in small arms is highly profitable, and the chances of being caught are relatively small. The money is especially good when the targeted group controls valuable natural resources—exemplified by UNITA's control over Angolan diamonds—that are used to finance weapons purchases.

The 1990s saw the emergence of the European Union as an important sender of economic sanctions. The European Union (often joined by the United States) has suspended aid and restricted trade in response to threats to international security and egregious human rights violations, especially in Africa and Yugoslavia. In the process,

2. In recent years, numerous studies have been conducted on the humanitarian impact of economic sanctions on Iraqi civilians. The United Nations Children's Fund (UNICEF), the World Food Program (WFP), the Food and Agricultural Organization (FAO), and several research institutions have issued reports drawing attention to the suffering of ordinary Iraqis, in particular of children.

the European Union has emerged as a political actor with an identity distinct from its member states. However, most EU sanctions involve only minor aid cutoffs and have not been particularly effective.

About the Authors
Kimberly Ann Elliott is a senior fellow, Gary Clyde Hufbauer is the Reginald Jones Senior Fellow, and Barbara Oegg was a research associate with the Institute for International Economics in Washington, D.C.

Further Reading
Baldwin, David A. *Economic Statecraft*. Princeton: Princeton University Press, 1985.

Carter, Barry E. *International Economic Sanctions: Improving the Haphazard U.S. Legal Regime*. New York: Cambridge University Press, 1988.

Cortright, David, and George A. Lopez. *The Sanctions Decade: Assessing UN Strategies in the 1990s*. Boulder, Colo.: Lynne Rienner, 2000.

———, eds. *Smart Sanctions: Targeting Economic Statecraft*. Lanham, Md.: Rowman and Littlefield, 2002.

Doxey, Margaret P. *International Sanctions in Contemporary Perspective*. New York: St. Martin's Press, 1987.

Hufbauer, Gary Clyde, Jeffrey J. Schott, and Kimberly Ann Elliott. *Economic Sanctions Reconsidered*. Rev. ed. 2 vols. Washington, D.C.: Institute for International Economics, 1990.

Knorr, Klaus. *The Power of Nations: The Political Economy of International Relations*. New York:, Basic Books, 1975.

Lenway, Stefanie Ann. "Between War and Commerce: Economic Sanctions as a Tool of Statecraft." *International Organization* 42, no. 2 (1988): 397–426.

Malloy, Michael P. *Economic Sanctions and U.S. Trade*. Boston: Little, Brown, 1990.

O'Sullivan, Meghan. *Shrewd Sanctions: Statecraft and State Sponsors of Terrorism*. Washington, D.C.: Brookings Institution Press, 2003.

Weiss, Thomas, ed. *Political Gain and Civilian Pain: Humanitarian Impacts of Economic Sanctions*. Lanham, Md.: Rowman and Littlefield, 1997.

Saving

Laurence J. Kotlikoff

Saving means different things to different people. To some, it means putting money in the bank. To others, it means buying stocks or contributing to a pension plan. But to economists, saving means only one thing—consuming less out of a given amount of resources in the present in order to consume more in the future. Saving, therefore, is the decision to defer consumption and to store this deferred consumption in some form of asset.

Saving is often confused with investing, but they are not the same. Although most people think of purchases of stocks and bonds as investments, economists use the term "investment" to mean additions to the real stock of capital: plants, factories, equipment, and so on.

Between 1990 and 2005, the annual rate of U.S. net national saving (net national income less private consumption expenditures less government consumption expenditures, all divided by net national income) averaged only 5.3 percent. In contrast, the nation's saving rate was 7.6 percent in the 1980s, 10.3 percent in the 1970s, and 13.0 percent in the 1960s.

The 2004 rate of U.S. saving of just 2.2 percent is remarkably low, not only by U.S. standards, but also by international standards. Differences in how the statisticians in different countries define income and consumption make comparisons across nations difficult. But, corrected as well as possible for such data problems, America's saving rate is significantly lower than that of other industrialized countries. This explains, in large part, why the United States has run a very large current account deficit in recent years. The U.S. current account deficit measures the amount that foreigners invest in the United States net of what Americans invest abroad. Because Americans are not saving very much, they do not have much to invest in the United States, let alone abroad. Foreigners are making up the difference by investing heavily in the United States.

Why do countries save at different rates? Economists do not know all the answers. Some of the factors that undoubtedly affect the amount people save are culture, differences in saving motives, economic growth, demographics, how many people in the economy are in the labor force, the insurability of risks, and economic policy. Each of these factors can influence saving at a point in time and produce changes in saving over time.

Motives for Saving
The famous life-cycle model of Nobel laureate Franco Modigliani asserts that people save—accumulate assets—to finance their retirement, and they dissave—spend their assets—during retirement. The more young savers there are relative to old dissavers, the greater will be a nation's saving rate. Most economists believed for decades that this life-cycle model provided the main explanation of U.S. saving. But in the early 1980s, Lawrence H. Summers of Harvard and I showed that saving for retirement explains less than half of total U.S. wealth. Most U.S. wealth accumulation is saving that is ultimately bequeathed or given to younger generations. The motive for bequests and gifts

from older to younger Americans is unclear. A very large component of the bequests may be unplanned, simply reflecting the fact that many people do not spend all their savings before they die. In this case, people save to consume, not bequeath, but end up bequeathing nonetheless.

In recent years, a much larger fraction of the retirement savings of the American elderly has been annuitized. That is, the savings take the form of company pensions or Social Security that pay regular checks until death, with no payments after the person dies. Having your retirement finances come in the form of an annuity eliminates the risk of living longer than your money lasts. One possible result of the increased annuitization of retirement assets may be that people, especially those who have already retired, have less incentive to save more in case they "live too long."

The precautionary motive—that is, the motive to save in order to be prepared for various future risks—is one of the key reasons people save. Besides the risk of living longer than expected, people save against more mundane risks, such as losing their job or incurring large uninsured medical expenses. Computer simulation studies show that the amount of precautionary saving can be very sensitive to the availability of insurance against these and other kinds of risks. For example, the decision not to insure low-risk but high-cost health expenditures such as nursing-home care can lead to a 10 percent increase in national saving.

Another issue related to motives and preferences for saving is the role of the rich in generating aggregate saving. Do rich Americans account for most of U.S. saving? Not really. Relative to their incomes, some of the rich save a lot, and some dissave. So, too, for the poor. There is considerable mobility of wealth in the United States, at least over long periods of time (see HUMAN CAPITAL). The fact that the ranks of the rich are continually changing suggests that some of those who are initially rich dissave and dissipate their wealth, while others who are not initially rich save considerable sums and become rich. Former heavyweight champion Michael Tyson, for example, grossed an estimated $400 million during the heyday of his boxing career but ended up declaring bankruptcy. Sam Walton, who started Wal-Mart, started life in poverty and ended as one of the richest people in the world.

Economic Growth and Demographic Change

A country's saving rate and its economic growth are closely connected. This follows from the life-cycle model. If there are more young people around than old people because the population is growing, there will be more workers saving for their retirement than there will be retirees who are dissaving, that is, spending down their assets. This will leave overall net saving positive. The higher the population growth, other things equal, the higher will be the saving rate. The same is true of technical change. Suppose there are the same number of young people around as old people, but the young earn more than did the old because of technological change. Then the young will save more than the old dissave, which, again, will imply a positive saving rate.

In an economy not experiencing growth in technology or population, one would expect, at least in the long run, saving to be zero, with the exception of the saving needed to replace depreciating capital. If there is no engine for growth, in the long run the saving the young do for retirement, to leave bequests, or for any other reason would exactly offset the dissaving of retirees, leaving the economy's total saving at zero. The economy would have positive assets (claims to capital) but would experience no increase or decrease in the level of these assets over time.

That an economy's overall long-run saving rate is zero does not mean that no one saves or dissaves. Rather, it means that the positive savings of those accumulating assets exactly balance the negative savings of those decumulating assets. For growing economies, long-run saving is likely to be positive to ensure that the stock of capital assets keeps pace with the number and productivity of workers.

Recent years have seen a large increase in the number of workers and in productivity per worker. The increase in the number of workers is due to baby boomers entering the workforce. The increase in productivity is due to the fact that baby boomers are in their peak years of productivity, and also due to a growing capital stock and to technological improvement, especially in information and communications technology. The fact that these factors did not suffice to raise U.S. saving rates means that other forces, to be discussed below, reduced national saving.

Labor-Supply Decisions

National saving is the difference between national income and national consumption. Labor income represents about three-quarters of national income. So changes in labor income, if not accompanied by equivalent changes in consumption, can greatly affect an economy's saving rate. Take, for example, the recent remarkable increase in U.S. female labor force participation. In 1975 half of the women age twenty-five to forty-four participated in the labor force; by 1988 more than two-thirds were in the labor force. This increase in the female labor supply is a major reason, if not the main reason, for the rise in U.S. per capita income since 1975.

If the additional net-of-tax income these women earned had all been saved, the U.S. saving rate after 1980 would have exceeded 20 percent. Because much of the increase in labor supply was by women age eighteen to thirty-five, particularly married women, one would expect them to have saved some portion of that income for their old age. Assuming this did occur, we need to look elsewhere to understand the puzzle of why U.S. saving fell.

Adding to the puzzle is the ongoing increase in the expected length of retirement. More and more Americans, particularly men, are retiring in their late fifties and early sixties. At the same time, life expectancies continue to rise. Today's thirty-year-old male can expect to live to age seventy-six, 5.3 years longer than the typical thirty-year-old could expect in 1960. If he retires at age fifty-five, today's thirty-year-old will spend almost half of his remaining life in retirement. Economic models of saving suggest that aggregate saving should depend strongly and positively on the length of retirement. Thus, with the retirement age decreasing and life expectancy increasing, economists would expect people to save a lot more—not a lot less.

Economic Policy

Government policy also can have powerful effects on a nation's saving. To begin with, governments are themselves large consumers of goods and services. In the United States, federal, state, and local governments account for more than one-fifth of all national consumption. More government consumption spending does not, however, necessarily imply less national saving. If the private sector responds to a one-dollar increase in government consumption by reducing its own consumption by one dollar, aggregate saving remains unchanged.

The private sector's consumption response depends critically on who pays for the government's consumption and how the government extracts these payments. If the government assigns most of the tax burden to future generations by borrowing in the present and repaying principal plus interest on the borrowing in the future, current generations will have little reason, other than concern for their offspring, to reduce their consumption expenditures.

If current generations are forced to pay for the government's spending, the size of the private-sector consumption response will vary according to which generation foots the bill. The older the people who are taxed, the larger will be the reduction in consumption. The reason is that older people, being closer to the ends of their lives, consume a higher share of their remaining lifetime resources than do younger ones. Thus, taxing retirees, say, instead of forty-year-old workers, will reduce private-sector consumption and increase national saving.

Finally, different taxes have different incentive effects. For example, the government might raise its funds with taxes on capital rather than taxes on labor income. By lowering the

after-tax return to saving, taxes on capital income discourage saving for future consumption and thus reduce saving.

Explaining the Decline in U.S. Saving

What explains the recent decline in U.S. saving? One cause that can quickly be dismissed is increased government consumption. In the 1960s, when the national saving rate was 13.0, the ratio of government consumption to national income was 18.6 percent. Since the 1990s, the government's consumption rate has been 17.5 percent but the saving rate has averaged only 5.5 percent.

Could disincentives to save be responsible for the decline in U.S. saving? Not likely. Marginal personal tax rates on taxable capital income have fallen dramatically over the past two decades. In addition, the effective marginal tax on capital income earned on saving done within a retirement account, such as an Individual Retirement Account, is zero.

The main explanation for the decline in national saving appears to be the major and ongoing government policy of taking an ever larger share of resources from young and future Americans and giving them to older Americans. Because the elderly are close to the ends of their lives and have much higher propensities to consume than younger people and the unborn, redistributing from young and future U.S. generations to older generations raises national consumption and lowers national saving.

The distribution of resources across generations arises through a host of fiscal policies, including deficit finance, the pay-as-you-go finance of Social Security and Medicare benefits, shifts in the tax structure away from consumption and capital income taxation toward wage taxation, and even capital depreciation and expensing provisions. In recent decades, increased distribution to the current elderly has come primarily in two forms. The first is giving the elderly additional medical benefits under the Medicare and Medicaid programs. The elderly receive these benefits in kind, which means the only way they can get the benefits is to use them; one cannot "save" a Medicare payment. The second is cutting the taxes the elderly pay.

The Implications of Low Saving for Baby Boomers

Americans used to save at a fairly high rate. As a consequence, the collective stock of U.S. wealth holdings is still quite large—roughly thirty-five trillion dollars. This is enough to finance all Americans' consumer expenditures for about five years. But about 60 percent of this wealth is owned by people who are fifty or older, who appear to be spending a good deal of it on themselves. If the elderly do end up spending rather than bequeathing the bulk of existing U.S. wealth, will younger Americans, particularly baby boomers, accumulate enough savings to maintain the standard of living they currently enjoy in their old age?

Based on current evidence, the answer appears to be *no*. Compared with their parents, baby boomers can expect to retire earlier, live longer, rely less on inheritances, receive less help from their children, experience slower real wage growth, face higher taxes, and replace a smaller fraction of their preretirement earnings with Social Security retirement benefits. Unless baby boomers change their saving habits substantially and relatively quickly, they may experience much higher rates of poverty in their old age than those currently observed among U.S. elderly.

About the Author

Laurence J. Kotlikoff is a professor of economics and chairman of the Department of Economics at Boston University, a research associate with the National Bureau of Economic Research, and president of Economic Security Planning, Inc. He was previously a senior economist with President Ronald Reagan's Council of Economic Advisers.

Further Reading

Ando, Albert, and Franco Modigliani. "The Life Cycle Hypothesis of Saving: Aggregate Implications and Tests." *American Economic Review* 53, no. 1 (1963): 55–84.

Auerbach, Alan J., and Laurence J. Kotlikoff. *Dynamic Fiscal Policy.* New York: Cambridge University Press, 1987.

Bernheim, B. Douglas. "Taxation and Saving." In Alan J. Auerbach and Martin S. Feldstein, eds., *The Handbook of Public Economics.* Amsterdam: North-Holland, 2002. Vol. 3, pp. 1173–1249.

Kotlikoff, Laurence J. *Essays on Saving, Bequests, Altruism, and Life-Cycle Planning.* Cambridge: MIT Press, 2001.

———. *Generational Accounting: Knowing Who Pays and When for What We Spend.* New York: Free Press, 1992.

———. *What Determines Savings?* Cambridge: MIT Press, 1989.

Kotlikoff, Laurence J., and Scott Burns. *The Coming Generational Storm.* Cambridge: MIT Press, 2004.

Kotlikoff, Laurence J., and Lawrence H. Summers. "The Adequacy of Saving." *American Economic Review* 72, no. 5 (1982): 1056–1069.

———. "The Role of Intergenerational Transfers in Aggregate Capital Formation." *Journal of Political Economy* 89, no. 4 (1981): 706–732.

Savings and Loan Crisis

Bert Ely

Years later, the extraordinary cost of the 1980s S&L crisis still astounds many taxpayers, depositors, and policymakers. The cost of bailing out the Federal Savings and Loan Insurance Corporation (FSLIC), which insured the deposits in failed S&Ls, may eventually exceed $160 billion. At the end of 2004, the direct cost of the S&L crisis to taxpayers was $124 billion, according to financial statements published by the Federal Deposit Insurance Corporation (FDIC), the successor to the FSLIC. Additionally, healthy S&Ls as well as commercial banks have been taxed approximately another $30 billion to pay for S&L cleanup costs. Finally, the federal courts are still resolving the so-called goodwill cases stemming from regulatorily inspired mergers of failing S&Ls into healthy S&Ls in the early 1980s (discussed below). Resolving these cases will probably cost taxpayers another $5–$10 billion.

The bankruptcy of the FSLIC did not occur overnight; the FSLIC was a disaster waiting to happen for many years. Numerous public policies, some dating back to the 1930s, created the disaster. Some policies were well intended but misguided. Others had lost whatever historical justification they might once have had. Yet others were desperate attempts to postpone addressing a rapidly worsening situation. All of these policies, however, greatly compounded the S&L problem and made its eventual resolution more difficult and much more expensive. When disaster finally hit the S&L industry in 1980, the federal government managed it very badly.

Fifteen public policies that contributed to the S&L debacle are summarized below.

Public Policy Causes with Roots Before 1980

Federal deposit insurance, which was extended to S&Ls in 1934, was the root cause of the S&L crisis. Deposit insurance was actuarially unsound from its inception, primarily because all S&Ls were charged the same insurance premium rate regardless of how safe or risky they were. That is, deposit insurance provided by the federal government tolerated the unsound financial structure of S&Ls for decades. No sound insurance program would have done that. Congress tried to rectify this problem in 1991 when it directed the FDIC to begin charging risk-sensitive deposit-insurance premiums. However, because those who should pay the most would scream the loudest to Congress, the FDIC's premium structure still does not charge the riskiest banks and S&Ls enough. Much of the time, the "drunk drivers" of the S&L and banking world pay no more for their deposit insurance than do their sober siblings. Those who do pay more still do not pay enough.

Borrowing short to lend long was the financial structure that federal policy effectively forced S&Ls to follow in the aftermath of the Great Depression. S&Ls used short-term passbook savings to fund long-term, fixed-rate home mortgages. Although the long-term, fixed-rate mortgage may have been an admirable public-policy objective, the federal government picked the wrong horse—the S&L industry—to do this type of lending because S&Ls funded themselves primarily with short-term deposits. The dangers inherent in this "maturity mismatching" became evident every time short-term interest rates rose. S&Ls, stuck with long-term loans at fixed rates, often had to pay more to their depositors than they were making on their mortgages. In 1981 and 1982 the interest rate spreads for S&Ls (the difference between the average interest rate on their mortgage portfolios and their average cost of funds) were −1.0 percent and −0.7 percent, respectively.

Regulation Q, under which the Federal Reserve since 1933 had limited the interest rates banks could pay on their deposits, was extended to S&Ls in 1966. Regulation Q was price fixing, and like most efforts to fix prices (see PRICE CONTROLS), Regulation Q caused distortions far more costly than any benefits it may have delivered. Regulation Q created a cross subsidy, passed from saver to home buyer, that allowed S&Ls to hold down their interest costs and thereby continue to earn, for a few more years, an apparently adequate interest margin on the fixed-rate mortgages they had made ten or twenty years earlier. Thus, the extension of Regulation Q to S&Ls was a watershed event in the S&L crisis: it perpetuated S&L maturity mismatching for another fifteen years, until it was phased out after disaster struck the industry in 1980. A remnant of Regulation Q remains—banks are still barred from paying interest on business checking accounts.

Interest rate restrictions locked S&Ls into below-market rates on many mortgages whenever interest rates rose. State-imposed usury laws limited the rate lenders could charge on home mortgages until Congress banned states from imposing this ceiling in 1980. In addition to interest rate ceilings on mortgages, the due-on-sale clause in mortgage contracts was not uniformly enforceable until 1982. Before, borrowers could transfer their lower-interest-rate mortgages to new homeowners when property was sold.

A federal ban on adjustable-rate mortgages until 1981 further magnified the problem of S&L maturity mismatching by not allowing S&Ls to issue mortgages on which interest rates could be adjusted during times of rising interest rates. As mentioned above, during periods of high interest rates, S&Ls, limited to making long-term, fixed-rate mortgages, earned less interest on their loans than they paid on their deposits.

Restrictions on setting up branches and a restriction on nationwide banking prevented S&Ls, and banks as well, from expanding across state lines. S&Ls, unable to diversify their credit risks geographically, became badly exposed to regional economic downturns that reduced the value of their real estate collateral. In the 1980s, S&Ls began branching across state lines; in 1994, Congress authorized interstate branching for banks.

The dual chartering system permitted state-regulated S&Ls to be protected by federal deposit insurance. Therefore, state chartering and supervision could impose losses on the federal taxpayer if the state regulations became too permissive or if state regulators were too lax.

The secondary mortgage market agencies created by the federal government—Fannie Mae and Freddie Mac—undercut S&L profits by using their taxpayer backing to effectively lower interest rates on all mortgages. This helped home buyers, but the resulting lower rates made S&L maturity mismatching even more dangerous, especially as interest rates became more volatile after 1966.

Public Policy Causes That Began in the 1980s
Disaster struck after Paul Volcker, then chairman of the Federal Reserve Board, decided in October 1979 to restrict the growth of the money supply, which in turn caused interest rates to skyrocket. Between June 1979 and March 1980 short-term interest rates rose by more than six percentage points, from 9.06 percent to 15.2 percent. In 1981 and 1982 combined, the S&L industry collectively reported almost $9 billion in losses. Worse, in mid-1982 all S&Ls combined had a negative net worth, valuing their mortgages on a market-value basis, of $100 billion, an amount equal to 15 percent of the industry's liabilities. Specific policy failures during the 1980s are examined below.

An incomplete and bungled deregulation of S&Ls in 1980 and 1982 lifted restrictions on the kinds of investments S&Ls could make. In 1980 and again in 1982, Congress and the regulators granted S&Ls the power to invest directly in service corporations, permitted them to make real estate loans without regard to the geographical location of the loan, and authorized them to hold up to 40 percent of their assets as commercial real estate loans. Congress and the Reagan administration naïvely hoped that if S&Ls made higher-yielding, but riskier, investments, they would make more money to offset the long-term damage caused by fixed-rate mortgages. However, the 1980 and 1982 legislation did not change how premiums were set for federal deposit insurance. Riskier S&Ls still were not charged higher rates for deposit insurance than their prudent siblings. As a result, deregulation encouraged increased risk taking by S&Ls.

Capital standards were debased in the early 1980s in an extremely unwise attempt to hide the economic insolvency of many S&Ls. The Federal Home Loan Bank Board (FHLBB), the now-defunct regulator of S&Ls, authorized accounting gimmicks that violated generally accepted accounting principles. In one of the most flagrant gimmicks, firms that acquired S&Ls were allowed to count as goodwill the difference between the market value of assets acquired and the value of liabilities assumed. If a firm acquired an S&L with assets whose market value was five billion dollars and whose liabilities were six billion, for example, the one-billion-dollar difference was counted as goodwill, and the goodwill was then counted as capital. This "push-down" accounting—losses were pushed down the balance sheet into the category of goodwill—and other accounting gimmicks permitted S&Ls to operate with less and less real capital. Thus just as S&Ls, encouraged by deregulation, took on more risk, they had a smaller capital cushion to fall back on and, therefore, less to lose by making bad decisions.

Inept supervision and the permissive attitude of the FHLBB during the 1980s allowed badly managed and insolvent S&Ls to continue operating. In particular, the FHLBB eliminated maximum limits on loan-to-value ratios for S&Ls in 1983. Thus, where an S&L had been limited to lending no more than 75 percent of the appraised value of a home, after 1983 it could lend as much as 100

percent of the appraised value. The FHLBB also permitted excessive lending to any one borrower. These powers encouraged unscrupulous real estate developers and others who were unfamiliar with the banking business to acquire and then rapidly grow their S&Ls into insolvency. When the borrower and the lender are the same person, a conflict of interest develops. Also, because developers, by nature, are optimists, they lack the necessary counterbalancing conservatism of bankers.

Delayed closure of insolvent S&Ls greatly compounded the FSLIC's losses by postponing the burial of already dead S&Ls. Figure 1 shows how losses in insolvent S&Ls grew during the 1980s as the closure of insolvent S&Ls was delayed. Mid-1983 would have been the optimum time to close hopelessly insolvent S&Ls. Instead, Congress chose to put off the eventual day of reckoning, which only compounded the problem. Over half of these losses reflect the pure cost of delayed closures—compound interest on already incurred losses. The rest of the cost, except for the part that went to owners of S&Ls, represents the waste of real resources—building unneeded shopping centers and office buildings and keeping open S&L branches that should have been closed. However, there would have been little, if any, of this real waste if all of the then-insolvent S&Ls had been closed by mid-1983; they would not have been around to make all the bad loans they made after 1983 or to incur wasteful operating expenses.

Lack of truthfulness in quantifying the FSLIC's problems hid from the general public the size of the FSLIC's losses.

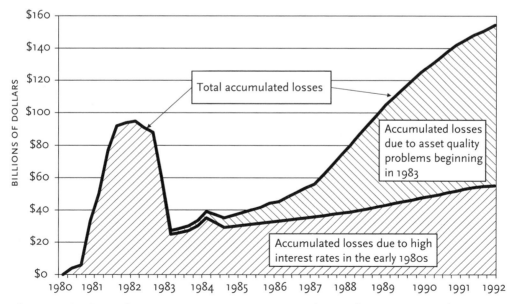

Figure 1 FSLIC/Resolution Trust Corporation's Accumulation of Losses During the 1980s and Early 1990s (quarterly estimates—June 30, 1980, to June 30, 1992)

Neither the FHLBB nor the General Accounting Office (GAO), now called the Government Accountability Office, provided realistic cost estimates of the problem as it was growing. On May 19, 1988, for example, Frederick Wolf of the GAO testified that the FSLIC bailout would cost thirty to thirty-five billion dollars. Over the next eight months, the GAO increased its estimate by forty-six billion dollars.

Congressional and administration delay and inaction, due to an unwillingness to confront the true size of the S&L mess and anger politically influential S&Ls, prevented appropriate action from being taken once the S&L problem was identified. The 1987 FSLIC recapitalization bill provided just $10.8 billion for the cleanup, even though it was clear at the time that much more—possibly as much as $40 billion—was needed. The first serious attempt at cleaning up the FSLIC mess did not come until Congress enacted the Financial Institutions Reform, Recovery, and Enforcement Act of 1989 (FIRREA). Even FIRREA, however, did not provide sufficient funds to completely clean up the S&L mess. Eventually, in fits and starts, Congress did appropriate sufficient funds to finish the job.

Flip-flops on real estate taxation first stimulated an overbuilding of commercial real estate in the early 1980s and then accentuated the real estate bust when depreciation and "passive loss" rules were tightened in 1986. The flip-flop had a double whammy effect: the 1981 tax law caused too much real estate to be built, and the 1986 act then hurt the value of much of what had been built.

What Did Not Cause the S&L Disaster

Some highly publicized factors in the S&L debacle—criminality, a higher deposit-insurance limit, brokered deposits, and faulty audits of S&Ls—did not cause the mess. Instead, these factors are symptoms or consequences of it.

Crooks certainly stole money from many insolvent S&Ls. However, criminality costs the taxpayer money only when it occurs in an already insolvent S&L that the regulators had failed to close when it became insolvent. Delayed closure is the cause of the problem, and criminality is a consequence. In any event, criminality accounted for only five billion dollars, or 3 percent, of the cost of the FSLIC bailout.

Raising the deposit-insurance limit in 1980 from $40,000 to $100,000 did not cause S&Ls to go haywire, but it did make it slightly easier to funnel money into insolvent S&Ls. Put another way, had the deposit-insurance limit been kept at $40,000, a depositor intent on putting $200,000 of insured funds into insolvent S&Ls paying high interest rates would have had to deposit his money, in $40,000 chunks, into five different S&Ls. Because of the higher limit, two $100,000 deposits would keep the $200,000 fully insured.

Brokered deposits became an important source of deposits for many S&Ls in the 1980s. Brokered deposits allowed brokerage houses and deposit brokers to divide billions of dollars in customers' funds into $100,000 pieces, search the country for the highest rates being paid by S&Ls, and deposit those pieces into different S&Ls. Brokered deposits, though, were the regulators' best friend because this "hot money," always chasing high interest rates, kept insolvent S&Ls liquid, enabling regulators to delay closing these S&Ls. Regulators, therefore, were the true abusers of brokered deposits. Only in this regard did brokered deposits contribute to the S&L crisis. In the years since then, brokered deposits have become an acceptable funding source for banks and S&Ls since only sound institutions can now accept brokered deposits.

Certified public accountants (CPAs) have been blamed for not detecting failing S&Ls and reporting them to the regulators. However, CPAs were hired by S&Ls to audit their financial statements, not to backstop the regulators. Federal and state S&L examiners, working for the taxpayer, were supposed to be fully capable of detecting problems, and often did. Interestingly, CPA audit reports often disclosed financial problems in S&Ls, including regulatory accounting practices that were at odds with generally accepted accounting principles. The regulators, however, usually failed to act on those findings. The CPAs were scapegoats for known problems the regulators should have quickly acted on.

Junk-bond investments by S&Ls were often cited in the press and by politicians as a major contributor to the industry's problems. In fact, junk bonds played a trivial role. (JUNK BONDS are securities issued by companies whose credit rating is below "investment grade.") A GAO report issued just five months before the passage of FIRREA cited a study by a reputable research group that showed junk bonds to be the second most profitable asset (after credit cards) that S&Ls held in the 1980s. The report also pointed out that only 5 percent of S&Ls owned any junk bonds at all. Total junk-bond holdings of all S&Ls amounted to only 1.2 percent of their total financial assets. Even so, Congress mandated in FIRREA that all S&Ls sell their junk-bond investments—which they did, often at a significant loss.

The Future of S&Ls

In 1989, Congress started knocking down the barriers separating commercial banks from S&Ls. Since then, much of the S&L industry has been absorbed into the broader banking industry, through outright mergers as well as bank holding company acquisitions of S&Ls. Statutory and regulatory changes have largely, but not completely, eliminated differences between bank and S&L charters. For all practical purposes, both types of institutions operate today under the same regulatory regime. Yet at the end of 2004, 886 S&Ls remained, with total assets of $1.35 trillion. While many of the largest S&Ls are now owned by bank holding companies, two independent S&Ls—Washington Mutual Bank and World Savings Bank—each had more than $100 billion of assets while numerous other independent S&Ls had assets exceeding $1 billion. The number of S&Ls most likely will continue to decline, but it may be many years before they disappear completely. Whether or not S&Ls do disappear is no longer a public-policy concern because they now are so similar to banks.

About the Author

Bert Ely is head of Ely and Company, a financial institutions and monetary policy consulting firm in Alexandria, Virginia. He was one of the first people to publicly predict FSLIC's bankruptcy.

Further Reading

Ely, Bert. "Technology, Regulation, and the Financial Services Industry in the Year 2000." *Issues in Bank Regulation* 12, no. 2 (1988): 13–19.
Ely, Bert, and Vicki Vanderhoff. *Lessons Learned from the S&L Debacle: The Price of Failed Public Policy.* Report No. 108. Lewisville, Tex.: Institute for Policy Innovation, 1991.
Fand, David. "The Savings and Loan Debacle." Paper presented at the George Edward Durell Foundation Conference, "American Money and Banking: Fiscal Fitness in the 1990s?" May 21–22, 1991.
Hector, Gary. "Where Did All Those Billions Go?" *Fortune,* September 10, 1990.
Kane, Edward J. *The Gathering Crisis in Federal Deposit Insurance.* Cambridge: MIT Press, 1985.

Social Security

Thomas R. Saving

Social Security, or, to be precise, Old Age, Survivors and Disability Insurance (OASDI), is the U.S. government program that pays benefits to workers after retirement, to spouses and children of deceased workers, and to workers who become disabled before they retire. In 2003, the program had 47 million recipients, of whom 32.6 million were retired workers and their dependent family members, 6.8 million were survivors of deceased workers, and 7.6 million were disabled former workers and their dependent family members. Social Security is financed through a payroll deduction (FICA) tax that is more than adequate now, but soon will be less than the amount needed to pay benefits.

The first social security program originated in Germany in 1889 under Chancellor Otto von Bismarck. By 1935, when President Franklin Delano Roosevelt signed the U.S. Social Security law, thirty-four European nations operated some form of old-age retirement plan based on transfers from workers to retirees. The U.S. Social Security system remained a retirement and survivor benefit program until 1957, when Congress began changing it significantly. The only previous changes had been increases in benefits and in taxes. In 1957, Congress broadened the program to include disability insurance benefits for severely disabled workers. In 1972, Congress approved automatic cost-of-living adjustments (COLAs) and in 1977 changed the benefit formula to provide a constant percentage of work income. Then, in 1983, in response to a funding crisis, Congress raised the payroll tax rate to its current level, increased the retirement age, and started to tax benefits.

In spite of and, in some cases because of, these changes, the system faces serious challenges in the future. In 1945, the United States had more than forty workers per retiree, so a minimal tax on workers could support all retirees. However, the system that began with few receiving benefits had to mature, and this maturation process meant that more and more individuals would become eligible for benefits. Thus, this idyllic world could not last. The combination of increased life expectancy from sixty-one years for those born in 1935 to seventy-six for those born in 2004, increased benefits, and falling birthrates has reduced the number of workers per retiree to three. By 2030, only two workers will be available to support each retiree.

U.S. Social Security comprises two distinct programs, each covering a separate population and each with its own method of financing. Old Age and Survivor Insurance (OASI) provides two types of benefits: retirement benefits for retired workers and benefits to the spouses and children of deceased workers. Disability Insurance (DI) provides benefits for disabled workers and their dependents on the same basis as retirement benefits are determined.

Social Security retirement benefits are based on average indexed monthly earnings for the thirty-five highest earnings years prior to retirement. The benefit formula is set up to favor lower-income workers. For example, in 2004, someone with average monthly earnings of $624 received a benefit that replaced 90 percent of earnings. Someone whose average monthly earnings were $3,760 received a benefit that replaced 42 percent of earnings, while someone with monthly earnings at the then-taxable maximum of $7,325 received a benefit that replaced only 28 percent of earnings. Early retirement—retirement between age sixty-two and the full-benefit age—results in a deduction from full benefits based on the actuarial assumption that early retirees will collect benefits for a longer period of time. The full-benefit age was sixty-five until 2000, when it began a two-month-a-year rise. It reached sixty-six in 2005, where it will remain until 2017; it will then rise by two months each year until it reaches sixty-seven in 2022.

Social Security's survivors' benefits are granted to the children and spouses of individuals who worked for at least ten years. Children and surviving spouses with children under sixteen years of age each receive an amount equivalent to 75 percent of the deceased's benefits, subject to a family maximum. Older surviving spouses are also eligible for benefits.

Disability benefits are granted to individuals who worked for at least ten years prior to disability, although younger workers with fewer than ten years of work may qualify for some benefits. Benefits are determined by a worker's earnings, ability to work in previous employment, ability to adjust to another job, and the expected duration of the disability. Children and spouses of disabled workers may also be eligible for benefits.

Many people believe that the FICA taxes they pay are placed in an account in their name at the Social Security Administration. In fact, these funds arrive at the U.S. Treasury and are used for current retirees' benefits and other government expenditures. If, at the end of the year, revenue from FICA taxes exceeds total benefits paid, which it has every year since 1983, the Treasury issues special government bonds to the Social Security Administration. These bonds prove that the Treasury used Social Security's money for other purposes and promise that when FICA revenues are too small to pay benefits, the Treasury will redeem the bonds. These bonds are, in essence, an IOU from the federal government to itself. It matters little whether the IOUs amount to zero, $100 billion, or $10 trillion.

The OASDI's revenues are expected to be relatively stable, growing from 12.71 percent of payroll in 2004 to 13.39 percent in 2080, with the modest rise attributable to increased revenues from the taxation of Social Security benefits. Costs will rise rapidly from 10.8 percent of payroll, when the first of the baby boomers become eligible for early retirement in 2008, to 17 percent in 2031, when the last of the baby boomers reach normal retirement age. Even after the last baby boomer retires, costs will continue to rise steadily for the indefinite future. While the program's current tax revenues are expected to exceed its costs until 2018, in every subsequent year thereafter, the program will face a funding deficit that will continue to grow in dollar terms and as a percentage of payroll.

Traditionally, media reports have summarized Social Security's financial health by reporting two numbers, the seventy-five-year actuarial deficit and the year of Trust Fund

exhaustion. For 2004, these two numbers were 1.89 and 2042. The 1.89 actuarial deficit means that if the OASDI tax rate were raised in 2004 from its 2004 level of 12.4 percent of payroll to 14.29 percent of payroll, Trust Fund exhaustion would occur exactly seventy-five years later—in this case, 2078. Even if this payroll tax increase were enacted immediately, however, the system would go into deficit in 2023, just five years later than is currently forecast. Furthermore, there would be large deficits after 2078. The last time the Social Security system was brought back into actuarial balance was 1983, when a combination of an increased tax rate, gradual increase in full retirement age, and partial taxation of benefits reduced the actuarial deficit from 1.82 to − 0.02. However, the government anticipated in 1983 that the actuarial deficit would be high again twenty years later.

The relevance of the 2042 Trust Fund exhaustion date is that the Treasury is not legally obligated to fund benefit payments that exceed Social Security revenues once there are no Trust Fund bonds to redeem. That date is artificial, though. Starting in 2018, paying benefits will require transfers from the rest of the federal budget. While the Trust Fund is an asset to Social Security, it is a Treasury obligation, not a Treasury asset, and provides no revenue to the Treasury for the payment of benefits. Thus, the redemption of Trust Fund assets will require some combination of increased federal taxes, reduced federal expenditures on other programs, or increased debt sales to the public.

Because Social Security is popular, it is difficult to change; without change, however, the program is financially doomed. As the Social Security trustees repeatedly point out, by 2018, Social Security will no longer be able to contribute to the Treasury revenue that, in 2003, equaled 7 percent of total income tax revenues. In fact, by 2024, the payment of Social Security benefits will require a transfer from the Treasury of more than 7.5 percent of total income tax revenues; by 2042, this transfer will grow to more than 15 percent of total income tax revenues.

Further, if Congress chooses to cover the looming deficits by raising the existing payroll tax, the tax rate required to pay benefits will grow from its current level of 12.4 percent of payroll to 17.8 percent of payroll by 2042 and to 19.4 percent by 2080, the end of the trustees' normal seventy-five-year horizon. Given that current Social Security replaces on average 42 percent of earned income, if in the long run there are two workers per retiree—the level expected by 2030—the required tax rate will be 21 percent. To the extent people view payroll taxes as pure taxes rather than as generating future benefits, such taxes reduce the supply of labor and result in a deadweight loss to the economy. At best, the current tax rate, if invested at the 3 percent rate assumed by the trustees, would just yield the benefits currently promised. Thus, the current payroll tax could be viewed by participants as buying them their promised benefits. However, the ultimate 21 percent payroll tax could not be so viewed and would result in a real reduction in the nation's output.

If currently scheduled Social Security benefits are paid, other government spending will have to be reduced or income taxes increased by almost 15 percent of projected income tax revenue. The Medicare program faces similar financial shortfalls. By 2030, maintaining currently scheduled Social Security and Medicare benefits would require all the payroll taxes and other revenues earmarked for these programs, plus more than 50 percent of all projected income tax revenues. This burden would fall on future workers, who would have to pay much higher payroll taxes.

To put the Social Security problem in perspective, the trustees calculated that the debt the system owed its current participants (those fifteen years old and older) at the close of 2003 was thirteen trillion dollars. If the government continued paying scheduled benefits and collecting only scheduled taxes from current participants, all new entrants to the workforce would have to pay off this thirteen-trillion-dollar debt in their lifetime. This is the equivalent of saddling each newborn with a substantial mortgage for which he will receive nothing in return.

With the Medicare debt added to the Social Security debt, new entrants to the workforce owe current participants almost forty-two trillion dollars. Because these debts are so enormous, they cannot and will not be honored. If the government solves the problem well and soon, the solution will be less painful. The required changes will cost something, but doing nothing will cost even more and will pass that cost on to future generations.

Even if benefits currently scheduled for the future are paid, the participants in Social Security will have received a rate of return on their taxes that is near zero. This low rate of return has formed the basis for increasing calls for reform. In 2001, President George W. Bush established the President's Commission to Strengthen Social Security (CSSS), of which I was a member. The CSSS considered alternative ways of dealing with the thirteen-trillion-dollar debt and suggested adjusting the benefit formula and allowing workers to invest part of their FICA taxes in individual retirement accounts. Thus, part of each worker's FICA would be deposited to an account in his or her name and would not become part of general Treasury revenue.

Currently, benefits are scheduled to increase with the increase in real wages. The CSSS benefit formula adjustment would fix the real purchasing power of benefits at the level that would be achieved in 2009. The individual accounts would replace future benefit increases, so that the benefit structure would remain virtually unchanged. These changes would pay off about $4.4 trillion of the $13 trillion Social Security debt, largely through a significant reduction in the level of future promised benefits. Even with this reform, however, future generations would be saddled with $8.6 trillion in extra debt. Several other reforms are being considered, ranging from retaining much of the current pay-as-you-go financing to completely privatizing the system. To the extent that we replace a system in which individuals depend on future generations to pay for their retirement with one in which each generation saves for its own retirement, the U.S. capital stock will grow. Further, contributions to private accounts, even if equal to current tax rates, would correctly be viewed by participants as buying direct benefits and would have little negative effect on labor supply. Thus, the reform path that is ultimately chosen will have long-run implications for capital growth and income growth, and, ultimately, will determine which generation bears the burden of financing retirement.

About the Author

Thomas R. Saving is the director of the Private Enterprise Research Center at Texas A&M University and University Distinguished Professor of Economics at Texas A&M. In 2000, President Bill Clinton appointed Dr. Saving a public trustee of the Social Security and Medicare Trust Funds. In May 2001, President George W. Bush named Dr. Saving to the bipartisan President's Commission to Strengthen Social Security.

Further Reading

Board of Trustees of the Federal Old-Age and Survivors Insurance and Disability Insurance Trust Funds. *Annual Report of the Board of Trustees of the Federal Old-Age and Survivors Insurance and Disability Insurance Trust Funds.* Washington, D.C., March 2004.

Feldstein, Martin. "The Missing Piece in Policy Analysis: Social Security Reform." *American Economic Review* 86, no. 2, (1996): 1–14.

———, ed. *Privatizing Social Security.* Chicago: University of Chicago Press, 1998.

Kotlikoff, Laurence J., and Jeffrey Sachs. "It Is High Time to Privatize." *Federal Reserve Bank of St. Louis Review* 80, no. 2 (1998).

Mitchell, Olivia S., Robert J. Myers, and Howard Young, eds. *Prospects for Social Security Reform.* Philadelphia: University of Pennsylvania Press, 1999.

Murphy, Kevin, M., and Finis Welch. "Perspectives on the Social Security Crisis and Proposed Solutions." *American Economic Review* 88, no. 2 (1998): 142–150.

President's Commission to Strengthen Social Security.

Strengthening Social Security and Creating Personal Wealth for All Americans. Washington, D.C., December 21, 2001.

Schieber, Sylvester J., and John B. Shoven. *The Real Deal: The History and Future of Social Security.* New Haven: Yale University Press, 1999.

Social Security and Medicare Boards of Trustees. *Status of the Social Security and Medicare Programs: A Summary of the 2004 Annual Reports.* Washington, D.C., March 2004.

Socialism

Robert Heilbroner

Socialism—defined as a centrally planned economy in which the government controls all means of production—was the tragic failure of the twentieth century. Born of a commitment to remedy the economic and moral defects of capitalism, it has far surpassed capitalism in both economic malfunction and moral cruelty. Yet the idea and the ideal of socialism linger on. Whether socialism in some form will eventually return as a major organizing force in human affairs is unknown, but no one can accurately appraise its prospects who has not taken into account the dramatic story of its rise and fall.

The Birth of Socialist Planning

It is often thought that the idea of socialism derives from the work of Karl Marx. In fact, Marx wrote only a few pages about socialism, as either a moral or a practical blueprint for society. The true architect of a socialist order was Lenin, who first faced the practical difficulties of organizing an economic system without the driving incentives of profit seeking or the self-generating constraints of competition. Lenin began from the long-standing delusion that economic organization would become less complex once the profit drive and the market mechanism had been dispensed with—"as self-evident," he wrote, as "the extraordinarily simple operations of watching, recording, and issuing receipts, within the reach of anybody who can read and write and knows the first four rules of arithmetic."

In fact, economic life pursued under these first four rules rapidly became so disorganized that within four years of the 1917 revolution, Soviet production had fallen to 14 percent of its prerevolutionary level. By 1921 Lenin was forced to institute the New Economic Policy (NEP), a partial return to the market incentives of capitalism. This brief mixture of socialism and capitalism came to an end in 1927 after Stalin instituted the process of forced collectivization that was to mobilize Russian resources for its leap into industrial power.

The system that evolved under Stalin and his successors took the form of a pyramid of command. At its apex was Gosplan, the highest state planning agency, which established such general directives for the economy as the target rate of growth and the allocation of effort between military and civilian outputs, between heavy and light industry, and among various regions. Gosplan transmitted the general directives to successive ministries of industrial and regional planning, whose technical advisers broke down the overall national plan into directives assigned to particular factories, industrial power centers, collective farms, and so on. These thousands of individual subplans were finally scrutinized by the factory managers and engineers who would eventually have to implement them. Thereafter, the blueprint for production reascended the pyramid, together with the suggestions, emendations, and pleas of those who had seen it. Ultimately, a completed plan would be reached by negotiation, voted on by the Supreme Soviet, and passed into law.

Thus, the final plan resembled an immense order book, specifying the nuts and bolts, steel girders, grain outputs, tractors, cotton, cardboard, and coal that, in their entirety, constituted the national output. In theory such an order book should enable planners to reconstitute a working economy each year—provided, of course, that the nuts fitted the bolts; the girders were of the right dimensions; the grain output was properly stored; the tractors were operable; and the cotton, cardboard, and coal were of the kinds needed for their manifold uses. But there was a vast and widening gap between theory and practice.

Problems Emerge

The gap did not appear immediately. In retrospect, we can see that the task facing Lenin and Stalin in the early years was not so much economic as quasi military—mobilizing a peasantry into a workforce to build roads and rail lines, dams and electric grids, steel complexes and tractor factories. This was a formidable assignment, but far less formidable than what would confront socialism fifty years later, when the task was not so much to create enormous undertakings as to create relatively self-contained ones, and to fit all the outputs into a dovetailing whole.

Through the 1960s the Soviet economy continued to report strong overall growth—roughly twice that of the United States—but observers began to spot signs of impending trouble. One was the difficulty of specifying outputs in terms that would maximize the well-being of everyone in the economy, not merely the bonuses earned by individual factory managers for "overfulfilling" their assigned objectives. The problem was that the plan specified outputs in physical terms. One consequence was that managers maximized yardages or tonnages of output, not its quality. A famous cartoon in the satirical magazine *Krokodil* showed a factory manager proudly displaying his record output, a single gigantic nail suspended from a crane.

As the economic flow became increasingly clogged and clotted, production took the form of "stormings" at the end of each quarter or year, when every resource was pressed into use to meet preassigned targets. The same rigid system soon produced expediters, or *tolkachi*, to arrange shipments to harassed managers who needed unplanned—and therefore unobtainable—inputs to achieve their production goals. Worse, lacking the right to buy their own supplies or to hire or fire their own workers, factories set up fabricating shops, then commissaries, and finally their own worker housing to maintain control over their own small bailiwicks.

It is not surprising that this increasingly Byzantine system began to create serious dysfunctions beneath the overall statistics of growth. During the 1960s the Soviet Union became the first industrial country in history to suffer a prolonged peacetime fall in average life expectancy, a symptom of its disastrous misallocation of resources. Military research facilities could get whatever they needed, but hospitals were low on the priority list. By the 1970s the figures clearly indicated a slowing of overall production. By the 1980s the Soviet Union officially acknowledged a near end to growth that was, in reality, an unofficial decline. In 1987 the first official law embodying *perestroika*—restructuring—was put into effect. President Mikhail Gorbachev announced his intention to revamp the economy from top to bottom by introducing the market, reestablishing private ownership, and opening the system to free economic interchange with the West. Seventy years of socialist rise had come to an end.

Socialist Planning in Western Eyes

Understanding of the difficulties of central planning was slow to emerge. In the mid-1930s, while the Russian industrialization drive was at full tilt, few raised their voices about its problems. Among those few were LUDWIG VON MISES, an articulate and exceedingly argumentative free-market economist, and FRIEDRICH HAYEK, of much more contemplative temperament, later to be awarded a Nobel Prize for his work in monetary theory. Together, Mises and Hayek launched an attack on the feasibility of socialism that seemed at the time unconvincing in its argument as to the functional problems of a planned economy. Mises in particular contended that a socialist system was impossible because there was no way for the planners to acquire the information—"produce this, not that"—needed for a coherent economy. This information, Hayek emphasized,

Heilbroner on Who Predicted Socialism's Demise

But what spokesman of the present generation has anticipated the demise of socialism or the "triumph of capitalism"? *Not a single writer in the Marxian tradition!* Are there any in the left centrist group? None I can think of, including myself. As for the center itself—the Samuelsons, Solows, Glazers, Lipsets, Bells, and so on—I believe that many have expected capitalism to experience serious and mounting, if not fatal, problems and have anticipated some form of socialism to be the organizing force of the twenty-first century.

. . . Here is the part hard to swallow. It has been the Friedmans, Hayeks, von Miseses, *e tutti quanti* who have maintained that capitalism would flourish and that socialism would develop incurable ailments. Mises called socialism "impossible" because it has no means of establishing a rational pricing system; Hayek added additional reasons of a sociological kind ("the worst rise on top"). All three have regarded capitalism as the "natural" system of free men; all have maintained that left to its own devices capitalism would achieve material growth more successfully than any other system.

From Robert Heilbroner.
"The World After Communism."
Dissent (Fall 1990): 429–430.

emerged spontaneously in a market system from the rise and fall of prices. A planning system was bound to fail precisely because it lacked such a signaling mechanism.

The Mises-Hayek argument met its most formidable counterargument in two brilliant articles by Oskar Lange, a young economist who would become Poland's first ambassador to the United States after World War II. Lange set out to show that the planners would, in fact, have precisely the same information as that which guided a market economy. The information would be revealed as inventories of goods rose and fell, signaling either that supply was greater than demand or demand was greater than supply. Thus, as planners watched inventory levels, they were also learning which of their administered (i.e., state-dictated) prices were too high and which too low. It only remained, therefore, to adjust prices so that supply and demand balanced, exactly as in the marketplace.

Lange's answer was so simple and clear that many believed the Mises-Hayek argument had been demolished.

In fact, we now know that their argument was all too prescient. Ironically, though, Mises and Hayek were right for a reason they did not foresee as clearly as Lange himself. *"The real danger of socialism,"* Lange wrote, in italics, *"is that of a bureaucratization of economic life."* But he took away the force of the remark by adding, without italics, "Unfortunately, we do not see how the same or even greater danger can be averted under monopolistic capitalism" (Lange and Taylor 1938, pp. 109–110).

The effects of the "bureaucratization of economic life" are dramatically related in *The Turning Point,* a scathing attack on the realities of socialist economic planning by two Soviet economists, Nikolai Smelev and Vladimir Popov, that gives examples of the planning process in actual operation. In 1982, to stimulate the production of gloves from moleskins, the Soviet government raised the price it was willing to pay for moleskins from twenty to fifty kopecks per pelt. Smelev and Popov noted:

> State purchases increased, and now all the distribution centers are filled with these pelts. Industry is unable to use them all, and they often rot in warehouses before they can be processed. The Ministry of Light Industry has already requested Goskomtsen [the State Committee on Prices] twice to lower prices, but "the question has not been decided" yet. This is not surprising. Its members are too busy to decide. They have no time: besides setting prices on these pelts, they have to keep track of another 24 million prices. And how can they possibly know how much to lower the price today, so they won't have to raise it tomorrow?

This story speaks volumes about the problem of a centrally planned system. The crucial missing element is not so much "information," as Mises and Hayek argued, as it is the motivation to act on information. After all, the inventories of moleskins did tell the planners that their production was at first too low and then too high. What was missing was the willingness—better yet, the necessity—to respond to the signals of changing inventories. A capitalist firm responds to changing prices because failure to do so will cause it to lose money. A socialist ministry ignores changing inventories because bureaucrats learn that doing something is more likely to get them in trouble than doing nothing, unless doing nothing results in absolute disaster.

In the late 1980s, absolute economic disaster arrived in the Soviet Union and its Eastern former satellites, and those countries are still trying to construct some form of economic structure that will no longer display the deadly inertia and indifference that have come to be the hallmarks of socialism. It is too early to predict whether these efforts will succeed. The main obstacle to real perestroika is the impossibility of creating a working market system without a firm basis of private ownership, and it is clear that the creation of such a basis encounters the opposition of the former state bureaucracy and the hostility of ordinary people who have long been trained to be suspicious of the pursuit of wealth. In the face of such uncertainties, all predictions are foolhardy save one: no quick or easy transition from socialism to some form of nonsocialism is possible. Transformations of such magnitude are historic convulsions, not mere changes in policy. Their completion must be measured in decades or generations, not years.

About the Author

Robert Heilbroner, a socialist for most of his adult life, was the Norman Thomas Professor of Economics (emeritus) at the New School for Social Research and author of the best-seller *The Worldly Philosophers.* He died in 2005. The editor of this volume, David R. Henderson, edited this article slightly, but only to adjust it for developments in the formerly socialist countries, not to change any of its other substantive content.

Further Reading

Hayek, Friedrich A. "Socialist Economic Calculation: The Present State of the Debate." In Hayek, *Individualism and Economic Order.* 1942. Reprint. Chicago: University of Chicago Press, 1972.

Heilbroner, Robert. "After Communism." *New Yorker,* September 10, 1990.

———. "The Triumph of Capitalism." *New Yorker,* January 23, 1989.

Lange, Oskar, and Fred Taylor. *On the Economic Theory of Socialism.* New York: McGraw-Hill, 1938.

Mises, Ludwig von. "Economic Calculation in the Socialist Commonwealth." In Friedrich A. Hayek, ed., *Collectivist Economic Planning.* London: Routledge and Sons, 1935.

Smelev, Nikolai, and Vladimir Popov. *The Turning Point.* New York: Doubleday, 1989.

Spatial Economics

Wolfgang Kasper

Producers and buyers are dispersed in space, and overcoming the distances between them can be costly. Much commercial activity is concerned with "space bridging," and much entrepreneurship is aimed at making good use of locational opportunities and cutting the costs of transport and communication. Spatial economics is the study of how space (distance) affects economic behavior.

The Costs of "Space Bridging" Have Fallen

Throughout history, transport costs have hampered specialization, and improvements in transport and communications have been among the main driving forces of economic progress. In medieval Europe and China, most ordinary people never moved farther than twenty miles from their birthplaces, and before the advent of book printing, most people knew very little about what happened beyond those narrow horizons. Firms that depended on heavy inputs, such as steel makers, used to locate near the source of major inputs—coal mines, in particular. By contrast, firms that interacted intensively and frequently with customers tended to locate near the demand. Thus, gasoline stations are still found near busy intersections.

In recent decades, technical and organizational progress has caused the costs of transport to fall steadily and communication costs to plummet. Between 1950 and 2000, the price of bulk sea freight and port handling dropped, on average, by 0.9 percent annually, of long-distance passenger air transport by 2.6 percent annually, and of trans-Atlantic phone calls by an astounding 8 percent annually. The inflation-adjusted price of a long-distance phone call from New York to London is now less than 1 percent of what it was in 1950. Fax machines, portable video cameras, satellite TV, computers, and cell phones have all cut communication costs greatly. More recently, the Internet has made global communication so cheap and user friendly that words and images can be distributed by almost anyone globally, without delay and at near-zero cost. These technologies have opened new, easily accessible channels of communicating, so that entirely new forms of the division of labor between different locations have become feasible.

This reduction in transport costs has revolutionized decisions about where goods and services are produced. The relative costs of employing immobile production factors, such as land and labor, have become relatively more important in influencing the spatial arrangement of industries, irrespective of national borders. Yet, most businesses still take account of transport and communication costs (and the risks of disruptions) between the locations from which their inputs are supplied and the locations where they find their market demand.

Globalization

In the wake of these changes, globalization has become a tough political issue. Lower transport and communication costs have thrown many firms and their workers into global competition. Now, with concerns about competitors in faraway places entering the local market, locals must control costs more tightly, remain innovative, and sell at lower prices than before. Manufacturers have long known that foreign producers can make inroads into local markets and that their own market is increasingly the world, rather than simply the national market. Thus, there are now steel plants in China, Japan, and South Korea, far from iron and coal mines but near ports; the falling cost of shipping has made it possible to transport coal and iron ore to seaside locations, from where steel is sold around the world. What matters more for capital-intensive industries is whether the capital owners enjoy secure property rights where they invest. Consequently, locations now have to compete by providing good property-rights protection and other such trust-inspiring institutions.

Because the Internet now makes it possible to provide many services over long distances and even globally, service providers—in accounting, finance, and managerial supervision, for example—have also become more mobile. Thus numerous low-skill service jobs have begun to migrate from high-wage locations to low-cost locations overseas. Established service providers are now often coming under competitive pressure from new, low-cost competitors in distant places, such as call centers and software developers in Ireland or India. By the same token, engineers in New York offices are now supervising construction work in Brazil in real time, and academics in California are delivering lectures and tutorials via computer terminals throughout East Asia, adding high-skill job opportunities in America.

The Thünen Model

The work of nineteenth-century German economist Johann Heinrich von Thünen explains the economic effects of falling space-bridging costs. Thünen became the father of spatial economics when he laid out the basic logic of how producers distribute themselves in space. He explained that the owners of mobile production factors, such as capital and technical knowledge, have to be paid the same return whether their assets are employed in the center of activity or on the periphery, at a distance from the central marketplaces. Otherwise they engage in "locational arbitrage"—that is, move from places where they are paid less to places where they are paid more.

The story for owners of immobile production factors such as land and labor is different. If they are in remote locations, then, to stay in business, they must absorb the entire transport-cost disadvantage. Landowners and workers in the center of markets, on the other hand, can earn a premium. In short, the prices of immobile land and labor vary inversely with the distance from the central marketplaces. This "Thünen principle" can be demonstrated at various levels of locational analysis:

A. In a city or region, real estate rents drop as one moves

away from the center of activity. In the center, enterprises use a lot of capital to build high-rises, thus saving on land costs, and only space-saving offices are located there. Cheap land on the periphery is devoted to space-intensive uses, such as manufacturing plants, logistics centers, and dumps. If landowners on the periphery were to raise their rents, they would soon be out of business.

B. Within a nation, landowners and workers can earn high "location rents" if they operate in the central areas of economic activity, such as Chicago or Los Angeles. There, mobile factors crowd in and make intensive use of land and labor, and people earn high incomes. High rental prices for the immobile inputs determine what is produced in the central cities. If the differentials in land and labor costs between central regions and more remote areas exceed the transport cost of products from the remote locations to the central markets, enterprises migrate. That is how industry has spread from historic centers such as New York and Boston to new industrial regions.

C. On a global scale, North America, northwest Europe, and northeast Asia are now the central locations. Because they are the major gateways to global economic networks, these central locations are where world-market prices and product standards are determined and the highest incomes are earned. Mobile and immobile inputs are combined there most intensively and with the highest productivity. Farther away in economic space are new industrial countries, such as Mexico, Taiwan, and Malaysia, where immobile laborers and landowners earn lower incomes. And still farther afield, on the periphery of global economic networks, are the underdeveloped countries where locals earn very low incomes. As wages in the new industrial countries rise, producers have to raise productivity to retain footloose industries. Otherwise, mobile capital, know-how, and enterprise move to newer and cheaper locations.

Since Thünen's days, government administration has become another important immobile production factor. The cost-benefit ratio of government administration can nowadays play a major role in decisions about where to locate activities, both within a nation and globally. Reliable property rights, expedient and transparent regulations, impartial law enforcement, and relatively low taxation attract new investments, which causes industrial locations to expand. Governments in remote locations must keep taxes particularly low and provide good, small government if they want to attract capital and enterprise. In this sense, they are not completely sovereign; instead, they face a strong incentive to act like other immobile production factors in the "Thünen system," offering competitive support services to local workers and landowners. In the past, government administrators on the periphery of the global economy, who realized that they had to compete indirectly with their counterparts elsewhere, were crucial in creating new industrial centers. Thus, the governments of Singapore, Hong Kong, and Taiwan offered tax concessions, developed industrial land, and simplified regulations to attract foreign capital and enterprises, and were spectacularly successful in raising their populations' living standards.

Another aspect of spatial economics, one that has become increasingly contentious in recent years, is the legal and illegal migration of workers across borders. This aspect of globalization is now putting social strain on some societies. A potentially less disruptive measure would be to reduce government barriers to mobility of capital and goods. As international trade economists have known for a long time, to the extent that governments restrict free trade and the free movement of capital, they create incentives for people to move. For example, the stronger are the U.S. government's restrictions on imports from Brazil and the Brazilian government's restrictions on investment from the United States, the stronger is the inducement for Brazilians to migrate to the United States.

Institutions and Attractiveness

The freer flow of information and new transport and communications technologies have now raised the mobility of capital—human, financial, and physical—entrepreneurs, and entire firms to unprecedented levels. The owners of these mobile production factors, who wish to supply world markets, are increasingly "shopping around" for the labor, work attitudes, and style of government administration that promise them high rates of return and low risks. Many companies are becoming "locational innovators" and multinationals. Lack of economic freedom and well-working government institutions makes some countries unattractive to mobile factors of production. However, low labor-unit costs and an expedient administration, which keep transaction costs and business risks low, are market signals that aspiring industrial countries can use to make themselves highly attractive. The influx of multinationals will then raise productivity and further enhance the attractiveness of such new locations, even if wage rates are gradually rising. In addition, originally peripheral places can address their transport-cost disadvantages by investing in efficient transport infrastructures. Understanding and correcting the "Thünen disadvantage" has rewarded Singapore, Hong Kong, and Taiwan with spectacular success.

Coping with Globalization

The rising global mobility of products, people, capital, and enterprise poses new competitive challenges to producers and workers in the established economic centers, who are losing some of their relative advantage. They can react to the emergence of competitive new economies in one of two ways. They can "Japan/Korea/China bash" to extract subsidies and political patronage, or, instead, they can be competitive and innovative, raising productivity in the traditional central production places and specializing in goods and services that still incur high transport costs, so that they still enjoy a degree of locational advantage. They can also draw on cheap imported inputs to produce end-products competitively for domestic and world markets. The mature, high-income economies at the center of the global system enjoy an important asset in the dynamic game of global competition: their innovative capacity. On that score, they are more likely to succeed if they reject political and social regulations that hamper innovative enterprise and cause high costs of transacting business, such as a legal system that raises the risks of innovation (see LIABILITY). Competitive producers in the old centers are also discovering that the new industrial countries buy many goods and services that the advanced economies are still best able to produce.

Economic theory suggests—and history amply confirms—that defensive political responses are rarely sustainable over the long term, whereas the competitive, open response of enterprises generates opportunity for most. Globalization is a positive-sum game, one reason being that economic openness to trade and factor mobility has been the most powerful antidote to political "RENT-SEEKING" (the use of political restrictions to secure artificial market niches). In open economies, political and bureaucratic energies are channeled to support mobile producers and to create an investment climate in which all production factors can thrive by cooperating. Openness was the reason modern industrial development took off in Western Europe. There, small, open states had to attract footloose merchants and industrialists by providing the rule of law, secure private property rights, and other economic freedoms, protected by expedient, impartial courts of law. By contrast, the closed worlds of Imperial China and Mughal India had no reason to abandon arbitrary, despotic rule. They had little innovative enterprise and experienced relative economic decline for centuries, despite their often much more advanced technical know-how.

In recent decades, this has, of course, changed: now that China and India are opening up, they are using progress in transport and communications to thrive. With time, they may well shed the former periphery handicaps and become new industrial centers in their own right, changing the global economic space.

About the Author

Wolfgang Kasper is an emeritus professor of economics at the University of New South Wales, Australia. He served on the staff of the German Council of Economic Advisors, the Kiel Institute of World Economics, the Malaysian Treasury, the Reserve Bank of Australia, and OECD.

Further Reading

Andersson, Åke E., and David E. Andersson, eds. *Gateways to the Global Economy.* Northampton, Mass.: Edward Elgar, 2000.
Blaug, Mark. *Economic Theory in Retrospect.* 4th ed. Cambridge: Cambridge University Press, 1985. Chapter on Thünen.
Giersch, Herbert. "Labor, Wage and Productivity." In Giersch, *Openness for Prosperity: Essays in World Economics.* Cambridge: MIT Press, 1993.
Kasper, Wolfgang. *Global Competition, Institutions, and the East-Asian Ascendancy.* San Francisco: ICS Press, 1994.
Kasper, Wolfgang, and Manfred E. Streit. *Institutional Economics, Social Order and Public Policy.* Northampton, Mass.: Edward Elgar, 1998. Chaps. 11 and 12.

Sportometrics

Robert Tollison

Until recently, economists who analyzed sports focused on such things as the antitrust exemption, the alleged cartel behavior of sports leagues, and the player draft (see SPORTS). Sportometrics is different. It is the application of economic theories to the behavior of athletes to explain what they do and to see if what they do can help to explain the behavior of people in other professions and settings. Instead of being about the "economics of sports," sportometrics introduces the idea of "sports as economics."

In other words, sportometricians view sports as an economic environment in which athletes behave according to incentives and constraints. Economists have, for example, shown how incentives and costs can explain how much effort runners exert in a footrace (see Higgins and Tollison 1990; Maloney and McCormick 2000). Using data from sprint events of the modern Olympics from 1896 to 1980, Richard Higgins and Robert Tollison (1990) found that running times were faster when there were fewer contestants in a race. This makes sense. With fewer runners, each runner's chance of winning is greater, and, therefore, each runner's expected gain from putting out additional effort is greater. This cannot be attributed to decreased congestion: because each runner is given a lane, congestion does not diminish when the number of contestants falls.

Higgins and Tollison also found that the harder an Olympic record is to break, the less effort contestants will expend to break it. Can any fan ever forget Carl Lewis's pass on a third attempt to break Bob Beamon's long-jump record in the 1984 Olympics? Horse racing is an even better contest to analyze because the prerace odds were used to control for the differential abilities of the racers. The study found similar results: an increase in the number of competitors leads to an increase in average race times.

The economic activity called arbitrage also enters into sports. Arbitrage is what economists call the exploitation of price differences for the same commodity. For example, if wheat sells for $3.00 a bushel in Chicago and $3.30 in Indianapolis, and if it can be transported to Indianapolis for twenty cents per bushel, then an arbitrageur can make ten cents on each bushel he buys in Chicago and sells in Indianapolis.

What does this have to do with professional basketball? A lot. Each player has an incentive to build up his individual performance statistics, particularly the number of points he scores. But a good coach enforces a regime in which shots are allocated—arbitraged—among players to maximize the probability that each shot taken will be made. Players who make a higher percentage of their shots should thus be given more chances to shoot. Moreover, the value of three-point shots must be traded off against two-point shots. Using data from the National Basketball Association, Kevin Grier and I found that coaches who are better at enforcing such an allocation of shots—better arbitrageurs—are more likely to win games and to have longer tenure as head coaches. Among the better coaches, we found, was Cotton Fitzsimmons, the former coach of the Phoenix Suns. He became head coach of the Kansas City Kings in 1977 and, in his first full season, led the Kings to forty-eight wins and a shooting efficiency rating of 66 percent, a very high statistic in the NBA.

In each case studied, economists gain insight not only on the behavior of athletes and coaches, but also on more general economic problems. The behavior of runners is analogous to that of bidders for a government contract: a bidder will expend more effort—lobbying and the like— the fewer competitors it has for a contract. Coaching a team is analogous to managing a company: within a company, managers "arbitrage" tasks among employees.

Analyzing sporting events, moreover, provides insights into the workings of all competition within well-defined rules—just as we see in our economy. Incentives and constraints are spelled out clearly; players behave as rational economic actors; sporting events and seasons can be seen as the operation of miniature economies—and so on. One of the first sportometrics analyses done (see McCormick and Tollison 1984) showed, for example, that basketball players respond rationally when an additional referee is on the court. Using data on the Atlantic Coast Conference Basketball Tournament, the study found that, other things being equal, adding one referee reduced the number of fouls per game by about seventeen, a reduction of 34 percent. A more general application of this research is to the issue of how we can reduce the number of crimes by adding police officers to our police forces.

Most economic analysis is based on the idea that when the incentive to do something increases, people will do more of it. Kenneth Lehn, formerly chief economist at the Securities and Exchange Commission, showed that this idea applies even to the amount of time baseball players spend on the disabled list. After players were signed to multiyear, guaranteed contracts with no extra pay for each game played, their incentive to play diminished. Sure enough, Lehn found that the amount of time players spent on the disabled list increased from 4.7 days in the precontract period to 14.4 days after—an increase of 206 percent.

Sports data have been used to understand other interesting issues. Brian Goff, Robert McCormick, and I analyzed the process of racial integration in Major League Baseball and college basketball (Goff et al. 2002). We wanted to know what type of teams integrated first—winners or losers. Using data on team rosters and other information about teams and schools, we found that winning teams were the first to acquire and use the more productive black players. Thus, entrepreneurship and not competitive pressure played the key role in the racial integration of sports.

Goff, William Shughart, and I analyzed the designated hitter rule in the American League of Major League Baseball (Goff et al. 1997). Under this rule, in force since 1973, American League pitchers do not have to bat. Thus, a pitcher in the American League does not have to fear direct retaliation for hitting a batter on the other team. In economic jargon, the pitcher's cost of plunking a batter is lower in the American League. As economists would have predicted, after the rule change there was a significant increase in hit batters in the American League.

Yet other studies have examined sports data to test hypotheses from GAME THEORY. P. A. Chiappori, Steve Levitt, and Tim Groseclose (2002) studied penalty kicks in soccer to see if goalies and kickers play a "mixed-strategy equilibrium"—that is, one in which the direction of the kick and the initial movement of the goalie are random. Such a result had previously been difficult to find in experimental studies, but they found it on the soccer field. Mark Waller and John Wooders (2001) found a similar result for the placement of tennis serves at Wimbledon.

Finally, in what has been hailed as a general contribution to managerial economics as well as being a book about sports, Michael Lewis recounts the story of what he calls

Moneyball. This is a story about Billy Beane, general manager of the Oakland Athletics since 1997. By following principles of sabermetrics (the statistical analysis of baseball), Beane has been able to field excellent, competitive teams for far lower expenditures on players than other baseball franchises. Beane and sabermetrics are an example of sportometrics in action.

About the Author

Robert D. Tollison is a professor of economics at Clemson University. His specialty is in using economic analysis to explain the behavior of politicians and of athletes.

Further Reading

Chiappori, P. A., Steve Levitt, and Tim Groseclose. "Testing Mixed-Strategy Equilibria When Players Are Heterogeneous: The Case of Penalty Kicks in Soccer." *American Economic Review* 92 (September 2002): 1138–1151.

Goff, Brian L., Robert McCormick, and Robert Tollison. "Racial Integration as an Innovation: Empirical Evidence from Sports Leagues." *American Economic Review* 92 (March 2002): 16–26.

Goff, Brian L., William Shughart, and Robert Tollison. "Batter Up! Moral Hazard and the Effects of the Designated Hitter Rule on Hit Batsmen." *Economic Inquiry* 35 (July 1997): 555–561.

Goff, Brian L., and Robert D. Tollison, eds. *Sportometrics.* College Station: Texas A&M Press, 1990.

Higgins, Richard S., and Robert D. Tollison. "Economics at the Track." In Brian L. Goff and Robert D. Tollison, eds., *Sportometrics.* College Station: Texas A&M Press, 1990.

Lehn, Kenneth. "Property Rights, Risk Sharing, and Player Disability." *Journal of Law and Economics* 25 (October 1982): 343–366.

Lewis, Michael. *Moneyball: The Art of Winning an Unfair Game.* New York: Norton, 2003.

Maloney, Michael, and Robert McCormick. "The Response of Workers to Wages in Tournaments: Evidence from Footraces." *Journal of Sports Economics* 1 (May 2000): 99–123.

McCormick, Robert E., and Robert D. Tollison. "Crime on the Court." *Journal of Political Economy* 92 (April 1984): 223–235.

Waller, Mark, and John Wooders. "Minimax Play at Wimbledon." *American Economic Review* 91 (December 2001): 1521–1538.

Sports

Gerald W. Scully

Major league sports, as every reader of the sports pages knows, is a major league business. As a result, economics has a lot to say about how players, teams, and leagues will act under different circumstances. But would you believe that economics can be used to predict which teams will win and which will lose? It can.

How good a professional sports team is depends, of course, on the quality of its players. Because teams compete for better players by offering higher salaries, the quality of a team depends largely on how strong it is financially. The financially stronger teams will, on average, be the better teams. And they will also, on average, be the ones in bigger cities, because more revenues can be made in bigger cities. In baseball, equivalent win records in New York, Los Angeles, or Chicago yield three times the revenue as in Kansas City, Milwaukee, or Pittsburgh. That is why professional sports teams in cities with large populations tend to have records above .500, while teams in cities with small populations tend to have records below .500.

Exceptions to the rule that financially stronger teams are better are some small-market teams, such as Oakland and Montreal, that, for certain periods of time, develop high-quality players in their farm-team system. These "diamonds in the rough" are better than the market. Such a strategy can produce relatively competitive teams in a small market while keeping player salaries relatively low. Of course, the exception proves the rule. Once these players win substantial salary increases through arbitration or become free agents, big-market teams often hire them away.

It is easy to see why large-market teams do better in the era of free agents, when a star player can move to whichever team will pay him the most. But, as I will explain below, this differential between large- and small-city teams also existed when teams "owned" player contracts and players were not free to accept a higher offer.

One factor that matters for team revenues and for competitive balance is the league's rule for dividing the gate receipts. In basketball and hockey, the home team gets all of the gate receipts and the visitor gets nothing. The gate division is 85:15 in baseball and 60:40 in football. When the home team gets to keep more of the gate receipts, the teams in bigger cities get more of the benefit from their inherent financial advantage. When the split is more equal, the financial advantage of being in a bigger market is less. Partly for this reason, financial disparity is least in the National Football League (NFL).

But in all sports, revenues from national television contracts have grown as a percentage of total revenues, and TV revenues are divided equally among the clubs. As a result, the differences in the financial strength of teams have narrowed. Big-city domination, though not completely eliminated, has diminished.

By their very nature, sports leagues are cartels that exclude competition from other companies. You cannot start a baseball team and hope to play the Yankees unless you can get Major League Baseball (the cartel) to grant you a franchise. The antitrust laws prohibit cartels, but professional sports is the only private business in the United States that is largely exempt from those laws. Ever since a 1922 court decision (*Federal Baseball Club of Baltimore* v. *National League et al.*), baseball has been totally exempt. No other sport enjoys such a blanket exemption from antitrust, but all professional team sports have a labor exemption and, since the Sports Television Act of 1961, a broadcast exemption.

All of the leagues have collusive agreements that govern the selection, contractual arrangements, and distribution of players among the teams. Collectively, these agreements grant a degree of monopsony power (monopoly power over the right to buy something—in this case, player services) to owners. The owners exploit this power by paying the players less than their incremental contribution to revenue.

Athletes enter most professional team sports through a drafting procedure. The common feature of the drafts is that they grant one team exclusive bargaining rights with each prospective player. Once drafted, the athlete negotiates with that team alone, and others cannot offer higher salaries to get him. In some instances, signing bonuses for draft choices are very high. Such instances are relatively rare and depend on the quality of the player and the labor-market structure of the sport. In baseball, where drafted players usually are assigned to the minor leagues, face relatively long careers on average, are not constrained by a salary cap, and are paid their salaries for the length of their contracts—which can be for several years—large signing bonuses for amateurs are rare. In football, where players face a salary cap, careers are short—less than three years, on average—and salary is not guaranteed if the player fails to make the team or is injured during the season, signing bonuses can be high for impact players. The rules affecting the amateur draft have been weakened somewhat over the years, but competitive bidding for beginning players remains impeded. Once the player has come to terms with the drafting team, he must sign a uniform player's contract that allows him to sell his services only to the team holding the contract. Although player contracts vary from sport to sport, all contain some basic prohibitions against player-

initiated moves to other teams. That is, owners are free to "trade" (sell) players to other teams, but players are not totally free to offer their services to competing teams.

Owners claim that restrictions on player movement are necessary to maintain competitive balance and prevent financial powerhouses such as the old Yankees from buying up all the best talent and completely dominating the sport. That, owners say, would make the sport duller for fans and hurt everyone. Economists have always been skeptical about the owners' motives—and about the evidence. There never was any disagreement over the fact that star players would wind up on big-city teams. But economists believe that this would happen regardless of whether or not leagues restrict moves initiated by players. If players were free to move between teams, then, assuming they were indifferent about location, they would play for the team that pays the most. The team that pays the most is the one that expects the largest increment in revenue from that player's performance. Since an increment in the win-loss record yields more revenue in, say, New York than in Kansas City, the best players go to New York rather than to Kansas City.

That point, which is made by those who justify restrictions on mobility, is correct. But limiting the ability of players to initiate moves should not have any effect on where players end up playing. When players are not free to move, does a small-city team that acquired a star player in the draft keep him? For a small-city franchise, the team holding the player's contract expects him to contribute, say, one million dollars in incremental revenue to the club. In a large city, that same player's talents might contribute three million dollars. Because the player is worth more to the big-city team in either case (and the big-city team will pay more for him), the small-city franchise has an incentive to sell the player's contract to the big-city team, and thereby make more money than it could by keeping him. Thus, players should wind up allocated by highest incremental revenue, with or without restrictions on player-initiated movement.

The evidence supports that conclusion. Since the advent of free agency, which made it easier for players to jump from one team to another, the total movement of players (trades, sales, minor league transfers) has been about the same as it was before. So, although restrictions on player-initiated movement should not affect the allocation of player talent within a league, they substantially affect the division of income between owners and players. Under free agency, the players earn what they contribute to incremental revenue; under league restrictions on player-initiated transfers, the owners keep more of the revenues. The dramatic rise in player salaries since the mid-1970s, notably in baseball and basketball, is largely the result of the relaxation of restrictions on player-initiated transfers.

The most important antitrust issue in sports today relates to the formation of new leagues. The collusive arrangement in the allocation of broadcast rights between the television networks and the existing leagues constitutes a formidable barrier to entry for a new league. In particular, football programming is very valuable because football games attract large audiences. Large audiences mean high advertising revenues and, therefore, large network television revenues to the NFL. By allocating games to several networks instead of just one, the NFL has become a partner with the networks in the broadcast enterprise. Further, the contract stipulates that the networks cannot broadcast another professional football league's games within forty-eight hours of an NFL game. This relegates any competing league's games to midweek, which is hardly attractive to the networks.

Television, by building fan recognition and loyalty, builds attendance and gate receipts. Thus, a competing league may not be able to exist without access to television. The NFL has an exclusive, multiyear contract with the networks that is a barrier to entry for a competing league. Only when the network-NFL contract expires is there the possibility of a point of entry. But for that to happen, the networks would have to consider a new league's games suitable substitutes for NFL games. Because teams in new leagues are inferior to established teams (the established teams already have the best stars), the networks have little incentive to make such a substitution. Partly because of the broadcast exemption to antitrust law, and partly because of the judicious expansion of the leagues in all of the professional team sports, fans are unlikely to see competing sports leagues arise.

Some seventy-three million fans attended major league baseball games in 2004, and fan interest remains high in other professional team sports. The explosion of new sport facilities since 1990 has contributed to increased attendance. These expensive facilities, usually financed by taxpayers, are leased to the teams at relatively low prices. These implicit annual subsidies to teams are about ten million dollars or so per team, and a new facility adds twenty million or more to a team's revenue. These added revenues and subsidies add to a franchise's value.

Economists have found that the benefits from the government subsidies, such as increased employment, expanded consumer leisure spending, economic development, or other economic effects, are a fraction of the subsidies. Proponents of public spending on sports facilities claim that income generated in the community is ten dollars for every one dollar spent by the team's fans. Econ-

omists are skeptical that the impact is more than twice that of club revenues. Many other public projects rank well above sport facilities in generating benefits for a given subsidy. But politicians and bureaucrats are in a poor bargaining position relative to the monopoly leagues. These leagues keep one or more sites open and threaten to relocate or deny expansion to the locality that will not build a new facility. Politicians want to provide popular projects that their constituents favor, and a sports team is considered part of the local culture and quality of life. Often, special bond elections are held to approve public spending for sport facilities. Such elections seldom draw voter turnouts of more than 10 percent. Relatively more fans turn out to vote than the general public. Moreover, these facilities often are financed by increased taxes on tourists. But one must also turn to psychological and sociological explanations for the popular support of sports monopolies.

One important area of economic activity that this article leaves out is that of amateur sports. The economic importance of amateur sports, measured by the value of time and other resources spent by participants and fans, is comparable in order of magnitude to the importance of professional sports.

About the Author

Gerald W. Scully is emeritus professor of economics at the University of Texas at Dallas.

Further Reading

Lewis, Michael. *Moneyball: The Art of Winning an Unfair Game.* New York: Norton, 2003.

Noll, Roger G., and Andrew Zimbalist, eds. *Sports, Jobs and Taxes: The Economic Impact of Sports Teams and Stadiums.* Washington, D.C.: Brookings Institution Press, 1997.

Quirk, James, and Rodney D. Fort. *Pay Dirt: The Business of Professional Team Sports.* Princeton: Princeton University Press, 1992.

Scully, Gerald W. *The Market Structure of Sports.* Chicago: University of Chicago Press, 1995.

Standards of Living and Modern Economic Growth

John V. C. Nye

Judged by the huge strides that people all over the world have made in overcoming poverty and want, it is only a slight exaggeration to say that little of economic consequence happened before the last three centuries. Before that, most of the world not only took poverty for granted, but also assumed that little could be done about it. Even the most optimistic early writers could not imagine that more than a few percent of the population would ever be well off; they thought that the best we could do for the masses would be to minimize their suffering on Earth. Growth, if it could have been measured, was probably not 3 percent a year but, at the most, only a percent or 2 per decade. Increases in the size of population were typically accompanied by declines in the average income. Yet the last few centuries have seen us banish starvation and famine from a large part of the Earth. In the most successful countries, the average citizen now enjoys a material standard of living that would have made the greatest king of two hundred years ago turn green with envy.

The official measurement of national output—gross domestic product—shows that the average American's annual income in 2000 was five times as high as the annual income of his counterpart in 1890, and twelve times as high as the average American's income in the middle of the nineteenth century.

Even for the poorer areas of the Earth, the growth of the last fifty years has been quite remarkable. Excluding the developed nations of North America, Western Europe, and Japan and focusing only on the so-called Third World, we find that per capita economic growth, improvements in life expectancy, and declines in mortality from disease and malnutrition outstripped the performance of the most advanced nations of Europe, Britain, and France, during the Industrial Revolution of 1760–1860 (see Williamson 1993, p. 12). Indeed, the economic growth of China, South Korea, and Taiwan has been so rapid since the 1960s that their people have seen material improvements in thirty or forty years that took the British, French, and Germans a century or more to attain.

When we read about the great civilizations of ancient Egypt and Rome or of the Aztecs and the Incas, we tend to compare them with the empires of Britain or the growth of the United States. This comparison, judged in economic terms, is highly misleading. Although the great civilizations in Egypt and Rome were able to construct big buildings, the vast majority of their citizens, by today's standards, were dirt poor.

What is unusual about the developed world since the 1700s is that—beginning with Britain and then spreading to all of Western Europe, North America, and much of Asia—the population rose dramatically and was accompanied by an even more sustained rise in income per person. At first, particularly in the eighteenth and early nineteenth centuries, this was more a matter of rising population without falling per capita incomes. Overall improvements in material prosperity seemed so modest that

even contemporaries such as Adam Smith did not appear to notice that they were living through what historians would later label the Industrial Revolution. Eventually, the changes were so dramatic that everyone could see that the daily lives of even the common laborers of Britain, France, Germany, and the United States had been greatly transformed. The reason for this transformation was the accumulation of capital, which was due in turn to technological improvement and to the fact that these societies had large doses of economic freedom. The twentieth century saw this transformation spread to a large part of the world.

The United States has been especially remarkable: here, real per capita income has grown by about 2 percent a year for two centuries (Maddison 1982, p. 44). This has meant an astounding improvement in well-being not just for the richest, but even for the poorest. Not only is per capita income up, but mortality is down (see, e.g., Fogel 2004). Contrary to popular wisdom, the air and water are cleaner than they were a century or two ago (cf. Baumol and Oates 1995). Both the quantity and the quality of food have improved. And even outside the United States, famine has been virtually eradicated.

To see how much more an American worker can buy today, compare the number of hours he would have had to work to obtain various items in 1895 versus 2000 (Table 1). Whereas a one-hundred-piece china set would have

Table 1 Multiplication of Productivity 1895–2000: Time Needed for an Average Worker to Earn the Purchase Price of Various Commodities

Commodity	Time to Earn in 1895 (hours)	Time to Earn in 2000 (hours)	Productivity Multiple
Horatio Alger (6 vols.)	21	0.6	35.0
One-speed bicycle	260	7.2	36.1
Cushioned office chair	24	2.0	12.0
100-piece dinner set	44	3.6	12.2
Hair brush	16	2.0	8.0
Cane rocking chair	8	1.6	5.0
Solid gold locket	28	6.0	4.7
Encyclopedia Britannica	140	33.8	4.1
Steinway piano	2,400	1,107.6	2.2
Sterling silver teaspoon	26	34.0	0.8

Source: 1895 Montgomery Ward catalog.

taken 44 hours of labor income in 1895, a twenty-first-century American would need to work 3.6 hours or less for it. The numbers are 28 versus 6 hours, respectively, for a gold locket; and 260 versus 7.2 hours for a one-speed bicycle (taken from De Long 2000, based on prices in the 1895 Montgomery Ward catalog). Comparing the prices charged in the Montgomery Ward catalog with prices today—both expressed as a multiple of the average hourly wage—provides an index of how much our productivity in making the goods consumed back in 1895 has multiplied.

The productivity multiple for the *Encyclopedia Britannica* is vastly understated in the table because the Internet has made the encyclopedia far cheaper. A banquet for the wealthy in the mid-1800s might have consisted of roast beef and chicken, ham, potatoes, fried fish, heavy soups, different types of beans, and perhaps some cake. Today, this type of meal is consumed in the Midwest's all-you-can-eat restaurants for $8.99 a person, with special $2.00 discounts for senior citizens. The only difference is that today's meal has fresher fruits and vegetables, which, in the 1800s, could often not have been obtained at any price out of season, as well as juice, both diet and nondiet soft drinks, and cake and ice cream.

Even these comparisons understate the increases in our well-being over the past century. The official statistics do not reflect the enormous range of goods and services widely consumed today that were not available at any price in earlier times. This is most obvious for medicine. Prior to antibiotics, the common cold or flu was not a mere inconvenience but often a life-threatening disaster. A small wound, if improperly cared for, might have become infected and resulted in the loss of an arm or leg. While still in office, President Calvin Coolidge saw his younger son die of a blood infection from a blister incurred while playing tennis on the White House lawn without socks. Absent the polio vaccine, tens of thousands of children became handicapped every year, and parents everywhere worried that their living environments were not clean enough to forestall the infection. More recently, triple bypasses and even heart transplants have gone from being an unattainable miracle to being the perquisites of a very rich or very fortunate few, to almost routine procedures in the developed world. On a more mundane level, can any medicine have done as much good for as little cost as aspirin? This simple and inexpensive product not only reduces headaches and fevers, but also lowers the likelihood of heart attacks and, perhaps, some cancers. This improvement is due to product availability and better knowledge.

Less than 150 years ago, controversy still existed over whether doctors and nurses should wash their hands and disinfect their instruments before performing operations and delivering babies. Ignaz Semmelweis discovered that, indeed, they should—a discovery, incidentally, that gained him no fortune and drew great resentment.

Moreover, we can scarcely go a day without using inventions and innovations that were once the stuff of science fiction. Cell phones, flat-screen TVs, airbags and antilock brakes, CT scans, digital video players, portable computers, and, of course, the World Wide Web were completely unavailable a few decades ago.

Most of the growth indexes that economists use calculate improvements by comparing the cost of standardized, comparable bundles of goods in different time periods. But the price indexes do not adjust adequately for new goods or for quality improvements (see CONSUMER PRICE INDEXES). And the quality of almost every good has improved. Compare, for example, a 2007-model car to its 1988 counterpart. The 2007 model is much more likely to have power doors and windows, dual airbags, antilock brakes, a more powerful and fuel-efficient engine, a built-in CD player, environmentally friendly air-conditioning, better and more durable paint, often greater passenger space, and substantially fewer defects.

One final example: Before radio, television, or musical recordings, one could not hear Beethoven's Fifth Symphony without attending a live concert. Today, for a fraction of a day's wages, most anyone in the United States can hear any of Beethoven's nine symphonies performed by some of the greatest orchestras and conductors that have ever lived. That sort of improvement in our standard of living is what the statistics do not fully capture.

There is one main downside to improvements in productivity, and it is small compared with the upside. The downside is that goods that require human input, especially specialized, highly skilled human input, are likely to increase in price over time. After all, the flip side of saying that human incomes have risen is to say that human labor has become more costly. We get a glimpse of what life was like for the middle class one hundred years ago, when real wages were lower, by looking at the middle class in poor countries today, where wages are substantially lower than in the rich countries. In poor countries today, even middle-class families, though less able than our middle class to afford stereos and nice cars, can hire servants and maids. As long as servants and maids are still available, the prices they command allow us to correct our statistics accordingly. The problem is more complicated where the quality of the good or experience has been diminished in some way as improved technology and more costly labor have led to substitutions in the good provided. A trip to the beach, for example, may not feel the same if ten thousand other tourists are competing for the same strip of sand.

Moreover, differences in preference may cause losses for those with unusual tastes. Although most people may prefer ballpoint pens to fountain pens, the few that prefer the older technology may lose out as people switch to the newer, cheaper product. This lessens the economies of scale to be enjoyed by the traditional pens and may drive out those skilled workers with special skill in making these pens.

Also, luxury goods that are valued for their exclusivity as well as their quality complicate the story further because the widespread availability of the product may actually degrade its value even if the object is nominally the same.

But for all this, the news is undoubtedly positive. The greatest losers from these trends are likely to have been either the very rich or those with unusual tastes that have not been supported by the market. The difficulties that arise from the universal spread of high incomes throughout the population are hardly disasters. Even if money does not buy happiness, raising as many people as possible to a middling level of prosperity is still an important first step.

About the Author

John V. C. Nye is professor of economics at Washington University in St. Louis, professor of economics at George Mason University, and holder of the Bastiat Chair in Political Economy at the Mercatus Center. He was a founding member of the International Society for the New Institutional Economics (ISNIE) and is a specialist in Western economic history.

Further Reading

Baumol, William J., and Wallace E. Oates. "Long Run Trends in Environmental Quality." In Julian L. Simon, ed., *The State of Humanity.* Oxford: Blackwell, 1995.

De Long, J. Bradford. "Cornucopia: Increasing Wealth in the Twentieth Century." 2000. Unpublished manuscript online at: http://www.j-bradford-delong.net/TCEH/2000/TCEH_2.html.

Fogel, Robert William. *The Escape from Hunger and Premature Death, 1700–2100.* Cambridge: Cambridge University Press, 2004.

Maddison, Angus. *Phases of Capitalist Development.* Oxford: Oxford University Press, 1982.

Nye, John V. C. "Economic Growth and True Inequality." 2002. In Library of Economics and Liberty, online at: http://www.econlib.org/library/Columns/Nyegrowth.html.

———. "Irreducible Inequality." 2002. In Library of Economics and Liberty, online at: http://www.econlib.org/library/Columns/Nyepositional.html.

Williamson, Jeffrey. "How Tough Are Times in the Third World?" In D. N. McCloskey, ed., *Second Thoughts: Myths and Morals of U.S. Economic History.* New York: Oxford University Press, 1993.

Stock Market

Jeremy J. Siegel

The price of a share of stock, like that of any other financial asset, equals the present value of the sum of the expected dividends or other cash payments to the shareholders, where future payments are discounted by the interest rate and risks involved. Most of the cash payments to stockholders arise from dividends, which are paid out of earnings and other distributions resulting from the sale or liquidation of assets.

The cash payments available to a shareholder are uncertain and subject to the earnings of the firm. This uncertainty contrasts sharply with cash payments to bondholders, the value of which is fixed by contractual obligation and is paid in a timely manner unless the firm encounters severe financial stress, such as bankruptcy. As a result, the price of stocks normally fluctuates more than the price of bonds.

Over time, most firms pay rising dividends. Dividends increase for two reasons. First, because firms rarely pay out all their earnings as dividends, the difference, called retained earnings, is available to the firm to invest or buy back its shares. This, in turn, often produces greater future earnings and, hence, higher prospective dividends. Second, a firm's earnings will rise as the price of its output rises with inflation, as demand for its products grows, and as the firm operates more efficiently. Firms with steadily rising dividends are sought after by investors, who often pay premium prices to own such firms.

Cash payments to shareholders also result from the sale of some of the firm's assets, outright liquidation, or a buyout. A firm may sell some of its operations, using the revenues from the sale to provide a lump-sum distribution to stockholders. When a firm sells all its operations and assets, this total liquidation results in a cash distribution after obligations to creditors are satisfied. Finally, if another firm or individual purchases the firm, existing shareholders are often eligible to receive cash distributions.

Stock Markets

In the United States, most stocks are traded either on the New York Stock Exchange (NYSE, or "Big Board") or on NASDAQ, an electronic market that grew out of the "over-the-counter" market in 1970. The NYSE, founded in 1792, trades most of the large U.S. stocks through a series of specialists who are assigned stocks and facilitate trading on the floor of the exchange. In contrast, the NASDAQ has no specialists and no specific physical location since market makers and traders operate wholly through electronic systems.

In addition, there is a smaller exchange, also located in New York, called the American Stock Exchange (Amex), which trades in small stocks that are not large enough to qualify for trading on the NYSE. Many of the newly issued ETFs, or exchange-traded funds, that are designed to match the major stock market indexes are traded on the Amex.

Stock Indexes

The aggregate movement of individual stocks is measured by stock indexes. The world's most famous stock index, and the one that has the longest continuous history, is the Dow Jones Industrial Average, which dates from 1897 and currently contains thirty large firms. The S&P (Standard and Poor's) 500 Stock Index contains five hundred stocks and is a value-weighted price index that was founded in 1957. It is considered the benchmark index for large stocks traded and contains about 80 percent of the value of all U.S. stocks.

The Nasdaq index represents stocks traded on the NASDAQ market (see above). This index is also value-weighted and is heavily influenced by the large technology stocks (such as Microsoft and Intel) that trade on the NASDAQ market.

There are also indexes of smaller stocks and international stocks. The best known small-stock index is the Russell 2000, which contains the smallest two thousand of the top three thousand stocks traded. Standard and Poor's also publishes mid-cap and small-stock indexes. Morgan Stanley has developed many indexes for international stock markets abroad, including the EAFE (Europe, Australasia, and Far East), which contains almost all non-U.S. stocks.

Returns on Stocks

The total return from owning stock arises from two sources: dividends and capital gains. A total return index for stocks can be computed by assuming that all dividends are reinvested by buying additional shares of the stock. A total return index would be akin to the accumulation of a pension plan that reinvested all dividends and capital gains back into the market, or to a mutual fund that reinvested all distributions back into the fund.

Over time, the total return on stocks has exceeded that of any other class of asset. This is shown in Figure 1, which compares the total returns to stocks, long- and short-term government bonds, gold, and commodities (measured by the Consumer Price Index, or CPI.). One dollar invested in stocks in 1802 would have grown to $8.8 million in 2003, in bonds to $16,064, in treasury bills to $4,575, and in gold to $19.75. The CPI has risen by a factor of 14.22, almost all of it after World War II.

The average compound after-inflation rate of return on stocks from 1802 through 2002 was 6.8 percent per year, and this number has remained remarkably steady over time. A 6.8 percent annual rate of return means that if all dividends are reinvested, the purchasing power of stocks has doubled, on average, every ten years over the past two centuries. This return far exceeds that of other financial assets. This evidence shows that, over long periods of time, the price of stocks fully compensates stockholders for any inflation, as the real return on stocks since World War II is virtually identical to that prior to that war.

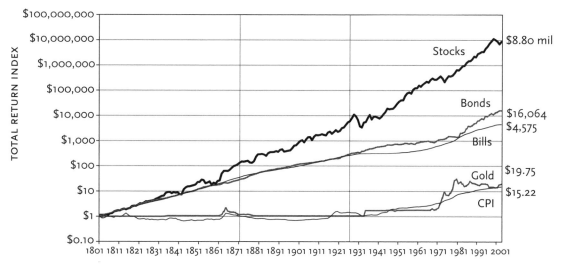

Figure 1 Total Nominal Return Indexes, 1802–2003

Factors Affecting Stock Prices

Two major factors affect stock prices: earnings, which determine the dividends on the stocks; and interest rates, which "discount" future cash payments to the present.

As interest rates rise, all other things being equal, stock prices will fall. However, interest rates often rise in an environment of increasing economic activity and, hence, higher expected earnings. Therefore, stock prices may not fall and may actually rise when interest rates rise. Notwithstanding, low-interest-rate environments are usually deemed good for the stock market, and stocks usually respond favorably when the Federal Reserve lowers rates and unfavorably when it raises rates.

Stock prices are quite variable in the short run. The annual standard deviation of after-inflation returns has averaged about 18 percent, which means that about two-thirds of the time, stock returns will be in a range from −12 percent to +24 percent over a twelve-month period. However, the worst average annual real return for stocks over any twenty-year period has been 1.0 percent, and the worst return over all thirty-year periods is 2.6 percent per year after inflation.

Over twelve-month periods, stocks outperform bonds only about 60 percent of the time. But as the holding period becomes greater, the frequency of stock outperformance becomes very large. Over twenty-year periods, stocks outperform bonds about 95 percent of the time. We recently passed through a rare twenty-year period in which bonds outperformed stocks as recently as 2002. But since 1872, stocks have always outperformed bonds over thirty-year periods.

The stock market almost always falls before recessions. In fact, thirty-nine of the forty-two recessions the United States has experienced from 1802 through 1990 were preceded or accompanied by declines of at least 10 percent in the stock index. In the postwar period, the peak of the stock market preceded the peak of the business cycle by between six months and eight months, but this is quite variable. In 1990, stocks and the economy peaked in the same month, but in the 2001 recession, stocks peaked about one year earlier.

Stock prices can move dramatically even within a day. Over the past 120 years, there have been about 120 days when the Dow Jones Industrial Average changed by at least 5 percent. In only about one-quarter of these periods has there been an identifiable cause of such a change. On other occasions, stock movements were caused by accumulated optimism or pessimism of investors.

The largest one-day drop in stock-market history occurred on Monday, October 19, 1987, when the Dow Jones Industrial Average fell 508 points, or 22.6 percent. No significant news event explains the decline, although rising interest rates and a falling dollar began to weigh on a market that had become temporarily overvalued after a five-year bull run.

Because a recession did not follow this huge decline and stock prices subsequently recovered to new highs, many pointed to "Black Monday," as that day was called, as a confirmation of the "irrationality" of the stock market.

Stock prices, however, are determined by expectations of the future, which must, by definition, be unknown. Shifts in sentiment and psychology can sometimes cause substantial changes in the valuation of the market. Despite occasional false alarms, the stock market is still considered an important indicator of future business conditions.

About the Author

Jeremy J. Siegel is the Russell E. Palmer Professor of Finance at the University of Pennsylvania's Wharton School.

Further Reading

Bogle, John C. *Common Sense on Mutual Funds: New Imperatives for the Intelligent Investor.* New York: Wiley, 1999.

Ellis, Charles D. *Winning the Loser's Game: Timeless Strategies for Successful Investing.* 4th ed. New York: McGraw-Hill, 2002.

Graham, Benjamin, and Jason Zweig. *The Intelligent Investor: The Definitive Book on Value Investing.* Rev. ed. New York: HarperBusiness Essentials, 2003.

Malkiel, Burton. *A Random Walk down Wall Street: The Time-Tested Strategy for Successful Investing.* New York: Norton, 2003.

Shiller, Robert J. *Irrational Exuberance.* 2d ed. Princeton: Princeton University Press, 2005.

Siegel, Jeremy J. *Stocks for the Long Run: The Definitive Guide to Financial Market Returns and Long-Term Investment Strategies.* 3d ed. New York: McGraw-Hill, 2002.

Supply

Al Ehrbar

The most basic laws in economics are the law of supply and the law of demand. Indeed, almost every economic event or phenomenon is the product of the interaction of these two laws. The law of supply states that the quantity of a good supplied (i.e., the amount owners or producers offer for sale) rises as the market price rises, and falls as the price falls. Conversely, the law of demand (see DE-MAND) says that the quantity of a good demanded falls as the price rises, and vice versa. (Economists do not really have a "law" of supply, though they talk and write as though they do.)

One function of markets is to find "equilibrium" prices that balance the supplies of and demands for goods and services. An equilibrium price (also known as a "market-clearing" price) is one at which each producer can sell all he wants to produce and each consumer can buy all he demands. Naturally, producers always would like to charge higher prices. But even if they have no competitors, they are limited by the law of demand: if producers insist on a higher price, consumers will buy fewer units. The law of supply puts a similar limit on consumers. They always would prefer to pay a lower price than the current one. But if they successfully insist on paying less (say, through price controls), suppliers will produce less and some demand will go unsatisfied.

Economists often talk of "demand curves" and "supply curves." A demand curve traces the quantity of a good that consumers will buy at various prices. As the price rises, the number of units demanded declines. That is because everyone's resources are finite; as the price of one good rises, consumers buy less of that and, sometimes, more of other goods that now are relatively cheaper. Similarly, a supply curve traces the quantity of a good that sellers will produce at various prices. As the price falls, so does the number of units supplied. Equilibrium is the point at which the demand and supply curves intersect—the single price at which the quantity demanded and the quantity supplied are the same.

Markets in which prices can move freely are always in equilibrium or moving toward it. For example, if the market for a good is already in equilibrium and producers raise prices, consumers will buy fewer units than they did in equilibrium, and fewer units than producers have available for sale. In that case producers have two choices. They can reduce price until supply and demand return to the old equilibrium, or they can cut production until the quantity supplied falls to the lower number of units demanded at the higher price. But they cannot keep the price high and sell as many units as they did before.

Why does the quantity supplied rise as the price rises and fall as the price falls? The reasons really are quite logical. First, consider the case of a company that makes a consumer product. Acting rationally, the company will buy the cheapest materials (not the lowest quality, but the lowest cost for any given level of quality). As production (supply) increases, the company has to buy progressively more expensive (i.e., less efficient) materials or labor, and its costs increase. It charges a higher price to offset its rising unit costs.

Are there any examples of supply curves for which a higher price does not lead to a higher quantity supplied? Economists believe that there is one main possible example, the so-called backward-bending supply curve of labor. Imagine a graph in which the wage rate is on the vertical axis and the quantity of labor supplied is on the horizontal axis. It makes sense that the higher the wage rate, the higher the quantity of labor supplied, because it makes sense that people will be willing to work more when they are paid more. But workers might reach a point at which a higher wage rate causes them to work less because the higher wage makes them wealthier and they use some of that wealth to "buy" more leisure—that is, to work less. Recent evidence suggests that even for labor, a higher wage leads to more hours worked.[1]

Or consider the case of a good whose supply is fixed, such as apartments in a condominium. If prospective buyers suddenly begin offering higher prices for apartments, more owners will be willing to sell and the supply of "available" apartments will rise. But if buyers offer lower prices, some owners will take their apartments off the market and the number of available units will drop.

History has witnessed considerable controversy over the prices of goods whose supply is fixed in the short run. Critics of market prices have argued that rising prices for these types of goods serve no economic purpose because they cannot bring forth additional supply, and thus serve merely to enrich the owners of the goods at the expense of the rest of society. This has been the main argument for fixing prices, as the United States did with the price of domestic oil in the 1970s and as New York City has done with apartment rents since World War II (see RENT CONTROL).

Economists call the portion of a price that does not influence the amount of a good in existence in the short run an "economic quasi-rent." The vast majority of economists believe that economic rents do serve a useful purpose. Most important, they allocate goods to their highest-valued use. If price is not used to allocate goods among competing claimants, some other device becomes necessary, such as the rationing cards that the U.S. government used to allocate gasoline and other goods during World War II. Economists generally believe that fixing prices will actually reduce both the quantity and the quality of the good in question. In addition, economic rents serve as a signal to bring forth additional supplies in the future and as an incentive for other producers to devise substitutes for the good in question.

---

1. Finis Welch, "In Defense of Inequality," *American Economic Review* 89, no. 2 (1999): 1–17.

About the Author

Al Ehrbar is a principal in EVA Advisers LLC, an investment advisory firm. He formerly was editor of *Corporate Finance* magazine and a senior editor of *Fortune* magazine.

Further Reading

Alchian, Armen. "Costs and Outputs." In *Choice and Costs under Uncertainty.* Vol. 2 of *The Collected Works of Armen A. Alchian.* Indianapolis: Liberty Fund, 2006. Pp. 161–179.
Robinson, Joan. "Rising Supply Price." *Economica* 8 (1941): 1–8.

Supply-Side Economics

James D. Gwartney

The term "supply-side economics" is used in two different but related ways. Some use the term to refer to the fact that production (supply) underlies consumption and living standards. In the long run, our income levels reflect our ability to produce goods and services that people value. Higher income levels and living standards cannot be achieved without expansion in output. Virtually all economists accept this proposition and therefore are "supply siders."

"Supply-side economics" is also used to describe how changes in marginal tax rates influence economic activity. Supply-side economists believe that high marginal tax rates strongly discourage income, output, and the efficiency of resource use. In recent years, this latter use of the term has become the more common of the two and is thus the focus of this article.

The MARGINAL TAX RATE is crucial because it affects the incentive to earn. The marginal tax rate reveals how much of one's *additional* income must be turned over to the tax collector as well as how much is retained by the individual. For example, when the marginal rate is 40 percent, forty of every one hundred dollars of additional earnings must be paid in taxes, and the individual is permitted to keep only sixty dollars of his or her additional income. As marginal tax rates increase, people get to keep less of what they earn.

An increase in marginal tax rates adversely affects the output of an economy in two ways. First, the higher marginal rates reduce the payoff people derive from work and from other taxable productive activities. When people are prohibited from reaping much of what they sow, they will sow more sparingly. Thus, when marginal tax rates rise, some people—those with working spouses, for example—will opt out of the labor force. Others will decide to take more vacation time, retire earlier, or forgo overtime opportunities. Still others will decide to forgo promising but risky business opportunities. In some cases, high tax rates will even drive highly productive citizens to other countries where taxes are lower. These adjustments and others like them will shrink the effective supply of resources, and therefore will shrink output.

Second, high marginal tax rates encourage tax-shelter investments and other forms of tax avoidance. This is inefficient. If, for example, a one-dollar item is tax deductible and the individual has a marginal tax of 40 percent, he will buy the item if it is worth more than sixty cents to him because the true cost to him is only sixty cents. Yet the one-dollar price reflects the value of resources given up to produce the item. High marginal tax rates, therefore, cause an item with a cost of one dollar to be used by someone who values it less than one dollar. Taxpayers facing high marginal tax rates will spend on pleasurable, tax-deductible items such as plush offices, professional conferences held in favorite vacation spots, and various fringe benefits (e.g., a company luxury automobile, business entertainment, and a company retirement plan). Real output is less than its potential because resources are wasted producing goods that are valued less than their cost of production.

Critics of supply-side economics point out that most estimates of the elasticity of labor supply indicate that a 10 percent change in after-tax wages increases the quantity of labor supplied by only 1 or 2 percent. This suggests that changes in tax rates would exert only a small effect on labor inputs. However, these estimates are of short-run adjustments. One way to check the long-run elasticity of labor supply is to compare countries, such as France, that have had high marginal tax rates on even middle-income people for a long time with countries, such as the United States, where the marginal rates have been persistently lower. Recent work by EDWARD PRESCOTT, corecipient of the 2004 Nobel Prize in economics, used differences in marginal tax rates between France and the United States to make such a comparison. Prescott found that the elasticity of the long-run labor supply was substantially greater than in the short-run supply and that differences in tax rates between France and the United States explained nearly all of the 30 percent shortfall of labor inputs in France compared with the United States. He concluded:

> I find it remarkable that virtually all of the large difference in labor supply between France and the United States is due to differences in tax systems. I expected institutional constraints on the operation of labor markets and the nature of the unemployment benefit system to be

more important. I was surprised that the welfare gain from reducing the intratemporal tax wedge is so large. (Prescott 2002, p. 9)

The supply-side economic policy of cutting high marginal tax rates, therefore, should be viewed as a long-run strategy to enhance growth rather than a short-run tool to end recession. Changing market incentives to increase the amount of labor supplied or to move resources out of tax-motivated investments and into higher-yield activities takes time. The full positive effects of lower marginal tax rates are not observed until labor and capital markets have time to adjust fully to the new incentive structure.

Because marginal tax rates affect real output, they also affect government revenue. An increase in marginal tax rates shrinks the tax base, both by discouraging work effort and by encouraging tax avoidance and even tax evasion. This shrinkage necessarily means that an increase in tax rates leads to a less than proportional increase in tax revenues. Indeed, economist Arthur Laffer (of "Laffer curve" fame) popularized the notion that higher tax rates may actually cause the tax base to shrink so much that tax revenues will decline, and that a cut in tax rates may increase the tax base so much that tax revenues increase.

How likely is this inverse relationship between tax rates and tax revenues? It is more likely in the long run when people have had a long time to adjust. It is also more likely when marginal tax rates are high, but less likely when rates are low. Imagine a taxpayer in a 75 percent tax bracket who earns $300,000 a year. Assume for simplicity that the 75 percent tax rate applies to all his income. Then the government collects $225,000 in tax revenue from this person. Now the government cuts tax rates by one-third, from 75 percent to 50 percent. After the tax cut, this taxpayer gets to keep $50, rather than $25, of every $100, a 100 percent increase in the incentive to earn. If this doubling of the incentive to earn causes him to earn 50 percent more, or $450,000, then the government will get the same revenue as before. If it causes him to earn more than $450,000, the government gets more revenue.

Now consider a taxpayer paying a tax rate of 15 percent on all his income. The same 33 percent rate reduction cuts his rate from 15 percent to 10 percent. Here, take-home pay per $100 of additional earnings will rise from $85 to $90, only a 5.9 percent increase in the incentive to earn. Because cutting the 15 percent rate to 10 percent exerts only a small effect on the incentive to earn, the rate reduction has little impact on the amount earned. Therefore, in contrast with the revenue effects in high tax brackets, tax revenue will decline by almost the same percentage as tax rates in the lowest tax brackets. The bottom line is that cutting all rates by a third will lead to small revenue losses (or even revenue gains) in high tax brackets and large revenue losses in the lowest brackets. As a result, the share of the income tax paid by high-income taxpayers will rise.

As the Keynesian perspective triumphed following World War II, most economists believed tax reductions affect output through their impact on total demand. The potential supply-side effects of taxes were ignored. However, in the 1970s, as inflation pushed more and more Americans into high tax brackets, a handful of economists challenged the dominant Keynesian view. Led by Paul Craig Roberts, Norman Ture, and Arthur Laffer, they argued that high taxes were a major drag on the economy and that the top rates could be reduced without a significant loss in revenue. They became known as supply-side economists. During the presidential campaign of 1980, Ronald Reagan argued that high marginal tax rates were hurting economic output, but contrary to what many people think, neither Reagan nor his economic advisers believed that cuts in marginal tax rates would increase tax revenue.

The 1975–1985 period was an era of great debate about the impact of supply-side policies. The supply siders highlighted the positive evidence from two earlier major tax cuts—the Coolidge-Mellon cuts of the 1920s and the Kennedy tax cut of the 1960s. Between 1921 and 1926, three major tax cuts reduced the top marginal rate from 73 percent to 25 percent. The Kennedy tax cut reduced rates across the board, and the top marginal rate was sliced from 91 percent to 70 percent. Both of these tax cuts were followed by strong growth and increasing prosperity. In contrast, the huge Hoover tax increase of 1932—the top rate was increased from 25 percent to 63 percent in one year— helped keep the economy depressed. As the economy grew slowly in the 1970s and the unemployment rate rose, supply-side economists argued that these conditions were the result of high tax rates due to high inflation.

Keynesian economists were not impressed with the supply-side argument. They continued to focus on the demand-side effects, charging that it was irresponsible to cut taxes at a time when inflation was already high. They expected the rate cuts to lead to larger budget deficits, which they did, but also that these deficits would increase demand and push the inflation rate to still higher levels. As Walter Heller, chairman of the Council of Economic Advisers under President John F. Kennedy put it, "The [Reagan] tax cut would simply overwhelm our existing productive capacity with a tidal wave of demand." But this did not happen. Contrary to the Keynesian view, the inflation rate declined substantially from 9 percent during the five years prior to the tax cut to 3.3 percent during the five years after the cut.

Economists continue to debate the precise effects of the 1980s tax cuts. After extensive analysis of the 1986 rate reductions, both Lawrence Lindsey and Martin Feldstein concluded that for taxpayers previously facing marginal tax rates of 40 percent or more, the drop in tax rates caused such a large increase in taxable income that the government was collecting even more revenue from taxpayers in these top brackets. This would mean that tax rates of 40 percent had had a highly destructive impact on economic activity. Joel Slemrod argued that Lindsey's and Feldstein's estimates of the extra income due to tax rate cuts are too high because they inadequately reflect people's shifting of personal income from high-tax-rate years to low-tax-rate years and of business income from regular corporations to partnerships and Sub-S corporations in response to the lower personal tax rates. According to Slemrod, only a small portion of the increase in the tax base resulted from improvements in efficiency and expansion in the supply of labor and other resources.

Even though economists still disagree about the size and nature of taxpayer response to rate changes, most economists now believe that changes in marginal tax rates exert supply-side effects on the economy. It is also widely believed that high marginal tax rates—say, rates of 40 percent or more—are a drag on an economy. The heated debates are now primarily about the distributional effects. Supply-side critics argue that the tax policy of the 1980s was a bonanza for the rich. It is certainly true that taxable income in the upper tax brackets increased sharply during the 1980s. But the taxes collected in these brackets also rose sharply. Measured in 1982–1984 dollars, the income tax revenue collected from the top 10 percent of earners rose from $150.6 billion in 1981 to $199.8 billion in 1988, an increase of 32.7 percent. The percentage increases in the real tax revenue collected from the top 1 and top 5 percent of taxpayers were even larger. In contrast, the real tax liability of other taxpayers (the bottom 90 percent) declined from $161.8 billion to $149.1 billion, a reduction of 7.8 percent.

Since 1986, the top marginal personal income tax rate has been less than 40 percent, compared with 70 percent prior to 1981. Nonetheless, those with high incomes are now paying more. For example, more than 25 percent of the personal income tax has been collected from the top 0.5 percent of earners in recent years, up from less than 15 percent in the late 1970s. These findings confirm what the supply siders predicted: the lower rates, by increasing the tax base substantially in the upper tax brackets, would increase the share of taxes collected from these taxpayers.

Supply-side economics has exerted a major impact on tax policy throughout the world. During the last two de-cades of the twentieth century, there was a dramatic move away from high marginal tax rates. In 1980, the top marginal rate on personal income was 60 percent or more in forty-nine countries. By 1990, only twenty countries had such a high top tax rate, and by 2000, only three countries—Cameroon, Belgium, and the Democratic Republic of Congo—had a top rate of 60 percent or more. In 1980, only six countries levied a personal income tax with a top marginal rate of less than 40 percent. By 2000, fifty-six countries had a top marginal income tax rate of less than 40 percent.[1]

The former socialist economies have been at the forefront of those moving toward supply-side tax policies. Following the collapse of communism, most of these countries had a combination of personal income and payroll taxes that generated high marginal tax rates. As a result, the incentive to work was weak and tax evasion was massive. Russia was a typical case. In 2000, Russia's top personal income tax rate was 30 percent and a 40.5 percent payroll tax was applied at all earnings levels. If Russians with even modest earnings complied with the law, the tax collector took well over half of their incremental income. Beginning in January 2001, the newly elected Putin administration shifted to a 13 percent flat-rate income tax and also sharply reduced the payroll tax rate. The results were striking. Tax compliance increased and the inflation-adjusted revenues from the personal income tax rose more than 20 percent annually during the three years following the adoption of the flat-rate tax. Further, the real growth rate of the Russian economy averaged 7 percent during 2001–2003, up from less than 2 percent during the three years prior to the tax cut.

Ukraine soon followed Russia's lead and capped its top personal income tax rate at 13 percent. Beginning in 2004, the Slovak Republic imposed a flat-rate personal income tax of 19 percent. Latvia and Estonia also have flat-rate personal income taxes.

Supply-side economics provided the political and theoretical foundations for what became a remarkable change in the tax structure of the United States and other countries throughout the world. The view that changes in tax rates exert an impact on total output and that marginal rates in excess of 40 percent exert a destructive influence on the incentive of people to work and use resources wisely is now widely accepted by both economists and policymakers. This change in thinking is the major legacy of supply-side economics.

1. These figures are from James Gwartney and Robert Lawson, *Economic Freedom of the World, 2003 Annual Report.*

About the Author

James D. Gwartney is a professor of economics and director of the Gus A. Stavros Center for the Advancement of Free Enterprise and Economic Education at Florida State University. He was previously chief economist of the Joint Economic Committee of the U.S. Congress.

Further Reading

Canto, Victor A., Douglas H. Joines, and Arthur B. Laffer. *Foundations of Supply-Side Economics.* New York: Academic Press, 1983.

Federal Reserve Bank of Atlanta. *Supply-Side Economics in the 1980s.* Westport, Conn.: Quorum Books, 1982.

Gruber, Jonathan, and Emmanuel Saez. "The Elasticity of Taxable Income Evidence and Implications." NBER Working Paper no. 7512. National Bureau of Economic Research, Cambridge, Mass. 2000.

Lindsey, Lawrence. *The Growth Experiment: How the New Tax Policy Is Transforming the U.S. Economy.* New York: Basic Books, 1990.

Prescott, Edward C. "Richard T. Ely Lecture: Prosperity and Depression." *American Economic Review,* Papers and Proceedings, 92, no. 2 (2002): 1–15.

Slemrod, Joel, ed. *Does Atlas Shrug: The Economic Consequences of Taxing the Rich.* New York: Russell Sage Foundation, 2000.

U.S. Congress. Joint Economic Committee. *The Mellon and Kennedy Tax Cuts: A Review and Analysis.* Washington, D.C.: Government Printing Office, 1982.

Surface Freight Transportation Deregulation

Thomas Gale Moore

History of Regulation

With the establishment of the Interstate Commerce Commission (ICC) to oversee the railroad industry in 1887, the federal government began more than a century of regulating surface freight transportation. Railroad regulation was strengthened several times in the early part of the twentieth century. Those changes stifled price competition between railroads by prohibiting rebating, discounting, and secret price cutting. The federal government nationalized the railroads during World War I, and by the end of the war had provided about $1.5 billion (1919 dollars) in subsidies to the ailing railroads. The major concern after the war was to make the railroads profitable. The Transportation Act of 1920 essentially cartelized the railroad industry and mandated that the Interstate Commerce Commission establish rates to provide a "fair rate of return." The ICC was given complete authority over entry, abandonment, mergers, minimum rates, intrastate rates, and the issuing of new securities.

Even during the prosperous 1920s, railroad earnings never reached what the act indicated might be a fair rate of return. New competition from the growing trucking industry presented a major problem for the railroads. With the advent of the Great Depression, earnings plummeted and, for the first time, became negative for the whole railroad industry. In an attempt to improve their profitability, leaders of the railroad industry, together with the ICC, urged Congress to regulate these competitors.

The trucking industry also suffered during the Depression and began to favor allowing the ICC to restrict competition. With the major spokesmen for a number of large truckers arguing for controls to prevent "cutthroat competition," Congress moved to control motor carriers and inland water carriers.

The Motor Carrier Act of 1935 required new truckers to seek a "certificate of public convenience and necessity" from the ICC. Truckers already operating in 1935 could automatically get certificates, but only if they documented their prior service—and the ICC was extraordinarily restrictive in interpreting proof of service. New trucking companies found it extremely difficult to get certificates. In 1940, Congress extended ICC regulation to include inland water carriers, another competitor of the railroads. Thus, with pipeline regulation, which originated with the Hepburn Act of 1906, the ICC controlled all forms of surface freight transportation (air freight was controlled separately).

From 1940 to 1980, new or expanded authority to transport goods was almost impossible to secure unless an application was completely unopposed. Even if no existing carriers were offering the proposed service, the ICC held that any already certified trucker who expressed a desire to carry the goods should be allowed to do so; new applicants were denied. The effect was to stifle competition from new carriers.

By reducing competition the ICC created a hugely wasteful and inefficient industry. Routes and the products that could be carried over them were narrowly specified. Truckers with authority to carry a product, such as tiles, from one city to another often lacked authority to haul anything on the return trip. Regulation frequently required truckers to go miles out of their way.

During the first three-quarters of the twentieth century, the ICC kept a stranglehold on railroads, preventing them from abandoning unprofitable lines and business. Regulations restricted rates and encouraged price collusion. As a result, by the end of this period many railroads faced bankruptcy, and Congress faced the prospect of having to take over the railroads to keep them operating.

Regulation's Costs

Studies show that regulation increased costs and rates significantly. Not only were rates lower without regulation, but service quality, as judged by shippers, also was better. Products exempt from regulation moved at rates 20–40 percent below those for the same products subject to ICC controls. Regulated rates for carrying cooked poultry, compared with unregulated charges for fresh dressed poultry (a similar product), for example, were nearly 50 percent higher.

A number of economists were critical of the regulation of motor carriers right from the beginning. James C. Nelson, in a series of articles starting in 1935, led the attack. Walter Adams, a liberal Democrat, followed in 1958 with a major critique in *American Economic Review*. In 1959, John R. Meyer of Harvard, Merton J. Peck of Yale, John Stenason, and Charles Zwick coauthored an influential book, *The Economics of Competition in the Transportation Industries,* spelling out the harm regulation caused.

In 1962, John Kennedy became the first president to send a message to Congress recommending a reduction in the regulation of surface freight transportation. In November 1975, President Gerald Ford called for legislation to reduce trucking regulation. He followed that proposal by appointing several procompetition commissioners to the ICC. By the end of 1976, those commissioners were speaking out for a more competitive policy at the ICC, a position rarely articulated in the previous eight decades of transportation regulation.

President Jimmy Carter followed Ford's lead by appointing strong deregulatory advocates and supporting legislation to reduce motor carrier regulation. After a series of ICC rulings that reduced federal oversight of trucking, and after the deregulation of the airline industry, Congress, spurred by the Carter administration, enacted the Motor Carrier Act of 1980. This act limited the ICC's authority over trucking.

Over the last quarter of a century, Congress has sharply curtailed regulation of transportation, starting with the Railroad Revitalization and Regulatory Reform Act of 1976 (the 4-R Act), the Motor Carrier Act of 1980, the Household Goods Act of 1980, the Staggers Rail Act of 1980, the Bus Regulatory Reform Act of 1982, the Surface Freight Forwarder Deregulation Act of 1986, the Negotiated Rates Act of 1993, the Trucking Industry Regulatory Reform Act of 1994, and the ICC Termination Act of 1995. Those acts deregulated successively, either totally or in large part, trucking, railroads, bus service, and freight forwarders,

and lifted most of the remaining motor carrier restrictions, including those imposed by the states.

Deregulation of motor carriers became complete—except for household movers—at the end of 1995 with the ICC Termination Act of 1995, which also established the Surface Transportation Board as part of the Department of Transportation to continue to monitor the railroad industry. The act transferred truck licensing, mainly for safety purposes, to the Federal Highway Administration. At that time, the federal government also preempted state regulation of trucking, eliminating the last controls over price and service in the motor carrier industry. It eliminated the need for motor carriers to file rates and authorized truckers to carry goods wherever they wanted to serve. Railroads were given more freedom to price, except when "captured shippers" could show that they faced a single carrier without significant alternatives.

The Success of Deregulation

Deregulation has worked well. Between 1977, the year before the ICC started to decontrol the industry, and 1982, rates for truckload-size shipments fell by about 25 percent in inflation-adjusted terms. The General Accounting Office found that rates charged by LTL (less-than-truckload) carriers had fallen by as much as 10–20 percent, with some shippers reporting declines of as much as 40 percent. Revenue per truckload-ton fell by 22 percent from 1979 to 1986. A survey of shippers indicates that they believe service quality improved as well. Some 77 percent of surveyed shippers favored deregulation of trucking. Shippers reported that carriers were much more willing to negotiate rates and services than they had been prior to deregulation.

The Surface Transportation Board reports that railroad rates fell by 45 percent in inflation-adjusted dollars from 1984 to 1999. The demise of the ICC at the end of 1994 eliminated many of the statistics collected on the motor carrier industry. However, limited data show that revenue per ton-miles, adjusted for inflation, continued to decline, falling by 29 percent from 1990 to 1999. How much of this is due to deregulation and how much might be attributed to technological improvements, improvement in roads, and other factors is difficult to determine.

In arguing against deregulation, the American Trucking Associations predicted that service would decline and that small communities would find it harder to get any service at all. In fact, service to small communities improved, and shippers' complaints against truckers declined. The ICC reported that, in 1975 and 1976, it handled 340 and 390 complaints, respectively; in 1980, it dealt with only 23 cases, and in 1981, with just 40.

Deregulation has also made it easier for nonunion workers to get jobs in the trucking industry. This new competition has sharply eroded the strength of the drivers' union, the International Brotherhood of Teamsters. Before deregulation, ICC-regulated truckers paid unionized workers about 50 percent more than comparable workers in other industries. In 1997, the median wage for union and nonunion drivers was $43,165 and $35,551, respectively, while the median wage in the United States for that year was only $25,598. Thus, union drivers still commanded a premium of roughly 21 percent, but even nonunion drivers make more than the wage earned by half the labor force. The number of unionized workers in the industry has fallen considerably, with only 13 percent of the drivers and warehouse workers belonging to the union in 2002, down from around 60 percent in the late 1970s.

The number of new firms has increased dramatically. In 2004, the American Trucking Associations, the largest trade association for the motor carrier industry, reported having nearly thirty-eight thousand members, considerably more than double the number licensed by the ICC in 1978. While the ICC used to license carriers for specific routes, now all carriers can go wherever their business takes them. The value of operating rights granted by the ICC, worth hundreds of thousands of dollars when such authority was almost impossible to secure, has plummeted to zero now that operating rights are easily obtained.

Intermodal carriage surged sharply from 1981 to 1986, but has since leveled off. The ability of railroads and truckers to develop an extensive trailer-on-flatcar network is a direct result of the Motor Carrier Act of 1980 and the Staggers Act (1980), which partially freed the railroads. Table 1 shows the market share of the principal modes of freight transportation in the United States for the year 2003.

Domestic water carriers, which operate primarily on the Mississippi and its tributaries, the Columbia River system, the Sacramento and San Joaquin rivers connecting to the San Francisco Bay, and the Great Lakes, have not suffered

Table 1 Volume and Revenue Shares in 2003 (in percentages)

Mode	Share of Tons	Share of Revenue
Trucks	68.9	86.9
Rail	12.9	5.1
Intermodal	0.9	1.1
Air	0.1	1.9
Water	7.7	1.1
Pipeline	9.4	3.9

Source: American Trucking Associations, April 28, 2004, press release.

from burdensome federal controls, but have benefited from taxpayers' subsidies. Through the Army Corp of Engineers, the waterways have been kept open and improved, locks have been built and maintained, and dams constructed. For a long time the industry paid nothing toward maintaining and improving the waterways, but since 1980 the government has required barge traffic to pay fuel taxes, the proceeds of which have gone into the Waterways Trust Fund. The revenues, however, are not adequate for the updating that the industry believes is necessary.

The Interstate Commerce Commission was never very active in overseeing pipelines, so the Congress established the Federal Energy Regulatory Commission in 1977 to regulate oil and gas pipelines. The Surface Transportation Board (STB) regulates all other pipelines, such as those that carry anhydrous ammonia, carbon dioxide, coal slurry, phosphate slurry, and hydrogen. In 1997, only twenty-one pipelines were under the STB's jurisdiction. Those pipelines are treated as common carriers that must have rates that are reasonable and nondiscriminatory. The abolition of the ICC eliminated the requirement of pipelines to report the rates.

Savings

Since 1980, air carriers have been the fastest-growing segment of the freight industry, expanding by 193 percent in terms of ton-miles from that year to 2001. Truck traffic and rail transportation have surged by 89 percent and 63 percent, respectively. Water transportation and oil pipelines have declined. Although the Staggers Act, which partially freed the railroads, enabled them to carry more goods a longer distance, it was less successful in increasing their profits. From 1980 to 1995, revenue ton-miles grew by 42 percent while total revenues inched up by only 19 percent. The greater freedom the railroads experienced allowed them to improve their productivity by reducing labor costs and consolidating their activities.

The "Railroad Rate Study" conducted in 2000 by the Surface Transportation Board's Office of Economics, Environmental Analysis, and Administration reported that "numerous academic studies have confirmed that rail economic regulatory reform resulted in significant economic efficiency benefits, most notably rapid productivity growth, that enable railroads to become financially stronger while lowering average rate levels."[1] The study claims that shippers gained nearly $32 billion more in 1999 than they gained in 1984.

1. Surface Transportation Board, Office of Economics, Environmental Analysis, and Administration, *Rail Rates Continue Multi-Year Decline*, December 2000, p. 2, online at: http://www/stb.dot.gov/stb/docs/RI.pdf.

Between 1984 and 1999, an index of real railroad freight rates fell by 45 percent. On the other hand, the number of class 1 railroads (the largest companies, with operating revenues above $250 million) shrank through mergers from thirty-nine in 1980 to eight in 2001. In many markets in which it operates, the railroad industry is a duopoly (a market with only two sellers) and yet is intensely competitive.

One of the economy's major gains from trucking deregulation has been the substantial drop in the cost of holding and maintaining inventories. Since truckers are better able to offer on-time delivery and more flexible service, manufacturers can order components just in time to be used, and retailers can have them just in time to be sold. The Department of Transportation estimated that the gains to consumers were $15.8 billion (in 1990 dollars).[2] This does not include the annual benefits to industry of reduced inventories, which have been estimated to be as high as $100 billion.

Current Issues

With the virtually total deregulation of motor carriers—household movers must still file rates—railroads alone remain under control. For certain shipments, railroad pricing is still regulated. If the railroad has a shipper who has no good alternative means of moving his product, the railroad cannot charge more than 180 percent of variable costs. In those "captive shipper" cases, the shipper can bring a case before the STB asking the board to force the railroad to lower its charges. The STB must then estimate variable costs and determine whether the rates are unreasonable. Coal and grain companies have exploited this provision to gain lower rates. Thus the government forces the railroads to subsidize coal and grain companies at the expense of other shippers, the railroads' stockholders, and investments in maintenance and new facilities. Captive shippers represent about 20 percent of the railroad business and do face higher rates, but the cost to the economy is very small and the gain from using the market much greater. In a recent Brookings paper, Clifford Winston and Curtis Grimm argue that the STB should be abolished along with the remaining controls over rates and that antitrust jurisdiction over the railroads should be turned over to the Antitrust Division of the Justice Department.

The Congress should also refrain from adding more regulation. Some shippers and legislators have been urging the government to require "open access"—that is, requiring one railroad that has the only tracks to a particular shipper to let other railroads service that customer over its tracks. The other proposal is to require railroads to quote

rates to any two points on their lines ("bottleneck rates"). Both of these steps would force the STB to regulate rates and determine costs of service, a step backward in freeing the railroads from government controls. Railroads were freed of much regulation because it was strangling the industry; additional regulation might easily eliminate the small profit margins the roads currently earn, leading to reduced maintenance, bankruptcies, or both.

Final Thoughts

The writings of economists have driven the deregulation of airlines, motor carriers, and railroads. Right from the beginning of trucking regulation, economists questioned the need and desirability of government control over rates and service. Research showed how costly those regulations were to the economy. In a 1973 study done for a Brookings Institution conference, this author estimated that the costs imposed on the U.S. economy by ICC regulation were somewhere between $3.8 and $8.9 billion yearly, in 1968 dollars. In 1974, President Ford organized an economic summit meeting dealing with inflation, to which he called some of the leading economists in the country. Although many people believe that economists never agree, twenty-three economists signed a statement at that meeting recommending deregulation of transportation. The result has been all that economists predicted.

About the Author

Thomas Gale Moore is a senior fellow at the Hoover Institution at Stanford University. Between 1985 and 1989 he was a member of President Ronald Reagan's Council of Economic Advisers.

Further Reading

Grimm, Curtis, and Clifford Winston. "Competition in the Deregulated Railroad Industry: Sources, Effects, and Policy Issues." In Sam Peltzman and Clifford Winston, eds., *Deregulation of Network Industries, What's Next?* Washington, D.C.: Brookings Institution Press, 2000.

Long, Stanley G., ed. *Transport at the Millennium.* Thousand Oaks, Calif.: Sage Publications, 1997.

Moore, Thomas Gale. "Rail and Truck Reform: The Record So Far." *Regulation* (November/December 1988): 57–62.

Organization for Economic Cooperation and Development. International Conference: "Road Transport Deregulation: Experience, Evaluation, Research." November 1988.

U.S. Congress. House Committee on Government Operations. *Consumer Cost of Continued State Motor Carrier Regulation.* House Report 101–813, 101st Congress, 2d session, October 5, 1990.

U.S. Congress. House Committee on Public Works and Transportation. Subcommittee of Surface Transportation.

2. U.S. Department of Transportation, *Transportation Statistics Annual Report,* 1995.

Hearings on Economic Regulation of the Motor Carrier Industry. 100th Congress, 2d session, March 16, 1988.

U.S. Department of Transportation. *Moving America: New Directions, New Opportunities. A Statement of National Transportation Policy, Strategies for Action.* Washington, D.C.: U.S. Department of Transportation, 1990.

Taxation

Joseph J. Minarik

In recent years, taxation has been one of the most prominent and controversial topics in economic policy. Taxation has been a principal issue in every presidential election since 1980—with a large tax cut as a winning issue in 1980, a pledge of "Read my lips: no new taxes" in the 1988 campaign, and a statement that "It's your money" providing an enduring image of the 2000 campaign. Taxation was also the subject of major, and largely inconsistent, policy changes. It remains a source of ongoing debate.

Objectives

Economists specializing in public finance have long enumerated four objectives of tax policy: simplicity, efficiency, fairness, and revenue sufficiency. While these objectives are widely accepted, they often conflict, and different economists have different views of the appropriate balance among them.

Simplicity means that compliance by the taxpayer and enforcement by the revenue authorities should be as easy as possible. Further, the ultimate tax liability should be certain. A tax whose amount is easily manipulated through decisions in the private marketplace (by investing in "tax shelters," for example) can cause tremendous complexity for taxpayers, who attempt to reduce what they owe, and for revenue authorities, who attempt to maintain government receipts.

Efficiency means that taxation interferes as little as possible in the choices people make in the private marketplace. The tax law should not induce a businessman to invest in real estate instead of research and development—or vice versa. Further, tax policy should, as little as possible, discourage work or investment, as opposed to leisure or consumption. Issues of efficiency arise from the fact that taxes always affect behavior. Taxing an activity (such as earning a living) is similar to a price increase. With the tax in place, people will typically buy less of a good—or partake in less of an activity—than they would in the absence of the tax.

The most efficient tax system possible is one that few low-income people would want. That superefficient tax is a head tax, by which all individuals are taxed the same amount, regardless of income or any other individual characteristics. A head tax would not reduce the incentive to work, save, or invest. The problem with such a tax, however, is that it would take the same amount from a high-income person as from a low-income person. It could even take the entire income of low-income people. And even a head tax would distort people's choices somewhat, by giving them an incentive to have fewer children, to live and work in the underground economy, or even to emigrate.

Within the realm of what is practical, the goal of efficiency is to minimize the ways in which taxes affect people's choices. A major philosophical issue among economists is whether tax policy should purposefully deviate from efficiency in order to encourage taxpayers to pursue positive economic objectives (such as saving) or to avoid harmful economic activities (such as smoking). Most economists would accept some role for taxation in so steering economic choices, but economists disagree on two important points: how well policymakers can presume to know which objectives we should pursue (e.g., is discouraging smoking an infringement on personal freedom?), and the extent of our ability to influence taxpayer choices without unwanted side effects (e.g., will tax breaks for saving merely reward those with the most discretionary income for actually saving little more than they would without a tax break?).

Fairness, to most people, requires that equally situated taxpayers pay equal taxes ("horizontal equity") and that better-off taxpayers pay more tax ("vertical equity"). Although these objectives seem clear enough, fairness is very much in the eye of the beholder. There is little agreement over how to judge whether two taxpayers are equally situated. For example, one taxpayer might receive income from working while another receives the same income from inherited wealth. And even if one taxpayer is clearly better off than another, there is little agreement about how much more the better-off person should pay. Most people believe that fairness dictates that taxes be "progressive," meaning that higher-income taxpayers pay not only more, but also proportionately more. However, a significant minority takes the position that tax rates should be flat, with everyone paying the same proportion of their taxable income. Moreover, the idea of vertical equity (i.e., the "proper" amount of progressivity) often directly contradicts another notion of fairness, the "benefit principle." According to this principle, those who benefit more from the operations of government should pay more tax.

Revenue sufficiency might seem a fairly obvious criterion of tax policy. Yet the federal government's budget has gone from enormous deficit to large surplus, and back again, in just ten years. Part of the reason for the deficit is that revenue sufficiency may conflict with efficiency and fairness. Economists who believe that income taxes strongly reduce incentives to work or save, and economists who believe that typical families already are unfairly burdened by heavy taxes, might resist tax increases that would move the federal budget toward balance.

Likewise, other objectives of tax policy conflict with one another. High tax rates for upper-income households are inefficient but are judged by some to make the tax system fairer. Intricate legal provisions to prevent tax sheltering—and thus make taxes fairer—would also make the tax code more complex. Such conflicts among policy objectives are a constant constraint on the making of tax policy.

The U.S. Tax System

At the federal level, total tax collections have hovered in a fairly narrow range around 19 percent of the gross domestic product (GDP) since the end of the Korean War, though the percentage was down sharply in 2003 (see Table 1). The individual income tax has provided just under half of that revenue over the entire period. The corporation income tax was the source of almost a third of total revenue at the beginning of the period, but it has declined dramatically to under 10 percent today. In mirror image, the payroll tax for Social Security began at just under 10 percent of total revenue but increased sharply to about 40 percent as the elderly population and inflation-adjusted Social Security benefits grew and as the Medicare program was added to the system. The relative contribution of excise taxes (primarily on alcohol, tobacco, gasoline, and telephone services) has declined significantly.

One little-recognized aspect of the development of federal taxes is the gradual decline of revenues other than those earmarked for the Social Security and Medicare programs. Although total federal taxes are a roughly constant percentage of GDP, the Social Security payroll tax has increased significantly while other taxes have been cut in approximately equal measure. The result has been that federal revenues available for programs other than Social Security and Medicare have been squeezed from almost 17 percent of GDP in 1954 to as little as 10 percent in 2003.

States rely primarily on sales taxes, but income taxes are becoming increasingly important. Local governments rely most heavily on property taxes. Contrary to what many believe, any explosion in taxation has been at the state and local levels. Unlike federal taxes, state and local taxes have increased substantially—from about 6 percent of GDP in 1954 to 9 percent in 2002 (see Table 2).

Thus, although the level of federal taxes has been rela-

Table 1 Federal Tax Revenues by Type of Tax, Percentages of GDP for Selected Fiscal Years

Year	Individual Income	Corporate Income	Social Security	Excise	Other	Total
1954	7.8	5.6	1.9	2.6	0.5	18.5
1959	7.5	3.5	2.4	2.2	0.6	16.2
1964	7.6	3.7	3.4	2.1	0.7	17.6
1969	9.2	3.9	4.1	1.6	0.9	19.7
1974	8.3	2.7	5.2	1.2	1.0	18.3
1979	8.7	2.6	5.6	0.7	0.9	18.5
1984	7.8	1.5	6.2	1.0	0.9	17.3
1989	8.3	1.9	6.7	0.6	0.9	18.3
1994	7.8	2.0	6.6	0.8	0.8	18.1
1999	9.6	2.0	6.7	0.8	0.9	20.0
2003	7.3	1.2	6.6	0.6	0.7	16.5

Source: Office of Management and Budget.

Table 2 State and Local Tax Revenues by Type of Tax, Percentages of GDP

Year	Individual Income	Corporate Income	Property	Sales	Other	Total
1954	0.3	0.2	2.5	1.7	1.1	5.8
1959	0.4	0.2	2.9	2.2	0.9	6.7
1964	0.6	0.3	3.3	2.5	0.9	7.5
1969	1.0	0.4	3.3	2.9	0.8	8.4
1974	1.4	0.4	3.3	3.2	0.8	9.1
1979	1.5	0.5	2.5	3.0	0.7	8.3
1984	1.7	0.5	2.5	3.1	0.8	8.6
1989	1.9	0.4	2.7	3.1	0.7	8.9
1994	1.9	0.4	2.8	3.3	0.7	9.1
1999	2.1	0.4	2.6	3.3	0.7	9.1
2003	1.9	0.3	2.8	3.1	0.7	8.8

Source: Department of Commerce, Bureau of Economic Analysis.
Note: Data are not comparable to those in Table 1.

tively constant for nearly thirty years, total taxes have increased because state and local taxes have increased. (The data in Tables 1 and 2 are computed on different accounting years and procedures, and thus cannot be added together; the general picture they suggest is, however, accurate.) The increase in state and local taxes has added to the taxpayers' burden and has limited the federal government's ability to cut the federal deficit and to increase spending. It is true, though, that the federal government requires state and local governments to provide various government services.

Recent Tax Policy Changes

Much of the recent interest in tax policy has focused on the federal individual and corporate income taxes. Advocates of "supply-side economics" (most prominently, Arthur Laffer) believed that income taxes had severely blunted incentives to work, save, and invest and that the income tax burden had become excessive. Congress passed substantial income tax cuts in 1981, 2001, and 2003, which provided for substantial cuts in income tax rates along with significant tax inducements for business investment. In the face of a rapidly rising budget deficit, some of the 1981 tax cuts were partially repealed in 1982, 1990, and 1993.

An even more radical tax restructuring was passed in 1986. This law, like the 1981 law, also significantly reduced income tax rates. It was, however, radically different from the 1981 tax cuts in a more meaningful sense, in that all of the tax rate cuts were "paid for" by the elimination of tax incentives—including the remaining business investment inducements from 1981. While this tax "reform" simplified the tax law in some respects, it also included complicated provisions designed to prevent tax sheltering and provided significant tax relief for low-income taxpayers, especially families with children.

Tax scholars observed the experience of the 1980s closely to learn more about how taxes affect economic choices. While much controversy remains, certain results seem clear. First, as many economists expected, the two reductions of tax rates over the 1980s apparently did induce greater work effort, especially by married women. In 1988, according to Brookings Institute economists Barry Bosworth and Gary Burtless, men between the ages of twenty-five and sixty-four worked 5.2 percent more hours than they would have under the pre-1981 tax code; women aged twenty-five to sixty-four worked 5.8 percent more; and married women worked 8.8 percent more. These increased hours would translate into the equivalent of almost five million full-time jobs.

Second, household saving fell in the face of tax rate cuts and substantial targeted tax incentives for saving, strongly suggesting that taxes have a limited impact, at best, on saving. Studies by economists Steven F. Venti and David Wise (1987) suggest that individual retirement accounts (IRAs) were successful in encouraging new saving, but a study by William G. Gale and John Karl Scholz (1994) indicates that much of the IRA deposits came from households that had already accumulated considerable wealth and could simply transfer it into the tax-favored accounts.

Subsequent papers by James Poterba, Venti, and Wise (1996) and by Eric Engen, Gale, and Scholz (1996) reinforced these contrary positions, while more recent work by Orazio Attanasio and Thomas DeLeire (2002) found very little positive impact of IRAs on saving. And finally, while business investment did increase after the 1981–1982 recession (as documented by Harvard's Martin S. Feldstein), other economists (notably Barry P. Bosworth of Brookings) argue that this increase came primarily in assets (such as computers) that were not highly favored by the tax law. In fact, investment in equipment increased to a record percentage of GDP in the 1990s after the incentives were repealed in the 1986 tax reform, though Alan Auerbach and Kevin Hassett (1991) argue that it would have increased even more strongly if investment incentives had been continued.

Distribution of the Tax Burden

Many economists judge the fairness of the tax system largely on how the tax burden is distributed among different income groups. Further, some economists use the distribution of the tax burden as a major criterion of the success or failure of the tax changes of recent years. Despite considerable effort and innovative methods, however, estimates of the distribution of the tax burden are still limited by imperfect data and the differing perspectives of investigators.

Economists with the Congressional Budget Office have attempted to measure what percentage of overall income is paid in federal taxes of all kinds by various income groups. They assumed that all the corporate income tax is borne by owners of business capital and that the employer's share of the Social Security payroll tax is borne by workers, through lower wages. With these assumptions, they reached two important findings, both summarized in Table 3. First, the higher a family's income, the higher the percentage of income that family pays in federal taxes. In other words, the federal tax system as a whole is highly progressive. Second, between 1980 and 2000, the percentage of income paid in federal taxes of all forms decreased for the 80 percent of families with the lowest incomes taken as a group, and increased for the 20 percent with the highest incomes (see Table 3). The increases were small, with no identified group paying as much as one percentage point of their income more. Likewise, the declines among lower-income households were no more than two percentage points of income. Since 2000, there have been substantial new tax cuts, providing relatively more relief for upper-income households.

Although upper-income families paid a larger percentage of their income in tax in 2000 than they did in 1980,

Table 3 Federal Taxes as a Percentage of Family Income, 1980 and 2000

Quintile of Families (Ranked by Income)	1980	2000	Change
Lowest	7.7	6.4	−1.3
Second	14.1	13.0	−1.1
Third	18.7	16.7	−2.0
Fourth	21.5	20.5	−1.0
Highest	27.3	28.0	0.7
Top 10 percent	29.0	29.7	0.7
Top 5 percent	30.8	31.1	0.3
Top 1 percent	34.6	33.2	−1.4
All	22.2	23.1	0.9

Source: Congressional Budget Office.

they received a much larger share of total taxable income by the end of the period. One reason the taxable income of upper-income families is higher is that changes in the tax law, particularly in 1986, caused many upper-income families to reallocate their portfolios from nontaxable instruments like municipal bonds to assets that yield taxable income. But there also is evidence that the distribution of income simply became less equal. The net result is that upper-income families now pay a larger share of the total tax burden, but also have much higher after-tax incomes. So, for example, the 1 percent of households with the highest incomes paid 14.2 percent of all federal taxes in 1980 and 25.6 percent in 2000—and still saw their share of after-tax income more than double, from 7.7 percent in 1980 to 15.5 percent in 2000.

Current Tax Issues

Tax policy remains controversial, and some economists continue to argue for large-scale revision of the federal tax system. Princeton's David F. Bradford and Stanford's Robert E. Hall have advocated slightly different forms of a flat-rate tax on labor income coupled with immediate deduction ("expensing") of the cost of all investment for the corporate income tax. Some conservative economists, such as Charles E. McLure Jr., and some liberal ones, such as Alice M. Rivlin, argue for a broad-based federal tax on consumption, like the sales taxes imposed by the states or the value-added tax (VAT) widely used in Europe. A key issue to consumption-tax advocates is how the proceeds of the tax would be used. Some would insist that the money go to increase federal spending; some would demand that it be used to cut federal income taxes; and some would re-

quire that it reduce the deficit. Advocates argue that a tax on consumption would encourage saving; opponents claim that such a tax would unfairly burden low-income families.

In past years, some economists, including Princeton's Alan Blinder, argued that the income tax should provide a comprehensive adjustment ("indexation") for inflation to eliminate the inflationary mismeasurement of interest income and expense, depreciation of business investment, and capital gains. A few economists would maintain that indexation should be pursued today. However, an adjustment for inflation would be quite complex; and with inflation as low as 2 percent now, and with little short-term prospect of a substantial increase in inflation, many economists contend that the costs in complexity would exceed the benefits in precise measurement of income.

Some economists, including Martin S. Feldstein and R. Glenn Hubbard, argue for targeted tax cuts for capital gains (the profit from the sale of assets such as corporate stock or real estate) and dividends paid on corporate stock (to reduce or eliminate the so-called double tax on dividends, in which profits are taxed under the corporate income tax and then again when distributed to shareholders as dividends). Such initiatives are typically claimed to add to fairness (through attenuating "double taxation") and to increase economic growth. Opponents, such as Brookings's Henry J. Aaron, believe that they would be ineffective and would unduly benefit upper-income groups, who own the most capital assets and have the most discretionary income to save. The 2003 tax law cut the already reduced tax rates on capital gains and established similar reduced individual income tax rates for corporate dividend income. Because these provisions were both controversial and temporary, they will remain the subject of debate. Likewise, the general tax rate cuts enacted in 2001 and accelerated in 2003 remain temporary, expiring at the end of 2010.

Other, more conservative economists advocate greater incentives for household saving, such as allowing withdrawals of nondeductible deposits into designated savings accounts to be tax free. Advocates, such as Eric M. Engen, argue that greater freedom with respect to withdrawals from tax-favored savings accounts would encourage even people with modest incomes, who cannot risk "locking up" their limited funds until retirement, to save. Opponents, including Leonard E. Burman, William G. Gale, and Peter R. Orszag, fear that wealthy people would be able to shield past savings from taxation in perpetuity, thus increasing the federal deficit without undertaking any new saving.

The estate tax will be phased down until it is totally eliminated in 2010, only to return under its pre-2001 configuration in 2011. This provision has proved particularly controversial. Advocates of repeal, such as Council of Economic Advisers Chair N. Gregory Mankiw, argue that the estate tax, whose highest pre-2001 rate, at 55 percent, was significantly higher than the income tax, constituted double taxation and both discouraged effort and increased consumption on the part of older wealthy people. Advocates contend that successful small businesses and farms could be forced to shut down because of insufficient liquidity to pay the tax. Opponents, including William G. Gale, argue that efficiency concerns about the estate tax, whose exemptions were already so high as to excuse 98 percent of all decedents from any tax, were exaggerated. They maintain that much accumulated wealth (such as unrealized capital gains) might not be taxed at all upon death, that policies were already in place to postpone tax for estates with small businesses or farms that might have liquidity problems, and that the new law's phase-down, repeal, and reinstatement of the estate tax would make sound financial planning virtually impossible.

With taxpayers enjoying tax reductions today that are scheduled to fade away entirely in 2011—and with a sizable and possibly enduring budget deficit—these tax issues will surely remain prominent in the public-policy debate.

About the Author

Joseph J. Minarik is the senior vice president and director of research at the Committee for Economic Development. He was previously the Democratic policy director and chief economist of the Budget Committee of the U.S. House of Representatives. Prior to that, he was chief economist of the Office of Management and Budget under President Bill Clinton.

Further Reading

Attanasio, Orazio, and Thomas DeLeire. "The Effect of Individual Retirement Accounts on Household Consumption and National Saving." *Economic Journal* 112, no. 6 (2002): 504–538.

Auerbach, Alan J., and Kevin Hassett. "Investment, Tax Policy, and the Tax Reform Act of 1986." In Joel Slemrod, ed., *Do Taxes Matter? The Impact of the Tax Reform Act of 1986*. Cambridge: MIT Press, 1990.

Blinder, Alan. *Hard Heads, Soft Hearts: Tough-Minded Economics for a Just Society*. Reading, Mass.: Addison-Wesley, 1987.

Bosworth, Barry P. "Taxes and the Investment Recovery." *Brookings Papers on Economic Activity*, no. 1 (1985): 1–38.

Bosworth, Barry P., and Gary Burtless. "Effects of Tax Reform on Labor Supply, Investment, and Saving." Unpublished report prepared for the Brookings Institution.

Bradford, David F. *Untangling the Income Tax*. Cambridge: Harvard University Press, 1986.

Burman, Leonard E., William G. Gale, and Peter R. Orszag.

"Key Thoughts on RSAs and LSAs." Urban Institute, Brookings Institution Tax Policy Center, February 4, 2004.

Engen, Eric M. Testimony on the Economic Report of the President. U.S. Congress, Joint Economic Committee, February 26, 2003.

Engen, Eric M., William G. Gale, and John Karl Scholz. "The Illusory Effects of Saving Incentives on Saving." *Journal of Economic Perspectives* 10, no. 4 (1996): 113–138.

Feldstein, Martin S., and Joosung Jun. "The Effects of Tax Rules on Nonresidential Fixed Investment: Some Preliminary Evidence from the 1980s." In Martin S. Feldstein, ed., *The Effects of Taxation on Capital Accumulation*. Chicago: University of Chicago Press, 1987.

Feldstein, Martin S., Joel Slemrod, and Shlomo Yitzhaki. "The Effects of Taxation on the Selling of Corporate Stock and the Realization of Capital Gains." *Quarterly Journal of Economics* 94 (June 1981): 777–791.

Gale, William G. "Estate Tax: Tax Needs Reform, but Repeal Would be a Giveaway to the Wealthy." *Spartanburg Herald-Journal*, July 27, 2003.

Gale, William G., and John Karl Scholz. "IRAs and Household Saving." *American Economic Review* 84, no. 5 (1994): 1233–1260.

Goode, Richard. *The Individual Income Tax*. Rev. ed. Washington, D.C.: Brookings Institution, 1976.

Hall, Robert E., and Alvin Rabushka. *The Flat Tax*. 2d ed. Stanford, Calif.: Hoover Institution Press, 1995.

Hubbard, R. Glenn. Testimony Before the Joint Economic Committee. U.S. Congress, January 30, 2003.

Lindsey, Lawrence. *The Growth Experiment: How the New Tax Policy Is Transforming the U.S. Economy*. New York: Basic Books, 1990.

Mankiw, N. Gregory. Remarks at the National Bureau of Economic Research Tax Policy and the Economy Meeting. National Press Club, November 4, 2003.

McLure, Charles E. Jr. *The Value-Added Tax: Key to Deficit Reduction?* Washington, D.C.: American Enterprise Institute for Public Policy Research, 1987.

Minarik, Joseph J. "Capital Gains." In Henry Aaron and Joseph A. Pechman, eds., *How Taxes Affect Economic Behavior*. Washington, D.C.: Brookings Institution, 1981.

———. *Making America's Budget Policy*. Armonk, N.Y.: M.E. Sharpe, 1988.

Pechman, Joseph A. *Federal Tax Policy*. 5th ed. Washington, D.C.: Brookings Institution, 1987.

Poterba, James M., Steven F. Venti, and David A. Wise. "How Retirement Saving Programs Increase Saving." *Journal of Economic Perspectives* 10, no. 4 (1996): 91–112.

Rivlin, Alice M. "Strengthening the Economy by Rethinking the Role of Federal and State Governments." Distinguished Lecture on Economics and Government. *Journal of Economic Perspectives* 5, no. 2 (1991): 3–13.

Slemrod, Joel, ed. *Do Taxes Matter? The Impact of the Tax Reform Act of 1986*. Cambridge: MIT Press, 1990.

Venti, Steven F., and David Wise. "IRAs and Saving." In Martin S. Feldstein, ed., *The Effects of Taxation on Capital Accumulation*. Chicago: University of Chicago Press, 1987.

Telecommunications

John Haring

Telecommunications matters economically for two reasons. First, it plays a role perhaps second only to brain power in the operation and rapidly expanding productivity of the modern "information-based" economy; indeed, it supplies a primary technical means for productively harnessing the information and knowledge spread among individual economic actors throughout the global economic order. Second, the evolution of telecommunications from a "natural monopoly" to a more competitively structured industry has raised many challenging economic issues, the analysis and resolution of which are important in their own right and relevant to other sectors of the economy as well.

There's No "There" Anymore . . . Only "Here"

Information and communications technology plays an increasingly important role in the wealth of nations. Adam Smith's theory of economic growth emphasized the "division of labor" (i.e., productive specialization), and he argued that growth through the division of labor was limited by "the extent of the market." Thus, he favored extension of markets overseas and expansion of trade as practical methods of extending market boundaries, and thereby the scope available for further division of labor. Improvements in maritime navigation and the development of the steam engine and rail transport were important because they increased the size of economically relevant markets, thereby fostering greater productive specialization. Increases in market size also encourage economies of scale and scope and more intense competition among buyers and sellers.

Just as improvements in transportation during the Industrial Revolution expanded the breadth of markets, so also recent improvements in the availability of information and the ability to communicate are expanding markets by making buyers and sellers aware of each other. High-quality transportation and communications sometimes make physical distance irrelevant: a buyer and seller may be thousands of miles apart but still figuratively "next door" (see SPATIAL ECONOMICS).

At the turn of the twenty-first century, the U.S. economy experienced a jump in productivity growth, with productivity increases about 0.2 to 0.4 percentage points above the long-term trend. While the causes of this productivity surge are still debated, many economists believe it is due to the spread of increasingly economical and powerful information movement and management technologies throughout the economy.

A Network of Networks

The fundamental economic reform that has altered telecommunications is the introduction of competition into what had previously been a closed monopoly. In the United States, governments monopolized and regulated private telephone companies; in most other countries, governments owned and operated a monopoly telephone network.

Privatization and deregulation have produced substantial productivity increases, a proliferation of service offerings, and many service innovations. In the United Kingdom, for example, the British Post Office–run telephone company, prior to privatization, employed two to three times as many workers as were employed in the United States to maintain ten thousand access lines (a standard industry measure of productivity)—so there were huge gains to be reaped from privatization and deregulation simply by attaining productivity standards previously realized only by privately owned companies in the United States. Efficiency gains by U.S. telephone companies have also been quite substantial in the competitive era, although not as great as those experienced in many initially privatizing countries.

Before this revolution away from monopoly, governments typically sought to promote widespread ("universal") telephone service by keeping long-distance rates high—sometimes as much as 100 percent above cost in the United States and even more in some foreign countries—and using, or, in the case of private phone companies, requiring the phone companies to use, the revenues from long distance to subsidize line rentals. To put this into perspective, imagine that the government decided that everyone should have a fine automobile and subsidized a BMW purchase for every household—and then paid for this largesse by imposing an additional two-dollars-per-gallon gasoline tax. Everyone has a nice car under this program, but most cannot afford to drive it long distances; likewise, virtually everyone had a phone, but long-distance calls were a luxury item for most consumers.

The artificially high-priced service, long distance, supplied an attractive target for competition, which is where the initial competitive forays in telecommunications occurred virtually everywhere. The subsidized service—local line rentals—offered a less attractive target, although wireless services provided a means to offer a competitive service without the need to duplicate the existing wireline carrier's network of dedicated subscriber lines. U.S. regulators tried to have their cake and eat it too by attempting to promote competition for line rentals and related services at the same time they prevented the relevant service prices from rising to efficient levels. The result has been the proverbial "incomplete success" and a series of judicial reversals as the appeals courts have rejected the government's program.

Counterproductive Regulation

One method governments in most countries have used to spur competition is to require that different networks "interconnect" and exchange traffic with one another. Network interconnection requirements enable subscribers to use different, competing networks to communicate with one another. If subscribers to a new network cannot communicate with subscribers to the incumbent's network, and if most subscribers are on the incumbent's network, entry may be difficult.

But such requirements can also hobble competition, depending on the specific terms and conditions of interconnection adopted. When a new network service is introduced, one way firms may compete is by connecting subscribers and offering the ability to communicate with a larger number of people than competing networks offer. An interconnection requirement that does not adequately reward productivity (completing calls and/or providing effective service) can reduce rivalry and the incentive to extend network coverage. Why build out if others have already done so and must share what they have built on generous terms? Government requirements to interconnect for terms that are too generous to the user can thus actually deter deployment of competing facilities.

Indeed, this has been the principal flaw in U.S. government policy. U.S. regulators went far beyond simple interconnection requirements and attempted to give would-be competitors access to the incumbent operators' local network facilities and services on highly favorable terms. On the one hand, this encouraged many firms to try to compete with the incumbent network operators—indeed, so many that the market was effectively "spoiled" and most failed. On the other hand, the policy of low-priced access to the incumbent's facilities and services *discouraged* investments in new network facilities, including upgrades in the incumbents' own productive facilities. Why should a cable television system operator contemplating investment in a network upgrade that would allow telephone as well as cable services undertake such an investment when it might be undercut by competition from resale or repackaging of incumbent operator offerings at a huge discount? Or consider an incumbent telephone company that is considering deploying new "broadband" networks with huge information-carrying capacity; such a company could compete more effectively with the high-speed Internet and multichannel video services offered by cable system operators. But why would it do so if governmental "sharing" requirements make it effectively impossible to profit from such deployments?

The competitive revolution in telecommunications has placed substantial stress on the governmentally administered pricing structure. This pricing structure attempted to satisfy various political imperatives (notably, subsidized local service, especially to rural areas of the country) bearing little relation to economically efficient pricing. Such policies depend critically on *closed* markets; when markets are open, consumers can exercise "tax avoidance" strategies by turning to new, untaxed services. Voice-over-Internet-Protocol (VoIP) supplies a salient current example. VoIP supplies an increasingly effective substitute for telephony voice service, particularly for international long-distance calls whose prices in many instances remain wildly out of whack with relevant costs of production. VoIP permits users to complete telephone calls over the Internet without paying the taxes imposed on "plain old" telephone service. With widespread deployment of high-speed, broadband transmission capabilities, VoIP would supply an attractive substitute for conventional telephony and effectively doom the government's system of administered prices.

Policymakers typically recognize this sustainability problem, but often try to "solve" it by extending taxation to new services rather than withdrawing it from old ones. Indeed, "reform" in this area has often resulted in increases rather than reductions in tax burdens. One such example is the "Gore tax," named after former vice president Al Gore, that taxes users of various telecommunications services to subsidize installing computers in schools.

The Invisible Resource

While regulatory efforts to "create competition" through duplication or partial "socialization" of existing wireline networks have produced mixed results in the United States, "intermodal" competition, especially through development of wireless networks using the communications "carrying capacity" of the electromagnetic spectrum, has expanded tremendously. Here, too, it is difficult to credit the "visible hand" of government with a salutary influence. Jeffrey Rohlfs has *conservatively* estimated that the FCC's more than decade-long delay in licensing cellular telecommunications cost the U.S. economy more than *eighty-six billion dollars*—an amount that approximates the magnitude of the government's cost of the infamous savings and loan industry bailout (Rohlfs et al. 1991). Rohlfs's estimate results from measuring what the economic value of cellular telephony turned out to be and evaluating the worth of realizing those benefits sooner rather than later. Using a less conservative valuation procedure, MIT economist Jerry Hausman (1997) has estimated that regulatory delays in licensing cellular systems and in approving Bell company offerings of voice messaging in the United States cost consumers as much as fifty-one billion dollars per year for each year of regulatory delay.

Economic arrangements for spectrum management in the United States are similar to those adopted elsewhere: the FCC defines, assigns, and polices spectrum resource rights. These rights have two important characteristics. First, the government usually determines the use(s) to which operating rights may be put with a high degree of specificity. For example, a license might authorize a radio broadcast service or a microwave service. Significantly, the rights holder is legally precluded from using the assigned rights to supply a different service from the one(s) specified, although that might well be technically feasible and more valuable. The FCC has in recent years begun to afford more flexibility in use of assigned rights: it allowed Nextel, for example, to use spectrum operating rights designated for supply of various work-group communications services to provide a wireless telephony offering.

Second, government defines rights primarily in terms of the inputs that may be used. For example, a radio broadcaster is licensed to transmit from a specific location and height with a specific type of transmitter with a specific amount of power for a specific number of hours per day. There is often an active market in rights so defined. Allowing licenses to be bought and sold leads to productive efficiencies by encouraging investment and facilitating rights acquisition by those who can use them most productively.

However, these licenses are sold within a system of spectrum governance that remains substantially one of "command and control" similar to that of the now-defunct Soviet economy. The central government defines the ends to which specific means can be deployed, and it "solves" the problem of "chaos in the airwaves" through close coordination and control of the inputs used to exploit the resource space. Its ability to adapt to changes in demands for spectrum outputs and technological capabilities is severely limited. The relevant government bureaucracies have little incentive to adapt, and, similarly, the legal processes and administrative procedures are fairly inflexible. Also, the specific methods of rights definition and enforcement that have been adopted are inflexible.

For more than forty years, economists have advocated "market-based" reforms of this regime, ideas the FCC itself has now begun to entertain as the resource has be-

come more valuable and the government has begun selling it to the highest bidder. Rights might be "flexibly" defined, allowing a user to decide the uses to which they might be put. Just as a farmer can respond to perceived changes in prices and demands by altering the mix of crops produced, a spectrum owner might respond to changes in market conditions by altering the mix of outputs produced with given operating rights. Rights might also be subdivided and traded, so that "parts" as well as the "whole bundle" could be transferred through voluntary market exchanges.

Another suggested management innovation would designate some spectrum space for "unlicensed" usage. Instead of treating spectrum as if it were analogous to real estate, the idea would be to regard spectrum communications carrying capacity as more akin to roadways. Operating rights might be instantaneously assigned, as are rights-of-way on a highway, via various operating "etiquettes" or "protocols" and/or collection, using ingenious technical means, of usage tolls set to reflect instantaneous scarcity values.

The important advantage of these approaches is that they capitalize on "local" information about prevailing conditions of supply and demand and do not rely on a distant central authority believing that action is warranted in particular local circumstances. Just as it is inefficient for an economic czar to decide how many acres, and which acres, should be devoted to growing beans, it is also inefficient for a central authority to decide how much spectrum, and which spectrum, to use for, say, FM radio or the specific use of a particular communication path at a particular instant.

Flexibility and free exchange depend on the ability to define rights in terms of transmission effects (i.e., interference) rather than, or in addition to, specification of the permissible inputs that may be used, as is largely the current practice. While this redefinition may be difficult to implement, the potential payoffs from allowing a free-market allocation of the radio spectrum would be even larger. Consider the potentially burgeoning markets for various wireless communications service applications, including high-speed wireless Internet access, "third-generation" wireless, "wi-fi," and so on. Where will the spectrum "carrying capacity" to implement these applications be found? More effective husbanding of the "invisible" spectrum resource is one entirely plausible source of new supply. This is a case in which experimentation and implementation of test trials to gauge the market approach's efficacy would likely be far more illuminating than a plethora of paper pleadings before the FCC. The FCC's Spectrum Task Force has now arrived, in intellectual terms, where economists were forty years ago. As Mae West observed: "He who hesitates is a damned fool."

About the Author
John Haring is a consulting economist based in Great Falls, Virginia. He was formerly chief economist of the Federal Communications Commission and chief of the commission's Office of Plans and Policy.

Further Reading
Coase, Ronald. "The Federal Communications Commission." *Journal of Law and Economics* (October 1959): 1–40.

Gordon, Robert J. "Does the 'New Economy' Measure Up to the Great Inventions of the Past?" *Journal of Economic Perspectives* (Fall 2000): 49–74.

Hausman, Jerry. "Value the Effect of Regulation on New Services in Telecommunications." *Brookings Papers on Economic Activity, Microeconomics.* Washington, D.C.: Brookings Institution, 1997.

Jorgenson, Dale W. "Information Technology and the U.S. Economy." *American Economic Review* (March 2001): 1–32.

Jorgenson, Dale W., and Devin Stiroh. "Raising the Speed Limit: Growth in the Information Age." *Brookings Papers on Economic Activity.* Washington, D.C.: Brookings Institution, January 2000.

Kahn, Alfred E. *Whom the Gods Would Destroy, or How Not to Deregulate.* Washington, D.C.: AEI-Brookings Joint Center for Regulatory Studies, 2001.

Litan, Robert E., and Alice M. Rivlin. "Projecting the Economic Impact of the Internet." *American Economic Review, Papers and Proceedings* (May 2001).

Oliner, Stephen, and Daniel Sichel. "The Resurgence of Growth in the Late 1990s: Is Information Technology the Story?" *Journal of Economic Perspectives* (Fall 2000): 3–22.

Rohlfs, Jeffrey, et al. *The Cost of Cellular Delay.* National Economic Research Associates, Inc., 1991.

U.S. Federal Communications Commission. *FCC Spectrum Task Force Report.* November 2002.

Tragedy of the Commons

Garrett Hardin

In 1974 the general public got a graphic illustration of the "tragedy of the commons" in satellite photos of the earth. Pictures of northern Africa showed an irregular dark patch 390 square miles in area. Ground-level investigation revealed a fenced area inside of which there was plenty of grass. Outside, the ground cover had been devastated.

The explanation was simple. The fenced area was private property, subdivided into five portions. Each year the owners moved their animals to a new section. Fallow periods of four years gave the pastures time to recover from the grazing. The owners did this because they had an incentive to take care of their land. But no one owned the land outside the ranch. It was open to nomads and their herds. Though knowing nothing of Karl Marx, the herdsmen followed his famous advice of 1875: "To each according to his needs." Their needs were uncontrolled and grew with the increase in the number of animals. But supply was governed by nature and decreased drastically during the drought of the early 1970s. The herds exceeded the natural "carrying capacity" of their environment, soil was compacted and eroded, and "weedy" plants, unfit for cattle consumption, replaced good plants. Many cattle died, and so did humans.

The rational explanation for such ruin was given more than 170 years ago. In 1832 William Forster Lloyd, a political economist at Oxford University, looking at the recurring devastation of common (i.e., not privately owned) pastures in England, asked: "Why are the cattle on a common so puny and stunted? Why is the common itself so bare-worn, and cropped so differently from the adjoining inclosures?"

Lloyd's answer assumed that each human exploiter of the common was guided by self-interest. At the point when the carrying capacity of the commons was fully reached, a herdsman might ask himself, "Should I add another animal to my herd?" Because the herdsman owned his animals, the gain of so doing would come solely to him. But the loss incurred by overloading the pasture would be "commonized" among all the herdsmen. Because the privatized gain would exceed his share of the commonized loss, a self-seeking herdsman would add another animal to his herd. And another. And reasoning in the same way, so would all the other herdsmen. Ultimately, the common property would be ruined.

Even when herdsmen understand the long-run consequences of their actions, they generally are powerless to prevent such damage without some coercive means of controlling the actions of each individual. Idealists may appeal to individuals caught in such a system, asking them to let the long-term effects govern their actions. But each individual must first survive in the short run. If all decision makers were unselfish and idealistic calculators, a distribution governed by the rule "to each according to his needs" might work. But such is not our world. As James Madison said in 1788, "If men were angels, no Government would be necessary" (*Federalist*, no. 51). That is, if *all* men were angels. But in a world in which all resources are limited, a single nonangel in the commons spoils the environment for all.

The spoilage process comes in two stages. First, the nonangel gains from his "competitive advantage" (pursuing his own interest at the expense of others) over the angels. Then, as the once noble angels realize that they are losing out, some of them renounce their angelic behavior. They try to get their share out of the commons before competitors do. In other words, every workable distribution system must meet the challenge of human self-interest. An unmanaged commons in a world of limited material wealth and unlimited desires inevitably ends in ruin. Inevitability justifies the epithet "tragedy," which I introduced in 1968.

Whenever a distribution system malfunctions, we should be on the lookout for some sort of commons. Fish populations in the oceans have been decimated because people have interpreted the "freedom of the seas" to include an unlimited right to fish them. The fish were, in effect, a commons. In the 1970s, nations began to assert their sole right to fish out to two hundred miles from shore (instead of the traditional three miles). But these exclusive rights did not eliminate the problem of the commons. They merely restricted the commons to individual nations. Each nation still has the problem of allocating fishing rights among its own people on a noncommonized basis. If each government allowed ownership of fish within a given area, so that an owner could sue those who encroach on his fish, owners would have an incentive to refrain from overfishing. But governments do not do that. Instead, they often estimate the maximum sustainable yield and then restrict fishing either to a fixed number of days or to a fixed aggregate catch. Both systems result in a vast overinvestment in fishing boats and equipment as individual fishermen compete to catch fish quickly.

Some of the common pastures of old England were protected from ruin by the tradition of stinting—limiting each herdsman to a fixed number of animals (not necessarily the same for all). Such cases are spoken of as "managed commons," which is the logical equivalent of socialism. Viewed this way, socialism may be good or bad, depending on the quality of the management. As with all things human, there is no guarantee of permanent excellence. The old Roman warning must be kept constantly in mind: *Quis custodiet ipsos custodes?* (Who shall watch the watchers themselves?)

Under special circumstances even an unmanaged commons may work well. The principal requirement is that there be no scarcity of goods. Early frontiersmen in the American colonies killed as much game as they wanted without endangering the supply, the multiplication of which kept pace with their needs. But as the human population grew larger, hunting and trapping had to be managed. Thus, the ratio of supply to demand is critical.

The scale of the commons (the number of people using

it) also is important, as an examination of Hutterite communities reveals. These devoutly religious people in the northwestern United States live by Marx's formula: "From each according to his ability, to each according to his needs." (They give no credit to Marx, however; similar language can be found several places in the Bible.) At first glance Hutterite colonies appear to be truly unmanaged commons. But appearances are deceiving. The number of people included in the decision unit is crucial. As the size of a colony approaches 150, individual Hutterites begin to undercontribute from their abilities and overdemand for their needs. The experience of Hutterite communities indicates that below 150 people, the distribution system can be managed by shame; above that approximate number, shame loses its effectiveness.

If any group could make a commonistic system work, an earnest religious community like the Hutterites should be able to. But numbers are the nemesis. In Madison's terms, nonangelic members then corrupt the angelic. Whenever size alters the properties of a system, engineers speak of a "scale effect." A scale effect, based on human psychology, limits the workability of commonistic systems.

Even when the shortcomings of the commons are understood, areas remain in which reform is difficult. No one owns the Earth's atmosphere. Therefore, it is treated as a common dump into which everyone may discharge wastes. Among the unwanted consequences of this behavior are acid rain, the greenhouse effect, and the erosion of the Earth's protective ozone layer. Industries and even nations are apt to regard the cleansing of industrial discharges as prohibitively expensive. The oceans are also treated as a common dump. Yet continuing to defend the freedom to pollute will ultimately lead to ruin for all. Nations are just beginning to evolve controls to limit this damage.

The tragedy of the commons also arose in the savings and loan (S&L) crisis. The federal government created this tragedy by forming the Federal Savings and Loan Insurance Corporation (FSLIC). The FSLIC relieved S&L depositors of worry about their money by guaranteeing that it would use taxpayers' money to repay them if an S&L went broke. In effect, the government made the taxpayers' money into a commons that S&Ls and their depositors could exploit. S&Ls had the incentive to make overly risky investments, and depositors did not have to care because they did not bear the cost. This, combined with faltering federal surveillance of the S&Ls, led to widespread failures. The losses were "commonized" among the nation's taxpayers, with serious consequences to the federal budget (see SAVINGS AND LOAN CRISIS).

Congestion on public roads that do not charge tolls is another example of a government-created tragedy of the commons. If roads were privately owned, owners would charge tolls and people would take the toll into account in deciding whether to use them. Owners of private roads would probably also engage in what is called peak-load pricing, charging higher prices during times of peak demand and lower prices at other times. But because governments own roads that they finance with tax dollars, they normally do not charge tolls. The government makes roads into a commons. The result is congestion.

About the Author

The late Garrett Hardin was professor emeritus of human ecology at the University of California at Santa Barbara. He died in 2003.

Further Reading

Berkes, Fikret. *Common Property Resources*. London: Belhaven Press, 1989.

Hardin, Garrett. *Filters Against Folly*. New York: Viking-Penguin, 1985.

———. "Living on a Lifeboat." *BioScience* 24 (1974): 561–568.

———. "The Tragedy of the Commons." *Science* 162 (1968): 1243–1248.

Hardin, Garrett, and John Baden, eds. *Managing the Commons*. San Francisco: W. H. Freeman, 1977.

Hiatt, Howard H. *America's Health in the Balance*. New York: Harper and Row, 1987.

McCay, Bonnie J., and James M. Acheson, eds. *The Question of the Commons*. Tucson: University of Arizona Press, 1987.

McGoodwin, James R. *Crisis in the World's Fisheries*. Stanford: Stanford University Press, 1990.

Ostrom, Elinor. *Governing the Commons*. New York: Cambridge University Press, 1990.

Transition Economies

Anders Åslund

From 1989 to 1991, communism foundered throughout the former Soviet bloc in Europe and Asia. From Prague to Vladivostok, twenty-eight countries in the former Soviet Union and Eastern Europe abandoned similar political and economic systems.[1]

The Collapse of the Socialist System

At the end of communism, all these countries were experiencing great economic problems. The old, highly centralized socialist economic system had become ossified.

---

1. In both system and economic structure, these countries differed sharply from China and thus need to be discussed apart (Sachs and Woo 1994).

Although it had mobilized labor and capital for industrialization, it failed to keep up with modern economies. Its chronic shortcoming was shortages, as the centralized allocation system failed to balance supply and demand for the millions of goods and services characteristic of a modern economy. It was incapable of promoting efficiency or quality improvement because it focused on gross production, encouraging excessive use of all inputs. Its ability to innovate was very limited, too. The socialist economy suffered from a dearth of small enterprises and creative destruction (the destroying of the outdated by new and better products and services; see CREATIVE DESTRUCTION). As free resources dried up, growth rates started stagnating. In addition, an ever-larger share of the Soviet economy, about one-quarter of GDP in the 1980s, was devoted to military spending in the arms race with the United States. The stagnation of the standard of living bred public dissatisfaction, which in turn prompted excessive wage increases and held back necessary price rises. In Poland and the Soviet Union, budget deficits and the money supply grew rapidly toward the end of communism, causing HYPERINFLATION—more than 50 percent inflation during one month—drastic falls in output, and economic collapse (Kornai 1992).

Market economic transformation was initiated mainly by peaceful political revolutions heralded by a cry for "a normal society," meaning a democracy and a market economy based on private property and the rule of law. The causes of the collapse of communism were multiple, and their relative importance will remain in dispute. The economic failure was manifold and evident. Political repression and aspirations for national independence also helped cause the collapse. The multinational states—the Soviet Union, Czechoslovakia, and Yugoslavia—fell apart. The Soviet Union's inability to keep up with the United States in the arms race and in high technology was also a factor. The European Union attracted the East-Central European nations, which demanded a "return to Europe."

Differing Programs of Economic Transformation

At the beginning, the transition's direction was clear, but its final aims were not. Overtly, everybody advocated democracy, a normal market economy with predominant private ownership, a rule of law, and a social safety net, but their eventual goals ranged from the American-style mixed economy to a West European–style welfare state to market socialism. Instead of arguing about aims, people argued over whether the transformation to a market should be radical or gradual.

A radical program, "shock therapy" or "the Washington consensus," became the main proposal for how to undertake the systemic change. It amounted to a comprehensive and radical market reform. Key elements were swift and far-reaching liberalization of prices and trade, sharp reduction of budget deficits, strict monetary policy, and early privatization, usually coupled with international assistance conditioned on reform measures. The program's main advocate was Jeffrey Sachs of Harvard University, but mainstream Anglo-American macroeconomists; the International Monetary Fund (IMF); the World Bank; the Ministries of Finance of the G-7; and leading policymakers in Poland, the Czech Republic, the Baltic states, and Russia also supported it. Radical reform became the orthodoxy. Advocates used many arguments. The success of reform was in danger if a critical mass of market and private enterprise was not formed fast enough. A semireformed system would maintain major distortions that would cause people to seek privileges and subsidies, and would deter investment. The social and political costs of slow reform would be much greater because a semireformed system could not perform well. People were prepared to accept only a limited period of suffering (Fischer and Gelb 1991; Lipton and Sachs 1990; Shleifer and Vishny 1998). Shock therapy was applied in Poland, the Czech Republic, and the three Baltic states (Estonia, Latvia, and Lithuania).

In opposition to the radical reform program, numerous gradual reform programs were formulated. Some favored more gradual deregulation of foreign trade or prices. Others wanted more gradual reduction of inflation rates, budget deficits, and monetary expansion. Many argued that the quality of privatization was more important than its speed. The opponents of radical reform were diverse. Some were theoretical economists who believed that more gradual reform would minimize social suffering. Others, ranging from social democrats to communists, wanted to minimize the role of the market. The most important protagonists, however, were state enterprise managers, state officials, and political economists in the former Soviet Union. All gradualists maintained that the state was strong and capable of social engineering. Gradual reform came to dominate in Hungary, southeast Europe, and most of the former Soviet Union. Late in the day, Professor Joseph Stiglitz of Columbia University became the leader of the gradualists (Murrell 1992; Roland 2000; Stiglitz 2002).

Dramas of Reform

Debate is one thing and implementation is another. In practice, radical reformers were opposed initially by state enterprise managers and later by new businessmen, who were benefiting from transitional market distortions. Many of the anticipated stumbling blocks did not materialize. For instance, labor unrest and popular unrest were minimal, and the large military-industrial complex was

timid. Paradoxically, the problem was not the losers but the winners, who made fortunes on the large short-run subsidies garnered during the transition (Hellman 1998). Postcommunist transition is best understood as strife over these subsidies (Åslund 2002).

Many economists have undertaken ambitious multicountry regression analyses. Although statistics remain poor, economists widely agree that certain major market reforms increase real growth (Berg et al. 1999). Although the effects are often hard to disentangle because various reforms often occur simultaneously, decontrol of prices and foreign trade appears to have had the greatest impact. Also, inflation needs to fall below 40 percent a year to allow growth, and privatization is unequivocally beneficial. Governments that pursue such sound economic policies adopt more market-oriented legislation than less ambitious reformers do.

The liberalization of consumer prices and imports was surprisingly easily accepted, and many transition countries—for example, Poland, Estonia, and Russia—abolished all import tariffs to overcome the massive shortages. What proved harder was deregulating prices and exports of commodities because well-connected people wanted to purchase oil, metals, and grain at low prices fixed by the state and sell them on the free-world market at a multiple, making a huge profit. Usually, such decontrol was possible only after a major crisis.

Inflation was the main economic problem in the early transition. Thirteen countries had fourteen instances of hyperinflation, almost as many hyperinflations as had been registered in prior world history. Many countries entered their transition with high public expenditures boosted by populism. A flawed consensus held that these countries "needed" public expenditures as high as those of West European countries. The East-Central European countries have managed to collect such large state revenues, while most post–Soviet countries saw their revenues shrink in the midst of hyperinflation. Finance ministries had to be strengthened to bring government expenditures under control. Similarly, central banks had to be reinforced and had to tighten monetary controls and eliminate subsidized credits.

Only Central Europe and the Baltic states succeeded in their early stabilization efforts. Most of the other countries faced new financial crises, notably Bulgaria in 1996–1997 and Russia in 1998. These crises were caused by excessive budget deficits leading to untenable public debt. An underlying reason was usually semifiscal expenditures, such as public refinancing of loss-making banks in Bulgaria or tax rebates through barter payment of taxes in Russia. Under barter payment, companies paid their taxes in kind by agreeing to build roads or provide other products, extracting sweetheart deals. These renewed financial crises delivered great shocks, inspiring fiscal discipline. Policies on exchange rates have varied greatly. The first successful stabilizations, in Poland and Estonia, were based on pegged (temporarily fixed) exchange rates or currency boards with fixed exchange rates. Misalignment and financial crises, however, have led many countries to adopt floating exchange rates.

Privatization has been the most controversial reform because it is a conspicuous distribution of wealth, and all vie for a larger share. Moreover, privatization has been monumental and unprecedented in scope. Small-scale privatization of small shops has usually been undertaken relatively easily by selling them cheaply to their employees. Similarly, much of public housing has been sold for a nominal price to tenants. Agricultural land has been restituted in the Baltics and Central Europe. Land reform occurred early where agriculture is vital to the national economy, but later in other countries.

The privatization of large enterprises has been most controversial. The objectives have varied, including privatization for its own sake; for enterprise performance; for state revenues; for the attraction of foreign capital; for the satisfaction of employees, managers, or other domestic stakeholders; and for corporate governance. The debate has been polarized between advocates of early mass privatization and protagonists of piecemeal case-by-case privatization. The Czech Republic and Russia pioneered mass privatization of large enterprises through vouchers, which were distributed to all citizens and could be used to purchase shares of large enterprises. Hungary, Poland, and Estonia, by contrast, focused on case-by-case sales (Boycko et al. 1995; Stiglitz 2002). Economic analyses increasingly show that privatization has been beneficial. Start-ups and enterprises with foreign capital have performed the best to date, but enterprises that have participated in mass privatization are swiftly improving their records. Private ownership seems to matter in the long run.

The officially measured declines in output have been shocking. Fortunately, these huge drops are not credible because communist statistics exaggerated output, while capitalist statistics fail to cover much of what is going on in the economy. The quality of produce has radically improved, as substandard goods no longer find takers. Major structural changes have occurred. The prior overindustrialization has disappeared, and service sectors have expanded sharply. The huge military-industrial complex has shrunk to West European dimensions. In Russia, for example, military spending is now about 5 percent of GDP, falling from almost 25 percent of GDP in the former Soviet Union. Millions of new small enterprises have been created.

The decline in standard of living has been much less than the real contraction in output because consumption has grown sharply as a share of GDP and because much of the prior investment was forced and, therefore, not very valuable. A major concern, however, is that income differentials have risen sharply: in East-Central Europe to a West European level, in Russia to an American level, and in some post-Soviet countries even to a Latin American level. Curiously, pensions initially increased sharply as a share of GDP, while families with children have suffered disproportionate poverty. Complaints about deteriorating education and health care are standard, but in most transition countries their share of GDP has actually risen while these government-run systems appear to be in great disarray (Milanovic 1998). A few countries' governments have deregulated labor markets (Estonia, Latvia, and Kazakhstan), and many have reformed pensions, introducing a privately funded element. On the whole, though, these reforms are lagging.

International assistance has been greatly disputed. Jeffrey Sachs argues that the West should have done much more, and earlier, for the transition countries, while many others have complained about the IMF being too interventionist. In hindsight, international assistance has been significant, but not generous, and has played a crucial role in the success of the transitions. The IMF has played a key role in virtually every successful stabilization program, and it has been able to "graduate" many of the transition countries, as none has high inflation any longer. The World Bank and USAID have acted on a broader front, particularly assisting in privatization. Private philanthropist George Soros and his Open Society Institute have set an example for support of civil society, education, and much else.

A Great Divide
Outcomes have varied remarkably in terms of political system, economic system, and economic growth. Three trajectories are apparent. Radical reformers in Central Europe and the Baltics have built democratic and dynamic market economies with predominantly private ownership. Gradual reformers in southeastern Europe and most former Soviet republics have had greater problems achieving democracy. Their market economies are still marred by bureaucracy, though most property has been privatized. Three countries—Belarus, Turkmenistan, and Uzbekistan—have maintained their old dictatorship, state control, and dominant public ownership, doing little but ejecting the Communist Party.

These contrasting outcomes can be explained by the different goals of these regimes. While their dominant slogans were to build democracy, a market economy, and rule of law, postcommunist countries followed three starkly different policy paths. Radical reformers really wanted democracies and dynamic market economies. At the other end of the spectrum, a few autocrats desired little but the consolidation of their power. In the middle, countries pursued policies imposed by dominant elites who wanted to make themselves wealthy on transitional market distortions. Not surprisingly, the correlation between democracy, marketization, and privatization has been very strong.

Since 1999, economic development has taken another turn. By cutting government spending and introducing low or even flat tax rates, the former Soviet countries have excelled, with an average growth of 6 percent per year for five years and almost balanced budgets. The early successful reformers in Central Europe have stopped at a mediocre growth rate of 3 percent per year, with large budget deficits, current account deficits, and unemployment. Their public expenditures have stayed at a West European share of GDP. These countries have become, as Hungarian economist János Kornai put it, social welfare states "prematurely," with excessive taxes and social transfers impeding economic growth (Kornai 1992, p. 15). The picture of success appears to be partially reversed. Yet, the post-Soviet countries are lapsing into more authoritarian systems, while East-Central Europe remains democratic. Much of East-Central Europe acceded to the European Union in 2004,[2] and this appears to have stimulated democracy rather than economic growth.

Transition economics have brought a few new insights to economics. How to launch the transition mattered so much not because the workers or the people objected, but, it turns out, because the elite were the strong interest group that had to be mollified. Because much output under socialism was of so little value, whether real output declined during the transition is still in dispute. Privatization and enterprise restructuring have been the most pioneering areas, and the final verdict on their success is not yet in. Corruption is widespread, but this tends to happen in all countries where government officials have a large amount of discretionary power (see CORRUPTION), not just in transition economies. Macroeconomic stabilization and liberalization hardly offered anything very unexpected, apart from technicalities such as barter. As time passes, the peculiarities of transition economies wane.

About the Author

Anders Åslund is a senior fellow at the Peterson Institute for International Economics and was previously director of the Russian and Eurasian Program at the Carnegie Endowment

2. Estonia, Latvia, Lithuania, Poland, the Czech Republic, Slovakia, Hungary, and Slovenia.

for International Peace in Washington, D.C. He has been a senior economic adviser to the governments of Russia and Ukraine, and to the president of the Kyrgyz Republic.

Further Reading

Åslund, Anders. *Building Capitalism: The Transformation of the Former Soviet Bloc*. New York: Cambridge University Press, 2002.

Berg, Andrew, Eduardo Borensztein, Ratna Sahay, and Jeronim Zettelmeyer. "The Evolution of Output in Transition Economies: Explaining the Differences." IMF Working Paper no. 73. International Monetary Fund, Washington, D.C., 1999.

Boycko, Maxim, Andrei Shleifer, and Robert W. Vishny. *Privatizing Russia*. Cambridge: MIT Press, 1995.

European Bank for Reconstruction and Development [EBRD]. *Transition Report 2003*. London: EBRD, 2003.

Fischer, Stanley, and Alan Gelb. "The Process of Socialist Economic Transformation." *Journal of Economic Perspectives* 5, no. 4 (1991): 91–105.

Hellman, Joel S. "Winners Take All: The Politics of Partial Reform in Postcommunist Transitions." *World Politics* 50 (1998): 203–234.

Kornai, János. *The Socialist System: The Political Economy of Communism*. Princeton: Princeton University Press, 1992.

———. "The Postsocialist Transition and the State: Reflections in the Light of Hungarian Fiscal Problems." *American Economic Review* 82, no. 2 (1992): 1–21.

Lipton, David, and Jeffrey D. Sachs. "Creating a Market in Eastern Europe: The Case of Poland." *Brookings Papers on Economic Activity* 20, no. 1 (1990): 75–147.

Milanovic, Branko. *Income, Inequality, and Poverty During the Transition from Planned to Market Economy*. Washington, D.C.: World Bank, 1998.

Murrell, Peter. "Evolutionary and Radical Approaches to Economic Reform." *Economics of Planning* 25 (1992): 79–95.

Roland, Gérard. *Transition and Economics: Politics, Markets, and Firms*. Cambridge: MIT Press, 2000.

Sachs, Jeffrey D., and Wing Thye Woo. "Reform in China and Russia." *Economic Policy*, no. 18 (1994): 101–145.

Shleifer, Andrei, and Robert W. Vishny. *The Grabbing Hand. Government Pathologies and Their Cures*. Cambridge: Harvard University Press, 1998.

Stiglitz, Joseph E. *Globalization and Its Discontents*. New York: Norton, 2002.

Unemployment

Lawrence H. Summers

Few economic indicators are of more concern to Americans than unemployment statistics. Reports that unemployment rates are dropping make us happy; reports to the contrary make us anxious. But just what do unemployment figures tell us? Are they reliable measures? What influences joblessness?

How Is Unemployment
Defined and Measured?

Each month, the federal government's Bureau of Labor Statistics randomly surveys sixty thousand individuals around the nation. If respondents say they are both out of work and seeking employment, they are counted as unemployed members of the labor force. Jobless respondents who have chosen not to continue looking for work are considered out of the labor force and therefore are not counted as unemployed. Almost half of all unemployment spells end because people leave the labor force. Ironically, those who drop out of the labor force—because they are discouraged, have household responsibilities, or are sick—actually make unemployment rates look better; the unemployment rate includes only people within the labor force who are out of work.

Not all unemployment is the same. Unemployment can be long term or short term. It can be frictional, meaning someone is between jobs; or it may be structural, as when someone's skills are no longer demanded because of a change in technology or an industry downturn.

Is Unemployment a Big Problem?

Some say there are reasons to think that unemployment in the United States is not a big problem. In June 2005, for example, 33.5 percent of all unemployed people were under the age of twenty-four, and presumably few of them were the main source of income for their families. One out of six of the unemployed are teenagers. Moreover, the average duration of a spell of unemployment is short. In June 2005 it was 16.3 weeks. And the median spell of unemployment is even shorter. In June 2005 it was 7.0 weeks, meaning that half of all spells last 7.0 weeks or less.

On the basis of numbers like the above, many economists have thought that unemployment is not a very large problem. A few weeks of unemployment seems to them like just enough time for people to move from one job to another. Yet these numbers, though accurate, are misleading. Much of the reason why unemployment spells appear short is that many workers drop out of the labor force at least temporarily because they cannot find attractive jobs. Often two short spells of unemployment mean a long spell of joblessness because the person was unemployed for a short time, withdrew from the labor force, and then reentered the labor force.

And even if most unemployment spells are short, most weeks of unemployment are experienced by people who are out of work for a long time. To see why, consider the following example. Suppose that each week, twenty spells of unemployment lasting 1 week begin, and only one begins that lasts 20 weeks. Then the average duration of a completed spell of unemployment would be only 1.05 weeks. But half of all unemployment (half of the total of 40 weeks that the twenty-one people are out of work) would be accounted for by spells lasting 20 weeks.

Something like this example applies in the real world. In June 2005, for example, 42.9 percent of the unemployed had been unemployed for less than five weeks, but 16.9 percent had been unemployed for six or more months.

What Causes Long-Term Unemployment?

To fully understand unemployment, we must consider the causes of recorded long-term unemployment. Empirical evidence shows that two causes are welfare payments and unemployment insurance. These government assistance programs contribute to long-term unemployment in two ways.

First, government assistance increases the *measure* of unemployment by prompting people who are not working to claim that they are looking for work even when they are not. The work-registration requirement for welfare recipients, for example, compels people who otherwise would not be considered part of the labor force to register as if they were a part of it. This requirement effectively increases the measure of unemployed in the labor force even though these people are better described as nonemployed—that is, not actively looking for work.

In a study using state data on registrants in Aid to Families with Dependent Children and food stamp programs, my colleague Kim Clark and I found that the work-registration requirement actually increased measured unemployment by about 0.5 to 0.8 percentage points. If this same relationship holds in 2005, this requirement increases the measure of unemployment by 750,000 to 1.2 million people. Without the condition that they look for work, many of these people would not be counted as unemployed. Similarly, unemployment insurance increases the measure of unemployment by inducing people to say that they are job hunting in order to collect benefits.

The second way government assistance programs contribute to long-term unemployment is by providing an incentive, and the means, not to work. Each unemployed person has a "reservation wage"—the minimum wage he or she insists on getting before accepting a job. Unemployment insurance and other social assistance programs increase that reservation wage, causing an unemployed person to remain unemployed longer.

Consider, for example, an unemployed person who is accustomed to making $15.00 an hour. On unemployment insurance this person receives about 55 percent of normal earnings, or $8.25 per lost work hour. If that person is in a 15 percent federal tax bracket and a 3 percent state tax bracket, he or she pays $1.49 in taxes per hour not worked and nets $6.76 per hour after taxes as compensation for not working. If that person took a job that paid $15.00 per hour, governments would take 18 percent for income taxes and 7.65 percent for Social Security taxes, netting him or her $11.15 per hour of work. Comparing the two payments, this person may decide that an hour of leisure is worth more than the extra $4.39 the job would pay. If so, this means that the unemployment insurance raises the person's reservation wage to above $15.00 per hour.

Unemployment, therefore, may not be as costly for the jobless person as previously imagined. But as Harvard economist Martin Feldstein pointed out in the 1970s, the costs of unemployment to taxpayers are very great indeed. Take the example above of the individual who could work for $15.00 an hour or collect unemployment insurance of $8.25 per hour. The cost of unemployment to this unemployed person was only $4.39 per hour, the difference between the net income from working and the net income from not working. And as compensation for this cost, the unemployed person gained leisure, whose value could well be above $4.39 per hour. But other taxpayers as a group paid $8.25 in unemployment benefits for every hour the person was unemployed, and got back in taxes only $1.49 on this benefit. Moreover, they gave up $3.85 in lost tax and Social Security revenue that this person would have paid per hour employed at a $15.00 wage. Net loss to other taxpayers: $10.61 ($8.25 − $1.49 + $3.85) per hour. Multiply this by millions of people collecting unemployment, each missing hundreds of hours of work, and you get a cost to taxpayers in the billions.

Unemployment insurance also extends the time a person stays off the job. Clark and I estimated that the existence of unemployment insurance almost doubles the number of unemployment spells lasting more than three months. If unemployment insurance were eliminated, the unemployment rate would drop by more than half a percentage point, which means that the number of unemployed people would fall by about 750,000. This is all the more significant in light of the fact that less than half of the unemployed receive insurance benefits, largely because many have not worked enough to qualify.

Another cause of long-term unemployment is unionization. High union wages that exceed the competitive market rate are likely to cause job losses in the unionized sector of the economy. Also, those who lose high-wage union jobs are often reluctant to accept alternative low-wage employment. Between 1970 and 1985, for example, a state with a 20 percent unionization rate, approximately the average for the fifty states and the District of Columbia, experienced an unemployment rate that was 1.2 percentage points higher than that of a hypothetical state that had no unions. To put this in perspective, 1.2 percentage points is about 60 percent of the increase in normal unemployment between 1970 and 1985.

There is no question that some long-term unemployment is caused by government intervention and unions that interfere with the supply of labor. It is, however, a great mistake (made by some conservative economists) to attribute most unemployment to government interventions in the economy or to any lack of desire to work on the part of the unemployed. Unemployment was a serious economic problem in the late nineteenth and early twentieth centuries prior to the welfare state and widespread unionization. Unemployment then, as now, was closely linked to general macroeconomic conditions. The GREAT DEPRESSION, when unemployment in the United States reached 25 percent, is the classic example of the damage that collapses in credit can do. Since then, most economists have agreed that cyclical fluctuations in unemployment are caused by changes in the demand for labor, not by changes in workers' desires to work, and that unemployment in recessions is involuntary.

Even leaving aside cyclical fluctuations, a large part of unemployment is due to demand factors rather than supply. High unemployment in New England in the early 1990s, for example, was due to declines in computer and other industries in which New England specialized. High unemployment in northern California in the early 2000s was caused by the dot-com bust. The process of adjustment following shocks is long and painful, and recent research suggests that even temporary declines in demand can have permanent effects on unemployment, as workers who lose jobs are unable to sell their labor due to a loss of skills or for other reasons. Therefore, most economists who study unemployment support an active government role in training and retraining workers and in maintaining stable demand for labor.

The Natural Rate of Unemployment

Long before Milton Friedman and Edmund Phelps advanced the notion of the natural rate of unemployment (the lowest rate of unemployment tolerable without pushing up inflation), policymakers had contented themselves with striving for low, not zero, unemployment. Just what constitutes an acceptably low level of unemployment has been redefined over the decades. In the early 1960s an unemployment rate of 4 percent was both desirable and achievable. Over time, the unemployment rate drifted upward and, for the most part, has hovered around 7 percent.

Lately, it has fallen to 5 percent. I suspect that some of the reduction in the apparent natural rate of unemployment in recent years has to do with reduced transitional unemployment, both because fewer people are between jobs and because they are between jobs for shorter periods. Union power has been eroded by domestic regulatory action and inaction, as well as by international competition. More generally, international competition has restrained wage increases in high-wage industries. Another factor making unemployment lower is a decline in the fraction of the unemployed who are supported by unemployment insurance.

About the Author

Lawrence H. Summers is Charles W. Eliot University Professor at Harvard University. He was previously the president of Harvard University. Before that, he was secretary of the U.S. Treasury.

Further Reading

Feldstein, Martin. "The Economics of the New Unemployment." *Public Interest* 33 (Fall 1973): 3–42.
———. "Why Is Productivity Growing Faster?" NBER Working Paper no. 9530. National Bureau of Economic Research, Cambridge, Mass., 2003.
Friedman, Milton. "The Role of Monetary Policy." *American Economic Review* 58 (March 1968): 1–17.
Hall, Robert. "Employment Fluctuations and Wage Rigidity." *Brookings Papers on Economic Activity* 1 (1980): 91–141.
Summers, Lawrence H. *Understanding Unemployment.* Cambridge: MIT Press, 1990.
———. "Why Is the Unemployment Rate So Very High Near Full Employment?" *Brookings Papers on Economic Activity* 2 (1986): 339–383.
Summers, Lawrence H., and Kim B. Clark. "Labor Market Dynamics and Unemployment: A Reconsideration." *Brookings Papers on Economic Activity* 1 (1979): 13–60.

Unintended Consequences

Rob Norton

The law of unintended consequences, often cited but rarely defined, is that actions of people—and especially of government—always have effects that are unanticipated or unintended. Economists and other social scientists have heeded its power for centuries; for just as long, politicians and popular opinion have largely ignored it.

The concept of unintended consequences is one of the building blocks of economics. Adam Smith's "invisible hand," the most famous metaphor in social science, is an example of a positive unintended consequence. Smith maintained that each individual, seeking only his own gain, "is led by an invisible hand to promote an end which was no part of his intention," that end being the public interest. "It is not from the benevolence of the butcher, or the baker, that we expect our dinner," Smith wrote, "but from regard to their own self interest."

Most often, however, the law of unintended consequences illuminates the perverse unanticipated effects of legislation and regulation. In 1692 the English philosopher John Locke, a forerunner of modern economists, urged the defeat of a parliamentary bill designed to cut the maximum permissible rate of interest from 6 percent to 4 percent. Locke argued that instead of benefiting borrowers, as intended, it would hurt them. People would find ways to circumvent the law, with the costs of circumvention borne by borrowers. To the extent the law was obeyed, Locke concluded, the chief results would be less available credit and a redistribution of income away from "widows, orphans and all those who have their estates in money."

In the first half of the nineteenth century, the famous French economic journalist Frédéric Bastiat often distinguished in his writing between the "seen" and the "unseen." The seen were the obvious visible consequences of an action or policy. The unseen were the less obvious, and often unintended, consequences. In his famous essay "What Is Seen and What Is Not Seen," Bastiat wrote:

> There is only one difference between a bad economist and a good one: the bad economist confines himself to the *visible* effect; the good economist takes into account both the effect that can be seen and those effects that must be *foreseen*.[1]

Bastiat applied his analysis to a wide range of issues, including trade barriers, taxes, and government spending.

The first and most complete analysis of the concept of unintended consequences was done in 1936 by the American sociologist Robert K. Merton. In an influential article titled "The Unanticipated Consequences of Purposive Social Action," Merton identified five sources of unanticipated consequences. The first two—and the most pervasive—were "ignorance" and "error."

Merton labeled the third source the "imperious immediacy of interest." By that he was referring to instances in which someone wants the intended consequence of an action so much that he purposefully chooses to ignore any unintended effects. (That type of willful ignorance is very different from true ignorance.) The Food and Drug Administration, for example, creates enormously destructive un-

---

1. Online at: http://www.econlib.org/library/Bastiat/basEss1.html.

intended consequences with its regulation of pharmaceutical drugs. By requiring that drugs be not only safe but efficacious for a particular use, as it has done since 1962, the FDA has slowed down by years the introduction of each drug. An unintended consequence is that many people die or suffer who would have been able to live or thrive. This consequence, however, has been so well documented that the regulators and legislators now foresee it but accept it.

"Basic values" was Merton's fourth source of unintended consequences. The Protestant ethic of hard work and asceticism, he wrote, "paradoxically leads to its own decline through the accumulation of wealth and possessions." His final case was the "self-defeating prediction." Here he was referring to the instances when the public prediction of a social development proves false precisely because the prediction changes the course of history. For example, the warnings earlier in this century that population growth would lead to mass starvation helped spur scientific breakthroughs in agricultural productivity that have since made it unlikely that the gloomy prophecy will come true. Merton later developed the flip side of this idea, coining the phrase "the self-fulfilling prophecy." In a footnote to the 1936 article, he vowed to write a book devoted to the history and analysis of unanticipated consequences. Although Merton worked on the book over the next sixty years, it remained uncompleted when he died in 2003 at age ninety-two.

The law of unintended consequences provides the basis for many criticisms of government programs. As the critics see it, unintended consequences can add so much to the costs of some programs that they make the programs unwise even if they achieve their stated goals. For instance, the U.S. government has imposed quotas on imports of steel in order to protect steel companies and steelworkers from lower-priced competition. The quotas do help steel companies. But they also make less of the cheap steel available to U.S. automakers. As a result, the automakers have to pay more for steel than their foreign competitors do. So a policy that protects one industry from foreign competition makes it harder for another industry to compete with imports.

Similarly, Social Security has helped alleviate poverty among senior citizens. Many economists argue, however, that it has carried a cost that goes beyond the payroll taxes levied on workers and employers. Martin Feldstein and others maintain that today's workers save less for their old age because they know they will receive Social Security checks when they retire. If Feldstein and the others are correct, it means that less savings are available, less investment takes place, and the economy and wages grow more slowly than they would without Social Security.

The law of unintended consequences is at work always and everywhere. People outraged about high prices of plywood in areas devastated by hurricanes, for example, may advocate price controls to keep the prices closer to usual levels. An unintended consequence is that suppliers of plywood from outside the region, who would have been willing to supply plywood quickly at the higher market price, are less willing to do so at the government-controlled price. Thus results a shortage of a good where it is badly needed. Government licensing of electricians, to take another example, keeps the supply of electricians below what it would otherwise be, and thus keeps the price of electricians' services higher than otherwise. One unintended consequence is that people sometimes do their own electrical work, and, occasionally, one of these amateurs is electrocuted.

One final sobering example is the case of the *Exxon Valdez* oil spill in 1989. Afterward, many coastal states enacted laws placing unlimited liability on tanker operators. As a result, the Royal Dutch/Shell group, one of the world's biggest oil companies, began hiring independent ships to deliver oil to the United States instead of using its own forty-six-tanker fleet. Oil specialists fretted that other reputable shippers would flee as well rather than face such unquantifiable risk, leaving the field to fly-by-night tanker operators with leaky ships and iffy insurance. Thus, the probability of spills probably increased and the likelihood of collecting damages probably decreased as a consequence of the new laws.

About the Author

Rob Norton is an author and consultant and was previously the economics editor of *Fortune* magazine.

Further Reading

Bastiat, Frédéric. "What Is Seen and What Is Not Seen." Online at: http://www.econlib.org/library/Bastiat/basEss1.html.

Hayek, Friedrich A. *New Studies in Philosophy, Politics, Economics and the History of Ideas.* Chicago: University of Chicago Press, 1978.

Merton, Robert K. *Sociological Ambivalence and Other Essays.* New York: Free Press, 1976.

Urban Transportation

Kenneth A. Small

The defining trait of urban areas is density: of people, activities, and structures. The defining trait of urban transportation is the ability to cope with this density while moving people and goods. Density creates challenges for urban transportation because of crowding and the expense of providing infrastructure in built-up areas. It also creates certain advantages because of economies of scale: some transportation activities are cheaper when carried out in large volumes. These characteristics mean that two of the most important phenomena in urban transportation are traffic congestion and mass transit.

Traffic congestion imposes large costs, primarily in terms of lost time. (Economists measure the value of this time by examining situations in which people can trade time for money, such as by choosing different means of travel.) Researchers at the Texas Transportation Institute regularly estimate the costs of urban congestion; their estimate of annual congestion costs per capita in 2001 for seventy-five large U.S. metropolitan areas was $520, representing twenty-six hours of delay and forty-two gallons of fuel. This totals nearly $70 billion.[1]

But is the cost of congestion too high? Density dictates that we cannot expect to provide unencumbered road space for every person who might like it at 5:00 P.M. on a weekday—any more than one would expect to build a dormitory with a shower for every resident who wants to use one in the morning. Just as an architect might decide how many showers to provide for the dormitory, economists, by knowing how much people value their time and how much it costs to save time by increasing road capacity, can estimate the optimal amount of roadway capacity and the resulting level of congestion.

Virtually all economists agree that congestion in cities around the world is greater than this optimum. They also agree on the reason: driving in the rush hour is priced far below its real social cost. The social cost is the driver's cost to himself plus the congestion imposed on other drivers. People often drive, therefore, even when the social cost is more than the trip is worth to them because they do not bear the cost of the congestion they cause. Whereas this social cost varies by time of day and location, the individual's trip price (consisting of operating costs, fuel taxes, and the occasional toll) is more uniform. Even if the price covers the costs of providing road infrastructure, which it

probably does not in U.S. cities, it is not serving the purpose of allocating road capacity at peak hours to those who value it most.

These observations lead directly to the frequent recommendation for "congestion pricing": a system of prices that vary by time and location, designed to reduce congestion by encouraging people to shift their travel to less socially costly means, places, or times of day. Singapore has had congestion pricing since 1975. London adopted an ambitious pricing system in 2003, initially requiring five pounds (about eight U.S. dollars) to drive in its central area during weekdays. Singapore's tolls are now collected electronically, and London's through various off-site means, in both cases with enforcement by video recordings of license plates. In its first year, the London scheme appeared to have increased speeds to and in the central area by 15–20 percent and to have eliminated or diverted 67,500 weekday automobile trips there, with half of these shifting to public transit and another quarter diverting to less congested routes.[2]

A partial form of congestion pricing has recently been adopted in several U.S. locations. Known as "value pricing," it applies only to a set of "express lanes" that are adjacent to an unpriced roadway. This scheme has the advantage that paying the price is voluntary, but also the disadvantage that congestion is eliminated for only a fraction of travelers and is even greater for the others than would be the case if the express lanes were opened to everyone. Value pricing has been in place on State Route 91 in the Los Angeles region since late 1995 and on Interstate 15 near San Diego since late 1996.[3] Proposals have emerged for a nationwide network of such express lanes to replace the present system of intermittent carpool lanes.[4]

Since examples of congestion pricing are so few, the consequences of underpricing congested highways are far-reaching. People and businesses have rearranged themselves and their activities in time and place to lessen the

1. See David Schrank and Tim Lomax, 2003 *Urban Mobility Report,* available online at: http://mobility.tamu.edu/ums/.

2. See the Singapore Land Transport Authority Web site on electronic road pricing at: http://www.lta.gov.sg/motoring_matters/index_motoring_erp; and the Transport for London Web site on congestion charging at: http://www.tfl.gov.uk/tfl/cclondon/cc_intro. For other examples around the world, see the University of Minnesota's Value Pricing Homepage at: http://www.hhh.umn.edu/centers/slp/projects/conpric/.

3. See the operators' Web sites at http://www.91expresslanes.com/ and http://sandag.cog.ca.us/index.asp?classrd = 29 + fuseaction = home.classhome.

4. Robert W. Poole Jr. and C. Kenneth Orski, "HOT Networks: A New Plan for Congestion Relief and Better Transit," Reason Public Policy Institute, Policy Study 305, February 2003, available online at: http://www.rppi.org/ps305.pdf.

impacts of congestion, probably leading to more spread-out land-use patterns (although the land-use impact cannot be precisely predicted from theory). Furthermore, public authorities have responded by building more roadway capacity, including very expensive, wide expressways designed to allow high speeds, even though peak-period users cannot maintain those speeds. The result is a more spread-out urban area with bigger roads than would evolve if congestion pricing were in place.

The effectiveness of building capacity to relieve urban congestion is limited not only by its high cost, but also by the phenomenon of "latent demand" or "induced demand." Because many potential peak-hour trips are already deterred by the congestion itself, any success in reducing that congestion is partially undone by an influx of these previously latent trips from other routes, hours of the day, or travel modes. As a consequence, adding capacity may still provide considerable benefits by allowing more people to travel when and where they want to, but it will not necessarily reduce congestion. The same problem afflicts other anticongestion policies, such as employer carpooling incentives, mass transit improvements, and land-use controls; moreover, these policies usually provide only weak incentives to change travel behavior.

Now consider mass transit, where economies of scale are critical. Researchers who have compared the costs of serving passenger trips in a given travel corridor via various modes consistently find that automobiles are most economical at low passenger densities, bus transit at medium densities, and rail transit at very high densities. (There is some disagreement about exactly where these thresholds occur, but not about their existence.) As passenger density increases, it becomes worthwhile at some point to pay one driver to serve many passengers by carrying them in a single vehicle, and eventually to incur the high capital cost of building a rail line. However, many rail transit systems recently constructed in the United States are uneconomical because the passenger volumes they carry are too low.[5] An attractive alternative in such cases is "bus rapid transit," in which local bus transit is configured to offer rail-like service quality at costs between those typical of bus and rail. Bus rapid transit was pioneered in Brazil and also operates on selected corridors in Ottawa, Los Angeles, Seattle, Boston, and other cities.[6]

In addition to the transit agency's costs, scale economies have another dimension—costs incurred by its users. People using mass transit first have to access a station or bus stop and wait for the vehicle to arrive. Even if they know the schedule, they have to adjust their plans to match it, which is a cost to them. The more transit lines there are in a given area and the more frequent the service, the lower is each user's cost to reach the station and wait for a vehicle to arrive. Empirical evidence reveals that people care even more about avoiding time spent walking or waiting than about time spent inside a vehicle. So these access costs are quite significant, as are the scale economies that result when increased passenger density leads to greater route coverage and/or frequency of service.

Scale economies are behind proposals to use land-use regulation to bolster transit demand by creating areas of high-density residential, commercial, or industrial development. However, many analysts are skeptical about how effective a given measure would be and whether such "transit-oriented developments" can overcome the preferences for low-density living that accompany rising income levels.

Scale economies create a prima facie case for transit subsidies because the social cost of handling a passenger is lowered by the favorable effects on the average cost for everyone. Another argument for transit subsidies is to overcome the inefficiently low price on peak-hour highway travel, if congestion pricing is deemed infeasible. Countering these arguments is the well-documented tendency of transit subsidies to be partly absorbed in higher wages to transit workers, less efficient use of employees, and excessive capital expenditures. This problem could be alleviated by giving the subsidies in the form of fare discounts rather than as grants to transit agencies. If subsidies are justified because of economies of scale in transit, however, then they would be justified for the many other industries with scale economies: it is infeasible and probably unwise to subsidize them all.

Because of scale economies in mass transit, it makes sense to focus service on those few markets with potentially high passenger density, especially suburb-to-downtown commutes and local travel in densely populated low-income areas. Unfortunately, this dictum collides with the political balance typically achieved in metropolitan-wide transit systems, where every participating jurisdiction is eager to receive some service in return for its financial contribution.

5. See "The Public Purpose" Web site (http://www.public purpose.com/) for unabashedly critical and informative evaluations of many rail projects and other topics.

6. See the Bus Rapid Transit Policy Center Web site at: http://www.gobrt.org/; also Aaron Golub, "Brazil's Buses: Simply Successful," *Access* (University of California Transportation Center, Berkeley) 24 (2004), available online at: http://www.uctc.net/access/access.asp.

Scale economies might make a case for highway subsidies as well, but it is even less clear-cut. Scale economies exist in construction of a given highway, but somewhat less so in an entire network because the cost of intersections rises more than proportionally to their capacity. Furthermore, because highways occupy a significant fraction of scarce urban land, expanding them drives up land prices and/or requires expensive mitigation measures, offsetting any scale economies in constructing them. On balance, there is probably not a strong case for subsidizing urban highway travel.

Today, government provides most urban transportation services and facilities, but this is not necessary, nor was it historically always the norm. Privately built and financed canals, and later "turnpikes," were important in the industrialization of Britain in the eighteenth century and of the United States in the nineteenth century. And today, innovative private transit providers supply highly valued jitney service or specialized taxi service—sometimes illegally—in many cities around the globe, especially—but not exclusively—in the Third World. Ubiquitous private taxi fleets also play an important role in urban travel, and deregulating entry would bring down taxi fares substantially.

Private enterprise is making something of a comeback in infrastructure provision. A private company is completing Paris's A86 ring road via tunnels under Versailles, financed by tolls. A similar proposal may break a thirty-year impasse over completing the final link in the Long Beach Freeway near Los Angeles. London is undertaking a controversial privatization of its subway system. In 2004, Texas solicited proposals for private construction and operation of new toll roads, and in 2005 Chicago privatized operation of its Skyway, an important segment of Interstate 90 bringing traffic into the city from the east.[7]

Evidence suggests that the private sector can carry out transportation activities more cheaply than the public sector can. Many experiments with the private sector have been motivated by huge subsidy increases or evident inefficiency of public sector operations. During the 1980s, all of Britain's urban bus services outside London were privatized and the markets opened to free entry, resulting in cost savings but also some competitive problems. In most instances, some sort of regulation is needed to offset the market power that can accompany privatization. Success

depends on the specifics of the situation and the details of any accompanying regulatory or franchising arrangements.

Urban transportation has historically had a dramatic influence on land-use patterns. Upon the invention of horse-drawn and then electric streetcars, "streetcar suburbs" quickly arose along newly laid tracks. Following World War II, widespread construction of express highways had a similar but even stronger effect, especially in the United States, causing development to spread more ubiquitously because automobiles relaxed the need for proximity to a transit line. These developments provided many desired amenities to residents, but also created problems. Whatever one's judgment about the wisdom of those past decisions, the longevity of buildings makes such trends virtually impossible to reverse. In particular, a dispersed land-use pattern undermines the market potential of mass transit, making it ineffective as a means to counter the automobile's dominance, even if promoting mass transit might have been a better policy in the first place.

Urban transportation is a vital part of economic activity and responds to well-designed economic policies. Much can be accomplished to improve urban life by using our basic knowledge of economic incentives.

About the Author

Kenneth A. Small, research professor and professor emeritus of economics at the University of California at Irvine, specializes in urban, transportation, and environmental economics—especially highway congestion, air pollution from motor vehicles, and travel demand. Professor Small was a coeditor of the international journal *Urban Studies* for five years and is now associate editor of *Transportation Research B*. He received the Distinguished Member Award of the Transportation and Public Utilities Group of the American Economic Association in 1999 and is a Fellow of the Regional Science Association International.

Further Reading

Introductory

Altshuler, Alan, and David Luberoff. *Mega-Projects: The Changing Politics of Urban Public Investment.* Washington, D.C.: Brookings Institution Press, 2003. Insightful description and analysis of the political changes behind the extraordinary increase in costs of the large U.S. urban infrastructure projects that started around 1970.

Arnott, Richard, and Kenneth Small. "The Economics of Traffic Congestion." *American Scientist* 82 (1994): 446–455. Explanation of traffic paradoxes including induced demand, for a scientifically but not economically literate audience.

Downs, Anthony. *Still Stuck in Traffic: Coping with Peak-Hour Traffic Congestion.* Washington D.C.: Brookings Institution, 2004. A comprehensive look at numerous anticongestion

7. On privatization initiatives, see the periodicals *Public Works Financing*, and the Reason Foundation's *Privatization Watch* (http://www.reason.org/pw.shtml), especially "Urban Toll Tunnels Solve Tough Problems" by Robert W. Poole Jr. (http://www.rppi.org/urbantolltunnels.html).

policies and their effectiveness, concluding largely that the only ones that are effective are politically infeasible.

Klein, Daniel B., Adrian T. Moore, and Binyam Reja. *Curb Rights: A Foundation for Free Enterprise in Urban Transit.* Washington, D.C.: Brookings Institution Press, 1997. Policy-oriented analysis of how the public sector can establish property rights to encourage successful private transit.

Meyer, John R., and José A. Gómez-Ibáñez. *Autos, Transit, and Cities.* Cambridge: Harvard University Press, 1981. A thorough analysis of urban transportation policy for an educated lay audience.

National Research Council. *Curbing Gridlock: Peak-Period Fees to Relieve Traffic Congestion.* Washington D.C.: National Academy Press, 1994. Full report by a study panel on congestion pricing. Volume 1 is the report, aimed at a general audience; volume 2 is a collection of commissioned papers.

Pickrell, Don H. "Rising Deficits and the Uses of Transit Subsidies in the United States." *Journal of Transport Economics and Policy* 19 (1985): 281–298. Decomposes the dramatic increase in U.S. transit deficits into its sources, finding that about three-fourths of new subsidies were absorbed in higher costs.

White, Peter. "Deregulation of Local Bus Service in Great Britain: An Introductory Review." *Transport Reviews* 15 (1995): 185–209. Reviews results of British bus deregulation of 1980s.

Winston, Clifford. "Government Failure in Urban Transportaion." *Fiscal Studies* 21 (2000): 403–425. A nontechnical summary of inefficiencies in U.S. urban transportation policy drawing on the UK privatization experiment for perspective.

Advanced

Gómez-Ibáñez, José A., William B. Tye, and Clifford Winston, eds. *Essays in Transportation Economics and Policy: A Handbook in Honor of John R. Meyer.* Washington, D.C.: Brookings Institution Press, 1999. Collection of essays, some technical, on analytical and issue-oriented topics. Can serve as introductory textbook.

Santos, Georgina, ed. *Road Pricing: Theory and Evidence.* Elsevier: Oxford, 2004. Collection of scholarly articles about congestion pricing and related topics.

Small, Kenneth A. *Urban Transportation Economics.* Reading, Pa.: Harwood Academic, 1992, 2d ed. 2005. Advanced textbook and reference book.

Small, Kenneth A., and José A. Gómez-Ibáñez. "Urban Transportation." In Paul Cheshire and Edwin S. Mills, eds., *Handbook of Regional and Urban Economics.* Vol. 3. New York: North-Holland, 1999. Survey of selected topics, aimed at professional economists.

Winston, Clifford, and Chad Shirley. *Alternate Route: Toward Efficient Urban Transportation.* Washington, D.C.: Brookings Institution Press, 1998. Analysis of mass transit policy in the United States, with emphasis on quantifying

the inefficiencies of transit and highway investment and pricing.

Welfare

Thomas MaCurdy
Jeffrey M. Jones

The U.S. welfare system would be an unlikely model for anyone designing a welfare system from scratch. The dozens of programs that make up the "system" have different (sometimes competing) goals, inconsistent rules, and overlapping groups of beneficiaries. Responsibility for administering the various programs is spread throughout the executive branch of the federal government and across many committees of the U.S. Congress. Responsibilities are also shared with state, county, and city governments, which actually deliver the services and contribute to funding.

The six programs most commonly associated with the "social safety net" include: (1) Temporary Assistance for Needy Families (TANF), (2) the Food Stamp Program (FSP), (3) Supplemental Security Income (SSI), (4) Medicaid, (5) housing assistance, and (6) the Earned Income Tax Credit (EITC). The federal government is the primary funder of all six, although TANF and Medicaid each require a 25–50 percent state funding match. The first five programs are administered locally (by the states, counties, or local federal agencies), whereas EITC operates as part of the regular federal tax system. Outside the six major programs are many smaller government-assistance programs (e.g., Special Supplemental Food Program for Women, Infants and Children [WIC]; general assistance [GA]; school-based food programs; and Low-Income Home Energy Assistance Program [LIHEAP]), which have extensive numbers of participants but pay quite modest benefits.

Welfare reform, brought about through the passage of the Personal Responsibility and Work Opportunity Reconciliation Act (PRWORA) of 1996, significantly altered the rules for delivering income support, but it was narrowly focused on one program. The 1996 law replaced Aid to Families with Dependent Children (AFDC) with TANF. SSI and food stamps were also affected, but to a much lesser extent.

Key Programs

The accompanying figures summarize trends in the coverage and expenses of the six major federal safety-net programs over the past three decades. Figure 1 shows the percentage of the American population receiving benefits from each program, and Figure 2 presents the share of

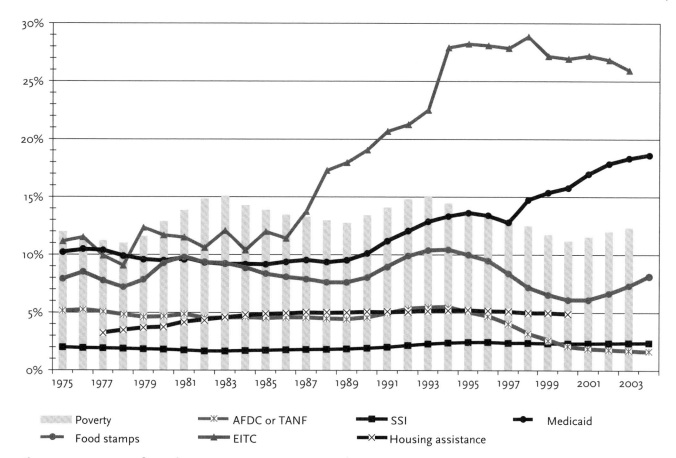

Figure 1 Percentage of Population Receiving Program Benefits

federal expenditures spent on each program. The bars in Figure 1 also plot the percentage of Americans classified as being in poverty. In addition to highlighting the evolution of these U.S. welfare programs, the following discussion briefly describes the forms of benefits paid out by programs, along with eligibility criteria.

Temporary Assistance for Needy Families pays cash assistance to single-parent or unemployed two-parent families for a limited term. The program also significantly funds job training and child care as a means to discourage welfare dependency and encourage work.

The origins of TANF are in the Social Security Act of 1935, which established the Aid to Dependent Children (ADP) program. ADP enabled state governments to help single mothers who were widowed or abandoned by their husbands. It was originally designed to allow mothers to stay at home and take care of their children, providing cash benefits for the basic requirements of food, shelter, and clothing. The program was expanded in the 1950s and 1960s to provide cash assistance to needy children and families regardless of the reason for parental absence. This expansion coincided with renaming the program Aid to Families with Dependent Children. While AFDC was prin-

cipally a federal program managed by the Department of Health and Human Services, it was administered through state-run welfare offices. Indeed, states were responsible for organizing the program, determining benefits, establishing income and resource limits, and setting actual benefit payments. With relatively little flexibility, an AFDC program in New York City looked a lot like its counterpart in Reno, Nevada, apart from differences in the maximum amount each state paid to a family for assistance. Funding for AFDC was shared between the federal and state governments, with the feds covering a higher portion of AFDC benefit costs in states with lower-than-average per capita income. As with many other welfare programs, AFDC's costs were not capped because the program was an "entitlement"—meaning that qualified families could not be refused cash assistance.

By the early 1990s, many policymakers were seeking alternatives to AFDC. Although the average monthly benefit in 1995 was only $376.70 per family and $132.64 per recipient, 40 percent of applicants remained on welfare for two years or longer. In response to this dependency, in 1996, Congress passed and President Bill Clinton signed the Personal Responsibility and Work Opportunity Rec-

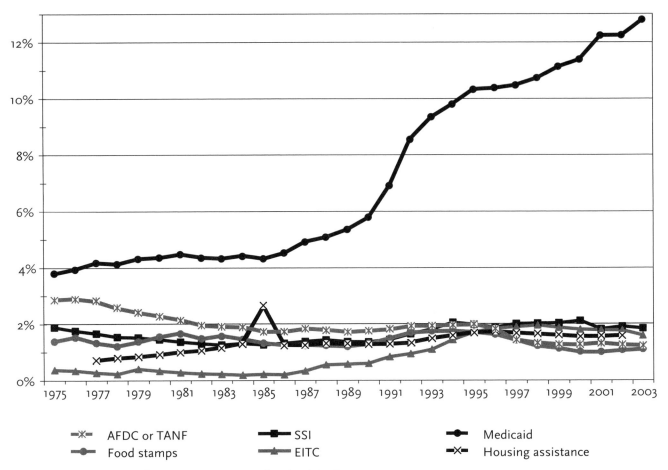

Figure 2 Program Spending as a Percentage of Federal Outlays

onciliation Act, which replaced AFDC with TANF. Under the new program, the federal government eliminated the entitlement to cash welfare, placed limits on the length of time families could collect benefits, and introduced work requirements. By law, a family cannot receive TANF benefits for more than a lifetime limit of five years, cumulative across welfare spells. Regarding work requirements, TANF mandated that at least 50 percent of recipients participate in "work" activities by 2002, with activities including employment, on-the-job training, vocational education, job search, and community service. Together, these activities must account for thirty hours per week for a single parent. Recipients who refuse to participate in work activities must be sanctioned, resulting in a loss of cash benefits. Enforcement of sanctions could include immediately suspending all cash payments, stopping support only after multiple episodes of noncompliance, or only partially reducing grants to families who fail to cooperate. States could, and in fact did, introduce more stringent requirements for families to work or participate in educational activities to qualify for cash payments. TANF cemented the primary emphasis on getting welfare recipients into jobs.

Figures 1 and 2 reveal that growth in neither costs nor enrollments motivated the passage of welfare reform in 1996. Program expenditures have accounted for less than 3 percent of the federal budget since 1975. The caseload remained relatively stable until the mid-1990s. After welfare reform, however, the welfare caseload and welfare spending as a percentage of government spending dropped sharply.

The Food Stamp Program, authorized as a permanent program in 1964, provides benefits to low-income households to buy nutritional, low-cost food. After 1974, Congress required all states to offer the program. Recipients use coupons and electronic benefits transfer (EBT) cards to purchase food at authorized retail stores. There are limitations on what items can be purchased with food stamps (e.g., they cannot be used to purchase cigarettes or alcohol). Recipients pay no tax on items purchased with food stamps. The federal government is entirely responsible for the rules and the complete funding of FSP benefits under the auspices of the Department of Agriculture's Food and Nutrition Service (FNS). State governments, through local welfare offices, have primary responsibility for administering the Food Stamp Program. They determine eligibility, calculate benefits, and issue food stamp allotments.

Welfare reform imposed work requirements on recipients and allowed states to streamline administrative procedures for determining eligibility and benefits. Childless recipients between the ages of eighteen and fifty became ineligible for food stamps if they received benefits for more than three months while not working. According to Figure 1, the FSP caseload has included between 6 and 10 percent of the U.S. population, following a cyclical pattern before welfare reform: during recessions, the caseload percentage was higher. Welfare reform caused a decline in the FSP caseload percentage.

Supplemental Security Income, authorized by the Social Security Act in 1974, pays monthly cash benefits to needy individuals whose ability to work is restricted by blindness or disability. Families can also receive payments to support disabled children or to help children whose parents have died. Although one cannot receive SSI payments and TANF payments concurrently, one can receive SSI and Social Security simultaneously. (In 2003, 35 percent of all SSI recipients also received Social Security benefits, and 57 percent of aged SSI recipients were Social Security beneficiaries.) The average SSI recipient received almost $5,000 in annual payments in 2003, with the average monthly federal payment being $417, and many state governments supplemented the basic SSI benefits with their own funds.

Welfare reforms and related immigration legislation in 1996–1997 sought to address three areas of perceived abuse in the SSI program. First, the legislation set up procedures to help ensure that SSI payments are not made to prison inmates. Second, the legislation eliminated benefits to less-disabled children, particularly children with behavioral problems rather than physical disorders. Finally, new immigrants were deemed ineligible for benefits prior to becoming citizens.

Medicaid became law in 1965, under the Social Security Act, to assist state governments in providing medical care to eligible needy persons. Medicaid provides health-care services to more than 49.7 million low-income individuals who are in one or more of the following categories: aged, blind, disabled, members of families with dependent children, or certain other children and pregnant women. Medicaid is the largest government program providing medical and health-related services to the nation's poorest people and the largest single funding source for nursing homes and institutions for mentally retarded people.

Within federal guidelines, each state government is responsible for designing and administering its own program. Individual states determine persons covered, types and scope of benefits offered, and amounts of payments for services. Federal law requires that a single state agency be responsible for the administration of the Medicaid program; generally it is the state welfare or health agency. The federal government shares costs with states by means of an annually adjusted variable matching formula.

The Medicaid program has more participants than any other major welfare program. More than 17 percent of the population received Medicaid benefits in 2002, up from about 10 percent in the 1970s and 1980s. Spending on Medicaid has risen steadily as a fraction of the federal budget, increasing from approximately 2 percent in 1975 to 13 percent in 2002. Total outlays for the Medicaid program in 2002 (federal and state) were $259 billion, and per capita expenditures on Medicaid beneficiaries averaged $4,291.

Housing assistance covers a broad range of efforts by federal and state governments to improve housing quality and to reduce housing costs for lower-income households. The Department of Housing and Urban Development (HUD) and the Federal Housing Administration (FHA) administer most federal housing programs. Under current programs, each resident pays approximately 30 percent of his or her income for rent.

In terms of welfare policy, there are two principal types of housing assistance for low-income families: subsidized rent and public housing. The federal government has provided rental subsidies since the mid-1930s and today funds the HUD Section 8 voucher program. Local governments commonly provide for subsidized housing through their building authority in that they require a portion of new construction to be made available to low-income families at below-market rents. Public housing (the actual provision of dwellings) is almost exclusively a federal program administered by local public housing agencies (PHAs), not private owner-managers. In contrast to the mid-1960s, public housing now accounts for a small fraction of overall housing assistance.

Earned Income Tax Credit, enacted in 1975, pays a refundable tax credit for working Americans with low earnings. The tax credit increases family income by supplementing earnings up to a fixed level. The program was initially designed to offset the impact of Social Security taxes on low-income individuals and to encourage individuals to seek employment rather than rely on welfare benefits. Because EITC is part of the regular federal income tax system, receiving benefits is private, unremarkable, and without stigma. In 2004, the EITC paid out $33.1 billion to approximately 18.6 million claimants—several billion dollars more than the amounts projected to be spent on other primary programs such as TANF and food stamps.

Table 1 Benefits, Taxes, and Disposable Income for a Family of Four

Earnings ($)	TANF	Food Stamps	SSI	Sec. 8 Housing	Federal EITC	Health Care	Federal Payroll Taxes	Federal Income Tax	Taxes, EITC	Taxes, EITC, TANF, FSP	Taxes, EITC, TANF, FSP, Sec. 8
0	8,148	5,988	9,660	10,800	0	MNP	0	0	0	12,663	20,611
4,000	7,498	5,510	8,170	9,400	1,600	MNP	−306	0	5,294	16,503	23,279
8,000	5,498	4,550	6,170	8,000	3,200	MNP	−612	0	10,588	19,317	25,393
12,000	3,498	3,590	4,170	6,600	4,300	MNP	−918	0	15,382	21,631	27,007
16,000	0	2,630	2,170	5,200	4,101	Child 6–19	−1,224	0	18,877	21,507	26,707
20,000	0	1,670	170	3,800	3,261	Child 1–6	−1,530	0	21,731	23,401	27,201
24,000	0	710	0	2,400	2,421	Child 1–6	−1,836	−190	24,395	25,105	27,505

EITC is one of the few programs that effectively reach the eligible population. Analysis of EITC claims in 1999 shows that 86 percent of eligible families with children received the credit. (In contrast, only 66 percent of eligible households with children received food stamp benefits in 1999.) Although the EITC is generally paid all at once as an annual refund, it can also be included with an employee's weekly, biweekly, or monthly paycheck.

Level of Benefits and Impacts on Work Incentives

How much do the above safety-net programs pay in benefits? Table 1 presents the benefit levels provided to a qualifying family whose annual earnings equal the amounts listed in the first column of the table. Calculations in this table assume that the family includes a father, a mother, and two children below the age of eighteen, and that this family lives in California.[1] According to the row in the table for a family that earns $8,000 a year, this family would be eligible to receive $5,498 from TANF, $4,550 from food stamps, $6,170 from SSI, $8,000 in housing benefits from the Section 8 program, and $3,200 from EITC, for a total of $27,418 in government assistance. Moreover, this family would qualify for Medicaid's Medically Needy Pro-

gram (MNP), wherein all family members would receive zero-price health care. On reaching $16,000 in earnings, the family would qualify for Medicaid's Children Ages 6 to 19 Program (Child 6–19), which provides zero-price health care to all children in the family; and at $20,000 in earnings, the family would qualify for Medicaid's Children Ages 1 to 6 Program (Child 1–6), which offers zero-price health care to all children ages six and below.

To determine the disposable income available to a family, one needs to add the family's earnings and the payments it receives in program benefits and then subtract the amounts paid in taxes. Any family faces three categories of taxes: Social Security payroll taxes, federal income tax, and state income tax. The eighth and ninth columns of the table show the amounts a family of four must pay in payroll and federal income taxes for the various levels of earnings—the negative values in these columns indicate payments that subtract from income rather than add to income. The table does not include a column for state taxes because none are paid for any of the income values considered in the table. The last three columns of the table report a family's disposable income for each level of earnings, assuming participation in the programs listed in the associated column. The family that earns $8,000 receives $10,588 in disposable income for the year when it chooses not to participate in any welfare program and obtains benefits only from EITC. This family's disposable income grows to $19,317 if it decides to take TANF and food stamps and to $25,393 if it also chooses to obtain assistance for rent.[2]

1. To qualify for low-income assistance, the family must have less than two thousand dollars in financial and housing assets. For the calculation of housing benefits, Table 1 assumes that the family pays nine hundred dollars in rent per month. In some circumstances, eligible benefit levels may be affected by dual-enrollment restrictions (e.g., cannot receive TANF and SSI concurrently).

2. In the calculation of food stamps and housing benefits, payments from TANF count as income: this lowers payments below

Does Welfare Help the Poor?

David Henderson

Economists believe that people tend to make decisions that benefit themselves, so the answer to the above question seems obvious. If welfare did not help the poor, then why would so many of them go on welfare? This self-interest among the poor could also explain a phenomenon noted by those who study welfare, namely that only about one-half to two-thirds of those who qualify for welfare programs are enrolled in them. Presumably, the others have decided that it is in their self-interest to refuse the money and keep the government from meddling in their lives.

So, while it seems clear that welfare helps the poor who accept welfare, that does not mean that welfare helps the poor generally. Two groups of poor people, not counted in the welfare statistics, are hurt by welfare. The first group consists of the future poor. Economists know that welfare is a disincentive to work, and, therefore, that its existence reduces an economy's output. If even some of this output would have been used for research and development, and if this forgone R&D would have increased growth, then welfare hurts growth by reducing R&D. If the annual growth rate of GDP in the United States had been just one percentage point lower between 1885 and 2005, then the United States today would be no richer than Mexico. The main thing that helps all poor people in the long run is economic growth. Even though the 1920s are thought of as a decade of prosperity, by today's standards almost all Americans in the 1920s were poor. Economic growth made almost all Americans richer than their counterparts of the 1920s. A reduction in economic growth, even a slight one, if compounded, causes more future poverty than would otherwise have been the case.

The second group hurt by U.S. welfare is poor foreigners. The welfare state acts as a magnet for poor immigrants to the United States. Because of this, there are various domestic pressures to limit immigration. Without the welfare state, the number of immigrants would likely rise substantially, meaning that many previously poor foreigners would become much richer. The welfare state limits this improvement.

Based on Tyler Cowen, "Does the Welfare State Help the Poor?" *Social Philosophy and Policy* 19, no.1 (2002) pp. 36–54.

Note, by looking at the "Taxes, EITC, TANF, FSP" column, that a family participating in these programs increases its disposable income by $5,294 when it raises its earnings from zero to $4,000. That means that, in this range of earnings, work is rewarded; the family actually increases its disposable income by more than $4,000. But if a family raises its earnings from $12,000 to $16,000, its government benefits fall so much that its disposable income literally *declines* by $124. This happens because program benefits fall as earnings rise. Families facing these latter circumstances (earning $12,000) clearly have no incentive to increase their work effort since they will see no enhancement of their spending power. If one alters the family's situation and also has it participate in housing programs, then the last column shows that raising earning from $12,000 to $24,000 yields merely $498 more in disposable income. Such features of our welfare system sharply reduce the returns of work, and in doing so discourage families from increasing their work activities. The U.S. welfare system enhances work incentives at low levels of earnings, but discourages work thereafter. To counterbalance such work disincentives, welfare reform in the mid-1990s introduced work requirements that required families to work above specific thresholds in order to qualify for benefits.

Future Directions

Welfare reform was enacted to promote self-sufficiency and to improve flexibility in the design of income-maintenance programs. To a large extent, these goals have been achieved. TANF has brought about substantial increases in the work activities of low-income families and enhanced states' flexibility to create welfare systems unique to their constituencies. States are using the monies they are allocated in a more efficient manner—focusing on job readiness, child care, education, and work placement.

What other policy trends characterize the evolution of welfare system in the United State today? Briefly, two key forces are changing the basic relationship between the government and welfare recipients in all programs.

First, welfare programs at all levels are being geared toward more work-related activities. Nearly every program gives priority to parents who show a willingness and commitment to work. At the same time, able-bodied adults who refuse to work now find themselves disqualified from many programs. The emphasis on work has gained strength only since 1996. Proposals for the reauthorization of wel-

the amounts listed in the table for the program. The program benefits listed in the first set of columns assume that the family participates only in that particular program.

fare reform all generally push for stricter work requirements and a longer work week.

Second, there has been a movement from pure in-kind provision to voucher-based systems. In-kind provision represents government efforts to both fund and directly serve the poor. Voucher systems are being emphasized not only for shelter but also for provision of food, health care, job training, and child care, among others. A cash-equivalent voucher is provided directly to the person served, who then redeems the voucher at any qualified/authorized service provider. This approach brings some of the advantages of market-based economics to the provision of welfare. The recipient spends dollars on the things he or she wants most. A classic example is public housing. HUD provides the funding for most public housing, and local government housing authorities use it to buy or build publicly owned residential units. This inefficient use of funds segregates low-income families into common facilities that typically duplicate housing resources that are widely available in the private market. Over the past decade, HUD and other government providers have been opting to fund more voucher-based, Section 8-type housing to meet the needs of the poor, thus allowing recipients greater choice in where they live.

Although welfare reform has achieved success in a short amount of time, more reform is needed. Of the many government assistance programs, only one, TANF, has seen any significant reform. The remaining programs (food stamps, SSI, housing assistance, Medicaid, and EITC) are about as inflexible as ever and generally ignore what is going on in the rest of the system. Future policy initiatives are likely to alter these programs toward the direction set for TANF in the 1990s welfare reform, with the two above trends continuing to influence new reforms.

About the Authors

Thomas MaCurdy is the Dean Witter Senior Fellow at the Hoover Institution and a professor of economics at Stanford University. He is a member of standing committees that advise the Congressional Budget Office, the U.S. Bureau of Labor Statistics, and the U.S. Census. Jeffrey M. Jones is a research fellow at the Hoover Institution. He was previously executive director of Promised Land Employment Service.

Further Reading

DeParle, Jason. *American Dream: Three Women, Ten Kids, and a Nation's Drive to End Welfare*. New York: Viking Books, 2004.

Jones, Jeffrey, and Thomas MaCurdy. "How *Not* to Mess Up a Good Thing." *Hoover Digest*, no. 2. Stanford, Calif.: Hoover Institution Press, 2003. Pp. 99–108. Online at: http://www.hooverdigest.org/032/jones.html.

MaCurdy, Thomas, and Frank McIntyre. *Helping Working-Poor Families: Advantages of Wage-Based Tax Credits over the EITC and Minimum Wages*. Washington, D.C.: Employment Policies Institute, 2004. Online at: http://www.epionline.org/studies/macurdy_04-2004.pdf.

Malanga, Steven. "The Myth of the Working Poor." *City Journal* (Autumn 2004). New York: Manhattan Institute, 2004. Online at: http://www.city-journal.org/html/14_4_working_poor.html.

Murray, Charles. *Losing Ground: American Social Policy 1950–1980*. New York: Basic Books, 1984.

O'Neill, June, and M. Anne Hill. "Gaining Ground, Moving Up: The Change in the Economic Status of Single Mothers Under Welfare Reform." *Civic Report*, no. 35 (March 2003). New York: Manhattan Institute, 2003. Online at: http://www.manhattan-institute.org/html/cr_35.htm.

Rector, Robert, and Patrick F. Fagan. "The Continuing Good News About Welfare Reform." Backgrounder no. 1620. Washington, D.C.: Heritage Foundation, 2003. Online at: http://www.heritage.org/Research/Welfare/BG1620.cfm.

Tanner, Michael. *The Poverty of Welfare: Fighting Poverty in Civil Society*. Washington, D.C.: Cato Institute, 2003.

2004 Green Book. Washington, D.C.: Committee on Ways and Means, U.S. House of Representatives, 2004. Online at: http://waysandmeans.house.gov/Documents.asp?section=813.

Biographies

Editor's Note

Any choice of whom to include in biographies is inherently subjective. I tried to make it less so by using two criteria. First, all economists who won the Nobel Prize in economic science up to 2004 are included. The reason is that those who were judged by their peers in Sweden to be worthy of the Nobel Prize should be written up in any encyclopedia of economics. Second, I omitted all economists who were born after 1920 and were still alive in June 1992 unless they had won the Nobel Prize. I chose this criterion be-cause there are too many noteworthy younger economists to do them all justice in a book of this length. Readers who are very familiar with the history of economic thought may well wonder why some famous dead economists, especially from the nineteenth century, are left out. This is where the subjectivity came in: I made judgments about their relative contributions. All biographies are written by me unless otherwise noted.

—DRH

George A. Akerlof (1940–)

George Akerlof, along with Michael Spence and Joseph Stiglitz, received the 2001 Nobel Prize "for their analyses of markets with asymmetric information." Although much of economics is built on the assumption of perfect information, various economists in the past had considered the effects of imperfect information. Two giants in this area were LUDWIG VON MISES and FRIEDRICH HAYEK, who predicted that socialism would fail because central planners could not possibly have the information they needed to plan an economy. One of the next steps in relaxing the perfect-information assumption was to assume, realistically, that one side of a market has better information than the other. That is what all three of the 2001 Nobel Prize winners did.

In his classic 1970 article, "The Market for Lemons," Akerlof gave a new explanation for a well-known phenomenon: the fact that cars barely a few months old sell for well below their new-car price. Akerlof's model was simple but powerful. Assume that some cars are "lemons" and some are high quality. If buyers could tell which cars are lemons and which are not, there would be two separate markets: a market for lemons and a market for high-quality cars. But there is often asymmetric information: buyers cannot tell which cars are lemons, but, of course, sellers know. Therefore, a buyer knows that there is some probability that the car he buys will be a lemon and is willing to pay less than he would pay if he were certain that he was buying a high-quality car. This lower price for all used cars discourages sellers of high-quality cars. Although some would be willing to sell their own cars at the price that buyers of high-quality used cars would be willing to pay, they are not willing to sell at the lower price that reflects the risk that the buyer may end up with a lemon. Thus, exchanges that could benefit both buyer and seller fail to take place and efficiency is lost.

Akerlof did not conclude that the lemon problem necessarily implies a role for government. Instead, he pointed out that many free-market institutions can be seen as ways of solving or reducing "lemon problems." One solution Akerlof noted is warranties, because these give the buyer assurance that the car is not a lemon, and the buyer is therefore willing to pay more for the car with a warranty. Also, the sellers who are willing to offer the warranty are those who are confident that they are not selling a lemon. Another market solution that has come along since Akerlof's article is Carfax, a very low-cost way of finding out a car's history of repairs. Akerlof also went beyond cars and showed that the same kind of issues arise in credit markets and health insurance markets, to name two.

Akerlof, along with coauthor Janet Yellen, also did some of the pioneering work in NEW KEYNESIAN ECONOMICS. They considered the case of firms with market power that follow a rule of thumb on pricing. The rule of thumb they considered was that firms do not increase price when demand increases and do not reduce price when demand falls. They showed that such a rule of thumb is "near rational"; that is, firms do not lose much profit from following this strategy relative to a strategy of immediately adjusting prices. They also showed, however, that if many firms followed this strategy, the effect on the overall economy was substantial. This lack of adjustment of prices, they noted, would mean that increases in money-supply growth would increase the growth of real output, and short-run drops in money-supply growth would reduce the growth of real output.

More recently, Akerlof has tried to explain the persistence of high poverty rates and high crime rates among black Americans. He and coauthor Rachel Kranton argue that many black people face a choice between going along with the mainstream culture and succeeding economically or acting in opposition to that culture and sabotaging themselves. The incentives are high, they argue, for doing the latter.

Akerlof earned his B.A. in economics at Yale in 1962 and his Ph.D. in economics at MIT in 1966. For most of his professional life, he has been an economics professor at the University of California at Berkeley. In 1973–1974, he was a senior economist with President Richard M. Nixon's Council of Economic Advisers; from 1978 to 1980, he was an economics professor at the London School of Economics.

Selected Works

1970. "The Market for 'Lemons'": Quality Uncertainty and the Market Mechanism." *Quarterly Journal of Economics* 84: 353–374.
1976. "The Economics of Caste and of the Rat Race and Other Woeful Tales." *Quarterly Journal of Economics* 90: 599–617.
1985 (with Janet Yellen). "Can Small Deviations from Rationality Make Significant Differences to Economic Equilibria?" *American Economic Review* 75: 708–720.
1985 (with Janet Yellen). "A Near Rational Model of the Business Cycle with Wage and Price Inertia." *Quarterly Journal of Economics* 100 (suppl.): 823–838.
1990. "The Fair Wage Hypothesis and Unemployment." *Quarterly Journal of Economics* 97: 543–569.
1996 (with Janet Yellen and Michael Katz). "An Analysis of Out-of-Wedlock Childbearing in the United States." *Quarterly Journal of Economics* 111: 277–317.
2000 (with Rachel Kranton). "Economics and Identity." *Quarterly Journal of Economics* 115: 715–753.

Armen A. Alchian (1914–)

Armen Alchian, an American economist born in Fresno, California, is in many ways like RONALD COASE. Like Coase, Alchian has published only a few articles, but very few are unimportant. And like Coase's, many of Alchian's articles are widely cited.

Many students and others who read economics are disturbed by economists' assumptions that companies maximize profits. One of their objections is that managers of companies do not know enough to be able to maximize profits. In 1950 Alchian presented a thoughtful response to this objection in his first major article, "Uncertainty, Evolution and Economic Theory." Alchian argued that even though all companies may not maximize profits, those that survive will be ones whose managers, by luck or by design, came close to maximizing profits. Therefore, those that we observe will have maximized profits. So for the long term at least, argued Alchian, for economists to derive the standard conclusions from the profit-maximization assumption, they do not need to show that all companies try to maximize profits.

While in the U.S. Army Air Forces during World War II, Alchian did some of the early work on the learning curve—the curve that relates unit costs to cumulative output. His article on the learning curve in aircraft production was based on statistical work he did during the war, but it could not be published until 1963 because it was based on classified information.

Alchian is also known for *University Economics* (now called *Exchange and Production*), coauthored with William R. Allen, a textbook that is unique in economics. It is much more literary and humorous than any other modern economics textbook that deals with complex issues for an undergraduate audience. Example: "Since the fiasco in the Garden of Eden, most of what we get is by sweat, strain, and anxiety." It also welcomes controversy rather than shying away from it, in the process daring the reader to disagree. Take, for example, the book's discussion of violence:

> Before condemning violence (physical force) as a means of social control, note that its threatened or actual use is widely practiced and respected—at least when applied successfully on a national scale. Julius Caesar conquered Gaul and was honored by the Romans; had he simply roughed up the local residents, he would have been damned as a gangster. Alexander the Great, who conquered the Near East, was not regarded by the Greeks as a ruffian, nor was Charlemagne after he conquered Europe. Europeans acquired and divided—and redivided—America by force. Lenin is not regarded in Russia as a subversive. Nor is Spain's Franco, Cuba's Castro, Nigeria's Gowon, Uganda's Amin, China's Mao, our George Washington.

Because of its literary quality and complexity, the textbook generally did not work with undergraduate or even M.B.A. classes. But its impact was out of all proportion to its sales. Many graduate students, particularly at the University of California at Los Angeles, where Alchian began teaching in 1946, and at the University of Washington (where Alchian student Steven Cheung taught), learned their basic economics from this book. Some of the University of Washington students went on to write best-selling textbooks that made many of Alchian and Allen's insights more understandable to an undergraduate audience. Alchian and Allen's textbook was truly a public good—a good that created large benefits for which its creators could not charge. And while Alchian played the role of selfish cynic in his class, some who studied under him had the feeling that he put so much care and work into his low-selling text—and into his students—because of his concern for humanity.

Other than through his text, Alchian's largest impact has been in the economics of property rights (he wrote the article on property rights in this encyclopedia). Most of his work in property rights can be summed up in one sentence: You tell me the rules and I'll tell you what outcomes to expect. In their textbook, for example, Alchian and Allen ask why the organizers of the Rose Bowl refuse to sell tickets to the highest bidders and instead give up wealth by underpricing the tickets. Their answer is that the people who make the decision on ticket prices do not have property rights in the tickets, so the wealth that is given up by underpricing would not have accrued to them anyway. But the decision makers can give underpriced tickets to their friends and associates. Thomas Hazlett, former chief economist at the Federal Communications Commission, used this same line of reasoning to explain why Rep. John Dingell blocked the Federal Communication Commission's early attempts to auction off the electromagnetic spectrum and instead favored giving it away.

Alchian also used the analysis of property rights to explain the incidence of discrimination. In a paper coauthored with Reuben Kessel, Alchian, who was himself subject to discrimination as an Armenian, and Kessel pointed out that discrimination was more pervasive in private firms whose profits were regulated by the government, and then explained that this is what the analysis of property rights would predict. Discrimination is costly—not just to those discriminated against, but also to those who discriminate. The discriminators give up the chance to deal with someone with whom they could engage in mutually beneficial exchange. Therefore, argued Alchian and Kessel, discrimination would be more prevalent in situations where those who discriminate do not bear much of the cost from doing so. A for-profit company whose profits are not regulated would see the cost of discrimination in its bottom line in the form of lower profits. A company whose profits are limited and that is already at the limit would face no cost from discriminating. Alchian and Kessel used this analysis to explain why regulated utilities discriminated against Jews and why labor unions discriminated against blacks. This analysis explains why Alchian has never trusted government—but has trusted free markets—to reduce discrimination.

Before teaching at UCLA, Alchian was an economist with the RAND Corporation.

Selected Works

1950. "Uncertainty, Evolution and Economic Theory." *Journal of Political Economy* 58 (June): 211–221.
1965. "Some Economics of Property Rights." *II Politico* 30: 816–829.
1972 (with W. R. Allen). *University Economics.* Belmont, Calif.: Wadsworth.
1977. *Economic Forces at Work.* Indianapolis: Liberty Press.

Maurice Allais (1911–)

In 1988 Maurice Allais became the first French citizen to receive the Nobel Prize in economics. He won it for his contribution to the understanding of market behavior and the efficient use of resources. Allais also showed that his insights could be applied to help set efficient prices for state-owned monopolies, of which France had many. Allais's work paralleled, and sometimes preceded, similar work done by English-speaking economists Sir John Hicks and Paul Samuelson. He also proved a result in growth theory in 1947 that had been credited to Edmund Phelps (in 1961).

Allais did not get credit as early as his English counterparts because his work was in French. "Had Allais' earliest writings been in English," commented Samuelson, "a generation of economic theory would have taken a different course." Allais also helped revive the quantity theory of money (monetarism). In utility theory, Allais discovered and resolved a paradox about how people behave when choosing between various risks that is now called the Allais paradox.

From 1937 to 1944, Allais worked in the French state-owned mine administration. In 1944 he became a professor at the Ecole National Supérieure des Mines de Paris and spent his career there. He is also the research director at the National French Research Council. He was named an officer of the Legion of Honor in 1977.

Selected Works

1965. "The Role of Capital in Economic Development." In *The Econometric Approach to Development Planning.* Amsterdam: North-Holland.
1966. "A Restatement of the Quantity Theory of Money." *American Economic Review* 56 (December): 1123–1157.
1969. "Growth and Inflation." *Journal of Money, Credit and Banking* 1, no. 3: 355–426.

Kenneth Arrow (1921–)

In 1972 American economist Kenneth Arrow, jointly with Sir John Hicks, was awarded the Nobel Prize in economics for "pioneering contributions to general equilibrium theory and welfare theory." Arrow is probably best known for his Ph.D. dissertation (on which his book *Social Choice and Individual Values* is based), in which he proved his famous "impossibility theorem." He showed that under certain assumptions about people's preferences between options, it is always impossible to find a voting rule under which one option emerges as the most preferred. The simplest example is Condorcet's paradox, named after an eighteenth-century French mathematician. Condorcet's paradox is as follows: There are three candidates for office; let us call them Bush (B), Clinton (C), and Perot (P). One-third of the voters rank them B, C, P. One-third rank them C, P, B. The final third rank them P, B, C. Then a majority will prefer Bush to Clinton, and a majority will prefer Clinton to Perot. It would seem, therefore, that a majority would prefer Bush to Perot. But in fact a majority prefers Perot to Bush. Arrow's more complicated proof is more general.

Arrow went on to show, in a 1951 article, that a competitive economy in equilibrium is efficient and that any efficient allocation can be reached by having the government use lump-sum taxes to redistribute and then letting the market work. One clear-cut implication of this finding is that the government should not control prices to redistribute income, but instead, if it redistributes at all, should do so directly. Arrow's insight is part of the reason economists are almost unanimously against price controls.

Arrow also showed, with coauthor Gerard Debreu, that under certain conditions an economy reaches a general equilibrium—that is, an equilibrium in which all markets are in equilibrium. Using new mathematical techniques, Arrow and Debreu showed that one of the conditions for general equilibrium is that there must be futures markets for all goods. Of course, we know that this condition does not hold—one cannot buy a contract for future delivery of many labor services, for example.

Arrow was also one of the first economists to note the existence of a learning curve. His basic idea was that as producers increase output of a product, they gain experience and become more efficient. "The role of experience in increasing productivity has not gone unobserved," he wrote, "though the relation has yet to be absorbed into the main corpus of economic theory." More than forty years after Arrow's article, the learning curve insight has still not been fully integrated into mainstream economic analysis.

Arrow has also done excellent work on the economics of uncertainty. His work in that area is still a standard source for economists.

Arrow has spent most of his professional life on the economics faculties of Stanford University (1949–1968 and 1980–present) and Harvard University (1968–1979). He earned his B.A. in social science at the City College of New York and his M.A. and Ph.D. in economics from Columbia University.

Selected Works

1951. *Social Choice and Individual Values.* New York: Wiley.
1954 (with Gerard Debreu). "Existence of a Competitive Equilibrium for a Competitive Economy." *Econometrica* 22, no. 3: 265–290.
1962. "The Economic Implications of Learning by Doing." *Review of Economic Studies* 29 (June): 155–173.
1971. *Essays in the Theory of Risk-Bearing.* Amsterdam: North-Holland.
1971 (with Frank Hahn). *General Competitive Analysis.* San Francisco: Holden-Day.

Frédéric Bastiat (1801–1850)

Joseph Schumpeter described Bastiat nearly a century after his death as "the most brilliant economic journalist who ever lived." Orphaned at the age of nine, Bastiat tried his hand at commerce, farming, and insurance sales. In 1825, after he inherited his grandfather's estate, he quit working, established a discussion group, and read widely in economics.

Bastiat made no original contribution to economics, if we use "contribution" the way most economists use it. That is, we cannot associate one law, theorem, or path-breaking empirical study with his name. But in a broader sense Bastiat made a big contribution: his fresh and witty expressions of economic truths made them so understandable and compelling that the truths became hard to ignore.

Bastiat was supremely effective at popularizing free-market economics. When he learned of Richard Cobden's campaign against the British Corn Laws (restrictions on the import of wheat, barley, rye, and oats), Bastiat vowed to become the "French Cobden." He subsequently published a series of articles attacking protectionism that brought him instant acclaim. In 1846 he established the Association of Free Trade in Paris and his own weekly newspaper, in which he waged a witty assault against socialists and protectionists.

Bastiat's "A Petition," usually referred to now as "The Petition of the Candlemakers," displays his rhetorical skill and rakish tone, as this excerpt illustrates:

> We are suffering from the ruinous competition of a foreign rival who apparently works under conditions so far superior to our own for the production of light, that he is flooding the domestic market with it at an incredibly low price. . . . This rival . . . is none other than the sun. . . .
>
> We ask you to be so good as to pass a law requiring the closing of all windows, dormers, skylights, inside and outside shutters, curtains, casements, bull's-eyes, dead-lights and blinds; in short, all openings, holes, chinks, and fissures.

This *reductio ad absurdum* of protectionism was so effective that one of the most successful postwar economics textbooks, *Economics* by Paul A. Samuelson, quotes the candlemakers' petition at the head of the chapter on protectionism.

Bastiat also emphasized the unintended consequences of government policy (he called them the "unseen" consequences). Friedrich Hayek credits Bastiat with this important insight: if we judge economic policy solely by its immediate effects, we will miss all of its unintended and longer-run effects and will undermine economic freedom, which delivers benefits that are not part of anyone's conscious design. Much of Hayek's work, and some of Milton Friedman's, was an exploration and elaboration of this insight.

Selected Works

Economic Harmonies. Translated by W. H. Boyers, 1964.
Economic Sophisms. Translated by A. Goddard, 1964. Includes "A Petition."

Selected Essays on Political Economy. Translated by S. Cain, 1964. Includes "What Is Seen and What Is Not Seen."
The Law. Translated by Dean Russell, 1995.
Articles by Bastiat in Lalor's *Cyclopaedia:*
  "Spoliation by Law"
  "Plenty and Dearth"
  Miscellaneous quotes, discussions, and references

Gary Stanley Becker (1930–)

Gary S. Becker received the 1992 Nobel Prize in economics for "having extended the domain of economic theory to aspects of human behavior which had previously been dealt with—if at all—by other social science disciplines such as sociology, demography and criminology."

Becker's unusually wide applications of economics started early. In 1955 he wrote his doctoral dissertation at the University of Chicago on the economics of discrimination. Among other things, Becker successfully challenged the Marxist view that discrimination helps the person who discriminates. Becker pointed out that if an employer refuses to hire a productive worker simply because of skin color, that employer loses out on a valuable opportunity. In short, discrimination is costly to the person who discriminates.

Becker showed that discrimination will be less pervasive in more competitive industries because companies that discriminate will lose market share to companies that do not. He also presented evidence that discrimination is more pervasive in more-regulated, and therefore less-competitive, industries. The idea that discrimination is costly to the discriminator is common sense among economists today, and that is due to Becker.

In the early 1960s Becker moved on to the fledgling area of human capital. One of the founders of the concept (the other being Theodore Schultz), Becker pointed out what again seems like common sense but was new at the time: education is an investment. Education adds to our human capital just as other investments add to physical capital. (For more on this, see Becker's article, "Human Capital," in this encyclopedia.)

One of Becker's insights is that time is a major cost of investing in education. Possibly that insight led him to his next major area, the study of the allocation of time within a family. Applying the economist's concept of opportunity cost, Becker showed that as market wages rose, the cost to married women of staying home would rise. They would want to work outside the home and economize on household tasks by buying more appliances and fast food.

Not even crime escaped Becker's keen analytical mind. In the late 1960s he wrote a trail-blazing article whose working assumption is that the decision to commit crime is a function of the costs and benefits of crime. From this assumption he concluded that the way to reduce crime is to raise the probability of punishment or to make the punishment more severe. His insights into crime, like his insights on discrimination and human capital, helped spawn a new branch of economics.

In the 1970s Becker extended his insights on allocation of time within a family, using the economic approach to explain the decisions to have children and to educate them, and the decisions to marry and to divorce.

Becker was a professor at Columbia University from 1957 to 1969. Except for that period, he has spent his entire career at the University of Chicago, where he holds joint appointments in the departments of economics and sociology. Becker won the John Bates Clark Award of the American Economic Association in 1967 and was president of that association in 1987.

Selected Works

1965. "A Theory of the Allocation of Time." *Economic Journal* 40, no. 299: 493–508.
1968. "Crime and Punishment: An Economic Approach." *Journal of Political Economy* 76, no. 2: 169–217.
1971. *The Economics of Discrimination.* 2d ed. Chicago: University of Chicago Press.
1975. *Human Capital.* 2d ed. New York: Columbia University Press.
1981. *Treatise on the Family.* Chicago: University of Chicago Press.

Jeremy Bentham (1748–1832)

British economist Jeremy Bentham is most often associated with his theory of utilitarianism, the idea that all social actions should be evaluated by the axiom "It is the greatest happiness of the greatest number that is the measure of right and wrong." Counter to Adam Smith's vision of "natural rights," Bentham believed that there were no natural rights to be interfered with.

Trained in law, Bentham never practiced, choosing instead to focus on judicial and legal reforms. His reform plans went beyond rewriting legislative acts to include detailed administrative plans to implement his proposals. In his plan for prisons, workhouses, and other institutions, Bentham devised compensation schemes, building designs, worker timetables, and even new accounting systems. A guiding principle of Bentham's schemes was that incentives should be designed "to make it each man's interest to observe on every occasion that conduct which it is his duty to observe." Interestingly, Bentham's thinking led him to the conclusion, which he shared with Smith, that professors should not be salaried.

In his early years Bentham professed a free-market approach. He argued, for example, that interest rates should be free from government control (see *Defence of Usury*). By the end of his life he had shifted to a more interventionist stance. He predated Keynes in his advocacy of expansionist monetary policies to achieve full employment and advocated a range of interventions, including the minimum wage and guaranteed employment.

His publications were few, but Bentham influenced many during his lifetime and lived to see some of his political reforms enacted shortly before his death in London at the age of eighty-four.

Selected Works

1787. *Defence of Usury.* London: T. Payne and Son.
1789. *An Introduction to the Principles of Morals and Legislation.* London: T. Payne and Son.
1802. *The Theory of Legislation.*
1818. *Defence of Usury.* 4th ed. London: Payne and Foss. (The fourth edition was the last published in Bentham's lifetime.)
1823. *An Introduction to the Principles of Morals and Legislation.* London: Clarendon Press, 1907. (This is a reprint of the 1823 edition, the last published in Bentham's lifetime, which was corrected and modified by Bentham.)

Eugen von Böhm-Bawerk (1851–1914)

Eugen von Böhm-Bawerk was one of the leading members of the Austrian school of economics—an approach to economic thought founded by Carl Menger and augmented by Knut Wicksell, Ludwig von Mises, Friedrich A. Hayek, and Sir John Hicks. Böhm-Bawerk's work became so well known that before World War I, his Marxist contemporaries regarded the Austrians as their typical bourgeois, intellectual enemies. His theories of interest and capital were catalysts in the development of economics, but today his original work receives little attention.

Böhm-Bawerk gave three reasons why interest rates are positive. First, people's marginal utility of income will fall over time because they expect higher income in the future. Second, for psychological reasons the marginal utility of a good declines with time. For both reasons, which economists now call "positive time-preference," people are willing to pay positive interest rates to get access to resources in the present, and they insist on being paid interest if they are to give up such access. Economists have accepted both as valid reasons for positive time-preference.

But Böhm-Bawerk's third reason—the "technical superiority of present over future goods"—was more controversial and harder to understand. Production, he noted, is roundabout, meaning that it takes time. It uses capital, which is produced, to transform nonproduced factors of production—such as land and labor—into output. Roundabout production methods mean that the same amount of input can yield a greater output. Böhm-Bawerk reasoned that the net return to capital is the result of the greater value produced by roundaboutness.

An example helps illustrate the point. As the leader of a primitive fishing village, you are able to send out the townspeople to catch enough fish, with their bare hands, to ensure the village's survival for one day. But if you forgo consumption of fish for one day and use that labor to produce nets, hooks, and lines—capital—each fisherman can catch more fish the following day and the days thereafter. Capital is productive.

Further investment in capital, argued Böhm-Bawerk, increases roundaboutness; that is, it lengthens the production period. On this basis Böhm-Bawerk concluded that the net physical productivity of capital will lead to positive interest rates even if the first two reasons do not hold.

Although his theory of capital is one of the cornerstones of Austrian economics, modern mainstream economists pay no attention to Böhm-Bawerk's analysis of roundaboutness. Instead, they accept Irving Fisher's approach of just assuming that there are investment opportunities that make capital productive. Nevertheless, Böhm-Bawerk's approach helped to pave the way for modern interest theory.

Böhm-Bawerk was also one of the first economists to discuss Karl Marx's views seriously. He argued that interest does not exist due to exploitation of workers. Workers would get the whole of what they helped produce only if production were instantaneous. But because production is roundabout, he wrote, some of the product that Marx attributed to workers must go to finance this roundaboutness, that is, must go to capital. Böhm-Bawerk noted that interest would have to be paid no matter who owned the capital. Mainstream economists still accept this argument.

Böhm-Bawerk was born in Vienna and studied law at

the university there. After teaching at the University of Innsbruck and serving in the civil service, he was appointed minister of finance during the years 1895, 1897, and 1900. He left the ministry in 1904 and taught economics at the University of Vienna until his death in 1914.

Selected Works

1890. *Capital and Interest*. London: Macmillan. Translated by William Smart. Reprint, 1959.
1891. *The Positive Theory of Capital*. London: Macmillan. Translated by William Smart.
1962. *Shorter Classics*. South-Holland, Ill.: Libertarian Press.

James M. Buchanan (1919–)

James Buchanan is the cofounder, along with Gordon Tullock, of public choice theory. Buchanan entered the University of Chicago's graduate economics program as a "libertarian socialist." After six weeks of taking Frank Knight's course in price theory, recalls Buchanan, he had been converted into a zealous free marketer.

Buchanan's next big conversion came while reading an article in German by Swedish economist Knut Wicksell. The obscure 1896 article's message was that only taxes and government spending that are unanimously approved can be justified. That way, argued Wicksell, taxes used to pay for programs would have to be taken from those who benefited from those programs. Wicksell's idea contradicted the mainstream 1940s view that there need be no connection between what a taxpayer pays and what he receives in benefits. That is still the mainstream view. But Buchanan found it persuasive. He translated the essay into English and started thinking more along Wicksell's lines.

One of the products of his thinking was a book he coauthored with Gordon Tullock titled *The Calculus of Consent*. In it the authors showed that the unanimity requirement is unworkable in practice and considered modifications to the rule that they called "workable unanimity." Their book, along with Anthony Downs's *An Economic Theory of Democracy*, helped start the field of public choice and is now considered a classic. Together, Buchanan and Tullock also started the academic journal *Public Choice*.

Perhaps Buchanan's most important contribution to economics is his distinction between two levels of public choice—the initial level at which a constitution is chosen, and the postconstitutional level. The first is like setting the rules of a game, and the second is like playing the game within the rules. Buchanan has proselytized his fellow economists to think more about the first level instead of acting as political players at the second level. To spread this way of thinking, Buchanan even started a new journal called *Constitutional Economics*.

Buchanan also believes that because costs are subjective, much of welfare economics—cost-benefit analysis, and so on—is wrongheaded. He spelled out these views in detail in *Cost and Choice*, an uncommonly impassioned economics book. Yet Buchanan has not persuaded most of his economist colleagues on this issue.

Buchanan was awarded the 1986 Nobel Prize in economics for "his development of the contractual and constitutional bases for the theory of economic and political decision making." Buchanan was born in Murfreesboro, Tennessee, and has spent most of his academic life in Virginia, first at the University of Virginia, then at Virginia Polytechnic Institute and State University, and most recently at George Mason University. In 1969 Buchanan became the first director of the Center for the Study of Public Choice. He was president of the Southern Economic Association in 1963 and of the Western Economic Association in 1983 and 1984, and vice president of the American Economic Association in 1971.

Selected Works

1962 (with Gordon Tullock). *The Calculus of Consent: Logical Foundations of Constitutional Democracy*. Ann Arbor: University of Michigan Press. Available online at: http://www.econlib.org/library/Buchanan/buchCv3Contents.html.
1968. *The Demand and Supply of Public Goods*. Chicago: Rand McNally. Available online at: http://www.econlib.org/library/Buchanan/buchCv5Contents.html.
1969. *Cost and Choice*. Chicago: Markham. Available online at: http://www.econlib.org/library/Buchanan/buchCv6Contents.html.
1973. "Introduction: L.S.E. Cost Theory in Retrospect." In James M. Buchanan and G. F. Thirlby, eds., *L.S.E. Essays on Cost*. London: Weidenfeld and Nicolson. Available online at: http://www.econlib.org/library/NPDBooks/Thirlby/bcthLS1.html.
1975 (with Robert P. Tollison). *The Limits of Liberty*. Chicago: University of Chicago Press. Available online at: http://www.econlib.org/library/Buchanan/buchCv7Contents.html.
1977. *Freedom in Constitutional Contract*. College Station: Texas A&M University Press.
1980 (with Geoffrey Brennan). *The Power to Tax*. Cambridge: Cambridge University Press. Available online at: http://www.econlib.org/library/Buchanan/buchCv9Contents.html.
The Collected Works of James M. Buchanan. Available online at: http://www.econlib.org/library/Buchanan/buchCContents.html.

Arthur Frank Burns (1904–1987)

Arthur F. Burns is best known for having been chairman of the Federal Reserve System from 1970 to 1978. His appointment by President Richard Nixon capped a career of empirical studies of the economy, and particularly of business cycles. In a 1934 study based on his Ph.D. dissertation, Burns had noted the almost universal tendency of industries to slow down after an initial growth spurt. Burns pointed out that this tendency did not imply slow growth for the whole economy because new industries continued to appear.

Measuring Business Cycles, coauthored with Wesley Mitchell and published in 1946 by the National Bureau of Economic Research (NBER), is a massive empirical study of previous business cycles. In it, Burns and Mitchell distilled a large number of statistical indicators of recessions and expansions into one signal of turning points in the U.S. business cycle. The NBER, a private nonprofit research institute, is now the organization that announces when recessions begin and end. Much of the institute's approach is based on work done by Burns and Mitchell. Their book, more than any other single accomplishment, gave Burns a reputation as an expert in business cycle forecasting.

Burns earned all his degrees at Columbia University and did all his teaching there. From 1953 to 1956 he was chairman of President Dwight D. Eisenhower's Council of Economic Advisers. He was president of the NBER from 1957 to 1967, and president of the American Economic Association in 1959. From 1981 to 1985 Burns was the U.S. ambassador to the Federal Republic of Germany.

Selected Works

1934. *Production Trends in the United States Since 1870.* New York: National Bureau of Economic Research.
1946 (with W. C. Mitchell). *Measuring Business Cycles.* New York: Columbia University Press.

Gustav Cassel (1866–1945)

Gustav Cassel, a Swedish economist, developed the theory of exchange rates known as purchasing power parity in a series of post-World War I memoranda for the League of Nations. The basic concept can be made clear with an example. If US$4 buys one bushel of wheat in the United States, and if 120 Japanese yen exchange for US$1, then the price of a bushel of wheat in Japan should be 480 yen

(4×120). In other words, there should be parity between the purchasing power of one U.S. dollar in the United States and the purchasing power of its exchange value in Japan.

Cassel believed that if an exchange rate was not at parity, it was in disequilibrium and that either the exchange rate or the purchasing power would adjust until parity was achieved. The reason is arbitrage. If wheat sold for four dollars in the United States and for six hundred yen in Japan, then arbitragers could buy wheat in the United States and sell it in Japan and would do so until the price differential was eliminated.

Economists now realize that purchasing power parity would hold if all of a country's goods were traded internationally. But most goods are not. If a hamburger cost two dollars in the United States and three dollars in Japan, arbitragers would not buy hamburgers in the United States and resell them in Japan. Transportation costs and storage costs would more than wipe out the gain from arbitrage. Nevertheless, economists still take seriously the concept of purchasing power parity. They often use it as a starting point for predicting exchange rate changes. If, for example, Israel's annual inflation rate is 20 percent and the U.S. inflation rate is 4 percent, chances are high that the Israeli shekel will lose value in exchange for the U.S. dollar.

Cassel was a professor of economics at the University of Stockholm from 1903 to 1936. His dying words were, "A world currency!"

Selected Works

1921. *The World's Monetary Problems.* London: Constable. A collection of two memoranda presented to the International Financial Conference of the League of Nations in Brussels in 1920 and to the Financial Committee of the League of Nations in September 1921.

Ronald H. Coase (1910–)

Ronald Coase received the Nobel Prize in 1991 "for his discovery and clarification of the significance of transaction costs and property rights for the institutional structure and functioning of the economy." Coase is an unusual economist for the twentieth century, and a highly unusual Nobel Prize winner. First, his writings are sparse. In a sixty-year career he wrote only about a dozen significant papers—and very few insignificant ones. Second, he uses little or no mathematics, disdaining what he calls "blackboard economics." Yet his impact on economics has been profound. That impact stems almost entirely from two of his articles, one published when he was twenty-seven and the other published twenty-three years later.

Coase conceived of the first article, "The Nature of the Firm," while he was an undergraduate on a trip to the United States from his native Britain. At the time he was a socialist, and he dropped in on perennial Socialist Party presidential candidate Norman Thomas. He also visited Ford and General Motors and came up with a puzzle: how could economists say that Lenin was wrong in thinking that the Russian economy could be run like one big factory, when some big firms in the United States seemed to be run very well? In answering his own question, Coase came up with a fundamental insight about why firms exist. Firms are like centrally planned economies, he wrote, but unlike the latter they are formed because of people's voluntary choices. But why do people make these choices? The answer, wrote Coase, is "marketing costs." (Economists now use the term "transaction costs.") If markets were costless to use, firms would not exist. Instead, people would make arm's-length transactions. But because markets are costly to use, the most efficient production process often takes place in a firm. His explanation of why firms exist is now the accepted one and has given rise to a whole literature on the issue. Coase's article was cited 169 times in academic journals between 1966 and 1980.

"The Problem of Social Cost," Coase's other widely cited article (661 citations between 1966 and 1980), was even more pathbreaking; indeed, it gave rise to the field called law and economics. Economists before Coase of virtually all political persuasions had accepted British economist Arthur Pigou's idea that if, say, a cattle rancher's cows destroy his neighboring farmer's crops, the government should stop the rancher from letting his cattle roam free or should at least tax him for doing so. Otherwise, believed economists, the cattle would continue to destroy crops because the rancher would have no incentive to stop them.

But Coase challenged the accepted view. He pointed out that if the rancher had no legal liability for destroying the farmer's crops, and if transaction costs were zero, the farmer could come to a mutually beneficial agreement with the rancher under which the farmer paid the rancher to cut back on his herd of cattle. This would happen, argued Coase, if the damage from additional cattle exceeded the rancher's net returns on these cattle. If, for example, the rancher's net return on a steer was two dollars, then the rancher would accept some amount over two dollars to give up the additional steer. If the steer was doing three dollars' worth of harm to the crops, then the farmer would be willing to pay the rancher up to three dollars to get rid of the steer. A mutually beneficial bargain would be struck.

Coase considered what would happen if the courts made the rancher liable for the damage caused by his steers. Economists had thought that the number of steers raised by the rancher would be affected. But Coase showed that the only thing affected would be the wealth of the rancher and the farmer; the number of cattle and the amount of crop damage, he showed, would be the same. In the above example, the farmer would insist that the rancher pay at least three dollars for the right to have the extra steer roaming free. But because the extra steer was worth only two dollars to the rancher, he would be willing to pay only up to two dollars. Therefore, the steer would not be raised, the same outcome as when the rancher was not liable.

This insight was stunning. It meant that the case for government intervention was weaker than economists had thought. Yet Coase's soulmates at the free-market-oriented University of Chicago wondered, according to George Stigler, "how so fine an economist could make such an obvious mistake." So they invited Coase, who was then at the University of Virginia, to come to Chicago to discuss it. They had dinner at the home of Aaron Director, the economist who had founded the *Journal of Law and Economics*.

Stigler recalled:

> We strongly objected to this heresy. Milton Friedman did most of the talking, as usual. He also did much of the thinking, as usual. In the course of two hours of argument the vote went from twenty against and one for Coase to twenty-one for Coase. What an exhilarating event! I lamented afterward that we had not had the clairvoyance to tape it.[1]

Stigler himself labeled Coase's insight the Coase theorem.

Of course, because transaction costs are never zero and sometimes are very high, courts are still needed to adjudicate between farmers and ranchers. Moreover, strategic behavior by the parties involved can prevent them from reaching the agreement, even if the gains from agreeing outweigh the transactions costs.

So, why were economists so excited by the Coase theorem? The reason is that it made them look differently at many issues. Take divorce. University of Colorado economist H. Elizabeth Peters showed empirically that whether a state has traditional barriers to divorce or divorce on demand has no effect on the divorce rate. This is contrary to conventional wisdom but consistent with the Coase theorem. If the sum of a couple's net gains from marriage, as seen by the couple, is negative, then no agreement on distributing the gains from the marriage can keep them together. All the traditional divorce law did was enhance the

---

1. George Stigler, *Memoirs of an Unregulated Economist* (New York: Basic Books, 1988), p. 76.

bargaining position of women. A husband who wanted out much more than his wife wanted him in could compensate his wife to let him out. Not surprisingly, divorce-on-demand laws have made women who get divorces financially worse off, just as the absence of liability for the rancher in our example made the farmer worse off.

Coase also upset the apple cart in the realm of public goods. Economists often give the lighthouse as an example of a public good that only government can provide. They choose this example not based on any information they have about lighthouses, but rather on their a priori view that lighthouses could not be privately owned and operated at a profit. Coase showed, with a detailed look at history, that lighthouses in nineteenth-century Britain were privately provided and that ships were charged for their use when they came into port.

Coase earned his doctorate from the University of London in 1951 and emigrated to the United States, where he was a professor at the University of Buffalo from 1951 to 1958, at the University of Virginia from 1958 to 1964, and at the University of Chicago from 1964 to 1979, when he retired.

See also: EXTERNALITIES.

Selected Works

1937. "The Nature of the Firm." *Economica* 4 (November): 386–405.
1938. "Business Organization and the Accountant." Reprinted in James M. Buchanan and G. F. Thirlby, eds., *L.S.E. Essays on Cost.* London: Weidenfeld and Nicolson, 1973. Available online at: http://www.econlib.org/library/NPD Books/Thirlby/bcthLS5.html.
1959. "The Federal Communications Commission." *Journal of Law and Economics* 2 (October): 1–40.
1960. "The Problem of Social Cost." *Journal of Law and Economics* 3 (October): 1–44.
1974. "The Lighthouse in Economics." *Journal of Law and Economics* 17, no. 2: 357–376.

Gerard Debreu (1921–2004)

Gerard Debreu's contributions are in general equilibrium theory—highly abstract theory about whether and how each market reaches equilibrium. In a famous paper coauthored with Kenneth Arrow and published in 1954, Debreu proved that under fairly unrestrictive assumptions, prices exist that bring markets into equilibrium. In his 1959 book, *The Theory of Value*, Debreu introduced more general equilibrium theory, using complex analytic tools from mathematics—set theory and topology—to prove his

theorems. In 1983 Debreu was awarded the Nobel Prize "for having incorporated new analytical methods into economic theory and for his rigorous reformulation of the theory of general equilibrium."

A native of France, Debreu spent most of his professional life at the University of California at Berkeley. He started as a professor of economics in 1962 and was appointed professor of mathematics in 1975. In 1976 Debreu was made a chevalier of the French Legion of Honor.

Selected Works

1954 (with Kenneth Arrow). "Existence of a Competitive Equilibrium for a Competitive Economy." *Econometrica* 22, no. 3: 205–290.
1959. *Theory of Value: An Axiomatic Analysis of Economic Equilibrium.* New York: Wiley. Reprint. New Haven: Yale University Press, 1971.
1981. *Mathematical Economics: Twenty Papers of Gerard Debreu.* Edited by W. Hildenbrand. Cambridge: Cambridge University Press.

Robert F. Engle (1942–)

In 2003, econometrician Robert Engle, along with econometrician Clive Granger, received the Nobel Prize in economics. Engle's prize was "for methods of analyzing economic time series with time-varying volatility (ARCH)."

ARCH stands for "autoregressive conditional heteroskedasticity." The name is complex, but the idea can be grasped. Many data vary randomly about a constant mean. For instance, the height of six-year-olds may come close to forming a normal distribution around its mean (or average) value. When these data are graphed, they form the so-called bell curve known to all students from their teachers' practice of "grading on a curve." But many economic time series (i.e., data recorded in calendar sequence, annually or at shorter or longer intervals) do not display a constant mean. GDP, for example, typically grows over time. Even if the econometrician estimates its trend rate of growth, he still finds that it varies around that trend—that is, is volatile. What is more, if GDP is above trend one quarter, it is likely to remain above trend the next quarter, and if it is below trend, it is likely to remain below trend. Such a time series is said to be "autoregressive." Effectively, it has a short-run mean and a long-run mean. Any random variation around the long-run mean raises or lowers the short-run mean; and even if there were no more random variations, the time series would adjust only slowly back toward its long-run mean. With GDP, autoregressive behavior implies extended periods of above-normal and below-normal economic activity—booms and slumps.

Although econometricians have long known that the variability in stock prices, GDP, interest rates, and other time series is not constant over time, before Engle they modeled the ever-changing mean, making the incorrect assumption that volatility around the short-run mean was constant (i.e., that the spread of the bell curve, measured by the standard deviation, was constant). When the volatility (measured by the standard deviation) is constant, statisticians call it "homoskedastic." But Engle realized that for many problems, such as calculating insurance premiums or the prices of options, the variability of a series around the mean is just as important as the variability of the mean itself, and that this variability is not always constant—it is "heteroskedastic." Just as with the mean of GDP, a time series (e.g., corporate profits or inflation rates) is sometimes best characterized as having a long-run and a short-run volatility. The volatility may rise or fall randomly around its long-run value. If, when it is high, it tends to stay high and, when it is low, it tends to stay low, adjusting only slowly back to the long-run value, then the volatility is itself autoregressive. Just as autoregressive variations in GDP describe the business cycle, autoregressive volatility in the prices of financial assets describes cycles of riskiness important to financial traders.

Engle figured out a way to formulate and estimate models that could describe these cycles adequately. The term "conditional" in ARCH implies that Engle's models also take account of the cycles in the mean. His ARCH model, first published in 1982, can be used to forecast volatility, something crucial for investors who want to limit the riskiness of their stock holdings. Engle's student, Tim Bollerslev, generalized the model, calling it, naturally, GARCH (generalized ARCH).[1]

GARCH has served a practical use in so-called value-at-risk analysis. Value-at-risk models are used to calculate capital requirements for compliance with the Basel rules that regulate risks in international banking. Using GARCH, economists can figure out how risky a portfolio can be while having only some specified small probability of a maximum loss. Individual investors can do likewise. In an example given on the Nobel committee's Web site, if you had $1 million in an S&P 500 index on July 31, 2002, there was a 99 percent probability that your maximum loss the next day would be $61,500, or about 6 percent.[2]

Engle earned his B.S. in physics at Williams College in 1964, his M.S. in physics at Cornell in 1966, and his Ph.D. in economics at Cornell in 1969. He was a professor at MIT from 1969 to 1974 and a professor at the University of California at San Diego from 1974 to 1999. Since 1999, he has been a professor at New York University's Stern School of Business.

Selected Works

1982. "Autoregressive Conditional Heteroskedasticity with Estimates of the Variance of U.K. Inflation." *Econometrica* 50: 987–1008.
1986 (with Tim Bollerslev). "Modeling the Persistence of Conditional Variances." *Econometric Reviews* 5: 1–50.

Irving Fisher (1867–1947)

Irving Fisher was one of America's greatest mathematical economists and one of the clearest economics writers of all time. He had the intellect to use mathematics in virtually all his theories and the good sense to introduce it only after he had clearly explained the central principles in words. And he explained very well. Fisher's *Theory of Interest* is written so clearly that graduate economics students can read—and understand—half the book in one sitting, something unheard of in technical economics.

Although he damaged his reputation by insisting throughout the Great Depression that recovery was imminent, contemporary economic models of interest and capital are based on Fisherian principles. Similarly, monetarism is founded on Fisher's principles of money and prices.

Fisher called interest "an index of a community's preference for a dollar of present [income] over a dollar of future income." He labeled his theory of interest the "impatience and opportunity" theory. Interest rates, Fisher postulated, result from the interaction of two forces: the "time preference" people have for capital now, and the investment opportunity principle (that income invested now will yield greater income in the future). This reasoning sounds very much like Eugen von Böhm-Bawerk's. Indeed, Fisher dedicated *Theory of Interest* to "the memory of John Rae and of Eugen von Böhm-Bawerk, who laid the foundations upon which I have endeavored to build." But Fisher objected to Böhm-Bawerk's idea that roundaboutness necessarily increases production, arguing instead that at a positive interest rate, no one would ever choose a longer period unless it were more productive. So if we look at processes selected, we do find that longer periods are more productive. But, he argued, the length of the period does not in itself contribute to productivity.

1. Tim Bollerslev, "Generalized Autoregressive Conditional Heteroskedasticity," *Journal of Econometrics* 31 (1986): 307–327.
2. See http://nobelprize.org/economics/laureates/2003/ecoadv .pdf.

Fisher defined capital as any asset that produces a flow of income over time. A flow of income is distinct from the stock of capital that generated it, although the two are linked by the interest rate. Specifically, wrote Fisher, the value of capital is the present value of the flow of (net) income that the asset generates. This still is how economists think about capital and income today.

Fisher also opposed conventional income taxation and favored a tax on consumption to replace it. His position followed directly from his capital theory. When people save out of current income and then use the savings to invest in capital goods that yield income later, noted Fisher, they are being taxed on the income they used to buy the capital goods and then are being taxed later on the income the capital generates. This, he said, is double taxation of saving, and it biases the tax code against saving and in favor of consumption. Fisher's reasoning is still used by economists today in making the case for consumption taxes.

Fisher was a pioneer in the construction and use of price indexes. James Tobin of Yale called him "the greatest expert of all time on index numbers."[1] Indeed, from 1923 to 1936, his own Index Number Institute computed price indexes from all over the world.

Fisher was also the first economist to distinguish clearly between real and nominal interest rates. He pointed out that the real interest rate is equal to the nominal interest rate (the one we observe) minus the expected inflation rate. If the nominal interest rate is 12 percent, for example, but people expect inflation of 7 percent, then the real interest rate is only 5 percent. Again, this is still the basic understanding of modern economists.

Fisher laid out a more modern quantity theory of money (i.e., monetarism) than had been done before. He formulated his theory in terms of the equation of exchange, which says that $MV = PT$, where M equals the stock of money; V equals velocity, or how quickly money circulates in an economy; P equals the price level; and T equals the total volume of transactions. Again, modern economists still draw on this equation, although they usually use the version $MV = Py$, where y stands for real income.

The equation can be a very powerful tool for checking the consistency of one's thinking about the economy. Indeed, Reagan economist Beryl Sprinkel, who was the U.S. Treasury undersecretary for monetary affairs in 1981, used this equation to criticize his colleague David Stockman's economic forecasts. Sprinkel pointed out that the only way Stockman's assumptions about the growth of income, the

inflation rate, and the growth of the money supply could prove true would be if velocity increased faster than it ever had before. As it turned out, velocity actually declined.

Irving Fisher was born in upstate New York in 1867. He gained an eclectic education at Yale, studying science and philosophy. He published poetry and works on astronomy, mechanics, and geometry. But his greatest concentration was on mathematics and economics, the latter having no academic department at Yale. Nonetheless, Fisher earned the first Ph.D. in economics ever awarded by Yale. After graduation he stayed at Yale for the rest of his career.

A three-year struggle with tuberculosis beginning in 1898 left Fisher with a profound interest in health and hygiene. He took up vegetarianism and exercise and wrote a national best-seller titled *How to Live: Rules for Healthful Living Based on Modern Science,* whose value he demonstrated by living until age eighty. He campaigned for Prohibition, peace, and eugenics. He was a founder or president of numerous associations and agencies, including the Econometric Society and the American Economic Association. He was also a successful inventor. In 1925 his firm, which held the patent on his "visible card index" system, merged with its main competitor to form what later was known as Remington Rand and then Sperry Rand. Although the merger made him very wealthy, he lost a large part of his wealth in the stock market crash of 1929.

Selected Works

1906. *The Nature of Capital and Income*. New York: Macmillan.

1907. *The Rate of Interest*. New York: Macmillan.

1911. *The Purchasing Power of Money*. New York: Macmillan.

1921. "Dollar Stabilization." *Encyclopedia Britannica* 30: 852–853. Available online at: http://www.econlib.org/library/Essays/fshEnc1.html.

1922. *The Making of Index Numbers*. Boston: Houghton Mifflin.

1922. *The Purchasing Power of Money*. New rev. edition. Available online at: http://www.econlib.org/library/YPDBooks/Fisher/fshPPM.html.

1930. *The Theory of Interest*. New York: Macmillan. Available online at: http://www.econlib.org/library/YPDBooks/Fisher/fshToI.html.

Robert W. Fogel (1926–)

Robert Fogel was corecipient (with Douglass C. North) of the 1993 Nobel Prize in economics "for having renewed research in economic history by applying economic theory

1. James Tobin, "Irving Fisher," in *The New Palgrave: A Dictionary of Economics* Vol. 2. Ed. John Eatwell, Murray Milgate, and Peter Newman. (New York: Stockton Press, 1987), pp. 369–376.

and quantitative methods in order to explain economic and institutional change."

Fogel earned his master's degree in economics at Columbia University in 1960, learning economics from GEORGE STIGLER and economic history from Carter Goodrich. He earned his Ph.D. at Johns Hopkins University in 1963, where he worked under SIMON KUZNETS. His interest, early on, was in understanding the factors that contribute to economic growth. Because of his training from Stigler and Kuznets, he was empirically inclined. His first major book, based on his Ph.D. dissertation, was *Railroads and American Economic Growth*. Fogel's work on railroads is a first-rate, extremely detailed application of one of the most important principles of economics: that there is a substitute for virtually everything. So rather than just accepting the idea that railroads were so important in economic growth because of their ubiquity, Fogel carefully considered where the extension of canals might have replaced railroads had the railroads never been built. He took account also of the cost of these hypothetical canals, along with the cost savings from not building railroads. Fogel concluded that almost all the agricultural land that became economically valuable because of railroads also would have been valuable had there been only an extended series of canals. The net contribution of railroads to gross national product (GNP) due to reducing shipping costs of agricultural products, concluded Fogel, amounted to only about 2 percent of GNP. Of course, Fogel recognized that his methods did not take account of the reduced cost of shipping nonagricultural goods by railroad.

Fogel, along with his University of Rochester colleague Stanley Engerman, generated much controversy in the early 1970s with their work on the economics of slavery. Fogel and Engerman claimed, in their fact-filled book, *Time on the Cross*, that slavery was economically viable before the Civil War and that economic factors would not have brought it down; an ethical commitment to ending slavery was required for that to happen. Fogel and Engerman also claimed that slavery was efficient, although other economic historians (including Gavin Wright, Peter Temin, Paul David, Richard Sutch, Roger Ransom, and, most recently, Jeffrey Rogers Hummel) have contested this claim.

In 1975, Fogel joined the faculty of the University of Chicago, where he remains. In the early 1980s, he began to study a burning question in economic demography: What accounts for the dramatic increase in life expectancy over the last two centuries? Between 1850 and 1950, for example, U.S. life expectancy at birth increased from about forty to sixty-eight years. Fogel found that less than half of the decrease in mortality could be explained by better standards of nourishment.

Selected Works

1964. *Railroads and American Economic Growth: Essays in Econometric History*. Baltimore: Johns Hopkins University Press.

1965. "The Reunification of Economic History with Economic Theory." *American Economic Review* 55, nos. 1/2: 92–98.

1974 (with Stanley L. Engerman). *Time on the Cross: The Economics of American Negro Slavery*. Boston: Little, Brown.

1981 (with James G. March). *Aging: Stability and Change in the Family*. New York: Academic Press.

1989. *Without Consent or Contract: The Rise and Fall of American Slavery*. New York: Norton.

2000. *The Fourth Great Awakening and the Future of Egalitarianism*. Chicago: University of Chicago Press.

2004. "Changes in the Disparities in Chronic Disease During the Course of the Twentieth Century." NBER Working Paper no. 10311. National Bureau of Economic Research, Cambridge, Mass.

2004. *The Escape from Hunger and Premature Death, 1700–2100: Europe, America, and the Third World*. New York: Cambridge University Press.

2004. "High Performing Asian Economies." NBER Working Paper no. 10752. National Bureau of Economic Research, Cambridge, Mass.

2005. "Reconsidering Expectations of Economic Growth After World War II from the Perspective of 2004." NBER Working Paper no. 11125. National Bureau of Economic Research, Cambridge, Mass.

Milton Friedman (1912–2006)

Milton Friedman was the twentieth century's most prominent advocate of free markets. Born in 1912 to Jewish immigrants in New York City, he attended Rutgers University, where he earned his B.A. at the age of twenty. He went on to earn his M.A. from the University of Chicago in 1933 and his Ph.D. from Columbia University in 1946. In 1951 Friedman received the John Bates Clark Medal honoring economists under age forty for outstanding achievement. In 1976 he was awarded the Nobel Prize in economics for "his achievements in the field of consumption analysis, monetary history and theory, and for his demonstration of the complexity of stabilization policy." Before that time he had served as an adviser to President Richard Nixon and was president of the American Economic Association in 1967. After retiring from the University of Chicago in 1977, Friedman became a senior research fellow at the Hoover Institution at Stanford University.

Friedman established himself in 1945 with *Income from Independent Professional Practice*, coauthored with Simon

Kuznets. In it he argued that state licensing procedures limited entry into the medical profession, thereby allowing doctors to charge higher fees than they would be able to do if competition were more open.

His landmark 1957 work, *A Theory of the Consumption Function,* took on the Keynesian view that individuals and households adjust their expenditures on consumption to reflect their current income. Friedman showed that, instead, people's annual consumption is a function of their "permanent income," a term he introduced as a measure of the average income people expect over a few years.

In *Capitalism and Freedom,* Friedman wrote arguably the most important economics book of the 1960s, making a case for relatively free markets to a general audience. He argued for, among other things, a volunteer army, freely floating exchange rates, abolition of licensing of doctors, a negative income tax, and education vouchers. (Friedman was a passionate foe of the military draft: he once stated that the abolition of the draft was almost the only issue on which he had personally lobbied Congress.) Many of the young people who read it were encouraged to study economics themselves. His ideas spread worldwide with *Free to Choose* (coauthored with his wife, Rose Friedman), the best-selling nonfiction book of 1980, written to accompany a TV series on the Public Broadcasting System. This book made Milton Friedman a household name.

Although much of his trailblazing work was done on price theory—the theory that explains how prices are determined in individual markets—Friedman is popularly recognized for monetarism. Defying Keynes and most of the academic establishment of the time, Friedman presented evidence to resurrect the quantity theory of money—the idea that the price level depends on the money supply. In *Studies in the Quantity Theory of Money,* published in 1956, Friedman stated that in the long run, increased monetary growth increases prices but has little or no effect on output. In the short run, he argued, increases in money supply growth cause employment and output to increase, and decreases in money supply growth have the opposite effect.

Friedman's solution to the problems of inflation and short-run fluctuations in employment and real GNP was a so-called money-supply rule. If the Federal Reserve Board were required to increase the money supply at the same rate as real GNP increased, he argued, inflation would disappear. Friedman's monetarism came to the forefront when, in 1963, he and Anna Schwartz coauthored *Monetary History of the United States, 1867–1960,* which contends that the GREAT DEPRESSION was the result of the Federal Reserve's ill-conceived monetary policies. Upon receipt of the unpublished manuscript submitted by the authors, the Federal Reserve Board responded internally with a lengthy critical review. Such was their agitation that the Fed governors discontinued their policy of releasing minutes from the board's meetings to the public. Additionally, they commissioned a counterhistory to be written (by Elmus R. Wicker) in the hope of detracting from *Monetary History.*

Friedman's book has had a substantial influence on the economics profession. One measure of that influence is the change in the treatment of monetary policy given by MIT Keynesian Paul Samuelson in his best-selling textbook, *Economics.* In the 1948 edition Samuelson wrote dismissively that "few economists regard Federal Reserve monetary policy as a panacea for controlling the business cycle." But in 1967 Samuelson said that monetary policy had "an important influence" on total spending. The 1985 edition, coauthored with Yale's William Nordhaus, states, "Money is the most powerful and useful tool that macroeconomic policymakers have," adding that the Fed "is the most important factor" in making policy.

Throughout the 1960s, Keynesians—and mainstream economists generally—had believed that the government faced a stable long-run trade-off between unemployment and inflation—the so-called PHILLIPS CURVE. In this view the government could, by increasing the demand for goods and services, permanently reduce unemployment by accepting a higher inflation rate. But in the late 1960s, Friedman (and Columbia University's Edmund Phelps) challenged this view. Friedman argued that once people adjusted to the higher inflation rate, unemployment would creep back up. To keep unemployment permanently lower, he said, would require not just a higher, but a permanently accelerating inflation rate (see Phillips curve).

The stagflation of the 1970s—rising inflation combined with rising unemployment—gave strong evidence for the Friedman-Phelps view and swayed most economists, including many Keynesians. Again, Samuelson's text is a barometer of the change in economists' thinking. The 1967 edition indicates that policymakers faced a trade-off between inflation and unemployment. The 1980 edition says there was less of a trade-off in the long run than in the short run. The 1985 edition says there is no long-run trade-off.

Selected Works

1945 (with Simon Kuznets). *Income from Independent Professional Practice.* New York: National Bureau of Economic Research.

1953. *Essays in Positive Economics.* Chicago: University of Chicago Press.

1956. Ed. *Studies in the Quantity Theory of Money*. Chicago: University of Chicago Press.

1957. *A Theory of the Consumption Function*. Princeton: Princeton University Press.

1962. *Capitalism and Freedom*. Chicago: University of Chicago Press.

1962. *Price Theory: A Provisional Text*. Chicago: Aldine.

1963 (with Anna J. Schwartz). *A Monetary History of the United States, 1867–1960*. Princeton: Princeton University Press.

1972. *An Economist's Protest: Columns on Political Economy*. Glen Ridge, N.J.: Thomas Horton and Daughters.

1980 (with Rose Friedman). *Free to Choose*. New York: Harcourt Brace Jovanovich.

Ragnar Frisch (1895–1973)

In 1969 Norwegian Ragnar Frisch, along with Dutch economist Jan Tinbergen, received the first Nobel Prize for economics "for having developed and applied dynamic models for the analysis of economic processes." Frisch received his prize for his pioneering work in econometric modeling and measurement; indeed, Frisch invented the word "econometrics" to refer to the use of mathematical and statistical techniques to test economic hypotheses. Frisch founded the Econometric Society in 1930.

Frisch believed that econometrics would help establish economics as a science, but toward the end of his life he had doubts about how econometrics was being used. "I have insisted that econometrics must have relevance to concrete realities," he wrote, "otherwise it degenerates into something which is not worthy of the name econometrics, but ought rather to be called playometrics."

In a paper on business cycles, Frisch was the first to use the words "microeconomics" to refer to the study of single firms and industries, and "macroeconomics" to refer to the study of the aggregate economy.

Frisch spent most of his professional life at the University of Oslo in Norway.

Selected Works

1933. "Propagation Problems and Impulse Problems in Dynamic Economics." In *Economic Essays in Honor of Gustav Cassel*. Reprinted in R. A. Gordon and L. R. Klein, eds., *Readings in Business Cycles*. London: Allen and Unwin, 1966.

1934. *Statistical Confluence Analysis by Means of Complete Regression Systems*. Oslo: University Institute of Economics.

1936. "Annual Survey of General Economic Theory: The Problem of Index Numbers." *Econometrica* 4, no. 1: 1–38.

1970. "Econometrics in the World of Today." In W. A. Eltis, M. F. Scott, and J. N. Wolfe, eds., *Induction, Growth and Trade: Essays in Honour of Sir Roy Harrod*. London: Clarendon Press.

John Kenneth Galbraith (1908–2006)

From the 1950s through the 1970s, John Kenneth Galbraith was one of the most widely read economists in the United States. One reason is that he wrote so well, with the ability to turn a clever phrase that made those he argued against look foolish. Galbraith's first major book, published in 1952, is *American Capitalism: The Concept of Countervailing Power*. In it he argued that giant firms had replaced small ones to the point where the perfectly competitive model no longer applied to much of the American economy. But not to worry, he added. The power of large firms was offset by the countervailing power of large unions, so that consumers were protected by competing centers of power.

Galbraith made his biggest splash with his 1958 book, *The Affluent Society*, in which he contrasted the affluence of the private sector with the squalor of the public sector. Many people liked that book because of their view that Galbraith, like Thorstein Veblen before him, attacked production that was geared to "conspicuous consumption." But that is not what Galbraith did. In fact, Galbraith argued that "an admirable case can still be made" for satisfying even consumer wants that "have bizarre, frivolous, or even immoral origins." His argument against satisfying all consumer demands is more subtle. "If the individual's wants are to be urgent," he wrote, "they must be original with himself. They cannot be urgent if they must be contrived for him. And above all, they must not be contrived by the process of production by which they are satisfied. . . . One cannot defend production as satisfying wants if that production creates the wants" (p. 124).

Friedrich Hayek made the most fundamental criticism of Galbraith's argument. Hayek conceded that most wants do not originate with the individual. Our innate wants, he wrote, "are probably confined to food, shelter, and sex." All other wants we learn from what we see around us. Probably all our aesthetic feelings—our enjoyment of music and literature, for example—are learned. So, wrote Hayek, "to say that a desire is not important because it is not innate is to say that the whole cultural achievement of man is not important."[1]

1. Friedrich Hayek, "The Non Sequitur of the 'Dependence Effect,'" *Southern Economic Journal* 27, no. 4 (1961): 346.

Galbraith's magnum opus is his 1967 book, *The New Industrial State*, in which he argued that the American economy was dominated by large firms. "The mature corporation," wrote Galbraith, has "readily at hand the means for controlling the prices at which it sells as well as those at which it buys. . . . Since General Motors produces some half of all the automobiles, its designs do not reflect the current mode, but are the current mode. The proper shape of an automobile, for most people, will be what the automobile makers decree the current shape to be" (p. 30).

The evidence has not been kind to Galbraith's thesis. Even our largest firms lose money if they fail to produce a product that consumers want. The U.S. market share of GM, for example, one of Galbraith's favorite examples of a firm invulnerable to market forces, had fallen from about 50 percent when Galbraith wrote the book to less than half that by 2005.

Galbraith was born in Canada and moved to the United States in the 1930s. He earned his Ph.D. in agricultural economics at the University of California at Berkeley. He was one of the chief price controllers during World War II as head of the Price Section of the U.S. government's Office of Price Administration. Unlike almost all other economists, Galbraith had defended permanent price controls. In 1943 Galbraith left the government to be on the editorial board of *Fortune*. After the war he directed the U.S. Strategic Bombing Survey, whose main finding was that saturation bombing of Germany had not been very effective at slowing down German war production. In 1949 he became an economics professor at Harvard, where he had been briefly before the war. Galbraith was also politically active. He was an adviser to President John F. Kennedy, Kennedy's ambassador to India, and president of Americans for Democratic Action. He was president of the American Economic Association in 1972.

Selected Works

1952. *American Capitalism*. Boston: Houghton Mifflin.
1952. *A Theory of Price Control*. Cambridge: Harvard University Press.
1958. *The Affluent Society*. Boston: Houghton Mifflin.
1967. *How to Get out of Viet Nam*. New York: New American Library.
1967. *The New Industrial State*. Boston: Houghton Mifflin.
1981. *Life in Our Times*. Boston: Houghton Mifflin

Henry George (1839–1897)

Henry George is best remembered as a proponent of the "single tax" on land. The government should finance all of its projects, he argued, with proceeds from only one tax. This single tax would be on the unimproved value of land—the value that the land would have if it were in its natural state with no buildings, no landscaping, and so on. George's idea was not new. It was largely borrowed from David Ricardo, James Mill, and John Stuart Mill.

In his heyday Henry George was very popular, with his ideas inspiring passionate debate among young intellectuals. After George published *Progress and Poverty* in 1879, a political movement grew in the United States around his work. He later narrowly missed being elected mayor of New York.

Most taxes, noted George, stifle productive behavior. A tax on income reduces people's incentive to earn income, a tax on wheat would reduce wheat production, and so on. But a tax on the unimproved value of land is different. The value of land comes from two components, its natural value and the value that is created by improving it (by building on it, for example). The value of a vacant lot in its natural state comes not from any sacrifice or opportunity cost borne by the owners of the land, but rather from demand for a fixed amount of land. Therefore, argued George, because the value of the unimproved land is unearned, neither the land's value nor a tax on the land's value can affect productive behavior. If land were taxed more heavily, the quantity available would not decline, as with other goods; nor would demand decline because of land's productive uses. By taxing the whole of the value of unimproved land, the government would drive the price of land to zero.

George was right that other taxes may have stronger disincentives, but economists now recognize that the single land tax is not innocent, either. Site values are created, not intrinsic. Why else would land in Tokyo be worth so much more than land in Mississippi? A tax on the value of a site is really a tax on productive potential, which is a result of improvements to land in the area. Henry George's proposed tax on one piece of land is, in effect, based on the improvements made to the neighboring land.

And what if you are your "neighbor"? What if you buy a large expanse of land and raise the value of one portion of it by improving the surrounding land. Then you are taxed based on your improvements. This is not far-fetched. It is precisely what the Disney Corporation did in Florida. Disney bought up large amounts of land around the area where it planned to build Disney World, and then made this surrounding land more valuable by building Disney World. Had George's single tax on land been in existence, Disney might never have made the investment. So, contrary to George's reasoning, even a tax on unimproved land reduces incentives.

George's argument also assumes that in setting taxes, the government can separate the raw value of land from the value of its improvements—a difficult, if not impossible, task, especially for a politically motivated government. Can the government tax the "unimproved rental value" of the land under an office complex in Los Angeles without creating any disincentive for the owner to increase its improved value?

Objections aside, Henry George may have been arguing for what is really the least offensive tax. As Milton Friedman said almost a century after George's death: "In my opinion, the least bad tax is the property tax on the unimproved value of land, the Henry George argument of many, many years ago" (Mark Blaug. *Economica*, New Series, 47, no. 188 [1980] p. 472).

Henry George was also a passionate advocate of free trade and opponent of protectionism. He saw clearly that protectionism is a misleading term for barriers to trade and identified whom "protectionism" hurts. George wrote:

> To every trade there must be two parties who mutually desire to trade, and whose actions are reciprocal. No one can buy unless he can find some one willing to sell; and no one can sell unless there is some other one willing to buy. If Americans did not want to buy foreign goods, foreign goods could not be sold here even if there were no tariff. The efficient cause of the trade which our tariff aims to prevent is the desire of Americans to buy foreign goods, not the desire of foreign producers to sell them. Thus protection really prevents what the "protected" themselves want to do. It is not from foreigners that protection preserves and defends us; it is from ourselves. (Henry George 1980, *Protection or Free Trade*, pp. 45–46)

About the Author

Charles L. Hooper holds an M.S. in engineering-economic systems from Stanford University and is a visiting fellow with the Hoover Institution.

Selected Works

1879. *Progress and Poverty.* 1912 ed. Garden City, N.Y.: Double-day, Page. Available online at: http://www.econlib.org/library/YPDBooks/George/grgPP.html.
1886. *Protection or Free Trade.* 1905 ed. New York: Doubleday, Page.

Clive W. J. Granger (1934–)

In 2003, econometrician Clive Granger, along with econometrician Robert Engle, received the Nobel Prize in economics. Granger's award was "for methods of analyzing economic time series with common trends (cointegration)."

Trained in statistics, Granger specializes in the behavior of time-series data (i.e., data that are recorded in calendar sequence, annually or at shorter or longer intervals). Early in his career, the best-developed statistics assumed that time series were stationary—that is, that they tended to vary randomly around a common long-run mean (or average) value or around a nonrandom trend. Many economic time series, however, appear to be nonstationary—to follow processes related to the random walk. The term "random walk" is suggested by the metaphor of a drunken man stumbling in the street—just as likely to go one way as another. A time series is a random walk when the next period's value is as likely to be higher as it is to be lower, so that the best forecast of the next period's value is just whatever today's value happens to be.

For lack of better techniques, economists often applied statistics designed for stationary data to nonstationary data. In 1974, Granger and coauthor Paul Newbold, building on the 1920s work of the English statistician G. Udny Yule, showed that pairs of nonstationary time series could frequently display highly significant correlations when there was no causal connection between them. For example, the U.S. federal debt and the number of deaths due to AIDS between 1981 and 2000 are highly correlated but are clearly not causally connected. Such "nonsense correlations" called into question the meaningfulness of many econometric studies.

Short-run changes in time series are frequently stationary, even when the time series themselves are nonstationary in the long run. So one strategy in the face of nonstationary data was to study only short-run changes. But Granger (working with Engle) realized that such a strategy threw away valuable information. Not all long-run associations between nonstationary time series are nonsense. Suppose that the randomly walking drunk has a faithful (and sober) friend who follows him down the street from a safe distance to make sure he does not injure himself. Because he is following the drunk, the friend, viewed in isolation, also appears to follow a random walk, yet his path is not aimless; it is largely predictable, conditional on knowing where the drunk is. Granger and Engle coined the term "cointegration" to describe the genuine relationship between two nonstationary time series. Time series are "cointegrated" when the difference between them is itself stationary—the friend never gets too far away from the drunk, but, on average, stays a constant distance back.[1]

Many economic time series are nonstationary. For example, over long periods, federal revenues and spending appear to be nonstationary, but they also appear to be cointegrated, in the sense that when they are far out of line, they tend to be drawn back into close proximity. Granger developed econometric methods for testing whether the relationships among these time series were genuine cointegrating relationships or nonsense, and for correctly estimating the genuine relationships.

In addition to his work on cointegration, Granger is famous for his earlier development of the concept of Granger causality, an idea with roots in the work of the mathematician Norbert Wiener. The current value of a time series is often predictable from its own past values. For example, GDP this quarter is imperfectly predicted from information about GDP over the past few years. A second time series is said to "Granger-cause" another if its past values improve the prediction one would get just from the past values of the first time series. Granger causality is related to cointegration. Granger and Engle demonstrated that when two variables are cointegrated, then at least one of them must Granger-cause the other. The first important application of Granger-causality to economics appears in a 1972 article by Christopher Sims in which he showed that money Granger-causes nominal GNP, apparently bolstering the monetarist idea that fluctuations in money are the major cause of business cycles (see MONETARISM and MILTON FRIEDMAN).[2] In the debate that followed, the limits of Granger-causality were clarified: the concept concerns predictability and not control, so that a finding that money Granger-causes GNP does not imply that the Federal Reserve has an effective instrument to steer the economy. While Granger himself had referred simply to "causality," the adjective "Granger" is now always attached to his idea to distinguish it from causality based on control.[3]

Granger was born in Wales. He attended the University of Nottingham, where he earned a B.A. in mathematics and economics in 1955 and a Ph.D. in statistics in 1959.

1. A fuller explication of the notion of cointegration is found in Kevin D. Hoover, "Nonstationary Time Series, Cointegration, and the Principle of the Common Cause," *British Journal for the Philosophy of Science* 54 (December 2003): 527–551.

2. Christopher Sims, "Money, Income, and Causality," *American Economic Review* 62 (September 1972): 540–552.

3. See Kevin D. Hoover, *Causality in Macroeconomics* (Cambridge: Cambridge University Press, 2001), esp. chap. 8.

He was on the faculty of the University of Nottingham until 1973, with occasional visiting positions at other universities. In 1973, he became a professor at the University of California at San Diego. He retired in 2003, just two months before winning the Nobel Prize. He was knighted in 2005. In reminiscing about his childhood, Sir Clive wrote, "A teacher told my mother that 'I would never become successful,'" which illustrates the difficulty of long-run forecasting on inadequate data."

About the Author

Kevin D. Hoover is professor in the departments of economics and philosophy at Duke University. He is past president of the History of Economics Society, past chairman of the International Network for Economic Method, and editor of the *Journal of Economic Methodology*.

Selected Works

1969. "Investigating Causal Relations by Econometric Models and Cross-Spectral Methods." *Econometrica* 37: 424–438.

1974 (with Paul Newbold). "Spurious Regressions in Econometrics." *Journal of Econometrics* 2: 111–120.

1981. "Some Properties of Time Series Data and Their Use in Econometric Model Specification." *Journal of Econometrics* 16: 121–130.

1987 (with Robert Engle). "Co-integration and Error-Correction: Representation, Estimation and Testing." *Econometrica* 55: 251–276.

Trygve Haavelmo (1911–1999)

In 1989 Norwegian economist Trygve Haavelmo was awarded the Nobel Prize "for his clarification of the probability theory foundations of econometrics and his analyses of simultaneous economic structures." He made two main contributions in econometrics. The first is a 1943 article that shows some of the statistical implications of simultaneous equations. The second is a 1944 article that bases econometrics more firmly on probability theory.

During the war years Haavelmo worked for the Norwegian government in the United States. He was a professor of economics at the University of Oslo from 1948 until his retirement in 1979.

Selected Works

1943. "The Statistical Implications of a System of Simultaneous Equations." *Econometrica* 11 (January): 1–12.

1944. "The Probability Approach in Econometrics." Supplement to *Econometrica* 12 (July): S1–S115.

1960. *A Study in the Theory of Investment.* Chicago: University of Chicago Press.

Roy F. Harrod (1900–1978)

Roy Harrod is credited with getting twentieth-century economists thinking about economic growth. Harrod built on Keynes's theory of income determination. The Harrod-Domar model (named for Harrod and Evsey Domar, who worked on the concept independently) is explained in *Towards a Dynamic Economics,* though Harrod's first version of the idea was published in "An Essay in Dynamic Theory."

Harrod introduced the concepts of warranted growth, natural growth, and actual growth. The warranted growth rate is the growth rate at which all saving is absorbed into investment. If, for example, people save 10 percent of their income, and the economy's ratio of capital to output is four, the economy's warranted growth rate is 2.5 percent (ten divided by four). This is the growth rate at which the ratio of capital to output would stay constant at four.

The natural growth rate is the rate required to maintain full employment. If the labor force grows at 2 percent per year, then to maintain full employment, the economy's annual growth rate must be 2 percent (assuming no growth in productivity).

Harrod's model identified two kinds of problems that could arise with growth rates. The first was that actual growth was determined by the rate of saving and that natural growth was determined by the growth of the labor force. There was no necessary reason for actual growth to equal natural growth, and therefore the economy had no inherent tendency to reach full employment. This problem resulted from Harrod's assumptions that the wage rate is fixed and that the economy must use labor and capital in the same proportions. But most economists now believe that wage rates can fall when the labor force increases, although they disagree about how quickly. And virtually all mainstream economists agree that the ratio of labor and capital that businesses want to use depends on wage rates and on the price of capital. Therefore, one of the main problems implied by Harrod's model does not appear to be much of a problem after all.

The second problem implied by Harrod's model was unstable growth. If companies adjusted investment according to what they expected about future demand, and the anticipated demand was forthcoming, warranted growth would equal actual growth. But if actual demand exceeded anticipated demand, they would have underinvested and would respond by investing further. This investment, how-ever, would itself cause growth to rise, requiring even further investment. Result: explosive growth. The same story can be told in reverse if actual demand should fall short of anticipated demand. The result then would be a deceleration of growth. This property of Harrod's growth model became known as Harrod's knife-edge. Here again, though, this uncomfortable conclusion was the result of two unrealistic assumptions made by Harrod: (1) companies naïvely base their investment plans only on anticipated output, and (2) investment is instantaneous. In spite of these limitations, Harrod did get economists to start thinking about the causes of growth as carefully as they had thought about other issues, and that is his greatest contribution to the field.

Harrod was a close colleague of Keynes, and his official biographer. *The Life of John Maynard Keynes* was a second, and only slightly less theoretical, product of Harrod's long association with Keynes.

Born in Norfolk, England, Roy Harrod graduated from New College, Oxford. After spending a term at King's College, Cambridge, where he came in contact with Keynes, Harrod returned to Oxford to administer and teach at Christ Church College until his retirement in 1967. Assar Lindbeck, the chairman of the Nobel Prize Committee, wrote that Harrod would have been awarded a Nobel Prize if he had lived longer. The backlog of other economists awarded the Nobel Prize caused Harrod to miss getting it.

Selected Works

1936. *The Trade Cycle: An Essay.* Oxford: Oxford University Press.
1939. "An Essay in Dynamic Theory." *Economic Journal* 49 (March): 14–33.
1948. *Towards a Dynamic Economics: Some Recent Developments of Economic Theory and Their Application to Policy.* London: Macmillan.
1951. *The Life of John Maynard Keynes.* London: Macmillan.

John C. Harsanyi (1920–2000)

John C. Harsanyi was corecipient (with John Nash and Reinhard Selten) of the 1994 Nobel Prize in economics "for their pioneering analysis of equilibria in the theory of non-cooperative games."

Harsanyi's interest in working on game theory was triggered when he read John Nash's contributions of the early 1950s. He took up where Nash left off. Nash had focused on games in which each player knew the other players' preferences. Harsanyi wondered how things would change when he introduced the (often more realistic) assumption that players have incomplete information about other players. He assumed that each player is one of several "types." Each type represents a set of possible preferences for the player and a set of subjective probabilities that that player places on the other players' types. Each player then chooses a strategy for each of his types. Harsanyi showed that for every game with incomplete information, there is an equivalent game with complete information.

The Nobel committee also noted Harsanyi's contributions to moral philosophy. As early as 1955, Harsanyi had pioneered the "veil of ignorance" concept (though not by that name) that philosopher John Rawls made famous in his 1971 book, *A Theory of Justice*. Harsanyi was a strong defender of the "rule of utilitarianism," the idea that the most ethical act is to follow the rule that will yield the most happiness.

During his early years Harsanyi escaped from two of the twentieth century's most vicious totalitarian regimes. He grew up in Hungary in the 1920s and 1930s. He had wanted to study philosophy and mathematics, but because he was of Jewish origin and saw Hitler's steadily rising influence, he took his parents' advice and became a pharmacy student, knowing that that would help him maintain a military deferment. In the language of game theory, he "looked forward and reasoned back." After the German army occupied Hungary, he worked in a "labor unit"—that is, he was a slave—from May to November 1944. When the German government tried to deport him to a concentration camp in Austria, he escaped from the railway station in Budapest.

Harsanyi earned his Ph.D. in philosophy at the University of Budapest in 1947 and became a junior faculty member at the University Institute of Sociology. He resigned from the institute in June 1948 because, he recalled, "the political situation no longer permitted them to employ an outspoken anti-Marxist as I had been." The fact that his wife "was continually harassed by her Communist classmates to break up with" Harsanyi "made her realize . . . that Hungary was becoming a completely Stalinist country." In April 1950, he and his wife escaped across the Hungarian border to Austria. "We were very lucky not to be stopped or shot at by the Hungarian border guards," he wrote.[1]

Harsanyi moved to Australia, where he spent most of the 1950s. He earned a master's degree in economics in 1953 and spent two years at Stanford, beginning in 1956,

where he earned his Ph.D. in economics. In 1964 he became a professor at the University of California at Berkeley.

Selected Works

1950. "Approaches to the Bargaining Problem Before and After the Theory of Games: A Critical Discussion of Zeuthen's Hicks's and Nash's Theories." *Econometrica* 24: 144–157.
1955. "Cardinal Welfare, Individualistic Ethics, and Interpersonal Comparisons of Utility." *Journal of Political Economy* 63: 309–321.
1967–1968. "Games with Incomplete Information Played by 'Bayesian' Players." Parts I–III. *Management Science* 14: 159–182, 320–324, and 486–502.
1973. "Games with Randomly Distributed Payoffs: A New Rationale for Mixed Strategy Equilibrium Points." *International Journal of Game Theory* 2: 235–250.
1975. "Can the Maximin Principle Serve as a Basis for Morality? A Critique of John Rawls's Theory." *American Political Science Review* 69: 594–606.
1985. "Does Reason Tell Us What Moral Code to Follow, and Indeed, to Follow Any Moral Code at All?" *Ethics* 96: 42–55.

Friedrich August Hayek (1899–1992)

If any twentieth-century economist was a Renaissance man, it was Friedrich Hayek. He made fundamental contributions in political theory, psychology, and economics. In a field in which the relevance of ideas often is eclipsed by expansions on an initial theory, many of his contributions are so remarkable that people still read them more than fifty years after they were written. Many graduate economics students today, for example, study his articles from the 1930s and 1940s on economics and knowledge, deriving insights that some of their elders in the economics profession still do not totally understand. It would not be surprising if a substantial minority of economists still read and learn from his articles in the year 2050. In his book *Commanding Heights*, Daniel Yergin called Hayek the "preeminent" economist of the last half of the twentieth century.

Hayek was the best-known advocate of what is now called Austrian economics. He was, in fact, the only major recent member of the Austrian school who was actually born and raised in Austria. After World War I, Hayek earned his doctorates in law and political science at the University of Vienna. Afterward he, together with other young economists Gottfried Haberler, Fritz Machlup, and Oskar Morgenstern, joined Ludwig von Mises's private seminar—the Austrian equivalent of John Maynard Keynes's "Cambridge

---

1. See http://nobelprize.org/economics/laureates/1994/harsanyi-autobio.html.

Circus." In 1927 Hayek became the director of the newly formed Austrian Institute for Business Cycle Research. In the early 1930s, at the invitation of Lionel Robbins, he moved to the faculty of the London School of Economics, where he stayed for eighteen years. He became a British citizen in 1938.

Most of Hayek's work from the 1920s through the 1930s was in the Austrian theory of business cycles, capital theory, and monetary theory. Hayek saw a connection among all three. The major problem for any economy, he argued, is how people's actions are coordinated. He noticed, as Adam Smith had, that the price system—free markets—did a remarkable job of coordinating people's actions, even though that coordination was not part of anyone's intent. The market, said Hayek, was a spontaneous order. By spontaneous Hayek meant unplanned—the market was not designed by anyone but evolved slowly as the result of human actions. But the market does not work perfectly. What causes the market, asked Hayek, to fail to coordinate people's plans, so that at times large numbers of people are unemployed?

One cause, he said, was increases in the money supply by the central bank. Such increases, he argued in *Prices and Production*, would drive down interest rates, making credit artificially cheap. Businessmen would then make capital investments that they would not have made had they understood that they were getting a distorted price signal from the credit market. But capital investments are not homogeneous. Long-term investments are more sensitive to interest rates than short-term ones, just as long-term bonds are more interest-sensitive than treasury bills. Therefore, he concluded, artificially low interest rates not only cause investment to be artificially high, but also cause "malinvestment"—too much investment in long-term projects relative to short-term ones, and the boom turns into a bust. Hayek saw the bust as a healthy and necessary readjustment. The way to avoid the busts, he argued, is to avoid the booms that cause them.

Hayek and Keynes were building their models of the world at the same time. They were familiar with each other's views and battled over their differences. Most economists believe that Keynes's *General Theory of Employment, Interest and Money* (1936) won the war. Hayek, until his dying day, never believed that, and neither do other members of the Austrian school. Hayek believed that Keynesian policies to combat unemployment would inevitably cause inflation, and that to keep unemployment low, the central bank would have to increase the money supply faster and faster, causing inflation to get higher and higher. Hayek's thought, which he expressed as early as 1958, is now accepted by mainstream economists (see PHILLIPS CURVE).

In the late 1930s and early 1940s, Hayek turned to the debate about whether socialist planning could work. He argued that it could not. The reason socialist economists thought central planning could work, argued Hayek, was that they thought planners could take the given economic data and allocate resources accordingly. But Hayek pointed out that the data are not "given." The data do not exist, and cannot exist, in any one mind or small number of minds. Rather, each individual has knowledge about particular resources and potential opportunities for using these resources that a central planner can never have. The virtue of the free market, argued Hayek, is that it gives the maximum latitude for people to use information that only they have. In short, the market process generates the data. Without markets, data are almost nonexistent.

Mainstream economists and even many socialist economists (see SOCIALISM) now accept Hayek's argument. Columbia University economist Jeffrey Sachs noted: "If you ask an economist where's a good place to invest, which industries are going to grow, where the specialization is going to occur, the track record is pretty miserable. Economists don't collect the on-the-ground information businessmen do. Every time Poland asks, Well, what are we going to be able to produce? I say I don't know."[1]

In 1944 Hayek also attacked socialism from a very different angle. From his vantage point in Austria, Hayek had observed Germany very closely in the 1920s and early 1930s. After he moved to Britain, he noticed that many British socialists were advocating some of the same policies for government control of people's lives that he had seen advocated in Germany in the 1920s. He had also seen that the Nazis really were National Socialists; that is, they were nationalists and socialists. So Hayek wrote *The Road to Serfdom* to warn his fellow British citizens of the dangers of socialism. His basic argument was that government control of our economic lives amounts to totalitarianism. "Economic control is not merely control of a sector of human life which can be separated from the rest," he wrote, "it is the control of the means for all our ends."

To the surprise of some, John Maynard Keynes praised the book highly. On the book's cover, Keynes is quoted as saying: "In my opinion it is a grand book. . . . Morally and philosophically I find myself in agreement with virtually the whole of it; and not only in agreement with it, but in deeply moved agreement."

Although Hayek had intended *The Road to Serfdom* only for a British audience, it also sold well in the United States. Indeed, *Reader's Digest* condensed it. With that book Hayek established himself as the world's leading classical liberal;

1. "Interview: Jeffrey Sachs," *Omni* 13, no. 9 (1991) p. 79.

today he would be called a libertarian or market liberal. A few years later, along with Milton Friedman, George Stigler, and others, he formed the Mont Pelerin Society so that classical liberals could meet every two years and give each other moral support in what appeared to be a losing cause.

In 1950 Hayek became professor of social and moral sciences at the University of Chicago, where he stayed until 1962. During that time he worked on methodology, psychology, and political theory. In methodology Hayek attacked "scientism"—the imitation in social science of the methods of the physical sciences. His argument was that because social science, including economics, studies people and not objects, it can do so only by paying attention to human purposes. The Austrian school in the 1870s had already shown that the value of an item derives from its ability to fulfill human purposes. Hayek was arguing that social scientists more generally should take account of human purposes. His thoughts on the matter are in *The Counter-Revolution of Science: Studies in the Abuse of Reason*. In psychology Hayek wrote *The Sensory Order: An Inquiry into the Foundations of Theoretical Psychology*.

In political theory Hayek gave his view of the proper role of government in his book *The Constitution of Liberty*. It is actually a more expansive view of the proper role of government than many of his fellow classical liberals hold. He discussed the principles of freedom and based his policy proposals on those principles. His main objection to progressive taxation, for example, was not that it causes inefficiency but that it violates equality before the law. In the book's postscript, "Why I Am Not a Conservative," Hayek distinguished his classical liberalism from conservatism. Among his grounds for rejecting conservatism were that moral and religious ideals are not "proper objects of coercion" and that conservatism is hostile to internationalism and prone to a strident nationalism.

In 1962 Hayek returned to Europe as professor of economic policy at the University of Freiburg in Breisgau, West Germany, and stayed there until 1968. He then taught at the University of Salzburg in Austria until his retirement nine years later. His publications slowed substantially in the early 1970s. In 1974 he shared the Nobel Prize with Gunnar Myrdal "for their pioneering work in the theory of money and economic fluctuations and for their penetrating analysis of the interdependence of economic, social and institutional phenomena." This award seemed to breathe new life into him, and he began publishing again, both in economics and in politics.

Many people get more conservative as they age. Hayek became more radical. Although he had favored central banking for most of his life, in the 1970s he began advocating denationalizing money. Private enterprises that issued distinct currencies, he argued, would have an incentive to maintain their currency's purchasing power. Customers could choose from among competing currencies. Whether they would revert to a gold standard was a question that Hayek was too much of a believer in spontaneous order to predict. With the collapse of communism in Eastern Europe, some economic consultants have considered Hayek's currency system as a replacement for fixed-rate currencies.

Hayek was still publishing at age eighty-nine. In his book *The Fatal Conceit*, he laid out some profound insights to explain the intellectuals' attraction to socialism and then refuted the basis for their beliefs.

Selected Works

1931. "Richard Cantillon." Translated by Micheál Ó Súilleabháin in the *Journal of Libertarian Studies* 7, no. 2 (1985): 217–247. Available online at: http://www.econlib.org/library/Essays/JlibSt/hykCnt1.html.

1935. *Prices and Production*. 2d ed. Reprint. New York: Augustus M. Kelley, 1975.

1937. "Economics and Knowledge." *Economica*, n.s., 4 (February): 33–54. Reprinted in James M. Buchanan and G. F. Thirlby, eds., *L.S.E. Essays on Cost*. London: Weidenfeld and Nicolson, 1973. Available online at: http://www.econlib.org/library/NPDBooks/Thirlby/bcthLS3.html.

1939. "Price Expectations, Monetary Disturbances, and Malinvestments." In Hayek, *Profits, Interest, and Investment*. Reprint. New York: Augustus M. Kelley, 1975.

1944. *The Road to Serfdom*. Chicago: University of Chicago Press.

1945. "The Use of Knowledge in Society." *American Economic Review* 35 (September): 519–530. Available online at: http://www.econlib.org/library/Essays/hykKnw1.html.

1948. *Individualism and Economic Order*. Chicago: University of Chicago Press.

1952. *The Counter-Revolution of Science: Studies on the Abuse of Reason*. Glencoe, Ill.: Free Press.

1960. *The Constitution of Liberty*. Chicago: University of Chicago Press. Reprint. Chicago: Henry Regnery, 1972.

1973. *Law, Legislation, and Liberty*. Chicago: University of Chicago Press.

1976. *Denationalization of Money*. London: Institute of Economic Affairs.

1977. Foreword to *Economics as a Coordination Problem: The Contributions of Friedrich A. Hayek* by Gerald P. O'Driscoll Jr. Kansas City: Sheed, Andrews, and McMeel.

1988. *The Fatal Conceit*. Chicago: University of Chicago Press.

1995. Introduction to *Selected Essays on Political Economy* by Frédéric Bastiat. Trans. from the French by Seymour Cain. Edited by George B. de Huszar. Princeton: Van Nostrand,

1995. Available online at: http://www.econlib.org/library/Bastiat/basEsso.html#Introduction,%20by%20F.%20A.%20Hayek.

James J. Heckman (1944–)

In 2000, James Heckman, along with DANIEL MCFADDEN, received the Nobel Prize in economics. Heckman won the prize for "his development of theory and methods for analyzing selective samples," highly technical work that it is difficult to explain to the layman. Nevertheless, the work rewarded by the Nobel committee has been valuable for economists' studies of many issues that laymen do care about. The main technical problem on which Heckman has spent much of his professional life involves self-selection. An economist who wants to know, for example, how male workers will respond to a higher wage rate can take microdata on wages and hours worked and find a relationship. This approach has a problem that economists have long recognized: some men will not work at all and, therefore, will not be in the data set. And, presumably, these men who do not work will be disproportionately from the group that, had they worked, would have earned low wages. They have "self-selected" out of the workforce. So the economist's estimates on the effect of wages on hours worked will be biased. How is the economist to deal with this fact if he wants to generalize from his sample to the male population in general?

Enter Heckman. Heckman came up with a clever econometric approach to figuring out how to correct for this self-selection problem. In fact, empirical economists now know his correction as the "Heckman correction" or the "Heckit method." In 1985, using his own method to study the connection between work and wages noted above, Heckman found a bigger elasticity of labor supply among American men than had previously been thought to exist. That was because a given increase in wages did not just cause an increase in hours among those already working, but also caused relatively low-wage workers to reenter the labor market and get jobs.

In his Nobel lecture, Heckman laid out some important implications of self-selection for U.S. and European labor markets. One is that the vaunted diminution of the gap between black men's and white men's wages in the United States between 1940 and 1980 was due almost entirely to low-wage black men dropping out of the labor force. Another implication concerns the much-higher equality of wages in Europe compared with the United States that many economists and others have noted. Heckman pointed out that much of this difference is due to the fact that many low-skilled potential workers in Europe are not working. This is presumably because of high minimum wages, strong labor unions, and laws that make it hard for employers to lay people off (and therefore make the employers hesitant to hire).

The Nobel Web site refers to Heckman as "the world's foremost researcher on econometric policy evaluation." In 1999, Heckman and coauthors Robert LaLonde and Jeffrey Smith found that government programs to train workers are generally ineffective at increasing those workers' wages and long-term employment prospects. The reason they *appear* effective is that the average wage gain of people in these programs is high. But Heckman and his coauthors showed that this occurs because the trainees typically have lost or quit their jobs prior to entering the training program and that training is a form (albeit inefficient) of job search. Much of the improvement in their posttraining fortunes would have occurred without a government program in place. This would probably come as no surprise to people who have been in such programs. In 2002, with Pedro Carneiro, Heckman also showed that lack of credit is not a major constraint on the ability of young Americans to attend college. They found that credit constraints prevent, at most, 4 percent of the U.S. population from attending.

Heckman has also weighed in on the issue of racial discrimination in U.S. labor markets. In 1998 he wrote, "[M]ost of the disparity in earnings between blacks and whites in the labor markets of the 1990s is due to the differences in skills they bring to the market, and not to discrimination within the labor market."

Selected Works

1974. "Shadow Wages, Market Wages and Labor Supply." *Econometrica* 42: 679–693.

1975. "The Common Structure of Statistical Models of Truncation, Sample Selection and Limited Dependent Variables and a Simple Estimator for Such Models." *Annals of Economic and Social Measurement* 5: 475–492.

1976. "A Life Cycle Model of Earnings, Learning and Consumption." *Journal of Political Economy* 84: S11–S44.

1979. "Sample Selection Bias as a Specification Error." *Econometrica* 47: 153–161.

1981 (with Thomas MaCurdy). "New Methods for Estimating Labor Supply Functions." In Ronald Ehrenberg, ed., *Research in Labor Economics*. Vol. 4. Greenwich, Conn.: JAI Press.

1998. "Detecting Discrimination." *Journal of Economic Perspectives* 12, no. 2: 101–116.

1999 (with Robert LaLonde and Jeffrey Smith). "The Economics and Econometrics of Active Labor Market Programs." In Orley Ashenfelter and David Card, eds., *Handbook of Labor Economics*. Amsterdam: North-Holland. Chap. 31.

2002 (with Pedro Carneiro). "The Evidence on Credit Constraints in Post-secondary Schooling." *Economic Journal* 112: 705–734.

Walter Wolfgang Heller (1915–1987)

Walter Heller's claim to fame stems from his years as chairman of the Council of Economic Advisers (CEA) from 1961 to 1964, under presidents John F. Kennedy and Lyndon B. Johnson. Before that, and after, he was an economics professor at the University of Minnesota.

As chairman of the CEA, Heller persuaded President Kennedy to cut marginal tax rates. This cut in tax rates, which was passed after Kennedy's death, helped cause a boom in the U.S. economy. Heller's CEA also developed the first "voluntary" (i.e., enforced by veiled threats rather than by explicit laws) wage-price guidelines.

Heller's early academic work was on state and local taxation. In 1947 and 1948 he was tax adviser to the U.S. military government in Germany. He was involved in the currency and tax reforms that helped spur the German economic boom (see GERMAN ECONOMIC MIRACLE). In a 1950 article, Heller noted that the reduction in marginal tax rates helped "remove the repressive effect of extremely high rates."

According to tax economist Joseph Pechman, Heller was also one of the first economists to recognize that tax deductions and tax preferences narrow the income tax base, thus requiring, for a given amount of revenue, higher marginal tax rates.

Selected Works

1949. "Tax and Monetary Reform in Occupied Germany." *National Tax Journal* 2, no. 3: 215–231.

1966. *New Dimensions of Political Economy.* Cambridge: Harvard University Press.

1969 (with Milton Friedman). *Monetary vs. Fiscal Policy.* New York: W. W. Norton.

1975. "What's Right with Economics?" *American Economic Review* 65, no. 1: 1–26.

John R. Hicks (1904–1989)

The British economist John Hicks is known for four contributions. The first is his introduction of the idea of the elasticity of substitution. While the concept is difficult to explain in a few words, Hicks used it to show, contrary to the MARXIST allegations, that labor-saving technical progress—the kind we generally have—does not necessarily reduce labor's share of national income.

His second major contribution is his invention of what is called the IS-LM model, a graphical depiction of the argument John Maynard Keynes gave in his *General Theory of Employment, Interest and Money* (1936) about how an economy could be in equilibrium with less than full employment. Hicks published it in a journal article the year after Keynes's book was published. It seems safe to say that most economists became familiar with Keynes's argument by seeing Hicks's graph.

Hicks's third major contribution is his 1939 book *Value and Capital,* in which he showed that most of what economists then understood and believed about value theory (the theory about why goods have value) can be derived without having to assume that utility is measurable. His book was also one of the first works on general equilibrium theory, the theory about how all markets fit together and reach equilibrium.

Hicks's fourth contribution is the idea of the compensation test. Before his test, economists were hesitant to say that one particular outcome was preferable to another because even a policy that benefited millions of people could hurt some people. Free trade in cars, for example, helps millions of American consumers at the expense of thousands of American workers and owners of stock in U.S. auto companies. How was an economist to judge whether the help to some outweighed the hurt to others? Hicks asked if those helped could compensate those hurt to the full extent of their hurt and still be better off. If the answer was *yes,* then the policy passed the "Hicks compensation test," even if the compensation was never paid, and was judged to be good. In the auto example economists can show that the dollar gains to car buyers far outweigh the dollar losses to workers and stockholders, and therefore, by Hicks's compensation test, free trade is good.

In 1972 John Hicks and KENNETH ARROW jointly received the Nobel Prize for economics "for their pioneering contributions to general economic equilibrium theory and welfare theory." Educated at Balliol College, Oxford, John Hicks returned there as the Drummond Professor of Political Economy, a post he held until his retirement in 1965.

In 1935 he married the economist Ursula Webb. He was knighted in 1964.

Selected Works

1937. "Mr. Keynes and the 'Classics.'" *Econometrica* 5 (April): 147–159.

1939. "The Foundations of Welfare Economics." *Economic Journal* 49 (December): 696–712.

1939. *Value and Capital.* Oxford: Clarendon Press.

1940. "The Valuation of the Social Income." *Economica* 7 (May): 105–124.

1965. *Capital and Growth.* Oxford: Clarendon Press.

1973. *Capital and Time: A Neo-Austrian Theory.* Oxford: Clarendon Press.

1974. *The Crisis in Keynesian Economics.* Oxford: Basil Blackwell.

David Hume (1711–1776)

Though better known for his treatments of philosophy, history, and politics, the Scottish philosopher David Hume also made several essential contributions to economic thought. His empirical argument against British mercantilism formed a building block for classical economics. His essays on money and international trade published in *Political Discourses* strongly influenced his friend and fellow countryman ADAM SMITH.

British mercantilists believed that economic prosperity could be realized by limiting imports and encouraging exports in order to maximize the amount of gold in the home country. The American colonies facilitated this policy by providing raw materials that Britain manufactured into finished goods and reexported back to the colonial consumers in America. Needless to say, the arrangement was short-lived.

But even before the American Revolution intervened in mercantilistic pursuits, David Hume showed why net exporting in exchange for gold currency, hoarded by Britain, could not enhance wealth. Hume's argument was essentially the monetarist quantity theory of money: prices in a country change directly with changes in the money supply. Hume explained that as net exports increased and more gold flowed into a country to pay for them, the prices of goods in that country would rise. Thus, an increased flow of gold into England would not necessarily increase England's wealth substantially.

Hume showed that the increase in domestic prices due to the gold inflow would discourage exports and encourage imports, thus automatically limiting the amount by which exports would exceed imports. This adjustment mechanism is called the price-specie-flow mechanism. Surprisingly, even though Hume's idea would have bolstered Adam Smith's attack on mercantilism and argument for free trade, Smith ignored Hume's argument. Although few economists accept Hume's view literally, it is still the basis of much thinking on balance-of-payments issues.

Considering Hume's solid grasp of monetary dynamics, his misconceptions about money behavior are all the more noteworthy. Hume erroneously advanced the notion of "creeping inflation"—the idea that a gradual increase in the money supply would lead to economic growth.

Hume made two other major lasting contributions to economics. One is his idea, later elaborated by FRIEDRICH HAYEK in *The Road to Serfdom,* that economic freedom is a necessary condition for political freedom. The second is his assertion that "you cannot deduce ought from is"—that is, value judgments cannot be made purely on the basis of facts. Economists now make the same point by distinguishing between normative (what should be) and positive (what is).

Hume died the year *The Wealth of Nations* was published, and in the presence of its author, Adam Smith.

Selected Works

1752. *Political Discourses.* Edinburgh: A. Kincaid and A. Donaldson.

1875. *The Philosophical Works of David Hume.* 4 vols. Edited and annotated by T. H. Green and T. H. Grose. London: Longmans, Green.

1955. *Writings on Economics.* Edited by Eugene Rotwein. London: Nelson.

1987. *Essays: Moral, Political, and Literary.* Edited by Eugene F. Miller. Available online at: http://www.econlib.org/library/LFBooks/Hume/hmMPL.html.

William Stanley Jevons (1835–1882)

William Jevons was one of three men to simultaneously advance the so-called marginal revolution. Working in complete independence of one another—Jevons in Manchester, England; LEON WALRAS in Lausanne, Switzerland; and CARL MENGER in Vienna—each scholar developed the theory of marginal utility to understand and explain consumer behavior. The theory held that the utility (value) of each additional unit of a commodity—the marginal utility—is less and less to the consumer. When you are thirsty, for example, you get great utility from a glass of water. Once your thirst is quenched, the second and third glasses are less and less appealing. Feeling waterlogged, you will eventually refuse water altogether. "Value," said Jevons, "depends entirely upon utility."

This statement marked a significant departure from the classical theory of value, which stated that value derived from the labor used to produce a product or from the cost of production more generally. Thus began the neoclassical school, which is still the dominant one in economics today.

Jevons went on to define the "equation of exchange," which shows that for a consumer to be maximizing his or her utility, the ratio of the marginal utility of each item consumed to its price must be equal. If it is not, then he or she can, with a given income, reallocate consumption and get more utility.

Take, for example, a consumer whose marginal utility from oranges is 10 "utils," and from cookies 4 utils, when oranges and cookies are both priced at $.50 each. The consumer's ratio of marginal utility to price for oranges is 10/$.50, or 20, and for cookies is 4/$.50, or 8. Jevons would have said (and modern economists would agree) that this does not satisfy the equation of exchange, and therefore the consumer will change purchases. Specifically, the consumer could increase utility by spending $.50 less on cookies and using the money to buy oranges. He would lose 4 utils on the cookies, but gain 10 on the oranges, for a net gain of 6 utils. He will have this incentive to reallocate purchases until the equation of exchange holds (i.e., until the marginal utility of oranges falls and the marginal utility of cookies rises to a point where, as a ratio to their prices, they are equal).

Of course, as is true with most new developments in economic theory, one can always find earlier writers who said some of the same things. Jevons's role in the marginal revolution is no exception. Much of what he said had been said earlier by Hermann Gossen in Germany, Jules Dupuit and Antoine Cournot in France, and Samuel Longfield in Britain. Yet historians of economic thought are sure that Jevons had never read them.

Jevons put much less thought into the production side of economics. It is ironic, therefore, that he became famous in Britain for his book *The Coal Question,* in which he wrote that Britain's industrial vitality depended on coal and, therefore, would decline as that resource was exhausted. As coal reserves ran out, he wrote, the price of coal would rise. This would make it feasible for producers to extract coal from poorer or deeper seams. He also argued that America would rise to become an industrial superpower. Although his forecast was right for both Britain and America, and he was right about the incentive to mine more costly seams, he was almost surely wrong that the main factor was the cost of coal. Jevons failed to appreciate the fact that as the price of an energy source rises, entrepreneurs have a strong incentive to invent, develop, and produce alternate sources. In particular, he did not anticipate oil or natural gas. Also, he did not take account of the incentive, as the price of coal rose, to use it more efficiently or to develop technology that brought down the cost of discovering and mining (see NATURAL RESOURCES).

Born in Liverpool, England, Jevons studied chemistry and botany at University College, London. Because of the bankruptcy of his father's business in 1847, Jevons left school to take up the position of assayer at the Mint in Sydney, Australia. He remained there five years, resuming his studies at University College on his return to England. He was later appointed to the post of chair in political economy at his alma mater and retired from there in 1880. Two years later, with a number of unfinished books in process, Jevons drowned while swimming. He was forty-six.

Selected Works

1863. *A Serious Fall in the Value of Gold Ascertained, and Its Social Effects Set Forth.* 1863. Reprinted in Jevons, *Investigations in Currency and Finance.* London: Macmillan, 1884.

1865. *The Coal Question.* 1st ed. London: Macmillan.

1866. *The Coal Question.* 2d ed. London: Macmillan. Available online at: http://www.econlib.org/library/YPDBooks/Jevons/jvnCQ.html.

1871. *The Theory of Political Economy.* Reprint. Edited by R. D. Collison Black. Harmondsworth: Penguin Books, 1970.

1875. *Money and the Mechanism of Exchange.* London: C. Kegan Paul. Available online at: http://www.econlib.org/library/YPDBooks/Jevons/jvnMME.html.

1875. "The Solar Period and the Price of Corn." First published in Jevons, *Investigations in Currency and Finance.* London: Macmillan, 1884. Pp. 194–205.

1881. "Richard Cantillon and the Nationality of Political Economy." First published in the *Contemporary Review.* Available online at: http://www.econlib.org/library/NPDBooks/Cantillon/cntNT8.html.

1888. *The Theory of Political Economy.* 3d ed. Available online at: http://www.econlib.org/library/YPDBooks/Jevons/jvnPE.html.

1894. *Investigations in Currency and Finance.* Edited and with an introduction by H. S. Foxwell. London: Macmillan.

1906. *The Coal Question.* 3d ed. Revised and edited by A. W. Flux. London: Macmillan.

Harry Gordon Johnson (1923–1977)

Harry Johnson, a Canadian, was one of the most active and prolific economists of all time. His main research was in the area of international trade, international finance, and monetary policy.

One of Johnson's early articles on international trade showed that a country with monopoly power in some good could impose a tariff and be better off, even if other countries retaliated against the tariff. His proof was what is sometimes called a "possibility theorem"; it showed that such a tariff *could* improve the country's well-being, not that it was likely to. Johnson, realizing the difference between what could be and what is likely to be, was a strong believer in FREE TRADE. Indeed, he often gave lectures in his native Canada excoriating the Canadian government for its protectionist policies and arguing that Canada could eliminate some of the gap between Canadian and U.S. standards of living by implementing free trade.

In international finance Johnson's seminal 1958 paper named the growth in the money supply as one important factor that affects a country's BALANCE OF PAYMENTS. Before then, economists had tended to focus on nonmonetary factors. Johnson's article began what is now called the monetary approach to the balance of payments.

In the field of monetary economics Johnson made an early attempt to do for Britain what MILTON FRIEDMAN and Anna Schwartz were doing for the United States: measure the money supply over time. Although he did not achieve as much in this area as Friedman and Schwartz did, his work led to other, more careful and detailed studies of the British money supply. In 1959, after having been a professor at the University of Manchester in England, Johnson moved to the University of Chicago as the token "Keynesian." He learned a lot from monetarist Milton Friedman and others at Chicago, just as he had learned from Keynesians in England. Although never a monetarist himself, Johnson became increasingly sympathetic to monetarist views.

One of his classic articles, written in his early years at Chicago, is his 1962 survey, "Monetary Theory and Policy." The article is a graduate student's delight—tying together apparently disparate insights by other economists, pointing out their pitfalls, and laying out an agenda for future research—all in a clear, readable style that still manages not to sacrifice subtle distinctions.

In a relatively short career Johnson wrote 526 professional articles, forty-one books and pamphlets, and more than 150 book reviews. He also gave a prodigious number of speeches. According to PAUL SAMUELSON, when John-son died he had eighteen papers in proof. (Commented Samuelson: "That is dying with your boots on!") Johnson also earned many honors. In 1977, for example, he was named a distinguished fellow of the American Economic Association, and in 1976 the Canadian government named him an officer of the Order of Canada. Johnson graduated from the University of Toronto in 1943 and earned his Ph.D. from Harvard in 1958.

Selected Works

1953. "Optimum Tariffs and Retaliation." *Review of Economic Studies* 21, no. 2: 142–153.

1959. "British Monetary Statistics." *Economica* 26 (February): 1–17.

1961. "The 'General Theory' After Twenty-five Years." *American Economic Review* 51 (May): 1–17.

1963. *The Canadian Quandary: Economic Problems and Policies.* Toronto: McGraw-Hill.

1969. *Essays in Monetary Economics.* 2d ed. Cambridge: Harvard University Press.

1971. "The Keynesian Revolution and the Monetarist Counter-revolution." *American Economic Review* 61 (May): 1–14.

1972. *Further Essays in Monetary Economics.* London: George Allen and Unwin.

Daniel Kahneman (1934–)

In 2002, Daniel Kahneman, along with Vernon Smith, received the Nobel Prize in economics. Kahneman received his prize "for having integrated insights from psychological research into economic science, especially concerning human judgment and decision-making under uncertainty."

Kahneman did most of his important work with Amos Tversky, who died in 1996. Before their work, economists had gotten far in their analyses of decision making under uncertainty by assuming that people correctly estimate probabilities of various outcomes or, at least, do not estimate these probabilities in a biased way. Even if some people place too low a probability on an event relative to what was reasonable, economists argued, others will place too high a probability on that same event and the results would cancel out. But Kahneman and Tversky found that this is not true: the vast majority of people misestimate probabilities in predictable ways.

One bias they found is that people tend to believe in "the law of small numbers"; that is, they tend to generalize from small amounts of data. So, for example, if a mutual fund manager has had three above-average years in a row, many people will conclude that the fund manager is better than average, even though this conclusion does not follow from such a small amount of data. Or if the first four tosses of a coin give, say, three heads, many people will believe that the next toss is likely to be tails. Kahneman saw this belief in his own behavior as a young military psychologist in the Israeli army. Tasked with evaluating candidates for officer training, he concluded that a candidate who performed well on the battlefield or in training would be as good a leader later as he showed himself to be during the observation period. As Kahneman explained in his Nobel lecture, "As I understood clearly only when I taught statistics some years later, the idea that predictions should be less extreme than the information on which they are based is deeply counterintuitive."[1]

Another bias Kahneman and Tversky found to be common in people's thinking is "availability," whereby people judge probabilities based on how available examples are to them. So, for example, people overstate the risk from driving without a seat belt if they personally know someone who was killed while driving without. Also, repetition of various stories in the news media, such as stories about children being killed by guns, causes people to overstate the risk of guns to children (see RISK AND SAFETY).

Kahneman and Tversky also introduced "prospect theory" to explain some systematic choices most people make—choices that contradict the strictly rational model. Kahneman later admitted that their theory's name was meaningless, but that it was important for getting others to take it seriously, thus giving even more evidence that the framing of an issue matters. (See the next paragraph for an example.) Imagine, for example, that someone is given a chance to bet $40 on some outcome and that he is told, accurately, that his probability of winning $40 is 60 percent, which means that his probability of losing $40 is 40 percent. Most people will refuse such a bet. Kahneman and Tversky called this "loss aversion." This could be written off as simple risk aversion, which is certainly not irrational. What makes it strange, if not outright irrational, is that people act so differently with bigger gambles. Kahneman and Tversky found, for example, that seven out of ten people prefer a 25 percent probability of losing $6,000 to a 50 percent probability of losing either $4,000 or $2,000, with an equal probability (25 percent) for each. In each case the expected loss—that is, the loss multiplied by its probability, is $1,500. But here they prefer the bigger loss ($6,000) to the smaller one ($2,000 or $4,000). This choice demonstrates what economists calling risk-loving

behavior, the opposite of the risk aversion noted for the smaller bets.

Kahneman and Tversky also used prospect theory to explain other systematic behavior that departs from the economist's rationality assumption. Consider the following situation. Many people will drive an extra ten minutes to save $10 on a $50 toy. But they will not drive ten minutes to save $20 on a $20,000 car. The gain from driving the extra ten minutes for the car is twice the gain of driving the extra ten minutes for the toy. So a higher percentage, not a lower one, of people should drive the longer distance for the saving on the car. Why don't they? Kahneman's and Tversky's explanation is that the framing of the issue affects the decision. Instead of comparing the absolute saving in price against the cost of going the extra distance, people compare the percentage saving, and the percentage saving in the case of the car is very small.

Kahneman's and Tversky's work spurred a great deal of work by economists on systematic departures from rational behavior. See BEHAVIORAL ECONOMICS for an introduction to many of the issues.

Kahneman was born in Tel Aviv, Israel, and grew up in France. He earned his B.A. in psychology and mathematics at Hebrew University in 1954 and his Ph.D. in psychology from the University of California at Berkeley in 1961. He was a psychology professor at Hebrew University from 1961 to 1978, at the University of British Columbia from 1978 to 1986, at the University of California at Berkeley from 1986 to 1994, and has been a professor at Princeton University since 1993.

Selected Works

1972 (with Amos Tversky). "Subjective Probability: A Judgment of Representativeness." *Cognitive Psychology* 3: 430–454.

1973 (with Amos Tversky). "On the Psychology of Prediction." *Psychological Review* 80: 237–251.

1974 (with Amos Tversky). "Judgment Under Uncertainty: Heuristics and Biases." *Science* 185: 1124–1131.

1979 (with Amos Tversky). "Prospect Theory: An Analysis of Decision Under Risk." *Econometrica* 47: 263–291.

1986 (with Jack Knetsch and Richard Thaler). "Fairness and the Assumptions of Economics." *Journal of Business* 59: S285–S300.

---

1. See http://nobelprize.org/economics/laureates/2002/kahnemann-lecture.pdf.

Leonid Vitalievich Kantorovich (1912–1986)

Leonid Kantorovich shared the 1975 Nobel Prize with Tjalling Koopmans "for their contributions to the theory of optimum allocation of resources." Kantarovich was born and died in Russia and did all his professional work there. His first major breakthrough came in 1938 when he was consulting with the Soviet government's Laboratory of the Plywood Trust. Asked to devise a technique for distributing raw materials to maximize output, Kantorovich saw that the problem was a mathematical one: to maximize a linear function subject to many constraints. The technique he developed is now known as linear programming.

In *The Mathematical Method of Production Planning and Organization* (1939), Kantorovich showed that all problems of economic allocation can be seen as maximizing a function subject to constraints. Across the world, John Hicks in Britain and Paul Samuelson in the United States were reaching the same conclusion at around the same time. Kantorovich, like Samuelson, showed that certain coefficients in the equations could be regarded as the prices of each input.

Kantorovich's best-known book is *The Best Uses of Economic Resources,* in which he developed some of the points made in his 1939 book. He showed that even centrally planned economies have to be concerned with using prices to allocate resources. He also made the point that socialist economies have to be concerned about trade-offs between present and future—and therefore should use interest rates just as capitalist ones do. Unfortunately, as HAYEK has shown, the only way to use prices is to have a price system—that is, markets and private property.

Besides receiving the Nobel Prize, Kantorovich was awarded the Soviet government's Lenin Prize in 1965 and the Order of Lenin in 1967. From 1944 to 1960, Kantorovich was a professor at the University of Leningrad. In 1960 he became director of mathematical economic methods at the Siberian Division of the Soviet Academy of Sciences. In 1971 he was appointed laboratory chief of the Institute of National Economic Management in Moscow.

Selected Works

1939. Translated as "The Mathematical Method of Production Planning and Organization." *Management Science* 6, no. 4 (July 1960): 363–422.
1959. Translated as *The Best Uses of Economic Resources.* Oxford, N.Y.: Pergamon, 1965.

John Maynard Keynes (1883–1946)

So influential was John Maynard Keynes in the middle third of the twentieth century that an entire school of modern thought bears his name. Many of his ideas were revolutionary; almost all were controversial. Keynesian economics serves as a sort of yardstick that can define virtually all economists who came after him.

Keynes was born in Cambridge and attended King's College, Cambridge, where he earned his degree in mathematics in 1905. He remained there for another year to study under ALFRED MARSHALL and ARTHUR PIGOU, whose scholarship on the quantity theory of money led to Keynes's *Tract on Monetary Reform* many years later. After leaving Cambridge, Keynes took a position with the civil service in Britain. While there, he collected the material for his first book in economics, *Indian Currency and Finance,* in which he described the workings of India's monetary system. He returned to Cambridge in 1908 as a lecturer, then took a leave of absence to work for the British Treasury. He worked his way up quickly through the bureaucracy and by 1919 was the Treasury's principal representative at the peace conference at Versailles. He resigned because he thought the Treaty of Versailles was overly burdensome for the Germans.

After resigning, he returned to Cambridge to resume teaching. A prominent journalist and speaker, Keynes was one of the famous Bloomsbury Group of literary greats, which also included Virginia Woolf and Bertrand Russell. At the 1944 Bretton Woods Conference, where the International Monetary Fund was established, Keynes was one of the architects of the postwar system of fixed exchange rates. In 1925 he married the Russian ballet dancer Lydia Lopokova. He was made a lord in 1942. Keynes died on April 21, 1946, survived by his father, John Neville Keynes, also a renowned economist in his day.

Keynes became a celebrity before becoming one of the most respected economists of the century when his eloquent book *The Economic Consequences of the Peace* was published in 1919. Keynes wrote it to object to the punitive reparations payments imposed on Germany by the Allied countries after World War I. The amounts demanded by the Allies were so large, he wrote, that a Germany that tried to pay them would stay perpetually poor and, therefore, politically unstable. We now know that Keynes was right. Besides its excellent economic analysis of reparations, Keynes's book contains an insightful analysis of the Council of Four (Georges Clemenceau of France, Prime Minister David Lloyd George of Britain, President Woodrow Wilson of the United States, and Vittorio Orlando of Italy).

Keynes wrote: "The Council of Four paid no attention to these issues [which included making Germany and Austro-Hungary into good neighbors], being preoccupied with others—Clemenceau to crush the economic life of his enemy, Lloyd George to do a deal and bring home something which would pass muster for a week, the President to do nothing that was not just and right" (chap. 6, para. 2).

In the 1920s Keynes was a believer in the quantity theory of money (today called MONETARISM). His writings on the topic were essentially built on the principles he had learned from his mentors, Marshall and Pigou. In 1923 he wrote *Tract on Monetary Reform,* and later he published *Treatise on Money,* both on monetary policy. His major policy view was that the way to stabilize the economy is to stabilize the price level, and that to do that the government's central bank must lower interest rates when prices tend to rise and raise them when prices tend to fall.

Keynes's ideas took a dramatic change, however, as unemployment in Britain dragged on during the interwar period, reaching levels as high as 20 percent. Keynes investigated other causes of Britain's economic woes, and *The General Theory of Employment, Interest and Money* was the result.

Keynes's *General Theory* revolutionized the way economists think about economics. It was pathbreaking in several ways, in particular because it introduced the notion of aggregate demand as the sum of consumption, investment, and government spending; and because it showed (or purported to show) that full employment could be maintained only with the help of government spending. Economists still argue about what Keynes thought caused high unemployment. Some think he attributed it to wages that take a long time to fall. But Keynes actually wanted wages not to fall, and in fact advocated in the *General Theory* that wages be kept stable. A general cut in wages, he argued, would decrease income, consumption, and aggregate demand. This would offset any benefits to output that the lower price of labor might have contributed.

Why shouldn't government, thought Keynes, fill the shoes of business by investing in public works and hiring the unemployed? *The General Theory* advocated deficit spending during economic downturns to maintain full employment. Keynes's conclusion initially met with opposition. At the time, balanced budgets were standard practice with the government. But the idea soon took hold and the U.S. government put people back to work on public works projects. Of course, once policymakers had taken deficit spending to heart, they did not let it go.

Contrary to some of his critics' assertions, Keynes was a relatively strong advocate of free markets. It was Keynes, not ADAM SMITH, who said, "There is no objection to be raised against the classical analysis of the manner in which private self-interest will determine what in particular is produced, in what proportions the factors of production will be combined to produce it, and how the value of the final product will be distributed between them."[1] Keynes believed that once full employment had been achieved by fiscal policy measures, the market mechanism could then operate freely. "Thus," continued Keynes, "apart from the necessity of central controls to bring about an adjustment between the propensity to consume and the inducement to invest, there is no more reason to socialise economic life than there was before" (p. 379).

Little of Keynes's original work survives in modern economic theory. His ideas have been endlessly revised, expanded, and critiqued. Keynesian economics today, while having its roots in *The General Theory,* is chiefly the product of work by subsequent economists including JOHN HICKS, JAMES TOBIN, PAUL SAMUELSON, Alan Blinder, ROBERT SOLOW, William Nordhaus, Charles Schultze, WALTER HELLER, and ARTHUR OKUN. The study of econometrics was created, in large part, to empirically explain Keynes's macroeconomic models. Yet the fact that Keynes is the wellspring for so many outstanding economists is testament to the magnitude and influence of his ideas.

Selected Works

1913. *Indian Currency and Finance.* Reprinted in *Keynes, Collected Writings.* Vol. 1.

1919. *The Economic Consequences of the Peace.* Reprinted in Keynes, *Collected Writings.* Vol. 2.

1920. *The Economic Consequences of the Peace.* New York: Harcourt, Brace, and Howe. Available online at: http://www.econlib.org/library/YPDBooks/Keynes/kynsCP.html.

1923. *A Tract on Monetary Reform.* Reprinted in Keynes, *Collected Writings.* Vol. 4.

1925. *The Economic Consequences of Mr. Churchill.* Reprinted in Keynes, *Collected Writings.* Vol. 9.

1930. *A Treatise on Money.* Vol. 1: *The Pure Theory of Money.* Reprinted in Keynes, *Collected Writings.* Vol. 5.

1930. *A Treatise on Money.* Vol. 2: *The Applied Theory of Money.* Reprinted in Keynes, *Collected Writings.* Vol. 6.

1936. *The General Theory of Employment, Interest and Money.* Reprinted in Keynes, *Collected Writings.* Vol. 7.

1971–88. *Collected Writings.* London: Macmillan, for the Royal Economic Society.

1. *General Theory,* pp. 378–397.

Lawrence Robert Klein (1920–)

Lawrence R. Klein received the Nobel Prize in 1980 for "the creation of economic models and their application to the analysis of economic fluctuations and economic policies." Klein began model building while still a graduate student. After getting his Ph.D. from MIT, he moved on to the Cowles Commission for Research in Economics, which was then at the University of Chicago. While there he built a model of the U.S. economy, using JAN TINBERGEN's earlier model as a starting point, to forecast economic conditions and to estimate the impact of changes in government spending, taxes, and other policies.

In 1946 the conventional wisdom was that the end of World War II would sink the economy into a depression for a few years. Klein used his model to counter the conventional wisdom. The demand for consumer goods that had been left unsatisfied during the war, he argued, plus the purchasing power of returning soldiers, would prevent a depression. Klein was right. Later he predicted correctly that the end of the Korean War would bring only a mild recession.

Klein moved to the University of Michigan, where he proceeded to build bigger and more complicated models of the U.S. economy. The Klein-Goldberger model, which he built with then graduate student Arthur Goldberger, dates from that time. But in 1954, after being denied tenure because he had been a member of the Communist Party from 1946 to 1947, Klein went to Oxford University. There he built a model of the British economy.

In 1958 Klein joined the Department of Economics at the University of Pennsylvania. He has been a professor of economics and finance at the university's Wharton School since 1968. During his tenure there he built the famous Wharton model of the U.S. economy, which contains more than a thousand simultaneous equations that are solved by computers.

Klein was coordinator of Jimmy Carter's economic task force in 1976, but he turned down an invitation to join Carter's new administration. In 1977 he was president of the American Economic Association.

Selected Works

1950. *Economic Fluctuations in the United States, 1921–1941.* Hoboken, N.J.: Wiley.
1955 (with Arthur S. Goldberger). *Econometric Model of the United States, 1929–52.* Hoboken, N.J.: Wiley.
1966. *The Keynesian Revolution.* 2d ed. New York: Macmillan.
1975 (with Gary Fromm). *The Brookings Model.* Hoboken, N.J.: Wiley.

1983. *The Economics of Supply and Demand.* Baltimore: Johns Hopkins University Press.

Frank Hyneman Knight (1885–1972)

Frank H. Knight was one of the founders of the so-called Chicago school of economics, of which MILTON FRIEDMAN and GEORGE STIGLER were the leading members from the 1950s to the 1980s. Knight made his reputation with his book *Risk, Uncertainty, and Profit,* which was based on his Ph.D. dissertation. In it Knight set out to explain why "perfect competition" would not necessarily eliminate profits. His explanation was "uncertainty," which Knight distinguished from risk. According to Knight, "risk" refers to a situation in which the probability of an outcome can be determined, and therefore the outcome insured against. "Uncertainty," by contrast, refers to an event whose probability cannot be known. Knight argued that even in long-run equilibrium, ENTREPRENEURS would earn profits as a return for putting up with uncertainty. Knight's distinction between risk and uncertainty is still taught in economics classes today.

Knight made three other important contributions to economics. One is *The Economic Organization,* a set of lecture notes originally published in 1933. In it he laid out the circular flow model of the economy and emphasized that investments will be made until the returns to investments in each use are equal at the margin. These elements still survive in textbooks today.

Knight's famous article "Some Fallacies in the Interpretation of Social Cost," in which he took on ARTHUR PIGOU's view that congestion of roads justified taxation of roads, is another of his contributions to economics. Knight showed that if roads were privately owned, road owners would set tolls that would reduce congestion. Therefore, no government intervention was required.

Knight's final contribution is his work on capital theory in the 1930s. Knight criticized EUGEN VON BÖHM-BAWERK's view that capital could be measured as a period of production, and is widely thought to have won the debate over the Austrian concept of capital.

But Knight was much more than an economist. He was also a social philosopher, and most of his writings are in social philosophy rather than technical economics. A strong believer in freedom and a strong critic of social engineering, Knight worried that freedom would be undermined by increases in monopoly and income inequality. George Stigler tells of Milton Friedman challenging Knight's view that inequality would increase, and Knight's relenting, only to take the same position at the next lunch.

Knight often despaired at the general public's inability to understand even simple economic truths. In his 1950 presidential address to the American Economic Association, Knight said:

> Of late I have a new and depressing example of popular economic thinking, in the policy of arbitrary price-fixing. Can there be any use in explaining, if it is needful to explain, that fixing a price below the free-market level will create a shortage and one above it a surplus? But the public oh's and ah's and yips and yaps at the shortage of residential housing and surpluses of eggs and potatoes as if these things presented problems any more than getting one's footgear soiled by deliberately walking in the mud.

Interestingly, though, Knight was one of the signers of a 1946 letter to the *New York Times* urging that the price controls imposed during World War II be continued.[1]

Knight was an economics professor at the University of Chicago from 1927 until 1955, after which he was an emeritus professor until his death.

Selected Works

1921. "Cost of Production and Price over Long and Short Periods." *Journal of Political Economy* 29, no. 4: 304–335.

1921. *Risk, Uncertainty, and Profit.* Boston: Houghton Mifflin.

1924. "Some Fallacies in the Interpretation of Social Cost." *Quarterly Journal of Economics* 38: 582–606.

1935. *The Ethics of Competition, and Other Essays.* London: Allen and Unwin.

1947. *Freedom and Reform: Essays in Economics and Social Philosophy.* New York: Harper and Brothers. Reprint. Edited by J. M. Buchanan. Indianapolis: Liberty Press, 1982.

1951. *The Economic Organisation.* New York: Augustus M. Kelley.

Tjalling Charles Koopmans (1910–1985)

Tjalling Koopmans shared the 1975 Nobel Prize with Leonid Kantorovich "for their contributions to the theory of optimum allocation of resources." Koopmans, a native of the Netherlands, started in mathematics and physics, but in the 1930s switched to economics because it was "closer to real life." In 1938 he succeeded Jan Tinbergen at the League of Nations in Geneva and then left in 1940 when

Hitler invaded the Netherlands. In the United States, Koopmans became a statistician with the Combined Shipping Adjustment Board in Washington where he tried to solve the practical problem of how to reorganize shipping to minimize transportation costs. The problem was complex: the variables included thousands of merchant ships, millions of tons of cargo, and hundreds of ports. He solved it. The technique he developed to do so was called "activity analysis" and is now called linear programming. His first write-up of the analysis is in a 1942 memorandum. His techniques were very similar to those used by Kantorovich, whose work he discovered only much later.

Koopmans was also like Kantorovich in generalizing his approach from one sector of the economy to the economy as a whole. Koopmans showed the conditions required for economy-wide efficiency in allocating resources. He also, again like Kantorovich, used his activity analysis techniques to derive efficient criteria for allocating between the present and the future.

Koopmans was an economist with the Cowles Commission at the University of Chicago between 1944 and 1955, and then moved with the Cowles Commission to Yale University, where he became a professor of economics until he retired in 1981. Koopmans became an American citizen in 1946. He served as president of the American Economic Association in 1981.

Selected Works

1942. "Exchange Ratios Between Cargoes on Various Routes (Non-refrigerating Dry Cargoes)." Memorandum for the Combined Shipping Adustment Board. 1942. Reprinted in Koopmans, *Scientific Papers.* Berlin: Springer, 1970.

1947. "Optimum Utilization of the Transportation System." *Proceedings of the International Statistical Conferences* 5: 136–145. Reprinted in Supplement to *Econometrica* 17 (July 1949): 136–146.

1957. *Three Essays on the State of Economic Science.* New York: McGraw-Hill.

1970. *Scientific Papers of Tjalling C. Koopmans.* Berlin: Springer. Contains a bibliography through September 1969.

Simon Kuznets (1901–1985)

Simon Kuznets is best known for his studies of national income and its components. Prior to World War I, measures of GNP were rough guesses, at best. No government agency collected data to compute GNP, and no private economic researcher did so systematically, either. Kuznets changed all that. With work that began in the 1930s and

---

1. Hugh Rockoff, *Drastic Measures: A History of Wage and Price Controls in the United States* (Cambridge: Cambridge University Press, 1984), pp. 101–102.

stretched over decades, Kuznets computed national income back to 1869. He broke it down by industry, by final product, and by use. He also measured the distribution of income between rich and poor.

Although Kuznets was not the first economist to try this, his work was so comprehensive and meticulous that it set the standard in the field. His work was funded by the nonprofit National Bureau of Economic Research, which had been started in 1920. Kuznets later helped the U.S. Department of Commerce to standardize the measurement of GNP. In the late 1940s, however, he broke with the Commerce Department over its refusal to use GNP as a measure of economic well-being. He had wanted the department to measure the value of unpaid housework because this is an important component of production. The department refused, and still does.

Kuznets's development of measures of savings, consumption, and investment came along just as Keynes's ideas about how national income is determined created a demand for such measures. Thus, Kuznets helped advance the Keynesian revolution. Kuznets's measures also helped advance the study of econometrics established by RAGNAR FRISCH and JAN TINBERGEN.

Kuznets approached his work with a strict adherence to fact and a desire to understand economic phenomena through quantitative measurement. He had started early in his native Russia: he was head of a statistical office in the Ukraine under the Bolsheviks before moving to the United States at age twenty-one.

Many economists believe that Kuznets received the 1971 Nobel Prize for his measurement in NATIONAL INCOME ACCOUNTING, and certainly that was enough to merit the prize. But in fact, the prize was awarded for his empirical work on ECONOMIC GROWTH. In this work Kuznets identified a new economic era—which he called "modern economic growth"—that began in northwestern Europe in the last half of the eighteenth century. The growth spread south and east and by the end of the nineteenth century had reached Russia and Japan. In this era, per capita income rose by about 15 percent or more each decade, something that had not happened in earlier centuries.

One of Kuznets's more startling findings concerns the effect of economic growth on income distribution. In poor countries, he found, economic growth increased the income disparity between rich and poor people. In wealthier countries, economic growth narrowed the difference. In addition, Kuznets analyzed and quantified the cyclical nature of production and prices in spans of fifteen to twenty years. Such trade cycles, while disputed, are often referred to as "Kuznets cycles."

Kuznets was a professor of economics at the University of Pennsylvania (1930–1954), Johns Hopkins University (1954–1960), and Harvard University (1960–1971). He was president of the American Economic Association in 1954.

Selected Works

1934. *National Income, 1929–1932.* Senate document no. 124, 73d Congress, 2d session.

1937. *National Income and Capital Formation, 1919–1935.* New York: National Bureau of Economic Research.

1945 (with Milton Friedman). *Income from Independent Professional Practice.* New York: National Bureau of Economic Research.

1946 (assisted by Lillian Epstein and Elizabeth Jenks). *National Product Since 1869.* New York: National Bureau of Economic Research.

1953 (assisted by Elizabeth Jenks). *Shares of Upper Income Groups in Income and Savings.* New York: National Bureau of Economic Research.

1965. *Economic Growth and Structure: Selected Essays.* New York: Norton.

1966. *Modern Economic Growth: Rate, Structure, and Spread.* New Haven: Yale University Press.

1971. *Economic Growth of Nations: Total Output and Production Structure.* Cambridge: Belknap Press of Harvard University Press.

Finn E. Kydland (1943–)

Finn Kydland, along with EDWARD PRESCOTT, received the 2004 Nobel Prize in economic science "for their contributions to dynamic macroeconomics: the time consistency of economic policy and the driving forces behind business cycles." Because Kyland and Prescott worked so closely, this biography deals with their work on time consistency and Prescott's biography deals with their work on business cycles.

Although the issue of time consistency might sound arcane, it is crucial for economic policy. In their classic 1977 article, Kydland and Prescott pointed out that even governments that care deeply about their citizens often have "time-consistency" problems. A government may decide, for example, in the interest of all its citizens not to subsidize people's losses if they are flooded. The reason is that if people expect to be bailed out when flooded, they will locate in areas where it is inefficient for them to locate, because they are not bearing the whole cost of that location decision. So the government announces that it will not bail out people if their homes are damaged by floods. Then a flood comes, and the government decides that the optimal strategy *is* to bail people out: there is no danger of the bailout causing them to locate there because they already have. Here is the problem: people figure out that the government has this time-consistency problem—making a decision later that contradicts the earlier announced policy—and so do locate in the flood-prone area in the first place. Of course, people do not talk about the government in these terms, but they will try to estimate how likely it is that the government will cave in to political pressure and change its policy. If there is even some substantial likelihood, people's decisions to live in the flood-prone area will be distorted by it. In short, unless they can make a binding commitment regarding future policies, even governments that care about their people will have a credibility problem.

Kydland and Prescott modeled this problem mathematically and showed that it applies to many policy issues. For example, "time inconsistency" could explain why governments had trouble ending inflation. Although low or zero inflation is an optimal long-run policy, a government that announces a monetary policy to achieve it will be tempted to increase the growth rate of the money supply so as to reduce unemployment. But each year, government will find itself in that position and may never take the necessary painful short-run measures to end inflation.

Kydland's and Prescott's answer to the problem of persistent high inflation was to make central banks follow rules that would prevent them from inflating. But many economists and most government officials want the central bank to have some flexibility to deal with unanticipated events. The solution: structure the incentives so that central banks will care about keeping inflation low, but will still have the power to deal with unanticipated events. Economist Kenneth Rogoff,[1] building on Kydland's and Prescott's framework, showed that this optimal balance between credibility and flexibility could be achieved if monetary policy were delegated to an independent central bank and if the central bank were managed by someone more averse to inflation than the citizens in general. Interestingly, Alan Greenspan, an inflation "hawk," became chairman of the Federal Reserve Bank just two years after Rogoff's research. Also, reforms of central banks in New Zealand, Sweden, and the United Kingdom were based on academic economists' research that drew on the Kydland-Prescott framework—and the result was a substantial decline in inflation in those three countries.

Another example of the time-consistency problem is patents. Patents involve a trade-off between the short-term welfare loss from monopoly exploitation of a patent and the long-term welfare gain from the patent-induced incentive to innovate (see INTELLECTUAL PROPERTY). A government that does not credibly commit to enforcing patents will often violate the intellectual property rights of patentees. Many governments around the world are doing this with patents on drugs. Potential innovators, anticipating this, will innovate less. So a government that wants optimal innovation needs to figure out some way to lock itself in to protecting patents in the future.

One final example is tax policy. The incentive to accumulate capital will depend on the anticipated tax rate on capital in the future. A government may commit to a low tax rate in order to encourage capital formation. But once people have invested in capital, governments will be tempted to raise the tax rate on capital because the capital is already "formed." Again, though, many people will anticipate this and, unless the government is tied in to its commitments, will invest less in capital than otherwise. One can see the U.S. Constitution, along with an independent judiciary that enforces it, as a way of handling this credibility problem.

Kydland is a citizen of Norway. He earned his B.S. from the Norwegian School of Economics and Business in 1968 and his Ph.D. from Carnegie Mellon University in 1973. He is currently a professor at the University of California at Santa Barbara and at Carnegie Mellon University.

Selected Works

1977 (with Edward Prescott). "Rules Rather than Discretion: The Inconsistency of Optimal Plans." *Journal of Political Economy* 85: 473–490.
1982 (with Edward Prescott). "Time to Build and Aggregate Fluctuations." *Econometrica* 50: 1345–1371.
2002 (with Carlos E. J. M. Zarazaga). "Argentina's Lost Decade." *Review of Economic Dynamics* 5, no. 1: 152–165.

Oskar Ryszard Lange (1904–1965)

Polish economist Oskar Lange is best known for his contributions to the economics of socialism. His views on the feasibility of socialism changed back and forth throughout his life.

While teaching at the University of Kraków in 1934, he outlined, with coauthor Marek Breit, a version of socialism in which the government owned all plants and each industry, called a public trust, was organized as a monopoly. Workers would have a large say in running each industry.

Lange left Europe in 1935 to teach at the University of Michigan. In 1936 and 1937 he entered the debate with FRIEDRICH HAYEK about the feasibility of socialism. He

---

1. Kenneth Rogoff, "The Optimal Degree of Precommitment to an Intermediate Monetary Target," *Journal of International Economics* 18 (1985): 1169–1190.

presented "market socialism," in which the government would own major industries and a central planning board (CPB) would set prices for those industries. The CPB would alter prices to reach equilibrium, raising them to get rid of shortages and lowering them to get rid of surpluses. Hayek pointed out that having government set prices to mimic competition, as Lange suggested, seemed inferior to having real competition. Whether in response to Hayek's criticism or for other reasons, Lange modified his proposal, advocating that the government set prices only in industries with few firms.

In 1943 Lange moved to the University of Chicago. That same year he advocated that the Polish government socialize key industries, but that farms, shops, and many other small and medium-sized industries remain in private hands. A large private sector, he wrote, was necessary to preserve "the kind of flexibility, pliability and adaptiveness that private initiative alone can achieve."

In 1945, Poland's newly formed communist government appointed Lange ambassador to the United States, and in 1946 he became Poland's delegate to the United Nations. When Stalinist orthodoxy was imposed in Poland in 1949, Lange was recalled to Poland and given a minor academic job. In 1953, with Poland still under Stalinist oppression, Lange reversed himself and wrote an article praising Stalin's totalitarian economic control.

In 1955, after the political oppression had lifted somewhat, Lange was made a professor at the University of Warsaw and chairman of the Polish State Economic Council.

Selected Works

1936. "On the Economic Theory of Socialism, Part I." *Review of Economic Studies* 4, no. 1: 53–71.

1937. "On the Economic Theory of Socialism, Part II." *Review of Economic Studies* 4, no. 2: 123–142.

1942. "The Foundations of Welfare Economics." *Econometrica* 10, nos. 3–4: 215–228.

1943. *Working Principles of the Soviet Economy.* New York: Russian Economic Institute.

Wassily Leontief (1906–1999)

From the time he was a young man growing up in Saint Petersburg, Wassily Leontief devoted his studies to input-output analysis. When he left Russia at the age of nineteen to begin the Ph.D. program at the University of Berlin, he had already shown how LEON WALRAS's abstract equilibrium theory could be quantified. But it was not until many years later, in 1941, while a professor at Harvard, that Leontief calculated an input-output table for the American economy. It was this work, and later refinements of it, that earned Leontief the Nobel Prize in 1973.

Input-output analysis shows the extensive process by which inputs in one industry produce outputs for consumption or for input into another industry. The matrix devised by Leontief is often used to show the effect of a change in production of a final good on the demand for inputs. Take, for example, a 10 percent increase in the production of shoes. With the input-output table, one can estimate how much additional leather, labor, machinery, and other inputs will be required to increase shoe production.

Most economists are cautious in using the table because it assumes, to use the shoe example, that shoe production requires the inputs in the proportion they were used during the time period used to estimate the table. There's the rub. Although the table is useful as a rough approximation of the inputs required, economists know from mountains of evidence that proportions are not fixed. Specifically, when the cost of one input rises, producers reduce their use of this input and substitute other inputs whose prices have not risen. If wage rates rise, for example, producers can substitute capital for labor and, by accepting more wasted materials, can even substitute raw materials for labor. That the input-output table is inflexible means that, if used literally to make predictions, it will necessarily give wrong answers.

At the time of Leontief's first work with input-output analysis, all the required matrix algebra was done using hand-held calculators and sheer tenacity. Since then, computers have greatly simplified the process, and input-output analysis, now called "interindustry analysis," is widely used. Leontief's tables are commonly used by the World Bank, the United Nations, and the U.S. Department of Commerce.

Early on, input-output analysis was used to estimate the economy-wide impact of converting from war production to civilian production after World War II. It has also been used to understand the flow of trade between countries. Indeed, a 1954 article by Leontief shows, using input-output analysis, that U.S. exports were relatively labor intensive compared with U.S. imports. This was the opposite of what economists expected at the time, given the high level of U.S. wages and the relatively high amount of capital per worker in the United States. Leontief's finding was termed the Leontief paradox. Since then, the paradox has been resolved. Economists have shown that in a country that produces more than two goods, the abundance of capital relative to labor does not imply that the capital intensity of its exports should exceed that of its imports.

Throughout his life Leontief campaigned against "theoretical assumptions and nonobserved facts" (the title of a speech he delivered while president of the American Economic Association, 1970–1971). According to Leontief too many economists were reluctant to "get their hands dirty" by working with raw empirical facts. To that end Wassily Leontief did much to make quantitative data more accessible, and more indispensable, to the study of economics.

Selected Works

1941. *The Structure of American Economy, 1919–1929*. Cambridge: Harvard University Press.
1966. *Essays in Economics: Theories and Theorizing*. New York: Oxford University Press.

Abba Ptachya Lerner (1905–1982)

Abba Lerner was the MILTON FRIEDMAN of the left. Like Friedman, Lerner was a brilliant expositor of economics who was able to make complex concepts crystal clear. Lerner was also an unusual kind of socialist: he hated government power over people's lives. Like Friedman, he praised private enterprise on the ground that "alternatives to government employment are a safeguard of the freedom of the individual." Also like Friedman, Lerner loved free markets. He opposed minimum wage laws and other price controls because they interfered with the price system, which he called "one of the most valuable instruments of modern society."[1]

Both his clear writing and his hatred of authority are illustrated in the following defense of consumer sovereignty:

> One of the deepest scars of my early youth was etched when my teacher told me, "You do not want that," after I had told her that I did. I would not have been so upset if she had said that I could not have it, whatever it was, or that it was very wicked of me to want it. What rankled was the denial of my personality—a kind of rape of my integrity. I confess I still find a similar rising of my hackles when I hear people's preferences dismissed as not genuine, because influenced by advertising, and somebody else telling them what they "really want."[2]

Lerner, like Friedman, had a sharp analytical mind that made him follow an argument to its logical conclusion.

During World War II, for example, when JOHN MAYNARD KEYNES gave a talk at the Federal Reserve Board in Washington, Lerner, who was in the audience, found Keynes's view of how the economy worked completely convincing and challenged Keynes for not carrying his own argument to its logical conclusion. Keynes denounced Lerner on the spot, but Keynes's colleague Evsey Domar, seated beside Lerner, whispered, "He ought to read *The General Theory*." A month later, wrote Lerner, Keynes withdrew his denunciation.

Lerner was born in Romania and immigrated with his parents to Britain while still a child. He tried out several avocations: as tailor, Hebrew teacher, typesetter, and owner of a printing business that went bankrupt during the Great Depression. He turned to economics, enrolling in a night course at the London School of Economics in 1929, in order to discover why his business had failed. Lerner earned top honors and several scholarships for his logically reasoned essays, many of which were published while he was still an undergraduate. His appointment as assistant lecturer at the LSE in 1936 was the first of many teaching positions, the rest of which he held in the United States after 1937. PAUL SAMUELSON, in a tribute to Lerner on his sixtieth birthday, wrote that Lerner's experience "tempts one to advise students in Economics A to quit college, fail in business, marry and raise a family, and resist being overpaid."[3]

One of Lerner's first papers, published in 1934, is a clear diagrammatic exposition of international trade. Earlier, he had written, but not published, a proof of the conditions under which free trade in goods causes the prices of factors to be equal even when factors are mobile. Samuelson showed the same thing in an article much later. "After I had enunciated the same result in 1948," Samuelson later wrote, "Lord Robbins mentioned to me that he thought he had a seminar paper in his files by Lerner of a similar type. . . . He exhumed this gem, which appeared 17 years later in the 1950 *Economica*."[4]

Probably Lerner's best-known article is "The Concept of Monopoly and the Measurement of Monopoly Power." In it he laid out clearly why setting the price of a good equal to its marginal cost is important for efficiency. The amount by which the price exceeds marginal cost is a measure of MONOPOLY power in an industry. In 1964 Samuelson wrote: "Today this may seem simple, but I can testify that no one at Chicago or Harvard could tell me in 1935 exactly why $P = MC$ was a good thing."[5]

1. Tibor Scitovsky, "Lerner's Contributions to Economics," *Journal of Economic Literature* 22, no. 4 (1984): 1549.
2. From "The Economics and Politics of Consumer Sovereignty," p. 258.
3. Paul A. Samuelson, "A. P. Lerner at Sixty," *Review of Economic Studies* 31, no. 3 (1964): 169.
4. Ibid., p. 172.
5. Ibid., p. 173.

Lerner's main contribution to macroeconomic policy is his concept of functional finance. Lerner thought that if governments wanted to increase aggregate demand so as to maintain employment, and if the federal budget was balanced, the government should run a deficit by increasing government spending or decreasing taxes. If, on the other hand, the government wanted to decrease aggregate demand, it should, if the budget was balanced, run a surplus by decreasing government spending or raising taxes. These thoughts are often attributed to Keynes, and they do follow from Keynes's reasoning. But Keynes never stated them. It took Lerner's clear thinking to get from Keynes's model of the economy to these policy conclusions. Lerner's thoughts are attributed to Keynes because textbook writers, wanting to make Keynes's thinking clear, were immediately drawn to Lerner's thinking. As economist David Colander has written, Keynes could be considered just as much a Lernerian as a Keynesian.

Lerner was active in economic analysis until the day he died. In 1980, for example, he laid out a plan for breaking OPEC. In an article titled "OPEC—a Plan—If You Can't Beat Them, Join Them," Lerner advocated that the United States and other governments of oil-consuming countries impose a 100 percent excise tax on the difference between OPEC's price and the pre-OPEC price adjusted for inflation. In 1980 OPEC charged twenty-six dollars for a barrel of oil. The pre-OPEC price adjusted for inflation was six dollars. Therefore, at that price, the tax would have been 100 percent of 26 − 6, or twenty dollars. Lerner's plan, if followed, would have caused the price to consumers to rise two dollars every time OPEC raised its price one dollar. More important, it would have caused the price to fall by two dollars every time OPEC lowered its price by one dollar. Lerner's thinking, which was absolutely watertight, was that this plan would double consumers' elasticity of demand, causing them to demand less oil at higher prices and thus reduce the strength of the cartel. The plan was never adopted.

Lerner never developed a following. One reason, wrote Tibor Scitovsky of Stanford, was "Lerner's unrelenting logic," which "overruled whatever loyalties he started with" and "made him seem like a cold fish to just about everybody."[6] Another reason was that Lerner rarely stayed in one university long; he taught at Columbia, the University of Virginia, Kansas City, Amherst, the New School for Social Research, Roosevelt, Johns Hopkins, Michigan State, and the University of California at Berkeley. Another reason was that although he made major contributions in so many areas, he did not have a specialty. Also, Lerner made his insights so clear and so apparently obvious that people who

6. Scitovsky 1984, p. 1549.

adopted his ideas forgot where they learned them. Probably because he lacked a following, Lerner never received the Nobel Prize, although many economists think he should have.

Selected Works

1934. "The Concept of Monopoly and the Measurement of Monopoly Power." *Review of Economic Studies* 1: 157–175.
1934. "The Diagrammatical Representation of Demand Conditions in International Trade." *Economica*, n.s., 1 (August): 319–334.
1936. "The Symmetry Between Import and Export Taxes." *Economica*, n.s., 3 (August): 306–313.
1943. "Functional Finance and the Federal Debt." *Social Research* 10: 38–51.
1944. *The Economics of Control: Principles of Welfare Economics.* New York: Macmillan.
1972. "The Economics and Politics of Consumer Sovereignty." *American Economic Review* 62 (May): 258–266.
1980. "OPEC—a Plan—If You Can't Beat Them, Join Them." *Atlantic Economic Journal* 8, no. 3: 1–3.

W. Arthur Lewis (1915–1991)

In 1979, British citizen W. Arthur Lewis was awarded the Nobel Prize, along with THEODORE SCHULTZ, for "pioneering research into economic development . . . with particular consideration of the problems of developing countries." One of Lewis's major contributions to economics is a 1954 article that discusses his concept of a "dual economy" in a poor country. According to Lewis a poor country's economy can be thought of as containing two sectors, a small "capitalist" sector and a very large "traditional" (agricultural) sector. Employers in the capitalist sector hire people to make money. Employers in the traditional sector, on the other hand, are not profit maximizing and, therefore, hire too many people so that their productivity is very low. (The immediate question, of course, is why employers in the traditional sector would do this, and economists still debate Lewis's reasons for thinking this.) Lewis argued on this basis that the way to spur development in poor countries is to shift labor into manufacturing, where it is more productive. The capitalists save out of their profits and use this saving to expand, which then adds to growth. Lewis assumed that workers in agriculture save nothing, so that the only source of saving is the capitalists in manufacturing.

Lewis used his model to explain the pattern of growth in countries in general. This is how he explained the inverted-U-shaped growth according to a country's per capita income. For very poor countries like Bangladesh, growth is slow because the manufacturing sector is small or non-existent, and there is no large source of savings. For middle-income countries like Korea and Taiwan, growth is high because the manufacturing sector is growing and pulling labor out of agriculture, where it is underemployed. For high-income countries with a large manufacturing sector, like the United States, growth is slower because the gains from diverting labor out of agriculture are almost all exploited.

In the same 1954 article Lewis made a separate argument for poor countries engaged in trade, maintaining that poor countries would capture little or no benefit from increasing their exports. Instead, he claimed, they would confer benefits on consumers in the countries that import their exports. Take his example in which the richer countries produce steel (shorthand for manufactured goods) and food, and the poorer countries produce coffee (shorthand for exports of poor countries) and food. Assume that before exports are increased, ten pounds of coffee trade for one ton of steel. Now, because producers in the poor countries have a low opportunity cost of increasing exports of coffee (because the food that they could have produced is worth little), they will increase exports. But doing so will drive down the price of coffee. Say the exchange rate falls to twenty pounds of coffee per ton of steel. This is a good deal for coffee buyers, but not for coffee producers. In essence, Lewis was arguing that poorer countries had latent monopoly power in their exports that they were failing to exploit. These countries would do better, he argued, to divert their production into food and away from exports.

Lewis himself came from a poor British colony, Saint Lucia in the West Indies. He entered the London School of Economics on a scholarship at age eighteen. "I wanted to be an engineer," Lewis later said, "but neither the colonial government nor the sugar plantations would hire a black engineer." So he decided to study economics. He earned his Ph.D. from the London School of Economics in 1940. He began working on problems of the world economy at the suggestion of FRIEDRICH HAYEK, then chairman of the LSE's economics department. After World War II, when many former colonies became independent, Lewis began his study of economic development. Lewis had no sympathy for the view that poor countries should be run by dictators so that they could develop.

Lewis was a lecturer at the University of London from 1938 to 1948, then Stanley Jevons Professor of Political Economy at the University of Manchester from 1948 to 1958. He was vice chancellor of the University of West Indies from 1959 to 1963 and a professor of political economy at Princeton University from 1963 until his death.

Selected Works

1949. *Economic Survey 1919–1939.* London: Allen and Unwin.

1954. "Economic Development with Unlimited Supplies of Labour." *Manchester School* 22 (May): 139–191.

1955. *The Theory of Economic Growth.* London: Allen and Unwin.

1965. *Politics in West Africa.* London: Allen and Unwin.

1980. "The Slowing Down of the Engine of Growth." Nobel Lecture. Printed in *American Economic Review* 70, no. 4: 555–564.

John Locke (1632–1704)

Born in England, John Locke was a persistent champion of natural rights—the idea that each person owns himself and should have certain liberties that cannot be expropriated by the state or anyone else. When someone labors for a productive end, the results become that person's property, reasoned Locke.

Locke also believed that governments should not regulate interest rates. In a pamphlet titled *Considerations of the Consequences of the Lowering of Interest,* Locke opposed a bill before Parliament to lower the maximum legal interest rate from 6 percent to 4 percent. Because interest is a price, and because all prices are determined by the laws of nature, he reasoned, ceilings on interest rates would be counterproductive. People would evade the ceiling, and the costs of evasion would drive interest rates even higher than they would have been without the ceiling. Locke's reasoning on the subject, sophisticated for his era, has withstood the test of time: economists make the same objection to controls on interest rates today (see INTEREST RATES, PRICE CONTROLS).

Locke also sketched out a quantity theory of money, which held that the value of money is inversely related to the quantity of money in circulation. Locke erroneously believed that a country was in danger of falling into depression if its gold inflows from trade fell relative to those of its trade partners. What he did not realize, and what no one realized until David Hume pointed it out, was that gold flows cannot get out of line with trade flows. If "too little" gold came into Britain relative to gold inflows to other countries, for example (Locke assumed that the supply of gold would grow relative to the volume of trade), then British goods would become cheap relative to other countries' goods, causing more gold to flow to England from other countries.

Selected Works

1690. *Two Treatises of Government.*
1691. *Some Considerations of the Consequences of the Lowering of Interest and Raising the Value of Money.*
1696. *Several Papers Relating to Money, Interest and Trade, et cetera.*

Robert E. Lucas Jr. (1937–)

Robert Lucas was awarded the 1995 Nobel Prize in economics "for having developed and applied the hypothesis of rational expectations, and thereby having transformed macroeconomic analysis and deepened our understanding of economic policy." More than any other person in the period from 1970 to 2000, Robert Lucas revolutionized macroeconomic theory. His work led directly to the path-breaking work of FINN KYDLAND and EDWARD PRESCOTT, which won them the 2004 Nobel Prize.

Before the early 1970s, wrote Lucas, "two very different styles of macroeconomic theory, both claiming the title of Keynesian economics, co-existed." One was an attempt to make macroeconomics fit with standard microeconomics. The problem with this was that such models could not be used to make predictions. The other style was macroeconometric models (see FORECASTING AND ECONOMETRIC MODELS) that could be fit to data and used to make predictions but that did not have a clear relationship to economic theory. Many economists were working to unify the two, but economists themselves saw the results as unsatisfactory.

Lucas thought he could do better. His major innovation in his seminal 1972 article was to get rid of the assumption (implicit and often explicit in virtually every previous macro model) that government policymakers could persistently fool people. Economists MILTON FRIEDMAN and Edmund Phelps had pointed out that there should be no long-run trade-off between unemployment and inflation; or, in economists' jargon, that the long-run PHILLIPS CURVE should be vertical.[1] They reasoned that the short-run trade-off existed because when the government increased the growth rate of the money supply, which increased prices, workers were fooled into accepting wages that appeared higher in real terms than they really were; they accepted

jobs sooner than they otherwise would have, thus reducing unemployment. Lucas took the next step by formalizing this thinking and extending it. He pointed out that in standard microeconomics, economists assume that people are rational. He extended that assumption to macroeconomics, assuming that people would come to know the model of the economy that policymakers use; thus the term "RATIONAL EXPECTATIONS." This meant that if, say, the government increased the growth rate of the money supply to reduce unemployment, it would work only if the government increased money growth more than people expected, and the sure long-term effect would be higher inflation but not lower unemployment. In other words, the government would have to act unpredictably.

In a 1976 article he introduced what is now known as the "Lucas critique" of macroeconometric models, showing that the various empirical equations estimated in such models were from periods where people had particular expectations about government policy. Once those expectations changed, as his theory of rational expectations said they would, then the empirical equations would change, making the models useless for predicting the results of different fiscal and monetary policies. So, for example, if an econometric model showed that for some time period a three-percentage-point drop in inflation was accompanied by a two-percentage-point increase in unemployment, one could not use this correlation to predict the effect of a future three-percentage-point drop in inflation, because people's expectations would not be the same as they were in the time period for which this relation was estimated. One important implication of Lucas's work, which was confirmed by Thomas Sargent,[2] is that a government that is credible—that is, a government that makes itself understood and believed—can quickly end a major inflation without a big increase in unemployment. The reason: government credibility will cause people to quickly adjust their expectations. The key to that credibility, wrote Sargent, is fiscal policy. If governments commit to balanced budgets, then one of their main motives for inflation is gone (see HYPERINFLATION).

Not all macroeconomists have agreed with Lucas, but all have found themselves needing to confront his critique in some way. Although many economists in the 1970s, for example, thought that Lucas had pounded the final nail in the Keynesian coffin, Keynesians responded with models

1. Milton Friedman, "The Role of Monetary Policy," *American Economic Review* 58 (1968): 1–17; Edmund S. Phelps, "Money Wage Dynamics and Labor Market Equilibrium," *Journal of Political Economy* 76 (1968): 687–711.

2. Thomas Sargent, "The Ends of Four Big Inflations," chap. 3 in Sargent, *Rational Expectations and Inflation* (New York: Harper and Row, 1986).

that assume rational expectations (see NEW KEYNESIAN ECONOMICS).

In his Nobel lecture, one of the most readable Nobel economics lectures of the last twenty years, Lucas summed up his and others' contributions in the 1970s:

> The main finding that emerged from the research of the 1970s is that anticipated changes in money growth have very different effects from unanticipated changes. Anticipated monetary expansions have inflation tax effects and induce an inflation premium on nominal interest rates, but they are not associated with the kind of stimulus to employment and production that Hume described. Unanticipated monetary expansions, on the other hand, can stimulate production as, symmetrically, unanticipated contractions can induce depression.[3]

Lucas has also been one of the leaders in the field of economic growth. In "On the Mechanics of Economic Development" (1988), he helped break down the barrier that had existed between economic development economics (applied to poor countries) and economic growth (the study of growth in already rich countries). He argued that the same basic economic framework should apply to each and that it was crucial to understand how poor countries could grow. Lucas wrote:

> Is there some action a government of India could take that would lead the Indian government to grow like Indonesia's or Egypt's? If so, *what*, exactly? If not, what is it about the "nature of India" that makes it so? The consequences for human welfare involved in questions like these are simply staggering: Once one starts to think about them, it is hard to think about anything else. (Lucas 1988, p. 5; italics in original)

Lucas also did important work on the optimal tax structure. His work led him to change a fundamental belief. In the early 1960s, he had believed that "the single most desirable change in the U.S. tax structure would be the taxation of capital gains as ordinary income." By 1990 he believed that "neither capital gains nor any of the income from capital should be taxed at all." He estimated that eliminating capital income taxation would increase the U.S. capital stock by about 35 percent. This belief in low or zero taxation of capital gains is often attributed to believers in so-called supply-side economics. Lucas wrote, "The supply side economists, if that is the right term for those whose research we have been discussing, have delivered the largest genuinely free lunch that I have seen in

25 years of this business, and I believe we would be a better society if we followed their advice."[4]

Politically, Lucas is libertarian. Asked by an interviewer in 1982 whether there is social injustice, Lucas replied, "Well, sure. Governments involve social injustice."[5] Asked by another interviewer in 1993 to name the important issues on the economic frontier, Lucas answered, "In economic policy, the frontier never changes. The issue is always mercantilism and government intervention vs. laissez-faire and free markets."[6]

An interesting side note: when Lucas and his wife, Rita, got a divorce in 1988, she negotiated for 50 percent of any Nobel Prize money that he might receive, with an October 31, 1995, expiration date on this clause. He won the prize on October 10, 1995. Economists joked that Lucas's model applied to his wife: she had rational—or at least correct—expectations.

Lucas earned his B.A. in history in 1959 and his Ph.D. in economics in 1964, both at the University of Chicago. From 1963 to 1974, he was an economics professor at Carnegie Institute of Technology and Carnegie Mellon University. From 1974 to the present, he has been a professor of economics at the University of Chicago.

Selected Works

1972. "Expectations and the Neutrality of Money." *Journal of Economic Theory* 4: 103–124.

1976. "Econometric Policy Evaluation: A Critique." *Carnegie-Rochester Conference Series on Public Policy* 1: 19–46.

1981. *Studies in Business-Cycle Theory.* Cambridge: MIT Press.

1987. *Models of Business Cycles.* Oxford: Basil Blackwell.

1988. "On the Mechanics of Economic Development." *Journal of Monetary Economics* 22: 3–42.

1990. "Supply Side Economics: An Analytical Review." *Oxford Economic Papers* 42: 293–316.

1990. "Why Doesn't Capital Flow from Rich to Poor Countries?" *American Economic Review* 80: 92–96.

---

4. Lucas, "Supply-Side Economics," p. 314.

5. Arjo Klamer, *Conversations with Economists* (Totowa, N.J.: Rowman and Allanheld, 1983), p. 52.

6. Interview with Robert E. Lucas Jr., *The Region*, Federal Reserve Bank of Minneapolis (June 1993), online at: www.minneapolisfed.org/pubs/region/93-06/int936.cfm.

3. See http://nobelprize.org/economics/laureates/1995/lucas-lecture.pdf, p. 262.

Fritz Machlup (1902–1983)

Born in Austria, Fritz Machlup moved to the United States in 1933. He worked in two main areas: industrial organization, with particular emphasis on the production and distribution of knowledge, and international monetary economics.

One of Machlup's most famous articles in industrial organization is his 1946 defense of the economist's standard assumption that firms maximize profits. Economist Richard Lester had argued that businessmen do not know enough about their demand and cost conditions to maximize profits. Machlup agreed but maintained that the purpose of assuming profit maximization is not to predict everything a firm does, but instead to predict how it will react to changes in demand or in costs. For this purpose, argued Machlup, the assumption is appropriate. Machlup expanded on this argument in two later books, *The Economics of Sellers' Competition* and *The Political Economy of Monopoly*.

Machlup's 1949 book, *The Basing-Point System,* is said to have influenced President Harry S Truman's decision to veto a bill that would have forced cement producers to charge the same price irrespective of their buyers' locations. Machlup also wrote at length about the economics of the patent system.

Machlup studied economics at the University of Vienna in the 1920s under Ludwig von Mises and Friedrich Hayek. He wrote his doctoral dissertation under Mises on the gold-exchange standard. From 1922 to 1932 he worked in his family's cardboard-manufacturing business, and his interest in and insights into the economics of industry are often attributed to his experience there. Machlup taught at the University of Buffalo from 1935 to 1947, moved to Johns Hopkins in 1947, and moved to Princeton in 1960. After retiring in 1971 he joined the faculty of New York University, where he was active until his death. Machlup was president of the American Economic Association in 1966.

Selected Works

1949. *The Basing-Point System*. Philadelphia: Blakiston.
1952. *The Economics of Sellers' Competition*. Baltimore: Johns Hopkins University Press.
1952. *The Political Economy of Monopoly*. Baltimore: Johns Hopkins University Press.
1958. *An Economic Review of the Patent System*. Study of the Subcommittee on Patents, Trademarks, and Copyrights of the Committee on the Judiciary, U.S. Senate, study no. 15.
1962. *The Production and Distribution of Knowledge in the United States*. Princeton: Princeton University Press.
1976. *International Payments, Debts, and Gold*. 2d ed. New York: New York University Press.

Thomas Robert Malthus (1766–1834)

Malthus was interested in everything about populations. He accumulated figures on births, deaths, age of marriage and childbearing, and economic factors contributing to longevity. His main contribution was to highlight the relationship between food supply and population. Humans do not overpopulate to the point of starvation, he contended, only *because* people change their behavior in the face of economic incentives.

Noting that while food production tends to increase arithmetically, population tends to increase naturally at a (faster) geometric rate, Malthus argued that it is no surprise that people thus *choose* to reduce (or "check") population growth. People can increase food production, Malthus thought, only by slow, difficult methods such as reclaiming unused land or intensive farming; but they can check population growth more effectively by marrying late, using contraceptives, emigrating, or, in more extreme circumstances, resorting to reduced health care, tolerating vicious social diseases or impoverished living conditions, warfare, or even infanticide. Malthus was fascinated not with the inevitability of human demise, but with why humans do *not* die off in the face of such overwhelming odds. As an economist, he studied responses to incentives.

Malthus is arguably the most misunderstood and misrepresented economist of all time. The adjective "Malthusian" is used today to describe a pessimistic prediction of the lock-step demise of a humanity doomed to starvation via overpopulation. When his hypothesis was first stated in his best-selling *An Essay on the Principle of Population* (1798), the uproar it caused among noneconomists overshadowed the instant respect it inspired among his fellow economists. So irrefutable and simple was his illustrative side-by-side comparison of an arithmetic and a geometric series—food increases more slowly than population—that it was often taken out of context and highlighted as his main observation. The observation is, indeed, so stark that it is still easy to lose sight of Malthus's actual conclusion: that because humans have *not* all starved, economic choices must be at work, and it is the job of an economist to study those choices.

Malthus addressed many other issues. His *Principles of Political Economy* (1820) was the first text to describe a demand schedule as separate from the quantity demanded at a given price. His exposition of demand curves clarified the debate on Say's law and gluts (to which he objected in the long run on the grounds that markets self-adjust). His work centered on contrasting the long run, as exemplified by population growth, with the short run, reflected by cyclical events such as those affecting agriculture. Writing before the industrial revolution, Malthus did not fully appreciate the impact of technology (i.e., pesticides, refrigeration, mechanized farm equipment, and increased crop yields) on food production.

Malthus died in 1834, before seeing economics characterized as the "dismal science." That phrase, coined by Thomas Carlyle in 1849 to demean John Stuart Mill, is often erroneously thought to refer to Malthus's contributions to the economics of population growth.

About the Author

Lauren F. Landsburg is a private computer consultant. She is the editor of the Library of Economics and Liberty. Previously, she taught economics at the University of Rochester and was a senior economist with President Ronald Reagan's Council of Economic Advisers.

Selected Works

An Essay on the Principle of Population. 1st ed. 1798, online at the Library of Economics and Liberty, http://www.econlib.org/library/Malthus/malPop.html; 6th ed. 1826, online at the Library of Economics and Liberty, http://www.econlib.org/library/Malthus/malPlong.html.

1811. "Pamphlets on the Bullion Question." *Edinburgh Review* 18 (August): 448–470.

1820. *The Principles of Political Economy Considered with a View to Their Practical Applications.* London: John Murray.

Harry Markowitz (1927–)

In 1990, U.S. economists Harry Markowitz, William F. Sharpe, and Merton H. Miller shared the Nobel Prize "for their pioneering work in the theory of financial economics." Their contributions, in fact, were what started financial economics as a separate field of study. In the early 1950s Markowitz developed portfolio theory, which looks at how investment returns can be optimized. Economists had long understood the common sense of diversifying a portfolio; the expression "don't put all your eggs in one basket" is certainly not new. But Markowitz showed how to measure the risk of various securities and how to combine them in a portfolio to get the maximum return for a given risk.

Say, for example, shares in Exxon and in General Motors have a high risk and a high return, but one share tends to go up when the other falls. This could happen because when OPEC raises the price of oil (and therefore of gasoline), the prices of oil producers' shares rise and the prices of auto producers' shares fall. Then a portfolio that includes both Exxon and GM shares could earn a high return and have a lower risk than either share alone. Portfolio managers now routinely use techniques that are based on Markowitz's original insight.

Markowitz earned his Ph.D. at the University of Chicago. He has taught at Baruch College of the City University of New York since 1982.

Selected Works

1952. "Portfolio Selection." *Journal of Finance* 7, no. 1: 77–91.

1959. *Portfolio Selection: Efficient Diversification of Investments.* Reprint. Hoboken, N.J.: Wiley, 1970.

Alfred Marshall (1842–1924)

Alfred Marshall was the dominant figure in British economics (itself dominant in world economics) from about 1890 until his death in 1924. His specialty was microeconomics—the study of individual markets and industries, as opposed to the study of the whole economy. In his most important book, *Principles of Economics,* Marshall emphasized that the price and output of a good are determined by both supply and demand: the two curves are like scissor blades that intersect at equilibrium. Modern economists trying to understand why the price of a good changes still start by looking for factors that may have shifted demand or supply, an approach they owe to Marshall.

To Marshall also goes credit for the concept of price elasticity of demand, which quantifies buyers' sensitivity to price (see DEMAND).

The concept of consumer surplus is another of Marshall's contributions. He noted that the price is typically the same for each unit of a commodity that a consumer buys, but the value to the consumer of each additional unit declines. A consumer will buy units up to the point where the marginal value equals the price. Therefore, on all units previous to the last one, the consumer reaps a benefit by paying less than the value of the good to himself. The size of the benefit equals the difference between the consumer's value of all these units and the amount paid for the units. This difference is called the consumer surplus, for the surplus value or utility enjoyed by consumers. Marshall also introduced the concept of producer surplus, the amount the producer is actually paid minus the amount that he would willingly accept. Marshall used these concepts to measure the changes in well-being from government policies such as taxation. Although economists have refined the measures since Marshall's time, his basic approach to what is now called welfare economics still stands.

Wanting to understand how markets adjust to changes in supply or demand over time, Marshall introduced the idea of three periods. First is the market period, the amount of time for which the stock of a commodity is fixed. Second, the short period is the time in which the supply can be increased by adding labor and other inputs but not by adding capital (Marshall's term was "appliances"). Third, the long period is the amount of time taken for capital ("appliances") to be increased.

To make economics dynamic rather than static, Marshall used the tools of classical mechanics, including the concept of optimization. With these tools he, like neoclassical economists who have followed in his footsteps, took as givens technology, market institutions, and people's preferences. But Marshall was not satisfied with his approach. He once wrote that "the Mecca of the economist lies in economic biology rather than in economic dynamics." In other words, Marshall was arguing that the economy is an evolutionary process in which technology, market institutions, and people's preferences evolve along with people's behavior.

Marshall rarely attempted a statement or took a position without expressing countless qualifications, exceptions, and footnotes. He showed himself to be an astute mathematician—he studied math at St. John's College, Cambridge—but limited his quantitative expressions so that he might appeal to the layman.

Marshall was born into a middle-class family in London and raised to enter the clergy. He defied his parents' wishes and instead became an academic in mathematics and economics.

Selected Works

1890. *Principles of Economics*. Vol. 1. London: Macmillan.
1920. *Principles of Economics*. 8th ed. London: Macmillan.

Karl Marx (1818–1883)

Karl Marx was communism's most zealous intellectual advocate. His comprehensive writings on the subject laid the foundation for later political leaders, notably V. I. Lenin and Mao Tse-tung, to impose communism on more than twenty countries.

Marx was born in Trier, Prussia (now Germany), in 1818.

He studied philosophy at universities in Bonn and Berlin, earning his doctorate in Jena at the age of twenty-three. His early radicalism, first as a member of the Young Hegelians, then as editor of a newspaper suppressed for its derisive social and political content, preempted any career aspirations in academia and forced him to flee to Paris in 1843. It was then that Marx cemented his lifelong friendship with Friedrich Engels. In 1849 Marx moved to London, where he continued to study and write, drawing heavily on works by David Ricardo and Adam Smith. Marx died in London in 1883 in somewhat impoverished surroundings. Most of his adult life, he relied on Engels for financial support.

At the request of the Communist League, Marx and Engels coauthored their most famous work, "The Communist Manifesto," published in 1848. A call to arms for the proletariat—"Workers of the world, unite!"—the manifesto set down the principles on which communism was to evolve. Marx held that history was a series of class struggles between owners of capital (capitalists) and workers (the proletariat). As wealth became more concentrated in the hands of a few capitalists, he thought, the ranks of an increasingly dissatisfied proletariat would swell, leading to bloody revolution and eventually a classless society.

It has become fashionable to think that Karl Marx was not mainly an economist but instead integrated various disciplines—economics, sociology, political science, history, and so on—into his philosophy. But Mark Blaug, a noted historian of economic thought, points out that Marx wrote "no more than a dozen pages on the concept of social class, the theory of the state, and the materialist conception of history" while he wrote "literally 10,000 pages on economics pure and simple."[1]

According to Marx, capitalism contained the seeds of its own destruction. Communism was the inevitable end to the process of evolution begun with feudalism and passing through capitalism and socialism. Marx wrote extensively about the economic causes of this process in *Capital*. Volume one was published in 1867 and the later two volumes, heavily edited by Engels, were published posthumously in 1885 and 1894.

The labor theory of value, decreasing rates of profit, and increasing concentration of wealth are key components of Marx's economic thought. His comprehensive treatment of capitalism stands in stark contrast, however, to his treatment of socialism and communism, which Marx handled only superficially. He declined to speculate on how those two economic systems would operate.

1. Mark Blaug, *Great Economists before Keynes* (Highlander, N.J.: Humanities Press International, 1986), p. 156.

About the Author
Janet Beales Kaidantzis was assistant editor of *The Fortune Encyclopedia of Economics.*

Selected Works
1848. "Manifesto of the Communist Party." Reprinted in *Marx: The Revolutions of 1848.* Harmondsworth: Penguin Books, 1973.
1858. *Contribution to the Critique of Political Economy.* Reprint. London: Lawrence and Wishart, 1970.
1865. "Wages, Price and Profits." Reprinted in *Marx-Engels Selected Works.* Vol. 2. Moscow: Progress Publishers, 1969.
1867. *Capital: A Critique of Political Economy.* Edited by Friedrich Engels and reprinted in 1906, Chicago: Charles H. Kerr. Reprinted in 1976, New York: Penguin Books.

Daniel L. McFadden (1937–)

In 2000, Daniel McFadden shared the Nobel Prize in economics with James Heckman. McFadden received the prize for "his development of theory and methods for analyzing discrete choice." The award was given for very technical work that would be hard to explain to the layman, but it has been important for economists who want to study many important issues when the choices involve discrete rather than continuous choices. Before McFadden's work, empirical economists who studied various issues tended to assume that the variables they were studying were continuous. This works well when one studies, say, the demand for sugar, because people buy various amounts of sugar along a continuum. But what if one is studying the demand for refrigerators? Because most people have only one refrigerator, the choice of a refrigerator is a discrete choice. Or what if one is studying people's choice of travel modes for getting to work? Most people do not take the subway one day, a bus the next, and a car the day after that; most use one of those modes almost all the time. Economists needed a way to do empirical work on such discrete choices, but the tools to do so were missing.

That is where McFadden came in. In 1965, one of his graduate students at Berkeley was analyzing thesis data on the California state highway department's choices on where to put freeways and asked for his help. Freeway placement is an example of a discrete, rather than a continuous, choice. McFadden started to solve the problem but did not finish until 1968 (the paper was published in 1976), well after her thesis was done. In solving it, he created a technical method for dealing econometrically with discrete choices generally.

McFadden tested his model with data on people's trans-

portation choices before the Bay Area Rapid Transit (BART) system was built in the San Francisco Bay Area. While the official forecast was 15 percent, McFadden used his model to predict that only 6.3 percent of Bay Area travelers would use BART. The actual number turned out to be 6.2 percent.

McFadden has also used his own methods to analyze investments in telephone service and housing for seniors.

Selected Works
1974. "The Measurement of Urban Travel Demand." *Journal of Public Economics* 3: 303–328.
1976. "The Revealed Preferences of a Government Bureaucracy: Empirical Evidence." *Bell Journal of Economics and Management Science* 7: 55–72.
1978 (with Kenneth Train). "The Goods/Leisure Tradeoff and Disaggregate Work Trip Mode Choice Models." *Transportation Research* 12: 349–353.
1986. "The Choice Theory Approach to Market Research." *Marketing Science* 5: 275–297.
1987 (with Kenneth Train and Moshe Ben-Akiva). "The Demand for Local Telephone Service: A Fully Discrete Model of Residential Calling Patterns and Service Choices." *RAND Journal of Economics* 18: 109–123.
1994. "Contingent Valuation and Social Choice." *American Journal of Agricultural Economics* 74: 689–708.

James Edward Meade (1907–1995)

James Meade, an Englishman, was corecipient of the Nobel Prize in 1977, along with Bertil Ohlin, for their "path-breaking contribution to the theory of international trade and international capital movements." Much of Meade's work on international trade is in the two volumes of his *Theory of International Economic Policy,* which, writes Mark Blaug, "have become the bible of every trade economist." The book's first volume, *The Balance of Payments,* makes the point that for each of its policy objectives, the government requires a policy tool, a principle developed by Dutch economist Jan Tinbergen. Meade advocated using fiscal policy to achieve full employment and monetary policy to achieve the government's target on balance of payments.

The second volume, *Trade and Welfare,* examines conditions under which free trade makes a country better off and conditions under which it does not. Meade concluded that, contrary to previous beliefs, if a country was already protecting one of its markets from international competition, further protection of another market could be "second best." That is, although the ideal would be to eliminate all trade barriers, if for some reason this was not feasible, then adding a carefully chosen dose of protectionism could improve the nation's economic well-being.

Like Milton Friedman in the United States, Meade wanted to use economics to help make the world a better place and believed that government regulation often harmed an economy. He also believed that government should take strong measures to promote equality of income. "I have my heart to the left and my brain to the right," Meade said.

Meade also helped prepare the British government's set of national income accounts during World War II. Meade was a professor of commerce at the London School of Economics from 1947 to 1957 and then moved to Cambridge University, where he taught until he retired in 1974.

Selected Works

1951. *The Theory of International Economic Policy.* Vol. 1: *The Balance of Payments.* Vol. 2: *Trade and Welfare,* with "Mathematical Supplements." London: Oxford University Press.
1952. *A Geometry of International Trade.* London: Allen and Unwin. Reprint. New York: Augustus M. Kelley, 1969.

Carl Menger (1840–1921)

Carl Menger has the twin distinctions of being the founder of Austrian economics and a cofounder of the marginal utility revolution. Menger worked separately from William Jevons and Leon Walras and reached similar conclusions by a different method. Unlike Jevons, Menger did not believe that goods provide "utils," or units of utility. Rather, he wrote, goods are valuable because they serve various uses whose importance differs. For example, the first pails of water are used to satisfy the most important uses, and successive pails are used for less and less important purposes.

Menger used this insight to resolve the diamond-water paradox that had baffled Adam Smith (see MARGINALISM). He also used it to refute the labor theory of value. Goods acquire their value, he showed, not because of the amount of labor used in producing them, but because of their ability to satisfy people's wants. Indeed, Menger turned the labor theory of value on its head. If the value of goods is determined by the importance of the wants they satisfy, then the value of labor and other inputs of production (he called them "goods of a higher order") derive from their ability to produce these goods. Mainstream economists still accept this theory, which they call the theory of "derived demand."

Menger used his "subjective theory of value" to arrive at one of the most powerful insights in economics: both sides gain from exchange. People will exchange something they value less for something they value more. Because both trading partners do this, both gain. This insight led him to see that middlemen are highly productive: they facilitate transactions that benefit those they buy from and those they sell to. Without the middlemen, these transactions either would not have taken place or would have been more costly.

Menger also came up with an explanation of how money develops that is still accepted today. If people barter, he pointed out, then they can rarely get what they want in one or two transactions. If they have lamps and want chairs, for example, they will not necessarily be able to trade lamps for chairs but may instead have to make a few intermediate trades. This is a hassle. But people notice that the hassle is much less when they trade what they have for some good that is widely accepted, and then use this good to buy what they want. The good that is widely accepted eventually becomes money. Indeed, the word "pecuniary" derives from the Latin *pecus,* meaning "cattle," which in some societies served as money. Other societies have used cigarettes, cognac, salt, furs, or stones as money. As economies became more complex and wealthier, they began to use precious metals (gold, silver, and so on) as money.

Menger extended his analysis to other institutions. He argued that language, for example, developed for the same reason money developed—to facilitate interactions between people. He called such developments "organic." Neither language nor money was developed by government.

The AUSTRIAN SCHOOL of economic thought first coalesced from Menger's writings and those of two young disciples, Eugen von Böhm-Bawerk and Friedrich von Wieser. Later Austrian economists Ludwig von Mises and Friedrich Hayek used Menger's insights as a starting point, Mises with his work on money and Hayek with his idea of "spontaneous order."

Carl Menger was born in Galicia, part of Austro-Hungary (now southern Poland), to a prosperous family. He was one of three talented brothers; Anton was a legal philosopher and socialist historian, and Karl was a prominent mathematician. Carl earned his doctorate in law from the University of Kraków in 1867. As a result of publishing his *Principles of Economics* in 1871, he was given a lectureship and then a professorship at the University of Vienna, which he held until 1903. In 1876 he took a post as tutor for Crown Prince Rudolf of Austria. In that capacity he traveled throughout Germany, France, Switzerland, and England.

Selected Works

1871. *Principles of Economics*. Translated by J. Dingwall and B. F. Hoselitz, with an introduction by Friedrich A. Hayek. New York: New York University Press, 1981.

1892. "On the Origin of Money." *Economic Journal* 2 (June): 239–255.

Robert C. Merton (1944–)

Robert Merton, along with Myron Scholes, received the 1997 Nobel Prize in economics "for a new method to determine the value of derivatives" (see the biography for MYRON SCHOLES for a discussion of the significance of this contribution to knowledge).

In 1969, as one of his steps toward developing a formula for valuing options, Merton had written a paper with Paul Samuelson on the value of warrants. Merton, who was himself working on the options pricing issue in competition with his friend Myron Scholes, had planned to attend Fischer Black's and Scholes's presentation on option pricing at a July 1970 conference on capital markets sponsored by Wells Fargo Bank. But he overslept and missed the session. Maybe that was just as well, because he proceeded on his own and developed an alternate proof, published in 1973, of the option-pricing model. In his 1973 article, Merton generalized the Black-Scholes result by changing various assumptions on interest rates, dividend payments, and other variables.

In his Nobel lecture, Merton pointed out the wide applicability of the options-pricing framework. It can be, and has been, used to estimate the value of many things that can be seen as options—deposit insurance, pension insurance, guarantees of student loans, rights to drill offshore oil, development of pharmaceutical products, and others.

Merton also extended WILLIAM SHARPE's early work on the capital asset pricing model by developing an intertemporal capital asset pricing model.

Merton's academic interests were fueled strongly by his other interests. While a master's student at Cal Tech, he actively traded stocks, convertible bonds, warrants, and over-the-counter options at a local brokerage house before going off to his morning classes. These activities led him to a discovery that put him ahead of his later, more academic colleagues: the "institutional rigidities" that economists often claim are inviolate are more flexible in a free market. (Specifically, he found banks that would lend him up to 85 percent of the value of some of his convertible bonds rather than the usual 50 percent.) Also, his trading in warrants led him to work on warrant pricing with Sam-

uelson. And, finally, a section of his 1973 paper that helped win him the Nobel Prize was on pricing of a particular kind of call option that he had become aware of on a consulting job in Asia.

Merton's academic interests also fueled his other interests. In response to the large stock-market decline of 1973–1974, Merton and Myron Scholes started a mutual fund that used options to protect investors from losses. In 1993, he helped start Long Term Capital Management.

Merton earned his B.S. in engineering mathematics at Columbia University, his M.S. in applied mathematics at the California Institute of Technology, and his Ph.D. in economics at MIT. From 1970 to 1988, he was a professor at MIT, and from 1988 to the present he has been a professor at Harvard Business School. He is the son of sociologist Robert Merton (see UNINTENDED CONSEQUENCES).

Selected Works

1969 (with Paul A. Samuelson). "A Complete Model of Warrant Pricing That Maximizes Utility." *Industrial Management Review* 10 (1969) pp. 17–46. (Chapter 7 in *Continuous-Time Finance*.)

1973. "Theory of Rational Option Pricing." *Bell Journal of Economics and Management Science* 4 (Spring 1973): pp. 141–183. (Chapter 8 in *Continuous-Time Finance*.)

1977. "An Analytic Derivation of the Cost of Loan Guarantees and Deposit Insurance: An Application of Modern Option Pricing Theory." *Journal of Banking and Finance* 1: pp. 3–11.

1985. "Implicit Labor Contracts Viewed as Options: A Discussion of 'Insurance Aspects of Pensions.'" In D. A. Wise, ed., *Pensions, Labor, and Individual Choice*. Chicago: University of Chicago Press.

1992. *Continuous-Time Finance*. Rev. ed. London: Basil Blackwell.

1993 (with Zvi Bodie). "Pension Benefit Guarantees in the United States: A Functional Analysis." In R. Schmitt, ed., *The Future of Pensions in the United States*. Pension Research Council. Philadelphia: University of Pennsylvania Press.

John Stuart Mill (1806–1873)

The eldest son of economist James Mill, John Stuart Mill was educated according to the rigorous expectations of his Benthamite father. He was taught Greek at age three and Latin at age eight. By the time he reached young adulthood John Stuart Mill was a formidable intellectual, albeit an emotionally depressed one. After recovering from a nervous breakdown, he departed from his Benthamite teachings to shape his own view of political economy. In *Prin-*

ciples of *Political Economy*, which became the leading economics textbook for forty years after it was written, Mill elaborated on the ideas of David Ricardo and Adam Smith. He helped develop the ideas of economies of scale, opportunity cost, and comparative advantage in trade.

Mill was a strong believer in freedom, especially of speech and of thought. He defended freedom on two grounds. First, he argued, society's utility would be maximized if each person was free to make his or her own choices.[1] Second, Mill believed that freedom was required for each person's development as a whole person. In his famous essay *On Liberty*, Mill enunciated the principle that "the sole end for which mankind are warranted, individually or collectively, in interfering with the liberty of action of any of their number, is self-protection." He wrote that we should be "without impediment from our fellow-creatures, so long as what we do does not harm them, even though they should think our conduct foolish, perverse, or wrong."

Surprisingly, though, Mill was not a consistent advocate of laissez-faire. His biographer, Alan Ryan, conjectures that Mill did not think of contract and property rights as being part of freedom. Mill favored inheritance taxation, trade protectionism, and regulation of employees' hours of work. Interestingly, although Mill favored mandatory education, he did not advocate mandatory schooling. Instead, he advocated a voucher system for schools and a state system of exams to ensure that people had reached a minimum level of learning.

Although Mill advocated universal suffrage, he suggested that the better-educated voters be given more votes. He emphatically defended this proposal from the charge that it was intended to let the middle class dominate. He argued that it would protect against class legislation and that anyone who was educated, including poor people, would have more votes.

Mill spent most of his working life with the East India Company. He joined it at age sixteen and worked there for thirty-eight years. He had little effect on policy, but his experience did affect his views on self-government.

Selected Works

1844. *Essays on Some Unsettled Questions of Political Economy.* 2d ed., 1874.

1. The "her" is particularly appropriate. Mill strongly believed, possibly due to the influence of his wife, Harriet Taylor, whom he idolized, that women were the equals of men. His book *The Subjection of Women* attacked the contemporary view of women's inherent inferiority.

1848. *Principles of Political Economy, with Some of Their Applications to Social Philosophy.* 2 vols. London: John W. Parker.
1859. *On Liberty.* London: J. W. Parker. 4th ed., 1869.
1861. *Considerations on Representative Government.* London: Parker, Son, and Bourn.
1869. *The Subjection of Women.* London: Longmans, Green, Reader and Dyer, available online at: http://etext.library.adelaide.edu.au/m/mill/john_stuart/m645s/.

Merton H. Miller (1923–2000)

In 1990, U.S. economists Merton H. Miller, Harry Markowitz, and William F. Sharpe shared the Nobel Prize "for their pioneering work in the theory of financial economics." Miller's contribution was the Modigliani-Miller theorem, which he developed with Franco Modigliani while both were professors at Carnegie Institute of Technology. (Modigliani had earned the prize in 1985 for his life-cycle model of saving and for the Modigliani-Miller theorem.)

The Modigliani-Miller theorem says that under certain assumptions, the value of a firm is independent of the firm's ratio of debt to equity (see CORPORATE FINANCIAL STRUCTURE). Miller once gave a colorful analogy to try to simplify his and Modigliani's insight:

> Think of the firm as a gigantic tub of whole milk. The farmer can sell the whole milk as it is. Or he can separate out the cream, and sell it at a considerably higher price than the whole milk would bring. (Selling cream is the analog of a firm selling debt securities, which pay a contractual return.) But, of course, what the farmer would have left would be skim milk, with low butter-fat content, and that would sell for much less than whole milk. (Skim milk corresponds to the levered equity.) The Modigliani-Miller proposition says that if there were no cost of separation (and, of course, no government dairy support program), the cream plus the skim milk would bring the same price as the whole milk.[1]

Miller was a strong defender of the view that futures contracts, just like other products, are valuable to those who buy them. Therefore, he argued, government regulation of these contracts is likely to do more harm than good. His book *Merton Miller on Derivatives* is full of insights about derivatives.

Miller earned his undergraduate degree at Harvard University in 1944 and went on to work as a tax expert at the

1. From *Financial Innovations and Market Volatility*, p. 269.

U.S. Treasury Department. He later earned his Ph.D. in economics at Johns Hopkins University. He taught at Carnegie from 1953 to 1961, and in 1961 became a professor at the University of Chicago's Graduate School of Business, where he was the Robert R. McCormick Distinguished Service Professor. He became a public governor of the Chicago Mercantile Exchange in 1990.

Selected Works

1958 (with Franco Modigliani). "The Cost of Capital, Corporation Finance, and the Theory of Investment." *American Economic Review* 48 (June): 261–297.

1963 (with Franco Modigliani). "Corporate Income Taxes and the Cost of Capital." *American Economic Review* 53 (June): 433–443.

1991. *Financial Innovations and Market Volatility*. Cambridge: Blackwell.

1997. *Merton Miller on Derivatives*. New York: Wiley.

James A. Mirrlees (1936–)

In 1996 James Mirrlees and WILLIAM VICKREY were awarded the Nobel Prize in economics "for their fundamental contributions to the economic theory of incentives under asymmetric information." Mirrlees's main contribution was some highly complex mathematics that allowed him to solve a problem in taxation that William Vickrey had posed but had not been able to answer. Many economists, including Mirrlees, want to use the tax system to achieve a higher degree of equality than would otherwise obtain. This means taking a substantial amount of the additional income of high-income people, which would imply high marginal tax rates on them. But when the government imposes such high marginal tax rates on the highest-income people, it reduces the incentive of the most productive people to be productive. There is, in short, a trade-off between equality and efficiency. Economists have long wanted to figure out the optimum, but until Mirrlees's work no one had been able to solve it.

Mirrlees started with no presumption against high marginal tax rates. Indeed, he has been an adviser to Britain's Labour Party, which for decades imposed marginal tax rates in excess of 80 percent. But Mirrlees found that the top marginal tax rate should be only about 20 percent; and moreover, it should be about the same 20 percent for everyone. In short, Mirrlees's work justified what is now known as a "flat tax," more appropriately called a "flat tax rate."

Mirrlees wrote, "I must confess that I had expected the rigourous analysis of income taxation in the utilitarian manner to provide arguments for high tax rates. It has not done so."[1] Indeed.

Mirrlees also proved that the marginal tax rate on the highest-income person should be zero. This is the opposite of the way most noneconomists and most politicians think: marginal tax rates are typically the highest on the highest-income people. Mirrlees's reasoning is as follows. Imagine that the top tax rate is, say, 40 percent and that the top-earning person makes $500 million in a year before tax. If the government reduced the marginal tax rate to zero for all income over $500 million, it would not lose any revenue because no one was earning more than $500 million. But the individual currently earning $500 million might, because of the increased incentive to earn, decide to work more. He would be better off because he voluntarily chose to do something he did not do before, and the government would be no worse off. The net result is that society, which includes this individual, would be better off.

Mirrlees's work on consumption taxes produced another important finding. Working with American economist Peter Diamond, Mirrlees found that small economies should not impose tariffs on foreign trade and that taxation should be on consumption, not production.

Mirrlees also did highly theoretical work on another incentive problem: "moral hazard." As is well known to those who study insurance, insurance coverage gives the beneficiary an incentive to take more risks than would be optimal. This is called "moral hazard." Mirrlees's insight, based on a complex mathematical model, is that the problem can be solved with an optimal combination of carrots and sticks. Insurance payments are essentially a carrot. But "sticks" could be designed also, so that an insured person who takes risks pays a penalty for doing so. With this combination of carrots and sticks, the insured person acts almost as if he is uninsured, and the insurer acts almost as if he were the insured.

Mirrlees has a refreshing, understated sense of humor. Of his early years in university Mirrlees wrote: "It was regarded as morally dangerous to take philosophy at the beginning of one's university course." Reminiscing in 1996 on the advice one of his Cambridge teachers gave him to read Keynes's 1936 classic, *The General Theory of Employment, Interest and Money*, Mirrlees commented, "That may not have been the best advice, but it did no great harm, and one day I hope to finish it."

Born in Scotland, Mirrlees earned his M.A. in mathematics and natural philosophy from Edinburgh University in 1957 and his Ph.D. in economics from Cambridge University in 1963. He spent his early career at Cambridge, was an economics professor at the University of Oxford

1. Mirrlees 1971, p. 207.

from 1968 to 1995, and returned to Cambridge in 1995 as an economics professor.

Selected Works

1971. "An Exploration in the Theory of Optimum Income Taxation." *Review of Economic Studies* 38: 175–208.

1971 (with Peter A. Diamond). "Optimal Taxation and Public Production I: Production Efficiency, II: Tax Rules." *American Economic Review* 61: 8–27, 261–278.

1976. "The Optimal Structure of Incentives and Authority Within an Organization." *Bell Journal of Economics and Management Science* 7: 105–131.

1976. "Optimal Tax Theory: A Synthesis." *Journal of Public Economics* 6: 327–358.

Ludwig von Mises (1881–1973)

Ludwig von Mises was one of the last members of the original AUSTRIAN SCHOOL OF ECONOMICS. He earned his doctorate in law and economics from the University of Vienna in 1906. One of his best works, *The Theory of Money and Credit,* was published in 1912 and was used as a money and banking textbook for the next two decades. In it Mises extended Austrian marginal utility theory to money, which, noted Mises, is demanded for its usefulness in purchasing other goods rather than for its own sake.

In that same book Mises also argued that business cycles are caused by the uncontrolled expansion of bank credit. In 1926 Mises founded the Austrian Institute for Business Cycle Research. His most influential student, Friedrich Hayek, later developed Mises's business cycle theories.

Another of Mises's notable contributions is his claim that socialism must fail economically. In a 1920 article, Mises argued that a socialist government could not make the economic calculations required to organize a complex economy efficiently. Although socialist economists Oskar Lange and Abba Lerner disagreed with him, modern economists agree that Mises's argument, combined with Hayek's elaboration of it, is correct (see SOCIALISM).

Mises believed that economic truths are derived from self-evident axioms and cannot be empirically tested. He laid out his view in his magnum opus, *Human Action,* and in other publications, although he failed to persuade many economists outside the Austrian school. Mises was also a strong proponent of laissez-faire; he advocated that the government not intervene anywhere in the economy. Interestingly, though, even Mises made some striking exceptions to this view. For example, he believed that military conscription could be justified in wartime.

From 1913 to 1934 Mises was an unpaid professor at the University of Vienna while working as an economist for the Vienna Chamber of Commerce, in which capacity he served as the principal economic adviser to the Austrian government. To avoid the Nazi influence in his Austrian homeland, in 1934 Mises left for Geneva, where he was a professor at the Graduate Institute of International Studies until he emigrated to New York City in 1940. He was a visiting professor at New York University from 1945 until he retired in 1969.

Mises's ideas—on economic reasoning and on economic policy—were out of fashion during the Keynesian revolution that took over American economic thinking from the mid-1930s to the 1960s. Mises's upset at the Keynesian revolution and at Hitler's earlier destruction of his homeland made Mises bitter from the late 1940s on. The contrast between his early view of himself as a mainstream member of his profession and his later view of himself as an outcast shows up starkly in *The Theory of Money and Credit.* The first section, written in 1912, is calmly argued; the last section, added in the 1940s, is strident.

Mises had a strong influence on young people. The resurgent Austrian school in the United States owes itself in no small part to Mises's persistence.

Selected Works

1912. *The Theory of Money and Credit.* 3d English ed. Indianapolis: Liberty Classics, 1981.

1920. "Economic Calculation in the Socialist Commonwealth." Reprinted in *Collectivist Economic Planning: Critical Studies on the Possibilities of Socialism.* Edited by Friedrich Hayek. London: Routledge and Sons, 1935.

1921. The sections entitled "Finance and Banking" in two articles, "Austrian Empire" and "Republic of Austria," in the 12th edition of the *Encyclopaedia Britannica.*

1922. *Socialism: An Economic and Sociological Analysis.* 3d English ed. Indianapolis: Liberty Fund, 1981.

1944. *Omnipotent Government: The Rise of the Total State and Total War.* Reprint. Springs Mill, Penn.: Libertarian Press, 1985.

1949. *Human Action: A Treatise on Economics.* 3d ed. Chicago: Regnery. 1966.

1996. *Human Action: A Treatise on Economics.* 4th rev. ed. Irvington-on-Hudson, N.Y.: Foundation for Economic Education.

Franco Modigliani (1918–2003)

Franco Modigliani, an American born in Italy, received the 1985 Nobel Prize on the basis of two contributions. The first is "his analysis of the behavior of household savers."

In the early 1950s Modigliani, trying to improve on Keynes's consumption function, which related consumption spending to income, introduced his "life cycle" model of consumption. The basic idea is common sense, but it is no less powerful for that. Most people, he claimed, want to have a fairly stable level of consumption. If their income is low this year, for example, but expected to be high next year, they do not want to live like paupers this year and princes the next. So, Modigliani argued, people save in high-income years and spend more than their income (dissave) in low-income years. Because income begins low for young adults just starting out, then increases in the middle years and declines on retirement, said Modigliani, young people borrow to spend more than their income, middle-aged people save a lot, and old people run down their savings.

The second contribution that helped Modigliani win the Nobel Prize is the famous Modigliani-Miller theorem in corporate finance (see CORPORATE FINANCIAL STRUCTURE). Modigliani, together with Merton Miller, showed that under certain assumptions, the value of a firm is independent of its ratio of debt to equity. Although Modigliani claimed his two articles with Miller were written tongue-in-cheek, that is not how Miller, the Nobel Prize Committee, or financial economists took them. Their insight was a cornerstone in the field of corporate finance.

Modigliani also wrote one of the articles that started the RATIONAL EXPECTATIONS school of economics. In a 1954 article he and coauthor Emile Grumburg pointed out that people may anticipate certain government policies and act accordingly. Modigliani strenuously objected, though, to the lengths to which the rational expectations school has taken this basic insight.

Modigliani considered himself a Keynesian. A cartoon on his office door in 1982 said: "With your permission, gentlemen, I'd like to offer a kind word on behalf of John Maynard Keynes." Modigliani left fascist Italy in 1939 because he was both Jewish and antifascist. He earned his Ph.D. from the New School of Social Research in 1944. Modigliani taught at the New School from 1944 to 1949 and was a research consultant to the Cowles Commission at the University of Chicago from 1949 to 1952. He was a professor at Carnegie Institute of Technology from 1952 to 1960, at Northwestern University from 1960 to 1962, and at MIT from 1962 until his death. He was president of the American Economic Association in 1976.

Selected Works

1949. "Fluctuations in the Saving-Income Ratio: A Problem in Economic Forecasting." In *Studies in Income and Wealth*, no. 11. New York: National Bureau of Economic Research.

1954 (with Richard Brumberg). "Utility Analysis and the Consumption Function." In Kenneth Kurihara, ed., *Post-Keynesian Economics*. New Brunswick: Rutgers University Press.

1954 (with Emile Grumburg). "The Predictability of Social Events." *Journal of Political Economy* 62 (December): 465–478.

1958 (With Merton Miller). "The Cost of Capital, Corporation Finance, and the Theory of Investment." *American Economic Review* 48 (June): 261–297.

1963 (with Albert Ando). "The Life Cycle Hypothesis of Saving: Aggregate Implications and Tests." *American Economic Review* 53 (March): 55–84.

1963 (with Merton Miller). "Corporate Income Taxes and the Cost of Capital." *American Economic Review* 53 (June): 433–443.

Oskar Morgenstern (1902–1977)

Oskar Morgenstern is best known for his book, coauthored with physicist John von Neumann, *Theory of Games and Economic Behavior*. Morgenstern is also known for his skepticism about economic measurement. In a 1950 book, *On the Accuracy of Economic Observations*, Morgenstern challenged the easy use of data on national income to reach conclusions about the state of the economy and about appropriate policies, citing SIMON KUZNETS's finding that the measurement of national income is subject to a 10 percent margin of error. Morgenstern pointed out that economic policy advisers often proposed policies based on shifts in national income of 1 percent or less. Morgenstern reasoned that one cannot reach any conclusions based on small shifts that are well within the margin of error.

Morgenstern was born in Germany. After earning his doctorate, he became a professor at the University of Vienna in 1935. He was on leave in the United States in 1938 when the Nazis occupied Vienna. Dismissed from the university because he was considered "politically unbearable," Morgenstern became a professor at Princeton University, where he remained until his retirement in 1970.

Selected Works

1944 (with John von Neumann). *Theory of Games and Economic Behavior*. 2d ed. Princeton: Princeton University Press, 1947.

1950. *On the Accuracy of Economic Observations*. Princeton: Princeton University Press.

Robert A. Mundell (1932–)

Robert Mundell was awarded the 1999 Nobel Prize in economics "for his analysis of monetary and fiscal policy under different exchange rate regimes and his analysis of optimum currency areas."

In much of the work on macroeconomics before Mundell's work of the early 1960s, economists assumed—implicitly or explicitly—a closed economy, that is, an economy with no trade with other countries and no capital movements between countries. This was never a good assumption, and it became an even worse assumption as trade and capital flows expanded relative to various countries' gross national products. Possibly because he grew up in Canada (even then America's major trading partner) and did his undergraduate education at the University of British Columbia, Mundell was more aware than most American macroeconomists of the importance of international trade and international capital flows. The vast majority of Mundell's work over his lifetime has been on some aspect of trade or capital flows.

One of the first major questions Mundell addressed was how governments should stabilize economies—keeping them growing while avoiding high inflation—in a world of trade and capital flows. He showed that when the exchange rate is fixed, as it was throughout the 1950s and 1960s between all major trading countries, stabilizing the economy with monetary policy is futile. The reason is that a government that fixes its exchange rate against other currencies must be prepared to provide whatever amount of money is demanded at this fixed price. This means that monetary policy is essentially passive. A government that wants to stabilize the economy must thus use fiscal policy—that is, changes in taxes or government spending.

Mundell also considered the case of floating exchange rates. At the time this was regarded as a theoretical curiosum because, as mentioned, all major trading countries had fixed their exchange rates with each other. But Mundell's native Canada had floated its dollar from 1950 to 1962. Possibly for that reason, and possibly because Mundell had a sense of the future, he thought it worthwhile to consider the floating exchange rate case. (Major countries' exchange rates have floated since the early 1970s.) Mundell showed that if the country has a floating exchange rate, then the government has much more ability to use monetary policy. On the other hand, fiscal policy now becomes impotent. If the government wants to increase aggregate demand by increasing government spending, for example, then, if it does not change monetary policy, the increase in the exchange rate due to the increase in aggregate de-

mand reduces exports. Thus, all fiscal policy can do is change the composition of aggregate demand, not its level. The model Mundell used in 1960 to show this is now called the Mundell-Fleming model, after Mundell and Marcus Fleming,[1] who developed a similar, though less extensive, model around the same time.

Mundell also did some early work in what is now known as "the monetary approach to the balance of payments," which was actually laid out in rudimentary fashion by eighteenth-century economist David Hume. Mundell showed how, with fixed exchange rates, an economy will adjust as balance-of-payments surpluses or deficits cause changes in the money supply. Assume, for example, that capital moves across borders slowly. Then assume that the Federal Reserve increases the domestic money supply to reduce interest rates. With interest rates lower, domestic spending increases and imports increase. The resulting balance-of-payments deficit will cause money to leave the country, which in turn will cause domestic demand to fall, bringing the balance of payments back toward equilibrium. The net long-term result is a higher price level and no real economic effects.

Mundell also considered which government policy "tool" should be used on which policy "target." He showed, contrary to what many economists before him had believed, that when exchange rates are fixed, monetary policy should be used to ensure equilibrium in the balance of payments (also known as the "external balance"), and fiscal policy should be used to adjust aggregate demand to attain full employment ("internal balance").

In thinking through all these issues of assigning tools to targets and of fixed versus floating exchange rates, Mundell pointed out the so-called incompatible trinity: (i) unregulated mobility of capital, (ii) a particular fixed exchange rate, and (iii) a particular price level. Mundell showed that, at most, only two of these can be achieved. This has become standard thinking among economists and policymakers. It means that a government that wants, say, to keep inflation low and allow free capital movement must settle for a floating exchange rate, which is what most governments now do most of the time.

Mundell's other big idea in the 1960s involves optimum currency areas. Rather than take it as given that each country should have its own currency, Mundell noted that if states within countries all shared the same currency, more than one country could do the same. Again, this seemed

---

1. J. Marcus Fleming, "Domestic Financial Policies Under Fixed and Under Floating Exchange Rates," *IMF Staff Papers* 9 (1962): 369–379.

like a theoretical curiosum at the time (1961), but as the history of the euro has shown, it is anything but.

Mundell cited the reduction in transactions costs for trade across borders and the related ease of knowing various prices as the major advantages of a currency area (see MONETARY UNION). The major disadvantage, he noted, is the difficulty of maintaining full employment when one country suffers from some event that other members of the currency area do not suffer from. What if, for example, Canada and the United States are in a currency area, but the demand for softwood lumber suddenly declines? This would hurt Canada proportionally much more than the United States and, with a floating exchange rate, Canada could let the value of the Canadian dollar fall and save somewhat on the need for Canadian lumber workers' wages to fall. But with Canada and the United States in the same currency area—the ultimate in fixed exchange rates—the Canadian dollar cannot fall relative to the U.S. dollar because they are the same dollar. One immediate implication, noted Mundell, is that high labor mobility (i.e., allowing workers to move from one country in the currency area to another country in the area) is key so that workers can have an easier time finding jobs. Of course, the euro is now the world's largest currency area, and, in line with Mundell's thinking, many EU supporters are advocating that workers be free to move from one EU country to another. Opposition to such worker mobility, though, was strong among French voters who voted down the EU constitution in 2005.

The issue of mobility of labor also dovetails with another issue to which Mundell contributed. He showed that if labor and capital are mobile across national borders, then even if there are trade barriers, labor and capital can shift to equalize prices of tradable goods. This means that trade barriers lead to more movement of labor and capital.

Mundell was and is an ally of various supply siders who not only want to use fiscal policy to keep the economy growing—which is consistent with his original 1960s insight—but also want a *particular* fiscal policy: namely, keeping marginal tax rates low or cutting them to a low level. In his Nobel address,[2] Mundell highlighted the fact that inflation during the late 1960s and the 1970s had pushed people into higher and higher tax brackets, even when their real income had not increased. In the early 1970s, Mundell advocated that Canada's tax brackets be indexed to inflation so that inflation alone would not increase people's marginal tax rates, and the Canadian government adopted this policy. In 1981, President Ronald

Reagan and Congress also adopted indexing, effective in 1985.

Mundell earned his Ph.D. from MIT in 1956. His early positions were at Stanford University, the Johns Hopkins Bologna Center of Advanced International Studies, and the International Monetary Fund. From 1966 to 1971, he was a professor of economics at the University of Chicago. He has been on the faculty of Columbia University since 1974.

Selected Works

1960. "The Monetary Dynamics of International Adjustment Under Fixed and Flexible Exchange Rates." *Quarterly Journal of Economics* 84, no. 2: 227–257.
1961. "A Theory of Optimum Currency Areas." *American Economic Review* 51: 657–665.
1962. "The Appropriate Use of Monetary and Fiscal Policy for Internal and External Stability." *IMF Staff Papers* 9, no. 1: 70–79.
1963. "Capital Mobility and Stabilization Policy under Fixed and Flexible Exchange Rates." *Canadian Journal of Economics* 29: 475–485.
1968. *International Economics.* New York: Macmillan.

Gunnar Myrdal (1898–1987)

Gunnar Myrdal, a Swedish economist, made an international reputation with his 1944 book, *An American Dilemma,* today considered a classic in sociology. The book was the end product of a study that the Carnegie Corporation had commissioned about what was then called the "Negro question." Myrdal's damning critique of the "separate but equal" doctrine played a large role in the Supreme Court's 1954 ruling on *Brown v. Board of Education of Topeka,* which outlawed racial segregation in public schools. The book also contains solid economic reasoning. Myrdal, an egalitarian sympathetic to socialism, showed that Franklin Roosevelt's economic policies had badly hurt blacks. Myrdal singled out two New Deal policies in particular: restrictions on agricultural output and the minimum wage.

Myrdal opened a chapter titled "New Blows to Southern Agriculture During the Thirties: Trends and Policies" with the following:

Of all the calamities that have struck the rural Negro people in the South in recent decades—soil erosion, the infiltration of white tenants into plantation areas, the ravages of the boll weevil, the southwestern shift in cotton cultivation—none has had such grave consequences, or threat-

2. See http://nobelprize.org/economics/laureates/1999/mundell-lecture.pdf.

ens to have such lasting effect, as the combination of world agricultural trends and federal agricultural policies initiated during the thirties. (p. 254)

In an attempt to stabilize farm income, wrote Myrdal, the U.S. government restricted the production of cotton, putting hundreds of thousands of mostly black sharecroppers out of work:

> It seems, therefore, that *the agricultural policies, and particularly the Agricultural Adjustment program (A.A.A.), which was instituted in May, 1933, was the factor directly responsible for the drastic curtailment in number of Negro and white sharecroppers and Negro cash and share tenants.* (Ibid.; italics in original)

Myrdal also described how minimum wage legislation, ostensibly to improve working conditions, actually worsened blacks' economic standing:

> During the 'thirties the danger of being a marginal worker became increased by social legislation intended to improve conditions on the labor market. The dilemma, as viewed from the Negro angle is this: on the one hand, Negroes constitute a disproportionately large number of the workers in the nation who work under imperfect safety rules, in unclean and unhealthy shops, for long hours, and for sweatshop wages; on the other hand, it has largely been the availability of such jobs which has given Negroes any employment at all. As exploitative working conditions are gradually being abolished, this, of course, must benefit Negro workers most, as they have been exploited most—but only if they are allowed to keep their employment. But it has mainly been their willingness to accept low labor standards which has been their protection. When government steps in to regulate labor conditions and to enforce minimum standards, it takes away nearly all that is left of the old labor monopoly in the "Negro jobs."
>
> As low wages and sub-standard labor conditions are most prevalent in the South, this danger is mainly restricted to Negro labor in that region. When the jobs are made better, the employer becomes less eager to hire Negroes, and white workers become more eager to take the jobs from the Negroes. (p. 397)

Myrdal's analysis predated GEORGE STIGLER's classic 1946 article detailing the harmful effects of the minimum wage law. It supports the view that there truly is consensus among economists of various political persuasions when ideological loyalties are laid aside and clear economic analysis is undertaken.

Myrdal's other major classic is *Asian Drama: An Inquiry into the Poverty of Nations.* Its major message is that the only way to bring about rapid development in Southeast Asia is to control population, have a wider distribution of agricultural land, and invest in health care and education.

In 1974 Myrdal and Friedrich Hayek shared the Nobel Prize in economics "for their pioneering work in the theory of money and economic fluctuations and for their penetrating analysis of the interdependence of economic, social, and institutional phenomena."

Besides being an economist and a sociologist, Myrdal was also a politician. He was twice elected to Sweden's Parliament as a senator (1934–1936, 1942–1946), was minister for trade and commerce (1945–1947), and served as the executive secretary for the United Nations Economic Commission for Europe (1947–1957).

Selected Works

1944. *An American Dilemma: The Negro Problem and Modern Democracy.* Reprint. New York: McGraw-Hill, 1964.
1968. *Asian Drama: An Inquiry into the Poverty of Nations.* New York: Twentieth Century Fund.

John F. Nash Jr. (1928–)

John Nash, JOHN HARSANYI, and REINHARD SELTEN shared the 1994 Nobel Prize in economics "for their pioneering analysis of equilibria in the theory of noncooperative games." In other words, Nash received the Nobel prize for his work in game theory.

Except for one course in economics that he took at Carnegie Institute of Technology (now Carnegie Mellon) as an undergraduate in the late 1940s, Nash has no formal training in economics. He earned his Ph.D. in mathematics at Princeton University in 1950. The Nobel Prize he received forty-four years later was mainly for the contributions he made to game theory in his 1950 Ph.D. dissertation.

In this work, Nash introduced the distinction between cooperative and noncooperative games. In cooperative games, players can make enforceable agreements with other players. In noncooperative games, enforceable agreements are impossible; any cooperation that occurs is self-enforced. That is, for cooperation to occur, it must be in each player's interest to cooperate.

Nash's major contribution is the concept of equilibrium for noncooperative games, which later came to be called a Nash equilibrium. A Nash equilibrium is a situation in which no player, taking the other players' strategies as given, can improve his position by choosing an alternative strategy. Nash proved that, for a very broad class of games of any number of players, at least one equilibrium exists as long as mixed strategies are allowed. A mixed strategy is one in which the player does not take one action with certainty but, instead, has a range of actions he might take, each with a positive probability.

A simple example of a Nash equilibrium is the PRISONERS' DILEMMA. Another example is the location problem. Imagine that Budweiser and Miller are trying to decide where to place their beer stands on a beach that is perfectly straight. Assume also that sunbathers are located an equal distance from each other and that they want to minimize the distance they walk to get a beer. Where, then, should Bud locate if Miller has not yet chosen its location? If Bud locates one-quarter of the way along the beach, then Miller can locate next to Bud and have three-quarters of the market. Bud knows this and thus concludes that the best location is right in the middle of the beach. Miller locates just slightly to one side or the other. Neither Bud nor Miller can improve its position by choosing an alternate location. This is a Nash equilibrium.

Nash's other major contribution is his reasoning about "the bargaining problem." Before Nash, economists thought that the share of the gains each of two parties to a bargain received was always indeterminate. But Nash got further by asking a different question. Instead of defining a solution directly, Nash asked what conditions the division of gains would have to satisfy. He suggested four conditions and showed mathematically that if these conditions held, a unique solution existed that maximized the product of the participants' utilities. The bottom line is that how gains are divided depends on how much the deal is worth to each participant and what alternatives each participant has.

As readers of Sylvia Nasar's biography of Nash, *A Beautiful Mind,* know, Nash contended with schizophrenia from the late 1950s to the mid-1980s. As Nash put it in his Nobel autobiography, "I later spent time of the order of five to eight months in hospitals in New Jersey, always on an involuntary basis and always attempting a legal argument for release." His productivity suffered accordingly. But he emerged from his mental illness in the late 1980s. In his Nobel lecture, Nash noted his own progress out of mental illness:

> Then gradually I began to intellectually reject some of the delusionally influenced lines of thinking which had been characteristic of my orientation. This began, most recognizably, with the rejection of politically-oriented thinking as essentially a hopeless waste of intellectual effort.[1]

1. See http://nobelprize.org/economics/laureates/1994/nash-autobio.html.

Selected Works

1950. "The Bargaining Problem." *Econometrica* 18: 155–162.

1950. "Equilibrium Points in N-Person Games." *Proceedings of the National Academy of Sciences* 36: 48–49.

1950. "Non-cooperative Games." Ph.D. diss., Mathematics Department, Princeton University.

1951. "Non-cooperative Games." *Annals of Mathematics* 54: 286–295.

1953. "Two-Person Cooperative Games." *Econometrica* 21: 128–140.

John von Neumann (1903–1957)

"There are two kinds of people in the world: Johnny von Neumann and the rest of us." This quote is attributed to Eugene Wigner, a Nobel Prize–winning physicist. John von Neumann, whom people called Johnny, was a brilliant mathematician and physicist who also made three fundamental contributions to economics.

The first is a 1928 paper written in German that established von Neumann as the father of game theory. The second is a 1937 paper, translated in 1945, that laid out a mathematical model of an expanding economy and raised the level of mathematical sophistication in economics considerably. The third is a book coauthored with his Princeton colleague, economist Oskar Morgenstern, titled *Theory of Games and Economic Behavior,* after Morgenstern convinced von Neumann that game theory could be applied to economics.

In their book, von Neumann and Morgenstern asserted that *any* economic situation could be defined as the outcome of a game between two or more players. But the semicompetitive/semicooperative nature of most economic situations, in which the value of the outputs is greater than the value of the inputs, increased the complexity, and consequently, the two were unable to offer solutions. "Nash equilibrium" solutions have since been found, addressing the skepticism some economists had expressed about the applicability of game theory to economics.

In addition to game theory, the book gave birth to modern utility theory. Together, von Neumann and Morgenstern revived and mathematically structured the idea that individuals appear to be choosing among alternatives with probabilistic outcomes to maximize the expected amount of some measure of value termed "utility." This clarified Knight's concept of risk. The definition of utility they created led to the first coherent theory suggesting how we should make decisions when we know only the probabilities of some events.

The theory of games had been studied before, but after von Neumann and Morgenstern it received far more attention. Partly because of the enormous interest generated by their book, game theory has since been applied to economics, law, political science, and sociology.

Von Neumann was born in Hungary and published his first mathematical paper at age eighteen. He earned a degree in chemical engineering in Zurich and a doctorate in mathematics from the University of Budapest in 1926. In 1933 he joined the Institute for Advanced Study at Princeton. He was the youngest permanent professor of that institution and a colleague of Albert Einstein. In 1943 von Neumann was a consultant to the Manhattan Project at Los Alamos, New Mexico, where the first atomic bomb was built. His work on the bomb led to a presidential appointment to the Atomic Energy Commission in 1955. Von Neumann also helped develop the first electronic computer, the ENIAC, at the University of Pennsylvania.

Selected Works

1944 (with Oskar Morgenstern). *Theory of Games and Economic Behavior*. Princeton: Princeton University Press.
1945–1946. "A Model of General Equilibrium." *Review of Economic Studies* 13: 1–9.

Douglass C. North (1920–)

Douglass North shared the 1993 Nobel Prize in economics with ROBERT FOGEL "for having renewed research in economic history by applying economic theory and quantitative methods in order to explain economic and institutional change."

North earned his Ph.D. in economics at the University of California at Berkeley, but by his own admission learned how to reason like an economist from Donald Gordon, one of his colleagues at his first job at the University of Washington. In the early 1960s, North helped found cliometrics, which applies economics and quantitative methods to the study of economic history (named after Clio, the muse of history). One of his early major outputs from this work was his 1961 book, *The Economic Growth of the United States from 1790 to 1860*. In it he showed how one sector of the economy, cotton plantations, stimulated economic development in other sectors and led to specialization and interregional trade. In 1968 North published an article showing that organizational change was more important than technological change in increasing productivity in ocean shipping.

Throughout the 1970s, North published books and articles showing that institutions, especially well-developed property rights, are important in explaining economic growth. This field of study came to be called "the new institutional economics." North showed that England and the Netherlands industrialized more quickly because the guild system, which imposed restrictions on entry and work practices in various occupations, was weaker in those two countries than in other European countries. North went further, hypothesizing that when various groups in society see a chance to make higher profits that are impossible to earn within existing institutional arrangements, they will get together and change the institutions to make these higher profits possible. He showed that economic policy in agriculture, banking, and transportation fit this hypothesis.

In 1983 North moved to Washington University in St. Louis, where he is still on the faculty at this writing (2005). In the late 1980s and early 1990s, he came to question his earlier belief that progrowth institutional changes will necessarily occur. He argued that societies can sometimes be locked into dysfunctional institutions, such as absence of the rule of law and a judicial system that does a poor job of enforcing contracts and property rights. When that happens, reasoned North, it is often very hard to build the coalitions needed to reform these institutions.

Selected Works

1961. *The Economic Growth of the United States 1790 to 1860*. Englewood Cliffs, N.J.: Prentice Hall.
1968. "Sources of Productivity Change in Ocean Shipping 1600–1850." *Journal of Political Economy* 76 (September/October): 953–970.
1973. (with Robert P. Thomas). *The Rise of the Western World: A New Economic History*. Cambridge: Cambridge University Press.
1981. *Structure and Change in Economic History*. New York: W. W. Norton.
1990. *Institutions, Institutional Change, and Economic Performance*. New York: Cambridge University Press.
1990. "A Transaction Cost Theory of Politics." *Journal of Theoretical Politics* 2, no. 4: 355–367.
2005. *Understanding the Process of Economic Change*. Princeton: Princeton University Press.

Bertil Gotthard Ohlin (1899–1979)

Swedish economist Bertil Ohlin received the Nobel Prize in 1977, along with James Meade, for his "pathbreaking contribution to the theory of international trade and international capital movements." Ohlin's prize was based on his book *Interregional and International Trade,* published in 1933. With a 1919 article by his former teacher Eli Heckscher as his starting point, Ohlin showed that both interregional and international trade occur because goods can move more easily than the labor, capital, and land that produce them. Therefore, a country with a relatively abundant factor of production should export goods that intensively use that abundant factor, and should import those that intensively use the factor that is relatively scarce. Much later, economists showed that this would be true only for a world with just two goods. (See WASSILY LEONTIEF.)

In publications beginning in 1927 and ending in 1934, Ohlin also laid out theoretical reasoning and policy conclusions very similar to those in John Maynard Keynes's 1936 classic, *The General Theory of Employment, Interest and Money.* Unfortunately, Ohlin's contributions were published in Swedish and were never translated, and when he tried to get credit for them in a 1937 article in a British journal, the Keynesians did not believe him. Much later, though, his originality in this area was recognized.

Ohlin earned his Ph.D. at Stockholm University in 1924. He taught at the University of Copenhagen from 1925 to 1930 and at the Stockholm School of Business Administration from 1930 to 1965. Ohlin was also a member of the Swedish Parliament from 1938 to 1970 and the leader of the Liberal Party from 1944 to 1967.

Selected Works

1929. "Transfer Difficulties, Real and Imagined." *Economic Journal* 37 (March). Reprinted in H. S. Ellis and L. Metzler, eds., *Readings in the Theory of International Trade.* Philadelphia: Blakiston, 1949.
1933. *Interregional and International Trade.* Cambridge: Harvard University Press.
1937. "Some Notes on the Stockholm Theory of Saving and Investment." 2 parts. *Economic Journal* 47 (March): 53–69; (June): 221–240. Reprinted in G. Haberler, ed., *Readings in Business Cycle Theory.* Philadelphia: Blakiston, 1951.

Arthur M. Okun (1928–1980)

Arthur Okun is known mainly for Okun's Law, which describes a linear relation between percentage-point changes in unemployment and percentage changes in gross national product. It states that for every percentage point that the unemployment rate falls, real GNP rises by 3 percent. Okun's Law is based on data from the period between World War II and 1960, and he cautioned that the law is good only within the range of unemployment rates—3 to 7.5 percent—experienced in that time period.

Like many economic laws, Okun's is an observation of an empirical (real-world) regularity that is not based on any strong economic reasoning. Nevertheless, it has held up well, within the appropriate range of unemployment rates, since Okun discovered it. Yale's JAMES TOBIN, who was Okun's colleague both at Yale and on President John F. Kennedy's Council of Economic Advisers (CEA), called Okun's Law "one of the most reliable empirical regularities of macroeconomics."

Okun discovered the law while he was a senior economist with Kennedy's CEA. The CEA wanted to convince Kennedy that the economy-wide gains from lowering unemployment from 7 to 4 percent were greater than previously imagined. Okun's Law was a major part of the empirical justification for Kennedy's tax cuts. At the end of President Lyndon B. Johnson's administration, Okun was chairman of the CEA.

Okun believed that wealth transfers by taxation from the relatively rich to the relatively poor are an appropriate policy for government. But he recognized the loss of efficiency inherent in the distribution process. In *Equality and Efficiency, the Big Tradeoff* Okun introduced the metaphor of the leaky bucket, which has become famous among economists: "The money must be carried from the rich to the poor in a leaky bucket. Some of it will simply disappear in transit, so the poor will not receive all the money that is taken from the rich" (p. 91). Okun attributed these losses to the administrative costs of taxing and transferring, and to incentive effects. The poor who are receiving welfare or other transfer payments have less incentive to work because their transfer payments are reduced as they make more money. The rich have less incentive to work because high marginal tax rates take a large fraction of their additional income (top tax rates were between 50 and 70 percent at the time he was writing). The relatively rich also have more of an incentive to spend on tax-deductible items and on tax shelters as a way of avoiding taxes. "High tax rates," wrote Okun, "are followed by attempts of ingenious men to beat them as surely as snow is followed by little boys on sleds." For these insights, Okun can be considered one of the original supply siders (see SUPPLY-SIDE ECONOMICS).

Selected Works

1970. *The Political Economy of Prosperity.* Washington, D.C.: Brookings Institution.
1975. *Equality and Efficiency, the Big Tradeoff.* Washington, D.C.: Brookings Institution.
1983. *Economics for Policymaking: Selected Essays of Arthur M.*

Okun. Edited by Joseph A. Pechman. Cambridge: MIT Press.

Vilfredo Pareto (1848–1923)

Pareto is best known for two concepts that are named after him. The first and most familiar is the concept of Pareto optimality. A Pareto-optimal allocation of resources is achieved when it is not possible to make anyone better off without making someone else worse off. The second is Pareto's law of income distribution. This law, which Pareto derived from British data on income, showed a linear relationship between each income level and the number of people who received more than that income. Pareto found similar results for Prussia, Saxony, Paris, and some Italian cities. Although Pareto thought his law should be "provisionally accepted as universal," he realized that exceptions were possible; as it turns out, many have been found.

Pareto is also known for showing that the assumption that the utility of goods can actually be measured is not necessary to derive any of the standard results in consumer theory. Simply by being able to rank bundles of goods, consumers would act as economists had said they would.

In his later years Pareto shifted from economics to sociology in response to his own change in beliefs about how humans act. He came to believe that men act nonlogically, "but they make believe they are acting logically."

Born in Paris to Italian exiles, Pareto moved to Italy to complete his education in mathematics and literature. After graduating from the Polytechnic Institute in Turin in 1869, he applied his prodigious mathematical abilities as an engineer for the railroads. Throughout his life Pareto was an active critic of the Italian government's economic policies. He published pamphlets and articles denouncing protectionism and militarism, which he viewed as the two greatest enemies of liberty. Although he was keenly informed on economic policy and frequently debated it, Pareto did not study economics seriously until he was forty-two. In 1893 he succeeded his mentor, Leon Walras, as chair of economics at the University of Lausanne. His principal publications are *Cours d'économie politique* (1896–1897), Pareto's first book, which he wrote at age forty-nine; and *Manual of Political Economy* (1906).

A self-described pacifist who disdained honors, Pareto was nominated in 1923 to a senate seat in Mussolini's fledgling government but refused to become a ratified member. He died that year and was buried without fanfare in a small cemetery in Celigny.

Selected Works

1897. "The New Theories of Economics." *Journal of Political Economy* 5: 485–502.

Arthur Cecil Pigou (1877–1959)

Arthur C. Pigou, a British economist, is best known for his work in welfare economics. In his book *The Economics of Welfare* Pigou developed ALFRED MARSHALL's concept of EXTERNALITIES, costs imposed or benefits conferred on others that are not taken into account by the person taking the action. He argued that the existence of externalities is sufficient justification for government intervention. If someone is creating a negative externality, such as pollution, for instance, he is engaging in too much of the activity that generated the externality. Pigou advocated a tax on such activities to discourage them. Someone creating a positive externality—say, by educating himself and making himself more interesting or useful to other people—might not invest enough in education because he would not perceive the value to himself as being as great as the value to society. Pigou advocated subsidies for activities that created such positive externalities. These are now called Pigovian taxes and subsidies, respectively.

Pigou's analysis was accepted until 1960, when RONALD COASE showed that taxes and subsidies are not necessary if the people affected by the externality and the people creating it can easily get together and bargain. Adding to the skepticism about Pigou's conclusions is the new view, introduced by public choice economists, that governments fail just as markets do. Nevertheless, most economists still advocate Pigovian taxes as a much more efficient way of dealing with pollution than government-imposed standards.

Pigou studied economics at Cambridge and lectured at Cambridge until World War II. In 1908, at the age of thirty, he was appointed to Marshall's chair in economics. Pigou taught straight Marshallian economics, often insisting to his students that "it's all in Marshall."[1] Pigou was throughout his life an avid free trader.

Selected Works

1912. *Wealth and Welfare.* London: Macmillan.
1914. *Unemployment.* New York: Holt.
1921. *The Political Economy of War.* New York: Macmillan.

1. See Alfred Marshall, *Principles of Economics* (reprint, Amherst, N.Y.: Prometheus Books, 1997).

1932. *The Economics of Welfare.* 4th ed. London: Macmillan.

1933. *The Theory of Unemployment.* London: Macmillan.

1950. *Keynes's General Theory: A Retrospective View.* London: Macmillan.

Edward C. Prescott (1940–)

Edward Prescott shared the 2004 Nobel Prize in economic science with FINN KYDLAND "for their contributions to dynamic macroeconomics: the time consistency of economic policy and the driving forces behind business cycles." Because Prescott and Kydland worked together so closely, this biography deals with their work on business cycles. Kydland's biography deals with their work on time consistency.

In 1982 Prescott and Kydland wrote a paper that fundamentally challenged the Keynesian view that changes in aggregate demand for goods and services drive the business cycle. Prescott's and Kydland's article was squarely in the RATIONAL-EXPECTATIONS tradition of ROBERT LUCAS, who had demonstrated that a fundamental problem of standard Keynesian and monetarist models was that their posited relations between aggregate variables (say, consumption and income) were assumed to hold regardless of government policy. Prescott and Kydland speculated that changes in technology could generate many of the fluctuations in employment and output that had been noted in the past, and that changes in aggregate demand were not necessary to explain such fluctuations. In particular, they showed that if the elasticity of supply of labor is three, and if various "shocks" (i.e., unanticipated changes) in total factor PRODUCTIVITY (TFP) are persistent and of the right magnitude, their model could account for 70 percent of the fluctuation in output in the postwar United States.

The next step was to see if their key assumptions were reasonable. In 1986, Prescott did find that "shocks" in TFP productivity were persistent and of the right magnitude. But the posited labor supply elasticity of three seemed high. Prescott pointed out in his Nobel prize lecture, though, that this seemed implausible only because most people picture everyone working more in response to higher wages, when what really happens is that a small percentage of the population that was not working begins to work.[1] In the early 2000s, to check whether such a high responsiveness of work hours to wages was reasonable, Prescott studied work hours in various countries. His rea-

soning was that because workers would respond to wages net of MARGINAL TAX RATES, he could see how responsive hours were by studying countries with large differences in marginal tax rates. Canada, the United States, and Japan, he noted, have marginal tax rates of about 40 percent, whereas France, Germany, and Italy have marginal tax rates of about 60 percent. He showed that a labor supply elasticity of three would predict that Western Europeans would work about one-third less than North Americans and Japanese. The evidence confirmed his prediction. Moreover, his posited labor supply elasticity is consistent with the fact that hours worked per person were much higher in France and Germany in the early 1970s when marginal tax rates were substantially lower. It should be noted, though, that many economists still find an elasticity of three to be too high.

In his Nobel lecture, Prescott noted some important conclusions that follow from his and Kydland's research on business cycles:

> We learned that business cycle fluctuations are the optimal response to real shocks. The cost of a bad shock cannot be avoided, and policies that attempt to do so will be counterproductive, particularly if they reduce production efficiency. During the 1981 and current oil crises, I was pleased that policies were not instituted that adversely affected the economy by reducing production efficiency. This is in sharp contrast to the oil crisis in 1974 when, rather than letting the economy respond optimally to a bad shock so as to minimize its cost, policies were instituted that adversely affected production efficiency and depressed the economy much more than it would otherwise have been.

Prescott concluded that the gains in well-being from eliminating business cycles are small or negative, while the gains from eliminating depressions such as the Great Depression and from creating growth "miracles" are large. He noted work by Harold Cole and Lee Ohanian that is also consistent with this encyclopedia's article on the GREAT DEPRESSION, suggesting that Franklin Roosevelt's cartelization of U.S. industries in the early 1930s could have been the reason for the stunning reduction in hours worked per adult over that time.[2]

Prescott was born in the United States and earned his B.A. in mathematics from Swarthmore College in 1962, his M.S. in operations research from Case-Western Re-

---

1. See http://nobelprize.org/economics/laureates/2004/prescott-lecture.pdf.

2. Ibid.; Harold L. Cole and Lee E. Ohanian, "New Deal Policies and the Persistence of the Great Depression: A General Equilibrium Analysis," *Journal of Political Economy* 112 (August 2004): 779–816.

serve University in 1963, and his Ph.D. from Carnegie Mellon University in 1967. His main academic positions have been at the University of Pennsylvania from 1967 to 1971, Carnegie Mellon University from 1971 to 1980, the University of Minnesota from 1980 to 1998 and again from 1999 to 2003, and at Arizona State University since 2003.

Selected Works

1977. (with Finn Kydland). "Rules Rather Than Discretion: The Inconsistency of Optimal Plans." *Journal of Political Economy* 85: 473–490.

1982. (with Finn Kydland). "Time to Build and Aggregate Fluctuations." *Econometrica* 50: 1345–1371.

1986. "Theory Ahead of Business Cycle Measurement." *Federal Reserve Bank of Minneapolis Quarterly Review* 10 (Fall): 9–22.

1999. (with S. L. Parente). "Monopoly Rights: A Barrier to Riches." *American Economic Review* 89, no. 5: 1216–1233.

2002. "Prosperity and Depressions." *American Economic Review* 92, no. 2: 1–15.

2004. "Why Do Americans Work So Much More than Europeans." *Federal Reserve Bank of Minneapolis Quarterly Review* 28, no. 1: 2–15.

François Quesnay (1694–1774)

François Quesnay was the leading figure of the Physiocrats, generally considered to be the first school of economic thinking. The name "Physiocrat" derives from the Greek words *phýsis*, meaning "nature," and *krátos*, meaning "power." The Physiocrats believed that an economy's power derived from its agricultural sector. They wanted the government of Louis XV, who ruled France from 1715 to 1774, to deregulate and reduce taxes on French agriculture so that poor France could emulate wealthier Britain, which had a relatively laissez-faire policy. Indeed, it was Quesnay who coined the term "laissez-faire, laissez-passer."

Quesnay himself did not publish until the age of sixty. His first work appeared only as encyclopedia articles in 1756 and 1757.

In his *Tableau économique,* he detailed his famous zigzag diagram, a circular flow diagram of the economy that showed who produced what and who spent what, in an attempt to understand and explain the causes of growth. *Tableau* defined three classes: landowners, farmers, and others—called "sterile" classes—who consumed everything they produced and left no surplus for the next period. Quesnay believed that only the agricultural sector could

produce a surplus that could then be used to produce more the next year—and therefore help growth. Industry and manufacturing, thought Quesnay, were sterile. Interestingly, though, he did not reach this conclusion by consulting his table. Instead, Quesnay constructed the table to fit his belief. Indeed, he had to make his table inconsistent in order to fit his assumption that industry provided no surplus.

Although Quesnay was wrong about the sterility of the manufacturing sector, he was right in ascribing France's poverty to mercantilism, which he called Colbertisme (after Louis XV's finance minister, Jean-Baptiste Colbert). The French government had protected French manufacturers from foreign competition, thus raising the cost of machinery for farmers, and had also sold to wealthy citizens the power to tax farmers. These citizens had then used this power to the limit.

Quesnay advocated reforming these laws by consolidating and reducing taxes, getting rid of tolls and other regulations that prevented trade within France, and generally freeing the economy from the government's stifling controls. These reforms were much more sensible than his theorizing about the sterility of industry. As Mark Blaug writes, "It was only the effort to provide these reforms with a watertight theoretical argument that produced some of the forced reasoning and slightly absurd conclusions that invited ridicule even from contemporaries."[1]

Moreover, Quesnay's work paved the way for classical economics—in particular for Adam Smith, who latched on to Physiocratic notions of free trade and the preeminence of the agricultural sector.

That Quesnay had such a seminal influence on economics is all the more surprising in light of the fact that he served under Louis XV in Versailles not as an economist, but as a medical doctor.

Selected Works

1759. *Tableau économique.* 3d ed. Reprint. Edited by M. Kuczynski and R. Meek. London: Macmillan, 1972.

David Ricardo (1772–1823)

David Ricardo was one of those rare people who achieved both tremendous success and lasting fame. After his family disinherited him for marrying outside his Jewish faith,

1. Mark Blaug, *Great Economists before Keynes* (Atlantic Highlands, N.J.: Humanities Press International, 1986), p. 196.

Ricardo made a fortune as a stockbroker and loan broker. When he died, his estate was worth more than $100 million in today's dollars. At age twenty-seven, after reading Adam Smith's *The Wealth of Nations,* Ricardo got excited about economics. He wrote his first economics article at age thirty-seven and then spent the following fourteen years—his last ones—as a professional economist.

Ricardo first gained notice among economists over the "bullion controversy." In 1809 he wrote that England's inflation was the result of the Bank of England's propensity to issue excess banknotes. In short, Ricardo was an early believer in the quantity theory of money, or what is known today as monetarism.

In his *Essay on the Influence of a Low Price of Corn on the Profits of Stock* (1815), Ricardo articulated what came to be known as the law of diminishing marginal returns. One of the most famous laws of economics, it holds that as more and more resources are combined in production with a fixed resource—for example, as more labor and machinery are used on a fixed amount of land—the additions to output will diminish.

Ricardo also opposed the protectionist Corn Laws, which restricted imports of wheat. In arguing for free trade, Ricardo formulated the idea of comparative costs, today called COMPARATIVE ADVANTAGE—a very subtle idea that is the main basis for most economists' belief in free trade today. The idea is this: a country that trades for products it can get at lower cost from another country is better off than if it had made the products at home.

Say, for example, Poorland can produce one bottle of wine with five hours of labor and one loaf of bread with ten hours. Richland's workers, on the other hand, are more productive. They produce a bottle of wine with three hours of labor and a loaf of bread with one hour. One might think at first that because Richland requires fewer labor hours to produce either good, it has nothing to gain from trade.

Think again. Poorland's cost of producing wine, although higher than Richland's in terms of hours of labor, is lower in terms of bread. For every bottle produced, Poorland gives up half of a loaf, while Richland has to give up three loaves to make a bottle of wine. Therefore, Poorland has a comparative advantage in producing wine. Similarly, for every loaf of bread it produces, Poorland gives up two bottles of wine, but Richland gives up only a third of a bottle. Therefore, Richland has a comparative advantage in producing bread.

If they exchange wine and bread one for one, Poorland can specialize in producing wine and trading some of it to Richland, and Richland can specialize in producing bread. Both Richland and Poorland will be better off than if they had not traded. By shifting, say, ten hours of labor out of producing bread, Poorland gives up the one loaf that this labor could have produced. But the reallocated labor produces two bottles of wine, which will trade for two loaves of bread. Result: trade nets Poorland one additional loaf of bread. Nor does Poorland's gain come at Richland's expense. Richland gains also, or else it would not trade. By shifting three hours out of producing wine, Richland cuts wine production by one bottle but increases bread production by three loaves. It trades two of these loaves for Poorland's two bottles of wine. Richland has one more bottle of wine than it had before, and an extra loaf of bread.

These gains come, Ricardo observed, because each country specializes in producing the good for which its comparative cost is lower.

Writing a century before Paul Samuelson and other modern economists popularized the use of equations, Ricardo is still esteemed for his uncanny ability to arrive at complex conclusions without any of the mathematical tools now deemed essential. As economist David Friedman put it in his 1990 textbook, *Price Theory,* "The modern economist reading Ricardo's *Principles* feels rather as a member of one of the Mount Everest expeditions would feel if, arriving at the top of the mountain, he encountered a hiker clad in T-shirt and tennis shoes."[1]

One of Ricardo's chief contributions, arrived at without mathematical tools, is his theory of rents. Borrowing from Thomas Malthus, with whom Ricardo was closely associated but often diametrically opposed, Ricardo explained that as more land was cultivated, farmers would have to start using less productive land. But because a bushel of corn from less productive land sells for the same price as a bushel from highly productive land, tenant farmers would be willing to pay more to rent the highly productive land. Result: the landowners, not the tenant farmers, are the ones who gain from productive land. This finding has withstood the test of time. Economists use Ricardian reasoning today to explain why agricultural price supports do not help farmers per se but do make owners of farmland wealthier. Economists use similar reasoning to explain why the beneficiaries of laws that restrict the number of taxicabs are not cab drivers per se but rather those who owned the limited number of taxi medallions (licenses) when the restriction was first imposed.

Selected Works

1817. *On the Principles of Political Economy and Taxation.* In *The Works and Correspondence of David Ricardo.* 11 vols. Ed-

1. David D. Friedman, *Price Theory: An Intermediate Text,* 2d ed. (Cincinnati: South-Western Publishing, 1990), p. 618.

ited by Piero Sraffa, with the collaboration of M. H. Dobb. Cambridge: Cambridge University Press, 1951–1973.

Lionel Robbins (1898–1984)

Although recognized equally for his contributions to economic policy, methodology, and the history of ideas, Lionel Robbins made his name as a theorist. In the 1920s he attacked Alfred Marshall's concept of the "representative firm," arguing that the concept was no help in understanding the equilibrium of the firm or of an industry. He also did some of the earliest work on labor supply, showing that an increase in the wage rate had an ambiguous effect on the amount of labor supplied (see SUPPLY).

Robbins's most famous book is *An Essay on the Nature and Significance of Economic Science,* one of the best-written prose pieces in economics. That book contains three main thoughts. First is Robbins's famous all-encompassing definition of economics, still used to define the subject today: "Economics is the science which studies human behavior as a relationship between given ends and scarce means which have alternative uses" (p. 16). Second is the bright line Robbins drew between positive and normative issues. Positive issues are questions about what is; normative issues are about what ought to be. Robbins argued that the economist qua economist should be studying what is rather than what ought to be. Economists still widely share Robbins's belief. Robbins's third major thought is that economics is a system of logical deduction from first principles. He was skeptical about the feasibility and usefulness of empirical verification. In this view he resembled the Austrians—not surprising since he was a colleague of the famous Austrian economist Friedrich Hayek, whom he had brought from Vienna in 1928.

In 1930, when Keynesianism was starting to take over in Britain, Robbins was the only member of the five-man Economic Advisory Council to oppose import restrictions and public works expenditures as a means of alleviating the depression. Instead, Robbins sided with the Austrian view that the depression was caused by undersaving (i.e., too much consumption), and he built on this concept in *The Great Depression,* which exemplifies his anti-Keynesian views. Although he remained an opponent of Keynesianism for the remainder of that decade, Robbins's views underwent a profound change after World War II. In *The Economic Problem in Peace and War* Robbins advocated Keynes's policies of full employment through control of aggregate demand.

The London School of Economics was home to Robbins

for almost his entire adult life. He completed his undergraduate education there in 1923, taught as a professor from 1929 to 1961, and continued to be associated with the school on a part-time basis until 1980. During World War II he served briefly as an economist for the British government. Although Robbins was an advocate of laissez-faire, he made numerous ad hoc exceptions. His most famous was his view, known as the Robbins Principle, that the government should subsidize any qualified applicant for higher education who would not otherwise have the current income or savings to pay for it. His view was adopted in the 1960s and led to an expansion of higher education in Britain in the 1960s and 1970s.

Selected Works

1932. *An Essay on the Nature and Significance of Economic Science.* London: Macmillan.
1934. *The Great Depression.* London: Macmillan.
1934. "Remarks upon Certain Aspects of the Theory of Costs." First published in *Economic Journal* (1934). Reprinted in James M. Buchanan and G. F. Thirlby, eds., *L.S.E. Essays on Cost.* London: Weidenfeld and Nicolson, 1973.
1939. *The Economic Basis of Class Conflict.* London: Macmillan.
1939. *The Economic Causes of War.* London: Jonathan Cape.
1947. *The Economic Problem in Peace and War.* London: Macmillan.
1971. *Autobiography of an Economist.* London: Macmillan.

Joan Violet Robinson (1903–1983)

British economist Joan Robinson was arguably the only woman born before 1930 who can be considered a great economist. She was in the same league as others who received the Nobel Prize; indeed, many economists expected her to win the prize in 1975. *Business Week* was so sure of it that it published a long article on her before that year's prize was announced. It did not happen. Was the Swedish Royal Academy biased against Robinson? Many economists believe it was, but not because Robinson was a woman. Rather, her political views became more left wing as she aged, to the point where she admired Mao Zedong's China and Kim Il Sung's North Korea. These extreme views should not have affected her chances of getting an award for her intellectual contributions, but they probably did.

Robinson's first major book was *The Economics of Imperfect Competition.* In it she laid out a model of competition between firms, each of which had some monopoly power. Along with American economist Edward H. Chamberlin, whose *Theory of Monopolistic Competition* had appeared only a few months earlier, Robinson began what is known as the monopolistic competition revolution. Many economists believe that most industries are neither perfectly competitive nor complete monopolies. Robinson's and Chamberlin's books are what led them to that belief.

Robinson's first book and early articles show a distinctive writing style. She was clear and analytical, and she managed to put complex mathematical concepts into words.

Later in the 1930s Robinson became part of the "Cambridge Circus," a group of young economists that included later Nobel Prize winner James Meade; Roy Harrod; Richard Kahn; her husband, Austin Robinson; and Piero Sraffa. These economists met regularly to discuss their work and especially to discuss John Maynard Keynes's famous *General Theory of Employment, Interest and Money* (1936), both before and after it was published. Much of Robinson's work published at that time, especially her *Introduction to the Theory of Employment*, clarifies ideas that Keynes had not made clear. Robinson was the first to define macroeconomics, which became a separate field of inquiry only with Keynes's book, as the "theory of output as a whole."

In 1954 Robinson's article "The Production Function and the Theory of Capital" started what came to be called the Cambridge controversy. Robinson attacked the idea that capital can be measured and aggregated. This became the position in Cambridge, England. Across the Atlantic, Paul Samuelson and Robert Solow defended the by-then traditional neoclassical view that capital can be aggregated. Robinson won the battle. As historian Mark Blaug puts it, Samuelson made a "declaration of unconditional surrender." Yet most economists still think that aggregating capital is useful and continue to do it anyway.

Whether or not Robinson's gender prevented her from winning the Nobel Prize, it seems to have slowed her advance in academia. She taught at Cambridge University from 1928 until retiring in 1971, but in spite of a very productive career, she did not become a full professor until 1965. Perhaps not coincidentally, this was the year her husband retired from Cambridge.

Selected Works

1933. *The Economics of Imperfect Competition.* London: Macmillan. 2d ed., 1969.

1937. *Introduction to the Theory of Employment.* London: Macmillan.

1942. *An Essay on Marxian Economics.* London: Macmillan.

1956. *The Accumulation of Capital.* London: Macmillan.

1962. *Economic Philosophy.* London: C. A. Watts.

1970. *The Cultural Revolution in China.* London: Penguin Books.

1971. *Economic Heresies: Some Old-fashioned Questions in Economic Theory.* London: Macmillan.

Paul Anthony Samuelson (1915–)

More than any other economist, Paul Samuelson raised the level of mathematical analysis in the profession. Until the late 1930s, when Samuelson started his stunning and steady stream of articles, economics was typically understood in terms of verbal explanations and diagrammatic models. Samuelson wrote his first published article, "A Note on the Measurement of Utility," as a twenty-one-year-old doctoral student at Harvard. He introduced the concept of "revealed preference" in a 1938 article. His goal was to be able to tell by observing a consumer's choices whether he or she was better off after a change in prices, and indeed, Samuelson determined the circumstances under which one could tell. The consumer revealed by choices his or her preferences—hence the term "revealed preferences."

Samuelson's magnum opus, which did more than any other single book to spread the mathematical revolution in economics, is *Foundations of Economic Analysis.* Based on his Harvard Ph.D. dissertation, this book shows how virtually all economic behavior can be understood as maximizing or minimizing subject to a constraint. John R. Hicks did something similar in his 1939 book, *Value and Capital.* But while Hicks relegated the math to appendixes, "Samuelson," wrote former Samuelson student Stanley Fischer, "flaunts his in the text."[1] Samuelson's mathematical techniques brought a new rigor to economics. As fellow Nobel Prize winner Robert Lucas put it, "He'll take these incomprehensible verbal debates that go on and on and never end and just *end* them; formulate the issue in such a way that the question is answerable, and then get the answer."[2]

Samuelson is among the last generalists to be incredibly productive in a number of fields in economics. He has contributed fundamental insights in consumer theory and welfare economics, international trade, finance theory, capital theory, dynamics and general equilibrium, and macroeconomics.

1. Stanley Fischer, "Paul Anthony Samuelson," in John Eatwell, Murray Milgate, and Peter Newman, eds., *The New Palgrave: A Dictionary of Economics,* vol. 4 (New York: Stockton Press, 1987), p. 235.

2. Arjo Klamer, *Conversations with Economists* (Totowa, N.J.: Rowman and Allanheld, 1983), p. 49.

Swedish economist Bertil Ohlin had argued that international trade would tend to equalize the prices of factors of production. Trade between India and the United States, for example, would narrow wage-rate differentials between the two countries. Samuelson, using mathematical tools, showed the conditions under which the differentials would be driven to zero. The theorem he proved is called the factor price equalization theorem.

In finance theory, which he took up at age fifty, Samuelson did some of the initial work that showed that properly anticipated futures prices should fluctuate randomly. Samuelson also did pathbreaking work in capital theory, but his contributions are too complex to describe in just a few sentences.

Economists had long believed that there are goods that the private sector cannot provide because of the difficulty of charging those who benefit from them. National defense is one of the best examples of such a good. Samuelson, in a 1954 article, was the first to attempt a rigorous definition of a public good.

In macroeconomics Samuelson demonstrated how combining the accelerator theory of investment with the Keynesian income determination model explains the cyclical nature of business cycles. He also introduced the concept of the neoclassical synthesis—a synthesis of the old neoclassical microeconomics and the new (in the 1950s) Keynesian macroeconomics. According to Samuelson, government intervention via fiscal and monetary policies is required to achieve full employment. At full employment the market works well, except at providing public goods and handling problems of externalities. JAMES TOBIN called the neoclassical synthesis one of Samuelson's greatest contributions to economics.

In *Linear Programming and Economic Analysis* Samuelson and coauthors Robert Dorfman and Robert Solow applied optimization techniques to price theory and growth theory, thereby integrating these previously segregated fields.

A prolific writer, Samuelson has averaged almost one technical paper a month for more than fifty years. Some 338 of his articles are contained in the five-volume *Collected Scientific Papers* (1966–1986). He also has revised his immensely popular textbook, *Economics*, nearly every three years since 1948; it has been translated into many languages. Samuelson once said, "Let those who will write the nation's laws if I can write its textbooks."

In 1970 Paul Samuelson became the first American to receive the Nobel Prize in economics. It was awarded "for the scientific work through which he has developed static and dynamic economic theory and actively contributed to raising the level of analysis in economic science."

Samuelson began teaching at the Massachusetts Institute of Technology in 1940 at the age of twenty-six, becoming a full professor six years later. He remains there at the time of this writing (2006). In addition to being honored with the Nobel Prize, Samuelson also earned the John Bates Clark Award in 1947—awarded for the most outstanding work by an economist under age forty. He was president of the American Economic Association in 1961.

Samuelson was born in Gary, Indiana. At age sixteen he enrolled at the University of Chicago, where he studied under Frank Knight, Jacob Viner, and other greats, and alongside fellow budding economists Milton Friedman and George Stigler, who were then graduate students. Samuelson went on to do his graduate work at Harvard University.

Samuelson, like Friedman, had a regular column in *Newsweek* from 1966 to 1981. But unlike Friedman, he did not and does not have a passionate belief in free markets—or for that matter in government intervention in markets. His pleasure seemed to come from providing new proofs, demonstrating technical finesse, and turning a clever phrase.

Samuelson himself once said: "Once I asked my friend the statistician Harold Freeman, 'Harold, if the Devil came to you with the bargain that, in exchange for your immortal soul, he'd give you a brilliant theorem, would you do it?' 'No,' he replied, 'but I would for an inequality.' I like that answer."

Selected Works

1938. "A Note on the Pure Theory of Consumers' Behavior." *Economica*, n.s., 5 (February): 61–71.
1939. "Interactions Between the Multiplier Analysis and the Principle of Acceleration." *Review of Economics and Statistics* (May): 75–78.
1947. *Foundations of Economic Analysis.* Cambridge: Harvard University Press. 2d ed. 1982.
1948 (with William Nordhaus). *Economics.* 18th ed. New York: McGraw-Hill, 2004.
1948. "International Trade and the Equalization of Factor Prices." *Economic Journal* 58 (June): 163–184.
1954. "The Pure Theory of Public Expenditure." *Review of Economics and Statistics* (November): 387–389.
1958 (with Robert Dorfman and Robert Solow). *Linear Programming and Economic Activity.* New York: McGraw-Hill.

Jean-Baptiste Say (1767–1832)

French economist J. B. Say is most commonly identified with Say's Law, which states that supply creates its own demand. Over the years Say's Law has been embroiled in two kinds of controversy—the first over its authorship, the second over what it means and, given each meaning, whether it is true.

On the first controversy, it is clear that Say did invent something like Say's Law. But the first person actually to use the words "supply creates its own demand" appears to have been James Mill, the father of JOHN STUART MILL.

Say's Law has various interpretations. The long-run version is that there cannot be overproduction of goods in general for a very long time because those who produce the goods, by their act of producing, produce the purchasing power to buy other goods. Say wrote: "How could it be possible that there should now be bought and sold in France five or six times as many commodities as in the miserable reign of Charles VI?"[1] With this statement Say had the long run in mind. Certainly the long-run version is correct. Given enough time, supply does create its own demand. There can be no long-run glut of goods.

But Say also said that even in the short run there could be no overproduction of goods relative to demand. It was this short-run version that THOMAS ROBERT MALTHUS attacked in the nineteenth century and JOHN MAYNARD KEYNES attacked in the twentieth. They were right to attack it.

Say was the best-known expositor of Adam Smith's views in Europe and America. His *Traité d'économie politique* was translated into English and used as a textbook in England and the United States. But Say did not agree with Adam Smith on everything. In particular, he took issue with Smith's labor theory of value. Say was one of the first economists to have the insight that the value of a good derives from its utility to the user and not from the labor spent in producing it.

Say was born in Lyons. During his life he edited a journal, operated a cotton factory, and served as a member of the Tribunate under the Consulate of Napoleon. He was the first to teach a public course on political economy in France and continued his stay in academia first at the Conservatoire des Arts et Métiers, and then at the College de France in Paris. Say was a friend of Thomas Robert Malthus and DAVID RICARDO.

Selected Works

1803. *Traité d'économie politique.* Translated from the 4th edition of the French by C. R. Prinsep. *A treatise on political*

economy; available online at: http://www.econlib.org/library/Say/sayT.html.

Myron S. Scholes (1941–)

Myron Scholes, along with ROBERT MERTON, was awarded the 1997 Nobel Prize in economics "for a new method to determine the value of derivatives." The particular derivative they studied was stock options (see FUTURES AND OPTIONS MARKETS). A call option gives its owner the right to buy a stock at a particular price, called the strike price, during a set time period. A put option gives its owner the right to sell a stock at the strike price during a set time period. Scholes and his coauthor, the late Fischer Black, derived the formula for pricing a stock option in 1970. They submitted the article to the *Journal of Political Economy*, and it was rejected without even being reviewed. MERTON MILLER (who received the Nobel Prize in 1990) and Eugene Fama, two financial economists at the University of Chicago, where the journal is edited, persuaded the editors to take another look, and the journal published the article in 1973.

The issue of how to price stock options may sound unimportant, but it is hugely important. Stock options, like other financial derivatives, are attractive for one main reason: they allow people to reduce risk at a low cost. This has given huge benefits to major companies and even to small investors. Say you have invested in a stock index fund and you are comfortable with the risk of a 15 percent drop in the Standard and Poor's (S&P) 500 index, but you want to cover yourself in case the S&P 500 falls by more than 15 percent. Then you can buy a put on the S&P 500 with a strike price 20 percent below the current price. You have just used the options market to buy insurance. Virtually all major firms now use options and other derivatives to hedge against changes in exchange rates, raw-materials prices, and interest rates. Financial derivatives, in fact, have played an underappreciated role in making recessions less severe.

Before Scholes's and Black's work, no one knew how to value options precisely. Traders understood the basics. The higher the strike price, for example, the lower the value of a call option. The longer the time period in which the option could be exercised, the higher the value of an option. The higher the interest rate, the lower the value of an option. But how to handle risk? Scholes and Black worked away on the risk issue until they had a "Eureka" moment: they realized that the risk was already embodied in the price of the stock. They showed that risk canceled out of

<hr>

1. Say, *A Treatise on Political Economy,* book 1, chap. XV, para. 4.

the relevant equation, which means that they did not need to know risk in order to value the stock option.

Coincidentally, the Chicago Board Options Exchange (CBOE) was begun in April 1973, just one month after the Black-Scholes article was published. Now options traders had a tool for scientifically pricing options. The effect was electric—literally. By 1977, traders were roaming the CBOE floor with special financial calculators programmed with the Black-Scholes options-pricing model. In his Nobel lecture, Scholes told of his request to Texas Instruments for royalties. TI refused, citing the fact that the formula was in the public domain. Said Scholes, "When I asked, at least, for a calculator, they suggested that I buy one. I never did."[1]

Even though economists often have insights about the markets they study, rarely do the day-to-day players in those markets draw directly on what economists know. They usually do not need to. When an economist finds, for example, that an increase in the minimum wage causes employers to fire low-skilled workers, employers do not need to know that—they are already doing it. But the research on options pricing actually did improve the day-to-day activities of options traders. As economist J. W. Henry Watson and economic journalist Ida Walters wrote, "This marked the first time economic models became an explicit, integral part of a major market."[2] By 1984, the CBOE was second only to the New York Stock Exchange in the dollar value of financial assets traded.

Many important theories and findings in economics rely on options-pricing theory. These include the theory of the capital structure of a firm, analyses of the value of federal deposit insurance, decision making under uncertainty, and the value of flexibility.

Scholes was born in Canada. He earned his B.A. in economics at McMaster University in Hamilton, Ontario, and his M.B.A. (1964) and Ph.D. (1969) degrees at the University of Chicago. He was a professor at MIT from 1968 to 1973, at the University of Chicago from 1973 to 1983, and at Stanford University from 1983 to 1996. Since 1996 he has been a professor emeritus at Stanford. Along with co-winner Robert Merton, Scholes helped form Long Term Capital Management in 1993. LTCM exploited small arbitrage opportunities on a big scale; in Scholes's memorable phrasing, LTCM acted like a giant vacuum cleaner sucking up nickels that everyone else had overlooked. The strategy worked well for a few years but turned out not to be risk

free. The Federal Reserve Board helped arrange a bailout in 1998, and LTCM was liquidated in 2000.

Virtually all observers agree that had Fischer Black not died in 1995, he would have been a co-recipient of the 1997 prize.

Selected Works

1972 (with Fischer Black). "The Valuation of Option Contracts and a Test of Market Efficiency." *Journal of Finance* 27 (May): 399–418.
1973 (with Fischer Black). "The Pricing of Options and Corporate Liabilities." *Journal of Political Economy* 81: 637–654.
1976. "Taxes and the Pricing of Options." *Journal of Finance* 31: 319–332.
1992 (with Mark A. Wolfson). *Taxes and Business Strategy: A Planning Approach*. Englewood Cliffs, N.J.: Prentice Hall.
1996. "Global Financial Markets, Derivative Securities and Systemic Risks." *Journal of Risk and Uncertainty* 12: 271–286.

Theodore William Schultz (1902–1998)

In 1979 Theodore Schultz was awarded the Nobel Prize along with W. Arthur Lewis for their "pioneering research into economic development . . . with particular consideration of the problems of developing countries." Schultz's focus was on agriculture, a natural interest for someone who had grown up on a South Dakota farm. In 1930 Schultz began teaching agricultural economics at Iowa State College (now Iowa State University). He left in protest in 1943 when the college's administration, bowing to political pressure from some of the state's dairy farmers, suppressed a report that recommended substituting oleomargarine for butter. Schultz moved to the University of Chicago's economics department, where he spent the rest of his academic career.

Early on at Chicago, Schultz became interested in agriculture worldwide. In his 1964 book, *Transforming Traditional Agriculture,* Schultz laid out his view that primitive farmers in poor countries maximize the return from their resources. Their apparent unwillingness to innovate, he argued, was rational because governments of those countries often set artificially low prices on their crops and taxed them heavily. Also, governments in those countries, unlike in the United States, did not typically have agricultural extension services to train farmers in new methods. A persistent theme in Schultz's books is that rural poverty persists in poor countries because government policy in those countries is biased in favor of urban dwellers. Schultz was always optimistic that poor agricultural nations would be

1. See http://nobelprize.org/economics/laureates/1997/scholes-lecture.pdf.
2. J. W. Henry Watson and Ida Walters, "The New Economics and the Death of Central Banking," *Liberty* 10, no. 6 (1997): 21.

able to develop if this government hostility to agriculture disappeared. "Poor people in low-income countries," he stated, "are not prisoners of an ironclad poverty equilibrium that economics is unable to break."

Schultz was an empirical economist. When he traveled to serve on commissions or to attend conferences, he visited farms. His visits to farms and interviews with farmers led to new ideas, not the least of which was on human capital, which he pioneered along with Gary Becker and Jacob Mincer. After World War II, while interviewing an old, apparently poor farm couple, he noticed their obvious contentment. When he asked them why they were so contented even though poor, they answered that they were not poor because they had used up their farm to send four children to college and that these children would be productive because of their education. This led Schultz quickly to the concept of human capital—capital produced by investing in knowledge. Schultz was president of the American Economic Association in 1960, and in 1972 he won the Francis A. Walker Medal, the highest honor given by that association.

Selected Works

1950. "Reflections on Poverty Within Agriculture." *Journal of Political Economy* 43 (February): 1–15.
1961. "Investment in Human Capital." *American Economic Review* 51 (March): 1–17.
1963. *The Economic Value of Education.* New York: Columbia University Press. Translated into Spanish, Portuguese, Japanese, and Greek.
1964. *Transforming Traditional Agriculture.* New Haven: Yale University Press. Translated into Japanese, Korean, Portuguese, and Spanish. Reprint. New York: Arno Press, 1976.

Joseph Alois Schumpeter (1883–1950)

"Can capitalism survive? No. I do not think it can." Thus opens Schumpeter's prologue to a section of his 1942 book, *Capitalism, Socialism and Democracy.* One might think, on the basis of the quote, that Schumpeter was a Marxist. But the analysis that led Schumpeter to his conclusion differed totally from Karl Marx's. Marx believed that capitalism would be destroyed by its enemies (the proletariat), whom capitalism had purportedly exploited, and he relished the prospect. Schumpeter believed that capitalism would be destroyed by its successes, that it would spawn a large intellectual class that made its living by attacking the very bourgeois system of private property and freedom so necessary for the intellectual class's existence.

And unlike Marx, Schumpeter did not relish the destruction of capitalism. "If a doctor predicts that his patient will die presently," he wrote, "this does not mean that he desires it."

Capitalism, Socialism, and Democracy is much more than a prognosis of capitalism's future. It is also a sparkling defense of capitalism on the grounds that capitalism sparks entrepreneurship. Indeed, Schumpeter was among the first to lay out a clear concept of entrepreneurship. He distinguished inventions from the entrepreneur's innovations. Schumpeter pointed out that entrepreneurs innovate not just by figuring out how to use inventions, but also by introducing new means of production, new products, and new forms of organization. These innovations, he argued, take just as much skill and daring as does the process of invention.

Innovation by the entrepreneur, argued Schumpeter, leads to gales of "creative destruction" as innovations cause old inventories, ideas, technologies, skills, and equipment to become obsolete. The question is not "how capitalism administers existing structures, . . . [but] how it creates and destroys them." This creative destruction, he believed, causes continuous progress and improves the standards of living for everyone.

Schumpeter argued with the prevailing view that "perfect" competition was the way to maximize economic well-being. Under perfect competition all firms in an industry produce the same good, sell it for the same price, and have access to the same technology. Schumpeter saw this kind of competition as relatively unimportant. He wrote: "[What counts is] competition from the new commodity, the new technology, the new source of supply, the new type of organization . . . competition which . . . strikes not at the margins of the profits and the outputs of the existing firms but at their foundations and their very lives."

Schumpeter argued on this basis that some degree of monopoly is preferable to perfect competition. Competition from innovations, he argued, is an "ever-present threat" that "disciplines before it attacks." He cited the Aluminum Company of America as an example of a monopoly that continuously innovated in order to retain its monopoly. By 1929, he noted, the price of its product, adjusted for inflation, had fallen to only 8.8 percent of its level in 1890, and its output had risen from 30 metric tons to 103,400.

Schumpeter never made completely clear whether he believed innovation is sparked by monopoly per se or by the prospect of getting a monopoly as the reward for innovation. Most economists accept the latter argument and, on that basis, believe that companies should be able to keep their production processes secret, have their trademarks protected from infringement, and obtain patents.

Schumpeter was also a giant in the history of economic thought. His magnum opus in the area is *History of Economic Analysis,* edited by his third wife, Elizabeth Boody, and published posthumously in 1954. In it Schumpeter made some controversial comments about other economists, arguing that Adam Smith was unoriginal, Alfred Marshall was confused, and Leon Walras was the greatest economist of all time.

Born in Austria to parents who owned a textile factory, Schumpeter was very familiar with business when he entered the University of Vienna to study economics and law. He was one of the more promising students of Friedrich von Wieser and Eugen von Böhm-Bawerk, publishing at the age of twenty-eight his famous *Theory of Economic Development.* In 1911 Schumpeter took a professorship in economics at the University of Graz. He was minister of finance in 1919. With the rise of Hitler, Schumpeter left Europe and the University of Bonn, where he was a professor from 1925 until 1932, and emigrated to the United States. In that same year he accepted a permanent position at Harvard, where he remained until his retirement in 1949. Schumpeter was president of the American Economic Association in 1948.

Selected Works

1912. *The Theory of Economic Development.* Leipzig: Duncker and Humblot. Translated by R. Opie. Cambridge: Harvard University Press, 1934. Reprint. New York: Oxford University Press, 1961.
1939. *Business Cycles.* 2 vols. New York: McGraw-Hill.
1942. *Capitalism, Socialism and Democracy.* New York: Harper and Brothers. 5th ed. London: George Allen and Unwin, 1976.
1951. *Ten Great Economists.* New York: Oxford University Press.
1954. *History of Economic Analysis.* Edited by E. Boody. New York: Oxford University Press.

Reinhard Selten (1930–)

Reinhard Selten shared the 1994 Nobel Prize in economics with JOHN NASH and JOHN HARSANYI "for their pioneering analysis of equilibria in the theory of noncooperative games."

One problem with various Nash equilibria is that they are not always unique. Selten applied stronger conditions to reduce the number of possible equilibria and to eliminate equilibria that are unreasonable economically. In 1965 he introduced the concept of "subgame perfection,"

his term for this winnowing down of possible equilibria. "At that time I did not suspect that it often would be quoted, almost exclusively for the definition of subgame perfectness," Selten wrote in his Nobel autobiography.[1]

An example of subgame perfection is Selten's "chain store paradox." Imagine that firm A has a number of chain stores in various locations and that firm B contemplates entering in one or more of these locations. If firm A threatens a price war, then firm B might be dissuaded from entering, not just in a particular market, but in any of A's markets. In that case, it could well be worthwhile for A to threaten and, indeed, to carry out a price war in a single market. Knowing this, B does not enter. This is a Nash equilibrium. But Selten also saw that another Nash equilibrium was for B to enter. The reason: B would realize that A would have losses in each market in which B entered and A carried out a price war. These losses, cumulatively, would not be worthwhile. By looking forward and reasoning backward, B realizes that A will not carry on a price war, and therefore B enters. Which Nash equilibrium is the "right" one? Selten argued that it is the one where B enters because B thought through the whole sequence and realized that, from A's viewpoint, a price war would be irrational. B's strategy of entry and A's strategy of avoiding a price war are "subgame perfect."

Interestingly, this discussion of game theory was carried on long after economist Aaron Director, in 1953, offered a similar argument that "predatory pricing" is an irrational strategy. John S. McGee, following Director's hunch, examined the trial transcripts of *U.S. v. Standard Oil New Jersey,* which was thought to be one of the best-documented cases of "predatory pricing"—that is, pricing below a rival's costs to put the rival out of business. Sure enough, McGee found no evidence that Standard Oil of New Jersey had ever engaged in predatory pricing.[2] Indeed, the U.S. Supreme Court has accepted this reasoning and, in judging the antitrust laws, has given wide latitude to firms to cut prices in a price war.[3]

Selten realized, though, that there can be situations in which even the requirement of subgame perfection is insufficient. This led him to his next major contribution, the

1. Available online at: http://nobelprize.org/nobel_prizes/economics/laureates/1994/selten-autobio.html.
2. John S. McGee, "Predatory Price Cutting: The Standard Oil (N.J.) Case," *Journal of Law and Economics* 1 (October 1958): 137–169; see esp. p. 138, fn. 2, where McGee thanks Director for his strictly logical reasoning that predatory pricing makes no sense.
3. In *Matsushita Electric Industrial Co. v. Zenith Radio Corp.* (1986), the U.S. Supreme Court stated that "predatory pricing schemes are rarely tried, and even more rarely successful."

"trembling-hand" equilibrium. Imagine that each "player" thinks there is a small probability that a mistake will occur—that is, that someone's hand will tremble. A Nash equilibrium in a game is "trembling-hand perfect" if it obtains even with small probabilities of such mistakes.

Selten was born in Breslau, Germany, now the city of Wrocław, Poland. Growing up half-Jewish, he learned an important lesson from the virulent anti-Semitism he saw around him. As Selten put it, "I had to learn to trust my own judgment rather than official propaganda or public opinion."[4]

Selten became interested in game theory after reading about it in *Fortune* in the late 1940s. He earned his master's degree in mathematics at the University of Frankfurt in 1957 and his Ph.D. at the same school in 1961. He was a full professor of economics at the Free University of Berlin from 1969 to 1972. This was a period of student "unrest," which, wrote Selten, "made teaching difficult and sometimes impossible." For other reasons, though, he moved to the University of Bielefed in 1972 and stayed there until 1984, when he moved to the University of Bonn. He often collaborated with fellow future Nobel winner John Harsanyi.

Selected Works

1965. "Spieltheoretische Behandlung eines Oligopolmodells mit Nachfrageträgheit [An oligopoly model with demand inertia]." *Zeitschrift für die Gesamte Staatswissenschaft* 121: 301–324 and 667–689.

1975. "Reexamination of the Perfectness Concept for Equilibrium Points in Extensive Games." *International Journal of Game Theory* 4: 25–55.

1988. *Models of Strategic Rationality.* Dordrecht: Kluwer.

Amartya Sen (1933–)

In 1998, Amartya Sen received the Nobel Prize "for his contributions to welfare economics." Much of Sen's early work was on issues raised by KENNETH ARROW's "impossibility theorem." Arrow had shown, much more generally than Condorcet had in 1785, that majority rules often lead to intransitivities. A majority may prefer *a* to *b* and *b* to *c*, but it does not follow, as it does for an individual, that the majority prefers *a* to *c* (see PUBLIC CHOICE). If the majority prefers *c* to *a*, then there is an intransitivity. With coauthor Prasanta Pattanaik, Sen specified certain conditions that

eliminate intransitivities. He did later work on his own that resulted in a 1970 book that added to Arrow's initial insights. One major theme was his skepticism about utilitarianism. The Nobel committee cited this work in awarding the prize.

Sen also pointed out that the standard measure of poverty in a society, the proportion of people who are below a poverty line, leaves out an important datum: the degree of poverty among the poor. He came up with a more complicated index to measure not only poverty but also its degree.

Sen studied famines in various parts of the world and pointed out that they sometimes occurred even when there was no decline in food output. Some famines occurred when the real income of specific groups fell so that these groups could no longer afford to buy food. In such cases, most economists would advocate giving money to such people so that they could buy food and make their own trade-offs between food and other things. Along with coauthor Jean Drèze, Sen, though no strong believer in economic freedom, defended this standard economist's view and argued mildly against price controls on food because such controls would reduce the amount of food produced.

Sen was a moderate defender of free markets who sometimes put the moderate case brilliantly. He wrote:

> To be generically against markets would be as odd as being generically against conversations between people (even though some conversations are clearly foul and cause problems for others—or even for the conversationalists themselves.) The freedom to exchange words, goods or gifts doesn't need defensive justification in terms of their favorable but distant effects; they are a part of the way human beings in society live and interact with each other (unless stopped by regulation or fiat).[1]

Sen also wrote articles in 1990 and 1992 in which he argued that there were 100 million fewer females in China, India, and other Asian countries than there should have been. He assumed, reasonably, that this was because of discrimination against women by men and by governments. Many wondered if the Chinese government's one-child policy (which encouraged abortion when the expectant mother thought she was having a girl) might be one of the culprits behind this "missing women" phenomenon. More recent research, though, has found that about half of the female undercount can be explained without resort to female mortality. It turns out that women who are carriers of hepatitis B tend to have more boys than

---

4. See http://nobelprize.org/economics/laureates/1994/selten-autobio.html.

1. Amartya Sen, *Development as Freedom* (New York: Alfred A. Knopf, 1999), p. 6.

girls, and that the incidence of hepatitis B is high in these Asian countries.[2]

Sen was born in India. He completed his early academic education there and earned his doctorate from Cambridge in 1959. He was a professor at the University of Delhi from 1963 to 1971, at the London School of Economics from 1971 to 1977, at All Souls College in Oxford from 1977 to 1988, and at Harvard University from 1989 to 1997. He is now Master of Trinity College at Cambridge University.

Selected Works

1969 (with Prasanta K. Pattanaik). "Necessary and Sufficient Conditions for Rational Choice Under Majority Decision." *Journal of Economic Theory* 1, no. 2: 178–202.

1970. *Collective Choice and Social Welfare.* San Francisco: Holden-Day, 1970.

1976. "Poverty: An Ordinal Approach to Measurement." *Econometrica* 44, no. 2: 219–223.

1976. "Real National Income." *Review of Economic Studies* 43, no. 1: 19–39.

1977. "Starvation and Exchange Entitlements: A General Approach and Its Application to the Great Bengal Famine." *Cambridge Journal of Economics* 1, no. 1: 33–59.

1981. *Poverty and Famines: An Essay on Entitlement and Deprivation.* Oxford: Oxford University Press.

1989 (with Jean Drèze). *Hunger and Public Action.* Oxford: Oxford University Press.

1990. "Food, Economics, and Entitlements." In Jean Drèze and Amartya Sen, eds., *The Political Economy of Hunger.* Vol. 1: *Entitlement and Well-Being.* Oxford: Oxford University Press, 1990.

1990. "More than 100 Million Women Are Missing." *New York Review of Books,* December 20.

1992. "Missing Women." *British Medical Journal* 304: 587–588.

William F. Sharpe (1934–)

In 1990 American economists William F. Sharpe, HARRY MARKOWITZ, and MERTON H. MILLER shared the Nobel Prize "for their pioneering work in the theory of financial economics." Their early contributions established financial economics as a separate field of study. In the 1960s Sharpe, taking off from Markowitz's portfolio theory, developed the Capital Asset Pricing Model (CAPM). One implication of this model is that a single mix of risky assets

fits in every investor's portfolio. Those who want a high return hold a portfolio heavily weighted with the risky asset; those who want a low return hold a portfolio heavily weighted with a riskless asset, such as an insured bank deposit. A measure of the portfolio risk that cannot be diversified away by mixing stocks is "beta." A portfolio with a beta of 1.5, for example, is likely to rise by 15 percent if the stock market rises by 10 percent and is likely to fall by 15 percent if the market falls by 10 percent.

One implication of Sharpe's work is that the expected return on a portfolio in excess of a riskless return should be beta times the excess return of the market. Thus, a portfolio with a beta of 2 should have an excess return that is twice as high as the market as a whole. If the market's expected return is 8 percent and the riskless return is 5 percent, the market's expected excess return is 3 percent (8 minus 5) and the portfolio's expected excess return is therefore 6 percent (twice the market's expected excess return of 3 percent). The portfolio's expected total return would then be 11 percent (6 plus the riskless return of 5).

Sharpe was a Ph.D. candidate at the University of California at Los Angeles and an employee of the RAND Corporation when he first met Markowitz, who was also employed at RAND. Sharpe chose Markowitz as his dissertation adviser, even though Markowitz was not on the faculty at UCLA. Sharpe taught first at the University of Washington in Seattle and then at the University of California at Irvine. In 1971 he became a professor of finance at Stanford University. In 1986 Sharpe founded William F. Sharpe Associates, a firm that consulted to foundations, endowments, and pension plans. He returned to Stanford as a professor of finance in 1993 and is now a professor emeritus there.

Selected Works

1964. "Capital Asset Prices: A Theory of Market Equilibrium Under Conditions of Risk." *Journal of Finance* 19 (September): 425–442.

1977. "The Capital Asset Pricing Model: A 'Multi-Beta' Interpretation." In H. Levy and M. Sarnat, eds., *Financial Decision Making Under Uncertainty.* New York: Harcourt Brace Jovanovich, Academic Press.

Herbert Alexander Simon (1901–1985)

In 1978 American social scientist Herbert Simon was awarded the Nobel Prize in economics for his "pioneering research into the decision-making process within economic organizations." In a stream of articles, Simon, who

2. Emily Oster, "Hepatitis B and the Case of the Missing Women," Harvard University, August 2005, online at: http://www.people.fas.harvard.edu/~eoster/hepb.pdf.

trained as a political scientist, questioned mainstream economists' view of economic man as a lightning-quick calculator of costs and benefits. Simon saw people's rationality as "bounded." Because getting information about alternatives is costly, and because the consequences of many possible decisions cannot be known anyway, argued Simon, people cannot act the way economists assume they act. Instead of maximizing their utility, they "satisfice"; that is, they do as well as they think is possible. One way they do so is by devising rules of thumb (e.g., save 10 percent of after-tax income every month) that economize on the cost of collecting information and on the cost of thinking.

Simon also questioned economists' view that firms maximize profits. He proposed instead that because of their members' bounded rationality and often contradictory goals and perspectives, firms reach decisions that can only be described as satisfactory rather than the best.

Not surprisingly for one who believes that decision making is costly, Simon also worked on problems of artificial intelligence.

After earning his Ph.D. in political science from the University of Chicago, Simon joined the school's faculty. In 1949 he left for Pittsburgh, where he helped start Carnegie Mellon University's new Graduate School of Industrial Administration.

Selected Works

1957. *Models of Man*. New York: Wiley.
1958 (with James March). *Organization*. New York: Wiley.
1976. *Administrative Behavior*. 3d ed. New York: Macmillan. 4th ed., New York: Free Press. 1997.
1981. *The Sciences of the Artificial*. 2d ed. Cambridge: MIT Press.
1982. *Models of Bounded Rationality and Other Topics in Economic Theory*. 2 vols. Cambridge: MIT Press.

Adam Smith (1723–1790)

With *The Wealth of Nations* Adam Smith installed himself as the leading expositor of economic thought. Currents of Adam Smith run through the works published by David Ricardo and Karl Marx in the nineteenth century, and by John Maynard Keynes and Milton Friedman in the twentieth.

Adam Smith was born in a small village in Kirkcaldy, Scotland, where his widowed mother raised him. At age fourteen, as was the usual practice, he entered the University of Glasgow on scholarship. He later attended Balliol

College at Oxford, graduating with an extensive knowledge of European literature and an enduring contempt for English schools.

He returned home, and after delivering a series of well-received lectures was made first chair of logic (1751), then chair of moral philosophy (1752), at Glasgow University.

He left academia in 1764 to tutor the young duke of Buccleuch. For more than two years they traveled throughout France and into Switzerland, an experience that brought Smith into contact with his contemporaries Voltaire, Jean-Jacques Rousseau, François Quesnay, and Anne-Robert-Jacques Turgot. With the life pension he had earned in the service of the duke, Smith retired to his birthplace of Kirkcaldy to write *The Wealth of Nations*. It was published in 1776, the same year the American Declaration of Independence was signed and in which his close friend David Hume died. In 1778 he was appointed commissioner of customs. In this job he helped enforce laws against smuggling. In *The Wealth of Nations,* he had defended smuggling as a legitimate activity in the face of "unnatural" legislation. Adam Smith never married. He died in Edinburgh on July 19, 1790.

Today Smith's reputation rests on his explanation of how rational self-interest in a free-market economy leads to economic well-being. It may surprise those who would discount Smith as an advocate of ruthless individualism that his first major work concentrates on ethics and charity. In fact, while chair at the University of Glasgow, Smith's lecture subjects, in order of preference, were natural theology, ethics, jurisprudence, and economics, according to John Millar, Smith's pupil at the time. In *The Theory of Moral Sentiments*, Smith wrote: "How selfish soever man may be supposed, there are evidently some principles in his nature which interest him in the fortune of others and render their happiness necessary to him though he derives nothing from it except the pleasure of seeing it."[1]

At the same time, Smith had a benign view of self-interest, denying that self-love "was a principle which could never be virtuous in any degree."[2] Smith argued that life would be tough if our "affections, which, by the very nature of our being, ought frequently to influence our conduct, could upon no occasion appear virtuous, or deserve esteem and commendation from anybody."[3]

Smith did not view sympathy and self-interest as antithetical; they were complementary. "Man has almost con-

1. Smith 1759, part I, section I, chap. I, para. 1; available online at: http://oll.libertyfund.org/192/39008/908774.
2. Ibid., part VII, section II, chap. iii, para. 12; available online at: http://oll.libertyfund.org/192/39125/909478.
3. Ibid., part VII, section II, chap. iii, para. 18; available online at: http://oll.libertyfund.org/192/39125/909484.

stant occasion for the help of his brethren, and it is in vain for him to expect it from their benevolence only," he explained in *The Wealth of Nations*.[4]

Charity, while a virtuous act, cannot alone provide the essentials for living. Self-interest is the mechanism that can remedy this shortcoming. Said Smith: "It is not from the benevolence of the butcher, the brewer, or the baker, that we can expect our dinner, but from their regard to their own interest" (ibid.).

Someone earning money by his own labor benefits himself. Unknowingly, he also benefits society, because to earn income on his labor in a competitive market, he must produce something others value. In Adam Smith's lasting imagery, "By directing that industry in such a manner as its produce may be of greatest value, he intends only his own gain, and he is in this, as in many other cases, led by an invisible hand to promote an end which was no part of his intention."[5]

The Wealth of Nations, published as a five-book series, sought to reveal the nature and cause of a nation's prosperity. Smith saw the main cause of prosperity as increasing division of labor. Using the famous example of pins, Smith asserted that ten workers could produce 48,000 pins per day if each of eighteen specialized tasks was assigned to particular workers. Average productivity: 4,800 pins per worker per day. But absent the division of labor, a worker would be lucky to produce even one pin per day.

Just how individuals can best apply their own labor or any other resource is a central subject in the first book of the series. Smith claimed that an individual would invest a resource—for example, land or labor—so as to earn the highest possible return on it. Consequently, all uses of the resource must yield an equal rate of return (adjusted for the relative riskiness of each enterprise). Otherwise reallocation would result. George Stigler called this idea the central proposition of economic theory. Not surprisingly, and consistent with another Stigler claim that the originator of an idea in economics almost never gets the credit, Smith's idea was not original. The French economist TURGOT had made the same point in 1766.

Smith used this insight on equality of returns to explain why wage rates differed. Wage rates would be higher, he argued, for trades that were more difficult to learn, because people would not be willing to learn them if they were not compensated by a higher wage. His thought gave rise to the modern notion of HUMAN CAPITAL. Similarly, wage rates would also be higher for those who engaged in dirty or unsafe occupations (see JOB SAFETY), such as coal mining and butchering; and for those, like the hangman, who performed odious jobs. In short, differences in work were compensated by differences in pay. Modern economists call Smith's insight the theory of compensating wage differentials.

Smith used numerate economics not just to explain production of pins or differences in pay between butchers and hangmen, but to address some of the most pressing political issues of the day. In the fourth book of *The Wealth of Nations*—published, remember, in 1776—Smith told Great Britain that its American colonies were not worth the cost of keeping. His reasoning about the excessively high cost of British imperialism is worth repeating, both to show Smith at his numerate best and to show that simple, clear economics can lead to radical conclusions:

> A great empire has been established for the sole purpose of raising up a nation of customers who should be obliged to buy from the shops of our different producers all the goods with which these could supply them. For the sake of that little enhancement of price which this monopoly might afford our producers, the home-consumers have been burdened with the whole expense of maintaining and defending that empire. For this purpose, and for this purpose only, in the two last wars, more than a hundred and seventy millions [in pounds] has been contracted over and above all that had been expended for the same purpose in former wars. The interest of this debt alone is not only greater than the whole extraordinary profit, which, it ever could be pretended, was made by the monopoly of the colony trade, but than the whole value of that trade, or than the whole value of the goods, which at an average have been annually exported to the colonies.[6]

Smith vehemently opposed mercantilism—the practice of artificially maintaining a trade surplus on the erroneous belief that doing so increased wealth. The primary advantage of trade, he argued, was that it opened up new markets for surplus goods and also provided some commodities from abroad at a lower cost than at home. With that, Smith launched a succession of free-trade economists and paved the way for David Ricardo's and John Stuart Mill's theories of comparative advantage a generation later.

Adam Smith has sometimes been caricatured as someone who saw no role for government in economic life. In fact, he believed that government had an important role to

4. Smith 1776, book I, chap. 2, para. 2; available online at: http://oll.libertyfund.org/220/111839/2312795.

5. Ibid., book IV, chap. 2, para. 9; available online at: http://oll.libertyfund.org/220/111910/2313856.

6. Ibid., book IV, chap. VIII, para. 53; available online at: http://oll.libertyfund.org/200/111936/2316261.

play. Like most modern believers in free markets, Smith believed that the government should enforce contracts and grant patents and copyrights to encourage inventions and new ideas. He also thought that the government should provide public works, such as roads and bridges, that, he assumed, would not be worthwhile for individuals to provide. Interestingly, though, he wanted the users of such public works to pay in proportion to their use.

One definite difference between Smith and most modern believers in free markets is that Smith favored retaliatory tariffs. Retaliation to bring down high tariff rates in other countries, he thought, would work. "The recovery of a great foreign market," he wrote "will generally more than compensate the transitory inconvenience of paying dearer during a short time for some sorts of goods."

Some of Smith's ideas are testimony to his breadth of imagination. Today, vouchers and school choice programs are touted as the latest reform in public education. But Adam Smith addressed the issue more than two hundred years ago:

> Were the students upon such charitable foundations left free to choose what college they liked best, such liberty might contribute to excite some emulation among different colleges. A regulation, on the contrary, which prohibited even the independent members of every particular college from leaving it, and going to any other, without leave first asked and obtained of that which they meant to abandon, would tend very much to extinguish that emulation.[7]

Smith's own student days at Oxford (1740–1746), whose professors, he complained, had "given up altogether even the pretense of teaching," left him with lasting disdain for the universities of Cambridge and Oxford.

Smith's writings are both an inquiry into the science of economics and a policy guide for realizing the wealth of nations. Smith believed that economic development was best fostered in an environment of free competition that operated in accordance with universal "natural laws." Because Smith's was the most systematic and comprehensive study of economics up until that time, his economic thinking became the basis for classical economics. And because more of his ideas have lasted than those of any other economist, some regard Adam Smith as the alpha and the omega of economic science.

Selected Works

1759. *The Theory of Moral Sentiments*. Edited by D. D. Raphael and A. L. Macfie. Oxford: Clarendon Press; New York: Oxford University Press, 1976.

7. Ibid., book V, chap. I, para. 140 [OUP article ii, para. 12]; available online at: http://oll.libertyfund.org/200/111942/2316475.

1776. *An Inquiry into the Nature and Causes of the Wealth of Nations*. Edited by Edwin Cannan. Chicago: University of Chicago Press, 1976.

Vernon L. Smith (1927–)

In 2002, Vernon Smith and DANIEL KAHNEMAN were awarded the Nobel Prize in economics. Smith received his prize "for having established laboratory experiments as a tool in empirical analysis, especially in the study of alternative market mechanisms."

The dominant view among economists as recently as the 1970s was that economists, unlike chemists or biologists, would never be able to perform controlled experiments. Smith's work on experimental economics, which began in the mid-1950s, challenged that view. Today experimental economics is widespread and has been used to study electricity pricing, to allocate airplane landing slots, and to design auctions of operating licenses for pieces of the electromagnetic spectrum (see EXPERIMENTAL ECONOMICS).

In his first semester of teaching economics at Purdue, in the fall of 1955, Smith found it a challenge to present basic microeconomic theory to undergraduates. So the next semester, to make the theory more accessible, he ran a market experiment on the first day of class using rules that are laid out in the Experimental Economics entry. Smith, himself a skeptic about how quickly such an artificial market would reach equilibrium, was stunned by the results. More than anything he had learned in graduate school, these results convinced him that free markets work. From 1956 to 1960, he experimented further with various changes in the rules, and in 1962 he published his article on experimental economics.

In a market experiment, the experimenter must somehow control for the subjects' preferences. Of course, the subjects want to make more money—this preference is well-nigh universal. But how much utility does each person get from an increase in his or her wealth? This will vary from person to person. In 1976, Smith solved this problem with the "induced-value method," which has become a standard tool of economics.

Smith also used experimental economics to test for differences and similarities between various AUCTION systems. The most familiar auction system is the English system, in which buyers bid sequentially and in increasing order until no higher bid is submitted. Another auction system beloved by economists (see WILLIAM VICKREY) is the second-price sealed-bid system, in which the buyer pays only the second-highest bid. Smith found that English and sealed-bid second-price auctions produced similar experimental outcomes. Interestingly, though, Dutch auctions (in which a high initial bid by the seller is gradually lowered in fixed steps at fixed times until a buyer yells "buy") yielded lower prices than sealed-bid second-price auctions, which is contrary to the basic economic theory of auctions.

Experimental economics seems to have led Smith to delve into a more complex reality of human motivation than is outlined in standard economics texts and classes. Always the empiricist, he does not assume that markets work, but is open to seeing them work or fail. In his Nobel lecture, Smith laid out a number of examples of private enforcement of rules that seem to have worked well—in cattle ranching, mining, lobster trapping in Maine, and Eskimo polar bear hunting. Smith pointed out that these examples contradict the myth that a central function of government is to "solve" the free-rider problem in the private provision of public goods. In fact, he noted, the cattle-ranching example showed the reverse: private entities solved the public-good problem, and when governments came along and provided protection paid for by the taxpayers, cattle ranchers were quite happy to have the general taxpayer bear the cost of protecting their cattle. Smith also noted work by Robert Ellickson, who found that cattle ranchers in Shasta County have developed informal rules for handling the problem of stray cattle.[1] RONALD COASE had argued that with well-defined property rights and low transactions costs, people would handle such problems in an efficient way. Although the Shasta County ranchers' methods were not ones most economists would have thought of, in Smith's words, Ellickson "out-Coased Coase."[2] That is, Ellickson showed that private negotiations and sanctions worked to handle knotty problems without government intervention.

Smith earned his B.S. degree in electrical engineering from Cal Tech in 1949, his M.A. in economics at the University of Kansas in 1952, and his Ph.D. in economics from Harvard in 1955. He was a professor at Purdue University from 1955 to 1967, at Brown University from 1967 to 1968, at the University of Massachusetts from 1968 to 1975, and at the University of Arizona from 1975 to 2001. Since 2001 he has been a professor of economics and law at George Mason University.

Selected Works

1962. "An Experimental Study of Competitive Market Behavior." *Journal of Political Economy* 70: 111–137.

1. Robert C. Ellickson, *Order Without Law: How Neighbors Settle Disputes* (Cambridge: Harvard University Press, 1991).

2. See http://nobelprize.org/economics/laureates/2002/smith-lecture.pdf.

1965. "Experimental Auction Markets and the Walrasian Hypothesis." *Journal of Political Economy* 70: 387–393.
1976. "Experimental Economics: Induced Value Theory." *American Economic Review* 66: 274–279.
1991. *Papers in Experimental Economics.* Cambridge: Cambridge University Press.
2000. *Bargaining and Market Behavior: Essays in Experimental Economics.* Cambridge: Cambridge University Press.

Robert Merton Solow (1924–)

Robert Solow was awarded the Nobel Prize in 1987 "for his contributions to the theory of economic growth." His first major paper on growth was "A Contribution to the Theory of Growth." In it he presented a mathematical model of growth that was a version of the Harrod-Domar growth model (see ROY F. HARROD). The main difference between his model and the Harrod-Domar model lay in Solow's assumption that wages could adjust to keep labor fully employed. Out the window went the Harrod-Domar conclusion that the economy was on a knife edge.

Solow soon followed that paper with another pioneering article, "Technical Change and the Aggregate Production Function." Before it was published, economists had believed that capital and labor were the main causes of economic growth. But Solow showed that half of economic growth cannot be accounted for by increases in capital and labor. This unaccounted-for portion of economic growth—now called the "Solow residual"—he attributed to technological innovation. His article originated "sources-of-growth accounting," which economists use to estimate the separate effects on economic growth of labor, capital, and technological change.

Solow also was the first to develop a growth model with different vintages of capital. The idea was that because capital is produced based on known technology, and because technology is improving, new capital is more valuable than old capital.

A KEYNESIAN, Solow has been a witty critic of economists ranging from interventionists like Marxist economists and JOHN KENNETH GALBRAITH to relatively non-interventionist economists such as MILTON FRIEDMAN. Solow once wrote that Galbraith's disdain for ordinary consumer goods "reminds one of the Duchess who, upon acquiring a full appreciation of sex, asked the Duke if it were not perhaps too good for the common people." Of Milton Friedman, Solow wrote, "Everything reminds Milton of the money supply. Well, everything reminds me of sex, but I keep it out of the paper."

Solow earned his Ph.D. from Harvard, where he studied under Wassily Leontief, and has been an economics professor at MIT since 1950. From 1961 to 1963 he was a senior economist with President John F. Kennedy's Council of Economic Advisers. In 1961 he received the American Economic Association's John Bates Clark Award, given to the best economist under age forty. In 1979 he was president of that association.

Selected Works

1956. "A Contribution to the Theory of Economic Growth." *Quarterly Journal of Economics* 70 (February): 65–94.
1957. "Technical Change and the Aggregate Production Function." *Review of Economics and Statistics* 39 (August): 312–320.
1958 (with Robert Dorfman and Paul Samuelson). *Linear Programming and Economic Analysis.* New York: McGraw-Hill.
1963. *Capital Theory and the Rate of Return.* Amsterdam: North-Holland.
1967. "The New Industrial State, or Son of Affluence." *Public Interest* 9: 108.

Michael Spence (1943–)

Michael Spence, along with GEORGE AKERLOF and JOSEPH STIGLITZ, received the 2001 Nobel Prize "for their analyses of markets with asymmetric information." Spence's particular focus was on information about workers' productivity. Assuming that a worker knows more about his productivity than a potential employer knows, Spence showed how it can make sense for highly productive workers to "signal" their productivity by getting formal education. This insight may sound basic, but until Spence's work, economists had not had the insight—or at least had not thought through it rigorously. A large part of human behavior is signaling, whether it be in the clothes and watches we wear, the cars we drive, the beer we drink, or the degrees we earn.

Spence earned his B.A. in philosophy from Princeton University and his Ph.D. from Harvard in 1972. He was a professor at Stanford from 1973 to 1975, a professor at Harvard from 1975 to 1984, dean of arts and sciences at Harvard from 1984 to 1990, and dean of Stanford Business School from 1990 to 1999.

Selected Works

1973. "Job Market Signalling." *Quarterly Journal of Economics* 87: 355–374.
1974. *Market Signalling.* Cambridge: Harvard University Press.

George J. Stigler (1911–1991)

George Stigler was the quintessential empirical economist. Paging through his classic microeconomics text *The Theory of Price,* one is struck by how many principles of economics are illustrated with real data rather than hypothetical examples. Stigler deserves a great deal of the credit for getting economists to look at data and evidence.

Stigler's two longest-held positions were at Columbia University (1947–1958) and at the University of Chicago (1958–1991). From the early 1950s to the late 1960s, most of his research was in the field of industrial organization. A typical Stigler article laid out a new proposition with clear reasoning and then presented simple but persuasive data to back up his argument.

Take, for example, Stigler's "A Note on Block Booking." Block booking of movies was the offer of a fixed package of movies to an exhibitor; the exhibitor could not pick and choose among the movies in the package. The Supreme Court banned the practice on the grounds that the movie companies were compounding a monopoly by using the popularity of the winning movies to compel exhibitors to purchase the losers.

Stigler disagreed and presented a simple alternative argument. If *Gone with the Wind* is worth $10,000 to the exhibitor and *Getting Gertie's Garter* is worth nothing, wrote Stigler, the distributor could get the whole $10,000 by selling *Gone with the Wind.* Throwing in a worthless movie would not cause the exhibitor to pay any more than $10,000. Therefore, reasoned Stigler, the Supreme Court's explanation seemed wrong.

But why did block booking exist? Stigler's explanation was that if exhibitors valued films differently from one another, the distributor could collect more by "bundling" the movies. Stigler gave an example in which exhibitor A is willing to pay $8,000 for movie X and $2,500 for Y, and B is willing to pay $7,000 for X and $3,000 for Y. If the distributor charges a single price for each movie, his profit-maximizing price is $7,000 for X and $2,500 for Y. The distributor will then collect $9,500 each from A and B, for a total of $19,000. But with block booking the seller can charge $10,000 (A and B each value the two movies combined at $10,000 or more) for the bundle and make $20,000. Stigler then went on to suggest some empirical tests of his argument and actually did one, showing that customers' relative tastes for movies, as measured by box office receipts, did differ from city to city.

Stigler's thinking on government regulation was even more influential than his work on industrial organization. Because of Stigler's research, economists view regulation much more skeptically than their counterparts of the

1950s did. His first article on the topic, coauthored with longtime research assistant Claire Friedland and published in 1962, was titled "What Can Regulators Regulate? The Case of Electricity." They found that regulation of electricity prices had only a tiny effect on those prices. In the late 1970s, their finding was challenged by Gregg Jarrell, himself a Stigler student. But more important than this finding was their demonstration that one could examine the actual effects of regulation, and not just theorize about them.

Stigler devoted his entire 1964 presidential address to the American Economic Association to making this point. He argued that economists should study the effects of regulation and not just assume them. He twitted the great economists of the past who had given lengthy cases for and critiques of government regulation without ever trying to study its effects. In Stigler's view things were not much better in the twentieth century. "The economic role of the state," he said, "has managed to hold the attention of scholars for over two centuries without arousing their curiosity." Stigler added, "Economists have refused either to leave the problem alone or to work on it."

Many economists got the point. Since the mid-1960s, economists have used their sometimes awesome empirical tools to study the effects of regulation. Whole journals have been devoted to the topic. One is the *Journal of Law and Economics*, started at the University of Chicago in 1958. Another, the *Bell Journal of Economics and Management Science*, later the *RAND Journal*, started in 1970. As a general rule economists have found that government regulation of industries harms consumers and often gives monopoly power to producers. Some of these findings were behind economists' widespread support for the deregulation of transportation, natural gas, and banking, which gained momentum in the Carter administration and continued until halfway through the Reagan administration. Stigler was the single most important academic contributor to this movement.

Stigler was not content to examine the effects of regulation. He wanted to understand its causes. Did governments regulate industries, as many had believed, to reduce the harmful effects of monopoly? Stigler did not think so. In a seminal 1971 article, "The Theory of Economic Regulation," he presented and gave evidence for his "capture theory." Stigler argued that governments do not end up creating monopoly in industries by accident. Rather, he wrote, they regulate at the behest of producers who "capture" the regulatory agency and use regulation to prevent competition. Probably more important than the evidence itself was the fact that Stigler made this viewpoint respectable in the economics profession. It has now become the mainstream view.

Straight Talk from Stigler

Sears, Roebuck and Company and Montgomery Ward made a good deal of money in the process of improving our rural marketing structure, but I am convinced that they did more for the poor farmers of America than the sum total of the federal agricultural support programs of the last five decades.

Am I to admire a man who injures me in an awkward and mistaken attempt to protect me, and to despise a man who to earn a good income performs for me some great and lasting service?

Smith's intellectual heirs did little to strengthen his case for laissez-faire, except by that most irresistible of all the weapons of scholarship, infinite repetition.

Advertising itself is a completely neutral instrument and lends itself to the dissemination of highly contradictory desires. While the automobile industry tells us not to drink while driving, the bourbon industry tells us not to drive while drinking. . . . Our colleges use every form of advertising, and indeed the typical university catalog would never stop Diogenes in his search for an honest man.

When a good comedian and a production of *Hamlet* are on rival channels, I wish I could be confident that less than half the professors were laughing.

For his earlier work on industrial organization and his work on the effects and causes of regulation, Stigler was awarded the 1982 Nobel Prize for economics.

Stigler was an uncommonly clear and humorous writer. Economics from him never seemed like "the dismal science." With his sometimes biting wit, he could put a profound insight into one sentence. In discussing the benefits of capitalism, for example, Stigler wrote: "Professors are much more beholden to Henry Ford than to the foundation that bears his name and spreads his assets."

Not to be missed in a listing of Stigler's contributions is his research on information. His 1962 article "Information in the Labor Market" was a watershed for further studies on unemployment. According to Stigler, job seekers needed short periods of unemployment in order to search for a higher wage. Even in industries with a "going wage," variances in wage rates still exist. Therefore, the unemployed are as much information seekers as job seekers. His theory is now called the theory of search unemployment.

Information is also a problem for firms when they collude, implicitly or explicitly, to set prices. They do not know whether their competitors are secretly undercutting them. This uncertainty can be reduced, wrote Stigler, by spending resources to gather information. Stigler applied this insight to show that collusion is less likely to succeed if there are more firms in a market.

Also highly regarded as an economic historian, Stigler wrote numerous articles on the history of ideas in the early years of his career. His Ph.D. dissertation on the history of neoclassical production and distribution theories was highly acclaimed as a critical link in the chain of economic thought. Some of his articles in the area are collected in *Five Lectures on Economic Problems* (1950) and *Essays in the History of Economics* (1965). The entry on MONOPOLY in this encyclopedia is one of Stigler's last published works.

Selected Works

1950. *Five Lectures on Economic Problems*. New York: Macmillan.
1965. *Essays in the History of Economics*. Chicago: University of Chicago Press.
1966. *The Theory of Price*. 3d ed. New York: Macmillan.
1969. *The Organization of Industry*. Homewood, Ill: Irwin.
1975. *The Citizen and the State: Essays on Regulation*. Chicago: University of Chicago Press.
1986. *The Essence of Stigler*. Edited by Kurt R. Leube and Thomas Gale Moore. Stanford: Hoover Institution Press.
1988. *Memoirs of an Unregulated Economist*. New York: Basic Books.

Joseph E. Stiglitz (1943–)

Joseph Stiglitz, GEORGE AKERLOF, and MICHAEL SPENCE shared the 2001 Nobel Prize "for their analyses of markets with asymmetric information." The particular market with asymmetric information that Stiglitz analyzed was the insurance market. In 1976, Stiglitz and coauthor Michael Rothschild started from the plausible assumption that people buying insurance know more about their relevant characteristics than the insurance company selling it. They then showed that it would be in the insurance company's interest to "sort" its customers by risk category by offering a range of insurance products to all and letting the customers self-select. A low-premium, high-deductible health insurance policy, for example, would be attractive to healthy customers and unattractive to unhealthy customers. The unhealthy customers would be more likely to purchase a high-premium, low-deductible policy. In this way, the market would lead to what the authors called a "separating" equilibrium—that is, a market in which people's risk cate-

gory determined the kind of insurance they bought. Stiglitz and Rothschild also showed certain conditions under which there would be no equilibrium and the market would simply not exist.

Stiglitz realized that information asymmetry applies not just to insurance contracts, but also to much economic behavior. If there were no asymmetries in credit markets, for example—that is, if borrowers knew no more about their probability of repaying than lenders knew—then lenders would simply charge higher interest rates to higher-risk borrowers. But in 1981 and 1983, Stiglitz and Andrew Weiss showed that, to reduce losses, lenders have an incentive not only to charge higher rates to high-risk lenders, but also to ration credit to them. In fact, such rationing is widely observed in credit markets.

Stiglitz's work with Carl Shapiro on "efficiency wages" is another major contribution to the economics of asymmetric information. The basic idea is that firms may want to pay a wage higher than otherwise to give workers an incentive not to shirk. If wages are set so that there is no unemployment, a worker who is fired for shirking can simply get a job at the same pay elsewhere. So firms set wages higher than that. At a higher wage, each firm wants to employ fewer people, but more workers want to work at a higher wage than at a lower wage. The result: unemployment, even in the long run.

Stiglitz has also contributed to the theory of optimal taxation. In 1978, for example, he showed that, under reasonable assumptions, an estate tax will make incomes more, not less, unequal. His basic argument is that the estate tax may reduce savings, and the reduction in savings and capital accumulation will lead to a lower ratio of capital to labor; this greater scarcity of capital will increase the return to capital and, under certain assumptions, increase the share of income that goes to capital. Assuming that capital is more unequally distributed than labor, the result will be higher inequality of income.

From 1993 to 2000, Stiglitz entered the political arena, first as a member and then as chairman of President Bill Clinton's Council of Economic Advisers, and then as the chief economist of the World Bank. In this latter role he had major conflicts with economists at the International Monetary Fund (IMF) and at the U.S. Treasury over their views of government economic policy in Indonesia and other poor countries. Stiglitz objected to their advocacy of tax increases and tight monetary policy during times of recession, a policy that he called "market fundamentalism."

Over the years, Stiglitz has been critical of free markets, mainly because of the information asymmetries that exist in many markets. Stiglitz often called for government intervention to correct these market failures, but his arguments for these interventions were always what might be called "possibility theorems." He showed how it is possible for government to improve on markets but never explained the incentives that would lead government officials to do so. Possibly because of his experience in Washington, Stigler started to consider the incentives of government officials. In his conflict with IMF economists, for example, Stiglitz said, "Intellectual consistency should lead them to ask themselves, 'If we believe that government bureaucrats are always incompetent, then why are we an exception?'"[1] Stiglitz continued to question the incentives of government officials. In his Nobel lecture he took up the issue again:

> The problem is to provide incentives for those so entrusted to act on behalf of those who [sic] they are supposed to be serving—the standard principal agent problem. Democracy—contestability in political processes—provides a check on abuses of powers that come from delegation just as it does in economic processes; but just as we recognize that the take-over mechanism provides an important check, so too should we recognize that the electoral process provides an imperfect check. Just as we recognize that current management has an incentive to increase asymmetries of information in order to enhance its market power, increase its discretion, so to [sic] in public life.[2]

Stiglitz went on to compare government monopolies and private competitive firms:

> In the context of political processes, where "exit" options are limited, one needs to be particularly concerned about abuses. If a firm is mismanaged—if the managers attempt to enrich themselves at the expense of shareholders and customers and entrench themselves against competition, the damage is limited: customers can at least switch. But in political processes, those who see the quality of public services deteriorate cannot do so as easily.

While Stiglitz still puts his faith in government officials, it is a tempered faith. He suggests that getting rid of government secrecy would be a partial solution toward limiting the abuses of government.

Stiglitz earned his B.A. in economics at Amherst College in 1964 and his Ph.D. in economics from MIT in 1967. He has been a professor at MIT, Yale, Oxford, Prince-

ton, Stanford, and Columbia. He is currently a professor at Columbia University.

Selected Works

1976 (with Michael Rothschild). "Equilibrium in Competitive Insurance Markets: An Essay on the Economics of Imperfect Information." *Quarterly Journal of Economics* 90: 629–649.
1978. "Notes on Estate Taxes, Redistribution, and the Concept of Balanced Growth Path Incidence." *Journal of Political Economy* 86 (April): S137–S150.
1981 (with Andrew Weiss). "Credit Rationing in Markets with Imperfect Information." *American Economic Review* 71: 393–410.
1983 (with Andrew Weiss). "Incentive Effects of Terminations: Applications to the Credit and Labor Markets." *American Economic Review* 73: 912–927.
1984 (with Carl Shapiro). "Equilibrium Unemployment as a Worker Discipline Device." *American Economic Review* 74: 433–444.

John Richard Nicholas Stone (1913–1991)

British economist Richard Stone received the Nobel Prize in 1984 "for having made fundamental contributions to the development of systems of national accounts and hence greatly improved the basis for empirical economic analysis." Stone started his work during World War II while in the British government's War Cabinet Secretariat. Stone and his colleagues David Champernowne and JAMES MEADE were asked to estimate funds and resources available for the war effort. They did so, and their work was an important step toward full-blown national income accounts. Stone was by no means the first economist to produce NATIONAL INCOME ACCOUNTS. Simon Kuznets, for example, had already done so for the United States. Stone's distinctive contribution was to integrate national income into a double-entry bookkeeping format. Every income item on one side of the balance sheet had to be matched by an expenditure item on the other side, thus ensuring consistency. Stone's double-entry method has become the universally accepted way to measure national income.

Stone also did some important early work in measuring consumer behavior. He was the first person to use consumer expenditures, incomes, and prices to estimate consumers' utility functions.

Stone studied economics at Cambridge in the 1930s. After leaving the government in 1945, he became director of the newly formed Department of Applied Economics at

1. James North, "Sound the Alarm," *Barron's,* April 17, 2000, p. 34.
2. See http://nobelprize.org/economics/laureates/2001/stiglitz-lecture.pdf.

Cambridge. He was a professor there until he retired in 1980. Stone was knighted in 1978.

Selected Works

1942 (with David G. Champernowne and James E. Meade). "The Precision of National Accounts Estimates." *Review of Economic Studies* 9: 111–125.

1954 (with D. A. Rowe et al.). *The Measurement of Consumers' Expenditure and Behaviour in the United Kingdom, 1920–1938.* Vol. 1. Cambridge: Cambridge University Press.

1956. *Quantity and Price Indexes in National Accounts.* Paris: OECD.

1984. "Balancing the National Accounts: The Adjustment of Initial Estimates." In A. Ingham and A. M. Ulph, eds., *Demand, Equilibrium and Trade.* London: Macmillan.

Jan Tinbergen (1903–1994)

In 1969 Dutch economist Jan Tinbergen and Norwegian economist Ragnar Frisch shared the first Nobel Prize in economics "for having developed and applied dynamic models for the analysis of economic processes." Tinbergen, who held a Ph.D. in physics, had become interested in economics while working on his dissertation, "Minimum Problems in Physics and Economics" (1929). He began to apply mathematical tools to economics, which at the time was a relatively verbal and nonmathematical discipline. In 1929 he joined a unit of the Dutch Central Bureau of Statistics to do research on business cycles. He stayed there until 1945, taking a leave of absence from 1936 to 1938 to work for the League of Nations in Geneva.

Along with Frisch and others Tinbergen developed the field of econometrics, the use of statistical tools to test economic hypotheses. Tinbergen was one of the first economists to create multiequation models of economies. He produced a twenty-seven-equation econometric model of the Dutch economy, and his 1939 book, *Business Cycles in the United States, 1919–1932,* includes a forty-eight-equation model of the American economy that explains investment activity and models American business cycles.

Another of Tinbergen's major contributions was to show that a government with several economic targets— for both the unemployment rate and the inflation rate, for example—must have at least as many policy instruments, such as taxes and monetary policy.

Selected Works

1939. *Business Cycles in the United States, 1919–1932.* Geneva: League of Nations.

1951. *Business Cycles in the United Kingdom, 1870–1914.* Amsterdam: North-Holland.

1952. *On the Theory of Economic Policy.* Amsterdam: North-Holland.

James Tobin (1918–2002)

The American economist James Tobin received the 1981 Nobel Prize "for his analysis of financial markets and their relations to expenditure decisions, employment, production, and prices." Many people regard Tobin as America's most distinguished Keynesian economist. Tobin's most important work was on financial markets. He developed theories to explain how financial markets affect people's consumption and investment decisions.

Tobin argued that one cannot predict the effect of monetary policy on output and unemployment simply by knowing the interest rate or the rate of growth of the money supply. Monetary policy has its effect, he claimed, by affecting capital investment, whether in plant and equipment or in consumer durables. And although interest rates are an important factor in capital investment, they are not the only factor. Tobin introduced the concept of "Tobin's q" as a measure to predict whether capital investment will increase or decrease. The q is the ratio between the market value of an asset and its replacement cost. Tobin pointed out that if an asset's q is less than one—that is, the asset's value is less than its replacement cost—then new investment in similar assets is not profitable. If, on the other hand, q exceeds one, this is a signal for further investment in similar assets. Tobin's insight was also relevant to his ongoing debate with Milton Friedman and other monetarists. Tobin argued that his q, by predicting future capital investment, would be a good predictor of economy-wide economic conditions.

Tobin's portfolio-selection theory is another of his contributions. He argued that investors balance high-risk, high-return investments with safer ones so as to achieve a balance in their portfolios. Tobin's insights helped pave the way for further work in finance theory.

Tobin did his undergraduate and graduate work at Harvard University, with an interruption to serve in the U.S. Navy during World War II. In 1950 he became an economics professor at Yale University, taking a leave of absence to serve as a member of President John F. Kennedy's Council of Economic Advisers from January 1961 to July 1962. Tobin was quite proud of the 1962 *Economic Report of the President* that he helped to write. Tobin called the report, which was mainly written by chairman Walter Heller, along with Tobin, Kermit Gordon, Robert Solow, and Arthur Okun, "the manifesto of our [Keynesian] economics, applied to the United States and world economic conditions of the day." Its counterpart in the Reagan years was the 1982 *Economic Report*. Always the partisan, although an honest and thoughtful one, Tobin said: "It is interesting to compare the two; we have nothing to fear."

Tobin was also an adviser to 1972 presidential candidate George McGovern. Like most other economists across the political spectrum, Tobin believed that government regulation often causes damage. "We should be especially suspicious of interventions that seem both inefficient and inequitable," he wrote; "for example, rent controls in New York or Moscow or Mexico City, or price supports and irrigation subsidies benefiting affluent farmers, or low-interest loans to well-heeled students."

In 1970 Tobin was president of the American Economic Association. He is also the author of this encyclopedia's article on monetary policy.

Selected Works

1958. "Liquidity Preference as Behavior Towards Risk." *Review of Economic Studies* 25, no. 67: 124–131.
1965. "On Improving the Economic Status of the Negro." *Daedalus* 94, no. 4: 878–897.
1966. *National Economic Policy.* New Haven: Yale University Press.
1974. *The New Economics One Decade Older.* Princeton: Princeton University Press.
1988 (edited with Murray Weidenbaum). *Two Revolutions in Economic Theory: The First Economic Reports of Presidents Kennedy and Reagan.* Cambridge: MIT Press.
1990. "One or Two Cheers for 'The Invisible Hand.'" *Dissent* (Spring): 229–236.

Anne-Robert-Jacques Turgot (1727–1781)

Turgot was the French Adam Smith. His *Reflections on the Production and Distribution of Wealth,* which predated Smith's *The Wealth of Nations* by ten years, argues against government intervention in the economic sector. Turgot recognized the function of the division of labor, investigated how prices were determined, and analyzed the origins of economic growth. Like François Quesnay, Turgot was a leading Physiocrat who attempted to reform the most stifling of his government's economic policies.

Probably Turgot's most important contribution to economics was to point out that capital is necessary for economic growth, and that the only way to accumulate capital is for people not to consume all they produce. Most capital, he believed, was accumulated by landowners who saved the surplus product after paying the cost of materials and of labor. Turgot agreed with Quesnay's notion of the cir-

cular flow of savings and investment, where savings in one period become investment in the next.

In *Reflections,* Turgot analyzed the interdependence of different rates of return and interest among different investments, noting that interest is determined by the supply and demand for capital. Although the rates of return on each investment may vary, he argued, in a competitive free-market economy with capital mobility, rates of return on all investments will tend toward equality:

> As soon as the profits resulting from an employment of money, whatever it may be, increase or diminish, capitals turn in that direction or withdraw from other employments, or withdraw and turn towards other employments, and this necessarily alters in each of these employments, the relation between the capital and the annual product. (p. 87)

Turgot distinguished between a commodity's market price—determined by supply and demand—and its "natural" price, the price it would tend to if industries were competitive and resources could be reallocated. An increase in demand, for example, could increase a good's price, but if resources were free to enter that industry, the new supply would bring the price back down to its "natural" level. In this reasoning Turgot anticipated Adam Smith.

Turgot also predated Smith in recognizing the importance of the division of labor for an economy's prosperity, and he was the first economist to recognize the law of diminishing marginal returns in agriculture. Predating the Marginalists by a century, he argued that "each increase [in an input] would be less and less productive."

Turgot applied many of his laissez-faire economic beliefs during his thirteen-year appointment (1761–1774) as chief administrator for the Limoges district under Louis XV and as minister of finance, trade, and public works from 1774 to 1776 under newly anointed Louis XVI. In the latter job one of his first measures was to abolish all restrictions on sales of grain within France, a measure the Physiocrats had long advocated. He ended the government's policy of conscripting labor to build and maintain roads, and replaced it with a more efficient tax in money. Milton Friedman has called the replacing of taxes in kind with taxes in money "one of the greatest advances in human freedom." Turgot abolished the guild system left over from medieval times. The guild system, like occupational licensing today, prevented workers from entering certain occupations without permission. Turgot also argued against the regulation of interest rates.

Louis XVI did not welcome Turgot's reforms and dismissed him in 1776. Some historians claim that had Turgot's reforms been kept, the French revolution might not have erupted thirteen years later.

Turgot himself never lived to witness the upheaval his own reforms might have helped thwart. He died in Paris of gout at age fifty-four.

Selected Works

1766. *Reflections on the Production and Distribution of Wealth.* Reprinted in P. D. Groenewegen, ed. and trans., *The Economics of A. R. J. Turgot.* The Hague: Martinus Nijhoff, 1977.

Thorstein Veblen (1857–1929)

Thorstein Veblen was odd man out in late-nineteenth- and early-twentieth-century American economics. His position on the fringe started early. Veblen grew up in a Norwegian immigrant farming community in Wisconsin. He spoke only Norwegian at home and did not learn English until his teens. He studied economics under John Bates Clark, a leading neoclassical economist, but rejected his ideas. He did his graduate work at Johns Hopkins University under Charles Sanders Peirce, the founder of the pragmatist school in philosophy, and at Yale University under laissez-faire proponent William Graham Sumner. He repudiated their views as well.

Veblen is best known for his book *The Theory of the Leisure Class,* which introduced the term "conspicuous consumption" (referring to consumption undertaken to make a statement to others about one's class or accomplishments). This term, more than any other, is what Veblen is known for.

Veblen did not reject economists' answers to the questions they posed; he simply thought their questions were too narrow. Veblen wanted economists to try to understand the social and cultural causes and effects of economic changes. What social and cultural causes were responsible for the shift from hunting and fishing to farming, for example, and what were the social and cultural effects of this shift? Veblen was singularly unsuccessful at getting economists to focus on such questions. His failure may explain the sarcastic tone his writing took toward his fellow economists.

Veblen had to struggle to stay in academia. In the late nineteenth century many universities were affiliated in a substantial way with churches. Veblen's skepticism about religion and his rough manners and unkempt appearance made him unattractive to such institutions. As a result, from 1884 to 1891 Veblen lived on the largesse of his family and his wife's family. His big break came in 1892 when the newly formed University of Chicago hired his mentor, J. Laurence Laughlin, who brought Veblen with him as a teaching assistant. Veblen later became the managing editor of the *Journal of Political Economy,* which was and is edited at the University of Chicago. Veblen spent fourteen years at Chicago and the next three at Stanford. He died in obscurity in 1929.

Selected Works

1899. *The Theory of the Leisure Class.* New York: Macmillan.
1904. *The Theory of Business Enterprise.* New York: Charles Scribner's Sons.

William S. Vickrey (1914–1996)

William Vickrey and JAMES MIRRLEES shared the 1993 Nobel Prize in economics "for their fundamental contributions to the economic theory of incentives under asymmetric information."

One of the most important economic principles is that incentives affect people's behavior. It is also true that government officials virtually never know as much about the people their policies affect as the people affected know about themselves. In economics, the fancy term for this fact is "asymmetric information." How, then, does a government that is conscious of its ignorance set up incentives so that people will act in ways that are useful, not only to themselves but also to others? William Vickrey spent his career studying this issue, in areas ranging from income taxation to auction design to subway fares and highway tolls. In the process, he made some striking discoveries.

Consider income taxation. Vickrey, himself a strong believer in using the tax system to take from the rich and give to the poor, saw that such forced transfers would reduce people's incentive to work. His 1964 textbook, *Microstatics,* was one of the first economics textbooks to take this issue seriously. He wrote:

> There still remains the fact that money income from gainful work is subject to an income tax while imputed income from leisure is not taxed.... Accordingly, an income tax tends to make individuals choose leisure in preference to gainful work to an uneconomical extent. (p. 261)

For that reason, Vickrey favored fairly low marginal tax rates on high-income people. And what should the marginal tax rate on the highest-skilled person be? In 1987, Vickrey, drawing on work by Mirrlees, wrote:

> A somewhat disturbing result is that if the distribution of skills has a known upper limit, the marginal tax rate

should fall to zero at the top of the scale where there is only one taxpayer left, the argument being that there is no point to deterring him from earning the last dollar of income, since if he does not earn it there will be no revenue from it. (p. 1024)

Supply-side economist Arthur Laffer could not have said it better.

Vickrey also did early work in the theory of sealed-bid auctions. He showed that a second-price auction, whereby the highest bidder gets the item but pays only the price bid by the second-highest bidder, causes the good to be allocated to the person who values it most. The reasoning is as follows. The highest bidder knows that he can bid the true value of the item to him because he will not have to pay that value if he wins. This gives him an incentive to bid what the item is truly worth. Every bidder has this same incentive. So every person ends up bidding the true value of the item to him, and the item thus goes to the person who values it most. Under the standard first-price auction, by contrast, the person who values the good most might underbid and actually bid less than someone who values it less. Second-price auctions are now called Vickrey auctions.

Tolls on roads and bridges were common in nineteenth-century America and were discussed in economics textbooks of the time. But that insight was lost to the modern era until Vickrey brought it back, showing that tolls that were higher during times of peak use would lessen congestion. Always an empirical as well as a theoretical economist, Vickrey gave the following reasoning about the tolls (in 1963 dollars) he advocated for Washington, D.C.:

> It turned out that for each additional car making a daily trip that contributes to the dominant flow, during the peak hour, an additional investment of $23,000 was projected. In other words, a man who bought a $3,000 car for the purpose of driving downtown to work every day would be asking the community, in effect, to match his $3,000 investment with $23,000 from general highway funds. (Vickrey 1963, p. 456)

Vickrey's solution—higher tolls at peak times—would have obviated the need for many new highway-widening projects because many drivers, faced with tolls that reflected the true cost of such projects, would instead use carpools or buses. Those left would enjoy relatively uncongested roads but would pay for them. Vickrey even suggested a futuristic technology that has become standard: "equipping all cars with an electronic identifier." As early as 1948, Vickrey suggested pricing solutions for hotels and airlines that look a lot like the "yield management" that modern airlines practice.

Vickrey was born in Victoria, British Columbia, but moved to the United States at an early age. He earned his B.S. in mathematics from Yale in 1935, his M.A. in economics from Columbia University in 1937, and his Ph.D. in economics from Columbia in 1947. He spent his career as a professor at Columbia and died three days after winning the Nobel Prize.

Selected Works

1939. "Averaging of Income for Income Tax Purposes." *Journal of Political Economy* 47: 379–397.
1947. *Agenda for Progressive Taxation.* New York: Ronald Press.
1948. "Some Objections to Marginal Cost Pricing." *Journal of Political Economy* 56: 218–238.
1955. "A Proposal for Revising New York's Subway Fare Structure." *Journal of the Operations Research Society of America* 3: 38–68.
1960. "Utility, Strategy and Social Decision Rules." *Quarterly Journal of Economics* 74: 507–535.
1961. "Counterspeculation, Auctions, and Competitive Sealed Tenders." *Journal of Finance* 16: 8–37.
1962. "Auctions and Bidding Games." In *Recent Advances in Game Theory.* Princeton University Conference, pp. 15–27.
1963. "Pricing in Urban and Suburban Transport." *American Economic Review* 52, no. 2: 452–465.
1964. *Microstatics.* New York: Harcourt, Brace, and World.
1987. "Progressive and Regressive Taxation." In John Eatwell, Murray Milgate, and Peter Newman, eds., *The New Palgrave: A Dictionary of Economics.* London: Macmillan. Vol. 3, pp. 1021–1025.
1992. "Today's Task for Economists." *American Economic Review* 82: 1–10.
1993. "My Innovative Failures in Economics." *Atlantic Economic Journal* 21: pp. 1–9.

Jacob Viner (1892–1970)

Economics historian Mark Blaug called Jacob Viner "the greatest historian of economic thought that ever lived." One of Viner's greatest accomplishments is his book *Studies in the Theory of International Trade*. This work is not just a history of the theory of international trade but also a guidebook that tells where the early economists who studied trade were wrong and where they were right. In it Viner decisively refuted fallacies of MERCANTILISM. Viner also wrote a famous 145-page introduction to an edition of John Rae's *Life of Adam Smith*.

Viner was an international trade theorist in his own right. His book *The Customs Union Issue* introduced the distinction between the trade-creating and the trade-diverting effects of customs unions (see INTERNATIONAL TRADE AGREEMENTS). His earliest book, *Dumping,* is a comprehensive analysis of the subject.

Viner is known for his view that the long run matters. Some of his best articles are reprinted in a 1958 book, *The Long View and the Short*. "No matter how refined and how elaborate the analysis," Viner wrote, "if it rests solely on the short view it will still be . . . a structure built on shifting sands." One of the articles included in Viner's book, "Cost Curves and Supply Curves," lays out the short-run and long-run cost curves that still show up in microeconomics texts.

Viner, who grew up in Montreal, was an undergraduate student at McGill University, where he studied economics under the famous Canadian humorist Stephen Leacock. He earned his Ph.D. at Harvard, writing his dissertation under international trade economist Frank W. Taussig. He was a professor at the University of Chicago from 1916 to 1917 and from 1919 until 1946. He moved to Princeton in 1946, where he taught until retiring in 1960. For many of his years at Chicago, Viner, along with Frank Knight, edited the *Journal of Political Economy*. Viner is not considered part of the Chicago school as he was much less sympathetic to free markets than his Chicago school colleagues.

Selected Works

1917. "Some Problems of Logical Method in Political Economy." *Journal of Political Economy* 25, no. 3: 236–260.
1923. *Dumping: A Problem in International Trade*. Chicago: University of Chicago Press.
1937. *Studies in the Theory of International Trade*. New York: Harper.
1950. *The Customs Union Issue*. New York: Carnegie Endowment for International Peace.
1958. *The Long View and the Short: Studies in Economic Theory and Policy*. Glencoe, Ill.: Free Press.
1965. "Guide to John Rae's *Life of Adam Smith*." Introduction to *Life of Adam Smith*. New York: Augustus M. Kelley.

Leon Walras (1834–1910)

Separately but almost simultaneously with William Stanley Jevons and Carl Menger, French economist Leon Walras developed the idea of marginal utility and is thus considered one of the founders of the "marginal revolution." But Walras's biggest contribution was in what is now called general equilibrium theory. Before Walras, economists had made little attempt to show how a whole econ-

omy with many goods fits together and reaches an equilibrium. Walras's goal was to do this. He did not succeed, but he took some major first steps. First, he built a system of simultaneous equations to describe his hypothetical economy, a tremendous task, and then showed that because the number of equations equaled the number of unknowns, the system could be solved to give the equilibrium prices and quantities of commodities. The demonstration that price and quantity were uniquely determined for each commodity is considered one of Walras's greatest contributions to economic science.

But Walras was aware that the mere fact that such a system of equations could be solved mathematically for an equilibrium did not mean that in the real world it would ever reach that equilibrium. So Walras's second major step was to simulate an artificial market process that would get the system to equilibrium, a process he called "*tâtonnement*" (French for "groping"). *Tâtonnement* was a trial-and-error process in which a price was called out and people in the market said how much they were willing to demand or supply at that price. If there was an excess of supply over demand, then the price would be lowered so that less would be supplied and more would be demanded. Thus would the prices "grope" toward equilibrium. To keep constant the equilibrium toward which prices were groping, Walras assumed—highly unrealistically—that no actual exchanges were made until equilibrium was reached. If, for example, people who wanted to buy ketchup wanted more than sellers were willing to sell, then they would buy none at all. This assumption limits the usefulness of Walras's simulated process as an aid to understanding how real markets work.

Walras's sole academic job was as an economics professor at the University of Lausanne in Switzerland. This location was not ideal: because the dominant thinking in economics at the time was in Britain, it was difficult for Walras to affect the rest of the profession. Also, because his students were more interested in becoming lawyers than in becoming economists, Walras did not have disciples. Although his impact on economics was limited during his lifetime, it has been much greater since the 1930s. Historian of economic thought Mark Blaug wrote that Walras "may now be the most widely-read nineteenth century economist after Ricardo and Marx."[1]

Walras's father, the French economist Auguste Walras, encouraged his son to pursue economics with a particular emphasis on mathematics. After sampling several careers—he was for a while a student at the school of mines,

1. Mark Blaug, *Great Economists before Keynes* (Atlantic Highlands, N.J.: Humanities Press International, 1986), p. 262.

a journalist, a lecturer, a railway clerk, a bank director, and a published romance novelist—Walras eventually returned to the study and teaching of economics. In that scientific discipline Walras claimed to have found "pleasures and joys like those that religion provides to the faithful." Walras retired in 1902 at age fifty-eight.

Selected Works

1954. *Elements of Pure Economics.* Translated and annotated by William Jaffe. London: Allen and Unwin.

Max Weber (1864–1920)

Max Weber was one of the founding fathers of sociology. In his most famous book, *The Protestant Ethic and the Spirit of Capitalism,* he claimed that the seeds of capitalism were in the Protestant work ethic.

But Weber was also an economist who saw the distinctive feature of advanced capitalism, as in his pre–World War I Germany, in the extensive division of labor and a hierarchical administration that resembled the political bureaucracy. The two features together had created a new middle class whose position depended on neither physical capital nor labor, but on their HUMAN CAPITAL. Even in advanced capitalism, though, Weber considered the major source of progress to be risk taking by businessmen and entrepreneurs.

Weber accepted Ludwig von Mises's criticism of socialist economic planning and added his own argument. He believed that under socialism workers would still work in a hierarchy, but that hierarchy would be fused with government. Instead of dictatorship of the worker, he foresaw dictatorship of the official.

Like David Hume before him, Weber believed in the possibility of value-free social science. By that he meant that one could not draw conclusions about the way the world should be simply from studying the way the world is. Weber did not rule out normative analysis as being feasible or worthwhile—he believed in rational discussion of values—he simply wanted economists to distinguish between facts and values.

Born in Germany, Weber studied law and went on to do graduate work with a dissertation on medieval trading companies in Italy and Spain. He was appointed to a chair in political economy at Freiburg in 1894, and to another chair in political economy at Heidelberg in 1896. He suffered a nervous breakdown in 1898 and did not continue his scholarly work until 1904. From 1904 on he was a private scholar, mostly in Heidelberg.

Selected Works

1904. *The Protestant Ethic and the Spirit of Capitalism.* Reprint. London: Allen and Unwin, 1930.
1918. "Socialism." Reprinted in *Weber Selections in Translation.* Edited by W. G. Runciman. Cambridge: Cambridge University Press, 1978.

Knut Wicksell (1851–1926)

Economist Knut Wicksell made his name among the Swedish public with a series of provocative lectures on the causes of prostitution, drunkenness, poverty, and overpopulation. A MALTHUSIAN, the young Wicksell advocated birth control as the cure for these social ills. His image as a radical social reformer did much to attract the attention of the press and the Young Socialists with whom he sympathized. But his rejection of MARX and MARXISM limited his popularity.

Wicksell was not so much an innovator as a synthesizer. His integration and refinement of existing microeconomic theories helped earn Wicksell recognition as the "economists' economist." In his 1893 book, *Value, Capital, and Rent,* Wicksell analyzed and praised the Austrian theory of capital as elaborated by Eugen von Böhm-Bawerk. In the first volume of his *Lectures on Political Economy* Wicksell concluded that Böhm-Bawerk's idea of roundaboutness did not make sense, and agreed with Irving Fisher that waiting was a sufficient explanation for interest rates.

Wicksell also laid out marginal productivity theory, the theory that the payment to each factor of production equals that factor's marginal product. Economists Philip Wicksteed, Enrico Barone, and John Bates Clark had already elaborated this theory, but Wicksell's exposition of it was superior. Wicksell also emphasized that an efficient allocation of resources is not necessarily just, because the allocation depends on the preexisting distribution of income, and nothing guarantees that this preexisting distribution is just.

Wicksell is best known for *Interest and Prices,* his contribution to the fledgling field now called macroeconomics. In this book and in his 1906 *Lectures in Political Economy,* volume 2, Wicksell sketched out his version of the quantity theory of money (monetarism). The standard view of the quantity theory before Wicksell was that increases in the money supply have a direct effect on prices—more money chasing the same amount of goods. Wicksell focused on the indirect effect. In elaborating this effect, Wicksell distinguished between the real rate of return on new capital (Wicksell called this the "natural rate of interest") and the actual market rate of interest. He argued that if the banks reduced the rate of interest below the real rate of return on capital, the amount of loan capital demanded would increase and the amount of saving supplied would fall. Investment, which equaled saving before the interest rate fell, would exceed saving at the lower rate. The increase in investment would increase overall spending, thus driving up prices. This "cumulative process" of inflation would stop only when the banks' reserves had fallen to their legal or desired limit, whichever was higher.

In laying out this theory, Wicksell began the conversion of the old quantity theory into a full-blown theory of prices. The Stockholm school, of which Wicksell was the father figure, ran with this insight and developed its own version of macroeconomics. In some ways this version resembled later Keynesian economics. Among the young Swedish economists who learned from Wicksell were Bertil Ohlin, Gunnar Myrdal, and Dag Hammarskjöld, later secretary general of the United Nations.

For much of his adult life, Wicksell depended on several small inheritances, grants, and the meager income earned through public lectures and publications. Not until 1886, when he was awarded a major grant, did he begin to pursue economics seriously. With financial support secured, Wicksell traveled to universities in London, Strasbourg, Vienna, Berlin, and Paris. By 1890 Wicksell had returned to Stockholm, but being "too notorious" and unqualified to teach—he held degrees in mathematics, but economics instructors were then required to have formal degrees in law and economics—he returned to freelance writing and lecturing.

In 1900, when Wicksell was forty-eight years old, he was granted his first teaching position at the University of Lund, which he retained until his retirement in 1916. His quirky habits, friendly demeanor, and willingness to actively defend his beliefs earned him respect and popularity among his students. Throughout his lifetime Wicksell never lost his penchant for radicalism. He forfeited a professorship by refusing to sign the application with the conventional "Your Majesty's most obedient servant." In 1910 he was jailed for two months by the Swedish government for a satirical public lecture he delivered on the Immaculate Conception. In spite of his disdain for ceremony and fanfare, his common-law widow consented to an extravagant funeral upon his death at age seventy-four.

Selected Works

1893. *Value, Capital and Rent*. Translated by S. H. Frowein. London: Allen and Unwin, 1954. Reprint. New York: Augustus M. Kelley, 1970.

1901. *Lectures on Political Economy*. Vol. 1. Translated by E. Classen. London: Routledge and Kegan Paul, 1934.

1906. *Lectures on Political Economy*. Vol. 2. Translated by E. Classen. London: Routledge and Kegan Paul, 1935.

1907. "The Influence of the Rate of Interest on Prices." *Economic Journal* 17: 213–220.

Appendixes

Nobel Memorial Prize Winners in Economic Sciences

The Nobel Prize was established by the will of Alfred Nobel (1833–1896), the Swedish chemist who invented dynamite, to recognize humanitarian endeavors in physics, chemistry, physiology or medicine, literature, and peace. A prize in economics was introduced in 1969 after the Bank of Sweden donated funds for its monetary awards. In 1992 the economic prize carried a cash award of approximately $1.5 million.

Nominations for the prize are solicited by invitation only, with more than a thousand invitations per prize category, and require a written statement in support of the nomination. Committees then evaluate the nominees and make their recommendations to the appropriate prize-awarding organization. All the selection work for the Nobel Prize is conducted in secrecy. The prize in economics is awarded by the Royal Swedish Academy of Sciences. To date, thirty-two Americans have been honored with the prize.

The following individuals have been awarded the Nobel Prize in economics:

1969: Ragnar Frisch, Jan Tinbergen
1970: Paul Samuelson
1971: Simon Kuznets
1972: Kenneth Arrow, John Hicks
1973: Wassily Leontief
1974: Friedrich A. Hayek, Gunnar Myrdal
1975: Leonid Kantorovich, Tjalling C. Koopmans
1976: Milton Friedman
1977: James Meade, Bertil Ohlin
1978: Herbert Simon
1979: W. Arthur Lewis, Theodore Schultz
1980: Lawrence Klein
1981: James Tobin
1982: George Stigler
1983: Gerard Debreu
1984: Richard Stone
1985: Franco Modigliani
1986: James M. Buchanan
1987: Robert Solow
1988: Maurice Allais

1989: Trygve Haavelmo
1990: Harry Markowitz, Merton Miller, William Sharpe
1991: Ronald H. Coase
1992: Gary S. Becker
1993: Robert W. Fogel, Douglass C. North
1994: John C. Harsanyi, John F. Nash Jr., Reinhard Selten
1995: Robert E. Lucas Jr.
1996: James A. Mirrlees, William Vickrey
1997: Robert C. Merton, Myron S. Scholes
1998: Amartya Sen
1999: Robert A. Mundell
2000: James J. Heckman, Daniel L. McFadden
2001: George A. Akerlof, A. Michael Spence, Joseph E. Stiglitz
2002: Daniel Kahneman, Vernon L. Smith
2003: Robert F. Engle, Clive W. J. Granger
2004: Finn E. Kydland, Edward C. Prescott
2005: Robert J. Aumann, Thomas C. Schelling
2006: Edmund S. Phelps

Chairmen of the Council of Economic Advisers

The Council of Economic Advisers (CEA) is among the most prestigious groups of applied economists in the United States. Formed after World War II, the CEA advises the U.S. president on economic policy. Presidents tend to appoint the three members, including the chairman, from their own party; but the advice given is relatively nonpartisan. Below the chairman and the two members are approximately fifteen senior and junior economists who are appointed for their expertise in policy economics. On macroeconomics, the big difference between Democrat-appointed chairmen and members and Republican-appointed chairmen and members has been on the potency of monetary and fiscal policies. Although more and more economists, Republicans and Democrats alike, have over the last few decades come to believe that monetary policy is more potent than fiscal policy, Democrat-appointed chairmen and members have put more weight on fiscal policy than Republican-appointed chairmen and members. On many microeconomic issues, CEA economists at all levels and in Republican and Democrat councils agree. They favor free trade and free markets and tend to oppose price controls and regulation, although President Bill Clinton's first council chairman, Laura Tyson, was a notable exception on free trade.

Council chairmen and their dates of employment (with the president under whom they worked in parentheses) are listed below.

Edwin G. Nourse (Truman), 1946–1949
Leon H. Keyserling (Truman), 1950–1953
Arthur F. Burns (Eisenhower), 1953–1956
Raymond J. Saulnier (Eisenhower), 1956–1961
Walter W. Heller (Kennedy, Johnson), 1961–1964
Gardner Ackley (Johnson), 1964–1968
Arthur M. Okun (Johnson), 1968–1969
Paul W. McCracken (Nixon), 1969–1971
Herbert Stein (Nixon), 1972–1974
Alan Greenspan (Ford), 1974–1977
Charles L. Schultze (Carter), 1977–1981
Murray L. Weidenbaum (Reagan), 1981–1982

Martin Feldstein (Reagan), 1982–1984
Beryl W. Sprinkel (Reagan), 1985–1989
Michael J. Boskin (Bush), 1989–1993
Laura Tyson (Clinton), 1993–1995
Joseph E. Stiglitz (Clinton), 1995–1997
Janet Yellen (Clinton), 1997–1999
Martin N. Baily (Clinton), 1999–2001
R. Glenn Hubbard (Bush), 2001–2003
N. Gregory Mankiw (Bush), 2003–2005
Ben Bernanke (Bush), 2005–2006
Edward P. Lazear (Bush), 2006–

Presidents of the American Economic Association

The American Economic Association (AEA) is the largest organization of professional economists in the world. It was organized at Saratoga, New York, on September 9, 1885. The title of president of the AEA is one of the highest honors that can be bestowed on an economist. The following are the past presidents of the AEA and their years of service (with their university or institute affiliations in parentheses).

Francis A. Walker (MIT), 1886–1892
Charles F. Dunbar (Harvard), 1893
John B. Clark (Columbia), 1894–1895
Henry C. Adams (Michigan), 1896–1897
Arthur T. Hadley (Yale), 1898–1899
Richard T. Ely (Wisconsin), 1900–1901
Edwin R. A. Seligman (Columbia), 1902–1903
Frank W. Taussig (Harvard), 1904–1905
Jeremiah W. Jenks (Cornell), 1906–1907
Simon N. Patten (Pennsylvania), 1908
Davis R. Dewey (MIT), 1909
Edmund J. James (Illinois), 1910
Henry W. Farnam (Yale), 1911
Frank A. Fetter (Princeton), 1912
David Kinley (Illinois), 1913
John H. Gray (Minnesota), 1914
Walter F. Willcox (Cornell), 1915
Thomas N. Carver (Harvard), 1916
John R. Commons (Wisconsin), 1917
Irving Fisher (Yale), 1918
Henry B. Gardner (Brown), 1919
Herbert J. Davenport (Cornell), 1920
Jacob H. Hollander (Johns Hopkins), 1921
Henry R. Seager (Columbia), 1922
Carl C. Plehn (California), 1923
Wesley C. Mitchell (Columbia), 1924
Allyn A. Young (Harvard), 1925
Edwin W. Kemmerer (Princeton), 1926
Thomas S. Adams (Yale), 1927
Fred M. Taylor (Michigan), 1928
Edwin F. Gay (Harvard), 1929
Matthew B. Hammond (Ohio State), 1930
Ernest L. Bogart (Illinois), 1931
George E. Barnett (Johns Hopkins), 1932
William Z. Ripley (Harvard), 1933
Harry A. Millis (Chicago), 1934
John M. Clark (Columbia), 1935
Alvin S. Johnson (New School), 1936

Oliver M. W. Sprague (Harvard), 1937
Alvin H. Hansen (Harvard), 1938
Jacob Viner (Chicago), 1939
Frederick C. Mills (Columbia), 1940
Sumner H. Slichter (Harvard), 1941
Edwin G. Nourse (Brookings), 1942
Albert B. Wolfe (Ohio State), 1943
Joseph S. Davis (Stanford), 1944
I. L. Sharfman (Michigan), 1945
E. A. Goldenweiser (Institute for Advanced Study), 1946
Paul H. Douglas (Chicago), 1947
Joseph A. Schumpeter (Harvard), 1948
Howard S. Ellis (California), 1949
Frank H. Knight (Chicago), 1950
John H. Williams (Harvard), 1951
Harold A. Innis (Toronto), 1952
Calvin B. Hoover (Duke), 1953
Simon Kuznets (Pennsylvania), 1954
John D. Black (Harvard), 1955
Edwin E. Witte (Wisconsin), 1956
Morris A. Copeland (Cornell), 1957
George W. Stocking (Vanderbilt), 1958
Arthur F. Burns (Columbia), 1959
Theodore W. Schultz (Chicago), 1960
Paul A. Samuelson (MIT), 1961
Edward S. Mason (Harvard), 1962
Gottfried Haberler (Harvard), 1963
George J. Stigler (Chicago), 1964
Joseph J. Spengler (Duke), 1965
Fritz Machlup (Princeton), 1966
Milton Friedman (Chicago), 1967
Kenneth E. Boulding (Colorado), 1968
William J. Fellner (Yale), 1969
Wassily Leontief (Harvard), 1970
James Tobin (Yale), 1971
John Kenneth Galbraith (Harvard), 1972
Kenneth J. Arrow (Harvard), 1973
Walter W. Heller (Minnesota), 1974

Robert Aaron Gordon (California), 1975
Franco Modigliani (MIT), 1976
Lawrence R. Klein (Pennsylvania), 1977
Jacob Marschak (UCLA), 1978
Tjalling C. Koopmans (Yale), 1978
Robert M. Solow (MIT), 1979
Moses Abramovitz (Stanford), 1980
William J. Baumol (Princeton), 1981
Gardner Ackley (Michigan), 1982
W. Arthur Lewis (Princeton), 1983
Charles L. Schultze (Brookings), 1984
Charles P. Kindleberger (MIT), 1985
Alice M. Rivlin (Brookings), 1986
Gary S. Becker (Chicago), 1987
Robert Eisner (Northwestern), 1988
Joseph A. Pechman (Brookings), 1989

Gerard Debreu (California), 1990
Thomas C. Schelling (Maryland), 1991
William Vickrey (Columbia), 1992
Zvi Griliches (Harvard), 1993
Amartya K. Sen (Harvard), 1994
Victor R. Fuchs (Stanford), 1995
Anne O. Krueger (Stanford), 1996
Arnold C. Harberger (UCLA), 1997
Robert W. Fogel (Chicago), 1998
D. Gale Johnson (Chicago), 1999
Dale W. Jorgenson (Harvard), 2000
Sherwin Rosen (Chicago), 2001
Robert E. Lucas Jr. (Chicago), 2002
Peter A. Diamond (MIT), 2003
Martin S. Feldstein (NBER, Harvard), 2004
Daniel McFadden (California), 2005

Contributors

Armen A. Alchian, University of California at Los Angeles
Property Rights

Richard Alm, Federal Reserve Bank of Dallas
Creative Destruction (with W. Michael Cox)

Terry L. Anderson, PERC: The Property and Environment Research Center
Environmental Quality

Anders Åslund, Peterson Institute for International Economics
Transition Economies

Sue Ann Batey Blackman, Princeton University
Natural Resources (with William J. Baumol)

William J. Baumol, Princeton University; New York University
Natural Resources (with Sue Anne Batey Blackman)

Gary S. Becker, University of Chicago; Stanford University, Hoover Institution
Human Capital

Paul Bergin, University of California at Davis; National Bureau of Economic Research
Monetary Union

Jagdish Bhagwati, Columbia University; Council on Foreign Relations
Protectionism

George Bittlingmayer, University of Kansas, School of Finance
Advertising

Alan S. Blinder, Princeton University
Free Trade
Keynesian Economics

Walter Block, Loyola University
Rent Control

Peter J. Boettke, George Mason University
Austrian School of Economics

Michael D. Bordo, Rutgers University
Gold Standard

George J. Borjas, Harvard University, Kennedy School of Government
Immigration

Michael J. Boskin, Stanford University, Hoover Institution
Consumer Price Indexes

Donald J. Boudreaux, George Mason University
Comparative Advantage
Information and Prices

Bryan Caplan, George Mason University
Communism
Externalities

Don Coursey, University of Chicago, Harris School of Public Policy
Experimental Economics

Tyler Cowen, George Mason University
Arts
Public Goods

Braden Cox, Competitive Enterprise Institute
Airline Deregulation (with Fred L. Smith Jr.)

W. Michael Cox, Federal Reserve Bank of Dallas
Creative Destruction (with Richard Alm)

Robert W. Crandall, Brookings Institution
Pollution Controls

Andrew R. Dick, CRA International
Cartels

Avinash Dixit, Princeton University
Game Theory (with Barry Nalebuff)
Prisoners' Dilemma (with Barry Nalebuff)

Stanislav Dolgopolov, University of Michigan School of Law
Insider Trading

Al Ehrbar, EVA Advisers, LLC
Consumption Tax
Supply

Kimberly Ann Elliott, Institute for International Economics
Sanctions (with Gary Clyde Hufbauer and Barbara Oegg)

Bert Ely, Ely and Company
Financial Regulation
Savings and Loan Crisis

Alexander J. Field, Santa Clara University
Productivity

Leslie R. Fine, Information Dynamics Lab at HP Labs
Auctions

Jeffrey A. Frankel, Harvard University, Kennedy School of Government
Foreign Exchange

David D. Friedman, Santa Clara University, School of Law
Crime

Claudia Goldin, Harvard University; National Bureau of Economic Research
Gender Gap

John C. Goodman, National Center for Policy Analysis
Health Insurance

Linda Gorman, Independence Institute
Discrimination
Education
Minimum Wages

Kevin Grier, University of Oklahoma
Empirics of Economic Growth

James D. Gwartney, Florida State University
Supply-Side Economics

Arnold C. Harberger, University of California at Los Angeles; University of Chicago
Microeconomics

Garrett Hardin, University of California at Santa Barbara
Tragedy of the Commons

John Haring, Independant consultant
Telecommunications

Kevin Hassett, American Enterprise Institute
Investment

Thomas W. Hazlett, George Mason University
Apartheid

Robert Heilbroner, 1919–2005
Socialism

David R. Henderson, Stanford University, Hoover Institution; Naval Postgraduate School, Graduate School of Business and Public Policy
Demand
German Economic Miracle
Opportunity Cost
Present Value
Rent Seeking

Robert Hessen, Stanford University, Hoover Institution
Capitalism
Corporations

Paul Heyne, 1931–2000
Efficiency

Stephen R. C. Hicks, Rockford College
Ethics and Economics

Robert Higgs, Independent Institute
Government Growth

Jack Hirshleifer, 1925–2005
Disaster and Recovery

Charles L. Hooper, Objective Insights, Inc.
Pharmaceuticals: Economics and Regulation

Kevin D. Hoover, Duke University
New Classical Macroeconomics
Phillips Curve

Gary Clyde Hufbauer, Institute for International Economics
Sanctions (with Kimberly Ann Elliott and Barbara Oegg)

Saul H. Hymans, University of Michigan
Forecasting and Econometric Models

Douglas A. Irwin, Dartmouth College
International Trade Agreements

Christopher Jehn, Cray Inc.
Conscription

Jeffrey M. Jones, Stanford University, Hoover Institution
Welfare (with Thomas MaCurdy)

Steven L. Jones, Indiana University, Kelley School of Business
Efficient Capital Markets (with Jeffry M. Netter)

Wolfgang Kasper, University of New South Wales
Competition
Spatial Economics

George G. Kaufman, Loyola University
Bank Runs

Benjamin Klein, University of California at Los Angeles; LECG
Brand Names

Daniel B. Klein, George Mason University; Ratio Institute
Consumer Protection

Arnold Kling, Independent journalist and author
International Trade

Randall S. Kroszner, University of Chicago, Graduate School of Business; Federal Reserve Board
Corporate Governance

Laurence J. Kotlikoff, Boston University
Saving

Laura LaHaye, Illinois Institute of Technology
Mercantilism

Deepak Lal, University of California at Los Angeles; University College, London
Foreign Aid

Robert A. Lawson, Capital University
Economic Freedom

Dwight R. Lee, University of Georgia, Terry College of Business
"Redistribution"

Ronald Demos Lee, University of California at Berkeley
Population

Frank Levy, Massachusetts Institute of Technology
Distribution of Income

Stan Liebowitz, University of Texas at Dallas
Intellectual Property
Internet

Robert Litan, Kaufman Institution; Brookings Institution
Regulation

Jonathan R. Macey, Yale University, School of Law
Market for Corporate Control

Thomas MaCurdy, Stanford University, Hoover Institution
Welfare (with Jeffrey M. Jones)

Burton G. Malkiel, Princeton University
Interest Rates

N. Gregory Mankiw, Harvard University
New Keynesian Economics

Bennett T. McCallum, Carnegie Mellon University, Tepper School of Business
Monetarism

Fred McChesney, Northwestern University, School of Law
Antitrust

Henry McMillan, Pacific Life Insurance
Pensions

François Melese, Defense Resources Management Institute, Naval Postgraduate School
Corruption

Robert J. Michaels, California State University at Fullerton
Electricity and Its Regulation
Natural Gas: Markets and Regulation

Gregory J. Millman, Independent journalist and author
Futures and Options Markets

Jeffrey Milyo, University of Missouri, Columbia
Campaign Finance

Joseph J. Minarik, Committee for Economic Development
  Taxation
Stephen Moore, *Wall Street Journal*
  Capital Gains Taxes
Thomas Gale Moore, Stanford University, Hoover
  Institution
  Global Warming: A Balance Sheet
  Surface Freight Transportation Deregulation
Michael A. Morrisey, University of Alabama at Birmingham
  Health Care
Sendhil Mullainathan, Harvard University
  Behavioral Economics (with Richard H. Thaler)
Barry Nalebuff, Yale University
  Game Theory (with Avinash Dixit)
  Prisoners' Dilemma (with Avinash Dixit)
Clark Nardinelli, U.S. Food and Drug Administration
  Industrial Revolution and the Standard of Living
Jeffry M. Netter, University of Georgia, Terry College of
  Business
  Efficient Capital Markets (with Steven L. Jones)
Rob Norton, Independent author and consultant
  Corporate Taxation
  Unintended Consequences
John V. C. Nye, Washington University, St. Louis; and George
  Mason University
  Standards of Living and Modern Economic Growth
Barbara Oegg, formerly with the Institute for International
  Economics
  Sanctions (with Kimberly Ann Elliott and
  Gary Clyde Hufbauer)
Mack Ott, Independent international economic consultant
  International Capital Flows
  National Income Accounts
Robert W. Poole Jr., Reason Foundation
  Privatization
Paul R. Portney, University of Arizona, Eller College of
  Management
  Benefit-Cost Analysis
Annette Poulsen, University of Georgia, Terry School of
  Business
  Corporate Financial Structure
Benjamin Powell, San Jose State University; Independent
  Institute
  Housing (with Edward Stringham)
  Japan
David Prychitko, Northern Michigan University
  Marxism
Alan Reynolds, Cato Institute
  Marginal Tax Rates
Morgan O. Reynolds, Texas A&M University
  Labor Unions
Steven E. Rhoads, University of Virginia
  Marginalism
Sheldon Richman, Foundation for Economic Education
  Fascism

Russell Roberts, George Mason University
  Charity
Hugh Rockoff, Rutgers University
  Price Controls
Christina D. Romer, University of California at Berkeley
  Business Cycles
Paul M. Romer, Stanford University, Graduate School of
  Business
  Economic Growth
Murray N. Rothbard, 1926–1995
  Free Market
Paul H. Rubin, Emory University
  Law and Economics
Michael K. Salemi, University of North Carolina at
  Chapel Hill
  Hyperinflation
Timothy Sandefur, Pacific Legal Foundation, Economic
  Liberty Project
  Innovation
Thomas J. Sargent, Stanford University, Hoover Institution;
  New York University
  Rational Expectations
Thomas R. Saving, Texas A&M University
  Social Security
Isabel V. Sawhill, Brookings Institution
  Poverty in America
Anna J. Schwartz, National Bureau of Economic Research
  Money Supply
Gerald W. Scully, University of Texas at Dallas
  Sports
John J. Seater, North Carolina State University, College of
  Management
  Government Debt and Deficits
Jane S. Shaw, J. W. Pope Center for Higher Education Policy
  Recycling
William F. Shughart II, University of Mississippi
  Industrial Concentration
  Public Choice
Jeremy J. Siegel, University of Pennsylvania, Wharton
  School
  Stock Market
Kenneth A. Small, University of California at Irvine
  Urban Transportation
Gene Smiley, Marquette University
  Great Depression
Clifford W. Smith, University of Rochester, William E. Simon
  Graduate School of Business Administration
  Bonds
Fred L. Smith, Competitive Enterprise Institute
  Airline Deregulation (with Braden Cox)
Russell S. Sobel, West Virginia University
  Entrepreneurship
Seiji S. C. Steimetz, California State University at
  Long Beach
  Bubbles

Herbert Stein, 1916–1999
  Balance of Payments
George J. Stigler, 1911–1991
  Monopoly
Joseph E. Stiglitz, Columbia University
  Information
Edward Stringham, San Jose State University
  Housing (with Benjamin Powell)
Richard Stroup, Montana State University; PERC: The
  Property and Environment Research Center
  Free-Market Environmentalism
  Political Behavior
Lawrence H. Summers, Harvard University
  Unemployment
Daniel A. Sumner, University of California at Davis
  Agricultural Subsidy Programs
Jerry Taylor, Cato Institute
  Energy (with Peter Van Doren)
Richard H. Thaler, University of Chicago, Graduate School of
  Business
  Behavioral Economics (with Sendhil Mullainathan)
Lester C. Thurow, Massachusetts Institute of Technology,
  Sloan School of Management
  Profits
Richard H. Timberlake, University of Georgia
  Federal Reserve System
James Tobin, 1918–2002
  Monetary Policy

Robert Tollison, Clemson University
  Sportometrics
Marian L. Tupy, Cato Institute
  European Union
Peter Van Doren, Editor, *Regulation*
  Energy (with Jerry Taylor)
W. Kip Viscusi, Vanderbilt University
  Job Safety
  Liability
David N. Weil, Brown University
  Fiscal Policy
Lawrence H. White, University of Missouri at St. Louis
  Competing Money Supplies
  Inflation
Aaron Wildavsky, 1930–1993
  Risk and Safety (with Adam Wildavsky)
Adam Wildavsky, Google, Inc.
  Risk and Safety (with Aaron Wildavsky)
Glenn Yago, Milken Institute
  Junk Bonds
Richard Zeckhauser, Harvard University, John F. Kennedy
  School of Government
  Insurance
Benjamin Zycher, Manhattan Institute for Policy Research
  Defense
  OPEC
Todd J. Zywicki, George Mason University, School of Law
  Bankruptcy

Index

AAA (Agricultural Adjustment Act of 1933), 4, 173, 232–33

abortion, 325, 588

accidents: causes, 324; deaths, 446; rates, 327. *See also* job safety; tort law

accounting: internal controls, 91; sources-of-growth, 593; standards, 386

accounting firms: auditors, 91; regulation of, 91; savings and loan audits, 462

accounting scandals, 90, 98

acquisitions. *See* mergers; takeovers

activity analysis, 552

Adenauer, Konrad, 218

adverse selection, 282

advertising, 1–4; as barrier to entry, 2–3; competing with, 74; deceptive, 2; economic function, 1–2, 269; expenditures, 1; government, 3; history, 1; image, 2; price, 3; of quality, 82; ratios to sales, 1; regulation of, 3; relationship to profit, 3; seen as brainwashing, 59; television, 303–4; on Web sites, 303–4

AFDC (Aid to Families with Dependent Children), 408, 511. *See also* welfare system

affirmative action, 118–19, 216

Africa: average incomes, 146; economic freedom, 125; foreign aid, 194; government corruption, 99, 122, 194. *See also individual countries*

African Americans: civil rights movement, 119; effects of New Deal policies, 233, 572–73; poverty rates, 406; segregation, 118, 119, 572; strikebreakers, 321; wages, 117, 543

African National Congress Party, 18

Afrikaners, 15

Aftalion, Albert, 305

agency costs, 87–88, 89, 334, 335

Agent Orange, 327–28

aggregate demand: externalities, 379; fiscal policy influences, 183, 184, 185, 355, 483, 557; fluctuations and business cycles, 49; influences on, 316; Keynesian view, 376, 483, 550

aging. *See* elderly; retirement

Agricultural Adjustment Act (AAA) of 1933, 4, 173, 232–33

agricultural subsidy programs, 4–6; costs, 4, 438; criticism of, 4, 427; economic impact, 5, 166, 580; in European Union, 5, 166; forms, 4, 5; impact on international trade, 5–6; impact on prices, 166, 437; in OECD countries, 4–5, 427; parity prices, 344; reductions, 6; supporters, 4, 429, 438–39; in United States, 4, 5, 344, 437, 438–39; wool, 398

agriculture: cartels, 63; commodity futures, 207, 208, 209; in developing countries, 6, 557, 585–86; diminishing marginal returns, 599; effects of global warming, 220; employment, 102–3; in European Union, 5, 166; international trade, 5–6, 427; land rents, 580; New Deal programs, 4, 173, 232–33, 572–73; productivity growth, 102–3, 403; share of labor force, 403, 417–18; in Soviet Union, 66, 423; tenant farmers, 233; trade barriers, 5, 342, 427

Aid to Families with Dependent Children (AFDC), 408, 511. *See also* welfare system

aircraft: manufacturing, 326; military, 110

Air Force, U.S., 110

Airline Deregulation Act of 1978, 6

airline industry: cartel, 74; competition, 7; deregulation, 6–10, 60, 440; freight transportation, 487; growth, 7; hub-and-spoke system, 7, 8; low-cost carriers, 7, 8; mergers, 8; national ownership rules, 10; "Open Skies" agreements, 9–10; political control of grid, 8–9; profitability, 8; regulation, 6, 7–8, 9–10; subsidies, 10; yield management, 601

air pollution: controls, 170, 210, 399–400, 401–2, 441; effects of fuel efficiency standards, 153; futures, 210. *See also* environmental damage

airports, 9, 168–69

air traffic control, 9

Air Transport Association, 8, 9

Air Transportation Stabilization Board (ATSB), 10

Akerlof, George A., 521

Alchian, Armen A., 24, 522–23

Allais, Maurice, 523

all-volunteer forces (AVFs), 76, 77

altruism: actions based in, 34–35, 64; environmental quality and, 163; moral value, 162; among voters, 398. *See also* charity

aluminum: prices, 373; recycling, 162, 435

American Stock Exchange (Amex), 479

American Trucking Association, 486

Anchorage earthquake, 114

Angola, civil war, 455

antidumping duties, 426–27

antitrust, 11–14; criticism of, 11–13, 365; effects, 8, 13–14; enforcement, 12, 13–14, 62–63, 260, 366, 587, 594; exemptions, 13, 474; issues in sports, 474, 475; laws, 11, 13, 14, 58, 259; merger reviews, 260; origins, 11, 59; practices outlawed, 11; suspension of enforcement during Great Depression, 234. *See also* mergers; monopolies

apartheid, 14–19; colour bar, 15–17; created by white workers, 15, 16–17, 116; decline, 17–18; effects of international sanctions, 18, 452; implementation, 17; origins, 15–17

arbitrage: costs, 268; covered interest, 199; in foreign exchange, 528; locational, 469–70; price differences eliminated by, 268; in sports, 472

Arca/EX, 335

ARCH (autoregressive conditional heteroskedasticity), 530–31

Argentina: government debt default, 186; hyperinflation, 253; privatization, 414, 415

Army, U.S., 110

Army Corps of Engineers, 487

Arrow, Kenneth: biography, 523–24; impossibility theorem, 428, 523, 588

arts, 19–21; donations to nonprofit organizations, 19, 64; economic principles and, 19–21; innovations, 21; international trade in, 20; subsidies, 20

asbestos, 311, 326–28

Asia: average incomes, 147; male-female ratio, 588–89. *See also individual countries*

asset prices: based on present value of future cash flows, 138, 478; relationship to replacement costs, 598. *See also* efficient markets theory; stock prices asymmetric information: incentives under, 568, 600; in insurance market, 596; in markets, 88, 96, 268, 282, 521, 596–97; about stock values, 88, 96; on worker productivity, 594

AT&T, 366

athletes, behavior of, 471–73. *See also* sports

ATSB (Air Transportation Stabilization Board), 10

auctions, 21–23; of airport landing and takeoff rights, 168–69; definition, 21; Dutch, 21, 22, 168, 593; economic experiments, 168, 592–93; English, 21, 22, 168, 592–93; sealed-bid, 21–22, 592–93, 601; types, 21–22, 592–93, 601; Vickrey (second-price), 21–22, 601; of wireless bandwidth, 22–23

auditors, regulation of, 91

Audubon Society, 204

Australia: immigration, 256; minimum wages, 346, 347; trade embargo on France, 453

Austrian School of Economics, 23–27; business cycle theory, 26, 569; contemporary economists, 24; history, 23–24; leading figures, 23, 24, 526–27, 565, 569; propositions, 24–27; view of information and markets, 269. *See also* Hayek, Friedrich August; marginalism; Mises, Ludwig von

automatic stabilizers, 184

automobiles: accident rates, 327; electric, 150; emissions standards, 400; fuel efficiency, 153, 374; insurance, 281, 283; Japanese industry, 309, 426; safety regulation, 440; voluntary export restrictions, 426; warranties, 521

autoregressive conditional heteroskedasticity (ARCH), 530–31

AVFs (all-volunteer forces), 76, 77

baby boomers: in labor market, 403; retirements, 240, 458–59, 464

Bachelier, Louis, 138

balance-of-payments accounts, 27–29; capital account, 28–29, 290–91, 293, 297; current account, 28, 29, 290–91, 292–93, 297; deficits, 27; definitions, 27–28; discrepancies, 291, 292; money supply and, 547, 571; offsetting balances, 291; surpluses, 27; trade balance, 27, 28, 183, 297, 340; of United States, 27, 28, 29, 292

Bangladesh, effects of corruption, 98

Banking Act of 1935, 176

Bank of England: anti-inflation policies, 318; bullion controversy, 580; founding, 179; operation of gold standard, 223

bank runs, 29–31; in Great Depression, 232; illiquidity, 180; relationship to bank failures, 30; spillover effects, 29–30; as warning sign, 180

bankruptcy, 31–34; corporate, 31, 32–33, 181; costs, 33, 87, 89; enforcement of laws, 89; filing rates, 31, 32, 33; government, 185–86; history, 31; law, 31–33; pension plans and, 181; personal, 31, 32, 33

banks: antidiscrimination laws, 181; capital requirements, 179, 440, 531; checkable deposits, 71, 355, 356–57, 360, 361; crises in Great Depression, 175–76, 180, 232; currency issued by, 71; failures, 30, 180, 232, 310; free banking systems, 71–73; international, 181; national, 174; regulation, 174, 178–82, 440, 460; reserve requirements, 176, 177, 233, 351, 355, 357, 361; reserves, 356–57; runs on, 29–31, 180, 232; state charters, 174; too-big-to-fail, 180–81. *See also* financial institutions; investment banks

Bank Secrecy Act, 181–82

barriers to entry, 13, 258, 365

barriers to trade. *See* trade barriers

Barro, Robert, 318, 379, 435

barter, 200, 217, 252, 565

baseball, 472–73, 474

Basel capital standards, 179, 531

basketball, 472

Bastiat, Frédéric, 163–64, 505, 524–25

BCA. *See* benefit-cost analysis

Beane, Billy, 473

Bear Stearns and Company, 314

Becker, Gary Stanley, 323, 429, 525, 586

behavioral economics, 34–38; bounded rationality, 34, 35, 590; bounded selfishness, 34–35; decision making, 547–48; differences from traditional economic view of human behavior, 34–35; finance, 35–36, 140; loss aversion, 34, 548; mental accounting, 34; saving behavior, 36–37

benefit-cost analysis (BCA), 38–40; of environmental policies, 38–39, 441–42; estimation of benefits and costs, 38–39; issues, 39; use by governments, 39–40; value framework, 161

benefits, 347. *See also* health insurance; pensions

Bentham, Jeremy, 525–26

Berle, Adolf A., 60, 89, 97

Bernanke, Ben, 266

beta, 589

Bewley, Truman, 434

Black, Duncan, 428

Black, Fischer, 210–11, 566, 584–85

black markets, 410

Black-Scholes option pricing model, 210–11, 566, 584–85

Blinder, Alan, 54, 492

block booking of movies, 594

BLS (Bureau of Labor Statistics), 78, 79, 80, 262, 418, 503

Blue Cross, 241

Blue Shield, 241

boards of directors. *See* directors

Boers, 15

Boesky, Ivan, 315

Böhm-Bawerk, Eugen von, 23, 24, 526–27, 551, 587, 603

Bolivia, dollarization, 253

Bond Market Association, 86

bonds, 40–42; definition, 40; government, 224–27; interest payments, 289–90; issuers, 40; market values, 225; municipal, 42, 224; prices, 40, 289; ratings, 41, 313. *See also* corporate bonds; debt; government debt

booms. *See* expansions

Boserup, Ester, 404

Boulware, Lemuel, 319

Boulwarism, 319

bounded rationality, 34, 35, 590

brand names, 42–44; advertising, 1–2; economic function, 43–44; price premium, 42–43, 44; quality assurance function, 2, 43–44, 81

Bretton Woods system, 198, 222, 549. *See also* World Bank

bribery, 98, 99. *See also* corruption

Bridgestone, 43–44

brinkmanship strategy, 213

Britain. *See* United Kingdom

British Empire, 15, 591

Brock, William A., 434

brokerages: functions, 179; investor protection, 181; regulators, 179

Brunner, Karl, 350

bubbles, 44–47; debate on, 47; definition, 45; Internet stocks, 44–45, 140, 141, 301; irrational, 45, 47; Mississippi, 46–47; perpetuation, 45; rational, 45, 47; South Sea, 46–47; speculative, 198; tulip, 45–46

Buchanan, James M., 24, 332, 527

budget deficits: definition, 224; of European Union members, 186; fiscal policies, 182–83, 226–27, 355, 557; future taxes implied by, 226, 318, 378; as indicator of fiscal sustainability, 186; of United States, 40, 186

budget surpluses, of United States, 183

building industry. *See* construction industry

Bundesbank, 354

bureaucracies, 399, 429–30, 468, 603

Bureau of Engraving and Printing, 361

Bureau of Labor Statistics (BLS), 78, 79, 80, 262, 418, 503

Burma, international sanctions on, 452

Burns, Arthur Frank, 177, 528

Bush administration (1989–1993), 453

Bush administration (2001–2009): outsourcing of federal jobs, 416; Social Security reform proposals, 465; tax cuts, 83, 85, 355; tax proposals, 85–86; war on terrorism, 182; withdrawal from Kyoto protocol, 219–20

This book is printed on paper that is acid-free and meets the requirements of the American National Standard for Permanence of Paper for Printed Library Materials, z39.48-1992. ∞

Book design by Barbara E. Williams, BW&A Books, Inc., Durham, North Carolina

Typography by Apex Publishing, LLC, Madison, Wisconsin

Printed and bound by Edwards Brothers, Inc., Ann Arbor, Michigan

The typefaces used in this book, Scala and Scala Sans, were designed by Martin Majoor in 1990 for a commission from the Vredenburg Music Centre in Utrecht; they were named for La Scala, the famous opera house in Milan. For the roman fonts, Majoor was influenced by such humanist faces as Bembo; for the italics, he turned to models from the sixteenth-century Italian writing master Ludovico degli Arrighi. At the time it was introduced, Scala was one of the few serif faces with a companion sans serif for both the roman and the italic.